Great Britain and Ghana

DOCUMENTS OF GHANA HISTORY
1807–1957

Great Britain and Ghana

DOCUMENTS OF GHANA HISTORY

1807 – 1957

G. E. Metcalfe

INTEGRI PROCEDAMUS

Published on behalf of

The University of Ghana

by

Thomas Nelson & Sons Ltd

UNIVERSITY OF GHANA
Legon Accra Ghana
London Office
45 Gordon Square WC1

THOMAS NELSON AND SONS LTD
36 Park Street London W1
Parkside Works Edinburgh 9

10 Warehouse Road Apapa Lagos
P.O. Box 25012 Nairobi
117 Latrobe Street Melbourne C1

THOMAS NELSON AND SONS (CANADA) LTD
81 Curlew Drive Don Mills Ontario

THOMAS NELSON AND SONS
Copewood and Davis Streets Camden 3 N.J. USA

SOCIÉTÉ FRANÇAISE D'EDITIONS NELSON
97 rue Monge Paris 5

First Published 1964

Printed in Great Britain by
Richard Clay and Company Ltd,
Bungay, Suffolk

PREFACE

THIS selection of documents aims to illustrate, as fully as possible within the limits of a single volume, the development of British policy in Ghana between 1807 and 1957. The choice of period requires little explanation. Before 1807 British Governments had few direct dealings with the British settlements on the Gold Coast and no interest in Africans as such. From the time that Parliament decreed the ending of the British slave trade, however, the task of African 'civilisation', as it was called, became a more or less continuous element in British plans for that continent. However inadequately conceived or mistakenly pursued, however overlaid at times by other self-regarding motives, this concern for African welfare essentially distinguishes the period after 1807 from that earlier phase of Anglo-Ghanaian co-operation in the slave trade which, mutually profitable to the men of both races at the coast, was based on the devastation of the African and Ghanaian interior. It is this factor which through all their differences links MacCarthy and Maclean, Grey and Carnarvon, Guggisberg and Arden-Clarke, even those high priests of 'imperialism', Maxwell and Chamberlain.

Ghanaian policy is only a part of this wider programme and is only fully to be understood in its West African context. At times indeed the true context is global. The very shape of modern Ghana testifies to an adjustment of international Great Power rivalries in which the British order of priorities preferred Nigerian to Ghanaian goals, and subordinated both to British interests in eastern Africa for reasons that lay largely outside the continent altogether. The impact of two world wars, which had little or nothing to do with Africa in their origins, on the later development of British policy in Ghana is too obvious to require demonstration. Historical compartments are never water-tight; they still have to be resorted to as matters of convenience, and in the case of Ghana the dangers of treating it in isolation are much smaller than they would be in the case of Sierra Leone or the lands around the Niger. The colonial official in London might take the world for his parish, although even he tended to treat colonies severally on their merits; the colonial official in Cape Coast or Accra rarely saw beyond Kumasi and not often so far. He was blinkered involuntarily by the long obduracy of Ashanti (and Dahomey) as well as, later, by French and German ambitions. The Volta, unlike the Niger (whether approached from its upper or lower reaches), was no highway to the interior of the continent.

Essentially this is a documentation of official policy, although it should be made clear that it is in no sense an official undertaking. The sources used, including for the 19th century much unpublished material, are almost all official. The activities of private European agencies, trader and missionary are only recorded (in the latter case seldom) when they impinged on Government action. So too with African traditional society and modern Ghanaian 'nationalist' movements. Many of the fundamental documents of Ghanaian nationalism — those in which demands are made on British administrations — do indeed appear: but others of a more self-regarding nature, discussions of the African personality and the like, which might properly find a place in an anthology of nationalism, do not. Even so, the imperial factor was assuredly not the least in the making of modern Ghana; and it is, therefore, perhaps not immodest to hope that this compilation will be of use to students of modern Ghanaian and West African history, as well as to students of British colonial policy in general.

In order to print as many documents as possible the editorial arrangements are of the simplest, designed solely to make the collection comprehensible and manageable. The intention is to let the documents speak for themselves. No conscious attempt has been made to impose an interpretation, which would be quite foreign to the whole purpose of the work. The differentiation of four main phases of policy is admittedly subjective, but this may, if the reader wishes, be ignored altogether. The editor can only say that he embarked on this undertaking in a spirit of quite detached curiosity; he hopes that he has completed it in the same spirit.

ACKNOWLEDGEMENTS

THE editor gratefully acknowledges his indebtedness to the following: to the University of Ghana for meeting the costs of publication; to the Controller of H.M. Stationery Office for permission to reproduce Crown copyright material, without which the whole enterprise would have been impossible; the Ghana Government for permission to publish Gold Coast material; to the staffs of the Public Record Office and Rhodes House Library and especially to Mr. J. M. Akita and the staff of the Ghana National Archives, in whose unpretentious quarters in the old Secretariat at Accra most of the actual transcription was done; to his wife for shouldering some of the burden of typing; to the friends who helped with advice or information but are not to be held responsible for the use made of their counsel, among whom are Dr. D. S. Coombs, Professors Philip Curtin, J. D. Fage, G. S. Graham, G. W. Irwin, D. M. Kimble and Dr. W. Tordoff; and, finally, to his publishers for the skill and patience with which they have translated a formidable MS into so handy a volume.

CONTENTS

THE AGE OF EXPERIMENT, 1807–1852

BOOK II. THE FIRST PERIOD OF CROWN RULE, 1821–1828

Chapter 9   Maclean and the British Government, 1836–1840   147

Chapter 10   The Madden Mission and the Select Committee of 1842   160

Book IV.   The Resumption of Crown Rule, 1843–1852

Chapter 11   Lord Stanley and the Judicial System, 1842–1845   187

Chapter 12   Earl Grey and Lieut.-Governor Winniett, 1846–1849   201

THE AGE OF LAISSEZ–FAIRE, 1852–1886

Book V.   The Years of Uncertainty, 1852–1864

BOOK VII THE UNION WITH LAGOS, 1874–1886

THE AGE OF EXPANSION, 1887–1918

BOOK VIII   THE FIRST PHASE OF THE 'SCRAMBLE', 1887–1894

BOOK X   EXPANSION IN PEACE AND WAR, 1902–1918

THE AGE OF FULFILMENT, 1919–1957

BOOK XI   GUGGISBERG, 1919–1927

BOOK XII   MARKING TIME, 1928–1939

BOOK XIII   THE ADVANCE TO INDEPENDENCE, 1940–1957

APPENDIXES

1807–1852

THE AGE OF EXPERIMENT

BOOK I

The Last Years of the Company of
Merchants, 1807–1821

1 The abolition of the slave trade and the first clash with Ashanti 1807–1811

BEFORE the 19th century, the British Government had no direct dealings with the Gold Coast. From early Stuart times a succession of companies, of which the best known was the Royal African Company, enjoyed a monopoly of the British trade with the coast, and in return, maintained the forts, which were considered essential for the security of that trade. The monopolist companies were constantly criticised, especially after the revolution of 1688, and in 1750, largely owing to pressure from the rising port of Liverpool, the Royal African Company was replaced by a loose association of all the British Merchants trading to Africa (App. A1). This Company of Merchants trading to Africa was not itself a trading concern but simply a device for maintaining the forts and factories by means of a Parliamentary grant instead of a trading monopoly.

When Parliament passed the Act for the abolition of the slave trade, it made illegal some nine-tenths of the Company's trade with the coast. The Company, having failed to secure a postponement of the act (1), was obliged to apply to the Government for an increased grant (5), making a general tender of their services in the execution of whatever policy the Government should decide to pursue in that part of Africa in the future. In the circumstances, the British Government might well have decided that it had no further use for the Gold Coast forts. The Abolitionists, however, were strongly opposed to reducing the British interest in Africa. Zachary Macaulay, and those who thought like him, rather wished to see British influence extended to promote the civilisation of Africa, particularly by fostering new branches of 'legitimate' and less harmful trade (2). And it was in response to their prompting that the Government decided to send a commission of enquiry to collect information about the potentialities of West Africa (9). Macaulay was less certain of the fitness of the African Company, so long identified with the slave trade, for carrying out the new programme, and favoured a concentration of West African Governments at Sierra Leone (2). The Company of Merchants, for their part, protested, rightly as the event proved, against any attempt to manage the affairs of the Gold Coast from Freetown, and augured no good from the fact that the commissioners of enquiry appointed by the Government were all connected with that settlement (6). Nor did they conceal their belief that the abolition of the slave trade had not been an unmixed good (8).

The crisis initiated by this change in imperial policy coincided with another precipitated on the coast by the advance of the Ashanti armies to the sea (3), and their (unsuccessful) assault on Anomabu (4). Here, for the first time, was posed the most critical of all questions facing the British on the Gold Coast in the next seventy years: what was to be their attitude in the face of Ashanti aggression? Could they stand neutral? or if not, should they side with Ashanti or against it, assuming they had a choice? In 1807, Governor Torrane decided, rightly, that Ashanti was much the stronger party; he sought, and seems to have secured the friendship of Osei Bonsu. But when, in the following year, the Ashantis withdrew, the coast tribes fell to fighting among themselves (7, 8, 10). In 1811 the Ashantis were weakened by the defection of Akim, but they still held the advantage,

3

though they could not press it home. The result was a state of hostility and uncertainty (12, 13) very unfavourable to the development of trade (11).

1 AFRICAN COMMITTEE MINUTE
    AFRICAN OFFICE, 2 MARCH, 1807.

A committee this day by Special Summons. Present: Messrs Miles & French. Mr Cock and Mr Reed came after the hour.

There not being a number sufficient to form a Committee, the Secretary informed the members present that he had been directed to issue summonses for a meeting of the Committee this day, on account of the progress which has been already made in a Bill now before Parliament for the Abolition of the African Slave Trade,[1] for the purpose of considering whether any & what steps ought to be taken, for protecting the interest of the Company's servants in Africa. The Acts of the 23rd of Geo. the Second & the 5th of his present Majesty Cap. 44[2] having been read, Mr. Cock reported that he had had interviews with Lord Howick[3] one of His Majesty's principal Secretaries of State, in which great pains were taken for the purpose of introducing the following clauses into the said Bill viz.

And whereas certain persons subjects of His Majesty now resident in Africa have considerable Property in that Country and some of them a great proportion, or even the whole of what they may have been enabled to acquire by a long Residence there, and which cannot be realized unless special provision be made for that purpose, be it enacted that it shall & may be lawful for the Lords Commissioners of His Majesty's Treasury upon proof to their satisfaction being adduced, to grant Licences to such persons or their Representatives in this Country, to fit one or more ships for the purpose of bringing off such property in Slaves & to convey

[1] The Bill became law the same month.
[2] 23 Geo. 2, cap. 31. See Appendix A1. 5 Geo. 3, cap. 44 placed all forts and factories between Sallee and Cape Rouge under the Crown.
[3] Charles (later 2nd Earl) Grey (of the Reform Bill) 1764–1845, at this time Foreign Secretary in the Ministry of all the Talents.

the same to the West Indies for sale, at any time between the 1st Day of May 1807 & the 1st Day of May 1808.

But after all the Arguments which could be urged in favour of such a Measure, His Lordship could not be prevailed upon to admit the Introduction of any such Clause.

Resolved, that this Committee, though fully sensible of the hardship of the case, and the difficulty of realizing and conveying to Europe African property by any other than the long established usage of exporting slaves from the Coast to the West Indies; are fully convinced that it is utterly out of their power to obtain any relief to the parties interested by any measures which it is in their power to take for so desirable a purpose.   [T.70/149]

2 ZACHARY MACAULAY[1] TO LORD CASTLEREAGH[2]   8 MAY, 1807.

The British Settlements in Africa form at present a very loose and disjointed whole, subjected to great diversity of management and pursuing ends which widely differ from each other. Goree is a Military Government immediately under the directions of His Majesty, Sierra Leone is at present governed by the Sierra Leone Company by the authority of a Charter of Justice obtained from the King. Bance Island, a fortified settlement in the same river, is the property of Messrs John and Alexander Anderson of London who hold it by virtue of An Act of Parliament, and who have hitherto used it as a slave factory. The

[1] Zachary Macaulay (1768–1838): Governor of Sierra Leone 1793–9; Secretary of the Sierra Leone Company 1799–1808, and of the African Institute 1807–12; member of the Anti-Slavery Society from 1823.
[2] Robert Stewart, Viscount Castlereagh (later 2nd Marquis of Londonderry) (1769–1822); Secretary of State for War and the Colonies July 1805 to January 1806, and March 1807 to September 1809; Foreign Secretary 1812–22.

forts on the Gold Coast, seven or eight in number, are in the hands of the African Company, who receive annually from Parliament the sums required for their maintenance; and who continue a Company for the sole purpose of managing these forts, which were originally constructed and hitherto been supported for the protection and encouragement of the slave trade.

With a view both to the British interests in Africa, and to the improvement of Africa itself it appears to deserve consideration whether these Establishments, as well as any other which may hereafter be formed in Africa, should not be taken under the immediate government of His Majesty, otherwise it is not likely that any uniform plan of policy can be pursued with respect to that country, nor any liberal and concurrent efforts made to amend the condition of its inhabitants. It was also in that case naturally become a question, whether the different settlements on the coast of Africa should be independent of each other, and subject only to the direct controul and direction of which, the others might be placed. Supposing the latter, which seems the better plan, should be adopted, I should entertain no doubt, for reasons not now necessary to be specified, that Sierra Leone is the best situation for such a Presidency.

But whether the plan of uniting all our African Establishments under the Government of His Majesty is adopted or not, it appears to me that some steps might be taken, at the present moment which would be attended with advantage both to Africa and Great Britain. To these I will now take the liberty of briefly adverting, holding myself ready to furnish your Lordship with more detailed information, should your Lordship require it.

It appears to be in the first place desirable that for the course of the next year or two vessels of war should be stationed at different parts of the African Coast (vixt. at Goree, Sierra Leone, and the Gold Coast) with a view both of giving effect to the provisions of the Act for Abolishing the Slave Trade, and for other purposes of con-siderable moment. The Commanders of His Majesty's Ships are almost universally regarded with respect and deference by the native chiefs on the coast of Africa. Being recognised as the representatives and accredited agents of His Majesty they naturally possess a very considerable influence among those chiefs.

If such Naval Commanders therefore as may visit the Coast of Africa, were directed to convey to the chiefs to whom they may have an opportunity of communicating favourable views of the principles which have guided the British Government in abolishing the slave trade, and to point out to them the various means within their reach of improving the condition of their country, their representations, I have little doubt, would produce a considerable and very beneficial effect. And this is a remark which applies not only to the officers of His Majesty's Navy, but to all the servants of Government who reside on the coast. . . .

In particular it appears important to point out to them the advantage which they would derive from cultivating generally the *white* instead of the *red* rice, because in that case a vent might be easily obtained for their surplus produce of that article, either in Great Britain or the West Indies, the former species being a marketable article, while the other, though equally useful as food, would not find a sale out of Africa.

The other articles of exportable produce, the cultivation of which seems to me the best adapted to the present state of Africa are indigo, cotton and coffee, and these might be recommended to the attention of the chiefs. . . .

I have already expressed an opinion that the Settlement of Sierra Leone is better calculated than any other for the presidency of the African Coast. Its local advantages are great when compared either with Goree, or Cape Coast Castle, and without taking into account that Goree may be given up to France at a peace. The existence also of a Colonial Establishment at this place, together with a considerable extent of territory will afford facilities for promoting the great object of African civilization which are enjoyed in no other place on the Coast, particularly as the circumstances, which hitherto have chiefly impeded this object will be removed by the abolition of the Slave Trade, and the transfer of the Colony from the Company to Government. The example afforded by the Colony of a mild but firm and well-ordered Government, of rational liberty, and of secure and productive industry, would be of almost incalculable importance while the influence which its growing strength and respectability and its growing commercial importance must give it over the neighbouring chiefs, might be exerted in composing their differences, and inducing them to pursue plans of peaceful industry. . . .

The forts on the Gold Coast, if properly employed might be made very important engines of promoting the mutual benefit of Great Britain and Africa. In addition to those which we already possess, it might be advisable to obtain possession of two or three Dutch forts situated on the same coast, which I apprehend would be a work of little difficulty. If this were effected, we should possess almost the entire controul of that line of Coast which extends from Cape Three Points to the Rio Volta. It is important here to remark, that at this moment the laws of this district of Africa are administered in a great degree by the Governors of these forts, who ordinarily proceed in administering them on the principles not of British but of African legislation. That is to say, the guilt of African criminals is tried, not by the received rules of evidence, but by the application of some ordeal which is regarded according to [the] effect which it produces, as decisive of guilt or innocence. Persons thus found guilty being liable to be sold as slaves, and the Governors of the forts being generally slave traders, it might be presumed that some degree of oppression has arisen from this source. It is obvious, however, that the power which has been thus employed, and that without being resisted, may be converted into an instrument of great good to

Africa; and that the Governors who may now be appointed, being instructed to substitute equitable principles of law and benevolent maxims of policy, in place of those which have grown up under the former system, may by that change alone operate a very considerable amelioration in the civil condition of the inhabitants of a part of the coast which extends from three to four hundred miles in length. . . .

[C.O.267/24]

3 COLONEL TORRANE[1] TO THE LONDON COMMITTEE
CAPE COAST CASTLE, 12 JUNE, 1807.

Gentlemen,

The Aurora sails altogether unexpectedly. I can only write you a few hasty lines by her. We are all in health but involved in a series of war[s]. I have been at death's door, but that is past. I am actively employed in the most laborious manner throwing up works on the hill where Phipps Tower[2] originally stood, for the protection of this place. The King of Ashantee with a most powerful army has invaded the country. He has made rapid progress and actually cut his way through the heart of the Fantee country. The Fantees give way on every side & the Ashantees have taken Cormantyne Fort.

Mr. White is making active preparations at Annamaboe. They threaten the town and fort both. For the latter I am under no sort of apprehension: I shall do my best to protect the former. Mr. White's orders from me were on no account to suffer any armed force to approach within the reach of his guns, & to endeavour to send over to the [A]shantees the most conciliatory message, stating that we should be happy to consider both parties as friends and in becoming mediators, to which end we invite

[1] George Torrane after previous service with the Company (1785–92) was appointed Governor in September 1804 in the hope that he would be able to remedy the 'wretched and undisciplined state' of the Gold Coast forts (T.70/148). He died in December 1807.

[2] The modern Fort Victoria.

the [A]shantees headman over, observing at the same time that no body of men could be allowed to approach the garrison. Mr. White succeeded in sending a corporal and Company's slave, but for the interposition of one [A]shantee man of consequence, they would have been severely maltreated by the [A]shantees. By dint of perseverance, three of their inferior captains were persuaded to go to Annamaboe Fort where Mr. White treated them with great kindness, but their conduct was by no means conciliatory: quite otherwise & I have at present no prospect of peace. In fact the Ashantees meditate a settlement on the water side, but their hostilities to the forts astonishes me. If I do not receive a visit from them here under three or four weeks, I trust to giving a good account of them. Meantime, should the least opening offer of effecting a reconciliation between the parties I shall do my utmost to that effect. I trust, Gentlemen, you will approve the steps I am taking, that of doing everything for the protection of those poor fellows under our forts and who must be extirpated without powerful aid from me. To add to their calamities they are almost starved. A famine will most likely take place. Everything now is at an enormous price. Corn formerly bought at two & three ackies[1] pr. chest is now 12 acc. p. oz. & indeed cannot be got at that price. I am obliged to give additional aid to your Companies slaves or they must all perish.

I have &c

Geo Torrane. [T.70/35]

4 COLONEL TORRANE TO THE COMMITTEE
CAPE COAST CASTLE, 20 JULY, 1807.

Gentlemen,

In a short letter, in which I had the honour of addressing you on the 12th Ulto. by the Aurora, I mentioned the invasion of this coast by a numerous army of Ashantees, headed by the King in person. That letter also stated the threats they made of attacking Annamaboe Fort. This threat they put

[1] An ackie was worth five shillings sterling.

in execution on the 15th June. Mr. White's Garrison consisted of himself, Mr. Meredith,[1] Mr. F. L. Swanzy, Mr. Baines, Mr. T. A. Smith & 24 soldiers, Company's slaves and boys.

The Ashantee first took the town, and then rushed under the very walls of the garrison, for such of the town's people as had taken shelter there. Here the carnage was great — not less than from one to two thousand of the Ashantees fell by the fire from the fort. They made many fruitless attempts to force the gates, and fought with a bravery not to be excelled. In the conflict, after the engagement had continued about two hours, Mr. White received two shot, the one in the mouth and another by a ball which passed through his left arm.

Messrs Meredith, F. L. Swanzy & Baines were also slightly wounded, but not so as to lose the services of the two former gentlemen. Mr. White's wound was so severe as to deprive them of his further services. This was a considerable loss to a small garrison, some of whom were wounded, and and some killed. Here Mr. Meredith took the command, and the very gallant and cool conduct of this gentleman & Mr. F. L. Swanzy reassured the men, whose spirits were considerably depressed by the loss of Mr. White, to whom they all looked up with the greatest confidence.

The fire kept up by the enemy was so hot that they could no longer work the guns of the fort, the Ashantees picking off every man who appeared at an embrassure; they had therefore recourse to musquetry with which they did great execution. . . .

Immediately on receiving intelligence from Annamaboe of the engagement, I hastened to reinforce the garrison. The detachment was under the command of Captain Bold and embarked in the Colpoys, Capn. Coley, to which gentleman I have more than common obligations for the readiness he manifested in going on this service and for the judicious arrangement he

Meredith left his own account of these events in *An Account of the Gold Coast of Africa* (London), 1812.

made when at Annamaboe in landing the troops, by which every man was safely lodged in the fort: I have further to state the obliging manner in which he supplied the garrison with provisions and all other articles stood in need of.

At this period messengers were constantly passing in canoes between the Ashantees and the Governor of Elmina. A blacks' report reached me that the King had sent to Govr. Linthorst requesting he would write to me that he wished to be on terms with the English. With his wonted duplicity the Dutch Governor witheld this communication for many days, and previous to my receiving it, I directed Mr. White to send a flag of truce to the King immediately on his arrival at Annamaboe. This was done and had a most happy issue. 'Twas to signify to the King my astonishment at his hostile conduct, and the more so as our conduct to his messengers from Cormantine had been marked with kindness and attention. Mr. White himself was escorting them back as far as Agah to secure their safety, as he understood the Fantees would seize them.

Before I proceed, I will beg your patience in reading a short detail of the cause of this war.

The Assin country borders on that of Ashantee, and is divided into two states; the one commanded by King Cheboo [Tsibu] & Quacoe Apontay [Kwaku Apotai] the other by King Amon [Amo Adai]; Apontay though no king holds equal sway with Cheboo. These men are subordinate to the King of Ashantee. Cheboo & Quacoe Apontay were so involved in war some years past with different countries that they courted the aid of the King of Ashantee, and became subjects of his, on the condition of having his protection. This was granted.

A man of Amon's town of great property, died. It is a custom when rich men die to bury considerable riches with them. On this occasion a great treasure was interred with the deceased, and one of Cheboo's people happened to be present at the inter-

ment. He watched his opportunity, opened the grave and escaped with the treasure. Amon demanded redress of Cheboo and Quacoe Apontay, which they refused him. The affair was laid before the King of Ashantee, who summoned all the parties before him, and awarded in favour of Amon.

Cheboo being infirm, Quacoe Apontay only appeared, and tho' ordered to remain with the King till the affair was settled, he effected his escape and refused to refund the money; on this Amon attacked his town. They (that is Amon and Quacoe Apontay) afterwards, at the instigation of the King of Ashantee, met to settle the palaver. Quacoe sent messengers clandestinely to Cheboo, desiring he would send an armed force to him. The consequence was a fight, which concluded in the death of the man who stole the gold and the defeat of Quacoe Apontay and his men. The King of Ashantee, hearing this, sent two gold manillos, the one to Amon and the other to his adversary, directing they should cease all hostilities. Both parties took the manillos. Amon obeyed the King, but Quacoe Apontay attacked Amon suddenly, and drove him from his town. Amon represented this act to the King, obtained aid, & in turn defeated Quacoe Apontay, and drove him from their town.

The King then sent two gold swords, and a gold axe by messenger to Amon, directing him to be peaceable, and he would get Cheboo and Quacoe Apontay to return to their town and settle the affair. Amon obeyed, but in the night he being posted at the back of a river, was attacked and defeated, and the victors possessed themselves of even the King's gold swords, axe and messengers, killing every man who fell into their hands, not excepting the King of Ashantee's messengers. The natural consequence was a war with Ashantee, Quacoe Apontay and Cheboo fled to the Fantee country. The King of Ashantee sent a messenger to Accoom the Cabboceer of Assecoomah [Asikuma], accompanied by a present of twenty ozs. of gold, to represent the necessity of following these men into the Fantee country: to give assurances which he requested Accoom would do to all Fantees, of his peaceable disposition towards them, and that his only object was to possess himself of the persons of these two men. Accoom [Akumanin] sent a reply to Appoy Dongua [Apea Dankwa], the King's head captain to this effect: 'That he communicated to the Fantees the King's message, and laid before them the cause of the King's entering their territories, and their reply was that they would not interfere.' At this time Appoy Dongua commanded a large body of the King's forces. At the market town of Bimda, in Fantee, he gave battle to Cheboo and Quacoe Apontay and defeated them. The day following, the Ashantee army was attacked by a strong force whom they also defeated, and took many prisoners who proved to be Fantees. Among them was Atie the Cabboceer of Abrah [Abura], the principal town in Fantee. The Abrahs sent and offered any sum for his redemption. The King said he would give him up conditionally that his two gold swords and axe were restored to him, which were then in possession of the Abrahs, who had received them with other presents of large value from Cheboo & Quacoe Apontay, to engage them to espouse their cause and to direct the Fantees generally to join in their favour. In the meantime the King, placing implicit confidence in Accoom the Cabboceer of Assecoomah, sent Atie to him to remain in his custody. This trust Accoom betrayed, and liberated him. The King's captain took no immediate notice of this treachery further than to assure Accoom he would look to him hereafter to arrange that affair. At this period Quacoe Apontay then in the Fantee country, sent a message to the King of Ashantee, importing that though he had before refused his mediation, he would gladly accept of it if he would discharge the debts he (Quacoe) had contracted, when he would return to his town. On the receipt of this message the King sent presents of cloth and two gold manillos to Cheboo and

Quacoe Apontay, who again beheaded the King's messengers.

War therefore became inevitable. As Accoom the Cabboceer of Assecoomah had large supplies of provisions, the Ashantees applied to him for assistance. He gave them permission to come to his town, conditionally they had no arms with them. Six times he supplied them, the seventh, the Ashantees amounting to nearly one thousand had gone to his town for the purpose of getting provisions, he contrived to detach in separate parties. His measures being previously taken, he seized every one and these he sold or killed. [In] consequence he became involved in the war. A strong Ashantee force was sent against him and he was put to flight. From that period the King's progress to the waterside has been great. Those vile characters the Braffoes became an easy conquest to his army, and whatever the horrors of war, the destruction of such infamous characters makes great amends. I need not enlarge my subject by animadverting on their character. You will call to mind, Gentlemen, a former letter of mine respecting them, of the plunder they committed on the sea coast and finally my expelling them from our forts. . . .

The King in his career made Cheboo & Quacoe Apontay his sole objects. All towns wherein these men and their followers had taken sanctuary (and at many of them they gave him battle, aided by the Fantees) fell as a sacrifice to Ashantee resentment. They nevertheless defeated the King's main object; he never could make prisoners of them.

At length these men, driven from one town to the other, had only the sea-shore as a refuge. The Annamaboes [Anomabus], instigated by the Braffoes[1] were impudent enough to receive & protect them. Subjoined to the influence of the Braffoes, I may add the considerable bribes they got from Cheboo & Quacoe Apontay.

This proved fatal to them, & their town and property paid the forfeit of their act.

[1] Abura - fo = the people of Abura.

I attempted shortly after the messengers had been sent to Cormantyne by Mr. White, to send a soldier & head Company's slave with a flag of truce to the King of Ashantee, who was then at Abrah, a journey only of a day from Annamaboe, to enquire the motive of his coming; and to tender my services as a mediator between the contending parties, and these people I had in mind to forward by the Ashantees then at Cormantyne to Abrah, but as soon as they arrived at Annamaboe, they (the Annamaboes) were quite averse to the measure, and talked with the highest confidence; so that they fell by their own folly.

After the battle of Annamaboe, the Assins fled to this town with the small remains of their forces, consisting of about five hundred desperate men. The men of most power were bribed here by Cheboo & Quacoe Apontay to a very large amount. This came to my knowledge. I sent for those persons who had received the bribes, I represented to them the immense force of the Ashantees; that contending with them was absolutely impracticable — their town must fall; that the largeness of the sums given actually deceived them as to their true interest; that in lieu of keeping what these men had given, even their own property would become a prey to a conquering army, themselves destroyed or in slavery, their houses consumed by fire, and families butchered. This representation they affected to agree to, but with no very great sincerity. Meanwhile the town was in the greatest alarm. I had not less than 5,000 women in my garrison, their distresses came to the heart. In vain I called on the townspeople to seize the Assins, to look to their wives, their children; even their dead bodies would not remain unmolested in their graves. I urged them to rouse to a sense of their danger and not to suffer tamely a few men who had been corrupted by the Assins' gold thus to bring destruction on them. They had not the spirit to attend to me. The five hundred men alarmed them and thus they were on the point of becoming a prey to wretches who would have sacrificed

them all to a mere delusion. All eyes were directed to me. They looked to me if possible to avert the impending calamity.

I went into town accompanied only by Mr Fitzgerald the Chief Surgeon. After a walk reconnoitring for some time, our good fortune directed us to fall in with King Cheboo near the gates of the castle, and attended only by 8 or 10 men with musquets. There was no time to be lost. We rushed upon him, and being observed from the castle, a sergeant and two men came out, by which means Cheboo was made prisoner & I am happy to say without loss, as his people were panic struck, being altogether unprepared for the attack. My good fortune in possessing myself of Cheboo gave me hopes I might be equally fortunate in capturing Quacoe Apontay who I had discovered at a house on the outskirts of the town attended only by about sixty armed men . . . [but in this he failed]. Quacoe Apontay and his followers fled. I had however done sufficient to assure the king of Ashantee that war at Cape Coast with him was not the object of any one.

I sent to Annamaboe [as] the King was by this time arrived there. I invited his messengers to the Cape and acquainted him of my having his enemy King Cheboo a prisoner. This message changed the face of everything. 1300 poor unfortunate women who had sought security in Annamaboe Fort were in the greatest distress for provisions. 6 or 8 died daily. . . . By the steps I took I was enabled to open a treaty with the King and you may readily believe the first object was the removal to the Cape[1] of those unfortunate persons. . . .

Being sensible that my presence at Annamaboe would tend to reconcile all existing differences I sent an officer of rank to the King, intimating that if these poor people were allowed to come from Annamaboe and all dead bodies removed from under the fort walls, I would go down. The King was highly pleased at this and my terms agreed to. I accordingly went to Annamaboe the 23rd June. On the day follow-

[1] i.e. Cape Coast.

ing I sent an officer with Sackey the linguist whom I had ordered up from Accra, as being well known to the Ashantees, with presents of refreshments to the King & the day following I met him in an open place at the back of the town as he was averse to coming into the fort & of consequence I could not concede the point of waiting on him.

Our meeting was a mere matter of form only, of some hours [duration], much shew on the occasion, but we entered into the discussion of no business. The King spoke much of his loss by the fire kept up from the fort. . . . I represented the hostile language of his people who were invited and came over from Agah and who were told we wished to be on terms of amity with him, but that he would not be allowed to attack any town under a British fort. He lamented with much apparent sincerity Mr. White's wound.

I remained a fortnight at Annamaboe. The King has promised to avoid all towns under the British forts provided the inhabitants of those towns are not found in arms against him. I on my part have sent strict orders to Tantum & Winnebah on that subject, which orders I have the honor to send with this despatch. I had it not in my power to conclude my treaty with the King. The Fantees collected in some force to leeward of Cormantyne. The King went to give them battle. I witnessed the action which was decisive in favour of the Ashantees who, I am confident, must conquer wherever they go. They are both numerous and brave. The beach for miles is strewed with the dead in heaps of thousands. Their object of pursuit now is Accoom the Cabboceer of Assecoomah. . . . He is now with the Fantee army. If the King gets him, the war, I conclude, will cease. The King is accompanied by 12 kings, all men of power, but obliged to attend in person at his call, with such a force as he shall see fit to command.

The Ashantees fight both with musquets, bows and arrows. It doubtless was then the intention to place a large quantity of

gunpowder to the walls of the fort, and they had also a plan of cutting open the gates; the orders were given, and the day appointed, when my messenger acquainting him of my taking Cheboo, changed the face of affairs. I will not pretend to offer any opinion as to what success might attend either of these attempts; I will observe only, the king values not the lives of a few thousands, to carry any point in which he is determined. Their bravery I have more than once in this dispatch highly extolled; 'tis not to be surpassed; they manifest a cool intrepidity you gentlemen would look at with surprise and admiration. In all my negotiations with the king I had cause to remark what I have not experienced on the sea coast, to wit, the strictest regard to his word. In fact I look on King Zey,[1] so he is called, to be a high character. He is of middling stature, remarkably well built, and of a handsome open countenance. Indeed all the principal Ashantees seem half a century advanced in civilization to those people on the water side. He is attended with many Moors, and every Ashantee man has a gregory, or fetisch, which is a little square cloth, inclosing some little sentences of the Alcoran; some have many. In fact the Moors seem to have spread over the whole interior of Africa.

I have received a message from the king importing that as soon as the war shall be over, he will return and form his camp near Annamaboo, to the end that we may arrange all points for the future welfare of the country, and the regulation of the trade. And here let me observe that an intercourse securely opened with Ashantee, offers prospects of the highest advantage, and the more so as the slave trade is now at an end. The Ashantees have ivory and gold in great abundance, and the Fantees have ever thrown impediments in the way so as to prevent their intercourse with us: but it appears to hold out an object of more national importance, and one, if I can be

[1] Osei Tutu Kwamina Asibe (Osei Bonsu) became Asantehene c. 1800. He died in 1824.

the happy means of bringing about, I shall deem my services in Africa not altogether misapplied. I mean a thorough knowledge of the source of the Niger, and a direct and safe way of going to Timbuctu, should any more adventurers engage in that research. The conversation I have had with the Moors gives the fullest confidence of success in such an undertaking, and that confidence is not a little supported by the reflection of the influence I have with the King of Ashantee, the probable increase thereof, and the vast extent of country over which he rules, and the aid he can further give in such an enterprise. . . .

[T.70/35; Part printed in H.C.431 Accounts and Papers (1817) vi, 401]

5 S. Cock[1] to Lord Castlereagh
4 October, 1807.

During the continuance of the Slave Trade, the Committee were enabled to procure competent persons willing to encounter the climate of Africa, at salaries greatly inadequate to their service, by reason of the commercial advantages which those persons derived from a constant and extensive intercourse with vessels trading in slaves; but this trade now being abolished, the Committee are under serious apprehensions, lest their servants, incapable of supporting themselves upon their salaries only, and having no longer sufficient inducements to remain in Africa, should return to Europe, and the forts be abandoned. Although the primary and chief object of acquiring and maintaining the forts on the Gold Coast of Africa, has been to promote and render secure the commerce in slaves, yet the Committee conceive that several of their forts, being situated in that part of Africa in which gold (in any quantity) and ivory are to be procured, will still be found of the utmost importance, as the means of keeping up a secure intercourse with the Africans, in trading for those articles; and

they have therefore felt it a duty to submit to your Lordship, the necessity of their being authorized to give the earliest assurance to their servants, that such additions will be made to their salaries, during their continuance in their present situations, as may be deemed reasonable and just.

In making this representation the Committee venture an opinion, that five thousand pounds, in addition to the present grant of eighteen thousand pounds, will be required, and they entertain hopes that that sum will not be materially exceeded.[1]

The African Committee, in the present extraordinary era of their affairs, cannot allow a communication of this nature to be concluded, without making a general tender of their services, for the furtherance of such political and commercial objects as His Majesty's Government may now, or at any future period entertain; and this they do, under a well-founded conviction, that their general as well as local acquaintance with the affairs of the Coast of Africa, enables them (as experience has shown) to conduct the business of maintaining the forts on principles of the strictest economy, and with advantage to the interests connected with them.

I have etc.
S. Cock.

[H.C.506, A & P (1816) vii. 21.]

6 S. Cock to E. Cooke[2]
26 September, 1808.

Sir,

I have laid before the Committee of the Company of Merchants trading to Africa your letter of the 15th August last, acquainting them with the intention of Government to send out a Commission to the coast of Africa for the purpose of ascertaining

---

[1] Member, and from July 1808 until its disbandment Secretary, of the Committee of the Company of Merchants trading to Africa.

[1] Salaries were accordingly doubled. For details cf. Crooks, J. J., Records relating to the Gold Coast Settlements 1750–1874, Dublin, 1923, p. 105.

[2] Edward Cooke (1755–1820); closely associated with Castlereagh in Ireland and after; Under-Secretary for War and the Colonies 1804–6, 1807–9; Under-Secretary for Foreign Affairs 1812–17.

what measures may be most advisable in consequence of the abolition of the slave trade, and also communicating the desire of Lord Castlereagh to receive by a deputation from the Committee an explanation of their sentiments and object. . . .

His Lordship must be perfectly aware of the crisis to which the relative situations of the two countries have been brought by the abolition of the slave trade, and likewise the necessity of adopting speedy and judicious measures for preserving the existing intercourse with the natives, which has hitherto been almost wholly attributable to that branch of commerce. With this view, . . . the Committee feel it necessary to advert . . . to the situation of Sierra Leone for the purpose of stating their opinion of the impossibility of connecting that settlement with any plan embracing those parts of the coast which are under their management. . . .

With respect to the forts under the management of the Committee, they are not aware of any immediate change that is necessary: but they apprehend great evils will arise from the existence of the neighbouring forts in the hands of other nations, unless their co-operation in the abolition of the slave trade and the civilization of the country can be assured.

On this head it must be unnecessary to point out to his Lordship, the partiality which will inevitably be shown by the natives to those Europeans who favour their prejudices, and assist them in their accustomed pursuits. . . . Of the Dutch and Danish forts there are seventeen in number . . . which interesect the British forts on the whole range of the Gold Coast. The forts under the direction of the Committee are eleven in number, viz. — Apollonia, Dixcove, Succondee, Commenda, Cape Coast Castle, Annamaboe, Tantum Querry, Winnebah, Accra, Prampram, Whyday. . . . The nations in the towns under the several British forts acknowledge allegiance to this Government, and the principal of them receive stipends from the Committee out of the annual grant from Parliament, as do also some of the inland kings and other men of consequence.

The most important object which the Committee have now in view, in consequence of the abolition of the slave trade is to impress on the minds of the natives the utter impossibility of its renewal, and to attempt the substitution of other trades in its place. The chief articles which the Committee conceive may be made the subject of future trade with Africa are elephants teeth, gold dust, cotton, indigo, rice, indian corn, palm oil and timber. . . .

Elephants teeth have long been an article of import from Africa, but hitherto rather as an appendage to the slave trade, the ordinary method of conveying them from the interior having been by means of the slaves on their way to the coast. Gold dust has hitherto been imported into this country in very inconsiderable quantities, it being the policy of the natives to prevent the export. Cotton, being a plant well suited to the soil and climate of Africa, the Committee conceive that the utmost exertion should be made to introduce and encourage the cultivation of it. . . . [The Committee had already taken steps to encourage its cultivation.] Should their endeavours be attended with the success they anticipate, and such progress be made in the civilisation of the natives as shall favour the hope of security to European settlers, they have reason to think that lands may be hereafter employed in such plantations with very considerable advantage to the occupiers. . . .

On the subject of the commission, the Committee are unanimously of opinion that the persons composing it will be exposed to the greatest difficulties in the prosecution of their researches unless they are previously acquainted with the language, manners, prejudices and customs of the natives; and the Committee are very doubtful whether any information can be obtained through the means of such commission, more useful or correct than may be procured from gentlemen now in this country, to whom local residence and

practical observation has afforded opportunities of collecting such information, or
from the servants of the Committee now on
the coast of Africa. . . .

[Stipends to chiefs might be augmented
for promoting agriculture among their
subjects.] But still more important benefits
would arise from a reduction of those heavy
duties which attach to almost every article
that Africa produces. And if bounties
were granted upon the importation from
Africa into the British West India islands
of rice, indian corn and calavances, and the
vessels were permitted to return direct from
thence to Africa with rum, tobacco etc
under the protection of occasional convoys,
the Committee are persuaded that the importance of such trade would soon be
sensibly felt. There would be little difficulty, and in a short period, no difficulty in
procuring free black sailors to navigate
such vessels; and in process of time, the
Committee have no doubt that persons
would be found to emigrate from the coast,
who, on their arrival in the West Indies,
would either serve in the black regiments,
or hire themselves as labourers, and thus
fill up the chasm which otherwise may be
expected in the negro population.

I have etc.

S. Cock, Secretary.

[H.C.506 of 1816 pp. 110–13]

7 Governor E. W. White[1] to the African Committee   5 May, 1809.

. . . .

I am at a loss what answer to make to
your questions[2] respecting the disposal of
prisoners taken by the King of Ashantee,
all the information on that subject being
gained from hearsay, and that to the following effect: that some hundreds of men
women and children were carried up to the
Ashantee country; that some were sold to

[1] Governor, January 1808 to April 1816.
[2] In the Committee's letter to Governor and
Council, 20 September, 1808, in H.C.431 p. 53.
Torrane was supposed to have sold some of them
to slavers. His papers throw no light on this. But
cf. No. 63 below.

the shipping and traders, and that many
have been sacrificed at the several customs
made by the king, for relations and principal men killed in the war.

I am unwilling to venture an opinion of
the present intentions of the King of Ashantee, but little credit being due to the news-
mongers of this country. . . . Some time
past Mr Dawson[1] wrote me from Accra
informing me that the head general of the
army then residing at Accra had orders to
make proposals to the Fantees for peace;
that I was requested to send a message to
them to that effect; that if they were to
expect another visit from the king, he would
not return to his country without annihilat-
ing the Fantees.

I sent to Abrah where the chiefs of the
Fantees were assembled, adding to the
king's proposal my resolution to aid as
much as in my power the carrying into
effect so desirable an event. Their answer
was, that they were obliged to me, but that
as the king had injured them to the extent
of his power, they were determined on not
being friends with him. This answer was
sent to Accra.

The Fantees are a bad bullying people.
I am nearly certain they could not withstand
an army of 5,000 Ashantees. They are at
this moment exercising their utmost to
injure the people of Cape Coast, and only
(as I am informed) because the latter did
not suffer equally with themselves when the
Ashantees visited the waterside. . . .

[T.10/35. H.C.431 of 1817 pp. 39–40]

8 Governor & Council to the Com- mittee

Cape Coast Castle, 26 December, 1809.

The Annamaboes have confederated with
the people of Cape Coast, the Fantees in
general, and the Wassaws. They have a
large army at the back of Elmina, with the
inhabitants of which they are at war.
Some skirmishes have already taken place
at the skirts of Elmina town, and there can

[1] Joseph Dawson, Governor of James' Fort,
Accra; joined the Company's service in 1789.

be no doubt that it would be very soon destroyed if not protected by the Castle and Fort of St. Jago. Their anger is principally directed towards Mr. Neizer, whom they complain of as being the person who instigated the Ashantees to visit the water-side. The President has used every argument to dissuade the people of Cape Coast from interfering in this affair, but as there are but few of them in comparison to the Fantees &c., they were obliged to join them for their own security, the former having sworn to destroy them if they did not; and it would be the most easy thing in nature for them to prevent all provisions coming to this town, or the inhabitants having any communication with the interior. Indeed, they might with ease destroy the town itself by entering at the back of it, to which part the guns of this castle would not have effect.

The effect which the abolition of the slave trade may have produced is not clearly visible, as the bulk of the people are in a state of warfare. They condemn it along the coast, as it deprives them of the means of procuring those articles of luxury with that facility they were accustomed to do. How the inland people stand affected cannot be sufficiently ascertained on account of the present disturbed state of the country. We must, however, suppose that the men of consequence, being prevented from resorting to the mode of punishing their slaves, they were long accustomed to, wish for its revival. Industry is more visible, and there are not so frequent disputes in the different towns along the coast as formerly.

We cannot, however, refrain from observing that, although it may be productive of the most beneficial effects in a general sense, yet it has its attendant evils. The abolition having taken out of our hands the power of sending delinquents off the coast, we may now be robbed of property unless other modes of punishment than flogging and confinement are adopted. Some circumstances lately happened which called loudly for an exemplary punishment. Mr. Herbert had several pieces of cloth stolen from him by canoe-men. Another person

B

found base metal to the amount of several ounces to be mixed with his gold, which had been imposed on him by his gold-takers. Both of these crimes deserved hanging or transportation. We earnestly request, Gentlemen, that you will take this matter into consideration and obtain for us such authority as may insure a greater security of property.

We cannot proceed so rapidly with agriculture as wished until the disputes amongst the natives are ended. Commerce declines from the same cause, except at Accra where communication is preserved with the Ashantees. . . .

    [Signed] Edwd. William White
             Geo Richardson[1]
             Thomas Penny[2]
             Henry Meredith.[3]
[T.70/35. Part printed in H.C.431 p. 40]

9 MEMORANDA FOR THE GUIDANCE OF THE WEST AFRICAN COMMISSIONERS
               27 DECEMBER, 1809.
Captain Columbine to proceed to Sierra Leone with as little delay as possible, and after being joined by the other two Commissioners (Mr Ludlam and Mr Dawes) who are now at that place, to go on to the Gold Coast: after visiting all the forts on the Gold Coast, to proceed to Whydah, and thence to St Thomas's; from St. Thomas's to return to Sierra Leone; and after the Commissioners shall have closed their inquiries there and at Bance Island, to visit Goree and thence to return to England. [They were given discretion to visit other places.] . . .

The Commissioners to be instructed, first to keep a regular diary of their proceedings in which every remarkable occurrence may be noted.

2nd. To procure full and accurate information respecting the state of Africa in general, its commercial and agricultural capacities, and the social and civil condition of its inhabitants.

[1] Vice-President and Governor of Anomabu.
[2] Governor of Tantum.
[3] Governor of Winneba.

3rd. To make the state of the different British Settlements, vizt. Goree, Sierra Leone, Bance Island and the forts on the Gold Coast and at Whyday, the subject of minute and particular investigation.

4th. To endeavour to convey to the African Chiefs with whom they may have intercourse, a favourable impression of the principles which have produced the abolition of the slave trade, and to point out to them the means they enjoy of improving the condition of their country, and the various channels into which the industry of their people may be profitably directed.

5th. To turn the attention of British subjects resident on the coast as much as possible to the pursuit of agriculture, and of a trade in the natural productions of Africa, to the instruction of the natives in useful arts, and to the general improvement of our intercourse with that country.

6th. To consider and report their opinion respecting the expediency of procuring from the Portuguese Government the cession of the island of Bissao, with a view to the extinction of the slave trade on the windward coast.

7th. To consider and report their opinion as to the adviseableness and also as to the means of getting possession of the different forts on the African coast belonging to Powers in a state of hostility with this country; either with a view to the uses to which these forts may be applied, or to their demolition.

And, lastly, to consider and report with respect both to Africa generally and each particular place which they may visit; what measures may most advantageously be pursued for improving the state of the country; for enlarging the existing channels of commercial intercourse; and for opening new ones; in short, on all subjects involving the interests of Africa, more especially as these interests may be combined with those of this country. . . .

[C.O.268/18. Based on a draft by Zachary Macaulay dated 5 October, 1809 in C.O.267/24]

10 GOVERNOR WHITE TO THE AFRICAN COMMITTEE   7 NOVEMBER, 1810.

About a month past, two messengers arrived from the king of Ashantee. They were accompanied by the person who was sent with my message to the king.[1] . . . The king's message was as follows: 'That he did not mean to give offence by sending to me through the Dutch, that he regarded white men as his masters, and that he should be happy to keep in friendship with them; that it was his intention to send an army against the Assins; that their ill-treatment of the Ashantees some years back was the sole cause of his visit to the water side in the year 1807, as it would be that of the army he was about to send; that if the whites, Fantees or others protected his enemies, he should be obliged to wage war with them.'

I made the above message known to the head man of the Fantees, who sent the following declaration delivered in presence of myself, Mr. Meredith, Cabboceer and Pynims of this town [and] the Ashantee and Accra messengers: 'That they (the Fantees) were pleased to hear that the king's army was not intended to come against them; that as the king was anxious to be revenged on the Assins he could easily be so without sending his army very far, as they (the Assins) resided near to the borders of his own country; that they (the Fantees) were at war with the Elminas; that when the king's army in 1807 drove them to seek shelter at Elmina and other places, the people of Elmina sold a part of them, and caused others to be seized by the Ashantees.'

When the messengers were about to depart to Accra, I desired them to inform the king of Ashantee that it was the sincere wish of the English, as it would be their utmost endeavour, to keep in amity with all; that they came not to this country to make war but to promote trade and improve the country; that they had a great desire to obtain a free communication from and to

[1] Asking the Asantehene not to communicate with the English through the Dutch as he had done in the previous May.

the Ashantee country; that they (the Eng-lish) would be happy to aid in restoring peace and harmony, and that if the king would deliberate and make his sentiments known to them, they would do all in their power, in conjunction with him, to effect so desirable an event.

The messengers returned with a few presents for the king. The Fantees have not made another attack on Elmina. They remain encamped a few miles in the interior. . . .   [H.C.431 p. 42. T.70/35]

11 AN ACCOUNT of the real value of all Imports into and Exports from Great Britain from & to Africa from the Year 1805 to the Year 1810 inclusive.

YEARS	IMPORTS £		EXPORTS £
1805	193,034		1,156,955
1806	226,396	Exclusive	1,655,042
1807	242,747	of	1,022,745
1808	374,306	Gold	820,194
1809	383,926	Dust	976,872
1810	535,577		693,911

Upon the Imports it should be observed that many vessels having been lost or captured on their voyage home, the amount of their cargoes does not come into the above account of Imports. The Amount of Cargoes so lost must be at least one fifth or one sixth of the whole of the Return.

[T.70/73]

12 GOVERNOR WHITE TO THE COMMITTEE CAPE COAST CASTLE, 25 MARCH, 1811.
Since my last information respecting the Ashantees and Fantees[1] I have received news from Messrs Meredith and Smith[2] relative to their proceedings. A letter from the former gentleman dated the 1st of the month acquainted me . . . that an action had taken place between the Ashantees, Apams, Mumfords, Winnebahs, Adjuma-coons and Assins, the issue of which was a complete conquest on the part of the

[1] On 23 February he had informed the Com-mittee of a new invasion of Fante by the Ashan-tees.

[2] J. Hope Smith, then commandant at Tantum.

Ashantees. The Winnebahs in particular sustained a great loss. They were so appre-hensive the Ashantees would follow them to their town that they took to their canoes for safety.

Another letter from Mr. Meredith men-tions that two messengers had arrived at Winnebah who said that the Cabboceer of Akim, whose name is Attah,[1] and was formerly in the service of the King of Ashantee, was near Winnebah with 3,000 men. Attah had been very active in the attack on Annamaboe in the year 1807. On application to the King for the body of his brother who died in that town, he was told that it should not be given to him with-out he previously paid a considerable sum of gold dust. This with other acts of oppression so irritated Attah, that he deter-mined on taking the first favourable oppor-tunity of resenting them, which soon offered by the King's sending him 4 oz. gold, at the same time saying that as it was his intention to make a second attack on the Fantees, Attah must purchase powder and lead with the gold, and aid him. Attah took the gold and returned for answer that he would most certainly purchase powder and lead, but not for the purpose of fighting for him but against him.

An army was sent to subdue Attah, as well as the Cabboceer of the Aquapim [Akwapim] Country, who had revolted from the King of Ashantee and joined Attah. The Cabboceer was made prisoner and his people routed. Attah was more fortunate, having repulsed the Ashantees with considerable loss on their side, and but little on his own. Mr. Smith's letter of 4th present month stated that the Ashantees were at Lagou [Legu]. It seems, in their way from Winnebah to that town, they met with the Annamaboes and other Fantees; that after a severe contest the Ashantees became victorious, obliging their opponents to retreat, after having made prisoners of some of their captains. When Mr. Smith was certain of the Ashantees being at Lagou, he sent to them his sergeant, a

[1] Atta Wusu Yiakosan.

soldier, and his servant, with a flag of truce. The latter soon returned with two Ashantees. Mr. Smith endeavoured to get acquainted with their future intentions, but could gain no further information of consequence than that it was their determination to make their way to Elmina. They made Mr. Smith assurances of friendship towards the whites.

The day after, the Ashantee army took up their quarters near the wall of Tantum Fort, in which situation they did not remain for long, for hearing that Attah was fast approaching, they made off to the interior. Attah came up with them, fought, and obliged them to make a precipitate retreat, since which no further account has been gained of them. A week past, Attah sent messengers to myself and people of this town, with information of his being in pursuit of the Ashantees and of his intention to oppose them to the last, on account of the grievances he had experienced from their King.

I desired the messengers to tell Attah, that duty to my superiors, equally with my own inclination, made me extremely anxious to be in peace with all; that I could not interfere in his quarrel with the King of Ashantee further than as mediator, for the purpose of restoring tranquillity and commerce; that should I be solicited to act in that character, it would afford me considerable satisfaction and would, I was certain, be cheerfully sanctioned by you gentlemen. I further said that he as well as the King of Ashantee would find me ready at a moment to exert myself in the cause of humanity, it being the earnest wish of Englishmen to see this country in a civilised, peaceable and flourishing state.

Attah prior to meeting with the Ashantees, stopped at Apam, entered the Dutch fort, threw the guns over the walls, and released the Cape Coast canoemen who had been seized at the time Mr. Platt had been so cruelly treated by the people of Apam. The people of Akim commanded by Attah are reported to possess great courage; by living near the Ashantees, they are similar in their mode of fighting, and infinitely more capable of opposing their enemies with advantage than the Fantees are. . . .

P.S. I request to add, Gentlemen, that independent of the great security a Man-of-War would afford your settlements, smuggling would be annihilated. At present vessels under Spanish colours anchor without gunshot of this castle with impunity, as it is impossible for me to prevent slaves being sent to them by the natives, except myself and officers were to be on the look-out during the night.

Edwd Wm White.   [T.70/35]

13 GOVERNOR WHITE TO THE COMMITTEE
CAPE COAST CASTLE, 23 MAY, 1811.

Since the last information I had the honour to give you respecting Attah and the Ashantees, it has been reported to me that the former with the Fantees are preparing to march in quest of the Ashantees who are supposed to be at the back of Addah, to the amount of 20,000; that the Governor of Addah Fort, by name Flint, having been suspected of aiding the escape of Quow,[1] Cabboceer of Aquapim, an enemy of the Ashantees, had by them been inveigled from out of his fort, and made prisoner of.

One report states that the Ashantees had decapitated him — another that it is their intention to send him to their Country.[2] It is further said that should the Ashantees be conquered, Attah and the Fantees propose to attack the people of Accra, they being the friends of the Ashantees. Mr Minon, Governor of Cormantyne Fort stopped here a few days past on his way to Elmina. He informs me he was going to Governor De Veer to make known to him that it was the determination of the Fantees to destroy the fort, if the sum of 50 oz. was not paid to them. This conduct they declare to be on account of Mr. Neizer's having, as they say, prevailed on the King of Ashantee to send the late expedition against them. . . .

[T.70/35]

---

[1] Kwao Safrotwe.
[2] He was ransomed for £400.

2 The 1811 report and the peace settlement of 1815

OWING to the death of one of its members and the sickness of another, the Commission of Inquiry did not report until 1811.   It found the forts on the Gold Coast too numerous for any trade that there was, and recommended that some of them should be abandoned (14).   The Government, apparently, had hoped they would recommend a total abandonment of the coast (15).   The Commissioners were also shocked to discover that the slave trade still continued, and that the Africans to a man lamented the obstructions put in the way of it.

The Company had little difficulty in exposing the naïvety of these views (16), and pointed forcefully to the corollary: that unless the foreign as well as the British slave trade were abolished, nothing but ruin faced the British settlements. As long as the war in Europe lasted, British sea-power kept the trade within bounds; but the approach of peace raised the question of the future arrangements to be made with the Dutch and Danes (22), and made it important that the French should not be allowed to get a footing on the coast (23).   The Company itself had concluded local neutrality pacts with the Dutch in 1796 and 1805, and the British Government did not think the Dutch settlements worth an expedition in 1813. The possibility of taking over the Dutch settlements does not seem to have been even considered during the peace negotiations of 1814, perhaps because the Netherlands Government agreed to prohibit the slave trade in all its overseas possessions.   Both the Commissioners and the Company had favoured Britain taking over sole control of the Gold Coast forts, and the history of the settlements in the 19th century would have been much more satisfactory if that advice had been acted upon.

14 REPORT OF THE COMMISSIONERS OF AFRICAN INQUIRY. . . .   29 JULY, 1811.

The [Gold] Coast has been so repeatedly and thoroughly described, as to its soil, productions and inhabitants, that it would be a mere waste of time to enter again into a long detail on the subject.   The only points of importance which remain open to discussion are the European forts, and the influence which they may have towards the abolition of the slave trade.

The number of European forts here is very considerable, compared with the extent of coast which they occupy.   From Apollonia to Accra, a distance of about sixty-four leagues, there are no less than twenty-seven; five others are scattered over seventy-two leagues of coast down to Whyday [Wida]; and . . . it will be seen that the forts of the different nations intersect each other throughout.

None of them except Cape Coast, Elmina, Accra and Annamaboe are of any strength, or are capable of defence, except against the natives, and some of them not equal even to that.   Nor could the strongest ones make much resistance if any enemy should land cannon and be met with no molestation from the natives.

It must be evident from the numbers of them, that they are in general very trifling, unproductive concerns;   and indeed, it would appear that most of them have been erected more for the purpose of excluding a rival nation, and at the certainty of loss, rather than from the expectation of any positive good to be derived from a commerce which has never been found sufficient to defray the expenses of the companies engaged in it.   The expense attending the British settlements is understood to be about £24,000 or £25,000 annually; and whether the expenditure of such a sum of the public money produces an adequate return or not, may be worth consideration.

Most of the outforts, being utterly unable to protect any merchant ships (even from a privateer) which might be chased into their road, being so insignificant that they only exist in the country by the goodwill of the natives, and having their little trade exclusively in the hands of the Chief,[1] cannot be considered in any other light than as small private factories supported, at the public expense, for the sole benefit of the individuals who happen in rotation to succeed to the charge of them.

As to their trade, various causes give to these persons the entire and exclusive command of all that can be had in their vicinity. Being on the spot, and having a perfect knowledge of business, they can take advantage of times, scarcities &c, and as the natives round the fort are considered under its protection, they are expected in return to carry their trade there in preference to any other market. A ship can have none of these benefits. She must therefore enter the market at a great disadvantage, and find the presence of the British fort more injurious than beneficial. And, on the other hand, (putting trade out of the question), ships could derive no benefit from these forts as they could afford no protection.

Neither is the gain to the individual so great as to make the support of such places worth while to Great Britain, in order to secure the national benefit arising from large commercial returns. It is impossible to ascertain what these returns amount to; but the general profit to the Chief seems to be from £800 to £1,200 a year, exclusive of his salary; and to obtain this benefit from the individual, the public spend a greater sum, the average expense being about £1,400 or £1,500. Were any of the forts to be relinquished, it by no means follows that even the small returns which they now produce would be lost to our commerce, there being little doubt that they would be fully collected by occasional ships.

[1] i.e. Governor or Commandant of a fort.

It is therefore recommended that the following forts be given up, for the reasons above stated, to which may be added their great want of repairs — Succondee, Commenda, Tantum Querry, Winnebah, Pram Pram, Whyday. . . . But whether this entire reduction be adopted or not, the establishment of Whyday ought unquestionably to be given up. It is totally useless, being without any trade, and the ferocious king of Dahomey, in whose territories it is situated, so tyrannises over the Governor and the few people about him as to render such subjection utterly disgraceful to the British flag. . . .

The forts of Apollonia, Dixcove, Cape Coast, Annamaboe and Accra are sufficient to ensure as much influence to the British name as can be turned to any advantageous account. A part, or perhaps the whole of the first year's saving, which would accrue from the reduction above recommended, might be well applied to the effectual repair of these forts, and to furnishing them with new ordnance and carriages, of which they are greatly in want.

The Dutch forts demand the next attention, as it cannot be deemed advisable, whilst we are reducing our own establishment in so considerable a degree as is proposed, that we should allow our enemies to retain all their posts, although they are certainly by no means in a more respectable condition than our own, the Dutch capital excepted.

The situation of Elmina is the best on the coast for trade, defence and landing; and the castle itself is much larger than that of Cape Coast. But notwithstanding these great advantages . . . there are some considerable objections against our capturing it. Were we masters of it as well as Cape Coast, if we retained both we must have an establishment as expensive for Elmina as that of Cape Coast, to avoid which the seat of government would probably be removed to the former place, and Cape Coast be destroyed or let out upon lease to private merchants. All this would be most desirable, and even the expense of repairing

Elmina would not be worth consideration, provided there could be any reasonable expectation of our holding it in the event of a general peace. It is not presumed to give any opinion on this subject; but if the chance of our retaining Elmina should be judged to be against us, then it may not be advisable to take it, thereby to put ourselves to the expense of repairing or restoring the falling buildings, and of removing our present establishment, merely for the occupancy of a few years.

As to the Dutch forts [generally], if it should not be thought advisable to take the whole of them, we might limit ourselves to the reduction of the same number as we should lop off from our own establishment. The selection might be made so as to remove those which were nearest to our own; and upon this ground it is recommended to take Acquedah [Akwida], Boutree [Butre], Mouree, Cormantin, Bercoe [Senya Beraku], Crevecoeur (Dutch Accra); leaving them in possession of Axim, Succondee, Chamah [Shama], and Apam. . . .

The Governor of the Danish fort at Accra[1] having formed a plantation about fifteen miles up the country, it might be desirable not to molest him in the prosecution of a work which may, by the force of example, turn greatly to the benefit of Africa. It was commenced about three years past, and coffee is already brought to great perfection. It may, therefore, be thought right not to attack Christiansburg.

A treaty of peace and neutrality has been entered into between the British and Dutch settlements, the first article of which apparently would preclude ours from affording any assistance whatever in the proposed attacks on the latter, otherwise the Company's slaves would be of great use on such a service. It would, indeed, be proper that this treaty,[2] and the nature and extent of the sanction given to it by the British Government, should be fully considered before any of the Dutch forts were attacked.

Considered as a means of checking the slave trade, our forts on the Gold Coast do not appear to be of any further use than merely to prevent its being carried on within their own walls. Outside that small range they either have not, or do not exercise any jurisdiction.

[On] March 1st, 1810, the Anna, a brig from the Havanna, under Spanish colours, anchored in the road of Cape Coast where she took in a cargo of slaves. . . . She received her slaves . . . from a mulatto, educated in England, possessed of property, and carrying on a considerable trade, [who] lives a short quarter of a mile from the castle, and would undoubtedly receive its protection in case of danger. The proceeding was conducted without any interruption from Cape Coast Castle (except a threat to fire on the brig) as the Governor does not conceive that it lay within his jurisdiction. Yet the person thus violating the laws of Great Britain lives under the protection of the British flag; and as the natives themselves who reside close to our forts are stated by the African Committee to acknowledge allegiance to the British Government, it might seem that they are under some sort of tie to admit such interference as would be necessary to support a law enacted chiefly for the benefit of their own country, and for the maintenance of which Great Britain has shown herself so particularly solicitous. The word allegiance (used and repeated by the African Committee) ought surely even in its lowest and most vague sense, to bear some such meaning. It can hardly have been used to convey an idea of influence and power, which upon trial turn out to be nothing.

If this opinion of the Governor be binding, then the road of Cape Coast may become a most convenient resort for foreign slave ships, and Great Britain must either endure so gross an insult or give up the settlement; seeing that its long continuance has not been able to procure for it sufficient respect and authority to control or influence

---

[1] Chr. Schonning, Governor 1807–17. On his agricultural experiments cf. Adams, C. D., *Activities of Danish Botanists in Guinea 1783–1850*, in Trans. Hist. Soc. Ghana, 1957.

[2] Of May 1805 (in C.O.267/28/2); it extended an agreement made in 1796.

the savage natives living under its walls, in a point of such vital importance to Africa and so much insisted on lately by Great Britain.

The home direction of these settlements might admit of some alteration. Whilst the great business of the Gold Coast was the slave trade, the choice of the Committee by the three ports from which it was principally carried on (Liverpool, Bristol, and London) might be very suitable; But now that a total change has taken place in the trade of that coast, some change also might with propriety be made in the direction of its concerns. London, Liverpool and Bristol might be limited to a smaller number and the deficiency be supplied by other gentlemen whose long and public hostility to the slave trade had clearly proved their desire to ameliorate the state of Africa.

[H.C.506 pp. 135–8]

15 Treasury Minute
22 October, 1811.

My Lords, observing that the recommendation of the . . . Commissioners to dismantle, or dispose of to individuals, certain of the forts on the Gold Coast is made subject to certain suggestions relative to the Danish and Dutch forts in Africa, upon which my Lords are not at present competent to form a judgement, are of opinion that it is expedient to enable the African Company to maintain all of those forts for the present, with the exception of that at Whydah, which my Lords think ought immediately to be relinquished, and for the support of which my Lords cannot recommend to Parliament that any grant should be made beyond the present year; but as no vote was proposed to Parliament during the last session for the maintenance of any of the said forts, under an expectation that the said Report of the African Commrs., which it was hoped would have arrived before the close of the session, would recommend the discontinuance of the whole or a great part of them, my Lords have thought it necessary under this present impression, to direct a Warrant to be prepared

out of the Civil List for £10,000, to be issued to the said Company for the service of the current year; and my Lords will propose to Parliament, early in the next session, to replace the said sum, & also such further grant as may seem necessary, when His Majesty's Government shall have determined on the policy of retaining all or any of these forts.   [T.70/35]

16 The African Committee to the Lords of the Treasury   9 April, 1812.

. . . .

It is impossible for us not to hesitate in giving our assent to opinions so directly opposite to that system of policy which, during the last two centuries, has been adopted, not only by the Government of this country, but also by every other commercial state in Europe. . . .

Settlements on the coast of Africa have hitherto been deemed valuable on two grounds; first, as conferring an exclusive right of trade upon the Power possessing them; and, secondly, as the only medium through which it can be safely and advantageously carried on. The trade with the Gold Coast principally consists in a traffic of native merchants who travel from the interior, and frequently from very great distances, to exchange their goods for articles of foreign production. As these merchants cannot wait for the ships to arrive, nor the ships for them, it results that resident traders are necessary for their mutual accomodation; and that country will trade to the most advantage which has the greatest number of them established at convenient stations on the coast. For the sake of security, both to their persons and property, these traders must necessarily reside in forts, or under the immediate protection of them.

With a view to the preservation of order and good government, we have been obliged to make regulations for preventing competition between the officers at the different out-forts: but we have at all times been careful not to allow them to obstruct the trade of the shipping or the settlements of free traders. . . .

By the abolition of the slave trade, the commerce of Africa was rendered so insignificant that it may have appeared scarcely worth the maintenance of the settlements on the coast. But it must be recollected that those settlements which are supported at so trifling an expense, were originally formed with no view to the slave trade, which was then neither in existence nor in contemplation and that one of the chief arguments urged for the abolition of that trade was that on the adoption of that measure, a new, more desirable, and more extensive commerce would, in process of time, be established in Africa. We will not pretend to determine the precise extent to which these bright anticipations are likely to be realized; but that considerable progress has already been made will appear from the [fact] . . . that in the three years which have elapsed since the abolition, the average export to that country has been £830,325, and that the imports have rapidly increased until they amounted in the year 1810 to above half a million sterling, exclusive of gold, which has been imported in far greater quantities than during the slave trade.

It is a lamentable but certain fact that Africa has hitherto been sacrificed to our West India colonies. Her commerce has been confined to a trade which seemed to preclude all advancement in civilisation. Her cultivators have been sold to labour on lands not their own; while all endeavours to promote cultivation and improvement in agriculture have been discouraged by the Government of this country, lest her products should interfere with those of our more favoured colonies. . . .

Before any material improvement can be expected to take place in any district of Africa, the slave trade must be completely annihilated, or at least driven from that part of the coast; for so long as any people carrying on that trade are in possession of a single fort in the same neighbourhood, their influence will be superior to

ours, and we shall be considered as opposed to the interests of the natives and be regarded with feelings of enmity. It is, besides, unquestionable that the British trade will not be able to exist where the slave trade is carried on. Those engaged in the latter will monopolize the whole. Ships can always carry more goods than are required to purchase their complement of negroes, and with little additional expense and without loss of time, the surplus goods may be converted into gold, ivory, &c; whereas the British merchant must fit out his vessel expressly for the purpose of purchasing those articles.

The Commissioners complain that the forts, instead of preventing the slave trade, have permitted it to be carried on even in the towns under their walls, . . . which . . . we have stated to profess allegiance to us. . . . But we have never asserted that the dominion of the forts was absolute, nor led the public to expect anything so absurd as that about 35 Europeans, with a handful of men, half soldiers, half slaves, dispersed in eleven weak forts, along a coast of 350 miles in extent, could combat, and with force oppose, the wishes and interests of surrounding nations, or even of the towns in their immediate neighbourhood. The allegiance professed by the towns is founded, not upon power, but upon mutual advantage and security, and has always been understood to leave them in full possession of their native rights and privileges, and of the usages of that country by which they are entitled to carry on every description of trade.

But the Commissioners are the more astonished at the inability of the forts to suppress the traffic in question because . . . the abolition is for the interest of Africa itself and . . . therefore the towns should be particularly willing to admit such interference as may be necessary to carry it into effect.

Can these gentlemen be serious in such an observation? Can the wildest theorist expect that a mere act of the British Legislature should, in a moment, inspire with wisdom and refinement the unenlightened natives of the vast continent of Africa, and persuade them that it is for their interest to contribute to, or even to acquiesce in, the destruction of a trade, not inconsistent with their prejudices, their laws, or their notions of morality and religion, and by which alone they have been hitherto accustomed to acquire wealth, and to purchase all the foreign luxuries and conveniences of life? . . .

So long as the vessels of other countries are allowed to frequent the coast, the forts will be unable to prevent the trade in slaves. Until, therefore, we can interdict such intercourse by foreign vessels, good policy would forbid our imposing the impracticable duty of attempting it by force, upon those whose prospects of success in the great work of introducing cultivation and civilization so essentially depend on their preserving the friendship, confidence and respect of the natives.

We are aware of but one mode by which the slave trade can be entirely abolished in this part of Africa, and that, we feel it our duty to recommend. It is the occupation by this nation of the whole of the Gold Coast, . . . stationing good and respectable garrisons in the most commanding situation, [and,] at the rest, establishments sufficient to mark our possession. The sole right of external trade or internal being thereby vested in this country, two or three small ships of war, with some troops or an extra number of marines on board, should be kept constantly cruizing on the coast, to prevent the approach of all vessels not British. . . .

[The annexation of Holland by France makes it essential that we occupy the Dutch forts.] Great Britain, in the abolition of the slave trade, has made an immense sacrifice . . . of unparalleled liberality: but if the coast of Africa be allowed to remain in its present state, she will eventually feel that this sacrifice has been made, not to the cause of justice and humanity, but to France. . . .

Of the particular forts recommended by

the Commissioners to be abandoned, SUCCONDEE has a good landing place and considerable gold trade. . . . The natives are remarkably quiet and tractable, and more favourable to cultivation and improvement than any on the Gold Coast. As we have here only a settlement, and the Dutch a respectable fort, on the capture thereof, a mere mark of possession might be left at our own. COMMENDAH has some gold and ivory trade, furnishes corn and yams, . . . and . . . is the only place in our possession which furnishes canoes. TANTUM, valuable as a point of communication, is a place where the trade in slaves has been extensively carried on. It yields some gold and ivory, and abundance of provisions. WINNEBAH is useful in many respects. It is most fertile and a good corn country, has plenty of fish and stock, a good landing place, and should on no account be abandoned, as it is, in certain seasons, the only place on the Gold Coast which can supply fresh water to the shipping. It is also necessary to keep up the communication between Accra and Annamaboe, as must be evident to every person informed of the mode of travelling in that country. PRAM PRAM . . . has weaker claims to notice, but . . . should not be abandoned until a general peace shall have determined the footing that we are permanently enabled to retain in Africa. [Even Whydah should not be rashly abandoned.] . . .

That some of [the forts] are in bad repair and in an imperfect state of defence, we are ready to admit. . . . We have repeatedly represented to Parliament and pressed upon the consideration of His Majesty's Ministers . . . the insufficiency of the annual grant for their improvement, or even for their support. . . . During the existence of the slave trade, while a large number of ships were constantly trading upon the coast, the forts, although weak in themselves, were in security because the interest which the shipping had in their support made them always ready to join in their defence. But now, when the abolition has deprived them of this resource and the whole of the coast is involved in war, it becomes absolutely necessary that they should be substantially repaired and efficiently garrisoned, and two or three ships should be kept constantly cruising on the coast. . . .

In thus venturing to express our opinions, so much at variance with those of the Commissioners, we think it proper to observe that some of our members have resided many years at one or the other of all the forts, . . . while, from the very short stay of the Commissioners on the Coast, and the very limited part of it actually visited by them, they could have had but little personal means of ascertaining the expediency or probable effects of the measures which they have recommended.

In the concluding paragraph of their report, respecting the home direction of the settlements, the Commissioners seem to have travelled rather beyond the limits of their office. We have not understood that the expediency of altering the constitution of the African Company was submitted to their consideration. Nor could it have been necessary to send three Governors of Sierra Leone to the Gold Coast to ascertain the propriety . . . of transferring the direction of the settlements on that coast to themselves or their friends. . . .

[H.C.506 of 1816 pp. 104–8]

17 S. COCK TO GOVERNOR AND COUNCIL AFRICAN OFFICE, LONDON, 10 JULY, 1812.
Gentlemen,

By direction of the Committee I enclose you copies of a letter from Robert Peel Esqr.,[1] Secretary to Earl Bathurst,[2] and its enclosures; Vizt. 1st., Extract of a Letter to Mr. Croker from Commodore the Honble. F. P. Irby, dated Sierra Leone, 4th March, 1812, representing that great assistance had been given to the Portuguese

[1] Robert Peel (later Sir Robert) (1788–1850), Conservative statesman, and Prime Minister 1834–5 and 1841–6; entered Parliament 1809; Under-Secretary for War and the Colonies 1809–12.

[2] Henry Bathurst, 3rd Earl Bathurst 1762–1834; M.P. 1793; President of the Board of Trade 1807–12; Secretary of State for War and the Colonies 11 June, 1812, to 30 April, 1827.

carrying on the Slave Trade by the British Settlements on the Gold Coast, by supplying vessels with canoes and water.

2nd. A request from Captn. Irby, 'that the Governors of the Forts at the British Settlements will acquaint all Portuguese Vessels employed in the Slave Trade that they are liable to be captured if found trading at any places but such Settlements as are in the Possession of the Portuguese: and also that the Governors will not allow canoes to be supplied them from the Forts for the purpose of Slave Trading, all Persons assisting vessels in that traffic being liable to the Penalties of the Act of Parliament passed the 14th of May, 1812.'

Immediately on receipt hereof, you are to take the most effectual methods for procuring a compliance with what is required in the Papers herein referred to, at each of the Settlements in your charge; acquainting the several Governors, and other persons stationed thereat, that the Committee expect the most implicit obedience from them to the orders herein given.

I am directed further to require that you report to the Committee every instance that may come to your knowledge of disobedience of these orders, or of conduct on the part of any Persons in the employ of the Committee tending to promote or countenance the trading in slaves, in order that such measures may be adopted as shall appear to be expedient to prevent the recurrence of proceedings so contrary to law, and to the repeated order of the Committee.

[T.70/73]

18 THE AFRICAN COMMITTEE TO THE TREASURY   24 APRIL, 1813.
The Committee of the Company of Merchants trading to Africa beg leave to submit to their Lordships the . . . copy of a letter addressed to them, on the subject of guns and gunpowder being prohibited from exportation to Africa. The merchants interested in that trade are prepared to show to their Lordships . . . that guns and gunpowder are indispensably necessary

to the carrying on the trade between this country and Africa.

The Committee, after taking the best possible information on the subject, have no hesitation in respectfully recommending to their Lordships, a renewal of the order for the export of guns and gunpowder; being fully satisfied that those articles do not in any way tend, any more than others, to promote a contraband trade in slaves; the great expenditure being occasioned by the celebration of the funeral customs and in the amusements of the natives.

The Committee beg leave further to submit to their Lordships, that if the British merchants are not permitted to take a portion of their cargoes in guns and gunpowder, they must abandon the trade altogether, . . . which will throw it into the hands of neutral and other nations.

The Committee can assure their Lordships that since the abolition of the slave trade, the importation of African products has very materially increased, especially in the article of gold . . . which, they doubt not, is capable of being further extended, provided the merchants are permitted to regulate their cargoes suited to the demand of that country.

Guns and gunpowder are also essential in the purchase of rice and indian corn, of which (though this branch of commerce is but in an infant state) several cargoes have been carried to the Peninsula and to the West Indies. And if proper encouragement be given to the cultivation of these articles, that great continent will very soon become productive and useful. . . .

[H.C.431 p. 57]

19 G. BARNES TO EARL BATHURST
        AFRICAN OFFICE, 23 APRIL, 1814.
My Lord,

Although, in the important negotiations now pending for the re-establishment of the peace of Europe, we are convinced that the interests of every part of His Majesty's Dominions will be duly attended to, we trust we shall not be deemed intrusive in address-

ing your Lordship respecting the British Settlements on the coast of Africa, placed by Act of Parliament under our charge.

During the war, the absolute dominion of the sea enabled this country, not only to enforce the abolition of the slave trade upon her own subjects, and those of other states which have adopted the same system, but virtually to prevent almost every European nation from carrying on that traffic.

The return of peace will now restore, to states possessing settlements on the Coast of Africa, the power of renewing the trade in slaves; and our present object is to prevent, if possible, the injurious consequences likely to result, from this change, to the British settlements on the Gold Coast.

In a paper addressed, on the 14th of April 1812, to the Lords of His Majesty's Treasury, we pointed out to them the value of these settlements, and of the new trade which had already been established on the Gold Coast. We pressed also upon the consideration of their Lordships, the impossibility of this trade's continuing if the slave trade should be renewed in its vicinity; and strongly recommended that the Dutch forts which would interfere with our own should be taken possession of.

We take the liberty to annex extracts from that Paper of the parts to which we allude:—

The opportunity of preventing, by warlike means, the slave trade from interfering with the legitimate commerce which has been so successfully commenced, and which the public in this country have evinced so strong a desire to see extended in Africa, having been lost, it becomes our duty again to solicit the attention of His Majesty's Ministers to this object, while it may yet be effected by negotiation.

The first and most desirable point to be obtained is that all nations should be induced, like ourselves, to abolish the slave trade; and that each should grant to the other the power of enforcing the laws already existing or to be enacted for this purpose. If this cannot be gained, they should at least cede to us the exclusive possession of those parts of the Coast on which we have already established a different species of trade.

France does not of right possess any settlement on the Gold Coast, nor in its neighbourhood, except at Whydah; and although the British fort at this place has been abandoned, still the trade in slaves could not be carried on, either from Whydah, or from any part of the Bight of Benin, without the most serious injury to the British commerce on this coast. It would also be desirable that France should distinctly acknowledge our exclusive right of possession & trade on the Gold Coast and in the Bight.

The Dutch forts are interspersed with the British along the whole extent of this coast, and unless Holland can be induced entirely to abolish the slave trade, either their forts or our own must be abandoned. That trade, and the British commerce, cannot possibly exist together; nor will the lives even of the persons in charge of our forts be in safety if it is to be carried on upon the coast where they are resident and in avowed opposition to it; and if such is to be the result of our abolition law, that measure, instead of being a sacrifice of national interest to principles of justice and humanity, worthy the imitation of all nations, and the admiration of all ages, will be an act of equal folly and cruelty. We shall only have transferred to a rival a valuable trade, leaving the unfortunate African still to be sold as a slave, for the cultivation of a foreign soil, and to be transported at the unrestricted mercy of a Dutch merchant, instead of enjoying the protection of those mild laws, which, having been passed in this country before the abolition, insured to him all the comforts his unfortunate situation would admit of.

By the Committee &c.   [T.70/73]

20 S. COCK TO EARL BATHURST
21 JUNE, 1814.

My Lord,

We had the honour of addressing Your Lordship on the 23rd April, when the Treaty with France was under discussion, stating the conditions which, in our opinion, it appears to be necessary to obtain for the protection of the British Settlements on the Gold Coast of Africa. Since that date the Treaty has been signed and published, and we observe, with considerable alarm, that the 8th article, instead of specifying the Possessions and assigning the limits within which the French are to be allowed to carry on the slave trade on the coast of Africa, allows them generally to resume all the possessions which they held in the year 1792.

The French have at all times evinced the greatest anxiety to erect forts and to obtain a share of the trade upon the Gold Coast, while this Country has uniformly refused to grant to them any establishment there; and, even in time of peace, has driven off their ships and excluded them from all participation in that trade. By the general terms in which the above-mentioned Article of the Treaty is expressed, France will not only be enabled to renew her attempts upon the trade, but, unfortunately, the settlement of Amakow,[1] which, without any right, they established about the year 1786, [and] was, (notwithstanding the remonstrances of this committee and their application to Government for its removal) suffered to exist long subsequent to the year 1792, and its reestablishment may consequently be claimed under the present Treaty. At that time, the settlement was perhaps thought by Government too trifling to be worth a dispute with France, as it admitted them only to a small share of a trade in which we had a preponderating influence and control. Your Lordship will however perceive that the matter now stands upon very different ground. The French being allowed to renew the slave trade, which is interdicted to the subjects of this country, this station, in the very centre of the British possessions on the Gold Coast, will become immediately the emporium of that commerce; so that

[1] About a mile east of Saltpond, near the modern Ankaful. Cf. J. N. Matson, 'The French at Amoku' (*Transactions Ghana Historical Society*, vol. i, pp. 47–60).

the question now will be, whether we shall be compelled to relinquish settlements of long establishment, of considerable extent and value, and an infant trade, in which the Nation feels considerably interested, by suffering them to recover a settlement, formed in defiance of the rights of this country and of our existing treaties with the natives, and to renew (on a part of the Coast from which they have now been for some time excluded) a traffick declared by both nations to be repugnant to the principles of natural justice? We have before stated to Your Lordship, that this traffick and the British Commerce cannot exist together, and that the lives even of the persons in our forts will not be in safety while the slave trade is carried on in their neighbourhood. . . .

By the 1st additional Article of the Treaty, France engages that the slave trade shall, on her part, cease definitively in 5 years; although this stipulation of a definite period when the French slave trade shall cease does not appear to satisfy the wishes of the publick, it will, nevertheless, we apprehend, be found of incalculable importance, provided only that its performance can be relied upon; but it will be obvious to your Lordship, that France, at the expiration of 5 years (a period too short for the re-establishment of her Colonies, but sufficiently long to convince her of the value of this trade) will probably feel little disposed to pass laws for its abolition. . . . Under the existing circumstances, we submit to your Lordship, it will be extremely desirable that an agreement should be entered into between this country and France, that, after the expiration of 5 years, it shall be lawful for the ships of either power to capture vessels and cargoes engaged in the slave trade, unto the subjects of whichever state belonging. By this means, the onus of insisting on a termination of the French trade at the end of 5 years, will be removed from this country, and the performance of the stipulation will be most effectually secured. . . .

[T.70/73]

21 GOVERNOR WHITE TO THE AFRICAN COMMITTEE

CAPE COAST CASTLE, 30 APRIL, 1814. I beg to inform you that this part of the coast so immediately within my knowledge does not exhibit those signs of improvement my sanguine hopes led me to fancy were perceptible a few years past.

The people of Cape Coast are peaceably disposed and well behaved towards the whites. Quarrels between one part of the town and another occasionally take place, but they are easily terminated in an amicable manner by the interference of the Castle. Gold and ivory are brought from the interior in exchange for East India and Manchester goods, guns, powder, lead and iron. Cape Coast may be considered the emporium of trade, probably owing to the number of free traders residing in the town, and was peace established on a permanent basis, no doubt the trade would benefit very considerably. I have frequently exerted myself to effect so desirable an event, but from the obstinacy of the Fantees have as frequently failed. . . .

[Housebreaking is a serious problem.] I am the more particular, Gentlemen, in mentioning these circumstances to you as it may aid you in estimating the chance or probability there is of civilizing thousands of people, when those so immediately under our eye set such bad examples. I, and . . . many of your officers, give encouragement to industry and agriculture. To what permanent good does it tend? If any gentleman, who has been in the country, bears in his memory that the natives of Africa consider a Framfra soup and a little corn a luxurious meal (as they do to this day, and will, in my opinion, to the last) if such a gentleman will consider that a people so easily satisfied, so trained to idleness from their infancy as to allot to females the labour they themselves ought to perform; so bigoted as to the customs of their forefathers; I am inclined to think that he, with all others possessed of a knowledge of Africa, will be of opinion with me, that unsuccessful will be all endeavours to civilize or dispose to agriculture the natives of it, before they are conquered. If you take into consideration . . . the many hundreds of blacks there are to one white, and that our intercourse with them is but casual, you will not be surprised at the little progress (if, indeed, any can be allowed) they have made towards civilization. . . .

[T.70/36. Part printed in H.C.506]

22 OBSERVATIONS ON THE STATE OF TRADE AT THE SEVERAL BRITISH FORTS ON THE GOLD COAST

Annamaboe

. . . During a residence at Annamaboe these nine months, there appears no improvement in agriculture, but some in the construction of their houses. The blacks who live near the fort were very turbulent when I resided in the fort ten years ago. They appear at present much better disposed, and have less disputes among themselves. There is a stagnation in trade owing to the war between the Fantees and Ashantees, in consequence of which the paths are frequently intercepted. Some of the principal people of Annamaboe town for these three months past have been in the country negotiating for peace, and when that desirable end (peace) is accomplished among them, the trade will be considerable in ivory and gold dust, and there may be a change for the better in other instances. It is more than five years since the paths from Accra to Cape Coast were stopped, a distance of one hundred miles by land; but within these few months the Accras and Fantees have come to terms of peace and the roads from Accra to Cape Coast are free for travellers.

Joseph Dawson, 1 April, 1815.

Accra

The trade of British Accra consists of gold dust and elephants' teeth only, brought down by the Ashantees, and exchanged for gunpowder, rum, cowries, India goods &c. The gold trade is carried on to a greater extent here than at any other part of the coast when the country is in a settled state. This at present is not the case, as the Accras have been for the last three years in a continued warfare with the Fantees, indeed, more or less since the year 1807, at which period the king of Ashantee waged war against the latter people. . . . The abolition of the slave trade has made no alteration at Accra, except that it has lowered the circumstances of a few of the blacks. There is no improvement whatever in agriculture.

Joseph Dawson, 24 April, 1814.

Tantum Querry

The trade consists of gold, ivory and palm oil, which are given in exchange for British and East India manufactures. Cowries pass current, and are preferred by the natives of this part to gold. The population of Tantum is but small; 500 is the utmost. The inhabitants of a town $1\frac{1}{2}$ miles to the eastward called Lagoe, (the chief of which receives pay from the fort), are more numerous. They employ themselves in fishing and agriculture, the principal part in the former pursuit, and some few get a livelihood by trade. . . . The soil on the sea-side is not adapted for cultivation, and only during the rainy season will vegetation thrive. Previous to the rains commencing, the natives clear and cultivate a few spots along the sea-coast. After the crop (maize) is gathered, the wood soon grows up, and the country resumes the appearance of an immense forest. Yams, plantains, bananas and other indigenous plants are cultivated more in the interior, where the soil is richer, and where they are not exposed to the sea-breeze, so very injurious to vegetation. . . . The inhabitants . . . possess as little energy and enterprize as their neighbours, and are equally strangers to industry. All the necessaries of life are easily procured, and their wants are supplied without much labour. Certain kinds of work are performed by the men, but the drudgery devolves entirely upon the women. The gold and ivory trade is very inconsiderable. . . .

John Hope Smith, 25 April, 1815.

Apollonia

The trade of Apollonia has of late been very indifferent, owing to quarrels between the Caboceer and the surrounding inhabitants. It is expected soon to revive again. It consists in gold and ivory in exchange for East India and British manufactures, with powder, lead and iron.

Diggle Bayley, 1 April, 1815.

Dixcove

The trade consists of gold, ivory and palm oil for which you give in exchange, India and Manchester goods, also rum, gunpowder, iron and lead bars &c. There has been no material change since the last state and condition was rendered in.

Js. Mollan, 1 April, 1815.

Succondee

The trade consists chiefly in gold dust, for which are given British and India manufactures, rum, tobacco, iron, lead &c. The returns . . . continue at the old average.

Wm. Hy. Blenkarne.

Commenda

. . . The nature of the trade here is the barter of East India and Manchester goods, also powder, iron, lead and rum, for gold, ivory, palm oil and redwood boards. The extent of one year's trade would not exceed 100 oz. gold, 60 puncheons palm oil, half a ton of ivory, and 1,000 boards. The character of the people much the same as in the Fantee country, except not so addicted to drinking and pilfering. Conduct very peaceable towards the fort. The progress of agriculture has decreased since the abolition of the slave trade, there not being that vent for their commodities which there was when shipping had frequent recourse here. The abolition has not been attended with any visible effect, except making the natives poor and dissatisfied.

J. Mollan, 26 April, 1814.
[H.C.506 of 1816 pp. 15–17]

23 NAMES OF THE . . . KINGS AND CABBOCEERS . . . WHO RECEIVE MONTHLY STIPENDS . . . AT THE SEVERAL FORTS ON THE GOLD COAST   1814.

Cape Coast Castle.

Ando,[1] Dey of Fetue, 120 s.: Ahenebrah, king of Fetue, 40 s.

Cape Coast is in the kingdom of Fetue. The Dey has always received ground rent for the castle. It is from Fetue, and the neighbouring villages, that the natives and garrison are chiefly supplied with corn and other provisions. In case of disturbance with either Town or Castle, these people can prevent supplies from being brought down.

Braffoes and Curranteers of Fantee, for water custom, 60 s.

These people are the supreme chiefs of the Fantee country. By assembling the chiefs of Abrah and Murram they can at any time shut all communications between inland Fantee and the water-side.

Pynims and Cabboceers of Annaqua, Amissa and Annishan, 60 s.

These are little states on the sea-shore inhabited chiefly by fishermen, through which towns all communications must necessarily pass: but being situated at a distance from our forts, and those people much addicted to piratical acts, they have it in their power, upon any pretence, to stop messengers or others from passing and repassing. Their pay has been given to ensure a free communication, with the additional consideration that they acknowledge allegiance to the English nation. The British flag is hoisted in those towns.

At Annamaboe.

Amoony Commah, king of Annamaboe, 160 s. This is the most powerful prince we have to deal with, and one who has very great influence in all the Fantee towns near the sea-shore.

Coffee Sam, captain of the town, 40 s. The next man of most influence; of great use in cases of disturbance between the

[1] Probably Adoko.

natives and the garrison, or with the shipping.

Quacoe, ground landlord, 30 s. A Cabboceer who, independent of his situation as ground landlord, is otherwise a man of influence in the town.

Blankett, Cabboceer of Aggah, 40 s. Aggah [Eja] is a considerable town, situated at nearly an equal distance between the English fort at Annamaboe and the Dutch fort at Cormantyn. These people acknowledge allegiance to the English nation and hoist the British flag.

At James Fort, Accra.

Zey Coomah, King of Ashantee, 160 s. He receives pay as ground landlord and is a very powerful prince.

Quow, Caboceer of Accra town, 80 s. The principal man in the town, and the late Cudjoe's heir.

Abbe, Caboceer of Pram Pram, 20 s; Abraboe, same of the Upper Town. These persons are the principals, one of the Upper and the other of the Lower town of Pram Pram. . . .

At Tantum Querry.

Coffee Inchafoah, ground landlord, 80 s. And is otherwise a a man of influence in the Fantee country.

Eshow, king of Lagoe [Legu]; Coffee Mufer, Caboceer of Mumford, 20 s. (each). These people have always acknowledged allegiance to the English. Lagoe and Mumford are considerable trading towns, and many attempts have been made at different times by both the Dutch and Danes to obtain a settlement there, but they have failed through the attachment of these Caboceers who constantly hoist the British flag.

At Apollonia.

Sackey, king of Apollonia, 160 s. The king of Apollonia commands a great extent of country. His immediate predecessor, named Ammoniah, had been for many years first solicited by the Dutch to shut the river against the English, and was

then threatened that if he did not do so they would send a force and compel him; in consequence of which, on an application from him for protection, a representation was made by the Governor and Council to the African committee, and a fort was erected at that place under the sanction of Parliament.

Allumah, Town Caboceer, 160 s. This man's predecessor was the brother of Ammoniah, equally attached to the English, and the next in consequence to the king.

Quamino Amoa, River Caboceer, 30 s. Useful in facilitating communication over the river.

At Dixcove.

Quashie Bundy, ground landlord, 30 s.; Tando Cudjoe, principal Caboceer, 40 s. These persons have each great influence over the towns they reside in, and their predecessors have shown great attachment to the English in various disputes with the Dutch who have a fort immediately to windward, and another to leeward of Dixcove.

Attah, Caboceer of Atchuma [Achowa], 20 s. Atchuma has several times been attempted to be taken by the Dutch, but the Caboceer is wholly in favour of the English interest and hoists the British flag.

At Succondee.

Badu Quamino, ground landlord, 20 s; Quamino Gemfeah, Caboceer, 30 s; Quacoe Finn, same, 20 s. These persons are in like manner as other Caboceers, paid for the influence they have over the townspeople in preserving peace and good order.

At Commenda.

Quashie, king of the town, 60 s.; Gappea, Principal Caboceer, 40 s.; Baffoe, head of the fishing town, 20 s.; Quashie Bebeniah, captain-general, 20 s. Commendah fort is within gunshot of the Dutch fort. These Caboceers have on several occasions proved their attachment to the English, and in a very particular instance during the war in 1782 when the Dutch fort was taken and destroyed.   [H.C.506 pp. 100–1]

3 The Select Committees and the James–Bowdich Mission, 1816–1817

THE final defeat of Napoleon at last allówed the British Government to take the affairs of the Gold Coast into serious consideration. In 1816, and again in 1817, Select Committees of the Commons took evidence (24–5) which throws much light on the working of the African Company in its last years, but provided no clear guide to future policy. Their report (31) betrays some dissatisfaction with the Company's record, particularly with reference to African education and exploration, but did not go beyond recommending that the Governor should be appointed by the Crown.

The Company meantime planned to make good its shortcomings. A schoolmaster was appointed at Cape Coast, and in 1816, after another invasion had led to renewed negotiations with the Ashantis (26), it was decided to send a mission to Kumasi itself to place Anglo-Ashanti relations on a proper footing (27). Both Dutch and English were bidding at this time for the Asantehene's favour, and the former with their better supplies of gunpowder (18), and alleged readiness to encourage the slave trade (28), were in a strong position. The early days of the mission were critical, and Thomas Bowdich, nephew of the Governor of Cape Coast Castle, had to take over from his immediate superior (29, 32) before he succeeded in signing a somewhat equivocal treaty (33).[1] The Company made the most of this success (32), which in reality settled none of the problems at issue. The Asantahene looked to a speedy re-opening of the slave trade (34) and regarded the payment of 'notes' as token of his absolute sovereignty over the people of Cape Coast and Anomabu (30), a view which Governor Hope Smith declined to accept (38).

[1] For a recent discussion of the Ashanti Mission of 1817 see E. F. Collins, *The Panic Element in 19th c. British relations with Ashanti* in Trans. Hist. Soc. Ghana, 1962.

24 EVIDENCE OF SIMON COCK before the Select Committee on African Forts. . . .
1816.
The Committee observe, that the grant of Parliament for the maintenance of the forts on the Gold Coast is invested in the African Company here, upon goods which are sent out to the Coast; the Committee would be glad to know at what rate, or upon what terms, these goods are issued upon the coast, and in what manner they are there disposed of? — They are issued at what is termed a Company's price, which, upon an average, is about 50 per cent. dearer than they cost in England, but they are subject to the expense of freight, insurance, and different charges, which may amount to

about 12½ per cent., so that the public gain, by the manner of issuing, about 37½ per cent.; they are distributed in the payment of the salaries of the several persons in the Company's service on the Coast, but certain parts are used for repairing the forts and defending them, such as gunpowder, bricks, mortar, stone and so on. . . .

Then when you send out these articles, your officers select the articles they wish to have? — No, they do not; they send home, upon the return of the ship, a list of the cargo they wish to receive; we inquire at what prices the goods may be bought, and if we find we can comply with their wishes, and yet give the public an average of £50 per cent. profit, we then comply with their desire; but if not, we then send a small quantity of the goods which are dear, and a large quantity of those that are cheap. . . .

Do you not perceive, that if you were to send out an unusually large quantity of any article, it must lower its price? — No; the trade price in Africa never varies.

I suppose you mean by that, the merchants never sell the articles under this trade price? — I mean that a barrel of gunpowder upon the Gold Coast, has gone for fifty years at the same price that it does now. . . .

When you state that the price of gunpowder in Africa is always the same, do you mean the price at which you deliver it to your officers, or the real price the Africans will pay? — The nominal price to the Africans is always the same, but in buying it, he will give less of the article which he has to exchange it for. . . .

Do you apprehend that those goods which, having cost an hundred pounds in England, you give in payment £150 upon the Gold Coast, may not those goods probably obtain from the natives the price of £200? — That must depend very much upon the state of the trade at the time the goods arrived; but it is the particular care of the Committee, after they have determined upon the goods they will send, to secure proper profit to the public, and at the same time to give the utmost profit that it will admit of to their servants.

Do you not perceive, therefore, that while on the one hand it is possible that the nominal salaries of the servants of the Company may be considerably larger than the real salaries, on the other hand, the real salaries may be as considerably larger than the nominal salaries? — From a competition in trade, I think that scarcely possible; but I have always hoped and believed, that the goods we ship do give to our servants their salaries in sterling equal, or nearly equal to their nominal amount. . . .

25 EVIDENCE OF JAMES SWANZY.[1] . . .

Can you inform the Committee what proportion the slave trade bore to the total trade in which you were engaged? — Out of all proportion; I should conceive the slave trade was nine-tenths of the whole trade.

Do you know that the salaries of the Governors of the forts have been lately increased? — Yes.

To what amount, and what were the reasons for the increase? — I cannot exactly recollect the increase; it was probably 75 per cent. upon the salary, in consequence of the diminution of the profits arising from the abolition of the slave trade; they could not live upon their preceding salaries.

At the time that you was governor of the forts, were any judicial proceedings carried on by the respective governors and councils with regard either to the Europeans or to the natives? — They had no civil authority, no civil jurisdiction; they had no power of trial.

Did not civil offences frequently happen? — Frequently.

What then was the consequence? — Those offences with respect to the natives were left to their own laws. . . .

Did no instances occur in which disputes arose, or offences were committed between the Europeans and the natives? — Certainly.

In what manner, and by what authority were those disputes settled, or the grievances redressed? — By the authority of the Governor and Council, using their own discretion. . . .

Then if any European defrauded a native, how should you have acted? — I should have obliged him to give satisfaction to the injured party.

When you use the term obliged, by what means of compulsion would you have obliged him? — By our soldiers, if he chose to resist.

[1] 1767–1823. Resident on the Gold Coast 1789–99 and 1817–23: member of the African Committee, 1813–16. Cf. Henry Swanzy, 'A trading family in the 19th century Gold Coast' (*Trans. Ghana Hist. Soc.*, i, 87–120).

Did any such case ever occur? — I do not recollect any. . . .

Did the natives residing within the district attached to the fort, or in the neighbourhood, ever apply to the Governor and Council for their interference, either in disputes among themselves or in disputes with the Europeans? — Frequently; especially in disputes among themselves.

In what manner were such disputes settled? — In general, always indeed, by the mediation of the fort.

By that do you mean the Governor? — Yes, certainly.

And according to what law? — Their own discretion.

Did they uniformly submit to those decisions? — For the most part, but not uniformly.

In case of resistance, what measures were taken? — The Governor still continued his best offices, but never by force interfered. . . .

Has the African Committee taken any measures since the abolition of the Slave Trade to promote the civilization of the natives, and what is usually called the legitimate commerce of the country? — They have, as far as their limited means would allow, given every possible encouragement to trade, and steps are in progress towards the education of the inhabitants of that country.

What are such steps, and how long have they been taken? — About one year ago they appointed a schoolmaster, and associated with him two of their clerks, natives of the country, for the purpose of educating the natives of Cape Coast Town, and their means are too limited to extend that system.

Have any other means been taken besides those which you have mentioned? — We have also appointed a clergyman, who has not yet had an opportunity of going to Africa.

Of what nature is the accommodation which the forts afford to trade? — Very great; they keep open the communication with the interior, they are the depots for goods, they protect the British subjects residing near them; by these means the trade is collected day by day, and a collection of three months is shipped in 24 hours, without which no ship could profitably trade to the Gold Coast, as she would otherwise be obliged to stay for three months at each point to collect the same quantity of goods. I would wish to add also, that these forts give an exclusive trade, to a considerable extent, to the British subject.

Do free traders, not in the service of the Company, frequent the forts for the purpose of commerce? — Constantly. . . .

In your opinion they have as many opportunities of carrying on their trade to advantage as the resident servants of the Company in the forts? — Much greater . . . because they are wholly employed in their own business, whereas the Company's servants are employed the greater part of the day on public duties; they can also remove from place to place at pleasure; the Company's servant cannot remove without the permission of his superior, which is never granted for the purpose of trade.

Do those occasional free traders purchase goods immediately of the natives, or as they think fit, or only through the intervention of the Company's servants? — Always directly from the natives, and never through the Company's servants. . . .

Have the African Committee taken any measures to promote the success of the attempts now making to explore the interior of Africa? — Yes; but they have not been officially applied to; and I go further and say, I am clearly of opinion that to reach the Niger, the point from which the exploring of the interior of Africa should commence is the Gold Coast. Merchants from Howsee [Haussa], a large town on the Niger beyond where Mr. Park explored, were in the habit of coming down to the Gold Coast with trade; the journey then occupied about three months. . . .

Is it your opinion that if an additional sum were to be granted by Parliament to the

African Company, that great improvements would arise therefrom in the civilization of Africa, and in so far colonizing the inhabitants as to render Africa a source of profit to this country? — I have no doubt that if the means of the African Company were increased, they would very considerably improve that country; they would extend the benefits of education, civilization, and most materially increase the trade.

State to the Committee what would be, in your opinion, the sum requisite to attain the objects in view, and state those benefits in detail? — I would state £40,000 instead of £23,000; a sum that would enable the African Company to establish a school at each fort, to pay proper teachers, to subsist such of the children of the natives in the interior as would be inclined to send their children for education, but who would not pay anything towards the expense of it. It would enable them to fix a resident with the king of Ashantee, and thereby open a more direct intercourse, and make us better acquainted with that country.

You have stated the advantages to arise from this additional grant, chiefly, as it respects the civilization of Africa; do you not think that that very civilization would produce an increase of trade between this country and Africa? — That would be a necessary consequence; civilization must lead to cultivation, that must lead to a more extended use of British manufactures; it would ultimately lead to their dressing something in the British manner, and in time, would certainly consume a much larger proportion of our manufactures than at present. . . .

Have you any reason to believe that the king of Ashantee, or the other native chieftains would be willing to admit a resident from the African Company . . . ? — The King of Ashantee in particular applied to the Governor of Cape Coast Castle to send an officer to reside in his capital.

Was that ever made known to the British Government? — Never; not that I recollect.

When did that take place? — Probably six years ago.

Would this increased allowance enable the African Company to establish a system of civil jurisprudence, whereby justice might be done, not only to the Europeans, but to the natives of Africa? — That must emanate from Parliament; no money will give us power without an Act of Parliament. . . .

Do you not think that it is almost impossible successfully to civilize Africa without such institutions? — Certainly.

Therefore you hold that an application to Parliament to that effect is absolutely necessary to promote the objects in view? — I think it is a principal step towards effecting the objects in view. . . .

Is the ground upon which the fort stands considered as the territory of the African Company; and if so, what is the extent of their territory? — Our right to territory is very doubtful. We pay ground rents for the forts to the chief people of the town, or to the principal man of the country.

You recognize the sovereignty of the natives? — Yes, as lords of the soil, and entitled to rent; but not as possessing any other right of sovereignty. . . .

From what rank in life are [the Company's servants] usually taken? — From the middle class in life. . . .

What . . . is the nature and extent of the examination which the African Committee think it necessary to insist upon in the persons so sent out? — The extent of education that we look to is a perfect knowledge of arithmetic, writing a good hand, and possessing that fair education which is generally attained by youths of respectable connections at the age of 18. We do not make the classics a *sine qua non*. . . .

Do you appoint the Governors of Cape Coast Castle? — We do. . . .

If the Governor of Cape Coast Castle happens to die, who presides in that fort until you appoint another Governor? — The vice-president as a matter of course, as being second in command. The Governor of Annamaboe is vice-president of the Council. . . .

Who then succeeds to the government of Annamaboe? — The next senior officer in rank. . . .

You mean the commander of the fort that ranks next to Annamaboe? — They do not rank; Annamaboe is the only fort that ranks next to Cape Coast Castle; it is the individuals that rank, not the fort. . . .

Then, in point of fact, whenever a Governor of Cape Coast Castle dies there will be a change in all the other forts? — From the bottom to the top. . . .

Who are the members of the Council? — The Governors of Annamaboe, Accra, Tantum Querry and Commendah. . . .

Have the African Committee at present any intercourse with Government, so as to receive directions from them, and do they in fact receive any such? — They are not in the habit of applying to Government for instructions respecting the administration of their affairs in Africa . . . but upon important occasions they certainly communicate with Government.

Will you state upon what occasions such intercourse has taken place? — On one occasion in particular, respecting the war between the kingdom of Ashantee and the Fantee country, when they proposed to have the authority of Government to interfere for the purpose of settling that dispute, to which, I believe, they have not yet received an answer.

Have the African Committee, since the abolition of the slave trade, ever consulted Government as to what their views were with respect to the administration of the settlements? — I do not recollect that the African Committee have ever so consulted Government.

What orders then were given by the African Committee to their servants on the coast, respecting their conduct since the abolition of the slave trade? — The orders given were to use their utmost power to prevent any slave trade being carried on in and near their settlements. . . .

Have you heard of any other instances of the slave trade being assisted or permitted at any of our forts upon the coast of Africa? — I am fully persuaded that no slave trade has either been permitted or assisted among our forts, since I have been a member of the Committee. . . .   [H.C.506 of 1816]

26 THE ASHANTI INVASION OF 1816

(a) GOVERNOR AND COUNCIL TO THE COMMITTEE

CAPE COAST CASTLE, 27 MARCH, 1816.

The end of last month report was made to the Governor that the captain of the Ashantee army encamped at the back of Accra had determined on coming into the Fantee country for the purpose of possessing himself of the persons of Quow Saffaroutchie, Cudjoe Coomah and Coffee Ashantee[1] . . . whose conduct had given much displeasure to the King. He was met by the people of Adjumacoon [Ajumako] and Agoona [Agona] who, after fighting bravely, were entirely routed with the loss of many killed and several made prisoners. The Ashantees also had many killed.

The Fantees, hearing of the approach of the Ashantees, collected in great numbers to give them battle, but, ere they got sight of them, repented, and were happy to save themselves by flight. . . . On the 11th, information came that the Fantees had made a second attempt to stand their ground against the Ashantees, at that time near Abrah, but had fled from them in the most dastardly manner. On the 12th [we] sent two soldiers with a . . . flag of truce to the captain of the Ashantees near Abrah, inquiring the cause of his approaching so near this neighbourhood. The 13th . . . we were informed that a part of the Ashantees had moved to the back of Mouree. [The] afternoon [of the 14th] a great alarm in town from the appearance of one hundred Ashantees or Assins at the Salt-pond. Four thousand women and children at least slept in the castle this night. Friday 15th,

[1] Kwadwo Kuma was chief of Akim-Kotoku, and Kofi Asante chief of Akim Abuakwa.

the soldiers . . . sent . . . to the captain of the Ashantees . . . returned with the following message from the captain: 'That he was determined to pursue Quow Saffaroutchie, Cudjoe Commah and Coffee Ashantee to whatever place they might retreat; in fact, should they throw themselves in the earth, or secrete themselves in a rock, he would follow them.' . . . [We] promised that should it be in the Governor's power to seize the aforesaid men, he would do the same, as the means, he hoped, of restoring tranquillity. The town's people took fetish to the same effect, and a promise was given that the Governor would write to Mr Dawson to oblige his town's people to take similar fetish. . . .

E. W. White, F. James, W. Mollan.
[T.70/36 and H.C.431]

(b) THE SAME TO THE SAME
. . . 21 APRIL, 1816.

The affair with the Ashantees has been brought to a termination. A sum of 100 ounces of gold has been paid to them by the people of the town, and reciprocal oaths of friendship have been taken. . . .

(c) THE SAME TO THE SAME
. . . JUNE 1816.

On the 11th of May a letter was received from Mr. Sewell, Governor of Commenda, stating the apprehension his town's people were under of an attack from the Ashantees and Elminas. Messrs Hobart and Hutchison, with six soldiers, were immediately dispatched from this castle, but the report did not appear to be correct; and it is with much pleasure we inform you that there is perfect tranquillity between the Ashantees and all people under the protection of your forts. Part of the Ashantee army have marched towards Accra, and the remainder are expected to remove daily from their encampment in the Abrah country.

These two months past there has been considerable trade in gold dust and ivory, brought down by the Ashantees, and, as far as we can judge, there will be a much freer intercourse with them than hitherto, in consequence of their being in possession of the Fantee country, and in future the Fantees will be unwilling to dispute with them. . . .

(d) THE SAME TO THE SAME. . . .
4 OCTOBER, 1816.

A few days ago . . . the Ashantees . . . marched for their country, but after removing about thirty miles from their camp, they received orders from the king to return and proceed against a tribe called Crobos. . . . Since the departure of the Ashantee army from Abrah, several small parties have been down to this town and Annamaboe for the purpose of trading. . . . It is peculiarly gratifying to us to see an intercourse established which has not been known for sixteen years. . . .

The people of Winnebah have received the punishment which their infamous conduct merited.[1] On a moderate computation we may assert that one half of them have been carried away by the Ashantees. The solicitations of the remainder are strenuous to have the fort rebuilt. They have offered every service in their power on the occasion. [H.C.431]

27 AFRICAN COMMITTEE TO THE GOVERNOR AND COUNCIL

LONDON, 15 NOVEMBER, 1816.

The Committee are extremely anxious, (and in this respect the wishes of all classes of people in this country go with them), that no exertions should be spared to become better acquainted with the interior of Africa, and we consider the existing state of affairs to be most favourable for undertaking an exploratory mission into the dominions of the King of Ashantee.

If, therefore, nothing shall have transpired, in the interim of this despatch being received by you, to make the measure

[1] In 1812 the Winnebas had caused the death of their Governor (Meredith) for an alleged theft of gold. The Coast authorities retorted by destroying the fort. The Committee at home disapproved and gave orders for it to be rebuilt, but it never was. *Ibid.*

objectionable, we wish you to obtain permission from the King to send an embassy to his capital. If granted, you will select three gentlemen (one of them from the medical department) for that service; and let them be accompanied with a respectable escort, [to report in the fullest manner on Ashanti and the country beyond]. . . .

They should be directed also to procure and bring away (with the consent of the chiefs) any specimens of vegetable and mineral productions they may be able: and to ascertain where and how the natives collect the gold, and the extent to which the trade in that article and in ivory might be carried. It would, we conceive, be a most important advantage if the King of Ashantee and some of his chiefs could be prevailed upon to send one or more of their children to Cape Coast Castle, to be educated at the expense of the Committee, (to be attended by their own servants if required), under the guarantee of the Governor and Council for their personal safety, and that they should be sent back when required.

Another object would be to prevail upon the King to form and keep open a path, not less than six feet wide, from his capital, as far as his territories extend towards Cape Coast, you engaging, on the part of the Committee, to continue it from that point to Cape Coast; which we presume may be done at very small expense, by means of monthly allowances to the chiefs of such villages as lie in that line, upon condition that they shall not allow the paths to be overgrown with underwood or otherwise obstructed.

The gentlemen whom you may select, will, of course, be well advised by you not to interfere with any customs of the natives, however absurd, or in any way to give them offence; and they cannot too strongly impress upon the minds of the king and people of Ashantee, that the only objects His Britannic Majesty has in view are to extend the trade with that country; to prevent all interruption to their free communication with the waterside; and to instruct their children in reading, writing

&c, from which, as may be easily pointed out, the greatest advantages must arise to the Ashantees. . . . [T.70/74]

28 GOVERNOR AND COUNCIL TO THE AFRICAN COMMITTEE

CAPE COAST CASTLE, 5 MARCH, 1817.

We deem it our duty to inform you of the conduct of General Daendels[1] who is acting independent of his Government. We are aware that the desire of preventing the slave trade is a particular feature in the Dutch Government, but this traffic their representative in this country takes every opportunity of aiding and abetting. Portuguese vessels are furnished with canoes, and Spaniards supplied with water. The beginning of last month a large Spanish ship was four days at anchor in Elmina roads, receiving water and bartering dollars for such goods as were suited for the purchase of slaves. This vessel proceeded a short distance to leeward, and came to anchor off Apam . . . where the master purchased to the number of four hundred slaves, and carried them off the coast. A Spanish schooner also slaved from the same neighbourhood about three months ago.

During the time the Spanish ship was making her purchase, His Majesty's Ship 'Cherub' arrived, but to our very great disappointment we learnt from Captain Fisher that he was not legally authorized to interfere. The consequences of this continued intercourse with the natives of the Gold Coast made so serious an impression on the British residents . . . that they looked with unusual anxiety for the arrival of a Man-of-war, as the only means of reanimating their own hopes of inducing a commerce more congenial and valuable to Europe, by the prevention of a trade from which the natives can never be weaned. . . . They considered that the powers of British cruizers would speedily determine it, and their present disappointment is responsive to their previous confidence. . . .

It must be seriously impressed that this

[1] Governor of Elmina, 1816–18.

traffic is at present the only object of commerce congenial to the natives, or to which they are actively disposed. They will cling to it to the last moment. They may be deprived of it, but they cannot be diverted from it. They will quit it but from necessity, and make opportunities rather than neglect them.

The people of the coast are the brokers of those of the interior who supply the slaves; and as they are established from necessity as the sole medium betwixt the vessels and the sellers, they have every facility of adding to their regular profit by impositions which can neither be noticed by one party or detected by the other. This trade is consequently beyond all comparison so indolent and lucrative that even were there any appeal to their feelings, it would not influence in competition with such inordinate gain. Every other trade requires, comparatively, activity and exertion, and yields very inferior profit. It is unreasonable, therefore, to expect any conduct on the part of the natives but such as may be auxiliary to the slave traders.

The natives as well as the vessels have hitherto been cautious and confined in their conduct of the trade from their apprehension of British cruizers, yet still the most pernicious effects on the commerce and manners of Africa have been experienced from this secret intercourse. What then can be hoped for . . . from the confidence the restricted interference of British cruizers gradually confirms in both parties? The slave trade being invaluable to the natives, we must be viewed invidiously in comparison with those who still indulge in it. And this feeling we fear, may influence lasting connection with such foreign powers even in a different commerce. . . The Dutch, whose trading facilities, from their unlimited importation of powder, have already secured a large portion of the traffic of the coast, will further enjoy the advantage of supplying these slave ships for the market, from the reciprocal confidence and goodwill which has been observed in recent occurrences.

We view with regret this impunity of the trade, not only as fatal to our interests, but subjecting us to unmerited reflections affecting the languishing condition of commercial intercourse and civilisation, objects which . . . cannot be considerably advanced whilst a restricted slave trade is opposed to us. . . .   [H.C.431 pp. 51–2]

29 F. JAMES ESQ.[1] TO JOHN HOPE SMITH[2]
CUMMAZZEE.   22 MAY, 1817.[3]

After closing my letter of yesterday we were summoned to attend the King when the notes from Amooney and Aduco[4] were produced, and I was requested to explain their contents. This I did, with which the King appeared much displeased. He said that 'By right of conquest, whatever notes were held by the Fantees devolved to him and that their offering the pitiful sum of 4 [ackies] and your sanctioning such a transaction, was putting shame on his face and breaking his heart.' He deduced many instances of similar circumstances, where the notes had been transferred to him [notably after the conquest of Denkerah]. . . . He harped a good deal on the sum he received from Accra, an inferior fort, and that head-quarters should offer him 4 [ackies]. . . . Bearing in mind your conversation on the subject of these Notes, I endeavoured to parry the attack by stating that it was not you who offered him the sum of 4 [ackies] but the Fantee caboceers, who had requested you to make these Notes and deduct them from their pay, as an acknowledgement of the faith and allegiance towards him: that the pay he received from the British Government was that which had hitherto been paid at Accra, and which in future he would receive at headquarters.

He was far from satisfied with this explanation; said that your sanctioning

[1] One time Governor of Williams Fort, Whydah, and now Governor of James Fort, Accra.
[2] Governor-in-Chief from November 1816 to 1822.
[3] They arrived in Kumasi on 19 May.
[4] Amonu, chief of Anomabu, and Adoko, chief of Fante.

such a transaction belied our offers of friendship and convinced him that the English were wholly on the part of the Fantees against him, and asked if we should like to see the war with them renewed. I assured him, so far from it, our sole view was to establish friendship and amity, and that those Notes were of too trifling a nature to cause any disagreement between himself and the British Nation; that it was not on their account we visited him, but to establish a constant, friendly and free intercourse between himself and the forts; that if he would allow the Notes to remain until we returned, I would then convey his sentiments to you, and the affair could be amicably settled; recollecting your positively saying that Amoney and Aduco should not give up the whole of their notes, whatever might be the consequences, deterred me from offering to communicate with you immediately, as I conceived a refusal on your part might endanger our personal safety; at all events frustrate the whole intentions of the mission. He was still dissatisfied and assured us our presence alone prevented his despatching another army against the Fantees, and that unless the Notes were transferred to him, a renewal of the war was inevitable. Mr. Bowdich proposed an immediate communication, which I also saw was the only resource, but at that moment, like most blacks' palavers, there were too many talkers to get a word in. [Bowdich at this point expressed himself dissatisfied with James' conduct of the mission.] . . .

May 25th. This morning we were again summoned and the subject of the notes was again resumed. After some conference with the Cape Coast messengers and Amooney's, the whole of the generals and captains arose, and in a most solemn manner swore that unless the King was satisfied by the notes being given up, they would immediately proceed to the Fantee country and put every one to the sword, Cape Coast town included. Several of the captains, after swearing on the King, turned to us, and shook their cutlasses in a most threaten-ing manner. I have seen a good deal in Dahomey and other parts, but never did I experience a more alarming scene. . . .

There cannot be a moment's consideration how to act in so serious an affair. If the notes are not immediately given up, war will ensue, Cape Coast town will be attacked, the Castle will naturally defend it, a number of the enemy will be killed, and we shall fall a sacrifice to this enraged multitude of savages. Aduco, in my opinion, cannot be of any service to the British nation, nor, while we are friends with the King of Ashantee, can he do us any injury; therefore, depriving him of his note can be of little consequence, when so urgent a call demands it. Amooney is certainly entitled to a note which if given up can be renewed by the Company without the King knowing anything about it. . . . Any diminution of the notes will only make matters worse, as the King is already in possession of their amount from their own messengers. . . .   [T.70/40]

30 The King of Ashantee to Governor Hope Smith   Cumazee, 26 May, 1817.
The King of Ashantee, Zey, begs me to present his compliments to you and return his thanks to you and the King and Government of England for the presents which he considers very handsome. . . . He feels grateful also for you sending 4 officers to visit him. In answer to the offered friendship of the British nation, he returns them goodwill from his heart and wishes to consider them as brothers.

That the King of England has fought and conquered all Europe and consequently become the greatest monarch there; that he in like manner has conquered all the waterside, and therefore holds the command over them. He begs to know when an English army has taken a town, whether His Britannic Majesty would not expect the revenue of that town? That he has fought twice with the Fantees and that they voluntarily offered him vassalage. That the demand he made was the notes they received from the forts, which they have refused, and which hurts him much.

That in the slave trade the Fantees were not satisfied with cheating his people in their trade, but frequently seized and sold them, and that his respect for the whites made him remain quiet so long 'till at last he was obliged to send an army against them. That another cause of complaint against the Fantees was their giving protection to all runaways from this country, instead of giving them up to undergo the punishment due to their crimes. . . . That the cause of his sending an army a second time was their making war on the Accras and Elminas as his allies, after he had left the waterside. . . . That the Fantees sent for Cudjo Coomah from Akim, and wished him to join them against the king, which he did. . . . After this war the Fantis sent messages begging he would not send any more army against them; that they would acknowledge his superiority. These messengers were from the whole of the Fantee Country. That he returned for answer that if they would send the notes they held from the forts of Annamaboe and Cape Coast, he would come to terms with them, but not otherwise. . . . That in lieu of the notes in full he received those for 4 acs. . . . That he wishes the governor of Cape Coast to consider that the fort of Accra pays him 2 oz. [of gold][1] and that Annamaboe, a superior fort, and Cape Coast headquarters, whether it is correct to offer him 4 acs each? . . . That makes him think that our friendship is to the Fantees and not him. . . .

That the Fantees and Ashantees are not the same; that the Ashantees send good gold to purchase merchandize, and the Fantees mix bad with it. That the English give good powder, liquor and cloth; that the Fantees take some of the liquor out and put in water, cut Hf [?] off the cloth, and mix the powder with charcoal. . . . That if the English are really sincere in their friendship for him, they will give up the

[1] One gold ounce was worth £4 sterling, and contained 16 ackies.

two notes making his pay equal to that he receives from Elmina, which is 4 oz. per month. . . .

The king begs me to add that he has been informed *that the cause of the* abolition [of the slave trade] was his war with the Fantees, and that our idea was that the war ceasing, the other would naturally do so. This information I have denied, and given as a reason the slaves in the West Indies were already too numerous. He begs application may be made to the king of England to renew the trade. He has also been informed that the king of England not only refused to purchase slaves himself, but prevents the Dutch and other nations. That when he received this information it led him to believe everything else that was said to our prejudice; that our visit has in some degree removed those suspicions, and that the revewal of the slave trade will entirely do so.

The king begs you will not place too much dependence on the Fantees, as they are a deceitful set, but listen to him who is willing to supply anything that is wanted.
[T.70/40]

31 REPORT from the Committee on African Forts   25 June, 1817.
Your Committee have no difficulty in recommending that the same sum which the House has, for some years past, annually granted to the African Company — viz. £23,000 — be continued for the present year.

Your Committee, however, conceive that the more important part of the subject referred to them is the inquiry into the future policy which it may be expedient for Parliament to adopt in relation to this Company; and . . . they beg leave to submit their observations to the House under the following heads: — First, the past state; secondly, the present condition of the trade to the Company's settlements on the Gold Coast; thirdly, the probability of its future increases; fourthly, the state of repair and general condition of the forts and settlements; and, fifthly, the future policy which it may be most expedient to adopt in relation to this Company. . . .

1st. With respect to the trade to the Company's settlements on the Gold Coast antecedent to the present period. By far the principal part of that commerce was a trade in slaves, prior to the abolition of the slave trade by the legislature of this country, in 1807. The remaining articles of export from thence are stated to be chiefly gold dust, ivory, palm oil, and dye woods. Since the abolition of the slave trade, the total amount of commerce on the Gold Coast has consequently been materially diminished; but it is stated to your Committee, and there appears reason to think, that the trade in the remaining, or legitimate articles of commerce, above enumerated, may have increased. In proof of which, an account was given in by the African Committee to the Lords of the Treasury, in 1812.[1] . . . The exports, however, from this country to Africa, appear by the same account to have been materially diminished, as was to be expected, since the abolition. . . .

2nd. Your Committee now proceed to the actual state of the trade to the Company's settlements. This appears from all accounts to be inconsiderable; and your Committee see reason to believe that the trade in some of the minor settlements is confined to the governors and inferior officers there. It was stated by Mr. Banks, who went out to Africa in the Company's service, but resided some time as a free trader at Cape Coast Castle, which he left last in 1816, that at that time there were only five private traders at Cape Coast Castle, including himself, and scarcely any at the other forts.

It is stated by Mr. Bannerman, a native of Africa, who has been long resident as a free trader upon that coast, which he left only in November last, that at some of the outforts latterly, the only traders were the governors, who frequently made use of the boats and canoes as well as the slaves and

servants, kept at the public expense, for the purposes of their own trade. The Report of the Commissioners of Inquiry who went out to Africa in 1810 is to the same effect.

Your Committee, however, see reason to believe, from the evidence laid before them, that the prohibition to export gunpowder and firearms has been a main cause of the depression of trade to the British settlements, and of its transfer, in part, to foreign nations, to whom it has furnished increased facilities for reviving the slave trade; and the good effect of the removal of that prohibition which has taken place since your Committee were appointed, appears by the evidence of Mr. Cock, who says that since the permission to export was given by the Lords of the Council, several ships have been engaged to go to Africa, with an intention of loading on the coast with rice.

3rd. With regard to the probability of a future increase to any considerable extent, of the trade on the Gold Coast, beyond what may be expected from the recent permission to export gunpowder and arms, your Committee are unable to form a confident opinion. The witnesses who have represented the probability of such increase, have given that opinion upon the following suppositions: 1st, that the pecuniary means afforded by Parliament to the Company, should be increased with a view to enable them to establish a regular intercourse with the great interior kingdom of the Ashantees, and for other purposes. 2ndly, that the discouragements upon the imports of African produce should be removed. But, 3rdly, and principally, upon an end being put to the slave trade, which has, since the Peace, been revived, and is now carried on to an enormous extent by the Spaniards and Portuguese, and which all the evidence before the Committee concurs in representing as absolutely incompatible with and destructive of the legitimate commerce of Africa.

The degree to which the slave trade is now carried on by those nations, and its effect upon Africa, is so distinctly stated

---

[1] No. 11 above.

by . . . Sir James Yeo, in a letter . . . to the Admiralty, dated 7th November, 1816, that the Committee cannot forbear to lay before the House the following extract:

Though fewer negroes may have been enslaved since the Abolition Acts took place, with respect to this country, yet the cruelty to those now taken away by the Spaniards and Portuguese has increased quadruple, and these Acts appear to have had no other effect than that of transferring the slave trade to Spain and Portugal. . . . The profit they make is enormous. One of the schooners captured . . . off the river Lagos, having arrived but a few days on the coast, had only purchased ten slaves, for which the master gave 92 rolls of tobacco, each roll worth in the Brazils, 2,000 milreas, about twelve shillings sterling, making the cost of each slave to the Portuguese merchant, five pounds ten shillings, for which he would receive four hundred dollars. These facts will show that neither mountains, rivers or deserts will prove barriers to the slave trade, as the black chiefs will bring their slaves from every extremity of Africa as long as there is a nation that will afford them a slave market; and these circumstances will . . . clearly show, that the partial abolition of the slave trade is of little or no benefit, but that, on the contrary, the wretchedness of the natives is frequently increased by it; and I am convinced that the only means of promoting the happiness and civilization of Africa, will be to annihilate the slave trade in toto, for whilst there is such a facility in selling slaves, there will be no incentive to industry in that quarter of the world.

The increase of the legitimate trade may be considered in two points of view; 1st, an increase of the existing articles of trade before enumerated; 2ndly, an increase arising from the application of the labour of the natives to the culture of the soil, with a view to export. Scarcely anything appears yet to have been attempted for the latter object, the agriculture of the natives being almost entirely confined to articles of the first necessity for their own subsistence, and the cultivation of the Europeans to the limited extent of their own gardens. It appears, however, from the evidence of persons the best acquainted with that country, with very few exceptions, that the natives would be easily induced to raise and cultivate the articles of tropical produce to which their climate and soil are suitable, if they had adequate encouragement by a demand and market for them.

4th. The condition of the forts and settlements belonging to the Company appears to your Committee . . . to be by no means good, either as to repairs or means of defence. Of their eight forts and settlements, the greater part appear to want the means of defence even against an attack of the natives, the security derived from them consisting rather in opinion and in the interest which the natives have in trading with them, than in their intrinsic strength. It is evident, however, that such a security among tribes whose character is described by the servants of the Company, as selfish, unjust and perfidious, must be extremely precarious. A melancholy proof was afforded of this by the murder of one of their governors in 1812. . . .

The bad repair of the generality of their forts is admitted by the Company who ascribe it to the insufficiency of the annual parliamentary grant. This grant has varied in different years; on an average of fifty-eight years from 1750, when the present Company was established, to 1807 inclusive, it has been £13,431 per annum; since 1807 it has been £23,000 per annum. It follows, therefore, according to the statement of the Company, that without a considerable increase of the parliamentary grant, they will not be able to maintain their present establishments on a secure and respectable footing, much less to take any effectual steps towards maintaining and extending a communication with the interior, and introducing education and civilization among the natives.

5th. Your Committee now proceed to the last and most important subject for consideration; viz., the policy which it may be most expedient to adopt in future with regard to these settlements. This subject involves two questions; 1st, whether these settlements should be abandoned altogether; and 2ndly, whether, if continued, they should be maintained under the present system viz., the exclusive government and direction of the African Committee with the aid of Parliament; or whether, with a view to economy, to the interests of general trade, and to the ulterior objects of African civilization, a more advantageous system may not be adopted.

With regard to the first question; as the entire abandonment of the forts is understood to imply that of the trade also, and as this would not only be a present loss, though to an inconsiderable amount, to the country, but entirely cut up by the roots all chance of extending the existing trade, of opening new sources, and of improving the state of the country, and its inhabitants, by education and civilisation, your Committee can by no means recommend this policy to Parliament.

With regard to the second question your Committee feel more difficulty in deciding upon it.

The advantage of carrying on the trade by the medium of the Company is represented to be, 1st., a saving to the public in the pay of their officers and servants in Africa, who receive their salaries &c in goods, which are purchased by the African Committee of Management here, and sent out in a store-ship, freighted for that purpose; by which means it may be alleged that those officers receive them at a cheaper rate there than they could otherwise obtain them, and the public has the advantage of securing the payment of the salaries &c in British exports, at a commercial profit, instead of bills of exchange, which might perhaps [have] been employed in the purchase of foreign articles. As, however, it has not been suggested to your Committee

that free traders labour under any disadvantage from the want of this accomodation; and as Mr Banks . . . distinctly states that traders on that coast would find no difficulty in obtaining whatever goods they might order by private ships; added to which, Mr. Hutton states that he has himself received goods at as low a freight as the Company charge, your Committee are disposed to think it probable that the connections and skill of individual merchants might enable them to receive goods as cheap, or nearly as cheap, as the Company's merchants do under the present arrangement.

The second advantage arising from the management of the Company, is represented to be in the local experience of their governors, who rise to the chief command through subordinate stations in their service; which gives them an opportunity of becoming acquainted with the language, habits and manners of the natives and thereby enabling themselves the better to discharge the duties of their business.

Your Committee are not insensible to the advantage of employing persons of local and practical knowledge in these important situations; and they think that the present system, in that respect, is worthy of being adopted in any arrangement which it may be deemed expedient hereafter to make.

From the best consideration which they have been enabled to give to the subject, under the means of information which they possess, they are inclined to recommend that the Governor in chief should be appointed by the Government, with supreme authority extending over the whole of the British Settlements on the Gold Coast; that the number of those forts and settlements should be diminished by the disposal or abandonment of such as may, upon strict inquiry, appear not to be of service in a sufficient degree fully to compensate for their expense; that the inferior officers universally, including the chief officers of such out-forts as may be retained, should be appointed by the same authority, and according to the same routine of promotion as at present, subject to the control of the Governor in chief, with power of suspension by him in cases of misconduct, and of removal by the Government of this country; and that the number of the African Committee be reduced from the present number of nine to six, giving the chairman the casting vote. It is the opinion of your Committee that, by the reduction of some of the settlements and forts, a saving may be made, so that not only the remainder may be kept up, but the ulterior objects which your Committee have in view, of promoting the improvement of the country, may be pursued with a very small addition to the present expense to the country.

Your Committee cannot conclude their report without distinctly stating to the House, that a principal motive which induces them to recommend the continuance of an establishment on the Gold Coast, and the aid of Parliament for its maintenance, is the instruction and improvement of the natives of that country, in which but little, if anything, has been hitherto accomplished. As one method conducive to this purpose, they would recommend the establishment of schools at all the settlements which may be retained; and that in the selection of schoolmasters, a preference may be given to the writers and factors who will become supernumerary by the discontinuance of some of the factories and forts, so far as they may be properly qualified.

From a judicious application of a moderate Parliamentary grant, under the immediate direction and supervision of Government, and subject to a strict account either according to the provisions of 23 Geo. II and 23rd of the present King, or to such other as Parliament may deem it expedient to adopt, your Committee cannot but anticipate the most beneficial effects when the happy period of the total abandonment of the slave trade shall arrive. . . .

[H.C.431 of 1817]

32 GOVERNOR AND COUNCIL TO THE AFRICAN COMMITTEE

CAPE COAST CASTLE, 16 JULY, 1817.

Gentlemen,

We have now the satisfaction of forwarding you by the present conveyance of the schooner, 'Sir Henry Stanhope', the Ashantee correspondence. The letters received anterior to our despatch of the 22nd June we considered expedient to reserve until the affair of the Fantee notes was settled; as this and concurring circumstances might have inclined persons unacquainted with Africa to have judged unfavourably of the success of our embassy, and to have despaired of that which we had no doubt of accomplishing. We are now enabled to state that the hopes we entertained of its result have in every respect been amply realized, and although the expences of the mission have far exceeded our expectations, the termination has been proportionately adequate. The conclusion of the general treaty with the kings of Ashantee and Dwabin may justly be considered the accomplishment of a more important point, and the foundation to whatever future advantages may result from our connection with their dominions.

The settlement of the Commenda palaver before the mission arrived at Ashantee seemed to be invincible, and would most probably have proved so, from the circumstance of the king's messengers who were authorized to settle the affair having been ordered to negotiate it at Elmina, the people of which place being inveterate enemies of the Commendahs, prevailed on the Ashantees to insist on such extravagent terms, that a reconciliation could not have been effected.

Mr. Bowdich's representations to the king overcame this obstacle, and induced him to concede the point. The messengers were recalled from Elmina and an amicable arrangement has since been completed; a copy of the treaty concerning which we enclose. The king's ambassador is now waiting here to receive the sum which the Commendahs have agreed to pay. For the particulars of this affair we refer you to the Ashantee correspondence

The charges preferred against Mr. James by the other officers composing the mission were of such a nature as imperiously demanded our recalling him. This was immediately done and he arrived here in July last. The command of the mission consequently devolved on Mr. Bowdich . . . [who returned on the 3rd inst.]

Judging from the nature of the government and the disposition of the natives of Ashantee that it would be attended with some risk, leaving Mr. Hutchison as Resident, we deemed it prudent to order his return. The letter, however, did not arrive till after the treaty was concluded, prior to the ratification of which, Mr. Bowdich had perfectly satisfied himself that his personal safety would not be at all endangered. . . .[1]

J. H. Smith,
Jos. Dawson,
Wm. Mollan,
J. Gordon.

33 THE 'BOWDICH' TREATY WITH ASHANTI, 7 SEPTEMBER, 1817

Treaty made and entered into by Thomas Edward Bowdich, Esquire, in the name of the Governor and Council at Cape Coast Castle, on the Gold Coast of Africa, and on behalf of the British Government, with Sai Tootoo Quamina, King of Ashantee and its Dependencies, and Boitinnee Quama, King of Dwabin and its Dependencies.[2]

1st. There shall be perpetual peace and harmony between the British subjects in this country and the subjects of the Kings of Ashantee and Dwabin.

2nd. The same shall exist between the subjects of the Kings of Ashantee and Dwabin, and all nations of Africa residing

under the protection of the Company's Forts and Settlements on the Gold Coast, and, it is hereby agreed, that there are no palavers now existing, and that neither party has any claim upon the other.

3rd. The King of Ashantee guarantees the security of the people of Cape Coast from the hostilities threatened by the people of Elmina.

4th. In order to avert the horrors of war, it is agreed that in any case of aggression on the part of the natives under British protection, the Kings shall complain thereof to the Governor-in-Chief to obtain redress, and that they will in no instance resort to hostilities, even against the other towns of the Fantee territory,[1] without endeavoring as much as possible to effect an amicable arrangement, affording the Governor the opportunity of propitiating it, as far as he may with discretion.

5th. The King of Ashantee agrees to permit a British officer to reside constantly at his capital, for the purpose of instituting and preserving a regular communication with the Governor-in-Chief at Cape Coast Castle.

6th. The Kings of Ashantee and Dwabin pledge themselves to countenance, promote and encourage the trade of their subjects with Cape Coast Castle and its dependencies to the extent of their power.

7th. The Governors of the respective Forts shall at all times afford every protection in their power to the persons and property of the people of Ashantee and Dwabin who may resort to the water-side.

8th. The Governor-in-Chief reserves to himself the right of punishing any subject of Ashantee or Dwabin guilty of secondary offences, but in case of any crime of magni-

---

[1] The Asantehene demanded 2,000 ounces of the Komedas for offences against Elmina after the invasion of 1807, but agreed to accept 120 ounces, the Komendas on their part acknowledging fealty to him. This was ratified at Kumasi on 29 August, 1817. Text in Bowdich, Mission from Cape Coast to Ashantee, 1819, p. 113.

[2] Kofi Boaten, Juabenhene or chief of Juaben.

[1] 'I urged that the Fantee towns under the British Forts must be considered distinctly, and those only were viewed by the Government and the Treaty,' wrote Bowdich (Mission, p. 108): but owing to persistent efforts by the Asantehene to include a palaver with the town of Amissa in the negotiation, he agreed to modify this article 'by securing to you (the Governor) the opportunity of mediation (without attaching like responsibility) . . . not only [as] a precaution due to humanity but a prudent and legitimate extension of our influence.'

tude, he will send the offender to the Kings, to be dealt with according to the laws of his country.

9th. The King*s* agree to commit *their* children to the care of the Governor-in-Chief, for education, at Cape Coast Castle, in full confidence of the good intentions of the British Government and of the benefits to be derived therefrom.

10th. The King*s* promise to direct diligent inquiries to be made respecting the officers attached to the Mission of Major John Peddie and Captain Thomas Campbell[1] and to influence and oblige the neighbouring kingdoms and their tributaries, to befriend them as the subjects of the British Government.

Signed and sealed at Coomassie, this seventh day of September, in the year of our Lord, one thousand eight hundred and seventeen.[2]

The mark of Sai Tootoo Quamina X (L.S.)
The mark of Boitinnee Quama   X (L.S.)
Thomas Edward Bowdich.

In the presence of

William Hutchison, Resident.

Henry Tedlie, Assistant Surgeon

[et al, et al.]   [H. C. 412 (1865)]

34 Wm Hutchison to J. Hope Smith
           Cummasee, 11 October, 1817.

Sir,

I am this moment returned from the palace, being sent for by the king to hear a palaver, or rather a complaint, exhibited against the people of Cape Coast town by a special messenger sent by Sam Brew to charge them with an intention to kill him, as they have come against him in an armed manner to Amamfoo near Winnebah where he resides at present.

This insolent mulatto man, by presents to

---

[1] Peddie and Campbell landed in Sierra Leone in November 1815 intending to travel to Labi and Timbo in Futa Jalon and thence to the Niger to complete the work of Mungo Park. Both Peddie and Campbell died without ever reaching the Niger.

[2] This is the generally accepted form of the treaty. Dupuis, *Journal of a Residence in Ashantee*, 1824, xix ff. omits the passages italicised.

C

the king and his principal men, and being the chief support of the slave trade between this nation and the coast, has made the king interest himself in his favour in an improper degree. I have known for some days past of there being a slave ship under Spanish colours trading near Winnebah in that inhuman traffic. Specimens of guns, powder &c were sent up by Brew to the king as a present, and to induce him to send down slaves for sale; this I understand is invariably done. I hear the king sends down slaves to him today or tomorrow.

Sam Brew's messenger on being called to know why his master did not live at Cape Coast, made a long harangue; stated that he owed some white men money to the amount of 8 ounces, which caused the Guard to be turned out to take him and that he made his escape; since when the chief men at Cape Coast town have desired his death in solemn council, although Quamina Bura [?] settled his palaver with them.

Adocee[1] charged four messengers in the usual manner to speak the truth to you Sir, and to the pynims of the town. This was done with all the formalities of taking fetish and other ceremonies peculiar to great affairs, hereby giving it an importance that it does not merit. They are instructed to summon Sam Brew to Cape Coast to hear the cause of that town's going in a warlike manner to Amamfoo against him; whoever has broke the law to pay 110 peregrims gold to the king and 20 to the linguist. Previous to this I stated to the king before the chiefs assembled, that until Sam Brew made a proper submission to the Castle and behaved in a peacable manner, he would not be allowed to return to Cape Coast, that his conduct was such towards the officers that they could not put up with it.

On the breaking up of the assembly the king said he would send for me and dictate a letter to you which I must write. I beg leave to observe that all letters written in the palace are so hurried and entirely the sentiments of the king that I respectfully

---

[1] Edusei, 'Linguist' (i.e. Spokesman) of Osei Tutu Kwamina.

trust their tenor will not be imputed to my feelings.

We may conceive, Sir, that the grand focus of the slave trade on the Gold Coast, lies within 20 leagues (perhaps) to leeward of Accra, and as near to Annamaboe as vessels dare anchor with impunity. The present difference with the Wassaw states and the Ashantee King prevents the traffic further to windward. To prevent this it would be necessary to disable Sam Brew from carrying on his nefarious trade, as he has ever a supply of slaves ready, and an hour or little more is requisite to ship them, when the vessels stands out to sea for fear of capture. Were his Majesty's cruisers directed to that quarter, I humbly conceive it would be a means of stopping it altogether.

Since the departure of the mission the king invited me to accompany him at his public customs and ceremonies. I stated my willingness to do everything consistent with my character and station that the king wished, but that I must absolutely decline appearing where human sacrifices were offered, as contrary to my religion, my instructions, and my private feeling. I have only attended him twice until I know your sentiments, and also whether you wish me to accompany him to any kroom he may go to. I respectfully wait your pleasure and am &c.

Wm Hutchison.   [T.70/41]

35 HOPE SMITH TO HUTCHISON
CAPE COAST CASTLE, 21 NOVEMBER, 1817.

[Points out that Brew's palaver is with the British authorities and has nothing to do with the Cape Coast people.] . . .

It is not, as Brew has endeavoured to impress on the king, that he was banished the town merely because he owed a white man money. It is for his audaciousness in peremptorily refusing to obey my summons to come into the fort to answer a charge alleged against him: and on finding that he persisted in resisting my authority, I ordered out the guard to secure him, when he effected his escape from the town.

There is a most offensive paragraph in the king's letter which runs thus. 'Sam Brew sent me a present of several articles which make the Cape Coast people think he "dashed" them to him — but they as well as the Fantees all over the country are my slaves.' You will expressly state to the king, and in the most decided terms, that the Cape Coast people are not his slaves, nor have they ever been acknowledged as such; neither can they nor any of the natives residing under British protection be included in that most degrading title. . . . Any interference on the part of the king in matters concerning the people residing under the protection of the forts, cannot possibly be allowed. If they offend, the door of redress is open to him; but it is expected the complaints will not be of the frivolous nature of those that have already been exhibited, which have been mere pretexts for introducing arbitrary acts of oppression and the extortion of money.[1] . . .   [T.70/1606/2]

[1] Another palaver pending at this time concerned a Fantee who, apparently clearly in the wrong, to avoid being confined in the castle, 'swore on the King of Ashanti', i.e. appealed to Kumasi. Abropoo, a chief of Cape Coast, for ignoring this appeal and allegedly boasting that the Asantehene dared not interfere, was presented with a demand for 210 ounces of gold. Hope Smith finally agreed that a token payment should be made, but instructed Hutchison to get an additional article written into the treaty 'that no notice shall be taken of Ashantee oaths taken in any town under British protection'. — Letter of 23 December, 1817. *Ibid.*

4 The breach with Ashanti and the final campaign against the Company, 1818–1821

By the Bowdich Treaty, Osei Bonsu agreed to receive a British consul at Kumasi. It was perhaps a sign of waning confidence in the Company that the British Government decided itself to make the appointment to this post. On the other hand they gave the new consul, Joseph Dupuis, no instructions, simply referring him to the African Committee (37) without making plain what his standing was to be *vis à vis* the authorities at Cape Coast Castle. This culpable omission encouraged Dupuis to take an independent line, and when he finally got to Kumasi[1] he concluded a new treaty (43) which indeed settled the question of sovereignty over the peoples living beside the British forts, but on the Asantehene's terms. It was therefore promptly repudiated at Cape Coast (44) and Accra.

Governor Hope Smith already stood accused of a breach of the Bowdich treaty by his refusal to mediate in a new dispute between Ashanti and Komenda (40). His rejection of the Dupuis treaty, followed as it was by a further deterioration in Anglo-Ashanti relations exposed him to more criticism.[2] But quite apart from the fact that he can have had no conceivable interest in quarrelling with Kumasi,[3] his despatches (39, 42, 45) testify eloquently to the difficulties in the way of any real understanding between two Powers whose fundamental assumptions were so completely at variance: the Governor continuing to deny that Ashanti had any jurisdiction over Cape Coast; the Asantehene insisting that its inhabitants were as much his subjects as the rest of the Fanti.[4] The latter were an added complication. Resenting the relative immunity of Cape Coasters from Ashanti exactions (39) they plundered their farms and eventually goaded Hope Smith into sending an armed expedition to Mori to seize the Fanti paramount 'Paintri' (Yamfo Paintsil). This was in February 1821. Paintri's death aggravated an already tense situation. Trade at Cape Coast which had dwindled almost to nothing ever since the rejection of the Dupuis treaty now ceased altogether; and in Dupuis' view only positive negotiation at this stage could have averted open war with Ashanti.[5]

This failure in its 'foreign policy' coincided with mounting criticism of the Company's management of the forts. If trade was slow to develop it was because it was monopolised by the Company's officials (48); and if outside merchants were

---

[1] J. Dupuis, *Journal of a residence in Ashantee*, London 1824 and in T.70/1605/1 and T.70/1606/1 alleged that Hope Smith did his best to prevent him ever going to Kumasi.

[2] Dupuis, *op. cit.*, followed by W. W. Claridge, *A History of the Gold Coast and Ashanti*, 2 vols., London 1915, i, 327–30 and W. E. F. Ward, *A History of Ghana*, 3rd imp., London 1958, 170–4.

[3] This is the great weakness of Dupuis' diatribe against Hope Smith. He refers simply to the Governor's 'own secret interests, prejudices and animosities' without ever explaining what these could have been. *Loc. cit.* p. 207.

[4] Cf. Hutchison to Hope Smith, 16 November, 1817 (T.70/1603/2) for the Asantehene's view that the only difference between Cape Coast and the rest of Fante was that it had not been over-run by his armies, and this, not because he lacked the power but solely out of his consideration for the English.

[5] Dupuis regarded the Paintri expedition as the first blow in the Ashanti war. Others (e.g. James Swanzy) criticised the Governor's action mainly because it weakened 'our natural allies' the Fantes: but the Council as a whole, though only consulted *post eventum*, upheld Hope Smith. Dupuis would appear to exaggerate the effects of the incident. It did not begin, although it intensified the economic blockade of Cape Coast; and no armed hostilities followed for over two years. Hope Smith's defence (to the African Committee 3 March, 1821) is in C.O.267/54. For a recent criticism of his actions see the articles by E. F. Collins, 'The Panic element' in *Transactions of the Historical Society of Ghana*.

critical, the accounts for 1817 caused recriminations between the Committee and its own servants (38).   Sir James Yeo, not the first or last naval critic of merchant activities on the coast, condemned the whole system of financing the settlements (36) and supported earlier criticisms (17) with the damning indictment that the slave trade itself was still connived at, if not encouraged, at the British forts.   In October of the same year, 1818, Governor MacCarthy of Sierra Leone urged the Crown to take over.[1]   The Government which had hesitated, less from confidence in the Company than from uncertainty as to what to put in its place (49) at last decided to assume control of the Gold Coast forts itself (50).   The Bill abolishing the African Company was introduced in the same month (February 1821) that the Ashantis tightened their blockade of Cape Coast.

[1] MacCarthy to Bathurst 9 October, 1818, C.O.267/47.

36 SIR JAMES YEO[1] TO THE ADMIRALTY
12 MARCH, 1818.

. . . On my arrival on the Gold Coast, I observed several Spanish slave ships hovering about the forts, and on anchoring off Cape Coast Castle, I found a large ship of 600 tons at anchor off Mouree, only 5 miles from Cape Coast Castle, taking in slaves with all the coolness imaginable. This act of audacity in the Spaniard I was convinced proceeded from the confidence he had that at least no impediment would be thrown in his way by the officers of our forts.   This led me to make particular enquiries where he obtained his slaves from, and to my astonishment, I found the trade almost as active in the neighbourhood of our forts as at any time of the slave trade, and before my arrival, rows of poor wretches in chains were to be seen even in the very streets of our town of Cape Coast.   These slaves were embarked from the beach, which is as near the castle gate as the sally-port is to the sea at Portsmouth.   Thus many of the natives belonging to our towns and living under the protection of our guns, have been carried away as slaves.   I have been assured from good authority that this circumstance was reported to the Governor-in-Chief by the Captain of the Guard, Mr. Wm Colliver, and his reply was 'Very well.'

It is evident that this system must defeat all the views Government has so long been

[1] Sir James Lucas Yeo (1782–1818); entered the navy 1793; served in Europe, and America (1812); Commander of the West African squadron 1815–18.

studiously pursuing to improve and civilize Africa, and it is also clear that it must annihilate all legitimate trade.

In my former letter to you, Sir, dated November 1816, I have given it as my opinion that the present system is incompatible with the interest of the separate and free trader, and I now hope to show why it is so.   The improvement of our forts, and the security and extension of commerce does not depend on the amount of the annual grant by Parliament nor will improvement take place until there is a judicious and just expenditure and distribution of the public money.   At present Parliament grant a certain sum to the African Company.   With this they send out the stores and goods to pay their servants and keep our forts in repair.   Agreeable to an Act of Parliament 'To prevent any misapplication of the sums granted or embezzlement of the goods and stores by the servants of the Company, the Committee shall annually lay before Parliament an account of the disposal and application of those goods and stores attested upon oath.'   This has never been complied with, as will appear by Mr Cock's evidence before the Select Committee of the House of Commons last year.   The most probable & only cause to be assigned for the Act in question not being complied with, seems to be that all the governors of our forts and settlements on the Gold Coast have been in the habit from time immemorial of swelling out what is called a day book, in their 6 months accounts, which are audited twice a year by the chief governor. In these accounts all the charges they can think of are thrust in under [various heads[1]] . . . It is not surprising that the charges will be found enormous and the sums granted by Parliament appear to be expended. I am assured from good authority that the charges for Cape Coast Castle last year (1817) will not be much less than £8,000. . . .

The African Company wish it to appear that there is a great saving to the public by paying the officers in goods, and it seems to be alleged that these officers receive them at a cheaper rate than they could otherwise obtain them. This does not appear to me to be the case, neither is it acknowledged by the junior officers of the Company, and further, it is contradicted by the evidence of Messrs Hutton & Banks before the Select Committee. . . . So far indeed from the officers in their service receiving the goods at a cheaper rate, that Company lay on no less than the enormous sum of £82 pr. ct. and on some articles upwards of £100 pr. ct., & what is much worse, if any junior officer wishes £25 of his salary to be paid to his wife or his mother &c, the African Committee charge him the addition of £20. 6. 8., that is £45. 10., for £25 so advanced in England. It is therefore very evident that according to percentage they charge on the goods, £30,000 granted by Parliament would amount to the enormous sum of £54,640 Company's pay, that is, supposing such sum to be laid out in goods and necessaries for the payment of the officers' salaries.

It would be tedious in a letter to enumerate many articles. I will therefore confine myself to two. The Company pay for a gallon of rum 2/6d which is charged to the officer in Africa 6/-. Gunpowder in England is £3.10 per barrel, charged £8 10. Last year it was charged £12. 0. Again, if a gallon of rum is expended to pay the free canoe men, it is divided into 16 parts. Each man receives half a pint of rum and half a pint of water every time he goes off to a ship. Thus a 13 hand canoe is paid

[1] Citing those used in No. 38 below.

with less than one gallon of rum, which stands the Company 2s/6d & they charge Government in their day books . . . 19s for every 13 hand canoe that goes off. . . .

This enormous establishment of forts, governors, factors, writers, clerks &c is nothing more or less than a positive burden to the mother country who pay these men and provide them houses, canoes, servants and slaves for being merchants and thereby deprive the free and open trader of anything like a fair participation in the traffic. The governors of all our minor settlements do the whole of the trade, there not being a single free trader at any one except Accra; & at Cape Coast there are only two. . . .

Mr Swanzy is reported to have told the Select Committee . . . that . . . the Gold Coast produced 100,000 oz. of gold dust annually. I am of opinion it is much more likely £100,000. I know these last 3 years the ships-of-war have not taken home more than 8,000 oz. annually, & allow the like or even 12,000 oz. to have gone home in merchant-ships, the yearly remittance will only amount to 20,000 oz. which is about £80,000 sterling.

In the next place, what is the state of these forts, for which charges are made everywhere for military repairs? I maintain on the honor of an officer, that they are a positive burlesque as to real defence & nothing can cause them to be respected by the natives but their being sensible that it is their interest to live under them to protect them from their more powerful neighbours the Ashantees. This nation has now completely conquered the natives on the coast and as their capital is only 200 miles from Cape Coast, it is not improbable at a future period they may approach the coast. Consequently it behoves us, if we have forts here, that they should be in a proper state of defence . . . [He details defects]

As to roads, for which there are charges, there is no such thing to be seen in the country. There is, indeed, a foot-track from Cape Coast Castle to what is called the Com.y's Garden, which is a large piece of cleared ground with little or nothing in it, and tho' £50 a year is charged for a gardener it does not produce vegetables sufficient for the Governor's table.   This is the extent of the agricultural pursuits of the Company's officers, and if you express your surprize, they tell you the natives are idle, or the soil is bad, or the ants destructive.   The truth is that while we have men at the head of our affairs in Africa who make their own commercial pursuits the chief object of their attention, it cannot be expected agriculture will flourish or any permanent good result to the country, or the happiness & civilization of the natives. . . .

I feel it necessary now to mention our late mission to the king of the Ashantees, not only because it may be urged as a good reason for an additional grant; but because the public will shortly be amused with a long & specious account of this mission, both of which should, in my opinion, be received with due caution.

The officers first appointed on this service were Mr James, Governor of Accra Fort, Messrs Bowdich, Hutchison and Tedlie. The first of these gentlemen has been 17 years in the country.   I have seen much of him, & I am decidedly of opinion that he possesses a more perfect knowledge of the interior, speaks more of their languages, and is better acquainted with the customs & manners of the different nations than any officer in the Company's service, or indeed I may with safety add, any European now in Africa.   Mr James commanded in the first instance, but on the arrival at the capital of the Ashantees, Mr. Bowdich (who is nephew to the Governor in Chief) wrote some charge or complaint against his superior Mr. James, & in consequence of which the latter gentleman was recalled & the command devolved on Mr. Bowdich. This gentleman continued at Coomassey sometime.   At length he received a letter from his uncle informing him of the illness of his wife, on which he made known to the King that he must depart immediately. His Sable Majesty requested him to delay his departure, alleging with other reasons that he had not had time to collect suitable

presents for the King. . . . Mr. Bowdich accordingly attempted to depart by force. This, as may well be imagined was soon resented.   He and his embassy were stopped and on his drawing his sword the people beat and pelted him and his party back to their quarters, into which he was happy and most likely lucky to escape with his life.   The next day the King dismissed him most likely with no very favourable impression.   I mention these circumstances to show how very ill-calculated such a class of ambassadors are to impress on the minds of the African chiefs, that respect & admiration for the English character which it is evidently our interest & object to effect.

Mr Hutchison remained behind and that Gentleman only returned from Coomassee a few days before I left Cape Coast.[1]   Mr Hutchison appears a very intelligent young man & from everything I can judge from his testimony (as also that of Mr. James) the Ashantee king and his chiefs appear to be well disposed to be on friendly & commercial terms with us, but unquestionably very jealous & even averse to our possessing any knowledge of the interior.   Mr. James requested permission of the King to visit a river which runs a short distance at the back of Coomassee.   The King demanded what was his reason for wishing to see the river? Have you no river in your own country, said the King, and is not the water of your river like that of mine?

Mr Hutchison mentioned a large lake they have at the back of Coomassie 2 or 3 days' journey, about which they have a strange tradition 'That some day whitemen are to have ships on this lake, when their country will be conquered.'   They are therefore very particular in not allowing any whiteman to approach it.   They were always very uneasy and jealous whenever any messenger arrived from Cape Coast with letters for Mr Hutchison, and on one occasion the people threw stones at Mr Hutchison because he refused to write to the king of England to grant them a renewal of

[1] Hutchison left Kumasi on 4 February, 1818.

the slave trade. As to the treaty, it will stand good as long as convenient. . . .

The school at Cape Coast is at present a counterpart of their other absurdities, but which may look well in their report. When you visit this school (at which the king of Ashantee was invited to send his sons for education) you feel pleased to hear all the boys read English pretty clear & distinct, but you soon discover that they do not understand one word they utter, neither does the schoolmaster understand their language, the Fantee. So that when he has occasion to explain anything to his scholars, he is obliged to call a boy who understands both languages to interpret his meaning. . . .[1]   [T.70/1604/1]

37 S. Cock to Joseph Dupuis Esq.
African Office, 31 October, 1818.

Sir,

The Committee of the Company of Merchants trading to Africa have received a communication from the Right Honourable the Lords Commissioners of His Majesty's Treasury, importing that their Lordships desire that the intercourse which has been opened with the King of Ashantee should be kept up, and the advantages which may be expected to arise from it promoted to the utmost; and that, with this view, His Royal Highness, the Prince Regent has been pleased to appoint you, (your long residence at Mogadore and acquaintance with the Moorish language peculiarly qualifying you for the situation) to be His Majesty's Consul at Coomassie, the capital of Ashantee. Their Lordships further direct the Committee to make you an allowance of £500 sterling per annum from the period of your arrival in Africa and to pay for your

passage to Cape Coast and journey to Coomassie, furnishing you with an escort, and with such presents for the King as may be deemed most acceptable, not exceeding the value of £200; and with such instructions for your government as may be necessary for your own safety and useful to you in the promotion of the objects of confirming the friendly disposition of the natives of Ashantee and obtaining correct information of the kingdoms further inland.

Their Lordships have also intimated their opinion that, besides yourself, there should be stationed at Coomassie, one officer in the service of the African Company qualified to establish and conduct a school at that place, if the opportunity should be afforded, and also a surgeon with two or three subordinate officers, as the committee may think necessary . . . [Arrangements for his departure are complete.]

The Committee are however of opinion that previously to your going into the interior, you should take up your residence, for a considerable time, at Cape Coast, 1st in order that you may become seasoned to the climate; 2ndly that you may acquire a knowledge of the language and manners and customs of the natives; 3rdly that you may obtain the most satisfactory information from Coomassie, that yourself and attendants will be favourably received and permitted to reside there.

And in order that you may have a full insight into the Company's affairs and connections with the natives, whereby you may be enabled most effectually to promote the objects of His Majesty's Government in your appointment, the Committee propose that you should be admitted to a seat in Council. In concluding upon this last measure, the Committee are much influenced by the consideration of the extreme importance both to the service and to yourself, of your appearing to the natives to be a member of the Company, and wholly dependent upon the Governor and Council; since, were the natives to imagine that your situation was independent of the Company, you would be tormented with numerous

---

[1] This letter was forwarded to the Committee for their explanations on 30 November, 1818 Bowdich, in a letter of 26 December, alleged that Yeo only landed at Accra, where he got most of his information from a negro linguist who had been dismissed from the embassy for fraud and cowardice. As his own dissatisfaction with the Committee increased, however, Bowdich found substance in some of Yeo's charges. See his pamphlet, *The African Committee*, 1819.

applications, of various kinds, which, however improper, you would find it difficult, if not impossible to avoid; whereas by making it distinctly understood that you are subject to, and that your conduct must in all cases be regulated by the Governor and Council, you will be able, whenever you see proper, to evade coming to a decision by sending to Cape Coast for instructions. . . . [He is furnished with the papers of the Bowdich mission.]

One object most desirable to obtain, as it would essentially assist in the realization of the views of Government, might perhaps be a grant from the King of Ashantee, of a district about 25 miles from the coast, subject to a certain perpetual annual rent, with full liberty to clear and cultivate the same and to erect houses etc. Such a spot, judiciously chosen, might open an extensive field for the employment of the youth educated at the Company's schools and be the beginning of a system which might eventually extend to the cultivation and civilization of the whole coast. . . .

In every case in which you may require advice and assistance you may always rely upon the Governor and Council at Cape Coast, to the extent prescribed by their means — by the orders of Government — and by their sense of what is proper and just in the cases upon which you may apply to them. . . .[1]   [C.O.2/11]

38 AFRICAN COMMITTEE TO THE GOVERNOR AND COUNCIL

AFRICAN OFFICE, 13 NOVEMBER, 1818.

. . . We should be happy to comply with your request to be furnished with a gardener, bricklayer, carpenter and blacksmith if the state of our funds would admit of such an addition to the establishment, but your communication . . . that the cargo by the last store-ship was insufficient to cover the expenditure of the last year by the sum of £4,591, is so alarming that

[1] Dupuis' Commission is in C.O.268/19. It is printed in Dupuis, xxxvii, and in part by Claridge, i, 304–5.

instead of contemplating an extension of the establishment, our most anxious attention is directed to the consideration of the means by which the annual expenditure may be brought back to its proper limits.

Unfortunately, the accounts for 1817 received by the 'Cherub' only came to hand yesterday, and we have therefore, not had time for more than a cursory examination of them. We have, however, been exceedingly chagrined and concerned to observe the increased expenditure, under almost every head of the service, in the years 1816 and 1817, for which increase we are unable to account. Indeed, according to our present impression, knowing as you do the sum voted by Parliament, it is such as nothing can have occurred to justify, vizt.:—

	WHITE MEN'S SALARIES	BLACK MEN'S PAY	FREE CANOE MEN	FORTS REPAIRS
Average	£	£	£	£
1810–15	14,327	1,194	1,746	3,426
1816	15,911	1,133	2,202	4,514
1817	17,290	1,414	3,131	7,813

	EXTRA PRESENTS	SICK & WOUNDED	CANOES	WAR EXPENSES
Average	£	£	£	£
1810–15	338	400	796	—
1816	587	465	757	15,400
1817	570	573	1,165	—

In the difficulty to which we shall be subjected in making such a report to Parliament as shall satisfactorily account for an increase of the coast expenditure from the average of £26,300 to £35,700,[1] we shall wait your reply with much anxiety, since we cannot but feel that not only our credit, but your future welfare is involved in the explanation which you shall enable us to give. . . .[1]   [T.70/1603]

39 GOVERNOR & COUNCIL TO THE AFRICAN COMMITTEE

CAPE COAST CASTLE, 11 JANUARY, 1819.

[Reports the arrival of a messenger from Ashanti]. . . .

[1] Average expenditure for the 67 years before 1816 was £26,344. 14. 6.; expenditure in 1816 was £30,030. 2. 7 and in 1817, £37,983. 1. 10, not counting the expenses of the Ashanti mission, which were £2,227.

The principal errand on which the King deputed the messenger was to ask a present of rum, powder, and cloth from the Cape Coast people, to enable him to make a splendid entry into his capital,[1] which he was about making preparations for doing. This, however, was not believed to be the true motive of his request, but mere finesse on the part of the King to discover how the people were affected towards him, and whether they were attached to his cause or not.

The fortunate situation of the Cape Coast people in living under the protection of the castle, by which they are not subjected to the oppressive exactions which are too often practised by the Ashantees on the states which they have recently subdued, has excited considerable jealousy on the part of their neighbours, and created them many enemies; and the Fantees (from a circumstance which occurred lately) are not more favourably inclined towards them. The particulars of the affair alluded to are as follows.

The Fantees, in apportioning to the different towns the sums which were requisite to enable them to settle the King of Ashantee's demand, included Cape Coast and gave the people for their share the sum of.[2] This the Cape Coast people not only refused to pay but [declined] to contribute anything whatever towards the settlement of the claim, and at a meeting of the parties in the public hall, these people retraced the leading particulars of the war between the Fantees and Ashantees, and made it evidently appear that their connection with the former was never such as to authorize their now including them in the payment; which, if submitted to on this occasion, would subject them to the same imposition should any future claim be made on the Fantees. This circumstance was reported to the King with many additions on the part of the Fantees, both whom and

the Elminas have exerted themselves to poison his mind against these people, and wish to impress him with a belief that they are not his friends.

The arbitrary system and extreme oppression of the Ashantees when in power is such that they have but few real friends; and not only the natives of the town, but the Fantees and outside people in general, have recently entertained hopes of their meeting with a defeat. We believe, however, notwithstanding the repeated cautions which have been given them by the President on the subject, that some of the Cape Coast people, presuming on their situation, have not been sufficiently guarded in their expressions, and these have been magnified to the King. Being aware that he could not without sufficient grounds, make a direct demand on them, he adopted the expedient described, and they, seeing that it would be unwise policy to refuse the request, have sent him a present amounting to 50 oz. The return of the messenger is expected in about two months.

Both Portuguese and Spanish slavers continue to call at Elmina on their way to leeward, and the illegitimate trade which they are engaged in is considerably encouraged by the assistance they receive from the Dutch. The number of Portuguese vessels especially, have of late been much increased, and at Elmina they are supplied with canoes, without which they would be unable to prosecute their trade north of the line.

The trade carried on by natives with foreign vessels, to the great detriment of the free trader had arrived at such an alarming height, that the President considered it a matter of duty to interfere, and to revive a regulation which was formerly in force here prohibiting it. . . . Unfortunately, however, our Dutch neighbours do not cooperate with us in establishing a similar system, and a door is thereby left open for smuggling, which at times is partially carried on. We must, however, do the President of Elmina the justice to say that he has expressed a strong conviction of the

---

[1] On his return from the Bontuku War.
[2] Not given. Ricketts, *Ashanti War*, p. 8, says 50 ounces of gold. Hope Smith, letter of 3 March, 1821 (C.O.267/54) says 60 ounces.

necessity of the measure, but that his powers did not authorize its adoption. He has promised to write to his Government on the subject. . . .

    [Signed] J. H. Smith. Wm Mollan.
                         [T.70/1604/1]

40 GOVERNOR AND COUNCIL TO THE COMMITTEE   22 MARCH, 1819.

. . . Not long after the departure of the messengers who came here from the King to ask a present of the Cape Coast people, another messenger arrived who was employed on a similar errand to the people of Commenda. . . . The President immediately represented to the messenger the extreme poverty of the Commenda people, telling him there was no likelihood whatever of his obtaining anything from them that would be acceptable to the King, and that they had not even been able to discharge the debt due to the Cape Coast people for the things they had assisted them with in order to enable them to settle the King's former demand, seventy-two ounces having been advanced by the President at the solicitation of the Cape Coast people, they becoming guarantee. The messenger said he would proceed to Commenda and deliver the King's message, and requested that two of the pynims might be allowed to accompany him, which was acceded to. The Commenda people, it appears, met him outside of the town, and the knowledge of the nature of his visit so irritated them that they refused to permit him to enter it, declaring that they would rather perish than submit to such oppression. The man returned to Cape Coast, related the particulars of the treatment he had received from the Commendahs, and stated his intention of dispatching a messenger to the King to detail the circumstances to him, saying that, insulted as he was, he could not himself think of returning. A new messenger was accordingly sent to the King and arrived previous to the Cape Coast messengers, they having been detained a considerable time on their journey. The latter were after

a stay of thirty days in Ashantee, dispatched with other messengers belonging to the King to say that if the Cape Coast people did not give immediate satisfaction for the insult offered him by the Commendahs, he would send down an army and destroy their town.

The president replied that the Cape Coast people had not been guilty of any offence against the King; that they were by no means accessory to the conduct of the Commendas, nor should they suffer by their act of delinquency; and distinctly stated to the Ashantee messengers, that if the King commenced hostilities against them, he should consider him his enemy and would afford them all the protection in his power.

We are disposed to think that the King hastily credits any report to the disadvantage of these people. He considers them to be rich, and is eager to have an opportunity of plundering them. This will bring the matter to a crisis. He has now gone so far that he must either have recourse to arms, or, if on finding his demand resisted, he should deem it politic to shift his ground, it will be the means of making him more guarded in future.

In consequence of the King's unexampled insolence, the President has not intimated to his messengers the arrival of the presents, nor does he intend to do so until he becomes more civil, as they may perhaps be considered a peace-offering, not of choice but timidity.

[They recommend the abandonment of all forts save Dixcove, Cape Coast and Accra.] . . . We have for some years considered many of the outforts as a mere expense to Government without being of the least utility in any point of view whatever. Three of the forts . . . are in a state of dilapidation and it would be entirely a waste of money to attempt to repair them. . . .

The Governor of [Apollonia] fort and his garrison are completely in the power of an absolute and despotic chief. Whatever aggressions are committed on the part of this man are obliged to be submitted to, as from the insulated situation of the fort and the extreme badness of the landing, coercive measures cannot be resorted to. We well know that the British flag has too often been insulted at this place, and too often felt the disgrace of its being kept flying at a fort where its dignity cannot be preserved. Nor is there anything that can be urged in palliation of keeping up our establishment there. The gold trade is exceedingly trifling and even if it was considerable the abandonment of the fort would not occasion the loss of one ounce of it to the nation as the shipping would receive whatever was collected. . . . [Sekondi, Tantum and Komenda were equally useless.] Trade there is none. . . . Annamaboe . . . has nothing whatever to recommend it more than its being a fine fortification. It is too near headquarters to be valuable in the present day, and the expense attending its support is very considerable. The allowances to the natives alone form a principal item of the expenditure and exceed those of Cape Coast. These were granted them at a time when the slave trade was in existence and when the flourishing state of it here gave these people the ascendancy over any other. The fort constructed solely for the protection of the slave trade, a traffic now so universally and justly abhorred, is rendered useless in the present day. . . . The gold trade is very trifling. . . .

J. H. Smith, Wm Mollan, T. A. Adamson.
[T.70/1605/1[1]]

41 TREASURY TO AFRICAN COMMITTEE
27 OCTOBER, 1819.

I am commanded by the Lords Commissioners of His Majesty's Treasury to send you the enclosed copy of a 'Bill for the better regulation of the African Company' which was introduced into the House of Commons in the last session; and I am to acquaint you it is their Lordships' intention to bring the said Bill forward early in the next session and that on perusal thereof you will perceive that among other objects it is

proposed to reduce the number of the members of the Committee; to empower the Committee to abandon certain of the forts; to prohibit the members thereof from trading at them, or at any places in the neighbourhood; to regulate the method of appointing to the command of vacant forts; and to make provision relating to attesting the accounts of the coast expenditure. . . . [They are asked not to advertise any vacancies in the Committee, and to adopt measures for the abandonment of Apollonia, Komenda, Tantumkweri and Sekondi.] [T.70/1605/2]

42 J. HOPE SMITH TO J. DUPUIS
CAPE COAST CASTLE, JANUARY 1820.

[Recapitulates] the grounds which have led to the King's sending down the embassy which is at present here, to demand from this Castle 1600 ounces, equal to £6,400 and a similar sum from the caboceers and people of the town of Cape Coast.

These two points being entirely new ground could not be contemplated and of course could not be provided against by any instructions in your possession. They are of extreme importance and may on that account vitally affect the British interests in this country and as such they will require, and the Governor and Council have no doubt will receive your utmost attention.

On the first point 'The demand on the Castle of 1600 ounces' you are not under any circumstances to permit even its discussion, much less the payment of a single ounce on such a pretext or for the purpose of avoiding a war. Any payment so made would be a serious compromise of the British character and would also lay the Governor and Council open to repeated demands of a similar nature, until they would become so enormous that the whole allowance granted annually by Parliament would be insufficient to meet them. It would besides destroy at once that high opinion (and authority in this country is supported more by opinion than by the force possessed)

---

[1] A full account of the forts is included.

which the natives entertain of British power, the maintenance of which is so indispensable to the security of the service and for the protection of the important interests entrusted to the management of the Governor and Council.

On the second point 'The demand of Oz.1600 from the Cape Coast people', although this is a matter that might with more propriety be left for settlement to the respective parties, . . . the 5th Article of the treaty entered into with the King of Ashantee does unquestionably bind the Executive Government of this Country to entertain such questions and . . . such interference will have the effect of reducing enormous and unjust demand[s] to a sum within the means of the people of this town and which they are willing to pay rather than subject themselves to the inconvenience that would result from a dispute with the King of Ashantee, whose power they are altogether unable to cope with. And although they would find protection for their persons and property within the range of the Castle guns, yet, in the event of a war they must withdraw from the interior supplies for the necessaries of life. Their trade, the source of considerable profit would also be cut off. It is therefore obviously the interest of the people of Cape Coast to arrange their dispute with the King of Ashantee by the payment of a moderate sum of money. The Governor and Council though convinced that this will be the most politic proceeding as regards the townspeople cannot but sincerely regret the necessity of its adoption because they are sensible it will form a precedent for further exactions, and excuses will never be wanting to the stronger power when it has been resolved upon to extort money from the weaker. . . .

Should the King persist in demanding an exorbitant sum this Castle must interfere with its power to protect them, and . . . in fact the King's declaring war against these people will be considered as a declaration of war against the Castle as it never can be permitted to any power in Africa to oppress with impunity such people as reside under the British forts and claim British protection. . . . They trust 100 oz will satisfy the King. . . .

The Governor and Council are anxious to impress the necessity of not allowing the service of His Majesty and that of the Company to be separated in any negotiation whatever; they ought in all cases to be identified as one and the same: a contrary line of conduct would most certainly prove fatal to the influence of the Government in this country, would protract the settlement of the present dispute, and above all would create the most serious obstacles to the extension of our trade with the interior, which is indeed one of the principal objects of your embassy to Coomassie.

[T.70/1606/1]

43 THE 'DUPUIS' TREATY WITH ASHANTI
23 MARCH, 1820.

Treaty made and entered into by Joseph Dupuis Esq. — His Britannic Majesty's Consul for the Kingdom of Ashantee in Africa, in the name and on the behalf of the British Government, with O'Sai Tootoo Quamina, King of Ashantee and its Dependencies.

1st. The King of Ashantee agrees to receive and acknowledge Joseph Dupuis Esquire as His Majesty's Consul at Coomassie to the full intent and meaning of his commission; and if, at any time, ill-health should oblige the said Joseph Dupuis to leave this country, the King will receive and acknowledge any gentleman that he may appoint to succeed him.

2nd. The King of Ashantee having taken the *sacred oath of allegiance and fidelity* to the Crown of Great Britain in the person of the Prince Regent, make[s] known to all to whom these presents may come, that he will with all his power and influence, support, aid, and protect the British interests in this country and that he will, if necessary, on all occasions march his armies to any part of the country when the interests of Great Britain may require their aid and assistance.

3rd. The claim recently made by the King of Ashantee on the Governor of Cape Coast Castle, amounting to one thousand six hundred ounces of gold, or £6,400 is hereby acknowledged to be relinquished, and it is agreed that there are now no differences or palavers existing between the King of Ashantee and the Governor, or between the King and any other of His Britannic Majesty's subjects, collectively or individually.

4th. The King of Ashantee agrees and binds himself to encourage the commerce of this country with Cape Coast and its Dependencies by all the means in his power, and pledges himself not to allow any differences that may occur to interrupt the trade with the English merchants on the coast.

5th. The King of Ashantee claims the Fantee territory as his dominions, which the consul, on the part of the British Government accedes to, in consideration and on the express condition that the King agrees to acknowledge the natives residing under British protection entitled to the benefit of British laws and to be amenable to them in case of any act of aggression on their part.

6th. After the final adjustment of the present claims upon the natives of Cape Coast, the King binds himself to submit all future complaints to the consul only, and on no account whatever to make war with the natives at any of the English settlements without first allowing the consul an opportunity of settling such differences.

7th. The consul, on the part of the British Government guarantees all the protection in his power to the subjects of the King of Ashantee, who may have any connection with the British Settlements on the Coast.

8th. The consul binds himself on the part of the British Government and Governor and Council, to keep half the path that is at present made between Cape Coast and Ashantee well cleared and the King of Ashantee agrees to keep the other half of the path constantly in good order, so that there shall always be a free and easy communication with the Ashantee dominions.

9th. It is expressly agreed and understood that the consul shall at all times be at liberty to visit the capital of Ashantee and to take his departure therefrom whenever he may think fit without being subject to any interruption or detention; and that the consul's residence may either be at Coomassie or at Cape Coast as he may from time to time deem expedient for the public good, but if at any time during the consul's absence from Coomassie, the King of Ashantee has any complaint or palaver against the natives of the British Settlements, the same is to be submitted to the consul at Cape Coast and if it cannot be settled without his presence at Coomassie, it is agreed that the consul is to proceed to the capital on all such occasions.

10th. The King of Ashantee having publicly and repeatedly complained of the exorbitant prices charged on the notes he holds from the forts, of the goods he receives in payment of those notes, and in consequence of the manifest dissatisfaction expressed by the King on this subject in particular, the consul, in order to obviate any objection to the ratification of the present treaty, concedes this point to the King and agrees in future to take upon himself the payment of those notes, and the King declares he will not receive payment of the notes except through the medium of the consul.

11th. The King, on the part of his principal captains and counsellors, hereby acknowledges to their having also taken the oath of allegiance and fidelity to the crown of Great Britain.

12th. In virtue of this Treaty it is mutually agreed and expressly understood that all former treaties between the King of Ashantee and the authorities of Cape Coast Castle on behalf of His Majesty's Government, particularly the treaty of 1817, are from henceforth to become null and void, and are hereby declared so accordingly.

Given under our hand and seals at the King's palace at the capital of Coomassie, this 23rd day of March in the year of our Lord 1820, and in the fifty-ninth year of the reign of His Majesty George III.

The mark of O'Sai Tootoo Quamina.
Joseph Dupuis.

In the presence of

Benjamin Salmon
Francis Collins
David Mill Graves.

Supplementary Articles annexed to the General Treaty entered into this day between O'Sai Tootoo Quamina, King of Ashantee on the one part, and Consul Dupuis on behalf of His Britannic Majesty's Government on the other part, which articles are hereby considered and mutually admitted to be equally binding to the said contracting parties as if they were inserted in the primary or General Treaty itself.

Article 1

The King of Ashantee having by force of arms subdued the kingdom of Gaman or Buntooko, which he now governs in full and undisputed sovereignty — and whereas from political motives it has been deemed prudent to station troops in Amanaha on the banks of the Assinee River and other parts of the said kingdom to prevent the inhabitants from trading or holding any communication with the sea coast, the king now pledges himself in virtue of this article to remove the before-mentioned obstacles to the commerce of the kingdom of Buntooko or Gaman, and he guarantees the same privileges of trade to the natives of that country which the Ashantees themselves enjoy, provided their intercourse with the sea coast is confined to Cape Coast Castle or any other of the British forts and settlements on the Gold Coast. In promotion of this object, the King has already nearly completed a road forming a direct communication to the heart of the said country of Gaman, and he hereby binds himself to support, aid, and encourage the trade of that country.

Article 2

The King of Ashantee being decidedly averse to relinquishing his claim on the natives of Cape Coast Town, and in consequence of certain private negotiations which are now pending, through the medium of Mr. Smith, the Governor of Cape Coast Castle, on behalf of the parties concerned, and whereas the consul possesses no authority to guarantee payment to the King of any sum of money on behalf of the Natives of Cape Coast, beyond the limit of 100 ounces of gold, which has only tended to excite the King's anger and indignation, as well as for other reasons unnecessary to introduce in this treaty; it is hereby expressly stipulated that the natives of Cape Coast Town 'being subjects of the King of Ashantee' are excluded from participating in the benefits of either of the treaties, as the King is resolved 'to eradicate from his dominions the seeds of disobedience and insubordination.' Nevertheless, in consideration of the friendship existing between him and the King of England, and as the King of Ashantee is particularly anxious to convince the world of the sincerity of his regard for the honour and dignity, as well as the interests of the British Government and people, he will endeavour as much as possible to avoid giving offence either to the consul or to the authorities of Cape Coast Castle directly or indirectly, and therefore, whatever plans the King of Ashantee may think advisable to adopt in order to bring 'his people' under due subjection, he binds himself not to destroy the town of Cape Coast, nor will he allow a gun to be fired in the town, or suffer his troops to commit any act of hostility or depredation therein on the inhabitants or their property, and in particular as regards the white part of the population, to say all the free merchants and traders, he guarantees to them not only full security of person and property but also full protection in case of need. Moreover the King will not suffer his difference with the Cape Coast people to interfere with his plans for the promotion and extension of the commerce between the interior and the British settlements on the sea coast, which he promises shall be immediately restored.

Article 3

The King of Ashantee pledges himself for the security and protection in person and property to the missionaries or others, being subjects of His Britannic Majesty who may wish to establish themselves in any part of his territory for the purpose of propagating the Christian religion, and the King hereby cordially invites to his country such well disposed men.

Given under our hand and seal etc.

[C.O.267/52]

44 COMMODORE SIR G. R. COLLIER[1] TO J. W. CROKER[2]

CAPE COAST ROAD, 16 APRIL, 1820.

. . . .

The feelings of the whole body of merchants and Company's servants were so diametrically opposite to certain articles of Mr Dupuis' treaty that as a British officer employed on the coast for the protection of British commerce, I do not consider I can do otherwise than report the same for their Lordships's information. To this I must also add the entreaties of the native chief Aggery, king of Cape Coast, that the article of the treaty which guarantees his being delivered over as a slave or even as a subject to the king of Ashantee may not receive the sanction of His Majesty's Government. That living as he always has under the protection of the British flag, himself and his people have always avoided joining in any of the native wars, have carefully abstained from connecting themselves with the slave trade since its abolition by Great Britain and in all other ways have abided by the laws (as they understood) of England; for all which they have been in the custom of receiving certain annual pay from the

[1] Commander of the West African Squadron, 1818–21.
[2] John Wilson Croker (1780–1857); politician and *Quarterly* Reviewer; an outstanding Secretary of the Admiralty 1809–30.

British; and further, that although palavers have been repeatedly instituted by the king of Ashantee to excite Cape Coast to acts of hostility, he has upon all occasions carefully avoided giving offence, and in agreeing to pay any fine for the adjusting of a palaver it was done by the approbation and desire of the Governor and Council in the Castle.

I have &c.

[C.O.267/52]

45 GOVERNOR & COUNCIL TO THE COMMITTEE

CAPE COAST CASTLE, 19 MAY, 1820.

. . . We feel considerable anxiety respecting Accra. It is in fact our only vulnerable point, and should the Ashantees attain it in force, it would in all probability fall. The loss of life and property would be considerable and the injury to the British interests at that place would be most serious. Under these circumstances the Council at their last meeting felt the necessity of temporising, . . . at all events to gain time. They were for this reason induced to advise the people of this town to increase their offers in their negotiation with the Ashantee captain. This they have accordingly done (and in fact they have exceeded the sum fixed upon by the Council). Their offer amounts to Oz. 500 and the ambassador, conceiving it to be liberal has sent a messenger to the king recommending his acceptance of it. We therefore presume it will be agreed to.

The Council, considering the difficulties to which the Cape Coast people will be subjected in raising so large a sum and for the furtherance of the public interest, conceive it necessary they should be assisted to the amount of Oz. 200. Before, however, the king of Ashantee receives an ounce of this money, he must distinctly admit the people to be British subjects, and they are ready in the English acceptance of the word, to swear allegiance and fidelity to His Majesty George the Fourth. . . . [They were only to be advanced the money on condition they kept the town clean.]

The demand[1] of the king of Ashantee which forms the subject of Mr. Hanson's letter is a strong practical comment on the treaty just concluded with him by Mr. Dupuis . . . and the king's observation that 'all the blacks and whites are his subjects' are proof of the light in which he views the treaty. . . . To his [Dupuis'] want of spirit . . . to his apprehension of his safety, he has sacrified the British interests in this country. . . . No individual . . . has so much reduced the influence of Europeans as Mr Dupuis, and it will require years of a steady determined and well-conducted government to bring us back to the respectable footing on which we stood when he commenced his operations. . . .   [T.70/1606/1]

46 HOUSE OF COMMONS DEBATE
30 MAY, 1820.

Upon a petition being presented from the African Company, for the grant of £5,000.

Mr. Gordon expressed a hope that the prayer of this petition would not be acceded to until the establishments of the company from whom it proceeded should be inquired into by the House. These establishments were professedly instituted, in the first instance, with a view to the civilization of the inhabitants of Africa; but it was known that they were become mere commercial speculations, in which the interest of each of the speculators was much more consulted than the civilization of the negro. These institutions were, besides, not at all under the control of the British Government; and under these circumstances, they formed an anomaly which called for investigation, before any of the public money was voted for their use.

The Chancellor of the Exchequer[2] observed, that the proposed grant was to repay

monies already advanced by the company, in consequence of a proposition adopted by that House upon the recommendation of a committee, as well as upon the report of our admiral on the station. This, he hoped, would be the last year in which any proposition of this nature would be submitted to the House, and it would be satisfactory to the honourable gentleman to learn that all those British colonies or settlements on the coast of Africa were immediately to be placed under the direction of the executive government. . . .

[Hansard, New Series 1, cols 634–5]

47 J. GORDON[1] TO J. HOPE SMITH
JAMES FORT, 3 JUNE, 1820.

Sir,

I yesterday received a visit from the messenger the Ashantee king had sent to Mr Hanson and to the Danish Governor, on the subject of his monthly note. It appears his Majesty had pledged some gold in the hands of General Swanikuer[2] much about the same time he did the same thing with Mr James at this fort, and had lately insisted on its being restored to him, deducting the amount from his pay, for which it had been pledged. This proposal was refused, and finding all efforts to carry his point fail, this messenger stopped all trade to the Danish castle, by which he finally conquered the scruples of the Danish Governor, who yielded to the demand.

This success caused him to wait on me upon a similar thing, the king's pay and the gold left with Mr. James [and on his application being refused, trade with the English fort was stopped]. . . . It is really miserable to be insulted in this way by these rascally people. To allow them to act as this fellow has done without some punishment is making ourselves too submissive and shewing a want of spirit. . . . [But

---

[1] A demand for the payment of certain sums of money. Hanson was an African merchant of Danish descent, resident in British Accra, of which he was later commandant for a time under Maclean.

[2] Nicholas Vansittart (later first Baron Bexley, 1766–1851); Chancellor of the Exchequer from 20 May, 1812, to December 1822.

[1] John Gordon succeeded James as commandant of James Fort, Accra.

[2] C. Svanekjaer. Governor of Christiansborg Castle, 1819–21.

before defying them the garrison must be increased by at least 20 men.]

[T.70/1606/1]

48 M. FORSTER TO EARL BATHURST

4 JANUARY, 1821.

My Lord,

I am induced by various recent advices from the western coast of Africa and from communications with persons here engaged with myself in the trade to that quarter to address your Lordship with a view of calling your attention to the present state of the English trade on the Gold Coast. How far Government is aware of the effects of the civil and military administration in that quarter under the African company I know not, but all those who have been on that part of the coast (except perhaps the servants of the company) declare that the system hitherto pursued and now pursuing, is as discreditable to England as it is injurious to her commercial interests; and if possible still more ruinous in regard to the civilisation and trade of that part of Africa, by far the most important in a commercial point of view.

I should trespass too far on your Lordship's attention were I to enter into a detail of the causes by which that rich portion of the coast has been kept stationary in its trade and civilization for so many centuries; neither do I suppose it to be necessary, as I think your Lordship and Government cannot be entirely unacquainted with those causes, so obvious as they are now to every one at all acquainted with the affairs of the coast. I do not mean to attach any blame to those who have had and now have the management of the African Company's affairs. The principle upon which it stands is so bad that no better effects can be expected from it, although I have no doubt that those persons connected with it and who have an interest in perpetuating the system, will do all in their power to uphold it. This is natural on their part: but I am confident that if Government will institute an enquiry on the subject it will see the

absolute necessity of putting an immediate stop to it.

As a proof of what immense importance that part of the coast, so rich in valuable produce might now have been to England had Government taken its affairs out of the hands of the Company a few years ago, I may point out to your Lordship the increased and increasing trade of the Gambia and Sierra Leone although the natural resources of the latter places will not bear the slightest comparison with the Gold Coast.

As a proof of this, I beg to refer your Lordship to the Officers of Customs. Mr. Reid the Comptroller outwards has repeatedly lately expressed his surprise at the quantity of goods shipped to Gambia and Sierra Leone compared with former years; and had the administration of affairs on the Gold Coast been the same as at those places, there is no saying to what extent the trade of the former might have been carried ere this.

At present it is literally nothing and I consider the annual grant to the Company entirely thrown away as it regards the commerce of England and only beneficial to the servants of the Company who of course monopolise the whole of the trade, and I need not inform your Lordship that no trade labouring under such a monopoly (a demi-military and civil one) can be of the least benefit in a national point of view. The Governor is of course the chief trader and in addition to his proportion of the goods assigned to him for salary and purchased with the Government grant sent out recently in the store ship, there is now a large vessel, the 'George,' Captain Deeper, in the London docks ready to sail loaded entirely on his account. Of course no person can think of competing successfully with one who has all the stores and influence of the place at his command, and the consequences are such as might be expected; there is not one free trader, that I known of, at the place or near it; and the Dutch and Americans who hover on the coast in great numbers enjoy the best part of the trade. I lately intended to send an agent to Cape Coast, but was dissuaded from doing so by persons well aware of the prevailing system there who assured me my agent could do no good whilst it prevailed.

I do hope, my Lord, that Government will take the matter into immediate consideration, in order that this important district of the western coast of Africa may be rescued from a course of policy so destructive of its commerce and so alien to the interests of England. Were one uniform principle of government established on the coast, and the different settlements in dependency and communication with each other, the advantages to England would in a few years be incalculable. The officers of the Company are held in no respect by the natives, nor is their conduct or situation calculated to inspire any: their chief intercourse with the natives must necessarily be in a trading capacity. Such, my Lord, is the rank, and such the occupation of the representatives of England in that interesting quarter of the globe.

I have the honour etc.
M. Forster.
[C.O.267/55]

49 Commons Debates . . .

20 February, 1821.

Mr. Goulburn[1] rose to move for leave to bring in a bill to abolish the African Company, and to transfer to His Majesty all the forts and possessions belonging to them. He wished not to be understood, that by making such a motion, he cast any imputation whatever on the Company.

Mr. Marryat[2] observed, that though the object of this bill was not to impute any blame to the African Company the effect of it certainly was to cast an imputation upon it. The House had heard much of

[1] Henry Goulburn (1784–1856); M.P. 1808; Under-Secretary for War and the Colonies, August 1812 to December 1821; later Chancellor of the Exchequer (1828–30, 1841–6).
[2] Joseph Marryat; M.P. for Sandwich; Colonial Agent for Grenada; father of the novelist.

late of the impropriety of prejudging a case before a trial;[1] but the House, in acceding to this motion, was going to condemn a party which, on a former occasion, had been acquitted by a committee of its own selection. Gentlemen would recollect, that after the affairs of the African Company had been submitted to the consideration of a committee, the committee had declared itself satisfied with the manner in which they were administered, and had merely recommended that the governor of its settlements should be appointed by His Majesty, that the number of its forts should be diminished, and that the number of governors should be reduced from nine to six. What had occurred since that period to show the necessity for altering the manner in which the affairs of that settlement were regulated he did not know. The right hon. gentleman had not stated any cause for altering it, and a very deserving officer (Sir G. Collier) had spoken in high terms of the internal administration of it. He wished to remind the House that that company had opened a communication with the king of Ashantee, and with others of the native chieftains, from which there was a certainty of obtaining better intelligence respecting the interior of Africa than any which had yet been acquired; while two expeditions which had been sent out from Sierra Leone, at a cost of thirty or forty thousand pounds to the country, had entirely failed in the objects for which they had been fitted out.[2] He did not see why a company which was acknowledged on all hands to have acted meritoriously should be abolished without the necessity of the abolition of it being shown to a committee.

Mr. Gordon said, he had been a member of the committee to which the affairs of the African company had been referred, and had been instrumental in the drawing up of the report which it had presented to the House. When the committee recommended that the sovereignty of the settle-

[1] In the case of Queen Caroline.
[2] The expeditions of Peddie, Campbell and Gray to explore the course of the Niger.

ments on the Gold Coast should be continued to the African Company, it had done so from the difficulty of knowing how to avoid many evils which another system of government was certain to introduce. His Majesty's ministers had since laboured under the same difficulty; and he was informed that they had considered many plans for the administration of those settlements before they had determined on taking them under their own control and guidance.

That measure appeared to him to be wise and politic, and calculated to produce the most beneficial effects. He did not see what right the African Company had to complain of these forts being taken out of their hands. They were originally placed under their control to support the slave trade: and one would suppose that when the slave trade was abolished these forts would be abolished also. Besides, the country paid from £25,000 to £30,000 annually for their maintenance, and of this sum he thought the £1,200 paid in salaries to nine of its directors might at least be saved. He did not anticipate any increased influence to the Crown from this measure, for he thought that none of the candidates for office would wish to go out as Governor to Cape Coast Castle, and none of the aspirants in diplomacy to live as resident at the town of Tombuctoo, or other capital of the king of Ashantee. Leave was given to bring in the bill.

[Hansard, New Series 4, cols. 823–4]

50 An Act abolishing the *African* Company, and transferring to and vesting in His Majesty all the Forts, Possessions, and Property now belonging to or held by them. [7 May, 1821.]

'Whereas an Act passed in the Twenty-third Year of the Reign of His late Majesty King *George* the Second, intituled *An Act for extending and improving the Trade to* Africa:[1] and whereas another Act passed

---

[1] 23 Geo. 2, cap. 31.

in the Twenty-fifth Year of the reign of His said late Majesty King *George* the Second,[1] intituled *An Act for the Application of a sum of money therein mentioned, granted to His Majesty for making compensation and satisfaction to the Royal African Company of* England, *for their Charter, Land, Forts, Castles, Slaves, Military Stores, and all other effects whatsoever: and to vest the Lands, Forts, Castles, Slaves, and Military Stores, and all other their effects, in the Company of Merchants trading to* Africa; and for other Purposes in the Act mentioned: And whereas another Act passed in the Twenty-third Year of the Reign of His late Majesty King *George* the Third,[2] intituled *An Act for repealing an Act made in the Fifth Year of the reign of His present Majesty, intituled An Act for repealing the Act made in the last Session of Parliament, intituled "An Act for vesting the Fort of* Senegal *and its Dependencies in the Company of Merchants trading to* Africa:" *and to vest as well the said Fort and its Dependencies as well as all other the British Forts and Settlements upon the coast of* Africa, *lying between the Port of* Sallee *and* Cape Roque, *together with all the Property, Estate, and Effects of the Company of Merchants trading to* Africa, *in or upon the said Forts, Settlements, and their Dependencies, in His Majesty: and for securing, extending, and improving the Trade to* Africa: *and for vesting* James Fort *in the River* Gambia, *and its Dependencies, and all other the British Forts and Settlements between the Port of* Sallee *and* Cape Roque, *in the Company of Merchants trading to* Africa; *and for securing and regulating the Trade to* Africa: And whereas in pursuance of the said several recited Acts of Parliament, the whole of the Forts and Settlements upon the Gold Coast of *Africa*, held and occupied by His Majesty's subjects, have become vested in the Body Corporate of the Company of Merchants trading to *Africa*, created by the said first-recited Act of the Twenty-third Year of the Reign of His Majesty King *George* the Second, and

---

[1] 25 Geo. 2, cap. 40.
[2] 23 Geo. 3, cap. 65.

have been governed and managed by Officers and Servants appointed by them; but the whole Expense of such Management has, for many years past, been entirely defrayed by Sums granted by Parliament for the support of the said Forts and Settlements, the said Company having, in their corporate capacity, no funds whatever out of which any part of such expences could be defrayed, and having no beneficial interest in the said Forts or Settlements: And whereas it is expedient that the Company of Merchants trading to *Africa* should relinquish the Government and Management of the said Forts and Possessions, and should surrender the same to His Majesty; and it is therefore necessary that the said Company, created by the said recited Act of the Twenty-third Year of the Reign of His late Majesty King *George* the Second, should cease and be wholly abolished as a Body Corporate and Politic, and that all the said Forts and Settlements, and all the Property and Effects of the said Company therein, should vest in His Majesty, and that His Majesty should be enabled to grant such reasonable Allowances as He may see fit, to such of the Officers and Servants of the said Company who may not be retained in the Government or Management of any of the said Forts, or otherwise employed in His Majesty's Service, as His Majesty should deem just and reasonable, and for charging the Allowances so granted upon the Consolidated Fund of the United Kingdom of Great Britain and Ireland:'

May it therefore please Your Majesty that it may be enacted; and be it enacted by the King's most Excellent Majesty, by and with the Advice and Consent of the Lords Spiritual and Temporal, and Commons, in this present Parliament assembled, and by the Authority of the same, That from and after the Third Day of *July* One thousand eight hundred and twenty-one, the said corporation of the Company of Merchants trading to *Africa* shall wholly cease and determine and be abolished, and the said Company of Merchants trading to *Africa* shall no longer be or be deemed to be a Body Politic or Corporate; and all grants made to the said Company by or under or in pursuance of the said recited Acts of Parliament, or any or either of them, or in pursuance of anything therein contained, shall and the same are hereby declared to be henceforth null and void; and the said Company shall be and they are hereby divested of and from all Forts, Castles, Buildings, Possessions, or Estate or Rights, which were given to the said Company by or under or in pursuance of the said recited Acts, or any or either of them, or which have been since purchased or otherwise acquired by the said Company in addition thereto, or which now are possessed or claimed or held by the said Company, shall henceforth be, and the same and every one of them are and are hereby declared and enacted to be, fully and absolutely vested in His Majesty, His Heirs and successors for ever.

II.   And be it further enacted, That it shall be lawful for His Majesty to grant such reasonable Allowances as His Majesty may deem just and fit, to such of the Officers and Servants of the said Company as may appear deserving of the same, and may not be retained in the Government or Management of any of the said Forts, Castles, or Possessions of the said Company, or may not be otherwise employed in His Majesty's service, and to charge the same upon the consolidated Fund of the United Kingdom of *Great Britain* and *Ireland*: which Allowance, when so granted, shall commence from the Time of the respective Persons to whom the same may respectively be granted ceasing to be employed in the Management of any of the said Forts, Castles, or Possessions, or otherwise in His Majesty's Service, and shall be payable and paid quarterly after such Commencement respectively, at the Receipt of the Exchequer at *Westminster*, out of the said Consolidated Fund, free and clear of and from all Taxes, Charges and other Deductions whatsoever; but that no such Allowance shall be considered as finally and conclusively granted until the same shall have been first submitted to Parliament: Provided always, that if any Officer or Servant of the said Company, to whom any such Allowance may in the first instance be granted under the Provisions of this Act, should be afterwards appointed to any Office or Employment in His Majesty's Service, of equal or greater emolument, such Allowance shall, from the Date of such Appointment, altogether cease and determine; but if the said Office or Employment be of less emolument, a Deduction shall in such Case be made from such Allowance, equal to the amount of the Salary and Emoluments of such Office or Employment.

III. And be it further enacted, That from and after the passing of this Act it shall and may be lawful for His Majesty to order and direct that all or any of the Forts and Possessions on the West Coast of *Africa*, between the Twentieth Degree of North Latitude, and the Twentieth Degree of South Latitude, which now do or at any time hereafter shall or may belong to His Majesty, shall be annexed to or made Dependencies on the Colony of *Sierra Leone*; and that from the Date of their being so annexed or made Dependencies on the said Colony, they shall be subject to all such Laws, Statutes and Ordinances as shall be in force in the said Colony, or as shall at any Time thereafter be made, enacted, or ordained by the Governor and Council of the said Colony, and shall not be disallowed by His Majesty, in the same manner as if the said Forts, Possessions, Territories, or Islands had originally formed part of the said Colony of *Sierra Leone*.

IV. And be it further enacted, That this Act, or any of the Provisions thereof, may be altered, varied, or repealed by any Act or Acts to be made in this Session of Parliament. [1 and 2 George IV. cap. 28]

51 S. COCK TO EARL BATHURST
29 JUNE, 1821.

. . . .

The Committee are desirous of submitting to your Lordship, some remarks upon the change of the character of these settlements which will be produced by their annexation to 'and making them dependencies on the Colony of Sierra Leone, and subject to all such laws, statutes and ordinances, as shall be in force in the said Colony, or as shall at any time thereafter be made, enacted or ordained by the Governor and Council of the said Colony, and shall not be disallowed by His Majesty in the same manner as if the said Forts, Possessions, Territories or Islands had originally formed part of the said Colony of Sierra Leone.'

Upon these provisions of the Act (which formed no part of the Bill as laid before the Committee) they feel it proper to observe, that the Gold Coast settlements consist simply of forts, without any territory; and therefore, as the act describes Sierra Leone as a 'Colony', the operation of it will be to prevent their having any commercial intercourse whatever (even with the natives) but what may be carried on direct with the mother country, (with the exception of the article of wine by the Navigation Laws) except in those cases of urgent necessity, in which the governors of colonies are permitted to open their ports; and then only, subject to the orders of the Governor and Council of the Colony of Sierra Leone, 900 miles distant.

In the judgement of the Committee, the forts on the Gold Coast cannot be retained as 'Colonies' without the annihilation of their trade, unless the system of the laws by which the trade of the British colonies is governed, be relaxed in almost every essential point; and if that were to be done, the consequence could not fail to lead to much hardship, oppression, and injustice, for want of a rule for the regulation of commercial intercourse with them.

The Committee having had occasion to address the Right Honourable the Lords of the Committee of Privy Council for Trade, upon this subject in the month of May 1819, beg leave to enclose a copy of their said application, in further explanations of their opinions upon this point.

Upon the subject of the forts in relation to the African chiefs in whose territories they are situated, the Committee beg to point out to your Lordship the absolute necessity that those chiefs should continue to receive their monthly payment of goods, according to the agreements existing with them; and the Committee hope to be able to communicate to the Governor and Council, the early sanction of His Majesty's Government for their continuance. . . .

[C.O.267/54]

BOOK II

THE FIRST PERIOD OF CROWN RULE, 1821–1828

5 *Sir Charles MacCarthy, 1821–1824* [1]

THE difficulties implicit in the Crown taking over the Forts soon became apparent. As dependencies of Sierra Leone, the forts came under the Laws of Trade which, from the 17th century, had controlled the movement of shipping and commodities to and from the British colonies. These were scarcely appropriate to settlements which, possessing no territory, produced no trade goods and were besides interspersed with the forts of foreign Powers. The new Governor, MacCarthy, thought that the Navigation Laws would have to be relaxed (59) but this could not be done without the sanction of Parliament. The local merchants found the Sierra Leone customs duties, which MacCarthy imposed in order to raise some of the £17,000 required for the civil establishment, equally harmful to trade.

More serious was the question of slavery, illegal in Sierra Leone since 1808 (52). MacCarthy found it easier to declare the law than to apply it (53). He was the first to meet a problem which, more than any other, down to 1874, was to militate against any extension of British sovereignty over peoples among whom slavery was endemic.

Above all, though he was slower to appreciate this, MacCarthy inherited the strong probability of a war with Ashanti.[2] He arrived on the coast in March 1822 to find Cape Coast still under an Ashanti interdict, but believed this to be merely a local quarrel not affecting the British generally (54).

He made no overtures to Kumasi, for which he was perhaps to blame. But it is doubtful if they would have done any good, because on the fundamental issue of sovereignty over British subjects and protegées MacCarthy, and indeed all Crown officials, were much less inclined to compromise than their merchant predecessors. The arrest of a Fanti sergeant in the British service at Anomabu brought matters to a head (56). This unfortunate summed up the conflict in his own person. As a soldier he was a subject of King George. As an Anomabu he was claimed as a subject by the Asantehene. The prestige of either power was so involved that neither could admit the other's claim. For the British a climb-down would have condemned them to continue in the forts merely on sufferance: for the Asantehene it would have been the signal for defection amongst the recently conquered and still restless tribes.

There was strong local pressure in favour of a show-down with Ashanti (57) but eschewing these ambitious views (57n) MacCarthy thought it would be enough to put the forts in a posture of defence, for a firm remonstrance to secure satisfaction and better behaviour by the Ashantis (58). When the sergeant was put to death a punitive expedition was despatched to the scene of his execution at Dunkwa (60).

Badly bungled as it was, this military excursion brought offers of assistance from many neighbouring chiefs (60) who hoped to secure their independence (60n) with British help. The revolt, which soon included all the coastal states apart from

---

[1] Sir Charles MacCarthy (*c*. 1770–1824). After service in the West Indies he was given a Lieutenant-Colonelcy in the Royal African Corps and next year (1812) became Governor of Sierra Leone. He was knighted in 1820.

[2] But the year before (to Goulburn 16 August, 1821, C.O.267/53) he had referred to 'the war or misunderstanding now subsisting between the officers of the African Company and the King of the Ashantees'.

71

Elmina, spread inland (61) and after the repulse of a tentative Ashanti invasion in August 1823 (62) Wasaw and Denkyira also rebelled. While Britain's new allies took care to secure themselves against being abandoned to the tender mercies of Ashanti (63), MacCarthy continued to hope for an early peace with that country (64). He clearly underestimated both the political[1] and military implications of his policy; with the result that, instead of the decisive triumph which alone would have compelled Ashanti to recognise the independence of his allies, MacCarthy was himself defeated and killed at Adamanso in January 1824.

[1] E.g. he failed to notify the Colonial Office of the terms of his alliance with the Gold Coast chiefs, c.f. Nos 64 and 73 below.

52 EARL BATHURST TO SIR C. MACCARTHY
LONDON, 19 SEPTEMBER, 1821.

Sir,

By an Act which passed in the late session of Parliament of which a copy is enclosed, the several forts on the Gold Coast which have heretofore been in the occupation of the African Company have become vested in His Majesty's Government; and as His Majesty has been pleased to signify his Commands that they should be annexed to the Government of Sierra Leone, it becomes necessary for me to give you such instructions with respect to them as their change of circumstance appears to require.

As the Act of the last session to which I have referred has repealed the several statutes by which the condition of these forts was established and regulated; and as they are now made part of a British Colony, they will from the date of their annexation to Sierra Leone, fall under the provisions of the 7 & 8 Will. 3, cap. 22[1] by which no goods or commodities can be imported into or exported out of any Colony or Plantation in Asia, Africa or America to His Majesty belonging, but in a British built ship, owned by a British subject, and navigated according to law. You will also observe that the Act subjects these forts to all the laws in force at or applicable to Sierra Leone. The consequence will be that many local regulations and customs which have long prevailed in those forts will be altogether superseded and repealed: and you will find it necessary

[1] This act, the gist of which is sufficiently indicated in the text, consolidated the earlier laws of trade.

to make some general notifications to the inhabitants, in order to guard them against being implicated in any illegal proceeding by continuing to adhere to antient usages, which may now be inconsistent with the law. I mention this more particularly as applying to the state of slavery, which, being expressly prohibited in Sierra Leone by act of Parliament[1] cannot be permitted to exist in any of the forts now placed under your jurisdiction.

You are, I believe, aware that it is not His Majesty's intention to maintain all the forts hitherto occupied by the African Company. The dilapidated and undefensible state in which many of them are represented to be, renders it impossible, without a heavy and continued expense, to place them in such a state of efficiency as would ensure the respect of the natives, or even the security of the inhabitants; and there is moreover good reason to believe that every commercial advantage which settlements on that coast are capable of affording may be equally secured by retaining a more limited number of forts on a footing of greater respectability.

In order to decide upon the forts which

[1] 47 Geo. 3, cap. 44: An Act for transferring to His Majesty certain Possessions and Rights vested in the Sierra Leone Company . . . and for preventing any dealing or trafficking in the buying or selling of Slaves within the Colony of Sierra Leone (8 August, 1807) Para. 4 ran: That it shall not be lawful for any Persons or Persons whatsoever, inhabiting, or being, or who shall at any time hereafter inhabit or be within the said Peninsula or Colony of Sierra Leone, either directly or indirectly to deal or traffick in, buy or sell, or be aiding or assisting in the dealing or trafficking in the buying or selling of slaves, either within the said Peninsula or elsewhere.

it may be proper to retain permanently, it appears to His Majesty necessary that you should, with as little delay as possible, after your arrival at Sierra Leone, proceed to inspect their actual condition. And, as in the course of this inspection, many points may arise on which the advice and assistance of a distinguished naval officer may be useful, the officer who has been recently appointed[1] to succeed Sir Geo. Collier in the command on the coast of Africa, has been instructed to proceed direct to Sierra Leone for the purpose of taking you on board and accompanying you to the several forts on the Gold Coast. Your own observations on the spot, with the assistance of this officer, and with the information afforded by the reports of his predecessor, which are enclosed, will enable you to decide as to the forts which it may be proper to retain. The view which His Majesty's Government have taken of this subject is, that it may be proper ultimately to abandon all the forts with the exception of Cape Coast and Accra. For although temporary circumstances may have at the present moment given a degree of importance to Annamaboe[2] which may render its immediate abandonment inadvisable, it appears doubtful whether its permanent retention is necessary with a view to any political or commercial object. If, however, you should be satisfied that it is necessary to maintain this or some other minor fort in lieu of it, you will consider yourself invested with a full discretion to act as circumstances may appear to you to require; and should you deem it useful to His Majesty's service to retain a nominal command of the smaller forts as dependencies on those which I have specified, without, however, any military or civil establishment, I shall be prepared on your recommendation to submit such a measure to His Majesty's consideration: but before

adopting such a measure, I would seriously press upon your consideration, whether the British name and authority on the coast is not likely to suffer more from being exposed in these dependencies to be insulted with impunity, than the trade could gain by such additional channels of supply.

As soon as you shall have determined upon the forts which it may be proper either permanently or provisionally to retain, you will lose no time in abandoning the others. You will dispose, either by sale on the spot (if it be practicable) or by removal to the other forts, of any public property which may be found in them, and will give due notice to all persons resident there of the intention of His Majesty's Government, and of the period when they will be carried into effect.

The next point for your consideration will be the establishment of the forts permanently retained. In deciding upon this, you will bear in mind the necessity which at the present moment exists, of bringing the expense within the narrowest limits, and of making even some sacrifice of convenience to considerations of economy. Ultimately there can be no doubt but that the civil administration of them would be best conducted by placing it in the hands of the officer who may command the detachment of troops stationed for the military protection of each fort, and to the officer so employed an allowance of one pound a day might be made to cover his additional expenses. At present, however, I am aware that the force at Sierra Leone is too weak to make the necessary detachments for this service: until, therefore, it can be reinforced, it may be advisable for you to continue to employ such civil or military officers of the African Company as appear likely to be most efficient, together with such a number of their troops and mechanics as are adequate to the defence and maintenance of the several forts. To any civil officer so retained, you will assign such a fixed salary as may in your opinion, on a comparison

[1] Commodore Sir Robert Mends arrived at Sierra Leone to take up his duties on 18 February, 1822.

[2] See No. 54 below.

with those paid in Sierra Leone, be an adequate remuneration for the duties to be performed: but you will at the same time, in compliance with the 17th article of your instructions, restrict them from commercial pursuits and that trade on their private account which were permitted by the African Company and which were to a degree a consequence of the system which they pursued, but which are utterly inconsistent with the principles upon which His Majesty's Government is conducted. To such of the Company's troops as may be retained, you will continue to issue the same rate of pay and allowance as have been heretofore received by them from the Company; and you will give to the officers commanding them commissions until His Majesty's pleasure shall be signified with respect to them. It will be advisable also that you should report to me your opinion how far it might be practicable or convenient to incorporate these troops into the regiment serving at Sierra Leone, if such a mode of increasing the garrison of that colony should be judged expedient.

The abandonment of so considerable a number of forts and the reduction which will of necessity take place in the establishments of those which are retained, will necessarily involve the removal of several officers and servants of the African Company; and it will be a necessary part of your duty to investigate their several claims to consideration, and to report upon the amount of compensation to which you may consider them entitled. . . .
[C.O.268/19; H.C.551, A & P (1842), xii, p. 521]

53 SIR C. MACCARTHY TO EARL BATHURST
CAPE COAST CASTLE, 16 MAY, 1822.
. . . I gave a general notification to the native inhabitants with regard to their ancient usages, as to the state of slavery being contrary to law; but on this point I feel a considerable degree of difficulty in reconciling together the precise line of my duty and principles with the former established rights of the natives and Europeans on this coast. I have at present no means of ascertaining the number of persons who are held in a state of bondage by the native inhabitants. No census has, I believe, ever been taken, not even of the population of any of the towns living under the immediate protection of the guns, and I believe that almost every person of that description employed his slaves to cultivate the ground at krooms (small hamlets) situated from three to seven miles distant from each town, and, in the case of Accra, as far as 16 or 17 miles. I cannot at present even form a conjecture on that subject (slaves).

The inhabitants of each of the principal towns have not been thought to consider themselves British subjects, or amenable to the laws of England, except in those cases when difficulties have arisen between some of them and the Europeans, and the matter in dispute has been decided in their presence, after long 'palavers', by the person administering the government. In all other cases they have settled their differences among themselves, according to tradition. In general their decisions have been influenced by the grossest superstition or partiality. In some cases appeals have been made from those judgements to the governor, and his protection has often been claimed for the recovery of such of their relations or followers as have been 'panyarred' by the inhabitants of some kroom under the protection of a fort belonging to another power. 'Panyarring' is seizing a person on a 'man's head', either connected to a debtor, or belonging to his village or town. I had been given to understand that owing to the exertions of the late Governor-in-Chief, that baneful practice, contrary to all principles of rights and civilization, had ceased. Yet since I have taken the government several instances have occurred wherein I have been solicited to use my authority, either to order an inhabitant of this town to restore some free male or female from Accra, or other places, or where I have been obliged to request the assistance of the Governor of Elmina. So little do the inhabitants residing near or along the shores of the Gold Coast understand their own immediate interests, that although the greater number of the chiefs from Apollonia to Christiansborg have been compelled to surrender to the King of Ashantee a great proportion of their notes, and are frequently called upon to pay tribute to him upon the most frivolous pretences, yet the inhabitants of a town living under British protection will frequently panyar or purchase a person panyarred from another town living under the same protection.

I believe that since the abolition of the slave trade, the governors of the British forts have used every means to prevent the natives being under their immediate protection carrying on that odious traffic with Portuguese or Spanish slave vessels: but as they have no registry of slaves, and no control as to the mode of their treatment by the owners, they can only have acted in those cases (and they are very rare) when they received private information. I am not aware that they have been able to prevent the purchase of new slaves. A circumstance which occurred lately fully proves that no restrictions have been placed over them with regard to the treatment of their slaves; it having been stated to me that a man of colour had cruelly flogged several of his slaves residing on a kroom about four miles from this, and afterwards absented himself. I directed inquiries to be made into the circumstances, which caused some anxiety in the minds of the principal caboceers. They accordingly asked me the motives of the inquiries, and on my answering that it was in order to ascertain the correctness of the report against that man charged with flogging his people and absenting himself, they offered to stand his securities for his surrendering himself, which he did a few days later. . . . I appointed a day of hearing when, in the presence of the whole of the chiefs [and] of the principal inhabitants, he declared

that he had ordered four of his men to be punished; that in doing so he had merely followed the custom of the country; that they had not in any former cases been prevented from inflicting punishment on their slaves; and I am sorry to say that his statement was correct.

I took that opportunity to explain, as I had done before, my abhorrence of such criminal conduct. I stated that, according to the laws of England, no individual possessed the power of ordering summary punishment; that the lowest man was entitled to protection and to be heard in his own defence before a magistrate; that as he appeared unworthy of being considered as a British subject, he must return to the interior. I have had many applications for his forgiveness on the part of the chiefs, with promises that such a circumstance should never occur again: but I have not yet deemed it advisable to comply with their petition, although, in order to prevent a recurrence of the same nature, I propose assembling them before my departure, and to take their securities for his future good conduct, and promise that they will prevent anything of the kind.

I have, in every public and private meeting, declared that every individual who resided under the British flag must consider himself as amenable to British law.

In consequence of the declaration I made with regard to the state of slavery being contrary to our laws, I have had applications from two of the native merchants of Accra, educated in England and of English descent, to grant them indentures, for a certain number of years, of their slaves; and although I was much surprised at being informed that each of them possessed upwards of 200 persons of that description, as the Act of Parliament in abolishing the slave trade had sanctioned the indenture of liberated Africans, and as in fact most of these slaves are always employed several miles from town, I conceived that I would secure their emancipation, and accordingly granted indentures agreeably to the form I supposed most binding (one of which is herewith enclosed). I beg leave to solicit your Lordship's instructions on the subject. Several Europeans have since solicited the same favour, which I granted.

[H.C.551, A & P (1842), xii, 521–2]

54 SIR C. MACCARTHY TO EARL BATHURST CAPE COAST CASTLE, 18 MAY, 1822.

[Since the death of Governor Daendels, in 1818, the Dutch have reduced their Gold Coast establishments, now keeping up only Elmina and Axim] . . .

General Daendels . . . fomented the hatred of the King of Ashantee against the British merchants of the coast, and the two embassies of Messrs. Bowdich and Dupuis did not remove the strong prejudice of that chief. [Especially harmful was] the imbecility of the measure of the latter (Mr. Dupuis) who, in opposition to the evident policy of declaring the natives living immediately under the protection of the forts entitled to our support and not liable to the endless claims and impositions of the King, gave them up *en masse* as subjects of the Ashantees, conceiving that he had done a great deal by the declaration of the King and his oath of allegiance, which he never understood and none of his subjects would have dared to explain to him.

At present, however, as the Ashantee King is not so violent against the English in general, but merely reserves his hatred against this castle and people of Cape Coast, he permits his subjects to carry on their trade to Annamaboe and Accra, and these two places derive perhaps a larger share of the profits than even Elmina. He has strictly forbidden them to deal with our people at Cape Coast, and though they frequently take this path as the shortest cut to and from Elmina, our merchants have not been able to remove the injunction against them.

Some messengers with an insolent message to the late governor were here in January last. They wanted him to swear on White Man's Book (the Bible), and the people of Cape Coast to take fetish that they were the good friends of the King. They were sent back to settle their palaver on my arrival but have not returned, nor have I received any message.

From the circumstance of the Dutch not deriving any benefit from the trade on this coast and the whole advantage being engrossed by Americans, who pay no duties, it has been supposed that the Government of the Netherlands were disposed to sell or exchange their African possessions, and the Americans have spread the report of their Government being negotiating for that purpose. . . . Although Elmina and Axim in the hands of the government of the Netherlands is not very prejudicial to our commerce, I have no doubt they would prove highly so if occupied by the Americans. The fortress of Elmina and its situation near a river which, though small, allows of the entrance of boats and canoes at all times of the year, and of the repairs of small craft, is itself superior to all our establishments. . . . [The Dutch still supply canoes to slavers.]

With regard to Danish Accra (Christiansborg), I am satisfied from its present state and, indeed, from what I understood from Count B[ourke] . . . the Danish ambassador in Paris . . . that the Danish Government are disposed to give it to any Power that will take charge of it. In our hands it would become of importance, the fortress being much superior to our Accra. . . . The Danes keep their pretensions to some forts on the Volta. With that acquisition, and abandoning British Accra, — the Dutch fort being in ruins and the flag left to the charge of a black soldier, — a considerable extent of commerce would be obtained, and all ideas of traffic in slaves given up. . . . In the hands of the Americans, Christiansborg might become very troublesome.   [C.O.267/56]

55 EARL BATHURST TO SIR C. MACCARTHY LONDON, 20 AUGUST, 1822.

. . . I perfectly concur in your opinion that the possession of the neighbouring

Danish and Dutch forts would prove of great advantage to this country in a commercial point of view, and also enable us to oppose considerable obstacles to the prosecution of the slave trade on that part of the coast of Africa.

I have, therefore, directed a representation to be made on the subject to the Secretary of State for Foreign Affairs, but I fear the Powers to which those possessions belong will not be so ready to relinquish them as you seem to anticipate. . . .

[C.O.268/20[1]]

56 MAJOR CHISHOLM TO SIR CHARLES MACCARTHY

CAPE COAST CASTLE, 30 SEPTEMBER, 1822.

Sir,

I am extremely concerned to have to report to you that the serjeant stationed at Annamaboe was seized on the 16th ultimo by a party of Fantees at the instigation of the King of Ashantee, and brought to the principal town, Abrah, in the Fantee country, where he was confined in irons and placed at the disposal of an Ashantee chief.

I received a report of the occurrence from ensign Erskine on the following morning, but understanding that there was a large body of armed men at Abrah, I did not think it prudent to attempt a rescue. Nothing, therefore, remained to be done but to endeavour to procure his liberation by negotiation, and as I considered Mr. Williams, the Colonial Secretary, the best qualified person to conduct one, I dispatched him immediately to Annamaboe. My orders to him were, to convene the town's people in the public hall, and to demand from them a full disclosure of whatever they knew of the views by which the Ashantees were actuated in their violent proceedings towards the serjeant; to select one of the most respectable inhabitants to be sent to Abrah to treat in my name with the authorities at that place

for the serjeant's release, and to give him instructions to the following effect — viz.:

To state to the Ashantee chief and Fantee caboceers that he was sent by me to learn their reasons for committing so unjustifiable an act of aggression as the seizure of the serjeant:

To represent to them that he (the serjeant) was a subject of the King of England and was consequently amenable to the laws of that country only, and, therefore, that any complaints they might have to prefer against him ought to have been addressed to me:

To demand his immediate release, and to assure them that in the event of his being permitted to return to Annamaboe, I should be most ready (as I had always been) to listen to any complaints they might have to make, and to give them every justice.

Lastly, to say that if my communication was disregarded, I could not look on the proceedings in any other light than as a declaration of war against the King of England, and that under that impression I should keep in custody nine Ashantees who were secured by the officer commanding at Annamaboe on his hearing of the serjeant's detention.

In addition to this public action, I recommended to Mr. Williams to endeavour to interest the messenger to get information on other points by means of any influence he might possess amongst the Fantees, and as an inducement to act zealously, I authorised him to promise a reward proportionate to the advantages he should derive from any discovery he might make.

I was told by the linguist and others, that a messenger from Elmina had declared to the King of Ashantee that it was your intention, with the assistance of the Fantees, to destroy Coomassie, and that the attack was to be made on your return from Sierra Leone with troops. He stated that you had been refused aid by the Dutch Governor, and urgently pressed him to make a descent before you could arrive

---

[1] Bathurst's fears were justified and nothing came of this representation.

with the expected reinforcement. And it also appearing, from conversations I had with some of the merchants, that the purchases of ammunition made by the Ashantees during the preceeding three or four weeks were unusually great, I thought an attack was meditated, and, supposing they would esteem Accra our weakest post, from its great distance from the other settlements, the decayed state of the fort and the smallness of its garrison, I calculated on their attempting its conquest first, and therefore directed Captain Blenkarne to make every possible preparation for its defence.

Mr. Williams reported on his arrival from Annamaboe that my message had been delivered to the Ashantee chief and Fantee caboceers, and that the former had declined to restore the serjeant to me, observing that he was given into his hands by the Fantees for the purpose of being sent to Coomassie and that he would forfeit his existence by disposing of him otherwise. He hinted that he thought it probable I would wish to send a person to intercede with the King, and gave it out to be his intention to defer his departure for three or four days to enable him to join his party.

The Fantees told the messenger that they had apprehended the serjeant solely to avert a severe chastisement the King of Ashantee threatened to inflict on them because an obnoxious and forbidden expression had been used during an inquiry into a dispute between the serjeant and an Ashantee trader, in May last. They stated to him that the King considered the serjeant his subject, having ascertained that he was born in the Fantee country, and that the circumstance of his being in the British service could not screen him from punishment as the very ground upon which our forts stood belonged to the King and our jurisdiction in them was merely by sufferance. They would not permit him to see the serjeant and he was too narrowly watched to speak privately to any of his friends or acquaintances.

He saw at Abrah representatives from the Elminas, Accras, Wassaws, Assins and some other states tributary to Ashantee. The caboceers of Annamaboe were invited to join them, but they had declined doing so. It was understood that this assembly was convened to receive the commands of the King on various important points. One was said to be a demand of an additional tribute, and an alteration in the mode of payment. The slave trade was at its height when these states were brought under the Ashantee yoke, and the taxes imposed on them were receivable in slaves. The great reduction in the value of human beings and the want of purchasers for them of late years, have determined the King not to take them in payment hereafter. He requires gold or European goods in their stead, and as the quantities fixed by him are unreasonable in the extreme, the people have no hopes of being able to pay them, and consequently cannot be prevailed upon to accede to the proposed change. The chiefs have not yet dispersed, and the serjeant still continues at Abrah. Numerous reasons are assigned for his not being sent to Coomassie, but they are too contradictory and inconsistent to be worthy of credit. It was rumoured throughout the country until last week that his case had been inquired into by the chief and that a favourable report having been made to the King, he had ordered him to be liberated, and that as soon as some matters under discussion at Abrah should be settled, he would be brought to Annamaboe or here. A subsequent account made it appear that a day was fixed for the purpose, but that a difference of opinion arose as to who (whether Ashantee or Fantees) should accompany him; the Ashantee being understood to entertain an idea that he would be arrested and detained, I thought it right to set his mind at ease on that point, and a promise of security was given.

Late events fully convince me that the King has no thoughts of giving up the serjeant, but on the contrary is resolved to use every means in his power to injure the British establishments. I have been informed by a number of persons, some of whom are on intimate terms and in close correspondence with men of consideration at Coomassie, that he purposes attacking the town, and that, on the return of a part of his army employed on the banks of the Volta in subduing a small state which has revolted, the necessary dispositions will be made. A message he sent to the caboceers at Annamaboe on the 24th instant gives a countenance to these reports. He required them to declare whether they considered themselves his subjects or were disposed to take part with the Cape Coast people against him, and signified to them that the most acceptable proof of their fidelity would be their uniting themselves to the chiefs at Abrah. This they declined to do, and as their answer to the question respecting the people of this town was evasive, they expect nothing short of the severest vengeance at his hands.

I learn his present enmity proceeds from his not having received a present at the change of government similar to that given him by Mr. Dupuis on his arrival at his court as British consul. The homage paid to him by the late Company, and the uncontrolled authority they allowed him to exercise in their possessions, even to the extent of levying excessive fines in the towns protected by this and other forts, have given him a very unfavourable opinion of our national character. The immense presents he has at different times received, and the readiness with which Mr. Dupuis made an addition to his annual stipend and yielded several other important points, has led him to imagine that the commerce which he controls is absolutely necessary to our existence as a nation, and that we will ultimately concede dignity and every other consideration for the advantage of participating in it. His conduct to the Dutch who really have not either the means or inclination to make him presents, clearly shows that he considers us profitable subjects for his rapacity. Conceiving the

D

most effectual means to remove this impression would be to appear very indifferent as to his views, I have not adopted the measures which, under other circumstances I would have pursued, to get the serjeant back. There is no necessity for immediate interference in his behalf, as I am assured his life is in no danger.

You were here when the dispute at Annamaboe occurred and the particulars were made known to you by Mr. James Swanzy, but so ridiculous and unworthy of consideration must they have appeared to you that I conclude they have long ere this escaped your recollection, and I therefore proceed to detail them. The Ashantee trader, having got into an altercation with some person in Annamaboe fort, and the noise he made being very great, the serjeant desired him to be more ruly, observing that he was instructed by his master (meaning the officer) to preserve order and tranquillity, and that he could not permit him to violate these orders. The Ashantee immediately damned his (the serjeant's) master and said he did not care whether he was pleased or otherwise. The serjeant retorted in the same language, and his words being understood to apply to the King of Ashantee, the matter was made known to two of his captains then at Annamaboe. Mr. Swanzy heard of the affair and he caused it to be signified to the captains that a regular investigation would take place on the following day. They intimated it to be their intention to assist at the inquiry and accordingly attended at the appointed hour. The statements on both sides having been heard, the Ashantee was declared by all parties to be in fault, and being greatly irritated at the decision, he swore by the terms 'Cormantine and Saturday' that the serjeant was guilty to the extent he had asserted. The Ashantee chiefs, as if terror-struck by these expressions, declined to interfere further, saying that none but their King could now settle the business.

On hearing of the transaction, my curiosity was excited by the extraordinary and surprising degree of importance attached to the two words, and I, in consequence, made inquiries as to the cause of their being so much regarded. I have learnt that they refer to a signal defeat which the Ashantees suffered many years ago on a Saturday, and at a place in the interior called Cormantine,[1] and the recollection of the disgrace is so mortifying to the present prosperous and arbitrary king of Ashantee, that he has in the most positive terms prohibited any allusion to it. Such as are so unfortunate and incautious as to violate this order, or cause others to do so, generally atone for the offence with their lives. The few who escape are preserved by the payment of large sums of money to the avaricious monarch and his ministers. In addition to what he obtains in this way, he contrives to exact considerable amounts from parties concerned in the affair which may give rise to the infringement of his decree. . . .

I could adduce many other instances of imposture on the part of the Ashantees towards His Majesty's subjects in these parts, equally atrocious in their nature with the foregoing, but I feel satisfied that I have already said enough to show that the dignity and interests of our country and what we owe to a large population whose allegiance we claim, demand immediate and active efforts to check the proceedings of the ambitious author of our disgrace and their sufferings.

The humiliating and mortifying treatment the Ashantee tributaries are subject to and their excessive sufferings from plunder, must incline them to become parties to any measure likely to restore them to freedom, and as their several countries are very populous, a plentiful supply of arms and ammunition, with some money, would secure any number of allies we might wish for. . . . [The merchants have promised their full support.]

[C.O.267/56]

[1] This reference is to the death in ambush of Osei Tutu during a war against Akim Kotoku, c. 1731. Dupuis gives the village as Acromantie.

57 MEMORIAL OF THE CAPE COAST MERCHANTS   30 SEPTEMBER, 1822.

. . . It has long been the policy of the Ashantees who occupy a line between the great trading countries to the northward and the water-side never to permit a direct communication between the latter and the former. They monopolise to themselves the part of brokers to both, which to them has been the source of so much profit that they have in the course of very few years [e]merged from comparative obscurity and risen to a power of the very first rank in this part of Africa. Yet such is their rapacity, and so insolent and overbearing their deportment when they exact their extortionate tribute from the lesser states who have the misfortune to be subject to their yoke, that they have not a friend among the nations adjoining them, nor, we sincerely believe, an ally that would not forsake them and become their enemies should circumstances evince a reasonable prospect of freeing themselves from the thraldom of so galling a connection. . . .

[The seizure of the sergeant at Anamabu had only anticipated a conflict that was bound to come.] The act of aggresion may, therefore, be considered rather fortunate than otherwise as it affords an opportunity of destroying or humbling a power that must be destroyed or humbled before our footing in this country can be considered safe and respectable and before the leading object of His Majesty's Government in the increase of our knowledge respecting the unknown countries in the interior of this vast continent, the extension of our intercourse with the natives, the promoting their improvement and civilisation, and eventually the gradual diffusion of Christian knowledge, can ever be carried into effect.

You are aware, Sir, that to effect the overthrow of the king of Ashantee . . . considerable expense must be incurred and much time will be required. Of ultimate success we have no doubt, if active measures be adopted. . . . Unless his overthrow can be effected, or at all events his power greatly reduced, it will be better that the British force should be wholly withdrawn from the Gold Coast. One or other of these measures we feel satisfied His Majesty's ministers will, at no distant period, find it necessary to adopt.

Our own immediate personal interests would be considerably promoted by a speedy and friendly settlement of this dispute, but we prefer the sacrifice from the conviction that no such arrangements could be permanent or honourable. . . . We consider that the profits of an uncertain trade for a relatively short period, will be greatly overbalanced by a successful termination of a contest, the consequences of which must be to us, in the first instance, a great increase of commerce without any chance of interruption. . . .

We will take the liberty to touch on another subject . . . of no less importance to us . . . as it deeply affects . . . the trade with the mother country. . . . We allude to the peculiar circumstances which have tended to fetter the commerce of the British settlements, and materially to further increase that of the Dutch and Danes, who draw their trade from the same source, and have all their ports free, without any duties whatever being levied. The plain fact is that ships, not only of all foreign nations, resort to Elmina, but British vessels make a practice of doing their trade at that port in preference to Cape Coast, by which means they avoid paying any duties, and by which the Dutch are enabled to undersell us by 8 per cent., and some articles 12 per cent., which unintentionally makes the regulations of the Colonial Government a bounty to the foreign trade. . . .

There is another circumstance which gives the Dutch and Danes a decisive advantage over us, their being able to supply themselves with American rum, which by the natives is preferred to any other, in the proportion of four to five. This article they of course purchase free of duty and on such favourable terms otherwise as to bring it below the price at which we can import West India rum. Rum is indispensable to the trade here, and its importance may be judged of by the fact that at least 1,500 puncheons are annually disposed of in this part of Africa. . . .

[The best solution would be to purchase the Dutch and Danish possessions, which would also have political advantages.] No more effectual means could possibly be adopted to subvert or to control the power of the Ashantees. They would then be necessarily dependent on us for all their supplies both of warlike stores and articles of commerce, all of which they can now as readily procure as well at Elmina or Christiansborg Castle as at any of the British settlements. Thus subservient to us, and their power crippled, the Ashantees would be unable to exert the means of annoying us, and would no longer be capable of obstructing our intercourse with the nations in the interior who, there are strong reasons for believing, are a milder and better race.

The consolidation of the British authority on the sea coast would have a further beneficial tendency. The natives who are at present divided, jealous of each other and constantly embroiled, would, by being checked, forego their feuds and quarrels, and it is therefore reasonable to conclude that the march of civilisation would rapidly advance. . . .

We may be deemed sanguine, but we deliver it as our firm opinion that, in the space of a very few years, the revenue of this part of the colony would repay the sum to be expended in effecting the desired arrangements with the other powers. The amount necessary for that purpose we should conceive would not be considerable if we may judge by the trifling intercourse they have with their possessions here. For the last three years, the average of vessels from Holland to the Gold Coast has been one per annum, the average original value of the cargoes about £1,500 each. In fact, we can look upon Elmina in no other light than as a factory for the disposal of American and Portuguese produce. The only Danish vessel we have known to have visited this coast for the last three years was a ship (chiefly filled with government stores) which brought out a Governor for Christiansborg Castle, and immediately proceeded to the West Indies. . . . [Acquisition of these forts would also help to stop the slave trade.[1]]

(Signed) James Swanzy, Wm. Hutchison, Henry Swanzy, P. I. Fraser, F. L. Swanzy, Jas. Heddle, Edw. Jones, J. T. Pierce, John Hull, Pressich Dodd, J. W. Hanson, James Bannerman, Fredk. James.

[C.O.267/56]

58 SIR CHARLES MACCARTHY TO EARL BATHURST
CAPE COAST CASTLE, 14 DECEMBER, 1822.

My Lord,

I had the honour of stating to your Lordship in my letter of the 11th November, from Sierra Leone, that in consequence of the information I had received of Major Chisholm, commanding the troops on the Gold Coast, that the chief of the Ashantees had committed an act of hostility by causing a non-commissioned officer to be taken prisoner by some of his people and detaining him, and of the alarm such an act had caused in the country, as it was supposed that the said chief would proceed to attack the natives living under the protection of the forts, I had thought it my duty (although not impressed with the same feeling of alarm) to postpone my intended inspection of the settlement in the river Gambia, and to proceed to this place. . . .

I arrived here on the 9th instant only, after a long passage, and found the country

[1] Commenting on this, MacCarthy (to Bathurst, 11 November, 1822) hoped that matters would be arranged 'without a war on an extensive scale with the . . . Ashantees. I have, however, thought it advisable to be prepared for defence if necessary. . . . I am not ready to go the whole length of their suggestion with regard to the Ashantees and I have no hesitation in attributing the misconduct of this barbarian chief to the mistaken policy and weakness of measures pursued by the former Government of the Forts'. (C.O. 267/56; part in Crooks, *op. cit.*, p. 167.)

in the state I had anticipated. No further hostility has since taken place, and although the serjeant continues detained by the Ashantees, yet I believe from the report they have received, that they are inclined to apologise for their conduct and that matters will be made up in a manner that may impress him (the chief) with a better idea of the British nation, and prevent such an act in future. As the direct commercial intercourse with his people and our merchants is now at a stand, I am anxious to bring matters to a close as soon as possible. I will avail myself of an opportunity which will offer in the end of next month or February next to report my proceedings.

The Europeans are enjoying health and the native troops are improving in their discipline and appearance.

I have etc.   [C.O.267/5]

59 SIR C. MACCARTHY TO EARL BATHURST
CAPE COAST CASTLE, 11 FEBRUARY, 1823.

My Lord,

Having since my present visit on this station made several enquiries with regard to the commerce and the advantages and disadvantages which might attend the re-opening the intercourse with foreign vessels in the same manner as it was carried on before their being made dependencies of Sierra Leone; I am now led to believe that although several strong grounds may be urged for excluding foreigners in the same manner as they are at Sierra Leone, Bathurst in the Gambia, and the Isles de Los, yet, considering that Elmina and Danish Accra (Christiansborg) are in a great measure like American factories, more especially under the present circumstances (that of a long non-intercourse with the Ashantees) I think that it would give an opening to the British merchants for the disposal of their inferior African produce, such as the lowest class of ivory and palm oil, to permit for a short time, which might afterwards be extended if found advisable, the admission of foreign vessels at our forts, for the exchange of their merchandise for African produce.

I have also taken into the most serious consideration, the observations addressed to your Lordship on the part of the persons stating themselves as engaged in African commerce on this coast,[1] with regard to the duties raised in aid of the colonial service, and to which allusion was made in a memorial of the resident merchants addressed to me on the 30th September last. . . . I have availed myself of the latitude granted to me by your instructions, and no other duties have been collected but 6 per cent. on the invoice price of foreign goods and two per cent. on articles the growth of Great Britain and of her colonies including India, and even China, with regard to tea and silk.[2] These duties have not in one solitary instance prevented a vessel from unloading her cargo here when purchasers have been found, but as, unfortunately, for upwards of three years there has been a misunderstanding between this place and the Ashantees, as no other intercourse was allowed by that chief but the occasional passage of some of his traders through this path on their way to Elmina, and his own periodical sending for the receipt of his customs — commerce here has been at its lowest ebb, and the merchants, not finding customers among the natives, disposed of their goods to the merchants of Elmina. When vessels have called here not consigned to them they have declined purchasing. Under these circumstances, finding no market here and one open at Elmina, British vessels have naturally resorted there to sell, but not to avoid the payment of trifling duties.

In the event of your Lordship approving

of my suggestion with regard to the propriety of opening these ports to foreign vessels for a limited time, I beg to be honoured with your instructions as early as it may be convenient.[1]

I have etc. [C.O.267/58[2]]

60 SIR C. MacCARTHY TO EARL BATHURST

CAPE COAST CASTLE, 7 APRIL, 1823.

. . . Having ascertained that the intentions of the chief of the Ashantees were to follow up the murder which he had ordered to be committed on a sergeant of the Royal African Colonial Light Infantry,[3] by sending messengers not only to the whole of the Fantees, Accras, Winnebahs and other native chiefs, but even to those residing under the protection of the British forts, for the purpose of persuading them to take his 'fetish' (a supposedly indissoluble charm, which binds the person who drinks it to the interest of the giver); having further ascertained that his messengers had actually been for some days at Agar, a small native town within less than two miles of, and depending upon Annomaboe, . . . that they had held conferences with the chiefs and attempted to frighten them into a coalition against us, holding forth the murder committed on the unfortunate sergeant as a proof of the irresistible power of their chief who could soon destroy the British forts, that we were defenceless and therefore unable to protect them or ourselves: I deemed it my duty, in order to support in this part of Africa the undisputed character for honour and courage our country has for so many years maintained in Europe and elsewhere, not to delay any longer to carry into effect the only measures left to me.

---

[1] Petition of African merchants 16 July, 1822, is in C.O.267/57.

[2] And a duty of 3d a gallon on rum. For the imposition of these duties cf. MacCarthy to Bathurst in C.O.267/56. Except for the period 17 October, 1827, to 12 January, 1828, the duties remained unaltered until the Crown handed back the forts in June 1828. Cf. Lumley to Hay, private, 19 January, 1828, C.O.267/94.

[1] Bathurst pointed out (22 September, 1823, C.O.268/20) that this would require the sanction of Parliament.

[2] The matter was held over pending a review of the navigation laws by Parliament, which took place in 1825.

[3] Reported 10 February, 1823, C.O.267/58: precis in Crooks, pp. 168–9.

It was not in my power to prevent the commission of a crime, but I was satisfied that if I could, by sending a military force to Dunquah, make prisoners of those Ashantees caboceers who had been the principal instruments in the whole transaction, it would give an example as would prevent a similar occurrence. . . . [The expedition nearly miscarried, owing to the doubtful behaviour of the guides, but, after a stiff action, the Ashantees were put to flight.[1]]

Being the first enterprise of that nature by British soldiers it has had the happiest effects. It has dispelled the terror of the Fantee and other native tribes, who had, for several years, been held under the most abject state of oppression by the Ashantees and, in hopeless despair, considered them as invincible. Those very Fantees who . . . were compelled . . . to fight with the Ashantees at Dunquah, have seen those caboceers who had been foremost in tyranny and crime *run away* from the fire, and (although possessing every advantage of ground) leave . . . the Fantees and the lower class of Ashantees to bear the brunt of the action.

From that period to the present, not a day has elapsed without the arrival of messengers from all the native chiefs residing near the water-side as far down as Accra, requesting to be sworn on white man's book (the bible) that they would fight with us . . . [against] the Ashantees. Those Fantee chiefs who live near Dunquah and Abrah, being more exposed to an attack from the Ashantees, have also either come in person or sent confidential men to assure me that I had their best wishes. They have, however, been more reserved in their expressions, two of them being desirous, *if possible, to stand neutral*, whilst the others have declared that if the Ashantees should march towards the coast, they would instantly join our forces at Annamaboe.

[1] Dunkwa was at best a doubtful success. H. J. Ricketts, *A Narrative of the Ashantee War*, 1831, describes it as a reverse.

The Ashantees retired to Coomassie, and their chief, after uttering the most extravagent expressions of rage, and declaring, with repeated oaths to his captains, that he would kill every white and black man at Cape Coast and Annamaboe, has despatched messengers in all directions to claim the aid of the different chiefs. Those who came to Dunquah were received with great coldness by the Fantees, who advised the king to make up his difference, as they knew that he was wrong. Those sent to the English, Dutch and Danish Accras met with a worse reception. The caboceers told them that the king, who was pleased to call them his friends, had begun the war without their advice, that they wish him to sue for peace, and that, until his palaver with the English was made up, they would not permit any Ashantees to come to the Accras for the purpose of trade, or to purchase arms and powder. They have sent to me to say that when I fired they would fire.

I have reason to believe that, although the commandant of Elmina states, in a letter to me, that he is desirous to maintain a neutrality between us and the Ashantees, yet he avails himself, as the principal merchant of that fort, of what he considers a favourable opportunity to dispose of his powder and muskets.

With regard to the intended operations of the Ashantees, I have, at present, no means to give your Lordship a well-grounded opinion. It appears evident that though they have been blustering and threatening our forts, without any just cause, since last August, they were not prepared for war, but depended solely upon the terror of their name to bring us to seek a compromise, and, I suppose, to extort from the native people under our fort, as they had done in the year 1820, under some false pretence, a contribution of six hundred ounces of gold (£2,400). It is known they suffered very severe losses in their aggressions on the Crepees, Bontokoos and other nations, whom they have attempted to plunder and conquer.

I do not suppose they can move before what they term their Christmas (August).

Finding myself in a situation of extreme difficulty, having no option left between seeking to make peace with a ruffian who had committed an atrocious act, or to show to him and all the other African chiefs, that we would not leave such a deed unpunished, I preferred the last, in the persuasion that it would meet with our most gracious sovereign's approbation.

It is not unknown to your Lordship, that during the long period I have been employed on the coast of Africa (from 1812) it has been my most anxious desire to promote the civilisation and happiness of the people by persuading them to be at peace, encouraging them to agriculture and commerce, and, above other measures, impressing upon their minds the advantages they would acquire by embracing Christianity. The present case appeared to demand, with the same views a different conduct, and by chastisement to render the commission of crime hideous in their eyes. I scarcely need to mention that I shall embrace, with great pleasure, every opportunity which may lead to an honourable peace, and that I have declared so to all those chiefs who may make it known to the Ashantees. . . .[1]   [C.O.267/58]

61 MAJOR CHISHOLM TO SIR C. MacCARTHY

CAPE COAST CASTLE, 8 AUGUST, 1823.

. . . It was found that without the alliance of Appiah[2] the co-operation and, indeed, the fidelity of the other Fantee

chiefs could not be calculated upon, and I consequently thought it proper to send Captain Laing[1] with a detachment of the corps, the Annamaboe militia and as many of the natives as could be collected in the vicinity of Annamaboe, to endeavour to bring him to terms. After considerable hesitation he was prevailed upon to take an active part in the war, and, I am happy to say that he has given ample proofs of his attachment to us.

Measures were taken, at the same time, to put a stop to the intercourse between the Ashantees and the inhabitants of Elmina, and it is particularly satisfactory for me to have to report that they succeeded. Our active proceedings had the effect of inducing the Wassas to join us, and the Ashantees have, in consequence, been totally excluded from the waterside for nearly two months. . . . [Overtures to the Elminas were less successful.]

Information having been received, in the meantime, of the advance of three Ashantee armies of 10,000 each, towards our settlements . . . we received certain intelligence, in the beginning of last week, that a strong detachment of Ashantees was within six days' march of this, and it was currently reported that their object was to destroy the crops, to penetrate to Elmina, and, in conjunction with the inhabitants of that place, to attack Commenda, and otherwise to give us all the annoyance in their power.

The crops being too green to be cut, it was indispensably necessary to make an effort to save them, and I accordingly sent Captain Laing to the Fantee country with as many men as could be spared from the forts. About 600 of the Cape Coast militia proceeded to the borders of the Abisemoo country (adjoining Wassa) and instructions were dispatched to our allies in those quarters to concentrate their men

---

[1] On 16 May, 1823, MacCarthy reported the expulsion of Ashanti traders from Accra with considerable loss of life, and the swearing of a solemn oath of alliance by all the Fante chiefs save one, who promised to join. 'In addition to these men in arms for their own cause — the independence of their country from continued tyranny and oppression' the Asantehene was at war against Bontuku and Krepi. 'No moment could have been more favourable to bring his pretensions to a just level.' [C.O.267/58; precis in Crooks, op. cit., p. 175.]

[2] Aduonan Apea, chief of Ajumako, and collector of tribute for the Asantehene.

---

[1] Alexander Gordon Laing (1793–1826); after service in the West Indies, was given a company in the Royal African Corps in 1822. The same year he explored the headwaters of the Niger. He was murdered in the Sahara, after visiting Timbuctu, in 1826.

and to form a conjunction with us without delay. . . . Although the first accounts had represented the enemy to be little more than 1,000 strong, so panic struck were the people at the name of the Ashantee army that I really believe they would willingly have embraced an opportunity of submitting to their oppressors had the presence of the European officers amongst them not inspired them with confidence. . . . Various reports have reached this, within the last fortnight, representing that three armies, destined to attack the British settlements, are on the march, and some of them make the strength of each division 10,000 men; but those who profess to know something of the country consider the force to be greatly exaggerated. We have pretty positive accounts of the advance of 6,000 men in the direction of Wassa, but only two-thirds of them are armed. It is supposed that nothing of magnitude will be undertaken until the Crepee army returns. At any rate, the king will not take the field in person before them. . . . [C.O.267/58]

62 SIR C. MACCARTHY TO EARL BATHURST

CAPE COAST CASTLE, 12 DECEMBER, 1823.

My Lord,

I have the honour to report my return to this station on the 28th November, and it is with heartfelt pleasure that I have to state to your Lordship that I found the whole of the civil and military officers, European soldiers, native troops and inhabitants in good health, enjoying the same security as in a state of most profound peace. The harvest of yams, corn and other articles has been collected without any hindrance, and the only circumstance I have to regret is that commerce is not carried on as extensively as I should wish.

With regard to the trade of this place (Cape Coast), it is undoubtedly greater than at the time the forts were taken possession of by His Majesty's Government. The other stations, Accra and Annamaboe, are, for the present, not so

well situated, and as a state of good understanding and close alliance has now been established between our settlements and the whole of the tribes residing along the shore, from Apollonia to the Volta, that they are all in arms against the common enemy, except Elmina, I anxiously hope that I shall be justified in anticipating that on the termination of the Ashantee war, our commerce shall receive a vast increase, and His Majesty's subjects find the same protection, under the forts on the Gold Coast, as in his other possessions on the western coast.

It is with pleasure I have to state that the measures pursued by Major Chisholm, commanding the troops and administering the civil government at this station during my absence, deserve my approbation. It will be my duty to report in detail on the steps he followed and on the present state of the country.

The conjectures I had formed at Sierra Leone, on the receipt of letters from the Gold Coast, as expressed in my despatch of the 27th August . . . have been more than realised. The enemy had crossed, at that period (the end of July and early part of August), the Bosempra, with a force then magnified to 15,000 men; but [which] from subsequent information, and the observations of Captain Laing, did not exceed 9,000, for the purpose of laying waste the territory of our principal allies, the Fantee chiefs, and to intimidate all his then wavering adherents. The able manoevre and rapid movements of Captain Laing, who was directed by Major Chisholm to proceed forward with such of our troops as were at Annamaboe, with the militia of that station, commanded by some of the European British merchants, and our native allies, so disconcerted the Ashantees, unaccustomed to that mode of warfare, [that] they narrowly escaped being surprised in their encampment, and, after a rapid flight, leaving in their camp a considerable quantity of arms, some baggage of their chiefs, and provisions cooking on the fire, they recrossed the Bosempra, and sought shelter in Coomassie. On that occasion they lost a few prisoners.

The same success attended a movement executed by Captain Blenkarne some distance in front of Accra. The tributaries of the chief of Ashantee, finding themselves supported, attacked and dispersed several of his small parties. On the north was the chief of Denkera, who had been summoned by the king of the Ashantees to attend at Coomassie, [and] although narrowly watched, continued with a few brave fellows to regain his lost dominions, having concerted with his chiefs that they should draw near Coomassie and conceal themselves in the woods. The skill and gallantry displayed on that occasion are truly worthy of the cause he has eagerly embraced, to emancipate his country from the oppression of the Ashantees.

The Fantees have a large camp formed some miles in front of Dunquah, at Yan-Coomassie, on the main path leading to Coomassie. A party of militia, volunteers, and townspeople of Cape Coast, joined to several native chiefs, occupy a strong position, about sixteen miles to the north-west of this place. I visited them last Monday, and they appear determined in the cause, and anxious to move. I propose visiting, in like manner, the camp at Yan-Coomassie.

The success we have obtained has considerably lowered the influence of the Ashantees with the Elminas. A large proportion of the inhabitants have expressed themselves as anxious to join us, and are only detained by the tottering power of the European officers, who have now most strongly promised to adhere to a strict line of neutrality.

The communication of the Ashantees with the whole of the settlements on the waterside, without any exception, from Apollonia [to the Volta], has been cut off for some months, and they are deprived of receiving every description of arms and ammunition, and even the necessaries of life (salt). Various reports are in circulation of the death of Osai Tootoo Quamina,

[and of] disunion among themselves. On these reports, from the absolute non-intercourse between that country and our allies, it is impossible to form a correct opinion. It is a fact that our friends are increasing daily, and the Ashantee tributaries seeking shelter under the British flag.

I have within this two days received information that a party of Assins, who reside on the Ashantee side of the Bosempra, and his nearest tributaries, have brought their families to the camp of Yan-Coomassie. It has been supposed that my arrival, which was delayed much beyond the period that had been anticipated, will lead to some overtures of peace. As I have but one object, that of proving myself deserving of His Majesty's confidence by extending the protection of his arms to his subjects on this coast, I scarcely need to state to your Lordship, that, unelevated by the present position we hold, I most anxiously wish for an honourable peace. I shall go to Accra by the end of this month, in order to be enabled to form a correct opinion on the means for attack or defence, and not adopt on light grounds a definite measure.

I have etc.   [C.O.267/59]

63 THE OATH-TAKING AT NYANKUMASI
20 DECEMBER, 1823.

The whole of the native chiefs who joined . . . against the Ashantees were not satisfied until they had evinced their sincerity by swearing allegiance in their fashion, as follows. The person about to swear took a sword in his right hand and with great animation, whilst expressing his determination, called heaven to witness that he would be faithful to the cause, continually putting the sword upwards at the Governor's head, and flourishing it round his own, so near at times that His Excellency's eyes were frequently in imminent danger. They would also swear on the bible (white man's fetish as they termed it), but before any of them would consent to join in the war against the Ashantees, Sir Charles was obliged to assure them that he would never make peace with that tribe without acquainting them with his intentions, and that their interest would ever be considered.

The reason which they gave for this stipulation was that . . . in 1807 . . . [the Asin fugitives] arrived at Cape Coast, expecting to find protection, but on the contrary the governor, colonel Torrane, seized Chebboo their king, an old, infirm and blind man, and delivered him over to the Ashantees . . . at Annamaboe, where he was put to death with the most excruciating torture. Those of his people who had remained at Cape Coast . . . were taken prisoner, . . . lingered out a painful existence in the dungeons of the castle, many of them died, and the few that remained were brought to the hammer and sold as slaves to the best bidder. At Annamaboe, the treatment of the natives was equally dreadful. Even those who had found protection in the fort were claimed by Colonel Torrane, on the pretence that the king of Ashantee had made a present of them to him, and many of them were actually sold and put on board of slave vessels. . . .

[H. J. Ricketts, *op. cit.*, pp. 40–41]

64 SIR C. MACCARTHY TO COMMODORE FILMORE[1]

ASSAMACOU, W. WARSAW, 17 JANUARY, 1824.

Confidential.

Sir,

It having been reported in camp that His Majesty's Ship 'Owen Glendower' has arrived at Cape Coast, although I have no correct information to that effect, I beg to state that I had the honour of receiving

[1] Captain John Filmore was senior officer on the station after the death of Sir R. Mends on 6 October; took over command of his flagship the *Owen Glendower* and at the instance of Major Chisholm 'took upon himself to hoist the broad pennant' for the sake of the moral effect of having an admiral on the coast. He resigned owing to ill-health on 20 January.

by Captain Courtenay, on my arrival at Cape Coast Castle on the 27th Novr., the letter you had entrusted to his care. It affords me great satisfaction to return you my sincere thanks for the very handsome manner in which you were pleased to offer me your assistance; and to bear my testimony to the zeal evinced by Captain Courtenay. As I found the country in a perfect state of tranquillity, though at war with the Ashantees, and I was led to hope that that barbarian chief would be anxious to send messengers for peace, I conceived it unnecessary to avail myself of the instructions you had issued to Captain Courtenay to detain him on this station when I was satisfied that his services might be of the utmost importance to leeward, to check the traffic in slaves. He accordingly sailed the same day, for a cruise, as Captain Grace of H.M.S. 'Cyrene' for England, the 14th December.

Shortly after that time, when I was intending to go to Accra, I received information that the Ashantees had assembled a strong force and invaded the Dinkeras, and were proceeding by the Warsaws towards the waterside to renew their intercourse with the Dutch at Elmina. The conduct of the Governor of that fortress, and of his officers, under the plea of *neutrality*, has been such as to excite strong suspicions in my mind that at the same time that they did not think it expedient to declare openly in favour of the atrocious murder committed by the Ashantees, yet as they had supplied arms and ammunition to that chieftain long after the transaction, and continued doing so until the paths were closed by our allies, they would secretly encourage the invaders, and enable them, by the sale of arms and powder, to continue the war.

To counteract the plan of the enemy, I accordingly marched in the first instance to Djuquah, a camp about 15 miles from Cape Coast, and I have since moved here across the Bosempra, about 25 miles to the N.E. of Succondee. Major Chisholm with a part of the troops is at present on the Pra at Ampensasoo, upwards of 50 miles N.E. of Cape Coast. The main force of the enemy is encamped between 25 or 30 miles nearly due north of this post. I have not yet been able to ascertain its positive strength, which is reported at 10,000, but I believe exaggerated. I propose proceeding in that direction so soon as the troops who are on their march from our former camp have joined me.

I scarcely need to state my great anxiety to put an end to a war which is attended with considerable trouble and fatigue, and has put a stop to all my endeavours at improvement. With that view, I have directed the troops at Annamaboe and Accra to move forward, thus to threaten the enemy from various points.

Under these circumstances, the presence of H.M. Ship at Cape Coast and off Succondee cannot but be of great importance to the good of the service. Her appearance will retain the Elminas in their line of neutrality, if they were disposed to break through the solemn word of honour given by the Governor that he should scrupulously adhere to it, raise the confidence of our numerous allies, and may ultimately facilitate our return to Cape Coast when circumstances may render it expedient.

In requesting, accordingly, that you may remain on this station until matters are brought to a close, I entertain the most sanguine expectations that you will only be detained for a short period from the important objects you may have in view, and that success will crown your exertions in rescuing from slavery our unfortunate fellow creatures. . . .[1]

[Adm.1/1815]

[1] MacCarthy's distances and directions are only guesses. Ampensasoo (Mamponso) is about 35 miles as the crow flies north *west* of Cape Coast. The site of Nsamanko is uncertain. It is perhaps to be identified with the Manso (5.05 N, 1.50 W) of modern maps. The battle appears to have taken place some distance away, most probably on the banks of the Bonsa, in the vicinity of Adamanso (5.16 N, 1.52 W). C.f. Ricketts's eye-witness accounts in his *Narrative* and in his despatches printed by Crooks, *op. cit.*, pp. 83–8.

65 LIEUT. COLONEL A. GRANT[1] TO EARL BATHURST

CAPE COAST CASTLE, 31 JULY, 1824.
My Lord,

Finding no public documents of the late Sir Charles McCarthy here to enable me to judge how far he had put your Lordship in possession of his views and the policy he had adopted with respect to the native chiefs, with whom he had formed an alliance, I have the honour to state for the information of your Lordship the particulars which have come to my knowledge.

The seizure and murder of a sergeant belonging to the regiment at Anamaboe by an Ashantee chief, for an alleged offence committed against the king of Ashantee . . . led to the disastrous war we are now engaged in, the particulars of which your Lordship is already informed of. On this occasion, the late Sir Charles McCarthy solicited and obtained the alliance of the natives of the sea coast and inland chiefs who had been reduced under the power of the king of the Ashantees, and who readily embraced an opportunity to throw off his yoke. . . .

These chiefs, on declaring their willingness to make a common cause against the enemy and to act as directed by the authorities for the general good, were promised every possible assistance in establishing their independence, and as the Ashantees had made it a point to disarm the natives they had conquered, a considerable quantity of arms and ammunition were given them, and on my arrival here, I found many of these chiefs, with about six thousand men who on hearing of the approach of the enemy to attack this place had assembled to assist us.

Having received intelligence on the 20th

[1] Lt.-Col. A Grant of the Royal African Colonial Corps, Lieutenant-Governor of Sierra Leone, landed at Cape Coast with reinforcements on 17th July. He was the founder of Bathurst (1816) and of the post on Macarthy's island (1823); was then invalided home and only returned to the coast because of the emergency caused by MacCarthy's death.

that the enemy had moved in the direction of the Fantee country, I called together the chiefs, and after assuring them of my wish to continue the same friendly relations by supplying them with arms and ammunition for carrying on the war, they were directed to follow the enemy and protect their country. This was the policy I found established and which, under present circumstances, I am bound to adopt, and I would fain hope it may prove effectual in bringing the Ashantees to a more reasonable way of acting. Were the chiefs, our allies, more determined and more enterprising, they have at present means sufficient to crush the power of the enemy, but they want energy, nor can they be easily collected or brought to act in a body against them. They expect a strong regular force to co-operate with them, and that system, as far as circumstances would admit, has been acted on from December to May. Nearly the whole of the regular force on this part of the coast have been in the field, or, as it is more properly called in this country, the ' bush '. It is literally so, and the consequences have been disastrous beyond parallel both to officers and men, not so much from what they have suffered from the enemy as from the climate, excessive fatigue and privations that, with bad water and most uncomfortable accomodation in barracks here, brought on sickness and death.

I regret to state to your Lordship that, owing to the officers being so much occupied in the field, and from the number of casualties which have taken place in every department, I found the Colonial Commissariat and Regimental Accounts so much in arrear as to prevent the possibility of my being able to give your Lordship any idea of the expenses of the war. From the numbers of natives, our allies, who have necessarily been supplied with arms, ammunition, and various other articles, the sum must be great. I consider it, however, necessary to continue the supplies and to encourage them to harrass the enemy, already much distressed and

retiring to their country, particularly as the nature of the country is such, from its being one continued thicket, even to the skirts of the town, that no regular force could possibly act but with the greatest disadvantage. It is therefore only by encouraging and supporting the natives who have made it a common cause with us, that we can expect to make any impression on the enemy at a distance. And I have great pleasure in stating to your Lordship, that the chiefs our allies (with the exception of one 'Abagay', a Fantee, who in the outset, I understand, made himself very useful to us, but has since evinced a disposition to go over to the enemy) have conducted themselves well, and I have from themselves every assurance of a firm adherence to the cause.

From refugees and prisoners brought in we have various accounts of the motions of the enemy. All agree that they have suffered much, and that the King has determined on returning to Coomassie. Abagay is here a prisoner. He persists in declaring his innocence. I think it right to detain him till matters are settled and trust my doing so will meet with your Lordship's approbation. . . .

Conceiving it of the highest importance, nay, a measure of absolute necessity, to have a well-organised militia on this coast, ready to act on all occasions with the regular troops, I have to request that your Lordship may be pleased to take the same under consideration. His Excellency the late Sir Charles McCarthy had established a corps of militia here, at Anamaboe and Accra, but as they were not clothed by Government, and but badly paid, owing to the poverty of our colonial revenue, very few of them can now be mustered. The companies could be raised here and at other establishments, which, if clothed and paid at the rate of one shilling for a sergeant, 9d. for a corporal and sixpence for a private, when assembled to drill or other duties under arms, they would be an efficient force at no great expense to Government.

From the various reports I have heard, coupled with circumstances which have come to my knowledge, I have little hesitation in saying that the Elmina people encouraged the Ashantees to go to war with us. That they have supplied them with munitions of war and every other necessary, is a fact well established here, and corroborated by the testimony of the refugees whose statements I have the honour to enclose. To this great evil, I beg leave to call your Lordship's attention,

and to request you may be pleased to adopt such measures as may appear to your Lordship most expedient in laying the matter before His Majesty's Government, with a view to enforce the neutrality of the subjects of His Majesty the King of the Netherlands on this part of the coast.

I shall have the honour of forwarding copy of a correspondence which I am now carrying on with the Governor of Elmina on that subject.

I have etc.   [C.O.267/61]

6 Disengagement, 1824–1828

AFTER MacCarthy's debacle the British and their allies fell back on Cape Coast where the Ashantis were in turn repulsed early in July 1824 and soon afterwards withdrew across the Pra. The Government in England, very imperfectly informed as to MacCarthy's policy, now wished only to patch up a peace with Ashanti and reduce their coast establishments to Cape Coast Castle and Accra (66).

Major-General Turner, the new Governor-in-Chief, was doubtful if even these were worth keeping (67); thought that the only effective alternative to complete abandonment was to secure control of the whole coastline (68); and was very eloquent on the difficulties of trying to manage the affairs of the Gold Coast from Sierra Leone. The Colonial Office was not prepared for either total abandonment or new annexations (69). Bathurst thought the situation called for a new commission of inquiry (70), especially into the question of making the Gold Coast a separate Government (78).

Turner began by making the independence of the coastal states the basis of his peace offer to Ashanti[1] but when that failed reverted to a policy of neutrality, which, though not without its difficulties (71) was certainly more in line with his instructions from home (66). Subject always to his doubts about the expediency of staying on the Gold Coast at all, he regarded possession of Elmina as the key to success there: but before he could accomplish anything, he was called away to Sierra Leone, contracted fever in the Sherbro, and died in March 1826.

By the time the instructions to Turner's successor came to be drafted (74), the Ashantis were again on the offensive. Sir Neil Campbell was told, if possible to make peace, and if not, to defend the forts and leave the tribes to their own devices: but before he reached the coast, Lieutenant-Colonel Purdon, ignoring his own orders, (71), had taken the field and, with some of the eastern chiefs, won the decisive victory of Katamansu (75).

The allied chiefs did not think this a fitting moment to offer terms to Ashanti, preferring to turn their arms against Elmina (76). Campbell considered that this absolved Britain from further responsibility for them (77), and, as he found trade negligible and declining — a view in which he was soon supported by the findings of Commissioner Rowan, who besides questioned the whole policy of siding with the coastal middlemen against Ashanti (80) — he urged a drastic reduction of the scale of the local establishment, to the Dutch or Danish level.

Bathurst, by this time, was prepared to go further,[2] and gave orders for all the forts to be abandoned at the end of 1827 (78): but for this to be done without imperilling the British merchants, it was necessary that further efforts should be made to make peace on the coast (79). Campbell himself made no further moves before his death at Sierra Leone (14 August, 1827), but his deputy, Major Ricketts, managed to start peace talks, and in December 1827, the terms of a settlement were actually agreed upon (83). Then misunderstandings between the British

---

[1] Cf. his proclamation of 2 April, 1825, printed by Crooks, *op. cit.*, pp. 220–1: 'I will not make peace . . . until [the Asantehene] gives up every claim to tribute or subjection from surrounding nations.' This was not communicated officially to London.

[2] Bathurst was also influenced by the report of Captain Boteler, R.E., in December 1826, that it would cost £15,559 to make Cape Coast Castle and £47,637 to make James Fort, Accra, defensible. (H.C.570, A & P, 1833, vi, 207: precis in Crooks, *op. cit.*, 249–50.)

and Danish authorities (82, 84) and the Fante attacks on Elmina (85) caused the negotiation to be broken off. This failure caused the British Government, which had hitherto resisted pressure from various British commercial interests opposed to abandonment (81), to agree to devise some permanent arrangements whereby the local merchants might be aided to protect themselves.

66 EARL BATHURST TO MAJOR-GENERAL TURNER[1]   29 OCTOBER, 1824.
Sir,

As you have reported yourself ready to depart for your Government, I have received the King's commands to convey to you the following instructions for the guidance of your conduct with regard to the state of public affairs on the Gold Coast.

The recent successes which have been obtained,[2] with so much bravery, by His Majesty's forces over the Ashantee tribes, and the enemy's consequent retreat to Coomassie, which there appears no reason for doubting, afford strong grounds for entertaining the expectation that they will be anxious to put an end to an unsuccessful war, or at all events, that some considerable time will elapse before they may be again in a condition to renew their hostile attempts on His Majesty's forts and settlements.

Under such circumstances, you will have ample leisure to direct your attention to the condition of Cape Coast Castle and to the means of placing it in a state of adequate defence against future attack.

Upon your arrival at Cape Coast, you will endeavour to acquire a proper understanding of the views and pretensions which prompted the Ashantees to their unprovoked aggression against His Majesty's settlements.

Upon this subject I regret that no conclusive information has reached His Majesty's Government, and I anticipate that you may find it necessary to open a channel of communication with the Ashantee chiefs, in order to obtain some authentic

knowledge of their disposition and intentions. For this purpose, you might select some prisoner of war whose liberation might be acceptable to any person of influence at Coomassie; and as the circumstances under which you assume your government will enable you to resort with propriety to that or to any other convenient mode of communication with the enemy, I am not without hopes also that the death of the person who was recently considered as the chief ruler of the Ashantees[1] may have led either to the abandonment of, or to such a relaxation from the views with which the war was originally undertaken, as to induce the present ruler to enter readily into the spirit in which you will manifest your disposition to communicate with him.

In the event of this expectation being realised, an opportunity will be afforded to you for declaring that His Majesty disclaims all intentions of territorial aggrandisement and has never varied in his earnest desire that his subjects should cultivate the most friendly relations of peace and commerce with all the native powers of Africa and in particular with the Ashantee nation.

The victorious success obtained by His Majesty's troops with the assistance of the allied nations which have adhered to the British cause, has made no change in His Majesty's wishes and policy; and His Majesty is still desirous that those amicable relations should be renewed and perpetuated.

If these proposals should either be anticipated or favourably received by the chief of the Ashantees, it will be proper to invite him to send to Cape Coast Castle or to its vicinity, persons duly authorised to conclude a definitive treaty of peace: but

[1] Major-General Charles Turner entered the army in 1795; served in the West Indies and the Peninsula; Major-General, 1821; Governor of Sierra Leone, 5 February, 1825, to 7 March, 1826.
[2] i.e. the Ashanti repulse before Cape Coast on 11–12 July, 1824; cf. Crooks, *op. cit.*, 202 ff.

[1] By coincidence on the same day as MacCarthy.

it will for many reasons be convenient that such treaty should be formed without reference to any former treaty or convention which may have been concluded under the authority or sanction of the late African Company, with whose previous transactions and engagements with the Ashantees or with their allies it becomes the less necessary to identify His Majesty's Government, as the conduct of the enemy has virtually abrogated all pre-existing engagements of whatever nature they may have been, between His Majesty's subjects and the enemy.

I have further to desire that you will expressly stipulate that the native tribes which have sided with His Majesty's troops shall in no degree be disquieted or molested on account of the line of conduct which they have thought proper to follow during the existing contest: but you will, in general, feel it your duty to abstain as much as possible from interfering in any dissensions which may arise between those tribes and the enemy, or among themselves, respecting the supremacy which one may claim over the other.

A sum of five hundred pounds has been placed at your disposal for the purpose of enabling you to purchase such presents as you may consider calculated to assist you in the object of your negotiations with the chiefs of the native powers: but I desire that you will not consider yourself authorised, under present circumstances, to distribute the whole of these presents; and you will reserve not less than two-fifths of them in value until you shall have received my instructions for disposing of them.

I have etc.   [C.O.268/20]

67 MAJOR-GENERAL TURNER TO EARL BATHURST

CAPE COAST CASTLE, 24 MARCH, 1825.

. . . Upon the expediency of keeping up a moderate and reasonable establishment at Sierra Leone and the Gambia, I entertain no doubt, because I feel that under proper management these places will rise rapidly in importance, that they will become flourishing, that their expenses will not fall heavy on the Mother Country, and that the hopes and views of the reasonable part of the friends to Africa and humanity will not ultimately be disappointed.

But the expediency of keeping up our establishments on the Gold Coast is a question which I approach with doubt and hesitation, because I have been but a short time in the country and I feel that, notwithstanding the pains which I have taken, I do not yet possess sufficient knowledge to enable me to make up my mind to my own satisfaction. I believe that under the wisest system of management, it would have been found difficult to conduct the affairs of this intricate establishment as to make it a source either of public satisfaction or of profit: but under the system which has been pursued, the expensive and useless establishments which have been formed, and the difficulties into which the Government has been drawn by the transactions of the last eighteen months, I should be apprehensive that very little satisfaction or advantage would result from a continuance of the sacrifices [we are] making here.

It is always painful to me to allude to the acts of my predecessor, because my views evidently differ much from what his were, and his are unfortunately deprived of the advantage of explanations, and I trust that your Lordship will ascribe to a sense of duty alone any remarks which I may have occasion to make. . . .

Under what views or impressions the large and expensive civil establishment of this place was recommended to your Lordship I am utterly at a loss to imagine. Here we have no territory, sovereignty or subjects; consequently no right to administer laws, power to enforce them, or colonists to receive them. Therefore, when the Colony of Cape Coast is alluded to, it can only mean the fort. Yet there is a Colonial Secretary and Registrar at a salary of £500 per annum; an Accountant at £400, and *seven* writers, two of whom can neither read nor write, at various salaries. I am utterly at a loss to imagine the nature of the duties intended for these gentlemen. Under the African Company of Merchants, the case was widely different. The military commandant of the fort, with the assistance of a fort adjutant at seven shillings and sixpence per day, a situation which I would strongly recommend to your Lordship to provide for, with a collector and storekeeper as at present, would be quite sufficient to discharge the duties of this place.

The whole system of alliances with native chiefs is difficult and embarrassing in the ablest hands, but in inadequate ones dangerous. The Ashantee nation could easily be destroyed without much expense were it an object, but the people employed might afterwards be more troublesome than the Ashantees themselves.

I would recommend to your Lordship, under any circumstances, to abandon the forts of Dixcove and Annamaboe, thus concentrating the troops at Cape Coast and Accra: but I beg not to be understood as recommending the continuance of troops at any of the forts on the Gold Coast, because there are not, and there never can be, for want of harbours and many other causes, any adequate national recompense for the sacrifice, either as regards commerce, civilisation, or religious instruction. The Gambia and Sierra Leone must always be preferable for these objects, and by trying for too much, I fear that less real good is obtained. It is true that much money has been already laid out upon this place, but much more will be required if it is to be kept up.

The trade of this coast at present amounts to little or nothing, and there are only four or five merchants carrying it on. In the event of a peace with the Ashantees it might increase, but it must always be confined to a few articles such as gold dust and ivory, which may enrich individuals, but will not afford much employment for shipping or seamen. The Dutch station of Elmina being within seven miles, greatly hurts by its free ports and admission of American ships, the trade of this place. Even the people of Cape Coast go now to Elmina for their supplies.

Should your Lordship feel disposed to continue the establishment on this coast, I would recommend above all things to get Elmina from the Dutch, abandon all the places but that and Accra, except a nominal sovereignty, by keeping the English flag flying, and a paid native chief in each. This is the only arrangement under which, with the assistance of a steam-boat, I would venture to recommend the continuance of a British force upon the Gold Coast.

I do not know with what powers your Lordship has been pleased to invest Lt. Col. Grant, but he seems to consider himself authorised to dispose of all the public money voted for this station without any reference to the Governor. Such an arrangement is quite at variance with my instructions, and if tolerated could not but lead to great disorder and abuse, and involve the Government at home in difficulty, as in the recent occurrences in the Gambia. I consider the various stations on the coast as military detachments furnished from headquarters at Sierra Leone, and the officers commanding them, answerable to me, not only for the discipline of the troops, but for every shilling of public money which passes through their hands; and I hope to be honoured with the sanction of your Lordship to the orders which I have given to this effect. I will only take leave further to observe that without the aid of a steam-boat it is impossible that I can carry on the duties of the two stations, and I would therefore strongly recommend that the Gold Coast should have the advantage of a resident governor and separate corps. By trying for both I should do justice to neither. . . .   [C.O.267/65]

68 MAJOR-GENERAL TURNER TO EARL BATHURST   ACCRA, 9 APRIL, 1825.
. . . I have now had an opportunity of seeing all our stations on the Gold Coast,

and some little leisure to reflect upon their importance. I have no means of estimating the degree of importance which is attached to civilisation, to moral and religious instruction, and to the improvement of the condition of Africans, and were I to possess more information than I do, I doubt whether I should be a competent judge: but as far as the commercial concerns of the coast and the military protection are concerned, I feel that I shall be borne out in stating that neither the one nor the other are in a condition, or likely, under the present policy, to be in a condition to give satisfaction to those concerned in them, or to yield advantage to England.

The policy which was adopted at the transfer of these settlements to the Crown, coupled with the circumstances of other nations having settlements and free ports in their immediate vicinity, could not but have the effect, by attempting to levy heavy duties on English goods in our ports, to throw the trade into the hands of those who had free ports. Thus the English merchants themselves, in their distress, give the finishing blow to the trade of the British settlements by sending their own goods to these free ports to save duties and prevent their perishing in their hands by being unsold. But they only get money prices for them, and the valuable barter trade is lost to them as the natives go where the cheapest things are. It was overlooked, I presume, in imposing the Sierra Leone duties on this coast, that at the former place we have a country and a line of coast entirely to ourselves, from which we exclude foreigners and rivals, and that we force the natives to take our goods at our own prices: but here it is quite the reverse. Our rivals, Dutch and Danes, are, as it were, next door to us, and by their free ports carry away the trade from us.

The question, therefore, seems to be whether under all circumstances it is advisable to keep up these settlements at all, or, being kept up, whether they are to be maintained on the securest and most profitable footing? My belief is that the maintaining them will be to the Government a source of dissatisfaction, expense and waste of valuable public property, because there will always be much difference of opinion about them. Expense will be great because they are all in a ruinous and dilapidated state; whilst the want of harbours and the constant surf renders the landing of heavy stores hazardous, and at times impracticable, and the want of superintendence will always be felt in a place to which there is great dislike to reside.

But, on the other hand, should it be determined to keep up these settlements, the only policy under which there appears to be any chance of doing so successfully is to take a line of coast to ourselves by getting Elmina from the Dutch — (a place which I believe the Netherlands Government will not be found very unwilling to part with) — and purchasing from the native chiefs — (which can be done at a trifling expense) — a narrow territory, under five miles back, parallel to the sea all the way down from Elmina to this — (about 100 miles) — in order to give us a right to keep strangers off. We would command the whole trade of the coast, with the same expense or less than now, and there would be no risk of war with the native tribes because there would be no other place for them to go with their produce, or for means to carry on wars with. And there is no doubt but a very considerable trade could thus be pursued, and an intercourse opened with the interior of Africa, which under good management would become profitable to individuals and would prove a powerful agent in throwing open and civilising this part of Africa; and considerable duties might be safely collected by making all vessels call at a point [to] windward, show their manifests and pay on all the cargo. Gold dust and ivory are the only articles of trade on this coast worthy of notice.

The military force which I would recommend would be four hundred men, all natives, with a lieutenant-colonel Commandant, and four captains, the usual number of subalterns and regimental staff; this little corps to be quite distinct from the present African Corps which might then be reduced in strength, and the two companies now stationed on this coast be made over to the new corps, and a proportion of the officers also. The Lieut. Col. should be an officer of experience and abilities. . . . He should have the commission of Lieut. Governor under the Governor of Sierra Leone, but . . . transmit his own accounts to England. The situation would, in my opinion, for such an officer, be a very desirable and creditable one: but no officer should be selected for it who has been brought up in the African school. I never saw one of them worth employing.

I do not propose this plan to your Lordship with any view to save myself further trouble. I came to this country with no such feeling about me, but on the other hand, to work as long as my faculties will hold out, and it is perfectly indifferent to me where that work is done, whether on the Gold Coast or at Sierra Leone. But I would be grossly deceiving your Lordship and doing injustice to myself were I not to state unequivocally the impossibility of my attending to both, or doing justice to either if I attempted it.

Sir Charles McCarthy evidently looked at things through a flattering medium, and trusted much to the power of proclamations and fine words, as well as to those around him. The consequence has been that idleness, disorder and corruption to the greatest degree prevailed throughout the departments and no account whatever has been transmitted from the Gold Coast since its annexation in 1822. As to slavery, it nowhere exists to a greater degree than under the walls of our forts. . . . The discipline of the troops was at the lowest state I ever saw it anywhere, and the negligence of the officers beyond example.

The state of Cape Coast is wretched beyond description. Lieutenant-Colonel Sutherland caused a considerable portion of it to be burned down. The people have applied to me for remuneration, but I have no means of giving any, were I so inclined. The native chiefs around were also clamorous about their services, saying that they were drawn into the war, that they were promised great rewards if they joined, and that they did so at much expense and risk to themselves; that they have brought upon themselves the vengeance of the Ashantees, that they must have ammunition to defend themselves with, and that they must be remunerated for their losses. These are some of the difficulties into which the people wh urged poor Sir Charles McCarthy to undertake the war, brought upon their country. . . .

Of the Ashantees I have heard nothing since my last, nor have I considered it necessary to alter in regard to them the line of policy which I then laid down for myself. I find that the appearance of the transports and troops produced a great sensation throughout the country. . . . The object of their assembling was supposed to be Elmina, in which I by no means undeceived them, because the conviction of my being able to take it has greatly raised the estimate of our means. . . . It is under this impression alone that a good peace and terms can be procured and that we can regain our proper station. . . . Before I left England . . . I sent messengers to the Commander [of the Squadron] begging that he would assist me with part of his squadron in making a demonstration before Elmina, but he took no notice of me, and withdrew all the ships off the coast on my approaching it.

I regret the circumstance because I am satisfied that nothing short of the actual possession of Elmina could have so beneficial an effect as our anchoring before it and showing them and the Ashantees, who have an ambassador there, how easily we could take [it] from them, and how little dependence that nation must place on getting hereafter their warlike supplies from thence. . . . Should hostilities recommence, something of the kind must be done as they are almost all Ashantees without one European, and care nothing for their Governor, who was a cook in the same place with General Daendels. It is here alone that the Ashantees are vulnerable. By witholding powder from them and giving it to the other tribes, they could be at any time destroyed in a few months or humbled to anything we wished. I hope that I have satisfied your Lordship of the importance of Elmina to us, and that I will receive instructions respecting it.

This place is very small, but like the others much out of repair, and [has] no barracks but the cells where the slaves were kept. Still, if we keep the coast, I would recommend an economical post being kept up here. They are a better kind of people and the country is better.

I leave this for Gambia in a couple of days. . . . I fear that it will be a long time before I get back to Sierra Leone. The winds and currents make it necessary to go near 1,000 miles further from it than we are now before we get into a trade wind to carry us back. Indeed, the difficulties of communication between the two places are so great that it would be easier for the General Officer at Cork to take charge of Barbados than for me to take charge of the Gold Coast. . . . [C.O.267/65]

69 [COLONIAL OFFICE] MEMORANDUM ON THE GOLD COAST 2 JULY, 1825.
. . . General Turner, in describing the present state of the Gold Coast proposes three plans for the consideration of Lord Bathurst:

1st. To abandon the coast altogether as he apprehends that 'for want of harbours and many other causes, no adequate national recompense for the sacrifice either as regards commerce, civilisation or religious instruction'.

2ndly. To obtain possession of a line of coast 100 miles in extent and five miles in breadth in order to prevent the trade which is driven by high duties from our

ports from seeking the foreign ports contiguous to them, and

3rdly. To give up all the minor forts, retaining over them only a nominal sovereignty, to keep possession of Cape Coast and Accra alone, and to secure the fortress of Elmina, which he considers essential to the security of our trade on this coast, and which he apprehends may without difficulty be obtained from the Dutch.

In regard to the first proposition, it should be observed, that in deciding on the propriety of giving up any of our colonial possessions, it is necessary to consider not only the expense and embarrassment which may be saved by abandoning an unhealthy and insecure settlement, but also what is likely to be its future condition when so relinquished; and it is to be presumed that if the course recommended by General Turner were adopted, the Americans, who have been anxious to form an establishment lower down this coast, to indemnify themselves for their failure at Cape Mesurados, would most assuredly step in.[1] The danger of allowing these people to establish themselves on this coast is pointed out by Gen. McCarthy, and especially of permitting them to obtain from the Danes the cession of Christiansburg. (Desp. of 18 May, 1822.)

As General Turner does not point out any other position which could be occupied in order to further the objects for which the establishments on the Gold Coast have hitherto been kept up, it would appear that the propriety of not giving up one point d'appui until another has been secured, has not occurred to him, and the reasons which he has urged for abandoning this coast altogether are the less satisfactory as he does not partake of the general dread of the climate, and in proportion to the extent of blame which he attaches somewhat indiscriminately to all who have been entrusted with the direction of public affairs in these settlements since they have come

[1] The Settlement at Cape Mesurados, the future Monrovia, was in great difficulties at this time.

into the hands of the Government, a favourable expectation may be entertained of an improved order of things under a well-regulated, careful administration. . . .

The objections to the second proposal are numerous, but it is sufficient to observe that the removal of those duties which drive the traders from our ports would be a more simple mode of accomplishing the object in view than by entering into negotiation with the Dutch and Danes for the cession of forts over most of which they only hold a nominal sovereignty, or by the purchase of a long range of useless territory from the native chiefs.

The third scheme appears to be the most reasonable of all, at least as far as the selection of the points to be retained is concerned. These are clearly Cape Coast Castle and Accra, and it does not appear necessary that we should keep possession of any of the minor forts. The two of next importance are Dixcove and Annamaboe, but the chief recommendation of the former is its affording a port for the shipping the materials for building which are found in the neighbourhood, and Annamaboe is too near Cape Coast Castle to make its retention at all advisable.

It is proper, however, to state, in estimating the importance of these places, that Dixcove is considered both by Sir G. Collier, Sir R. Mends (successively commodores on this station) and by Governor McCarthy, as a position which ought to be retained, and that Governor McCarthy even recommended that Annamaboe should be kept.

Of the forts occupied by the Dutch and Danes, there are only two kept up in anything approaching to a respectable footing, Elmina and Christiansborg. The rest, such as Succondee, St. Sebastians, Commenda, and three or four other places of a minor description, are only garrisoned by a non-commissioned officer, stationed there for the purpose of hoisting the colours of the nation.

During the Ashantee War, the black population of Elmina appear to have taken a decidedly active part against us, by supplying our enemies with the means of annoyance — and although it may not be desirable to enter upon any negotiation with the Dutch for the cession of this place, yet they might fairly be required to impose such a check on the inhabitants of the town as to prevent their giving us fresh cause for complaint.

It is stated by Governor McCarthy 'that he understood from Mr. Bourke, the Danish Minister at Paris, that his Government would readily part with Christiansborg (or Danish Accra) if applied to on the subject' (18 May, 1822). It will depend upon the view which is taken of the different schemes submitted to Lord B. whether it is advisable to negotiate with the Danes for this purpose or not. The fort itself is said to be in good order and the soil within twelve miles distant to be favourable to the cultivation of coffee and cotton.

Accra is said to be the most healthy of all our settlements, but that is disputed by some of those . . . who have had the best opportunities of judging. It appears that the deaths on the Gold Coast among the better class of society may be estimated at 1 in 8; at Sierra Leone at 1 in 12. (Dr. Nicholls).

The Governors of forts should be restricted from being traders. The civil establishment upon this coast seems to be on a much larger scale than can possibly be required.   [C.O.267/65]

70 EARL BATHURST TO MAJOR-GENERAL TURNER   5 JULY, 1825.
[He regrets that the West African settlements were in so unsatisfactory a state, but says that no sudden or complete change of government should be undertaken before a special commission of inquiry had reported.] . . .

I have to acquaint you that after a full consideration of the present state of His Majesty's Possessions on the Gold Coast and the policy in regard to them which it would be most prudent to pursue, His

Majesty's Government have not deemed it expedient to abandon the coast altogether, to which measure your opinion seems in some degree to lean. It is reasonable to expect that under a better system of management, the evils which have been already experienced may not recur, and that some of those commercial advantages which have been anticipated from opening a communication with the interior of Africa may yet be realised, and may be hereafter extended by improving the friendly intercourse which has recently been established with the reigning power in Soudan and Bornou. Although, however, a general abandonment of our settlements on the Gold Coast has not been considered advisable, it has now been determined to reduce the number of points of which military possession shall be retained, in this quarter, to the two most important, which appear to be Cape Coast Castle and the fort at Accra, giving up entirely all military charge of the minor posts along the coast, of the greater part of which, indeed, for some time past only nominal possession has been enjoyed. And I have to desire that you will take the necessary steps for withdrawing from the smaller places to which I have alluded, any garrison there may be, together with such ordnance and ordnance stores as may be found at these stations, and that you will concentrate them in the two forts above mentioned. It will be necessary for you at the same time to make a correspondent reduction in the civil establishment belonging to this coast. It appears clearly to have been placed on much too large a scale, and you will make the best arrangements in your power for the employment of such individuals as it may be thought advisable to retain, reporting to me the manner in which you have temporarily disposed of the rest. [Officers will be sent out by the Board of Ordnance to put the forts in an efficient condition.] . . .

I cannot but anticipate that when placed on a proper footing, with a garrison of 300 men, and by remaining strictly on the defensive, the forts of Accra and Cape Coast Castle will prove sufficiently strong to keep in check any force which may be brought against them by the native powers, or to prevent any annoyance from the neighbouring fort of Elmina, should its inhabitants on any future occasion give colour to complaints similar to those which were brought against them during our late war with the Ashantees.

I have to signify to you His Majesty's approbation of your determination to abstain from all interference in the dissensions which appear to prevail among the nations and tribes inhabiting the countries adjacent to the Gold Coast.

There is no desire on the part of His Majesty's Government to obtain possession of any territory on the coast beyond that in the immediate vicinity of the two forts which have been named, and no advantage can be gained by entering into negotiations with the neighbouring chiefs which might have such accessions of territory for its ultimate object.

You have acted wisely in proposing the repeal of the act imposing a duty of six per cent. upon any goods imported into the colony which did not belong to merchants then residing in the colony, and which operated injuriously. . . . [He is urged to avoid all unreasonable expenditure.]

[C.O.268/20]

71 MAJOR-GENERAL TURNER TO LT.-COL. PURDON

SIERRA LEONE, 18 OCTOBER, 1825.

. . . In everything connected with Elmina there is much difficulty, as I have reason to apprehend that Earl Bathurst considers it a respectable Dutch settlement with European authorities and troops, and under that impression, entitled to all the respect of a garrison belonging to a friendly power. I will endeavour to explain to his Lordship that, although the flag of the Netherlands is flying there, that there are no European soldiers or merchants, that the people are all Africans (chiefly Ashantees) by whom, and not by the nominal Governor, all questions of importance are decided.

Regarding a place so singularly constituted, I cannot at this distance give you any other instructions than to observe the strictest neutrality, and by no means whatever to involve yourself either with that place or the native tribes without consulting your Government. I am well aware of the embarrassment into which the policy pursued during the Ashantee war has thrown you; and that it is very possible that your inability to fulfil promises so freely made at that time to the various tribes for their alliance, has already produced dissatisfaction and may ultimately lead to hostility. You will, without compromising your Government, do all you can to appease these irritations, but on no account are you to assume a hostile attitude, or go beyond the walls of your fort.

Should the war already begun between Elmina and Cudgoe Cheebo King of Dinkera, our best ally in the late war, still continue, you will have a very difficult part to act, as, on the one hand you must avoid, notwithstanding their late conduct towards us, giving any just cause of complaint to the commandant of Elmina, and, on the other hand, you must be equally careful not to give offence to your best ally. . . . Make the King of Dinkera your enemy and Cape Coast is lost. Your best and only chance of safety, situated as you are with Elmina, is by observing the strictest neutrality. . . .   [C.O.267/66]

72 INSTRUCTIONS TO THE WEST AFRICAN COMMISSIONERS   11 NOVEMBER, 1825.

. . . With respect to the Gold Coast, you are acquainted with the measures which it is proposed to adopt for reducing our establishments there to a very limited scale. . . .

The great delay which attends the communication by sea between Sierra Leone and the Gold Coast would appear to render it expedient that the officer appointed to administer the Government of this settlement should possess greater authority than is entrusted to him at present; and in deliberating upon this subject, you will consider whether the interests of the public service would not even require that the Government of the Gold Coast should be separated from the general Government of the Western Coast of Africa. . . .   [C.O.268/23]

73 EARL BATHURST TO MAJOR-GENERAL TURNER   20 DECEMBER, 1825.[1]

. . . There are no official documents in this Department which can throw any light on the promises and expectations which you seem to imagine were held out to our late allies on the Gold Coast. During the contest with the Ashantees, it may have been difficult to avoid, and even prudent to accede to the applications which came from such of the tribes as were disposed to take up arms against that nation; and I am aware that it may now be equally difficult not to admit that several of the native powers by their conduct at that time are entitled to our kindness and favourable consideration in any point where their demands can be reasonably complied with.

As, however, it would be highly impolitic to satisfy claims of this nature by furnishing these people with arms and ammunition by which they might be encouraged to make war upon each other, I am disposed to approve the instructions which you gave to Major Purdon, not to comply with the Queen of Akim's demand. But if she has any positive claim upon this country, which has not been already satisfied, and which is founded upon any agreement into which she may have entered with the British authorities on the

[1] On 19 October, 1825, Turner had asked Bathurst for 'instructions relative to the promises which were held out and the expectations of several of our late allies, particularly the Queen of Akim'. This was the great queen, Dokua, enstooled in 1817.

Gold Coast, you will instruct Major Purdon to acquaint me with the nature of such claims.

I have also to convey to you my approbation of the instructions which you gave to that officer for regulating his conduct during the contest between the chief of Dinkerah and the people of Elmina; and I should hope that by strictly adhering to that system of neutrality which you have directed him to pursue, no pretence for complaint will be afforded to either of the contending parties.

I have etc.   [C.O.267/66]

74 LORD BATHURST TO SIR N. CAMPBELL[1]   LONDON, 20 JUNE, 1826.
Sir,

I transmit to you . . . copies of two communications . . . which have been received from Lt. Col. Purdon, the officer Commanding on the Gold Coast.

These communications leave no room for doubting that an Ashantee force is approaching Cape Coast Castle and probably with hostile intention, although upon this point Lt. Col. Purdon has not transmitted any certain information. At all events, you will perceive that the Lt. Col. has taken measures for strengthening his position, in doing which he has acted wisely: but he has also issued ammunition to the native tribes, who appear, by an act of treachery, to have provoked attack from the Ashantees, and in this respect, the Lt. Colonel has not only, in my opinion, acted injudiciously, but, as you must be aware, in contravention to my instructions.

Under these circumstances, I have to signify to you the King's commands that you proceed forthwith in a ship of war

[1] Major-General Sir Neil Campbell (1776–1827) entered the army in 1797; served in the West Indies and the Peninsula, and with the Allied armies in Germany and France, 1813–14 — where he was severely wounded by a Cossack who mistook him for a Frenchman; knighted, 1814, and became a Major-General in 1825; appointed Governor of Sierra Leone, 13 May, 1825.

which has been appointed to convey you to Sierra Leone, where you will assume the Government of that Colony and of its dependencies, and you are then to repair immediately to the Gold Coast.

Upon your arrival there, you will make yourself acquainted with the real state of things, and if you should be enabled to satisfy yourself that the Ashantee nation does not meditate an attack against Cape Coast Castle, you will place yourself in communication with their rulers for the purpose of settling some definitive arrangement of peace with them, according to the spirit of the instructions which your predecessor received for his guidance upon his departure for Africa.

If, however, you should find the Ashantee rulers bent upon offensive views and projects, either against His Majesty's settlements on the Gold Coast, or against the neighbouring tribes, you will in that case concentrate your force at Cape Coast Castle, and abandon such of the other forts as it may appear to you inexpedient or impracticable to maintain against the enemy; and upon this subject you will in a great measure be guided by the opinions and advice of the commission of engineers which has been appointed to inquire into the state of those forts, and which will not, I trust, have left the coast before your arrival on the station.

You will, therefore, understand that, if you cannot make peace with the Ashantees, you are not, on that account, to undertake any military operations in the field against them, but you are to maintain possession of Cape Coast Castle, and without the assistance of the native tribes, whose total want of discipline renders them unworthy of confidence, and whose dissensions with the Ashantees arise out of local questions, which do not interest the policy of this country in maintaining a settlement on the Gold Coast.

I have etc.   [C.O.268/26]

75 LIEUT.-COLONEL PURDON TO EARL BATHURST

BRITISH ACCRA, 10 AUGUST, 1826.

My Lord,

In my last official despatch I made known to you my intention of taking the field to oppose the further progress of the enemy, and have now the honour to acquaint your Lordship that the arms of His Majesty and of his allies (under my command) have been crowned with success, by obtaining a signal victory over that of the Ashantee nation (headed by their King in person) in the plains of Dodowah, on the 7th instant.

Aware of the intentions and motions of the enemy, I collected all my force, amounting to nearly twelve thousand men, and marched from Accra on the 29th of last month to Abomassey, eighteen miles from hence. On the 4th of the present month I moved on to Achrooaland, three miles further in advance. For the events of the 6th, I arrived on the ground above alluded to, about forty miles from this station; picturesque and beautiful in the extreme, and sufficiently spacious to allow the largest armies that ever met in contact to decide on the fate of empires. The morning of the 7th ushered in a lovely day, a favourite fetish one for the King to fight on. It happened to fall on Monday, which his wise men prognosticated would render him invincible, and, no doubt confiding in their sorcery, he advanced to the attack, about half past nine a.m., in a most imposing and determined manner, and was met midway by the troops I had the honour to command, with corresponding bravery.

The fire that commenced was as impressive and animated as any I have ever yet witnessed, for upwards of an hour. But at the expiration of that time, a lull took place that caused me some uneasiness, and this originated in the left of my right-centre brigade giving way, and nearly the whole of my right wing. It was a critical moment . . . and necessary to redeem; and as soon as my centre reserve, composed solely of a company of the Royal African Colonial Corps (for reasons I shall hereafter explain) became uncovered by the refugees, I opened a destructive fire on the enemy, of rockets and of grape and canister, from my six and three-pounders, that made lanes thro' their columns and did infinite execution.

Perceiving them panic-struck and in the utmost confusion, I took advantage of it instanter, and moved forward to the attack with every man of my regiment present (save those with the field pieces) and cut through the enemy's centre. They immediately gave way in all directions, and the victory was our own. Here I must do justice to Accotoo, the King of Aquimboo[1] (who commanded a strong corps of observation on my extreme right, to protect that flank and watch the motions of the enemy), by acknowledging that he literally executed the orders I had given him in the morning; namely, to bring up his right shoulders the moment he heard the report of my great guns, and to attack the Ashantees on their left flanks. This movement, operating simultaneously in unison with my own, had a very happy effect, and decided the fate of the day.

Had the whole of our allies obeyed my orders, neither the King nor indeed few of his army, could possibly have escaped. But they are an opinionated, wild, mulish, undisciplined race, that will have their own way if possible, and will not attend to any system at variance with their own, or proper subordination. And the cause of their flight I attribute solely to their disobedience of my positive commands, by breaking from the line I had formed, and rushing to the contest in a savage manner, without any reserve to support or prudence to guide them in the case of a mishap. In such an undertaking I warned them of the consequence most forcibly and repeatedly, without effect. But when it was nearly too late — a touch and go concern — after getting well [frightened?] for their folly, they were glad to seek protection under our wings and acknowledge their error.

[1] Akoto, king of Akwamu.

Our loss from all the accounts I can collect, amounts to eight thousand[1] killed and two thousand wounded. That of the enemy, in killed, wounded and prisoners, to at least five thousand men. . . .

The whole of the King's camp equipage (I am informed of great value) and that of his army, have fallen into the hands of some of the least deserving of our allies and their followers. Among the plunder is, I learn, the state umbrella, the Golden Stool of state, and gold dust, ivory and other valuables, to a large amount. But what I consider (in a national point of view) of still greater importance, is that the head of the late Sir Charles McCarthy has been recovered (I have had it in my hands), and it is at this moment in the possession of Adonoqua, king of Aquapim, who asks a large sum for it. Should I be able to obtain possession without making too great a sacrifice, I shall have it interred with funeral honours. At present it is enveloped in two folds of paper, covered with arabic characters, tied up a third time in a silk handkerchief, and lastly, sewed up neatly in a leopard skin.

I should have mentioned that from the examination of many prisoners, (without any contradiction or a dissenting voice among them) it would appear that the army of the king of Ashantee amounted to at least 25,000 men, previous to the battle, and that of the allies, as before stated, to nearly 12,000, composed of the troops of Accatoo, King of Aquimbo, Adonaqua, King of Aquapim,[2] Dunqua, Queen of Aikim, Cudjoe Cheebo, King of Dinkera[3] young Cudjoe, King of Assin,[4] the King of Impil,[5] and many other caboceers and captains from different parts of the coast, with the whole of the British, Dutch and Danish Accras. This force I divided into five brigades and two strong corps of observation to protect each flank.

[1] Eight hundred is presumably meant.
[2] Ado Dankwa had been coerced into declaring against Ashanti in 1823.
[3] Kwadwo Tsibu of Denkyira.
[4] Tsibu Kuma of Asin-Atandaso.
[5] Probably Owusu Oko, king of Twifu.

The expense attending this campaign has been trivial beyond all comparison. I well knew it was not the wish of Great Britain to be involved in a war when it could be avoided with honour, but nolens volens, it was literally forced on us, and we had no alternative. . . . [Concludes with notices of individual services.]

[C.O.267/74]

76 CAMPBELL TO BATHURST
CAPE COAST CASTLE, 5 NOVEMBER, 1826.
My Lord,

It would far exceed the limit of an ordinary dispatch to submit to your Lordship a particular account of the distracted state into which this country, from Apollonia to the Volta, has been thrown since the late Sir Charles McCarthy meditated on war against the Ashantees; in which it still continues, notwithstanding the victory over them, which has produced a cessation of hostilities in the interior, and, as yet, has kept in concord the different powers who form a barrier between the Ashantees and the coast.

This peace is already on the point of being disturbed by demands from the native chiefs who fought on the 7th of August, for compensation or fine in money from others who did not send any men, but who were equally at war with the Ashantees. Messengers are now on their way from Accra, with others from the Queen of Akim, to make this demand from the King of the Fantees, near this on the right, and it is certain that the same was paid by the King of Warsaw, recently, to the King of Dinkerah (Cudjoe Chibboo), on the left. This state of peace and union among the confederates cannot continue long, for some of them were the constant allies of the Ashantees until they were bribed, cajoled or frightened, by threats of destruction from Sir Charles McCarthy, (and even stronger measures) to join his alliance. The greatest supporters of it since Sir Charles McCarthy's death, are the kings of Dinkerah and Tufil,[1] brothers

[1] Twifu.

and relations of the King of Ashantee, who were brought up at Coomassie, who can never expect forgiveness, and have a band of followers occupying a small tract of country 20 miles north of Elmina, which they threaten, and fall upon every pretext to attack others, or instigate them against each other and then plunder one of them. This has been the state of the coast between Elmina and Apollonia ever since Sir C. McCarthy's campaign ended by the retreat of the Ashantees in July, 1824. . . . By land the inhabitants of [Elmina] are in a state of very close blockade. Some Ashantee traders have not been able to get out, and the Governor assures me that ever since July 1824, there has been no communication by any individual to or from the Ashantees.

This account of the country will, I hope, induce your Lordship to estimate the difficulties which present themselves in opening any negotiation with the Ashantees, and which have defeated my efforts to fulfil . . . your Lordship's instruction. . . .

In consequence of the bad footing on which the late Major-General Turner was with the Dutch and Danish Governors, I endeavoured to remove it by studied attention. With the first it was quite successful [but not with the Danish Governor]. . . . He and some others, Europeans as well as native headmen, have obtained possession of a few of the principal Ashantees, including a favourite wife of the king and of his brother's, who are in perfect freedom and very well treated. With these, they expect, in case of peace with the Ashantees, to obtain advantages in trade; in case of [Ashantee] victory, to conciliate them; and to obtain favour with the present ruling tyrants during their prosperity, by encouraging the most violent opposition to peace.

As soon as possible after my arrival here I assembled all the kings and chiefs nearest this place, who were in the campaign, and others, but it was impossible to prevail upon them to unite with the king of England to open even the most indirect

communication with the Ashantees. I told them it was not to propose a peace, but to let it be understood by the Ashantees, that if they sent messengers here 'to ask for peace', they might pass in safety; that it would not be for the king of England alone or separately, but for all together, and that no peace would be granted without the strongest guarantees for the independence of every one of them. Councils were held with them in the formal manner peculiar to this country. They held several among themselves. Presents brought from Sierra Leone were distributed on a very liberal scale, but they would not yield. I then told them that as none of them could unite with the king of England or accept of his mediation, they could not any longer have claims for assistance in any future war; that he was resolved to be at peace with every nation in Africa who would remain peaceable, and wished them to follow the same course. . . .

[All attempts to open a negotiation failed at Accra as well as at Cape Coast.]

[C.O.267/74]

77 CAMPBELL TO BATHURST
CAPE COAST CASTLE, 12 NOVEMBER, 1826.
Confidential.

My Lord,

I have the honour in a confidential despatch to submit to your Lordship some observations respecting this dependency. . . .

1st. The merchants at Cape Coast are in number five, at Annamabu one (the commandant) at British Accra three, including the commandant and the other two are natives; at Dutch Accra none: so that *all* the Europeans (British) upon this coast amount to seven and one European clerk. There are none at the forts which have been abandoned, but, in the villages attached to a few of them nearest this, some of the merchants have a native factor who disposes of European goods by barter. This is, however, very limited, because every vessel from Europe carries on the same trade along the whole coast from

Apollonia, which is done by the master of the vessel on behalf of the owners at home. The goods for merchants at the British, Dutch and Danish settlements are landed in course of the voyage to leeward, and the vessel returns, perhaps more than once, to take on board the export barter from the natives as well as from the merchants.

2ndly. Some vessels bring out all their cargo for barter direct with the natives, and none for merchants. It is difficult to ascertain what proportion of the whole trade is carried on by each mode, but I am led, after every possible enquiry, to think that one fourth or one fifth only is carried on by the merchants. The collector thinks only one-tenth, but his estimate is probably erroneous.

3rdly. The whole of the merchants here trade upon their own accounts, and it cannot be very extensive or profitable when confined to so few, and no establishments of warehouses or of any kind that are observable.

4th. It is probable that the consumption of British manufactures and the exports would be the same without duties or establishments of government and without resident Europeans.

5thly. Nearly the whole of the imports and exports to and from the Dutch and Danish settlements are *British*. A man of war or merchant vessel comes out from the Netherlands once a year, or not so often, a store ship once in two years from Denmark. They do not levy any duties. Here, the support of the Netherlands' settlements is ascribed to the partiality of the king, in consequence of Elmina having never struck the Orange flag. It is obvious that neither the Dutch or Danish settlements are beneficial.

6thly. Their settlements are more upon a mercantile and colonial footing than the British. The troops are entirely colonial, excepting one or two officers and the governors. The present temporary governors are merchants and they, as well as all the officers, are engaged in trade. The Dutch draw for £4,000 sterling per year,

which the governor (ad interim) told me, includes the pay of the troops and every other expense, unless some unusual repair is required for the forts.

I do not think it possible to reduce the expenses of this dependency under the actual amount of them, upon the present footing, but from investigation here, and the proof of the Dutch settlements, I am induced to think that £4,000 per year would be enough for the British also, if they were placed upon the same footing, and that every officer and soldier of His Majesty's troops were withdrawn, which would then be indispensable.

Upon this point, I beg leave with every submission to state, upon the experience of my predecessors as well as my own, the utter impossibility of carrying on the duties of a regiment, and enforcing the care of regimental stores, between stations so separated as Sierra Leone and the Gold Coast, with such uncertain communication . . . which will now be much less frequent in consequence of the removal of the victualling department of the navy from Cape Coast to Ascension; a measure upon which I do not presume to offer any remark excepting that it will greatly injure this place by the loss of canoe hire and many other sources of expenditure circulated among the merchants and natives.

The arrangements already made for the two companies of the Royal African Corps stationed here, and for the garrisons of Accra and Annamaboe, would make it less difficult to carry into execution any changes which His Majesty's Government might please to order, for assimilating this dependency to the settlements of the other two Powers, with a view to economy, and to the efficiency of officers, by admitting coloured officers into these two companies, and separating them from the Royal African Corps, the duties of which at Sierra Leone and the Gambia fully require the whole of the officers and soldiers, independent of the disorganisation which is otherwise occasioned. The officers for this coast could easily be found here at present among the sons of the European merchants who have been educated in England and for whom there is no employment after the death of their fathers. They would not require much pay, no half-pay, no pension. . . .

The victory over the Ashantees has produced no results towards peace, commerce or civilisation. It has removed one tyrant for a time, and raised up several who are more barbarous and less amenable to any system, and who have nothing to offer for European manufactures. They have not the slightest information whatever since the day after the battle of the 7th August, respecting the Ashantees, not daring to enter their frontier. And as soon as the latter can recruit they will probably again venture forward, particularly if the confederates quarrel among themselves, as they will do in all probability.

From what I saw of the field of battle, and have ascertained here and at Accra, I am certain that the results of the battle have been grossly exaggerated. The Ashantees were not prepared to meet so large a force together, and some circumstance occasioned a panic, after the natives *had been repulsed* by them. It is impossible to say what occasioned it, but it must have been only in apprehension, and probably the fire of the rockets and opening of our guns, (although the det.ᵗ of the Royal African Corps saw only thirty men from the bushes to fire at), and the circuitous march of a native chief who at the same moment unexpectedly opened . . . fire in their rear.

These facts will enable your Lordship to appreciate what are the future prospects of this unhappy country. The only advantage which has been gained is that the natives have no longer any claim upon Great Britain for assistance in future or guarantees for the past, as I distinctly told them: but it will be very difficult to refuse them shelter if, at any time hereafter, they are driven under the walls of the [forts]. Such circumstances must again produce disease, famine, destruction of the well and

of the present arrangements for keeping the pond clean (by which abundance of good water is procured), as the garrison of two companies would be insufficient for more than the castle, which does not protect that supply of water, and only commands a very small part of the town. It deserves to be anticipated also, that this protection, or forbearance to fire upon one of the parties, will be considered a support by the other; as will the sale of ammunition by British merchants who will, if aggrieved, claim support from the commandant and involve him in a war and a very fatal blockade in spite of the most judicious conduct.

A message has been sent from the natives of British Accra to the confederates, to urge them to destroy any party sent from this to communicate with the Ashantees. These people receive an annuity from His Majesty's Government for the caboceers and headmen, but perceive that there is a termination to abuses and lavish expenditure of money and stores, by which they and the Europeans have had their greatest profits for some years past.

I have etc.   [C.O.267/74]

78 EARL BATHURST TO SIR N. CAMPBELL
LONDON, 21 MARCH, 1827.
[Opens with reference to the estimates for Sierra Leone.] . . .

You will perceive . . . that it is not proposed to apply to Parliament for more than a very limited and temporary grant on account of the forts on the Gold Coast, as it has appeared to His Majesty's Government that the interests of this country do not require that any civil government should be kept up there for the future, or that any garrison should be maintained there after the expiration of the present year.

It will be incumbent upon you, therefore, immediately upon the receipt of this despatch, to take measures for withdrawing such officers of Government as may be stationed at any of the forts; and I trust that you may not find it incompatible with your convenience to proceed in person to Cape Coast Castle for the purpose of concluding the other arrangements which must be adopted for giving effect to the views of His Majesty's Government.

Upon your arrival at Cape Coast Castle you will assemble such British merchants as may be residing there and with whom you appear already to have communicated on this subject; and you will announce to them that it is proposed to evacuate the forts altogether at the expiration of the year, or as soon after that period as a due attention to the security of the lives and properties of those who may be inclined to remain for mercantile purposes will permit. You will inform them also that if, in consequence of this measure, they should feel desirous of removing themselves and their establishments, you will be ready to afford them every assistance which they could reasonably expect for that purpose; and if they should propose to you to remove at once, you will then withdraw the troops and public stores, and cause the forts to be demolished, or at least rendered unfit for military occupation.

But if the merchants should on the contrary express their wish to remain on the coast, you are authorised to assure them that you will maintain military occupation of Cape Coast Castle during the present year, at the conclusion of which you will place them in possession of Cape Coast Castle and of the fort of Accra, if they should desire it, and assign to them a limited number of guns, together with two or three hundred stand of arms, a proportion of accoutrements and a moderate quantity of ammunition.

You will also acquaint them that if, in the event of their wishing to remain on the coast, they should think it expedient to embody themselves and their labourers into an armed militia, you could hold out to them the expectation that, for the first year, a sum not exceeding two thousand pounds, by way of outfit and pay, £1,500 for the second year, and £1,000 afterwards,

would be assigned to them and issued to them under proper regulations, for the support of such militia, which would be liable to be inspected from time to time by an officer whom you would despatch for that purpose. But you must distinctly apprize the merchants that, in the event of their preferring to remain in possession of the forts, it must be entirely at their own risk, and that they would under no circumstances have to expect any assistance from you for the purpose of carrying on hostile operations against the native tribes, nor any aid whatever beyond that which has been defined, for the purpose of protecting the forts against aggression. For although there might be an occasional appearance of a ship of war on the coast, in order to demonstrate to the native powers that the interests of the British residents in this quarter are not lost sight of by the Government at home, yet the captains of His Majesty's ships would receive strict orders to abstain from all interference in any contest which the merchants might be engaged in ashore.

It must also be explained to them that as the forts, when they shall have been evacuated, cannot be considered in any other light than as factories, and in no degree as dependencies of Sierra Leone, His Majesty's Government will not be considered responsible, after the expiration of the present year, for the payment of what is usually called the ground-rent of the castles, or for presents of any description, to the native authorities; nor will they be answerable for any further disbursement for repairs or improvements in these buildings beyond what it has been settled to contribute for that object in the present year. . . .

[Concludes with instructions for the disposal of the civil officers of government; pensions; native labourers; government stores; and the future relief of the merchants from customs duties.]

[C.O.268/26: H.C.57, A & P (1830)]

79 EARL BATHURST TO SIR N. CAMPBELL
23 MARCH, 1827.
Secret and confidential.
Sir,

I think it necessary to apprize you unreservedly of the view which His Majesty's Government have taken of the subject matter of your despatch No. 56 of the 5th of November last.

It appears from that despatch that the difficulties which you have had to encounter in your attempt to enter into communication with the Ashantees have their source in the distracted condition of the tribes who call themselves our allies; in the apparent disinclination of the British residents on the Gold Coast to assist in the accomplishment of an object which did not happen to coincide with their own opinion; and, to a certain degree, in the want of co-operation on the part of the commandant of the Danish settlement of Accra.

These obstacles combined during your short stay at the Gold Coast must have proved sufficiently formidable, I doubt not, to arrest the execution of your measures; but I cannot believe that you will find the same difficulties subsisting on your return to the coast.

The British merchants there (with whom it will be expedient that you should for the future communicate less unreservedly than you have hitherto done), if they intend (as is most probable) to remain on the coast, will hardly persist in considering that the pacification of the country is not the most desirable object which can be attained at present; and with respect to the commandant of Danish Accra, who appears to have at his disposal the only means by which it has always appeared to me that a communication could properly be established with the Ashantees, I should think that you will have no difficulty in making him understand that the same views of interest which led his predecessor to join in the general resistance against the aggression of the Ashantees, should now induce him to assist cordially in the

attempt to restore matters to a peaceful state. At all events, I would not have you construe unfavourably the refusal of that officer to convoke a meeting of the native chiefs at his fort; and I regret that you did not offer to remove the objection which he stated to you as his reason for not complying with your wishes, as nothing could have been more desirable than that you should have had a full communication with all those persons.

I do not understand from your despatch, who the chiefs are with whom you have already conferred, and how many there were whom you did not see. I am inclined to think, however, that when you shall have an opportunity of meeting them, you may find them more favourably disposed to listen to the explanation of your views than they appear to have been in the preceding autumn. They were then excited by the success which they had obtained over the Ashantees and it was not unnatural that they should wish that sufficient time should be given to enable the heads of all the different tribes concerned to attend at the meeting. It is reasonable, however, to suppose that time will have had some effect in moderating their pretensions; and the proposed evacuation of the forts will at least convince them that if they do not choose to make peace with the Ashantees now, they must be prepared to sustain for the future the whole pressure of the war.

I infer, indeed, from the statements which you have transmitted to me, that the personal situation of the chiefs of Dinkerah and Tufil precluded them from the expectation that they can ever accomodate their differences with the Ashantees. But as the other chiefs are not in a similar predicament, you must make it your endeavour to induce the latter to concur in your views, and to prevent the former from thwarting your measures.

You will be best able to devise upon the spot the arrangements which may be necessary for these purposes: but if, contrary to my expectations, you should find it utterly impracticable to induce the chiefs, when collected, to join you in your endeavours to pacify the country, it will be your duty to declare to them, in that case, that, deeply as His Majesty's Government would deplore their determination to reject the assistance offered to them, yet that you would thenceforth consider yourself absolved from any obligation to interfere in their affairs. It would then remain to be determined whether under such circumstances it might be expedient to carry into effect your instructions to evacuate the forts.

This is a very serious question, upon which I scarcely feel that I can at present convey to you any positive directions. You will bear in mind, however, that the merchants must not be left in a situation of peril; and, considering the disposition and conduct of the native tribes, I should be inclined to think that in the event of their continuing at war with their neighbours, it might not be safe to evacuate the forts within the time I have mentioned.

It will be necessary, however, to watch the proceedings of the merchants in their intercourse with the tribes; and if you should be enabled to obtain positive proof that any of the merchants have instigated the native chiefs to persist in rejecting all attempts to accomodate their differences with the Ashantees, you will not fail to acquaint me with the names of the parties and with their proceedings.

I have only further to acquaint you that I authorise you to carry with you to Cape Coast, the sum of £2,000 from the funds of the castle, which you will apply as may be most expedient, in payment of such necessary expenses as you may have to incur in establishing a communication with the Ashantees. And you will account to me separately and confidentially for the disbursement of the sum in question.

I am etc.   [C.O.268/26]

80 REPORT OF COMMISSIONER ROWAN ON HIS VISIT TO THE GOLD COAST JUNE, 1827.
[(a) Abstract of] the annual imports of the settlements of Cape Coast, Accra, Annamaboe and Dixcove . . . from the period of the transfer of these settlements to the Crown . . . to the 30th June, 1826. . . .

Year	Tonnage	Value of British;		Value of foreign imports	
1822[1]	2,647	£30,781 15s.	9½d.	£11,142 7s.	4d.
1823	4,238	27,101 2s.	9½d.	3,591 —	8d.
1824	5,110	13,898 5s.	½d.	4,289 17s.	8d.
1825	3,689	30,578 3s.	4½d.	2,916 13s.	2½d.
1826[2]	2,621	6,201 —	11d.	2,653 15s.	10d.

[1] From 1 April.   [2] To 30 June.

[(b) Abstract of exports. . . .]

Year	No. of ships	Tonnage	Gold Dust (ounces)	Ivory (tons)	Palm Oil (puncheons)	(tons)
1822[1]	9	1,428	10,896	18	1,202	480
1823	1	105	600	4	95	38
1824	6	610	2,011	20	638	255
1825	8	782	17,063	59½	650	260
1826[2]	6	895	7,071	29¾	590	217

[1] From 1 April.   [2] To 30 June.

[(c) Trade prospects.]

. . . A state of actual warfare, or of hostile preparation, has existed during the whole of the period since the forts were annexed to the crown. The amount of trade in these years, therefore, gives no idea of the extent to which it might be carried on under more favourable circumstances. It has been found impossible to ascertain on the coast, with any precision, or in a manner to be relied on, the amount of trade in the time of the African Company. An endeavour was made by the late Sir Charles McCarthy, to ascertain the imports for 1821. By information received from resident merchants on that occasion, it appeared that the total of the imports on the coast between Cape Palmas and British Accra, was computed to have been in that year, £166,136 currency, at 5 shillings the dollar. Of this amount £118,636 was imported in British, and £47,500 in foreign vessels. Though from the manner in which the information was obtained, it may be erroneous to a considerable extent, yet the amount so greatly exceeds the annual value of goods since imported on the Gold Coast that, after making large allowances, it will indicate a great diminution of trade. . . .

From April, 1822 to June, 1826, the value of British goods imported is £108,560. 7s. 10d., and that of foreign goods £24,593 14s. 8½d. . . . It is proper to remark, however, that the amount of imports here specified is that only upon which duties have been paid, but there is no question that the British have imported considerable quantities of goods the duties upon which have been evaded by means of the vicinity of Dutch possessions, where no duties are levied. . . . It is only requisite for the British merchant to have a store in the Dutch port where he can land his goods and afterwards dispose of them at leisure. Under the existing circumstances he has only the option of pursuing this course, or of relinquishing trade altogether. Foreign goods, that is spirits and tobacco imported in foreign vessels, are principal articles of trade, and these, in the British ports, if per- mitted at all, are subject to six per cent. duty. But the market of the Dutch and English trader being precisely the same, it is evident that the latter, if he pay six per cent. and 3d a gallon, in addition, for the spirits, cannot compete with the former. A similar dis- advantage would be experienced, but to a smaller amount, with regard to British goods, the duty upon these being only two per cent. The greater part of the European goods received upon the Gold Coast, and almost the whole of those received at Accra are British. Whether for Dutch, Danish or British Accra, they generally arrive in the same vessel, frequently from the same exporter, and always for the same market. The foreign trader thus has an advantage over the British trader to the amount of the duty paid by the latter. Whilst, therefore, the temptation to evade the duties, and the facility of evasion are so great, it will hardly excite surprise that the revenue derived from the imports should bear but a small proportion to the goods actually imported. . . .

[(d) Relations with Ashanti.]

As regards the Ashantees, they not only lay claim to the district [of the coastal tribes] as theirs by right of conquest, and to the consequent right of levying tribute customary with them: but find themselves cut off from the beneficial trade by the petty tribes between them and the coast. The extent to which this exclusion is experienced may be inferred from the circumstance of their having been obliged to substitute iron ore for leaden balls in their late action with the allied tribes, when so much depended upon their success.

In this point of view it seems unfortunate that, while the interests of the Ashantees and the British with reference to trade are the same, the latter should be so much identi- fied with those whose motives and objects are at variance with both. The principal obstacle to an extended trade with the interior is formed by the present allies of the British. Their object is to throw every impediment in the way of direct intercourse, in order that they may become exclusively the factors of each party and impose upon both. Formerly those tribes were disunited and weak, but they have been united by the policy of the British, and in proportion as they feel their strength, will the barrier which they

E

oppose be effectual in restricting the trade.   If this be the case, it would follow that the British have now only the choice of withdrawing their support from those with whom they have latterly been united, or of relinquishing the hope of extended commerce.

Without attempting to give an opinion as to the policy or expediency of the measures pursued upon the coast at the commencement of the present war with Ashantee, it is proper to state that it appears to have been considered from the first as altogether a British war, and every exertion was made to induce the various tribes to unite in the undertaking, with the solemn assurance that they should not be abandoned until the conclusion of a peace, in which their interests would be consulted and their safety guaranteed.   So far was this feeling carried that on General Sir Neil Campbell's arrival on the coast, soon after the action at Dodowah, several of the chiefs not only refused to be parties to any pacific negotiation, but absolutely adopted measures to frustrate the endeavours made by the General to open a communication with Ashantee.   Their avowed reason for this opposition was an apprehension lest the Ashantees, (being incapable of comprehending the motives of humanity which dictate a desire for peace), would construe any overture made with that view, either as an acknowledgement of past defeat, or dread of future hostility, and therefore rise in their demand, or at best subscribe to a hollow truce merely till it should suit their purpose to break it.   An opinion of this kind, being prevalent among the merchants, may have been sincerely entertained by some of the allied chiefs: but there is reason to suppose that the most influential of them were actuated in their opposition to overtures of peace by personal motives rather than by any regard for the general welfare.

How far such a proceeding may be considered as having cancelled all obligation on the part of the British Government with respect to the promise made at the commencement of the war, or the consequences in which, by this conduct, the allies may involve themselves, it is not for me to venture an opinion.   The circumstance is mentioned here only as it marks the disposition of the people.   It was in this spirit that *Cudjoe Cheebo*, one of the principal chiefs, sent a message to the acting governor of Elmina, to apprize him that in the action at Dodowah *he* had defeated the king of Ashantee, and driven him from the coast, and (accompanying the demand with a menace) that he expected payment of the sum which it was customary for the other to receive from the Dutch authorities. Many circumstances might be cited to justify an inference that power only is wanting to some of the allied tribes to render them as despotic and rapacious as those to whom they are now opposed.   This would be the result of their union and if divided they can never successfully cope with the Ashantees. . . .   [H.C.352, A. & P. (1826–7) vii, 267]

81 R. W. HAY[1] TO T. LACK[2]

DOWNING STREET, 27 JUNE, 1827.

Sir,

Having laid before Viscount Goderich[3] the memorial enclosed in your note of 21st

instant, from sundry manufacturers of the town of Birmingham, setting forth the great losses which will be sustained by them if the British settlements on the Gold Coast should be abandoned by His Majesty's Government; I have received his Lordship's directions to return to you the said memorial, and to acquaint you, for the information of the Lords of the Committee of Privy Council for Trade and Plantations, that His Majesty's Government have been mainly induced to come to the determination of withdrawing the garrisons and public establishments from the

[1] Robert William Hay; first Permanent Under-Secretary of State for the Colonies, 1825–36; Henry Taylor describes him as 'obtuse but bold'.

[2] Secretary to the Board of Trade.

[3] Frederick John Robinson, Viscount Goderich (later 1st Earl of Ripon) (1782–1859); M.P., 1806; Chancellor of the Exchequer, 1823–7; Secretary of State for War and the Colonies, 30 April–17 August, 1827, and 22 November, 1830–3 April, 1833; Prime Minister 1827–8; Cobbett's 'Prosperity Robinson' and 'Goody Goderich'.

forts on the Gold Coast, in consideration of the constant drain upon the troops and civil servants employed there, arising from the destructive unhealthiness of the climate and other local inconveniences, as well as of the great expense which, upon inquiry, was ascertained to be necessary in order to repair the forts and place them in a proper state of defence.[1]

Keeping in view, however, the interests of the merchants who reside there, the Governor of Sierra Leone has been directed not to abandon the forts without placing those merchants in possession of them, should they think it advantageous for themselves to remain on the coast, for which purpose it is proposed to grant them assistance in a moderate degree.

No accounts have as yet been received of the arrangements which the governor may have made with the merchants, in conformity with the views of His Majesty's Government, but Lord Goderich desires me to observe that the memorialists may rest satisfied that these views have not been adopted without the fullest examination of the subject in all its bearings, and that all those considerations which ought justly to influence His Majesty's Government in their deliberations on a question of so much importance were maturely weighed at the time.

As far as relates to the value of the trade between this country and the Gold Coast, and of which the memorialists are now apprehensive of being deprived, it would appear that the total amount of consignments to Cape Coast Castle, Accra, Annamaboe and Dixcove, have not, from the month of April, 1822 to 30th of June, 1826, exceeded the sum of £133,154 2s. 6¼d, of which £108,560 7s. 10d. was for the value of British manufactures and £24,593 14s. 8½d. for foreign manufactures. But whether this trade be so valuable as it is represented to be or not (and if it is of that importance which the memorialists assign to it, Lord Goderich has no reason to apprehend that

[1] Cf. Report by Captain Boteler on the Gold Coast forts, 1826 (H.C.570 of 1833).

the experience of the resident merchants will not enable them to maintain themselves on the coast), his Lordship is of opinion that His Majesty's Government would not be justified in purchasing such trade at a large sacrifice of human life and expense to the country.

I am etc.

[H.C.398. A & P (1874) xlvi, 1097]

82 Lt.-Col. LUMLEY[1] TO W. HUSKISSON[2]
CAPE COAST CASTLE, 15 JANUARY, 1828.
Sir,

In my despatch under date of the 3rd November, 1827, which I had the honour of addressing to the Right Honourable Lord Viscount Goderich, I informed his Lordship that I was then endeavouring to assemble the allied chiefs for the purpose of concluding a peace with the Ashantee nation, agreeably to the instructions communicated from time to time by the Right Honourable Earl Bathurst to the late Major-General Sir Neil Campbell.

I have the honour of now informing you that I succeeded in collecting, upon the 10th ultimo, all the chiefs claiming an alliance with us, and that they acceded, in a public conference held upon that day, to the terms upon which I proposed granting peace to the Ashantees. From the enclosed copy of these terms . . . you will perceive that a sum of money to be lodged in this castle by the king of Ashantee, as a pledge of his good faith and security for his future conduct, is the basis upon which it is proposed to rest the future peace and tranquillity of our settlements on the Gold Coast. . . .

The governor of the Danish settlements

[1] Officer commanding troops at Sierra Leone; Lieutenant-Governor and acting Governor-in-Chief, 1827–8; G. Maclean accompanied him as private secretary during his visit to the Gold Coast between October 1827 and March 1828. He died at Sierra Leone in June 1828.
[2] William Huskisson (1770–1830); M.P., 1796, and member for Liverpool, 1823–30; President of the Board of Trade, 1823–7; Secretary of State for War and the Colonies, 17 August 1872–30 May, 1828; killed at the opening of the Liverpool and Manchester railway.

at Accra sent an officer of the Danish navy to represent the interests of that settlement at the meeting. . . . He urged me strongly to propose that a portion of the money to be advanced by the Ashantees should be lodged in Christiansborg castle . . . as a security to the Danes against further aggression. To this, however, I would by no means consent, not only because it would have occasioned distrust and division among the native chiefs, but because each of them could, with equal justice, and would have advanced a similar claim, since the Danes were paid most liberally by the British Government for what services they rendered during the late war. The Danish officer . . . desired nevertheless . . . that 'Christiansborg Castle' should be included in the treaty, and at his own special request the words were written down in his presence. [The Danish governor, however, when he learned of this protested.] . . .

I expect the return of my messengers from Coomassie . . . on the 20th instant. . . . I have very sanguine hopes that the terms of peace will be acceded to, with the exception, perhaps, of the article which stipulates for the delivery of the two hostages who are persons of rank and consequence and nearly related to their sovereign.[1]

Upon that part of the Danish governor's letter in which he expresses his intention of concluding a separate peace for the Danish settlements and its dependent natives, with the Ashantees, I would remark that he is well aware that those whom he calls 'dependent natives' have sent deputations to Cape Coast Castle for the express purpose of requiring that they may be included in whatever arrangements the British Government may think proper to make with the Ashantees, and it is notorious that Great Britain alone of the European powers having establishments on this coast, possesses any influence among the

[1] This stipulation was inserted at the instance of the allied chiefs; cf. Lumley to Hay, 19 January, 1828, *ibid*.

native powers, with the exception, perhaps, of those towns which lie immediately under the guns of the Dutch and Danish forts. . . .

[C.O.267/94: H.C.412. A & P (1865) v]

83 TERMS UPON WHICH PEACE WILL BE GRANTED TO THE KING OF ASHANTEE
10 NOVEMBER, 1827.

1. That there shall be a perpetual peace between the subjects of His Britannic Majesty and the Ashantee nation.

2. That in like manner, peace shall exist in all time coming between the subjects of the king of Ashantee, and those of Aggery, king of Cape Coast; Adookoo, king of Fantee and Fantee chiefs; Amonoo, king of Annamaboe; Chibboo, king of Dinkira; Owosso Oko, king of Tufule; Annimini, king of Wassaw; the chiefs of Adjumacon and Essacooma; the Danish settlement of Christiansborg castle; British Accra, and all nations in alliance with His Britannic Majesty's subjects in this country.

3. That the king of Ashantee do renounce for himself, his heirs and successors for ever, all and every right to collect tribute (as a token of dependency) from any of the aforesaid nations in alliance with Great Britain, and that he do acknowledge each and all of these states to be free and independent.

4. That the king of Ashantee do engage to place in the castle of Cape Coast, a sum of money equal to 4,000 ounces of gold, there to be kept as a security for his preserving inviolate the provisions of a treaty of peace to be founded on these articles, by a breach of which treaty on his part, the aforesaid sum of money will be forfeited.

5. To prevent as much as possible any future war, it is agreed that in case of any of the parties subscribing to these articles committing an act of aggression, and complaint being made thereof to the Governor-in-chief of His Britannic Majesty's possessions on the coast (or, in the absence of the said Governor of Cape Coast, to the commandant of Cape Coast Castle, for

the time being, as his representative), any satisfaction which the circumstances of the case may require will be adjudged to the aggrieved party by the said Governor-in-Chief or his representative, who will also call to his assistance two or more of the adjacent kings or chiefs as a council.

6. If any of the allied kings or chiefs shall be the aggressor or aggressors as aforesaid, and if such aggressor or aggressors shall refuse to abide by the decision of the governor, or his representative, with the chiefs assembled with him in council, in that case he or they will no longer be considered as a confederacy, and must arrange his or their disputes as they best can.

7. In the event of the Ashantees becoming the aggressors and refusing to abide by the decision of the Governor (or his representative) and council, as aforesaid, then the sum of money lodged in Cape Coast Castle . . . shall be forfeited for ever, and the said sum of money may, if it be deemed expedient, be expended in the purchase of arms, ammunition and other warlike stores, for the purpose of carrying on war against the king of Ashantee and his people.

8. The king of Ashantee must signify his assent to the terms now proposed on or before [12] January next, and he must lodge the security required . . . on or before the same day.

9. The king of Ashantee must, as a further security, send to Cape Coast Castle two of the royal family of Ashantee named Osey Cudjoe and Apokoo, who are to remain in the said castle of Cape Coast for the space of four years as hostages. They must be sent to Cape Coast on or before the 12th day of January next.

10. The allies from the leeward coast, namely the Dutch and Danish Accras, the queen of Akim, the king of Akimbo, the king of Aquapim, &c &c, having neither arrived themselves nor sent persons to represent them, when these articles were agreed to in full assembly, although intelligence has been received that they are on their way to Cape Coast: be it provided, and it is hereby provided, that although the names of the above allies are not included with those of the other allies in the 2nd article in these terms, yet, if they or any of them shall signify their concurrence with and assent to these terms and proposals before the return of the messengers from Coomassie, then the party or parties so signifying their concurrence and assent shall be included in and entitled to all the benefits of the treaty in the same manner as if he or they had been present when the same was agreed upon.

[Enclosure in No. 82 H.C.412]

84 Lt.-Col. Denham[1] to R. W. Hay
H.M.S. Sybille, at sea, Bight of Benin. 1 February, 1828.
Private and confidential.

. . . The total abandonment of the forts at Cape Coast, Anamaboe and Accra is very much dreaded by the merchants, notwithstanding their conviction that they will be able to defend themselves and probably increase their profits, . . . and they would come into any reasonable arrangement that would prevent such an event. . . .

Even now the trade is important and might be protected by a few companies of militia. With a white or coloured commandant, about £2,000 per annum would pay all the expenses of the Gold Coast. If Government would arm and pay the militia, the merchants would clothe and feed them, and the heavy expense of a commissariate and medical staff would be thereby avoided. Bannerman house at Accra consumed 1,100 puncheons of rum during the last 17 months. 34,000 oz. of gold have been collected during the same

[1] Dixon Denham (1786–1828); Lieut.-Col.; served in the Peninsular and Waterloo campaigns; accompanied Clapperton and Oudney to Bornu in 1821; head of the Liberated African Department, Sierra Leone, January 1827, and at the time of writing the above was on his way to inspect the new liberated African settlement on Fernando Po; appointed Governor of Sierra Leone in December, he only assumed the government on 4 May and died on 9 June, 1828.

period and in the last six months, 10 tons of ivory and £7,000 worth of palm oil have been sent to England. . . .

The slave trade would, it is to be feared, flourish with additional strength on our giving up this part of the coast. All our allies would return to their old traffic, and they can move their victims to the neighbourhood of Whydah by land with great ease, where there is always a ready market, and they did after the defeat of the Ashantees at Dodowah. . . .

It is quite clear the Ashantees are desirous of peace . . . and nothing but the jealousy of the allies prevented a negotiation last year, which might have been overcome by Sir N. Campbell . . . if he had exercised a little patience. Captain Ricketts, who was left here by Sir N. Campbell as Commandant, and who has been nine years on the coast and [is] well acquainted with the natives, had opened a communication before Colonel Lumley's arrival at Cape Coast, and the messengers were in the town from the king of Ashantee several days before he landed. . . . Captain Ricketts' . . . removal from the command while any negotiation was pending between the Ashantees and the other native powers, to make way for an officer junior to himself and of very inferior merit, is a measure much to be regretted.[1] . . . If the peace with Ashantee should not prove permanent, it will be caused by 'hurrying the palaver', and the want of unanimity amongst the Europeans. The Danish governor, I hear, says that on his sending the next in command to himself to Cape Coast, in consequence of Captain Ricketts' invitation to be present at the palaver, Colonel Lumley told him the English were about to make peace for themselves and he might attend or not as he pleased. The Governor is in consequence in treaty with the queen of Akim in order to make a separate peace. . . .

[C.O.267/94]

---

[1] Ricketts was replaced by Hingston on 9 January, 1828; Denham made a point of sending him back to the Gold Coast in May.

85 KING OSEI YAW TO THE GOVERNOR OF CAPE COAST CASTLE   12 APRIL, 1828.

Honoured Sir,

I beg to acknowledge your letter of the 9th of last month, and on which I took into consideration of granting your request, but as I received some information that Fantees are already encamped for Elmina, so put me in great doubt with all my people. I thought when the peace was concluded [it] would [be] for all my subjects. Therefore I send your messenger, Mr. John Buckman,[1] with my messenger so that you will see into and settle them for peace. If such [be] made, [I] beg you will get some of the Ashantees that are at Elmina to come with Mr. John Buckman on his return.

I beg to inform you that the amount of the security of 4,000 ounces of gold . . . was too much, but, however, as my ancestors have lodged 400 ounces for the security of friendship in Elmina Castle, I beg to do the same, and as soon as Mr. Buckman will return I shall speedily return them to such amount.

[C.O.267/95]

86 CAPTAIN J. HINGSTON TO KING OSEI YAW   CAPE COAST, 1 MAY, 1828.

. . . I have to inform you that no other terms can be acceded to than those originally proposed, viz. 4,000 ounces of gold to be lodged in this castle, as well as two principal persons as hostages for the future tranquillity of the coast. . . . If the terms proposed are not acceded to by your Majesty within twenty days after the arrival of John Buckman and the messengers at Coomassie, you will order John Buckman and the other persons from Cape Coast to return; if you will Carr to remain [you will order] that some Ashantee chief be sent to reside at Cape Coast.

---

[1] Buckman was an issuer in Government service at Cape Coast, chosen by Maclean to take the agreed peace terms to Kumasi, whence he returned in April. He returned to Kumasi in May and remained there until 1830.

The dispute between the Fantees and Elminas cannot be allowed to interfere with the more important question between the British and the Ashantees. None of the Cape Coast [people] have joined in the war against Elmina. That on peace being concluded, every exertion will be made in conjunction with the Governor at Elmina to arrange the dispute between the Fantees and Elminas. . . . [C.O.267/95]

BOOK III

THE COMMITTEE OF MERCHANTS AND GEORGE MACLEAN, 1828–1842[1]

---

[1] The Committee continued to administer the settlements until February 1844. The dates above are of the documents in this section.

7 The framework of merchant rule, 1828–1830

THE arrangements for the future management of Cape Coast Castle and James Fort, Accra, by the resident merchants, were worked out in the course of 1828 (87–89). Making the most of the breakdown of the negotiations with Ashanti, the merchants got better terms for themselves than the Colonial Office originally intended to concede (118), though they were pretty much the same as those sketched by Campbell in 1826 (77). An annual grant of £4,000, subject to review by Parliament, was to be administered by a committee of three London merchants approved by Government. On the coast, the merchants were to elect from among their number a council of five, which in turn was to choose its President.

This was only a provisional arrangement, and in 1830 the regulations were amended (92) to allow of the appointment of a full-time, non-mercantile President in the person of George Maclean (93). The rules and regulations were intended to provide for the management of the two forts only (88), but, inevitably, the merchants remained involved in the affairs of their neighbours (90, 91).

87 R. W. HAY TO G. BARNES, R. BROWN, M. FORSTER

LONDON, 30 OCTOBER, 1828.

Gentlemen,

I am directed by Secretary Sir G. Murray[1] to acquaint you that he has had under his most attentive consideration the several papers and communications which have been successively received from you, as well as from the Gold Coast, upon the subject of the measures which it may be proper to adopt for the security of British trade, and for the protection of British residents in that quarter, in consequence of the determination to which His Majesty's Government have come of withdrawing the public establishments and garrisons from the forts of Cape Coast Castle and Accra; and I am further to acquaint you that Sir G. Murray is disposed to recommend that these forts be delivered over to the merchants residing there, and held by them under the following conditions, viz.:

1. That the forts of Cape Coast Castle and Accra shall continue to be dependencies of the Government of Sierra Leone.

2. That British law shall consequently continue to be in force in the said dependencies.

3. That the affairs of the forts shall be chiefly regulated by you as a committee, or by a committee of those merchants of London who shall be chosen by His Majesty's Government, as often as occasion may require.

4. That five of the resident merchants whose names may be approved by the Secretary of State, upon the recommendation of the committee of London merchants, be empowered to form themselves into a council of government, according to such rules and regulations as you or the committee of merchants for the time being, shall prescribe to the council, for the purpose of regulating the external and local affairs of the forts; and moreover that they shall be appointed Justices of the Peace, and empowered to form among themselves a court for the trial of all offences not amounting to felonies and misdemeanours; and that the said Justices be also authorised to exercise all such powers as may be legally conferred upon them, with a view to the preservation of the peace of the dependencies and to the protection thereof, against assault or rebellion, and

[1] Sir George Murray (1772–1846); entered the army, 1789; served in the Netherlands, West Indies, Ireland, Egypt and the Peninsula; M.P., 1823–32; Secretary of State for War and the Colonies, 1828–30.

for the repression of the slave trade within the limits or influence of the forts; it being understood that all crimes and misdemeanours committed within the limits of those forts shall be cognisable and punished by the courts of Sierra Leone.

5. That in order to enable the merchants residing at Cape Coast Castle and Accra to provide the means of regulating the affairs of the forts, and to maintain the buildings in repair, and to provide a sufficient garrison for their defence, an annual sum not exceeding four thousand pounds shall be placed at the disposal of you or of the committee of London merchants for the time being, on behalf of the merchants of Cape Coast Castle and Accra, from the 1st of July of the present year, it being understood that the merchants residing in the forts, or under the protection of the forts, shall be bound to keep them in repair, and carefully to preserve the guns and stores which have latterly been made over to them.

6. That the ports or harbours of Cape Coast Castle and Accra shall be open to all vessels without payment of any duty whatever.

7. That the money which may be voted by Parliament in conformity with the recommendations of His Majesty's Government for the maintenance of the forts, shall be appropriated under your direction, or that of the committee of London merchants for the time being, and duly accounted for at the expiration of every year to His Majesty's Principal Secretary of State for the Colonies, subject to the revision of the Lords Commissioner of His Majesty's Treasury, and that such account be accompanied by a detailed return of the origin, quantity and value of all goods, distinguishing British from foreign, which may be imported into the forts of Cape Coast Castle and Accra in the course of the year, and of the quantity and value of African produce which may be exported therefrom in British or foreign ships separately.

8. That the amount of the grant on account of the forts, for which applications may, from time to time be made to Parliament, shall in future be fixed by His Majesty's Government, after examining the reports from the coast respecting the state and value of the trade.

9. That although the transfer of the forts is to be considered as completely exempting His Majesty's Government from any further charge on account of them, it is to be expressly understood that it will be incumbent on yourselves and any future committee that may be chosen, to lay before His Majesty's Government, copies of such rules as it may be intended to lay down for the regulation of the establishments at Cape Coast Castle and Accra, and for ensuring the appointment of fit and proper persons at those places; and that no rules, regulations or appointments made by you or any future committee for such purposes shall be considered valid until they have received the formal sanction of His Majesty's Government.

Upon your signifying, in writing, your acceptance of these conditions laid down in the articles before-mentioned, Sir George Murray will be prepared to take the necessary measures for giving full effect to this agreement.

I am etc.

[C.O.268/27: H.C.551]

88 R. W. HAY TO BARNES, BROWN AND FORSTER   14 NOVEMBER, 1828.

. . . It is of course understood that the Government of Sierra Leone is not to interfere with the council of Cape Coast Castle or with you: but I am desired to explain to you distinctly that it is not the intention of His Majesty's Government that the council or magistracy of the forts should exercise any authority or jurisdiction 'over the persons and districts under the immediate influence or protection of those forts'.[1] The council and magistrates will only exercise authority and jurisdiction in the forts and roadsteads or harbours

[1] The phrase occurs in a letter of 11 November to which this is a reply.

thereunto adjoining, as well as over the persons who reside there.[1]

[C.O.267/97. H.C.551]

89 RULES FOR CONDUCTING THE AFFAIRS OF CAPE COAST CASTLE AND ACCRA AND SECURING THE APPOINTMENT OF FIT AND PROPER PERSONS FOR THE CHARGE AND MANAGEMENT OF THOSE FORTS.[2]

His Majesty's Government having come to the determination of withdrawing the public establishment and garrisons from the forts of Cape Coast Castle and Accra and delivering them over to the British merchants residing there, under an arrangement that the management of the forts shall be chiefly regulated by us, or our successors, as a committee, and that five of the said merchants shall be empowered to form themselves into a Council of Government according to such rules and restrictions as we or the committee for the time being may, with the sanction of His Majesty's Government, prescribe, the following have received the approbation of His Majesty's Government and are to be observed.

1. The President and Council who have been already elected at Cape Coast Castle to continue in office until the 1st of July, 1829.[3]

2. On the 24th June, or if that shall happen to be a Sunday, on the following day in the year 1829 and each succeeding year, the British resident merchants at Cape Coast Castle and Accra to meet and elect five persons to be the council in the following year, but no person to vote who shall not have completed one year's residence on the coast.

3. The British merchants at Accra to be allowed to vote in the election of members of council by proxy.

4. The Committee to transmit, for the approbation of His Majesty's Government, the names of those merchants who have resided not less than twelve months at Cape Coast Castle or Accra, and who are in their opinion, fit persons to be appointed magistrates and members of council, in order that commissions as magistrates may be granted to them.

5. The members of council to be chosen from the persons whose names have been so transmitted and approved of by His Majesty's Government and who are to enter upon their office on the 1st of July in each year, and to be competent to act immediately upon their election, but their names, as well as that of the President, are to be forthwith communicated to the Committee and by them to His Majesty's Government.

6. The council within three days after their election to choose a President upon whom the executive department shall more particularly devolve.

7. Any dispute arising at the election upon the right of voting or any other matter, to be settled by the existing President and Council, with a right, if their decision should be objected to, of appeal to the Committee in London, but the decision of the Council to be deemed valid until a contrary decision on such appeal to the Committee shall be received.

8. Any vacancy which may occur on the Council to be filled by election in the manner before-mentioned, three weeks' public notice of the day of election having been given.

9. The Council to meet the President for the dispatch of business once in every month on a fixed day, and on extraordinary occasions whenever summoned by him, or whenever a meeting shall be called for by at least three members of the Council.

---

[1] Later (29 November, 1828) Hay observed that although they had no jurisdiction beyond 'the forts and roadsteads', 'it will of course be competent for the Council . . . to exercise the influence of the authority which is entrusted to them in the adjacent districts'. [C.O.267/97.]

[2] The Rules were drawn up by the Committee and sent to Hay on 31 December, 1828.

[3] John Jackson (President), Wm Hutchison, J. T. Pierce, Robert Roberts and James Swanzy were elected on 24 June, 1828, and received charge of the forts next day. At the election a year later, R. F. Fry replaced Rbt. Roberts.

10. The President to vote in Council and to decide the question under consideration in cases where the votes are equal.

11. Any question decided by the casting vote of the President to be specially noted, and the original motion, with any amendments made upon it, entered in the minutes.

12. Neither the President nor any member of Council to vote in any matter in difference between himself and any other person or persons, or in any case in which his own conduct or personal interest is in question.

13. In every case of complaint to the President in Council, upon which they may be unable or unwilling to decide, *or on which their decision shall be appealed against*[1] the full particulars thereof to be transmitted to the Committee in London by the first convenient opportunity (if desired by the party complaining) with the President's report thereon, and a copy thereof given to the complainant, in order that he may at the same time transmit his observations, a copy of such observations being first delivered by him to the Council.

14. The number of acting magistrates to be limited to five, and vacancies in that number to be filled up by the President and Council from those gentlemen who, agreeably to Rule No. 4 have received their commissions.

15. The President and Council to transmit to the Committee every six months the names of any additional merchants who may have completed a residence of 12 months and who are in their opinion fit persons to be appointed magistrates and members of Council, in order that, if the Committee should concur in the same opinion, the names of such merchants may be submitted for the approbation of His Majesty's Government, that they may receive their commissions as magistrates.

16. A report of the state of the country,

[1] Clause in italics added in 1836.

the forts, trade, etc., signed in the same names, to be transmitted half-yearly.

17. The establishments at Cape Coast Castle and Accra and the pay and allowances for the persons comprising the same to be as stated in the annexed list.

18. The general principles of the establishment being voluntary service, the members of Council and other British merchants are to act without pecuniary reward in their several offices for the defence of the forts and preservation of order and good government on which depend their own personal safety and commercial prosperity.

19. The Secretary is restricted from trading, in order that his time be devoted entirely to the public service.

20. The Captain of the Guard is to perform the duties of captain and adjutant, attending personally to all the minutiae of the troops in which the lieutenants, receiving no pay, and having their own concerns to attend to, can afford him little assistance beyond that which may result from the portion of attendance necessary to qualify themselves for their offices. He is also to perform the duty of engineer or surveyor of the repairs of the castle, and deliver to the President and Council, for the purpose of being transmitted to the Committee, regular monthly returns, in duplicate, of the state and pay of the troops.

21. The Surgeon is to send similar returns of the casualties and health of the troops; he is also to superintend the schools and make returns of the number of children educated and of the state of the school establishment.

22. The Secretary is to be the accountant, deputy warehouse-keeper and general assistant to the President.

23. Copies of the accounts of expenditure to be transmitted to the Committee half-yearly in duplicate by every convenient opportunity, and of the proceedings of Council, also in duplicate, the said accounts and minutes to be signed by the

President, one member of the Council and the secretary.

24. A copy of the inventory of ordnance stores, furniture etc, at Cape Coast and Accra, the original of which has been already transmitted to H.M's Government, to be signed by the President and Council, and delivered by them to their successors every year, from whom they shall take a receipt for the several articles in the said inventory.

25. A copy of the said inventory to be sent home to the Committee and any alterations which may take place in it to be notified to them annually.

26. Fifty men in addition to the regular troops are to be provided by the resident merchants and traders in such manner and in such proportion as the President and Council may direct, to be trained and exercised as a militia, so as to qualify them to assist in the defence of the forts when required.

27. All appointments at Cape Coast Castle to be made by the President and Council, except when it may be required to send from this country a Captain of the Guard, Surgeon or Secretary to the Council, in which case the appointments to these stations are to be made by the Committee.

28. The President and Council to be empowered to suspend or dismiss any officer in their service for misconduct, incompetency or neglect of duty.

29. All judicial proceedings, both at Cape Coast Castle and Accra to be conducted publicly and in the presence of not less than two magistrates.

30. Apartments to be provided in the castle for the Captain of the Guard, Surgeon, Secretary and the persons in subordinate commands of the troops.

31. The President and Council may also allot apartments to other British residents upon their engaging to keep them in repair.

32. The fort of Accra to be a dependency on Cape Coast Castle under the management of the resident merchants; the officer to command the fort to be appointed by the President and Council to whom he shall be accountable for the due application of the monies issued to him, with a right of appeal to the Committee in all cases of dispute with the President and Council.

33. The salaries of President, Captain of the Guard, Surgeon and Secretary to be paid by bills drawn by them respectively upon the Committee, each bill to be marked with the signature of the Secretary as having been entered in the public accounts, and those drawn by the three last to be counter-signed by the President.

34. The remainder of the grant to be applied by the Committee to the purchase, shipment and insurance of goods for the pay of the troops and other necessary objects.

35. The passage-money of the officers sent from home to be paid by the Committee.

36. The existing regulations established by the instrument by which the forts were transferred to the merchants by Major Ricketts, dated the 25th June last, or so many of them as the President and Council may deem necessary for the security of the persons and property of the inhabitants, and the preservation of order and good government in the place, to be continued under the direction of the magistrates.

37. The Committee to be responsible to the Government for the due application by them of the monies voted by Parliament for the support of the forts.

[C.O.267/97.　H.C.551 (1842)]

90 COUNCIL MINUTE

CAPE COAST CASTLE, 1 JUNE, 1829.

At a meeting of the Council this day, present

　J. Jackson, Esquire, President.
　R. Roberts, Esquire ⎫
　　　　　　　　　　　 ⎬ Members.
　J. Swanzy, Esquire　⎭

. . . The President having stated to the Board [that] he had [been] applied to by the town people to take the case of Joe Aggrey into consideration:

Resolved: that Joe Aggrey for his past misconduct, in addition to the forfeit of his pay which is at this moment stopped, he do find and pay into the hands of the President, 5 oz. of gold, to be applied to the improvement of the town; that he and all others may in future be debarred from seeking those palavers that are of a tendency too likely to involve the whole community in trouble.

That he do take down the flag staff now erected before his house and substitute in its stead a similar one to that used by the Intins.

That he do deliver into the hands of the President the image of the king of Ashantee kneeling before him, Joe Aggrey, and the other image of the tiger and porcupine which he had made use of on top of his umbrella, to be dealt with as the President and Council may see fit; they have a political allusion to the unsettled dispute with the Ashantees and too likely to frustrate the much wished-for accomodation of those differences, if not even yet to be the subject of a complaint from the king of Ashantee, and the source of much trouble to himself and family and to the inhabitants of Cape Coast.

The President and Council can have not the slightest objection to his having images on the top of his umbrellas if it is his wish, provided always that he refrains from the use of [any of] an objectionable and mischievous tendency. That he is not, on leaving this, to parade the town as having gained a triumph, for, far from such being the case, he is to consider the favour now shown him as arising entirely from the leniency of the Council and not from the merits of his own case.

That he is not to put people in confinement on his own mere whim and fancy, many having been so confined by him for a very long period, and cost their families heavy expenses to obtain their release. All palavers are to be heard and determined in the presence of the pynims, and should

cases occur where it may be necessary to have the delinquent confined, such case will in every instance be reported to the Council.

By order of the President and Council.

[C.O.98/1A]

91 COUNCIL MINUTE
CAPE COAST CASTLE, 23 SEPTEMBER, 1829.

At a meeting of Council this day, present

> J. Jackson, Esquire, President.
> Wm. Hutchison ⎫
> J. Swanzy   ⎬ Esqr. Members.
> J. T. Pierce   ⎭

The President stated to the Board he had brought to an amicable conclusion the differences between the Warsaws and Dinkeras, and the latter had requested permission, through the Cape Coast people, to settle in the neighbourhood of Juquah, that, being removed from the Warsaws, they might avoid quarrels with them in future; and, having urged their request by reciting several cases with which they had cause to be aggrieved at the conduct of the Warsaws, the President, thinking it would be conducive to the quiet of the country, finding it also agreeable to the Juquah people, had complied with their wishes. — Acceded to.

The President stated that a like request from similar causes had been made by Amoo, a Warsaw chief, to become a resident at Cape Coast, which, meeting the wishes of the Cape Coast people, and the approbation of two members of the Council (Messrs. Swanzy and Roberts) as well as the sanction of the king and some of the chiefs of Warsaw, he had complied with the application in this case also. — Acceded to. . . . The Board then proceeded to take into consideration the propriety of again attempting to open a communication with the Ashantees. Resolved unanimously, that a reward of four ounces in goods, at gold prices, be offered to each of any two or three men who will volunteer to take a letter to Coomassie for the King of Ashantee; the said reward to be paid on the return of the parties, or, in the event of their falling a sacrifice, the reward will be paid to their relatives here, with the addition of the means requisite to perform their funeral rights, the messengers to be subsisted etc. for the journey. Resolved: that in the event of messengers being procured to go, the President do engage one of the Cape Coast chiefs to accompany and pass them through the Fantee and Assin countries. . . .   [C.O.98/1A]

92 Barnes, Brown and Forster to R. W. Hay

London, 14 October, 1829.

Sir,

Mr. John Jackson, President of the Council at Cape Coast Castle, being desirous of retiring from that situation, the state of his affairs requiring his presence in England, the merchants on the coast have expressed a wish that Mr. Maclean of the Royal African Corps, should be appointed to succeed him. We concur in opinion with them, that the safety of the forts would be best consulted by the appointment of a military man to that station, and that it would tend materially to promote the harmony and good government of the persons resident there if the President of the Council were not engaged in trade, and, consequently, free from all personal interest in any disputes which it might be his duty to adjust.

Mr. Maclean, having held the office of private secretary to the late Sir Neil Campbell and his successor, is well known to the merchants on the coast, by whom his appointment is solicited, and from the reports made to us of his character, talents and fitness for the station, we have great pleasure in being able to recommend him to Secretary Sir George Murray, for the office of President of the Council.

Being restricted from trading, we have no doubt that you will agree with us that as a compensation for the loss of this privilege, and towards enabling him to support without it the respectability of the office, some addition should be made to his salary.

The rules as at present framed do not provide either for such an appointment, or for the proposed compensation, and we beg leave to submit the annexed additional rules, which we trust will receive the approbation of Secretary Sir George Murray.

The whole body of rules and regulations have been necessarily framed without communication with the merchants on the coast. You will doubtless have anticipated the occurrence of some difficulties and the proposal of some alterations when they were transmitted to the persons who were to carry them into effect. Two, only, which we conceive to be admissible, have been desired, and as they appear to us to be unobjectionable, we avail ourselves of the present opportunity to submit them also for the approbation of Sir George Murray. . . .

Additional Rules [as approved by His Majesty's Government].

1. That it shall be competent for the Committee (in London) when so required by the merchants on the coast, to select the person who shall be appointed to fill the office of President of the Council of Government (on the Gold Coast); provided, however, that the person so selected and appointed by the Committee (in London) to preside over the Council of Government, shall be restricted from trading; that he shall receive no other salary or emoluments or advantages but what the Committee may assign to him, and that his appointment shall be revocable by the Committee (in London).

2. That the person so appointed shall receive (to enable him to support the respectability of the station), an addition to his salary of one hundred pounds per annum.

3. That the President and Council shall have the power of suspending any member

of the Council for misconduct, but shall submit the grounds upon which such suspension has been adopted, by the first conveyance, to the Committee (in London), who, if they think proper, may remove him altogether.

4. That the Members of Council shall retain their station so long as they continue to reside on the Gold Coast, and, in the event of their leaving it, their former residence shall be a sufficient qualification for their re-election in case of a vacancy.

[C.O.267/100][1]

[1] The Committee, in fact, forwarded four rules recommended by the coast merchants; the two referred to in their letter, after amendment by the Colonial Office, appear as 3 and 4 above.

8 The administration of George Maclean from 1830 to 1836

MACLEAN arrived on the coast on 19 February, 1830. He at once saw that it was impossible to eschew all political influence in the country (94), and caused Government to qualify its views (96), without, however, committing itself to any further financial outlay. The negotiations with Ashanti were resumed (95), and, largely through the services of the Ashanti princess Akiawa, whom Maclean redeemed from captivity (99), the treaty, which was to form the basis for Anglo-Ashanti relations for the next sixty years, was signed in April 1831. In August the Danes and the eastern states were included in the agreement (99).

Though the revolt of Juaben (101) caused some anxiety until Maclean mediated a settlement with a new Asantehene in 1835, there were no more serious differences with Ashanti. Taking his stand on the treaty, Maclean did his best to secure freedom of trade with the interior (98), in spite of Fante attempts to monopolise it (108). The mutual restitution of fugitives between the coast tribes and Ashanti was another aspect of his policy which excited some disingenuous criticism (116). Maclean was no doubt right in thinking some such arrangement essential to a good understanding with Ashanti (117), and for thirty years his successors, with occasional misgivings, maintained peace with that country by the same means.

As a result of the 1831 treaty, Maclean acquired or assumed large responsibilities for the other states who were parties to it. Both under the old Company (25) and under the Crown (134d), the British authorities had intervened in political and judicial disputes amongst the African population, usually at their request. Under Maclean, such interference was greatly extended. As far as his limited means would allow, he sought to preserve order, not merely at Cape Coast (97), where he took a lofty view of British rights (107, 117), but among the Wasaws (102), and, eventually, even in Nzima (103). The Apollonian agreement of February 1835 (104) was a dead letter as far as that country was concerned, but may be taken as illustrating the sort of goal towards which Maclean was working in his relations with the states generally. Human sacrifice particularly called for intervention (103, 111).[1] The President and Council found it impracticable to abide by their instructions, which ruled out any exercise of jurisdiction outside the forts, or in other than petty cases (100), and came to assume a share in the hearing of all capital cases (109); while the commandants of the out-forts which Maclean re-occupied, found their civil and criminal jurisdiction constantly growing (134b).

This great extension of influence was most insecurely based. As the agent of the merchants, Maclean was denied the backing normally accorded to a colonial governor — a title he was told not to assume[2] — while the merchants themselves were not unanimous in his support (94, 106), and sometimes encouraged African chiefs to oppose him (110, 111). The Rules and Regulations proved defective and ambiguous, and in 1835 the London Committee, disagreeing over their interpretation and over Maclean, had to be replaced (105). Like his predecessors, Maclean found his European neighbours on the coast something of an embar-

---

[1] For an earlier move against human sacrifice cf. Lumley to Osei Yaw, of 10 December, 1827 (Crooks p. 243) — a despatch which may well have been drafted by Maclean himself.
[2] Cf. Hay to Nicholls, 30 June, 1834 (Crooks, *op. cit*, p. 264).

rassment.   His differences with the Dutch were rare and unimportant (103) but the Danish Governor Morch made a determined effort to exclude the British from Akim and Akwapim (111–12).

93 THE AFRICAN COMMITTEE TO
G. MACLEAN   8 JANUARY, 1830.
[Conveys his instructions as President]. . . .

You will observe that the general principle of the Establishment is to vest the supreme authority in a Council of Government.   You are therefore, on all occasions to act in concert with your Council, of whom we think that not less than three members (two besides yourself) should be present on all occasions of importance.

The executive department will devolve upon the President of the Council, and this must more particularly be the case when the station is filled by a person whose time is to be devoted to the public service.   It will be your duty to superintend the whole of the Establishment and either to notice yourself, or bring under the consideration of the Council, any acts of delinquency or neglect which you may observe.

The command of the troops will belong entirely to yourself.   The appointment of the hours of parade and exercise, the relief number and station of the guard, and all the routine of military business, are to be arranged by you, and it will be the duty of the captain and lieutenants of the guard to pay implicit obedience to your orders in all military matters, and of the first mentioned officer to make his returns regularly to you.

We have mentioned the lieutenants of the guard who, we expect, will be appointed from amongst the merchants, and we beg that you will at your earliest convenience after your arrival, call their attention to the expediency of selecting two of their number for these offices, and also to the arrangements necessary for establishing the militia force of 50 men which they are required by the rules to furnish.   They must recollect the forts are held for their benefit, and if they do not exhibit reasonable activity and exertion in providing for their defence, they must expect that Government will shortly abandon them.   It will not be necessary for the 1st and 2nd lieutenants of the guard to devote their time to military business to the same extent as the captain of the guard who is to act as adjutant, but they must attend sufficiently to qualify themselves for duty in case of need.   Care should also be taken that the artificers and labourers are able-bodied men fit for military duty, and whose fidelity and attachment can be relied upon, and they should all in turn be trained and occasionally embodied, that your means of defence in case of danger may be as complete as possible.   Perhaps it might be expedient to provide them with some sort of cheap uniform dress to appear in on military duty.

[The duties of surgeon and secretary are adverted to.] . . .

It would be difficult to provide for all the cases which may occur on the coast from sickness or positive vacancies, nor is it indeed necessary, as the power of making all appointments is vested in the President and Council, who have no occasion ever to send to England for an officer if they have upon the coast a person competent and willing to act.   You will, therefore, make with them in all cases, such arrangements, either permanent or temporary, as may appear most expedient.   Officers requiring to leave the coast for the recovery of their health must resign their offices, but if they intend to return, the President and Council may provide for the performance of their duty during their absence, paying their salary, or such portion of it as may be necessary, to the person by whom the duty is performed, except in any case in which that duty shall be assigned to a person already receiving pay for another office. He must then receive only half the salary, and we wish it to be distinctly understood that any such arrangement must only be temporary, as it cannot be allowed that any person should permanently hold two offices. Although we require that persons leaving the coast should resign their offices, it is not our intention that a meritorious officer should be left without provision during the time necessary for the recovery of his health; but to prevent irregularities in this particular, we think it proper to reserve to ourselves the right of giving in all cases of this kind, such compensation or allowance as we may think proper. . . .   [C.O.267/126]

94 President and Council to the Committee of Merchants

CAPE COAST, 5 JUNE, 1830.

. . . We have at length some prospect of concluding a peace with the Ashantees. The great difficulty lies in inducing the native tribes, particularly those to leeward, over whom our influence is not so great, to be satisfied with the terms proposed, and the slowness of our communication with them and with Coomassie, causes the most vexatious delays. We would, however, fain hope that now a settlement of all differences is not far off.

The Ashantees, indeed, would have been glad to have submitted long since had they not been partially supplied with arms &c from the windward coast, principally sold by slave vessels, and it was our most anxious wish to have been able to put a stop to this traffic by maintaining and increasing our influence upon the windward part of the Gold Coast. And this we could have done very effectually by authorising British merchants to take possession of our windward forts, provided they did so at their own expense. One of our own number offered to take possession of Dixcove fort on those terms, the Council giving him in loan a few stand of arms &c. But here a difficulty arose. The Grant only specified Cape Coast Castle and Accra, and it was alleged by a person then living and trading in Dixcove that we had no power of any kind over these outforts, and that he

would keep possession of it. Unwilling to do anything rashly, we resolved to lay this case before you, viz., whether the abandoned forts be vested in the Government of Cape Coast Castle or not?

We are well aware that it is the wish and intention of Government that we should not exercise any political power, but it is impossible at once to alter a system which has been in force for two hundred years, and if any person *can* go into an abandoned fort, repair it, and call himself independent, and that too, in one instance, almost under the very guns of Cape Coast Castle, there will very soon be an end to that moral influence on which alone our personal safety and our value in a commercial point of view, depend. Mr. Hutchison has in this manner taken possession of Annomaboe fort within a very few miles of Cape Coast and denies that the Council of Government have any power over him; and when applied to to furnish a return of his imports and exports, he refused, and declared himself not amenable in any way to the Government of Cape Coast. Upon this principle, the British fort of Apollonia was changed into a slave factory. But there we thought ourselves justified in interfering, and granted our authority to a respectable native, formerly a sergeant in the Royal African Corps, to take possession of it.

We repeat we have no wish to exercise any political power, but we must possess it to a certain extent, otherwise the outforts on this coast will soon become little better than a series of slave factories, the country itself desolated with internal wars, and all legitimate trade put a stop to.
                                [C.O.267/106]

95 Council Minute

CAPE COAST CASTLE, 23 AUGUST, 1830.

At a meeting of Council held at Cape Coast Castle this day, present:

George Maclean, President.

James Swanzy. . . .

The President announced that after much labour and difficulty, besides incurring considerable expense, he had at length during his visit to Accra, succeeded in obtaining one of the royal family of Ashantee — a female who is understood to have much influence with the king, and who has declared that she will use every endeavour to bring about a peace betwixt the British settlements and Ashantee, provided she can be safely conveyed to Coomassie. The President reported that he had summoned the kings of Asin and Denkera and the other principal chiefs to attend at Cape Coast for the purpose of arranging the means of a safe conduct for 'Atianvah' (the Ashantee princess), through their several territories, but that he much feared, from what has been reported to him, that these chiefs would still endeavour to throw difficulties in the way of an amicable adjustment of our differences with Ashantee.

It was then resolved that every effort should continue to be made to keep open our communication with Coomassie, and by means of the woman Atianvah to induce the king to come into our arrangements for peace. . . .   [C.O.98/1A]

96 R. W. HAY TO THE AFRICAN COMMITTEE

LONDON, 23 SEPTEMBER, 1830.

Gentlemen,

I have received and laid before Secretary Sir G. Murray your letter of the 25th ultimo with the communication therein enclosed from the Council of Merchants at Cape Coast Castle . . . and calling his attention to the present state of the abandoned forts on the Gold Coast. . . .

Sir George Murray has directed me to acquaint you that the communication of the magistrates does not convey sufficient information to enable him to decide on the propriety of investing them with the control which they desire to possess over the abandoned forts.

Undoubtedly, H.M.'s rights of sovereignty and property to those forts remain unimpaired, and it rests, therefore, entirely with His Majesty's Government to dispose of them in any manner which may be conducive to the public interest.

It is needless, however, to remark that it never entered into the contemplation of Sir George Murray, that the magistrates of Cape Coast Castle should exercise any authority over those stations; nor does it seem necessary or expedient that they should exercise any interference with the trading operations of those merchants who have remained there at their own risk and charge. But if, on the other hand, it should appear that those individuals are either unable or unwilling to lend any useful co-operation in checking the unlawful proceedings of slave vessels resorting to that coast, Sir George Murray would not hesitate to authorise the magistrates to claim possession of the abandoned forts.

I am, therefore, directed to recommend that a communication in the spirit of the above observation should be made in the first instance to such merchants as may be residing at any of those forts; and with regard to those British stations where the public buildings are not occupied by British subjects, the magistrates may consider themselves fully authorised to take possession of them, and hold them on behalf of H.M.'s Government, with the understanding that, if it should be determined hereafter to reduce the Parliamentary grant for the Gold Coast, no allowance will be made for any expense which the magistrates may choose to incur for the occupation of those additional establishments.

I am &c.   [C.O.268/29]

97 COUNCIL MINUTE

CAPE COAST CASTLE, 8 NOVEMBER, 1830.

. . . The President stated that at length he had procured the attendance of the kings of Assin, Dinkera and the Fantee chiefs, and that after some difficulty they had acceded to the measures proposed.

It was then agreed that arrangements should be made for escorting Atianvah to

Ashantee and the President authorised to pay the necessary expenses.

The President reported that during the previous week an ancient and deeply-rooted quarrel betwixt two of the military quarters of Cape Coast had broken out into open warfare, and that it had become imperatively necessary for the security of the lives and property as well of the whites as of the natives, for him to take active measures and reduce them to order; that the troops had accordingly been ordered out and some prisoners taken, on which the people dispersed and agreed to return home and submit themselves.

To prevent such conduct in future, a fine of 17 ounces had been imposed, to be placed to the public accounts.

The Council approved of the measures that had been taken. . . .   [C.O.98/1A]

98 THE PEACE TREATY WITH ASHANTI
27 APRIL, 1831.

We, the undersigned — namely, the Governor of Cape Coast Castle and British settlements, on the part of His Majesty the king of England; the princess 'Akianvah' and chief 'Quagua', on the part of the king of Ashantee; 'Aggery', king of Cape Coast; 'Adookoo', king of Fantee; 'Amonoo', king of Annamaboe; 'Chibboo', king of Denkera; 'Ossoo Okoo', king of Tufel; 'Aminnie', king of Wassaw; 'Chibboo', king of Assin; the chiefs of Adjumacon and Essacoomah, and the other chiefs in alliance with the king of Great Britain, whose names are hereunto appended[1] — do consent to and hereby ratify the following treaty of peace and of free commerce between ourselves and such other chiefs as may hereafter adhere to it:—

1. The king of Ashantee having deposited in Cape Coast Castle, in the presence of the above-mentioned parties,

[1] The chiefs of Apollonia and Agah [Eja]. Ossoo Okoo was Owusu Oko, chief of Twifu; 'Aminnie' = Animiri, chief of Wasaw Amenfi; Essacoomah is the modern Asikuma. Quagua = okwakwa, the Asantehene's 'Linguist' or official spokesman.

the sum of 600 ounces of gold, and having delivered into the hands of the Governor two young men of the royal family of Ashantee named 'Ossor Ansah' and 'Ossoo Inquantamissah',[1] as security that he will keep peace with the said parties in all time coming, peace is hereby declared betwixt the said king of Ashantee and all and each of the parties aforesaid, to continue in all time coming. The above securities shall remain in Cape Coast Castle for the space of six years from this date.

2. In order to prevent all quarrels in future which might lead to the infraction of this treaty of peace, we the parties aforesaid, have agreed to the following rules and regulations for the better protection of the lawful commerce:—

The paths shall be perfectly open and free to all persons engaged in lawful traffic, and persons molesting them in any way whatever, or forcing them to purchase at any particular market, or influencing them by any unfair means whatever, shall be declared guilty of infringing this treaty, and be liable to the severest punishment.

Panyarring, denouncing and swearing on or by any person or thing whatever, are strictly forbidden, and all persons infringing this rule shall be rigorously punished; and no master or chief shall be answerable for the crimes of his servants, unless done by his orders or consent, or when under his control.

As the king of Ashantee has renounced all right or title to any tribute or homage from the kings of Dinkera, Assin, and others formerly his subjects, so, on the other hand, these parties are strictly prohibited from insulting, by improper speaking or in any other way, their former master, such conduct being calculated to produce quarrels and wars.

All 'palavers' are to be decided in the manner mentioned in the terms and conditions of peace already agreed[2] to by the parties to this treaty.

Signed in the great hall of Cape Coast

[1] Owusu Ansa and Owusu Kwantabisa.
[2] i.e. those in No. 83 above.

Castle, this 27th day of April, 1831, by the parties to this treaty, and sealed with the great seal of the Colony, in their presence.

[Signed] George Maclean, Governor. . . .

[H.C.412, A & P 1865, v, 446.]

99 COUNCIL MINUTE

5 SEPTEMBER, 1831.

At a meeting of Council held in Cape Coast Castle on the 5th September, 1831 there were present:

George Maclean, Esq. President
R. F. Fry Esq.
Wm. Hutchison Esq.
J. Swanzy Esq.
Robt. Roberts Esq.[1]

. . . The President laid upon the table an account of the expenses incurred in settling the Ashantee palaver at Accra, and in effecting a treaty of peace betwixt the leeward tribes and Ashantees. The President explained that the great excess of expenditure at Accra over that which had been necessary at Cape Coast Castle in effecting the same object was caused partially by a portion of the leeward tribes being under foreign influences, but chiefly in consequence of the lavish expenditure which had formerly been employed in inducing these tribes to join the alliance against Ashantee.

It was unanimously resolved that a fair proportion of the funds appropriated to the maintenance of Accra fort should be applied to the liquidation of the above expenses. . . .

The President was requested to prepare the bond which he had covenanted to give to the Danish government of Christiansborg, in lieu of the actual transfer of a moiety of the securities lodged [with] him by the king of Ashantee.

The President then stated to the Council that the whole of the king of Ashantee's family prisoners of war, whom by the original treaty of peace the British Government was obliged to restore free of all

[1] Re-elected to the Council on return from leave, vice J. T. Pierce who died 20 June, 1830.

ransom, had been procured and were now in Cape Coast and ready to proceed to Coomassie. Having, with the exception of Akianvah and her family, been all the property of whites, they had most liberally and handsomely been given up to the President, without any demand for compensation (although their owners, Messrs Bannerman and Richter, had expended large sums to rescue them from their original captors at Dodowah): but the princess Akianvah belonged to a native of Dutch Accra who had also paid a large sum for her redemption, and although he had given her up to the President (to his own great injury amongst the natives at that time), yet it was impossible that he should be asked to sustain so great a loss without compensation. The President therefore, before leaving Accra, had pledged himself that the sum of £80 should be paid to him. The question now was, how was that sum to be raised, since the public funds could not, from the great expense already incurred, afford it. It was unanimously resolved that a meeting of the merchants should be called and that it should be recommended to them to subscribe the necessary funds themselves. . . .

[C.O.98/1A]

100 COUNCIL MINUTE

CAPE COAST CASTLE, 11 APRIL, 1832.

At a meeting of Council held . . . this day, present:

George Maclean Esqr., President.
James Swanzy, Esqr. ⎫
Robert Roberts, Esqr. ⎭ Members.

The President stated that a murder attended with the most horrible and revolting atrocities had been committed near the town of Cape Coast on the 8th inst. by a notorious criminal who had escaped from the guard while working on the public roads the previous day, and that he had also on the 7th committed a rape and robbery on a Fantee woman about two miles from the castle. The morning after the perpetration of the murder, he was captured at Mouree by some inhabitants of that town and was with difficulty, on account of the fury of the natives, lodged in Cape Coast Castle.

The question now to which the President would direct the attention of the Council was whether or not they had the right to detain the prisoner and send him to Sierra Leone for trial, or whether he should be delivered up to the townspeople, to be tried by them according to the laws of the country?

The Council, taking into consideration

1st. That they are limited in their jurisdiction, according to the rules and regulations, merely to the forts and the persons residing therein;

2. That if the prisoner were sent to Sierra Leone he would on these grounds be acquitted;

3. That the prisoner, if detained here for the purpose of being sent to Sierra Leone might remain here for years before an opportunity might occur of transporting him thither, and

4. That the Council had not the means of defraying from their slender funds the expenses that would be incurred by sending him to Sierra Leone:

It was therefore unanimously resolved that the caboceers and chief people of the town should be summoned to try him according to their country laws, and that the Council, for the sake of humanity, should see the sentence carried into effect without allowing him to be exposed to the tortures to which by the custom of the country he would be subjected. . . .

[C.O.98/1A]

101 COUNCIL MINUTE

27 AUGUST, 1832.

At a meeting of Council held at Cape Coast Castle this day, present:

George Maclean, President.
James Swanzy, Esqr. Member.
Robert Roberts, Esqr. Member.

The President intimated that he had summoned the present meeting in consequence of his having received certain intelligence that a large marauding party of the rebel Ashantee chief Boatyn's people were scouting the paths betwixt this place and Ashantee and were plundering and insulting the traders on the path. If, therefore, they wished peace to be maintained throughout the country, some steps must be taken immediately to put an end to such practices; and as arrangements had already been made to send a party to Yancomassie,[1] he wished to have the consent of the Council to the measure before he despatched them. Such a step would not only be the means of dispersing the marauders, but would also tend to intimidate the adjacent tribes from attempting anything of the same kind.

The Council unanimously agreed to the measure and requested the President to despatch the party with all convenient speed.   [C.O.98/1A]

102 COUNCIL MINUTE

1 MARCH, 1834.

At a meeting of Council held at Cape Coast this day, present:

George Maclean, Esqr., President.
James Swanzy, Esqr., M.C.
John Jackson, Esqr., M.C.[2]
Wm. Topp, Esqr., M.C.[3]

The President announced that the present meeting had been summoned on account of the critical aspect which matters had now assumed in Wassaw. That the Council were already aware that the quarrel which had some time ago been settled in Cape Coast Castle, between the two rival Wassaw chiefs, had again broken out and now appeared to be approaching a crisis. In fact, the reports prevalent were that the one chief was marching with a strong force to attack the other. That this

[1] Nyankumasi-Fanti.

[2] Re-elected to the Council on return from leave (2 October, 1832) vice Hutchison (resigned).

[3] Secretary to the Council since March, 1830; elected to the Council vice Roberts (4 February, 1834).

was not the only evil dreaded from this internal dissension, but that various other chiefs throughout the country were beginning to arrange themselves on different sides and seemed anxious to take part in the dispute. If such should happen, a general war would then be inevitable. He therefore wished that, if possible, some measures should be adopted to prevent such a juncture from happening.

Mr. Jackson then proposed that messengers should be sent to the different chiefs likely to join in the quarrel, to endeavour to dissuade them from it. He also proposed that a meeting of the townspeople of Cape Coast should be held in the castle in order to ascertain their opinion on the subject, and to induce them to send messengers from the different quarters to accompany the messengers from the fort, and to join them in dissuading the various chiefs from joining the Wassaws.

To this proposition the Council agreed, and requested the President to call a meeting of the caboceers and pynims of the town for the purpose above-mentioned. . . .
                                                [C.O.98/1A]

103 COUNCIL MEETING
CAPE COAST CASTLE, 13 OCTOBER, 1834.
At a meeting of Council held . . . this day, present:

> George Maclean, Esqr., President.
> James Swanzy, Esqr., M.C.
> John Jackson, Esqr., M.C.
> W. Topp, Esqr., M.C. . . .

The President laid upon the table several letters from Governor Lans of Elmina, wherein he (Governor Lans) claimed certain portions of territory which had long been under the British flag, viz. Abremoo, Dhuguah[1] &c &c., upon which grounds he assumed the right of summoning these people before him and of settling differences which ought properly to belong to the decision of the Government at Cape

[1] Abremo and Ogua (if that is meant) lie northwest and north of Elmina.

Coast. It was agreed that the President should remonstrate with Governor Lans upon such conduct.

The President then adverted to the conduct of Cudjoe Chibboe,[1] who had been guilty of the most horrible atrocities during the 'custom' made for his deceased sister, and proposed, as a means of securing his person without trouble or expense, to threaten him with the retention of his prisoner (now in this castle) unless he should be forthcoming when ordered to appear.

The conduct of the king of Apollonia was then taken into consideration. It appeared that he had been guilty of wantonly killing some people belonging to Bassahini, who came peaceably to his country for the purpose of trade, and that on different occasions he had detained captains of vessels anchored there. The President said that he could no longer be an idle spectator of such enormities, and that if no other means of checking him could be found, he would be under the necessity of repairing to Apollonia and endeavour to put a stop to such proceedings. Agreed to. . . .   [C.O.98/1A]

104 RULES FOR THE GOVERNMENT OF APOLLONIA   FEBRUARY, 1835.
[Recounts the circumstances leading to the despatch of an expedition against Kwaku Aka, chief of Nzima (Apollonia)] . . .

And whereas the President, having overcome the said Accah, has ordered him to lodge in Cape Coast Castle the sum of 300 ounces of gold for the space of 15 years, as security for his conduct in future, which gold is now lodged accordingly; and whereas it is expedient and necessary that proper laws, rules and regulations should be laid down for the good government of Apollonia in time to come; wherefore, the President, taking all these matters into consideration, does hereby order that the said Accah, his chiefs and captains, do strictly obey and abide by the following laws.

[1] Kwadwo or Kojo Tsibu, chief of Denkyira.

First. No caboceer, chief or captain, or any other person whatever, shall presume to put any person to death, upon *any pretext whatever*; and any person so doing after this time shall be considered a common murderer, and punished accordingly. If anyone shall be guilty of a crime deserving death, he must be sent in irons to Cape Coast castle there to be judged and punished. This law strictly forbids all human sacrifices to the memory of the dead, or on any other occasion whatever. A breach of this law will be more severely looked into and punished than a breach of any other.

Second. No caboceer, chief, captain, or other person shall presume to cut, main or disfigure any person, whether a slave or freeman, upon any pretext whatever.

Third. The exportation of slaves from Africa being strictly prohibited by the laws of England, the chiefs, caboceers and people of Apollonia are hereby strictly forbidden to sell slaves for that purpose; nor shall they on any account, directly or indirectly afford assistance to slaving vessels towards obtaining their illicit cargoes.

Fourth. It having been agreed upon at Cape Coast Castle, in the year 1831, at which time a treaty of peace and commerce was concluded with the king of Ashantee, that in future all paths should be open to every person whatever, for the purpose of trade or other lawful business, in which agreement and treaty Apollonia was included; it is hereby ordered that no Apollonian shall presume to stop any path or to seize or panyar any person whatever who may be proceeding through Apollonia on lawful business. It is to be clearly understood that no one is allowed to panyar for debts or on any other pretext whatever. Any person guilty of this crime shall be severely punished.

Fifth. All debts are to be asked for and recovered in a quiet and peaceable manner and no violence must at any time be resorted to for that purpose. If a debtor positively refuses or evades payment of his just debts, then application must be made to the Governor who engages to recover the same with all expenses.

Sixth. . . . All laws and regulations now made must be observed by the Apollonians with regard to Dutch subjects equally as with regard to English subjects. . . .

Seventh. Small palavers may be settled by the Apollonians themselves, so long as they do not, in settling them, disobey any of the laws now made: but all great palavers must be referred to Cape Coast Castle.

Eighth. Every Apollonian who may be oppressed or injured, either by Quaqoh Accah or any other chief, is hereby invited to make his complaints to the Governor of Cape Coast Castle, who will take care that he is redressed, if his complaint be just; and no person need be afraid to do so, as the Governor will always afford him full protection. . . .

[C.O.267/131]

105 G. BARNES TO M. FORSTER
LONDON, 23 MARCH, 1835.

. . . Mr. Maclean is an active, zealous, able officer. His fort, his garrison and everything about him, are, I believe, in a state which do him great credit: but he has attempted to set aside the rules and to govern independently of the Council. . . .

So long as the rules remain unaltered, I shall continue my endeavours to enforce them, and I have no desire to see them altered, because I still think that they are well calculated for the accomplishment of their object. It is with this view that I expressed, as you state, an opinion that Government had acted wisely in placing the management of the forts in the hands . . . of those persons who are most interested in their preservation — the resident merchants, whose lives and property are dependent upon their condition and upon the efficiency of the garrison: but I have never said that an interested individual, who might have thousands depending on the personal good offices of the President, is the most fit person to superintend the conduct of that President and of the Council over which he presides. . . .[1]

[C.O.267/131]

106 COUNCIL PROCEEDINGS
CAPE COAST CASTLE, 28 JULY, 1835.

. . . We the undersigned British resident merchants at Cape Coast and Annamaboe, entitled by the rules and regulations for the Government of the settlements of Cape Coast and Accra to vote at the election of members of Council, solemnly protest against the whole proceedings in Council relative to the election of a member to fill the vacancy occasioned by the death of Joseph Ridley Esqr. deceased, as a partial and unfair election.

Partial and unfair, in so far as being well known to us that the President, for party and interested purposes, has exerted himself in the most unjustifiable manner by intimidating and holding forth promises . . . to influence the votes of the electors, in order to exclude a free and independent member, the choice of the colony, and gain their votes for his nominee, who will, he is aware, allow him still to revel in all the tyrannous misrule which has so long been carried on here, to the injury of the merchants, the ruin of commerce, the destruction of the welfare of the place, and the universal discontent of the native inhabitants.

Partial and unfair we pronounce it inasmuch that the President, after exerting

[1] Maclean applied in December, 1833 for leave of absence without vacating his appointment. The London committee divided over this. Barnes opposed the application, ostensibly because the rules and regulations laid it down that the President should be elected by the Council: but really (according to Forster), because he was the spokesman for Maclean's principal opponent on the coast — Mr. Jackson. Forster, the 'interested individual' of Barnes' letter claimed that the President should be appointed by and answerable to the Committee, subject to the approval of the Secretary of State. Lord Glenelg took advantage of this dispute to appoint a new committee, consisting of Joseph Reid, W. M. Hutton and J. G. Nicholls, cf. papers in C.O.267/126 passim.

himself as above stated, to gain his ends, pretends to deliberate without fear or favour on the fitness of the votes objected to, of deciding for or against himself, or acting the farce of judging his own cause, when we verily believe that his mind was previously resolved on the subject. . . .

Partial and unfair do we look upon the decision of the Council in this case, and incapable we must conceive them to decide upon it, constituted as it is only of the President, who had made himself so deeply interested in the event, and Mr. Topp, the proposer of the President's candidate. Indeed, until now we were not aware that two members could form a Council. . . . [The votes are examined in detail.]

[Signed] John Jackson [and seven others].

. . . We can make every allowance for the excited feelings of a defeated faction, but in bringing forward such heavy accusations as the above, some regard ought to be had for consistency and truth. But what is the fact? The greater number of the parties signing the Protest, not five months ago voluntarily appended their names (in the President's absence) to an address wherein the President is lauded for his equitable and just government, for the complete manner in which he has tranquillised the country and benefited commercial [activities]; (and here it is but justice to several of these gentlemen to say, that they have since declared that they thought they were merely making a protest but had no idea of making any attack on the President.)

To such vague and sweeping charges as the above, the President can only answer that their very authors knew them to be unfounded; that no administration could have been less tyrannical than that of the President; that he has invariably assisted the merchants, both in his public and private capacity, and . . . especially those from whom the protest has emanated. As to the ruin of commerce, the President can only refer to the facts that the very last vessel which sailed from the settlement for

England, carried home a freight of 5,250 oz. of gold and tons of ivory, and that the number of vessels anchoring in this road-stead and the gross quantity of imports, have increased during the President's administration 50 per cent. It is not easy to guess what is meant by the 'welfare of the place', but anyone having the use of their eyes can judge of its improved appearance since the present President arrived in this country.

If by the discontent of the native inhabitants . . . is meant that [of] such men as Cudjoe Chibboo and the chief of Apollonia, than it will be readily admitted that they are discontented, because the President has most justly punished them for their manifold and barbarous crimes, but that the mass of the native population are discontented we utterly deny. We do fearlessly assert that it will be a sorrowful day with them and for them, when they hear that the President is about to leave them. . . . An intelligent and wealthy native was asked lately . . . what the natives generally thought of the President. His immediate reply was that there never was so good a governor in the country, and that it would be a bad palaver when he left. . . . [The people of Cape Coast had offered to defend the President against the suspected designs of Captain Burgoyne.]

We trust that long ere this can reach England, the Committee will have given orders for the removal of the *real author* of the 'Protest', who has done more mischief within the few months that he has been in the settlement than may be cured in as many years. . . .[1]   [C.O.98/1A]

[1] There were two disputed elections in July, 1835, and a good deal depended on the verification of the qualifications of electors. The Committee in England felt that it was unfortunate that this duty devolved on Maclean and Topp, although this only happened because the other member of Council (Jackson) declined to attend. However, when new elections were ordered, the same men (James Swanzy and J. W. Hansen) were unanimously re-elected.

107 COUNCIL MINUTE

CAPE COAST CASTLE, 10 AUGUST, 1835.

At a meeting of Council this day, present:

> Geo. Maclean, President.
> William Topp, Esq., M.C.
> James Swanzy, Esq., M.C.[1]

. . . The President then stated that he wished to bring under the notice of the Council the subject of the quarterly allowances paid by the Castle to the caboceers and people of the town. From various parts of the correspondence which took place betwixt H.M. Government and the merchants when these establishments were placed upon their present footing, it would appear that erroneous ideas were entertained on this subject by the authorities in England, who seemed to suppose that the local Government were bound to pay these allowances in the name or in lieu of *ground rent*. This, as the Council well knew, was not the case — not only the ground on which the castle is built, but a very large extent of country having long been the actual property of the Crown — in proof of which, it may be sufficient to state that the greater part of even the native inhabitants, hold the ground on which their houses are built by grants from the Crown, which grants have always been given by the Governor for the time being, of which he (the President), has, during the last five years, given many, and [of] which a regular registry is kept in the Castle with ground plans annexed.[2] These periodical allowances, in fact, were formerly given, not only to the petty chiefs and natives residing under the guns of the forts on the Gold Coast, but to distant chiefs whose friendship it was considered expedient, for various reasons, to secure. Thus, previous to the late war with that country, the king

[1] For some reason not clearly stated in the minutes, Swanzy came up for re-election in 1835, and this apparently had the effect of causing him to rank after Topp. In fact he sat almost continuously from 1828 until his death in September 1842.

[2] Cf. Hackett to Newcastle, No. 50, 12 May, 1864 (C.O.96/64) for an account (with plan) of the Register of Town Lands dating from 1818.

of Ashantee received monthly pay from the Government, which pay or allowance had been originally granted to the chief of Fantee, but was transferred to the former when his power became predominant. In short, granting a monthly allowance to a chief was considered equivalent to securing his friendship and his services when required for warlike or other purposes. But the conditions upon which the allowance to the people of Cape Coast [was paid] were expressly stated in their monthly notes or 'pay books' as they are termed. These conditions are, that each quarter (district) of the town shall, besides rendering such services to the Government as may be from time to time required from them, keep in good and sufficient repairs certain streets, roads and defences appertaining to each district, which streets etc. are marked out by certain defined boundaries.

Now the Council was well aware that in no one instance had the townspeople performed any of the services which they had thus bound themselves to perform. He (the President) had repeatedly . . . remonstrated with them, but all in vain. Had no other means been used to repair the roads and clean the streets, the former would long [since] have become impassable, and the latter intolerable. He (the President) had found the people, as the Council well knew, equally impracticable when their services were required on extraordinary occasions. Their services had been only twice required by him; once when a large body of Ashantee traders had been stopped and plundered, about the distance of two days' march into the interior, which circumstance had nearly caused a total stoppage of communication with Ashantee; and again, on the occasion of the late expedition to Apollonia. On neither of these occasions had they rendered the slightest assistance, though in both cases the most liberal offers of reward were made to them. The Council would recollect that for his refusal to give any assistance in the first-mentioned case, the pay of the chief caboceer had been taken

from him, but afterwards restored by them. Their lenity on that occasion, however, appeared to have had no effect, for neither the caboceer nor townspeople had ever since that time performed any of the conditions on which their allowance had been granted. He, (the President), finding remonstrance vain, had subsequently tried the effect of suspending payment of their allowances, but equally without success. He therefore begged to place the whole matter in the hands of the Council, merely adding that he had employed a portion of the funds retained in effecting those repairs of roads etc. which were necessary.

The Council, after fully discussing the subject, are unanimously of opinion that, however expedient in the earlier periods of their settlements it might have been to make periodical allowances to the neighbouring chiefs and natives, such payments have long ceased to be either necessary or to be attended with any good effect; and that those granted to the people of Cape Coast ought to have been got rid of at the same time with those formerly made to several chiefs in the interior, the chiefs and people of Annamaboe etc.; that, in short, these payments are a most useless and unnecessary item of our expenditure.

As to the question immediately before them, the Council are of opinion that the funds now in store, arising from the suspended allowances, should be immediately employed in repairing the public roads to the various plantations. The Council are also of opinion that the President ought to remonstrate again with the head people of the town, and warn them if they persist in their line of conduct they will be in danger of losing their quarterly allowances entirely. . . .   [C.O.98/1A]

108 COUNCIL MINUTE

CAPE COAST CASTLE, 12 OCTOBER, 1835.

. . . The President laid upon the table two letters received from the king of Ashantee where he complained very much against the establishment by Fantee traders of a stationary market in his dominions, contrary to the understanding entered into when the treaty of peace and commerce was signed in 1831, and whereby his people were greatly injured. The Council requested the President to consult with the merchants generally on the subject, and if then deemed expedient, to call a public meeting of all the merchants upon the coast to take into consideration the present pernicious system of trade. . . .

[C.O.98/1A]

109 COUNCIL MINUTE
CAPE COAST CASTLE, FEBRUARY, 1836.
. . . The President stated that he was sorry to have to report to the Council that several instances of murder had lately taken place in the country, and that two persons accused of that crime were now in the castle, and the public mind was greatly exasperated and excited respecting these two cases.

Resolved: that the usual course be followed respecting these men; that the native authorities of the district to which they belong be summoned to try them, and that the President and Council do attend to see that no injustice be done, and that in the meantime every facility be given to the culprits to prepare for their defence. . . .

[C.O.98/1A]

110 COUNCIL MINUTE
CAPE COAST CASTLE, 8 FEBRUARY, 1836.
At a meeting of Council held this day, present:

Geo. Maclean, President.
William Topp, M.C.
Thomas Hutton, M.C.[1]

The President begged to recall the attention of the Council to the proceedings and result of the meeting of the pynims and townspeople on Saturday in presence of the Council and others. The Council

[1] Joined the Council in October 1835, in place of John Jackson.

would recollect that the whole of the caboceers and people, with the single exception of Joe Aggrey, had utterly denied all knowledge of or participation in the letter sent in their name to the Committee, and Aggrey being called on to explain how he had dared to make such a use of their names, acknowledged the fact, but thought he had some right to do so, as being caboceer. Aggrey also said that the letter had been written and brought to him to be acknowledged by him and that he had been adduced to authorise its transmission as he had been assured that it would do him good, but he declined to name the party who had manufactured the letter.

On being asked how, supposing he had understood the contents of the letter, he could authorise the insertion of a downright falsehood, namely that he had been 'suspended, excluded from coming into the castle'; he replied that he never authorised such an insertion, but merely meant to say that he was not looked favourably upon by the President.

The townspeople generally being invited to state publicly in that place, any grievances under which they might conceive themselves to labour, retired with their headmen to a consultation, and on their return declared that they had never made any note, nor had they any grounds to complain of, except the single circumstance of the stoppage of their pay: but on being asked whether the President had not assembled them as many as twenty or thirty times to represent to them the necessity of their doing something in return for their pay, and whether he had not repeatedly offered them their pay if they would even devote one day in the month to the performance of their contract, they acknowledged that such had been the case. On being further pressed, they admitted that for the last four, five or six years, they had not in any one instance performed their contract. . . .

Resolved, that it appearing from the previous minutes of Council that for a series of years the conduct of Joe Aggrey has been exceedingly bad, more particularly during the government of Mr. Jackson . . . when he was deposed and eventually fined £20, and to mark the Council's strong disapprobation of his late conduct in refusing to perform services required of him on the occasion of the late expedition to Apollonia . . . the said Joe Aggrey be suspended from his situation of chief caboceer until he prove by his conduct that he is in some measure worthy of being re-instated.   [C.O.98/1A]

111 COUNCIL MINUTE

CAPE COAST CASTLE, 15 MARCH, 1836.

. . . The President . . . called the attention of the Council to Cudjoe Chiboo's second memorial addressed to the . . . Secretary of State, and was proceeding to . . . prove to them the entire falsehood of the charges brought against himself personally in that memorial when he was interrupted by the Council, who stated that . . . it would be a mere waste of time for the President to disprove to *them*, or to any person acquainted with his administration, the absurd charges contained in the document on the table; a document which, though purporting to be a memorial from Cudjoe Chibboo evidently never could have emanated from him.

The President said that though he had resolved, in general, to treat such attacks with the contempt they merited, yet that he felt himself bound to give the fullest explanation respecting any document transmitted by the Secretary of State, more especially as it must be difficult for his Lordship to believe that charges so boldly put forward . . . could be so utterly destitute of foundation as they actually were. . . . The President could not help remarking that in this, as in former similar instances, the documents . . . had been forewarded directly to the Colonial Office. . . . This method of transmitting attacks on this Government had been persisted in, in direct defiance of the orders of the

Secretary of State himself, but he hoped that in future they would be returned to their authors unread, with directions to send them through the regular channels.

The President then stated that it now became the duty of the Council, in compliance with the recommendations of the Committee, to take into their serious consideration the expediency of restoring the security lodged by Cudjoe Chibboo for his future good conduct, and whether any portion of the fine imposed upon him might not be restored to him.

Whereupon after having fully deliberated and dispassionately considered the whole case, it was unanimously resolved:

1. That were the security given up or the slightest grace shown to Cudjoe Chiboo upon the present occasion, such act would be tantamount in the eyes of the whole country to a declaration on the part of His Majesty's Government, that human sacrifices are not only to be tolerated, but are legal, and that the local Government had acted unjustly and tyrannically in interfering to prevent them.

2. That no explanation or disclosure offered by the President and Council could prevent such an impression being firmly fixed in the minds of the natives, and that even Europeans are not wanting who would encourage and confirm such an impression.

3. That such an act would therefore be tantamount to the pronouncing of immediate sentence of death upon many hundreds and eventually thousands of our unfortunate fellow-creatures, since all the chiefs whom this Government has compelled long since to discontinue the practice of human sacrifices, would think themselves at liberty to resume those practices and even deem themselves bound to sacrifice innumerable victims to the *manes* of all those of their families who may have died since the practice has been abolished.

4. That instead of looking upon such an act as an act of grace on the part of this Government, Cudjoe Chiboo and others would look upon and proclaim it

solely as a triumph over the President and Council, and that therefore this Government would be deprived of all power to prevent such horrible practices in future.

5. That viewed merely in a political point of view, such an act would be fraught with the most pernicious consequences, because this Government, possessing but trifling physical power and very limited means, must govern almost entirely by the influence of opinion; and the high opinion entertained of its invariable justice and moderation, by the natives, being once shaken by the reversal of even one of its decrees would be lost, and its future decrees scorned and disobeyed.

6. That therefore the Council do deprecate interference with or reversal of its acts, except upon the strongest possible grounds and for the most urgent reasons. Even when the acts of the Council may appear to the Committee positively ill-judged, a direct reversal thereof is to be avoided if possible, since the great and permanent evil attendant upon such reversal must almost invariably much more than counterbalance the isolated and temporary benefit which might be derived therefrom.

7. Resolved that the above resolutions be recorded in the minutes as containing the sincere and conscientious opinion of the Council, after an impartial and dispassionate discussion of the whole case on its own merits, without reference to the language of the memorials or the party by whom they were prepared, and as two of the members are now absent, the secretary is hereby directed to send to them a copy of these resolutions, as well as the other documents relating to the affair, that the opinions of the whole Council may be recorded. . . .

The President then laid on the table the correspondence which had passed betwixt the Danish Governor and him on the occasion of his late visit to Accra. He said that with a view to bring[ing] the whole subject-matter of this correspondence before them, it would be necessary

F

that he should recapitulate the events wherein it originated.

The Council was aware that the Danish Government has, for a long time, evinced the greatest jealousy of the paramount influence exercised by this Government throughout the country. This jealousy was more particularly shown during the long negotiations which preceded the treaty of peace with Ashantee in 1831 and other late occasions. But while the manifestations of this jealousy were confined to mere correspondence, he (the President) had never taken the slightest notice of it, except when it might have been unavoidable. Of late, however, that is soon after the arrival on the coast of the present Danish Governor,[1] more decided symptoms of an inimical spirit towards us began to show themselves. The spirit was first evinced in an attempt to assert and even enforce an *exclusive* right to the extensive district of Akim and Aquapim.

These districts, the Council were aware, the Danish Government had, since the close of the war with Ashantee, been in the habit of calling Danish territory. And while their doing so had not interfered with the British commercial interests, no objections were offered, nor, had matters practically been allowed to remain as they were, would this Government ever have thought it necessary to agitate the question. The Danish Government had also of late claimed the district of Crobo, a tract of country bordering upon Aquapim and, as well as the latter, exceedingly valuable to the merchants of Accra, as from these districts they annually procure large quantities of palm oil.

Previous to the year 1823-4, Akim and Aquapim had formed integral portions of the Ashantee kingdom, having been first acquired by conquest and afterwards fully incorporated with Ashantee. In 1824, proposals were made by the British Government to the Akims and Aquapims, inviting them to join the British standard, and

[1] Frederick Siegfred Mörch (1800–39), Governor of Christiansborg Castle 1835-9.

promising them, in that case, emancipation from the Ashantee yoke. Those proposals were accepted, and eventually the hopes held out by this Government were realised, and those districts were rendered, entirely by means of British arms and British money, independent of Ashantee, which independence was acknowledged and secured to them by the treaty of 1831. In the war whereby these events were brought about the Danes were merely auxiliaries and paid as such by the British Government. . . .

The Danish Government, after the conclusion of the war, called the districts in question, Danish territory: but practically the British Government always exercised the same control over them as over its other territories (so called) and where necessary sent soldiers into them for the protection of their trade, and enforced redress of injuries etc, all without any opposition on the part of the Danish Government. Within the last twelve months, however, the present Danish Governor (Mr. Morck) did make objections to British messengers, soldiers, or others appearing in any of those districts, and more lately, assuming a higher tone, stated plainly that he had given positive orders to his soldiers to eject by force any British soldiers (who in this country are always the persons employed as messengers) that might appear there.

He (the President) was at first exceedingly unwilling to create any difference between the two Governments provided he could prevent or avoid it without compromising the interests of the British merchant. He therefore assured Governor Morck . . . that the soldiers sent by him . . . or the commandant of Accra, were merely messengers sent on special matters, who could do injury to no person, and that there could be no necessity or reason for any collision between the two settlements on that account. Apparently the moderate tone adopted by him (the President) had a contrary effect to what he had hoped for. . . . In the month of November last,

Governor Morck repaired to Aquapim, (betwixt which district and Crobo an ancient feud existed, which had only been settled by him, the President, about two years previously, after much trouble and expense) and there summoned the Crobos to come and do homage to him, as their lawful governor and master. . . .

[The Krobos declined this invitation and Mörch proceeded to Krobo with a large force. Akwapims and Krobos came to blows and there was considerable loss of life.] The Aquapims demanded assistance from the Danish Governor, which he refused to give, on which, the former suddenly withdrew from the camp and returned home. On the return of the Danish Governor to Christiansborg he sent for the chiefs of both Aquapims and Crobos to come to Danish Accra in order to settle their differences. The Aquapims flatly refused, saying — truly enough — 'that they owed no allegiance to Denmark', and adding that the Danish Governor had grossly deceived them by drawing them into a disastrous war and then treacherously leaving them to their fate. The Crobos evaded his summons.[1]

In the meantime he (the President) had gone to Accra on public business. Soon after his arrival, the Danish Governor . . . personally told him that in future he would permit no English soldiers or messengers to enter Akim or Aquapim, and stated that in one instance an English soldier had already been forcibly ejected from a district attached to Akim. The President requested that all communications . . . might be made by letter, whereupon the correspondence now on the table commenced. . . .

While this correspondence was going on, a deputation arrived from the Aquapim chiefs requesting to be formally, as they had long been in reality, received as British subjects. . . . In the meantime . . . in consequence of the ill-advised expedition

[1] Reindorf's account (*History*, 308–14) puts the chief blame on the Akwapimhene, Ado Dankwa.

of Governor Mörck, the merchants of British Accra would be deprived of at least 800 or 1,000 puncheons of palm oil this season, since at present not a Crobo can move down to the coast from the Aquapims having entire command of the paths.

The President was urged by many to receive the Aquapims and to take the whole matter betwixt them and the Crobos into his own hands: but he was unwilling to come into collision with a neighbouring settlement; and besides, it was not the wish of the British Government to acquire territorial rights, although it was certainly necessary for the protection of British commerce not to admit the absurd exclusive claims set up by the Danish Governor. He . . . had therefore acted in the manner stated in the papers on the table.

The Council . . . unanimously approved of the President's conduct in the matter, and urged the strong necessity which existed for affording protection to our valuable palm oil trade at Accra and Prampram. It was also resolved that a strong recommendation should be made to the Committee by the President in person on this subject. . . .

The possibility of settling the Wassaw differences was then discussed, and it was finally resolved that it was expedient that the President should proceed to Secondee with such force as might appear necessary to ensure respect paid to his messages and offers of mediation. . . .   [C.O.98/1A]

112 COUNCIL MINUTE
CAPE COAST CASTLE, 17 SEPTEMBER, 1836.
. . . The President[1] stated that he had requested the attendance of the Council at this time on account of information which Mr. Hanson had just received from Accra relative to the proceedings of the Danish Governor with the Aquapims. In this information it was affirmed that the Danes were still using all their influence by

intriguing with the headmen of that country, to withdraw them from their allegiance to Addo Donquah their rightful chief; that in addition to the chiefs of Addoman, regarding whom the Council were already aware that . . . the President had written to the Danish Governor, the heads of three more towns had revolted from Addo Donquah's authority and had been sent for to attend at Danish Accra in order that they might be bound over to support the authority of Quow Foom the person now raised by Governor Morck to the sovereignty of Aquapim.[1]

The Council, taking into consideration that these proceedings were in direct infringement of the agreement of the 8th of March, inasmuch as Addo Donquah has not since that date taken any hostile measures against the Danish Government, and that it was therein stated that so long as he did not do so he was to be free from all molestation; that Governor Morck, in opposition to this had not only set up another person in his place (thus certainly using every effort to molest him) but also, by endeavouring to withdraw the rest of the country from its allegiance to Addo Donquah, was using means which would no doubt bring on all the horrors of a civil war throughout the district of Aquapim; the Council, further considering that they were bound by every means in their power to avert such a state of affairs; that it was their duty to see Addo-Donquah, who had thrown himself upon them for protection, redressed, and his authority maintained, and to see the conditions of the above-mentioned agreement acted up to, were unanimously of opinion:

That as Mr. Hanson[2] was now about to

[1] William Topp, Esqr.

[1] Reindorf says that Adum was enstooled by the Danes as Akwapimhene. Kwafum, 'the old fox', seems to have taken the lead in getting Ado Dankwa to break with the Danes, and then persuading the Akwapim chiefs to desert him.
[2] Succeeded J. Ridley as commandant of Accra and member of Council in July 1835. (His election was declared invalid by the Committee, but he was unanimously re-elected in February 1836.) He died in 1840.

proceed to Accra, he be directed more fully to investigate the allegations made . . . and if he should find the truth of them confirmed, and that the Danish Governor had been using undue means to withdraw the Aquapims from their allegiance, that he remonstrate with him, pointing out to him the evils likely to result from these proceedings, and directly stating to him that the Council consider them a direct infringement of the above-mentioned agreement, which, since infringed by him, cannot be considered longer binding upon them. . . .   [C.O.98/1A]

9 Maclean and the British Government, 1836–1840

IN 1836, Maclean went on leave and was absent just over two years, returning to Cape Coast in August 1838.   He used this interval to press, through the Committee, for a revision of the regulations under, or in spite of which, he had to govern (113).   The Government declined any change that would have increased its own responsibility (114), and would not even restore the cuts made in the annual Parliamentary grant in 1832 (118).   On the other hand, Maclean succeeded in vindicating his administration against the charges of some of his critics (116–17), but failed to end the system of elections to the Council (115), which he, like the African Company before him, had found something of a stumbling-block in the way of efficient government (Appendix A 2).   He also raised the questions of domestic slavery and the surrender of fugitives to Ashanti, but without result as far as the Colonial Office was concerned (117).

His standing with the British Government was as high as it ever was to be in his lifetime on the eve of his return to Africa.   Even James Stephen, a strong critic of the policy of retaining the forts both before (119) and after 1838 (137) was, for a moment, impressed by their achievement in stopping the slave trade along the shores of the Gold Coast (120).   This was because Sir Thomas Fowell Buxton had just launched his campaign for more comprehensive measures to stop the West African slave trade.   Unfortunately for Maclean, the anti-slave-trade fervour was at its height when reports reached the Colonial Office, that vessels intended for the slave trade were in the habit of buying goods at Cape Coast.   Maclean, ordered to stop this and to institute proceedings against the guilty merchants, raised doubts as to his competency to do this (122–3).   Lord John Russell thereupon decided that the only security for the prompt application of the laws against the slave trade, was for the Government to resume control of the forts (124), but, at the instance of the Treasury (126), he agreed to defer acting on this conviction until after a special commissioner had visited West Africa and reported on the situation he found there.

113 G. MACLEAN TO THE COMMITTEE OF MERCHANTS

LONDON, 30 NOVEMBER, 1836.

. . . Under this Government, surrounded as it has been by difficulties both internal and external, with means the most limited, and with powers ill-defined, or rather, undefined, the British Gold Coast settlements have nevertheless attained to a degree of commercial and agricultural prosperity before unexampled in their history; while peace, order and perfect security of person and property have been established throughout the country.

Surely, then, I am justified in drawing . . . these inferences: 1st, that the Mother Country is bound, not less by justice than by distinct and positive engagements, to provide the means of good government and to encourage the prosperity of her Gold Coast settlements; and 2ndly, that these settlements possess within themselves in an eminent degree, the elements of prosperity. Having, I trust, satisfactorily established these points, I now proceed to point out those imperfections in the existing code of rules and regulations which render them inapplicable to the actual state of the settlements, and in many respects impracticable.

The great means whereby the local Government has been enabled during the last seven years to establish and maintain peace and order throughout so extensive a country with such feeble and apparently inadequate resources at its command, have been the strict and impartial administration of justice. It is this which has had the happiest effects in maintaining peace, encouraging agriculture and commerce and promoting the civilisation of the natives. Let but the local Government deny or cease to administer even-handed justice to the population for a single day, and the whole country would again become a scene of warfare, rapine and oppression.

Yet according to the rules and regulations, the powers of the local authorities do not extend a yard beyond the walls of the several forts; that is, the magistrates are empowered to exercise their functions on the only spot where their exercise is never required. The forts are only occupied by those in the employment of Government, who are governed by the regulations usual in all garrisons. It will be admitted that the chief object (though by no means the only one) of maintaining the forts and a local government, is to afford protection and encouragement to commerce. But no trade is carried on within the walls of the fort. The merchants or traders reside or have factories in the towns and at various stations throughout a considerable extent of country. According to the rules and regulations, therefore, they are beyond the pale of the protection afforded by the British flag, and the authorities embarrassed in performing the chief duty for which they were constituted.

But suppose, even, the authority of the Government to extend (as is, in the case of isolated forts in foreign countries, the general rule) as far as the guns of the fort can reach, still would its power thus limited, be utterly insufficient for the protection of trade. At present, traders resort to the several settlements from all parts of the country, in the full confidence that the British Government possess both the power and the inclination to protect their persons and property while journeying among the various intervening tribes; while the latter well know that certain punishment will follow any attempt to molest them. Were the case otherwise, constituted as that country is, all trade would cease. For example, the British resident merchants derive their chief trade (which is very extensive and lucrative) from Ashantee, the factories of which are about a hundred miles distant from any British settlements, the intervening districts being inhabited by several tribes, all of whom are the hereditary enemies of the Ashantees. With what prospect of safety could an Ashantee trader traverse such an extent of country, inhabited by people withheld by no moral restraint and personally hostile to him, if they were left to the guidance of their lawless passions? Moreover, the British Government has long been bound by the most positive and sacred engagements to protect these tribes (who have been taught to consider, and do consider themselves British subjects) not only from external aggression, but from the miseries of internal quarrels; and to recede from these engagements now would be to plunge the entire country into the most dreadful state of savage anarchy. . . .

But the extent of the judicial power conferred upon the local authorities by the rules and regulations is equally defective in another point of view. The very limited powers of a mere justice of the peace are but ill-calculated for the preservation of order and the repression of crime in an extensive and semi-barbarous country. Yet there is not, in that country, any court possessing powers more extensive than those possessed by a Court of Petty Sessions in England. How then, it may be asked, has the graver class of crimes been punished, or cases involving large amounts of property been decided heretofore? I answer that the absolute necessity of the case has hitherto compelled both myself and my colleagues to exercise judicial powers in all descriptions of cases, and that the same necessity has justified us to ourselves and others in so doing. But this manner of administering justice is neither satisfactory in itself, nor safe to the parties acting as judges.

To illustrate this I will suppose (a very common case) that one merchant owes another a large sum of money, say £1,000. The debtor is unwilling and refuses to pay this sum, and the creditor applies to the only authorities, the only court within his reach. How, in such a case, are these authorities to act? If they declare that they have no jurisdiction and decline to act, the natural and necessary consequence is that the injured party takes the law into his own hands, the debtor resists, and the matter becomes a mere question of physical strength betwixt the parties and their adherents. On the other hand, should the authorities act and compel the debtor to fulfil his engagements, either by distress or by personal imprisonment, it is plain that they are acting *ultra vires* and expose themselves to ruinous legal proceedings in the courts at home. Again, suppose a British subject should commit murder, or other felony, either within the fort walls or elsewhere, how in that case are the authorities to act? Justice and the interests of society equally demand that the criminal should receive the punishment due to his crime, but in whom is vested the power legally to award and execute that punishment? It may be said that Cape Coast Castle is in dependency upon Sierra Leone, and that persons guilty of grave offences ought to be sent there (where there is a competent court) for trial. But, practically speaking, this is impossible. We have no communication, or the means of communication with Sierra Leone, nor have we funds wherefrom the expenses of conveying prisoners and witnesses to Sierra Leone could be defrayed. Besides, witnesses neither would nor could absent themselves from their homes and business for many months whenever the ends of justice might require their presence at Sierra Leone; nor could such a sacrifice be required at their hands.

I have thus, I trust, shown the necessity of providing for the due administration of justice, either by authorising the existing magistrates to act judicially in all cases, or by the establishment of a separate and competent court. It requires, indeed, no arguments to prove that no well-regulated society can exist without possessing within itself the means of punishing and repressing crime, and of affording redress to the injured.

The next great defect in the present rules and regulations which I would notice, is the manner in which the election of members of Council is provided for. In the comparatively limited European society which exists on the Gold Coast, where each individual is intimately acquainted with all his fellow-residents, popular election is, at least on the Gold Coast, and has been, productive of the worst effects, where opposing candidates have appeared. It has had in those instances, the effect of producing bad feeling, lowering the Europeans in the eyes of the natives and of embarrassing the executive, and I speak with the sentiments of nine-tenths of the resident merchants in earnestly recommending that in future the members be appointed by the Committee under sanction of the Colonial Office.

The next defect, or rather perhaps it may be called an oversight, in the rules and regulations, is the omission of the names of Dixcove, Tantum and other settlements equally interested with Cape Coast Castle and Accra, and equally entitled to protection. . . .

Your intimate connection with the Gold Coast . . . will readily enable you to appreciate the truth of what I have advanced in this letter; and if convinced of the justice of the claims which I have attempted to advocate, I trust that you will most strenuously endeavour to impress the same conviction upon His Majesty's Government.   [C.O.267/136]

114 SIR GEORGE GREY[1] TO MESSRS REID, HUTTON AND NICHOLLS
LONDON, 30 DECEMBER, 1836.
. . . I have received and laid before Lord Glenelg[2] your letter of the 5th instant, with a communication therein enclosed from Mr. Maclean, on the subject of certain changes which he suggests should be made in the present constitution of the government of the settlements on the Gold Coast, and you request me to appoint an interview with you for the discussion of this subject.

Lord Glenelg has attentively perused the various propositions set forth by Mr. Maclean and desires to do justice to the zeal and ability with which they are supported: but without now minutely adverting to the particular sentiments contained in the letter, I am to offer a few general observations on its purport and character.

Mr. Maclean conceives, and proceeds to argue on the assumption that the forts on the Gold Coast are placed in the same relations with regard to Great Britain as those which are enjoyed by the regular colonial possessions of His Majesty. To such an opinion, however, it is impossible to subscribe. The forts in question have but few of the elements which constitute colonies, and can hardly be regarded as more than factories. When, therefore, Mr. Maclean states, 'That the mother country is bound . . . to provide the means of good government . . . of her Gold Coast settlements', the remark is inapplicable on two separate grounds; first as it implies

an undue estimate of the extent of the liability under which this country is placed in regard to those settlements; and secondly because it might be clearly shown that the utmost liberality has already been extended to them by the King's Government.

It further appears to Lord Glenelg, that the majority of Mr. Maclean's suggestions are of such a nature that a compliance with them could not fail to involve the British Government in an expense and expose it to a collision with the natives for the which no adequate justification could be offered.

With respect to the proposed change in the existing constitution of the Council, it is Lord Glenelg's desire, before offering any opinion on that subject, to be favoured with a statement in writing, of your own views in regard to its adoption, and of the points in which the present mode of election may be held to [defeat the] object in view. . . .   [H.C.551 of 1842]

115 JAMES STEPHEN[1] TO THE COMMITTEE OF MERCHANTS   LONDON 10 JULY, 1837.
. . . I have laid before Lord Glenelg your letter of the 15th ult. with the papers therein enclosed, relative to three distinct topics which you have been desirous of submitting for his Lordship's consideration.

With regard to the alteration of the rules and regulations for the management of the forts and castle on the Gold Coast, Lord Glenelg has directed me to state that he would be glad to be favoured by you with a distinct explanation of the particular import and object of each new rule as

---

[1] Sir George Grey (1799–1882); grandson of the 1st Earl Grey; Liberal M.P., 1832–74; Under-Secretary of State for the Colonies, June–December 1834, and April 1835 to February 1839; Home Secretary, 1846–52, 1855–8, 1861–6; he was the first Secretary of State for the Colonies, properly so called, from 10 June, 1854, to February 1855.

[2] Charles Grant, 1st baron Glenelg (1798–1866); son of one of Wilberforce's closest friends and himself closely identified with the humanitarians; his tenure of the secretaryship for war and the colonies (1835–9) coincided with the Canadian rebellion, in handling which he seemed to display a want of energy (cf. Brougham's gibe that the rebellion had cost Glenelg 'many a sleepless *day*'), which led Howick and Russell to demand his resignation in 1839.

[1] James Stephen (later Sir James) (1789–1859); son of James Stephen, friend and brother-in-law of Wilberforce; counsel to the Colonial Office, 1813; abandoned private practice to become permanent counsel to the Board of Trade and the Colonial Office, 1825; assistant Under-Secretary of State for the Colonies, 1834; Permanent-Under-Secretary, 1836–47; (cf. Henry Taylor's dictum that 'for more than twenty-five years . . . he more than any other man, virtually governed the Colonial Empire'; his influence was probably at its height under Glenelg); Professor of Modern History at Cambridge, 1849–59.

amended by you. The principal alteration relates, as you have observed, to the mode of appointing the President of the Council of magistrates; an appointment which you propose to vest in yourselves, instead of leaving it to the selection and vote of the Council. The question therefore arises whether any and what practical inconvenience has arisen, what advantage would be gained by placing the selection of the President beyond the control of the Council?

Lord Glenelg would, moreover, wish to be apprised whether you have reason for believing that the alteration which you have suggested of the mode of appointing the Council would be acceptable to the majority of the traders resident on the coast. On this point his Lordship would naturally incline to think that their interests would best be secured by consulting their wishes: but if it should be their desire that the Council should be filled up on the principle of seniority of residence, it would still remain to be well considered whether that principle is calculated to secure able and zealous service. His Lordship does not presume that it has entered into your contemplation that any but subjects of Her Majesty should be qualified for seats in the Council, but it will occur to you as desirable that no misunderstanding should exist on that point.

With reference to the proposal which has been made to you that some legal remedy should be provided for protecting the merchants who are engaged in trade with the Gold Coast against fraudulent or insolvent debtors, Lord Glenelg has directed me to state that he will readily consider any suggestion which you may have to offer with a view to that object. It appears, however, to him, so far as he is at present advised, that no effectual remedy of that nature can be provided, which would not involve the establishment of a court of judicature; and his Lordship does not suppose that it would enter into your views to appropriate any portion of the grant which Parliament has assigned for the maintenance of the forts to the support of judicial officers. His Lordship therefore apprehends that the only remedy against the inconvenience of which the merchants complain, must be found in their own prudence and caution. . . .[1]

[C.O.267/144]

116 G. MACLEAN TO THE COMMITTEE OF MERCHANTS

LONDON, 14 OCTOBER, 1837.

[Captain Burgoyne, on being dismissed from his post of Captain of the Guard, turned champion of the 'deeply injured and oppressed race of Africans' and brought a series of charges against Maclean. The first related to the death of a slave (Kobina) after a flogging at Accra.] . . .

Mr. Burgoyne's second charge is that a system of 'pawning' the natives, and thence one of coercive labour, prevails on the Gold Coast.

The prevalence of this system, even if there were (which there is not) anything morally wrong or illegal in it, cannot be charged against the Government of Cape Coast Castle, since it has prevailed in that country from time immemorial and the local Government possesses neither the right nor the power to interfere with it. This system (which under different names and modifications, prevails more or less in every country in the world) is peculiarly adapted to a state of society so constituted as that on the Gold Coast of Africa, and Mr. Burgoyne might as well exclaim against the system of apprenticeship in England, as it also induces a system of 'coercive' labour. The system which Mr. Burgoyne impotently attempts to make a handle in order to excite a prejudice in this country against the resident merchants on the Gold Coast, is simply this.

A man owes a debt, perhaps, which it is

[1] W. M. Hutton observed (H.C.551, Q.3842): 'We interpreted that letter as a sort of intimation that we should proceed with the administration without altering the rules, and that matter then dropped.'

utterly out of his power to pay. He thereupon applies to a person of property and offers to serve him as a labourer or domestic servant, as the case may be, at a low rate of wages, provided he (the person of property) will pay the debt, the debtor binding himself to serve his new employer until he shall have saved enough or otherwise acquired property sufficient to repay the sum advanced on his account. But his master has no more power over his 'pawn' than he has over any other servant. If he were to ill-use him, the servant has only to apply to the next magistrate and the master would at once be punished, or, if the 'pawn' is dissatisfied with his situation, he has only to apply to anyone whom he would prefer as his master, and he will, in nine cases out of ten, pay his debt (which his former master is obliged to accept) and take him as his servant. Many persons become 'pawns' when there is no necessity for this step merely for the purpose of securing regular and steady employment. In short, to relieve a debtor of his obligations and to accept of his services in lieu of the debt, is not uncommon, I presume, in England or in any country in the world, and the system of 'pawning' in Africa is nothing more or less. At all events, as I have already said, the local Government is not answerable for it.

[The third charge was that Maclean owned a slave and sold one to the Dutch for a soldier. The fourth accused the Gold Coast Government of recognising the purchase of a slave by a British subject.] . . .

I am anxious to meet this question on the broadest grounds, not for the purpose of refuting Mr. Burgoyne's absurd accusation, but for the purpose of having the question of domestic slavery on the Gold Coast set at rest.

I must premise that the local Government on the Gold Coast can in no respect be held answerable for a system or state of society which has existed in those settlements for upwards of two hundred years and which has been sanctioned . . . by each succeeding government. Previous to the year 1807, Cape Coast Castle and its dependencies formed the grand emporium whence the British West India Colonies were supplied with slaves. The Slave Trade Abolition Act of that year, while it expressly prohibited the exportation of slaves, in no respect interfered with the system of slavery existing *within* the settlements. Even in 1822 when the final abolition of the late African Company's charter took place and the settlements were, politically speaking, annexed to Sierra Leone, Sir Charles McCarthy . . . did not feel himself warranted in interfering with the rights of those individuals, whether European or native, who possessed domestic slaves. In fact, during the Ashantee war, the Home Government expressly sanctioned those rights by employing the domestic slaves of individuals as militia, and paying their masters for their services as such.

But although the local Government on the Gold Coast has never been vested with power to interfere with the previously-existing rights of individuals, I will boldly assert that no person has ever more zealously or more successfully opposed the slave trade than myself. I will assert, without fear of contradiction, that from the early part of 1830, when I entered upon my duties as Governor of Cape Coast Castle, until I left the coast last season, not a single slave was exported from any part of the immediate line of coast which is studded with the English castles and factories; an assertion which I will be bold to state could not have been made by any preceding governor.

But I have gone even further than the prevention of the exportation of slaves. I have invariably prevented, upon my own responsibility, the transmission of domestic slaves from the settlements to the interior, by native owners, for the purposes of sale. And I have even, as far as in me lay, prohibited the transfer of domestic slaves under any circumstances from one person to another. And in many instances where it has been proved before me and my brother magistrates that a slave has been treated with undue severity by his master, I have enfranchised him. In short, while as President of the Council I had no authority to interfere with the system of domestic slavery which I found in existence when I entered upon my duties, I uniformly did everything in my power to modify and mitigate it, and in point of fact, domestic slavery, when I left the coast, existed in little more than name. . . .

Mr. Burgoyne next proceeds to accuse me of having been instrumental in restoring fugitive slaves to their owners, in contravention of a circular of Earl Bathurst's dated the 31st December, 1825. Of this circular I am entirely ignorant, none such having ever been sent to Cape Coast Castle. . . . It is quite true that from time immemorial the uniform rule and practice has been on the Gold Coast and adjoining territories for independent chiefs and the European local governments mutually to surrender fugitive criminals and slaves, and Mr. Burgoyne well knows that had I dared on my own responsibility to depart from this practice and thus broken faith with Ashantee, instant and severe retaliation by the seizure and slavery of hundreds of innocent victims would have been the consequence. But I deny — utterly and indignantly deny — that I ever allowed a fugitive to be given up without first receiving ample security for his (or her) personal safety. And wherever I have entertained the most distant doubt on the subject, I have in every such case redeemed, at my own expense, and enfranchised such person. I know even that in pursuance of this system I have frequently screened criminals from well-merited punishment. . . .

Mr. Burgoyne, aware that the British Government and public are justly sensitive on the subject of the slave trade, artfully attempts to excite odium against the Government or resident merchants on the Gold Coast, by accusing them of encouraging that vile traffic, the former by permitting slave vessels to visit the forts, and the latter by trading with them. You are well aware, gentlemen, that in 1828, Cape Coast Castle was declared a free port by the Home Government and that the local Government possesses no power whatever to shut out from the port the ships of any nation. But it is utterly false to say that a single vessel actually engaged in the slave trade ever (at least since I have been Governor) visited any of our roadsteads on the Gold Coast.

It is possible enough that vessels eventually destined to be employed in that trade may have visited not only our settlements on the Gold Coast, but the Gambia, Sierra Leone, as well as the French, Dutch and Danish African colonies, but it is absurd to suppose that any vessel with slaves on board, or even fitted out for that purpose, would dare to visit a British port. You well know, gentlemen, that had I dared to interfere with a vessel merely because I might suspect that she was eventually intended to carry off a cargo of slaves, I should most probably have been instantly dismissed from my office. I have frequently known Her Majesty's cruisers to lie at anchor in Cape Coast roadstead, alongside of vessels which both the commander of the former and myself had every reason to think were about to be employed in the slave trade, but with which we had no power to interfere. . . .

[C.O.267/144]

117 G. MACLEAN TO THE COMMITTEE OF MERCHANTS

LONDON, 16 DECEMBER, 1837.
. . . I now proceed to the second point touched upon in Sir George Grey's communication,[1] the system, namely, of 'pawns', as to the propriety of which Lord Glenelg expresses considerable doubts.

[1] Sir George Grey (to the Committee, 5 December, 1837), asked for more details about the Kobina case, pawning and the restitution of negro deserters.

That the system in question is liable to abuse, as remarked by his Lordship, is doubtless true, but . . . it is a system which has existed throughout the Gold Coast and adjoining territories from time immemorial, and with which the local Government has never hitherto been authorised to interfere.

On the contrary, the authorities, both under the African Company and subsequently . . . under the Colonial Office, have invariably recognised and enforced, where necessary, the rights of the 'pawn' owners. Whether any and what new regulations applicable to this system shall be framed is a subject solely for the consideration of the Right Honourable the Secretary of State.

The above remarks are also applicable to the system of domestic slavery. . . . When in 1822–3 the settlements were annexed (politically) to Sierra Leone, almost every resident merchant possessed a greater or less number of domestic slaves. . . . Their right to hold this species of property was fully recognised by the Government of that day; they were considered, in fact, to be on the same footing as the proprietors of slaves in the West India colonies. . . . When in 1828 the local Government was placed upon its present footing, no alteration took place in the system of domestic slavery, nor, when the legislature subsequently abolished slavery in the West India and other colonies, were any instructions on the subject transmitted to the authorities on the Gold Coast. . . . Yet I can with truth allege that I uniformly exerted the whole power and authority which I possessed . . . towards the amelioration of the condition of the slaves, and to prevent any increase in their number. No person connected with the government was allowed to acquire slaves, and in cases where owners were proved to have been guilty of cruelty towards their slaves, I have deemed myself warranted in ordering their manumission. The whole subject is one of considerable difficulty, and well merits, I humbly think, the consideration of Her Majesty's Government. I feel fully warranted in saying that, during the last eight or ten years, great and perceptible advances in civilisation have been made among the native population on the Gold Coast — that is, since the actual abolition of the export slave trade — and I feel equally warranted in saying that it would greatly conduce to the further advancement of civilisation were the question under discussion finally set at rest.

[Another] point alluded to in Sir George Grey's communication, relates to the practice pursued by the British and other local governments of mutually giving up fugitive criminals and others. Although for this system or practice I am in no respect personally responsible, as it had existed for many years previous to my administration, yet I deem it one with which it would be unwise and even dangerous to interfere.

I will suppose that a party of Ashantees arrive at Cape Coast Castle and claim my protection, stating that they have been cruelly used by their master (or owner) and are anxious to escape from further persecution. I will suppose (a case, however, which seldom if ever occurs) that this is their sole reason for deserting their master, and that they have committed no crime whatever. Were I, on these fugitives being claimed by the king of Ashantee, to decline to give them up, the immediate result would be the seizure by him of perhaps double the number of some tribe living under the protection of the British flag, and in this he would conceive himself fully justified.

Practically speaking, however, I have seldom known any but criminals to seek the protection of the British flag, and even these I have very rarely delivered, having almost always made it a matter of personal favour with the king that he should allow them to be redeemed for a sum of money. In no case whatever have I ever delivered up a fugitive without receiving undoubted security for his personal safety. I almost always, indeed, stipulate for the personal appearance before me of the party, at stated periods. Moreover, no person is given up merely because he is the subject of a foreign chief. It must be shown he has been guilty of some crime, or that there exists against him some just claim.

But this system is absolutely necessary, considered in another point of view. Were it once promulgated throughout Ashantee and elsewhere that runaways would, under any circumstances, receive protection from the British authorities, our settlements would speedily be inundated by hundreds and thousands of the off-scourings of those countries. How then could these men be maintained, or how kept in order? The result would necessarily be not only the hostility of foreign tribes, but loud complaints on the part of our own people who must, in some way or another, be burdened with the support of the fugitives. . . .

[C.O.267/144; H.C.551 of 1842]

118 Minute by D. S[mith, for] Mr. Stephen

Colonial Office, April 1838.
[On 23rd April, 1838, the Committee asked that their annual grant be restored to its original level of £4,000.]

I am inclined to think that this application should be resisted.

Mr. Huskisson, who took the determination to withdraw the establishments of government from the Gold Coast, had, in the first instance, resolved to grant nothing for the maintenance of the forts, because he considered that if the trade were sufficiently valuable to induce the merchants to remain, they might very well afford the expense of defending themselves; and Lord Glenelg, who then presided over the Board of Trade, gave it as his opinion that the trade was not of sufficient importance in a national point of view to justify the expense of any special establishments for its protection. Mr. Huskisson, however, thought proper to yield to the solicitations of the merchants

and proposed to allow them £2,000 for the first year, £1,500 for the second and £1,000 for the third. I am not sure whether he did not intend to make a larger grant, but it was fixed by Sir George Murray at £4,000, with the understanding that the Government reserved to themselves the right of regulating it every year on a [re]view of the actual extent of the trade. I believe that the total value of the imports at that time was under £70,000.

Shortly after Lord Ripon came to this office, he reduced the grant to £3,500, much to the dissatisfaction of the Committee, and now they have, as far as they can, shown good grounds for asking to have it restored to its former amount. But I cannot help thinking that the Committee are professedly undertaking too much, with reference at least to the object for which the grant was made.   [C.O.267/150]

119 J[ames] S[tephen for] Mr. Smith

Colonial Office, 26 April, 1838.
If it be not presumption to say so, I should avow my opinion that it was a great error to attempt any compromise of this kind originally. What a government is, conducted by merchants for their own benefit, and what a government is, maintained by the state for the public good, we sufficiently know. But a colonial administration, conducted by merchants with contributions from the public treasury, was an experiment which it was, I think, obvious enough, could issue in nothing but a constant attempt to encroach more and more on the part of the grantees, who would soon lose sight of the distinction between commercial factories and government colonies, and whose officers would, as a matter of course, aspire to the rank and consideration of Governors.

I should entirely subscribe to your opinions and should think this letter should be answered by a refusal, in which the attention of the merchants should be recalled to the original basis of the arrangement, had I not lately seen a paper from the Foreign Office on the subject of the slave trade, which very strongly advocated the policy of enlarging and even multiplying our settlements on the western coast of Africa. I wish you would read that paper which is at present in Lord Glenelg's hands. I think you will agree with me that though it should not prevent the writing an answer to this letter, co-inciding substantially with your proposal, it would require the exercise of considerable caution as to the terms of that letter, so as to make it clear that there would be no inconsistency if hereafter the refusal should be modified or even retracted.   [C.O.267/150]

120 Minute by J. S[tephen]
      Colonial Office, 20 June, 1838.
. . . I think that if the statement as to the suppression of the slave trade is true,[1] it would be a short-sighted and most lamentable parsimony to refuse any little increase of the grant which is really required for the extension of that service. Any one of the ships which are now employed off Cuba, rather to witness than to arrest the slave trade, costs the nation incomparably more than the whole expense of the Gold Coast establishment.   [C.O.267/150]

121 James Stephen to the Committee of Merchants
      London, 22 October, 1839.
Sir,
   I have laid before Lord John Russell[2] your letter of the 11th instant, with the copy therein enclosed of a communication which the Gold Coast Committee have received from Captain Maclean[1] in explanation of the circumstances under which vessels destined for the slave trade are in the habit of trading with the forts on the Gold Coast.

His Lordship has directed me to observe on this subject, that the Slave Trade Abolition Act, 5 Geo. 4 cap. 113, s. 10, in the most comprehensive terms which it is possible to employ, prohibits, under the most severe penalties, every act done within Her Majesty's dominions in furtherance of the slave trade. For example, the use of any ship for accomplishing any object or contract relating to that trade is declared a felony, and the ship is subject to forfeiture. From the statement of Captain Maclean, it appears that vessels fitted up for the slave trade, and afterwards employed in carrying slaves, habitually come to Cape Coast Castle to purchase goods to enable them to carry on the slave trade to the leeward. As administrator of the government of that settlement, Captain Maclean has an undoubted right to seize all such vessels, and to send the masters and crews to Sierra Leone for trial. He observes that we are at war with neither Spain, Portugal nor Brazil, and inquires by what authority could he prevent vessels belonging to those countries from anchoring at any of our ports? The answer is, by the authority of the British statute to which, within the British dominions, all persons, aliens as well as denizen, friends not less than enemies, are bound to yield obedience.

Lord John Russell deeply regrets to learn that slave-trading vessels have been allowed to anchor at Cape Coast Castle and to purchase goods. It is of the utmost importance that the most decisive instructions should be immediately given for the discontinuance of this practice, and it will be the duty of Captain Maclean to enforce such instructions vigilantly and severely.

                    I am &c.   [H.C.551 of 1842]

---

[1] On 18 June the Committee renewed its application, making the claim that their (or Maclean's) administration had stamped out the slave trade along 260 miles of coast.

[2] Lord John Russell (later (1861) Earl), (1792–1878); 3rd son of the 6th Duke of Bedford; M.P. 1813; Secretary of State (for War and the Colonies), 30 August, 1839, to 3 September, 1841, and (for the Colonies) 23 February to 21 July, 1855; Foreign Secretary, 1852–3, 1859–65; Prime Minister, 1846–52, 1865–6.

[1] Maclean's letter, dated 17 June, 1839, is printed in H.C.551 of 1842.

122 COUNCIL MINUTE

CAPE COAST CASTLE, 12 NOVEMBER, 1839.

At a meeting of Council held this day, present:

George Maclean Esquire, President.
James Swanzy   ”   Members.
Thomas Hutton   ”

The President laid before the Council a despatch[1] which he had received from the Marquis of Normanby,[2] Colonial Secretary, stating that it appeared from a report of the proceedings taken before the Courts of Mixed Commission at Sierra Leone, that a vessel named the 'Dos Amigos', recently condemned as having been engaged in the slave trade, had been supplied by a merchant . . . of Cape Coast with a quantity of guns and gunpowder. Lord Normanby, in calling his (the President's) attention to this fact, reminds him that trafficking with persons engaged in the slave trade is contrary to the municipal laws of Great Britain, and directs that it be strictly prohibited in future.

The Council, having taken into consideration the above-mentioned despatch, came to the following resolutions:

1. That the British authorities on the Gold Coast, having never been until the present time, instructed or authorised to interfere with vessels which they might suspect of being destined to be engaged in the slave trade, have never felt themselves warranted in doing so, when such vessels, on visiting any of the various ports under their control, have strictly complied with the port regulations and confined themselves to legitimate traffic.

2. That the regulations of the British ports on the Gold Coast require all vessels anchoring therein to deliver in their certificates of registry, and to furnish a full and faithful account of their cargoes to the local authorities before being permitted to

open trade or to ship or land merchandise.

3. That in the case of the vessel Dos Amigos . . . the above regulations were strictly complied with before that vessel was permitted to have any commercial communication with the colony.

4. That although the authorities might have suspected or even known from intrinsic information that the Dos Amigos was destined for the leeward slave trade, yet after she had complied with the port regulations . . . the authorities [could not] prevent her from engaging in legitimate trade . . . and that the same observation applies to many other vessels which have traded at the British Gold Coast settlements under circumstances precisely similar to those under which the Dos Amigos did so.

5. That ever since the government of these settlements was placed upon its present footing, the authorities have shown themselves most anxious to suppress and discourage the slave trade by every means which they conceived they could legitimately use, which is proved by the fact that during the last ten years, the exportation of slaves has been effectually stopped along the whole line of coast subject to their control.

6. That in order to give effect to the instructions conveyed in the Secretary of State's despatch upon this subject, the President be requested to take such steps as will in future prevent vessels which he may have just reason to suspect of being about to embark in the slave trade, carrying on any description of traffic at any of the Gold Coast British settlements, and that he be further requested to prepare, print and circulate a proclamation warning all persons against holding any communication with interdicted vessels. . . .

[C.O.98/1A]

[1] Dated 29 August, 1839 (in C.O.267/155: H.C.551).

[2] Constantine Henry Phipps, Marquis of Normanby (1797–1863); Secretary of State for War and the Colonies, 20 February–30 August, 1839; ambassador in Paris, 1846–52.

123 MACLEAN TO RUSSELL

CAPE COAST CASTLE, 27 JANUARY, 1840.

[Acknowledges the Marquis of Normanby's instructions to prevent further supplying of suspected slavers, and Russell's instructions (of 3 October, 1839) to institute proceedings against the merchant who supplied the Dos Amigos, and states that the Council does not think he has power to do this.] . . .

It would be quite impossible for me to prove a guilty knowledge against Mr. Thompson, or even to adduce legal proof that the vessel to which the purchaser of the goods belonged was, in effect, intended or fitted out for the slave trade. . . .

But in point of fact, if Mr. Thompson has exposed himself to legal punishment by his conduct in the instance referred to, I know of no merchant in the whole colony, including, of course, the members of Council themselves, who has not in like manner and in many instances, rendered himself liable to similar criminal proceedings being taken against him. Nor is it pretended to be denied that in a general sense all these merchants knew or suspected that such vessels as the Dos Amigos were connected, directly or indirectly, with the slave trade. At least I have never seen a Spanish, Portuguese or Brazilian vessel on this coast, (and I have seen hundreds) that was not so engaged. But they (the merchants) have always considered themselves fully justified as merchants in selling their merchandise to any person who might come to their warehouse prepared to pay them money or other equivalent for their goods; nor have I ever imagined for a moment that I could legally interfere with such traffic. But wherever I thought I could legitimately interfere, I have always done so. I have uniformly interdicted canoes or canoe-men being supplied to suspected vessels, and these are essentially necessary to the prosecution of their illicit traffic throughout a great part of the leeward coast. . . .
[C.O.267:162/H.C.551]

124 MINUTE BY LORD JOHN RUSSELL
3 APRIL, 1840.
There can be no doubt that the merchants supply vessels trading in slaves with all that they require from our own settlements!

To prove the offence, i.e. that anyone knowingly and wilfully did so, must be very difficult. Nor do I see that the removal of Mr. Maclean would prevent a recurrence of the same evils.

If it is possible to take the whole concern into our own hands, and make ourselves responsible for the utmost vigilance in future, to prevent such infractions of acts of Parl[iament] . . . I should wish to know how, by what law or prerogative, we can make such a change? [C.O.267/162]

125 MINUTE BY STEPHEN
3 APRIL, 1840.
I believe nothing to be more easy than to make the change which would transfer the management of these settlements from the merchants to the Crown. The existing committee has no charter as a corporation, nor any other constitutional character. They would be most aptly described as a body of persons who have contracted for a certain annual sum of money to superintend the government of these settlements. On their advice the various public officers are appointed. The Parliamentary grant is paid over to them, and they engage to keep down the expense within the limits of the grant. Now if Mr. Maclean or any other person were appointed by the Queen to be Lieut. Gov., and the merchants were told that their services were to be dispensed with, the whole business would fall into the ordinary channel of a correspondence between the Lieut. Gov. and the Sec. of State. . . . This is an arrangement which the Government, as I conceive, may terminate at their pleasure. [C.O.267/162]

126 THE TREASURY TO THE COLONIAL OFFICE   10 JUNE, 1840.
Sir,
The Lords Commissioners of Her Majesty's Treasury, having had under

their consideration your letter dated 6th ultimo, transmitting copies of communications from the Secretary of the Admiralty, and Rear-Admiral the Hon. George Elliot, with a report from Captain Tucker on the state of the forts of Cape Coast Castle and Accra, I am commanded to acquaint you, for the information of Lord John Russell, that my Lords concur in the opinion that the system at present prevailing of supplying slave-trading vessels from these forts should be put a stop to by Her Majesty's Government.

With respect to the course proposed to be adopted,[1] their Lordships would suggest how far it would be practicable to stop the evil effectually without taking the government of the forts into the hands of the Crown and reverting to a system which, when it existed, was the subject of so much animadversion in the House of Commons.

At present an allowance of £3,500 per annum (to which £500 per annum has been added for the last and present years) is made to the merchants for the keeping up of these forts. My Lords apprehend that this grant would never be made if the country were aware that the protection of these forts is given to the slave trade. My Lords, therefore, consider that the parties should be informed that no grant will be recommended to Parliament in a future year if the system continues, and that some agent or officer should be appointed to reside at Cape Coast Castle, or in some other proper situation, to report to Her Majesty's Government the proceedings of the merchants and others in reference to this subject.[1]

I am &c.

C. E. Trevelyan.

[H.C.551]

---

[1] 'That these forts shall be resumed by the crown, and that an officer shall be appointed by Her Majesty to conduct the government of the forts.'

[1] Russell decided (C.O. to Treasury, 17 June, 1840) that the above proposal was unacceptable, but proposed to send out a commissioner of enquiry to report.

10   The Madden Mission and the Select Committee of 1842

THE Commissioner selected by Lord John Russell was Dr. R. R. Madden,[1] one of the most exalted of the anti-slavery zealots, who, in the temper of 1840, was hardly likely to do justice to Maclean's achievements. Moreover, before he landed at Cape Coast, it had been further reported that British subjects — a very nebulous term on the Gold Coast — were possessed of slaves in British territory — another uncertain quantity. This had resulted in further correspondence and differences between the merchants and the British Government (127–31). If the British Government was less than fair to Maclean, it was largely because, in these exchanges, they appeared to accept Maclean's own valuation of the Gold Coast settlements; that they really were a colony and not merely trading factories.

Madden's report (132), though marred by evident bias, drew attention for the first time to Maclean's exercise of judicial powers among the coast tribes, and assembled a good deal of information on the economic progress of the settlements under merchant rule, mostly supplied by Maclean himself. But the Colonial Office, now directed by Lord Stanley, was so little impressed by Madden's qualities as a reporter, that it declined to act on his recommendations (133) before a Select Committee of the House of Commons had gone into the whole question of West African affairs.

In the meantime the Niger expedition had failed disastrously. In the reaction against what *The Times* called 'brainless Buxtonian benevolence', a juster appraisal was possible of Maclean's work on the Gold Coast. The Select Committee, unlike that of 1865, did not enter on its enquiries with any preconceived solutions of its own, and as a result provided much useful evidence on a number of aspects of Gold Coast affairs (134). And though it agreed with Madden that Government should resume responsibility for the settlements there, it also recommended that Maclean's jurisdiction over the surrounding tribes should be continued and put on a regular and permanent footing (135).

[1] Richard Robert Madden (1798–1886); doctor, traveller and writer; became very unpopular on account of his abolitionist zeal while serving as a Special Magistrate in Jamaica (1833–4) and as judge in the Mixed Commission Court at Havana (1836–40); friend and biographer of Lady Blessington, who is said to have been responsible for his appointment as West African Commissioner of Inquiry; in later life took up the cause of the Irish peasantry.

127 PROCLAMATION

SIERRA LEONE, 4 MARCH, 1841.

By his Excellency Sir John Jeremie[1] Knt., Captain-General and Governor-in-Chief of the Colony of Sierra Leone and its dependencies between the 20th degree of north and the 20th degree of south latitude, Vice-Admiral, Chancellor and Ordinary of the same &c &c.

Whereas undoubted information has been conveyed to us that the practice of holding persons in slavery prevails in certain parts of the British territories in Africa, within the limits of this government . . . as aforesaid:[1]

Now therefore be it known that by the

[1] Sir John Jeremie (1795–1841); born in Guernsey; both as Chief Justice of St. Lucia and Public Prosecutor in Mauritius (1824–33) made himself very unpopular on account of his abolitionist views; judge in Ceylon, 1836; Governor of Sierra Leone, October 1840; died 23 April, 1841.

[1] By Commander Wm. Tucker. Cf. Tucker to Jeremie, 3 March, 41, C.O.267/163.

several acts of Parliament, viz., 5 Geo. 4, cap. 113, and 3 & 4 Will. 4, cap. 73, commonly called the Slave Trade Abolition Act and the Slave Emancipation Act, it is unlawful for any person to hold slaves in any country whatever,[1] except India, Saint Helena and Ceylon; and that in all such cases the holders are liable to severe punishment and the persons thus unlawfully held in slavery to seizure and confiscation:

And whereas undoubted information has been further conveyed to us, that it is not unusual for traders to take persons in pawn within the said limits: Be it therefore also known that such holding in pawn is a holding in slavery within the meaning of those Acts.

And we do hereby strictly enjoin and require all officers civil and military, all officers of customs, and others Her Majesty's loyal subjects, to aid and assist in the execution of the law.

Given at Government House, Freetown, in the said Colony, this 4th day of March, in the year of our Lord 1841, and of Her Majesty's reign the fourth. . . .

[H.C.551 (1842)]

128 PETITION OF THE PRINCIPAL MULATTO FEMALES OF THE GOLD COAST TO THE RIGHT HONOURABLE LORD JOHN RUSSELL
CAPE COAST CASTLE, 29 MARCH, 1841.

The humble Petition of the undersigned natives of the Gold Coast residing under the protection of the British settlements, showeth,

That your petitioners, natives of Africa, are the proprietors of a number of slaves, agreeably to the laws and customs of this country, established from time immemorial, and which they learn are in many respects similar to those in the East Indies where slavery to a certain extent is still recognised by the British Government, and the same having been invariably acknowledged, countenanced and protected by all the European governments

---

[1] Properly, in any British territory.

established upon the Gold Coast, British, Dutch and Danes.

Your petitioners have been surprised to find, by a proclamation issued by His Excellency Sir John Jeremie . . . dated the 4th March, 1841 and made known and promulgated here by the government of this settlement and by Her Majesty's Commissioner, Dr. Madden, on the 19th March,[1] 1841, that they were without the least warning to be deprived of their rights and property, and in one moment to lose the services of the whole of their slaves: but having been given to understand that the British Government, desirous of granting to all slaves their freedom, wherever they have influence, power or authority, have, in equity and justice to the proprietors, in all cases hitherto, awarded compensation for the slaves so liberated:

Your petitioners therefore humbly pray that in submitting to the will and wishes of the British Government, their cases may meet with like consideration, and that compensation be awarded them as in every other instance.

And your petitioners will ever pray.

[Marks of] Fanny Smith, Mary Jackson, Elizabeth Swanzy, Mary Hutton, Sarah Crosby, Catherine Bannerman, Helen Colliver. Certified by J. Jackson, J.P.

[H.C.551 (1842)]

129 G. MACLEAN TO LORD JOHN RUSSELL
CAPE COAST CASTLE, 13 APRIL, 1841.

My Lord,

I had the honour of receiving on the 21st February last, your Lordship's letter of the 7th of December, 1840, transmitted by Her Majesty's Commissioner of Enquiry, Doctor Madden. He arrived here on the 19th February, during my absence at British Accra, to which station I had been hastily summoned in consequence of the death of the late commandant.

On being made acquainted with Doctor Madden's arrival, however, I lost no time in repairing to Cape Coast Castle for the

---

[1] Actually on 23 March.

purpose of affording him every assistance in my power towards the prosecution of the objects of his mission. Unfortunately he had been only a few days engaged in prosecuting his enquiries when he was attacked by the ordinary remittent fever of the country, which compelled him entirely to suspend his labours until within the three or four days preceding his departure on the 26th ultimo.

The points to which his attention was chiefly directed while here were, first, the system of domestic slavery which has always existed in these settlements; 2ndly the system of persons holding what are termed 'pawns', that is to say, free persons who voluntarily bind themselves to serve for low wages in consideration of receiving in the first instance, a certain sum of money, the service to continue until the sum of money be repaid; and 3rdly, the administration of justice by the local authorities.

The two former of these points more particularly engaged Doctor Madden's attention in consequence of the arrival, four days previous to his departure, of a Proclamation issued by His Excellency the Governor in Chief, specially bearing on the points in question. . . . As its promulgation has caused considerable excitement among those of the native population who have always considered themselves, and have been considered, British subjects, and as I have been requested to forward a petition on the subject from a few of the principal mulattos here, I feel it necessary to trouble your Lordship with a few remarks upon each of the points above enumerated.

In my correspondence with the African Committee, during the last eight years, I have repeatedly alluded to the existence of domestic slavery in these settlements, not only among the more purely native population of the inland districts, but among those living under the guns of the forts, and intimately connected with the Europeans, among natives of this country educated in Europe, and even, in some instances,

among the European residents. I would refer more particularly to a letter under date of the 14th October, 1837. . . . The reply to this letter, while it acquitted me of all blame with respect to that and other matters, contained no specific instructions for enforcing the Slave Emancipation Act on this coast. In point of fact, until the arrival of Sir John Jeremie's Proclamation three weeks ago, I possessed no official notice of the Act 3 & 4 Will. 4, chap. 73, therein referred to, nor am I at this moment acquainted with its specific provisions, or how it is to be enforced. . . . Being anxious to carry [the] Proclamation into effect, but feeling the necessity, situated as this Government is, of acting with prudence and caution in the matter, and having no means of communicating with the Governor-in-Chief on the subject, I am induced earnestly to request from your Lordship, to instruct me *how far* the 'Slave Emancipation Act' is applicable to these settlements, and in what manner I ought to proceed in enforcing it?

With regard to the European residents, no difficulty has occurred or will occur. Immediately after the promulgation of the Proclamation, those resident in Cape Coast met and at once agreed to comply with its terms so far as they personally were concerned: but they deprecated in the strongest manner, interference with the rights of the natives. . . .

The next class of persons whose interests would be materially affected by the Proclamation, but to whom Dr. Madden thought it was certainly applicable, are the principal mulattos and others, several of whom are on a footing, in every point of view, with the European merchants. These, in general, are ready to emancipate their slaves, but demand compensation. From a few of them in this neighbourhood I have received the accompanying petition, which I have now the honour to transmit to your Lordship. Many of this class, though natives of the country, are superior in education and habits to those around them, and as most of them have little to depend on save the expenses of their domestic and predial slaves, their claim for compensation is reasonable.

The next class are the less educated native chiefs and others, living more immediately under the guns of the several forts, and these have distinctly refused to emancipate their slaves unless compelled by force, or largely compensated for them. Some of them, indeed, when remonstrated with, threatened to withdraw into the country with their people, and to raise the whole population of the interior against the forts, or at least to stop all communication betwixt them and the interior.

The last class are the bulk of the native population of the inland districts who have practically been subject to the British forts since peace was concluded with Ashantee. These, however, are not, strictly speaking, British subjects, the Government having in 1828 disclaimed the territorial rights formerly possessed by the forts. The great majority of this population would resist any attempt to emancipate their slaves, nor has this Government any means of enforcing the Emancipation Act as against them.

'Pawns' also are stated in the Proclamation to be slaves within the meaning of the Act, but I think it would be impolitic to enforce it too strictly as regards them, as the doing so would be, and indeed has already been, productive of great misery to the people themselves. Those people who have been directed to dismiss their pawns have, of course, demanded the money lent them, and have thus caused great trouble and inconvenience to the pawns and their families. In general, pawns may be described as servants voluntarily serving for an indefinite length of time, but who can at any moment leave their masters, either by paying their debts from their own resources, or by procuring other masters . . . I have invariably, in cases of persons dying intestate, or becoming insolvent, emancipated their slaves on condition of their becoming pawns — so favourable do I consider that condition to

be. That is to say, instead of allowing slaves to be sold, I have classed them as debtors to the estates, in very moderate amounts, according to their respective abilities to earn their money — which money they have readily found parties to advance to them on condition of their serving them at low wages until they should become able to repay the money advanced. Still, the system is liable to abuse, and I should recommend, in the first place, that the term 'pawn' should be abolished; secondly, that no contract of this kind should be held good unless entered into before a magistrate; and, lastly, that the term of the contract should be definite.

The last point by which Dr. Madden's attention seemed particularly arrested, was the circumstance of [the] local Government exercising jurisdiction over a large extent of territory and a numerous population to whose allegiance [the] British Government lays no claim. Upon this point my opinions are strong and decided, and have been expressed at length in my letter dated the 30th November, 1836, and transmitted through the African Company to the Colonial Office. . . .

[H.C.551 (1842)]

130 MINUTE BY JAMES STEPHEN
COLONIAL OFFICE, JUNE, 1841.

The Gold Coast Committee . . . distinctly admit[1] that in defiance of the act for the abolition of slavery, there exists to this moment a large body of persons held in slavery in the African forts. They further admit that they have all along been aware of this, and that so long ago as 1837 a formal report on the subject was made to them by Captain Maclean. *Yet it is now for the first time that that Report has reached this Office.*[2] They admit that their own officers have continued to be

[1] Cf. Committee to R. Vernon Smith (7 June, 1841) in H.C.551.
[2] This, of course, was an error. See (116) above, which Stephen evidently had not seen.

proprietors of slaves. They admit that the practice prevails of sending back fugitives into slavery. . . . I cannot but repeat an opinion I have already expressed to you that this Gold Coast Committee are utterly unworthy of confidence, and that the management by commercial men of such a trust, simply because they have contracted to do it cheaply, was a great error originally, and cannot be too soon or too effectually abandoned.

Dr. Madden has, indeed, to report on these affairs, but it would seem almost superfluous to await any man's report in order to reach the conclusion that a systematic and concealed, if not a corrupt opposition to the unequivocal law of the land, disqualifies those who have practised it, for the further discharge of their delegated powers. Difficulties, of course, there are and will be, in obeying the law, and these gentlemen and their agent, Capt. Maclean, make the most of them. But if such apprehensions are to neutralise the act of Parliament on the Gold Coast, they might have been attended with exactly the same effect in every other British Settlement where slavery existed. . . .

[C.O.267/168]

131 LORD JOHN RUSSELL TO G. MACLEAN
LONDON, 14 JULY, 1841.

Sir,

I have the honour to acknowledge the receipt of your despatch of the 13th of April last, relating to the Proclamation which was issued . . . by the late Governor of Sierra Leone, Sir John Jeremie. . . . The Proclamation . . . is nothing more than the affirmation of a principle of law regarding which it is impossible that any doubt should arise. Perhaps, indeed, the mere words of the Proclamation may not have been accurately chosen. It declares it to be unlawful for any person to hold slaves in a British territory. To that extent it is indisputably correct. The additional declarations that it is unlawful for a British subject to hold slaves in any country whatever, except India, St. Helena and Ceylon, is a wider assertion than, I apprehend, can strictly be made. For the laws of Great Britain are, of course, binding only within the British Dominions, except in a few particular cases . . . [such as] treason. . . . But I do not understand that a British subject would incur any penalty by holding men in slavery within the limits of any country by the law of which slavery is permitted.

This distinction is of great practical importance in reference to the British forts on the Gold Coast. Her Majesty's dominion on that coast is, as I understand, of very narrow local range. If I am correctly informed, it extends only to the forts themselves. . . . It follows that within the fort of Cape Coast Castle, a different rule of law regarding slavery may prevail from that which exists beyond those limits; within them the statute 3 and 4 William 4, cap. 73 is unquestionably in force; beyond it is not. . . . Whether it was or was not an oversight that the Slavery Abolition Act was not published at Cape Coast Castle, it admits of no dispute or doubt that it is and has been the law for several years past, so far as the place itself is within the dominion of the British Crown. Sir John Jeremie had no choice but to insist on the exact obedience to that law. No power in the state, except the Legislature itself, can dispense with the observance of it. Whether the residents within Her Majesty's dominions on the Gold Coast are European, mulattos or natives, the rule of law that no man can be holden in slavery there is peremptory and inflexible and must be strictly enforced.

With regard to persons living in vicinity but not within the British dominions, the same rule does not apply. If the laws and usages of those countries tolerate slavery, we have no right to set aside those laws or usages, except by persuasion, negotiation and other peaceful means.

With regard to the case of persons called 'pawns', your statement appears to confirm Sir John Jeremie's declaration that such holding in pawn is a holding in slavery within the meaning of the Acts of Parliament. . . . It appears to me that the distinction between a pawn and a slave is little more than nominal, and that Sir John Jeremie rightly pronounced both systems an infringement of the Act of Parliament. . . .

In answer to your first question, Against whom is the Slavery Abolition Act to be enforced, I therefore answer: it is to be enforced against any person holding another in slavery, or in pawn, within the dominions of the British Crown.

To your second question, What steps ought you to take in enforcing it, my answer is, that you should announce immediately, and in the most public manner, that the Act for the Abolition of Slavery extends to and is in force within the British forts on the Gold Coast, and all territories there, so far as the limits of the Queen's dominions extend. . . .

With regard to the claim for compensation, made by the seven persons who have signed the petition of the 29th of March last, you will inform the petitioners that it cannot be admitted; first, because in no case has it been given except by the enfranchisement of slaves duly registered; and second, because Her Majesty's Government do not admit that it was ever lawful to hold any person in slavery in Her Majesty's dominions on the western coast of Africa, although the existence of slavery there, at a former period, may, as a mere matter of fact, not be capable of contradiction.   [H.C.551 (1842)]

132 DR. R. R. MADDEN'S REPORT ON THE GOLD COAST

. . . At present, no judicial establishment exists on the Gold Coast: but all classes of crimes and offences are taken cognisance of by the magistrates; summarily disposed of by committal to gaol (and for periods of unlimited extent), or punished by fines, and, in some cases, I am informed by Captain Tucker of Her Majesty's Ship 'Wolverine',

to his own knowledge, by death. This awful responsibility of the Governor and his Council should be removed, and in every case of crime for which a capital punishment is called, elsewhere. The exercise of the functions of judge and jury should never devolve on a colonial governor, or the merchants who may happen to compose his council.

The extent of the exercise of judicial powers, conferred not by law but by passing exigencies, goes to a very extraordinary extent here. I was informed by the President of the Council of Government that he had to take cognizance of cases where application for divorce had been made to him, and once, in the instance of a female, now mistress of the school at Cape Coast, married to a European, . . . he had pronounced a formal sentence of divorce, and had the sentence duly recorded in the archives of his office.

The difficulties and evils that arise from the present anomalous system of government, and the total absence of a judicial establishment, can only be judged of by actual observation, or by reference to the . . . list of prisoners confined in Cape Coast Castle, made out in the month of April last, when I called for an examination into every individual case before the Council and magistrates. On that examination there proved to be no less than 91 persons in confinement; some who had been immured for upwards of four years, others for terms of one, two and three years; and in no instance but one, a definite term of imprisonment was recorded in the book in which the prisoner's name, date of committal, or the crime or amount of debt for which the person had been confined, was stated. A great number of these cases were those of natives from adjoining districts, for crimes committed, or debts contracted in places in which we had no territorial rights, and, consequently, over the natives of which we had no jurisdiction.

In reply to my applications for the release of a number of these prisoners, the presiding magistrate and member of Council argued that the influence of the Government was extended more widely and beneficially for the natives by the means that were adopted for the repression of crime and the prevention of injustice on the part of the pynims or native judges, who are notoriously corrupt and litigious; that it conciliated the native chiefs to take cognizance of those cases which they sent to the authorities at Cape Coast for adjudication or punishment; and that in many cases it was an act of mercy to the culprits to take them out of the hands of their own chiefs, whose anger they might have incurred.

I admitted that such might be the case, but that authorities of Cape Coast were not justified in becoming the ministers of the vengeance of the barbarous chiefs in their vicinity, or the dispensers of their laws, however mildly they might administer them; that lengthened periods of imprisonment, limited to no legal term, and the confinement at all of persons over whom we had no legal authority, was an infraction of the second stipulation in the compact entered into with the Government, namely: 'That British law should continue in force in these forts', and likewise of the fourth: that 'The magistrates shall not exercise authority or jurisdiction over the districts and natives under the immediate influence or protection of the forts'. The magistrates, however, were of opinion that British law was not applicable to the state of a settlement like that of Cape Coast; and that it would be impossible to carry that law into execution, and to exercise, at the same time, the great influence which they had over a district extending some 30 miles inland, and which they had no military force sufficient to secure or to control. If British law was not applicable to the people who lived under our protection on the Gold Coast, I begged to be informed under what code, Russian or Turkish, justice was administered here, and by what authority, the law, which was exclusively directed by the compact already cited to

be in force in these settlements, had been set aside?

The presiding magistrate informed me that they had a written authority for dispensing with it: but this authority was not produced, and it only remained for me to demand the liberation of those prisoners whose cases I considered those of greatest hardship and injustice. . . .   [This was refused.]

The controversies of the natives of the adjoining districts are frequently referred, by the consent of both parties, to the President of the Council, for decision. There can be no question but the natives find their advantage in bringing these palavers before Captain Maclean, the justice of whose decisions is acknowledged by all parties, rather than in placing themselves in the hands of their chiefs or kings, whose rapacity and venality is but too familiar to all their subjects.

But, independently of the great loss of time occasioned by the settlement of these disputes, and the neglect, of necessity, of other official duties of higher importance, the imposition of heavy fines on the persons against whom an unfavourable decision is given, seems to me very objectionable. Having called for a statement of the amount of fines levied on the natives, and the disposal of them, I found they amounted, from June 1839 to December 1840, to £187. 5s. sterling, and were expended for the purchase of public stores and the defrayment of the expenses of the militia service. . . .

The authorities at Cape Coast exercise their influence over the whole of the country from Dixcove to Accra, an extent of 120 miles; and the President of the Council, in reply to a question of mine on this subject, states: 'That the territory belonging to it' (speaking of the local Government) 'is understood to comprehend the entire colony from Dixcove to Accra.' This way of understanding the matter, I think, has led to an exercise of authority over the native, whose soil we seem to consider ours, yet where we positively have no territorial rights.

It is very true the exercise of that authority has tended to repress the slave trade in those parts, and for the last ten years the slave trade may be said to have ceased on the whole line of coast from Apollonia to Accra: but this has been accomplished, I think, at the expense of our character for strict justice with the natives. They consider us as seeking after our own advantages, and endeavouring to become masters of the country, on the pretence of putting down this trade. They are repressed by the fear of punishment, from carrying it on: but our right to punish them they do not acknowledge. . . . I never spoke to one of their chiefs, who did not speak of the cessation of the slave trade with regret. The old King Aggery, at Cape Coast, openly boasted to me of the active part he had taken in it; and, in defending the custom of making and holding slaves, he said: 'We would wish to have nothing to do here with English laws. We like to have the English here, but not to make laws for us. The country is ours, and we are the allies of England: but we do not want to be made its subjects. The fort belongs to you, but the country belongs to us.'

The fact is, the rights of the people are kept in abeyance between the claims of their own chiefs and the pretensions of our local Government; and the influence of fear, and to a certain extent, that of the character of the present Governor, for the impartiality of his decisions in their 'palavers', is the only hold we have on the natives. With the exception of the impediments thrown in the way of the native chiefs sacrificing human beings, for which object great praise is certainly due to Captain Maclean, civilization has certainly not advanced one step beyond the precincts of the castle, nor has the cessation of the slave trade been attended with those beneficial results which ought to have been expected from it. There are no appearances of increased cultivation. The whole country about Cape Coast is one great wilderness of verdure, where nothing is found to grow, that needs cultivation, except, here and there, at long and distant intervals, a patch of ground on which the bush has been burnt [and] a small quantity of yams or maize has been planted. . . . It is only about 15 or 20 miles from the sea-side, where cultivation is carried on to any extent. . . .

Mr. Swanzy, one of the principal merchants at Cape Coast, has made an attempt to introduce the growth of coffee and cotton, and has expended a great deal of time and money on the experiment. . . . The plantation called Napoleon is situated . . . about four miles from Cape Coast. Formerly a garden was made here by Governor Torrane. . . . At his death, however, it appears to have been neglected, and when Mr. Swanzy undertook to establish his plantation, the place was like the surrounding jungle. It is unfortunately the lot of all agricultural improvements in these countries, to die with the individual who commenced and carried them on. . . . [Swanzy] employs about 100 negroes in the field. . . . I found, on inquiry, that the majority of these labourers were slaves, hired from their owners, and the wages paid for them was at the rate of 5s. a month, sterling, paid in 'romauls' of cotton cloth, or 1s 3d a week, and about one third of that sum for children, a great many of whom I saw employed there, apparently well contented and well fed. . . . The negroes here, it is said, can support themselves on $2\frac{1}{2}$d a day tolerably well; and from $1\frac{1}{2}$d to $2\frac{1}{2}$d or 3d a day, I was informed, was the ordinary rate of wages all along this coast, paid to the natives when employed by Europeans.

The first cotton crop grown here by Mr. Swanzy proved very abundant, but exception was taken, in the English market, to the shortness of the staple. It fetched a low price and proved an unprofitable speculation. The cotton trees are now growing wild, and the cultivation of them entirely given up.

The coffee here has been planted from slips brought from Prince's Island, about two years ago. It looked extremely well, and promised to yield an ample crop in a few months more. So long, however, as African coffee pays a duty of 1s 3d per pound, while West India is introduced at 6d, there can be no hope of this cultivation . . . being prosecuted at all in Africa. . . . It is a folly to expect to see cultivation increased to any extent in Africa whilst we shut out those products for which her soil is best fitted. . . .

The trade of Cape Coast has considerably increased of late years. The cessation of warfare between the Ashantee and Fantee nations has caused the paths to be opened, from the interior to the coast; and the merchants of Ashantee now come down from Coomassie . . . to Cape Coast or Anamaboe, without let or hindrance. This journey, which formerly was considered one of great peril and difficulty, is now easily performed in 60 hours' travelling. . . .

All our settlements on the Gold Coast are badly situated, both for trade and health. There is no harbour on any part of the Gold Coast, except at Dixcove, where vessels of 20 or 30 tons burthen may enter. Cape Coast, like Anamaboe and Accra, is an open roadstead. The landing at these places is difficult and dangerous, especially at Accra. The surf on the beach is at all times considerable, but at particular seasons it is so heavy that for periods of two or three weeks, all communication is cut off between the ships and the shore.

In the year 1840, 38 British vessels arrived at Cape Coast, and nine vessels of war. During the last nine or ten years, the trade has gone on steadily increasing. In the year 1831, the imports into Cape Coast were £130,851. 3s 11½d., and in 1840 they amounted to £423,170. The same steady increase is to be noted in the exports. These from Cape Coast Castle in 1831 amounted to £90,282 9s 6d, and in 1840 they had increased to £325,008. . . . In 1816, the exports from the coast of Africa into England amounted only to £127,320 10s 3d., and the imports from England into Africa of British and foreign produce,

£158,559 10s 3d. In 1836, the latter had increased to £620,000, and of this amount, those to Cape Coast and Accra amounted to £75,000, while the exports from Africa into England for that year were, in round numbers, £800,000, and of these, £160,000 were from the Gold Coast. . . . The description of goods imported into the British settlements on the Gold Coast are the following: Manchester goods, guns, powder, lead, and iron bars, flints, rum, pipes, tobacco, beads, cowries, brass wire, earthenware, soap, tallow, glass ware, wine, provisions and perfumery. The commodities we received from our settlements on this coast are gold dust, ivory, dye-woods, palm-oil, and ground nuts. . . . It is impossible to get any certain information of the quantity of gold dust exported from the Gold Coast, as it is not entered at the custom-house when sent home by vessels of war. . . . The greatest part of what comes to England is from Cape Coast and Accra. For five years previously to June 1834, the exports of gold from Cape Coast averaged 18,226 ounces a year, and now, probably, from all our settlements on the western coast of Africa, not above 25,000 ounces are exported, or to the value of about £85,000 a year.

To give some idea of the relative commercial advantages of our different settlements at Cape Coast, Sierra Leone and the Gambia, I have drawn up the following table of the total exports and imports for the year 1839:—

	Exports from	Imports into
Cape Coast	£194,576	£354,460
Sierra Leone	58,440	103,086
Gambia	162,789	153,903
	415,805	611,449

In the above table, the total exports and imports are given, but of this a large portion is to and from foreign countries. . . . The exports from the Gambia to Great Britain amounted only, that year, to £70,809, and the imports from Great

Britain, to £67,474, so that more than one-half of the trade of the Gambia is with foreign states. I was not able to obtain any return of the amount of trade with foreign states at Cape Coast, but I should think two-thirds of the imports and exports are to and from Great Britain. . . .

The decrease in the value of cotton goods in the markets on the Gold Coast has considerably affected the profits of the merchants there. They are still, however, probably greater than they are in any other part of the world. I do not believe the people of any other country pay so dearly for our manufactures as the people of Africa. . . . Mr. Maclean . . . attributes the diminution of the merchants' profits here to the increased number of competitors since 1817. The number of resident merchants has doubled since that period.

The invoice value of 100 dollars is estimated by Captain Maclean to be about £13 or £14 sterling, exclusive of charges. This estimate can only apply to certain Manchester goods, in which trade there is a great competition, but, to my own knowledge, the common muskets which are purchased for the trade in England at 10s. a piece are sold to the natives along the coast for five or six dollars; and where I have seen iron bars, spirits and gunpowder, bartered for rice and other provisions, the calculation I made on the spot was that the profit charge on these articles could not fall much short of 150 per cent.

The British merchants on the Gold Coast complain very much, and it seems to me, with a great deal of reason, of the injury done to British commerce by foreign vessels and by transient traders who visit these places, and who are enabled to undersell the resident merchants who have expensive establishments to support and who have an interest in upholding the government of the place where they carry on their trade. In the month of October 1840, the merchants of Cape Coast addressed a memorial to the Governor, to be forwarded to the London Committee, on this subject. . . . They state that a duty of

half per cent upon the invoice amount of such goods as may be landed, without any distinction of flag, is the only impost upon the commerce of that place; that foreigners have consequently imported large quantities of merchandise at a lower rate than the merchants can do from England, so that in point of fact they are to some extent excluded from their own markets. Of the foreign vessels, American, Hamburg and French are those which chiefly frequent our settlements. . . . The remedy which the merchants suggest, and which I think ought to be applied to this evil, is the revival of the foreign and transient duties which were once in force here, on a reduced scale; say five per cent, in addition to the half per cent now levied, on the invoice price of all goods landed from foreign vessels; and a transient duty of $2\frac{1}{2}$ per cent in addition to the half per cent now levied, on the invoice amount of all goods landed by persons who are not residents of the colony, or who are not possessed of lands and houses within it. . . .

SLAVERY ON THE GOLD COAST prevails to a greater extent among the natives than on any other part of the coast which I have visited. Like all slaves, however, which are chiefly for domestic service and not for predial labour, the treatment is mild and the slaves comparatively happy. . . . I was not aware, however, that slavery existed in any part of the British Empire or of its settlements, except in India, Ceylon and St. Helena, which were specially exempted from the operation of the general Act of Emancipation of 1834, till I visited the Gold Coast. There I found English subjects holding slaves and pawns, buying, selling and disposing of them as property at their deaths, and the official sanction of the authorities even given to this system.

This was the first matter to which I called the attention of the President of the Council. . . . I called on Captain Maclean to take steps to put it down. . . . [He] did not think it necessary or advisable to do so. . . . I found it impossible to move

Captain Maclean from the opinion he entertained that the Government was aware of the existence of slavery there, and was not disposed to meddle with it. Having had more recent opportunities of knowing the opinions now entertained on this subject in England than Captain Maclean, I endeavoured, though fruitlessly, to change his opinion, and to convince him that whatever apathy in former times might have been felt with respect to the existence of slavery in British settlements, the deepest interest was now taken in the question of emancipation; and wherever it was connived at and suffered to exist, the moment its existence was known, the authorities would surely be instructed to prosecute the parties who were engaged in it.

In the course of three or four weeks subsequent to this application to Captain Maclean . . . Sir John Jeremie transmitted to me . . . copies of his proclamation prohibiting slavery, under severe penalties, on the part of British subjects in any of our settlements on the coast. These proclamations I lost no time in having posted by my servant in all public places of the town. . . . I explained the necessity of obeying the law to such of the people as were British subjects, and some of these persons of colour immediately consented to give up their slaves. But the effect produced on the white inhabitants was such as could hardly have been expected to be occasioned by . . . any matter which was not one of life and death. . . . I was informed if it was attempted to be carried into execution, the natives would rise in rebellion; there would be an end of all subordination; that Ashantees would come down with fire and sword to reclaim their fugitive slaves; the Dutch of Elmina would make war on us for theirs; . . . slavery had never been abolished in our settlements on the Gold Coast because there was no mention of our African settlements in the Emancipation Act . . . and because they had never received any compensation for their slaves.

I replied . . . that I believed they might dismiss all their fears with respect to the natives at once; that the proclamation was never intended to apply to them; that where we had no territorial rights, it never could be imagined our laws were to be enforced; . . . that the proclamation applied solely to British subjects living in British settlements, and not beyond the soil belonging to them. . . .   [H.C.551]

133 Dr. Madden's summary of his recommendations

1. That the maintenance and administration of the affairs of these settlements should be taken out of the hands of the Committee of Merchants and re-assumed by the Home Government.

2. That no Governor or other Public Servant in these settlements should be permitted to carry on trade.

3. That steps should be taken and instructions issued to our authorities on the Gold Coast to prosecute, under the Emancipation Act, any person buying, selling, or holding slaves, either in his own name or that of any native woman with whom he is connected, and that it be distinctly explained to our authorities that every man held for any period to compulsory labour, whether under the name of 'pawn' or 'debt' is to be considered a slave.

[4–7. Measures to be taken against London firms for aiding the slave trade.]

8. That whenever a new form of government is adopted, a Chief Justice should be appointed to reside at Cape Coast, to visit at stated periods all the other settlements on the Gold Coast.

9. That the President of the Council of Government be immediately instructed to release all persons confined in the jail of Cape Coast, who are not amenable to our laws and do not reside within our jurisdiction; and to abstain in future from exercising legal or military control over such persons; and that the question be set at rest as to the extent of our jurisdiction beyond the soil on which our

forts are situated, and whether the native towns within reach of their guns are to be considered subject to us.

10. That the number of black soldiers in all these settlements be increased by 100 men; the employment of militia to be discontinued; and the pay of the soldiers fixed at 12/6 a month and paid in money and not in goods; and that no payment in goods to those persons employed under Government be permitted.

11. That small forts or block-houses be established at Whydah, Winnebah, Apollonia, and one also erected at the Bonny, to complete a chain of posts from the Bights of Benin and Biafra to Apollonia (whose influence would extend to Cape Palmas).

12. That a Normal School be established in England or the West Indies for the training up of fit coloured persons for the office of native teachers in our settlements on the western coast of Africa.

13. That a small colonial schooner should be stationed at Cape Coast for affording the authorities the means of communication between our settlements on the Gold Coast and of detaining or sending to Sierra Leone slave trade vessels or those engaged in aiding and abetting them.

14. That notwithstanding the objections raised to the general principle of duties on imports being levied at our settlements in Africa, that the great advantage now derived from the casual foreign traders over our own merchants established in our settlements would render it necessary to impose a duty of 5 per cent on all goods imported in foreign vessels. . . .

[C.O.267/170]

134 PROCEEDINGS OF THE SELECT COMMITTEE ON WEST AFRICAN FORTS 1842.

[a. Evidence of Mr. J. G. Nicholls.]

104. *Chairman*)[1] By what tenure does the present governor hold his office? — He is

[1] Ryder, Dudley, Viscount Sandon (later (1847) 2nd Earl of Harrowby (1798–1882)); Conservative M.P. and philanthropist.

appointed by the Committee of Merchants.

105. How is he removable? — He is not removable, unless there is cause of complaint against him: then the Committee are under the necessity of removing him.

106. He holds his office at the pleasure of the Committee? — It is not a limited period of service; it is an indefinite period of service.

107. The Committee have the power of recalling him? — Certainly. . . .

161. *Mr. Forster*) The profits of the merchants are referred to in the report? — Dr. Madden has stated that the natives pay too much for their goods.

162. Are you aware of the rate of profit at those settlements? — During the period I was an African merchant and outfitted ships to that coast, which is a trade carried on solely by barter (and it is the only trade [of that kind] I believe now, except a small . . . barter trade with China) . . . I never considered that a ship could make a good voyage unless we realized 60 per cent on our original invoice; and the reason partly is this: gold dust in that country is current, and it is £4 an ounce: when it is brought here it sometimes does not realise 70s. Then . . . there is a great loss from leakage of palm oil, and there is a great loss in leakage upon part of the outward cargo, in rum particularly, and there is also a considerable loss, in the course of trading, by the cockroach and other insects who destroy the cotton goods. . . .

176. No man is more familiar than yourself with the trade of the coast of Africa, and every person engaged in that trade; in your opinion have not a greater number of merchants become bankrupt in that trade within the last 25 years than [in] any other trade within your knowledge? — I believe there has, since the abolition of the slave trade. . . .

[b. Evidence of Francis Swanzy.]

383. *Chairman*) Where was your principal residence? — Dixcove Fort, where I resided nearly eight years.

384. There you have exercised official functions, have you not? — Yes, as a magistrate.

385. What do you consider to have been the physical limit of your jurisdiction? — My jurisdiction as a magistrate I exercised over all the people living on the Dixcove territories, although not properly authorized to do so. That territory consists of five miles of sea-coast and extends 20 miles inland: but the influence of the fort reaches further. The Dutch claim the rest of the Ahanta country. The limit of my jurisdiction must necessarily be very undefined.

386. Do you consider your direct authority to be limited by the walls of the fort? — No; there has never been any defined authority.

387. What was the nature of the jurisdiction you did exercise there, morally and civilly? — At first when I went to Dixcove, I had but little experience or knowledge of the country; consequently the natives did not bring many of their palavers to the fort for settlement, except small cases of debt, and cases of no difficulty: but afterwards they brought palavers of all kinds, law-suits, complaints of servants against their masters, masters against their servants, wives against their husbands, and law-suits relating to the owning of ground &c. I was called upon to interfere in preventing the people from being panyarred or ill-used by the chiefs of the interior, and recovering such people or goods panyarred; and, in short, in settling and arbitrating in palavers of all kinds, and of almost every nature, which they brought to the fort in preference to settling them among themselves.

388. You settled those on principles of natural equity? — Yes, on the simplest possible code, with a very strict regard to justice.

389. According to the natural principles of right and wrong, without reference to written law? — Yes, it was impossible to have written law, the manners and customs of the natives are such.

390. With reference to laws of their own? — . . . Of course.

391. You allowed them to plead their own laws and customs before you? — Partly so; those . . . suitable to the country, which could not be done away with.

393. The natives came by their own consent? — Yes.

394. When your decision was announced, was it always acquiesced in? — Universally so. . . .

397. Did you find that [jurisdiction] established when you first arrived there, or did you create this influence? — It was partially established but it has been gradually increasing the last 10 years by the consent of the natives themselves; in fact they have forced it upon us. . . .

404. Suppose a complainant comes before you; in what way do you bring the defendant before you; suppose he claims a debt arising 30 miles inland? — In Dixcove, if any man comes before me and states that such a person owes him a debt, I ask him if he has personally applied to that man for payment of the debt. If he answers, 'No', I tell him to do so, more than once, and to give the man a little time. If his application has been ineffectual, he comes to the fort again and I then make use of my power to issue a summons, which I give to the constable. He goes into the town and finds this man who is summoned and told to appear at the fort at such an hour. On his appearance, I inquire into the nature, the justice and amount of the debt; and if the man is of a known good character and known family, according to the amount of the debt, I give him a week, or a month, or six weeks to pay it in.

405. Suppose the defendant resides inland, at a distance from the town; do you still exercise jurisdiction? — I send a message to his chief (if he lives under one) by a messenger, constable, or soldier, accompanied perhaps by the creditor; and if the defendant is of good character, the chief will perhaps interfere for him, and promise to see that he pays the debt in a month,

or any given time; or he sends the debtor down for examination. I use my own discretion as to giving him any time; or, if a bad character, detain him in the fort till he gives security for the payment, or till his friends appear and interfere in his behalf, and take him out of the fort. . . .

407. *Viscount Courtenay*) Are the headmen or caboceers always present during those inquiries? — No; in important cases the captains of the towns are present. . . .

411. *Chairman*) Do they pay no fees in your court? — In taking out a summons they pay one dollar, which is paid by the party in fault, which goes to the expense of paying the constable. . . .

425. You never had to coerce any of the chiefs into assistance to your summons? — No; I had occasion to interfere about forty miles off. The people injured the Dixcove and water-side people generally in their transactions with them. When they went up to dig for gold, and to trade and sell fish, they were ill-treated. I went up with some of the chiefs of Dixcove and some of the complainants, and we established a code of laws between the water-side and this chief . . . called Armoo. . . .

432. *Mr. Wood*) What number of hours do you, on the average, find the administration of justice occupy? — There is generally a case or two in the morning, sometimes more, at other times eight or ten. I have been occupied two hours a day on the average.

441. *Chairman*) Do they ever wish you to inflict punishments such as would be repugnant to English feeling? — They have done so, and I cannot say that they are very merciful among themselves towards their own people. I have heard frequent complaints made of the smallness of the punishments inflicted, or the letting out of debtors, or giving them a month or two months when they would wish to have them confined in the fort. I have heard them complain, when time has been given to debtors, saying, 'Ah, if I were to take the law into my own hands, I should soon get paid by panyarring.' . . .

457. You only settle such cases as are brought before you by the voluntary submission of the parties? — Yes: but if I heard of a case of a chief, in the interior 50 miles back, acting with cruelty and injustice, I should send a messenger to remonstrate with that chief, and I have no doubt that such remonstrance would be effectual to prevent that cruelty and injustice being repeated. . . .

815. You do not admit that the statements that 'The authorities of Cape Coast were not justified in becoming the ministers of the vengeance of the barbarous chiefs . . .' is a correct picture of the sort of jurisdiction which the magistrates of Cape Coast exercise? — Certainly not: they are far from acting as the ministers of the vengeance of the barbarous chiefs in their vicinity . . . but prevent the chiefs from taking such vengeance and following their barbarous laws. . . . [Dr. Madden] also states, 'They consider us as seeking after our own advantages, and endeavouring to become masters of the country, on the pretence of putting down this trade.' I beg to state they do not consider us as . . . endeavouring to become masters of the country at all, and that it has not been accomplished at the expense of our character for justice, but the contrary. . . .

817. You think they would be most unwilling to see us withdraw our influence? — I am certain they would be most unwilling; it would be a total loss to them. . . .

901. Is [Apollonia] entirely in the hands of the natives, without any interference from foreign authorities? — It is in the hands of a chief who commits great cruelties, and treats the people in a most oppressive and tyrannical manner. Human sacrifices are frequent there. He refuses to listen to any communication from Cape Coast or the other forts. The people are in a state of the most abject slavery. In short, it is a little Ashantee on the beach. Those doings are carried on on the very beach, under the walls of the British fort almost. . . .

911. Do you think the condition of

Apollonia is a very fair specimen of what many other parts of the Gold Coast would be, but for the interposition of the European authorities? — I do, certainly. . . .

942. Do you conceive that an English fort is of very great advantage as a control over the conduct of European vessels? — I do. I have heard of conduct on the part of captains of merchant vessels on the windward coast which is very disgraceful, and for which they would incur heavy penalties if they were prosecuted, and the natives have no means of getting redress; and I am surprised we do not hear oftener of vessels being taken, plundered, and crews murdered by the natives, for which they have sometimes sufficient justification. . . .

[c. Evidence of Robert Roberts.]

1222. Mr. Forster) . . . You had an opportunity of seeing the system pursued under the Crown and the system pursued under the Committee of Merchants? — I had. . . .

1228. Did the system under the management of the merchants, at the time you were there, appear to you to work well for the advantage of the natives and the Europeans on the coast? — It did under the government of Mr. Maclean and the Council.

1229. Would you recommend the settlements to be placed under the Crown, in preference to remaining under the management of the merchants? — I think they would be better under the Crown [provided] . . . there was a governor appointed, fit for the duties there.

1230. You think that a great deal would depend upon the appointment of the governor? — Yes, and I think it ought to be managed by a council, with the governor, as it is at present; that the governor should not have the sole power, as used to be the case in the Government time. . . .

1233. In the event of the settlements being transferred to the Crown, would you recommend any material change from the present form of government? — I think there might be a person appointed to decide between the natives in any palaver, such as debts and petty offences, and that it should not be necessary to bring them within the fort. . . .

1235. *Chairman*) To separate the judicial functions from those of the executive? — Yes, except the larger questions such as people going to war. These should be settled in the fort by the governor and council. I think there should be a person appointed for the former purpose. . . .

1239. *Mr. Forster*) Do you think that the person governing the colony of Sierra Leone would be sufficiently well acquainted with the wants of the settlements on the Gold Coast and the character and habits of the natives, to interfere beneficially with the government of those settlements? — I think the governor of Sierra Leone can know nothing about the Gold Coast. . . .

1301. *Chairman.*) You were in the country at the time of the transfer of the administration from the Government to the Committee of merchants. What difference in the mode of management was effected by that transfer? — The governor acted with the advice of the Council; there was nothing else changed.

1302. Is not the governor able on any occasion to act on his own responsibility? — He does sometimes, but, generally speaking, he summons his council. . . .

1304. Have they extended in any way their jurisdiction or their interference, further inland from the coast? — I believe not: since the peace [with] Ashantee, Governor Maclean has, of course [a] greater field to go over.

[d. Evidence of William Bircham Sewell.]

1356 . . . The [African] company did not adjudicate between native and native, but exercised its authority exclusively for the protection of merchants? — Almost exclusively; it interfered to a small extent in order to preserve the peace of the country, by preventing the practice of panyarring . . . which often led to ruinous lawsuits by which whole families had been sold into slavery. . . .

1368. When the forts were taken possession of by the Crown, what was the immediate change in the character of the government? — That magistrates were appointed and commissioners of the Court of Requests. . . .

1370. Will you explain what the difference was? — Before 1822 . . . there were no magistrates excepting the governors of forts, who were considered magistrates *ex-officio*: on my return to Cape Coast in 1825, I found there were justices of the peace and commissioners of the court of requests; and I think the effect was very beneficial. The people appeared much disposed to bring their cases, both civil and criminal, for adjudication, finding that they were decided promptly and without expense, and no doubt considering that magistrates were free from that local connection and bias which may be supposed often to influence the decisions of their own chiefs and elders. . . .

[e. Evidence of G. C. Redman.]

3319. *Mr. Forster*) You stated . . . that you have been 30 years engaged in different branches of the African trade; has the African trade been carried on during that period by all the merchants on the same general system? — The trade is carried on in the same way as formerly in the floating trade.

3320. *Mr. W. Patten*) Is there any difference in the other trade from what it was formerly? — Formerly every house in London had a house either at the Gambia or at Sierra Leone: but some 25 years ago, Mr. Forster introduced the system of sending out goods on commission; it became a commission house, and it has been very prosperous, arising from that system, and we, who have not gone upon that system, have not been so prosperous. . . .

3325. *Chairman*) What is the system of trading on commission? — Any gentlemen who wish to go out to seek their fortunes in West Africa, apply to a house to supply them with goods upon credit. That house

G

charges them a commission, and, by having a great many correspondents, one is set against the other. It is like a sort of insurance, whereas, if you only have one house, as in former times, in case of any accident happening to the .parties in the trade, great loss accrues. . . .

3327. *Mr. W. Patten*) Will you explain the term you made use of just now, that the house in London charges a commission? — When the house in London charges a commission, it does not take the responsibility of the trade upon the coast of Africa, whether it be profit or loss; the party who goes out runs the risk of that himself, not the party in London; they have their commission. . . .

3333. Will you describe the other mode of carrying on the African trade which existed before this system was introduced? — A merchant in London had a house at Sierra Leone, and there were two or three clerks and a head clerk at so much a year. He sent out the goods, and kept open house, which was the fashion originally at Sierra Leone, for the officers both of the army and navy; and at the same time opened a retail store for the natives to come and purchase the goods, and what produce they collected for the goods, or what bills they got from the government officers were remitted to the merchant in London, he taking to himself all the proceeds . . . and perhaps obtaining large profits: but he took the risk at the same time; the parties in the establishment had fixed salaries. . . .

3340. *Mr. Wood*) Will you describe what you mean by the floating trade? — The merchant puts on board a ship a certain quantity of goods, under charge of the captain, to sell upon the coast for produce, or for gold or ivory . . . and he remains out till he disposes of that cargo, and he brings home the proceeds. He goes from port to port. The goods are never landed to be sold; they are sold out of the ship. Lately they have given credit to the natives, which is a very bad system. . . .

3347. *Mr. Evans*) What extent of credit

is commonly given. . . ? — Sometimes from £5 to £100.

3348. What length of credit? — Perhaps it may be a few weeks, or two or three months. When a ship is going down the coast, they leave the goods on shore, and when she comes back, they are paid in palm-oil; and sometimes, of late, when the ship has a small quantity of goods remaining, they have left it with the natives to be paid the next voyage. . . .

[f. Evidence of Rev. J. Beecham.[1]]

3604. *Chairman*) How many missionaries have you upon the Gold Coast? — We have missionaries stationed at Dixcove, Commenda, Cape Coast Castle, Annamaboe, Cormantine, Salt Pond, Tantum, Lago, Mumford, Winnebah, and British Accra, and we are now extending our missionary operations to Badagry on the Slave Coast. In the interior we have stations at Abasa, Donquah, Domonassi, Yankumasi, Mansu and several other places.

3605. What is the total number of persons employed in the mission? — The whole number of English missionaries at present employed is six, and a considerable number of native teachers. We have recently extended our missionary operations to Ashantee. In the year 1839, Mr. Freeman, our missionary at the Gold Coast, made a visit of observation to Coomassie . . . and . . . had a very kind reception from the king. He told the king what was the object of his journey; that the society of which he was the agent were anxious to commence Christian schools in Coomassie. . . . The king told him that it was a subject that required very grave consideration, but that if he would come up again after the rainy season was over, or send some properly accredited person, he would make known to him his views upon the subject.

Mr. Freeman was then instructed by the missionary committee to visit this

---

[1] Secretary of the Wesleyan Methodist Missionary Society.

country for the purpose of communicating the fullest information relative to the state of things in Ashantee. . . . He remained a few months in England . . . visiting many of the principal towns in the country, received very liberal . . . donations . . . and returned to the Gold Coast with a reinforcement of missionaries. In the course of last autumn he went up again to Coomassie. . . . He . . . has been permitted to commence religious services in the capital. . . . The king has granted permission . . . to build a mission house, and has given a piece of land for that purpose. Mr. Freeman was not able to remain long at Coomassie, but left his colleague, Mr. Brooking, with several native agents. . . . When Mr. Freeman was at Coomassie, the king appeared to hesitate respecting the establishment of a school. We have this morning, however, received a letter from Mr. Freeman in which he states . . . that the king has given his free consent to the establishment of a school and that a Christian school is now commenced . . . in the capital of Ashantee.

3608. *Sir T. D. Acland*) You have stated that there are six European missionaries employed in your mission, but that you have a number of other stations: how are those filled; are they filled with natives? — We have six English missionaries with native assistants. We have also 10 mission schools, two of which are in part supported by the local Government. Three of those schools are for girls. The schools contain 224 boys and 92 girls; . . .

3610. Are they along the coast under the protection of the forts? — They are all on the coast with the exception of the one at Coomassie. We have seven chapels on the Gold Coast. . . . The entire cost of our mission establishment . . . is about £4,000. . . .

3614. Have [the native agents] been drawn from the schools which have been founded at Cape Coast? — All the native agents that we employ upon the Gold Coast received the elements of their education in the Government school. Of course they have been instructed by the missionaries since they were taken into connexion with the Society, but I believe the whole of them received their elementary education there. . . .

3649. *Chairman*) Can you state the nature of the difficulties which the missionaries have experienced in promoting the improvement of the natives? — I would observe that the degradation of the female sex is one of the great obstacles with which the missionaries have to contend. . . . The women are treated as inferior beings, as mere creatures of convenience, and are grossly ignorant. . . . The superstitions of the people present a great obstacle. I speak more especially with regard to the influence of those superstitions in preventing regular industry among the natives. The natives can engage in no undertaking whatever, of any moment, without first consulting their priests or fetish men. . . . They are greatly obstructed by their notion respecting lucky and unlucky days [on the latter no work being done]. . . . Many of their mines and trees and hills are considered sacred to their deities; the mines must not, therefore, be worked, the trees must not be cut down, the hills must not be cleared of the bush and cultivated. . . .

I would also remark on the ruinous funeral customs of the people. . . . Many individuals under the influence of this system are reduced to the necessity of selling their services as 'pawns' to others. . . .

3656. . . With regard to slavery, I would observe that it is fostered to a great extent by the people themselves; a spirit of rational independence and freedom cannot be found among the heathen population of this country. . . . The love of liberty seems to give way to a desire for security; and a person generally prefers to attach himself in a state of dependence to some chief for the sake of the protection and other privileges which the dependents of chiefs enjoy. . . .

With the permission of the Committee, I will read an extract from the instructions of our committee to our missionaries on the subject of slavery. . . . 'On the subject of slavery, the missionaries are called upon . . . to exercise the greatest care and watchfulness. While they strictly adhere to their printed instructions, and avoid all political intermeddling whatever, they are scrupulously to guard against anything which could possibly be construed into a connivance at one of the worst evils which have ever afflicted and degraded mankind. The great principles of the Gospel must be so maintained with mildness, constancy and firmness, as to make it appear that slavery in every form is altogether opposed to the spirit and precepts of Christianity; and this will be the more necessary from the consideration that the native chiefs are not amenable to British law, and that they therefore can only be acted upon by moral means.'

Now in carrying out those instructions, the missionaries attend in the first place to the inculcation of the great principle that all souls are equal in the sight of God, and they endeavour to impress on the chiefs what are the inalienable rights of their dependents as human beings. Another method they adopt, is to protect, as far as lies in their power, the slaves from injurious treatment by the chiefs. . . . Then again, in building chapels and houses . . . the missionaries . . . do not employ slaves by hiring them of their masters, but they take care to hire the individuals themselves, and to pay them their wages. . . .

3665. Do you think that it would be possible to carry on emigration from Africa to the West Indies, without producing a real or seeming slave trade? — I think it would be extremely difficult to adopt any safe plan. The difficulty would be increased by the unwillingness of the Africans to leave their native soil and go to the West Indies. . . . Love of country is a very strong and governing principle in the African. . . . But if it were practicable, . . I doubt much whether, taking a large view of the question, it would be desirable; because I think the removal of any considerable number of free and enlightened Africans (if you could meet with them) to the West Indies would be injurious to the work of civilization in Africa itself. . . . It would be removing the very agents whose services are required in Africa in promoting the elevation of Africa itself. . . . It is not that I have any undue bias in favour of Africa, because as a missionary society we have as deep an interest in whatever concerns the West Indies as we have in what relates to the interest of Africa.[1] . . .

[h. Evidence of Dr. R. R. Madden.]

9054. *Mr. Milnes*) You say in your Report, 'There can be no question but the natives find their advantage in bringing palavers before Captain Maclean . . .'? — I am quite of that opinion.

9055. On what grounds then do you think it is injurious to the character of British justice, that this British jurisdiction should be exercised over the natives? — It struck me that in the first place it is contrary to every principle of justice that capital punishments should be carried into effect without any of those legal forms which, in every other part of the world where British rule exists, are observed.

9056. But in civil transactions you think it is clearly beneficial to the natives? — Yes, I think it is in civil cases: and in criminal cases where the angry passions of the chiefs are excited very much against the prisoners, I think it would be a benefit for them to come before the Governor of Cape Coast. . . .

9059. Is it not of particular importance that in criminal cases such as would be likely to excite the angry feelings of the chiefs, the English jurisdiction should be allowed to be exercised? — It might be better for the natives, but it would be very injurious to our character if a British

[1] The Wesleyans were blamed for the small interest shown at Sierra Leone in this favourite object of the 1842 Committee. Cf. Qs. 6384 ff.

Governor were allowed to put people to death without the forms of British law.

9060. Do you mean to say that the technical forms of English law are not observed, or that the principles and spirit of English law are not observed? — I mean that the technical forms of English law are entirely lost sight of in those criminal cases; that there is neither judge nor jury properly speaking. There is a judge, but he acts in the capacity of jury also.

9061. Are the proceedings conducted in the presence of the persons accused? — They ought to be. The courts are held in the Governor's house, assisted by a certain number of magistrates. There was no such court held before the Governor while I was there, but he had several palavers while I was there. The manner in which they were gone through was this. Mr. Maclean went into his office and walked about the room. . . . The negroes were sitting down either side, delivering their charges, and those who were accused making their defence. . . . He listened very patiently to them, and then decided their cases, and the party who was cast was, in some cases, mulcted or fined. . . .

9069. *Chairman*) Do you think there are materials for a jury consisting of persons sufficiently free from local impressions and prejudices to ensure a better administration of justice than would take place by leaving it in the hands of the governor? — I am satisfied that there are sufficient persons to be found in those settlements to act as jurors, and that it would tend a great deal to enhance our influence with the people if there were such forms.

9070. What was the nature of the palavers at which you were present? — I did not understand the nature of them; I did not understand the language. Mr. Maclean is conversant, I believe, with the language. . . .

9137. *Viscount Ebrington*) A sort of compromise is effected between the English and the native law in India? — Exactly, and I would have the same in Africa, where it did not sanction any barbarous customs. . . .

9141. *Mr. Aldam*)   Do you not know that in India they follow nearly the reverse of your plan, observing the Indian law in civil cases, and to a considerable extent, the English law in criminal? — I was not aware of that. . . .

9196. *Viscount Courtenay*)   Do you believe that any unfavourable impression existed with regard to the fairness of Mr. Maclean's conduct on the Gold Coast in consequence of . . . his alleged connexion with the house of Forster and Smith? — The impression made upon my mind was that the merchants there, whose dealings were with other houses, would not be so favourably treated as a merchant immediately connected with Mr. Forster. . . .

9201. *Mr. Forster*)   Do you mean that he received consignments of vessels and goods, and that he sold those goods, receiving a commission? — No; my impression is this, that those vessels that were consigned to him, were put under his especial charge, so far as directing the captains to what place it would be most advisable for them to go to dispose of their cargoes. . . .

9213. You must have observed or heard that the great bulk of the vessels frequenting Cape Coast Castle from the house of Forster & Smith are vessels on freight, and that they do not go there for the purpose of seeking a market at all.   That being the case, how can any advice and information from Mr. Maclean on the subject of a market, be of any use to them? — But the vessels of Forster & Smith constantly go to Cape Coast Castle although they do not sell their goods there. . . .

9214. Are you aware that the house of Forster & Smith has . . . for . . . perhaps . . . 20 years had only one vessel engaged in the floating trade, and that therefore it can only be that single vessel that could apply to the Governor for any information of the kind you allude to? — I was not aware of that fact, and there is a very different impression on my mind. . . .

9224. *Mr. Aldam to Mr. Swanzy*)   Is it your opinion that he would have refused his assistance and advice to any other house? — He would not.

[H.C.551, A & P (1842) xi]

135 REPORT OF THE SELECT COMMITTEE ON WEST AFRICA   1842.

The SELECT COMMITTEE appointed to inquire into the state of the British Possessions on the West Coast of Africa, more especially with reference to their present relations with the neighbouring native tribes, and who were empowered to report their observations, together with the minutes of evidence taken before them, to the House: — Have considered the matters referred to them, and have agreed to the following Report: . . . [The report recapitulates the events leading to Dr. Madden's mission.]

The reports which were the result of this gentleman's inquiries, involving materially the interests of humanity and of commerce, and impeaching gravely the characters of individuals engaged in the British trade with Africa, in a manner which seemed to call for further investigation before any conclusion could be fairly come to upon the questions at issue, have been laid before your Committee, have in fact formed the basis of their proceedings, and are published with this report: but in publishing them, your Committee beg to state that while they do full justice to the value of much of the information contained in them, and to the zeal and diligence of Dr. Madden, they do not concur in all his conclusions, or intend to warrant the accuracy of his statements.   His inquiries were conducted over a vast surface of coast in a short period, and under circumstances of considerable interruption from health disordered by the climate, and in many instances he apparently found himself compelled to take his information from third parties, the accuracy of whose statements and the correctness of whose opinions he had not the opportunity of testing.

In many of his recommendations they

concur: on some, and those of no slight importance, they have come to an opposite opinion; but thinking it would be more convenient that they should give their own conclusions upon the whole subject submitted to them in a consecutive form, rather than in the shape of a commentary upon his reports, they beg to submit the following statement and recommendations to the House, as the conclusions at which they have themselves arrived.

Gold Coast

In the first place, then, we recommend that the Government of the British forts upon the Gold Coast be resumed by the Crown, and that all dependence on the Government of Sierra Leone should cease.

We fully admit the merits of that administration, whether we look to the officer employed, Captain Maclean, or to the Committee under whom he had acted, which, with the miserable pittance of between £3,500 and £4,000 a year, has exercised, from the four ill-provided forts of Dixcove, Cape Coast, Annamaboe, and British Accra, manned by a few ill-paid black soldiers, a very wholesome influence over a coast not much less than 150 miles in extent, and to a considerable distance inland, preventing within that range, external slave trade, maintaining peace and security, and exercising a useful though irregular jurisdiction among the neighbouring tribes, and much mitigating and in some cases extinguishing some of the atrocious practices which had prevailed among them unchecked before. We would give full weight to the doubts which Captain Maclean entertained as to his authority, until specifically so instructed, to prevent vessels suspected of being intended for the slave trade, but not having slaves on board, from trafficking in lawful goods within his jurisdiction; and we do not infer from the circumstance, that the Government of these forts had any partiality for an abominable traffic which, on the contrary, they have done much to check: but we think it desirable, for the

sake of enlarging the sphere of usefulness of these settlements, and of giving greater confidence in the character and impartiality of their Government, that it should be rendered completely independent of all connection with commerce, by a direct emanation of authority from the Crown, and that it should be placed, with increased resources, in direct and immediate communication with the general government of the Empire.

We recommend, further, the reoccupation of several of the forts, such as Apollonia, Winnebah and Whydah, abandoned in 1828 . . . and the reconstruction of others, on however small a scale, on other similar points. In some cases the climate will be found not worse, in others better, than on other parts of the coast of Africa; but this evil may be very much mitigated, if not entirely removed, by the employment of such Europeans only as are already enured to a tropical climate, and of British subjects of African descent, who, we believe, may now be found, either within our African settlements or our West India Colonies, fitted for almost every branch and grade of service; and we look upon such establishment as of high importance, not for the extension of territory, but of that control over the slave trade, and wholesome moral influence over the neighbouring chiefs, which we have described as having been exercised by the existing forts, and which is much needed at those places to which we have particularly alluded, as well as others.

The judicial authority at present existing in the forts is not altogether in a satisfactory condition; it resides in the Governor and Council, who act as magistrates and whose instructions limit them to the administration of British law, and that, as far as the natives are concerned, strictly and exclusively within the forts themselves; but practically and necessarily and usefully, these directions having been disregarded, a kind of irregular jurisdiction has grown up, extending itself far beyond the limits of the forts, by the voluntary submission of the natives themselves, whether chiefs or traders, to British equity; and its decisions, owing to the moral influence, partly of our acknowledged power, and partly of the respect which has been inspired by the fairness with which it has been exercised by Captain Maclean and the magistrates at the other forts, have generally, we might almost say, uniformly, been carried into effect without the interposition of force. The value of this interposition of an enlightened, though irregular authority (which has extended in some cases, and with advantage to humanity, even to an interference in capital cases) is borne witness to, not only by parties connected with the Government of the settlements, who might be suspected of a bias in its favour, but also by the Wesleyan missionaries, and even by Dr. Madden, who, objecting to its undefined extent, and to the manner in which, in some respects, it has been carried out, yet still bears high testimony to its practical value, to its acknowledged equity, and to its superiority over the barbarous customs which it tends to supersede. Even the duration of imprisonment, of which he complains, has been usually adjudged to offences which would have incurred a severer penalty in most civilized countries, and would certainly, if left to the arbitrary decision of native chiefs, or to the 'wild justice' of private revenge, have been punished by death, and that frequently of the most cruel kind. Still, however, it is desirable that this jurisdiction should be better defined and understood, and that a judicial officer should be placed at the disposal of the Governor, to assist, or supersede partially or entirely, his judicial functions, and those now exercised by the Council and the several commandants in their magisterial capacity: but we would recommend, that while he follows in his decisions, the general principles, he be not restricted to the technicalities of British law, and that altogether he should be allowed a large discretion.

It is to be remembered that our compulsory authority is strictly limited, both by our title and by the instructions of the Colonial Office, to the British forts, within which no one but the Governor, his suite, and the garrison reside; and that the magistrates are strictly prohibited from exercising jurisdiction even over the natives and districts immediately under the influence and protection of the forts. All jurisdiction over the natives beyond that point must, therefore, be considered as optional, and should be made the subject of distinct agreement, as to its nature and limits, with the native chiefs, and it should be accommodated to the condition of the several tribes, and to the completeness of the control over them, which by vicinage, we are enabled to exercise. Their relation to the English Crown should be, not the allegiance of subjects, to which we have no right to pretend, and which it would entail an inconvenient responsibility to possess, but the deference of weaker powers to a stronger and more enlightened neighbour, whose protection and counsel they seek, and to whom they are bound by certain definite obligations.

These obligations should be varied and extended from time to time, and should always at least include (as many of the treaties now in existence on the coast already do) the abolition of the external slave trade, the prohibition of human sacrifices and other barbarous customs, such as kidnapping under the name of 'panyarring', and should keep in view the gradual introduction of further improvements as the people become more fitted to admit them.

In this arrangement we should find the solution of our difficulty in regard to domestic slavery, and a modification of it under the name of 'pawns', which has prevailed within these settlements, not actually within the forts, but within their influence, and even in the hands of British subjects. To them, indeed, they have been already prohibited: but although the system of pawns, which is properly an engagement of service voluntarily entered into for debt, and terminable at any time by the payment of the debt, is one which 'does not seem abstractedly unjust or unreasonable', yet as liable to much abuse, and much resembling slavery, it should be the object of our policy to get rid of it even among the natives; and in the places more immediately within the influence of British authority, we believe there will be no difficulty in limiting it at once, both in extent and duration, and probably, ere long, in abolishing it, by arrangements such as we have above suggested. Some caution, however, must be exercised in this matter on account of the close intermixture of Dutch and Danish with the British settlements, though perhaps it might be possible to induce them to cooperate in such arrangements as might be thought desirable for the improvement of the neighbouring tribes; and great facility and advantage would certainly arise from such co-operation, if it could be secured.

With regard to the judicial arrangements, a plan has been suggested by which a supreme judicial officer might be placed at Ascension, at Fernando Po (where no authority of any kind exists, and one is much needed), or at some other island off the coast, visiting, with the aid of a steamer, the various settlements on the Gold Coast periodically, as well as the trading stations in the Bight of Benin and Biafra, and exercising in the latter a very wholesome influence in the adjustment of disputes with the natives, which for want of such interposition, occasionally lead to consequences injurious to the British character and to the interests of commerce. But your Committee are aware that difficulties might arise in carrying out this suggestion, more especially on account of the necessity for prompt decision in most cases in which natives are concerned, and therefore are not prepared at present to do more than call attention to the suggestion.

We would here acknowledge the great services rendered to religion and civilization on this coast by the Wesleyan body; they have even established a friendly communication with the barbarous court of Ashantee, which promises results important in every way; and, indeed, little in the way of religious instruction would have been done without them. But we would recommend that further provision should be made for these objects by the appointment of a Colonial Chaplain, and by the encouragement of schools of a higher class than any which are found there at present; to which, among others, the neighbouring chiefs should be invited to send their sons to receive an education which might fit them to be of benefit to their own people directly, if they returned to their families, or indirectly if they remained, by entering into connection with British interests.

Some officer should also be appointed whose duty should be to take care of the effects of intestate persons, to verify the character of vessels entering the ports, and to attend generally to the fiscal regulations of the settlements.

We beg also to call attention to the suggestion that we should endeavour to secure the co-operation of our Dutch and Danish neighbours in licensing the canoes which ply along the coast, as they seem to afford considerable facilities to such slave trade as still exists along the leeward coast. The Military also should be somewhat increased in number, and their condition, as recommended by Dr. Madden, should be improved. . . .

All the objects which we have been recommending may be attained at an expense far short of that which was incurred for these settlements when they protected, instead of, as now, controlling the slave trade, or even when they were last under the direct management of the Crown. Indeed, in itself, it is of but trifling amount when compared with the objects to be attained, and we are confident that the increased expense will be well repaid, both directly by the diminished necessity for naval forces upon the leeward coast, and indirectly by the increase of commerce, which will be the certain consequence of extended influence over very important nations, including the kingdoms of Dahomey and Ashantee, of an improving population; and of the continued and still more complete suppression of the slave trade on that coast, once infamous as the principal scene of its operations. . . .

[The report then discusses the promotion of emigration to the West Indies.] It would be well for the African, in every point of view, to find himself a free labourer in the free British West India Colonies, enjoying there, as he would, higher advantages of every kind than have fallen to the lot of the negro race in any other portion of the globe. [But on the Gold Coast where there was apparently no surplus labour, they would not encourage emigration.

They then review measures against the slave trade.] . . .

Happily in this great work we need not despair. The measures lately adopted have done much. . . . North of the Line, the slave trade, with the exception of a few points in the neighbourhood of Sierra Leone and the Gambia, is virtually extinct. . . . [More might be done with faster ships and steamers.] Encouragement and ample protection, at the same time, should be given to lawful trade in every shape, and the settlements which we hold, or which we may form upon the coast, should be kept open indifferently to all nations as to ourselves, that they may see and be compelled to acknowledge, that in all we are attempting for Africa, we are only endeavouring to provide a feast of which all may equally partake, and seeking, as the reward of our exertions, no advantage to ourselves, save that which may fairly fall to our lot from a proportionate share of a more abundant table, spread out for the common benefit of all.

[H.C.551, A & P (1842) xi, pp. iii–xxi]

BOOK IV

THE RESUMPTION OF CROWN RULE, 1843–1852

11 Lord Stanley[1] and the Judicial System, 1842–1845

LORD STANLEY did not accept all the Select Committee's recommendations (136). He determined to try to maintain the forts on much the same restricted footing as under the Committee of Merchants (142), but agreed to appoint a judicial officer to exercise jurisdiction outside the forts, and nominated Maclean to the new office. This, however, meant that Maclean now took second place, and Stanley's first choice for Lieutenant-Governor was not a happy one. The preparation of the necessary legal instruments (139, 141, 148) was a matter of some difficulty, and Stephen never liked continuing Maclean's system (137, 151). On the coast, in accordance with the Committee's recommendation, the chiefs were persuaded to state their acceptance of British jurisdiction (144) in the document known as the 'Bond' (145), which, in the later nineteenth and twentieth century came to be regarded alternately as the Magna Carta (483) and the Munich (506b) of Gold Coast history.

Maclean continued to administer the Gold Coast settlements until the new Lieutenant-Governor arrived in February 1844. For a time he even hoped to see their boundaries extended by the effective occupation of Apollonia,[2] by the purchase of the Danish forts (138), and by the re-occupation of Whydah (140). As far as Dahomey was concerned he was much too sanguine (152), though in effect he set in train the negotiations which were ultimately to result in the British occupation of Lagos. After 1844, Maclean was in the background[3] and relations with Ashanti became rather strained as a result (146, 153).

[1] Edward George Stanley (later 14th Earl of Derby) (1799–1869): entered Parliament as a Whig in 1822; Under-Secretary for the Colonies, 1827–30; Secretary of State for War and the Colonies, March 1833–May 1834 and from September 1841 to December 1845; joined the Conservatives in 1835; later three times Prime Minister.
[2] Maclean to Stanley, 17 September, 1843, in C.O.96/2 (and in Crooks).
[3] He went on leave in July 1844, and died on 22 May, 1847, not long after returning to his post.

136 G. W. HOPE[1] TO JAMES STEPHEN
COLONIAL OFFICE, 3 DECEMBER, 1842.

I send you with this a copy of the Report of the Committee upon the West Coast of Africa. Of the recommendations contained in that Report, Lord Stanley proposes as soon as it can be done, to carry into effect some, abandoning or postponing others. . . .

As to the Gold Coast

1st. Lord Stanley proposes to resume the Government into the hands of the Crown as recommended: but does not adopt the further proposal of making it independent of Sierra Leone, considering

[1] George William Hope, Parliamentary Under-Secretary for the Colonies, 1841–45.

the Settlements as forts or factories rather than Colonies.

2nd. He is prepared to appoint a Judicial Officer as well as a Governor (it must be a Lt. Gov.), such Judicial Officer to have the jurisdiction, or rather the duty proposed by the Committee, of trying cases beyond the actual British Dominions, by consent of the natives. The range of British dominion he proposes to confine, as at present in strictness it is, to the walls of the fort.

3rd. He considers the appointment of a chaplain and of some one to take charge of intestate estates advisable. Possibly this latter duty might be combined with the judicial office.

4th.   He proposes to make the pay of the troops really in amount what it is now only nominally — being paid in merchandise: but otherwise he does not wish materially to increase the establishments at first. . . .

On the further alterations suggested by the Committee he is, I think, inclined to suspend his judgement until he shall have a report from whoever is sent out as Governor. . . .

On the advisability of the changes proposed, however, and on the question how they can be legally affected, Lord Stanley wishes, before proceeding further, to have your views. . . .   [C.O.96/2]

137 MEMORANDUM BY JAMES STEPHEN
LONDON, 3 DECEMBER, 1842.

. . . The Judicial Officer who is to execute, beyond the precincts of the Queen's Dominions, justice rather than law, would be encumbered rather than aided by any form of legal appointment. There is no apparent good reason why a judicature, which in its exercise is to be quite independent of all positive law, should in its institution seek a legal basis. All the manuscripts and seals which legal subtlety could bring together would of course be unavailing to legalize the appointment of an English judge beyond the Queen's Dominions, except indeed as an Act of Parliament might be said to render it legal within the local range of the authority of Parliament. But how to frame such an act is, I suppose, an insoluble problem. We are about to make an usurpation which the goodness of our motives and the necessity of the case are to justify, and I suppose such a justification would not be improved by an abortive attempt to give a semblance of law to that which, ex hypothesi, is to be lawless. If the arbiter judge is fit for the employment, he will not be critical about his Commission. . . .

[After discussing various points of detail, he goes on:]

It could answer no good purpose to trouble Lord Stanley or you with an argument to prove that the recommendations of the Committee are wrong not in detail but in their essence. Yet such is the only opinion which I could express on the 'advisability' of these changes if I wrote what I really thought. . . . But to what end trouble you with a discussion to prove that the value of these African settlements to our commerce is enormously exaggerated; that in fact they are nothing else than factories kept up at the expense of the nation at large for the profit of half a dozen inconsiderable merchants, who avail themselves of our national sensibility on every subject on which the commercial wealth or the national importance of Great Britain are concerned, — that the trade of them all put together is of less value to us, present or prospective, than the trade with the Isle of Skye — that we are recklessly increasing and dispersing our Colonial Empire in all directions, and creating a demand for naval and military force which there are no means of meeting, except by weakening that force where its presence is most needed — that, in short, neither the Gambia nor the Gold Coast are worth retaining, or that, if retained, they should be placed exclusively in the hands of the mulattoes or negroes from the West Indies, and left to maintain themselves like the American settlement of Liberia? . . .   [C.O.96/2]

138 J. BANNERMAN TO M. FORSTER
BRITISH ACCRA, 19 DECEMBER, 1842.

My dear Sir,

The principal object of my writing to you by this opportunity is to apprize you of a report brought here a few days ago by the Danish store ship, to the effect that the Danish Government had come to the determination to dispose of their settlements on this coast and in the West Indies, and that the French Government are likely to become the purchasers of Christiansborg Castle and its dependencies, and that the French Ministers are to propose the measure at the next meeting of the Chambers.

I need not point out to you the mischief that would accrue to British interests if such an arrangement is carried into effect. You have had some experience of French encroachments and jealousies at the Gambia and Portendic. What then must we expect if they establish themselves within two miles of us! If there is any truth in this report, I trust you will use your influence with your friends to avert the evil. You are well aware of the great extent of territory presumptuously claimed by the Danes here, and if they make this over to the French we must very soon be involved in serious disputes with the latter. It is from this disputed territory that *all* our palm oil and live stock come; and if they (the French) are in possession of it, they will soon prohibit the natives from bringing their produce to the British settlements.

Forty thousand pounds is said to be the price set upon these settlements by the Danes, and if the French become the purchasers, the English Government will soon have to expend four times that sum in protecting themselves from the encroachments of the new-comers. . . .[1]

[C.O.96/3]

139 THE BRITISH SETTLEMENTS ACT
APRIL 1843.

Anno Sexto Victoriae Reginae

Cap. XIII

An act to enable Her Majesty to provide for the Government of Her Settlements on the Coast of Africa and in the Falkland Islands — 11 April 1843.

Whereas divers of Her Majesty's subjects have resorted to and taken up their abode and may hereafter resort to and take up their abode at divers places on or adjacent to the coast of the continent of Africa and on the Falkland Islands: And whereas it is necessary that Her Majesty should be enabled to make further and better provision for the civil government of the said settlements: Be it therefore enacted by the Queen's Most Excellent Majesty, by and with the advice and consent of the Lords Spiritual and Temporal, and Commons, in this present Parliament assembled, and by the authority of the same, That it shall be lawful for Her Majesty, by any order or orders to be by Her made, with the advice of Her Privy Council, to establish all such laws, institutions, and ordinances, and to constitute such courts and officers, and to make such provisions and regulations for the proceedings in such courts and for the administration of justice, as may be necessary for the peace, order, and good government of Her Majesty's subjects and others within the said present or future settlements respectively, or any of them; any law, statute, or usage to the contrary notwithstanding.

And be it enacted, That it shall be lawful for Her Majesty, by any commission or commissions under the Great Seal of the United Kingdom, or by any instructions under Her Majesty's signet and sign manual, accompanying and referred to in any such commission or commissions, to delegate to any three or more persons within any of the settlements aforesaid respectively the powers and authorities so vested in Her Majesty in Council as aforesaid, either in whole or in part, and upon, under, and subject to all such conditions, provisoes, and limitations as by any such commission or commissions or instructions as aforesaid Her Majesty shall see fit to prescribe: Provided always, that notwithstanding any such delegation of authority as aforesaid, it shall still be competent to Her Majesty in Council, in manner aforesaid, to exercise all the powers and authorities so vested as aforesaid in Her Majesty in Council: Provided also, that all such Orders in Council, commissions, and instructions as aforesaid, and all laws and ordinances so to be made as aforesaid, shall be laid before both Houses of Parliament as soon as conveniently may be after the making and enactment thereof respectively.

---

[1] The Danes denied any intention of selling, but said Britain should have the pre-emption when they did. Cf. Wynn to Aberdeen, 21 August, 1843. Copy in C.O.96/3.

And be it enacted, That this Act may be amended or repealed by any Act to be passed in this Session of Parliament.

140 G. MACLEAN TO LORD STANLEY
          CAPE COAST CASTLE, 20 MAY, 1843.

My Lord,

I have the honor herewith to forward for your Lordship's information, a copy of a letter addressed to me by the Reverend T. B. Freeman, Superintendent of the Wesleyan Missions on the Gold Coast, together with a communication addressed by the King or Chief of Dahomey to Her Majesty the Queen of England.

Mr. Freeman having been instructed to plant a missionary station at Badagry, in the kingdom of Dahomey, found that it would be necessary to secure the countenance and protection of the king of that country; and in the month of March last, he succeeded, after encountering many difficulties and delays, arising chiefly from the jealousy of the Portuguese residents at Whydah, in penetrating to the capital of Dahomey and in procuring an interview with the king. His reception by the latter was exceedingly kind and flattering and he held several long conversations with him respecting the objects which England had in view respecting the slave trade. The result was that the king expressed his entire readiness to co-operate with England in this matter, provided some steps should be taken to substitute a legitimate traffic in lieu of that (the traffic in slaves) to which the people of Dahomey had hitherto solely devoted themselves, and from which alone they had hitherto derived their supplies of foreign products and manufactures.

Your Lordship is probably aware that the sea-board of the kingdom of Dahomey comprises a great portion of what is emphatically termed the 'slave-coast' extending from Popo to Lagos; and that from the several ports embraced in it there have, perhaps, been more slaves exported during the last thirty years than from any other portion of the coast of similar extent. At present, three cruisers are unceasingly employed in watching this line of coast: yet notwithstanding their vigilance, cargoes of slaves are not unfrequently exported without detection. It seems, therefore, to me, of the greatest importance that immediate advantage should be taken of the present favourable disposition evinced by the king of Dahomey.

By re-occupying the British fort at Whydah and stationing out-posts at Popo and Lagos, I am convinced that we should by negotiation and other peaceful means, speedily effect the entire suppression of the slave trade along the Dahomey coast. So convinced am I of the expediency, practicability, and safety of re-occupying Whydah fort, that under ordinary circumstances, I should not hesitate — having been already assured of the cordial concurrence and co-operation of Captain Foote, the senior naval officer on this station, at once to re-hoist the British flag at Whydah and Badagry, which I could do at a very trifling expense. But having lately received official notice from the African Committee that I am speedily to be superseded in the administration of this Government, I, of course, do not feel myself at liberty to take any active steps in the matter. I shall not fail, however, to state my views on the subject to my successor on his arrival. . . .

Captain Foote, commanding Her Majesty's Ship 'Madagascar' having lately visited Cape Coast Castle, Mr. Freeman and myself had an opportunity of laying before him a detailed statement of the whole of the circumstances connected with the former's late mission to Dahomey. Captain Foote was so struck with the facility with which, by the most simple means, the slave trade might be suppressed in the Bight of Benin, and the expense of three cruisers saved, that he prepared and signed two treaties or conventions which Mr. Freeman has been authorized on his next visit to Dahomey to propose for the king's acceptance. The first of these documents is a treaty of amity and commerce, and is conceived in the usual terms; the other binds the king of Dahomey to abandon and prohibit the slave trade within his dominions, on condition of his receiving from the British Government an annual payment of seven hundred pounds sterling, payable in merchandise of the king's selection, for the space of seven years from the date of the ratification of the treaties by the British Government. This annual indemnification to the King for the loss of his present revenue derived from the slave trade, is only to be paid on the presentation of authentic annual certificates from competent parties, that the conditions of the treaty have been strictly fulfilled.

I may add that the king of Dahomey not only granted the fullest assurance of his protection for the Christian missions at Badagry, but expressed an anxious wish that a missionary station and school should be established at Whydah.

I have etc.

[C.O.96/2]

141 THE FOREIGN JURISDICTION ACT, 1843.

Anno Sexto & Septimo Victoriae Reginae
Cap. XCIV

An Act to remove Doubts as to the Exercise of Power and Jurisdiction by Her Majesty within divers Countries and Places out of Her Majesty's Dominions, and to render the same more effectual — 24th August, 1843.

Whereas by treaty, capitulation, grant, usage, sufferance, and other lawful means, Her Majesty hath power and jurisdiction within divers countries and places out of Her Majesty's dominions: and whereas doubts have arisen how far the exercise of such power and jurisdiction is controlled by and dependent on the laws and customs of this realm, and it is expedient that such doubts should be removed: Be it therefore enacted by the Queen's most Excellent Majesty, by and with the advice and consent of the Lords Spiritual and Temporal, and Commons, in this present Parliament assembled, and by the authority of the same,

that it is and shall be lawful for Her Majesty to hold, exercise, and enjoy any power or jurisdiction which Her Majesty now hath or may at any time hereafter have within any country or place out of Her Majesty's dominions, in the same and as ample a manner as if Her Majesty had acquired such power or jurisdiction by the cession or conquest of territory.

2. And be it enacted that every act, matter and thing which may at any time be done, in pursuance of any such power or jurisdiction of Her Majesty, in any country or place out of Her Majesty's dominions, shall in all courts ecclesiastical and temporal and elsewhere within Her Majesty's dominions, be and be deemed and adjudged to be, in all cases and to all intents and purposes whatsoever, as valid and effectual as though the same had been done according to the local law then in force within such country or place.

3. And be it enacted, that if in any suit or other proceedings, whether civil or criminal, in any court ecclesiastical or temporal within Her Majesty's dominions, any issue or question of law or of fact shall arise for the due determination whereof it shall, in the opinion of the judge or judges of such court, be necessary to produce evidence of the existence of any such power or jurisdiction as aforesaid, or of the extent thereof, it shall be lawful for the judge or judges of any such court, and he or they are hereby authorized to transmit, under his or their hand and seal or hands and seal, to one of Her Majesty's Principal Secretaries of State, questions by him or them properly framed, respecting such of the matters aforesaid as it may be necessary to ascertain in order to the due determination of any such issue or question as aforesaid: and such Secretary of State is hereby empowered and required, within a reasonable time in that behalf, to cause proper and sufficient answers to be returned to all such questions, and to be directed to the said judges or their successors; and such answers shall, upon production thereof, be final and conclusive evidence, in such suit

or other proceedings, of the several matters therein contained and required to be ascertained thereby.

4. And whereas it may in certain cases be expedient that crimes and offences committed within such countries or places as aforesaid should be inquired of, tried, determined, and punished within Her Majesty's dominions; Be it enacted, that it shall and may be lawful for any persons having authority derived from Her Majesty in that behalf, by warrant under her hand and seal, to cause any person charged with the commission of any crime or offence the cognizance whereof may at any time appertain to any judge, magistrate, or other officer of Her Majesty within any such country or place as aforesaid, to be sent for trial to any British colony which Her Majesty may by any Order in Council from time to time appoint in that behalf; and upon the arrival of such person within such colony it shall and may be lawful for the Supreme Court exercising criminal jurisdiction within the same to cause such person to be kept in safe and proper custody, and so soon as conveniently may be, to inquire of, try, and determine such crime or offence, and upon the conviction of the person so charged as aforesaid, to correct and punish him according to the laws in force in that behalf within such colony, in the same manner as if the said crime or offence had been committed within the jurisdiction of such Supreme Court: provided always, that before any such person shall be sent for trial to any such colony as aforesaid, it shall be lawful for him to render for examination to the judge, magistrate, or other officer of Her Majesty to whom the cognizance of the crime or offence with which he is charged may appertain, within the country or place where the same may be alleged to have been committed, any competent witness or witnesses, the evidence of whom he may deem material for his defence, and whom he may allege himself to be unable to produce at his trial in the said colony; and the said judge, magistrate, or other officer shall thereupon proceed in the examination and

cross-examination of such witness or witnesses in the same manner as though the same had been tendered at a trial before such judge, magistrate or other officer, and shall cause the evidence so taken to be reduced into writing, and shall transmit a copy of such evidence to the Supreme Court before which the trial of such person is to take place, together with a certificate under his hand and seal, of the correctness of such copy; and thereupon it shall be lawful for the said Supreme Court, and it is hereby required, to allow so much of the evidence so taken as aforesaid as would have been admissible according to the law and practice of the said Supreme Court, had the said witness or witnesses been produced and examined at the trial before the said court, to be read and received as legal evidence at such trial. . . .

[In case the laws of the place in which the Act was committed vary from those of the colony the Court may give effect to them. Nothing herein to alter any law respecting crimes committed out of Her Majesty's dominions.[1]

5. Power to send convicts for execution or imprisonment to a British Colony[1]

6. Power to transport convicts[1]

7. Limitation of actions[1] (as under) 24 Geo. 2 cap. 44[2]]

142 LORD STANLEY TO LIEUT.-GOVERNOR H. W. HILL   16 DECEMBER, 1843.
Sir,

Your detention in this country during the present year, caused by circumstances over which you had no control[3] rendered it necessary for Her Majesty's Government to defer the arrangements which they had proposed to make at an earlier period for resuming to the Crown the Government of

---

[1] Marginal summary of the Act.
[2] 'An Act for the rendering Justices of the Peace more safe in the execution of their office and for indemnifying constables and others acting in obedience to their warrants.'
[3] Hill, who had served in the West African Squadron, was required as a witness in certain slave trade cases which were expected to come before the courts in 1843.

the British forts and settlements on the Gold Coast. . . .

As the forts and settlements on the Gold Coast are dependencies on the Government of Sierra Leone, you will be guided, so far as they may be applicable to the circumstances of your Government, by the Royal Commission and Instructions which are furnished to the Governor of that Colony, and I therefore transmit to you a copy of those Instruments by which you will be appraised of the general powers and functions with which that officer is invested.

On your arrival at Cape Coast Castle, you will cause Her Majesty's Commission appointing you Lieutenant Governor of the forts and settlements to be publicly read and promulgated, and you will take oaths prescribed for the occasion, administering them afterwards to such persons employed in the public service as you may think proper.

You are aware that Mr. Maclean, the officer at present in charge of the forts, has expressed his willingness to accept the office of Judicial Assessor and magistrate. The power of this officer within British territory (so long as no court is established with civil and criminal jurisdiction) must be derived from his commission as a Justice of the Peace, which he already holds from the Governor of Sierra Leone, or from a renewed commission to the same effect from yourself. . . . In the event of a Council being constituted by Her Majesty, it would be right to consider whether the members should not be vested with [similar] powers . . . and authorized to form a court over which Mr. Maclean would preside as chairman. For the present, Mr. Maclean will receive such general assistance as he may require in the exercise of his magisterial functions as well from those who already hold commissions of the Peace from the Governor of Sierra Leone as from others to whom you may think proper to issue such commissions.

As regards any powers to be exercised by Mr. Maclean among tribes not within British territory, as proposed by the Select Committee . . . I need scarcely observe that it must rest with the sovereign power in each territory to authorize or permit the exercise of any jurisdiction within that territory, whether according to British laws or the laws there prevalent. . . . The provisions of the Foreign Jurisdiction Act of last session . . . will, I have no doubt, assist Her Majesty's Government in executing the plan proposed by the Select Committee more fully than can be done by the mere appointment of the Assessor, which, however, has been made with reference to its provisions.

To this act, as affecting the two cases of murder at Winnebah, Mr. Maclean's attention has already been called in a despatch dated the 29th September last. The reply to that despatch may possibly afford sufficient information to enable me to advise Her Majesty as to the propriety of conferring general powers on the Assessor, under it. In any case, I have to request that you will call upon Mr. Maclean for a report with that view, specially adverting to the circumstances which under the first section of the act are required to enable Her Majesty's Government to apply its provisions. . . .

In the meantime, however, I would not be understood as desiring that the exercise of that jurisdiction which has been established by Mr. Maclean in the case of crimes and misdemeanors committed among neighbouring tribes should be abandoned or interrupted. On the contrary, it is my wish that it should be maintained. To take the opposite course would, according to the concurrent testimony of all persons conversant with the habits of the natives, not only be most detrimental to the maintenance of order and civilization at the moment, but render its restoration at a future period very difficult.

The present Council will necessarily cease to exist as a body legally constituted, and I should wish you to take into your earliest consideration, and to report to me whether it would not be advisable that you should have the aid of a Council duly constituted by Her Majesty. . . .

I do not propose to apply to Parliament for a grant of more than four thousand pounds for the maintenance of the forts and settlements for the year 1844, but the grant will be relieved from the charge which it has hitherto borne for the military force employed on the coast. The scale of establishment which Her Majesty's Government have sanctioned is as follows:—

Lieutenant Governor	£800
Table allowance	200
Judicial Assessor and Magistrate	500
Special allowance to Mr. Maclean	120[1]
Secretary to Lieutenant Governor	200
Clerk to Judicial Assessor	100
Chaplain	300
Surgeon	300
Commandant at Accra	100
	2,620

It is proposed that the Judicial Assessor should be charged with the care of the estates of deceased persons, unrepresented, whether testate or intestate, but this duty must be vested in him by an enactment of the local Legislature of Sierra Leone. . . .[2]

With the view of limiting, as far as may be practicable, the future expenditure on account of the forts within the scale at which they have been maintained under the management of the African Committee, no provision is made on the Estimate for an establishment at any of the forts except Cape Coast Castle and British Accra. It will be proper, however, that a merchant or other resident at each of the forts should be furnished with a Commission as Justice of the Peace.

The re-occupation of the abandoned fort at Whydah, as recommended by Mr. Maclean, must depend on the terms of the

[1] This was to prevent Maclean suffering a loss of income from the change in status.

[2] By some oversight this was not done, with serious consequences for Maclean's successor as Judicial Assessor; cf. the papers in H.C.433, 245, 182. Correspondence relating to J. C. Fitzpatrick. A & P (1856) xlii, A & P (1857 ii) xxviii, and (1859 ii) xxii.

treaty which it is proposed to conclude with the king of Dahomey. I stated in my despatch to you of the 25th ultimo, that I had no objection, as a temporary measure, to the arrangement made by Mr. Maclean, of sending a sergeant of the garrison at Cape Coast Castle to reside at Badagry, but I have desired you to report to me your opinion, in regard to the expediency of occupying the fort at that place.

I have only to observe, in conclusion, that it will be your duty to report to me most fully on all matters connected with your Government so soon after your arrival on the coast as you may be able to form a correct opinion of the state of affairs in that quarter. [C.O.96/2]

143 MACLEAN TO STANLEY
CAPE COAST CASTLE, 2 FEBRUARY, 1844.

. . . In obedience to your Lordship's instruction,[1] I have attentively considered the [Foreign Jurisdiction] Act . . . and am clearly of opinion that its provisions are precisely and strictly applicable to such cases as those reported by me to the African Committee, as well as to the civil and criminal jurisprudence of these settlements generally. . . .

The sovereignty of [the Gomoa] district as well as of all those over which I exercise control, was formally ceded to the British Crown either previously to, or during the Ashantee war, and although this sovereignty was said to be renounced by the British Government when the forts were transferred to the merchants in 1828, yet, in point of fact and practically speaking it never was renounced, simply because such renunciation must have proved ruinous to the settlements and been fraught with misery to the natives themselves. My warrants and summonses, therefore, are, and always have been executed in those districts with as much authority and assumption of rights as an English judge's warrant would be in Yorkshire; and I and my brother magis-

[1] Conveyed in Stanley to Maclean, 29 September, 1843, C.O.96/2.

trates have uniformly exercised both civil and criminal jurisdiction over their population. It appears to me, therefore, that whether the British Government shall resume its sovereign rights over these districts or not, the first clause of the Foreign Jurisdiction Act clearly renders it competent to Her Majesty's duly authorized officers and magistrates to exercise both civil and criminal jurisdiction over the inhabitants of them.

But though, under the provisions of this Act, the competency of the Queen's authorized officers to exercise jurisdiction over every part of the Gold Coast territory, which is and has been for a series of years *de facto* under British control, seems to be indisputable: yet it does not appear to me that there are any magistrates or officers at present on the Gold Coast who can be said, strictly speaking, to possess sufficient authority derived from Her Majesty to try and condemn persons accused of capital offences. My own powers as a magistrate, and those of the members of Council, are derived from the Governor of Sierra Leone, and are, strictly speaking, limited to those of a justice of the peace. Your Lordship is aware, from the Report of the late Committee of the House of Commons on the British West African Possessions, of the mode in which, justified by the absolute necessity of the case, we have on several occasions exercised the highest criminal jurisdiction. But this mode, though admirably adapted to the present condition of this country, and though it [has] worked extremely well, and been attended with the best results, yet is, I apprehend, of too irregular a nature to be sanctioned in a colony whose Government derives its authority directly from the Crown. I would therefore respectfully submit to your Lordship whether it would not be expedient that a court competent to exercise the highest criminal jurisdiction should be constituted in this colony.

I have &c.   [C.O.96/4]

144 HILL TO STANLEY

CAPE COAST CASTLE, 6 MARCH, 1844.

Private and confidential.

My Lord,

An opportunity offering for England tonight, I am induced thus hurriedly to acquaint your Lordship, that several of the chiefs from different parts of the country adjacent to Cape Coast, have visited me today in great state to pay their respects on the transfer of the Government.

I have for some days been aware that an idea was believed by the natives of its being the intention of Her Majesty's Government to pronounce freedom to all slaves within the limits over which jurisdiction has been exercised. I need not tell your Lordship that an attempt to carry any such measure would cause a revolution.

The chiefs were delighted on my informing them that it was quite an idle report, and that the export slave trade was all that we prohibited. They expressed satisfaction on my telling them they were not at liberty to ill-use their domestic slaves, and if a person inherited a slave, that person was not at liberty to sell the slave again, but such slave was to be considered a member of the family.

I considered it a good opportunity of establishing an agreement to their being under our jurisdiction, and drew up the document of which the enclosed is a copy, and which the chiefs readily signed. This will, I hope, my Lord, meet with your approbation, and I think it quite sufficient to establish the powers of the Foreign Jurisdiction Act. I beg to mention the chiefs expressed great satisfaction at the appointment of Captain Maclean to preside over the trial of offenders.

I shall take the earliest opportunity of visiting Accra and the other forts, and I have already applied to the senior naval officer for a vessel of war to convey me to the different stations, when I shall endeavour to get the chiefs of those districts to sign a similar agreement. . . .   [C.O.96/4]

145 DECLARATION OF THE FANTE CHIEFS
(THE 'BOND') 6 MARCH, 1844.

1. Whereas power and jurisdiction have been exercised for and on behalf of Her Majesty the Queen of Great Britain and Ireland, within divers countries and places adjacent to Her Majesty's forts and settlements on the Gold Coast, we, the chiefs of countries and places so referred to, adjacent to the said forts and settlements, do hereby acknowledge that power and jurisdiction, and declare that the first objects of law are the protection of individuals and property.

2. Human sacrifices and other barbarous customs, such as panyarring, are abominations and contrary to law.

3. Murders, robberies and other crimes and offences will be tried and inquired of before the Queen's judicial officers and the chiefs of the district, moulding the customs of the country to the general principles of British law.

Done at Cape Coast Castle, before his Excellency the Lieutenant Governor on this 6th day of March, in the year of our Lord, 1844.

[The marks of:]

Cudjoe Chibboe, king of Denkera
Quashie Ottoo, chief of Abrah
Chibboe Coomah, chief of Assin
Gebra, second chief of Assin[1]
Quashie Anka, chief of Donadie[2]
Awoosie, chief of Domonassie
Amonee, chief of Annamaboe
Joe Aggrey, chief of Cape Coast. . . .
[C.O.96/4][3]

146 HILL TO STANLEY
CAPE COAST CASTLE, 2 APRIL, 1844.

My Lord,

In obedience to the instructions conveyed to me in your Lordship's despatch no. 10

[1] Gabiri, chief of Asin Apemanim.
[2] Quashie Anka, a sub-chief of the Dominasi state, formerly in Maclean's service, signed his name.
[3] For later signatories cf. Appendix C.

of the 16th of December, and no. 3 of the 30th of September last, apprizing me of the importance of maintaining friendly relations with the king of Ashantee, and authorizing me to send messengers to the king as soon as possible after my arrival here, and to forward him the presents which had been supplied me for that purpose: I have the honour to inform your Lordship that I despatched messengers to Coomassie with the presents for the king on the 28th of February, and beg to transmit a copy of my letter to the king on that occasion, with his reply; from which your Lordship will observe that there is no appearance of an interruption to the friendly communications that at present exist with that country.

On my arrival here, I heard some disquietude existed in Ashantee on account of the change of Government of these forts, and that the king was assembling his captains for council, but I now hope all idea of dispute has subsided. The king's messenger brought me a young tiger and delivered a message from the king respecting the Assin people offering some interruption to the Ashantees when passing through the country the Assins are residing in — which is mentioned in the king's letter also — but did not make any direct complaint.

These Assins were formerly Ashantees, and left that country for Fantee, where they have resided under their own chiefs for several years, in alliance with the other Fantee chiefs; and were contracting parties to the articles of peace signed with Ashantee on the 7th of April 1831.

The king of Ashantee has long wished to induce the Assins to return to his dominions, but they were among the first chiefs to come here on my arrival and to acknowledge the Queen's power and jurisdiction over them; and showed not the slightest desire to return to Ashantee.

I am under the impression the king of Ashantee had contemplated making the Assins a subject of contention, and I think he would lose no opportunity of attempting to use compulsion over them: but the river Prah which separates the two countries is too good a boundary to be passed without committing a direct violation of the agreement of peace.

I have &c.   [C.O.96/4]

147 HILL TO STANLEY

CAPE COAST CASTLE, 5 AUGUST, 1844.

. . . It is most necessary [that] the administration of justice should be uniform and advancements or improvements timely and cautiously introduced, and that records should be punctually kept and periodically transmitted of all cases heard and judgments given.

It is impossible to expect that merchants who happen to be carrying on their business at the different settlements, will sacrifice their time and take an interest in the performance of duties of this nature under the Crown without remuneration: but even with remuneration, merchants are not likely to perform the duty [as well] as Government officers.

The appointment of one Judicial Assessor is merely provision for Cape Coast. The other stations are left to the chance of a merchant finding it convenient to attend a case or not. I beg strongly to submit to your Lordship the necessity of stipendiary officers or assistant assessors being appointed, quite separated from all mercantile business. These officers might be the civil commandants of the forts and collect what dues or moneys that may become payable to the Crown at their stations.

Four of these officers and a clerk for each, I think are required for Cape Coast, Accra, Anamaboe and Dixcove, and if a fifth were introduced for Winnebah and Tantum, it would be of great service. The Chief Judicial Assessor or Chief Justice, I would recommend to have the management and arrangement of the whole course of judicial proceedings, to sit as judge on all criminal trials and higher civil cases, and with the governor to constantly visit each

station. It is quite astonishing the number of cases that are daily brought forward to be heard, and it is very essential the natives should have a speedy settlement of their disputes. . . .

I hope my Lord, you will pardon me for offering an opinion; and with all deference to the decision of the Committee of the House of Commons, I am firmly impressed with the belief that it would be more advantageous to the Government, and to these settlements also, that the Government establishment should be withdrawn, and that the settlements should recede under the control of a Committee of Merchants, in all things subject to the approval of the Crown.

Such a measure would be of much less expense than a Government establishment under the Crown. For instance, the Company of the 1st West India Regiment now here are at a cost of £5,000 per annum; the Parliamentary Grant for the forts is £4000 a year, and quite inadequate to maintain a Government, making together the sum of £9,000 a year.

I would humbly suggest a Committee of Merchants should name for the approval of the Government, a President of the Council, a Judicial Assessor, and a secretary, these officers ex-officio to be in the Council, and with one resident merchant form the Council and be empowered to make their own local laws, subject of course to the Home authorities. The officers I have named, I think, should be most decidedly prohibited from being concerned in trade, either directly or indirectly, or acting as agent or adviser. . . .

A government conducted by a Committee of Merchants would unite the co-operation of the resident traders and give them some interest in the advancement of the Government views; and in the performance of their judicial duties, the constant superintendence of the Assessor, together with the check of keeping records and making returns, they would adopt a uniform system of acting. . . .   [C.O.96/4]

148 ORDER IN COUNCIL APPOINTING CAPE COAST CASTLE a place for the trial of offenders brought there under 6 & 7 Vict. cap. 94.

At the Court of Windsor, the 3rd day of September 1844.

Present:

The Queen's most Excellent Majesty in Council . . .

[Cites 6 Vict. cap. 13 and 6 & 7 Vict. cap. 94]

And whereas Her Majesty hath power and jurisdiction within divers countries and places adjacent to Her Majesty's forts and settlements on the Gold Coast in Africa; Her Majesty is pleased, by and with the advice of Her Privy Council to order, and it is hereby ordered, that all judges, magistrates, assessors and other officers duly appointed to exercise the said power and jurisdiction in the name and on behalf of Her Majesty, within the countries and places aforesaid, shall in the exercise thereof observe, until further order, such of the local customs of the said countries and places as may be compatible with the principles of the law of England, and in default of such customs shall proceed in all things as nearly as may be according to the said law of England; and in further pursuance of the powers by the said Acts of Parliament vested in Her Majesty, Her Majesty is pleased, by and with the advice of Her Privy Council, to appoint the settlement of Cape Coast Castle and the colony of Sierra Leone as British colonies to which it shall be lawful for any person having authority derived from Her Majesty in that behalf, by warrant under his hand and seal, to cause any person charged with the commission of any crime or offence, the cognizance whereof may at any time appertain to any judge, magistrate or other officer of Her Majesty within the countries and places aforesaid, to be sent for trial, or in order that sentences passed within such countries and places as aforesaid may be carried into effect within such colonies.

And the Right honourable Lord Stanley, one of Her Majesty's Principal Secretaries of State, is to give the necessary directions herein accordingly.

[Signed] C. C. Greville.

[H.C.383, A & P (1854–5) xxxvii]

149 STANLEY TO HILL

22 NOVEMBER, 1844.

. . . I have to acquaint you that upon the Report of the Law Officers of the Crown, Her Majesty has been pleased to pass an Order in Council . . . under the Acts 6 and 7 Vict. cap. 94, appointing Her Majesty's settlement of Cape Coast Castle a place to which persons coming within the operation of . . . those Acts may be sent for trial and punishment.

The order, you will perceive, provides for two distinct classes of cases. The one, that of persons whom it may be deemed expedient to send from the neighbouring countries to be tried within Her Majesty's settlements. The other, that of persons who may have been tried in the neighbouring countries but whom it is considered advisable to send into Her Majesty's settlements for the purpose of undergoing their sentence.

As regards the first class of cases, you will, of course, bear in mind that in any trial which takes place, the provisions of the 6th and 7th Victoria cap. 94, applicable to that event, must be strictly observed and also that as the jurisdiction for the trial of offenders sent under the provisions of the Act is given to the Supreme Court of the Colony only to which they are sent, that in the present state of the Judicial Institutions on the Gold Coast, such offenders would require to be forwarded thence to Sierra Leone for trial.

For practical purposes, therefore as yet at all events, this power is not likely to be of any general utility. The powers, however, given under the second head will, I apprehend, greatly facilitate the working of the system which has grown up in our relations with the tribes surrounding the forts under your Government.

It being necessary to provide for the appointment of persons to be specially empowered to exercise the powers conferred by the different sections of the 6th and 7th Victoria c. 94, I send you additional instruction under the Sign Manual, giving you the requisite authority both to act yourself, and to nominate others for the same purpose, and I have, as you will perceive, taken the opportunity of providing for Mr. Maclean's absence or inability to discharge the duties of Assessor to the sovereigns and chiefs of the neighbouring tribes by making a fresh appointment to that office, including yourself and others with him as such assessors, having power to act either jointly or severally. . . .

You will bear in mind that the power of the Assessor in his judicial capacity is not derived from . . . the Acts of Parliament above referred to, or from the Order in Council, and further, that it cannot be exercised by him as such within Her Majesty's dominions. It must be founded on the assent and concurrence of the sovereign power of the state within which it is exercised, either express, as in the case of the Treaty transmitted by you in your Private and Confidential Despatch of the 6th of March last, or implied from long usage, as in the case of the long and general acquiescence which can be shown in many districts, in the authority hitherto exercised by Mr. Maclean.

You will understand that the system upon which Mr. Maclean has proceeded in the exercise of judicial powers over the natives is to be taken as the guide for the exercise of the powers of the Assessor for the future. It consists, in fact, in combining with an impartial investigation of the cases brought before him, a mitigation of the severity of the sentences which in most such cases would be awarded by the native judges in the event of conviction. I need not, therefore, instruct you to caution the Assessor of the necessity for a lenient exercise of the discretion entrusted to him, but in the event of his deeming capital punishment in any case inevitable, you will instruct him that the execution must be carried into effect by the native authorities, and take place in the country in which the offender is tried.

Having thus, as far as possible, brought the very peculiar case of the jurisdiction exercised among the tribes in the neighbourhoods of the forts on the Gold Coast within the operation of the Acts of Parliament referred to in the commencement of this despatch, it only remains for me further to observe that I am not to be understood as affirming that the exercise of that jurisdiction is not capable of being justified and maintained independently of any such express sanction of the Legislature. . . . I must guard myself against being supposed, because I endeavour to give it the aid of the forms I have adverted to, to assume that the general principles of the law of England are not comprehensive enough to allow for the necessities which such a state of circumstances as exists in the Gold Coast unavoidably creates, and to justify those measures by which such necessities when created can alone be adequately provided for.

[C.O. 96/4: H.C.412, A & P (1865)v]

150 STANLEY TO HILL

30 DECEMBER, 1844.

. . . You recommend that with a view of providing for the due administration of justice in the several forts and settlements, a separate assessor should be appointed at each fort with a clerk attached to each of these functionaries. This arrangement would cause a considerable increase of expense, which I could not sanction without further proof than I now possess of the necessity of such appointments. My opinion is that occasional visits by the Chief Assessors to all the forts would suffice for attaining the ends of justice.

With respect to your suggestion that the management of the forts should be re-transferred to a committee of merchants at a charge of double the amount of that which was assigned to the last committee for that purpose, I need only observe that such a step would not be justifiable so soon after the adoption of the arrangements recommended by a committee of the House of Commons, and before sufficient time has elapsed to enable Her Majesty's Government to form an opinion of the advantages likely to result from the new system of government. [C.O.96/4]

151 MINUTE BY JAMES STEPHEN[1]
COLONIAL OFFICE, 28 JANUARY, 1846.

I cannot but think that it was an error to countenance the establishment of this singular jurisdiction, and the transmission to this office of these reports of what is done in exercise of it. An English officer, in an adjacent, barbarous country (of which the Queen is not the sovereign) presides in courts held by the natives, and administers to them a kind of law made up of native customs and of English forms and maxims. I think it likely enough that he does much good. But I never could find out by what law he does it. If the proceedings were allowed to pass silently, one might rejoice that the good was done, and waive any inquiry how far it was lawfully done. But these singular trials are all reported to the Head of this Office, and by him those reports are silently laid aside. This is, I believe, the only thing that can be done with them. Still, the mere receipt of such reports fastens on the Head of this Department a responsibility of which he cannot acquit himself by mere silence and inaction. I cannot but doubt whether it would not be the best course to say frankly . . . that it will, hereafter, be useless to report them unless some new and extraordinary question should arise which it might appear to the

[1] On Acting-Governor James Lilley's despatch of 6 October, 1845, transmitting reports of cases heard before the Judicial Assessor's Court.

Governor to demand the interference of Her Majesty's Government. [C.O.96/7]

152 MINUTE BY D. SMITH
COLONIAL OFFICE, 14 MAY, 1846.

It seems to me that there is no evidence to warrant the conclusion that the king of Dahomey is at all disposed to lend his assistance in putting down slave trade, but on the contrary that there is every reason for supposing that he is not inclined to surrender the practical advantages which he derives from his present pursuits. I can scarcely, therefore, conceive the utility of making any proposition to him which should not be founded upon the offer of solid and tangible benefits in substitution for the profits which he might be required to renounce.

With regard to the re-occupation of Whydah, I can perceive no Colonial interest in the question. It is reasonable to suppose that the establishment and display there of British authority will have the effect of raising some additional trade, but not probably to an extent that would compensate for the expenditure to be incurred for rebuilding the fort and supporting it. I think it a great mistake to suppose that a petty trade of such a description is calculated to put down the traffic in slaves. Why is the king of Dahomey anxious for the re-occupation of Whydah? Because he wants more trade, or more abundant supplies of bafts, tobacco, muskets and gunpowder. From the slave dealers he can only obtain dollars. . . .[1] [C.O.96/8]

[1] The truth of Smith's observations was borne out by twenty years of futile missions to the court of Dahomey. King Gezo actually signed a treaty abolishing the slave trade, in 1852, but it never came into force.

12 Earl Grey[1] and Governor Winniett, 1846–1849

WHEN the Whigs assumed office in July 1846, many questions of Gold Coast administration remained to be settled by the new Secretary of State, the 3rd Earl Grey. Stephen, in his last year at the Colonial Office, was still a convinced opponent of jurisdiction over the tribes (154). The merchants connected with the coast, who had evidently worked on Governor Hill earlier (147), urged Grey to set up a council in which they would have a majority (156–7). In Commander Winniett, the settlements had an energetic governor who pursued a vigorous 'foreign policy'. He visited Dahomey in March 1847, urged Grey to buy out the Danes (158), led an expedition against Apollonia (160), and, in October 1848, visited the Asantehene in Kumasi (163) — the first and last British Governor to do so before 1896.

Grey was at first non-committal. If he would not abandon the 'Protectorate' (155), he would not extend it (159), and strongly disapproved of any move that appeared to add to British responsibilities (161). Winniett's reports in 1847 and 1848 on the commercial and fiscal prospects of the settlements, and still more on the progress of civilisation among the African population, were so favourable that Grey was won over to considering how to extend the good work (164). It was a question of money. Winniett thought the Dutch would co-operate in a joint scheme of customs duties. Grey himself favoured direct taxation, and discussed with Winniett how best to introduce it (167–8).

[1] Henry George Grey, Viscount Howick, later 3rd Earl Grey (1802–94): son of Earl Grey of the Reform Bill; entered Parliament as Whig member for Winchelsea, 1826; Under-Secretary for the Colonies, 1830–3; Secretary at War, 1835–9; with Lord John Russell was chiefly responsible for forcing Glenelg to resign in 1839; Earl, 1845; Secretary for War and the Colonies, 1846–52; published *The Colonial Policy of Lord John Russell's Administration* in 1853.

153 G. MACLEAN TO B. CRUICKSHANK
CAPE COAST, 19 DECEMBER, 1846.

. . . About a week ago we were alarmed by information from the interior stating that the King of Ashantee had stopped all the paths, made prisoners of all Fantees etc then in Ashantee, and had attacked and destroyed a village situated on our side of the frontier, and further, that our allies in the interior of Fantee, Assin, Akim, etc., had, in retaliation, seized and detained all the Ashantee traders passing through their respective districts. This intelligence has since proved to be substantially correct; and the present state of affairs is precisely one of those crises which I have so often predicted would occur, and with which the Government as now constituted, is utterly powerless and unable to deal. This day three years, I would, with the power and

influence which I then wielded, have set matters right again in ten days' time. As things stand now, the result may be a new Ashantee war. The Governor being in his 'seasoning' and unable to attend to business, I have taken such steps as will, I trust, re-open the paths and restore confidence: but I cannot now, as I once could have done, guarantee the success of my exertions — although I hope the best. This interruption to trade will, I fear, interfere seriously with the amount of the remittances which would otherwise have gone home. . . [C.O.96/12]

154 MINUTE BY JAMES STEPHEN
COLONIAL OFFICE, 15 FEBRUARY, 1847.[1]

We have, as you know, at the Gold Coast [no] sovereignty properly so called beyond

[1] Commenting on Winniett to Grey (No. 74) of 23 November, 1846.

the precincts of the several forts we occupy there. But Mr. Maclean has been appointed to the office of Judicial Assessor, by which, as far as I can understand, is meant that he is to administer justice according to no fixed law, but pretty much at his discretion, among all the savage tribes in the neighbourhood. His sentences, when they are reported, are invariably such as no principle of English law could sustain. They rest on the apology that he must do the best he can to make justice respected. The resource of receiving, in silence, reports of all his anomalous proceedings, has always been resorted to, as the only means of escape from the dilemma of sanctioning what was clearly illegal, or of condemning what was clearly unavoidable. But in the present case, Mr. Maclean, finding that the natives would not obey his orders (which they were under no obligation that I know of to obey), obtains a party of 25 soldiers and deliberately records his intention to destroy the town[1] and plantations of the disobedient chief, if he should persist in refusing to surrender. He also reports having levied a fine on the contumacious district, which he says they had hard work to get together.

So long as Mr. Maclean holds a commission to administer justice, in his own way, among these barbarous people, it would be idle to be very strict with him as to the modes in which he sets himself to execute such a task. Burning towns, levying fines on districts, and marching soldiers up and down the country, are, I suppose, the only legal process of the slightest avail in such a place and amongst such a people. But why we should think it necessary to interfere at all in their affairs, as administrators of justice, is the question, to afford an answer to which I have long sought in vain. It may be our interest to trade with them, and our duty to convert them, if possible, to Christianity, and to repress and punish their slave trading in opposition to their treaties with us. We may be bound also to repel and, if possible, to

[1] Tantum.

anticipate any attacks which they may meditate on our own settlements. But why we should take upon ourselves to be judges over them, I know not. Why we should not assume that office is sufficiently evident. Every exercise of it brings us more and more into danger of a war, than which none could be more utterly absurd, or, in proportion to its extent, more costly. I believe it was thought that Great Britain was bound to take care that barbarous crimes should be punished, and barbarous punishments prevented, in the immediate vicinity of our own settlements. It is an obligation of which I do not perceive the basis, and a policy of which I could never discover the wisdom. However, if it is still to be maintained, the reported proceedings of Mr. Maclean must, I suppose, be approved.　　　　　　[C.O.96/9]

155 MINUTE BY EARL GREY
16 FEBRUARY, 1847.

I understand the principle upon which we have hitherto acted to be that, by the exercise of the jurisdiction we have assumed, we prevent the petty disputes, which arise among the natives, from being settled in the only way they could be settled, in the absence of some impartial authority, i.e. by arms. It is said that if we were to abstain from exercising this power, the whole country would be given up to anarchy and the most grievous oppression practised; that, on the other hand, by the system which has been adopted, a great deal of security for life and property has been established in the neighbourhood of our forts, and that civilization is thus beginning to take root in this region, whence it may become widely diffused in Africa. This view of the subject was, I believe, adopted by the Committee of the House of Commons which sat upon this subject 4 or 5 years ago. It certainly is that of the merchants who trade to the coast, and, without more information than I at present possess, I am not prepared to reject it. The subject is one, however, into which I should wish hereafter to look more closely. . . .

[C.O.96/9]

156 J. Bannerman, B. Cruickshank and J. Clouston to M. Forster, M.P.[1]

London, 12 February, 1847.

. . . Our proposition simply is:—

That a Council of Government, presided over by the Lieutenant Governor, and composed of six members, be established at Cape Coast.

That this Council consist of the Lieutenant-Governor, the Judicial Assessor and four merchants residing within the Settlements.

That the qualifications required in a member be that he holds a Commission of the Peace and that he has resided three years in the country.

That the members be appointed by election.

That the electors be composed of the Judicial Assessor, the Colonial Secretary and the merchants residing at the different settlements; that the Lieutenant-Governor have the casting vote; and that he and the Judicial Assessor decide upon the right of the claimants to vote.

That the Council meet on a fixed day once a month, and that a requisition to the Lieutenant-Governor, signed by four members, shall at any time be sufficient for calling an extra-ordinary meeting.

That an unanimous negative on the part of the Council to any of the Governor's measures shall have the effect of suspending such measures, until the sanction of Her Majesty's Government has been obtained for them.

That this Council be empowered to make Regulations for their own guidance and for the general government of the Colony, and that such Regulations shall be binding until sanctioned or disapproved of by Her Majesty's Government. . . .   [C.O.96/12]

[1] Enclosure in No. 157 below.

157 M. Forster to Earl Grey

London, 22 March, 1847.

. . . The remarkable success of the Government of the Gold Coast under the merchants, for the fourteen years they conducted it, upon a principle which enabled them not only to repair the evils which had arisen from the six years of disastrous government by the Colonial Office, but to raise the country to a state of prosperity unexampled in its history, and unexampled in any other part of the coast, is a sufficient proof . . . of the soundness of the scheme proposed by Messrs Bannerman, Cruickshank and Clouston,[1] which, as respects the election of the Council, is virtually the same that obtained under the system of self-government to which I allude.

Indications have already been given that the present machinery of government on the Gold Coast, which has superseded that system, is too cumbrous for efficiency. It appears to involve a formula of reference and reports, utterly unsuited to the exigencies of the country, where action is required. Promptitude and decision are above all things necessary to establish and maintain our moral influence with the natives, and these attributes are unfortunately alien to the spirit of the form of government now established in that quarter. . . .

A Governor inexperienced in his office and unaided by the advice of a council, will naturally be slow to undertake duties which entail responsibility. Associated with a council composed of the officers of Government, as little conversant as himself with the native character, he would be released from responsibility without gaining assistance; while, aided by a council selected as has been proposed, he would at once have the safest advice and the readiest and most efficient co-operation. . . .   [C.O.96/12]

158 Commander W. Winniett to Earl Grey

Cape Coast Castle, 31 December, 1847.

[Governor Carstenson reports that the Danes want to sell their Gold Coast

[1] No. 156 above.

Settlements. It is important that Britain should buy them, to keep out the French and to enable a closer watch to be kept on the export of slaves east of the Volta.] . . .

These settlements contain six fortifications at different points as follows:

1. Christiansborg Castle at Danish Accra, which building is about two-thirds the size of Cape Coast Castle. It is in a good state of repair, and many of the guns on the battlements are new, having been recently sent out from Europe, and some of them are brass.

2. The redoubt, a small building, mounting 10 or 12 guns, situated on the western side of the town towards English and Dutch Accra. This is also in a good state of repair.

3. Tacia Fort — situated about eight miles below Danish Accra. It is not in a good state of repair, but part of it is tenable.

4. Ningo Fort — situated about thirty-five miles below Danish Accra and six miles below Prampram. This fort is in ruins and quite untenable.

5. Quittah Fort — situated about eighty-five miles from Danish Accra. It has recently undergone partial repair and is therefore tenable.

6. Addah Fort — situated on the banks of the Volta, about eight miles from its mouth and consequently about seventy miles from Danish Accra. This fortification is, I understand, in a dilapidated state, though tenable.

The average size of all these forts, with the exception of Christiansborg Castle and the Redoubt, is about that of our fort at Dixcove.

In addition to these buildings, there are in Danish Accra four of the largest and best water-tanks in the Country, and at Fredericksborg, about half a mile inland from Danish Accra, on a rising ground, and consequently in a very healthy situation, two substantial houses for officers' quarters; and a large dwelling-house and a coffee plantation, about fifteen miles into the interior behind Danish Accra, to which the Danish local Government has opened easy communication by a good road. All the buildings — forts, houses etc, consist of stone, and are now worth, in their present state, at the lowest just valuation, £30,000.

The Danes also claim fealty from the various tribes in the interior, bordering on the line of coast under their flag, namely, the Aquapims, Akims, Croboes, Aquamboes,[1] and Crepees, occupying territory extending on an average one hundred miles inland, and containing perhaps from 75,000 to 100,000 inhabitants: but that claim has never, I believe, been acknowledged by the British Government, and it seems that some of these tribes, if not all, have a decided preference for British jurisdiction. There can be no doubt that the Danish settlements on the Gold Coast could revert to the British Crown, not merely without opposition on the part of the native tribes . . . concerned, but with their ready concurrence and entire satisfaction. . . .   [C.O.96/11]

159 Grey to Winniett
LONDON, 6 MARCH, 1848.
Sir,

I have received your despatch of the 31st of December last . . . submitting for my consideration the expediency of effecting a purchase from the Danish Government of their Settlements on the Gold Coast and in the Bight of Benin, which, in the present state of the forts and buildings, you estimate on the lowest just valuation at £30,000.

Her Majesty's Government do not consider the attainment of the objects which you contemplate by this purchase to be commensurate with the outlay of so large a sum, and they are not prepared, therefore, to entertain the proposal.   [C.O.96/13]

160 Winniett to Grey
CAPE COAST CASTLE, 22 MARCH, 1848.
[Announces his decision to lead an expedition against the chief of Apollonia.]
. . . The accompanying documents from Mr. F. Swanzy, the Civil Commandant of

_____
[1] Akwamus.

Dixcove, from Mr. Cruickshank, the present acting Judicial Assessor, and from his Excellency Governor Van der Eb of Elmina . . . will show that the insubordination and tyranny, insolence and intrigue of this chieftain, have now exceeded all bounds; and that [not] to direct *at once* against him, for the purpose of crushing rebellion and establishing good order, the energies of the local government there, with whatever aid I can secure from Her Majesty's squadron, would be to temporize with a case pregnant with incalculable mischief to the well-being of the British settlements here; and to compromise British honour in the eyes of the natives of the country, and the French and Netherlands Governments, whose subjects have suffered from these outrages.

The documents to which I have referred, furnish against the Apollonia chieftain, the following well-substantiated charges:

1. His disregard for, and his contempt of the British Government, as shown most strongly in his contemptuous detention (if nothing worse) of messengers sent to him on the most friendly terms; and his insolent answer to the inquiry made respecting the fate of those messengers.

2. His profanation of the British flag. . . .

3. His uniformly bad treatment of the masters of British vessels.

4. The murder of the French commandant of Assinie and his boat crew.

5. His stopping of the path and waylaying and murdering Wassaw people while on their way to Cape Coast.

6. His piratical attack upon the Dutch canoes at Axim, and capture of twelve Dutch subjects.

This, my Lord, is indeed a grievous list of wrongs, to say nothing of the seventh and last charge furnished, namely *intrigues with Ashantee*, which, while it is, from its very nature, less clearly provable than the others, is, if true, the most important of all as it regards its bearing on the welfare of the British settlements on this coast. . . .

Finding that I have with me the unanimous voice of all classes and orders of the people of the Colony, both European and native . . . I have determined to proceed *at once* with a force of *four thousand, five hundred men*, against this monster of Apollonia. Her Majesty's Brigantine 'Dolphin' accompanies me, and I have chartered the brig 'Governor Maclean' — a vessel belonging to Messrs. Forster and Smith of London — as a transport. . . . It may be reasonably hoped that the cash which I am now compelled to draw on Her Majesty's Treasury, for the purpose of providing subsistence for the army, and to meet other unavoidable expenses connected with this important movement, will be eventually paid back by the king of Apollonia. . . .[1]   [CO.96/13]

161 GREY TO WINNIETT

LONDON, 3 JULY, 1848.

Sir,

I have received your Dispatch, No. 12 of the 22nd March, reporting that you were preparing a hostile expedition against the king of Apollonia.

From a correspondence which has been forwarded to this Office by the Lords Commissioners of the Admiralty, I find that you had applied for a naval force to co-operate with you in this expedition, and that Commodore Sir Charles Hotham had declined to afford you that assistance. . . . It was clearly your duty to have reported this circumstance to me, especially as you had decided upon acting against the advice of an officer of such high character, and that the proposed hostile operations should be postponed until they should have received the express sanction of Her Majesty's Government.

Nothing but a case of very great necessity would have warranted you in taking this course, but in the present instance there was no such urgency. . . . [A year had elapsed since the insult to the messengers, who should not have been sent in the first place.]

[1] The king was taken prisoner, tried and found guilty on all charges, and imprisoned for life in Cape Coast Castle, where he died in 1851.

I perceive by your despatch that you mention the territory of Apollonia as being part of your Government and within British jurisdiction, and you describe the chief as being guilty of insubordination. The British claim to the territory of Apollonia is one which, however valid, does not appear for several years to have been in any manner practically asserted, and this being the case, I regard the step you have taken, in bringing it forward, as highly injudicious, since it is not our policy to extend our territories or our responsibility on the coast of Africa.   On the contrary, it is expedient that as Lieutenant-Governor of the settlements on the Gold Coast, you should avoid, as regards these barbarous chiefs so far from Cape Coast Castle, entering into relations with them which are likely to lead to our receiving insults it might be difficult to pass over. . . .

I cannot consider that any of the other charges against the chief are of a nature to justify our interference. If you suppose, as you seem to do, that the British Government is to undertake the general maintenance of order amongst the barbarous inhabitants of the west coast of Africa, you have fallen into a great and dangerous error, and it is this impression apparently which has led you to adopt measures against the king of Apollonia of which I entirely disapprove. . . .   [C.O.96/13]

162 MINUTE BY EARL GREY
COLONIAL OFFICE, JULY 1848.

[The fact that the Apollonian expedition was approved of by the merchants, among them Forster, was no recommendation of it.]

Mr. Forster, like all other merchants, has no objection to urging the Government to undertake warlike operations whenever it is fancied their own interests can be promoted by doing so, but a great objection, as a member of the House of Commons, to provide the means of meeting the expense such a system occasions. Such advice in favour of the expedition I consider of very little value.

163 GOVERNOR WINNIET AT KUMASI
OCTOBER 1848.

October 24 . . . After briefly adverting to the kindly feelings of Her Majesty's Government towards [the Ashantehene], I embraced the favourable opportunity offered for speaking to him on the subject of human sacrifices. I told him of the anxious desire on the part of Her Majesty that these sanguinary rites should be abolished, and begged his serious attention to a question so important to the cause of humanity.

In answer to these remarks, he inquired whether I had seen any instances of human sacrifice taking place since I had entered his dominion. I certainly had not seen or heard of any, and therefore expressed myself to that effect; and he then observed, that although human sacrifices were the custom of his forefathers, he was reducing their number and extent in his kingdom, and that the wishes of Her Majesty should not be forgotten.

He then adverted to the refugee Assins, who took shelter under the British flag in 1826, and observed that as permanent peace was now established and confirmed by my coming to pay him so friendly a visit, he hoped I would allow some of the Assins to come up to Kumasi and visit him, and that, should any of them wish to return and settle under his government, I would consent to their doing so.

Matters relative to the Wesleyan mission in Kumasi were then referred to, and I was much gratified to find how completely the mission has secured his confidence and esteem. . . .

[From Governor Winniett's journal. H.C.399, A & P (1849) xxxiv]

164 GREY TO WINNIETT
LONDON, 20 JANUARY, 1849.
Sir,

Various circumstances have, till lately, rendered it impossible for me to give the attention I could have wished to the subjects adverted to in your despatch No. 48

of the 27th of May, 1847,[1] but I have now been able to consider these questions in connection with your very interesting and valuable report on the present state and prospects of the Colony, which accompanied the Blue Book for 1847[2] and which reached me in the spring of last year. A careful consideration of these despatches and of such information as I have been able to obtain from other sources, has led me to the conclusion that the British settlements on the Gold Coast are capable of being rendered conducive, in a far greater degree than they have yet been, to the extension of British commerce and to the improvement and civilization of the barbarous inhabitants of this portion of Africa.

With this view, I am of opinion that the formation of a local military corps, on the plan you have recommended, would be attended with great advantage, more especially if combined, as I conceive that it might be, with measures for increasing the number of posts where a military force is maintained, and for improving the means of communication between them. Experience has proved that military discipline is a powerful engine for introducing, amongst barbarous tribes, the habits of civilization, while, by extending security over a wider district, and by the improvement of the means of communication, additional facilities would be afforded to commerce, which would tend still more directly to the improvement of the population. But measures of this kind cannot be adopted without occasioning an expense which ought not, in the judgement of Her Majesty's Government, to be charged upon the revenue of this country, and which would be justifiable only if defrayed by the colony. Nor does it appear to be impracticable to draw from the colony the resources required for its own improvement, though it would be almost a necessary preliminary to any steps to be adopted for

that purpose, that British jurisdiction should be more clearly established and more regularly exercised over the territory adjoining our forts, in order that the inhabitants of the district, who have the advantage of British protection, may be subjected to the corresponding obligation of contributing to the expense of the establishment maintained for their benefit, by taxation.

It appears from the report already quoted that the population of these districts which acknowledge and are amenable to the jurisdiction of this Government is not less than 275,000. And the account of their condition and character appears to show that they raise or traffic in the valuable products of the country to a great extent, and consume a very considerable quantity of British manufactures. These people, as I understand, have been brought gradually under British jurisdiction, by the operation of treaties to which their chiefs have successively given their assent; and all that is needed appears to be to convert this qualified supremacy into complete dominion.

If the necessary steps for the purpose could be taken, I have little doubt, judging from the account which you have given of the capabilities of the Gold Coast, the numbers and circumstances of its inhabitants, and the ease with which they are able to maintain themselves, that additional revenue might be raised, sufficient to cover the expense of the proposed corps and also of the other measures which might, by degrees, be adopted for the extension of the blessings of civilization.

In the stage of society in which the tribes of our neighbourhood are at present placed, there are, in my opinion, strong reasons for supposing that the best method of raising revenue is by direct taxation. On this point, I have to refer you to a despatch which I have recently addressed to Lord Torrington, the present Governor of Ceylon, and of which an extract accompanies this despatch.[1]

---

[1] Approving suggestions for the appointment of civil Commandants at Dixcove, Anomabu and Accra; a properly qualified agent at Kumasi, and the raising of a local military force. In C.O.96/11.
[2] Cf. A & P (1847) xxxvii.

[1] Cf. *The Colonial Policy of Lord John Russell's Administration*, i, 81–3.

H

A moderate house tax, commutable by those who are unable to pay in money, for labour on roads or public works, would probably be the best adapted for the purpose. Such a tax might equitably be imposed upon those who seek the protection of the British Government, in return for the security that they obtain, and it would afford a sufficient revenue to enable the Government, besides maintaining a local military force, to adopt various other measures calculated to promote the progress of civilization, and especially to undertake the construction of roads and the extension and improvement of schools, in which industrial might be combined with intellectual education.

But as no increase of establishment can take place unless the expense of it is thus defrayed by the Colony, the first step must be a clear definition of its limits, and the complete establishment, within those limits, of British authority, in the manner above suggested. What local reasons there may be, for or against that extension, in particular directions, I am, of course, unable to judge. But, regarding the subject in a general point of view, I am aware of no objection to comprehending the whole of the large population, now partially owning British jurisdiction, completely under the authority of the Colonial Government.

I feel great confidence in entrusting this important subject to your hands, and shall be glad to receive from you, as early as you can make it, a report of the practicability of obtaining from its chiefs and inhabitants, a cession of the territory in question to Her Majesty. The establishment of a separate legislature for the settlements on the Gold Coast would, probably, be the necessary consequence of such an extension of the rights of sovereignty.   [C.O.96/11]

165 I. C. FITZPATRICK[1] TO EARL GREY CAPE COAST CASTLE, 25 FEBRUARY, 1849. My Lord,

I have the honour to enclose your Lordship a copy of a letter which I have

_____
[1] Judicial Assessor 1848–53.

addressed to the king of Ashantee this day. That your Lordship may understand the nature of the king's object, I beg leave to mention a few facts connected with it.

In the year 1829, certain chiefs of Ashantee left their country and joined the Fantees and English, then at war with the king of Ashantee. In 1830 peace was made, and in the treaty then entered into, the independence of those chiefs, who had settled at a place called Assin, on the Fantee side of the Ashantee border, was guaranteed, and they were declared under British protection. Since then they have occupied this Assin territory, and, being warlike and powerful chiefs . . . as well as at enmity towards the king of Ashantee, they act as a formidable barrier to this barbarous king or his succession, if either should ever wish to renew their predatory incursions into the Fantee country. The king of Ashantee has from time to time made unavailing efforts to induce these chiefs to return, or in some way to get them into his power. He applied to Lieut. Gov. Hill when administering the Gold Coast to 'take his hands off them'; that is, cease to afford them British protection, in order that he might punish them. I believe Lieut. Gov. Hill replied that he would consider any interference with these Assin chiefs on the part of the king, as a declaration of war. This put an end to the matter then; but on the occasion of the late visit of Lieut. Gov. Winniett to Kumassi, the subject was renewed, as your Lordship will perceive on reference to the journal transmitted by His Excellency.

I do not know the nature of His Excellency's reply, but I believe he promised to speak to the Assin chiefs on the subject, as I find in the letter-book a letter written to his Majesty after Lieut. Gov. Winniett's return from Kumassi, of which I have the honour to enclose a copy. Since Lieut. Gov. Winniett left the coast, I received a communication from the King of Ashantee renewing the subject, and I was waited on at the same time by the Wesleyan missionary resident at Kumassi, and by the Revd. Mr. Freeman, who severally informed me that the king was cherishing the hope that he might possibly get these people into his power, and that they (the chiefs) were very much alarmed and discontented at hearing that the question was entertained at all. Under these circumstances, I wrote the letter at first referred to, and I humbly trust it may meet with your Lordship's approbation. My object was in a firm, and at the same time, inoffensive manner, to set the question at rest, and to put an end to hopes which, if indulged in, would ultimately result in subjecting the English authority on the coast to insult, or involve it in a contest with a barbarous and inhuman chief, in which much blood and treasure would be wasted, and from which no honour or advantage could possibly be gained.

I have &c.   [C.O.96/16]

166 M. FORSTER TO B. HAWES[1]

LONDON, 30 APRIL, 1849.

Private.

Sir,

You are aware that Denmark has been for some time anxious to divest herself of her possessions on the Gold Coast; and no wonder, seeing that they cost her about £3,000 a year, while she has no commerce or other advantage from them since she abolished the slave trade, half a century ago.

The question now is, into whose hands should they fall? This question would be of comparatively small importance to us if our own possessions did not adjoin them. But the commercial prosperity and peace of our own settlements are intimately bound up with them. In the hands of Denmark we have nothing to fear from them, and the country dependent on them may be considered safe from the revival of the slave trade. But should they fall into other hands, a different policy might be pursued, and the consequences might be serious. A

[1] Benjamin Hawes (later Sir Benjamin) (1797–1862); Whig M.P. from 1832; Under-Secretary for the Colonies, 6 July, 1846, to 31 October, 1851; retired from Parliament in 1852 to become Permanent Under-Secretary of State for War.

bad example, so near our own door, could be mischievous, both in a commercial and moral point of view. I hold it, therefore, of the greatest importance, if Denmark is to give them up, that they should be secured to this country. Some power or other must succeed Denmark, or the whole country would be thrown into confusion.

I have been repeatedly applied to by . . . the financial agent of the Danish Government, on this subject, and have also seen the Danish Minister, at his request, about it. About three years ago, I found they were in negotiation with France, when I suggested a difficulty to Lord Aberdeen, which, I believe, stopped the treaty at that time. I know that Belgium is very anxious for some possession on the coast, the Rio Nunez having been spoken of for that purpose: but it is to England that the Danish Government is most anxious to transfer them.

She began by asking forty thousand pounds for them, which was the sum asked, I believe, of France. Now I have reason to think she would take a fourth of that sum, at which France might think them a bargain, even without the exclusive sovereignty of that portion of the territory claimed by Denmark as belonging to the forts. At all events, something must now be done, as Denmark seems resolved to sell or lease them, or otherwise get rid of them. . . .

I enclose, for the information of Lord Grey, the plans and inventory of the forts and territory, placed in my hands by Count Reventlow. The mere buildings and stores far exceed the sum he asks for them — viz. £10,000. Compared with their importance to this country, the sum is a bagatelle.

At the same time, I am fully aware of the narrow views which obtain, both at the Treasury and with a portion of the public, on such matters. The late, patched-up, hollow peace with the Punjab, was a consequence of this feeling, and we now see that it has cost us four or five millions of money and many thousand lives. There is no help for this folly and weakness, yet I would appeal to Lord Grey, whether he cannot successfully overcome the difficulty in so small a matter as this. We are spending half a million a year on the squadron, while we utterly neglect the more effectual and permanent remedies applicable on shore. One vessel of the squadron costs annually as much as Denmark asks for the fee simple of these forts.

If Government should refuse them, I tell you frankly, that I shall feel bound to propose an alternative to the Danish Government, which, while it relieves Denmark from the expense of maintaining them, shall (temporarily at all events) prevent them passing into the hands of a foreign power. . . .

Perhaps you will consult with Lord Grey, and let me know his opinion on the subject. I have told the Danish ambassador that I would first communicate with his Lordship. At the same time, I must not be understood as assuming any official authority in the matter as between the two Governments. . . .   [C.O.96/17]

167 MEMORANDUM BY SIR WILLIAM WINNIETT   LONDON, 1 AUGUST, 1849.

. . . The country or district between Cape Coast, or the line of sea coast, and the river Boossum Pra, which separates the Fantee from the Ashantee country, is composed of many tribes of people, each tribe being headed by a chief who is called a caboceer. There are about twelve of these caboceers over the country between Cape Coast itself and the Pra — the distance being from 80 to 100 miles. On all matters of importance affecting the general welfare, they assemble and consult together: but each rules absolutely over his own tribe and district. One of their caboceers would not yield his territory or authority without the consent of the others, and to avow a direct intention on the part of the Government at Cape Coast to assume territorial rights, would create suspicion and alarm amongst the body of caboceers. The Government at Cape Coast should, in fact, only proceed with caution and take advantage of circumstances as they arise. . . .

To collect a direct tax of any description from the caboceers would occasion difficulty. It might bring the Government at the Castle into direct collision with the caboceers, or, in case a caboceer was a willing agent, it would put the people under him in opposition to his rule, and the soldiers of the fort would be continually required to enforce the payment of the taxes due to the caboceers. Such, I fear, would be the result of an attempt at direct tax on the natives.

In so rude a state of society as the country now is, escape into what is called the bush, is of such facility, that to avoid payment of taxes very many would resort to it, and so render it almost impossible of collection.
[C.O.96/19]

168 GREY TO WINNIETT

HOWICK, 6 AUGUST, 1849.
Private.

[Winniett's memorandum has convinced him that] . . . the plan for imposing direct taxation on the native population . . . ought not to be attempted in the form in which I proposed it. But I still retain the opinion that such taxation, provided it were very moderate in amount, and that its proceeds were applied to proper objects, would be of very great service.

I would propose that on your return to the coast you should call together the caboceers and that, pointing out to them the great benefit the people have derived from the schools at Cape Coast and from the medical assistance afforded by the Colonial Surgeon, . . . you should induce them to consent to endeavour to increase the number of schools, and also to establish a few dispensaries, where medical men might be stationed to give advice and assistance to those who needed it. You might point out to them that these benefits could only be obtained by their assistance, and that of their people, but that a very moderate amount of contribution by them would be sufficient. I would suggest that, in the first instance, the caboceers should be advised to agree to the imposition of a tax of only 5s or 6s a year upon each head of a family. . . . The tax I would recommend to have levied by the caboceers, to whom, for the purpose of giving them an interest in the measure, I would allow a percentage on the amount levied. . . . I think it of great importance that, while the expenditure of the money should take place mainly under the direction of the Lieutenant Governor, the caboceers should be made to join in the management of this business, and with that view, I would endeavour to form them into a kind of committee, or into two or three committees for different parts of the districts, which should meet periodically, and have laid before them the proposed expenditure of the money available for the objects above described, and also statements of past expenditure. . . . It should be made a rule that none but those who have paid the tax should be allowed the benefit of these institutions. . . . Those who could not pay in money should be required to pay in labour valued at so low a rate that it should be their interest to pay in money instead. . . . There would be no difficulty in turning the gratuitous labour thus obtained to good account in improving roads, in building school-houses or dispensaries etc.

The great danger to be guarded against would be that of abuse of their power by the chiefs in collecting the tax, and to prevent this, I would suggest that the Judicial Assessor, or some officer to be appointed for the purpose, should, with two or three of the neighbouring chiefs investigate every complaint. . . .

It would, I think, be of the utmost importance that the schools established should be *industrial* schools. . . . In Africa, ignorance of the common industrial arts contributes almost as much as intellectual ignorance, to keep the people in a state of poverty and barbarism, and I am quite convinced that intellectual and industrial instruction should go hand in hand. . . . Whenever the funds available for the purpose would admit of it . . . a portion of them should be set apart to pay for sending

to England to finish their education some of the most intelligent of the youths brought up in the schools . . . to finish [their] education here, either in the Normal schools as a teacher, or in one of the Medical Colleges.

If [the new duties][1] succeed in raising the revenue you anticipate, this might be employed in further measures for the improvement of the population and for giving a more settled and regular character to the Government of the district. In attempting the latter object, I would carefully preserve whatever is capable of being rendered useful in the existing customs and institutions of the people, and aim rather at improving and developing the existing system, than at substituting another. I would accordingly endeavour to render the meetings of the caboceers, which you say now take place, more regular and frequent, and by degrees to invest them with greater authority, and I would also try to give the caboceers the character rather of responsible public officers than of absolute chiefs. This might be accomplished by assigning to them moderate stipends (when the revenue will admit of it) and by gradually establishing a right on the part of the people, to appeal to the Lieutenant Governor against any abuse of authority on the part of the chief. Such abuse, on being proved, might be followed at first by depriving him only of part of his stipend, but ultimately I should look to acquiring the power of deposing a caboceer who should misconduct himself, and of exercising some considerable influence, at least, in the choice of a new one. . . .

Though it is desirable to look forward and to have a clear idea of the objects to be aimed at, much of what I have now suggested cannot be attempted at once, and . . . the success of such designs depends upon their being very cautiously and gradually pursued. . . . [C.O.96/19]

---

[1] Winniett proposed (to Grey, No. 44 of 20 May, 1847: C.O.96/11) a duty of 3d. a gallon on gin and rum, the consumption of which he estimated at two million gallons.

13 Earl Grey and the Gold Coast, 1850–1852

IN 1850 Grey decided to separate the Gold Coast from Sierra Leone. The new constitution, embodied in the Charter (169) and the Governor's Instructions (178), did not satisfy the merchants (172). In 1851, however, they dropped their idea of an elective council (177). Some of them urged that the chiefs be brought into association with Government, by means of a deliberative council (174), a proposal which Grey eagerly welcomed (176).

It was a sign of Grey's changed temper that in 1849 he accepted a renewed proposal for the purchase of the Danish forts (166), and thanks to vigorous support from Palmerston, saw it carried (173) in spite of strong and able opposition in the House of Commons (171).

Unfortunately, Winniett died in December 1850, and the most crucial innovation of all, the introduction of direct taxation, fell to the management of his successor (180). Grey himself was out of office before the Poll Tax 'Ordinance' was passed (181). Although in several particulars this measure departed from Grey's original intentions, he hailed it with extravagant optimism and parental pride as an important step in the direction of a civilised African form of self-government (184); a goal in which few, if any, of his British contemporaries, believed.[1]

[1] Compare the views of the radical Cobden (171) and the conservative Adderly (p. 311 n. below).

169 CHARTER under the Great Seal of the United Kingdom, to provide for the Government of Her Majesty's Forts and Settlements on the Gold Coast.

Victoria R. — Letters Patent, dated 24 January, 1850. Victoria, by the grace of God, of the United Kingdom of Great Britain and Ireland, Queen, Defender of the Faith, to all whom these presents shall come, greeting: [Recites 1 & 2 Geo. IV. cap. 28.] . . .

And whereas, in pursuance of the Act of Parliament aforesaid, his Majesty King George the Fourth did by certain letters patent under the Great Seal of the United Kingdom of Great Britain and Ireland, bearing date at Westminster, the 17th day of October, in the second year of his reign, order, direct and appoint that all and every of the forts and possessions theretofore . . . . held by the corporation of the company of merchants trading to Africa . . . should be annexed to and made dependencies on, the said colony of Sierra Leone. . . .

And whereas by certain other letters patent under the Great Seal . . . bearing date at Westminster the 16th day of April 1846 . . . we did constitute and appoint our trusty and well-beloved Norman William Macdonald, Esquire, to be our Captain-General and Governor-in-Chief in and over the peninsula of the said colony of Sierra Leone, and of all territories, islands and possessions annexed to or depending on the said colony . . . [and cites 6 Vict. cap. 13]

We do by these presents revoke the said respective letters patent of his said late Majesty King George the Fourth and of the 16th day of April 1846 respectively, so far as the same shall apply to all and every the territories, islands and possessions situate in or adjacent to the Gold Coast on the West Coast of Africa, which now belong to us, and are commonly designated as our forts and settlements on the Gold Coast.

And we do hereby order, direct and appoint, that all and every our said forts, territories, islands and possessions on the said Gold Coast do forthwith cease to be annexed to and be dependencies on the said colony of Sierra Leone. And further know you, that in pursuance and exercise of the powers so vested in us as aforesaid, by the said recited Act of Parliament passed in the sixth year of our reign, we, of our especial grace, certain knowledge, and mere motion, by this commission, under the Great Seal of the United Kingdom aforesaid, delegate to the persons hereinafter named, within the said forts and settlements on the Gold Coast and their dependencies, the powers and authorities so vested in us in our Privy Council as aforesaid, but upon, under and subject to all such conditions, provisoes and limitations as by this our commission or by the instructions under our signet and sign manual accompanying the same, are prescribed: and we do declare our pleasure to be, and do hereby declare and grant, that the Governor for the time being of the said forts and settlements on the Gold Coast, and such other persons, not being less than two, as are hereinafter designated, shall constitute and be a Legislative Council for the said forts, territories, islands and possessions: and we do hereby direct and appoint that the persons other than the said Governor, constituting the said Legislative Council, shall be such public officers within the said forts and settlements as shall be designated, or such other persons within the same as shall from time to time be named for that purpose by us, by any instrument or instructions, or warrant or warrants, to be by us for that purpose issued under our signet and sign manual, and with the advice of our Privy Council, all of which councillors shall hold their places in the said Council at our pleasure.

2. And we do hereby authorise, empower and enjoin such Legislative Council to make and establish all such laws, institutions, and ordinances as may from time to time be necessary for the peace, order and good government of our subjects and others within our said present or future forts and settlements on the Gold Coast comprised between the 10th degree of west longitude and the 10th degree of east longitude; and our pleasure is, that in the making and establishing all such laws, institutions, and ordinances, the said Legislative Council shall conform to and observe all such rules and regulations as shall be given and prescribed in and by such instructions as we, with the advice of our Privy Council, shall from time to time make for their guidance therein: Provided nevertheless, and we do hereby reserve to ourselves, our heirs and successors, our and their right and authority to disallow any such ordinances in the whole or in part, and to make and establish from time to time, with the advice and consent of Parliament, or with the advice of our or their Privy Council, all such laws as may to us or them appear necessary for the order, peace, and good government of our said present and future forts, settlements and their dependencies, as fully as if these presents had not been made.

3. And whereas it is expedient that an Executive Council should be appointed to advise and assist the Governor of our said forts and settlements on the Gold Coast for the time being in the administration of the government thereof, we do by these our letters patent, authorize the Governor of our said forts and settlements to summon as an Executive Council such persons as may from time to time be named or designated by us in any instructions under our signet and sign manual, addressed to him in that behalf.

4. And we do hereby authorise and empower the Governor of our said forts and settlements on the Gold Coast for the time being, to keep and use the public seal appointed for the sealing of all things whatsoever that shall pass the seal of our said forts and settlements.

5. And we do hereby give and grant to the Governor of our said forts and settlements for the time being, full power and authority in our name and on our behalf, but subject nevertheless to such provisions as may be in that respect contained in any instructions which may from time to time be addressed to him by us for that purpose,

to make and execute in our name and on our behalf, under the public seal of our said forts and settlements, grants of land to us belonging within the same, to private persons for their own use and benefit, or to any persons bodies politic or corporate, in trust for the public uses of our subjects there resident or of any of them.

6. And we do hereby authorise and empower the Governor of our said forts and settlements on the Gold Coast for the time being to constitute and appoint judges, and in cases requisite, commissioners of oyer and terminer, justices of the peace, and other necessary officers and ministers in our said settlements, for the due and impartial administration of justice, and for putting the laws into execution, and to administer or cause to be administered unto them such oath or oaths as are usually given for the due execution and performance of officers and places, and for the clearing of truth in judicial matters.

7. And we do hereby give and grant unto the Governor of our said forts and settlements on the Gold Coast and their dependencies for the time being, full power and authority, as he shall see occasion, in our name and on our behalf, to remit any fines, penalties or forfeitures which may accrue or become payable to us, provided the same do not exceed the sum of £50 sterling in any one case; and to respite and suspend the payment of any such fine, penalty, or forfeiture exceeding the sum of £50 until our pleasure thereon shall be made known and signified to such Governor.

8. And we do hereby give and grant unto the Governor of our said forts and settlements on the Gold Coast for the time being, full power and authority, as he shall see occasion, in our name and on our behalf, to grant to any offender convicted of any crime in any court, or before any judge, justice, or magistrate within our said forts and settlements, a free and unconditional pardon, or a pardon subject to such conditions as by any law or ordinance hereafter to be in force in our said settlements may

be thereunto annexed, or any respite of the execution of the sentence of any such offender for such period as to such Governor may seem fit.

9. And we do hereby give and grant unto the Governor of our said forts and settlements on the Gold Coast full power and authority, upon sufficient cause to him appearing, to suspend from the exercise of his office within our said forts and settlements, any person exercising any office or place under or by virtue of any commission or warrant granted or which may be granted by us, or in our name, or under our authority, which suspension shall continue and have effect only until our pleasure therein shall be made known and signified to such Governor. And we do hereby strictly require and enjoin the Governor of our said forts and settlements for the time being, in proceeding to any such suspension, to observe the directions in that behalf given to him by our instructions, under our signet and sign manual, accompanying his commission of appointment as Governor of the said forts and settlements.

10. And in the event of the death, incapacity or absence out of our said forts and settlements on the Gold Coast and of their dependencies, of such person as may be commissioned and appointed by us to be the Governor, we do hereby provide and declare our pleasure to be, that all and every [of] the powers and authorities herein granted to the Governor of our said forts and settlements on the Gold Coast, shall be and the same are hereby vested in such person as may be appointed by us by warrant under our signet and sign manual to be the Lieutenant-Governor of our said forts and settlements, or in the event of there being no person upon the place commissioned and appointed by us to be Lieutenant-Governor thereof, then our pleasure is, and we do hereby provide and declare, that in any such contingency all the powers and authorities herein granted to the Governor or Lieutenant-Governor of our said forts and settlements shall be and the same are granted to the judicial assessor for the time

being of our said forts and settlements, or in the event of his death, incapacity or absence, to the senior justice of the peace for the time being, for our said forts and settlements and their dependencies.

11. And we do hereby require and command all our officers and ministers, civil and military, and all other the inhabitants of our said forts and settlements on the Gold Coast, to be obedient, aiding and assisting to such person as may be commissioned and appointed by us to be the Governor of our said forts and settlements on the Gold Coast, or in the event of his death or absence, to such person as may, under the provisions of these our letters patent, assume and exercise the functions of such Governor.

12. And we do hereby reserve to us, our heirs and successors, full power and authority from time to time to revoke, alter or amend these our letters patent as to us or them shall seem meet. . . .

Given at our Court at Windsor, this 19th day of January 1850, in the 13th year of our reign.

By Her Majesty's Command
[Signed] Grey.
[H.C.383 of 1855, A & P (1854–5) xxxvii]

170 Sir W. Winniett to Earl Grey
Cape Coast Castle, 4 June, 1850.

My Lord,

I believe your Lordship is perfectly aware that since the close of the war with Ashantee, an understanding has existed between the British Local Government and the King, to the effect that all runaways from Kumassie are to be delivered back to the King, upon application made by him to the Officer-Administering the Government. This arrangement has frequently given rise to serious doubts in my mind, how I might be considered blamable in delivering up individuals who had sought the protection of the Government: but however reluctant I have felt in acknowledging the necessity of adhering to this arrangement, considerations for the peace of the country have had

so much weight with me that I have not hesitated to incur the risk of blame from adoption of a course so much opposed to English ideas.

My reason for calling your Lordship's attention to this subject is that a case has lately occurred where a runaway Ashantee was demanded by the King, and it was thought justifiable, on account of the bad treatment which he had received, to oppose the demand. The King, however, has renewed it, with a threat to close the paths, and to prevent any intercourse with our Settlements if compliance with his request be not granted. Under these circumstances, and foreseeing the utter ruin to trade, with every chance of the country being involved in war, by a persistence in the course originally adopted in this case, I have considered it most prudent to adhere to the arrangements heretofore existing in the Settlements.

I shall not cease, however, to use every precaution in my power, consistent with the maintenance of the peace of the country, to secure for all such refugees, a kind and humane treatment, and, by using the weight of my influence, I hope to be able to succeed in making such arrangements with the King, as may tend to improve the condition and liberty of his people.

I have etc.   [C.O.96/19]

171 House of Commons: Committee of Supply   19 July, 1850.

. . . Motion made, and Question proposed:—

'That a sum not exceeding £24,080 be granted to Her Majesty to defray the charge of the Civil Establishments on the Western Coast of Africa, to the 31st day of March, 1851; also for the purchase of stores &c, on the Gold Coast, from the Danish Government.'

Mr. Cobden said he should have thought it probably more in order if some member of the Government had explained the grounds upon which the Committee were called upon to vote this sum.   It was proposed to vote £10,000 for five settlements on the coast of Africa. . . . He asked himself, what were the grounds on which they proposed to extend their territory on the coast of Africa . . . and so far as he could understand it, they were, first of all to extend their operations on shore for the suppression of the slave trade — next, they were to extend their trade, and then there was a general plan for the diffusion of civilization on the continent of Africa. . . .

They had always some fresh plan for the suppression of the slave trade.   First they had steam vessels, then they had the Niger expedition, with its horrible loss of life, and now they were to have martello towers which were to put an end to the slave trade in two years and a half, according to Governor Winniett's opinion. . . .[1] If they could not abolish the slave trade . . . by means of steam vessels, it was futile to think of abolishing it by means of stationary forts on land.

The next object for which these forts were to be purchased, was to extend their trade on the coast of Africa.   Now he, as a free trader, maintained that if they removed the obstacles on trade, it was not their business to purchase land for the promotion of agriculture or trade.   They had petitions from Manchester and Liverpool in favour of the purchase of these forts; but he maintained that they should not vote the money of the tax-payers at large to promote the interest of particular traders in a particular locality. . . .

[The sum involved was insignificant in itself, but it would lead to heavier commitments.]   There were very magniloquent terms used with regard to the extension of civilization and the promotion of Christianity on the coast of Africa. . . . That showed that he was right in viewing this not merely as a vote of £10,000.   They aimed at nothing short of the civilizing and Christianising the vast coast of Africa.   But he held that they had a great deal to do at

home, within a stone's throw of where they were, before they embarked on a scheme of redeeming from barbarism, the whole coast of Africa. . . .

If they extended their territory, they would involve themselves in endless obligations. . . . Governor Winniett . . . speaks of the natives wishing to offer fealty to the Queen. . . . He spoke of a tract of country one hundred miles in the interior, and bordering the territory of the king of Ashantee.   A very formidable tribe possessed that country.   They had engagements with them before; and if they were to occupy this country, who was to guarantee that they would not find themselves embarked some fine morning in a war with the Ashantees. . . . If they were not going to buy any territory, but merely the forts, with the land under the range of their guns, what was to be the character of their relations with the native tribes? Were they to be dependent on this country?

But they were told that there was a probability of raising a revenue from the natives.   He never knew a case in which territory was to be purchased or acquired, in which they were not told that it would bring a revenue.   But the result generally was, that it was a source of money going out, instead of coming in. . . . He exhorted the House not to trust in this revenue till they saw how it was to be raised.

He exhorted the Committee to pause before they recognised the principle of extending possessions in tropical climates. He said tropical climates, because there was a great difference between acquiring territory where the race might become indigenous, so as to extend commerce and to spread the principle of self-government over the world, and taking possession of tropical territory, where their own race was not indigenous, where government must be upheld by force, and where there was no prospect of being able to disembarrass themselves of the responsibility of governing the people. . . .

Another consideration why they should pause before they sanctioned the purchase

---

[1] In his evidence before the Lords' Committee on the Slave Trade in 1849 (A & P (1850) ix).

of these forts was that the climate was most prejudicial and fatal to the health of white men. We should be told, perhaps, of the great benefits to civilization and humanity in our taking steps to abolish the slave trade. But was there not some consideration due to our own race, to those whom we should be sending to the coast of Africa, 'the white man's grave'? . . . He recollected that he denounced [the Niger] expedition at a public meeting in Manchester, as little short of murder, and he gave offence to many persons by doing so [but he had been justified by the event]. . . . He called on those who professed the principles of humanity, as well as the political economist and the mere politician, on no grounds to sanction the extension of this system to the coast of Africa. . . .

Mr. Forster: . . . The honourable member for the West Riding [Mr. Cobden] might be considered the author of the whole transaction, for it had been in consequence of the outcry raised by the financial and colonial reformers, that Earl Grey was rendered anxious to decrease every possible expense, and, on coming to the Gold Coast, and finding there certain expenses without any revenue being raised to meet them, adopted the present arrangement as a means of raising some local revenue. Our settlements on the coast being situated between those of the Dutch and of the Danish, it was impossible to raise any revenue without coming to some arrangement with them. . . . Denmark [desiring] . . . to get rid of their forts and to sell them to England . . . and Holland having agreed to come to an arrangement with us for enabling us to raise a revenue,[1] the negotiation for the sale of the forts was finally arranged, and in this way, it was now proposed to lessen the expenditure of the British establishment. In effect, the measure was one of economy, and on that ground he was prepared to defend it. It would at all events be the

fault of the Colonial Office if it was not so. . . .

In his experience of forty years with respect to the coast of Africa, this was the first vote he had ever seen which was likely to be attended with any beneficial effects to the trade and commerce of this country. He could sum up millions that had been completely thrown away on the coast [as on the expeditions of Peddie, Gray, Laing, Tuckey, and that to the Niger] . . . The Colonial Office seldom did anything right; for thirty-five years he had opposed their proceedings on the coast of Africa, but he was glad to see they were ready to listen to reasonable advice, and he would support them fully on this vote. . . .[1]

[Hansard 3rd series/113/37–43, 44–6]

172 H. SMITH AND F. SWANZY TO EARL GREY   LONDON, 16 AUGUST, 1850.

. . . Your Lordship has been pleased to establish a Council which [is] . . . to consist of the Governor, the Judicial Assessor, the Collector of Customs (only just arrived from England, and knowing nothing of the country), the Commandant of Christiansborg, Mr. Bannerman, and of only one non-official member, Mr. Cruickshank. . . .

The Council as at present constituted cannot possibly give satisfaction to the inhabitants, or answer the purpose for which it was doubtless created. . . . Neither the merchants or inhabitants generally are properly represented. . . . Council in its present form will very often be composed of the Governor, the Judicial Assessor and the Collector, who, all inhabiting the Castle, may there meet and pass new measures unknown to the inhabitants. . . . [They will have a personal interest in voting customs duties to pay their own salaries.]

---

[1] This was a slight, if pardonable exaggeration. The Dutch Government had agreed in principle to co-operate in imposing customs duties, but in November 1850 changed its mind, owing to the opposition of Dutch trading interests.

[1] Bright, Milner Gibson, Hume, Hutt and Molesworth all spoke, and Gladstone voted, against the purchase. Its principal defender was Palmerston who chided his opponents with acquiescence in the slave trade. Cobden's motion to reduce the vote by the £10,000 needed to buy the forts, was lost by 42 votes to 138, and the original question was then put and agreed to.

As long as the Council is composed chiefly of executive officers resident in the castle, having few and faint sympathies with the people, and to whom the welfare of the country is, by the circumstances of their appointment, subordinate to their own direct pecuniary interests, who are utterly ignorant of the trade and nature of the country, who, looking upon their residence there merely as a stepping stone to a better appointment somewhere else, and longing for the day when they shall finally quit the shores of Africa, feel little interest in its prosperity, and who do not possess that respect and confidence on the part of the inhabitants, which long residence and continued intercourse with them confer — the co-operation of the merchants and people will not be obtained. . . . [They urge the addition of four members to be elected by the merchants and respectable inhabitants.]

The qualification of voters can be managed without much difficulty. The payment of a certain amount of customs dues annually, or the possession of a house valued at a certain fixed sum, might be held to confer the right to vote at the election of members of council; and the town councils and several town companies might be allowed a certain number of votes. . . .

There is a possibility of the inhabitants, if the council is continued in its present unsatisfactory shape, forming a separate chamber, unconnected with the Government, wherein to debate on the public and local affairs of the countryside. Your Lordship is aware that many chiefs and kings . . . consider themselves under the influence, though not the subjects, of the British Government, and . . . form what may be called a federal union. . . . We think it would be very beneficial if the chiefs of all these states and tribes could be persuaded to meet annually at Cape Coast and Accra, or to send their representatives, and thus to form a General Council, representing all the separate peoples forming the federation under the influence of the British flag. This would bind them all

together and teach them that the good of each is the good of all. Laws could then be introduced, approved . . . and made general. . . . All quarrels between the different tribes would be ended. The probability of an Ashantee war . . . would be removed.

[a.] MINUTE BY GREY
5 NOVEMBER, 1850.

I am certainly not prepared to place in the hands of a few merchants (whose interests or at least what they believe to be such, are by no means necessarily identical with those of the population) the power of controlling the Government, with which they would be invested, if a majority of the Council were to be appointed in the manner now contended for, but (with the present council) it may not unreasonably be complained that there is no security that the measures of the Government will always be guided by a proper amount of local knowledge. . . .
[C.O.96/21]

173 CONVENTION . . . FOR THE CESSION OF THE DANISH POSSESSIONS ON THE COAST OF AFRICA TO GREAT BRITAIN
SIGNED AT LONDON, 17 AUGUST, 1850.

. . . In consideration of the sum of ten thousand pounds sterling, to be paid by Her Majesty the Queen of the United Kingdom of Great Britain and Ireland to His Majesty the King of Denmark, on the exchange of the ratifications of the present convention, His Danish Majesty cedes to Her Britannic Majesty, her heirs and successors, in full property and sovereignty, all the forts belonging to the Crown of Denmark, which are situated on that part of the coast of Africa called the Gold Coast or the Coast of Guinea, and which comprises Fort Christiansborg, Fort Augustaborg,[1] Fort Fredensborg,[2] Fort Konegsteen,[3] and and Fort Pridsensteen,[4] with their appurtenances and all the guns and stores con-

---

[1] At Teshie. [2] At (old) Ningo.
[3] At Ada. [4] At Keta.

tained therein; together with all other possessions, property, and territorial rights whatever belonging to His Danish Majesty on the said coast. . . .

Done at London, the 18th August 1850.

(L.S.) Palmerston
(L.S.) Reventlow.
[H.C.1298, A & P (1851) lvii]

174 J. BANNERMAN AND B. CRUICKSHANK TO SIR W. WINNIETT

C.C.C., 22 AUGUST, 1850.

[They do not believe the people prefer merchant to Crown rule[1].] . , .

The murmurs of the privileged classes at the decline and extinction of their privileges . . . . instead of being a reproach to the Government, is an incontestable proof of its efficient amelioration of the condition of the native population. . . .

We cannot conceal from you, however, the opinion, which hourly experience is more forcibly impressing upon our minds, that the time has arrived for modifying, in a great measure, our system of administration . . . and we would respectfully submit for your serious consideration, the suggestions which we now venture to offer upon the subject.

The natural consequence of a more general diffusion of wealth by means of trade, and of a more extensive dissemination of justice by the local Authorities, has been to give increased liberty to the masses, and to diminish proportionately the authority of chiefs and masters. The removal of former restraints has given free scope to individual action, thus leaving men more exposed to the wild guidance and the rash impulse of their own passion, which must necessarily result in the introduction of crimes scarcely known in a simple and primitive state of society. This entails upon the Government, the exercise of a

[1] This seems to be borne out by the memorial of Gold Coast native merchants of August 1850 to the effect 'that the existing form of government that we now enjoy under the Queen is the best, and it is our wish that it remains unaltered'. In C.O.96/19.

more extensive and subdivided watchfulness over the people. The obedience which the slave formerly unhesitatingly yielded to his master, the dependent and feudal retainer to his chief, and the general body to their superstitious observances and obligations, concentrated the controlling power within such a narrow compass, and at the same time maintained this power in such perfect efficiency, that the Government had only to keep a watchful eye over these directing influences, to ensure the peace of the country. But while all these restraints have been gradually weakened, no attempt has yet been made to meet the altered relations of the people. We are still acting as a police force at haphazard, according to the views and ideas of individual magistrates, without any approach to an uniform system of laws; and more indebted, certainly, to the appreciation of the English protectorate and the quiet docility of the people for the general tranquillity, than to any prudent measures of prevention. The great bond of attraction which unites the people to us, is the value of our support against the Ashantees. To this may be added the acknowledged advantages of our administration of justice; but the result of this latter cause . . . being a more minute and daily increasing jurisdiction, a more systematic course of administration is rendered absolutely necessary for its proper exercise.

At present there is no legally acknowledged medium of communication between the Government and the people, if we except proclamations, orders to individual chiefs, and the intervention of the police. The former are little comprehended by the body of the people. The Chiefs frequently plead the disobedience of their people as an excuse for the non-execution of the orders given, and are rather anxious to parade this disobedience as a proof of the injurious effect of the levelling character of our justice; and to govern entirely by means of constables, would render necessary a force far beyond anything which we could bring to bear upon them. Neither have we any established mode of obtaining the sentiments of the people upon measures which it may be considered necessary to adopt, and which cannot efficiently be carried out without their concurrence.

With regard to the levying of duties, and other subjects of legislation affecting the general body of the people, we feel the necessity of having the assistance and co-operation of the native authorities to enable us to carry them into practice; and yet, at present we could not get that co-operation without the most dilatory and clumsy process of personally consulting a number of parties scattered through the country in various directions, whom it might be difficult also to bring to an unanimous opinion.

For all these reasons and many others with equal claims to our consideration, which we could adduce if necessary, we are of opinion:

1st. That as it would be perfectly impossible to govern the immense population of the Gold Coast without the instrumentality of the chiefs, it is an imperative duty, incumbent upon the Government, to endeavour to elevate the moral standard of native jurisdiction by such a general code of Regulations as may be found necessary to meet the exigencies of the country.

2nd. That for this purpose, a legally constituted deliberative assembly, to be called 'The Assembly of Native Chiefs', be appointed to meet at Cape Coast Castle twice every year for the purpose of framing with the assistance of the Judicial Assessor and other magistrates such laws as shall, when sanctioned and confirmed by the Governor, become generally binding upon the natives of the country; and,

3rd. That the members of this Assembly receive a small annual stipend from the Government.

We do not think it necessary at present to indicate more particularly, the duties of such an Assembly, or the great advantage which it will hold out to the Government as an efficient instrument of disseminating a more universal system of justice. It is sufficient to point out the necessity for some such legalized organ of communication with the people and to leave its construction and the rules for its guidance for more matured consideration.

Finally, we beg leave to assure your Excellency, that you appear to us to possess in an eminent degree the attachment of the people, which must always be a sufficient guarantee for the peace of the country: but we believe that you will immeasurably increase this esteem, and confer a lasting benefit upon Africa, by laying the foundations of a system of Government so essentially necessary to the march of social progress.   [C.O.96/19]

175 EARL GREY TO SIR W. WINNIETT
LONDON, 19 SEPTEMBER, 1850.
Sir,

I have received your despatch No. 45 of June 4th last, in which you report that you had surrendered a runaway Ashantee to the king of that country under an arrangement made since the close of the war with it.

I have considerable difficulty in giving you any definite instructions on this subject in the absence of more complete information.

There can be no objection, as far as I am aware, to the execution of an agreement to surrender to the king of Ashantee, persons who have fled from his country, charged with the commission of crimes or offences against Ashanti law and usage, so far as their surrender does not involve any breach of the laws of humanity.

But with regard to runaway slaves from Ashantee, I have to direct your attention to two despatches of my predecessor, Lord Stanley, of the 29th and 30th December 1844. Lord Stanley pointed out that any such surrender, where the slave had taken refuge on British territory (as in Cape Coast Castle), would be absolutely illegal, under the statute 3rd & 4th Geo. IV, cap. 113; and that, if the slave was found on territory not British, but under British protection, such surrender, although not strictly illegal, as in the former case, was equally contrary to the spirit of English law, and not to be sanctioned.

I fully concur in these views of Lord Stanley. If, therefore, it is for the advantage of the settlements, that such an agreement as that you have described, with the king of Ashantee, should be maintained, it is desirable that the class of persons to whom it is to apply, and the terms on which their surrender is to take place, should be defined.

I have &c.   [C.O.96/19]

176 MINUTE BY EARL GREY
16 NOVEMBER, 1850.

I entirely approve of the proposal to have a half-yearly meeting of chiefs to make laws and regulations for the districts, and that these chiefs should be paid. I think the salaries should be sufficient for their maintenance in a respectable manner, according to the notions of the people as to the manner in which chiefs ought to live, and that, in return for these salaries, they should undertake the duty and responsibility of maintaining the laws and enforcing order in their respective districts.

For this purpose, they should have the assistance of a certain number of constables, from the inhabitants of the district. They should not have the power of inflicting punishments for offences, by their own authority, but should be required to bring offenders before the nearest magistrate. To provide for these salaries, and for the establishment of public dispensaries and hospitals (see despatches lately written respecting the natives in N.S. Wales[1] and the tribes to the north of the Cape of G. Hope), a small house tax or poll tax should be imposed.

With regard to the legislative council, I think, upon the whole, it will be better to maintain it unaltered, but that a chamber

[1] An error for Natal: cf. despatches to Sir H. G. Smith of 30 November, 1849, and 7 January, 1851, on the affairs of Natal and British Kaffraria, printed in Earl Grey's *Colonial Policy*, ii, pp. 488–508.

of commerce should be created and that by requiring the drafts of laws to be made public before they are passed, this body would be enabled to advise upon them.

[C.O.96/19]

177 LEGISLATIVE COUNCIL MINUTE
CAPE COAST, 1 APRIL, 1851.

At a meeting of the Council held at Cape Coast, this day, present:

His Excellency, Lieut. Governor Bannerman
The Honourable B. Cruickshank
The Honourable F. Swanzy } Members of
The Honourable T. Hutton } Council ad interim.

Mr. Swanzy stated that he would ask His Excellency to bring forward a measure for the establishment of an elective Council.

Mr. Cruickshank confessed that he had, at one time, the same opinion on these points: but his recent and more immediate intercourse with the people and their government, satisfied him that his opinion had not been well grounded. In as far as referred to the [claim of] merchants of the highest respectability to vote, he would not object; but he was convinced that enlightenment and civilization would always be left out of sight when native authorities could carry it by numbers; and that it was contrary to all experience to believe that, without the coercing influence of a more intelligent Power, anything would be done by the native authorities to advance themselves in the scale of civilization.

This view being generally allowed to be correct, and no one advocating Mr Swanzy's measure, it was set aside.

Other matters connected with the local affairs of the town occupied the attention of the Council, but the general opinion was that, in its present stage, all that was practicable was the extension of British justice, which was silently working a very happy change upon the social condition of the natives.

[Adm.14/1.   Ghana National Archives]

178 GOVERNOR'S INSTRUCTIONS
1 APRIL, 1851.

Victoria R.   INSTRUCTIONS to Our Trusty and Well-beloved Stephen John Hill, Esquire, Brevet-Major in Our Army, Our Governor and Commander-in-Chief in and over Our Forts and Settlements on the Gold Coast, or, in his absence, to

(Seal)   Our Lieutenant-Governor, or the Officer administering the Government of Our said Forts and Settlements for the time being. Given at Our Court at Buckingham Palace, this 1st day of April 1851, in the Fourteenth year of Our Reign

Whereas in pursuance and exercise of the powers in us vested, in and by a certain Act of Parliament, made and passed in the sixth year of our reign [6 Vict. cap. 13] . . . by a Commission under the Great Seal of our United Kingdom of Great Britain and Ireland, bearing even date herewith, at Westminster, We have constituted and appointed you, the said Stephen John Hill, to be our Governor and Commander-in-Chief in and over our said present and future forts and settlements on the Gold Coast, comprised within the 10th degree of west longitude and the 10th degree of east longitude. . . :

Now, therefore, by these Our Instructions under our Royal sign manual and signet . . . do declare our pleasure to be, that you shall, with all due solemnity, cause our . . . Charter, together with our said Commission, to be read and published in the presence of our chief officers and other the principal inhabitants of the said forts and settlements and their dependencies, you shall then and there take the oaths appointed to be taken. . . .

2. And we do authorise and require you from time to time, and at any time hereafter, by yourself, or by any other to be authorised by you in that behalf, to administer and give to all and every such person or persons, as you shall think fit, who shall hold any office or place of trust or profit, or who shall at any time or times pass into our said settlements or be resident therein, the oath commonly called the oath of allegiance, save only in cases wherein any other oath or oaths is, or are prescribed by the statutes in that behalf made, or by any of those statutes; in which cases, it is our pleasure, and we do hereby direct that you do administer to such persons such other oath or oaths as aforesaid.

3. And whereas by the said recited Charter, made in pursuance and exercise of the powers in us vested, in and by the said recited Act of Parliament, we have authorised the Governor or Lieutenant-Governor for the time being of our said forts and settlements on the Gold Coast, and such other persons, not being less than two, as are in the said Charter designated, to constitute and be a Legislative Council for the said forts and settlements: And we have by the said Charter further declared that in addition to the said Governor or Lieutenant-Governor, the said Council shall be composed of such public officers within the said forts and settlements, or of such other persons as shall from time to time be named or designated by us, by any instruction or instructions, warrant or warrants, to be by us for that purpose issued under our signet and sign manual, and with the advice of our Privy Council, and that all such councillors shall hold their places in the said Council at our pleasure, with full power and authority to make and establish all such laws, institutions, and ordinances as may be required for the peace, order, and good government of our said present or future forts and settlements, and that in the making of all such laws, institutions, and ordinances, the said Legislative Council shall conform to and observe all such rules and regulations as should be given and prescribed in and by such instructions as we, with the advice of our Privy Council, shall from time to time make for their guidance therein:

Now, therefore, by these our instructions under our signet and sign manual, and with the advice of our Privy Council . . . we do nominate and appoint the public officers and persons hereinafter named, to be members of the said Legislative Council, who shall hold their places in the said Council at our pleasure; that is to say, the Judicial Assessor . . . for the time being, the Collector of Customs[1] . . . for the time being, and our trusty and well-beloved James Bannerman and Brodie G. Cruickshank, Esquires.

And we do hereby further order and appoint that, upon the death, incapacity or absence from our said forts and settlements, of the said James Bannerman and Brodie G. Cruickshank, or of such other persons as we may hereafter appoint to be members of the said Legislative Council, it shall be competent for you, or the Governor for the time being . . . by a Commission, to be for that purpose issued, under the public seal of our said forts and settlements, to nominate and appoint any fit and proper person or persons to such vacancy or vacancies in the said Council, who shall hold their appointments only until our pleasure shall be known.

4. And in further exercise of the powers and authorities in us vested . . . we have, with the advice of our Privy Council, thought fit to make, and do hereby make and ordain, the following regulations for the guidance of the said Legislative Council, in the making such Laws and Ordinances as aforesaid; (that is to say) we do declare our pleasure to be, that the said Legislative Council shall not be competent to act in any case unless two members, at the least, of such Council, in addition to the Governor for the time being, or to the member who may preside therein in his absence, shall be present at and throughout the meeting of such Council.

5. And we do authorise and require you, or the Governor of our said forts and settlements on the Gold Coast and their

dependencies, for the time being, to preside in the said Council.

6. And we do further declare our pleasure to be that all questions proposed for debate in the said Council shall be decided by the majority of votes; it being our pleasure that the Governor for the time being, or the member presiding in his absence, shall have an original vote, in common with the other members of the Council, as also a casting vote, if upon any question the votes shall be equally divided.

7. And for ensuring punctuality of attendance of the members of the said Council, and for the prevention of meetings of the said Council being holden without convenient notice to the several members thereof, it is our pleasure and we do hereby direct, that you or the Governor . . . for the time being, do frame and propose to the said Council for their adoption, such standing rules and orders as may be necessary for those purposes, with such standing rules and orders as may be best adapted for maintaining order and method in the despatch of business, and in the conduct of all debates in the said Council, which rules and orders (not being repugnant to the said recited Act of Parliament and Charter, or to these Instructions, or to any other Instructions which you may receive from us) shall at all times be followed and observed, and shall be binding upon the said Council, unless the same, or any of them, shall be disallowed by us.

8. It is our pleasure, and we do hereby direct, that no Law or Ordinance shall be made or enacted by the said Council, unless the same shall have been previously proposed by yourself, and that no questions shall be debated at the said Council, unless the same shall first have been proposed for that purpose by you: Provided nevertheless, and it is our pleasure, that if any member of the said Council shall deem any law fit to be enacted by the said Council, or any question proper there to be debated, and shall of such his opinion transmit a written statement to you, it shall be lawful for any such member of the said Council,

---

[1] In Additional Instructions of 12 February, 1853, replaced by the Colonial Secretary.

to enter upon the minutes thereof, a copy of any such statement, together with the reasons, upon which such his opinion may be founded.

9. And we do further direct that minutes be regularly kept of the proceedings of the said Council, by the Clerk of the said Council, and that the said Council shall not ever proceed to the despatch of business until the minutes of the last preceding meeting shall have first been read over and confirmed or corrected as may be necessary.

10. And we do further require and enjoin you, twice in each year, to transmit to us, through one of our principal Secretaries of State, a full and exact copy of the minutes of the said Council for the last preceeding half-year.

11. And it is our further pleasure, that you do not propose or assent to any Ordinance whatever respecting the constitution, proceedings, numbers, or modes of appointing any of the members of the said Legislative Council, or otherwise in relation to any of the matters mentioned or referred to in the said Charter and in these our 'Instructions, which shall be in anywise repugnant to or inconsistent with such Charter or Instructions, or repugnant to the said recited Act, or to any other Act of Parliament, but that any such Ordinance, or pretended Ordinance, shall be absolutely null and void to all intents and purposes.

12. And you are expressly enjoined not to propose or assent to any Ordinance whatever, whereby any person may be impeded or hindered from celebrating or attending the worship of Almighty God, in a peaceable and orderly manner, although such worship may not be conducted according to the rites and ceremonies of the Church of England.

13. And we do further enjoin you not to propose or assent to any Ordinance whatsoever, whereby our revenue might be lessened or impaired, or whereby our prerogative might be diminished or in any respect infringed, or whereby any increase or diminution might be made in the number,

salary or allowances of any public officers, which have or shall have received our sanction, without our special leave and command therein first received.

14. And we do further direct that you do not propose or assent to any Ordinance whatever, whereby bills of credit or other negotiable securities, of whatever nature, may be issued in lieu of money, on the credit of the said forts and settlements on the Gold Coast and their dependencies, or whereby any government paper currency may be established therein, or whereby any such bills or any other paper currency, or any coin, save only the legal coin of the realm, may be made or declared to be a legal tender, without special permission from us in that behalf first obtained.

15. And we do further enjoin and command you not to propose or assent to any Ordinance whatever by which persons, not of European birth or descent, might be subjected and made liable to any disabilities or restrictions to which persons of European birth or descent would not also be subjected and made liable.

16. And it is our further pleasure, that you do not propose or assent to any Ordinance whatever for raising money by the institution of any public or private lotteries.

17. And it is our further will and pleasure that you do not propose or assent to any Ordinance whatever for the divorce of persons joined together in holy matrimony.

18. And we do further direct that you do not propose or assent to any Ordinance whatever by which any tax or duty might be imposed upon the trade or shipping of the United Kingdom, or whereby any tax might be imposed upon transient traders, or upon persons residing and carrying on business for a short time within our said forts and settlements on the Gold Coast and their dependencies, from which other traders and persons carrying on the like business would be exempt.

19. And we do further direct that you do not propose or assent to any Ordinance whereby any grant of money or land, or

other donation or gratuity may be made by the Legislative Council to you.

20. And we do further direct that you do not propose or assent to any private Ordinance whatever whereby the property of any individual may be affected, in which there is not a saving of the rights of us, our heirs and successors, and of all bodies politic and corporate, and of all other persons excepting those at whose instance and for whose special benefit such Ordinance may be passed, and those claiming by, from, through, and under them.

21. And it is our will and pleasure that you do not propose or assent to any Ordinance whatever to which our assent has once been refused, without express leave for that purpose first obtained from us.

22. And it is our further will and pleasure that all Laws and Ordinances to be enacted by the said Legislative Council shall henceforth be styled, 'Ordinances enacted by the Governor of our Forts and Settlements on the Gold Coast, with the Advice and Consent of the Legislative Council thereof'; and that no other style or form shall ever be observed in any such enactment, and that all such Laws and Ordinances be drawn up in a simple and compendious form, avoiding, as far as may be, all prolixity and tautology.

23. And we do further direct, that when any Ordinance shall have been passed by you, with the advice of the said Legislative Council, the same shall forthwith be laid before us for our final assent, disallowance, or other direction thereupon, to be signified through you; for which purpose, we do hereby require you, with all convenient speed, to transmit to us, through one of our Principal Secretaries of State, a transcript in duplicate of every such Ordinance, as aforesaid, duly authenticated under the public seal of the said forts and settlements and their dependencies, and by your own signature; and we do direct that every such transcript to be so transmitted by the earliest occasion next after the enactment of the said Ordinance, and that no such Ordinance be made to take effect until our pleasure

thereupon be first made known and signified to you, and by you to the inhabitants of the said forts and settlements, excepting only in the case of Ordinances for raising the annual supplies for the service of the said forts and settlements and their dependencies, and in any other cases in which the delay, incident to a previous communication with us, would be productive of serious injury or inconvenience; in which several cases, we do hereby authorise you, with the advice of the said Council, to determine the time at which any such Ordinance shall take effect and come into operation within the said forts . . . which proceedings, with the reasons thereof, you shall, on the earliest occasion, report to us through one of our Principal Secretaries of State: And we do hereby reserve to us, our heirs and successors, full power and authority to confirm and finally enact or disallow any Ordinances which may be passed by you with the advice and consent of the said Council, either in whole or in part, such confirmation or disallowance being from time to time signified to you through one of our Principal Secretaries of State.

24. And we do further declare our pleasure to be, that in the month of January, or at the earliest practicable period at the commencement of each year, you do cause a complete collection to be published, for general information, of all Ordinances enacted during the preceding year.

25. And we do further direct that all Ordinances, made by you with the advice of the said Legislative Council, be distinguished by titles, and that the Ordinances of each year be also distinguished by numerical marks, commencing in each successive year with the number one, and proceeding in arithmetical progression to the number corresponding with the total number of Ordinances enacted during the year, and that every such Ordinance be divided into successive clauses or paragraphs, distinguished in like manner by numerical marks, and that to every such clause be annexed in the margin a short summary of its contents.

26. And we do further declare our pleasure to be, that in the passing of all laws, each different matter be provided for by a different law, without intermixing into one and the same Act such things as have no proper relation to each other; and that no clause or clauses be inserted in or be annexed to any Act, which shall be foreign to what the titles of such Act imports; and that no perpetual clause be part of any temporary law; and that no Act whatever be suspended, altered, continued, revived or repealed by general words, but that the title and date of such Act, so suspended, altered, continued, revived, or repealed, be particularly mentioned and expressed in the enacting part.

27. And it is our express will and pleasure, that no law whatsoever be made to continue for less than two years, except only in cases where it may be necessary, upon some unforeseen emergency, to make provision by law for a service in its nature temporary and contingent.

28. You are also to take care that in all Laws or Ordinances to be passed by our said Legislative Council, in any case for levying money or imposing fines, forfeitures, and penalties, express mention be made that the same are granted or reserved to us, our heirs and successors, for the public uses of the said forts and settlements and their dependencies, and the support of the government thereof, as by the said Law or Ordinance shall be directed.

29. And whereas, by the said recited Charter, we have authorised the Governor . . . for the time being, to summon as our Executive Council such persons as should from time to time be named or designated by us in any instructions under our signet and sign manual, to be addressed to him in that behalf: Now we do, by these our Instructions, nominate and appoint the undermentioned persons to be the members of the said Executive Council; that is to say, the Judicial Assessor . . . for the time being, and the Collector of Customs . . . for the time being. And we do hereby further ordain and appoint, that upon any

special occasion on which you, or the Governor for the time being . . . shall judge it advisable to obtain the advice of persons residing there, touching our affairs in that quarter, it shall be competent for you, or for such Governor, by a commission to be for that purpose issued under the public seal of our said forts and settlements, to summon for any such special occasion only, any such persons as aforesaid, as extraordinary members of our said Executive Council.

30. And we do declare our pleasure to be that you do forthwith communicate to our said Executive Council, these our Instructions, and likewise all such others from time to time, wherein their consent and concurrence are requisite, and as you shall find convenient for our service to be imparted to them.

31. And we do hereby declare that it is our pleasure, that our said Council shall not proceed to the despatch of business, unless duly summoned by your authority, and unless two members at least, exclusive of yourself, be present and assisting throughout the whole of the meetings at which any such business shall be despatched.

32. And it is our pleasure that you do attend and preside at the meetings of our said Executive Council.

33. And we do further direct and command, that a full and exact journal or minute, be kept of all the deliberations, acts, proceedings, votes, and resolutions of our said Executive Council; and that, at each meeting of the said Council, the minutes of the last preceding meeting shall be read over and confirmed or amended, as the case may require, before proceeding to the despatch of any other business.

34. And it is our further will and pleasure, and we do hereby command, that in the execution of the several powers and authorities granted and committed to you, by our said Charter and Commission, and these our Instructions, or by any additional Instructions hereafter to be given to you by us, you do in all things consult and advise

with our said Executive Council, and that you do not exercise the powers and authorities aforesaid, or any of them, except by and with the concurrence and advice of our said Executive Council, save and except only in such cases as are hereinafter saved and excepted; (that is to say) Provided always, that nothing herein contained shall extend to prevent your exercising, without the advice and consent of our said Executive Council, the several powers and authorities, or any of them, which may be of so urgent and pressing a nature as not to admit of the delay unavoidably incident to the deliberations of our said Council. It is nevertheless our pleasure that the measures adopted by you, without the advice of our said Executive Council upon any such emergency, shall with all convenient speed be by you brought before our said Executive Council for their revision and sanction: Provided also, that nothing herein contained shall prevent your exercising the several powers and authorities aforesaid, or any of them, without the advice and concurrence of our said Executive Council, in any case, or upon any occasion, which may not appear to you to be sufficiently important to require their assistance and advice, or which may be of such a nature that in your judgement our service would sustain material prejudice by consulting our said Executive Council thereupon.

35. And it is our further will and pleasure, that no question shall be brought before our said Executive Council for their advice or decision, excepting only such questions as may be proposed by you for that purpose: Provided nevertheless, and it is our will and pleasure, that if any member shall deem it expedient that any question should undergo the deliberation of the said Executive Council, and shall, by application in writing to you, request and propose that such question should be so discussed, it shall be competent to any such member to enter upon the minutes of the said Executive Council such his written application to you, together with the answer which may be returned by you to the same; and it is

our will, and we do further direct, that if in any case you see sufficient cause to dissent from the opinion of the major part, or of the whole of our said Executive Council, upon any question brought by you under their consideration, it shall be competent to you, upon any such occasion, to execute the powers and authorities vested in the Governor of our said forts and settlements on the Gold Coast . . . in opposition to such their opinion; it being nevertheless our pleasure, that in every case it shall be competent to any member of our said Council, to record at length, on the minutes of the said Council, the grounds and reasons of any advice or opinion he may give upon any question brought under the consideration of such Council; and it being also our pleasure, that in the event of your acting upon any occasion in opposition to the advice of the whole or the major part of the said Executive Council, you do, by the first opportunity, transmit to us, through one of our Principal Secretaries of State, a full explanation of the grounds of every such measure, together with complete copies of the minutes, if any, of the said Executive Council relating thereto. And we do further direct, that twice in each year, a full transcript of all the minutes of the Executive Council of the preceding half-year, be transmitted to us, through one of our Principal Secretaries of State.

36. And whereas we have . . . authorised the Governor . . . upon sufficient cause to him appearing, to suspend from the exercise of his office within our said settlements and their dependencies, any person exercising the same, under and by virtue of any commission or warrant granted or to be granted by us, or in our name, or under our authority: Now we do charge and require you, that before proceeding to any such suspension, you do signify, by a statement in writing to the person so to be suspended, the grounds of such your intended proceeding against him, and that you do call upon such person to communicate to you, in writing, a statement of the grounds upon which he may be

desirous to exculpate himself, which statement and exculpation you will lay before the Executive Council; and having consulted them thereupon, you will cause to be recorded in the minutes of the said Council, whether they, or the majority of them, do or do not assent to the said suspension; and if you thereupon proceed to such suspension, you are to transmit both of the said statements, together with the Minutes of Council, to us, through one of our Principal Secretaries of State, by the earliest conveyance. But if, in any case, the interests of our service shall appear to you to demand that a person shall cease to continue to exercise the powers and functions of his office instantly, or before there shall be time to take the proceedings hereinbefore directed, you shall interdict such person from the exercise of his powers and functions, preserving to him, however, until such proceedings shall have been taken, the emoluments and advantages of his office.

37. And it is our pleasure that all commissions to be granted by you to any person or persons, for exercising any office of employment in or concerning our said forts and settlements on the Gold Coast and their dependencies, be granted during pleasure only; and that whenever you shall appoint, to any vacant office or employment, any person not by us specially directed to be appointed thereto, you shall at the same time expressly apprise such person that such appointment is to be considered only as temporary and provisional until our allowance or disallowance thereof be signified.

38. And whereas . . . we have given and granted unto the Governor . . . full power and authority, as he shall see occasion, in our name and in our behalf, to grant to any offender convicted of any crime in any court, or before any judge, justice, or magistrate, within our said settlements and their dependencies, a free and unconditional pardon, or a pardon subject to such conditions as by any law or Ordinance hereafter to be in force in our said forts . . . may be thereunto annexed, or any respite of the sentences of any such offender for such period as to such Governor may seem fit: Now we do hereby require and enjoin you to call upon the judge presiding at the trial of any such offenders, to make to you a written report of the cases of all persons who may from time to time be condemned to suffer death by any sentence of any court within the said settlements . . . and such reports of the said judge shall by you be taken into consideration at the first meeting thereafter, which may be conveniently held, of our said Executive Council, where the said judge shall be especially summoned to attend, and you shall not pardon or reprieve any such offenders as aforesaid, unless it shall appear to you expedient to do so, upon receiving the advice of our Executive Council therein; but in all such cases, you are to decide either to extend or to withhold or pardon or reprieve, according to your own deliberate judgement, whether the members of the said Executive Council concur therein or otherwise, entering, nevertheless, on the minutes of the said Council a minute of your reasons, at length, in case you should decide any such question in opposition to the judgement of the majority of the members thereof.

39. And whereas you will receive, through one of our Principal Secretaries of State, a book of tables in blank (commonly called 'The Blue Book'), to be annually filled up with certain returns relative to the Revenue and Expenditure, Militia, Public Works, Legislation, Civil Establishments, Pensions, Population, Schools, Course of Exchange, Imports and Exports, Agricultural Produce, Manufactures, and other matters, in the said 'Blue Book' more particularly specified, with reference to the state and condition of our said forts and settlements: Now we do hereby signify our will and pleasure, that all such returns be accurately prepared, and punctually transmitted to us, from year to year, through one of our Principal Secretaries of State, and that no officer in our said settlements and their dependencies, within whose department it may be to contribute any return or returns for the purposes aforesaid, or to

prepare the same when so contributed, shall be entitled to receive or shall receive from you any warrant for the payment of his official salary which may become due and payable to him, so long as such duty as aforesaid shall be in arrear, or remain unperformed.

40. And it is our further will and pleasure that you do, to the utmost of your power, promote religion and education among the native inhabitants of our said forts and settlements and their dependencies, or of the lands thereto adjoining, and that you do especially take care to protect them in their persons, and in the free enjoyment of their possessions, and that you do by all lawful means prevent and restrain all violence and injustice, which may in any manner be practised or attempted against them, and that you take such measures as may appear to you to be necessary for their conversion to the Christian faith, and for their advancement in civilization.

41. And we do hereby declare our pleasure to be, that the preceding Instructions shall be taken and understood as addressed to the Governor for the time being of our said forts and settlements and their dependencies, or to the officer for the time being administering the Government thereof, notwithstanding the same or any part thereof may be in terms addressed to you, the said Stephen John Hill.

42. And we do hereby reserve to ourselves, our heirs and successors, full power and authority, from time to time, to revoke, alter, renew, or explain these our Instructions or any part thereof.

V.R.   [H.C.383 of 1855]

179 JAMES BANNERMAN TO EARL GREY
CAPE COAST CASTLE, 6 MAY, 1851.

. . . It is possible that . . . the proposal of forming the Legislative Council into a Court of Appeal may not have been explained in sufficiently explicit terms.[1] At

[1] The proposal was made in the opening part of the despatch from which extract No. 174 has been taken. It was rejected by Grey in a despatch to Winniett (18 December, 1850) to which No. 179 forms a reply.

present, the judgement of the Judicial Assessor is supreme. The Governor may remit or commute a punishment, but he cannot reverse a decree. In cases of appeal to the Governor, the only course hitherto open to him has been to summon a full Bench of Magistrates, with the Judicial Assessor as President. In the ordinary discharge of his duty, the latter superintends the other magistrates in their official functions, and may have cause to admonish, to reprimand, and even to impose fines for a neglect of, or any undue severity in, the exercise of their authority. He will not easily be over-ruled by his subordinates, and, in fact, in his capacity purely of Assessor to the Native Chiefs, he may decline to permit their interference at all, as, strictly considered, the mere magistrate has no jurisdiction beyond our forts. There have not been many appeals, but they have been made principally by those beyond the jurisdiction of a magistrate, and in the especial province of the Judicial Assessor.

Your Lordship may be inclined to think that, where an English magistrate sits in judgement with the Native Chiefs, to assist them in the administration of ustice, there could not arise any necessitv for appeal against that magistrate, as the chiefs themselves are professedly judges. But your Lordship is to understand, what may possibly be already known to you, that the Assessor, instead of being assistant and adviser, has, owing to the deference paid to his superior sense of justice, been elevated into the supreme judicial authority, even where purely native law is administered; and so much has this become the practice, and so generally is it acknowledged and admitted, that he holds his court more frequently without the presence of a single native ruler than otherwise. From this explanation, your Lordship will readily comprehend how the chiefs may themselves become the appellants. The Governor might certainly entertain the appeal, but he could only do so by telling the Judicial Assessor that he had assumed an authority beyond his commission, by dictating where he had only a right to counsel. But this would be to overturn at once all the influence which has been acquired and established by this very assumption of justice.

What is wanted, is an Appeal Court, of sufficient dignity in the eyes of the natives to give them confidence, and composed of men whom it would be no derogation to the Judicial Assessor to have his decisions, appealed against, referred to; the members of Council being his equals in rank, and the Governor, his superior. A professional man acting as Judicial Assessor might object to have his decisions revised by un-professional men; but almost invariably he acts as an Equity Judge, and your Lordship is aware that not much legal knowledge is necessary for the comprehension of what is or what is not justice. When, therefore, it was proposed to constitute the Legislative Council into a Court of Appeal, it was not meant in its capacity of a Legislative Council, but as being composed of the persons on the coast holding the highest official rank, and, on that account, in much respect with the people.

I may not perceive all the difficulties attending a measure of this kind, which may readily occur to your Lordship, not being so conversant as your Lordship is with the obstacles in the way of its formation: but there cannot be any doubt about the importance of having, on the spot, an appeal from the decision of a single man with such extraordinary powers as rest in the hands of the Judicial Assessor. . . .   [C.O.96/22]

180 S. J. HILL TO EARL GREY
CAPE COAST CASTLE, 27 OCTOBER, 1851.
Confidential.
My Lord,

Having . . . taken into consideration . . . your Lordship's views respecting the benefit that would probably arise from convening a meeting of the chiefs of the different tribes under the control of this Government, I consulted with Messrs Bannerman and Cruickshank . . . on this subject, and

it is their opinion that, in the present state of society, it would not be judicious to call together such general meetings, for the following reason.

As each king or chief moves attended by a very large and imposing body of followers, fully armed, a general meeting, under such circumstances, would be the means of showing them their great physical power, as compared to ours, and therefore might defeat the object we should have in convening the assembly, and possibly be productive of the most serious consequences, should it have the effect of weakening the influence now possessed by the authorities here; added to which, each king or chief, according to custom, would expect a suitable present, and, the number being very great, the expenditure to satisfy all would necessarily be a larger outlay than your Lordship might be disposed to sanction.

Under these circumstances, my Lord, I have determined, with your sanction, not to proceed in the matter unless I see my way more clearly, as I should be particularly guarded against any chance of a retrograde movement, as a bad principle in dealing with the people of this country. . . .

I believe, my Lord, I am justified in expressing a hope that I will be enabled to raise a House rate, but this change also must be very gradual. All the persons to whom I have spoken on the subject, seem to think that it would be a desirable tax, and that no serious opposition will be offered to such a measure. It is therefore my present intention to feel my way with all parties, and when secure, to commence the experiment at this place, extending it to Accra, Annamaboe, and the principal forts, and from each seabord station, gradually work the measure on through the different villages under British protection. . . .
[C.O.96/22]

181 THE POLL TAX 'ORDINANCE'
19 APRIL, 1852.

At a general meeting of the chiefs and head-men of the towns and districts upon the

Gold Coast under British protection, held at Cape Coast Castle on the 19th day of April, 1852, in the presence of his Excellency, Major Hill, Governor and Commander in Chief, and the civil and military officers of his Government, it was unanimously resolved and agreed upon: —

1. That this meeting, composed of his Excellency the Governor, his Council, and the chiefs and headmen of the countries upon the Gold Coast under British Protection, constitutes itself into a Legislative Assembly with full powers to enact such laws as it shall seem fit, for the better government of these countries.

2. That this Assembly be recognised by Her Majesty's Government as legally constituted; that it be called the Legislative Assembly of Native Chiefs upon the Gold Coast; that it be presided over by his Excellency, the Governor, who shall have the power to assemble, prorogue, and adjourn it at pleasure; and that its enactment, sanctioned and approved of by the Governor, shall immediately become the law of the country, subject to the approval of Her Majesty the Queen, and be held binding upon the whole of the population being under the protection of the British Government.

3. That this Legislative Assembly, being thus duly constituted, having taken into consideration the advantages which the chiefs and natives derive from the protection afforded them by Her Majesty's Government, consider it reasonable and necessary that the natives generally should contribute to the support of the Government by submitting, from time to time, to pay such taxes as may be determined upon by the majority of the chiefs assembled in Council with his Excellency the Governor.

4. That it appears to the chiefs at present assembled in Council, that the most productive, the least burthensome, and the most equitable tax, which, in the present state of the country, can be levied, would be a poll tax upon the gross amount of the population enjoying the protection of the British Government.

5. That entertaining the views here expressed, the chiefs and headmen do, for themselves and their people, voluntarily agree to pay annually to the Government the sum of 1s sterling per head, for every man, woman and child residing in the districts under British protection.

6. That the collection of this tax be confided to officers appointed by his Excellency the Governor, assisted by the chiefs, who, in consideration of annual stipends to be paid to them by the Government, agree to give, in their several districts, their cordial assistance and the full weight of their authority in support of this measure, and to aid the tax-gatherers in taking a census of the population and in collecting the tax.

7. That pay-notes specifying the services to be rendered and the amount of pay to be given to each chief or headman, be immediately granted under the hand and seal of the Governor, payable annually after the collection of the tax, upon certificates given by the tax-gatherer of the district, that the services specified have been duly performed.

8. That it shall be competent for the tax-gatherer to sue any person refusing to pay the tax, before the native chief of the district, or an English magistrate, as for common debt, and that the master of a house or the head of a family be considered responsible for the whole of the inmates of the house.

9. That any obstruction offered to the tax-gatherer, or assault made upon him in the execution of his duty, shall be punished by fine or imprisonment, one half of all such fines to be paid to the chief of the district or town.

10. That it shall be competent for the tax-gatherer and chief of a district, subject to the approval of the Governor, to make such local arrangements for facilitating the collection of the tax as may be found expedient.

11. That the revenue derived from this tax, after payment of the stipends of the

chiefs and other expenses attending its collection, be devoted to the public good, in the education of the people, in the general improvement and extension of the judicial system, in affording greater facilities of internal communication, increased medical aid, and in such other measures of improvement and utility as the state of the social progress may render necessary, and that the chiefs be informed of the mode of its application, and entitled to offer such suggestions on this point as they may consider necessary.

12. That a proclamation based upon these resolutions be issued by his Excellency the Governor, to carry them into full effect during this current year, and that such proclamation, issued with the full concurrence of the Legislative Assembly of the Native Chiefs upon the Gold Coast, shall have in every respect the force of a law, and be held binding upon the whole of the native population being under the protection of the British Government.

[The marks of]

George Fynn Aggrey chief of Cape Coast
Eddoo   „   Fantee
Ammoney   „   Annamaboe
Quahi Ephraim   „   Denkera
Chibboo Arbarbeo „   Dixcove
Quanim Deawool   „   Secondee
Quacoe Yarkey   „   Secondee
Quabina Ammoah   „   Abrah
Chebboo Coomah   „   Domonassie
Bondeguay   „   Winnebah
Quow Cootooacoo „   Mumford
Quamina Menasah „   „
Quashie Eccoom   „   Agoonah
Yow Dodoo   „   Agoonah
Eddom Ashantee   „   Aseam
Quammo Ahwih   „   Agah.
     [C.O.96/25[1]: H.C.412, A & P (1865) v]

---

[1] For later adherents to these resolutions, see the Governor's despatches of 2 August and 22 October, 1852. As far as these can be identified, it may be said that all the chiefs west of the Volta (as far as and including Nzima), and only Krepi to the east of it, agreed to pay the tax.

182 S. J. HILL TO EARL GREY[1]
CAPE COAST CASTLE, 23 APRIL, 1852.
Confidential.

My Lord,
    With reference to my despatch of this day's date, forwarding to your Lordship certain Resolutions signed by the chiefs, engaging that the natives under British protection should pay a yearly Poll Tax of one shilling for every man, woman and child throughout the settlements, I consider it necessary to explain that, finding, on agitating a 'House Tax' that the people generally would prefer paying a Poll Tax, and were averse to the former levy, I gave up the first idea and adopted the latter, as being the most popular with the masses of the people, and affording a larger revenue.

    The great difficulty that I found in my Government, was the impossibility of getting at the chiefs, to secure their support in carrying out any measures of utility; added to which, certain educated natives, with no real pretension to any power, were in the practice of assuming an authority which did not belong to their position; by such means exercising an undue influence with the chiefs and headmen, and generally opposing, in an underhand manner, the efforts of the Governor. And I am quite aware, in my own case, they have done all in their power to induce the natives not to agree to the proposed Poll Tax. This opposition is now quite overcome by the chiefs being placed in their proper position, and brought into direct communication with the Executive; and I have no doubt, my Lord, that this measure will be the means of producing the most happy results as respects the future welfare of the natives enjoying the protection of Her Majesty's Government, as I find the chiefs very docile and willing to listen to reason.

    Your Lordship will perceive that this new constitution, if approved of, will place the Governor in a better position for carrying into effect any changes that may be submitted for future legislation, at the same

---

[1] Grey had left office in February 1852.

time be most popular with the chiefs of the country, and accelerate the march of civilization and consequent social improvement of the natives generally.

I have &c.   [C.O.96/25]

183 HILL TO GREY
CAPE COAST CASTLE, 24 APRIL, 1852.
My Lord,

With reference to my despatch of the 23rd instant, I have the honour to inform your Lordship, that the collection of the Poll Tax agreed upon will be a matter of much trouble and difficulty, more particularly as it is almost impossible to procure, within this Government, such persons for collectors as can be recommended or depended upon, and the imperfect means of communication and great extent of country, must add to the difficulty to be overcome. It is true, I might leave the collection to the chiefs, but then I should fear that, acting under the authority of the Government, and knowing that the natives would be afraid to show any opposition, they would be induced to increase the amount of the levy, thereby oppressing the people and enriching themselves. . . .

It is my intention, with your Lordship's approval, to appoint the best men I can procure as sub-collectors, dividing the masses of the people under British protection into 12 districts, with one sub-collector to each, at a salary of one hundred pounds per annum, including his travelling expenses.   And in order to secure a check on these sub-collectors, I would appoint a General Collector, at a liberal salary, say six hundred pounds per annum, to supervise the whole. . . . [Without such an appointment] I am inclined to believe that much of the revenue will be lost or appropriated to private purposes.

On making a calculation of the probable expense for collecting this tax, together with the sum that should be paid to each chief, I am of opinion that it will take £25 per cent on the gross total to defray these charges, which, deducted from the probable

amount of the levy will leave £15, annually, for the purposes specified in t.. Resolutions signed by the chiefs. . . . When your Lordship takes into consideration that, throughout the Western Division of the Government, the shillings will be paid in gold dust, which must take time to test and weigh, and again, that in the Eastern Division, the tax can only be received in cowrie shells, at the rate of forty to every penny, requiring time and trouble in the counting, the percentage for securing this revenue may not appear unreasonable. However your Lordship may be assured that I will do all in my power to make the expenses on this head as light as possible. . . .   [C.O.96/25; H.C.412]

184 EARL GREY'S COMMENT

I cannot but regard with great satisfaction the success which, in three different countries so widely removed from each other as Ceylon, Natal and the Gold Coast, has thus far attended the experiment of imposing direct taxation on an uncivilized population, with a view to their improvement. The experiment is a novel one in modern colonial administration, and is the practical realization of views which I was led to form more than twenty years ago when Under-Secretary of State, and on which at that time, I earnestly, but in vain, recommended that the measure for the abolition of slavery should be founded.

But even the imposition of the tax . . . is of less importance, and less full of promise for the future, than the steps which have been taken in order to obtain an authority for its collection, which should be regarded by the people as binding upon them [in the Legislative Assembly of Chiefs]. . . .

I am persuaded that I do not overrate the importance of the establishment of this rude negro Parliament, when I say, that I believe it has converted a number of barbarous tribes, possessing nothing which deserves the name of a government, into a nation, with a regularly organized authority, and institutions, simple and unpretending, but suited to the actual state of society. I trust that those whose duty it may be to watch over the future progress of the nation, which has thus, as I may say, been created, will endeavour to guard it carefully from the dangers to which it will be exposed, either by an attempt on the one hand to force too rapidly into existence, before the people's minds are prepared for them, the more regular government and more perfect laws of civilized nations, or by neglecting, on the other hand, to proceed, steadily but cautiously, with those many social and legal reforms which must be successively adopted before the traces of recent barbarism and its evils can be got rid of.

The true policy I believe to be . . . to keep constantly in sight the formation of a regular government on the European model, and the establishment of a civilized polity, as the goal ultimately to be aimed at: but in the endeavour to arrive at it, taking care that each successive step shall appear to the people themselves as nothing more than the natural mode of providing for some want, or remedying some evil,

which they practically feel at the moment. . . .

The real interest of this Country is gradually to train the inhabitants of this part of Africa in the arts of civilization and government until they shall grow into a nation capable of protecting themselves and of managing their own affairs, so that the interference and assistance of the British authorities may by degrees be less and less required. Orderly and civilized communities cannot grow up in a country capable of yielding such valuable productions without our carrying on with them a large and mutually advantageous trade: but in a climate so uncongenial to European constitutions, it is not desirable that the maintenance of order and the progress of civilization should continue to depend on the exercise of authority by white men, or that the duty of governing and protecting the inhabitants of western Africa should be thrown upon this Country longer than can be avoided.

[*Colonial Policy of Lord J. Russell's Administration*, ii, 284–7]

1852–1886

THE AGE OF LAISSEZ-FAIRE

BOOK V

The Years of Uncertainty, 1852–1864

14 The Poll Tax experiment and troubles with the tribes, 1852–1856

GREY'S brave words had scarcely appeared in print before the difficulties implicit in maintaining the Protectorate began to make themselves felt. First and most serious was an Ashanti crisis. While Maclean was developing the Protectorate, and even when Grey was formulating his plans for it, the Ashantis had been generally quiescent. There had, indeed, been minor alarms, particularly after 1844 when the Ashanti were uneasy at seeing Maclean superseded (146), and Maclean himself had found it more difficult to adjust disputes (153). The question of what to do with fugitives from Ashanti had been brought before Grey (170), and by him put aside with some misgivings (175). And the Asantehene had sounded in turn Hill (146), Winniett (163) and Fitzpatrick (165) on the subject of the Asins, over whom he was anxious to recover his control.

It was the intrigues of certain Asin chiefs with Kumasi that provoked a major crisis in the autumn of 1852 (185–6), followed by an Ashanti invasion in the April of 1853 (188). Eventually the Ashantis withdrew without fighting, in the face of the determined efforts of Governor S. J. Hill to put the Protectorate in a state of defence, but not before the British Government had been made aware of new and unwelcome responsibilities (190). George Blankson was sent to Kumasi on a largely futile mission (192), which, however, seemed to reveal that there was no immediate threat from that quarter. The want of a satisfactory agent at Kumasi was more readily felt than supplied (194). Disputes continued, and in 1855 once more invasion seemed not unlikely (202).

Relations with the Protected States were scarcely better; and here Grey's own projects came into question. It was perhaps more surprising that the chiefs had ever been brought to vote the poll tax in the first place than that they soon objected to paying it. The former Danish districts rose in rebellion in 1854 (193) and although other causes were not wanting (and the local authorities made the most of them) there is no doubt that the tax touched off the rising. The bombardment of Christiansborg and Labadi brought little improvement in the tax returns (198), and the Colonial Office, very properly, became uneasy about continuing a levy that could apparently only be collected by force (199).

At Cape Coast also, the authorities, British and African, found themselves at variance. Here too the Poll Tax contributed to the unrest, though the first victim of the agitation was the Judicial Assessor, Mr. Fitzpatrick, who was obliged to retire. This was to assail the Protectorate in its most fundamental aspect, and at a time when steps were being taken to strengthen the judicial system by the enactment of a Supreme Court Ordinance (189).

A few months later, there was a difference between the chief of Cape Coast and the head of a court he had inaugurated, which resulted in a movement to destool the chief. Rightly or wrongly, the official tendency was to attribute these opposition movements to the intrigues of the merchants (191) or to the activities of the new 'Half-caste and half-civilized' elements that were now coming to the fore (196). And while the Home Government was as anxious as ever to repudiate political responsibilities (187), the fracas at Cape Coast was deemed, not altogether wisely perhaps,[1] to call for a statement of the British position *vis à vis* the protected chiefs (197).

Largely for want of effective leadership, the Protectorate was drifting out of control; and when that old critic of colonial administration, Sir William Molesworth, found himself, in the last three months of his life, in charge of the Colonial Office, he decided that there was a case for investigation by an independent observer (200). Major H. St. George Ord, who was eventually selected for this duty, received his instructions from the Prime Minister (Palmerston) himself (201). In view of the Government's evident reluctance to believe that Grey's experiment was to be written off as a failure, it is perhaps not surprising that Ord sought to explain the continuing alienation of the tribes, less in terms of the Poll Tax (though he had reforms to propose there), than in a failure to take the chiefs and headmen into the confidence of Government (203).

[1] Ord (to Labouchere, 14 February, 1856; in C.O.96/40) thought the destoolment justified.

185 S. J. HILL TO SIR JOHN PACKINGTON[1]
CAPE COAST CASTLE, 23 OCTOBER, 1852.

Sir,

I have the honour to bring under your notice the following circumstance which has occurred in these settlements, and should, in my opinion, be reported for your information.

Cudjoe Chibboo, chief of Assin, a country under the protection of Great Britain, has been tried by a court composed of chiefs, the judicial body, with myself presiding. After a fair and impartial investigation he was convicted of the following serious charges, viz.:

1st. Sending a man as a prisoner to the King of Ashantee, well knowing that the life of such person thus sent would be sacrificed.

2nd. For receiving a bribe in gold from the King of Ashantee, and endeavouring to induce his captains to accept proportions of the same, in order to bring them under the authority of that monarch; the rule in this country obliging every man taking such a present to serve the donor.

3rd. For setting my authority as Governor at defiance, by detaining the soldier stationed in the Assin country, and

[1] John Somerset Packington (later first Baron Hampton) (1799–1880): Conservative M.P. for Droitwich, 1837–74; Secretary of State for War and the Colonies in Derby's 'Who? Who?' administration.

stating to such soldier that it was his intention to throw off his allegiance to the English and join the king of Ashantee, and he did not care for what I could do.

With the unanimous consent of the chiefs, magistrates, and in accordance with my own opinion, I deposed Cudjoe Chibbo, and he is now confined in this Castle, a prisoner for life.

It may be necessary for me to explain that the Assin nation formed for many years one of the confederate states subject to the Ashantee rule, and were in time of war the advance guard of the army of that monarchy, and fought against the English on several occasions; but being tired of the oppression exercised by the Ashantees, they crossed the frontier river between Ashantee and Fantee, swearing allegiance to Great Britain, [and] have been under the protection of our flag since. The people of Ashantee have often tampered with the Assins to induce their return but hitherto without effect; and even in this case, I am happy to say, the captains generally refused the bribe offered, declaring that no quantity of gold could induce them to leave the protection of a flag under which they had enjoyed so many privileges and such liberty. . . . I was most anxious to prevent this chief's intention of joining the Ashantees, as I had reasons for believing, if such move had occurred, [that] the King of Ashantee, feeling himself compromised by the consequent breach of treaty, might have been induced to listen to the strong war party existing in his dominions, and possibly commit some act of aggression on the nations under our protection, which would lead to a war; as I believe it is only the peacable disposition of the present King that prevents a collision between Ashantee and the Fantee States. . . . I am glad to say, that so far as promises may be relied upon, and to all appearance, the most perfect understanding exists between the King of Ashantee and myself, and from all I can learn, provided no untoward event takes place, we may hope for peace during the lifetime of the present monarch. . . .

[H.C.703 of 1853, A & P (1852–3), lxv]

186 HILL TO PACKINGTON
CAPE COAST CASTLE, 27 OCTOBER, 1852.

Sir,

With reference to my despatch on the 23rd instant . . . I have the honour to inform you that, the Fantee and Assin chiefs and captains having petitioned me to restore Cudjoe Chibbo to his former position as chief of the Assins, I have been induced to grant their request on the following terms:

1st. That all the nephews or heirs apparent to the different headmen in the Assin country be delivered up as hostages, and placed under the care of the Fantee chiefs.

2nd. That several Assins, now on the Ashantee side of the river Prah, cross that boundary, and settle with the rest of their nation under the rule of the English flag.

3rd. That the Assins and Fantees conjointly undertake to make such a military road as I may approve of, opening the whole country from Cape Coast Castle to the river Prah, a distance of some 90 miles, in order that the Government may have easy access to the interior of the country. . . .   [H.C.703 of 1853]

I

187 THE DUKE OF NEWCASTLE[1] TO
S. J. HILL   LONDON, 5 JANUARY, 1853.

Sir,

I have to acknowledge your despatch No. 50 of 18th October last, in which you apply for the approval and authority of my predecessor to your marching a force into the territory of the king of Augua,[2] in order to enforce obedience to your authority.

If you are yourself satisfied that this chief has assumed an attitude of defiance towards the British Government, and that it is necessary that this measure should be adopted, in order that satisfaction may be obtained for injuries done to British subjects, I feel that it is incumbent upon me, in reliance on your judgement, to give the authority required; always under the provision that the expenses of the expedition are to be defrayed by the Colonial Government.

But I must distinctly inform you that Her Majesty's Government have no intention of claiming any territorial rights over Augua, or any other native district in the neighbourhood of the British forts.[3] Whatever claims of this kind the Danish Government may have advanced, I must instruct you not to enforce them. The possession of the Danish forts and ground actually occupied by the Danes is all which it was intended to acquire by the Convention of 1850 as British territorial dominion.

The influence to be exercised over the native tribes is that of protection, as heretofore, in the neighbourhood of the old British forts, not of dominion. You will therefore take no steps, in pursuance of your military operations against the chief of Angua, which may involve the conquest

[1] Henry Pelham Fiennes Pelham Clinton, 5th Duke of Newcastle (1811–64); M.P., 1832–51, first as a Tory and later as a Peelite; Secretary of State for War and the Colonies, December 1852 to June 1854; Secretary for War until February 1855; Secretary of State for the Colonies, 1859–64.

[2] i.e. Awunah, or mod. Anlo.

[3] Hill spoke of the Anlos as swearing and therefore owing allegiance after the transfer of the Danish forts.

or permanent occupation of any portion of his territory.

I have &c.   [C.O.96/25]

188 S. J. HILL TO THE DUKE OF NEWCASTLE

CAPE COAST CASTLE, 8 APRIL, 1853.

My Lord Duke,

It becomes my duty to report for your Grace's information, an untoward event which has caused me much anxiety, as I have every reason for supposing it will lead to a war with the Ashantees.

On the morning of the 22nd ultimo, I received a message from a chief in the interior, to the effect that an armed body of Ashantees had crossed our frontier, and were in the Assin territory for the purpose of taking away the chiefs of that country, Chibboo and Gabril.[1] I immediately selected an officer, who is also a magistrate, and well known to the Assins, as he had been superintending a military road through their country, and ensign Brownell, with a party of 40 soldiers, marched the same afternoon.

On Mr. Brownell's arrival in Assin, he found the report to be correct, and on communicating with the captain of the Ashantee forces, and asking the reason of this invasion, he was informed that the king of Ashantee had sent them for the purpose of making what is called 'custom' for old Chibboo, the late king of Denkera, who had been formerly a subject of Ashantee, but during the late war, placing himself and people under the protection of Great Britain, had fought stoutly throughout against his former master, the king of Ashantee. . . . [This] was intended as a blind to deceive me, while the Ashantees took measures to carry out their object in securing the Assin chiefs and as many of their people as could be seized. . . .

Chibboo and Gabril were sent into Cape Coast by the native chiefs, but previous to the latter being sent, Mr. Brownell con-

[1] Kwadwo (Kojo) Tsibu and Gabiri, chiefs of Asin Atandaso and Asin Apimenim respectively.

fronted him with the Ashantee captain who, throwing off the mask, declared the plot, and accused Chibboo and Gabril of having deceived his master, the king of Ashantee, from whom they had received a bribe of 400 ounces of gold, which Gabril could not deny. . . .

Mr. Brownell then, agreeably to my instructions, informed the Ashantee captain [that] his country and that under my protection, were at peace; [that] it was my great desire to cultivate friendly relations between their people and mine; and although he should not have crossed the frontier with an armed force, yet as the object of their visit had failed, I requested that he would, with his men, return into their own country, and the palaver could be settled between the king of Ashantee and myself. This captain made many excuses, to gain time whilst a large force of Ashantees were crossing the Prah river to his support, and Ensign Brownell found, from the report of the Assins, who had to retire, that a strong force of Ashantees had established themselves at a place called Foosooway, a day's march at our side of the river.

[Reinforcements were sent up with strict orders not to fire, except in self-defence. Brownell went to the Ashanti camp and promised restoration of plundered Ashanti property, provided the Ashanti left the Protectorate peacefully.] . . .

The Ashantee captains agreed to retire, and it was all arranged that their army should march on the morning of the 5th. However, when the morning came, a fresh pretext for delay presented itself, and as the Ashantees were now adding to their strength daily, their army now numbering some 7,000 men, with a supporting force of probably as many more under the command of the king's son in their rear, but within the Assin territory, I found it was useless to hope for a peaceful termination to this gross act of aggression. . . . It is just possible the Ashantees may be induced to retire, and hostilities be avoided: but from the restless, warlike disposition of those people, and taking into consideration the opinion of all best acquainted with their character, I regret to think that they will never be satisfied without bloodshed. . . .

[He made defensive arrangements accordingly.] All the natives on our frontier are prepared for defence, and I have posted in front of the Ashantee army, a native force of armed men under the command of Captain M'Court of the Gold Coast Corps, with one officer and one hundred men of the Gold Coast Corps, two light field-pieces, and four rocket guns. . . . Every path leading to the sea coast is guarded with outposts. . . . Scouts are out in every direction to watch the movements of the Ashantees. My orders to all, are not to fire a shot . . . excepting in self-defence.

I submit a copy of a letter received from the merchants at Cape Coast, urging me to precipitate matters, [and] my reply thereto, and I trust [that] in my anxiety to avoid, if possible, the horrors of war, your Grace will not consider I have used too much forbearance with those uncivilized people, nor in any way compromised the honour of the British flag. Had Ensign Brownell first reported his intention to me, he should not have entered the Ashantee lines, but as he did so, and from a noble motive, to prevent hostilities, risking his own life for the cause of peace, I had no alternative left but to faithfully carry out all his promises made to the Ashantee chiefs. . . . The whole onus now rests on the Ashantees. . . .

As it is the opinion of all classes of persons that war is inevitable, I have asked for soldiers to be sent to my aid from Sierra Leone and the Gambia, but as those garrisons have only a weak force, I cannot hope for much assistance. Could the native allies be depended upon in case of collision, all might end well, and few soldiers be required: but they had been kept down for so many years by the Ashantees, and the prestige of the Ashantee name in war is such as to make it doubtful how far they would stand close conflict

with them, so that a reserve of disciplined men, in any action that may take place, is absolutely essential.

In case of war, and in order to draw the enemy as far as we can from their resources, and, if possible, bring them down under the guns of the forts, I have instructed the officers in command of outposts, if attacked by superior numbers, to retire steadily on Cape Coast Castle, and only to give battle when the opportunity may appear favourable to our arms. It is also my intention to take the command in person, as my presence may give confidence to our allies.

As it will be necessary, at the lowest estimate, to keep a native army in the field, of at least 20,000 men, to defend these settlements, and the subsistence alone of such a number would, at the rate of 2½d. per diem for each, amount to £208. 6. 8d. per diem, independent of contingent expenses, I have to beg your Grace's instructions as to the manner in which this expenditure is to be procured; the funds at the disposal of the local Government being totally inadequate to afford any extra outlay.

If I may be permitted to offer an opinion, I would respectfully suggest, that for greater efficiency and economy, a disciplined force should be sent here to put an end to this war, as I am perfectly satisfied that 1,000 men from the West India Regiments, with their bayonets, would do more than ten times that number of natives, imperfectly armed and undisciplined; and, indeed, without such a reinforcement, it is impossible to calculate when hostilities may cease, as the last Ashantee war lasted many years.

The mercantile loss from continued hostilities would be immense, as the stoppage of trade in consequence of the present position of affairs, up to this time, is supposed to have caused a deficit of some £30,000 or £40,000. All trade, improvements, etc., are at a standstill; a ruinous state of affairs, for which it is satisfactory to know [that] not the slightest semblance of a reason can be offered by our aggressors. . . .[1]   [H.C.703 of 1853]

189 THE SUPREME COURT ORDINANCE
26 APRIL, 1853.

An Ordinance for the establishment of a Supreme Court of Civil and Criminal Jurisdiction within Her Majesty's Forts and Settlements on the Gold Coast.

Whereas it is expedient to make provision for the better administration of justice within Her Majesty's forts and settlements on the Gold Coast:

1. Be it therefore enacted, by His Excellency Stephen John Hill, Governor and Commander-in-Chief of Her Majesty's Forts and Settlements on the Gold Coast, by and with the consent of the Legislative Council thereof, and by authority of the same, that a court of jurisdiction, to be styled 'The Supreme Court of Her Majesty's Forts and Settlements on the Gold Coast,' be and hereby is constituted and established.

2. And be it further enacted that the said Supreme Court shall be holden and presided over by a Chief Justice, to be hereinafter nominated and appointed, who shall at the time of his appointment, be a barrister-at-law of one of the Inns of Court at Westminster, of Dublin, or an Advocate of the Court of Session in Scotland.

3. And be it further enacted, that the said Supreme Court shall be a court of record, and shall within the said forts and settlements, and within this jurisdiction, have cognizance of all pleas, civil and criminal, and jurisdiction in all cases whatsoever, as fully and amply, to all intents and purposes, as Her Majesty's Courts of Queen's Bench, Common Pleas and Exchequer, at Westminster, or either

[1] The Ashanti retired the following week without fighting. The question of reinforcements therefore had not to be faced, and Newcastle was able to approve the Governor's 'moderation and forbearance, combined with watchfulness and a firm maintenance of the rights of British territory and of our native allies'. Cf. Crooks, pp. 333–7.

of them, lawfully have or exercise; and the said court shall also, at all times, be a court of oyer and terminer and general gaol delivery, in and for the said forts and settlements; and the said Chief Justice, so to be appointed, shall have and exercise such and the same jurisdiction and authority in the said forts and settlements as the Judges of the Courts of Queen's Bench Common Pleas and Exchequer in England, or any of them, lawfully have and exercise, and as shall be necessary for carrying into effect the several jurisdictions, powers and authorities committed to the said court.

4. And be it further enacted, that the said Supreme Court of Her Majesty's Forts and Settlements on the Gold Coast, shall and may inquire of, hear and determine all treasons, piracies, murders, conspiracies, and such other offences, of what nature or kind whatsoever committed, or that shall be committed, upon the sea, or any haven, river, creek or place where the Admiral or Admiralty have authority, power or jurisdiction, according to the common course of the laws of the realm of England, and not otherwise; and that all persons convicted of the offences to be inquired of, heard and determined in the said court, shall be subject and liable to, and shall suffer all such and the same pains, penalties and forfeitures, as by any law or laws now in force, persons convicted of the same would be subject and liable to, in case the same were respectively inquired of, tried, heard, determined and adjudged in England, any law, statute or usage to the contrary notwithstanding.

5. And be it further enacted, that the said court shall be held at Cape Coast Castle, or such other of Her Majesty's forts on the Gold Coast, and at such times and so often as the Governor and Commander-in-Chief of Her Majesty's forts and settlements for the time being, may direct and appoint.

6. And be it further enacted, that any action of law to be brought in the said Supreme Court, when the parties, plaintiff and defendant, shall join issue on any

matter of fact, the trial of such issue or issues, may be heard by the said Chief Justice, and a jury of not less than six men; and that on the trial of any person or persons upon any charge or information before the said court, such trial may be heard by the said Chief Justice, and a jury of not less than six men, whose unanimous verdict shall, to all intents and purposes, be as valid and binding as the verdict of 12 men would have been in the same case.

7. And be it further enacted, that it shall not be necessary before bringing any person or persons to trial before the said Supreme Court, to present any bill of indictment to any grand jury against such person or persons, or to have or hold any preliminary inquiry before any other tribunal, save and except such inquiry as any justice of the peace may deem it necessary to make before committing such person or persons for trial before the said court.

8. And be it further enacted, that it shall and may be lawful for persons to serve as jurors on the trial of said issues or persons before-mentioned, in the said Supreme Court, who are not or shall not at the time of such trial be inhabitants of any of Her Majesty's forts or settlements on the Gold Coast: Provided always, that such persons shall either be the subjects of Her Majesty the Queen, or inhabitants of those countries adjacent to Her Majesty's forts and settlements on the Gold Coast, which are under Her Majesty's protection.

9. And be it further enacted, that the Honourable James Colman Fitzpatrick, now filling the office of Judicial Assessor, or assistant to the native sovereigns and chiefs of the countries adjacent to Her Majesty's forts and settlements on the Gold Coast, be and hereby is nominated and appointed Chief Justice of the said Supreme Court, and that the said Chief Justice shall receive the sum of £300 sterling per annum, in addition to his present salary as Judicial Assessor as aforesaid.[1]

[1] An amending ordinance to provide for the appointment of successors to the office was passed in 1854.

10. And whereas it is expedient to provide means for the revision of decrees or judgements pronounced by the said Judicial Assessor in certain cases: And whereas a suitor before the native tribunals would be entitled to appeal from the decision of his chief to a council of wise men and captains; be it further enacted, that in all cases wherein the matter in dispute between the parties is of the value of £300 sterling, or upwards, it shall and may be lawful for any person interested in the case, and who feels aggrieved by the decision of the said Judicial Assessor, within 10 days of the pronouncing of such decision, and upon lodging in court the sum of £50 to cover any costs or damages the respondent may incur therein, to appeal to the Governor and Council for reversal of the same.

11. And be it further enacted, that it shall and may be lawful for the Governor and Legislative Council of Her Majesty's forts and settlements on the Gold Coast, to entertain, hear, and determine such appeals, and to measure the costs and damages aforesaid, and they are hereby required to do so: Provided, that on the hearing of such appeals, there shall be present, in addition to the Governor and Judicial Assessor, at least one other member of Council; and provided also, that no member of Council who is interested in any way in the result of such appeal, shall sit on the hearing thereof; and that in the event of the number of voices being agreed in the determination of judgement upon such appeal, the Governor for the time being shall have two voices.

12. And be it further enacted, that notwithstanding the lodging of such appeal as aforesaid, and pending the hearing thereof, the original decree of the court of the Judicial Assessor shall be in operation and full force, as if no appeal had been lodged: Provided, nevertheless, that all money and property levied under or in virtue of such decree, shall remain in the custody of the court until the decision on such appeal shall be made known.

13. And be it enacted that this Ordinance shall come into operation immediately on the passing thereof.

H.C.383 of 1855]

190 B. CRUICKSHANK TO THE DUKE OF NEWCASTLE   LONDON, 18 MAY, 1853.

. . . The Governor's obligations to assist the Fantees in repelling the advance of an armed Ashantee force into the country south of the Prah are based:

1st. Upon the treaty concluded at the end of the war.

2nd. Upon a bond which the Fantee chiefs (Assins included) signed . . . in 1844. . . .

3rd. Upon the enactment authorising the imposition of a poll tax, which was made upon the express understanding of the continued protection of the Government:

And lastly, and generally, upon the acknowledged practice of the kings of Ashantee, who have, during the last 25 years, invariably sought redress of injuries done by the Fantees and Assins, from the Governor, who, in like manner, has stood between these and any encroachment on the part of the Ashantees.

Upon the present occasion, the king knew that his underhand dealings with the Assins deprived him of any right to apply to the Governor, and hence he has added to his original breach of good faith, the violation of the Fantee territory, with the view of obtaining redress for himself for the trickery of the Assin chiefs. . . .

While I conceive that Her Majesty's Government is bound by every consideration of honour and good faith, to protect the Fantee territory from hostile invasion, I am strongly opposed to any aggressive measure, even in retaliation. All that is required of us, and all that it is prudent for us to seek, is to maintain the boundary of the Prah. In the account given in the 'Times' of the 14th, the conquest of Ashantee is hinted at. I need scarcely say that this is absurd, nor do I believe that

Major Hill could, for a moment, entertain any such project. The capital of Ashantee is fully six days' march from the Prah, through an almost impenetrable forest, and over steep and rugged hills. If we could over-run the country, which is very doubtful, it would be utterly impossible to maintain, by force, our position in it. My views, therefore, in seeking an interview with your Grace, extended no farther than to entreat your support for the Governor's measures to preserve the independence of the Fantees. . . .

[C.O.96/29: H.C. 703]

191 MINUTE BY H. M. MERIVALE[1]
COLONIAL OFFICE, 5 NOVEMBER, 1853.

You are aware of the ancient feud between the mercantile interest at Cape Coast, i.e. the mercantile firms in London which trade there and their agents and dependents in the Colony and neighbourhood, and the local Government. The dissatisfaction of the merchants has been pressed on this office in many ways (ever since the government was taken out of their hands some years ago . . .) and particularly in a series of complaints against Mr. Fitzpatrick, the Judicial Assessor. These have been repeatedly investigated and found to rest (as far as his dealings with the natives are concerned) on very insubstantial information. The two successive Governors and other local authorities have borne the highest testimony to his impartiality, firmness, and knowledge of the native policy and character.

Mr. Brodie Cruickshank, the now acting Governor, is (or was until he became Acting Governor) agent to Messrs Forster and Smith, the chief of these London Houses. He is also a man of much ability and influence on the coast. He has moreover, a violent personal quarrel with

[1] Herman Merivale (1806–74) was Professor of Political Economy at Oxford before he succeeded Stephen as Permanent Under-Secretary in 1847. He left the Colonial Office in 1859.

Mr. Fitzpatrick (on the subject of the administration of estates).[1]

Mr. Brodie Cruickshank was sworn in on the 27th August, and in ten days he had got rid of his Chief Justice and Judicial Assessor, the means being, giving him leave of absence on full salary, on account of his 'unpopularity', which convinced Mr. C. that the Government could not be carried on while he continued to deal justice to the natives.

This unpopularity merely rested on the natives' 'belief that they had grievances' — a belief which, no doubt, Mr. C's employers and friends have done their utmost to encourage. The acts alleged against him are of the most trifling nature. He is accused of inflicting exorbitant fines, but if the only specific instance is one of a fine of 100 dollars for sacrificing five human victims, it scarcely seems a very oppressive act. The only exception I can see, to the trivial character of these complaints, is the charge of having brought king Coffee Amissah to trial (in a civil action) before an ordinary jury; which might, no doubt, be an improper shock to native feelings, if he were a real king or chief: but if he is only one of those shams, who are constantly raised up, in these native towns close to British settlements, as tools, for various purposes, of the real native leaders (as Mr. Fitzpatrick asserts . . .), then he was probably rightly treated.

But the charge of unpopularity, which is the real one, is made out, not by any remonstrance of the chiefs of the many native tribes along the coast, among whom Mr. Fitzpatrick's jurisdiction is exercised, but merely by a petition from the 'Chiefs, caboceers' etc etc of Cape Coast, — a native town inhabited, as we know, by traders etc of a very suspicious character, many of them implicated in that mitigated slave trade or 'pawn' system, against which Mr. Fitzpatrick has been repeatedly instructed to proceed, and, most of them, commercial dependents of Messrs Forster and Smith. . . .

[1] References p. 194 n. above.

It is to be noticed that throughout all these proceedings there is no notice whatever (that I have found) of any part taken in them by the executive council. Yet that body was expressly constituted by Lord Grey, in general accordance with the wishes of the merchants, to be a check upon the Governor, and it was clearly the Lieutenant Governor's duty to take no steps in such a matter as this without consulting it.

The 'leave of absence' cannot, of course, continue. For a suspension, I can see no ground whatever. . . . It is, of course, competent to the Sec. of State to cut the knot by making some other provision for Mr. Fitzpatrick . . . but I own I should entertain much doubt of the policy of such a concession to such a rabble as the four 'representatives'[1] and their followers, whom, I believe, the slightest show of firmness would probably silence at once. On the other hand, it seems very doubtful whether, if the mercantile body are not to be restored altogether to their ancient authority (which would be difficult since Lord Grey's great extension of the Protectorate), it is possible to maintain Mr. Brodie Cruickshank as Lieut. Governor. . . .[2]   [C.O.96/28]

192 B. CRUICKSHANK TO THE DUKE OF NEWCASTLE
CAPE COAST, 12 JANUARY, 1854.

My Lord Duke,

With reference to my despatch No. 82, in which I reported to your Grace that I had sent Mr. Blankson,[3] a native merchant, to Coomassie, for the purpose of obtaining a renewal of the treaty of Peace with the

[1] Henry Barns, Joseph Smith, Thomas Hughes and Wm. de Graft.

[2] Newcastle (to Cruickshank, 24 November, 1853) administered a sharp censure for his concession to popular clamour 'of which you were the first to recognize the utter injustice', as discreditable and bound to weaken authority.

[3] George Kuntu Blankson (1809–98); a member, in the 1830s, of the Cape Coast Society for promoting Christian knowledge; in 1834 was sent by Maclean on a mission to Kumasi; connected, through Cruickshank, with the firm of Forster & Smith; M.L.C. 1862–73; went on a further mission to Kumasi in 1866.

king of Ashantee; I have the honour to inform your Grace that Mr. Blankson returned to Cape Coast on the 2nd instant, accompanied by messengers from the king; and bearing a letter from his Majesty, giving a detailed account of his reasons for not signing the new treaty which I had proposed to him. . . .

Although the king has refused to sign the treaty which I submitted to him . . . he has acknowledged himself to be bound by the former treaty, and has only abstained from a formal renewal of it, lest, by so doing, he should convict himself of a breach of the former agreement. . . . He appears also to place great importance upon the restriction put upon the sale and transport of munitions of war to his country after Governor Hill's invitation to him to renew commercial intercourse with the settlements. This measure was adopted by Acting-Governor Fitzpatrick, and seemed necessary to force the king into a distinct understanding respecting his intentions. It has had much weight in calling forth the very pacific tone of his communication to me, and had already obtained your Grace's approval.

Apart from the untenable ground which the king has assumed in many of his arguments, I regard his letter as perfectly satisfactory, in as far as it is a full and explicit declaration of his pacific intentions, for which our best guarantee is in the respect with which the very spirited conduct of the natives under our protection, and the vigorous measures of Governor Hill have [inspired] him. He has declared in his letter that if he had seen any means of recovering the Assins without an application to Governor Winniett, he would not have scrupled to have attained his object. This desire may possibly still continue to influence him; but peace is ensured in the meantime, founded too much upon a much higher respect for our means of resistance than the kings of Ashantee have ever before acknowledged.

I hope these explanations will be satisfactory to your Grace, and that you will approve of my having removed all restrictions upon the sale of warlike stores, and having returned to our former amicable relations with the king; as well as of my general proceedings throughout this affair. Governor Hill, rather as a suggestion than as a demand, requested the king to give some compensation to the Assins for the destruction of some of their villages: but his reply, which arrived after the Governor's departure for England, clearly indicated that this could not be insisted upon without risking a war. I therefore confined myself solely to a renewal of our friendly relations; and the Assins . . . considered themselves indemnified by such protection as they received after the first outbreak, and by a remission of the Poll Tax during the past year. . . .

[C.O.96/30: H.C.456, A & P (1854–5) xxxvi]

193 HILL TO NEWCASTLE
ACCRA, 29 JANUARY, 1854.

[Reports that the people of Christiansborg and Labadi had refused to pay the Poll Tax and had taken up arms.] . . .

I found on my arrival at this fort, that the disaffection had spread as far as the Volta river, and the natives from all the intermediate sea villages, were in arms, having Danish flags flying, and menacing the fort with an armed force of about four thousand persons. Unwilling, before all negotiations had failed, to proceed to hostilities, and as I considered it most probable that this force, composed of the inhabitants of so many towns, must, in a few days, separate, if not proceeded against, I refrained from taking any notice of their menacing attitude, more particularly as Mr. Cruickshank had given them until Thursday, the 19th instant, to come in and express contrition for their misconduct. As I foresaw, the hostile army separated on Friday, and I have permitted those refractory people to return to their towns, after paying a fine to cover the expense consequent on the movement of the troops, and coming into the fort to beg pardon for their misconduct.

I can only attribute this spirit of resistance to the fact that our stringent rules respecting the sale or transfer of slaves for transportation, are strictly enforced, whereas under the Danish Government, too weak to control them, those people did whatever they pleased, and committed many acts of barbarity, without notice or punishment. Indeed, one of their complaints is that under British rule they are not allowed to torture their women, or indulge in any of their cruel customs, and the present rising was also a struggle against any advancement in civilization, as in some of the towns they took their children from school and obliged the missionary teachers to leave. . . . The whole of the tribes transferred from the Danish Government, are most uncivilized, excitable, and difficult to manage, as their former rulers could never keep them down under any authority, and they would gladly shake off their sworn allegiance to the British Government, if it were not for the protection afforded them against more powerful tribes. . . .[1]

[C.O.96/30: H.C.456]

194 HILL TO NEWCASTLE
CAPE COAST, 4 MARCH, 1854.

My Lord Duke,

I have had the honour to receive your Grace's despatch, No. 75 of the 19th January, relative to the contemplated appointment of a British consul at Coomassie, and requesting that I would furnish a report of my own views on this subject.[2]

Agreeably to your Grace's desire, I beg leave most strongly to recommend that an agent under the control of the local Government, should be stationed in the

[1] A more serious rising in September, touched off by the seizure of smuggled rum, was only suppressed by bombarding Osu, Labadi and Teshi.
[2] The question had been discussed during Hill's leave (Hill to Merivale, 4 October, 1853). Hill at that time insisted that the consul be a European. [C.O.96/27]

capital of Ashantee, as I quite agree with Mr. Cruickshank,[1] that any officer placed at Coomassie under the immediate orders of the Secretary of State for Foreign Affairs, and acting independently of the Governor of these Settlements, must tend to weaken the respect of the Ashantee king for the authority of the local Government, and prove detrimental in maintaining peace with that potentate.

On my arrival here, I found that the Lieutenant-Governor had already made arrangements, in the absence of a European, for sending an educated native[2] at a salary of £100 per annum, as a medium of communication between the king of Ashantee and this Government; which arrangement I have carried out, subject to your Grace's approval.

I have etc.

[C.O.96/30; H.C.456]

195 HILL TO NEWCASTLE
CAPE COAST CASTLE, 31 MAY, 1854.

. . . I have to inform your Grace that I found on my arrival that the Poll Tax collection had not commenced, nor do I believe the natives would have paid it under Mr. Cruickshank's management. Indeed, they intimated as much to that gentleman, complaining that the promises made to the chiefs, that they should receive salaries and yearly pay tickets, had not been kept; which, I regret to say, was but too true, as, until I assembled the chiefs on the 15th instant, laid before them a copy of the return which I now forward to your Grace, paid them their salaries, and gave them the promised pay tickets, only those chiefs at Cape Coast and Denkera had been settled with by the Lieutenant-Governor, causing discontent and jealousy in the minds of all the others.

I am now happy in being able to report that the collection of the tax is proceeding

[1] Cruickshank had been instructed to sound the Asantehene about the appointment of a consul (Newcastle to C., 22 October, 1853).
[2] George Musgrove.

satisfactorily, and I have no doubt that the revenue of the present year will equal that of the past: but I consider it my duty to inform your Grace, that I met the greatest opposition from the Cape Coast chiefs and headmen, who, after trying every dodge in vain, to postpone the collection, intimated that it was their intention to repudiate it altogether; when I was compelled to inform them that I would enforce the payment, and punish, according to the law made by the Native Assembly, any person who resisted payment, and that they might think it over next day, and on the following one the collection must commence. Finding me determined on the subject, they altered their tone, agreed to pay, and we parted on a better understanding.

I should inform your Grace, that these oppositionists are the same clique to whose tumultuous clamour Mr. Cruickshank gave way, and by an act of weakness, led them to believe they could over-rule the Government. . . .   [C.O.96/30]

196 MINUTE BY H. M. MERIVALE

COLONIAL OFFICE, 29 FEBRUARY, 1855.

The more general question of the position of the British Government on this coast, is raised by these papers.[1]

You are aware that the kind of Protectorate now established over a coast peopled by more than 400,000 natives, was a favourite object of Lord Grey's policy, and was carried out by him through the purchase of the Danish forts. The scope of his Lordship's policy cannot be so well explained as it is by himself, in his 'Colonial Policy of Lord John Russell's Administration.' And from all I understand, it has had, even in a short time, remarkable effects. The influence of the

[1] Acting Governor Connor's report (18 December, 1854) of an attempt to destool Kofi Amissah, chief of Cape Coast. The recap. was for the benefit of the new Secretary of State (Lord John Russell). There were five different Secretaries within the year, and intervals when the Prime Minister had to act.

British power has been greatly extended, and with it, the spread of Christianity — successful nowhere in West Africa except on this very coast — and here, as I am informed, principally through the great exertions and influence of the Wesleyans. If, in short, any beginning has been made in accomplishing the objects of British policy for these 50 years past, it is precisely here — and the experiment therefore deserves to be sedulously watched over.

But its difficulties of course grow with its success. The relation of 'protectorate' is obviously very undefined. So far as this country is concerned, it is pretty well fixed by a remarkable Act of Parliament of 6 & 7 Vict., commonly called Mr. Hopes' act (introduced by Mr. G. Hope and drawn up by Mr. James Hope). And though the blacks do not understand the refinements of that act, they have, I do not doubt, a very fair comprehension of the general relations between a protecting and a protected community. But there is growing up an intermediate class — half caste and half civilized — men with a certain amount of English knowledge and ideas derived from the missionaries or elsewhere — and they seem to exert an influence among the Africans by insisting on their anomalous state of dependence — assuring them that they are not 'subjects' of Great Britain, and therefore owe no obedience — which results in movements like this at Cape Coast, of which more are to be expected.

The favourite remedy with Governors etc. is 'annexation' of the particular territory. That is, in other words, founding a new empire in Western Africa. Supposing this out of the question — I will not trouble you with arguments pro or con — I see no great difficulty at present in maintaining the Protectorate. The recent defeat of the insurgents near Christiansborg, will probably strengthen our hands. The steamer 'Dover' and any additional assistance the Adm[iral]ty could give us, will be of more value than additional regiments without the means of locomotion, which are so aided by the conformation of this coast.

There is, however, a weak point in our position. The keystone of Lord Grey's policy was the levy of the 'Poll Tax'. This seems to be falling behind. I was not aware, though it may have been reported, that the late Mr. Cruickshank had thought proper to remit five months of it during his short government. On this point, the Acting-Governor should, I think, be told that though the Secretary of State recognizes the great importance as well as justice, of devoting this fund to native objects, the first of those objects is that protection, without which their advance in civilization cannot be secured at all, and that therefore, it is the full intention of Her Majesty's Government that expense occasioned by such outbreaks as this shall be defrayed from it. . . .

Cape Coast *Town* has always been under the influence of half-caste traders, men of a certain substance and intelligence, connected with the two or three trading firms which carry on the commerce of this part of Africa with England; mercantile bodies which governed these forts until Parliament in 1842 thought it proper that Government should take the control out of their hands. They have never been reconciled to the change. There has always been a contest between the officers representing Government and this trading interest. And Cape Coast *Town*, being out of British *jurisdiction*, and only under British *protection*, they have had a most convenient fulcrum for their opposition. . . .

[He suggests writing on the lines of No. 197 following.]   [C.O.96/31]

197 SIR GEORGE GREY TO H. CONNOR
LONDON, 3 MARCH, 1855.

[After expressing satisfaction at the restoration of order in Cape Coast]:

. . . You are aware, from the repeated instructions of former Secretaries of State, that Her Majesty's Government have no intention of extending the dominions of the Crown in that portion of Africa in which the forts under your Government are situated, and do not consider that any reasons have been advanced sufficient to justify the adoption of such a change of policy.

But on the other hand, they are determined on maintaining the protectorate over the native tribes adjoining the forts, which has now been for so many years established, with the consent, and indeed at the desire of the great mass of the people who enjoy the advantages of the Crown's controlling authority. When they find that even parties, engaged in memorializing the Secretary of State against the conduct of the local authorities, express themselves so strongly as the writers of the letter of the 5th ultimo, as to the benefit derived by the African race from the present system . . . they cannot hesitate in believing that the policy, thus deliberately pursued, is in accordance with the best interests of humanity.

But there can be no more obvious result of the right of protection, than that the authority of chief or king cannot be conferred or taken away, except with the concurrence of the Chief Representative of the Crown's authority on the coast. Her Majesty's Government have every wish, and indeed recognize it to be their duty, to conform to the laws and customs of the native tribes in this matter, as far as they can be ascertained: but subject always to this necessary ratification.

It follows, therefore, that they must pronounce against the claim on the part of the memorialists, to elect and depose the chief who is termed the King of Cape Coast Town, without the concurrence of the Governor. The line of conduct adopted by Governor Hill and yourself in reference to the disputes between Coffee Amissah and Mr. Thompson, are founded upon a due observance of this principle; and I am confident that in carrying it into execution, you will conform yourself as nearly as circumstances will allow to the recognized usages of the people, as well as to their interests. If the misconduct alleged against Coffee Amissah be such as to warrant his deposition, it is before you that the fact must be established, and by you that the deposition must be sanctioned.

[C.O.96/33]

198 HENRY CONNOR TO SIDNEY HERBERT[1]

CAPE COAST CASTLE, 7 APRIL, 1855.

. . . The circumstances connected with the Poll Tax are many of them known to the Colonial Office: its institution in 1852; the late Lieutenant Governor Cruickshank's unfortunate surrender in 1853 to a clamour of the town of Cape Coast of five months of the tax, changing the period of its becoming due, from 1st August to the 1st January following; then the two disturbances in Accra in 1854, hindering any collection (beyond between £20 and £30 in James Town) that year in the Leeward district, which had, the previous year, paid more than £3,000. . . .

Part of this Leeward district — the country called Akim — had been prompt in paying the tax previously. I endeavoured, therefore, first to get a collector for it. You will observe in Governor Hill's despatches, lament of his difficulty in getting fit collectors. . . . Their former collector, a coloured man, had, they said . . . plundered them and robbed the Government. I made three attempts to send Englishmen as collectors, but failed, as I did in respect of a higher class of native. I at last appointed a fairly educated Cape Coast native, and sent him off the first week in January. After some delay, I sent another collector to what is properly the Accra district, and including James Town. I did this against the advice of the civil commandant there, an old officer of the Government, but timid, and, I am afraid, prejudiced against the Poll Tax, by his

connection with parties in the town. . . . He said the attempt to collect would cause a rebellion. I replied that I must make the attempt, and asked where I could hope to succeed, if I failed under the guns of our forts?

It is true, some merchants and traders of James Town, sent to the Civil Commandant, for transmission to me, what they called a Protest, against the collection of the tax. . . . I was led . . . to believe that the leaders among the aforesaid merchants were also leaders of the opposition to the Government; and a private letter, from an officer on the spot, also stated that the Europeans merchants were determined to oppose the collection of the tax. Part of my directions had been that the officer commanding the adjacent fort of Christiansborg, should be ready with military assistance, if required, and he was directed to take to James Fort a couple of mountain howitzers.

Happily . . . all opposition has melted away, and the tax is in process of peaceable collection, in the town, and everyone gives me to hope that the country will follow the example of the town, which is looked upon as a kind of headquarters.

This, however, has not yet been realised, for while matters were trembling in the balance at James Town, the Akim collector, who had already been guilty of delay in going to his post, deserted it, without having collected the tax, and went to James Town, where, of course, his unsuccessful return at once became known. [He was sentenced to imprisonment.] . . .

[C.O.96/33]

199 MINUTE BY H. M. MERIVALE

COLONIAL OFFICE, 28 JULY, 1855.

This[1] is a very serious account.

Out of a receipt scarcely equalling £4,000 — not much more than half what was at

---

[1] Sidney Herbert, later first Baron Herbert of Lea (1810–61) nominated by Palmerston as Secretary of State for the Colonies 7 February, 1855, had in fact resigned on 21 February, 1855.

[1] Henry Connor's reports of 4 and 16 May, on the proceeds of the Poll Tax, and announcing his intention to use force, if necessary, to quell the growing opposition to the tax in the Leeward district.

one time anticipated — we pay £850 for salaries of commandants, who may be partially useful to the natives as magistrates; £190 for a surgeon for them, whose services they do not use; £200 for roads, buildings and 'superintendence', whatever that may mean. And besides these sums, I do not see any item, of the smallest kind, which can be set down as for the public good of the natives. In fact, almost the whole goes, in one shape or another, in what may be termed expenses of collection.

Unless, therefore, on the Acting-Governor's ingenious theory that the visit of the tax-gatherer in the bush itself advances civilization, I do not see what good, results from the Poll Tax. It may be very true that the produce would be greater, and the expense of collection much less, had it not been for the opposition of the mercantile party to a tax which, whether usefully spent or not, is assuredly not an onerous one. But unless we are prepared with such moral or material discouragement to that opposition, as may establish our power on a secure basis, there seems no safe alternative short of endeavouring to reconstruct the old mercantile system of government, which would probably result in a new appeal to Government, for protection.   [C.O.96/33]

200 MINUTE BY SIR WILLIAM MOLESWORTH[1]

COLONIAL OFFICE, 31 JULY (?), 1855.

If I am correctly informed, the object with which our establishments on the Gold Coast are maintained, is mainly the hope of improving the condition of the natives, and replacing the slave trade by legitimate traffic. The indirect tendency of commerce, is looked to, as the most effectual preparative for the more direct agency of education (religious and intellectual), and our protection is extended over the native tribes as a security for commercial inter-

[1] Sir William Molesworth (1810–55); Radical M.P. and Colonial reformer; Secretary of State for the Colonies, 21 July to 17 November, 1855.

course as much as for the sake of training the natives gradually in the principles of British law, and giving them access to opportunities of improvement.

We have reason to suspect that the merchants (as a body) are ill-disposed to the present regime, which has, no doubt, interfered with their influence, formerly almost supreme, at the establishments on the coast; and this circumstance creates doubt as to the confidence which should be placed in their statements. At the same time, it is not satisfactory evidence of the success of establishments which exist for the promotion of commerce, that the whole mercantile body should so strongly express their dissatisfaction with the present system of administration.

It might be somewhat a set-off to this, if the natives appeared to be well satisfied and improving, but, whether it be from the machinations of the merchants, as has been suggested, or from real or imagined grievances, the natives are evidently far from contented, and at one fort,[1] a sanguinary collision, leading to a very serious loss of life, has already occurred. I have already, in a former minute, adverted to some indications, given in the correspondence, which seem to show that the opposition to the poll tax was connected with that outbreak, and which qualify my admiration for the conduct of the military, who seem to have been not reluctant to the use of violent measures.

Some of the objections to the Poll Tax are directed against the tax itself; others against the administration of the funds raised by its imposition. I feel great difficulty in expressing any opinion, either as to the alleged hardships involved in the collection, or as to the practical difficulties that may supervene in the application of the money, and the excessive amount of salaries said to be charged upon it.

On all these points, I continue to think that the opinion of a highly qualified person, *on the spot*, is requisite, as a guide for the future policy of these settlements.

[1] Christiansborg.

If reduced to conjecture, I should be disposed to prefer a hut tax, at a fixed rate on each dwelling, to the present poll tax, but I should not like to abandon a measure, so lately adopted, without having ample means for decision.

The acting Governor seems to be a man of energy and some ability, but he could not be looked to for an impartial opinion upon the policy, to which he seems to have committed himself, of ruling these settlements with a high hand, and setting at naught the remonstrances of the mercantile body.   [C.O.96/33]

201 LORD PALMERSTON TO MAJOR H. ST. G. ORD

LONDON, 31 OCTOBER, 1855.

[Transmits his instructions as 'Commissioner to inquire into certain matters affecting the condition of the . . . Settlements on the Gold Coast'.]

. . . The voluntary recognition of British influence by a large native population, the submission of their disputes to the decision of British magistrates, and the gradual progress of education, are circumstances which favourably distinguish the settlements on the Gold Coast, and which have encouraged an expectation that further efforts might lead to still more extensive improvements.

But it must be borne in mind, that all measures directed to the improvement of the native tribes, must exclusively depend, for their success, upon the voluntary concurrence of the natives in the requisite measures. It is not the desire of Her Majesty's Government to extend Her Majesty's territorial sovereignty beyond its present limits for the sake of mere extension of territory, nor to impose, by compulsion, institutions of which the natives are not prepared to appreciate the value.

By the application of this principle, Her Majesty's Government are desirous to test the conflicting statements, which have been laid before them, in respect to a new system, which was introduced, in the year 1852, in pursuance of the views of Earl Grey, then Secretary of State for the Colonies. . . .

During the past year, certain merchants, and other persons connected with the Gold Coast, have forwarded numerous complaints, affecting the administration of affairs in our settlements, but, more especially, directed against the maintenance of the poll tax. Into the allegations contained in these complaints, it will be your duty carefully to enquire, distinguishing between those which are directed against the system itself, and those which relate to the mode in which the proceeds of the tax are at present appropriated.

Her Majesty's Government would, with great regret, learn that a plan, designed in a spirit of enlightened benevolence, and, at least in the first instance, willingly accepted by the natives, had encountered such serious obstacles, as to render expedient its total abandonment. But if the statements recently made, were proved to their full extent; if it should appear that the maintenance of the Poll Tax is likely to lead to sanguinary collisions with the native population, and to an interference with the ordinary operations of trade, thus endangering the essential objects for which the settlements themselves are retained, Her Majesty's Government would have to consider whether they must not lay aside, for the present, the expectations which were entertained as to the useful results of the measures of 1852.

But Her Majesty's Government indulge a hope that . . . the defects in the existing system of administration may admit of correction, without weakening those institutions which, if properly administered, must so practically contribute to the welfare of the African population. . . .

It will be your duty to enquire, what foundation there is for the statements made as to the inability of the natives to pay the tax. . . . It may . . . be a matter for consideration, whether the levy would be facilitated by the exemption of children below a certain age, or by the substitution of a hut tax for a poll tax (as in British Kaffraria).

A matter of greater difficulty is the question how far the tax could be made to preserve a voluntary character, not, of course, as regards each separate individual, but as regards tribes, or considerable sections of the natives, without compromising the objects for which it is maintained. For Her Majesty's Government have seen, with regret, that the Acting Governor has recently thought it necessary to announce that if, in certain districts, the tax were not duly paid, it should be levied by force. It did not clearly appear whether this announcement was confined to the inhabitants of the territory adjacent to James Town, Accra, which is actually under British rule, and where such an announcement, if rendered necessary, might properly be enforced: but it would be altogether contrary to the views of Her Majesty's Government to employ coercion for the purpose of levying such a tax from the people in the protected territory.

It would be desirable that you should consider carefully, how far the natives may be induced to persevere regularly in the payment of the tax, by making them feel that the continuance of the benefits, accruing therefrom, is dependent on its payment; as, for instance, whether, in case of default in payment by any tribe, the medical officer, the magistrate (would this be safe?), the schoolmaster of the district, might be usefully withdrawn and employed elsewhere? . . .

The Secretary of State will be desirous to receive your report in respect to each of the separate objects to which the poll tax revenue has hitherto been applied, together with your opinion upon the fitness of each charge, in itself, as a legitimate item of expenditure, and also upon the value and efficiency of the services which are afforded to the natives in return for this expenditure. . . .

It appears to have been contemplated by Governor Hill, that a meeting of the chiefs should be annually convened, under the presidency of the Governor, whereat any question connected with the levy and expenditure of the tax, might be considered and decided. Such a meeting, has not, however, been summoned in the present year, and Her Majesty's Government learned with regret, that the cause assigned by the Acting-Governor for his decision, was the apprehended disaffection of many of the native chiefs.[1]

It may be somewhat doubtful whether such an assembly could be maintained as a permanent institution, but if it were advisable to secure the attendance of the native chiefs, that object might probably be attained, by reserving the payment of the whole or part of the allowance made to them out of the poll tax revenue, until after the annual meeting. This, as well as other points connected with the payments to the chiefs, will require your consideration.

[He was also to report on the Accra disturbances, but without holding a formal inquiry which might 'renew excited feelings'.] . . .

Another system which will demand notice, is the system of 'pawns'; that is to say, of domestic slavery endured in discharge of debt. . . . To eradicate the evil of slavery, even in this modified form, throughout the protected territory, should be the policy of those who represent Her Majesty in the Settlements on the coast. It will be an important portion of your duty, to examine fully into the facts, and to report fully as to the measures which may appear to you best calculated to secure [this] object. . . .

You will observe, from the correspondence which I annex, that some of the merchants connected with the Gold Coast,

[1] Cf. Connor to Herbert (4 May, 1855). Commenting on Hill's meeting with the chiefs on 15 May, 1854, Connor wrote: 'I was told that the chiefs from the interior did not attend; that it was, in fact, a meeting of the factious misled chiefs or so-called chiefs of the town of Cape Coast who after having been insolent and equivocating and objecting at last flatly refused to continue paying the tax.' Connor thought it easier to circulate a statement of accounts to the chiefs.

are not satisfied with the present form of government established there, and that they claim to have a greater share of influence in public affairs. It must, however, be borne in mind, that it was after Parliamentary inquiry, and . . . with the advice of a Committee of the House of Commons, that the management of the Settlements was transferred from the hands of the merchants to Her Majesty's Government: but this circumstance need not preclude those merchants from having their proper influence in all matters of local public concern, if, by education and character, they are entitled to claim a share in legislation. [He was to ascertain if Grey's instructions for the publication of draft ordinances, had been carried out.] . . .

[C.O.96/37]

202 MEMORANDUM BY SIR G. BARROW[1]
COLONIAL OFFICE, 21 DECEMBER, 1855.

. . . There is no doubt that, in a barbarous country like Ashantee and the adjoining countries, when suspicions are entertained of the conduct of the chiefs, and especially if they are of the same kind as led to evil on former occasions, the Governor must naturally regard them as more serious than they would appear to be to those who judge of them at a distance.

The first complaint of the king of Ashantee (which was as far back as Oct. 1854), was that one of his subjects, who had gone down to Cape Coast with gold to purchase goods, had been robbed in the house in which he slept. Proper measures were taken by the local Govt. and the owner of the house was arrested, as the responsible person, and imprisoned: but in default of the usual payment being made, for his maintenance in gaol, by the party who had caused his arrest, he was released. The king then demanded that his property should be sold — but it was found that he had no property, so that, considering that no theft was brought home to him, and he

[1] Sir George Barrow (1806–76); entered the Colonial Office in 1825.

was imprisoned only because he was the owner of the house, the local Govt. seems to have gone to the full length of its power, to satisfy the king: but he continued to harp on this subject for some time after.

A more serious affair took place in February 1855. The king of Ashantee complained that a captain of the king of Akim's, had called land in Ashantee his own, and taken gold from it, and had sworn the great Ashantee Oath, that the Ashantee living on that land should leave it. The local Govt. ordered enquiries to be made on this subject. . . .

It would appear that on each bank of the Prah river, which is the boundary between Akim and Ashantee, there is a 'kroom', the inhabitants of which are in the habit of digging gold dust, the Ashantees paying a tax to king Aggaman (of Akim),[1] for the privilege. It must be inferred from this that the Ashantees must have crossed the river for the purpose of digging gold, and not worked on their own side of the river; but the account of this is confused.

King Aggaman, however, sent one of his messengers to the Ashantee side of the river, to collect the tax, but his cap (of office) was torn off his head, one half sent to the king of Ashantee, the other to king Aggaman, with a message that if he sent 100 people with such caps, they would do the same to them, as no one was allowed to wear the gold cap in any part of Ashantee, but the king's messenger.

A second messenger from King Aggaman, accompanied by two soldiers, was treated in the same way, and King Aggaman swore by his sword, that if he had not bound himself to the English Govt., he would march that day and fight the Ashantees.

The Actg. Governor pointed out to King Aggaman, that he was wrong in sending two soldiers over the river; that his complaint ought to have been made to the British Agent at Coomassie, and that his messengers ought to have been sent to

[1] Agyeman of Akim Kotoku.

the king of Ashantee.   The king of Ashantee seems to have been most offended at the great Ashantee Oath, which had been taken, and thought the Actg. Gov. had not taken sufficient notice of it.

The Actg. Gov. caused the king to be informed that he was aware of the greatness of the crime of swearing the king of Ashantee's oath, and that if the king wished it, he would, although not now acting as judge,[1] hear the case himself; but it would be requisite that he should know the name of the person accused, and that there should be witnesses of the fact.

The rest of the papers[2] are taken up with the alleged attempts of the agents of the king of Ashantee to bribe the Assins to place themselves under his power.   That money was given to certain parties in Assin, there can be no doubt.   The . . . declaration . . . of his Majesty [that he would not have attempted bribery with such trifling sums] is not worth much.

The Actg. Gov. doubts the policy of having a British agent at Coomassie, and he certainly ought to be a discreet man, if there is to be one at all.   Mr. Musgrove, who is at present there, told the king that 'there is a great difference now, between the time when the late George Maclean Esq. was President and yielded to some of his customs and laws, and this present time in which the British Government has taken the administration of affairs on the Gold Coast into its own hands; for the British Govt. is not to follow the customs and laws of others nations, except such as agree with the laws and customs of the British nation — which the Actg. Gov. pointed out to him as being entirely incorrect.   He would prefer an agent from the king of Ashantee, to reside at Cape Coast, with respect to which, he is to consult Major Ord. . . .

[C.O.96/35]

[1] Henry Connor was Chief Justice and Judicial Assessor from July 1854 to May 1856.
[2] Connor to Molesworth, of 11 and 15 October, which were so voluminous that the copyist was unable to complete them before the mail sailed. On 13 November Connor reported that the danger of invasion had passed.

203 H. St. G. Ord to H. Labouchere[1]
LONDON, 16 MAY, 1856.

[Finding opposition to the poll tax was general, he summoned two meetings of chiefs and headmen, to discuss it.] . . .

A general feeling of soreness and irritation, an impression that they were despised and neglected, was universal among them, and to this, more than to any specific evil in the Poll Tax itself, I became convinced their hostility was due.

The result of these inquiries brought me to the conviction that, admitting, as the natives readily did, the propriety of their contributing, in some manner, towards the local revenue, for their own immediate benefit, there was no form of tax that presented so many advantages and so few evils, and that, if the details of its imposition were somewhat modified, and its appropriation regulated, in strict conformity with the original expressed intention of its promoters, it could not fail to be of great benefit to the country, and ought to do more towards its gradual civilization than any other engine of which the Government could avail itself. . . .

[He found it useless to interview individual chiefs from the interior.] . . . It soon became evident that on the chiefs and headmen of Cape Coast they relied almost implicitly for counsel; that from their position in constant association with the white people, they inferred that they must understand, better than themselves, what was advisable and expedient, and that, in short, they would be guided in all their decisions by the opinion of the people of Cape Coast. . . .

I found, however, that this influence was entirely repudiated by the local Government, and that great offence had thus been given to the chiefs of Cape Coast, who asserted that the Government, by ignoring the power that they possessed, were injuring them in the eyes of the

[1] Henry Labouchere (later Baron Taunton), 1798–1869. M.P. 1826–59; Under-Secretary for War and the Colonies, Feb.–Aug. 1839; President of the Board of Trade, 1841, 1847–52; Secretary for the Colonies, 1855–8; uncle of his namesake, the later editor of *Truth*.

le. I spoke to the Governor, on the subject, and pointed out to him that it was quite clear certain chiefs in the town possessed considerable influence over the minds of a large body of the people, and that policy would dictate the expediency of endeavouring to make them exercise that influence to further the measures of Government, and that to attempt to ignore it could only irritate the chiefs, whilst it deprived the Government of a very powerful and useful agent. His Excellency . . . explained that his system had always been the reverse of this, and that, . . by not recognizing any power in the Cape Coast Chiefs, beyond their own legitimate authority in their districts, he was taking the best measures to weaken the influence which, it was alleged, they possessed. . . .

[At a conference with the Cape Coast chiefs] . . . I promised, on behalf of the Government,

1st. That the tax should be remitted on all infants.

2nd. That where it could be shown that persons had died since the tax was collected, no charge should be made by the collectors for them.

3rd. That poor women, having no husband or head of family to pay for them, should be exempted.

4th. That aged persons, unable to work, and having no relative or head of family to pay for them [should be exempted]. . . .

[At Christiansborg, the Krobos did not attend the meeting, and Chief Dowuona withdrew, after his demand for compensation for the destruction of his town, had been refused. James Town, in a very disorderly meeting, refused to pay, though Akwapim said it would pay if the others did. The Governor thought his language too conciliatory.] . . .

To make the collection voluntary amongst the tribes . . . would be . . . to make the chiefs . . . responsible for the tax; a measure which would tend to exalt the power of the chiefs, which it is part of our policy to endeavour to lower, and would give them opportunities for exaction and extortion. . . .

Should the tax continue to be paid, I consider that the efforts of the Government should be directed, in the first instance, to objects calculated to benefit the towns on the coast. It may seem unfair that a tax, paid equally by the coast people and those from the interior, should be distributed more for the benefit of one than the other: but from the dependent relation in which the latter stand to the former, it is very necessary that the advantages conferred should be felt and appreciated first by the coast people. . . . At the meeting, whilst complaints were made by the coast tribes, that the promises made them had not been fulfilled, in respect to the improvement of their towns and roads etc., the bush chiefs made no objections whatever, of this character. In fact, they seemed readily to admit, that any improvements should be first commenced in the town, and then extended to the country. . . .

[More magistrates were needed, including fewer military men and more educated natives. Industrial education should be stressed instead of the present system which produces a superfluity of clerks, with very exaggerated notions of their ability, and a contempt for manual work. Domestic slaves, who are really more like clansmen, cannot be liberated; but something might be done to reduce the interest rate for the redemption of pawns. We must either buy out the Dutch, or get a customs agreement with them.]

I think it highly important that the Legislative Council should contain some members of the mercantile body, and I recommend that the names of two merchants resident at Cape Coast, and one at Accra . . . be now added to the Council; and as the various contingencies of the climate render their absence at times unavoidable, power should be given to the Governor to summon temporarily to the Councils, such gentlemen as he may consider duly qualified.[1] . . .   [C.O.96/40]

[1] The full report covers 168 pages.

15 Sir Benjamin Pine: Abandonment or Reform?
1856–1858

ORD's report directed the attention of Government to two other problems which required to be solved if the Gold Coast Settlements were to prosper. The first was the need for a customs agreement with the Dutch, and, in the course of 1856, Ord was himself employed in negotiations at the Hague, to this end. After a promising start, however, the mission ended in failure. The second problem was the question of domestic slavery, and it was this, above all else, that dominated the thinking of the next Governor of the Gold Coast.

Sir Benjamin Pine, who took up his duties in March 1857, was born in 1809. He had entered the Colonial Service, as Queen's Advocate for Sierra Leone, in 1841, and after eight years in that colony, during two of which he was Acting-Governor, he was appointed, in 1849, Governor of the newly formed Colony of Natal. His services there won him a knighthood, and recommended him to Labouchere for the task of restoring order to the Gold Coast Settlements.

The fourteen months Pine spent on the coast (23 March, 1857 to 11 May, 1858) may be considered as falling into two roughly equal periods. Down to October 1857, his first, very unfavourable, impressions of the country, found expression in a series of trenchant despatches — which Merivale found more clever than consistent — culminating in the discovery that 'the Protectorate of England over these countries involves the violation of English law, and the moment that law is fully observed by our officers, that moment our jurisdiction is brought to an end' (207). This referred, of course, to the tacit recognition of domestic slavery. Put like this, there was only one logical conclusion, that the Protectorate ought to be abandoned forthwith; and Pine did not hesitate to say so (208). Though not accepted without demur (209–10), his words made a considerable impression on at least two Secretaries of State, one of whom remembered to confront Pine with them in 1865.[1]

Government and Cabinet changes, however, caused both Labouchere and Stanley to postpone acting on Pine's recommendations.[2] And, in the meantime, the Governor's own views were modified. Faced with a series of practical problems, in the administration of the poll tax (211), the best course for the courts to adopt in slavery cases (213), the unsatisfactory recruitment of the Gold Coast Corps (215), the shocking state of the towns (216), and the perennial problem of the Dutch (214), Pine was ready with bold, if not always practical, remedies (221).

He worked closely with T. B. Freeman (207), whose visits to Akim and Krobo, and (immediately after Pine's departure) to Akwamu and Krepi (217), wrought a great improvement in the Eastern Districts. Pine, however, did not enjoy good health, and had pleaded for sick leave for some time before he finally got away in May 1858.

In subsequent discussions with the Colonial Office, he retracted his earlier views about the Protectorate, but two of his recommendations were to have

[1] See H.C.412 of 1865, Questions 3094 ff.
[2] Palmerston's Government fell in February 1858, and Labouchere gave way to Lord Stanley (later 15th Earl of Derby). In May, Stanley handed over to Sir E. Bulwer (later Lord) Lytton.

unfortunate consequences. One was in favour of an exchange of territory with the Dutch, if his earlier (and better) idea of buying them out of their eastern forts, failed.[1] The other was for a re-union of the West African Settlements under one Government. Lord Carnarvon was favourably impressed by this suggestion, and urged it on his chief, Bulwer Lytton (218b): but the Governors concerned were against it,[2] and so was the Duke of Newcastle, who took over from Lytton in June 1859 (218c). Pine went off to apply the federal recipe in the more congenial field of the Leeward Isles.

[1] Memorandum of 20 May, 1859, in C.O.96/46. But Pine made two provisos that were later overlooked: that all the states east of Wasaw should remain under British protection, and that the Dutch should enter a defensive alliance with Britain against Ashanti. Cf. Nos. 257 and 263 below.
[2] Memorandum by Barrow, of 29 June, 1859, ibid.

204 H. LABOUCHERE TO SIR B. PINE
DOWNING STREET, 30 SEPTEMBER, 1856.
[Transmits Ord's report on the Gold Coast.] . . .

I should wish you to give your earliest attention to the present system of appointing magistrates on the Gold Coast. The exertions which you made, during your administration of the Government of Natal, to establish an efficient magistracy over the natives of that Colony, show that you are sensible of the great importance of that object. The general practice at the Gold Coast, has been to appoint officers of the Gold Coast Corps as magistrates, and it may be feared that officers so appointed do not always possess a competent knowledge of the local customs upon which, in many instances, their decisions ought to be based. . . . I approve of Major Ord's suggestions, in regard to newly appointed magistrates not being allowed, at first, to administer justice singly, and to the selection, in each of the large towns, of one or two of the native merchants, who may be qualified, by education and position, for appointments to the Commission of the Peace, and to sit with the paid magistrates, on certain days, in a kind of petty sessions. . . .

I am also willing to assent to the gradual and cautious introduction of a more important change, suggested by Major Ord; viz. that some of the native merchants should be added to the Legislative Council, and that the Governor should have the power of making appointments to the Council temporarily, during the absence of any of its members: but on these points I should be glad to receive your deliberate opinion when you have had some experience of the practical working of the existing system. . . .

Major Ord has urged, very strongly, and apparently with great justice, the necessity of a greater degree of conciliation towards the natives than has been generally shown by the local Government, together with a juster appreciation of the native character. The local Government may, no doubt, have had much to contend with, in their intercourse with some of the merchants, who, from a desire to revert to the former system of administration, or a desire to ingratiate themselves with the natives, may oppose themselves to the Government, and incite others to the same course: but I entertain no doubt that a forbearing but firm course of administration, directed impartially to secure the general well-being, will, on the Gold Coast as well as elsewhere, secure the general support of the community. . . .

The question of domestic slavery and 'Pawns', which Major Ord brings under notice, is one of extreme difficulty. Any measure which may tend, in practice, to ameliorate the condition of those who are in a state of servitude, provided that they did not implicate Her Majesty's Government in a direct sanction of usages to which they are altogether opposed, would receive my cordial support: but I apprehend that the adoption of Major Ord's suggestions on this subject would be far too direct a recognition of an evil which is only tolerated because we have not the means of suppressing it. If you should gradually succeed in inducing the native chiefs to put an end to the existing practice of domestic slavery, I should regard it as a most important step gained in the civilization and advancement of the natives.

A negotiation is now pending, between the British and the Netherland Governments, for the imposition of moderate duties on imports into the settlements of the two countries on the West Coast of Africa; and the Dutch Government has determined to send out a special commissioner to report on the proposed measure. If this negotiation should prove successful, a considerable increase of revenue may be anticipated, and this will supply the additional means for improving and civilizing the people. . . .   [C.O.96/40]

205 PINE TO LABOUCHERE
ACCRA, 30 APRIL, 1857.
. . . For some years past, the greater part of the people of [the Leeward] districts have refused to pay the Poll Tax, and last year, all the tribes refused to pay it. With the exception of the inhabitants of James Town and Pram Pram, the portion of the Accra race under our protection have practically repudiated our authority, by ceasing to appeal to our courts of justice. This example has been followed by a considerable part of the Oji, or Ashantee, tribes of the Leeward districts, including the Aquapims and Aquamboos. Among these people, the most barbarous fetish rites — trials for witchcraft and human sacrifices — have been carried on with impunity.

This state of affairs dates from the period of the disputes between the Government and a large part of the Accra race, which resulted in the bombardment of Christiansborg. There has been some difference of opinion, as to the causes of these disputes. Major Ord traces them chiefly to the wild and lawless character of the natives who had lately been under Danish rule (the result of the limited authority exercised over them by that Government), and to their impatience of the greater amount of control which they experienced under our Government, and, further, to the imposition of the Poll Tax, upon a people theretofore accustomed to receive gifts, instead of making payments. Major Ord considers that, from these circumstances, these people became so excited against their rulers that it required only a very trifling cause to induce an outbreak, and that the cause was found in a dispute about the collection of the local revenue, and the seizure of a cask of smuggled rum.

This view of the subject contains much truth, but it does not, I think, fully embrace all the causes which led to the outbreak. In regard to the character of the natives lately under Danish rule, Major Ord's opinion is, to a certain extent, opposed to that of Mr. Bannerman, the Civil Commandant, an unexceptionable authority, who states that for two years after those people were handed over to us, their conduct was, in every respect, quiet and obedient.

My own opinion is, that the character given to these people by Major Ord is partially correct, but that they would never have rebelled against the Government, had they been ruled carefully and justly; and that the cause of these outbreaks must be traced to injudicious acts of the local Government, affecting the people generally, but more keenly felt and resented by the late Danish subjects, who were less submissive and amenable to rule than their fellow countrymen, who had long been under our protection.

The chief object of complaint was the Poll Tax, but more especially the manner in which it was expended. There is no doubt that, as regards the people of the protected territory generally, the manner in which the Poll Tax fund has been administered is open to considerable objection, but it seems to me that these Leeward districts have, in this respect, especial cause of complaint. . . .

The whole of the tax . . . has been paid into one common fund. The accounts of its expenditure . . . in other respects un-intelligible, are especially so in this, that it is impossible . . . to discover, with any approach to accuracy, what part of the money has been spent in the Windward, what in the Leeward districts. . . . At a low estimate, however, it may be considered that . . . out of about £4,350, collected in the Leeward districts, only about £900, or less than a fifth part, has been there expended on the object for which it was given, even allowing that the increase of Mr. Bannerman's salary (£500) may be fairly considered as among those objects.

[This] . . . has left impressions on the minds of the natives, not to be easily effaced. It has made them think that the Government only condescends to consult them for the purpose of taking their money, and, that obtained, it regards their humble counsel as useless. It has brought into suspicion and disrepute, those meetings between the Government authorities and the chiefs and headmen, which might have been so fruitful of good, in working out a gradual change for the better in the laws and customs of the country. However, by using the chiefs merely for the purpose of imposing taxes, without giving them any sort of control over the expenditure, it has lowered them in the eyes of the people, and, in some places, almost destroyed their power. As they have a percentage on the proceeds of the tax, the people have re-garded them as mere instruments of extor-tion. The consequence has been, that in some places the power exercised by the chiefs has fallen into the hands of the dregs of the people. In this country it is a serious evil to destroy the power of the chiefs until we can supply an efficient substitute for it. . . .

The bombardment and destruction of Christiansborg has naturally left, in the minds of a large number of people, feelings of resentment against the Government. I believe that the people of this place, in common with the people of these districts generally, had much cause of complaint against the local Government. When, however, they attempted to right themselves by force . . . the authorities were, in my opinion, absolutely driven into the painful measures which they adopted. The ani-mosity caused by these sad measures, was made much more bitter by the deplorable, though unavoidable, circumstance that they involved many innocent persons in the ruin brought on by their guilty neigh-bours. Unfortunately, the chastisement has not produced such an impression of the fear of our military force as to compensate for the misery it caused. The natives here are sufficiently acute to observe that the destruction of a town by the guns of a fort, assisted by those of a man-of-war in the roads, is no proof of our superiority over them in their own mode of war-fare. . . .

Whilst the dispute was going on in 1854, between the Government and the people of Christiansborg, Governor Hill called in the chiefs and the headmen of Dutch Accra, to mediate between himself and these people. The mediation was rewarded by presents, given from time to time during the disputes. Under the circumstances, the native magistrates of Dutch Accra were, as it may be supposed, in no haste to terminate negotiations which brought them profit and increased importance. This mediation was useful, so far as concerned its immediate object . . . and it was mis-chievous in its after consequences. For the position in which these men were, at that time, placed by the Local Government, has emboldened them since, to exercise a most prejudicial influence over the natives under our protection. Not only have they assumed authority over a great part of the Accra race, of which . . . their chief claims to be paramount head (although under Mr. Maclean's government and since, his authority over natives under our rule was jealously excluded), but they have even exercised the rights of sovereignty

over the Aquapims and others of the Ashantee race, with whom they have no kind of
connection, and have extorted from them
large sums of money under the name of fines.

The want of magistrates in these districts
is another cause of their present state.
Mr. Bannerman at James Town . . . is
the only paid magistrate within the whole
of them. A further cause . . . is the in-
frequency of the visits of the Judicial
Assessor. I find . . . that for the past
three years, the average interval between
the visits of that officer to Accra, has been
ten months. . . .   [C.O.96/41]

206 Pine to Labouchere
Cape Coast Castle, 12 June, 1857.
Sir,

Referring to that part of your despatch
to me, No. 2 of 30th September last, in
which you state that you are willing to
assent to Major Ord's suggestions that
some of the native merchants should be
added to the Legislative Council, but expressed your desire to receive my opinion
upon the point, I have now the honour to
lay before you my views on the subject.

The present Legislative Council consists
of the Governor, the Chief Justice, the
Colonial Secretary and the Officer Commanding the Gold Coast Corps. A
council so constituted is, in my opinion,
extremely unsatisfactory. . . . As a body
entrusted with the duty of framing laws
suited to the wants of the country, it fails
and must fail to command the confidence
of the people, from the feeling that it does
not possess within itself that intimate
knowledge of the nature of the country,
the condition of the people, their institutions, their habits of thinking, and their
prejudices, without which knowledge, no
man can safely legislate for any country,
more especially for one in so anomalous a
state as that of these settlements and the
protected territory. . . .

I believe . . . that, under almost any
circumstances whatever, the people would
have no confidence in a Legislative Council
composed of a few Government officials.
I had, for some years, painful experience
of this in Natal, where such a council
formed my very greatest difficulty. . . .
But this community has seen, practically,
the inconvenience arising from such a body.
Several ordinances have been passed, utterly
unsuited to the state of the country, and
mistakes have occurred in some, which
would doubtless have been avoided had any
intelligent inhabitant been in the council.

I would therefore advise that the
council should be extended in the following
manner. Four merchants and two civil
commandants of forts should be added
to the council at once, but not for life.
Nominee councillors, appointed for life,
soon become separated from the rest of
the people, and lose their confidence. I
would propose, therefore, that they should
be appointed for three years only. At the
end of that time, the Governor might reconstruct the council by the re-appointment
of any of these gentlemen whom he found
to possess the confidence of the people, and
for those who had not that qualification,
he might substitute others who had.

In exercising this duty, however, the
Governor should be guided by no narrow
partisan feelings. He should not consider
whether a man is, as it is called, a Government man, or an Opposition man. He
should look upon every one as a loyal
subject of the Government, who honestly
and temperately tendered him his advice
as to public affairs, however much that
advice might differ from his own views. . . .
The only objections that should, in the
Governor's view, exclude a man from a seat
in council, are badness of character, want
of sufficient intelligence, and the promulgation of opinions inconsistent with the
maintenance of Her Majesty's authority
and the [preservation] of order.[1]

---

[1] The three year rule (recently proposed and
rejected in Hong Kong) was not deemed advisable.
'At the end of 3 years the choice will be forced on
the Governor of continuing as councillors men
of good character, but troublesome opponents, or
of dismissing them and making them martyrs'
H.M.7/11 (C.O.96/41).

I should advise the exclusive right of the Governor to introduce Ordinances; his veto, and that of the Crown, and all other regulations of the council should be retained.

By these arrangements, which are, I think, the nearest approach that can safely be made to a representative system, the Government will have little risk of passing laws which cannot be executed, or which do not generally harmonise with the feelings of the people. . . .   [C.O.96/41][1]

207 PINE TO LABOUCHERE
SIERRA LEONE, 31 AUGUST, 1857.

Confidential.

Sir,

Referring to my despatch of the 10th ultimo, marked confidential, in which I informed you that I had arrived at the conclusion that, for some years past, the condition of these settlements had been retrograding, I . . . now . . . proceed to consider the causes of this decline. . . .[2]

Since my arrival here, I have been painfully impressed by the great difficulty of obtaining anything like correct information regarding the people of the interior of the protected country, and of holding satisfactory intercourse with them. Situated as we are, on the coast, we seem to be separated, as by an impenetrable screen of bush and of language, from the interior people. We can only receive their messages through imperfect interpretation. We cannot, without great risk of life and health, visit them in the bush. I have never decided any important question referred to me from the interior, without a feeling of painful uncertainty as to whether I really understood its merits; a feeling that the sword of justice was descending in

[1] Pine's nominations were J. Bannerman (C.C. Accra); R. Clarke (C.C. Anomabu); R. Hutchison and J. Smith (merchants of Cape Coast); and J. E. P. Moffat and J. C. Hansen (merchants of Accra).

[2] The despatch is written in the form of a commentary on a memorandum on the causes of the decline of British influence, submitted, at the Governor's request, by T. B. Freeman.

the dark, and might strike the wrong party. This is more especially felt in disputes relating to land, where local knowledge is necessary. I know that this is an inconvenience which cannot be wholly avoided in the peculiar position of this Government. I cannot, however, help thinking that it might, to some extent, be lessened, by our having an efficient native police at our disposal. . . .

[This is called for by] the manner in which the Government exerts its authority over the country. In purely judicial matters, the person complaining takes out a summons from a court against the defendant. This has frequently to be served far in the interior, and if it is not obeyed, constables, or, in some cases, a military party, are sent to enforce it. In criminal cases, especially in important ones, it is frequently necessary to send military parties to bring down the offenders. Again, in cases of a political character, such as a question between chiefs as to the right to the succession of the stool (i.e. the chiefship), and matters of a similar nature, in which the Governor is called upon, or otherwise feels compelled to interfere, it is sometimes necessary to send armed parties to the spot, not for the purpose of actually using force, but to prevent violence, and ensure the prompt and peacable obedience to the Governor's decision. Moreover, in order that the Government may fully understand the nature of these questions, it is very desirable to send persons to make enquiries on the spot. A few soldiers are also always sent with the Poll Tax collectors, to enforce due obedience to their authority.

I think it must be evident . . . that, for the proper discharge of these duties, an armed police is required, the non-commissioned officers of which should be selected on account of their intelligence and integrity, as well as on account of their military qualifications. Such a force, Mr. Maclean seems to have possessed in his militia, small parties of which, under non-commissioned officers, were stationed in several parts of the interior, especially at the residence of important chiefs. This arrangement was very agreeable to the chiefs, and extremely convenient to the Government, by enabling it to hold easy and satisfactory intercourse with them, and to give correct information. Several of the chiefs have expressed to me their wish for a revival of this system, which, they say, will prevent their proceedings from being misrepresented to me. Mr. Maclean's militia system might have been defective in some respects, and probably required reform; but to abolish it, and to substitute a purely military corps in its place, was, in my opinion, a very grave error. . . .

The Gold Coast Corps . . . is, in fact, the only police force which the Government has to enforce its authority. . . . It is no disparagement to a Corps of regular soldiers, to say it is not fitted for police purposes [but] . . . has been a source of embarrassment and weakness. . . .

Mr. Freeman mentions among the causes of discontent, that it has been usual, of late, to refer almost all cases, in which chiefs were concerned, to the police courts of the coast towns . . . for the decision of questions which ought to be, and in former times were, settled by the friendly arbitration of the Governor himself.

I certainly think that cases in which important chiefs are concerned, and especially disputes or misunderstandings between such chiefs, ought not, at all events in the first instance, to be referred to a court of law; but that, as to them, the Governor should act as the mediator, or, as the natives would call him, the Father. A few kind and judicious words from him will, almost always, settle such disputes, which might otherwise disturb the peace of the country. . . .

I may say here, once for all, that I consider that, of late years, there has been too much interference with the authority of the native chiefs, and this is one of the causes of the decline of our influence. This interference has been exerted by ignoring the native tribunals, and by allowing the chiefs to be summoned before our courts in comparatively trivial cases. The theory that all subjects are equal in the eyes of the law requires modification in this country. We must never forget that our position required [us] to uphold, while we control, the native authorities. . . . But to proclaim throughout these countries, that kings and great chiefs may be summoned before our courts by their subjects, for any petty debt or trivial wrong; what is this but at once to abrogate their authority? Doubtless, by not interfering in such cases, complete justice is not done. Some wrongs go unredressed. But we are not in a position to establish such a complete jurisdiction, and by attempting it, we throw the country into disorder, thereby causing more wrongs and greater oppression. If the country were directly subject to the Crown, and British magistrates were scattered all over it, the sooner the native authority [were] destroyed, the better. But as this is not the case, we must be content to keep peace, to put down practices revolting to humanity, to protect life, to punish important crimes, to prevent flagrant violation of the rights of property, and, for the rest, to protect the people against minor oppressions by generally controlling the authority of the chiefs. But we shall not effect this without very great difficulty; if we attempt more, we shall assuredly do far less.

Our jurisdiction here is doubtless one of extreme difficulty and perplexity, and what renders it more so, is that it is not equally strong, and cannot be exerted to the same extent in all the countries under our protection. For instance, while, in the towns on the coast, our judicial tribunals can take cognizance of the most trifling matters, our authority over the powerful kingdoms of Akim and Aquapim, even at the best of times, requires to be exercised with great caution. The exercise of the judicial authority, in these countries, requires the ability of a stateman rather than the learning of a lawyer; and I cannot help thinking that Mr. Maclean, with his great tact and knowledge of native character, was better fitted to exercise it, than the most learned lawyer sent direct from England.

This seems a proper place to speak of the machinery of the administration of justice. This is in a state far from satisfactory. In Mr. Maclean's administration, he personally exercised the judicial function. He was constantly travelling from place to place, hearing and deciding cases. Although, therefore, his jurisdiction was not exercised according to the forms of English law, so desiderated by Dr. Madden, yet there was a certain unity about it. Emanating from a single mind, while it adapted itself to the varied conditions of the several countries over which it extended, it yet preserved a harmony of action. Of late years, however, the chief justices have not perambulated the country sufficiently often to control the proceedings of the civil commandants and magistrates and ensure an uniform administration of justice. No general rules have been laid down for the guidance of these latter functionaries, so that the practice of their courts has been extremely conflicting and contradictory. So little have the simplest principles of the judicature been understood that the magistrates at Cape Coast Castle have constantly been in the habit of hearing appeals from the decisions of other magistrates. The judicial records have, in several places, been kept in so imperfect a manner as to be unintelligible. All this has produced a confusion and irregularity in the administration of justice, which has been sensibly felt by the people.

The practice which has prevailed latterly of hearing cases in which natives were concerned, before the 'Supreme Court' instead of the 'Judicial Assessor's Court' has also occasioned discontent, by giving the chiefs the impression that we wish to ignore their authority, as the foundation of our own, and to assume a direct control over the country which they are not prepared to admit. In another respect I think the practice very inexpedient. There

are native cases brought before our courts, which no purely British tribunal ought to entertain. . . .   [C.O.96/41]

208 Pine to Labouchere, Sierra Leone
1 October, 1857
Confidential.

. . . One of the conditions, expressed or implied, of our exercise of the Protectorate, is that we shall not interfere with the rights of the native chiefs and headmen, as to slavery. We have been tacitly allowed to violate this condition to a certain extent, by manumitting slaves, in cases of decided cruelty, and by helping discontented slaves to procure new masters. I am convinced that we can go no further. If, except in the cases mentioned, we were to emancipate slaves who came before our courts without compensating their masters, there would at once be a resistance to our authority which we have no means of overcoming.

It may be said that we should only take cognizance of slave cases in which the slave has been treated with such cruelty as enabled us to liberate him. This is the course which, in my difficulty, I have in the meantime ordered to be pursued. I fear, however, when it is fully known, it will cause great trouble, and be found impracticable. It is altogether a one-sided administration of justice. The chiefs and headmen will justly say that our courts are only open to decide cases against them, never for them. Besides, in order to discover whether it is a case for our interference, we must hear both parties. If we decide that it is not such a case, I am at a loss to know what we can do with the slave. If we drive him out of the fort, we virtually deliver him to his master. If we allow him to remain inside (which in other respects is impracticable), we really take him from his master. . . .

Even if we escape from these difficulties as to direct interference between master and slave, I cannot see how we can exercise our jurisdiction without recognizing slavery. Slaves have been shown to compose the bulk of the property, 'the staple currency' of the country. Our courts could not decide a case of disputed succession, or scarcely any other case in which property is concerned, without taking cognizance of slavery. Slavery meets us at every point. . . . It is as impracticable to exercise judicial authority over these countries without recognizing slavery, as it would be for a Court of Chancery to perform its functions in England without taking cognizance of the existence of real and personal property. . . . The anomaly of our position . . . cannot be more forcibly stated than by saying, that the Protectorate of England over these countries involves the violation of English law, and the moment that law is fully observed by our officers, that moment our jurisdiction is brought to an end. . . .

Even as to executive and fiscal matters, our Government there is in a false position in regard to slavery. . . . To afford the protection of our flag and authority to nations so deeply immersed in the sin of slavery, as these are, is to some extent to give it our sanction. In particular, I think, to collect a Poll Tax from people composed only of slave-owners and slaves, is in this respect objectionable, especially as all pecuniary payments in these countries directly or indirectly involve the selling or pawning of human beings. The Poll Tax collectors have mentioned to me more than one case where people were compelled to pawn their children to pay the tax. . . .

We have been struggling between two antagonistic principles. One of these principles is non-interference with the native rights as to slavery; the other is the great principle of the empire, the non-recognition of slavery in any form. Mr. Maclean's administration sacrificed the latter principle, and so, in this respect, was at harmony with itself. Our Government has embraced both principles, and tried to reconcile them. It has singularly failed to do so, while it has offended both of them.

The conflict meets us at every point. It meets us in our intercourse with the chiefs, in the administration of justice, in the collection of the Poll Tax; in every measure we undertake. It was strikingly seen in raising the Gold Coast Corps. . . . Nor have our efforts sensibly diminished slavery. On the contrary, some think, and among them, Mr. Freeman, that it has increased. It is, in the nature of things, not improbable that such has been the case. Other institutions have been preserved by removing their abuses. Why should it be otherwise with slavery? By checking some of the cruelties and other evils of this system, we may probably have prolonged its existence. The effect of our interference may have been to smooth and varnish it for its preservation. . . .

[C.O.96/41]

209 PINE TO LABOUCHERE
    SIERRA LEONE, 10 OCTOBER, 1857.
Confidential.

. . . After having arrived at the conviction that our protectorate over the countries on the Gold Coast necessarily involved the recognition of slavery and pawning, I can have no hesitation in advising that it should at once be withdrawn. There are, however, other reasons for this step.

1st. The efficient exercise of the Protectorate will require an expense which we have no certain means of getting without an increase of the Parliamentary Grant. I regard the Poll Tax as, in several respects, an objectionable impost, and I do not think its continued collection by any means certain. It must be remembered that it is a voluntary tax, depending on the fickle will of barbarians. The customs duties, I also regard as a very insecure source of revenue, unless we can make an arrangement with the Dutch on the subject, which at present . . . does not seem very probable. . . .[1]

[1] The $\frac{1}{2}\%$ a.v. duties, imposed in 1839 by an act of the Sierra Leone Legislative Council, were increased to 2% a.v. by Ordinance 2 of 1855. Cf. Conran to Russell, 2 July, 1855, C.O.96/34. Judging by the revenue returns (Appendix D) Pine's doubts as to their efficacy were fully justified.

2nd. It must, I think, be evident to you, from the statements I have made in former despatches, that for the efficient administration of this Government, a man of very great and peculiar abilities is required. Everything depends, in these settlements, on the character of the Governor. In most other possessions of the Crown, this point is not of such vital importance. In colonies where a regular machinery of government can be applied and is established, the Governor for the time being, 'tho' capable of doing some good or evil, cannot in general seriously compromise the interests of those colonies. . . . Not so with respect to the Gold Coast. . . . There the hand of the Governor is distinctly felt everywhere; any serious mistake on his part is instantly productive of widespread mischief. . . .

I believe that the services of a man capable of governing these settlements cannot be obtained, even by the offer of a far higher salary than that given at present. It will be almost equally difficult to procure a sufficient staff of able subordinate officers. The climate, even for the western coast of Africa, is so extremely unhealthy that no man even seasoned in the other colonies there, of the most moderate prospects and ability, will offer his services for the Gold Coast.

It may be said that the Government once had a competent administrator in Mr. George Maclean. He was altogether a peculiar case, not likely ever to occur again. . . . There are sufficient causes to account for the decline of our influence without adverting to this subject, but it cannot be [denied] that the inferiority to him of Mr. Maclean's successors has been one of the causes of that decline. But I am bound to say that from what I have seen or heard of the rest of these gentlemen, I do not consider them unequal to the government of many other colonies.

It remains to be considered what should be done after withdrawing the protectorate.

It seems to me doubtful whether the Crown should even keep the forts and retain any settlements on the Gold Coast. In a commercial point of view I think the value of these settlements has been overrated. The coast is harbourless and washed by a terrific surf. There are no navigable rivers. The staple production of the country, palm oil, is not to be compared either in quantity or quality with that produced on other parts of the coast further south. Moreover it is doubtful whether our Government on the Gold Coast does not impede rather than benefit such commerce as there is. By far the greater part of our trade on the coast is carried on with countries not under our jurisdiction, and it does not appear that it suffers on that account. The trade in the Bight of Benin, for instance, has increased of late years more in proportion than that of all our possessions on the coast.

If, however, Her Majesty's Government think it right to retain some jurisdiction on the coast, two courses are open to them. 1st. They may retain possession of the forts by means of moderate garrisons, and exercise a consular jurisdiction for the protection of our commerce, and for the protection, as far as practicable, of the natives against the Ashantees. In this case it ought to be understood that no coloured or other native merchants should be entitled to the protection of our influence, who directly or indirectly hold slaves or are in any way concerned in the traffic.

2nd. Her Majesty's Government might, by purchase or free cession, acquire territorial jurisdiction over small [areas] of country adjacent to the forts. These spots should be directly subject to English law. Slavery should not there be tolerated. They should be the asylums of freedom. No slave who took refuge within them should on any account be restored to his master. A simple code of laws founded on the law of England, but suited to the state of the people, should be framed for their government. Order and cleanliness should be introduced into the towns, and practices revolting to humanity and decency abolished. Should the population, owing to the influx of slaves, inconveniently increase, it might be drained off by promoting emigration to the West Indies, which in that case would be free from all objection.

In a philanthropic point of view this is by far the most desirable course we can adopt. A few small, free colonies on the coast would do more to abolish slavery and spread true civilization than the largest protectorate we could exercise, tolerating and sanctioning the barbarous institutions of the people. Slave owners would be far more careful not to ill-treat their slaves when they knew that they could run into our colonies and be free, than they are now when they know that, except in extreme cases, their slaves will either be restored to them by us, or be paid for. I feel sure that such little colonies would do far more to advance civilization in a few years than our Protectorate would do in a century. The Gold Coast Settlements are, I believe, older than the Gambia, and far older than Sierra Leone, yet I have no hesitation in saying that the former are as far behind the latter in civilization as the latter are behind Great Britain. . . .

The new colonies might have to encounter some hostility on the part of the native chiefs, but if their limits were at first not extended much beyond the range of the guns of the forts, there would be no great difficulty in repelling such hostilities. The refugees from the chiefs would, of course, have a personal interest in fighting against them.

The government of these settlements might be very simple. The local management of each of them might be committed to some kind of municipality. The civil establishment need only consist of a Lieutenant Governor, a Secretary, a couple of clerks and two or three paid magistrates. The whole government might with great advantage then be placed under the paramount control of the Governor of Sierra Leone, who, it may be presumed, would in general be a superior man to anyone who could be provided exclusively for the

Gold Coast. From the facilities afforded by the steamers, he could easily proceed to visit the settlements two or three times a year, and direct the general policy of their government. This plan, moreover, would render the military resources of the two governments common to both, without any difficulty or clashing of authority, and would give rise to an intercourse between them decidedly favourable to the advancement of the newer settlements. . . . [The need for a poll tax or a local corps would disappear.]   [C.O.96/41]

210 COLONIAL OFFICE MINUTES
BY H. M. MERIVALE

(a)

16 NOVEMBER, 1857.

The experiment which [Governor Pine] considers to have failed was a favourite idea with Lord Grey. And reference to his book shows that he considered the recognition of domestic slavery as a fundamental and indispensable part of it. No man was more thoroughly opposed to slavery than Lord Grey: but he was quite [explicit] that its suppression in this portion of Africa was impracticable; and he thought its recognition, with a view to ultimate improvement, better than to abandon the whole project.

If he was wrong in this, and Sir B. Pine right, as a matter of principle, then there is an end of the case; nor can I say that the success of the experiment has been hitherto so brilliant as to make its abandonment a matter of very great regret. And one difficulty does not appear to have struck Lord Grey himself — which is, that under existing circumstances, any increase of commerce or of production, such as the growth of cotton, which his Lordship particularly wished to encourage, must inevitably entail an increase of slavery and of the internal slave trade.

I think, moreover, experience has gone against Lord Grey in another particular. He determined on maintaining this Protectorate on a very trifling Parliamentary estimate, not only from motives of economy, but also because he relied on the poll tax to make it 'self-supporting'. But the poll tax is in the first place an instrument for increasing slavery, as Sir B. Pine points out — in the next place, the half-caste merchants seem able and willing to prevent the people from paying it without disturbance; at all events, it cannot be augmented. We are therefore trying a great experiment with wretchedly inadequate means — not the least of our errors being the keeping up a Governor on £800 a year, in a place where, Sir B. Pine most truly says, a man of ability and influence is the chief thing wanted.

If these reasons are thought sufficient to justify abandoning the experiment, I can only say that I think the abandonment should be complete — i.e. preserving only the forts, and concerning ourselves no further in native affairs than to extend some protection against Ashantee invasion, to which, I suppose, we stand committed by former proceedings.

I cannot but think the plan of appropriating (in event of abandonment) small portions of territory round the guns of the forts very undesirable, except, perhaps at Cape Coast Castle itself, and possibly Accra.

But for my own part, though with no great hopes from the Protectorate, I cannot say I think the time for giving it up has arrived. Good has been done, though not to the extent philanthropists may have wished — evil, probably, averted to a greater extent. . . .

As to the question of illegality in the proceedings of British magistrates abetting slavery, I am afraid it is a real difficulty. You will see by the minutes on 4620 of 1855[1] that it was not overlooked, but that Lord John Russell thought it best to leave the matter alone.   [C.O.96/41]

[1] Connor to Herbert (7 April, 1855), arguing that a special act was necessary to indemnify officials on the Gold Coast for their recognition of domestic slavery, by their routine exercise of jurisdiction.

(b) BY CHICHESTER-FORTESCUE[1]
19 DECEMBER, 1857.

[Governor Pine] is influenced solely by a morbid fear of doing wrong in the recognition of domestic slavery, for which we are not responsible, which we cannot suppress, but the evils of which we can and do mitigate. I confess I have no sympathy with the state of mind which would refuse to touch this unclean thing — even for the purpose of doing good — in order to satisfy that kind of conscientiousness.

As far as I can judge, I believe Sir B. Pine's comparison of the Gold Coast with Sierra Leone and the Gambia, so much to the disadvantage of the former, to be unsound. In the two latter cases we enforce our laws and prohibit all practices contrary to them, within very narrow limits — in the former we exercise a very imperfect but far more important influence over a great region of Africa. . . .
[C.O.96/41]

211 PINE TO LABOUCHERE
ACCRA, 4 DECEMBER, 1857.
Sir,

Referring to . . . my despatch of 30th April last containing certain suggestions for the better administration of the Poll Tax Fund, I have now the honour to inform you of the measures which I have, subject to your approval, adopted for carrying those suggestions into effect.

1st. I have laid it down as a rule that the proceeds of the tax collected in the Western Districts, should be paid into the public chest at Cape Coast Castle, and that collected in the Eastern Districts into the chest at Accra; and that the same shall be expended in the District in which it is collected.

2ndly. I have established it as a rule that two-thirds of the fund shall be

[1] Samuel Chichester Fortescue (later Baron Carlingford) (1823–98), Liberal M.P. for Louth County, 1847–74; Under-Secretary of State for the Colonies, 1857–8 and from June 1859 to October 1865; served on the Select Committee of 1865; Baron Carlingford, 1874.

expended in the extension of the magistracy and the establishment of schools and hospitals, and the remaining third in physical improvements, such as roads, bridges and the like.

3rdly. I have directed that the funds shall be thus expended under the general supervision of local councils appointed by the Governor, to consist of native chiefs, merchants and other inhabitants. The one-third devoted to local improvements is to be under the direct control of the local councils, and an account of the expenditure of the other two-thirds is to be laid before them periodically. The Governor, or in his absence, the Civil Commandant of the District, is to be president of each of the councils. . . . [An ordinance would be prepared to establish them.]

For the purpose of these regulations, I have established three districts or divisions in the settlements: one extending from the western boundary to a spot a few miles east of Cape Coast Castle, called the Cape Coast district; another extending from the latter point to the Secoom River, called the Anomaboe district; and a third including the country between that river and the river Volta, called the Eastern or Accra district. The country east of the Volta, which . . . never agreed to the Poll Tax, I have not noticed. For each of these divisions I have appointed a local council composed of the principal chiefs and merchants, and one or two missionaries.

The councils of Cape Coast and Accra have had several meetings, and I have agreed to some very useful by-laws for cleaning and improving the towns, and establishing police regulations. The people seem extremely pleased with this measure, and it has tended to give them greater confidence in the administration of the poll tax fund, and to render the impost more popular than it has been for some time past.

In the document called the Poll Tax Ordinance, it was stated that the accounts of the expenditure of the Poll Tax should be submitted to an annual assembly of the chiefs and headmen of the countries under our protection. I have however already informed you, in the despatch already referred to . . . that no such general assembly ever took place . . . but that there were on that occasion district assemblies for the several main divisions of the country. In point of fact, a general assembly of all the chiefs and headmen of the protected countries, except perhaps in case of war, is a thing which never had any existence and is utterly impracticable. The stipulation in question was therefore incapable of being observed. It might indeed have been possible to call annual meetings of the chiefs of the principal districts, but in the first place such meetings . . . would be attended with an expense of upwards of £500, and in the second place, such large tumultuous assemblies would be very unfit to audit accounts and discuss financial details. In short, it would be a mere mockery and delusion on the part of Government to employ them for any such purpose. On the other hand, at a council where numbers should not exceed 20, and composed of one or two kings or principal chiefs from each of the countries in the districts, and of the principal merchants, the amount of the tax fund can be carefully examined; and thus a substantial check against improper expenditure is placed in the hands of the people. At the same time, the Government will be freed of that suspicion as to the faithful administration of the fund which has been the cause of so much heartburning and discontent. . . . I should remind you that Lord Grey, who suggested this tax, perpetually laid great stress on its being administered by some kind of municipal institutions, and I am convinced that if his Lordship's view had been carried out as far as practicable, much of the trouble which this impost has occasioned would have been spared.

I cannot, however, conceal from myself . . . that there are no strong grounds for hoping that these or any other measures I am adopting will, under present circumstances, effect any permanent and substantial improvement in the condition of these people. But whilst I have laid freely before you my strong objections to the present jurisdiction over these countries, I feel it my duty to carry out what I conceive to be the views of Her Majesty's Government, to the utmost of my ability, as far as I can conscientiously do so.[1]

[C.O.96/41]

212 PINE TO LABOUCHERE
ACCRA, 29 DECEMBER, 1857.

. . . To free our courts from a recognition of slavery, I have issued the rules, a copy of which I . . . enclose. In order to avoid any inconvenience which might result from the sudden announcement of these regulations, I have directed the individual authorities not to go out of their way to promulgate them, but quietly and firmly to act upon them as occasions arise.

What effect these regulations will have on the native mind when they become fully known remains to be seen. I do not, however, think that, with the increased confidence lately felt in the Government, they will produce so much hostility as I had anticipated. . . . The mode of dealing with the case of a slave who, without being able to prove any ill-usage, enters our forts, insists on claiming their protection . . . [has] yet to be provided for. . . .

I beg, however, to submit to you a measure which, while it may to some extent meet the specific difficulty I have named, will be a decided step towards freedom. You will observe that if a slave cannot prove ill-usage, I have directed the magistrate simply to decline all interference on either side. It seems to me, however, that there would be no impropriety in such a case if the magistrate offered to apprentice the slave to the master for five years, or shorter time, according to his age, giving him letters of manumission . . . at the end of the period, and registering his case in a book to be kept for the purpose. . . .

[1] Labouchere signified his approval on 23 January.

There is in this no forcible interference with native rights, if such they can be called. We simply say to the master, If you want our intervention in the matter, you have it on these terms or not at all. I am inclined to think that in a short time, many masters would avail themselves of this arrangement, for it will give them the advantage of being able to call on the Government to compel the quondam slave to work on fair terms. . . . The registration of the apprentice would be perfectly easy, as it would take place only as the cases were brought before the magistrate, and if the magistrates perambulate their districts, as I have directed, the supervision and control of the system would not be attended with great difficulty. . . .

[C.O.96/41]

213 MEMORANDUM FOR THE GUIDANCE OF THE COURTS AS TO CASES INVOLVING SLAVERY AND PAWNING [Enclosure in the above]
CAPE COAST CASTLE, 30 OCTOBER, 1857.

1. No Judicial Assessor, Commandant, or Justice of the Peace, shall on any account whatever, compel or order a slave or pawn to return to his master.

2. In cases where it is proved that the master has been decidedly guilty of cruelty towards his slave, the slave may be emancipated and protected; in all other cases the Courts must simply decline to interfere.

3. In pawn cases, if the person pawned is other than the person who contracted the debt, the debt itself is not to be enforced by our Courts of Law, as founded on an immoral and unlawful consideration; but if the pawn is the person who contracted the debt, it is to be enforced like any other kind of debt.

4. Any British subject who directly or indirectly is implicated in slavery or pawning, is guilty of felony; and in any such case, the above-mentioned officers must, under all circumstances, emancipate any slaves or pawns belonging to the offender, and take prompt steps to have him brought

to justice under Statutes 5 Geo. 4, cap. 113, and 6 & 7 Vict., cap. 98.

By order.

Edward B. Andrews,
Colonial Secretary.
[C.O.96/41: H.C.412 of 1865]

214 PINE TO LABOUCHERE

ACCRA, 30 DECEMBER, 1857.

Sir,

In several of my former despatches, I have adverted to the difficulties to which the close intermingling of the Dutch settlements on this coast with our own, has given rise; and I now beg to submit to you some suggestions for the partial removal of this obstacle.

You will observe that, with one exception, all the places practically occupied by the Dutch lie to the westward of Cape Coast Castle. To the eastward of the latter, Dutch Accra is the only place they really occupy, although between these two places, they have several small settlements, one or two of which are garrisoned, if I may call it so, each by a single soldier, whose duty is confined to keeping the Dutch flag flying. To the eastward of Accra, the Dutch have no settlements whatever.

I was at one time disposed to think that in order to consolidate the possessions of the Crown here, it would be advisable to exchange Dixcove and the other British Possessions west of Cape Coast and its neighbourhood, for Dutch Accra and the few other Dutch places east of Cape Coast. By this arrangement, the Sweet River, which is about six miles west of Cape Coast, would become the boundary between the Settlements of the two countries — all the westward becoming Dutch; all the eastward British.

To this plan, however, though recommended by its geographical simplicity, there are great objections. The people of Dixcove and the other British places on that side of Cape Coast are extremely attached to our Government. They have readily paid the Poll Tax, and have seldom

K

given us any trouble. On the other hand, they have a great antipathy to the Dutch. It would therefore be cruel to transfer such a people to a Government they dislike, and, moreover, I feel sure they never would submit to it unless compelled to do so by main force.

An arrangement not open to the same objections and which at the same time would give us most of the advantages of that I have mentioned, is to induce the Dutch Government to sell Dutch Accra and the rest of their places east of Cape Coast. The only place of any real value is Dutch Accra, and its value almost entirely consists in its proximity to our settlements.

That place and James Town, or British Accra, in fact form one town, only separated by an ideal line, actually in one part running through the middle of a house. The Dutch part of the town lies to the east of the British, and beyond it, only two miles off [is] the British castle of Christiansborg, so that Dutch Accra is closely wedged in between two British settlements.

The Dutch garrison consists of five soldiers only, while James Fort and Christiansborg have together nearly 100 men. The Dutch settlement is thereby really entirely protected by our forces, without which they could not, among this warlike people, keep their position a single hour, for they have no hold on the [affections] of the people. A few years ago their commandant would have been murdered in his fort but for our interference. They are, in point of fact, maintaining the place at our expense and to our very great inconvenience and annoyance. In this state of affairs it will always be impossible for us to collect any duties worth mentioning at Accra. . . . In every other respect the Dutch settlement is a nuisance to us. Their people are some of the most troublesome in the country, and they are under no wholesome control. I have [already] pointed out the mischief they do by interfering with the people under our protection. In fact, this place is the greatest difficulty in the way of the government of these eastern districts by the Crown. . . . I have heard the Dutch authorities here say that the chief value of their settlements consists in their close proximity to ours, and that their government could not and would not keep them up if we were to abandon ours; . . . and yet . . . the Dutch Government will come to no understanding with us even as to the collection of duties. Their settlements may all, in my opinion, be likened to parasitical plants living on the British oak. . . .

The Dutch Government on this coast has attempted to do next to nothing for the improvement of the people. It is in some respects tyrannical and oppressive. It boasts that it does not levy a poll tax on its people, as we do, but it does not care to remember that it is in a great measure maintained by the presence of the British Government; that it economizes its expenditure by the expedient of allowing its officers to trade instead of properly paying them; and that it partly ekes out the amount it is compelled to spend by inflicting heavy fines on its people for various offences. In short, I consider the Dutch Government on this coast as an anti-civilizing element. . . .   [C.O.96/41]

215 PINE TO LABOUCHERE
CAPE COAST CASTLE, 10 FEBRUARY, 1858.
. . . I have in other despatches pointed out that the [Gold Coast] Corps is in fact the police of the country. This it must continue to be unless an armed police, fully 200 strong, under strict military discipline, is established in addition. . . . Our resources are quite unable to bear the expense of such a police . . . and if they were . . . I see no necessity for keeping up two corps when one would suffice. Besides, the two military corps in the same forts under separate commands would lead to endless difficulties. . . .

I have shown [the Corps'] present unfitness as a police. This arises chiefly from the adoption of the ordinary military mode of recruiting, a mode wholly unsuited to the circumstances of the country. The mass of the people are slaves, so that the chances are that 9 out of 10 men enlisted belong to that class. Thus a two-fold source of evil is produced. First, the chiefs and upper classes are deprived of their slaves without their consent and without remuneration. Secondly, these same slaves, generally bad characters, are sent back to them with red coats on their backs, to enforce the orders of Government; which they, of course, do with all the insolence natural to their sudden change of fortune.

Again, the Corps thus recruited is necessarily composed of the off-scourings of the country; of men who have plundered their masters or committed other atrocities. The conduct of such men acting as police may well be imagined. Wherever they are sent into the bush on service, they pillage or maltreat the people. Even the presence of their officers cannot restrain them. Every time I have taken excursions into the interior accompanied by an officer and a few soldiers, well-founded complaints have been made of the lawless conduct of the men.

This is not all. Deserters from the Corps, and men discharged at the end of their term of service, for the most part betake themselves to the bush. Besides plundering in the ordinary way, they not infrequently extort money under the name of fines which they impose on the people under pretence that they are armed with the authority of the Government. They even form themselves and the refuse of the people around them, into armed bands, and carry on their depredations on a more ambitious scale. A particularly flagrant case of this kind occurred lately, in which a party of these ruffians, after plundering the people under our protection about Apollonia, actually attacked the French settlement at Assinee, where they were fortunately beaten and several of them taken prisoner.

All this has caused the greatest irritation

among the chiefs and people, and I am only surprised that they have borne it so long. Fortunately, the most serious of these outrages have taken place in the most peaceable and loyal part of the country. Had they occurred in the Eastern districts, I believe widespread insurrection would have been the result. . . .

This can only be [cured] by abolishing the present mode of recruiting, substituting the following plan. The kings and chiefs should each be requested to furnish a given number of the most respectable men they can spare. It should be impressed upon them that the Queen's uniform cannot be worn by thieves and vagabonds, and that we have neither the desire to take their slaves from them, nor the power to pay for them. I am sure that the chiefs would fall in with this arrangement. I have already spoken to two very important chiefs on the subject, and they expressed their readiness to co-operate with us, provided the present obnoxious system of recruiting were abolished. Great care should be taken that the Corps should contain men of the various tribes and nations in proper proportions, so as to keep each other in check and prevent combination. . . .

Another circumstance, equally injurious . . . is that the present articles of war are utterly unsuited to the people and country. At best, the Corps will be composed of savages. . . . To apply the articles of war to such men is like attempting to bind a tiger with the chain of a lap dog. The guard room and the black hole have no terrors for the savage negro, whose life is an alternation of brutal excitement and apathy. . . . As a soldier in his own country he can only be ruled by the sternest discipline. I should think that the rules of war applicable in the presence of the enemy would be found scarcely too stringent for this Corps. . . .

There is another point. . . . It seems that one of the objects had in view when the formation of this Corps was first proposed, was that the men should be taught some mechanical art and employed in effecting local improvements. This object seems to have been lost sight of, and yet I am sure that had it been carried out, something better might have been made even of the wretched materials of which the Corps is now composed. As it is, these runaway slaves look with disdain upon such works, saying that they enlisted only as soldiers. In fact, a species of sepoyism . . . has been established without a tithe of the excuse which existed for it in India. . . .[1]

As to the conversion of the Corps into artillery, some artillery force is certainly required, both to defend the forts and to take the field against the Ashantees, especially as the natives themselves attach importance to that arm. I do not, however, see why the men could not have been taught enough of gunnery for the purpose required without converting the Corps into a purely artillery one. The great object for native warfare should be to make the men completely master of the simple manoeuvres likely to be actually required in the field, and expert riflemen. . . . I would recommend . . . that about 100 men should be drilled as artillerymen . . . and the remaining 200 should be chiefly drilled in the manner I have mentioned, and employed as the police of the country. . . .

I come now to the question of the separation of the command of the Corps from the Governor's office. Seeing that the Corps, or the greater part of it, is now, and must be the police of the colony, I do not see how this division of authority can be kept up. Moreover . . . the circumstances of these settlements where civil and military live in the same forts, the latter nearly all employed in the civil service, render such an arrangement extremely inexpedient. I am sure that it is the opinion of all the officers . . . in these settlements that the two services should be under one head. The only difference of opinion is as to how this union is to be brought about.

[1] The Indian Mutiny was, of course, still raging when Pine wrote.

My own opinion is that the Governor . . . whether a military man or not, should be ex officio Colonel of the Corps; the practical command of it as to details being retained by a military officer. . . . The circumstances of the settlements are peculiar and require a departure from ordinary rules.   [C.O.96/43]

216 PINE TO STANLEY[1]

7 MAY, 1858.

My Lord,

The disorderly and filthy state in which I found the towns under the walls of the forts has been described in a former despatch. . . . One of the immediate causes of this unsatisfactory state . . . is their peculiar position. In them the inconvenience incidental to the division of authority between the Protecting and the Native Governments are especially felt. They have weakened each other. The immediate presence of the former has overshadowed and depressed the power of the chiefs, which, however, has still vitality enough to hamper its direct control over the towns. . . .

I . . . tried various expedients for remedying the state of the towns. . . . I soon found that chiefs, however willing, had not the power to effect any permanent good. . . . The district councils . . . composed of the chiefs and principal men of large districts extending far into the interior . . . could only attend to the coastal towns as parts, and not considerable parts of their jurisdiction. . . . By increase of the town members . . . they came to degenerate into town councils having . . . control of the whole of the portion of the tax fund of the entire district applicable to the local improvements. . . . The tax fund of the towns themselves was

manifestly insufficient to enable the district councils to put them in order. . . . They had no executive to carry out their measures except the Government itself. In fact they were never designed to be more than legislative bodies. . . . For the Government to assume the direct control of the towns was out of the question. Such a measure would increase our difficulties as to slavery, and . . . the expense . . . would be far beyond our means. Moreover, the measure seemed wrong in principle. The best government is that which teaches people to govern themselves, and certainly the object of this government was not to clean out dirty towns, but to direct the people to that and other objects by controlling and modifying their own governments.

It was evident that some strong native government must be established in the towns themselves. The question was, what this should be? To restore the authority of the chiefs in its integrity was out of the question. Opposed as I am to the reckless destruction of the power of the chiefs where we have no authority to substitute for it, I know far too much of their system of rule to desire to restore it when it has fallen, and when anything short of pure anarchy can be put in its place. At any rate, the restoration of the power of the chiefs in these towns was impossible. There are parts of the population over which they could never acquire control. There has grown up a large class of native merchants and traders, the greater part of whom are in advance of them in wealth and intelligence. There are also in these towns a few European merchants.

It seemed, under these circumstances, that the only practicable way of regulating these towns was to combine these elements together, and out of them to form a kind of government which should not directly supersede, but incorporate within itself, the authority of the chiefs, while it should be strengthened and extended by the influence of the more intelligent natives and of the Government itself. A simple kind

---

[1] Edward Henry Stanley (later 15th Earl of Derby) (1826–93); Conservative M.P. for King's Lynn, 1848–69; Secretary for the Colonies, February to May 1858; Foreign Secretary under Disraeli, 1874–8; Secretary for the Colonies under Gladstone, 1882–5, when he was credited with saying 'We don't want any more black men.'

of municipal corporation appeared best suited for this purpose.

I had frequently discussed this project with the principal men of Cape Coast town and James' Town Accra, and had gradually brought them to understand and approve of it. The former of these towns has been until lately in so divided a state, owing to dissensions between the king and his chiefs, that it would have been difficult to carry such a plan into effect. In James Town however, which seemed so unpromising a field for the experiment, the measure has been called for and introduced. . . . I was urged, now that the people were in the mood, to bring the measure into effect at once. . . . I thought it better to comply . . . and have our proceedings afterwards confirmed by law.

A meeting of the chiefs and people was therefore held in the hall of the fort. After Mr. Freeman and I had briefly explained the general features of this law, the assembly proceeded to choose the seven members of the town council. The people voted in classes through their respective chiefs, as provided for in the Ordinance. The chiefs voted for none of their own number, but for merchants of their own colour. The merchants, with very good taste, voted for and brought in the most intelligent of the chiefs. The results of the election . . . gave general satisfaction. After this election, the councillors chose for Mayor, Mr. James Bannerman, son of the late commandant.

The council have commenced their duties with energy. They have passed several by-laws for the suppression of nuisances, some of them of rather a stringent nature. . . . The town has been assessed on a scale descending from £3 per annum for first class houses, to five shillings for the worst class. . . . It is calculated that this tax will produce about £200 per annum. . . . The poll tax of the town only produced . . . about £55. The Government is still to receive two thirds of this sum from the council. . . .

The Ordinance itself requires . . . few remarks. . . . The 9th chapter is important. It establishes a court to be held before the mayor and one of the councillors, to which it gives jurisdiction in civil cases when the matter in dispute does not exceed £50, and in criminal cases when the matter in dispute does not exceed 6 months imprisonment with hard labour. It may at first sight seem that this is a large jurisdiction for such a court, but I would remind your Lordship that native tribunals of this country . . . do enjoy quite as large, if not larger powers, and that our mission is not to supersede native authority, but to teach it its right exercise. . . . The establishment of a regular native court, acting according to prescribed rules, and whose decisions are subject to the instant review of our own courts on the spot, is one of the best modes of teaching this lesson. . . .   [C.O.96/43]

217 T. B. FREEMAN EXPLAINS THE IMPLICATIONS OF THE PROTECTORATE TO THE KREPIS

22 JUNE, 1858.

I. The Poll Tax.

1. The assembled chiefs were warned that in all financial business transactions between the supreme Government and the Krepees, the current value of cowries at Accra, the head-quarters of the Eastern District, is to be the public standard. (. . . The Krepees have a different standard for cowries. . . .)

2. Public improvements. The chiefs were informed that after the first payment of the tax on the 1st of December next, the Government will be glad to listen to any suggestions they may wish to offer on this head. They answered that they clearly understood and that they agreed to the arrangement.

II. Judicial Business.

1. The Government will support the great chiefs in their lawful authority over their people.

2. The Governor will protect the people against tyranny and oppression on the part of their native rulers.

3. All ordinary judicial cases are left in the hands of the great chiefs, to make such arrangements in every town and village as will secure the due and impartial administration of justice.

4. An appeal lies from any and all other native courts to the court of the chief paramount (Kujo Dai).

5. An appeal lies from the court of the chief paramount to the court of the commandant of the Eastern District.

6. No great chief can be summoned, but any of his people can, by respectful complaint, appeal to the court of the commandant.

7. Cases of murder, or any cases involving *life* and *death* can only be adjudged in the court of the Commandant.

8. Constables and policemen sent into Krepee on duty will always when practicable, serve summonses &c through the respective chiefs of towns and districts.

9. Human sacrifices forbidden and declared to be murder. n.b. It was solemnly declared that Her Majesty's Government will not extend her protection over any country or tribe which admits human sacrifices among its public institutions.

10. Panyarring under any and all circumstances forbidden on pain of punishment.

III. Recent Proclamations explained and enforced.

1. Contracting and limiting the time employed in customs for the dead.

2. Prohibiting the putting of people into fetish.

3. Prohibiting the harbouring and encouraging runaway subjects of the king of Ashantee in the Protected Territories. . . .[1]

[C.O.96/43]

---

[1] Freeman was instructed by Pine to proceed to Akwamu, whose chief had signified his willingness to pay the Poll Tax, and by Bird, to visit Krepi. The report from which the above extract is taken covers 126 pages.

218 COLONIAL OFFICE MEMORANDA
1858–9.

(*a*) Minute by H. M. Merivale
5 March, 1858.

. . . Mr. Labouchere considered this subject a great deal. He was at first much struck with Sir B. Pine's views: but on further reflection and consultation with African authorities, especially Dr. Livingstone, he came round to the opinion that it was better to persevere in Lord Grey's experiment. But he preferred leaving the ultimate decision to his successors. . . .

[C.O.96/44]

(*b*) Memorandum by the Earl of Carnarvon[1]   11 November, 1858.

It is impossible to read [Governor Pine's] despatches without coming to one and only one conclusion, viz. that a complete abandonment of the Protectorate was our best course. Lord Stanley was considerably influenced by them, and when leaving this office was under serious doubts as to the propriety of giving up the Gold Coast.

But the time when Sir B. Pine wrote the despatches in question was apparently a turning point in the condition of that country, and since he has been in England, and I have had an opportunity of talking over this subject with him, I have become aware of his very altered views.

I do not think that an entire abandonment of the Gold Coast was ever contemplated of late years: but several schemes for a partial abandonment or a modification of the existing system had been discussed. There were two main proposals of this nature.

1. An abandonment of the Protectorate and the formation of small colonies to be acquired by purchase or cession, where we should exercise full rights of sovereignty. . . . But I have never seen very clearly the

---

[1] Henry Howard Molyneux Herbert, 4th Earl of Carnarvon (1831–90); Conservative statesman; Under-Secretary for the Colonies, February 1858–June 1859; Secretary of State for the Colonies, June 1866–March 1867, and from February 1874 to January 1878.

advantages of this plan. It would, perhaps, relieve us of some of our existing responsibility — or rather sense of responsibility — in exercising a virtual sovereignty, and yet being obliged to tolerate slavery and many other objectionable practices. But it would still impose upon us the careful and anxious maintenance of our foreign and intricate relations with the native races; and whilst by asserting an actual sovereignty over these colonies we should pledge ourselves to defend and hold them, we should be less capable than ever, as I think, of resisting attack.

We should change our whole position by becoming the holders of territory. There would be a constant risk of those territories growing by cession, by conquest, and by individual rapacity, or, if indeed this should not occur, we should be open to the suspicion of it, and jealousy of our intentions would soon supplant the confidence which is now apparently felt in us, and which is the best reason of our occupation of the coast.

Our policy also would necessarily change, and I doubt whether for our advantage. Now we rely simply upon the force of our example and influence; we should in such a case be tempted to lean more upon the material strength of our colonies, which after all would probably betray us on the first emergency.

The second proposal has been to withdraw entirely from the Protectorate, and, retaining the forts for commercial reasons, leave the country to itself. I doubt the morality of this in the first place. We have established ourselves in that country, and have undoubtedly affected the native mind by our presence, if for good, also probably for evil. We are hardly at liberty thus to throw down the system of good and evil for them to make their choice, and, having disturbed their own system and organisation, to withdraw ourselves from all further responsibility because we find that the task upon which we imprudently entered is a more severe one than we expected. The only consequence of our withdrawal,

to the native races, would be a more complete anarchy and more bloody wars than existed before we appeared on the coast.

But if indeed we withdraw from the Protectorate, better also to withdraw from the forts. It would be an ineffective solution of our difficulties and it would fairly expose us to the reproach of sacrificing all considerations of what is due to humanity and Christian obligations whilst we retained all that commercially is profitable; and it would be disgraceful to us as a civilized Power, to see within a hundred yards of the forts, bloodshed, misrule and abominable practices in full play. . . .

[He recommends putting all the West African Governments under Sierra Leone.]

[C.O.96/44]

(c) Minute by the Duke of Newcastle
31 August, 1859.

. . . Our position on the Gold Coast, whether viewed in a philanthropic or commercial light, is very unsatisfactory, and must be reviewed as soon as a new Governor is appointed. We have done, or attempted to do, either too much or too little. I do not, however, think it is possible to recede. The attempts now making by Foreign nations to revive the slave trade would, if no other consideration interfered, render abandonment of our position on the coast impossible. The purchase of the Dutch forts, if Holland would entertain the proposal, would be the first great step towards effecting the objects which brought us to this unhealthy region, and would before long so increase the pecuniary resources of the Colony, by rendering moderate customs duties possible as to relieve the Parliamentary grant altogether, if the Governor were not tempted to launch into premature and ill-calculated expenses.

The first, and present question, however, is the amalgamation of the Governorships of the three settlements. The only object, as I conceive, for which this proposal is made, is to obtain a better man as Governor-in-Chief by the inducement of a better salary. I do not think the object attainable. In the first place, the increase proposed . . . is so small. . . . Considering the risks of health and life and the social privations they suffer, it is wonderful that such good men have been found to go there — but we must not forget that the demand in this country for superior men for all situations exceeds the supply, and no salary within reason would tempt such men from other employment to the w[est] coast of Africa.

My main objection, however, is that supposing such a man obtained, the advantage would all fall to S. Leone, and nothing but detriment to Gambia and G. Coast. The distance apart is great. The visits of the Governor could not be frequent. In his absence the subordinate officers would possess but small authority with the natives. They would look to the Governor-in-Chief alone and would appeal from the Lt. Governor on all occasions. Thus authority would be weakened and justice delayed. . . .   [C.O.96/46]

16 The Krobo war and the failure of the Dutch negotiations, 1858–1862

THE recovery under Sir Benjamin Pine was short-lived. In September 1858 the authorities were obliged to intervene in Krobo (219), and their forces were repulsed in an attack on Krobo Hill. The military consequences were not serious, as the Krobos submitted in the following month. As usual, they were fined to pay the costs of the expedition sent against them, but, to save trouble, as he thought, the Acting-Governor farmed out the collection of the fine to a Cape Coast merchant, who hoped to recoup himself in Krobo palm oil (220). This questionable expedient was the cause of constant disputes which gravely dislocated trade and impaired the influence of Government for years, until they were finally terminated in 1866.

When Pine's successor finally arrived at Cape Coast in April 1860, he was met by difficulties on all sides. There was war in Akim, the Ashanti were rumoured to be preparing to invade the Protectorate, the Labadis wanted no interference in their affairs, there was a series of riots at Cape Coast, and the municipal government introduced by Pine had collapsed.

Governor Andrews, formerly Colonial Secretary at Cape Coast, was hardly equal to his task. His rambling despatches were 'a melancholy waste of time and paper'; his projects at times 'so wild as to be dangerous'.[1] In the circumstances, he decided to withdraw from all commitments beyond the Volta (224). Demands for more effective government (229) were singularly inappropriate at a time when Andrews was saying that without more money, British jurisdiction would have to be confined to the forts;[2] and the Treasury, as always, was making difficulties over every application for its assistance (228).

The crucial need for money explains why the Home Government put its hopes and energy into reaching an understanding with the Dutch. After the negotiation was broken off in 1857 (223), an attempt was made in 1859 to reach a local agreement on the coast, but this broke down over the Dutch demand for Wasaw (222). At the Hague the following year, the same obstacle was encountered, but the offer of the Dutch to accept a common system of import duties (225) in return for the withdrawal of the British protection from Wasaw, was 'very tempting'[3]. Andrews was instructed to see if he could get the consent of the Wasaws to the exchange (226), but there was no comfort in his reply (227). A solution of the financial question was as far off as ever.

[1] C.O.96/49.   [2] To Newcastle, 25 April, 1861, in C.O.96/52.
[3] Chichester Fortescue's comment (11 August, 1860). He went on: 'But I think we are bound in good faith not to hand over Wasaw to the Dutch without their own consent' (C.O.96/50).

219 MAJOR H. BIRD TO SIR E. BULWER LYTTON[1]

CHRISTIANSBORG, 10 NOVEMBER, 1858.

[1] Edward George Earle Lytton Bulwer Lytton, later 1st Baron Lytton (1803–73); novelist and M.P., first liberal (1831–41) and then conservative (1852–66); Secretary of State for the Colonies, May 1858–June 1859.

Sir,

With reference to my despatches . . . of the 9th September and . . . 8th October last, reporting that a rebellion had broken out in Crobboe, and that I had taken active measures to repress the same, I have now the honour to submit to you the following report and to state the expedition has been crowned with entire success.

The Crobboe country consists of a vast, extended, rich and undulating plain, with several isolated ranges of rocky hills of varying height and extent, rising abruptly out of it, one of which is the Crobboe mountain. . . . Crobboe is situate from 50 to 60 miles distant from this station, the river Volta forming its boundary on the north-eastern side; is about 20 miles square, containing, according to Mr. Freeman's estimate, a population of not less than 20,000 souls. It is divided into north-eastern and south-western Crobboe. The former is governed by Odonkor Ossu, the latter by Ologoo Pattoo. Both districts are pretty equally balanced with regard to power and population. Each chief has his stronghold provided by nature on the mountain or hill, to which they resort in times of disturbance or war, and on which are two well and substantially built towns. Odonkor Ossu's is called Magnya and Ologo Pattoo's 'Nilo'.[1] I am told that during the Ashantee invasions the Crobboes resorted to their hill and kept the invaders at bay by detaching and rolling down huge masses of granite whenever they made the attempt to scale the heights and take the towns by storm. Crobboe has been of late years the principal seat of the palm oil trade of this district.

The inhabitants, like the Christianborg, Labadi, Tacia[2] and Ningo people, were formerly under the rule of the Danish Government. They speak the Adampa[3] language, which is a dialect of the Ga or Accra language. The king of Christianborg seems to possess a kind of suzerainty over them, and to him they look for counsel in time of difficulty.

For years past, the Crobboes, in common with all the former Danish subjects, have shown a restless and turbulent disposition, and a strong desire to get rid of the controlling power of the British Govern-

ment. . . . The chiefs have certainly felt, what they never experienced under Danish rule — themselves being governed, and their extortions being curtailed. Like the nobles of feudal times, some of them have all along steadfastly striven to resist what they consider as an invading authority, and shake off the galling yoke.

Before the poll tax ordinance was passed, this irritation was confined to the kings and chiefs. They, however, by accepting the ordinance and complying, for the first year, with its provisions, have probably used it as an engine to excite dissatisfaction among the mass towards the new government. For what were the immediate results? Rebellion amongst the Christiansborg inhabitants, and the subsequent destruction of their town; disaffection among the whole of the Adampe race . . . including the interior districts of Crobboe and also those of Aquambo and Krepee . . . amounting almost to a positive negation of British rule. . . .

The turbulent and refractory Adampe race have hitherto cared little for British protection, for this reason; they, under any circumstances would be protected from Ashantee invasion indirectly through the protection afforded to the countries lying to the north and west of them. To have, therefore, withdrawn our protection from the rebellious Crobboes, would, I hold, have been wrong and positively unjust to other people who have all along acknowledged allegiance to the British flag. To have remained neuter on this occasion would have been a declaration of weakness, the destruction of the prestige of the Government, and the yielding over the country to anarchy and bloodshed. . . . I felt too it was one of those cases in which, if Government interfered, that interference could scarcely be too prompt, and that had I delayed taking active measures until I had received the sanction of Her Majesty, the danger would have been most imminent, not only of jeopardising the peace of the neighbouring districts, but of the country at large. . . .

[1] Manya and Yilo Krobo.
[2] Teshi.
[3] Adangbe.

[The immediate occasion for intervention was the rebellion of Tenu, one of the chiefs of north-eastern Krobo, backed by Ologo Patu. Pine had contemplated an expedition against Patu in 1857, but Freeman in 1857 had got that chief to accept British jurisdiction. Then Tenu rebelled, Patu sent him help, and began raiding on his own account. Freeman was sent with full powers and a military force, to secure the submission of the tribe, peacefully if possible. On 18th September a first attack miscarried, but by the 20th October, when the tribes had put 20,000 men into the field to help the Government, Patu saw that resistance was hopeless, and surrendered. He was fined 15,000 heads of cowries (£1,875) and was destooled; his captains were fined 20,000 heads (£2,500) and gave hostages. Tenu was imprisoned for 12 months and fined 6,000 heads (£750).][1]

I am very desirous, if possible, to establish a commandant's station at Crobboe; for I am impressed with the idea that this Government cannot be successfully carried on except inland stations are maintained. The hasty visit of a magistrate every six months or every year, to the interior districts, is not likely to effect sufficient good to compensate for the expense the colony must necessarily be put in affording him the means of transport. To benefit the people, to make them respect our laws, and love our institutions, it is essential that European magistrates should live amongst them, and thus enable them to learn something of our principles of government.

Hitherto we have been led to believe the inland districts were too unhealthy for the European constitution. This expedition has proved the fallacy of that belief. . . . I feel satisfied . . . [that] the prestige of the English stands higher . . . at this moment than it has done at any other period in the history of the eastern district. At all events, the auxiliaries as well as the Crobboes, have had fully demonstrated to

[1] 24 pages in original.

them that rebellion against the British Government, although carried on 50 miles in the interior, is a losing game; and further, that the Government has the will and power to support and maintain the rightful authority of all those chiefs who are under its protecting care. The reaction in our favour consequent on the conquest of the Crobboes, has been so great that Dowoonah, the king of Christiansborg, whose authority extends over the refractory people of Labady, Tacia and Ningo etc., holds out strong hopes to Mr. Freeman, that all the people over whom he possesses a kind of suzerainty, will for the future own allegiance to Her Majesty and pay the poll tax. He pithily assigned his reason by saying, 'For we see we have now a master.' . . . [C.O.96/44]

220 BIRD TO BULWER LYTTON
CAPE COAST CASTLE, 11 DECEMBER, 1858.

. . . I have just completed . . . the necessary arrangements for the payment of the fine inflicted on the rebels. Mr. Hutchinson of Cape Coast, an extensive merchant in this country, and agent to Mr. Swanzy of London, who does very extensive business in this country, has become security for the payment of the whole amount within the space of six months, to be paid by installments, and which are being paid by that gentleman, who, in turn receives value in palm oil from the late rebel chiefs. . . . I have permitted the Crobboe chiefs and captains to return to their country . . . [except Tenoo] by which means the payments in palm oil . . . will be facilitated. . . .

I propose to spend the surplus money, first in making, as far as practicable, a good road from Accra to [Kpong] on the banks of the Volta in Crobboe, and adjoining the Aquambo frontier. This road, covering a distance of sixty miles, will be a very great boon to the inhabitants of those districts as also to the Krepees, as it will greatly facilitate the carriage of palm oil from Crobboe to the coast, as also cotton from thence, and the neighbouring countries of Aquambo, Aquapim and Crippee. . . . I have been promised assistance in . . . this work from the German missionaries who have several stations in that part of the country, lying between Accra and Crobboe.

Second, I would propose, should there be any funds left . . . that it be laid out in local improvements . . . such as the sinking of wells for the natives, the want of which is much felt in this country. . . .[1]

[C.O.96/44]

221 NEWCASTLE TO BIRD
LONDON, 17 SEPTEMBER, 1859.

Sir,

With reference to Sir Benjamin Pine's despatch No. 40 of the 29th April, 1858, transmitting 'An Ordinance to establish District Assemblies', I have to acquaint you that after careful consideration of that Ordinance Her Majesty's Government are impressed with the conviction that the state of society on the Gold Coast is not yet ripe for an enactment of the kind.

I have therefore advised Her Majesty to disallow the same, and it is disallowed accordingly; although, I need scarcely add, I fully appreciate the good intentions of the framers, and it is not without regret that I have come to the decision above stated.

Should the question of its re-enactment ever be reconsidered, I am inclined to think that it will be safest to confine the operation and power of such assemblies to questions regarding the Poll Tax, or any other tax on natives which may by and by be substituted for it. I think it would also probably be essential to render the meeting of such assemblies not more frequent than

[1] He was warned (20 January, 1859) that the farming out of fines should not be repeated. In fact increasing difficulty was found in exacting payment, until it was finally wound up in 1866. Cf. espc. Memo. on the Crobo fine by Sir G. Barrow (9 October, 1861). The article by Dr. Wolfson in the Economic History Review, 2nd series, vol. 6 (1953), p. 68, 'A price agreement on the Gold Coast, 1858–66', appears to me to read more into this episode than the facts warrant.

once a year. These, however, are only suggestions with a view to the future. At present I think such legislation undesirable.

I have etc.   [C.O.96/45]

222 BIRD TO NEWCASTLE
CAPE COAST CASTLE, 12 NOVEMBER, 1859.

My Lord Duke

I have the honour to acknowledge the receipt of your Grace's despatch No. 7 of the 7th July, with reference to an exchange of territories with the Dutch Government on this coast.

In reply thereto, I beg to state that in accordance with the instructions therein contained, I immediately communicated with the Dutch Governor at St. George d'Elmina (Lt. Col. Nagtglas) and made the following proposition to him: viz., that we should both draw up, independent of each other, as a basis for discussion, the terms on which we would propose the exchange of territory to be effected, and . . . then exchange our views, previous to an interview.

This was accordingly done, and I enclose copies of the proposals made by each party respectively, and, agreeably to an arrangement, Lt. Col. Nagtglas visited me at Cape Coast Castle on the 5th of September last. The result of this day's discussion was that we agreed on all points but one, and that a very essential one, viz., the boundary line to the interior, from the mouth of the Sweet River.

His Excellency Lt. Col. Nagtglas wished that Her Majesty's Government should give up the protection and jurisdiction over the inland countries of Eastern and Western Wassaw, an extensive district extending from that of Cape Coast to the Ashantee frontier, and governed by two principal chiefs; to which I considered it my duty to object for the following reasons:

1st. I consider the sole object in the exchange to be that of getting rid of the present entanglement of Dutch and English territory on the coast . . . which, in my humble opinion, can be fully attained without giving up the Wassaws, who are a numerous race and have always paid our government a considerable amount of poll tax . . . and whose country abounds in gold, which may in after years turn out very profitable to our government.

The reason His Excellency expresses for wishing to get possession of Wassaw is that he will then have free communication with the interior tribes. It appears to me that this reason is foreign to the object entertained by both Governments, as, after the exchange, on the plan proposed by me, the Dutch Government will have the same facilities of communicating with the interior tribes through Wassaw as they have at present, and by the acquisition of Apollonia, will acquire the means of communicating with the interior without passing through any district under British protection. Our giving up Wassaw would, in addition to the loss of its present and prospective value to us, give rise to very serious disturbances, as they (the Wassaws) will never willingly be ruled by Dutch authority.

2ndly. I consider that the districts of Dixcove, Apollonia and Commenda, which, if an exchange should take place on the terms proposed by me, would be given up by Her Majesty's Government, would be fully equivalent to the Dutch possessions we would receive in exchange. . . .

I have so far entered on this negotiation in obedience to your Grace's instructions, as I did not consider myself justified in delaying the preliminaries while I communicated with your Grace upon the principle: but I most respectfully request that I may be understood as not recommending the measure. . . .

I fear that under the peculiar circumstances of this Government, the difficulties in the way of withdrawing the protection of the British Government from any of the districts which have accepted it, without compromising the honour and good faith of the protecting power, are almost insuperable; as I do not imagine that there is the least chance of the people accepting the protection of the Dutch Government,

or in any way submitting to it, except under compulsion.

Notwithstanding every care that could be taken to keep the negotiation secret, rumours of the proposed change have got abroad, in consequence, I am told, of some paragraphs on the subject in the English newspapers; and the people have everywhere within the British settlements proposed to be exchanged, expressed a determination that whatever the two Governments may agree on, they never will submit to the authority of the Dutch.

If then, the protection of Great Britain be withdrawn from them, they will be left open to such measures of conquest and compulsion as the Dutch authorities may choose to adopt; and that such measures are in contemplation, I conclude from the desire expressed and avowed, to have the Wassaw country in particular, abandoned by the British Government, as a means of extending their possessions towards the interior.

In case of those measures being taken, the natives of the districts would be sure to claim the protection of the British Crown, which could not be accorded to them consistently with the proposed treaty with the Government of the Netherlands, or, I fear, consistently with the maintenance of the honour and good faith of the British nation. . . .   [C.O.96/45]

223 ORD TO BARROW

LONDON, 16 MAY, 1860.

. . . The remedies that have been proposed are first, that the Dutch should join us in the imposition of a system of import duties on all goods imported into Dutch waters. . . . Secondly that we should exchange certain forts and posts so as to give the Dutch all the coast to the west and take ourselves all to the east of our respective capitals. . . .

This . . . would not remove [one] cause of complaint urged by the trader, inasmuch as goods would continue to be, as they still are, introduced duty free into St. George d'Elmina, smuggled thence into Cape Coast Castle and the immediate neighbourhood and sold there to the prejudice of the British fair trader. . . .

The imposition of duties by the Dutch in conjunction with ourselves was . . . first proposed in 1855, and in 1857 when at the Hague . . . our then minister and myself succeeded in inducing the Dutch Government to put forward proposals for regulating such a scheme, and to draft a treaty for giving it effect: but the termination of the negotiation was, by the express desire of the [Dutch] Ministry, deferred to a more favourable moment, the position they then occupied with the Chambers rendering it highly unadvisable that they should bring forward any measure to furnish additional points of attack to the Opposition, which, in their weak condition, could hardly fail to entail their complete defeat.

Since that time, this question has not been revived . . . [except] that a proposal [was] made by the Dutch and English Governors last year for the mutual imposition of duties, and was rejected by the Dutch Government. . . .

To [the] proposal by which the Dutch seek a transfer of any rights, territorial or otherwise, which we may possess on the coast, I trust Her Majesty's Government will not be induced to give its assent, except as far as relates to the forts and posts. The grounds upon which they have sought to obtain this transfer are altogether untenable, and the transfer itself would be inconsistent with fair dealing towards the tribes, who, I have very little doubt would indignantly repudiate it. Our protectorate over the Wassaw and Denkera countries was created by the mutual arrangement of the chiefs and ourselves, and unless the chiefs are consenting parties to the transfer, it could not take place.

Moreover, the transfer is unnecessary and the reasoning of the Dutch Government on the subject incorrect and illogical. They can give us no rights which we cannot now exercise, and their allegation of

being placed in a worse position by our retention of the Wassaw protectorate is equally untenable. It is no impediment to their trade from their existing possessions on that coast, and when they become possessed of all the coast, their influence over the natives, and consequently their power, would naturally become greater.

If, therefore, the Government be firm in its determination to allow of no transfer but that of the forts, I think that in communicating this resolve, a very favourable opportunity would be afforded for reopening the original negotiation. . . .

[C.O.96/50]

224 E. B. ANDREWS TO THE DUKE OF NEWCASTLE

CAPE COAST CASTLE, 4 JULY, 1860.

My Lord Duke,

My despatch No. 53 of the 29th May last, wherein I allude to the probability of circumstances occurring, rendering it necessary to withdraw the protection and jurisdiction of the local government over certain districts taken over from the Danish Government, will, in some measure, prepare your Grace for the communication I have now the honour to make. . . .

On my arrival here I found the Eastern Districts in a most disturbed state. . . . On the 14th ultimo I received a communication from the chief Civil Commandant of the Eastern Districts, acquainting me that serious contentions were going on between two great chiefs in the Krepee district beyond the Volta. With the rumours still existing, and circumstances occurring rather to bear out the reports with reference to the evil intention of the king of Ashantee, I considered [there was need to act] before meeting the chiefs of the Eastern Districts in September.

On the 19th ultimo, I summoned the Executive Council, specially calling in Mr. Hutchison, the mayor of Cape Coast, and Mr. Grant, a town councillor, both gentlemen being occupied in commercial pursuits: and having laid before the members the letters of the Chief Civil Commandant of the Eastern Districts . . . [I observed] that the local Government was not in a position, from the state of our finances, as well as our military force, to extend the Protectorate. Therefore, the best course, I held, was to withdraw entirely and not to collect any more poll tax in that country; keeping a strict account of what had been paid, preparatory to repaying the amount if no equivalent had been rendered. The Council unanimously agreed that the course suggested was the correct one, and it was accordingly decided that the jurisdiction and protection should be withdrawn.

It was evident to my mind that the Protectorate on this side of the Volta was not ruled over; that certain tribes, more in particular the Labady and Tacia people, were rebellious; and here was the local Government making vain attempts to rule over places 200 miles away from the seat of government, in a country where the journeys had to be performed by hammock at the rate of 25 miles per day, with numerous obstacles in the way, and when tribes close to Christiansborg were not yet subject to our rule. I considered that collecting Poll Tax from the Krepe people, who would at the most contribute some £300, might at any moment involve the Government in a military expenditure of ten-fold the amount, independent of other perplexing difficulties that we were not called upon to run the risk of incurring. . . .

[Pine himself did not want to interfere in the trans-Volta area but had been persuaded into it by Freeman.] . . . In a conversation I had with Mr. Freeman, I made this observation. 'It appears to me that, . . . contrary to what may be called a political axiom, that commerce is the precursor to government . . . you are working to plant a government where no commerce exists, for this is one of your arguments for exercising jurisdiction and protection over these districts. If they be so important for the cotton trade, and such grand results are to be derived, com-mercial men are keen enough to undertake their development, provided it will pay. It is not for the local Government to take up commercial speculations. We have no money to forward such undertakings, and I hold it would be highly improper if ever we had.' Mr. Freeman at length admitted my views in a great measure to be correct.

This cotton question is a purely mercantile operation, and as to its success . . . that all depends whether the cotton when brought down to the coast can be shipped at a price sufficiently remunerative to find a ready market in Liverpool. Every information in the power of the local Government has been afforded to the Cotton Supply Association, and I shall by this mail inform the Association that they must now judge for themselves whether the development of the country in this branch is worth undertaking; and to do this their own experienced agent will have to come out, for on his judgement they will have to be guided. . . .[1]

I am in hopes that taking these steps of withdrawing from these districts beyond the Volta and Quittah fort likewise, will have a good effect on other districts. . . .

[C.O.96/49]

225 Lord Napier[2] to Lord John Russell

THE HAGUE, 1 AUGUST, 1860.

My Lord,

Since I had the honour of addressing your Lordship . . . Colonel Ord and Colonel Nagtglas have held repeated conferences respecting the exchange of the British and Netherland settlements on the Gold Coast, especially with a view to the

[1] The Cotton Supply Association of Manchester had urged the need for Government action (12 October, 1858) by the occupation of Kpong and the construction of a road thence to Prampram. They were told by Carnarvon (28 October, 1858) that there were no imperial funds available for such a purpose.

[2] Francis Napier, 9th Baron Napier of Murchiston (1831–1905); British Ambassador at the Hague; subsequently ambassador at St. Petersburg and Berlin.

discovery of some interior division line which might be acceptable to the Netherland Government without involving too great a sacrifice on our part. . . .

These inquiries did not prove to be successful. It was recognised that the region of Wassaw, though nominally divided into two districts — eastern and western — at present forms one political community which cannot be severed; and the only choice offered is either to abandon the protectorate over the whole of that country to the Dutch, or to retain the whole. As the former alternative is not contemplated by the instructions of Her Majesty's Government, and as Colonel Nagtglas appeared more disposed to concession than the Colonial Minister, it was hoped by renewed representation . . . that M. de Rochussen might be brought to . . . accede to the proposals of Her Majesty's Government by consenting to the exchange of our respective possessions on the seaboard, leaving our position in the interior unaltered. In order that the subject might be fully debated, I yesterday procured a meeting at the Colonial Department at which the Colonial and Foreign Ministers . . . two gentlemen belonging to the Colonial Office, Colonel Nagtglas, Colonel Ord and myself were present.

In opening the discussion I stated the inconvenience attached to the present intermixture of our possessions. . . . I asserted that these embarrassments were equally experienced by both parties, and that they were most sensibly felt on the coast. The evils complained of, could be remedied by a mutual consolidation of territory on the seaboard, and by the adoption of a common system of import duties. . . . I remarked that the exchange was virtually reduced to the cession of Apollonia and Dixcove on our part, and to that of Accra on the part of the Netherlands. I asserted that Apollonia, if we regarded its extent and eventual value, and Dixcove, if we considered its port, formed a just equivalent for Dutch Accra, and I appealed to Colonel Nagtglas in confirma-

tion of my opinion. . . . Colonel Nagtglas frankly allowed that the former places might be regarded as an equivalent for Accra, though he held the latter on the whole to be the better settlement. He did not, however, think that the mere exchange of the places on the seabord would remedy all the existing evils. The juxtaposition of the British protected territory, Wassaw, behind the Dutch coast, would open the door to many contests respecting jurisdiction and revenue.

Having thus, as I conceived, obtained from the person best informed on the opposite side, an avowal that the overture of Her Majesty's Government for an exchange of the places on the coast was equitable, I then applied myself to show that the Netherlands government ought not to desire, and could not expect the acquisition of Wassaw. The chief object, I observed, in protecting the tribes of the interior, was to maintain them as a barrier against the Ashantees. . . . The protection of the intermediate tribes was onerous and expensive; the exercise of that protection by Great Britain was therefore in so far advantageous to the Netherlands, for the rear of their sea-board was thus defended for them; nor did the British protectorate in any degree operate to their prejudice . . . for the intermediate country was totally unavailable for colonial settlements, and was open for commercial access equally to all parties. But even, I continued, if the Dutch could profit by the acquisition of Wassaw, they could not justly obtain it from Her Majesty's Government for they had no equivalent to offer for it. . . . The Colonial Minister warmly repudiated the notion that the Netherlands required or desired English assistance to protect their settlements against the Ashantees. They could protect themselves. He disputed my assertion that the intermediate country was useless for colonial settlement; he thought the interior was the important part, not the coast. The existence of a British Protectorate behind the Dutch sea-board would be an endless source of disputes. . . . He deprecated the idea of treating this question as one of mere equivalents, and . . . also hinted that the authority of Great Britain in Wassaw was not incontestable. The chiefs of that country had recognised Dutch protectorate in former times, adopted the Dutch flag, and contracted engagements with the Netherlands Africa Company. . . .

In demonstration of the rights of Her Majesty's Government over Wassaw, I here exhibited the revenue act of 1852, by which the supremacy of Great Britain is recognised by the signature of King Ennimil. . . . With regard to the value of the interior for the purposes of colonial settlement . . . Colonel Nagtglas . . . on being appealed to, declared . . . that centuries must probably elapse before it could be available for those purposes. . . .

Colonel Ord strongly urged the expediency of not dividing Wassaw from the other districts between Ashantee and the sea. He considered it most important to hold the intermediate country concentrated under one authority for the protection of the sea-board. . . . If Wassaw were ceded to the Netherlands, the barrier against Ashantee would be divided and weakened, and our common interest would be impaired.

Notwithstanding the[se] arguments . . . M. de Rochussen remained unshaken. . . . He maintained the importance of Wassaw to the Netherlands, and . . . repeated that he could not submit to the legislature a treaty by which the Dutch settlements would be debarred from eventual expansion. . . .

[The Dutch were asked for their proposals.]

After some discussion upon the subject, it became apparent that the Netherlands cabinet would be disposed to negotiate upon the following terms:

1. The cession of all British settlements to the west of the Sweet River to the Netherlands, and the cession of all Dutch settlements to the east of the same point to Great Britain.

2. The abandonment [by] Great Britain of all protectorate over the country interposed between the Dutch sea-board, thus consolidated, and the Ashantee frontier, the line of demarcation to be laid down in conformity with local natural boundaries by commissioners on the spot.

3. The establishment of a common system of import duties, affecting arms, gunpowder, tobacco, spirituous liquors, and perhaps on other merchandise: but in the latter respect the Colonial Minister spoke with some hesitation.

4. The maintenance of the capitation tax in those districts ceded by Great Britain where it is at present levied. . . . M. de Rochussen declared his inability to negotiate for the imposition of a common system of import duties without a territorial partition. [C.O.96/50]

226 SIR G. C. LEWIS[1] TO E. B. ANDREWS

LONDON, 22 SEPTEMBER, 1860.

. . . It appears that the Dutch Government make the termination of the protectorate exercised by Great Britain over Wassaw, an indispensable preliminary of any settlement, but that if that point be conceded, they are willing to consent to an exchange of forts, east and west of the Sweet River; to impose duties corresponding to those imposed in British territory; and to enter into an alliance for the protection from the Ashantees of the tribes lying between that people and the coast.

These terms seem in many respects to be advantageous, but, as at present advised, I am not prepared to agree to the abandonment of the protectorate over Wassaw, without the consent, or at all events against the wishes of its inhabitants, nor without a reasonable expectation that they will not be materially injured by that abandonment.

[1] Sir George Cornewall Lewis (1806–63); at this time Home Secretary in Palmerston's 2nd Cabinet; author of The Governance of Colonies (1841).

I have accordingly to instruct you to report fully upon the advantages and disadvantages of the arrangement which alone the Dutch Government is prepared to accept, and particularly as to whether the protectorate of Wassaw can be abandoned with justice to its inhabitants, and without exposing the British Government to the charges of vacillation and bad faith; whether any substantial injury would be inflicted on the Wassaws by their transfer to the Dutch; and what terms of transfer would be most likely to secure to them the advantages which they at present possess under British protection.

I should also be glad to learn whether the transfer would increase the difficulty of keeping peace on the frontier of the two protectorates.

I have further to instruct you to report whether the consent of the Wassaws would be likely to be obtained, and if you should deem it prudent to do so, you have my authority for endeavouring to obtain such consent, taking care that it shall be of a bona-fide character.

You will have the goodness to lose no time in making the desired report, as it is expedient that there should be no delay in coming to an understanding on the subject with the Dutch.

I have etc.   [C.O.96/49]

227 ANDREWS TO NEWCASTLE
CAPE COAST CASTLE, 8 NOVEMBER, 1860.
. . . To the solemn assertion of the Dutch Colonial Minister . . . that Holland warmly repudiated the notion of aid from England to ward the Dutch settlements from the aggression of the Ashantees, because the Dutch had the strength to defend themselves, there can be but one reply. . . . But for the presence of our ships-of-war and of our troops, the power of the Dutch would be a mere nullity in this country.

The ill-blood cherished for many years and prevailing today between the people of Dutch Accra and the Dutch public authorities, is so undisguised that, if the rumour were to get into circulation that the British Civil Commandant at James Fort had orders not to lend assistance to the Dutch officer under any circumstances, a riot would immediately ensue . . . the Dutch commandant would be driven beyond the precincts of the town, and the Dutch ensign would be torn down and replaced by our own. . . .

The Dutch Government may not be in awe of an attack from Ashantee, because the general impression on the Gold Coast . . . is that the Dutch Government at Elmina pays tribute to the king of Ashantee for the lease of that fort, just in the same way as, antecedently to the Ashantee War, we paid tribute of a similar bearing and title to that monarch.

At any rate it is undeniable that the Dutch Government draws the recruits for its forces in Java from Ashantee, and to the king of Ashantee a certain sum is paid by the Dutch Government for each recruit.

Having written thus generally . . . I will address myself . . . to the four conditions on which Lord Napier has averred that the Netherlands Cabinet would be ready to treat.

The first condition provides that all British settlements on this coast to the west of the Sweet River shall be ceded to Holland, and that all Dutch Settlements to the east of the same stream shall be ceded to England.

I must say at the outset, that such a cession of our territory will entail separation from the most loyal and peaceable dependents of the British Crown on the Gold Coast; dependents who have not only cheerfully and regularly contributed their quota to the . . . revenues of the local Government, but who have never hesitated to avow their bitter hostility to the Dutch, and their determination not to submit to the Dutch sway. The establishment and enforcement of the cession to the Netherlands of [these] settlements . . . will lead to difficulties which must be still more complicated by the fact that the

Dutch Government has openly professed to hold its present territory by the right of conquest.

I apprehend, your Grace, that the protection of our flag ought not to be withdrawn from the people of Apollonia and Dixcove without their consent; but, under any circumstances, England should be chary of parting from a tractable and industrious people who are thriving under her tutelage and are unwilling to secede from the supervision of her laws.

The second condition . . . provides that Great Britain shall abandon all protectorate over the country interposed between the Dutch seaboard thus consolidated, and . . . the frontier of Ashantee. As it stands, this proposition would involve the division of Denkerah, Ohifful,[1] and probably of Assin and Wassaw,[2] into two parts. To divide these countries without any deference being paid to local natural boundaries would be impracticable; and even if practicable, the attempt to cut a tribe or nation in twain, and to allot one half to this sovereign and the other half to that sovereign, would be fruitful of internal mischief and external feud.

The objections to the withdrawal of the English Protectorate from Wassaw are nearly as cogent as the objections to the abandonment of Apollonia and Dixcove. . . . Moreover Wassaw is well known to be rich in auriferous deposits. It offers itself in that guise as a temptation to the subjugation of the Dutch sword; and that the Dutch are not averse to . . . conquest may be gathered from the term 'eventual expansion' which the Dutch Minister could not refrain from uttering before Lord Napier. There was no necessity for [this] allusion . . . because the Dutch, equally with ourselves, have free access to and free passage from Wassaw.

[1] Twifu.
[2] In actual fact Denkyira, Twifu and Wasaw lay entirely west of the mouth of the Sweet River; Asin alone would have been partitioned. In the absence of any reliable map of the interior districts, Andrews' assumptions were generally accepted.

The third condition provides that there shall be a common system of import duties affecting arms, gunpowder, tobacco, spirituous liquors, and perhaps 'other' merchandize. Lord Napier notes . . . that the Colonial Minister 'spoke with hesitation' of the establishment of import duties on other merchandize. . . . Unless import duties shall be levied on *all* goods the third condition must be . . . [rejected]. To exclude hardware and Manchester goods from the payment of equal duties would be playing . . . into the hands of the Dutch and be leaving every existing difficulty in full operation against ourselves.

The fourth condition provides that the capitation tax shall be maintained in districts ceded by Great Britain. I conceive, your Grace, this is a matter for the . . . consideration of the Dutch alone. . . . As long as the poll tax shall be maintained within the districts under the protection of Great Britain, no harm, but rather a benefit will arise out of the retention of the tax in those districts which may be abandoned by England. I am nevertheless . . . [hopeful] that if the proposed exchange should be accomplished, the increase of the import duties will admit of the absolute remission or abrogation of the poll tax. . . .

I may conclude by remarking that one main objection . . . to the scheme of an equitable exchange . . . is [that] the Dutch can tender no equivalent for any tract of soil or principle of jurisdiction which the English may be called on to give up or waive. They may offer us a few forts; but these forts would turn out to be an encumbrance. They are in ruins [and we already have] more forts than we can properly occupy or can possibly keep in decent repair. . . . If even it should be conceded that the Dutch Government is entitled to the sovereignty of the districts which are occupied by its wretched military contingent, the English Government cannot accept that sovereignty, for it is a sovereignty over slave states.

[He would prefer: 1st. To buy the

eastern forts, or 2ndly To draw the demarcation line along the southern and western boundaries of Denkerah and Wassaw; or 3rdly. To offer to leave the Dutch a clear field, or ask them to do the same for us. Liverpool and Manchester would find the money to buy them out.]   [C.O.96/49]

228 MINUTE BY T. F. ELLIOT[1]
COLONIAL OFFICE, 19 FEBRUARY, 1862.

The fact is that for the sake of a favourite object of national policy, we maintain on the coast of Africa a variety of small and needy settlements, which cannot pay their own way: that the Treasury, on the other hand, is too apt to view them as if they were or ought to be able to pay their own way — nay, as if they ought to be able to pay for the conflicts with native tribes, which arise out of the general British policy in western Africa; so that when we apply to the Treasury to concur with us in asking Parliament for the aid indispensable to meet any unusual demand on such colonies, they reply by desiring us to call on the Governor for further proof of the necessity. The real proof is the knowledge we possess of the state and capabilities of these settlements.

If the Treasury think that the measures of Great Britain for the suppression of the slave trade are unwise, or cost more than the object is worth, the issue ought to be raised in a different arena, and it should be ascertained whether Parliament and the

[1] Sir T. Frederick Elliot; Assistant Under-Secretary of State for the Colonies, 1847–68.

country will reverse their policy. But so long as that policy is adhered to, it is purely vexatious to insist on treating these African settlements as if they were flourishing and independent, and to try to stave off, from one session to another, items which we all know to be necessary, by useless demands upon the Governor for further explanation.   [C.O.96/59]

229 FROM THE *African Times*[1]
LONDON, SATURDAY, 22 MARCH, 1862.

[Kwaku Mensah, chief of Wasaw Amenfi had just defied the Government over a case of human sacrifice.] . . .

We demand an effective Government for the Gold Coast. . . . But who is to blame? Who but ourselves? In neglecting to use the means by which alone the great resources of those districts can be developed, we are equally without those which are necessary for enforcing respect and obedience. What pacified the Highlands of Scotland — put an end to the wars among the clans — prevented depredations on the Lowlands — made the Government authority to be respected — and developed the resources of the country? . . . Roads — good military roads were the indispensable means for making the sovereignty a fact instead of a mere idea. . . . Quacoe Mensah would not have dared to insult the Government had there been a good road from the coast into his district. . . .

[1] This paper, which commenced publication in London in January 1862, made itself the mouthpiece of African demands for economic and political advance.

17 The Ashanti War of 1863–1864

GOVERNOR RICHARD PINE, a younger brother of Sir Benjamin, was appointed to succeed Andrews on 30 August, 1862. He arrived on the coast on 18 October, to find the forts at Accra demolished by an earthquake, and the Gold Coast Artillery, the only upholders of law and order, in a state of mutiny. These formed a fitting prelude to the events of 1863.

Like most of his predecessors, Pine found it difficult to know how to act in the matter of fugitives from Ashanti, and in two cases which came before him at the end of 1862, he declined to return them to Kumasi (230). If he erred in so doing, he was nevertheless upheld by the British Government (231), which thereby rendered itself responsible for active defence measures when invasion resulted. The Asantehene, appealing to established practice, invoked a supposed agreement (232) which Pine was naturally unable to find as it had never existed (233). In March 1863, the Ashantis invaded the Protectorate (234), the defence of which was so mismanaged (235) that they were able to ravage it and ultimately withdraw with complete impunity.

The bad effect of this failure effectively to protect the Protectorate, could, in Pine's view, only be repaired by a counter-invasion of Ashanti (235). The Duke of Newcastle, not unnaturally, was not prepared to sanction so hazardous a step without expert military advice (236). On the other hand he could not deny that the situation might arise in which an offensive would prove the best defence (237), and Pine was eventually given reinforcements to defend the frontier on the Pra, with a conditional permission to cross it (238). Defences were duly organised on that river to await an attack which never came. This and the mounting casualties from disease, placed the Government in a painful dilemma (239) which was ultimately resolved by withdrawing all reinforcements, not merely from the Pra, but from the country.

Edward Cardwell[1] who took over the Colonial Office in the midst of these troubles, was reduced to hoping that the demonstration would somehow deter the Ashantis from further aggression. But he was insistent that the chiefs should do more for their own defence than they had attempted in 1863 and 1864, and laid down a strictly defensive role for British troops in any future operations on the Gold Coast (240–1). Cardwell doubtless intended no more than to bring back British policy to what he believed it to have been before Pine put a force on the banks of the Pra. But explaining this to the chiefs was no easy matter (242), and the 'retreat' of 1864 was the prelude to various projects for African self-government. The bulk of the chiefs, however, while presenting particular grievances, had no desire to see the protectorate withdrawn (243).

[1] Edward Cardwell (later 1st Viscount Cardwell) (1813–86); M.P., 1842–74; President of the Board of Trade, 1852–5; Chief Secretary for Ireland, 1859–61; Chancellor of the Duchy of Lancaster, 1861–4; Secretary of State for the Colonies, 1864–6; Secretary of State for War, 1868–74.

230 RICHARD PINE TO THE DUKE OF NEWCASTLE

CAPE COAST CASTLE, 10 DECEMBER, 1862.

. . . The refuge afforded to runaway slaves and pawns under the British flag has, during my long experience[1] proved the source of the greatest irritation and

[1] Pine had served on the Gambia since 1855.

annoyance to native kings and chiefs, and the wound the most difficult for Her Majesty's representative to heal; and unfortunately I find here such questions of every-day occurrence.[1]

While addressing these lines to your Grace, I have two claims from the powerful and much-dreaded king of Ashantee for the restoration of his subjects.

The first case is that of a slave boy who some weeks since escaped from his master on his way back to Ashantee, and took refuge in the kingdom of Assin under this Protectorate. As has been the custom, I desired the king of Assin to restore the boy to his sovereign, and he is immediately sent down to me with special messengers. An inquiry takes place in the hall of this castle, when the runaway boy avows himself to be a slave; that he was overloaded, and otherwise cruelly ill-treated by his master; that he has taken the King's Oath, not to return to Ashantee; that death will be the penalty for his offence; and that by force alone will he leave the Protectorate. The master admits the boy to be a slave, but declares that, for my sake, the king of Ashantee will not take his life.

The second case is that of an old man (not a slave) who is claimed by the axe-bearer, sword-bearer and followers of the king of Ashantee, who exhibit their symbols of office with much ceremony, and are considered of more than ordinary importance. This old man is accused of having received and converted to his own use a piece of (so called) rock gold, which, by the law of the country, must be accounted for to the king. There is not a tittle of evidence, except the remotest hearsay, in support of the allegation, and the accused solemnly denies the charge. He is a man of property, and declares that the king desires only to entrap him, take his head, and afterwards, possession of his property. The king's messengers offer to swear that the accused will be fairly tried,

[1] See, e.g., Bird to Bulwer Lytton (27 August, 1858) in C.O.96/43; and Nos. 170 and 175 above.

and, even if found guilty, will not lose a hair of his head. The old man imploringly cries to me, 'Kill me if you like; that will be better than giving my head to the king.' And no one can assure me that I may rely upon the king's word; yet all would be delighted for me to restore to him his subjects.

Gladly would I try an experiment, and send back these subjects of Ashantee, for if confidence were once created between this Government and Ashantee, the greatest obstacle in the way of amicable relations between us, would be removed; and if against the old man there were the slightest shadow of a prima facie case of criminality, my course would be clear: but as it is, I dare not deliver him up, much less the runaway boy. Their blood would be upon my head. And yet I feel that I am estranging, if not exasperating, the most powerful king on this coast, and upon whom, according to his ideas, I am committing a gross injustice. . . .

[C.O.96/58. H.C.385, A & P (1864) xli, 133]

231 MINUTE BY THE DUKE OF NEWCASTLE   14 FEBRUARY, 1863.

The questions here discussed are some of the most painful and embarrassing which arise out of our well-intentioned but ill-advised system of 'protecting' certain native tribes on the west coast of Africa. I imagine that the only advantage we claim or desire from this 'protection' is that the tribes protected should abstain from slave-dealing and resort to legitimate commerce. But what are the *responsibilities* we incur? In the first place, the defence of the tribe against such enemies as their obedience to our humane views entails upon them. Are we further bound to insist upon compliance by the protected tribe with such moral laws as regulate, or ought to regulate, our own conduct? Are we bound to prevent them from giving up to the vengeance of a master, a runaway slave, or to the punishment of death by a savage king, a subject who has committed some political offence?

It is clear to me that in the two cases here mentioned . . . nothing could justify the Governor in surrendering them after they had entered our forts. . . . The king of Ashantee can surely have no right to expect from us what we deny to the United States! But the question is, ought we to *make* the king of Assin conform to our high standards of justice and humanity? It would be well if we could *induce* all these tribes to do so, but how far are we to carry our *interference*, and does interference to this length promote, in the long run, the cause of freedom and civilization?

I fear we must leave these protected tribes, for the present, to take their own course in these matters. . . .

[C.O.96/58][1]

232 The Asantehene[2] to Governor Pine
Kumasi, 9 February, 1863.

. . . In poor George Maclean's time, I made agreement with him in certificate, the one in Cape Coast Castle, and another in my hand, therein stated, that any Fantee person run up to me to deliver him and to bring him to Cape Coast. And if any slave of mine also run away to Cape Coast, you are to deliver him back also to me, as all the Governors that take charge of Cape Coast Castle did not move from this agreement, but always [ful]filled the rules of the said poor George Maclean, except your time has destroyed the agreement. But little time before your coming, about 70 persons of Wassaw, your own subjects, ran away to my country, and the Governor of Cape Coast Castle sent a soldier to me for them, and I tried as much as possible, and got them for the soldier to deliver them to him. These persons I subsisted them 4oz. 8 acs. gold dust to maintain them in the way, because the Governor being a good friend to fore-

[1] Pine's action was approved in a despatch of 4 March, 1863.
[2] Kwaku Dua I, Asantehene, 1835–67.

shown agreement, and also to me. But when you came, any of my slaves run to Cape Coast, you and your subjects take them, and would [not] bring him to me, so you have taken more of my subjects and even my grandson, and now you are going to take Quashie Gainie also. So you must not blame me for keeping my subjects from coming down to Cape Coast, but when disturbances arise, then all the blame is upon you, because you have broken the rule of agreement. . . .

[C.O.96/60. H.C.385 of 1864]

233 Pine to Newcastle
Cape Coast Castle, 10 March, 1863.
[Announces the arrival of an embassy from Ashanti.] . . .

Early on [the 20th February] the Governor of Elmina informed me that he had received a letter and message from the king of Ashantee, complaining of my conduct, nearly in the same terms as that he addressed to myself. The Governor appeared much alarmed, admitting that a large quantity of munitions of war had been sold to the people of the king of Ashantee very recently, but that he had at Elmina prohibited a further supply at my request. He expressed his regret that he was unable to do more than remain neutral, as the king of Ashantee was his ally. He, however, offered to despatch an officer to the king of Ashantee as mediator between us, which offer I did not accept; and I then returned to Cape Coast Castle to hold my palaver with the king's emissaries.

At the meeting were present all officers, civil and military, merchants, and as large a portion of the inhabitants of the town as could be accomodated in the hall. When I had read aloud the long-expected letter of the king of Ashantee, the treaties and other documents connected with our relations with Ashantee were laid upon the table for inspection, and every person of long residence and experience in the settlements was invited to give information on the subject. The more the validity of the claim of the king of Ashantee to the restoration of his subject unconditionally, by treaty, was investigated, the more apparent it became that it was invalid; and it was the unanimous opinion of all present, that my compliance with the king's request for the delivery of his chief, Quasi Gainie, to death and plunder, was impossible.

The whole of these proceedings were carefully explained to the king's emissaries; and they were asked whether they had been molested on their way down to Cape Coast Castle. When they replied that they had not, but that a small quantity of gunpowder and guns had been seized from them in the town of Cape Coast, and that some of their countrymen had been similarly treated by the different tribes through whose countries they had passed, I explained to them that the seizure in Cape Coast was in accordance with my proclamation, but that the other wrongs of which they complained, were utterly without my sanction or approval, and had doubtless occurred (if at all) in consequence of the prevailing impression that the king of Ashanti meditated hostile proceedings against the Protectorate; an impression which had been created by the acts of the king himself.

Throughout the whole of this long interview, the chief captain behaved with the utmost self-possession and politeness, conversing freely on all subjects, but most assiduously avoiding all information or allusion to his king's intentions. . . .

[C.O.96/60. H.C.385 of 1864]

234 PINE TO NEWCASTLE

CAPE COAST CASTLE, 15 APRIL, 1863.

. . . The tribes of the Protectorate have been arming and preparing themselves for the expected invasion, and have advanced to the support of those nearest the supposed enemy, one in the district of Assin, and the other in the district of Akim.

I have supplied our allies with small quantities of ammunition, but have en-joined them in the strictest manner to abstain from hostilities, unless in case of absolute necessity. Still, from time to time, rumours have been prevalent that large parties of Ashantees have crossed the boundary and invaded the Protectorate, pillaging and over-running the country, and compelling the allies to fall back: but until within the last few days, it was not universally believed that invasion was imminent, and that the intentions of the king of Ashantee were warlike. . . .

On the 13th instant I summoned an Executive Council, Commodore Wilmot and other officers assisting as members, when it was unanimously decided that Major Cochrane should take the field this day, not for the purpose of attacking the Ashantees, but with the view of observing their movements, concentrating the allies, encamping his little army in an advantageous position, so as to command access to that point of the Protectorate the most sorely pressed, and to which camp I purpose proceeding in person as soon as it is established.

Major Cochrane has my strictest injunction to be well assured that the movements of the Ashantees are organized, sanctioned and approved by their king; and to avoid, if possible, and by every means in his power, a conflict.

Our whole regular force does not exceed 400 men, which is indeed a small body to meet the enormous army which it is said the king of Ashantee has at command. But it is to be hoped that some 15,000 or 20,000 of our allies may be depended upon, and I have by this mail, made requisitions for assistance upon the Governor of Sierra Leone and the Gambia.

It is impossible to convey to your Grace any idea of the difficulties which surround me in this vast country under existing circumstances, amongst others, the impossibility of procuring reliable information as to the actual state of affairs, and I have strictly avoided sending forth military officers or parties, under the fear of their being cut off, and thus increasing my anxieties; and for the same reason, it is deemed inexpedient that our force should be divided. . . .

[C.O.96/60. H.C.385 of 1864]

235 PINE TO NEWCASTLE
CAPE COAST CASTLE, 12 MAY, 1863.
My Lord Duke,

On the evening of the day in which I had last the honour to address your Grace, Major Cochrane, having received information that Annamaboe, where a small force was stationed, was threatened by the Ashantees, marched with his whole force for that place, with a view to meet the enemy.

After waiting three days without any result, the Officer Commanding marched to a place called Mankessim, about fifteen miles in the interior, in the direction of the alleged position of the enemy, where he remained until the 5th instant, but without meeting with any opposition. . . . In the neighbourhood of Mankessim were encamped some thousands of native allies who are supposed to send out spies under the direction of the Commanding Officer, for observation, and yet . . . nothing but insignificant skirmishes [had] taken place . . . between the spies of either party.

On the 7th instant, Major Cochrane proceeded some two miles distant to a place called Denkera, and the last information I received was from Barng, a little further on. . . . It is exceedingly unsatisfactory for me to be able to afford your Grace a vague and meagre account only, of the military proceedings within the Protectorate: but your Grace is aware of the somewhat anomalous position of a Civil Governor in time of invasion, when the Officer Commanding the troops becomes 'responsible . . . for the defence and security of the Colony — the power of the Civil Governor to issue orders being suspended.' While at Mankessim, Major Cochrane kept me advised of his movements, or to use his own words, non-movements, . . . but of late I have no knowledge of his proceedings. . . .

Much dissatisfaction has lately been expressed by the inhabitants of this town and our allies, at the inactivity of Major Cochrane with the regulars and a large native force at his command; and that, within so short a distance of one body of the enemy's army, he should not have sought him out, as the invaders can be no longer permitted to overrun the country at their will. . . .

Independent of the army which Major Cochrane is supposed to be watching in the Winnebah district, there is another body of Ashantees in the Assin district, where some 8,000 or 10,000 native allies have for some weeks been collecting. . . . The district of Accra is also threatened by an army of Ashantees . . . and as all the military have been removed from thence, and it is undefended, I contemplate despatching a detachment of seamen to garrison the town — a duty at present performed by a small number of volunteers. . . .

It is with the deepest regret that I find myself involved, in spite of all my precautions, in a serious, and I fear, lingering war: but such being the case, I will not conceal from your Grace the earnest desire that I entertain that a final blow shall be struck at Ashantee power, and the question set at rest for ever, as to whether an arbitrary, cruel, and sanguinary monarch shall for ever be permitted to insult the British flag, and outrage the laws of civilization.

This desirable object can be attained only by the possession of such a force as I fear the Governor of these settlements can never hope to command, unless your Grace should be pleased to urge upon Her Majesty's Government, the policy, the economy, and even the mercy of transporting to these shores an army of such strength as would, combined with the allied native forces, enable us to march to Coomassie, and there plant the British flag.

To a stranger, the course I point out may appear a visionary one; but I am convinced that, even with all the disadvantages of climate, the expedition would not be so dangerous, so fatal, or accompanied with such loss of life, as have attended expeditions in other, and apparently more genial climates; and with 2,000 disciplined soldiers,[1] followed by upwards of 50,000 native forces, who require only to be led and inspired with confidence by the presence of organised troops, I would undertake (driving the hordes of Ashantee before me) to march to Coomassie.

As the case now stands, the most I can hope is to drive the Ashantees from the Protectorate, without the chance of administering that chastisement, or demanding that retribution, which is so justly due to its inhabitants, and remain in constant dread of subsequent incursions of a powerful enemy.

Although I am not sanguine, the allies, now in arms, amount [ing] to upwards [of] 50,000 men, declare that with the smallest additional military force they would attempt to reach Coomassie, if permitted; and I only hope that the assistance I have demanded from Sierra Leone and the Gambia, as I advised your Grace by the last mail, may arrive and be in such force as to embolden me to sanction such an enterprise, for I feel that any other measure must necessarily be incomplete.

[C.O.96/61.   Part printed in H.C.385]

236 NEWCASTLE TO PINE
LONDON, 22 AUGUST, 1863.
. . . [To] allude to your former despatch . . . of the 12th of May, in which you submitted a plan of organising a very large force, to consist of 2,000 disciplined soldiers, followed by upwards of 50,000 natives, and of making with that army a regular invasion of the territory of Ashantee:

I am not insensible to the encouragement

[1] With the reinforcements which arrived on the day Pine wrote, there were already 700 regulars of the 2nd and 3rd West India Regiments on the coast. Four hundred men of the 4th West India Regt. landed in August. A final reinforcement of 670 officers and men arrived in April 1865.

which the unfortunate inaction of the troops and native allies under Major Cochrane's command may afford to fresh aggressions by the Ashantees; but the proposal of a regular invasion to be made upon that nation, and of a march upon their capital, is too serious to admit of my encouraging it. I will merely say, at present, that I should feel very averse to its adoption, except in case of overruling necessity, and also after the report of some more competent military commander than anyone from whom there has yet been an opportunity of obtaining an opinion at the Gold Coast. . . .

[C.O.96/61.   H.C.385 of 1864]

237 COLONIAL OFFICE TO WAR OFFICE
LONDON, 18 DECEMBER, 1863.
[States that it is necessary to send additional reinforcements to the Gold Coast.] . . .

In expressing this opinion, his Grace would be understood to continue to maintain, as he has always maintained, that the principle of all military proceedings on the West Coast of Africa should be that of defence and not of aggression. It is upon this principle alone that the Government are authorized to make war; and no invasion of neighbouring territories can be sanctioned, unless it can be shown that it is a defensive measure, safer, less costly in blood and money, and more likely to be decisive in its results, than waiting for an attack which is being prepared, and which no peaceful measure can ward off, without loss of that dignity and position which are essential to our security. It cannot be denied that in dealing with savage nations such may be the case; and although his Grace is by no means prepared to affirm with certainty that such is the case on the Gold Coast at the present moment, yet he regards it as quite possible, either that it is so, or that it may shortly become so, owing to the loss of military reputation consequent on recent occurrences, and the spirit of presumption and audacity which has been generated among the Ashantees.

His Grace feels, therefore, that he cannot refuse to Governor Pine, a conditional authority to strike a blow within the Ashantee territory, if such a blow can be struck without making other or further advance than, in his own opinion, and that of the officer in command, may be consistent with the utmost consideration for the safety of the troops; and provided also he can satisfy himself that the result will be to remove the disastrous impressions caused by the impunity of the Ashantees when they last ravaged the protected territory, and to obtain reparation and secure the peace of the Protectorate. His Grace will impress upon the Governor that these results, and not the gratification of revenge on the part of the protected tribes, or the love of glory of the black troops, would constitute the only justification of an aggressive movement. . . .[1]

[C.O.96/63, H.C.71, A & P (1865) xxxii]

request that you will guide yourself by the principles therein stated.

In case the expected Ashantee invasion takes place, my hope is that you and the officer in command will be able to inflict so severe a punishment upon the invaders as will remove the disastrous impressions caused by their impunity when they lately ravaged the Protected Territory, and will deter them from any further aggression.

But should no opportunity be found of striking such a blow without entering the Ashantee territory, you are not to regard yourself as absolutely prohibited from doing so under any circumstances, and from advancing as far as the utmost consideration for the safety of the troops would permit, for the purpose of obtaining reparation and securing the peace of the Protectorate. . . .

[C.O.96/63. H.C.385 of 1864]

238 Sir F. Rogers[2] to R. Pine
London, 21 December, 1863.

Sir,

With reference to your despatch No. 92 of the 12th October, in which you state your views with regard to the expediency of organizing a force to attack the Ashantees, even supposing that the latter should not take the initiative, which you consider the more probable, and suggesting that another regiment should be sent to the Gold Coast, I transmit for your information an extract of a letter which by my desire has been addressed to the War Office,[3] explaining the grounds on which I have recommended that your application should be complied with, and I have to

[1] It took some time to collect the reinforcements. The *Tamar* left England on 8 January, 1865, but did not make up its complement (chiefly of the 1st and 4th W.I. Regts.) until March. By the time these troops reached Cape Coast (9 April) the local military authorities were already on the point of calling off the projected offensive.
[2] Sir Frederick Rogers, later 1st Baron Blachford (1811–89); entered the Colonial Office in 1846; baronet, 1851; Permanent Under-Secretary, 1859–71.
[3] No. 237 above.

239 Minute by Sir George Barrow
Colonial Office, 12 May, 1963.[1]

An enormous expense[2] has been incurred to no purpose, and the Ashantees may well imagine that we only made a show of attacking them. But the worst seems to be that we are leaving under the protection of two companies[3] — which may be prostrated by sickness — at the Prah, a large accumulation of food and other requirements — ammunition and guns — a prize which may tempt the Ashantees.

Is . . . the main expense of these preparations to be allowed to continue till October next, with the poor satisfaction, at the utmost, of destroying Coomassie, after the Ashantees have removed

[1] Probably inspired by the appearance in *The Times* that morning of a letter from an officer serving on the coast, appealing for an inquiry into conditions on the Pra. It was the first of several strongly critical letters and on 20 May there were questions in Parliament which may have prompted No. 240.
[2] Some £700,000.
[3] Of the five companies moved up to the Pra in January, three had already been withdrawn in March because of the mounting sick lists.

everything, and which they will rebuild after we have retired?

On the other hand, if the expedition is given up altogether, what effect will a second failure (for so it would be regarded) have upon the protected tribes, and still more, on the Ashantees themselves. . . ?

[C.O.96/64]

240 E. CARDWELL TO W. HACKETT[1]

23 MAY, 1864.

[In the absence of Governor Pine who is reported to have left the Colony to recover his health] . . . I feel it is my duty to instruct you to take measures in concert with the Officer in Command of the Troops, for handing over to the Native chiefs, whose interest it is to defend the frontier of their own territory, the stockades which have been erected to guard the passes of the River Prah; to remove to the coast such portion of the stores as, considering the difficulty of transport, it may be desirable to remove; to give to the friendly chiefs such stores as it is impossible or not worth while to remove, or such as may be especially useful to them in their defensive measures; and to bring down the whole of the Queen's Forces as rapidly as possible, to the healthier quarters on the coast. . . . You will above all things take especial care, in concert with the Officer in Command, that no stores of any kind are left in such an exposed state as to be likely to fall into the hands of the Ashantees, and so afford them a sense of triumph. This remark especially applies to guns of all kinds, and other military stores.

It appears that the number of troops upon the coast will now be more than double the number for which the buildings will afford accomodation, and that the removal of a considerable number will be necessary for their own health and comfort, and for the health and comfort of those who are left behind. Immediate arrangements, therefore, are intended to be made by the War Department for

[1] Chief Justice and Judicial Assessor since 1861.

reducing the force at your disposal to its normal strength, and removing the remainder from the coast.

It may be hoped that the display of force made during the last few months will not have been without its due effect, both on the Ashantee enemy and on the friendly native chiefs, and that the cessation of the rains may not bring with it the necessity for a renewal of warlike preparations on your part to defend yourself or the friendly native population from wanton attack. Under the now altered circumstances of the case, I do not propose to renew the conditional permission given by the Duke of Newcastle to Governor Pine, to strike a blow within the territory of Ashantee.

To take immediate steps for securing, as far as possible, the health and comfort of the officers and men, is now the first and paramount duty for the Government.

You will keep me fully informed of everything which tends to show the disposition of the Ashantees, and as no military operations on our part will now be possible for several months, I content myself, at present, with instructing you to use your best efforts to avert the renewal of the war, to induce the native chiefs to rely on their own power and energy to a much greater extent than appears to have been their habit of late, and to avoid the necessity of again bringing to the Settlement a number of the Queen's Troops too great to be properly accomodated on the spot, with the certainty that all who go inland will be exposed to the most serious risk of health and life.

[C.O.96/64, H.C.41, A&P (1864) xlv]

241 CARDWELL TO PINE

23 JUNE, 1964.[1]

. . . The unfortunate circumstances of the present year may encourage the Ashantees

[1] *The Times* (16 and 17 June) joined in criticism of the policy which had led to the debacle. On 17 June a motion of censure was only defeated in the House of Commons by 233 votes to 226 — a phenomenal attendance for a West African debate.

in the design they appear to have entertained of renewing their invasion when the season for military operations shall return. I think it right, therefore, to convey to you the general views of Her Majesty's Government upon the measures which, in concert with the Officer Commanding the Forces, you should take to provide against that danger.

The duty of defending the extensive territory in the Protectorate can only be satisfactorily discharged if the chiefs to whom it belongs are united and resolute in their own defence. If they are not united, and will not take upon themselves the principal part of the exertions necessary, it will not be possible to defend them without exposing the Queen's Forces to the risks of a deadly climate, and to the hazard of being virtually defeated by the disastrous consequences of that climate, before they have been able to bring the native enemy to the issue of arms.

The proper course, therefore, is to take every possible means for bringing the chiefs to a united and decided system of defence, and for this purpose, to give them advice, to supply them judiciously with military stores, and, in concert with the Officer in Command of the Forces, to furnish them with such assistance as he may be able to afford, without exposing his officers and men to any protracted residence in the interior, especially at the unhealthy season, and without weakening his force upon the coast so as to endanger the safety of the Settlements themselves. I must repeat the caution which I conveyed to you in my despatch of 23rd ultimo, that you should avoid, if it be in your power, the necessity of bringing to the Settlement a number of the Queen's troops too great to be properly accomodated on the coast.

Instructions to the same effect will be sent by the Secretary of State for War to Lieut. Colonel Conran, and I shall request the Lords Commissioners of the Admiralty to direct the attention of the Commodore on the station to the possibility that you may find yourself again engaged in measures of defence against an invasion by the king of Ashantee. Since, however, the experience of the past year has exhibited in so strong a light the great difficulties which attend operations on the part of Her Majesty's forces, I rely on your using every exertion to avoid a renewal of the war.

You have already received from the Duke of Newcastle the full expression of his approval of your conduct in respect of the origin of the late war — I mean your refusal to surrender to a cruel death two refugees demanded by the king of Ashantee; but that approval I now desire to repeat, and I take the opportunity of impressing upon you the great importance of your being clearly in the right in any case of difference which may hereafter arise. I trust that you will be careful to assure yourself that you are acquainted, as far as possible, with all the circumstances which may be alleged on either side, and that you will not permit yourself to become involved in any hostile operations until you shall have first exhausted every legitimate means of preserving peace.

[C.O.96/64, H.C.266, A & P (1873) xlix]

242 PINE TO CARDWELL

CAPE COAST CASTLE, 13 JULY, 1864.
Sir,

With reference to your despatch No. 151 of the 23rd May, addressed to the officer administering the Government, I have the honour to state that on the 5th instant I assembled a meeting of the chiefs of Cape Coast and others who had since my arrival sought an interview for the purpose of understanding the proceedings which had followed since the arrival of the last mail, with respect to the withdrawal of the troops and munitions of war from the camps.

It is well to mention that immediately on receipt of your instructions, the Lieutenant Governor had desired the chiefs to take possession of the provisions and other things which might be useful to them, in accordance with your despatch; which order was only partially obeyed by reason of the surprise which arose at the unexplained withdrawal of the troops; so that the difficult and delicate task of explanation devolved upon me. I requested the attendance of the principal merchants and inhabitants of the place, and to the best of my ability I endeavoured to soften the disappointment which you anticipated might be felt by the chiefs at the necessary withdrawal of the Queen's troops.

I think I may say that I succeeded beyond the expectation of many and certainly my own, in smoothing the difficulties which surrounded the declaration that the British Government had withdrawn so vast a proportion of the protection which had been accorded to the tribes under its rule.

The great grievance appeared to be the fact of the Col. Commanding having destroyed the guns and ammunition, which, according to their ideas would have been useful to them. Prepared for this complaint, I met it at once by saying that Col. Conran believed these stores to be useless to the native tribes, and feared their falling into the hands of the enemy; but that if necessary, and [if] the Protectorate should be re-invaded, supplies for defence could be redoubled; with which they appeared satisfied, but feared that those who were most inimical to Ashantee and who had fled hither from thence for protection would not be so easily satisfied. . . .

The chiefs, upon the whole, behaved exceedingly well, and although grave and sad in their deportment, said that they would be patient, provided the Colonel, myself, and the original garrison did not leave. But undemonstrative as are notoriously the natives of this country, I am not free from anxiety that a feeling of discontent and dissatisfaction pervades the Protectorate.

I take a deep interest in this country, and although I flatter myself that I enjoy the fullest confidence of the people, I cannot but see that our uncertain tenure of power here, which has been pushed to the extreme with impunity, is very considerably jeopardized; and I candidly confess that unless the Administrator of this Government be armed with fuller powers and more extensive pecuniary means, that we shall be compelled to shut up our courts and refuse that influence and protection which have been so long eagerly sought by the natives. For, deprived of the boon which they were led to hope would be conferred upon them by the subjugation of their powerful enemy, I fear to press the payment of poll and other taxes, of which I have given notice and intended to have enjoined, for I am not sure that resistance will not take the place of cheerful obedience.

Had it not been for my continued anxiety now to watch over what I conceive to be a critical state of things, I should have adopted . . . medical [advice] to visit England, and there sought the honour of an interview . . . [to] bring under your notice a more comprehensive idea of my anomalous and singular position.

I have not the slightest reliable information to convey with respect to our relations with the King [of Ashantee]. . . . I shall use my best efforts to avert the renewal of the war and to induce the native chiefs to rely more on their own powers and energy than (you are pleased to observe) they have lately done. And here I think it behoves me to record the sense I entertain of the support, cheerful and willing obedience which has been accorded to me by every tribe within the Protectorate, with the exception of the Accras, who refused to advance without subsistence. . . .

[C.O.96/64]

243 Grievances of the Gold Coast Chiefs 9 August, 1864.

First. That they are as it were deprived of the power of holding domestic slavery, which has greatly reduced their power and dignity as kings and chiefs, their influence destroyed and then rendered them helpless.

They agree to follow agricultural pursuit if they will be permitted to hold domestic slavery for reasons assigned by them. . . .

Second. That they are for very trifling cause now and then cast into prison by the officials, which insures to them great disgrace, and places them upon the same par with their subjects.

Third. That it had been the custom of the former officials to create a court consisting of native kings and chiefs, to sit and adjudicate cases in which kings and chiefs are involved. But this is not the case now. Therefore they want his Excellency to remedy that.

They observed also that the country in sixty or seventy years past was in a thriving position when domestic slavery was valent, but now since the great alterat that has taken place with reference to the slave holding, the country is totally deprived of its wealth. That the kings and chiefs are not to convert themselves to shepherds, farmers and such like. They further remarked that if they had been allowed to hold domestic slavery, they would have given the Government for the transport corps, at least each fifty men, without any expense to the Government but that of subsistence alone.

They lastly, in an urgent manner, begged of the Governor not to tender the method of peacemaking to the enemies until they (the enemies) asked for it, because it will add more shame to the British flag.   [C.O.96/64]

BOOK VI

THE YEARS OF RETREAT, 1865–1873

18   *The Select Committee of 1865*

If Cardwell had hoped that by insisting on a strictly defensive policy he would disarm critics of the Gold Coast Protectorate, he was disappointed.   The Conservative Opposition, led by Adderley and Stanley, carried a motion for a Select Committee of inquiry into the West African Settlements, calling for special attention to the Gold Coast (244).   The findings of the Committee (247) reflected the views of Adderley and Stanley rather than those of the witnesses examined by it, though the recommendations for future policy (248), thanks partly to Cardwell, did not go beyond a pious hope that at some future time the tribes could be left to manage their own affairs.

The emphasis was, however, clearly on reducing commitments, wherever possible. The Colonial Office apparently discussed plans for confining occupation to Cape Coast (252), and the new Governor-in-Chief (at Sierra Leone), worried about the Ashantis, would have liked to abandon that post as well (256).   On the other hand, if they stayed at all, the British were bound to interfere to some extent in local affairs (253).   The question was, within what limits were they to interfere? Not, obviously, in remote and disturbed parts of the protectorate, like the Volta lands (249), where it was comforting to believe, with Colonel Conran, that traders were themselves to blame for 99 per cent of their difficulties[1] and therefore should be left to their own devices (250).

Conran, who became Acting-Governor on 19 August, 1865, seems to have advocated firmer rule within a more confined area, and on 16 September, issued a Proclamation defining the limits of British territory.   This was disallowed by Cardwell as an extension of obligations (which, in form, it was), not a reduction, as Conran probably intended.   Similarly he recommended a division of the coast with the Dutch (257), hoping that thereby the task of managing and defending the Protectorate would be halved.   For on the coast the effects of the Select Committee were making themselves felt among the African population (254), and chief Aggery of Cape Coast, obstreperous ever since his enstoolment in February 1865 (245), became so elevated that Conran decided to have him deported to Sierra Leone (258).

[1] Conran to Blackall, 9 June, 1866.   (C.O.96/71)

244 House of Commons Debates
21 February, 1865.

[A] Mr *Adderley*[1] in moving for a Select Committee to consider the state of the British Establishments on the western coast of Africa, said that . . . he wished for

[1] Sir Charles Bowyer Adderley, later 1st Baron Norton (1814–1905); Conservative M.P. for North Staffordshire, 1841–78; interested in Colonial questions; co-operated with E. G. Wakefield in founding Canterbury, N.Z., and the Colonial Reform Society; opposed transportation; Under-Secretary for the Colonies, June 1866 to December 1868.

inquiry in order to see whether these settlements were well ordered and regulated and whether they attained their object, or, on the contrary, did not rather obstruct it.

On the first point he thought there was sufficient reason for inquiry from the recent experience of one of these settlements.   It was only last Session that the House was filled with alarm, and some members of it exposed to the bitterest suffering,[1] owing to

[1] Sir John Hay, Conservative M.P. for Wakefield, lost a brother in the 1864 campaign.   He moved the vote of censure of June 1864 and served on the Select Committee of 1865.

the Governor of the Gold Coast . . . having nearly run us into a third war with the Ashantees, the most warlike of the African tribes. Governor Pine said, 'The silence of the king of Ashantee must be broken by some steps taken on our part.' Troops were reluctantly furnished to that Governor, and many gallant lives were lost, not in conflict with any enemy, but by contact with this pestilential climate, and through being brought into that contact without due preparations having been made. The troops were withdrawn only in time to save them from utter destruction, and in order to prove that the war, which was not precipitated by their withdrawal, could not have called for their appearance at all.

They were told by the Governor that wars and commotions of this kind, when they occurred, involved a total suspension of the objects for which these settlements were made.[1] He said that the seaboard of his extensive government lay exactly outside the cruizing ground of the squadron, so that whenever war took place, the squadron had to be withdrawn from the cruizing ground in order to maintain the war. The Governor also stated that these wars must be expected in the neighbourhood of such tribes, from time to time, if Englishmen would settle there, and that whenever they did occur, this country must be prepared to bear all the brunt of such wars, both in men and money: 'For,' said the Governor, 'my government is not a colony but a protectorate, so that I cannot call upon the natives or the inhabitants to supply either their labour or their money.' The Governor added that he had neither hope nor heart to press the people for any tax, and he had recently run the settlement almost into a revolution by proposing even a licence duty on the sale of rum. Not only was it impossible to levy a tax upon the natives, but also their services could not be made use of, inasmuch as the Gold Coast Artillery, the only native force which had been raised, had become mutinous and in-

[1] See H.Cs. 3364, 385, 393, A & P (1864) xli *passim* for the references in this paragraph.

subordinate, and has since been disbanded. That was the local corps which was considered by Lord Grey as an essential part of the system which he established for the consolidation of our government.

The Governor went on to describe his own position as anomalous and untenable, for whenever war threatened, as was almost continuously the case, his authority as Civil Governor became suspended, the sole responsibility falling upon the military commander, with whom he had quarrelled and held no communication whatever. The military commander had been removed from the colony since the period referred to, and the danger which then existed had ceased, but the Colonial Secretary told the House, only last Friday, that Colonel Conran, accompanied by troops, was at this moment making a military progress among the neighbouring warlike tribes for the purpose of opening a friendly intercourse with them which was not unlikely to replace the Government in its usual confusion. He saw by the papers that the residents considered Colonel Conran understood their interests far better than the Civil Governor, and the measures he had adopted were certainly more likely to promote the speculations of the settlers than the objects for which civil Governors were put there by this country.

He might mention, lastly, that the Government of the Dutch Settlement at Elmina, in the immediate neighbourhood, were now, and always had been, unfriendly to this country, and were always in intimate alliance with our constant enemies the Ashantees. Under such circumstances an inquiry into the state of the Government of the Gold Coast could not be entered into a moment too soon. . . .

[The other settlements were in nearly as bad a case. Their chief function was to stop the slave trade, the end of which was at last in sight.] But suppose that day had arrived, it was well to consider now with what other object the four settlements . . . should be maintained. Two other objects had been assigned. One was for the promotion of legitimate commerce, and the other for the civilization of the native races. . . .

The last quotation which he would make was with regard to the influence of our West African Governments upon commerce, and it was as follows:

'There is probably more trade in palm oil in the Bights of Benin and Biafra, and in ground nuts on the coast between Sierra Leone and the Gambia, where no colony exists, than in all the British settlements put together.'

Indeed, there was pretty good proof that as the Governments were conducted now, they were obstructing rather than promoting commerce.[1] Colonel Conran trailing the British flag round the territories of warlike chiefs gave bad encouragement to peaceful trade.

Now as to the second object, civilization, he doubted whether it was right to tax this country for civilization, even for the high object of civilizing barbarous tribes in Africa. If the efforts hitherto made had been successful, perhaps nobody in that House would be found to complain. But had we any encouragement to hope that the civilization of Africa would be effected through the agency of that House? The missionary work was noble, but it was not subsidised. Voluntary action had been to a great extent successful, but governments had done little to help it and much to disturb it. It was the opinion of an eminent (Basel) missionary . . . that the governments maintained by Great Britain upon that coast, as now conducted, were no assistance to the efforts of the missionaries for the civilization of the country.

If that was the case, what was to be done? He thought it quite clear that we must either go on or go back, that we must do a great deal more or a great deal less than at present. We must either render every Government secure by larger forces, or else stand out of the way of the native chiefs, who, if we were not there, would have a

[1] Cf. No. 209, p. 266, above.

much greater control over their own subjects. Our commerce will find its way there without any civil or military establishments to protect it, and will indirectly civilize the country. . . .

[B] *Lord Stanley:* The real question is whether there are not some at least among these settlements which involve us in great outlay and risk, and the maintenance of which serves no useful purpose. When I say serve no useful purpose, I mean they do not answer the end of promoting our trade; because I suppose nobody imagines we increase our political influence or our military power by retaining them. . . .

As to that . . . which I may call the philanthropic part of the question — I think we are in that respect acting in some degree under a delusion. Whenever that matter is discussed . . . it is constantly assumed that in some way or other we are responsible for the fortunes and destiny of the African race. Now I confess that I do not see that that is in any manner the case. . . . The slave trade was not created by England or by any European country. . . . We do not know of any time when it did not exist in the interior of Africa. The Englishmen found it there and used it; and I do not deny that they aggravated its evils. But they did not originate it. . . . And now, thirty years after the extinction of slavery, and sixty years after the legal extinction of the slave trade, I think we may fairly hold that whatever debt we owed to the people of Africa has by this time been paid off. . . .

Therefore, I say, we ought to view this simply as a matter of trade. We have only, or at least mainly, to consider whether the trade that is carried on at these various points which we occupy is increasing or diminishing, and whether there is any reason to think that at any point it would be greater or less if our occupation were to cease. . . .

One word only upon the question of the expense of these settlements. I have no doubt we shall hear whatever is to be said in their defence, and it may be stated that, as far as civil government goes, they cost very little, and that even their military expenses are not very considerable. As to civil government, I would point out that, with the exception of the Imperial forces, which stand in a different class, these are the only colonies which entail on us any charge whatever for their civil government, excepting, perhaps, one or two of the smaller West India Islands. . . .

The real burden is the responsibility you have undertaken, and the limit of which you do not know and nobody knows. Recollect how the matter stands. You cannot afford to send out as governers or persons in authority in these colonies, in any sense your best men. No man will go out to Africa who can find employment elsewhere. . . . You must take . . . the men whom you can get . . . and in the hands of these men, placed there with no influence brought to bear upon them such as a large British population can always bring to bear on those who govern — in the hands of men surrounded by negroes, having everything their own way about them, you are compelled, to a great extent, to leave the power of peace and war, and an authority the exercise of which may at any moment involve the sacrifice of thousands of lives and many millions of money.

I do not wish it to be inferred from what I have said that I am ready to commit myself at once to the absolute abandonment of these posts. But I think there is a prima facie case made out for inquiring as to whether they are worth retaining. And holding that opinion to some extent with regard to them all, I think it does more particularly apply to that one of which we know the least and with which the business we do appears to be decreasing, the Gold Coast, where, in a country extending over some 300 miles, you are surrounded on all sides by utterly savage and warlike tribes, and have constituted yourselves, so to speak, the head of a confederation over which you have very little material power. That settlement is in so peculiar and

anomalous a position that I think it might deserve to be a special subject of inquiry. . . .   [Hansard 3/177/535 ff.]

245 JOHN AGGERY[1] TO RICHARD PINE
CAPE COAST, 16 MARCH, 1865.

. . . Governor Captain Maclean . . . in a peculiar, imperceptible, and unheard of manner, wrested from the hands of our kings, chiefs and headmen, their power to govern their own subjects. The Governor, placing himself at the head of a handful of soldiers, had been known himself to travel to the remotest parts of the interior for the purpose of compelling kings, chiefs and headmen . . . to obey His Excellency's summons, or to comply with His Excellency's decrees. A blow was thus firmly, slowly and persistently struck, and the supreme authority, power, and even influence of the kings, chiefs and headmen, gave way to the powerful Governor Maclean. . . . A white face, a red jacket, was in consequence a terror on the Gold Coast, and very kings were frightened into making concessions, compliances and obeisances as degrading in the regal office as affecting the royal character, authority and income. In order to gain his point . . . the Governor spared no efforts to adopt measures calculated to breed disaffection, disloyalty, disobedience and consequent estrangement in the subject towards his lawful king. A king was regarded as not above the reach of the then established Court of Justice, and any one individual subject was placed on a footing with his sovereign, as equally as the 'King is less than all', perhaps forgetting that it is only when the king has violated the fixed and essential principles of the constitution of a nation that a people,

[1] John Aggery was enstooled as king of Cape Coast in February 1865, and proceeded to set up his own court presided over by Joseph Martin. An African agent of one of the European firms, summoned before it, refused to recognise its authority, and successfully resisted arrest. Governor Pine said he was prepared to recognise properly organised 'country' courts, saving always a right of appeal to the British courts. Aggery replied by denouncing the Protectorate ab initio.

in the absence of any higher tribunal to appeal to, might lawfully do themselves right.

The Governor constituted himself as the people. Complaints of every description from the subject were sustained against the king; and the king was not infrequently placed in the dock and fined or imprisoned or (hardly credible) flogged for trivial offences. Many a subject was encouraged and countenanced to throw off with impunity their very allegiance — an allegiance which could not well be disowned and ignored and denied without endangering the security of the king. . . . Hence the threatened overthrow of the rights of the native kings and chiefs, hence the 'servility and delusion and puerile confidence in Governors and the indifference to liberty, deep-seated in the natives here and on the Gold Coast generally; and hence the alleged continued practice . . . that the decisions of . . . the kings and chiefs of Cape Coast and of the interior have been and are invariably subject of reversal . . .'

If all the proceedings and all the witnesses as required be transferred from my court to your Excellency and your Judicial Assessor, your Excellency or your Judicial Assessor may be both party and judge. . . . The [king's] court . . . is not irresponsible. It is responsible to the king for its acts. Well has it been said over and over again, that Cape Coast, in the eyes of the law, is not British territory. It is therefore necessary for me to be given to understand whether the proceedings complained of as unlawful are repugnant to Christianity and natural justice. . . .

Your Excellency [suggests] . . . 'that so soon as the pending matter is disposed of, an interview take place . . . with a view to our coming to a mutual understanding on the subject of the establishment of a court to be called the king's court, upon such a basis as I can recognise.' But the king's court is not of yesterday. From time immemorial it has existed, and it even existed before Cape Coast Castle itself was erected, and the ground on which the castle

stands was originally taken from my ancestors at an annual rent. . . .

We have already protested against. . . the inhabitants of Cape Coast and other places being regarded as British subjects. . . . On what grounds your Excellency holds George Blankson Wood as a British subject, I cannot say and perhaps I dare not ask.

If, as the Queen of England's representative, you are intended to act as my adviser, and if, as a special adviser, you had acknowledged George Blankson Wood as my subject and tender[ed] counsel where the proceedings complained of were repugnant to Christianity and natural justice, I might have conscientiously fallen into your views. . . .

I cannot but apprehend that serious results are likely to arise from the policy adopted by your Excellency. . . . Meanwhile I feel obliged to refer the matter to Her Majesty's Government in England . . . especially as we understand a Committee of the House of Commons will be assembled this session . . . to inquire into the state of affairs on the Gold Coast. . . .[1]

[C.O.96/67]

246 W. HACKETT TO R. PINE

LONDON, 22 MAY, 1865.

Sir,

I read with much pain the papers relating to the suit Wood against Martin in the Judicial Assessor's Court at Cape Coast. I say with pain because it is the first instance within my recollection in which the supremacy of British tribunals on the Gold Coast has been disputed.

With regard to the course which it is now proper to pursue, and I may say I give my

[1] Martin was summoned before the Judicial Assessor's Court in the face of protests from Aggery and the Cape Coast Companies. Aggery refused to attend with the other chiefs when they met Pine prior to his departure to England, but sent messengers to the interior chiefs, alleging that all native courts were to be suppressed and slaves to be set free, and asking for money to send an ambassador to England. The ambassador was Martin, who did not speak English.

opinion with all due deference to that of Her Majesty's Government, I think that the decree obtained in the Court at Cape Coast Castle should be carried into effect. Without entering into the question as to whether the plaintiff in the suit was a British subject, I think it is sufficient to observe that the jurisdiction now claimed by the British Court is one which has been enjoyed and exercised by it, certainly ever since the time of Mr Maclean, if not longer, and that the chiefs, headmen and natives of the Protectorate generally have always acknowledged this jurisdiction. If the claims of the king of Cape Coast be conceded in this case, British influence in the Protected Territories is at an end, and the office of Judicial Assessor becomes practically useless.

With regard to the manner in which Her Majesty's Government has viewed this question, I may mention that a despatch was written (I think in the year 1853) by the late Duke of Newcastle when Colonial Secretary, on the subject of some complaints made against Judicial Assessor Fitzpatrick, in which his Grace distinctly laid down the responsibility of the native chiefs — (in that case it was, I think, the king of Cape Coast who complained) as before the British tribunals. I can only regard this attempt to set up the irresponsibility of the native courts as the fruit of the intrigues of a few discontented spirits among the townspeople, and I am convinced that the people of the Protectorate generally submit cheerfully to British authority. Indeed the more important chiefs are those who show most docility and respect for British rule.

In conclusion, I think that whatever may be decided hereafter as to the mode and extent of the jurisdiction to be exercised by British magistrates on the Gold Coast, that the decree given in this particular case should remain in force; and I do so on the ground that it was given by virtue of a jurisdiction now exercised for upwards of thirty years, and never before, at least successfully, disputed.

I have etc.   [C.O.96/67]

247 DRAFT REPORT OF THE SELECT COMMITTEE ON AFRICA (WESTERN COAST)
22 JUNE, 1865.

. . . The protectorate of tribes about our forts on the Gold Coast assumes an indefinite and unintelligible responsibility on our part, uncompensated by any adequate advantage to the tribes. It is even the opinion of the Colonial Secretary of that Government[1] that it has enervated and disunited the protected chiefs, and that so far from training the chiefs to a better conduct of their own affairs, it only leads them to lean on the English.

It rests on no documentary evidence or conditions; excites vague expectations among the chiefs, and practically engages the English Government in maintaining weak tribes against their former sovereigns, and in keeping peace among them all, or even in compensating for losses mutually occasioned by invasion, and generally in administering a territory which we cannot even tax as subject. . . .

In the hope of a speedy termination of the slave trade [the Committee][2] conceive that it would be wise at once to forbid any steps being taken by any officers of the Crown in West Africa, to retrace which might be difficult though desirable upon such an event.

All further extension of territory or assumption of government in West Africa, or any new treaty implying protection of native tribes, should be peremptorily prohibited and carefully prevented.

It may be impossible at present to withdraw from settlements and engagements already made; but even these may be capable of immediate reduction and consolidation; and when their chief object, the suppression of the slave trade, is achieved, and the protection of commerce becomes their sole remaining object, they may be still further modified and partially abandoned. Immediate reduction will be an overt act, duly notifying this intention, and most effectually checking the extension,

[1] W. A. Ross, Colonial Secretary of the Gold Coast, 1860–5. (Cf. H.C.412 Qs 1865–6.)
[2] 'They' in original.

without hazarding the efficiency of the present governments. . . .

On the Gold Coast there is no possibility of raising a sufficient revenue while the Dutch remain and thwart our policy.

The forts we now retain, to say nothing of the Danish forts which we added by purchase in 1851, are, with the exception of Cape Coast Castle, more or less in ruins, and in some cases subject to earthquakes. The cost of putting them in habitable order would be considerable, even without fortifying them, and the whole cost would fall on the Home Treasury. None of these forts should be restored, but barracks should be made tenantable at Accra, and perhaps one other healthy site besides Cape Coast Castle.

The protectorate should only be retained while the chiefs may be as speedily as posisible made to do without it. Nothing should be done to encourage them to lean on British help, or trust to British administration of their affairs, whether military or judicial. The judicial assessor does not fulfil the first intention of the office, assisting the chiefs in administering justice, but supersedes their authority by decisions according to his own sole judgement. This office, instituted with the best intentions, seems, by the evidence of a Commissioner from the native king of Cape Coast,[1] to have led to the introduction of needless technicalities and expense, and the employment of attorneys, when the natives had better speak for themselves. The chiefs should be rather left to exercise their own jurisdiction, with only an appeal, when necessary, to the English magistracy. Queen's Advocates seem wholly unnecessary, and trials by jury inapplicable in many cases.

The forts on the Gold Coast should be under the command of a Lieutenant Governor at Cape Coast Castle, under the orders of the Governor of Sierra Leone, with a small council, legislative and executive, subject to his sanction of their proceedings; and the exercise of his govern-

[1] Joseph Martin.

ment should be as much as possible confined to the forts actually occupied.

Three companies now stationed on the Gold Coast may be reduced to two, and police should be organised to supersede part of this reduced force as speedily as possible.

The judicial establishment should consist only of magistrates, important cases being reserved for the Chief Justice's circuit from Sierra Leone.

The whole of this reduced establishment would be paid for by little more than the present Parliamentary Grant, and all attempts at raising a revenue, whether by taxes or customs, futile as both have proved, would be spared, as well as the assumption of partial sovereignty over the neighbourhood, implied in such attempts. . . .

[H.C.412, A & P (1865) v]

248 RESOLUTIONS OF THE SELECT COMMITTEE   26 JUNE, 1865.

Resolved:—

That it is the opinion of this Committee:

That it is not possible to withdraw the British Government, wholly or immediately, from any settlements or engagements on the West African Coast. . . .

That all further extension of territory or assumption of Government, or new treaties offering any protection to native tribes, would be inexpedient; and that the object of our policy should be *to encourage in the natives the exercise of those qualities which may render it possible for us more and more*[1] to transfer to them the administration of all the Governments, with a view to our ultimate withdrawal from all, except, probably, Sierra Leone.

[1] The clause in italics was added in Adderley's original resolution at the instance of Mr. Cardwell. In 1869 (in his *Review of the Colonial Policy of Lord John Russell's Administration*) Adderley, who was 'quite sure that no miracle can set up the European model in Africa' explained that he understood the resolution to mean 'that we should get out of the scrape in which we have involved ourselves, as speedily as we honourably can, leaving the tribes in a fair way of being able to hold their own and govern themselves'.

That this policy of non-extention admits of no exception, as regards new settlements, but cannot amount to an absolute prohibition of measures which, in peculiar cases, may be necessary for the more efficient and economical management of the settlements we already possess.

That the reasons for the separation of West African Governments in 1842 having ceased to exist, it is desirable that a Central Government over all the four settlements should be re-established at Sierra Leone, with steam communication with each Lieutenant Government.

That the evidence leads to the hope that such central control may be established with considerable retrenchment of expenditure, and at the same time with a general increase of efficiency. . . .

[H.C.412 of 1865]

249 E. CARDWELL TO COL. E. CONRAN
LONDON, 1 SEPTEMBER, 1865.

Sir,

I have received Acting Governor Mockler's despatch No. 67 of the 12th of July, accompanied by a correspondence on the subject of recent disturbances on the banks of the Volta, and of Commander Richard's operations there.

The Lords Commissioners of the Admiralty are of opinion, in which I concur, that, under the circumstances, and with the information in Commander Richard's possession, he acted with prudence and discretion.

There is no doubt that the territory of the Protectorate extends along the east coast as far as Quittah, which is some distance beyond the Volta, where these disturbances took place. But as a general rule, it has been judged advisable in the management of the affairs of the Coast to avoid, as far as possible, the exercise of any authority amongst the natives in this situation.

In consequence of a communication from Governor Andrews that on those parts of the Coast where the natives were unwilling to live under British protection, the policy

of the Government should be one of non-interference, except for the purpose of preventing human sacrifice, the Secretary of State, in a despatch No. 33 of the 14th of September, 1860, intimated his readiness to leave the matter to the discretion of the Governor.

It is desirable to act in accordance with the view which was then expressed, and to continue to avoid, as far as possible, any interference in the remote parts of the territory, with the natives who do not yield willing obedience to British authority.

I enclose for your information, a copy of a letter received on this subject from the Admiralty.

I have etc.   [C.O.96/68]

250 W. G. ROMAINE[1] TO SIR F. ROGERS
ADMIRALTY, 29 AUGUST, 1865.

. . . Commodore Wilmot will be directed to inform officers under his command that it is not the policy of Her Majesty's Government to afford protection to traders who may settle among savage tribes within the Protectorate of the Gold Coast, at a distance from any British establishment. My Lords consider that traders should be informed that, if they choose to establish themselves in such places, it must be at their own risk, and that the officers of Her Majesty's Ships are ordered on no account to commence any hostile acts against the tribes on the Coast in consequence of treatment such traders may meet with.

Any cases of forcible interference with European traders by the natives on the coast will be reported to the Commodore, who will always be in possession of the views and directions of Her Majesty's Government. . . .   [C.O.96/69]

251 MINUTE BY T. F. ELLIOT
22 NOVEMBER, 1865.

I am in great hopes that we shall be able to submit for your approval a scheme for

[1] William Govett Romaine (1815–93); 2nd Secretary at the Admiralty, April 1857–June 1869.

withdrawing all the outlying stations on the Gold Coast and concentrate at Cape Coast Castle. . . .   [C.O.96/68]

252 CARDWELL TO CONRAN
LONDON, 23 NOVEMBER, 1865.
Sir,

I have to acknowledge your dispatch No. 114 of 7th October, enclosing the copy of a notice[1] which you have issued, in which you define the limits of Her Majesty's possessions on the Gold Coast.

I am unable to approve the step which you have taken in declaring the territory within five miles of eight separate British forts to be British territory, and I have to instruct you to recall the notice in which this is done.

Whatever influence you may be able to exert in encouraging or repressing barbarous customs leading to the loss of life, will be very proper, and I shall be happy to approve your exercise of it: but the extension of British territory is a different matter, and cannot receive my sanction.

I have etc.

[C.O.96/68, H.C.198, A & P (1867) xlix]

253 MINUTE BY T. F. ELLIOT[2]
19 DECEMBER, 1865.

Efforts to get rid of filth and pigs and other consequences of barbarism in the town which is under the very walls of the castle, are very laudable and necessary. If we are to sit in our fort, as if we were stalled oxen or pigs ourselves, contented witnesses of all the evils of savage life at our very door, I cannot help thinking that we should not only be doing no good but great harm, and that the sooner we went away altogether, the better. It may be doubtful whether or not we ought to be on the coast at all, but

[1] The Notice is printed by Crooks, *op. cit.*, pp. 371–2. Four of the forts were in Cape Coast, the others being Dixcove, Anomabu, James Fort Accra and Christiansborg Castle.

[2] Cf. Governor's notice of 1 November, 1865, and Cardwell's despatch of 22 December, 1865. Crooks, *op. cit.*, pp. 372–4.

it seems to me perfectly certain that we ought not to be there if, instead of diffusing the blessings of civilization, we are to afford the spectacle of a civilized Power lending itself to all the faults of a childish African chief who only exists by its sufferance.

[C.O.96/68]

254 CONRAN TO CARDWELL
CAPE COAST CASTLE, 5 FEBRUARY, 1866.

[The chief of Abremu Agona had threatened to invade Dutch territory.] . . .

The fact of Elmina and the other Dutch settlements being surrounded at seven or eight miles distance by the tribes under our protection, affording an instance like Agomah, should be enough to [urge] our making further effort for the settlement of affairs on the Gold Coast.

Whilst a division such as that proposed would be the means of placing an equal responsibility with England on the Dutch, as regards the protection of the natives, [it would] relieve our Government from embarrassment which I can foresee approaching. . . . Since the West African Inquiry held in the House of Commons last year, the greatest change appears evident in many of our districts on the sea-shore, through the efforts made by King Aggery and his councillors to spread reports amongst the natives, on Mr Martin's return from England in September last; endeavouring to influence the minds of the so-called scholars (those natives who can read and write) and petty native lawyers, who cling like leeches to the skirts of their more ignorant kings and chiefs, for the sake of gain, for the mere writing of the commonest of letters to the Government and especially the Chief Justice's department, giving the greatest trouble, and causing, what is much worse, the greatest discontent.

King Aggery and his councillors are led to believe by Mr Charles Bannerman, a native advocate possessing much talent, but totally devoid of principle, that the time has arrived when they themselves should govern the coast: but that the English should also remain as their advisers and directors in all things. To which scheme, the merchants of all colours, and others of fixed ideas and principles, strongly object, fearing that without the protection of England, themselves and their connections should be by such means plunged back to the former condition of their ancestors. . . .

[C.O.96/70]

255 E. CARDWELL TO MAJOR S. W. BLACKALL[1]

LONDON, 23 FEBRUARY, 1866.

Sir,

I send you a Commission appointing you Governor-in-Chief in and over all the Settlements on the West Coast of Africa. I place full confidence in the discretion with which you will exercise these powers, and I feel that you will be the better able to give effect to the views of Her Majesty's Government in consequence of the share you have had in the deliberations which have taken place in this country.

The first great use of these Settlements has been the extinction of the slave trade at all places within reach of their influence. The object next in importance is the promotion of legitimate commerce, which not only affords the most powerful discouragement of slave-trading, but also softens the manners and alleviates the condition of the neighbouring native tribes. These are purposes, however, which ought not to require any cumbrous or expensive forms of Government. Our aim should be to provide for them by a very few functionaries adequately remunerated at each separate post, concentrating at the seat of the Government in Chief any institutions which require higher authority or more complicated establishments.

Proceeding to this view, I duly considered the question whether at places where the population and the transactions are so

limited as at the Gambia and the Gold Coast, and where experience has shown that the number of laws required in each year is so small, it might not be superfluous to keep up separate legislatures. But it must be remembered that the power of the Crown to create and define Legislative bodies is derived from the Act 6 & 7 Victoria, cap. 13 and the language of the first clause of this act is such that it appears to require a distinct Legislature in each Settlement on the coast of Africa. Nor, upon the whole, do I regret this restriction. If a general legislature were to have been clothed with the power of making laws binding upon the Gambia and the Gold Coast I should have felt it indispensable that it should include members from those places, an arrangement which might have entailed practical inconveniences in the necessity of their resorting to the principal seat of Government. Again, the great distance of Lagos from Sierra Leone, and the possibility of its becoming the seat of an extensive commerce, would have precluded the idea of depriving that place of a power of local legislation. Such a change therefore could not have been made general for the whole coast of Africa, and I am content that each settlement should retain its existing powers of legislation.

The principal officers of each of the outlying settlements will be the Administrator of the Government,[1] the Collector of the Revenue, and the Magistrate. These will represent the Executive, the Fiscal and the Judicial branches of Administration. The Administrator of the Government will combine in his person the duties of Colonial Secretary, with the requisite clerical assistance. The Collector of Revenue will collect all public revenue, whether of customs or derived from other sources, and will also perform the duty of Treasurer. He will be next in rank to the Administrator and unless otherwise specially provided, will fill his place in case of death or absence. On the

[1] Major Samuel Wensley Blackall, born 1809; entered the army 1827; M.P. for Longford, 1847–61; Governor of Dominica; Governor of Sierra Leone, 1863; Governor-in-Chief West African Settlements, February 1866–February 1868.

[1] Conran's commission as Administrator of the Gold Coast was forwarded by Cardwell to Blackall on 22 February, 1866.

other hand, in the event of the death or absence of the Collector, the Administrator will assume the direction and responsibility of that office. The Magistrate will dispose of all cases except such as may be reserved for the Circuit or other Supreme Court, to be hereafter substituted for the existing Supreme Court. Until that change be made by law, the existing Courts must of course remain in the exercise of their present jurisdiction.

But it appears evident that the outlying settlements do not require the complicated machinery of an English superior court of justice. I shall be glad to receive a report from you, with any assistance which you may find it expedient to seek from your legal adviser . . . on the definition of the civil and military causes which shall be excepted from the jurisdiction of the Resident Magistrate, and reserved for the Circuit Court. It will be desirable, I think, that only the gravest criminal cases, and only civil cases involving large amounts, should be so reserved. I shall also be glad to have your opinion on the number of circuits in the year, and to learn whether the Sierra Leone Bench can furnish the required visits to the Gold Coast and to Lagos, as well as to the Gambia. . . .

Into the subject of the minor offices at the various settlements, as well as into that of the clerical aid required in the three principal offices, I have not entered because these can only be effectively dealt with on the spot. But I rely on your making a searching review of them, and upon your sparing no effort to render them as economical as possible.

I transmit to you a copy of the estimates laid before Parliament this year, which provides for a sum of £39,000 for the service of the West Coast of Africa. Besides this, application will have to be made for debts amounting to £21,880, so that the total sum applied for will be no less than £61,380. If such liberal aid should be granted by Parliament, it will be the more incumbent on the Government to take care that there should be no fresh excess of expenditure

beyond the resources of the Settlements. You will observe that £10,000 is the amount of aid allotted to the current Civil Estimates of the three minor settlements, vizt.

to the Gambia £3,400
to the Gold Coast £3,300
and to Lagos   £3,300.

It is absolutely indispensable that the expenditure of these Settlements should be so restricted this year as to fall within the present amount of the Colonial Revenue and of the aid granted by Parliament.

Active measures are in progress for the purpose of furnishing you as soon as possible with at least one of the two steamers which form so important a part of the scheme for carrying on the new Government in Chief.

Some difficulties may unavoidably occur in the first transition from one system to another, but I rely upon the zeal of yourself and of the several Administrators, for shortly bringing the new plan into successful operation.

I have etc.   [C.O.96/71]

256 CARDWELL TO BLACKALL
LONDON, 23 JUNE, 1866.

Sir,

I have your despatch No. 6 (Gold Coast) of the 19th ultimo, forwarding a copy of a despatch of the Administrator of the Gold Coast, describing a second visit from emissaries of the king of Ashantee on a peaceful mission, and tracing the proceedings of the local Government with regard to Ashantee in previous years as well as on the last occasion.

You remark that Colonel Conran's statement shows the perpetual danger to which we are exposed by maintaining the Protectorate, and that we do so without any adequate result; and you submit whether, under such circumstances, the retention of Cape Coast, at all times an unhealthy station, is desirable.

After hearing several very competent

witnesses, including yourself, the Committee on the West African Settlements came to the conclusion that it would not be possible to withdraw the British wholly or immediately from any settlements or engagements on that coast. But in maintaining our settlements we must bear in mind the objects which the Committee had in view; vizt. to encourage in the natives such qualities as would gradually enable them to govern themselves without the continuance of our intervention, and by the establishment of a central government to effect a considerable retrenchment of expenditure, and at the same time an increased efficiency.

In pursuance of these recommendations, Her Majesty's Government have taken measures for diminishing the expenditure, civil and military, in all the settlements, for impressing on the natives on the Gold Coast, the necessity of relying on their own exertions for their self defence; and for leaving to the chiefs in the Protectorate, in a greater degree than heretofore, judicial decisions in which British subjects are not concerned.

In a Proclamation dated the 16th January last, Colonel Conran impressed upon the kings and chiefs of the Protectorate, their obligation to abstain from any acts which might lead to hostilities. I hope he will take every suitable opportunity to renew this caution, especially to the chiefs bordering on Ashantee, and to explain to them that they would not be sheltered from the consequences of such acts by expeditions of British troops into the interior.

I have etc.   [C.O.96/71]

257 CONRAN TO BLACKALL
CAPE COAST, 6 SEPTEMBER, 1866.

Confidential.

. . . A division of the coast and protectorate between the Dutch and English . . . would in my opinion be the simplest and safest plan that might be adopted for the removal of all difficulties; the Dutch taking charge and the government of all between

Sweet River . . . and Assinee, while we take from same spot all down to Quittah, in the centre of which stands Accra, which for various good reasons should be our headquarters. This plan once established, we should be relieved from the protection and responsibility of the most awkward portions of the Protectorate,[1] as the Dutch would be compelled to share in the common defence of the country which has hitherto devolved upon us. . . . As there are but two modes through which the Ashantees . . . can receive supplies from the coast during war, the Assinee and Volta, there could be no difficulty in cutting them off at any moment by a combined effort in these places, in the event of hostilities being hereafter resorted to on their part; whilst the revenue to be raised . . . would not amount to less than from £12,000 to 15,000 per annum for each Government, and enough to render them self-supporting without troubling the Treasury. . . .

Surely it is better to try half courses than to throw up the Protectorate altogether [in view of] the consequences that would be sure (in my opinion) to follow that step; the natives not having the slightest prospect of self-government, and even if they had, the total want of union which has from time immemorial existed . . . and will for ever exist, I fear, renders the prospect of their being able to govern so remote that we must either adopt some plan such as I have suggested, or content ourselves with the prospect of having a most difficult and unsatisfactory task to labour under, in governing the Gold Coast. . . .

British law should be solely maintained in the towns of Cape Coast, Accra and Anamaboe where we have magistrates and courts available for the administration of justice, and to the extent of about two miles all round each place, to the exclusion of native courts. . . . All cases arising outside should be freely left to their own settlement, murder and the like offences, of course, being subject to the decision of the

---

[1] Apollonia (Nzima) and Wasaw were, in Conran's view, particularly troublesome.

Administrator, whose powers should resemble those originally intended for the Judicial Assessor; whilst the appearance in our courts of native lawyers, the curse of the place, should upon no account be tolerated. . . .   [C.O.96/72]

258 CARNARVON TO BLACKALL
                LONDON, 23 FEBRUARY, 1867.
Sir,

I have received your dispatch No. 62 of the 24th of December last, reporting that John Aggery, commonly called King of Cape Coast, had been sent away by Colonel Conran, the Administrator of the Gold Coast, from that place to Sierra Leone, on account of what appeared to be seditious and menacing proceedings, and that you had set Aggery free at Sierra Leone on parole with an allowance of five shillings a day for his maintenance, until you receive instructions from me as to his ultimate disposal. I have also received your dispatch, No. 2 of the 15th of January, transmitting further papers from Colonel Conran in explanation of his measures, and enclosing a proclamation in which he had pronounced the deposition of Aggery.[1]

Alluding to the recent attempt of another petty chief to imprison and torture some people close to the British fort at Annamaboe, you express the general conviction that nothing but a firm enforcement of British authority over chiefs who are situated on our very border, will prevent a return amongst the Fantee tribes to their cruel and barbarous customs. At Cape Coast you represent that an attempt at divided authority must lead to constant collision. You see no objection to recognizing a Head man, but under the control

of Her Majesty's representative. You report to me that Aggery knows very little English, and that it was only with difficulty, and through the medium of an interpreter, that you could make him understand your communications to him about his threatening letter to Colonel Conran. Your conclusion is, that his presence at Cape Coast with the title of King, being an ignorant man in the hands of artful persons, must be a source of constant danger; and assuming him to be deposed, you think that he could not complain if, upon giving security for his future good behaviour, he were permitted to return to Cape Coast, enjoying his private means, and with a pension for his own life of £100 per annum.

I much regret that the injudicious course taken by Aggery under bad advice has brought affairs to the present crisis. The anomalous position of the British Government on the Gold Coast affords no general principles for the decision of such questions as the present. I can only look to the history of the place for my assistance in endeavouring to arrive at a just conclusion.

The town of Cape Coast is contiguous to, and inseparably united with Cape Coast Castle. The Government House and the market are both situated outside the fort and within the precincts of the town.[1] From time to time a chief was elected who, being approved by the Governor, received the title of King, according to what may be a somewhat injudicious practice of white people in designating chiefs on the African coast. In 1856 the king of Cape Coast at that time was deposed by Colonel Ord, Her Majesty's Commissioner, in compliance with the wish of his people, who were dissatisfied with him. An interval followed of nine years, during which there was no king at all: but in February 1865, Governor

---

[1] See H.C.198 of 1867: Papers relating to the Deportation of King Aggery. (A & P (1867) xlix.) Conran (to Cardwell, 23 October, 1865, *loc. cit.*) wrote: 'I do not consider the King a bad man, but I think he is very badly advised by a set of part educated councillors, who resemble Chartists . . . and have nothing to lose, but everything to gain by any change that they may effect in this place, which they could not govern for a week in our absence, as no king or chief in the Protectorate deigns to acknowledge Aggery.'

[1] The Governor's House at this time was immediately north of the Methodist church, at the junction of Chapel (now King) Street and Hughes (now Garden) Street, and is today the C.C.P.'s Court. Cf. the map in Hackett to Newcastle No. 50 of 12 May, 1864 (C.O.96/64). All the area between Fort Winniett (William) and the Castle was locally held to be the property of the Crown, according to Hackett.

Pine permitted and ratified the election of John Aggery. I find it stated in Colonel Conran's evidence before the Parliamentary Committee of 1865, that Governor Pine refused to admit his right to hold courts or appoint magistrates, and similar evidence in substance was given by Colonel Ord.

Aggery sent an agent named Martin to give evidence before the Committee of the House of Commons; and after that agent's return, erroneous accounts are said to have been circulated, of the proceedings before the Committee. There certainly has been a greater disposition than had appeared before, to dispute the Governor's authority, and to set up the native against the English courts, which had been resorted to for many years by the natives with great benefit. After various other differences, Aggery, on the 15th March 1866, addressed a Memorial to Governor Blackall, which revealed the false ideas that he had been taught to entertain. He complained that the Governor passed British laws without making them known to Aggery beforehand, and obtaining the consent of the people; that the British Government received the revenues of customs and all other public revenues, whilst none of them went to King Aggery; and he ended by announcing that he was about to form a corps of natives, to be trained to arms, for what he called the benefit of the country, and for purposes of self-defence.

These pretensions need no comment. They are simply a claim to set aside the sovereignty and the power of the Queen at Cape Coast Castle itself, which is the chief seat of Government on the Gold Coast. My predecessor replied that Aggery's pretensions must be effectually discountenanced; that he must be told that, in return for protection, we expect deference to our authority, and that he would not be permitted to make himself an exception to that rule. Aggery, however, did not alter his course. He appears to have fallen into the hands of a European or man of colour, who had been lately dismissed from the office of churchwarden; and after, growing

indications of disrespect for the Government, Aggery wrote his menacing letter to Colonel Conran, having previously held a meeting of his followers, at which, as reported by Colonel Conran, no fewer than 2,500 persons were assembled.

These are the circumstances under which Colonel Conran, believing, as he sets forth in his address of the 10th of December to the principal European and native inhabitants of Cape Coast, that there was grave public danger, resolved upon immediately sending off Aggery by the mail steamer to Sierra Leone, with a view to the ultimate decision of the case by you or by Her Majesty's Government.

I have already said that I regret the absence of any settled law by which I could dispose of the matter. The practical question seems to be whether there are sufficient grounds for depriving Aggery of the title and position which was accorded him by Governor Pine in the beginning of 1865. Whilst I regret that the affair should have been thus forced by him to such an issue, it is clear to me, on a review of the foregoing facts, that it would be inconsistent with the proper precautions to be observed at Cape Coast, and with that resistance, which it is our duty to offer, to the renewal, under the very walls of our forts, of the cruel punishments and exactions of native chieftains, to allow Aggery to resume his former position. I have therefore to express my approval of his deposition. I agree with you, that it will be better to avoid conferring a title so calculated to mislead as that of King, on the next person who may be elected by the people, and approved by the Governor, as the leading native authority in the town. The designation which you propose of Head man, is far more appropriate. . . .

[Aggery himself was to be treated with 'all reasonable consideration' and allowed a modest pension, but to be required to reside at Sierra Leone 'for one or two years, until the memory of recent transactions has passed.']

[C.O.96/74. H.C.198 of 1867]

19   The Turning Point, 1867–1870

ACTING on Conran's welcome advice, the Home Government (Lord Derby's) lost no time in concluding with the Dutch an agreement to divide the coast and impose a common customs system (259).   The consequences in Africa were disastrous, and during the next two years, the Protectorate almost foundered completely. Dutch attempts to occupy the abandoned British forts were everywhere resisted by the local people (261), while the western chiefs marched against Elmina, and, failing to take it by storm, sat down to invest it.

Administrator Ussher, and his deputy Simpson, were in a difficult position. They disapproved of the agreement with the Dutch, and to that extent understood the determination of the chiefs to oppose it (262–3): but they had no confidence in the wisdom or motives of the self-appointed advisers of the Fante chiefs at Mankessim (261–2).   To attack Elmina was to invite an Ashanti invasion, but it was easier for the Secretary of State in London (270) than for Ussher on the coast (265) to say that he would wash his hands of the States if they refused to listen to British advice.   Simpson tried a different tactic; to work with the Fantee chiefs and so wean them from the influence of the 'scholars' (266); but even he was convinced 'that so long as the British Government is represented at all it must be paramount, and take the lead'. (267).

In these difficult years, there is, in fact, apparent, a divergence between the men on the spot, convinced of the need for bolder measures, and the Secretary of State, standing rigidly by the tenets of the Select Committee.   This is particularly evident in the discussion on the policy to be adopted in the eastern districts, where confidence in the Government was unaffected by the Anglo-Dutch exchange, but where the policy of non-intervention, inaugurated by Governor Andrews, and endorsed by Cardwell, had only given freer rein to tribal animosities and warfare; Akwamu against Krepi, and Anlo against Ada, with Ashanti on the one side, and Accra on the other, only too ready to join in.

Conran himself had sent an expedition to the Volta in 1866, believing that he had thereby disposed of all difficulties,[1] but Ussher had to do the same in 1867 (260), and peace treaties negotiated with the Akwamu and Anlo, proved of little value.[2]   In 1869, the acting-Administrator (Simpson) made a further attempt at mediation, found himself for a few critical days a prisoner in the hands of the Akwamu, and brought on his head a massive rebuke from Lord Granville (268).

In after years this despatch was to be quoted as the classic statement of the policy of non-intervention.   But the logic of events was too strong.   Another expedition went to the Volta in 1870 (271), and, in the face of another, though less emphatic, rebuke, from another Secretary of State (272), the Governor-in-Chief himself, whose post had been created, at the instance of the Select Committee, for the precise purpose of curbing such local military excursions, defended the intervention (273).

---

[1] Conran to Cardwell (8 March, 1866), C.O.96/70.
[2] T. B. Freeman made treaties with Akwamu (28 August) and Anlo (14 November) in 1867, but Sir A. E. Kennedy had to make another treaty with Anlo in November 1868.   It too did not last.

319

259 Convention between Her Majesty and the King of the Netherlands, for an exchange of Territory on the Gold Coast of Africa.

Signed at London, 5 March, 1867. [Ratifications exchanged at London, 5 July, 1867.]

Her Majesty the Queen of the United Kingdom of Great Britain and Ireland, and His Majesty the King of the Netherlands, being of opinion that an interchange of territory on the West Coast of Africa would conduce to their mutual advantage, and would promote the interests of the inhabitants, have resolved to conclude a Convention for that purpose, and have therefore named as their Plenipotentiaries . . . [the Earl of Carnarvon and Lord Stanley; and Baron Bentinck and M. C. J. M. Nagtglas] who . . . have agreed upon the following articles:—

Article I.

Her Britannic Majesty cedes to His Majesty the King of the Netherlands, all British forts, possessions, and rights of sovereignty or jurisdiction, which she possesses on the Gold Coast, to the westward of the mouth of the Sweet River, where their respective territories are conterminous; and His Majesty the King of the Netherlands, cedes to Her Britannic Majesty, all Netherlands forts, possessions, and rights of sovereignty or jurisdiction, which he possesses on the Gold Coast, to the eastward of the mouth of the Sweet River. . . .

The boundary between the possessions of Her Britannic Majesty and those of His Majesty the King of the Netherlands, will be a line drawn true north from the centre of the mouth of the Sweet River, as far as the boundary of the present Ashantee Kingdom, but with such deviations within three English miles of the coast, as shall be necessary to retain within British territory, any villages which have been in habitual dependence on the British Government at Cape Coast, and within Netherlands territory, any villages which have been in habitual dependence on the Netherlands Government at St. George d'Elmina.

Article II.

The two High Contracting Parties agree that the following Tariff of duties of Customs shall be enforced in their respective Possessions upon the Gold Coast [see Table below]:

Article III.

In order to prevent frauds in the importation of goods, the High Contracting Parties engage to empower the officers of their respective Customs on the Gold Coast, to require the masters of vessels, to make declarations of the nature, quantity and value of any goods which they may be allowed to land.

If the officers shall be of opinion that the value so to be declared is insufficient, they shall be at liberty to take the goods on public account, on paying to the importer the amount of his valuation, with the addition of ten per cent thereon, and returning any duty which may have been already paid.

Article IV.

The Tariff of Customs duties, specified in Article II, shall be put into operation from and after a day to be agreed upon[1] between the two Governments, and shall remain in force for a period of ten years; and further, until the expiration of twelve months after either of the two Contracting Parties shall have given notice to the other of its desire for a revision or termination thereof.

[1] 1 January, 1868.

	British Possessions	Netherlands Possessions
Ale, beer, wine and all spirits or spirituous liquors	Sixpence per old wine gallon	Eight cents per litre
Cigars, snuff or tobacco in any shape	One penny per pound	Ten cents per kilogramme
Gunpowder	do. do.	do. do.
Firearms of every description	Each one shilling	Each sixty cents.

Article V.

The Tariff of Customs duties may be enforced or relaxed by the local authorities, at their own discretion, or according to the orders of their respective Governments, in respect of articles imported for the use of those authorities, or for the personal use and consumption of officers in the actual service of the Government.

Article VI.

The mutual transfer of forts, possessions, and rights of sovereignty, or jurisdiction, stipulated in Article I of the present Convention, is dependent upon and subject to the establishment of the proposed Tariff, and shall not take effect until the Government of each country shall have procured the enactment of any Laws or Regulations necessary in order to establish that Tariff for the term and under the conditions hereinbefore described, and shall have actually put the same into operation.

Article VII.

After the transfer alluded to in the foregoing Article shall have been made, a map shall be drawn of the new boundary division according to the terms of Article I. Two copies of the said map, duly attested by the Governments of either side, shall then be appended to this Convention, for the purpose of showing the boundary, which shall undergo no alteration, even should any of the villages mentioned at the end of Article I be subsequently abandoned, or the Tariff be modified or withdrawn.

Article VIII.

The present Convention, after receiving, so far as may be necessary, the approval of the legitimate authority, shall be ratified, and the ratifications shall be exchanged at London within a period of four months, or sooner if possible. . . .

[H.C.3900, A & P (1867) lxxiv]

260 H. T. Ussher to Major S. W. Blackall   Accra, 9 March, 1867.

Confidential.

Sir,

I have the honour to report to your Excellency that the detachment under Lieutenant Phelps, 2nd W.I. Regiment, consisting of 25 men, reached Addah in safety, having been conveyed thither in Her Majesty's Ship 'Dart', Commander Lowther, R.N.

The reports I have received, directly and indirectly, from Addah, confirm me in my supposition that this step has been attended with excellent results. An impression had gone forth that Her Majesty's Government intended to remain perfectly passive, under any circumstances but those of a direct attack upon the Forts upon the Gold Coast.

I have every reason to believe that the Ashantees have given up their ideas of intriguing in the trans-Volta district. A serious defeat sustained by John Tay, chief of Jellah Coffee, at the hands of the Agotims (a tribe friendly to us, although not under our protection), had doubtless contributed to this result.

At the same time, I cannot conceal from Your Excellency, that a very great depression exists in the Eastern Districts, on account of the total stoppage of trade. A demonstration on the part of Her Majesty's Navy on the seaboard from the Volta to Jellah Coffee, cannot fail to exact from the Ahunas an engagement to enter into peaceful relations, and perhaps, if made in a determined manner, may result in compensation to the anxious traders under our protection, who have been insulted, plundered, and maltreated by these people. It is also of the utmost importance that the impression should be removed from the minds of the Ahunas that they will be tacitly supported in their aggressions by Her Majesty's vessels of war in the Bights. That this impression exists there can be no doubt; and at present, the curious spectacle is presented, of Her Majesty's Navy being on friendly and intimate terms with the leaders of the movement against British influence and supremacy.[1]

I am also of opinion that Geraldo, the notorious slave dealer, and the ring-leader in the whole of these troubles, can easily be captured, and that too with the neutrality of the Ahunas. . . .[2]

Reports are rife respecting a contemplated invasion by the Ashantees, of our territory, this year. In support of this, I beg to enclose Governor Van Idsinga's confidential communication to Colonel Conran, on the subject. The king of Ashantee is doubtless bent upon capturing Gaynin and Adjeman, chief of Akim, if possible; and I am in duty bound to confess that the constant disgraceful conduct of this latter chief is of such a nature that we shall never be on friendly terms with Ashantee until he is removed. I am writing to his fellow chief Attah, on the subject of the barbarities practised on unoffending Ashantees by Adjaman, and, if necessary, will concert measures with Attah for his removal to Cape Coast.

A large trade has however been doing with Ashantee during the last fortnight, through the medium of the Assins. About 400 of these people have come down to purchase brass rods and other articles of peaceful commerce; and many are still in town. The behaviour of the Assins contrasts favourably with the turbulence and bad feeling of Adjaman and his adherents.

I have &c.   [C.O.96/74]

[1] The navy at this time drew supplies from Jellah Coffee (Dzelukofe).
[2] Geraldo, freed slave of Cesar Cerquira Lema, a Brazilian slaver, took over his master's name, property and wife, at his death in 1862. In 1865, having been driven out of Adah for grossly ill-treating one of their chiefs, he persuaded the Anlo to take up his quarrel with that town. After keeping the Volta lands in a state of confusion for over twenty years, he eventually died at Keta, from injuries received when he tripped over a small child.

261 H. T. Ussher to Sir A. Kennedy[1]
Cape Coast Castle, 19 March, 1868.

. . . The complications which have arisen between the Fantees and the Dutch become daily more alarming, and threaten to involve the Protectorate in ruin.

The Fantees appear, from their present tone towards me, inclined to throw off British allegiance. They are aided and abetted in their conduct by self-interested mulattos, who doubtless aspire eventually to the reins of government, should Great Britain abandon her position. The Council at Mankessim held lately, appears to have resulted in a series of resolutions amongst the Fantee chiefs, to support and protect themselves, regardless of British interests or protection. Their loyalty has been shaken to its foundations . . . by the provisions of the Convention of 5th March, by which, they assert, the English have sold them and their brothers to the Dutch, and subsequently, as they say, to the Ashantees.

The Apollonians, who quietly accepted Dutch protection at first, are now said to have risen to join the Denkeras and Wassaws. The feeling of the natives appears to intensify in hatred against the Dutch, and a determination appears to exist, not only to resist their assumption of authority, but to expel them, if possible, from the coast.

The measures taken by myself to endeavour to secure neutrality have been almost useless. . . . Every attempt has been made by me to dissuade the Fantees from their present course, but in vain; and as my messengers appear now to be only insulted and detained, I am resolved to remain perfectly quiet. . . .

[C.O.96/76]

[1] Sir Arthur Edward Kennedy (1810–83); served in the army, 1827–48; Governor of the Gambia (1851), Sierra Leone (1852), Western Australia (1854–62), Vancouver Island (1863); Governor-in-Chief of the West African Settlements February 1868–January 1872; Governor of Hong Kong (1872–7), and Queensland (1877–83).

262 USSHER TO KENNEDY

CAPE COAST CASTLE, 6 APRIL, 1868.

. . . The natives . . . cannot understand how a Power for so many years their ally and protector, and in whose strength and greatness they possess unbounded confidence, can, as they insist has been done, 'sell them . . . to Ashantee.' They look upon the Dutch as feudatories to Ashantee; and this opinion is unfortunately strengthened by the fact of the payment to the king at Coomassie, of a yearly tribute by the Dutch for the ground upon which Elmina stands, and also by the uniform deference and friendship exhibited by the Dutch to that great native power, the mortal and traditional enemy of the Fantee race. They also look upon the Dutch with contempt for their apparent want of power, and contrast their cautious policy with the vigorous and determined attitude so long maintained by Great Britain against Ashantee.

Finally, the association of so many years with Commendah, Denkera, Dixcove, Tchuful, Wassaw, as allies of Fantee, have raised a determination which I would scarcely have credited in these people, not to part from them, nor to permit them, did they wish, to become Dutch subjects.

But unfortunately, another and less creditable movement has been secretly at work, and threatens at this crisis entirely to undermine British influence. A small class of discontented and unprincipled natives, principally mulattos and semi-educated blacks (who appear to be an evil inseparable from all negro communities), is active in its endeavours to persuade the ignorant, impressionable, and childlike Fantees, that the time has come to govern themselves and to throw off our rule, retaining us here as advisers only. They cunningly and wilfully [mis]represent the Parliamentary Resolutions of 1865 to these people, and I can trace their evil effects too plainly in the disrespect I have received lately from the central Fantee tribes at Mankessim. . . . They undoubtedly urged the chiefs to assemble a solemn council at Mankessim, avowedly to collect money and concert measures to repel an Ashantee invasion (of which there was then no chance), but in reality to foster the great scheme of armed opposition to the provisions of the treaty of interchange. . . .

In the face of the apparent unflinching determination of the interior tribes to resist the Dutch . . . it is plain that the Netherlands Government cannot hope to retain their possessions except at a great expenditure, and by the aid of a large and disciplined force. Should the Dutch Chambers, as appears probable, be disinclined to expend further treasure on these, to them, unprofitable settlements, I presume they would be willing to dispose of them by sale. I would suggest to Her Majesty's Government the consideration of this course, with a view to their acquisition by us, as a means of solving this question. But it should first be distinctly ascertained that the chiefs of the entire Protectorate not only desire our rule, but that they are willing to enter into a formal obligation with us, to receive and respect it. . . .

An argument in favour of such a course appears to me to be the unusual activity of the French upon this coast, exhibited of late, particularly during the past year. . . . Should the Dutch resolve to sell their possessions, they would find, I fancy, a willing purchaser in France, whose acquisitions of coast-line from Assinee to Elmina would be dangerous to our influence . . . [though] it is possible that . . . the Imperial Government would prove good and faithful, and, what is better, powerful allies to us. . . .   [C.O.96/76]

263 USSHER TO KENNEDY

CAPE COAST CASTLE, 7 MAY, 1868.

. . . Since the date of my last despatch . . . Mr. T. B. Freeman has been engaged at the Fantee camp in ascertaining the real state of feeling of the chiefs, and in endeavouring to remove from their minds the erroneous impression which he found existed with regard to the policy and intentions of Her Majesty's Government . . .

that I have been intriguing to bring down Ashantee, and . . . that the British Government is quite indifferent to the fate of the tribes hitherto composing the Protectorate. . . .

If the Dutch, or rather the Elminas, would consent to an offensive and defensive alliance against Ashantee, everything would be at an end. Upon such a proceeding the Dutch Governor places his formal veto, and will not hear of any approach to such a step. . . . [This] is an insuperable obstacle to any peaceful arrangement. . . .

It is quite evident, by a reference to Colonel Conran's despatch of 6th September 1866, that he, in recommending the partition of the Protectorate, was quite ignorant of the policy of the Netherlands Government upon this coast. He assumes as a matter of course, that they would take measures for protecting the tribes against Ashantee, in concert with this Government; whereas, being tributaries of, and bound by ties of interest to that Great Power, their object has ever been to improve and foster communication with it from the coast. This great scheme would be attained by the submission of Wassaw and Denkera, who would undoubtedly be in great danger from Ashantee; but I venture to state that the Dutch will never be able to reap the benefit of the Convention, short of an armed force and continued military occupation of the districts in question. . . .   [C.O.96/76]

264 USSHER TO KENNEDY
CAPE COAST CASTLE, 7 AUGUST, 1868.
. . . In accordance with my many . . . warnings to the Fantees, they now find themselves in a precarious position; at enmity with the Dutch, on unfriendly terms with Her Majesty's Government, divided amongst themselves, and finally threatened by Ashantee. This latter hostile power has driven in the whole of Western Wassaw and is now attacking Denkera and Tchuful, all these countries being beyond the line of British protection.

The kings of Denkera and Tchuful each sent me messengers, with Ashantee jaw-bones (a sign of war), and implored my forgiveness for the past, and assistance against their enemy. I referred them to their allies, the Fantee chiefs, who had brought them to this strait, and told them that I could not help them, and that their best chance of security lay in opening friendly intercourse with the Dutch. . . .

Our position, although not satisfactory, is much simpler than heretofore. Our relations with the interior, for the present at least, have ceased; and there remains now only the supervision of our trading posts along the sea-board and the collection of our revenue, which appears to be . . . improving. . . .   [C.O.96/77]

265 H. T. USSHER TO T. F. ELLIOT
BOULOGNE, 7 NOVEMBER, 1868.
Sir,

From private sources I learn that the king of Ashantee has sent messengers to the Acting-Administrator of the Gold Coast, laying down certain terms, the compliance with which will alone cause him to forego his intention of immediate invasion.

As his terms are not at all likely to be complied with by the disordered and divided assembly calling itself the Council of the Fantee Nation, I think it right to remind you, in case you should not know it, that I have on many occasions of unprovoked outrage on Ashantee by the Fantees, as well as during their suicidal attack upon the Dutch, the friends and almost the allies of Ashantee, warned them most solemnly of the extreme danger they were incurring, of hostile invasion from Ashantee.

I have also informed them most emphatically, that in cases where the hostilities of Ashantee would be provoked by them, the Fantees, Her Majesty's Government would neither support nor countenance them in their difficulties, actively or morally.

The events I anticipated appearing likely to be fulfilled, I have thought it my duty to inform the Duke of Buckingham and Chandos of the repeated warnings the

Fantees have received, and to express my opinion that the Ashantees have received insults and provocation from the Fantees, generally under the pretext of avoiding the chance of invasion; accomplishing this desirable object by stopping inoffensive traders 'en masse', and by detaining and robbing ambassadors from the Ashantee king to myself and Colonel Boers, and despoiling them of their despatches.

At the same time, the king of Ashantee, although always reassured by me, in my correspondence with him, that the British Government did not countenance, and would not support such acts on the part of Fantee, does not cease to regard the local Government as responsible for these acts in a measure, and can scarcely understand or believe in the alteration of our policy, as regards military aid and alliance with Fantee, since 1863–4. . . .

It is therefore of course to be anticipated that the forces of the king, in case his projected attack be carried out, will be directed eventually against Cape Coast and Accra, as the strongholds of the Fantee coalition; and it will, in my opinion, be difficult, if not impossible, to avoid coming into collision with the king, unless, by careful diplomacy, this monarch may be made to understand and respect our position upon the coast. . . .   [C.O.96/78]

266 W. H. SIMPSON[1] TO SIR A. E. KENNEDY
ACCRA, 5 DECEMBER, 1868.

[Messengers had been sent to invite the interior chiefs to a conference on the affairs of the Protectorate, to be held at Cape Coast in January.] . . .

I conveyed through these messengers my intention to consider on that occasion, the general state and affairs of the Protectorate, with the view more especially of openly recognizing and supporting the council of the kings assembled at Mankessim; of substituting thereat the authority and influence of the Administrator, for the interested

[1] Collector of Customs; Acting Administrator, August 1868 to November 1869.

services and pernicious interference of the 'scholars' or semi-educated natives, hitherto in uncontrolled ascendancy; and of devising (if feasible) some simple scheme, consistent with the prerogatives of the Crown, whereby a union for self-defence may be practically effected between the different nations within the Protectorate, and the first step to be taken by them, under the guidance and instruction of the British Government, for testing their fitness to approximate in any way towards self-government.

I am aware Sir, of the difficulty and delicacy of the task proposed, but if I have rightly understood as well the temper of these people and times, as the policy of the Home Government, an attempt at political advancement will be made within these Settlements. That it should be anticipated, therefore, by the executive, and its course controlled at the very outset, has appeared to me to be within the strict limits of the responsibilities and duties of my position. . . .   [C.O.96/77]

267 SIMPSON TO KENNEDY
CAPE COAST CASTLE, 5 MAY, 1869.

[As the chiefs declined his offer of a conference at Cape Coast, he visited them at Mankessim.] . . .

Judging from all that I have seen and heard during my expedition, I have but little faith in any permanently good results arising from the Council, in the matter . . . of self-government. So long as an exciting cause exists, like the Elmina question and the threatening attitude of Ashantee, there may, and I think will be an increased cohesion among the members of it: but so soon as that ceases, and the kings individually experience a diminution of their power through the Council, it will die a natural death.

Self-government, in the sense understood by civilized nations, is impossible so long as slavery exists, and as the kings and chiefs derive their power from that institution, they will undoubtedly maintain it to the death. There is, moreover, no class here, whether native or foreign, educated or not, capable, or sufficiently honest if capable, of giving any aid whatever to help forward an advance in civilization amongst the lower orders; and these latter, if they were emancipated tomorrow, would either starve or sell themselves again as slaves to their old masters.

I have therefore, while humouring those who believe that the regeneration and independence of their country is at hand, never lost sight of the necessity, which I believe to exist, that so long as the British Government is represented at all, it must be paramount and take the lead in the direction of the native national affairs. It cannot throw off its responsibilities at a moment's notice, although an incurrence of the former heavy military expenditure in defence of the Protectorate would certainly be a reckless waste of money, and wholly undesired and unlooked for by the natives. Should the Government be withdrawn, human sacrifices would recommence in Cape Coast within a week, and the country return to a state of utter barbarism and ruin. This result has followed even the partial disruption of relations with the Fantees in the interior, and I have now some three or four cases of brutal murder arising from fetishism, which demand my earliest attention and the infliction of a prompt and summary punishment. One undoubted immediate and direct benefit has however been gained by the meeting, viz. the re-establishment of the influence of the Government over the whole of the western division of the Protectorate. . . .

[C.O.96/80, H.C.171, A & P (1873) xlix]

268 EARL GRANVILLE[1] TO SIR A. E. KENNEDY   LONDON, 17 MAY, 1869.
. . . In my despatch of the 10th instant, I stated that I should address you more fully

[1] Granville George Leveson-Gower, 2nd Earl Granville (1815–91); Liberal M.P., 1837–55 and then Leader in the House of Lords; Secretary of State for the Colonies, December 1868 to July 1870, and February to August 1886; Foreign Secretary, 1870–4 and 1880–5.

on the subject of your despatches of 14th and 16th April last, respecting the relations between the Government of the Gold Coast and the neighbouring African tribes.

Although the apprehensions suggested by the first of these despatches are in some degree qualified by the intelligence, or rather the absence of intelligence, reported in the second, it is plain that the affairs of the Gold Coast are in an exceedingly anxious, and I must add, unsatisfactory state.

You cannot be unaware that the recent war with the Ashantees was a subject of great regret to Her Majesty's Government, that the recurrence of such a war would be viewed as a great calamity, and that the renewed employment in it of British troops, including, of course, the West India regiments, would be wholly contrary to the policy of this country.

These considerations impose on yourself and the Administrator, the necessity of great caution in holding out expectations to the friendly tribes beyond what you will be able to fulfil, and of great forbearance in dealing with an unfriendly nation, against whom you can prosecute no effectual hostilities.

It is under these circumstances that the events described by Mr. Simpson have occurred.

You have elsewhere reported to me that the Fantees . . . have adopted certain hostile proceedings against the Elminas, a portion of their own tribe under the control of the Dutch, almost on the express ground that they are allied with the king of Ashantee, with whom the British Government is, and desires to remain at peace. The Government of the Gold Coast has attempted to appease this quarrel, and to a certain extent has succeeded in doing so, but in a manner not unlikely to give umbrage to the Ashantees.

With this cause of discontent already in existence, a quarrel has broken out between certain tribes in the neighbourhood of the Volta, at some distance from our principal settlements. Over some of these tribes, who are on the other side of the river, we have never hitherto affected to exercise any influence. If we now claim to exercise any, it is in consequence of the former cession by Denmark of their settlements in that neighbourhood.

You had yourself visited these tribes, and had persuaded them to sign a treaty which, I [re]collect, they disregarded as soon as you had left the river. Mr. Simpson, if I rightly understand what has passed, appears to have considered himself bound, or at liberty, to follow up what he supposed to be your policy, by proceeding to the scene of the dispute and endeavouring to repeat or supplement your work. He found that the Ashantees had been beforehand with him, and that the tribes whom he had hoped to persuade were inaccessible to argument. They detained him for some days by something like force, and he hardly escaped from their hands.

It is plain that he had adopted a very hazardous course, without a clear apprehension of the state of the facts, or a just calculation of his own power; a serious error in an officer occupying so responsible a position. Such a step, if it did not succeed in averting hostilities, was obviously calculated to precipitate them. To meet that probability, Mr Simpson had recourse to menace on the one hand and offers of protection on the other. I select some passages from his letters.

To the king of Ashantee he writes, that if his troops should attack the Crepees, [Krepis] he, Mr. Simpson, will 'lend every assistance, moral and physical, to the Crepees in the defence of their country and independence.' He states that the tribes about the Volta acknowledge the British title by purchase, and that the soil itself of these countries is British soil, and that, although the British Government do not adopt this view, they will not acquiesce in the occupation of that part of the banks of the river by a foreign power, and that the control of Great Britain over those parts has revived and will not be suffered to abate.

He adds that if the Ashantees will withdraw from Aquamoo [Akwamu], he will guarantee the Aquamoos against attack by the Crepees, or a chief called Domfrey [Dompre], who is acting at present in favour of the Creppes, and is accused of various outrages on ambassadors.

The substance of these messages, Mr Simpson communicated to the king of Akim, encouraging him to hope that he will have the co-operation and assistance of the British Government in giving the Ashantees 'such a lesson as will conclude at once and for ever, the constant and unreasonable dread with which that power has been hitherto regarded.'

He informs the king of Ahwoolah [Awuna] that his orders are peremptory to secure peace and the freedom of the river; that if the Crepees are attacked they will have as allies the Protectorate and the British Government, and that he will render them assistance in every way possible, in money, men, and munitions of war.

He writes to a chief in arms called Domfrey, promising assistance in case of an attack on him, and he informs a king, apparently of doubtful friendliness, that if his loyalty is made clear he shall be first king of Crepee, but that if he assists the enemy, just measures of retribution will be taken against him, adding that the Ashantees, if they made an attack on the Crepees, 'will have to fight the British Government as their allies.'

I have quoted these passages at length in order to make the effect of what Mr Simpson has done, perfectly clear. That effect is, as matters now stand, to make the British Government not a neutral, nor even an ally, but a principal in the quarrel or complication of quarrels which are arising between the kingdom of Ashantee and the neighbouring tribes, so that the defeat or ill-success of those tribes, is the defeat or ill-success of the British Government, and that their destruction, from default of adequate assistance, will be chargeable on the British Government if it have authorised, or should adopt, the acts of its officers; or on that officer personally if his proceedings are not so authorised or approved.

The statement I have made will, I think, convince you that Her Majesty's Government have never authorised, so that they are not at liberty to confirm the threats or promises to which Mr Simpson has resorted.

The announcements which I have selected from his letters, so far as they are addressed to allies, must be effectually recalled; and those allies must be made clearly to understand that although the British Government, so long as they conduct themselves satisfactorily, may be ready to give them some assistance in the way of arms, ammunition, and money, yet the wars in which they engage are their wars, and not the wars of this country; that they must rely on themselves for success in those wars, and that the British Government is unable to make itself responsible for their defence in case they should prove unable to defend themselves. . . .

If, unhappily, war shall have broken out, it is impossible for me to foresee that state of things which may exist when this despatch reaches you, or to measure the obligations which the steps taken by Mr Simpson may have imposed on the British Government.

I can only say that by the opening or stoppage of trade, by advice and countenance, by the supply of arms, stores, or money, any reasonable assistance should be given to those who will have embarked in a very perilous war in reliance on pledges given by a British officer. But in giving this assistance, they should, if possible, be made clearly to understand that this is all they have to expect; that Mr Simpson's promises, so far as they go beyond this, are not confirmed by Her Majesty's Government; that British troops cannot be employed in their aid; and that their safety must depend upon their own exertions.

[C.O. 96/79, H.C.266, A & P (1873) xlix]

269 H. T. Ussher to Sir A. E. Kennedy
Cape Coast Castle, 2 December, 1869.
. . . Should serious complications arise [with Ashanti], which I do not anticipate,

they will be caused by the action of the so-called 'Fantee Confederacy'. This small knot of men, consisting of three or four chiefs, with a semi-educated black at their head as President, is quite powerless for good in the country. But although their orders are ridiculed by the other chiefs, their constables beaten, and their attempts at collecting revenue met with defiance, they are still supported and approved by Fantee opinion in any acts, which they may commit, hostile to Ashantee or Elmina; and it is possible that they may refuse to deliver up the Ashantees in their power. No other course would be left to me, under such circumstances, but to return the sword-bearer and crier to the king, disavowing the acts of the Fantee chiefs.

On the 30th ultimo, an Ashantee captain, captured some time ago, with 100 traders and about 200 oz. of gold, by the Assins, escaped from confinement and took refuge with me. It appears that Mr. Ghartey, the nominal President of the Confederacy, was about to inflict the cruel punishment of the log upon . . . the Ashantee chief. He is now in my charge and will be cared for with the others. He states that the 'Confederacy' is persistent in endeavouring to impress the Ashantees with the idea that Mr Ghartey, as President, is the Governor of the Gold Coast, and he stated to me that until now he had begun to share this opinion, adding, however, that the king of Ashantee would never believe that such was the case. . . .   [C.O.96/81]

270 Granville to Kennedy
London, 31 December, 1869.
. . . Her Majesty's Government were aware of the intention of the Dutch Government to take steps to establish their authority in the settlements on the Gold Coast. It will be extremely unfortunate if the Administrator takes any steps calculated to throw any suspicion on our friendly feelings towards the Dutch Government or on our desire to see them in peaceable possession of that which we have handed

over to them. And I am sorry to infer from the papers before me, that the Fantees who are expected to attack them are receiving gun-powder through Cape Coast town. If the Administrator can prevent this, he ought to do so; and particularly to take care that arms and ammunition intended for use against the Dutch are not obtained on the pretext that they are necessary [for use] against the Ashantees.

I observe in one of Mr Ussher's despatches that he apprehends reprisals 'on Fantee and consequently British territory'. Nothing is British territory but the forts and their immediate neighbourhood. And if persons who profess to be under our protection, choose without our advice or consent to attack a friendly power, or aid those who are in revolt against it, they must not expect the British Government to use its authority to shield them from the consequences. Reprisals though involving an invasion of Protectorate Territory cannot, in this case, be treated as violations of British territory.

You will take care that Mr. Ussher understands this.

I have etc.

[C.O.96/79, H.C.171, A & P (1873) xlix]

271 USSHER TO KENNEDY
ACCRA, 8 JULY, 1870.

[Reporting on an expedition to the Volta.] . . .

It would appear that the Ahunahs, as a consequence of their quarrel with Addah, aided and abetted by Geraldo, the cause of that quarrel, have from the commencement conspired with the Aquamoos, who are tributary to Accra, to bring down the Ashantees, and to invade and destroy the splendid districts of Crepee and Agotim. That their expressed intention was that when this junction should be effected and the Ashantees in full possession of the eastern bank, they . . . should proceed . . . to invade the Protected districts which would have thus been placed entirely at their mercy. . . .

It was also evident that but for the exertions of Domprey, aided by the Crepees, this event might have been expected to take place long since. With a small force of not more than 400 men, this captain held in check a large body of Ashantees, aided by the Aquamoos. But this could not last for ever, and Domprey's resources appear to have been failing, although he would not admit it on our arrival.

I also ascertained that the Ahunahs were breaking and evading the treaty entered into by them with your Excellency in 1868. . . . It does not appear that they have committed of late any direct hostilities against the Addahs themselves, it being a part of their scheme to maintain a show of inactivity . . . along the seaboard, in order thereby to retain their trade with the white man, whilst they should levy war up the river, in alliance with the bitter enemies of the Accra and Addah nations.

It must not be supposed that the king of Ahunah is really responsible himself for this. Ahunah is actually a republic; the king, as in nearly all these districts, being a very convenient scape-goat, and being obeyed or not as may suit the purpose of the real movers in the affairs, i.e. the war chiefs and fetish priests. . . .

It further appeared that the actual, and, to the native allies, insurmountable difficulty in the way of opening the river, was the island of Doffo and the town of Volo situated nearby. The inhabitants of these places, actually within the protectorate, . . . had declared against the Accras, and for five long years, a comparatively small band of these piratical rebels, aided from time to time by the presence of Aquamoos and Ashantees, have closed the river, plundering every canoe attempting to pass, and slaying or taking captive the crew; . . . their position being impregnable to any native force, however large, on account of the hopelessness of any attempt to cross the deep and rapid water surrounding their stronghold. I pass over their ill-treatment and derision of Her Majesty's Commissioner in 1867, but proceed to state that they destroyed not long since the town of Asuchary and burnt it to the ground, and that they have in addition driven the people of the latter town from their fishing grounds. . . . The Accras have not been immaculate throughout this war . . . but the heavy balance of aggression . . . lies with the Ahunas and their allies. . . .

[The Accras with the aid of Glover in the steamboat 'Eyo', reduced Dofo, and the allies were then left to continue the war. Their indiscipline may yet lead to disaster. The Anlos must also be dealt with.]

It is quite impossible that peace can exist on the seaboard and war on the river. . . . If . . . a Government steamer could be placed at once on the river, the matter is at an end. Our resources justify me in pressing the adoption of this course, which, if carried, will in due time bear remunerative fruits in the revenue of Addah. But should the river again unfortunately be neglected, the prestige of the Government be suffered to be neutralized by inaction, and the undeniable disaffection of many of the riverside towns be permitted again to take a tangible shape, matters will soon lapse into the abnormal state in which they had for so long been suffered to remain. . . .

With regard to the capabilities of the river Volta for trade, there can be no doubt about the matter. During at least four months of the year the draught of water over the shallowest parts will accomode vessels of some size: but taking it during the dry season, any steamer for river work will have to be of light draught, similar to boats employed, I am informed, on the Indian rivers, and carrying considerable cargo. The fertility of Crobboe in palm oil, and of Crepee in cotton, will in time of peace develop industry and civilization to a great extent; and the natives will naturally soon learn the advantages of water communication, as compared with a laborious process of walking immense distances with heavy burdens on their heads. There can be no doubt that the moment the fact becomes established that the river is safe, a

settlement will be formed at the Volta mouth. . . .   [C.O.96/85]

272 THE EARL OF KIMBERLEY[1] TO SIR A. E. KENNEDY

LONDON, 1 AUGUST, 1870.

[Expresses concern at the loss of life on the expedition, and at the fact that no quarter was given by our native allies.] . . .

The expedition was described by you as one of demonstration and survey, and was, of course liable to attack and bound to be prepared against it. But in this case it was intended from the beginning, with the aid of the native allies 'to open the upper river by dispersing the piratical and rebellious tribes of Doffo and Volo', as stated in Mr. Ussher's despatch.

I have to request that you will instruct the Administrators of the Gold Coast and Lagos, not to undertake in future any hostile operations against the natives without referring home for instructions, except in cases of real and urgent necessity for the protection of the British Settlements. . . .

[C.O.96/85]

273 KENNEDY TO KIMBERLEY

SIERRA LEONE, 20 SEPTEMBER, 1870.

. . . It is necessary that it should be clearly understood that the Doffos and Volos are barbarous and bloodthirsty pirates who live by plunder alone, which their commanding position in the river enabled them to carry on with comparative impunity. They have no industry of any kind, and are inferior to the Accras in all but violence and lawlessness.

The alternative lay between punishing these people, or abandonment of the river and loss of prestige. It is well to look

[1] John Wodehouse, 1st Earl of Kimberley (1826-1902); Liberal statesman; as Lord Wodehouse was Under-Secretary for Foreign Affairs, 1852-6 and 1859-61; Earl of Kimberley (Norfolk), 1866; Secretary of State for the Colonies, 1870-4 and 1880-2; Secretary of State for India, February-June 1886 and August 1892-March 1894; Foreign Secretary March 1894-June 1895.

African difficulties in the face. Firmness and promptitude in punishing evil-doers is the most merciful course in the end. No well-established act of aggression should be overlooked. If it is, other and greater outrages are sure to follow, which will render more serious hostilities unavoidable. The native African does not understand inactivity or hesitation on the part of the injured; he attributes them to fear and so becomes bolder. . . .

[C.O.96/85]

20   The Fanti federation and the cession of the Dutch forts, 1871–1872

IF the British authorities had their difficulties, they were nothing to those of the Dutch who, in spite of being reinforced during 1869, were no nearer to establishing their rule in the ceded British stations; while their control over Elmina itself was weakened by the arrival there of an Ashanti force under a peculiarly bloodthirsty leader, named Akyampon.   They decided to cut their losses and leave the coast to the British.   For their part, the British were very willing to take over the Dutch forts, if they could be sure that this would not involve them in trouble with Ashanti (275).   They secured from the Dutch an assurance that Elmina was not subject to the Asantehene (274), but required them also to secure an avowal of this from Kumasi, before they would ratify the treaty of cession.   Accordingly Kwesi Plange went to Kumasi and brought back the renunciation asked for, and though the validity of this document was not above suspicion, the forts were duly taken over by the British in April 1872.[1]   The greatest single cause of disturbance in the Protectorate was thereby removed.

Disastrous as the exchange project had proved politically, even in 1868 it had been justified financially by a substantial increase in the revenue, as a result of the new customs duties it imposed.   Thenceforward, as their resources increased so did the confidence of the British authorities, and by 1871 they were thinking seriously about re-establishing their influence in the Protectorate at large (276–7).

At this inauspicious moment a small group of Fantis at Mankessim announced their intention of making good the short-comings of the British by promoting economic and educational progress in the Protectorate (278), at the same time promulgating a constitution for the government of the inland districts (279).   The acting-administrator promptly arrested the leaders (280) but the Colonial Office disavowed his action, while insisting that it would have to be consulted before it gave its support to any projects of reform (281).   The real strength of the movement seems always to have been a good deal less than it claimed (282), and after the British had taken over Elmina, its position was weaker still.   This much is apparent in the very different tactics employed in April 1872, when the spokesmen of the Federation asked for British financial support for their government (285).   With the Elmina question out of the way, the chiefs generally hoped for a re-affirmation of British influence, and not even Pope-Hennessy, whose extreme readiness to reverse any pre-existing policy left a trail of confusion across the Colonial Empire from Freetown to Sarawak, thought it wise to accept the federation at its own valuation (286).

[1] This is the usually accepted (and official Colonial Office) version of the sequence of events: but cf D. S. Coombs, *The place of the Certificate of Apologie in Ghanaian History* (Trans. Hist. Soc. of Ghana iii, p. 182) where it is pointed out that the British Government apparently declared themselves satisfied about the Dutch title to Elmina in March 1871, i.e. before Plange went to Kumasi.   It is certainly the case that little or no notice was paid to the Apology in the Colonial Office when it finally found its way there, which seemed to the present editor a sufficient reason for omitting it from this collection.   Plange's mission, in Dr. Coombs' view originated with the Governor of Elmina, Nagtglas, not with the Dutch Government which, understandably, declined the invidious task of asking for a certificate of its own credentials from the ruler of Ashanti.   Dr. Coombs also gives strong grounds for believing that any dissimulation connected with the Document emanated from the Asantehene rather than from Plange. The Apology is printed in Crooks, *op. cit.*, p. 400.

274 C. T. M. NAGTGLAS TO H. T.
USSHER   ELMINA, 20 DECEMBER, 1870.

. . . The Netherlands Government pays a yearly stipend to the king of Ashantee of 20 ounces or fl.960, £80.

Why? In 1791 the West India Company which was the owner of the forts paid that amount to the king of Ashantee. When the forts &c went over to the Crown, the Government was bound to maintain the payment, which has been done hitherto.

Tradition says that in former times, 150 years ago, the West Indian Company paid the chief [of] Dinkirah 20 ounces of gold to encourage the trade for slaves, gold dust and ivory; that the king of Ashantee conquered Dinkirahs, and that also the pay note came into his hands. So he asked the king to pay him, as he was now in possession of the note, to which request the Company agreed to save some troubles.

The king of Ashantee has no recognised claim upon the territory or people of Elmina. . . .

[C.670, A & P (1872) lxx]

275 COLONIAL OFFICE TO FOREIGN
OFFICE   LONDON, 3 FEBRUARY, 1871.
Sir,

With reference to former correspondence on the subject of the transfer of the Dutch Possessions on the Gold Coast to Great Britain, I am directed by the Earl of Kimberley to transmit to you for the consideration of Earl Granville, copies of despatches . . . from the Governor in Chief of the West African Settlements, on several matters which require the attention of Her Majesty's Government.

His Lordship will perceive that the king of Ashantee claims Elmina as his own by right,[1] and it is admitted that an annual payment of about £80 (which he represents as tribute) has long been paid him. . . . Although it would be impossible for Her

[1] Cf. letter of the Asantehene to Ussher, 24 November, 1870 (printed *ibid.* and in Crooks, *op. cit.*, pp. 388–9) in which he hopes that Elmina will not be included in the impending exchange 'for it is mine by right'.

Majesty's Government to sanction the annual payment to the king of Ashantee of £80, which the Dutch Government have paid to him, if it is to be considered as an acknowledgement of any political superiority or territorial ownership, there is no reason why it should not be paid him by the Government of the Gold Coast, as an inducement to maintain peace and encourage trade, and continued to him so long as he acted properly toward the British Government and the tribes under our protection.

Lord Kimberley, however, considers it necessary, before proceeding further with the Convention, that the Dutch Government should procure, by such means as they think fit, the renunciation of the claim of the king of Ashantee to Elmina, else this Government may find itself involved in a war with the Ashantees.

Colonel Nagtglas remarks, in his statement on the subject, that he can readily understand that the king of Ashantee will be very much annoyed by the transfer of the Dutch possessions, as he will lose the free intercourse not only with Elmina, but with the people on the seaside from Assinee to the Volta.

Lord Kimberley does not see what is to prevent the Ashantees from having a continued free intercourse with Elmina, nor how the transfer can affect their present position with respect to access to the seaside: but his Lordship has no doubt that it would be a happy circumstance if the Ashantees could have direct access to the sea for purposes of trade, and he would readily instruct our Authorities on the coast, not only to offer no obstruction to such a movement, if conducted by peaceful means and under safe conditions, but to facilitate it as far as lies in our power.

The documents transmitted by Sir A. Kennedy prove the absolute necessity that the Dutch Government should, before the completion of the transfer, remove the Ashantee chief Atjiampon and his followers from the Elmina country. That chief was present at the meeting held at Elmina to consider certain proposals which the Administrator of the Gold Coast had authorized Mr. Bartels to submit to the king and chiefs, for establishing peace between the Elminas and the Fantees, in anticipation of the transfer, and on that occasion Atjiampon told the meeting that Mr. Bartels had said what did not please the Elmina people, adding 'We don't want the English flag and will not have it.' . . .

It would likewise appear . . . that [Colonel Nagtglas] has not received instructions to prepare the people for the transfer, or at any rate, that he has not understood his instructions in the same way as the British Authorities have understood the corresponding instructions addressed to them, and Lord Kimberley would recommend that this should be pointed out to the Dutch Government.

The promise made by Mr Bartels at the meeting, that violence on the part of the Fantees should be put down if necessary with a high hand and by force, was not justified by the instructions conveyed to the Administrator, who will be informed that such an improper promise must not be repeated, and that steps must be taken to disengage Her Majesty's Government from any liabilities attaching to it.

[C.670 of 1872]

276 USSHER TO KENNEDY

ACCRA, 6 MARCH, 1871.

. . . With regard to the definition of purely British territory and of territory supposed to come under British protection, I should not recommend that any territory should be declared to be purely British beyond the actual limits of the forts. The acquisition of any additional land as territory, even short of the absolute annexation of the entire Protectorate, would necessitate the immediate abolition of domestic slavery within that acquired territory, and might induce grave complications with the natives: whilst the action of the law, as it at present stands, would be crippled by the anomaly of the Chief Magistrate exercising the func-

tions of a Judicial Assessor to native chiefs, and dealing with native questions according to an undefined mixture of British and native law, within the limits of territory absolutely declared to be British and where native law would be null and void. The present assumption that every act done by Her Majesty's Government on the Gold Coast, is in the name of, and by and with the consent of the natives, is, in my opinion, at least, sufficient for all practical purposes.

As regards the definition of British jurisdiction, there can be little doubt that, if the Volta is to be utilized, and this distracted border or debateable land to be converted into a prosperous trading country, the sea coast . . . to three miles beyond the old fort of Quittah should be reoccupied [to prevent smuggling.] . . .

Our jurisdiction in the interior districts must, I apprehend, remain as it is. And it will diminish or increase according to the firmness or otherwise with which the local Government is enabled to deal with the native chiefs. In 1866 and 1867, in fact up to 1869, our orders were not respected in the interior, and great lawlessness prevailed: but from the gradual cessation of active hostilities, and from the increased power of the local Government (derived from its improved revenue) that lawlessness is rapidly diminishing. Of late, I have brought down and punished chiefs from the interior, who have for many years set the Government at defiance.

The actual assumed jurisdiction of the protected districts should, I apprehend, be (after the cession of the Dutch Settlements) from Apollonia in the windward or western districts, to Quittah [Keta] on the Ahuna coast. The interior jurisdiction in a northerly direction would be generally asserted with more or less effect up to the boundaries of Ashantee; with the exception of the territory between the river Volta and Quittah, where I should only recommend that a strip or tongue of land bounded on the north by the Ahuna 'Songo' or lagoon, should be declared within British jurisdiction. The more northerly trans-Volta districts of Krepee and Aquamoo, the latter not well disposed to the British, will be effectually neutral or rather friendly, as soon as a steamer makes her appearance on the river. . . .   [C.O.96/87]

277 KENNEDY TO KIMBERLEY
SIERRA LEONE, 8 NOVEMBER, 1871.

My Lord,

I have had the subject of stipending the native chiefs . . . of the Gold Coast Protectorate under my consideration for the last year,[1] and I feel convinced that as a measure alike of economy and justice, it ought to be done at once.

My experience of the system of giving stipends to native chiefs surrounding this settlement has proved [it] beyond doubt to be the cheapest and most effectual mode of keeping peace and keeping roads open for commerce. I can now send a single person armed with authority three or four hundred miles into the interior, with perfect safety. Any message of this Government is respected and protected by the native chiefs through whose territory they may pass.

The same system on the Gold Coast would prove economical, because presents must be and are given under existing circumstances, and this system of 'dashes' is nearly as expensive and not at all as effective as a permanent stipend of equal value. Fifty or one hundred pounds paid to a native chief would go further in maintaining peace and order throughout the country than ten times the amount expended on the police. Indeed, law and order cannot be maintained for long on this coast by other than moral control. The very fact of bringing the chiefs or their messengers face to face with the Queen's representatives, once or twice a year, to receive their stipends, would have the best moral effect.

It must be remembered that, the slave trade at an end, the chiefs and kings in the interior have no means of living or supporting their barbarous dignity save by contributions, either voluntary or forced, from their own people and traders passing through their country. Nothing can be more obstructive, or indeed, destructive of trade than this levying of toll. A condition of the stipend should be to keep the roads 'open' or free.

Day by day, the kings and chiefs become more enlightened, and several have said to me, with great truth, 'The Government takes all the money, and we never taste any.' It is the worst possible policy to lower or 'belittle' native kings or chiefs in the estimation of their dependents. They can at a small cost be made the best and cheapest supporters of law and order. . . . I feel perfectly confident that if a sum of about £500 a year were paid in the Cape Coast or Western district and a like sum in the Accra or Eastern district, we should never have any difficulty in getting the kings and chiefs to do the bidding of the Government. . . .[1]   [C.O.96/89]

278 QUASSIE [KWASI] EDOO AND OTHERS TO SIR A. E. KENNEDY
MANKESSIM, 24 NOVEMBER, 1871.

Sir,

We, the kings and chiefs and others assembled at Mankessim, beg most respectfully to forward you the enclosed copy of a Constitution framed and passed by us after mature deliberation.

We have united together for the express purpose of furthering the interests of our country.

In the Constitution it will be observed that we contemplate means for the social improvement of our subjects and people, the growth of education and industrial pursuits, and, in short, every good which British philanthropy may have designed for the good of the Gold Coast, but which we think it impossible for it at present to do for the country at large.

---

[1] He raised it in a despatch to Kimberley of 10 October, 1870.

M

[1] Kimberley minuted (3 December, 1871) — 'I quite agree.'

Our sole object is to improve the condition of our peoples, not to interfere with, but to aid our benefactors on the sea coast, and we count upon your Excellency giving us at times that assistance which may be necessary to carry out our humble efforts.

We beg to forward a copy of the Constitution . . . for the information of the Right Honourable the Secretary of State for the Colonies.

(Signed) Quassie Edoo   (his X mark)
   Anfoo Otoo   (his X mark)
    Kings President . . .

   Qow Yanfoo   (his X mark)
   king of Ayan.

Thomas Solomon (his X mark)
chief of Dominassie.

W. E. Davidson, Vice-President.

J. F. Amissah,   Secretary.

For the kings and chiefs assembled at Mankessim and all the members of the Confederation.   [H.C.171 of 1873. Papers relating to the Fanti Confederation]

279 Constitution of the New Fante Confederacy.

To all whom it may concern.

Whereas we, the undersigned kings and chiefs of Fanti, have taken into consideration the deplorable state of our peoples and subjects in the interior of the Gold Coast, and whereas we are of opinion that unity and concord among ourselves would conduce to our mutual well-being, and promote and advance the social and political condition of our peoples and subjects, who are in a state of degredation, without the means of education and of carrying on proper industry; we, the said kings and chiefs, after having fully discussed and considered the subject at meetings held at Mankessim on the 16th day of October last and following days, have unanimously resolved and agreed upon the articles hereinafter named.

Article 1. That we, the kings and chiefs of Fanti here present, form ourselves into a committee with the view of effecting unity of purpose and of action between the kings and chiefs of the Fanti territory.

2. That we, the kings and chiefs here assembled, now form ourselves into a compact body for the purpose of more effectually bringing about certain improvements (hereinafter to be considered) in the country.

3. That this compact body shall be recognised under the title and designation of the 'Fanti Confederation'.

4. That there shall be elected a president, vice-president, secretary, under-secretary, treasurer and assistant-treasurer.

5. That the president be elected from the body of kings, and be proclaimed king-president of the Fanti Confederation.

6. That the vice-president, secretary and under-secretary, treasurer and assistant-treasurer, who shall constitute the ministry, be men of education and position.

7. That it be competent to the Fanti Confederation thus constituted to receive into its body politic any other king or kings, chief or chiefs, who may not now be present.

8. That it be the object of the Confederation:

 i. To promote friendly intercourse between all the kings and chiefs of Fanti, and to unite them for offensive and defensive purposes against their common enemy.

 ii. To direct the labours of the Confederation towards the improvement of the country at large.

 iii. To make good and substantial roads throughout all the interior districts included in the Confederation.

 iv. To erect school-houses and establish schools for the education of all children within the Confederation, and to obtain the service of efficient schoolmasters.

 v. To promote agricultural and industrial pursuits, and to endeavour to introduce such new plants as may hereafter become sources of profitable commerce to the country.

vi. To develop and facilitate the working of the mineral and other resources of the country.

9. That an executive council be formed, composed of [the ministry] . . . who shall be ex-officio members thereof, together with such others as may be hereafter from time to time appointed.

10. That in order that the business of the Confederation be properly carried on during the course of the year, each king and principal chief shall appoint two representatives, one educated, the other a chief or headman of the district of such king and principal chief, who shall attend the meetings which the secretary may deem necessary to convene for the deliberation of state matters.

11. That the representatives of the kings and chiefs assembled in council shall be known under the designation of the 'Representative Assembly of the Fanti Confederation' and that this assembly be called together by the secretary as state exigency may require.

12. That this representative assembly shall have the power . . . of exercising all the functions of a legislative body.

13. That the representatives of each king and chief be responsible to the nation for the effectual carrying out of the bills, resolutions &c passed at such meetings and approved of by the king-president. . . .

15. That the National Assembly shall appoint an educated man to represent the king-president, and act as vice-president of the Confederation; and that the vice-president shall preside over all meetings convened by the secretary.

16. That there shall be in the month of October of each year, a gathering of the kings, principal chiefs, and others within the Confederation, when a recapitulation of the business done by the Representative Assembly shall be read, and the programme of the ensuing year discussed.

17. That at such meetings the king-president shall preside, and that it be the duty of the king-president to sanction all laws &c passed by the Representative Assembly, so far as they are compatible with the interests of the country.

18. That the king-president shall not have the power to pass any, or originate any laws . . . &c nor create any office or appointment, excepting by and under the advice of the ministry.

19. That the representatives of the kings and principal chiefs hold office as members of the Representative Assembly for three years, at the expiration of which it shall be competent for the kings and chiefs to re-elect the same or appoint other representatives.

20. That the members of the Ministry and Executive Council hold office for three years, and that it be competent to the National Assembly to re-elect all or any of them and appoint others. . . .

[Articles 21–27. Details of school and road-building programme.]

28. That a site or town, unanimously agreed upon, be chosen as the nominal capital of the Confederation, where the principal business of the State should be conducted.

29. That provincial assessors be appointed in each province or district, who shall perform certain judicial functions and attend to the internal management thereof. . . .

[Articles 30–33. Duties of Secretary and Treasurer.]

34. That it be the duty of the under-secretary . . .

To hear and determine, with an assistant appointed by the Secretary, cases which may be brought from the provincial courts.

To arrange important appeal cases for the hearing of the Executive Council, which shall constitute the final court of appeal of the Confederation. . . .

[Articles 35–6. Duties of assistant-treasurer and provincial assessors.]

37. That in each province or district, provincial courts be established to be presided over by the provincial assessors.

38. That it be the duty of the Ministry and Executive Council:

To advise the King-President in all state matters. . . .

To hear, try and determine all important appeal cases brought before it by the under-secretary, option being allowed to any party or parties dissatisfied with the decision thereof to appeal to the British Courts. . . .

39. That three of the 'ex-officio' members of the Executive Council, or two ex-officio and two non-official members of the Executive Council shall form a quorum of said Council. . . .

40. That one-third of the members composing the Representative Assembly shall form a quorum.

41. That all laws . . . &c be carried by the majority of votes in the Representative Assembly or Executive Council, in the latter the Vice-President possessing a casting vote.

42. That it be the duty of the National Assembly, held in October of each year . . .

To elect from the body of kings the President for the ensuing year. . . .

To consider all programmes laid before it by the Executive Council. . . .

To place on the 'stool' in cases of disputed succession thereto, the person elected by the Executive Council, with the concurrence of the principal inhabitants of the town, croom or district.

43. That the officers of the Confederation shall render assistance as directed by the executive in carrying out the wishes of the British Government. . . .[1]

[H.C.171 of 1873]

[1] The list of adherents is given as consisting of the chiefs of Mankessim, Abrah [Abura], Ayan [Anyan], Coomendah [Komenda], Edjumacoo [Ajumako], Incoosoocoom [Nkusukum], Assin, Dominassie [Dominasi], Donnassie [Odonasi?], Saltpond, Tuarcoh [Tuakwa?], Abrarsempah [Abakrampa], Batdazah [?], Quarman [Kwamang], Aduddzi [?], Trupessedardir [Mpesedadi?], Bookah [?], Adoomanoo [?], Ampinafoo [Apimanim?], Abbankrome [Obakrom?], Acrofome [Akrofuom?], Arnum [?], Abiror [?], Ichafu [Eduafu?]. But cf. Nos. 280 and 282 below.

280 C. S. Salmon[1] to Sir A. E. Kennedy

Cape Coast Castle, 4 December, 1871.

. . . The Constitution was handed to me in Government House by Mr. Davison the Vice-President and Mr. Brew Assistant-Secretary. I refused to forward it officially to your Excellency on their part. The parties have never applied for any sanction to their proceedings. I officially proclaimed them to be illegal some time since. . . .

The people of the country, the merchants and traders, and all the kings and chiefs, except those immediately interested, are one and all utterly opposed to this new Confederacy. Kings Edoo of Mankessim and Otoo of Abrah are the only two cognisant of the actual proceedings, and even they have been partially imposed on. . . . Four of these mentioned as kings are very small chiefs. The majority of the names appended to the Constitution have been put down without the knowledge or consent of the parties themselves.

I have arrested all the Ministry except Grant. Warrants are out against the other members of the Executive Council. I have sent for the judge. The parties will be tried in the Judicial Assessor's Court. . . . If the kings come down I shall send a magistrate to Mankessim . . . to make enquiries and to obtain the seal.

This dangerous conspiracy must be destroyed for good, or the country will become altogether unmanageable. The people could not stand a double taxation. The Government have for a long time been attempting to do what this Confederation states to be its object; but they, the originators of it have, more than all else, hindered us, by keeping up a state of feuds and destroying unity and confidence. . . .

[H.C.171 of 1873]

[1] Colonial Secretary and Acting Administrator of the Gold Coast.

281 KIMBERLEY TO KENNEDY
LONDON, 16 JANUARY, 1872.

Sir,

I have received your despatch of the 16th ult. transmitting despatches from the Administrator of the Gold Coast, reporting the proceedings of the so-called Fantee Confederation, and the steps which he had taken to check what he regarded as a dangerous conspiracy.

As the information before me does not lead me to attach so much importance to this movement, I cannot but regret that persons claiming to hold office under the Confederation should have been arrested, although they were subsequently, and apparently after a short interval, released on bail; and if on the receipt of this despatch, the proceedings which the Administrator contemplated in the Judicial Assessor's Court should not have taken place, you will instruct him to stay all proceedings and to free the parties from bail.

But whilst I feel it necessary to give these directions, I fully recognise that the Administrator acted under a strong conviction that it was incumbent upon him to take the promptest and most effective measures for putting down a movement which, in his judgement, infringed the conditions of the British Protectorate, and was likely to prove delusive and injurious to the natives who would be affected by it.

There is hardly room for question that some of the articles in the constitution of the Confederation were practically inconsistent with the jurisdiction of the British Government in the protected territory. I think that the Administrator might have confined himself to issuing a proclamation warning British subjects from taking office under the Confederation and stating that those who did so would be held responsible for their acts. He would have been quite right also in declining to recognize in any way the 'Constitution' until the articles had been approved by Her Majesty's Government, and in publishing Mr. Grant's disavowal of participation in the proceedings of the Confederation.

Her Majesty's Government have no wish to discourage any legitimate efforts on the part of the Fantee kings and chiefs to establish for themselves an improved form of government, which, indeed, it is much to be desired that they should succeed in doing; but it is necessary that all parties concerned should understand, that so long as they live under the protection of Great Britain, the protecting Government must be consulted as to any new institutions which may be proposed.

The manner in which the new 'Constitution' was brought into operation and certain acts performed under it, without any previous communication with the British authorities, would be more likely to tend to discord and disorder than to further the ends which the promoters of the Constitution profess to have in view.

[H.C.171 of 1873. The minutes on which the despatch was based are in C.O.96/89]

282 C. S. SALMON TO J. J. KENDALL [1]
CAPE COAST CASTLE, 20 JANUARY, 1872.

. . . The Confederacy is at present confined to the small district of Mankessim and the larger one of Abrah; but the Abrah people are discontented at their king residing so long at Mankessim, and have sent for him. . . . When the king returns to Abrah, the last and only prop of the new Confederacy will have fallen, and the palaver may then be considered at an end.

The duplicity with which the promoters of the Constitution of the new Confederacy acted throughout is well illustrated by an extract from a letter of Major Brownell's dated the 17th instant: 'At a meeting of the chiefs and headmen at Winnebah, they told me they have been summoned some time since to go to Mankessim. This they refused to do, stating that they did not approve of the Confederation, and would not join it in any way.' The Constitution

[1] Captain J. J. Kendall; served in the Crimea and under Maximilian of Mexico, 1865–7; Colonial Secretary, Sierra Leone; Acting Governor-in-chief West African Settlements, August–December 1869 and January–February 1872.

apparently attempted to leave the British coast towns out, but the above extract demonstrates that the promoters intended differently. . . .

The worst feature in the new constitution is the complete manner in which all power is taken from the native kings and placed in the hands of the 'Ministry' and 'Executive Council', composed of young men, some of doubtful respectability, and none with any means, or holding any position in the country. After deep and searching inquiries, I am perfectly convinced that the two kings, and the few chiefs under them, that really formed the new confederacy, were misled by the Cape Coast young men, both as to the ends to be attained by the so-called constitution, and as to its scope.

The movement as regards the people of the Protectorate is now virtually at an end. It never reached the Eastern District. The Ashantee ambassadors watched the proceeding with interest, and no doubt kept the king well informed of our divisions.

[C.O.96/92 H.C.171 of 1873]

283 THE EARL OF KIMBERLEY TO J. POPE-HENNESSY [1]

LONDON, 12 FEBRUARY, 1872.

Sir,

The Convention for the cession of the Dutch forts on the Gold Coast is now awaiting the formal exchange of ratifications which may be expected to take place in the course of a few days, and it therefore becomes my duty to give you the necessary instructions as to the transfer of the forts.

As you will have in the first instance to go through the formalities connected with the assumption of the temporary administration of the West African Settlements, it appears desirable that you should proceed forthwith to Sierra Leone. It will prob-

---

[1] John Pope-Hennessy (later Sir John) (1834–91); Governor of Labuan, 1867; Acting Governor in Chief of West African Settlements, February 1872–February 1873; later Governor of Bahamas (1873), Windward Is. (1875), Hong Kong (1876), and Mauritius (1882–9).

ably not be advisable that you should go on to the Gold Coast until you receive from me intimation that the treaty is finally ratified; unless any intelligence should in the meantime reach you from that settlement, leading you to believe that your presence there is required sooner. You will, however, in any case abstain from all action until you are informed of the ratification.

Her Majesty's Government, in concluding this treaty, have done so in reliance on the power of the Dutch Government to transfer the forts to the British authorities peaceably, and without giving rise to any acts on the part of the native tribes under Dutch protection, on the occasion of the transfer, which might lead to open hostility, as unhappily occurred in 1868, when certain forts were exchanged between the British and Dutch.

Her Majesty's Government have no intention of assuming a British Protectorate over those native tribes without their consent. It is probable that the natives of Denkera and the two Wassaws, who were formerly under the British Protectorate before the exchange of forts, may be desirous of becoming so again: but I wish to call your particular attention to the Elminas, a small tribe, numbering about 12,000 or 15,000, in the immediate neighbourhood of the Dutch fort at St. George d'Elmina, who were originally a portion of the Fantee nation.

The Elminas have hitherto been under the protection of the Dutch, and are also in alliance with the king of Ashantee, avowedly for protection against the Fantees, with whom they have lately had constant feuds, which the British authorities have had great difficulty in appeasing.

The position of affairs with respect to this tribe will require your earliest and most serious attention; and after your arrival at Cape Coast, you will endeavour to ascertain, in conjunction with the Governor of Elmina, whether the departure of the Dutch, and the occupation of the forts by the British, are likely to cause any movement on the part of the Elminas, which might lead to open violence. They should be distinctly told that they will not be required to place themselves under British protection against their will, and a similar communication should be made to all the tribes over whom the British Protectorate, which was relinquished in 1868, formerly extended. Her Majesty's Government wish you likewise to ascertain what is the present temper of the Fantee kings and chiefs in the neighbourhood of Cape Coast; whether they are well-disposed towards the British authorities, and would be willing to prevent their followers from molesting the Elminas, whether the latter place themselves under British protection or not.

The objects which Her Majesty's Government have throughout had in view in negotiating this treaty, are not the acquisition of territory, or the extension of British power, but the maintenance of tranquillity and the promotion of peaceful commerce on the coast; and nothing could be further from their wish than that a treaty made with these objects should be carried into effect by violent measures. At the same time they trust that, by judicious and cautious management, the excitement which may possibly arise upon an event of so much importance as the retirement of the Dutch from the coast, may not lead to any difficulties; and I need not say that they would greatly regret that arrangements which they believe are calculated to be of much benefit to the whole population, by putting an end to old feuds and difficulties inseparable from the division of authority which has hitherto prevailed on the coast, should be frustrated by the jealousies of the native tribes.

But you will on no account employ force to compel the natives to acquiesce in the transfer of the forts; and if you should find that the attempt to assume possession of the forts on the part of the British authorities would probably be followed by resistance on the part of the surrounding native tribes, you will not accept the transfer of the forts, but will report the circumstances to Her Majesty's Government, and await further instructions.

[H.C.266, A & P (1873) lxix]

284 Convention between Her Majesty and the King of the Netherlands for the transfer to Great Britain of the Dutch Possessions on the coast of Guinea.
Signed at the Hague, 25 February, 1871[1] ...

Article I.

His Majesty the King of the Netherlands transfers to Her Majesty the Queen of the United Kingdom of Great Britain and Ireland, all the rights of sovereignty, jurisdiction and property which he possesses on the coast of Guinea.

Article II.

Her Majesty the Queen of the United Kingdom of Great Britain and Ireland accepts those rights and the obligations resulting from them towards the populations hitherto placed under the authority of the King of the Netherlands.

The British Authorities will take care, as far as possible, that no person belonging to these populations, who may, during the dominion of the Netherlands, have participated in quarrels or hostilities with independent tribes or tribes dependent on Great Britain, shall be annoyed or troubled on that account.

Any person who, within a period of six years after the actual transfer of the aforesaid possessions, may wish to remove to other Netherland possessions or to foreign places, shall be considered at liberty to do so by the British authorities.

Article III.

In the transfer are comprised all the forts, buildings and premises with the grounds appertaining thereto, owned by the Netherlands Government, as also all the stores or

[1] Final ratifications were exchanged at the Hague on 17 February, 1872.

ordnance, weapons, ammunition and the like, besides furniture and all other movable objects, with the exception of those articles which the Netherland Authorities at the coast may deem unfit for transfer.

For the stores and movable articles to be thus transferred, there shall be paid to His Majesty the King of the Netherlands, a fair price, not exceeding twenty-four thousand pounds. . . .

Article IV.

The Africans freed from military service in the Netherlands trans-atlantic possessions, and who have not made use of the liberty mentioned in Article II to remove from the coast, shall, provided they conform themselves to the laws and regulations introduced or established by the British authorities, be allowed to continue to dwell by themselves, in the manner adopted by a large number of them, in any part of the present Netherland Guinea.

Article V.

Netherland subjects, provided they conform themselves to the laws and regulations of the British Government, shall be treated on the coast of Guinea on the same footing as British subjects, in regard to their right to proceed thereto or to travel therein, or to establish themselves within the same; or to hold temporarily therein any houses, manufactories, warehouses, shops and premises, which may be necessary for the purpose of their residence or trade, by wholesale or retail, carried on either in person or by any agents whom they may think fit to employ.

Netherland subjects, Netherland vessels and goods imported or exported in Netherland vessels, shall be treated on the coast of Guinea on the same footing as British subjects, vessels, and goods, in all that regards commerce, navigation, duties of import or export, local dues, trade duties, prohibitions, impositions, warehousing, bounties and draw-backs, without any distinction as to the respective flags under which articles of lawful commerce may be imported or exported, or as to place of origin, departure or destination.

Article VI.

The present Convention, after receiving so far as may be necessary, the approval of the States General, shall be ratified, and the ratifications shall be exchanged at the Hague as soon as possible. . . .

[H.C.474, A & P (1872) lxx]

285 PROPOSALS OF THE LEADERS OF THE FANTI FEDERATION

ELMINA, 16 APRIL, 1872.

[A long historical introduction purports to show that Britain had abandoned the Protectorate after 1864.[1]] . . .

1. In the first place, for the Fanti Confederation to be of real practical use in the amelioration, development and civilization of the country, it must have the recognition . . . and support . . . of Her Majesty's Government. . . . We do not for one single moment pretend to be able to carry on a government in the interior without such recognition and assistance; for without that, the interests of both might clash, and a collision with the Local Government could not in any way further our object, and could have but one result, the breaking up of the Confederation, and the checking of all further progress towards the material improvement of the country for some years. It is therefore imperative that the Confederation[2] should not countenance, uphold, or protect any king or chief or other person who has once joined the Confederation, in any acts or deeds against its laws and customs.

2. That the jurisdiction of the Fanti Confederation shall be recognized and acknowledged to exist, and be exercised over all tribes, peoples, provinces, or districts choosing to join it, and that its authority and jurisdiction and that of the local

---

[1] Cf. Crooks, *op. cit.*, pp. 423–8.
[2] This reads as if it were a mistake for 'Local Government'.

Government, be clearly and strictly defined in judicial and other matters.

3. That any person or persons, committing any offence or crime within the jurisdiction of the Confederation, and escaping into the sea-coast towns, shall, on representation, be handed over by the local authorities to be tried in the courts of the Confederation, if the offence or crime be within their jurisdiction; if not, the person or persons so escaping shall be tried in the courts of the Local Government, on evidence being furnished; and, in like manner, any person or persons committing an offence in British jurisdiction and escaping into that of the Confederation, shall on representation from the local authorities, be handed over to them for trial. . . .

4. That the courts of the Confederation be recognized as the courts of first instance in matters or disputes between its subjects; option being allowed to parties dissatisfied with the judgements of such courts to appeal to the British Courts as provided for in the 4th section of Article 38 of the Constitution.

5. That in cases of any complaints against any officials of the Confederation being made to the British Authorities, the complaints so made to be referred in the first instance to the Executive of the Confederation, and to report thereon to the Local Authorities.

6. That the Vice-President of the Confederation and four other gentlemen, natives or residents of the Gold Coast, be appointed members of the Legislative Council, in addition to the present members, and that these gentlemen be elected by the people, and not nominees of the Administrator. . . . These elections should be made in the eastern and western districts of the protectorate, so that the interests of all might be fairly represented.

7. We come now to the question of questions, the financial. . . . On drawing up a rough estimate, and considering the vast improvements to be made in the country, and the great extent of the Confederation, if recognized by Her Majesty's Government, . . . we find that the Confederation must have a revenue of some £20,000. It is proposed that one half of this sum should be placed at the disposal of the Confederation out of the revenue of the Gold Coast, and that the other half be raised by the Confederation itself.

The amount to be raised by the Confederation would be by way of court fees, fines, &c, the Confederation paying the kings and chiefs certain stipends in lieu of the fees and fines received by them, in consideration of the kings and chiefs foregoing same, and giving up their right of settling palavers or disputes of any kind; and it has been rudely estimated that a revenue of some £10,000 would be derived from this source. The Confederation would establish courts of justice in each district, and dispense justice far more impartially, expeditiously and at less cost, than the present native courts, in which suitors, as is well known, are generally mulcted in twice or thrice the amount in dispute.

As regards the sum to be placed at the disposal of the Confederation by the Local Government, the Government would by it be relieved of the trouble and expense of governing the interior of the Protectorate, of making the improvements necessary therein . . . and yet be able to check any reckless or useless expenditure, by appointing some one to audit the accounts of the Confederation at stated periods.

The only other point we were requested to submit to you was as regards the liability already incurred by the Confederation, which was said to amount to some two thousand ounces of gold, equal to £7,200. Chief Acquainoo stated that the kings and chiefs were desirous of ascertaining from your Excellency whether Her Majesty's Government would place them in possession of funds to liquidate that liability, since the Government was opposed to their imposing any taxes or duties. . . .

If Her Majesty's Government will not furnish [the Confederation] with pecuniary aid out of the revenue of the settlements, nor on the other hand permit it to levy such taxes and duties for the purpose of obtaining a revenue, as are necessary, then Her Majesty's Government will have to take over the whole country, and govern it as vigorously and on the same principles as it does her other colonies; but not to permit us to be governed and ruled in the shameful and neglectful way in which we have been for years past, and give free scope for our legitimate aspirations to raise our benighted country to the same height of civilization as other more favoured nations have attained to. . . .   [C.O.96/94. H.C.171 of 1873]

286 POPE-HENNESSY TO KIMBERLEY
SIERRA LEONE, 29 OCTOBER, 1872.

. . . When it became known that I was not disposed to sanction the policy of the Administrator, a number of native gentlemen connected with the Confederation, called upon me with a request that they might be allowed to submit their views to Her Majesty's Government. To this I readily agreed and had more than one interview with them in the castle of Elmina. . . . As far as I could observe, every educated native at Cape Coast sympathised with the Confederation. . . . [On the other hand, the transfer of the Dutch forts had radically altered the outlook of the chiefs who all sent assurances of their attachment to British rule.]

The existence, throughout the Protectorate, of such a widespread desire for more intimate relations with the British Government, cannot be overlooked in considering the feasibility of the 'Fantee Confederation'. Whatever may have been the case before the transfer, there is no doubt whatever now, that the majority of the chiefs in the whole Protectorate as it exists at the present, would rather see British rule extended and made more of a reality. . . .

It is evident that the present judicial system is undefined and far from satisfactory. The Fantee Confederation are right in saying that the judicial authority of the chiefs has been usurped and nothing

tangible put in its place. The Administrator at Cape Coast appears to have broken as far as he could, the authority of the chiefs, and not to have substituted anything for it. Hence of late years, the frequent stoppage of roads and the natural uprising of a spirit such as that of the Fantee Confederation.

I therefore concur with the members of the Confederation that an important change is required: either a scheme of native government, with certain financial and judicial powers, should be recognized, or steps should be taken to gradually introduce throughout the Protectorate the same system of Government that exists in the other Crown Colonies.

Up to this, the Gold Coast differed from all other colonies in one important respect . . . that is, in the absence of the first element of government — power. The West Indian troops in Cape Coast Castle gave the Government no real power in the Protectorate. Experience shows that they were not physically fit for any operations in the interior. As Imperial troops, an Administrator ran great risk in using them. The chiefs in the interior have not been slow to learn this; and when, of late years, an Administrator was weak enough to utter threats, the chiefs have laughed at them. Immediately before my arrival on the coast, two native chiefs treated with contempt summons issued under Mr. Ussher's proclamation.[1]

In my despatch, No. 56 of the 31st May, I took the liberty of suggesting a remedy for this by substituting an irregular force of armed police for the West Indian troops; and your Lordship has so far approved of the scheme as to sanction the withdrawal of the moiety of the Imperial troops now on the Gold Coast. Since then, Mr Salmon states that the formation of a mixed force,

---

[1] Ussher on 9 March issued a Proclamation warning chiefs against taking part in the Confederation and threatening proceedings against those who did. At the same time he signified to the chiefs of Mankessim and Abura his willingness to discuss the formation of a council of *chiefs*. (H.C.171, p. 44.)

partly Mahommedans and partly pagans, that is, made up of Houssas and of the Fantee police, is steadily going on, and will soon admit of the total withdrawal of the troops. . . . It is clear that the local Government are obtaining, for the first time, some real power, independent of the precarious and costly imperial troops. With that power at his disposal, the Administrator can establish district magistrates in the interior, by whom trade can be protected and something like an administration of justice secured, in concert with the native chiefs.

Of the alternatives presented by the members of the Fantee Confederation, I therefore recommend your Lordship to adopt that of extending the system of Colonial Administration. I therefore make no observations on the details of the scheme that they propose themselves. At the same time, I think it fair that another native should be placed in the Legislative Council, and some attempt made to establish municipal institutions in the chief towns on the coast. For a seat on the Legislative Council, I venture to recommend Mr. F. C. Grant, the leading native merchant of Cape Coast, a gentleman who seems to have the confidence of the educated natives as well as of the chiefs.

As to further utilising the native element, I enclose for your Lordship's information a copy of a document addressed to me by the chiefs of Cape Coast, together with my reply, and a copy of a memorandum I transmitted to them with a scheme for establishing a municipal council. Instead of giving such a council the power of local taxation (to which the failure of Sir Benjamin Pine's plan some years ago is attributed) I propose to give them one hundred pounds a month out of the sum annually voted for the Public Works Department. [He had found Cape Coast in a disgraceful condition.] . . . The hundred pounds a month . . . would be well laid out even if it were all spent on sanitary objects alone. But I believe it will not only clean the town and keep it clean,

but will also enable the principal streets to be lighted and some beginning of roads attempted in the vicinity.

In conclusion, therefore, whilst for the great object of government throughout the whole territory, old and new, on the coast of Guinea, I venture to recommend a firm extension of Her Majesty's authority, I think there might be advantageously combined with it, a certain amount of native self-government in the towns, and of judicial power by chiefs in the interior, in concert with district magistrates.

[C.O.96/94. H.C.171 of 1873]

287 COLONIAL OFFICE MEMORANDUM[1]
n.d. (DECEMBER ?) 1872.

. . . Unless Mr. Ussher, Mr. Simpson and Sir Arthur Kennedy and others (including now, it would appear from recent despatches, Mr. Pope-Henessy himself) are all mistaken in their estimate of these men, it is impossible to believe that any benefit would accrue to the kings and chiefs of the Protectorate from Messrs. Brew and Co's supervision. Most of these 'scholars' are mulattos, handsome, clever and specious, but, if report is to be trusted, thoroughly unprincipled, and the kings-president (Abrah and Mankessim) would be mere tools in their hands. . . .

The proposed addition of the Vice-President and four other natives to the Legislative Council could not be entertained, nor could the 'scholars' be entrusted with the disposal of £10,000 out of Gold Coast funds towards the support of the confederacy. The application for £7,200 to pay the expenses of their abortive attempt in 1871 because they were discountenanced by the British Government, is a cool request.

Mr. Ussher's views appear sensible and his long experience at Cape Coast cannot be disregarded. He would confine any change to a native council of chiefs, whom

---

[1] On Pope-Hennessy's despatch (No. 286 above).

he would place in direct relation with the Government, and he would ignore the 'educated natives' altogether; and he would stipend the chiefs.[1]

Mr. Ross . . . recommends the native council and a meeting with the Governor

annually, to debate on the administration of the Protectorate. This would not controvert the recommendation of the Select Parl. Committee in 1865 [against assuming new responsibilities]. . . .[1]   [C.O.96/94]

[1] Cf. Ussher to Pope-Hennessy (4 May, 1872) in H.C.171 of 1873.

[1] Kimberley postponed deciding pending repulse of the Ashanti invasion (to Keate, 10 March, 1873) ibid.

21   The 'Sagrenti' War, 1873–1874 [1]

THERE had been no real peace with Ashanti since 1864, and though there was no open conflict, Ashanti forces had moved into Krepi in 1869, and hovered about Wasaw and Nzima during the Elmina war. In spite of their precautions, the British had scarcely occupied Elmina, not without trouble, before the Ashanti armies were on the move, and the Protectorate, early in 1873, found itself faced with a full-scale invasion. The rights and wrongs of the Elmina question were conveniently obscured by the demand of the new Asantehene [2] for a return to his allegiance of all the Protected tribes (290) and (67) his evident determination to fight.

In face of this new threat, the Fanti federation disappeared without trace, leaving the British authorities and the chiefs to work out their own salvation. Starting from Cardwell's instructions of 1864, Administrator Harley found it difficult to stand strictly on the defensive (289), and after the inevitable defeat of the Fantes, which did not occur without a stiff resistance at first, Lord Kimberley himself had to promise the help of West Indian troops (291) and even began to look for easy ways of attacking Ashanti (292).

From the moment the Government nominated Sir Garnet Wolseley ('our only soldier', as Disraeli called him) the initiative in deciding military policy passed gradually into his hands. To avoid the unfortunate dualism of 1863, Wolseley was vested with supreme civil as well as military command. Required to strike an effective blow against Ashanti (294), he saw from the first that this would entail the use of European troops, and might involve an advance to Kumasi (295). He won his point at last (296), and in a campaign planned to beat the rains as much as the Ashanti (297), fought his way to Kumasi, which was destroyed. On his way back to the coast, he received the Asantehene's agreement to peace terms (299).

[1] Sagrenti, an African rendering of Sir Garnet, is the local name for what is conventionally reckoned the sixth Ashanti war.
[2] Kofi Karikari, Asantehene 1867–74.

288 MINUTE BY SIR E. H. KNATCHBULL-HUGESSON [1]   27 FEBRUARY, 1873.

[Neither Harley's [2] severity nor Pope-Hennessy's indulgence were really responsible for the war.[3]] . . .

[1] Edward H. Knatchbull-Hugesson, 1st Baron Brabourne (1829–93); entered Parliament as a Liberal in 1857; Under-Secretary for the Colonies, 1871–4; then went to the Lords, where he sat as a Conservative.
[2] Colonel (later Sir) Robert William Harley; entered the army in 1847; served in the Gold Coast (1863) and Gambia (1864) expeditions; Administrator of British Honduras, 1871–2; Administrator of the Gold Coast, 1872–3; Acting Governor-in-Chief West Africa, March–August 1873; later Lieutenant Governor of Tobago (1875), Grenada (1877) and British Honduras (1883–4).
[3] See the voluminous papers on the Transfer of the Dutch Possession and Alleged Ashanti

I rather incline to think that the king of Ashantee who laid claim to Elmina as soon as he heard the Dutch were about to leave it, has thought the present a propitious moment to prosecute his claim by force, when there might be supposed to be some dislike to the change of masters on the par

Invasion, of 1873, from which Crooks prints copious extracts, *op. cit.*, pp. 404 ff, especially C.801 (A & P (1873) xlix). The chief of Elmina, re-instated by Pope-Henessy, in spite of his declared opposition to British rule, and assured by him that there would be no British interference with local customs, was ordered by Harley to take the oath of allegiance and on refusing was arrested. At the same time Harley told the Elminas that many of their customs would have to cease. An acrimonious correspondence ensued between Harley and Pope-Henessy.

of some of the transferred people, and that uncle Adjempon has stirred him up to action, having done all in his power to foment disaffection to British rule during his long residence in Elmina, and having possibly even gone there at first for this purpose. However the Ashantees must now receive a severe lesson — the more severe and effectual it is, the better chance of avoiding future inroads.   [C.O.96/96]

289 R. W. HARLEY TO THE EARL OF KIMBERLEY

CAPE COAST, 15 MARCH, 1873.

. . . The tribes of the Protectorate are now assembling at Dunquah, and I have issued a fresh supply of ammunition, which has had to be purchased from the merchants, as the supply available from the imperial magazine is nearly exhausted. But it is difficult to resist the demands which are made as a right, not as a favour, on the part of the native kings and chiefs, for munitions of war, men, and money, as they state that they are and have been loyal subjects of the Queen, and as such should receive protection. I confess that the position is one of some embarrassment; for while on the one hand, the instructions of the Secretary of State (vide despatch of the 23rd June 1864) are definite and specific as to the extent of the assistance to be given to the tribes of the Protectorate upon such an emergency rising as the present, it is difficult to find that these instructions have been impressed [on] or even communicated to the people after the close of the war of 1864; so that ten years of an indolent ease has been allowed to pass without the tribes taking any active measures, so far as I can ascertain, for their defence. Indeed, the fact declares itself openly, as they are as helpless now as they were found to be in 1863. . . .

There can be no doubt that they require leaders capable of directing them, and above all, staying, for the present, the angry and bitter jealousies which exist among them so as to prevent a united and decided course of action. With this in view, I have felt disposed to sanction the employment of the Houssas under Lieutenant Hopkins, around whom they would probably rally, and thus effect a determined resistance, which, if not made now at Dunquah, there will be nothing to prevent the Ashantees coming to the coast, as they are within thirty miles of it at Yancoomassie, the Fantee position and camp from which they drove them on the 10th instant.

The probability is that Elmina is the next point of attack of the Ashantees. I have little doubt, if any, that the king of Elmina is privy to their objects and aims, and that he and some of his chiefs and a small portion of his people are prepared to join them on their appearance before the town. He has now with him at Elmina several Ashantees, among whom are two sons of Atjiempon, who was recently sent back to his country from Cape Coast, in accordance with a promise given by Mr. Pope Henessy, but who is now said none the less to be taking the most active part in this war against the protectorate. Feeling that in this crisis of affairs it was indispensable to ascertain beyond a doubt, the loyalty of the king . . . I deemed it advisable to instruct the military commandant at Elmina to summon the king and his chiefs to the palaver hall of the Castle, and to represent that at such a time as the present, when so much rumour was about, that the loyalty of the king and his chiefs should not be a matter of doubt or question, and that I wished him and them to take the oath of allegiance to Her Majesty, and to set an example of loyalty and goodwill to his subjects.

It will be seen by the report of Captain Turton, that the king and two of his chiefs refused to take it; and that the king, when asked to subscribe the oath, became violent, and admitted 'having taken the fetish oath to oppose the English Government coming to Elmina, and that he has not broken that oath yet.' . . . The military commandant, in accordance with my instructions, then arrested the king and the two chiefs who with him had refused to take the oath of allegiance, and had them placed on board H.M.S. 'Seagull', which I had requested to go round to Elmina, and they arrived the same evening at Cape Coast . . . and are now accomodated with separate rooms in the Castle. . . .   [H.C.266 of 1873]

290 KING KOFI KALKAREE TO GOVERNOR HARLEY   COOMASSIE, 20 MARCH, 1873.

. . . His Majesty states that he, being the grandson of Ossai Tutu, he owns the Elminas to be his relatives, and consequently the fort at Elmina and its dependencies being his, he could not understand the Administrator-in-Chief's sending Attah, *alias* Mr. H. Plange, to tell him of his having taken possession of them for Quake Fram, and notifying him also that in four months he, the Administrator, would come to Ashantee to take away power from him.

He states that he has been made angry by this, and it was this which led to his sending his great captains and forces to bring him Quake Fram of Denkerah, who dares to take his Elmina fort &c, and also the Assins and Akims who are his own slaves, and who have united with the Denkerahs to take power from him.

His Majesty further states that your Honour's restoring him these tribes, viz., Denkerahs, Akims and Assins back to their former position as his subjects, and also restoring the Elmina fort and people back in the same manner as they were before, will be the only thing or way to appease him, for he has no quarrel with white men: but should your Honour come in to interfere, as he hears you are, that you have not to blame him, because he will then start himself.

That his Majesty having heard of some false information being brought to your Honour respecting your messengers and the white captives, he has requested their attesting this letter with their own signatures, of their being in health. . . .

[Signed by the Asantehene and three linguists]
Joseph Dawson, the writer.
Fr. Ramseyer for himself, his wife and child.
G. Kuhn.
M. J. Bonnat Sen.[1]
H. Plange, to testify my being alive.
                    [C.890, A & P (1874) lxvi]

291 KIMBERLEY TO HARLEY
                    LONDON, 29 JULY, 1873.

[Approves measures for the defence of Dixcove and Sekondi.] . . .

Every exertion should be made to make timely arrangements for the defence of such points as you may determine, in consultation with the officer commanding the troops, to hold with an armed force. . . .

You will no doubt have considered, in conjunction with the officers commanding Her Majesty's Naval and Military forces, after the arrival of the reinforcements in the 'Himalaya', whether it would be advisable to strike a blow at the Ashantees, who, it appears, are encamped at a short distance from Elmina and Cape Coast.

But much must depend upon the extent to which you can succeed in re-organizing the native forces, and I trust you have directed your particular attention to the importance of obtaining the co-operation of the tribes in the neighbourhood of Accra. As that part of the country has not yet been invaded by the Ashantees, I apprehend that the action of those tribes, if they are willing to come forward, might have a decisive effect upon the war.

You should impress upon them and all the friendly tribes, that nothing can be more disastrous than the protracted occupation of the country by the Ashantees, and that if they will unite in a general effort to drive out the invaders, Her Majesty's Government will give them active support, not only by supplying them with arms and

[1] The missionaries, Ramseyer and Kuhne and the trader Bonnat had been captured by the Ashanti in Krepi in 1869. Negotiations for their ransom had been going on almost ever since.

ammunition and money where it can be expended to real advantage, and by sending them officers to improve their organisation, but also by the aid, where it can be given, of the armed forces of Her Majesty.

After the severe reverses which the Fantees and their allies have experienced[1] it cannot be expected that they will recover confidence unless they are assured that the British Government will take every reasonable measure to assist them in the arduous conflict in which they are engaged; and it is essential to our interests that they should feel that in such an emergency, the Power to whom they look for protection is able and willing to assist them effectually. . . .

In case any movement should be determined upon in the vicinity of the Prah river, it is essential that full information should be obtained as to the extent to which that river is navigable, and I have to desire that you will procure and remit home, as soon as possible, all the information which you can procure on that subject, and also as to whether there is more liability to sickness on the river than on land.

I have etc.

[C.O.96/100, C.891, A & P (1874) xlvi]

292 THE EARL OF KIMBERLEY TO CAPTAIN J. H. GLOVER[2]

LONDON, 18 AUGUST, 1873.

Sir,

Her Majesty's Government have determined to accept the offer made in your letter of the 30th ultimo, and a commission will be transmitted to you, appointing you Special Commissioner to the native chiefs of the eastern districts of the Gold Coast, who, it is hoped, will resort to energetic measures for driving the Ashantee invaders from the protected territory. You will be

[1] Nyankumasi Asin (9 February, 1873), (Fanti) Nyankumasi (10 March, 1873), Dunkwa (9 April, 1873) and Jukwa (5 June, 1873).

[2] John Hawley Glover (later Sir John) (1829–85); accompanied Baikie's 2nd Niger expedition; Administrator (1863) and Colonial Secretary (1864) of Lagos, of which he was again Administrator from 1866–72; later Governor of the Leeward Isles and then of Newfoundland.

subject to the general control of the officer administering the Government of the Gold Coast. [Sir G. Wolseley has been appointed to this post.] . . .

The general object which you will keep in view is to create such a diversion in the flank and rear of the Ashantees as may force them to retreat from the Protectorate, or at all events, to so far harass and alarm them as to enable an attack to be made on them in front with better prospect of success.

The facilities which are afforded by a river navigable as the Volta is, to a long distance from the coast, for carrying the war into the Ashantee territory, are unquestionable, and it is stated that the country in the neighbourhood of that river is comparatively free from bush, and is therefore less unhealthy, and can more easily be penetrated than the district lying directly between the Gold Coast and the Ashantee country.

It would be impossible to suggest any particular line of operations . . . and . . . it must be left to you to judge for yourself, on the spot, according to circumstances, how far it may be prudent to attempt to penetrate into the Ashantee territory in the direction of Coomassie, and whether it may be practicable to march upon Coomassie itself. You will, of course, bear in mind, that the resources of the Ashantees are said to be very considerable, and that an advance to a great distance from the Volta must necessarily be attended with much risk, unless, indeed, you should succeed in obtaining assistance from the tribes in the eastern part of the Ashantee dominions. So little is known of that part of Africa, that opinions on this point amount to little more than conjecture. If it be true, however, that the population is to a considerable extent Mahommedan, decisive successes gained against the Ashantees might cause some disruption of the ties which unite it to the government of Coomassie. But Her Majesty's Government . . . must not be understood as giving an opinion that a march upon Coomassie is an operation which it would in any case be prudent to take.

It will be advisable that you should seize any opportunity which may present itself, of opening communications with the tribes on the north of Ashantee. It is known that from time to time, severe wars have been carried on between those tribes and the Ashantees, and news of an invasion of Ashantee from the east might possibly cause some movement to be made from the north.

Lastly, I have strongly to impress upon you, the necessity of using your utmost efforts to prevent the natives who take part in the movements, from putting to death captives and unarmed men, and committing the other barbarities which are too often the concomitants of native warfare. Her Majesty's Government, when furnishing the tribes of the Protectorate with effective means to defend themselves against their enemies, have a right to require that those means shall not be used for purposes abhorrent to humanity and the usages of civilized nations. . . .

[C.O.96/101 : C.891]

293 THE EARL OF KIMBERLEY TO MAJOR-GENERAL SIR G. WOLSELEY[1]

10 SEPTEMBER, 1873.

Sir,

Her Majesty's Government wish to leave you a large discretion as to the terms which you may think it advisable to require from the king of Ashantee, but I may point out to you that the treaty which was concluded with Ashantee in 1831 . . . seems to afford a reasonable basis for any fresh convention.

It would certainly be desirable to include in such a convention, an explicit renewal by the king of Ashantee, of the renunciation contained in the treaty of 1831, of all claims to tribute or homage from the native kings

[1] Sir Garnet Joseph (later 1st Viscount) Wolseley (1833–1913); Commissioned, 1852; served in Burma, the Crimea, India, China and Canada, and after a period at the War Office under Cardwell, subsequently served in Zululand and Egypt.

who are in alliance with Her Majesty, and further, a renunciation of all pretensions on his part to supremacy over Elmina, or over any of the tribes formerly connected with the Dutch, and to any tribute or homage from such tribes, as well as to any payment or acknowledgement in any shape by the British Government, in respect of Elmina or any other of the British forts or possessions on the coast.

The king should also, for his own interest, no less than with a view to the general benefit of the country, engage to keep the paths open through his dominions, to promote lawful commerce to and through the Ashantee country, and to protect all peaceful traders passing through his dominions to the coast; and it might be expedient that a stipulation should be made that a resident British consul or agent should be received at the Ashantee capital, if Her Majesty should think fit at any time to appoint one.

You will, of course, be careful to avoid as far as possible, anything which may endanger the lives of the European missionaries and their families who have so long been held in captivity at Coomassie, without any fault of their own, so far as Her Majesty's Government are aware, and you will use every effort to secure their safe release. You will also endeavour to procure the surrender of all the prisoners taken by the Ashantees from the tribes in alliance with Her Majesty.

It is a usual practice with the native tribes to demand hostages for the faithful performance of treaties of peace. This was done in 1831, when two hostages of high rank were delivered over to the British Government by the king of Ashantee. If you should find it advisable to make a similar demand on the present occasion, you will bear in mind that the hostages should be men of high rank and position in Ashantee.

It would be reasonable to exact from the king, the payment of such an indemnity as may be within his means, which are said to be considerable, for the expenses of the war, and the injuries inflicted on Her Majesty's allies.

Lastly, the opportunity should not be lost for putting an end, if possible, to the human sacrifices and the slave-hunting which, with other barbarities, prevail in the Ashantee kingdom.   [C.O.96/101: C.891]

294 KIMBERLEY TO WOLSELEY
LONDON, 6 OCTOBER, 1873.
Sir,

The preparations which have been made by the Military and Naval Departments to place you in full possession of all the means necessary for success in your important mission, have given rise to very numerous conjectures and speculations as to the intentions entertained by Her Majesty's Government. It is not necessary for me to warn you against being misled by expressions . . . of these unauthorised anticipations. . . .

Previous instructions have given you authority as to the immediate use of the forces under your command, with a view to a speedy peace or to striking an effective blow at the Ashantees. A satisfactory state of things will be attained if you can procure an honourable peace, or can inflict, in default of such peace, an effectual chastisement on the Ashantee force.

Unless and until one of these objects shall have been gained, you will understand that the primary purpose of military operations will be to drive the enemy from that district of country, their presence within which, endangers or seriously menaces the security of the British settlements upon the coast. To procure their withdrawal from the large and ill-defined territory which may be included within the loose description of the Protectorate, is an object which, however desirable, must depend upon a variety of considerations, among which a main one is the union and force of the tribes who inhabit that country. This question should be reserved for the consideration of Her Majesty's Government. . . .

[C.O.96/102: C.892, A & P (1874) xlvi]

295 WOLSELEY TO CARDWELL
CAPE COAST CASTLE, 13 OCTOBER, 1873.[1]

. . . There is, Sir, but one method of freeing these settlements from the continued menace of Ashantee invasion, and this is to defeat the Ashantee army in the field, to drive it from the protected territories, and, if necessary, to pursue it into its own land, and to march victorious on the Ashantee capital, and show not only to the king, but to those chiefs who urge him on to constant war, that the arm of Her Majesty is powerful to punish, and can reach even to the very heart of their kingdom.

By no means short of this can lasting peace be insured; one truce after another may be made, but they will again and again be broken, for the Ashantees have learnt to believe that they may with impunity invade and lay waste the protected territory, and dwell there unmolested by the white man, till they arrive under the very walls of our forts.

If the history of former wars with the Ashantees be examined, it will be found that every sign of weakness, and every unsuccessful effort of ours, has been followed by renewed hostilities on their part; and on the other hand, that the show of military strength alone has brought peace. It was thus that the Ashantee advance to Annamaboe in 1807 was followed by the invasion of 1811, this again by the advance to Cape Coast Castle in 1817, when the Ashantees were bought off; and this by the insult and invasion of 1823. The sad failure of Sir Charles Macarthy's expedition in 1824 brought the enemy to the walls of our forts, and again in 1826 they renewed their attacks. Now for the first time, they were not only defeated but routed, and the signal victory of Dodowah freed the country for many a long year. . . . For twenty-five years . . . this lesson had its effect.

But in 1853 the restless chiefs again urged on the king to war, and the perpetual dread of invasion was renewed. Though happily staved off by the judicious measures of Governor Hill, and a show of strength, the

[1] Wolseley reached Cape Coast on 2 October.

invasion was kept hanging over the heads of the protected tribes . . . [until 1863 and Pine's disastrous expedition in 1864]. From that day to this there has been no peace between the Ashantees and England. No strength has been shown by England. . . . Our Fanti allies . . . have disbanded and become demoralised. They have lost their confidence in the English power of protection, and in proportion the Ashantees have grown bold and confident. Their forces lie in security within nine miles of our forts, and for six months they have lived on the produce of the land said to be protected by us.

Her Majesty has confided to me the task of insuring a lasting peace. Past history, the experience of those who have watched the condition of the coast, and my own observation of the actual state of affairs, alike convince me that by no method but such signal chastisement as I have described, can such peace be insured; and that such punishment cannot be inflicted without the assistance of British troops.

It cannot, I think, be doubted that under the influence of civilization and European protection, the Fanti tribes have grown less warlike and more peaceful than formerly. Yet even in their best times they were no match for the Ashantees. . . . I have held interviews with the kings. I have seen the greedy mercantile spirit in which the war is viewed by them, and the excuses made to delay their departure for the field. They tell me they have little influence in raising their men; that their men prefer trading to fighting, and have gone into far countries to hide. The Cape Coast people actually claim the privilege of being the last to turn out to fight the invaders of their country.

In the face of these facts . . . and the hour having arrived when on account of the advancing season, my decision as to the need for European troops must be made, it is impossible for me to say that my prospects are such that I dare undertake to carry out my mission with native forces only, nor would the Government or the Country hold me excused were the valuable lives of the British officers who have volunteered for this expedition sacrificed, and the prestige of our country lowered, by the desertion of those native forces, a result which I foresee is too likely were I to rely solely on them. . . . Under no circumstances, it appears to me, could I rely on such native troops alone to pursue the war into the enemy's country. Nor would their presence serve to show the power of Her Majesty as would that of a body of English soldiers. . . .

But, Sir, I should still not apply for these troops . . . were it not that I am convinced that the service for which I demand the European soldiers can be performed by them without undue risk. . . .

Two months, or nearly two months, must elapse before the troops can arrive off Cape Coast Castle. In that time, the road which is now complete to Yancoomassie, will, unless the Ashantees have been more successful than hitherto in preventing its construction, be complete, at least as far as the Prah; the native troops will have attained such organization as I can give them; the transport will be prepared for an advance; and I may even hope, with the aid of the Houssas and these forces, to have cleared the country on this side of the Prah.

I may therefore say that on the arrival of the troops in these roads, about the middle of December, all will be ready for their immediate advance into the enemy's country, and that they shall not be kept inactive for one single day. . . . The troops would arrive soon after the commencement of that season of the year which your instructions[1] describe as the most healthy, viz., the months of December, January, February and March; and as I guarantee that the operations in which they would be engaged would not last more than about six weeks, or at the most, two months, they might re-embark on board ship by the beginning or middle of February, and under no circumstances would they be required to remain on

[1] Cardwell to Wolseley, 8 September, 1873; Crooks, *op. cit.*, pp. 460–2.

shore after the commencement of the unhealthy season. . . .

It now remains for me only to repeat my
request that as soon as possible after the
receipt of this despatch, the troops . . .
may be embarked for this station, and to
add that I attach the greatest possible importance to the men being selected for this
service, and to good accomodation being
provided for them on board ship, so that
they may arrive here in thoroughly healthy
condition. . . .   [C.892 of 1874]

296 WOLSELEY TO KIMBERLEY
CAPE COAST CASTLE, 4 NOVEMBER, 1873.
. . . The forces now under my command
consist simply of about 200 of the 2nd West
India Regiment, very much under-officered.
I can therefore only strike blows against
detached fractions of the enemy and cannot
venture to bring his whole army to action,
or strike an effective blow against him. . . .
The most serious result . . . for which I
am seeking is a unanimous rising of the
tribes. Nothing tends so much to bring
this about as the policy of constantly
engaging the enemy in partial skirmishes,
attacking his foraging parties and alarming
his camps by threatened attacks upon
them. . . .

In this matter of the rising of the tribes,
two entirely different questions are involved.
I have throughout assured them that the
war was their war, not Her Majesty's, and
that unless they put forth all their strength
in their own cause, we could do nothing for
them. I should not think of suggesting any
measure which would tend to relieve the
natives from the duty of fighting for themselves.

But . . . it is not enough for us that they
should be willing to do their utmost. They
must also do it within a given time. And
seeing that we left them almost entirely to
themselves at the beginning of this contest,
it is scarcely to be expected that without
something more than mere verbal assurances, the whole of a much dispersed and
dispirited people will suddenly come to

believe in our serious intention vigorously
to aid them. To get the people to act with
that rapidity which for our own purpose is
essential, we must act energetically ourselves. . . .

I fully understand the reluctance of Her
Majesty's Government to send any English
regiment here. If I believed that it was in
the least possible for me to dispense with
their service [s] . . . I should feel at least an
equal reluctance myself. . . . But I desire
most urgently to urge that if European
troops are despatched to me, it is indispensable that they should be sent at once. . . .
Experience gained during the past eight or
nine days,[1] when I have so frequently
engaged portions of the enemy without the
assistance of any marines or sailors, clearly
proves that the Fantee levies cannot be
induced to face the Ashantees, and that
consequently no serious blow can be struck
against the enemy without the contingent of
English troops that I have already felt it
necessary to ask for.

I have steadily kept before myself in all
that I have done, the fact that the one great
purpose of my coming was to procure a
permanent and satisfactory peace. . . . I
have demanded of [the Asantehene] nothing which I was not required by the
express terms of my instructions to exact.
. . . I have endeavoured to leave him a
loop-hole by which he may escape from the
necessity of acknowledging that he has
done wrong. . . . The blows which I have
struck were expressly directed to . . . the
object pointed out by your Lordship as the
primary one to be attained. They have
been most successful . . . causing the
enemy to retreat from the menacing position they had occupied for so many months
at Mampon and Effootoo [Efutu], so that
I believe I may safely assert that the British
settlements upon the coast are for the
present secure.

I must, however, remind your Lordship
that the ultimate security of those settlements must depend upon one of two things.

[1] The actions at Iscabio (27 October) and
Dunkwa (3 November).

Either forces must be retained here and paid by Her Majesty, expressly with a view to this security; or . . . the tribes must be induced to act vigorously and in union, for their own defence. All the more warlike tribes, and those which can give us the most valuable assistance, border upon Ashantee, and are comparatively distant from the settlements themselves. . . . If it were to be supposed among these tribes, that our sole object in the contest would be the mere security of our own settlements, and that as soon as that had been secured, we should abandon them, and repudiate the treaty of 1831, my sole chance of permanently securing the settlements themselves, would disappear. If I had now to wait for two months for the decision on this point of Her Majesty's Government, my present position would also be untenable. . . .

[C.892]

297 WOLSELEY TO CARDWELL

AGEMMUM,[1] 7 FEBRUARY, 1874.

Sir,

On the 5th instant I had the honour to address you from Coomassie, and to inform you that if the king refused to come in I should destroy his capital. I now regret to have to report that all my efforts to induce him to come himself, or send a prince of the royal blood to treat with me, failed; and that the king only continued that policy of falsehood and deception which have marked all his dealings with me. Messengers who arrived throughout the 5th were abusing the liberty which I allowed them, by carrying off arms and ammunition from the town; and on the evening of that day I decided upon withdrawing my troops and destroying Coomassie.

My decision to withdraw immediately was strengthened by the fact that tornadoes appeared to have set in, and that the passage of the rivers in my rear might be rendered more difficult by delay. . . .

[1] The Ashantis retired across the Pra in mid-December. Wolseley's counter-invasion of Ashanti began the following month. After heavy fighting (from 31 January) he entered Kumasi on 4 February. Ajumam is some 12 miles south of Kumasi.

Early on the 6th our homeward movements commenced, headed by the Naval Brigade, and covered by a rear guard of the 42nd Highlanders, which did not retire till the town had been set on fire in every quarter, and the mines in the palace fired. A tornado had raged during the previous day and night, but the destruction of the town by fire was complete. . . .

My . . . mission I conceive I have now fulfilled by the aid of the troops which Her Majesty's Government confided to me for its accomplishment. Yet I can truly state that no means were left untried by me to bring about a peacable solution of the campaign. Up to the last hour, I left the king's palace untouched, in hopes that he would return. The troops refrained with the most admirable self-control from spoliation or plunder. . . .

All the troops have now reached or passed this point. The return march was not made without difficulty. The streams and rivers had become so swollen from the effect of the tornadoes of the last few days, that the shallow swamps had become waist deep, and the water in the River Ordah had yesterday submerged the bridge constructed on the night of the 3rd instant, and was still rising when the troops passed the river. . . . I shall continue my homeward march to-morrow by as rapid stages as the nature of the country will allow, and with every military precaution.   [C.922]

298 WOLSELEY TO KIMBERLEY

FOMMANAH, 13 FEBRUARY, 1874.

[Reports the arrival of Ashanti envoys and discussion of peace terms.] . . . They made objections to two clauses only.

1st. They professed not to have understood that the sum of money demanded was so large as 50,000 oz. When, however, I informed them that the king had already expressly agreed to this sum, they withdrew the objection. I fancy that it is very doubtful whether the whole of the money will ever be obtained by Her Majesty's Government, but as the payment of a few thousand pounds cannot be a matter of relatively so great importance as the maintenance of peace, I have caused the wording to be . . . so framed . . . that the whole question of the money . . . will . . . be open for solution in any way Her Majesty's Government may think fit.

The second point to which objection was raised is one which has caused me much more anxiety. As I have already explained in my despatch No. 37 of this same date, I have not felt myself justified in refusing absolutely to allow the king of Adansi and his people, on their earnest petition, to join with the Wassaw people and occupy their lands together.

I considered therefore that it was indispensable, in order to avoid future trouble, that the king of Ashantee should distinctly acknowledge the independence of this people. I carefully explained to the envoys at the same time, that I had taken no steps whatever myself in this matter; that the action on the part of the Adansi people was purely voluntary, and that it was one with which it was impossible for me to interfere.

It has been agreed that within a fortnight the king shall send to Cape Coast the treaty, signed by himself. I incline to believe that the danger of breaking up, to which his kingdom is exposed, unless we are on friendly terms with him, will induce him to fulfil, with as much punctuality as he is capable of, the conditions of the treaty.

For not only have the Adansi people begged to be allowed to migrate, but I have heard, through the king of Adansi, that the much more powerful Becquah tribe is quite as anxious to do the same, and only awaits my decision on the case of the king of Adansi, before declaring its intention to oin some tribe nearer to the coast.

These and other indications that only very slight action on our part is required to cause the complete dissolution of his kingdom, will, I believe, be for the fulfilment of the engagements he has now entered into, better securities than any others we could have. [C.922]

299 THE TREATY OF FOMENA
13 FEBRUARY–14 MARCH, 1874.[1]

TREATY OF PEACE BETWEEN MAJOR-GENERAL SIR GARNET JOSEPH WOLSELEY, C.B., K.C.M.G., ACTING ON BEHALF OF HER MAJESTY VICTORIA, QUEEN OF GREAT BRITAIN AND IRELAND, AND SAIBEE ENQUIE, ACTING ON BEHALF OF HIS MAJESTY KOFFEE KALKALLI, KING OF ASHANTEE.

Article 1.

There shall be hereafter perpetual peace between the Queen of England and her allies on the coast on the one part, and the King of Ashantee and all his people on the other.

Article 2.

The King of Ashantee promises to pay the sum of fifty thousand ounces of approved gold, as indemnity for the expenses he has occasioned to Her Majesty the Queen of England by the late war; and undertakes to pay one thousand ounces of gold forthwith, and the remainder by such instalments as Her Majesty's Government may from time to time demand.

Article 3.

The King of Ashantee, on the part of himself and his successors, renounces all right or title to any tribute or homage from the Kings of Denkera, Assin, Akim, Adansi, and the other allies of Her Majesty formerly subject to the Kingdom of Ashantee.

Article 4.

The King, on the part of himself and his heirs and successors, does hereby further renounce for ever, all pretensions to supremacy over Elmina, or over any of the tribes formerly connected with the Dutch Government, and to any tribute or homage from such tribes, as well as to any payment or acknowledgement of any kind by the British Government in respect of Elmina or any other of the British forts and possessions on the Gold Coast.

[1] 14 March was the date of ratification at Cape Coast.

Article 5.

The King will at once withdraw all his troops from Apollonia and its vicinity, and from the neighbourhood of Dixcove, Secondee, and the adjoining coast line.

Article 6.

There shall be freedom of trade between Ashantee and Her Majesty's forts on the coast, all persons being at liberty to carry their merchandise from the coast to Coomassie, or from that place to any of Her Majesty's possessions on the coast.

Article 7.

The King of Ashantee guarantees that the road from Coomassie to the river Prah shall always be kept open and free from bush, to a width of fifteen feet.

Article 8.

As Her Majesty's subjects and the people of Ashantee are henceforth to be friends for ever, the King, in order to prove the sincerity of his friendship for Queen Victoria, promises to use his best endeavours to check the practice of human sacrifice, with a view to hereafter putting an end to it altogether, as the practice is repugnant to the feelings of all Christian nations.

Article 9.

One copy of this treaty shall be signed by the King of Ashantee and sent to the Administrator of Her Majesty's Government at Cape Coast Castle within fourteen days from this date.

Article 10.

This treaty shall be known as the Treaty of Fommanah.   Dated at Fommanah, this 13th day of February 1874.

[Signatures of Coffee Jutin and eight others for Kumasi, and by representatives of Juabin, Bekwai, Kokofu, Kuntanase, Nsuta, Mampon[g] and five others.]

[C.922]

BOOK VII

THE UNION WITH LAGOS, 1874–1886

22 Carnarvon's New Course, 1874–1876

GLADSTONE's Liberal Cabinet had been forced by the Ashanti invasion of 1873 to modify their military policy on the Coast. Whether they would also be driven to political changes had not been decided before their defeat at the General Election of 1874. To the officials in the Colonial Office at least it was by now clear that the recommendations of 1865 had not made for firm government (300), and that the Select Committee's attempt to evade the obligations of the Protectorate could not be persisted in (301). The effects of the growing trade and revenue of the settlements became apparent in the new House of Commons in May 1874, when a motion was introduced, though not pressed to a division, 'That this House is of opinion that . . . it would not now be desirable to withdraw from the administration of affairs on the Gold Coast.'[1]

It fell to the new Conservative Secretary for the Colonies, the Earl of Carnarvon, who nearly twenty years before had been its warmest advocate, to announce the end of Gold Coast dependence on Sierra Leone. Instead, the Gold Coast was united with Lagos in one independent Government (302). For the rest, his Gold Coast policy exhibits, not so much the stirrings of a new 'imperialism' — still nearly twenty years in the future — as the first resolute attempt to grapple with the practical implications of the Protectorate as it had developed in the thirty years since the treaties of 1844. In that period, the functions and duties of the British Authorities had been silently but inexorably growing, until they went far beyond the scope of the never very adequate 'Bond' (304); until, in everything but name, the British authorities were, in fact, the Government. Carnarvon was for frankly recognising this, and replacing the Bond by a clearer definition of the powers he meant to wield (305); while ensuring that the men on the spot had the necessary administrative, judicial (311) and financial resources to govern effectively. In some ways it was perhaps unfortunate that he allowed himself to be dissuaded from publicly scrapping the 'Bond' (312). And a more important check was his failure to come to an understanding with France (316), which might have profoundly modified the development of West Africa, although as far as Carnarvon was concerned the object of the negotiation was not to acquire territory but to secure more ample revenues and better control of the arms traffic.

On one point, however, Carnarvon was adamant: the Protectorate could no longer tolerate the recognition of Domestic Slavery (306). Here, indeed, he held that 1874 had made a change. By assuming, almost unaided, the defence of the Coast peoples against Ashanti, Britain had earned the right to insist that her wishes in this matter should be respected by them. And once the Local Government had decided on the best scheme of emancipation (308) and proceeded to carry it out (309), African protests were very brusquely pushed aside (310).

One consequence of the 1874 expedition was to bring the British Authorities for the first time into contact with the internal politics of Ashanti, and with the tribes of the Ashanti hinterland. But their desire to see Ashanti weakened (307), or for

[1] Parl. Debates 3/218/1204. This debate marked a reaction in other ways. One member hoped 'that there would be no endeavour on the part of the Colonial Office to extemporise a Negro Government and a Negro Parliament. They had seen enough of Negro Parliaments in Hayti and elsewhere, and he could not understand how a statesman like Earl Grey could support the establishment of a Negro Parliament.' *Ibid.* (Speech of Mr. Mills.)

direct trade with Salaga and beyond (313), was tempered by their anxiety to avoid becoming implicated in new difficulties (314). Carnarvon was perhaps bolder than his agents on the Coast, or his immediate successors in London, in stressing 'the great importance of encouraging commercial relations with those tribes of the interior which have hitherto been debarred from access to the coast, whether by material difficulties or by the jealousy of the dominant king of Ashanti', and regretting a missed opportunity of closer relations with Gyaman and Sefwhi.[1]

[1] Carnarvon to Freeling, 9 March, 1877 (C.O.96/120).

300 COLONIAL OFFICE MEMORANDUM
MARCH 1874.

. . . Although a great preponderance of opinion in favour of the concentration of the Settlements under a Central Government, was presented to the Committee [of 1865], yet subsequent experience has shown that, at all events as regards the Gold Coast, it may be questioned whether the system has succeeded. Colonel Ord who strongly advocated its adoption, considered the fact that it had for a length of time been in successful operation in the West Indies, was a sufficient ground for proposing its trial in the Settlements, but the circumstances in the two cases are so very different as materially to lessen the force of the argument.

In the West Indies there is no vague and undefined jurisdiction like the Protectorate on the Gold Coast, neither are there powerful savage neighbours like the kings of Ashantee and Dahomey, with whom an error of judgement or lack of discretion on the part of the Administrator may involve Great Britain in difficulties and war. Besides, it may be observed that the West India Islands which are subordinate to Barbados and Antigua, are none of them at more than a day's steaming from the seat of Government, and the majority are much nearer. It does not seem as if, in weighing the evidence in favour of a central government, and the placing of it at Sierra Leone, sufficient account had been taken of the position of constant hazard and danger in which we have always stood on the Gold Coast. So far as regards the consequences which might result from mal-administration, the Gold Coast is incomparably the most important of all the Settlements, and

requires the constant presence of an officer of experience and position, who is able and willing to act on his sole responsibility. This responsibility, it is but reasonable to suppose, a subordinate officer, not invested with that authority which justifies free action, would often hesitate to assume, and thereby lose opportunities and incur dangers which a decided policy would have turned to advantage, or averted.

It is true that whenever an emergency arises it is the duty of the Governor-in-Chief to proceed immediately from Sierra Leone to the Settlement threatened, but the shortest time involved in communicating with Sierra Leone from Cape Coast and receiving an answer, is nine or ten days. Moreover, the great point to be aimed at is to prevent the emergency from arising, and it is here that the value at the Gold Coast of a Governor having sole authority, and responsible only to Her Majesty's Government, would be shown. There are probably few places in the world where so much depends upon the action of single public servants, and it is, therefore, desirable that there should be on the spot a strong controlling power.

Another, and not less serious drawback to the system of dual Government, may be found in the difficulties which at once result from want of harmonious action or cordial relations between the Governor-in-Chief and the Administrator. When this is the case, the authority of the latter is at once weakened; his decisions, when it is known that they are liable to be overruled by an edict from headquarters, lose their influence, and he himself is placed in a position of doubt and difficulty.

In such cases, the Governor-in-Chief is

apt to complain that he is not furnished with full and proper information, whilst the Administrator considers that he does not receive that support and countenance which he has a right to expect from his superior officer. There can be little moral doubt but that Colonel Harley's hands were weakened at a critical time by the want of confidence shown towards him by Mr. Henessy, which was reflected in the conduct of some of the subordinate officers of the Government.

No stronger proof, however, of the inherent weakness of the present system of Government could be found than the fact that as soon as matters on the Gold Coast became serious, it was deemed necessary to relieve the Administrator from the control of the Governor-in-Chief and place him in direct communication with the Secretary of State.

If it is not thought advisable to place each of the Settlements under a separate Government, the natural arrangement would seem to be that Sierra Leone and the Gambia should form one Government, and that the Gold Coast and Lagos should be united to form another. These two settlements are only 300 miles apart, and similar questions of native policy are likely to occur in each, so that it would seem desirable that they should be governed by an official well acquainted with native matters, who could adopt a uniform system of dealing with such subjects.

The Resolutions of the Committee pointed most clearly and strongly to the restriction within the narrowest possible limits of all interference with the native tribes, and the relinquishment, so far as could be, of all engagements or responsibility to protect or aid them. The effect of these Resolutions may, perhaps, best be gathered from a perusal of the . . . despatch addressed by Earl Granville to the Governor-in-Chief in 1869.[1] . . . The line of policy indicated in this despatch is very different to that pursued by Captain Maclean . . . and in the direction of non-

[1] No. 268.

intervention even goes beyond the principles laid down by Mr (now Viscount) Cardwell in 1864.[1] . . .

With regard to the Resolutions deprecating any new acquisition of territory, it may be a question whether they were not violated in principle by the transfer of the Dutch Settlements in 1872, though on the other hand, it might, perhaps, fairly be contended that this measure was one of those which were 'necessary for the more efficient and economical administration of the Settlements we already possess.'

The fact is that the Resolutions were altogether vague and inconclusive, and while they declared it to be impossible for this country to withdraw from any of its engagements on the West Coast of Africa, they at the same time fettered the hands of H.M.'s Government, and hampered its action in pursuing a firm and distinct policy towards the natives.

A. W. L. Hemming[2] [C.O.806/3]

301 MINUTE BY E. FAIRFIELD[3]

COLONIAL OFFICE, 24 MARCH, 1874.

The policy of withdrawal from interference . . . is most clearly expressed in the . . . despatch from Lord Granville of the 17th May 1869. . . . The line of policy there indicated is that the tribes may make what wars and provoke what enemies they please, but are not to hope for any help, or at most not more than money, arms and advice, from the protecting Government.

The policy of Mr Maclean would have been to forbid them to make any wars he did not approve of, but to aid them substantially when they were unavoidably led into hostilities.

[1] No. 241.
[2] Augustus W. L. Hemming (later Sir Augustus); entered the Colonial Office, 1869; British delegate at the Berlin Conference, 1884; on West African boundary commissions in Paris, 1889–90 and 1894; Governor of British Guiana (1896) and Jamaica (1898–1904).
[3] Edward Fairfield; entered the Colonial Office, 1866; Secretary of the London South Africa Conference of 1876; Assistant Under-Secretary for the Colonies, 1892–7.

Viscount Cardwell's despatch of June 1864 remained the leading instruction on the subject of our duties to the protected tribes until the outbreak of the late Ashanti war, and on the 28th of February 1873 Lord Kimberley [endorsed it]. . . .

The events of the following months led Lord Kimberley to reconsider our position and policy. The Ashantees . . . were in military possession of the whole Protectorate. The question was whether Great Britain could allow a savage enemy to pillage and depopulate a country which, though not legally British territory was substantially a part of the Queen's dominions; whether, as we had assumed every other duty of Government, we were not bound to fulfil the most elementary duty of all; whether we were not bound to defend a people from destruction, whom we had so handled that they had lost the ability to defend themselves. Two whole generations of men had passed away since a Fantee tribe had been permitted to engage in war. They had lost the art of native warfare, and we had not supplied them with civilized discipline.

These were the elements of the question before H.M.'s Government last summer, and their decision was to despatch such an expeditionary force to the coast as should clear the Protectorate and effectually curb Ashantee power.

The recent exertions of this country, great as they have been, do not seem to have relieved us from further duty in relation to the defence of the Protectorate, supposing British jurisdiction is to be maintained there. The duty arises from the fact that our presence renders the protected tribes less able to defend themselves, whilst our peculiar policy has exposed them to the undying hatred of their most powerful enemies, although, of course, the cost of providing such defence is primarily chargeable to local resources, and can, it may be hoped, be usually defrayed in full from that source.   [C.O.806/3]

302 SPEECH BY THE EARL OF CARNARVON HOUSE OF LORDS, 12 MAY, 1874.

. . . Her Majesty's Government feel that they are acting in accordance with the instinct of Parliament and the country when they come to the conclusion that at such a moment as this especially, it is impossible for us to terminate our residence at Cape Coast Castle and abandon it (Hear, Hear). Having stated that, I shall now explain what are the conditions under which in future we propose to administer affairs there. . . . At present the Gold Coast is administered in connection with three other settlements. . . . Now the distances between these settlements are far too great; and . . . the politics of these places differ. The politics of Lagos are different from those of Sierra Leone. Now we propose to consolidate Lagos and the Gold Coast into one colony, and to consolidate them very much on the principles of the organization of the Straits Settlements. When I was before at the Colonial Office that organization was established[1] and I think it has worked in a satisfactory manner. I never heard of any complaints of it. We propose then to apply, with some slight modifications, the same principle to Lagos and the Gold Coast. We propose to have an Executive and Legislative Council of small numbers at the Gold Coast, but to require that it should hold its councils three times a year at Lagos. We have at the Gold Coast a small squadron of three vessels, which will keep up the communications between the two places. The difficulty will be to find a Governor. We intend . . . to give him great power, and to exact from him great responsibility.

I hope to effect a reduction in the number of officers, but to increase their salaries in cases in which we think they are underpaid. We propose that for the consolidated settlements there shall be appointed one Colonial Secretary; one Treasurer for both, with a sub-treasurer at Lagos, as there will be separate accounts; one Auditor; one Chief Justice; a Queen's

[1] In April 1867.

Advocate; one officer of armed police, which we propose shall be enlisted for each Colony; one Colonial Engineer, and one Chief Surgeon. . . . I think I may say that the increase of salaries will not in the aggregate exceed £6,000 or £7,000 a year. This will not be regarded as a heavy additional expenditure, seeing that the revenue of the Colony, which in 1870 was not more than £11,000, had, according to Sir Garnet Wolseley's belief, risen within the last year to £52,000. [Recruitment would be improved by putting the civil service on the tropical pension rates and assuring them passages to England.] . . .

The next question is, where should the seat of Government be placed? . . . There are three considerations — the military, the commercial and the sanitary. So far as the military consideration is concerned, I am not aware that Cape Coast Castle has any special advantages. So far as its sanitary features [are concerned] . . . it is perhaps one of the very worst places that could have been selected. The soil is saturated through and through with sewage. There is decaying vegetable matter everywhere about, and the houses are crowded on one another. . . . Even cattle cannot exist at Cape Coast Castle. It deserves more than perhaps any other place the appellation of the white man's grave. (Hear!) This being the case, there must be a change; the seat of government must be moved, but for obvious reasons it must be on the sea coast. Now there is a choice of one or other of two places — Accrah on the east and Elmina on the west. Accrah appears to be a desirable place as regards health. Horses and cattle will live there; and as we are proposing the consolidation of the Lagos and Gold Coast settlements, it has this advantage — that it is about midway between the two. As against these advantages, the landing-place is bad. On the other hand, Elmina is in a hilly district, there is a good water supply there, and the port, which at present admits craft of 40 or 50 tons, may be made available for much larger vessels. At present I

am not prepared to say to which place we shall be disposed to give the preference.[1]

My Lords, while some town on the coast must be the nominal seat of the Government always, and its real seat in time of war, I think there would be a very great advantage in the Governor and his staff being able to go to the hills. At a distance of some 30 miles from Accrah is a country with hills [where] . . . missionaries have lived for a long time, and their children have been born and grown up there. I think that in these hills, which would be to Accrah or Elmina what Simla is to Calcutta, it would be possible to erect a station for the Government of the Colony. Simple buildings which might be stockaded, could be constructed, and a detachment of armed police might be kept there. The place might be connected with the seat of government on the coast by roads and the telegraph. . . .

As to expenses connected with roads and such works, I see no reason why they should not be defrayed by the natives, very much as is the case in India. One of the complaints made by the Ashantees was that their traders when on their way to the coast, have been constantly molested by the Fantees. Therefore I shall propose to have certain stations on the road and detachments of armed police to hold the country, to maintain the roads, and to punish with inflexible severity any attempt on the part of lawless people to disturb those who are engaged in trade. In that way we should secure health for the Government and peace for the trade of the country. At the same time, we should keep up communications between different parts of the country, and this is the great secret of administrative success in a wild and barbarous region.

And now I will say a few words on the question of the military force. There, as everywhere else, we must have an actual military force in the background, and to

[1] Local opinion favoured Accra, the transfer to which was effected early in 1877, cf. Strahan to Carnarvon, confidential, 5 March, 1875 (C.O.96/ 115) and the memorandum in C.1343, p. 68 A & P (1875), liii.

economise that military force would be the very worst economy of which we could possibly be guilty. (Hear, hear.) The question, however, is what that force shall be? . . . I am clearly of opinion that the English troops are wholly misplaced in the Gold Coast. In the same way, I doubt whether the West Indian troops are very much more suitable, for whenever they have been tried, they have been found to succumb to the influence of climate as rapidly, if not more rapidly, than English soldiers. Therefore I come to the conclusion that, on the whole it is the wisest policy to dispense altogether, as soon as possible, with English troops, and to rely entirely upon native forces. (Hear, hear.) I think these native forces will be found to be efficient and inexpensive. Speaking roughly, I may say that of late years we have never had fewer than 300 West Indian soldiers on that Coast. Now a West Indian costs £100 a year, whereas a Houssa costs only £30. Consequently we could maintain 1,000 Houssas, who would be more effective, for the same amount that 300 West Indian troops now cost. I should be sorry to have the native force selected from one single tribe, for I think the soldiers ought to be taken from all the best fighting tribes. This is an experiment which I think must be tried, as it is essential to our occupation of the Gold Coast. There ought, however, to be a full proportion of English officers attached to this force — rather a larger proportion than is now attached to Indian irregular regiments — and if a few more are wanted at any time, they can be made available for political and general service.

This nearly exhausts what I have to say on the external administration of the Gold Coast, but I should like to make a few remarks on internal questions. The life-blood of a colony must be its trade and its commercial system. A great deal of evidence has been given on this subject, and yet I candidly own I am not satisfied in my own mind as to the results. It seems clear that a change has occurred on the Gold Coast, not dissimilar to that which has happened in many other parts of the world. Formerly there were a few influential and wealthy merchants, men of education and ability, who by their residence there, greatly strengthened the hands of the Government. At present, I believe, a different class exists. There are many and there are small traders, and this tells no doubt, in a less satisfactory degree, on Government.

We have applied the English law there in all its technicalities and in all subtle processes. Now it is a mistake, and almost an absurdity, to apply to negroes the English law of bankruptcy. (Hear, hear, and a laugh.) Yet this has been done with, I am told, the most dismal results, as fraud and dishonesty are the only consequences. Therefore I look forward to a great simplification of this and other branches of law on the Gold Coast.

It is said by some that there is very little trade to be expected from the interior. I venture, however, to doubt that. At all events, the revenue is a rising one, and I trust that, with proper care and management, it will continue to rise considerably. There is one point with regard to our trade which I cannot refrain from mentioning on this occasion — namely the importation of arms. This is a very serious question. The arms supplied to the Ashantees were for the most part transported into the interior when the coast was closed. They were imported from the west through a village where the French have a claim and used to exercise some jurisdiction. With the greatest friendliness on their part, it was impossible to prevent the importation of those arms to the Ashantees. . . . But how different it would have been if, instead of old Birmingham guns, they had been supplied with breech-loaders and arms of precision, which they might have employed in the bush with deadly effect. (Hear, hear.) How the importation of arms is to be controlled from without, I am not at present prepared to say, but it is a point which deserves very grave consideration, because it is very important with reference to our preponderance on the Coast, that we should have the means of stopping the supply. (Hear, hear.) Along our own frontier it is comparatively easy to do this, and I should be inclined to give the Government a monopoly of the sale of arms. The Government could then supply weapons of such type as they might deem to be most advantageous to the natives, each firearm bearing a particular stamp, and each being issued to a native only on the recommendation of his own chief. In this way we may be quit of one great danger. (Hear, hear.)

As regards the administration of justice, changes will, of course, be necessary. At this moment there is on the Gold Coast no Court of Appeal, no Public Prosecutor, and only one judge. Now I propose to have one Chief Justice for the two settlements, one Chief Magistrate or Judge resident at each settlement, but applicable to either, and one Queen's Advocate or Public Prosecutor. Besides that, I hope to extend, as far as possible, the principle of separate administration. There are many cases where it is easier to bring a tribunal to the persons interested than it is to bring the persons interested to a tribunal, and this was the principle we adopted in re-organizing Jamaica. Besides that, I am bound to say, I entertain very considerable doubts as to whether the jury system ought to go on without some material modification. (Hear, hear.) Though it is the palladium of English liberty, I doubt whether it is essential to liberty on the Gold Coast. It seems to be true that Gold Coast juries, partly through tribal jealousies and partly through interested motives, cannot be thoroughly entrusted with the adjudication of the cases which are brought before them.

It is impossible to forget that domestic slavery exists. Slavery in this form is so utterly repugnant to all our principles that it must be the object of any Minister as soon as he can to extinguish it. It has proved a source of difficulty on more than one occasion. Though difficulties are brought about by native slavery, on the other hand the difficulties involved in a

N

compulsory emancipation of slaves would be still greater. (Hear, hear.) Unless Parliament is prepared in such case to do that which is fair, to look upon the slave as property, and vote heavy compensation, which probably would not be far short of a million sterling, I hardly see how you can deal with that subject. If slavery were immediately abolished, the necessary results would be an increase of our obligations and of the complications in these territories. . . . I would gladly lay down such rules as would pave the way to the ultimate and indeed the early extinction of slavery: but anything sweeping in the way of compulsory emancipation, seems to me at this moment more calculated to enhance the difficulties with which we have to deal, and even to worsen the lot of the slave, than a gradual and cautious way of dealing with it.

Your Lordships will see that Her Majesty's Government are inclined to retain, as far as territorial jurisdiction goes, the Protectorate pretty much as it stands. On the whole it seems to me that the present limits of our territorial power should not be enlarged more than is absolutely necessary. . . .

Lastly, I wish to say, both for myself and for Her Majesty's Government, that it will be open to us at any future time to reconsider our position on this coast. . . . I have read that you ought to pave the way to an abandonment of this coast. I can only say that sentiment betrays a very gross mis-apprehension of the facts of the case. The moment you begin to pave the way for abandonment, you will provoke further agressions and render the government of the coast almost impossible. If ever the time should come to make preparations to abandon the coast, the sooner those preparations are executed the better. . . .

I have given the abstract of the scheme we propose and which I hope without increasing materially our obligations, will give us a fair and reasonable chance of maintaining more efficiently than hitherto has been the case, our position upon the

Gold Coast. It will always be a task full of difficulty, and possibly of danger. . . . It is certainly not a desire of further territory or further empire, which bids us remain on the West Coast of Africa; it is simply a sense of obligations to be redeemed and duties to be performed. But . . . as long as we do stay there, whether it be long, or whether it be short, we should exercise an effective control — a control beneficial to the natives themselves, and worthy of the history and position of this country.

[*The Times*, 13 May, 1874]

303 ORDER IN COUNCIL

6 AUGUST, 1874.

Order in Council for determining the mode of exercising the Power and Jurisdiction acquired by Her Majesty within divers countries on the West Coast of Africa near or adjacent to Her Majesty's Gold Coast Colony.

. . . At Osborne House, Isle of Wight. . . .

WHEREAS by an Act made and passed in the session of Parliament holden in the sixth and seventh years of Her Majesty's reign, intituled 'An Act to remove doubts as to the exercise of power and jurisdiction by Her Majesty within divers countries and places out of Her Majesty's dominions, and to render the same more effectual,' it was, amongst other things, enacted that it should be lawful for Her Majesty to hold exercise and enjoy any power or jurisdiction which Her Majesty then had, or might at any time thereafter have, within any country or place out of Her Majesty's dominions, in the same and as ample a manner as if Her Majesty had acquired such power or jurisdiction by the cession or conquest of territory. And whereas by certain Letters Patent under the Great Seal of the United Kingdom of Great Britain and Ireland, bearing date at Westminster, the 24th day of July 1874, in the thirty-eighth year of Her Majesty's reign, Her Majesty's settlements on the Gold Coast and Lagos were constituted and erected into one colony, under the title of

the Gold Coast Colony, and a Legislative Council was appointed for the said Colony, as by the said Letters Patent, reference being had thereto, will more fully appear. And whereas Her Majesty hath acquired power and jurisdiction within divers countries on the West Coast of Africa near or adjacent to Her Majesty's said Gold Coast Colony, and it is expedient to determine the mode of exercising such power and jurisdiction. Now, therefore, it is hereby ordered, with the advice and consent of Her Privy Council, as follows:—

1. It shall be lawful for the Legislative Council for the time being of the said Gold Coast Colony, by ordinance or ordinances, to exercise and provide for giving effect to all such powers and jurisdiction, as Her Majesty may, at any time, before or after the passing of this Order in Council, have acquired in the said territories adjacent to the Gold Coast Colony.

2. The Governor for the time being of the said Colony shall have a negative voice in the passing of all such ordinances as aforesaid. And the right is hereby reserved to Her Majesty, her heirs and successors, to disallow any such ordinances as aforesaid, in whole or in part; such disallowance being signified to the said Governor through one of Her Majesty's Principal Secretaries of State, and also to make and establish from time to time, with the advice and consent of Parliament, or with the advice of her or their Privy Council, all such laws or ordinances as may to her or them appear necessary for the exercise of such powers and jurisdiction as aforesaid, as fully as if this Order in Council had not been made.

3. In the making and establishing all such Ordinances, the said Legislative Council shall conform to and observe all such rules and regulations as may from time to time be appointed by any instruction or instructions issued by Her Majesty with the advice of her Privy Council, and until further directed, the instructions in force for the time being as to Ordinances passed by the said Legislative Council, for the peace, order and good government of the said

Gold Coast Colony shall, as far as they may be applicable, be taken and deemed to be in force in respect of Ordinances passed by the said Council by virtue of this Order in Council.

4. In the construction of this Order in Council, the term 'Governor' shall include the officer for the time being administering the Government of the said Gold Coast Colony.

And the Right Honourable the Earl of Carnarvon, one of Her Majesty's Principal Secretaries of State, is to give the necessary directions herein accordingly.

[Signed] Arthur Helps.

[C.1139, A & P (1875) lii]

304 THE EARL OF CARNARVON TO CAPTAIN G. C. STRAHAN[1]

LONDON, 20 AUGUST, 1874.

Sir,

In my despatch of the 20th instant, I had the honour to forward to you an Order made by Her Majesty in Council, which delegates to the Legislature of the Gold Coast, the exercise by ordinance or ordinances of such power and jurisdiction as Her Majesty has or may at any time have acquired in the territories adjacent to the Gold Coast Colony.

The Legislature of the Gold Coast Settlements has from time to time enacted Ordinances which were intended to take effect beyond the local limits of the British Settlements of the Gold Coast. Doubts, however, have been entertained as to the validity and force of such legislation, and in 1855 the Law Officers reported that such assumption of authority was not justified.

Her Majesty's Government, having decided to establish a new Colony and Legislative Council for the settlements of the Gold Coast and Lagos, vesting in that Council the power to legislate for the pro-

[1] Captain G. C. Strahan; entered the army, 1857; Colonial Secretary, Bahamas, 1867; Administrator of Lagos, 1873; Governor of the Gold Coast Colony, 1874-6; Governor of the Windward Isles, 1876.

tected territories on the Gold Coast, the Law Officers were requested to report upon the subject, and, in accordance with their opinion . . . the Order in Council already transmitted to you, was passed. By this Order, the Local Legislature is (subject to the conditions and reservations therein specified) clothed with whatever legislative authority Her Majesty has or may hereafter claim to exercise on the Gold Coast.

This having been done, it becomes advisable to define as clearly as may be, the extent of Her Majesty's power and jurisdiction, so as to prevent misunderstandings in future, and to enable the Colonial Legislature to know on what subjects it may properly legislate.

I need not examine here in detail the origin and history of the peculiar jurisdiction exercised by this country in the protected territory of the Gold Coast. Carried to its highest development under Governor Maclean, its existence is first authoritatively recorded and recognized in the Report of the House of Commons' Committee of 1842, which, in recommending the continuance of the system, suggested that it should be made the subject of distinct agreement with the native chiefs. That recommendation resulted in the negotiation with the native chiefs of the document called the Bond, of the 6th of March 1844, which is the only document purporting to define the extent of the Queen's jurisdiction on the Gold Coast in other than strictly political matters. But that definition, either from being an inadequate representation of the facts as they then existed, or from change of circumstances, no longer truly expresses what Her Majesty's Government believe to be the extent and scope of Her Majesty's power.

The Bond grants to Her Majesty's officers, the right to try and punish crimes and offences and to repress human sacrifices, panyarring, and other unlawful acts and barbarous customs. It is silent as to the Queen's right, by her officers and delegates, to collect customs, to administer civil justice, to legislate for the public health, to

erect municipalities, to provide for education, to construct roads, and regulate the
industrial and social economy of the
Protectorate. On all these matters the
Legislature or Government of the Settlement have, with or without the co-operation of the native rulers, exercised authority
to an extent which, strictly speaking, could
only be justified on the assumption (the
justice of which I am satisfied is not open
to question) that these matters have by
usage and by the sufferance and tacit assent
of the natives, fallen within the province of
the Queen's authority.

The necessity of some more adequate
definition of the Queen's authority than the
obsolete Bond of 1844 being thus apparent,
it remains to be considered whether that
definition should take the form of a Bond
to be negotiated with the chiefs, as in 1844,
or a Proclamation emanating from the sole
authority of the Queen.

In 1844, the methods of proceeding by
negotiation was recommended by obvious
considerations of prudence. But in the
thirty years which have since elapsed, the
power and resources of the British Government have been gradually increasing, until,
by the recent victories of the British forces,
they have been so strengthened and consolidated as to render an act of sovereign
power, such as a Proclamation of the
Queen, the only appropriate mode of proceeding for the attainment of the desired
object. It may be added that there are
many objections of policy to proceeding by
way of negotiation. It is not for Her
Majesty to take as a grant what is already
claimed and held as a right; whilst, looking
to the number of petty chiefs on the coast,
and the obscurity in which their relations
with one another are involved, there would
be some danger of not inviting the concurrence of chiefs who might afterwards allege,
and with a certain show of reason, that
their consent was as requisite as that of
others whose co-operation had been asked
and given. Besides this, the Government
would be placed in a position of much
embarrassment if any considerable body of

chiefs refused their consent in part or in
whole to the proposed Treaty.

On the other hand, I should be anxious
to avoid the risk, if any, attendant upon
this manner of proceeding, of alienating the
feelings of the natives, and I am fully alive
to the importance of their willing co-
operation in the work of promoting the
civilization and prosperity of the Protectorate. The nature of the proposed terms
are such as, if not fully and clearly explained, might excite the alarm and aversion
of the less intelligent rulers, whilst a too
hasty assumption of authority might create
a feeling of discontent, and possibly lead
them to seek alliances beyond the Protectorate with tribes hostile to our power.
. . . [He invites Strahan's views on this.]

In defining the nature of the Queen's
Protectorate on the Gold Coast, it may be
well also to define and limit the local extent
of that Protectorate.

What may be termed the natural boundaries of the Protectorate to the north and
east are, to a great extent, marked out by
the course of the Prah and the Volta, and
the lagoon dividing Quittah from the sea
[sic]; but considerations connected with
the protection of trade and the collection of
revenue, may compel your Government to
plant establishments or exercise jurisdiction
in parts of the Ahoonah country lying to the
east of the Volta and behind the lagoon.
The question of the northern limit of the
Protectorate towards the Croboe and
Aquamoo country will also call for careful
examination in connection with the request
of the Aquamoo people to be included in
the Protectorate, recently reported by Dr.
Gouldsbury, and it may be worthy of consideration whether some limitation should
not be put on what are usually regarded
as the boundaries of British jurisdiction
in the little-known regions of the north-
west. . . .

The history of our relations with the
protected territories of Lagos differs entirely
from that of our relations with the protected
territories in the Gold Coast. . . . I am
inclined to think that the Queen's authority

as a protecting power need not, under present circumstances, be declared to extend to the Protectorate of Lagos. . . .

[C.1139, pp. 2–5]

305 [Proposed] Proclamation defining the Nature and Extent of the Queen's Jurisdiction on the Gold Coast.

. . . And whereas it is expedient for the guidance and information as well of the Legislature of Our said Gold Coast Colony, as for that of the native chiefs and rulers living under our protection in the said territories, that the nature of Our power and jurisdiction as well as their local limits be declared by Us.

Therefore We do declare as follows:—

Our power and jurisdiction which We have acquired as aforesaid extends amongst other things to —

I. The preservation of the public peace and the protection of individuals and property.

II. The administration of civil and criminal justice, including —

1. The constitution and regulation of a Superior Court of Justice such as that which has been hitherto known as the Judicial Assessor's Court, of District Magistrates' Courts, Native Courts, and such other Courts as it may from time to time be deemed expedient to create.

2. The enactment of laws relating to crimes, wrongs, personal rights, contracts, property rights, and fiduciary relations similar to those prevailing in Our Gold Coast Colony, but framed with due regard to native law and customs where they are not repugnant to justice, equity and good conscience.

3. The determination of appeals from native tribunals to magistrates or to some superior court.

4. The apprehension and trial of criminals and offenders of all kinds, in any part of the said territories.

5. The supervision and regulation of native prisons.

III. The extinction of human sacrifices, panyarring, judicial torture and other immoral, barbarous and cruel customs.

IV. The abolition of slave-trading.

V. Measures with regard to domestic slavery and pawning.

VI. The protection and encouragement of trade and traders, including the construction, maintenance and improvement of roads, paths, bridges, harbour works, water ways, telegraphs, and other public works which benefit trade and promote civilization.

VII. The maintenance of an armed police force for the preservation of internal order and the prevention of foreign aggression, and the organization of the military forces of the native rulers in alliance with Her Majesty.

VIII. The settling by the authority of the Governor of Our Gold Coast Colony, of disputes arising between different chiefs and rulers in the said territories.

IX. The promotion of the public health, including the imposition, with the assent of the native chiefs, of sanitary rates in the towns and villages.

X. The establishment of municipalities.

XI. The raising of a revenue by licences and customs, and by such direct imposts as the native chiefs and rulers or a major part of them may agree to.

And further, We declare that the undermentioned territories are those within which at the present time, We have power and jurisdiction as aforesaid. [List of territories to be inserted by the local authorities in the first instance.] . . .

[C.1138, pp. 5–6]

306 Carnarvon to Strahan

21 August, 1874.

. . . I now desire to address you on the subject of slavery and slave-dealing in the protected territories of the Gold Coast.

Her Majesty's territorial dominion is of narrow local range. It extends merely to the forts, or at most to so much of the lands immediately adjacent as may be required for defensive, sanitary, or other purposes essential to the maintenance of the British position on the coast. All beyond that is foreign territory.

Within British territory, slavery has, I need scarcely say, no existence. It ceased by virtue of the Act of Parliament of 3rd and 4th Will. IV, cap. 73. But in the territories which lie beyond that range, the rule is otherwise. That country is foreign soil, divided amongst native chiefs and rulers, standing in no relation of allegiance to Her Majesty, independent of one another, and each presumably sovereign within the local limits of his own domain.

But within the territory of each such ruler, the English sovereign has, by cession or sufferance, acquired a varying degree of authority, and over the whole an undefined and somewhat anomalous jurisdiction.

Hitherto that authority has not been regarded as entitling the Crown to interfere directly with the system of slavery and slave-dealing which has existed by law and custom in those territories from time beyond the memory of man. The eminent statesman who was then Secretary of State for the Colonies, in 1841 did not hesitate to lay down this doctrine: 'If the laws or usages of these countries . . . tolerate slavery, we have no right to set aside those laws or usages, except by persuasion, negotiation, and other peaceful means.'[1]

Whilst I am not prepared to dispute the political wisdom of this proposition, viewing it, as is only just, in reference to the circumstances and possibilities of the time when it was laid down, I would observe that even then, the British Government, through the Judicial Assessor, and the general administration of the settlement, exercised though an indirect yet a powerful influence upon slavery, as well as upon the other barbarous customs of the Gold Coast, and mitigated, in a material degree, its miseries and injustice. . . .

Further than this, however, the Government did not attempt to go. The right was not claimed, and the duty was denied,

[1] Cf. No. 131 above.

of making any more direct attack on this ancient institution of the country.

But the time has now come when it appears to me possible to lay aside the somewhat timid attitude which was, in a great measure, imposed upon my predecessors by the force of circumstances, and even to incur some risk, for the sake of removing the dishonour and moral taint which is incurred by a toleration of slavery, when once that toleration ceases to be a matter of absolute necessity.

At the beginning of last year, the tribes of the Fantee Protectorate were invaded by an Ashantee army estimated at 40,000 men, and led by a general of the king's family. This army defeated and broke up the united armies of the Fantee tribes in two pitched battles, laid the whole country waste by fire and pillage, and proceeded even to attack the fortified British Settlements on the seaboard. That attack was, indeed, easily repelled by the disciplined English forces, armed as they were with weapons of precision: but the whole of the Protectorate, as before, lay helpless and unresisting at the mercy of the conqueror. . . .

The Fantee chiefs and people did little or nothing for their own deliverance. But the Queen's troops and seamen, aided by native levies from Sierra Leone, Lagos and Bonny, fought the battles of the Fantees, cleared the Protectorate of their enemies, followed the army of the king of Ashantee into his own territory, defeated it in three pitched battles, possessed themselves of his capital city, and compelled him to agree to a Treaty of Peace which it may be hoped will effectually secure the Protectorate from annoyance on the part of their old enemies.

I have been thus particular in recapitulating the events of the late war, because I hold and am desirous of pressing on the Fantee chiefs, that as, by the costly and unaided efforts of the Queen, they have been raised from the abyss of misery and defeat in which they lay to a position of peace and security, so Her Majesty, as their deliverer, is entitled to require of them a greater degree of deference and conformity to the known desires of herself and her people than she has in former times exacted.

Nor is it intended that Her Majesty's title to their co-operation should rest upon their rescue and protection only. It is hoped so to influence their internal affairs and their relations with their neighbours as to promote greatly their trading interests and bring them prosperity as well as peace.

The chiefs and the inhabitants of the Protectorate should be frankly informed that in return for the benefits thus conferred, their co-operation is required in the pursuit of one principal and paramount object, which Her Majesty's Government will employ their unremitting efforts to accomplish, and this is the immediate abolition of slave-dealing and the importation of slaves, to be followed by such regulation of the relations between master and slave as shall ultimately, and in no long course of time, effect the extinction of slavery itself.

In making this avowal, care should be taken to excite no needless fears such as might arise if it were to be supposed that what is contemplated is some sudden and ruinous subversion of the existing social relations depending upon slavery, without regard to the various interests which have grown up and are closely connected with it. But Her Majesty's Government desire that their abhorrence of slavery and their determination to take measures for its ultimate abolition, as well as for the immediate abolition of slave-dealing by importation, should be declared at once, because it is now, when the impression made by recent events is fresh and strong, that such a declaration will be opportune, supported as it must be, in the minds of the natives, by a sense of what has been done for them . . . and by a lively consciousness, on the part of the owners of slaves themselves, that it is owing solely to the British nation that they are not themselves slaves of a foreign Power.

Under such circumstances, it is not in mere acknowledgement of indefeasible rights of property, impossible as it would be wholly to ignore, under the circumstances of the case, that there are certain rights of property vested in the owners of slaves on the Gold Coast, as there were forty years ago in the West Indies, that Her Majesty's Government abstain from enforcing their immediate emancipation; it is also from a sense of the evils and sufferings that might be occasioned to the slaves themselves, as well as to other classes, by an abrupt dissolution of ties by which the whole fabric of society has been hitherto held together, and which are interwoven with all their traditional sentiments and usages.

But there are no such considerations to dissuade the immediate abolition of slave-dealing by importation. This is an outrage and a crime, and must be punished as such wheresoever the authority of the British Crown can avail to bring it to justice. I have to request, therefore, that in concert with your legal adviser, you will prepare, for submission to Her Majesty's Government, the draft of an ordinance by which full punishment shall be awarded for this offence and by which every person brought under compulsion within the Protectorate from beyond its bounds for the purpose of being sold or otherwise dealt with as a slave, shall be declared free.

Slave-dealing, by the sale or pawning of slaves who are natives of the Protectorate or already within its limits, is a matter of more difficulty. The Doncos or slaves of foreign extraction, may perhaps be dealt with on a different footing from the others. They are said to be treated with much more harshness than the native slaves, . . . and at the same time, their isolated condition may render their liberation a matter of less difficulty than the liberation of native slaves. . . . I suggest for your consideration, the question whether they or their children might not be emancipated at once, by payment to their owners, by the Government, in fixed annual instalments, of the total sum of £8, as the established price of each of the adult slaves, with such additions for children, if any, as their estimated value might justify, on such slaves contracting with the Government to give their daily labour to the making of roads or other public works, for such a term of years and at such a rate of wages as would provide for their subsistence and that of the children, if any, and at the same time re-imburse the Government, wholly or in part, the sums paid for the slaves and their families. The practicability of this scheme would depend, amongst other things, on the means which the Government might have of inducing or coercing the performance by these liberated slaves of their contract to supply the required amount of labour. . . . The means of coercion should certainly not be by corporal punishment.

I proceed now to the still more intricate question, in what way to provide for the abolition of native and domestic slavery. . . . This . . . resembles rather the patriarchal institutions of former, or the Turkish system of modern times, than the predial slavery of our West Indian Colonies previously to 1834. But whatsoever external aspect of mildness and moderation slavery may put on under one form or another, it is never to be forgotten that its internal workings, could they be seen either in their general or in their exceptional character, would disclose an amount of miseries and sufferings, of injustice and cruelty, not experienced in any other condition of life, which defines all niceties of adjustment and regulation, and for which no Christian Government, if it has the power, ought to make itself responsible. Further, we must bear in mind that, in proportion as we succeed in promoting the commercial and industrial prosperity of the country, we add new temptations to the slave-owner to abuse his power, and we aggravate the sufferings of the slave. . . . If labour in the Gold Coast should become, as we hope it may, much more productive and profitable than it is at present, the inevitable consequence will follow that it will be extorted in larger measure and by severer means.

But I am further led to consider that . . .

were a scheme of emancipation adopted which involved compensation in money to the slave-owner, the compensation, if left to be computed according to the current market price of the time, would become more costly in proportion as the country became more prosperous. It is therefore important that the existing price of slaves should be ascertained as nearly as may be. . . . At the same time, it will not be desirable at present to hold out publicly to the owners of slaves, an expectation that a claim to compensation in money will be admitted as a necessary condition of emancipation. Various projects of emancipation have been suggested . . . some of which do, and others do not, contemplate compensation for the slave owners. . . .

My attention has been directed . . . to the course taken by Lord William Bentinck nearly fifty years ago, in treating the question of slavery in India, which was that of simply forbidding slave dealing, and providing that no court should take cognizance of any right over the liberty or person of a servant, otherwise than under the ordinary rules of English law applicable to contracts for service between free men. . . . There was no disturbance of labour relations. Where the slaves were content, they went on serving. There was no excitement and no occasion for compensation. But the emancipation was far more complete and immediate than in any other country, and probably affected many more millions of men than in the Americas and the West Indies put together. . . . It is scarcely conceivable that the abolition of Gold Coast slavery can be thus simply and easily accomplished.

[An alternative would be the apprenticeship scheme, or that put forward by Lord Howick, but not adopted, in 1833.] . . . There may be other measures which may be better suited to the circumstances with which we have to deal . . . but however this may be, I would wish you to prepare at once for an early declaration that all children born after the end of this year shall be born free. This can entail no practical hardships on the present holders of slaves; it is possible; it is right as a matter of policy; and it will remove from the next generation the sufferings and bondage which have cast a shadow upon English institutions on the West Coast of Africa. . . .

I desire . . . that . . . you will look into these matters in all their bearings and report to me [your] conclusions . . . always bearing in mind that the question at issue is not whether the legal existence of slavery shall or shall not cease, nor indeed whether emancipation shall be deferred to some indefinite and distant date, for on those questions the mind of Her Majesty's Government is made up; but by what modes of proceeding the many difficulties in the way may be surmounted without sacrifice to those objects which are essential to public order and the peace of society on the Gold Coast.

There is one further observation which I think it necessary to make for your guidance. In [past] accounts . . . of the structure of society . . . the patriarchal position of the chief has been dwelt upon as the mainstay of society. I am very imperfectly informed as to the alteration wrought by the events of last winter in the position of the chiefs and in the other elements of social organization: but of one thing there can be no doubt, that the importance to be attached to the views and sentiments of the chiefs is not to be measured by their claims or their deserts, inasmuch as both are wholly insubstantial, but by the value of their co-operation, whatever that may be, in giving beneficial effect to the changes we purpose to bring about.

[C.1139, pp. 6–13]

307 STRAHAN TO CARNARVON
CAPE COAST CASTLE, 3 SEPTEMBER, 1874.

. . . Your Lordship will have learnt from my despatch No. 172 of the 13th of July, that soon after the late expedition, the people of Krachie, who were soon afterwards followed by the Juabins, had determined to throw off their allegiance to King Coffee Calcalli; a determination which was openly expressed by the Juabin portion of the embassy, before the Coomassie ambassadors, at the interview which formed the subject of the despatch above referred to; that there were rumours that others of the tribes were following the lead given to them by Juabin; that King Coffee Calcalli endeavoured, through his ambassadors, to obtain my interference to bring back the tribes who had already left him, and to prevent a further defection of his people; that failing in this, the Coomassie ambassadors confined themselves to a request (in which the Juabin ambassadors joined them) that I would send some one to Coomassie and Juabin to prevent war; and that . . . I arranged that Captain Lees[1] should proceed to Coomassie on the 14th of July last.

Your Lordship will now observe from Captain Lees' report that, at the time of his arrival at Coomassie, the state of affairs in Ashanti was such as to leave no doubt in his mind that an outbreak of hostilities was imminent; that King Coffee Calcalli, after many unsuccessful attempts to induce Captain Lees to exert an influence to bring back the defected tribes to their allegiance, accepted the suggestion that such concessions should be made by Coomassie with regard to Juabin as to render an amicable arrangement possible; that as a result, the independence of Jabin has been agreed to by King Coffee Calcalli; and that both kings swore to maintain peace, to keep open roads, to give up prisoners then in their hands, and to allow old disputes to die out.

The object of Captain Lees' mission, viz. to avert a war, having thus been attained, he left Coomassie on the 17th of August, arriving at Cape Coast on the 25th.

[1] Charles Cameron Lees (later Sir); served in the army, 1854–67; Civil Commandant, Accra, 1867; Collector of Customs, Lagos, 1872; Colonial Secretary, Gold Coast, 1873; Administrator of Lagos, 1874, and Lieutenant-Governor of the Gold Coast to 1879; subsequently served in Labuan, Mauritius and the West Indies.

The Coomassie ambassadors have waited upon me on several occasions since Captain Lees' return. In the first interview they expressed their thanks for the peaceful arrangement of affairs as brought about by Captain Lees. At the second, they . . . requested that I would send someone to Coomassie — they suggested a policeman — who should be instructed to report to me from time to time how things were going on.

I replied, much in the same terms as those used by Captain Lees before the king at Coomassie, that I could not mix myself up in the disputes of tribes outside British jurisdiction; that in the interests of peace I had agreed, at the request of both Coomassie and Juabin, to mediate between them to prevent a war which was said to be imminent, and at a time when communication between them had ceased; that both kings had now sworn to maintain peace, and that here ended the part which I had consented to play. As to sending a policeman, they were not slow to see that a man in this position would neither have my confidence nor theirs, and that influences might be brought to bear upon him to induce him to act beyond his instructions. I endeavoured further, in reply to their persistent requests to regain for the king his lost authority, to impress upon them that they must at once abandon any hope of my interference with a view to bringing back the disaffected tribes to their allegiance.

At a third interview, held yesterday, which was resumed today, they brought me a message, purporting to be from the King (for I place little reliance on anything the ambassadors say) that he begged me to ask the Queen to send someone in authority to live at Coomassie and 'arrange matters for him.' On being questioned as to what was meant by the last expression, they stated, with a coolness which was half amusing, half irritating, and as if the subject was being brought forward for the first time and was to be treated *de novo*, irrespective of anything that had passed before — that the King wished someone to 'bring his people back, as everyone was leaving him and he must starve.' [They were again told that this was impossible.] . . .

It is impossible to forsee, with any degree of certainty, what will be the fate of King Coffee Calcalli, but from all I can learn of his character, which appears to be treacherous, bloodthirsty and tyrannical, the loss of his power is certainly not to be regretted. Indeed, when the ambassadors urged the wholesale desertion of his people as a ground for my interference, I pointed out that the rule of the King must indeed have been a hateful one, when the tribes, one after another, were casting off his yoke on the first opportunity which they had of doing so with success.

The Juabins, who of all the Ashanti tribes appear to be the most given to trade, will probably now become the most powerful: but however this may be, I believe that, adhering to the broad principle of non-interference, the wisest policy, in the altered state of affairs in Ashanti since the date when the treaty was signed, will be to watch the course of events and take advantage of our prestige to turn them to the best account in the interests of peace and civilization.

Your Lordship will be pleased to learn that large numbers of traders are arriving daily at Cape Coast, from all parts of Ashanti, and that so good are the prospects of trade that large orders have been sent to England to meet the expected increase in transactions with the interior. . . .

[C.O.96/113]

308 STRAHAN TO CARNARVON
CAPE COAST CASTLE, 19 SEPTEMBER, 1874.

. . . After due consideration of the several schemes indicated by your Lordship, I have decided on recommending a proposal, the main features of which are: —

1. The immediate and absolute prohibition of slave-dealing in every form, including the prohibition of the importation into the Protectorate of slaves and persons

to be sold as slaves, and a declaration of the unconditional freedom of such persons.

2. Provision that no Court, English or Native, shall give effect to any right or claim affecting personal liberty, except such rights as by the law of England may arise under contracts of service, and as, without being repugnant to that law, may arise out of the family and tribal relations which exist among the native inhabitants of the protected territories.

3. A declaration that all children born on or after a certain date (to be named) shall be free persons. . . .

As a preliminary measure, I have already sent to summon the kings and chiefs of the western and eastern districts, the former on the 16th of October, and the latter on the 5th of November next, when I propose to explain to them the views and intentions of Her Majesty's Government with regard to slave dealing and the early abolition of slavery throughout the Protectorate. . . .

The scheme which is now submitted is in substance identical with that referred to by your Lordship as having been followed by Lord William Bentinck in India, with such good results. . . . I . . . believe that under this scheme, the great end of emancipation may be speedily or almost at once obtained. . . .

As regards compensation by the Government, I am bound to say that I think it is excluded from consideration for one reason, to say nothing of others, viz., that the conditions and materials are wanting which would afford the slightest hope of its being honestly carried out. The numbers of the slave and of the free population, and their relative distribution in different districts, are not known, and as registration and other checks are impossible, I am convinced that claims for compensation, which it would be quite impossible to disprove, would be repeated again and again for the same individual.

In the same way, the recovery of any reimbursement from the manumitted slaves . . . by their employment on Government works, would, I fear, prove illusory. They would desert whenever more remunerative employment offered, or a love of idleness prompted them; severe punishment would become necessary without being effectual.

Besides these considerations, it is not to be expected that the slaves in any large numbers would avail themselves of opportunities of self-redemption, and only very slowly would this method operate (if ever it sufficed) to wipe out the reproach of slavery in the Protectorate. . . .

I do not anticipate that the slaves will immediately, in any large numbers, leave their masters. The influence of habit and established association, and the difficulty of obtaining a livelihood in other than the accustomed modes, will combine to prevent any general or widespread exodus. . . . It may be expected that . . . in the great majority of instances they will continue, at least for some time, to give their labour for an equivalent maintenance, and when the time comes when contracts of hiring shall have become the rule, the risks attendant on emancipation may be considered at an end. . . .

It might be a formidable contingency if any combination should take place in resistance to the change, as for instance by the masters combining with the slaves, both being misled or in ignorance of its real nature; but combination for resistance, or indeed for any purpose, except by the intervention of a civilized Power, is foreign to the disposition of the people. . . . Besides which, the recent expedition has left so strong an impression of Her Majesty's power and resources, that I do not regard any general or organized opposition, even if that might have taken place at some former time, as being now even a possible danger. . . . [C.1139, pp. 13–17]

309 PROCLAMATION BY HIS EXCELLENCY GEORGE CUMINE STRAHAN, CAPTAIN ROYAL ARTILLERY, GOVERNOR AND COMMANDER-IN-CHIEF OF THE GOLD COAST COLONY.

WHEREAS the Queen's Most Excellent Majesty has resolved to abolish slave-dealing in Her Protectorate of the Gold Coast and the importation thereinto of slaves and persons intended to be dealt with as slaves, and also to provide for the emancipation of persons holden as slaves within the said Protectorate:

And whereas the Governor and Legislative Council of the Gold Coast Colony have by Her Majesty's command, enacted an Ordinance bearing date 17th December 1874, by which all selling, buying, or dealing in slaves is declared unlawful, and is absolutely and forever abolished, prohibited and made penal, and another Ordinance also bearing date 17th December 1874, providing for the emancipation of persons holden in slavery:

Now I do hereby proclaim, publish and make known the said Ordinances to all persons whom it may concern.

And further, in order and to the intent that all the Kings, Chiefs, Headmen and other persons throughout the aforesaid Protectorate and elsewhere may the more readily understand and obey the laws now made and enacted, I hereby require every person to take notice and observe that now and from henceforth:

It is unlawful to sell or purchase or transfer or take any person as a slave.

It is unlawful to sell or purchase or transfer or take any person so as to make such a person a slave.

It is unlawful to put or take any person in pawn for or on account of any debt.

It is unlawful to bring any person, whether slave or free, into the Protected Territory from Ashantee or elsewhere in order that such person should be sold or dealt with as a slave or pawn.

It is unlawful to take or send any person out of the Protected Territories in order that such person should be sold or dealt with as a slave or pawn.

It is unlawful to make any contract or agreement for buying, selling, or pawning any person, or for bringing any person into or out of the protected Territories to be sold or dealt with as a slave or pawn.

It is unlawful that any King, Chief, Headman, or other person should, in any palaver, or by any means whatsoever, force or constrain any person for the purpose of compelling him to remain at any place or serve any master contrary to the will of such person.

Whosoever offends against these laws shall be punished with imprisonment and hard labour and may also be fined.

If in any contracts hereafter made, it should be agreed that any person shall be put in pawn, or bought or sold or transferred, the whole contract shall be null and void.

And further, let all persons whom it may concern, take notice that all children whom after the 5th day of November 1874, have been or shall be born in the Protectorate, have been declared free. But it is not intended by any of the aforesaid laws, or otherwise, to offer inducement to any persons to leave any master in whose service they may be desirous of remaining, or to forsake the krooms where they have been accustomed to inhabit, and that it is intended to permit the family and tribal relations to continue in all respects according as used and wont, except only that of slavery and such customs as arise therefrom and are thereon necessarily dependent.

Given at Government House, Cape Coast Castle, this 17th day of December, in the year of Our Lord, 1874, and of Her Majesty's Reign the 38th.

By command,
W. Owen Lanyon,
Acting Colonial Secretary. . . .
[C.1139, pp. 42–3]

310 CARNARVON TO STRAHAN
19 FEBRUARY, 1875.

Sir,

I have the honour to acknowledge the receipt of your despatches of the 3rd January and of the 8th of the same month, transmitting and commenting upon certain petitions purporting to be signed, or in most cases to be certified by the marks of kings, chiefs, ladies and others within the

Gold Coast Protectorate, in which it is urged that the steps taken by you in pursuance of the statement which you made on the 3rd of November in last year to the assembled kings and chiefs, should be annulled, and that the holder of slaves and pawns should be permitted to retain them unless upon proof of cruelty or maltreatment; or, in the event of this request not being acceded to, that compensation should be paid. . . .

I cannot doubt you are right in attributing these documents to some one or more of the educated Fantis who have on previous occasions . . . (as for example in the case of the well-known scheme for a Fanti Confederation) . . . undertaken, without sufficient authority, to make proposals and representations . . . which could be seriously entertained only if they emanated directly from the kings and other persons in authority. . . . It is with the kings and chiefs, not with irresponsible natives, however clever or well educated, that Her Majesty's Government must deal. . . .

The reply which it is my duty to advise the Queen that you should be directed to give . . . is a very simple one . . . that . . . this Government cannot for a moment listen to any arguments in favour of compromise or further delay. . . .

The kings and chiefs appear to have throughout shown a proper sense of the great benefits conferred upon them by the Queen in the rescue of their country from invasion . . . and I at once absolve them from any conscious participation in so ill-advised and unworthy a sentiment as that contained in the seventeenth paragraph of the petition to the Queen, in which they are made to say that 'the late war was not a war of their own, and that the British Forces fought more to uphold and maintain the dignity of the British Empire than in defence of the people of the Gold Coast.' These words will be generally repudiated, but they unfortunately represent too correctly that lamentable want of patriotism and public morality which have in times past characterised too many of the Gold Coast natives,

and have rendered it so difficult either to govern or to defend the Fantis. . . .

The only other point to which I think it necessary to refer is the suggestion that compensation should be granted to the Petitioners for the loss of their slaves and pawns. . . . You will now inform the Petitioners . . . that in view of all that has been done for them, they will find more than the equivalent of such sacrifices as some of them may now be called upon to make, and that it is difficult for the Queen to entertain seriously a request for money compensation from slave-holders who, but for Her generous and prompt interference, would now be either dead or themselves subjected to a most cruel slavery. . . .

[C.O.96/115]

311 CARNARVON TO STRAHAN
16 APRIL, 1875.

[Transmits] . . . Instructions as to the mode in which the several jurisdictions now existing on the Gold Coast and at Lagos might best be fused into one harmonious system.

There is at present for each of the British Settlements . . . a separate Chief Magistrate's Court, from which appeals lie to the Supreme Court of Sierra Leone. There is besides for the Protectorate on the Gold Coast, the Judicial Assessor's Court, the jurisdiction of which is primarily exercised by the Chief Magistrate of the Gold Coast sitting generally with native chiefs as assessors, and also by several magistrates and commandants at the out-stations, subject to appeal.

The union of the Settlements of Lagos and the Gold Coast under one government and legislature, points obviously to the union of the two British Courts, and the new attitude which has been imposed upon Her Majesty's Government in their relations to the Protectorate, since the Queen's Forces reconquered and rescued the country, suggests the abolition of the distinction hitherto observed in the treatment of cases coming before the Judicial

Authorities of the Gold Coast in their distinct capacities as administrators of British law and assessors to the native kings in administering native law.

Her Majesty's Order in Council of the 6th of August last, delegating to the local Legislature Her powers of legislation in the protected territories, is a sufficient warrant to that body for proceeding to deal with this matter, and the measures adopted for abolishing slave-dealing and slavery of themselves suggest the necessity of making the influences of British jurisdiction accepted as widely as possible over the territories in which these measures have force, as their success must not be imperilled by entrusting their administration to the native courts.

An Ordinance should be submitted to your Council creating a Supreme Court for the Gold Coast and Lagos and for the Gold Coast Protectorate. [The question of its applicability to the Lagos Protectorate is for consideration.] . . . With respect to the legal jurisdiction of the Supreme Court, it might be well that the Ordinance should enact that the Court shall have the same jurisdiction as Her Majesty's Court of Queen's Bench, Common Pleas and Exchequer, have in England, and shall be a Court of Oyer and Terminer, and Gaol Delivery, Assize and Nisi Prius — and that it should also have the same jurisdiction as Her Majesty's Courts of Equity in England, with all the powers and authorities of the Lord Chancellor as to the appointment and control of Guardians of Infants and Committees of Lunatics and their Estates.

The Court should also be empowered to exercise the same Jurisdiction as Her Majesty's Court of Probate, and (if it should be considered desirable) to exercise the same jurisdiction as Her Majesty's Court for Divorce and Matrimonial causes. A jurisdiction in Bankruptcy or Insolvency should be conferred upon the Court by a separate Ordinance, the provisions of which might be specially framed with reference to local circumstances.

The Courts should consist of a Chief Justice and two Puisne Judges — one of the Puisne Judges residing generally on the Gold Coast and the other generally at Lagos; the Chief Justice . . . moving from post to post as the business of the Courts or the necessities of the public service might require. . . . The Court should have power to appoint any Magistrate or Commandant to be in his district a Commissioner of the Court. [He defines the general powers of Commissioners.] . . .

When the Supreme Court is established I should hope that its influence might be so widely extended as to supersede in most districts of the Protectorate the courts of the native kings, which are in themselves open to grave objections, and which, in view of the present policy towards the native rulers, there is no political reason to encourage. The natives do not place a high value on time, and those living at a moderate distance from the coast would probably repair for justice to the nearest Magisterial Post on the sea-coast. With British magistrates at the several British ports from Axim to Quittah, I should hope that British justice might be effectually made accessible to the people of Apollonia, the two Wassaws, Elmina, Denkera, Fanti, Abrah, Aquapim, Adampe, and the Ahuna country between the lagoon and the sea. If the sanatorium is established at Akropong, justice might be administered by British magistrates to the people in Croboe and the neighbouring country.

Wherever the Colonial Courts can be made to meet the requirements of the people of any district, I should, as I have intimated, be prepared for the suppression of the native courts of that district. Understanding always this to be done prudently and with proper regard to existing circumstances and considerations, where this cannot be effected the native courts should be regulated on the principles . . . [of] the Memorandum on slavery and the Jurisdiction of the Judicial Assessor, which I forwarded to you confidentially in my despatch of the 6th of November.

With regard to the substantive system of

law to be administered in the court, the Ordinance should lay down for its guidance that all civil and criminal jurisdiction in the Colony should be exercised, so far as circumstances permit and subject to local legislation, upon the principles of and in conformity with the common law, the rules of equity and the statutes of general application in force in England at the date of the Colonial Charter. As regards natives who have not adopted the usages of civilization and Christian life, native law and custom, as declared by the kings and chiefs sitting with the Judges as their assessors, should prevail if not contrary to natural equity and right, especially with respect to the laws of marriage, of testamentary dispositions and inheritance, and of the tenure, transfer and devolution of property. In cases between natives and Europeans, where it may appear to the Court that substantive injustice would be done to either party by a strict adherence to the rules of English law, native laws and customs should be considered and the principles of natural equity and good conscience should be applied.

[Procedure should be as simple as possible. Sample colonial acts are enclosed for guidance.] . . . In furnishing you with codes which recognise and regulate a system of Trial by Jury, I do not, of course, wish to be understood as desiring to revive the practice of Trial by Jury in civil cases on the Gold Coast, though I consider that the judges may usefully continue, when trying cases between natives involving native custom, to associate with themselves the intelligent native chiefs of the district.

The question of Trial by Jury in criminal cases presents a somewhat difficult question. A jury composed of either white men or black men would each be open to objections of its own, especially when trying a prisoner of a different colour. In the Judicial Assessor's Court there has never been any system of Trial by Jury, and as the new Court must in a large measure be regarded as succeeding to the jurisdiction of the Assessor's Court, there might seem the less

necessity to establish Jury Trial, were it not for the fact, as stated by Mr. Chalmers, that of late years a practice has grown up of transferring important criminal cases arising in the Protectorate for trial in the Court of the British Settlement where the system of Jury Trial prevails. On the whole, and looking to the very peculiar state of circumstances and society in the Colony, I should be inclined to confine trial by jury to capital cases. Perhaps the system in force in India for the trial of natives by the Court with the aid of assessors, might be adopted with advantage, and you will observe that the drafts of a Criminal Procedure Ordinance which I enclose, and which was lately prepared for Fiji, contains clauses providing for this mode of trial. . . .

[Appeals to Sierra Leone will cease as soon as the new Supreme Court is established.]   [C.O.96/115]

312 MEMORANDUM BY D. P. CHALMERS[1]
29 JUNE, 1875.

. . . Of those objects,[2] the one which might in August 1874 have been considered more likely than any other to meet with opposition, inasmuch as, far more than any other, it contradicts native traditions and their former practice, has been fulfilled, the Ordinances Nos. 1 and 2 of 1874 having entirely suppressed the legal existence of slave-trading and pawning, and abolished slave-holding as respects all *post nati*, and eviscerated it as respects *ante-nati*, by reducing it to an arrangement which is only maintainable if and so long as the domestic acquiesces.

The administration of civil and criminal justice has been dealt with in its principal features.

The abolition of human sacrifices and other barbarous practices, the preservation of the peace, the protection of individuals

---

[1] David Patrick Chalmers (later Sir); magistrate in Gambia, 1867; Judicial Assessor, Gold Coast, 1869; Queen's Advocate, Sierra Leone (1872) and Gold Coast (1874); Chief Justice, Gold Coast (1876) and British Guiana (1878–94).
[2] Those set out in No. 305 above.

and property, have been dealt with implicitly through the general incorporation of the laws of England as the laws of the Protected Territories made by the Supreme Court Ordinance.

A Customs Tariff Ordinance and an Inland Licensing Ordinance have been passed and promulgated.

The 'Public Lands Ordinance' has assumed large rights in the Crown as respects the land of the Protected Territories when required for the service of the Crown.

Labour Contracts have been regulated.

The enactments which have been passed and promulgated are such as usually emanate from Sovereign Authority. On the promulgation of each enactment and its acquiescent reception, a confirmation of Her Majesty's asserted right is secured, of as strong, or (more properly) of stronger force than would arise from acquiescence in the same right asserted merely as a potentiality in the Proclamation.

We have thus obtained much of the effect of the Proclamation already, and there is no reason to suppose we shall not equally well obtain what remains of its enumerated purposes, as well as others not enumerated, as to which *specificatio unius exclusio alterius* was always a difficulty as respects the Proclamation.[1] . . .   [96/117]

313 STRAHAN TO CARNARVON
CAPE COAST CASTLE, 25 OCTOBER, 1875.

. . . With reference to the scheme which Monsieur Bonnat[2] endeavoured to carry out, viz., to obtain the goodwill and assistance of Coomassie and Juabin to enable him to reach Salaga and from there to open up trade with the coast, placing factories or depots at various points along the banks of

[1] Enclosed in Carnarvon to Strahan (7 July, 1876), stating that he has decided not to proceed with the Proclamation (No. 305).

[2] M. Bonnat, born near Mâçon, was agent for a French firm in the Volta districts, where he was captured by the Ashanti in 1869; released by the British in 1874 he returned to Kumasi the next year, on the trading venture here described; in 1877 he turned to gold prospecting in the Ancobra valley and discovered the Tarkwa reef, where he died in 1881.

the Volta, your Lordship is aware that Monsieur Bonnat received only the support of Coomassie, which he did by swearing allegiance to the king, and entering into an agreement to pay to the king a percentage on all goods from the interior which passed through his hands, the king undertaking on his part to secure to Monsieur Bonnat, the monopoly of the trade of the upper Volta.

This was an arrangement which . . . in my opinion amounted to a farce, inasmuch as the king of Coomassie's guarantee of a safe passage was worth nothing when beyond a few miles of his capital. To get to Salaga, Monsieur Bonnat and his Coomassie escort had to pass through tribes which had thrown off their allegiance to Coomassie and had cast in their lot with Juabin. Monsieur Bonnat had been unsuccessful in securing the goodwill of Juabin. As regards these tribes the king of Coomassie was powerless, the tribes who before the war had been in the habit of paying tribute to Ashanti having since its close paid none. . . . [Salaga itself was hostile to Kumasi.]

So far as is known of Salaga, it would appear to be situated in a north-east direction from Coomassie at a distance of about 8 days' journey. In two days' journey from Salaga the Volta is reached. Salaga seems to be one of the markets or trade centres to which articles of commerce, chiefly ivory, are brought from the far interior, and is probably capable of absorbing a considerable quantity of European manufactures in exchange. Its population, I understand to be a fluctuating one in which there is a large Mahommedan element.

The people of Salaga have, I understand, been long anxious to have direct intercourse with the coast. Before the late war their trade with the coast was carried on through Ashanti. All other routes were shut to them, inasmuch as the tribes along these routes were under Ashanti rule and were allowed to do nothing which could have the effect of diverting trade from Coomassie. Now that Coomassie's power over these tribes has ceased, the people of

Salaga are doubtless desirous of having free and friendly intercourse with the power which conquered Ashanti.

To have a free intercourse with Salaga through Ashanti would doubtless be a great advantage to this Colony, but to my mind the question arises, would not Coomassie, if allowed to establish itself in its former power, act as a barrier to the opening up of trade with the interior, re-imposing perhaps four to ten-fold the extent of the tribute which was exacted from the interior tribes. . . . [On the other hand, if Ashanti remains divided, that will not foster trade either.] The prospects, therefore, of opening up the trade of the interior through Ashanti is not encouraging.

But I am strongly of opinion that the trade of the interior may come down to the coast without reference to Ashanti, viz, from Salaga by way of a country called Bayim,[1] through Crepee to the Volta near Kpong. A deputation of the chiefs of Bayim, a tribe who, according to the deputation, are in friendly and frequent intercourse with Salaga, waited upon me some time ago, during one of my visits to Accra, asking, as they expressed it, 'to belong to England and to hold the English flag.'

It was only in passing through Crepee, which, as your Lordship is aware, was once included in the Protectorate, that the Bayims had any obstacle placed in the way of their progress to the coast, and that only in the shape of having a large toll exacted from them for a passage across the Volta, which, I may inform your Lordship, was reduced, on their return, in consequence of a representation which I made to the king of Crepee on the subject.

To this deputation I replied that although I could not accede to their request, I desired to be on friendly terms, and I trusted that they would prove the genuine nature of their message by coming to trade with the coast, and that I would use my best efforts to prevent their being molested on the way.

This is, in my opinion, the route which all our efforts ought to be directed to open

[1] Buem.

up. There would in this way be the main line by Bayim and one or more subsidiary lines through Ashanti; for the Ashantis, being powerless to maintain themselves by raids or by taxes upon the industry of the interior, would only have the resource of trade upon which to rely. . . .

[C.O.96/115]

314 CARNARVON TO STRAHAN
29 DECEMBER, 1875.
Sir,

I have the honour to acknowledge the receipt of your despatches No. 220 of 13th November and No. 221 of 16th November, forwarding reports from Dr. Gouldsbury, and conveying the intelligence of the defeat of the Juabins by the army of Coomassie, their retreat towards Akim, and the steps which you had taken, in consequence, for preventing any violation of the territory of the Protectorate by the pursuing forces.

It is with regret that I have received the information of these renewed disturbances of the peace, and of the success of the king of Coomassic, which, as you observe, will probably tend to revive the power and prestige of the Ashanti kingdom, a result which can scarcely be regarded without anxiety.

I do not doubt that you weighed well and carefully the risks attending upon the dispatch of the Houssas into a territory[1] which, though nominally neutral, I understand to be so connected with the two belligerents as to be liable to be easily drawn into the quarrel, and I am so well aware of the difficulties in dealing with these questions, and the dangers which result from hesitation quite as much as from over-promptitude to act, that I am quite disposed to believe that the course which you took was, under the circumstances, the wisest and best that was open to you. But I shall await, with some anxiety, your further reports on this subject,

[1] They were sent to Kibbi in Akim, in case the Kumasis followed the Juabins across the frontier. It was decided to invite the Juabins to settle inside the Protectorate, preferably away from the frontier. In 1877 the chiefs of Akim Abuakwa and Akwapim made available the lands which became New Juaben.

which I trust will be satisfactory. I need not, I know, remind you of the necessity of a constant and minute watchfulness in a case where the elements of disorder abound.

I approve of your instructions to Dr. Gouldsbury, and of your having declined to accede to his proposal for a force of Houssas to be stationed at Juabin. I have every confidence that you will continue to avoid committing the Government of the Colony unnecessarily to any share in quarrels beyond the Protectorate.

[C.O.96/115]

315 F. & A. Swanzy to the Earl of Carnarvon

London, 12 February, 1876.

My Lord,

We have received your Lordship's letter of the 9th instant, and as the proposed exchange of territory on the West Coast is of great importance to us, we address your Lordship at once on the subject.

We have been many years connected with the trade of West Africa, and have establishments at all the principal places from Grand Bassam to Whydah inclusive. We should be glad to see the Gold Coast and Lagos Colonies extended as far as proposed in the Government scheme, provided there was no opposition on the part of the native populations of the French settlements and free towns of the Gold Coast and Bight of Benin who would object to British rule on account of the heavy duties likely to be imposed, the probable abolition of slavery, and stoppage of trade in guns, gunpowder, etc.

The French withdrew the whole of their staff from Grand Bassam, Assinnee and that part of the coast, during the Franco-Prussian war, when the only duty levied, vizt., ¼ per cent. on exports, was suspended. Their establishments were placed at the disposal of the merchants at the nominal rent of £24 per annum and were to become their property absolutely if not claimed before the expiration of five years. The Government gave notice lately that the establishment would again be occupied, but

up to the date of our last advices from there they had not been claimed. Grand Bassam is notoriously the most unhealthy place on the West Coast of Africa and the Government lost the greater portion of the officers sent there. There are only two firms established in the French settlements alluded to, our own and that of Messrs Verdier and Co. of La Rochelle, other merchants having withdrawn on account of the unhealthiness of the climate and the small amount of business to be done. There has been no improvement in trade for years past, and since the Ashanti war, it has diminished rather than increased. The Government establishments are mostly in ruins, the merchants having had very little use for them, and therefore no occasion to keep them in repair. The Ashantis and interior tribes have no access to the French coast and they trade with middlemen on the borders of the Assinee territory.

Porto Seguero, Little Popo, Aghuey and Grand Popo are independent native towns with a king or headman of each, and they are in no way connected with each other. Whydah and Godomey are the only coast towns of Dahomey. We are not aware that the French have any more right to Whydah than have Her Majesty's Government. There are three or four old slave forts there, one known as French and occupied by a French merchant whose agent is French consul; one known as British and occupied by ourselves until lately, for trading purposes, but now in ruins; and the other known as Portuguese is occupied by a Portuguese Government staff, consisting of a Commandant, priest, and six or eight black soldiers. It would therefore appear that the Portuguese have more right to the town than any other European Power, but they do not interfere in any way with the native authorities, and the French merchants pay the same duties as others to the king of Dahomey.

We maintain, my Lord, that there can be no comparison between the value of the Gambia and that of the places proposed to be transferred to Great Britain in exchange, and we cannot believe that Her Majesty's Government will be willing to give up a river which is navigable for 400 miles and which leads through a healthy climate to the heart of the vast continent of Africa, for the pursuance of a policy fraught with much danger and of very doubtful benefit to this country or the Gold Coast or Lagos Colonies. Thousands of loyal British subjects in the Gambia, and the inhabitants of every place proposed to be transferred, will be found opposed to the change. The French merchants at Whydah and other places proposed to be placed under the British flag are strongly opposed to the scheme, and we, in common with others, protest against it, knowing as we do, that if nothing worse follows, great loss of trade and depreciation of our property must result if it is followed out.

We beg to remind your Lordship that only a few years ago, the transfer of Dixcove by the British to the Dutch Government against the will of the inhabitants, led to difficulties which caused the plunder and destruction of our property, and that up to the present time we have not been able to recover any compensation for our loss which amounts to £8,000. We now fear that similar difficulties and loss may arise if the scheme is carried out.

We believe the present revenue of the Gold Coast is sufficient for all purposes, and that it is not affected to any great extent by the free ports, where the trade is insignificant in comparison. But if the revenue is not sufficient, we would respectfully suggest a further increase in the tariff, rather than an extension of coast line in opposition to the will of the inhabitants. We would further suggest that proposals be made to the French Government for fiscal arrangements in their Settlements such as exist in the Gold Coast Colony; and that negotiations for annexation be opened with the native authorities of places between Quittah and Lagos.

The Djuabins would doubtless have been able to hold their own against the Ashantis if they had not been deprived of the means of defence; and we seriously question the policy of stopping the trade in arms and gunpowder along the Gold Coast, directly after the conquest of Ashanti, when the people of that country were able to get supplies from the free ports. . . . [C.O.96/119]

316 SPEECH OF THE EARL OF CARNARVON, HOUSE OF LORDS, 17 FEBRUARY, 1876.

. . . The Gambia settlement, going back from the coast, is in proximity to the French colony of Senegal, and may be described as the outlying part of the national estate. . . . In 1866 proposals [for its transfer to France] were made by the French Government to Lord Clarendon. In 1867 they were renewed; and in 1868 the French colony of Senegal made certain advances of territory abutting on Sierra Leone, which led to apprehensions of difficulty to our colony. In 1868 and 1870 the negotiations were still continued; and the only point to which I need direct your Lordships' attention, is that up to that time what this country proposed to do was to extinguish the rights which the French had in the neighbourhood of Sierra Leone. . . .

The Franco-German war caused an interruption in the negotiations, and though they came before us from time to time, nothing tangible was proposed till 1874. By that time, circumstances as regards our possessions had very much altered; the Gold Coast colonies had been consolidated, and thus what might have been desirable had become almost a necessity, looking at it in the way of revenue.

The substance of the proposals made by the French Government to me may be briefly stated as follows:—

First, that the French should abandon all their rights and establishments in and around the territory of Sierra Leone;

Secondly, that they should abandon their posts of Assinie and Grand Bassam, and all their posts further down the coast on the other side [of Sierra Leone];

Thirdly, that they should abandon all territory claimed by them between the Gold Coast and Lagos; and

Fourthly, that they should abandon any pretensions or rights they may have east of Lagos to their own settlement of the Gaboon.

Your Lordships will see that by this arrangement not only all French claims between Sierra Leone and the easternmost extremity of Lagos, would be swept away, but we should acquire exclusive rights at the mouths of the Niger, if we like to use them.

When I say that the French surrender these rights and pretensions, it does not follow that we acquire fresh territory. So far from increasing our responsibilities in these quarters, I am prepared to contend that by such an arrangement as that proposed, we should be diminishing them; because we should be making the territory that belongs to us more compact and more consolidated, and therefore more manageable for political and fiscal purposes. What I think the transfer would do is this: it would remove all French rights, claims and pretensions in the places I have named, and thereby prevent the conflict of authority which now exists, and which is extremely injurious to our interests.

There has been . . . much misunderstanding, and I may say . . . much misrepresentation with regard to this exchange. . . . [It does not mean dismembering the Empire. The Gambia is not really an old colony — its effective settlement dates only from 1821. The 14,000 natives are quite indifferent to the exchange: the European population numbers 20. The trade has passed to France. There is a growing debt. The hinterland is occupied by warlike and fanatical Mahomedans.]

It has been estimated that if the transfer can be effected, the revenue of Sierra Leone will be enormously increased, and that the revenue of the Gold Coast, which is now £70,000 a year . . . may be doubled. Now what is meant by revenue? Revenue on the Gold Coast means everything. It means good government; it means the health of the English officers who are employed there; it means the civilization of the natives on the coast; and it means security against attack. I say we are not in a position of security on the Gold Coast, and to put us in that position, increased expenditure is necessary. There are but two ways in which revenue for such a Colony may be obtained. On the one hand it can be found from within; and I believe the resources of the Gold Coast and Lagos are such as to secure for us a revenue which will enable us to secure the great objects to which I have just adverted. On the other hand, if you do not get a revenue from within, there is one other source from which it can be had, and that is a Parliamentary vote in aid. . . . [Earl Grey had stated the case against that twenty years ago.]

Parliament deliberately decided to retain the Gold Coast Colony. It did so undoubtedly in the belief that good government could be established in that Colony, and for the improvement and civilization of the native races. In a great part the intentions of Parliament have been carried out, but owing to the climate and other causes, this has been at a much greater expenditure than would otherwise have been called for. If the customs duties can be made available by such protection against smuggling as this transfer would secure to us, then I believe the revenue will be sufficient to meet all the requirements. If not, then I see no alternative other than that Parliament should step in. . . . [The Exchange will also make it easier to control the import of precision guns.]

The exchange now proposed is, in my opinion, more favourable to this country than any previously offered; secondly, as it is more favourable, so it is more important at this moment, because there is now a greater necessity than ever before for some such arrangement. . . .

[Hansard, 3/227/374–83[1]]

[1] There was some opposition to the transfer, particularly in the Commons, who decided to appoint a Committee of Inquiry. On 31 March, however, Carnarvon announced the abandonment of the negotiation, because the French were apparently no longer willing to give up 'that entire and exclusive control of the coast', which alone justified the exchange. (Parl Deb. 3/228/265).

23 The Problem of Native Administration, 1877–1880

CARNARVON'S demand for a more effective government of the Protectorate ushered in a debate on how best this was to be achieved. Carnarvon's own resignation in February 1878 did not expedite an answer to what was in any case a difficult problem. At the coast, the British ruled directly, closely supervising the chiefs where they did not supersede them altogether. In the interior, however, in Governor Freeling's views, they could only work through the chiefs (317). And in 1878, a Native Jurisdiction Ordinance was passed, on lines he had recommended, but not for five years was any attempt made to put it into force (319).

In part the delay was due to the fact that the proposal to pay stipends to the chiefs (320), favoured by most of the men on the spot, was bound up with projects for re-introducing direct taxation (321) which none of them cared to contemplate (328). Governor Ussher, however, went further, in arguing that the chiefs were not fit for the work assigned to them by the Ordinance, without supervision by European commissioners. 'The only road to improvement' he wrote 'is to bring the European into immediate contact with the natives of the Interior' (328). Only after the introduction of special commissioners into the interior districts would it be wise to go on with schemes for native administration.

Economic developments were pointing in the same direction. From 1875 dates the beginning of serious mining prospecting in the western districts. Freeling viewed this development with some distrust, as a likely source of land disputes (318), since he did not believe that the chiefs could or would alienate their lands on the only terms likely to satisfy the mining interests. The Home Government, however, was anxious to foster such enterprise (324), and Governor Ussher agreed, while deprecating any special favours for the mines (326). But in his view, the coming of the European prospector or trader called for a parallel advance by the European administrator, if order was to be maintained. In 1880, accordingly, the first two commissoners for districts away from the coast were posted where they could best scrutinise the activities of Europeans and their agents — at Tarkwa and Odumase — (330): but the Government still jibbed at the expense and responsibility of direct rule over the Protectorate as a whole (331).

---

317 S. FREELING[1] TO THE EARL OF CARNARVON

CAPE COAST, 10 FEBRUARY, 1877.

[Discusses proposals for furthering Carnarvon's policy of developing the Protectorate.] . . .

To get roads constructed, which is most necessary, at a comparatively small cost, it will be necessary either to enforce labour ourselves, or to strengthen the power of the

[1] Sanford Freeling (later Sir); entered the army, 1847; Colonial Secretary of Gibraltar, 1859; Lieutenant-Governor of Dominica (1868), Granada (1871); Governor of the Gold Coast (1876–8) and Trinidad (1880–4).

kings and chiefs, or to speak more correctly, to restore to them a portion of the authority over their own people which various causes have gradually tended to diminish.

The latter is the best course to be pursued, and it is most desirable that it should be effected for many reasons. It will be impossible, except at an enormous cost in money and probably in valuable lives, to have a sufficient number of resident commissioners in the interior districts of the Protectorate to carry out our laws. Besides, this would tend still more to teach the people to lean only upon Government. I have proposed, therefore, to Sir D. Chalmers, that the authority and powers of the different kings and chiefs should be clearly defined, and then that they should be informed that they would be supported by Government in upholding this authority as long as it was not abused. These kings should receive a stipend, according to their status and power and the functions with which they may be charged by the Government; and I feel convinced that such course will be the best and cheapest mode of governing the Protectorate and will aid materially in obtaining practicable roads. Sir D. Chalmers is already occupied in defining these powers etc., and the result of his labours I shall communicate to your Lordship before taking further action.

In connection with roads will come the erection on them of some forts or stockades, which in certain places might be deemed advisable. It is quite possible that the day may again arrive when the Ashantees may overcome the neighbouring tribes and be as powerful or more so than ever and give trouble. I therefore think that no effort should be spared to place the Protectorate, by degrees, on such a footing that another invasion, if attempted, could be crushed at the outset; and a few advanced forts on . . . selected sites might be useful.

Certain main roads should be constructed from existing forts on the sea-board to the extremity or nearly so of our boundaries on the north; such as, for example, one from Elmina where I propose there shall be a strong Houssa force with stores, ammunition, etc, to the town of Denkera, leading through the district of Eastern Wassaw and Denkera. From Cape Coast, where two companies of the West India Regiment are quartered, there is, as your Lordship is aware, a fair road to Prahsue. The bush, however, on each side, should eventually be more cleared.

With regard to the eastern district, from Accra, which is to be the headquarters, a road is in course of construction to Aburi. A branch from this should be carried to Kpong on the Volta, bearing eastward, and another branch should be made through Eastern Akim to the westward. The[se] roads should be constructed in the first instance and information should be obtained as to what others it would be advisable to make both for strategical and trade purposes.

To this end, I venture to make the following suggestions. That the services of an officer of experience in native affairs. . . should be obtained solely for the purpose of travelling within the Protectorate. He should visit the different districts within and adjacent to the boundary . . . explain to the kings and chiefs the objects in view and how it was proposed they should be carried out . . . the part which would devolve upon them in supplying materials and labour, and that their authority as native rulers in doing so would be supported. Accompanying the Commissioner, who would be charged with the political portion of the business, should be one or two officers of Royal Engineers [who] . . . would lay out the position of the roads, select sites and make plans for bridges and forts. . . . [The Commissioner might also review the able-bodied men of each district and supervise the formation of a native militia.]   [C.O.96/120]

318 FREELING TO CARNARVON
ACCRA, 29 MAY, 1877.

[There is need for great caution in promoting mining enterprise.] . . .[1]

The influx of Europeans for mining purposes, to have a chance of success, would entail the assumption of the soil by the Government, for the tribes would never alienate it willingly even if a large payment were made, and it would therefore be unjust to the rightful owners.

The rightful owners of the soil in the Protectorate are the kings and chiefs and

[1] Carnarvon (to Freeling, 21 April, 1877) had asked if, in the changed circumstances of the Protectorate, some encouragement might not be given to mining enterprise.

their people, and not the Government. I consider that Her Majesty's Government have no territorial rights whatever over the various districts of the Protectorate. The limits of British territory are even now somewhat indefinite, and had better remain so; but strictly speaking are, I believe, only the forts. The right of jurisdiction exercised by the Crown does not rest upon any claim of sovereignty, but upon a course of long-continued general and undisturbed usages and acquiescence, and no similar usage has established in the Crown any seigneurial rights over the land.

There is no land absolutely unoccupied, in the sense of being without an owner; it is either the property of the occupant of the Stool or of certain chiefs and headmen. These may allow others to occupy and do so on payment of a certain portion of the yield, whether of gold or provisions: but the occupier obtains no fixed tenure, and the duration of his occupancy is purely arbitrary on the part of the owner. It is always associated with the Stool, the immediate possessor of which can lease or dispose of land as he or she will, during possession of the Stool, but on death or removal, such lease or disposal falls through, as the land reverts to the Stool and is inherited by the successor.

Land cannot be entirely alienated. It is held with tenacity and there is no subject which gives rise to disputes of so much acrimony and pertinacity as disagreements relating thereto. At present there is a disagreement of the kind which has for many years past been a source of trouble and anxiety to the Government, and at times has led to inter-tribal war between the Aquapims and Croboes. I hope soon, however, to be able to settle the matter satisfactorily.

It is asked[1] (and for gold-mining to have a chance of success, it would be necessary) whether the mines will be protected by the Government and be able to secure rights of

[1] By Fitzgerald, editor of the *African Times* (to Carnarvon, 8 April, 1877), pointing out that there was no hope of increased gold output by the natives who only usefully occupy one twentieth of the surface area.

ground and water for working the mines; and it is also stated that there will be an absolute need of important facilities and important protection, and further that the working of gold mines ought to be placed beyond the caprice of any native king or chief.

My answer to this is that it would be impossible without injustice to the rightful owners of the soil; and the more ignorant and savage the people are, the more just we ought to be in our dealings with them. . . . I look with alarm and apprehension to the influx of miners in the present state of the Protectorate. . . . I think that any such influx will be full of difficulties and perils [for] the miners themselves and may lead to grave difficulties to Government. . . . Miners could only by the consent of the kings and chiefs, obtain a temporary occupancy, and there would be a very great difficulty in procuring trustworthy interpreters. Disputes would probably arise and some act of violence be committed, perhaps by the miners themselves, which would lead to their being tried by native law, and if the miners were in any number, and armed, this might lead to grave consequences.

But even supposing Her Majesty's Government were willing, and thought it desirable and just to enforce the sale to the Crown of a certain supposed Gold District, what would be the consequence? In the first place, a district commissioner would have to be appointed with judicial court and a staff of officers, and this, as regards the Wassaw and Akim districts, our principal gold fields, is a notably unhealthy country. . . . The expense to Government would be very great and all for a problematical result. Natives work . . . very little, labour could not be enforced, and no Europeans could stand the work in such a climate. . . . The time may come when the kings and chiefs may see that it is for their own good that the land should be worked, and natives may be induced to labour, but it certainly has not arrived as yet. . . .

[C.O.96/121]

319 THE NATIVE JURISDICTION ORDINANCE[1]
24 JUNE, 1878   *15 January, 1883.*
⟨No. 8, 1878⟩ . . . *No. 5, 1883.* An Ordinance to facilitate and regulate the exercise in the Protected Territories of certain powers and jurisdiction by Native Authorities.

Whereas it is expedient to facilitate and regulate the exercise in the Protected Territories of certain powers and jurisdictions by Native Authorities:

Be it enacted by the Governor of the Gold Coast Colony, by and with the advice and consent of the Legislative Council thereof, as follows:—

I. Preliminary.

1. This Ordinance may be cited as the 'Gold Coast Native Jurisdiction Ordinance, ⟨1878⟩ *1883.*'

2. In this Ordinance unless the context otherwise requires —

> 'Head Chief' means a Chief who is not subordinate in his ordinary jurisdiction to any other Chief, and includes the Chiefs known as Ohen, Ohene, Manche and Amagah;
> Head Chiefs 'Division' means the portion of the Protected Territories under the supervision of a Head Chief;
> 'Chief' includes Head Chief;
> 'Natives' or 'Native' includes Mulattos, and all persons resident in the Country other than those commonly known as Europeans;
> 'Native Tribunal' means a Head Chief, or the Chief of a sub-division, or village, as the case may be, sitting with the Captains, Headmen, and others who by Native Customary law are the Councillors or Assistants of such Head Chief or Chief;
> ⟨'The Court' includes any Divisional Court of the Supreme Court of the Gold Coast Colony, and such of the

[1] The 1878 Ordinance was never put into effect, but repealed and substantially re-enacted by Ordinance No. 5 of 1883. Passages of the 1878 Ordinance which then disappeared are bracketed: ⟨   ⟩: new wording in 1883 in italics.

Commissioners of the said Court as may in the manner prescribed by the Supreme Court Ordinance 1876, or Criminal Procedure Ordinance 1876, be authorised to exercise jurisdiction in Appeals and References, Civil or Criminal, from Native Tribunals.⟩
'Commissioner' means the Secretary for Native Affairs, or other officer appointed by the Governor for the consideration of all or any matters relating to or in dispute respectively in the Native Tribunals:
'The Court' means the Divisional Court over which the Chief Justice presides, or any other Divisional Court designated by him.

3. It shall be lawful for the Governor, with the advice of the Executive Council, by Proclamation to be issued by him for that purpose, to declare from time to time as he may think desirable, that any Head Chief's Division or part thereof, shall be brought from a time to be named therein, within the operation of this Ordinance. On such Proclamation being issued, and in force, the said Division or part thereof, shall be subject to the provisions of this Ordinance, and the powers and jurisdiction of all Native Authorities therein shall be exercised under and according to the provisions of this Ordinance and not otherwise.

4. Every Head Chief's division or part thereof so brought within the operation of this Ordinance may be subdivided, if the Governor thinks fit, into such convenient groups of villages under the supervision of such Chiefs, subordinate to the Head Chief, as the Governor, with the advice of the Executive Council shall appoint. It shall be lawful for the Governor with the like advice from time to time to alter and amend any such sub-division. Except in so far as expressly so altered, all Native subdivisions of territory and grouping of villages for purposes of jurisdiction existing at the commencement of the Ordinance shall continue.

II. Power of making Bye-laws.

5. It shall be lawful for the Head Chief of every division brought within the operation of this Ordinance, with the concurrence of the Chiefs, Captains, Headmen, and others who by Native customary law are the Councillors of his Stool, to make such bye-laws, consistent with the laws of the Gold Coast, and subject to the provisions of this Ordinance, as he may deem expedient for promoting the peace, good order, and welfare of the people of his division, and also by the bye-laws so to be made to annex and appoint penalties in respect of the breach of any such bye-laws.

The matters respecting which such bye-laws may be made, and the nature and extent of the penalties which may be imposed for their enforcement shall be such as are declared by the Rules. . . . The concurrence mentioned in this section and in section seven may be given by such majority of the said Chiefs, Captains, Headmen and others, or in such other manner as is sanctioned and authorised by Native customary law. . . .

6. The Bye-laws so prepared shall be forthwith reported to the Governor for the approval or disallowance thereof by the Governor in Council, and such of the Bye-laws as shall be so approved shall be published in the Gazette, and shall thereupon become as valid and effectual as if the same had been enacted in this Ordinance. No Bye-law which the Governor in Council disallows shall have any force or effect whatsoever. . . .

7. [Bye-laws may be amended or revoked][1] in the same manner as is prescribed by this Ordinance with respect to Bye-laws. . . .

8. [Disallowed Bye-laws not to be re-enacted without Governor's assent.]

9. [Saving existing native laws] not being repugnant to natural justice, equity or good conscience, nor incompatible, either directly

---

[1] Most of the following sections bracketed [   ] contain the marginal summaries of the Ordinance itself.

or by necessary implication, with any enactment of the Colonial Legislature. . . .

III. Native Tribunals.

10. The Head Chief of any Division which shall have been brought under the operation of this Ordinance, and the Chiefs of sub-divisions or villages shall with their respective Councillors, authorized by Native law, form Native Tribunals, having power and jurisdiction to try breaches of any Bye-laws made and approved in the manner in this Ordinance beforementioned, or existing at the commencement of this Ordinance, and to exercise Civil and Criminal jurisdiction in the causes and matters aftermentioned, in which all the parties are natives, or in which any party not a native, consents in writing to his case being tried by the Native Tribunal.

11. The said Civil jurisdiction shall extend to the hearing and determination of —

All personal suits in which the debt, damage, or demand does not exceed seven ounces of gold or twenty-five pounds sterling, or such other sum as may from time to time be fixed by the Rules, and the defendant is within the particular jurisdiction of the Tribunal;

All suits relating to the ownership or possession of lands held under native tenure, and situated within the particular jurisdiction of the Tribunal;

All suits and matters relating to the succession to the goods of any deceased person who had at the time of his death his fixed place of abode within the particular jurisdiction of the Tribunal, where the whole value of the goods of such deceased person does not exceed fourteen ounces of gold or fifty pounds sterling, or such other sum as may from time to time be fixed by the rules.

12. The Criminal jurisdiction shall extend to the hearing, trial and determination of all criminal charges and matters in which any person is accused of having, wholly or in part within the particular jurisdiction of

the Tribunal, committed or been accessory to the committing of any of the offences which may from time to time be described in the Rules.

13. [Power of punishment.] . . . The extent of the fines and the periods of personal detention shall be such as may from time to time be prescribed by the Rules.

14. [Compensation to aggrieved persons.]

15. [Restoration of property in unlawful possession.]

16. The Governor may, with the advice of the Executive Council, restrict the jurisdiction of any particular Chief or Native Tribunal so as such Chief or Tribunal may exercise only a part of the jurisdiction, Civil and Criminal, authorized generally by this Ordinance. . . .

17. [No jurisdiction if Crown a party.]

18. [Jurisdiction to be exclusive. Proceedings not void for errors as to venue. Courts may remit certain cases to Native Tribunals.]

19. [Judgements not impeachable for errors in constituting Tribunal.]

20. No Counsel, Advocate, Solicitor, Proctor, or Attorney shall appear or act for any party before a Native Tribunal, nor in any proceedings removed from a Native Tribunal to *the Commissioner or to* the Court, by appeal or otherwise, except by special leave of *the Commissioner or of* the Court, and under the conditions contained in the first Schedule to the Supreme Court Ordinance, 1876: . . . [Exceptions in certain cases.]

References and Appeals to the Court.

21. [Cases beyond native jurisdiction to be referred to the ⟨Court⟩ *Commissioner*.]

22. The Governor, *the Commissioner*, the Queen's Advocate, or any officer or officers whom the Governor may from time to time designate in that behalf, may stop the hearing or further hearing of any civil or criminal case commenced or brought before any Native Tribunal and direct the case to be enquired of and tried *by the Superior Native Tribunal, if any, or* by the Court, *as he shall deem expedient.*

23. The defendant in any case . . . brought before any Native Tribunal may apply to the ⟨Court⟩ *Commissioner* for removal of the proceedings, and if the ⟨Court⟩ *Commissioner* sees sufficient reason . . . ⟨it⟩ *he* may stop the hearing or further hearing of the case before such Tribunal . . . and direct the trial to be by the Court. . . .

24. [Appeals and rehearings.]

25. [Security and . . . procedure in appeals.]

IV. Miscellaneous.

26. [Chiefs to have power of (a) Conservators of peace; (b) of carrying laws and orders of Court into effect; (c) of apprehending offenders.]

Withdrawal of Powers.

28. [Governor in Council may withdraw privileges of Ordinance.]

29. [Governor in Council may suspend or dismiss Chiefs.]

Penalties for certain Offences.

30. [Unauthorized persons not to act in Native Tribunals.]

31. [Taking reward for corrupt influence.]

32. Whoever falsely pretends to be a messenger from or to hold any office or authority from the Governor, *the Commissioner*, or from the Supreme Court, or wears any garb, or carries any badge or token with the intention that it may be believed . . . that he is such messenger, or holds such office or authority, and in such assumed character does, or attempts to do, or to procure any Chief or Native authority to do or abstain from doing any act whatsoever, shall be punished with imprisonment with or without hard labour which may extend to two years or with fine which may extend to fifty pounds, or with both.

33. [Evidence as to false witness.]

Supplemental Rules.

34. The Rules in the Schedule to this Ordinance shall come into operation at the

commencement of this Ordinance and shall have the same force and effect as if enacted in the body of this Ordinance. . . .

35. The Governor may from time to time by any order approved by Resolution of the Legislative Council make and alter, amend or revoke, Rules consistent with this Ordinance . . . requisite for regulating all or any of the following matters:—

The fees to be received by Chiefs and Native Tribunals;

The process to be issued by them and the mode of executing the same;

The recording or reporting of judgements made by them;

The execution of judgements pronounced by them;

The form and conditions of prosecuting applications to the Court for relief;

The form and mode of giving jurisdiction under section ten in cases not ordinarily triable by Native Tribunals;

and generally all such rules as may be requisite for the further or better execution of any of the provisions of this Ordinance. . . .

Contents of the Schedule.

Bye-Laws.

Rule 1. Purposes for which Bye-laws may be made:—

Roads, wells, springs, water courses, watering and bathing places;

Unoccupied lands and forests;

Land marks and fences;

Public fisheries;

Preventing accidents;

Abating nuisances;

Clearances at towns &c;

Burial grounds and burials;

Mines and mining;

2. Punishments for breaches of Bye-laws.

Criminal Jurisdictions.

3. Offences within Native Jurisdiction:—

Petty assaults;

Slander;

Putting in Fetish;

Keeping poisons with intent to injure &c;

Spreading infectious diseases;

Causing nuisances;

Fire raising;

Disobeying lawful orders of Chiefs;

Disobeying or neglecting oath of Chiefs;

Insulting Chiefs;

Seduction;

Theft, extortion and cheating;

Panyarring;

Unlawful possession of property.

4. Fines and their extent, and alternative penalties. . . .

Enforcement of Judgements in Civil Cases.

5. By execution against property &c.

Chiefs' Oaths.

6. Lawful oaths.

7. Unlawful oaths.[1]

8. Persons to be punished for doing unlawful acts under oaths.

Appeals and Applications to the Court.

9. Procedure on seeking relief.

10. Security as the Court directs.

11. Process to be issued.

12. Limits of appealable value, &c.

320 C. C. LEES TO SIR MICHAEL HICKS-BEACH[2] NO. 230.

ACCRA, 18 NOVEMBER, 1878.

Sir,

I have the honour to bring before your notice the subject of stipends to native kings in the Protectorate.

It is desirable to grant these stipends for

---

[1] Oaths which involve a curse or depreciation against the life of any person, or an excessive pecuniary penalty.

[2] Sir Michael Edward Hicks-Beach, 9th Bt. (later 1st Earl St. Aldwyn) (1837–1916): Conservative M.P., 1864–1905; Secretary of State for Colonies, 1878–80; Chancellor of the Exchequer, 1885–6; 1895–1902.

many reasons, and among them I offer for your consideration the facts that the granting them would tend to increase the influence of this Government by attaching the kings, who, as a rule, having very little command of money, would be very sensible of the stipend; and at the same time it would tend to increase the feeling of a community of interests between the kings and the Government. It would also tend to increase the influence of the kings over their people as well by the aid given by the possession of the money, as by the evidence it would afford of their being substantially recognized by the Government.

It is also a measure commended by justice, since the English rule has closed sources of gain — not necessarily oppressive — which but for it would have been open to the kings; and as they are expected and required to co-operate with the Government, they ought to be encouraged to do so cheerfully. The precedents of Sierra Leone and the Gambia are in favour of the measure.

Besides these reasons, in my opinion, any scheme of direct taxation — and one is under consideration — would depend for its success in a great measure on the disposition of the kings, and I think it would be better to give them an interest in the revenue before attempting to increase it directly at the expense of their subjects.

I have not seen my way clearly hitherto to proclaiming the Native Jurisdiction Ordinance, as the parts of the Protectorate in which it is most required are those furthest removed from the seat of Government, and I have not had at my disposal an officer of sufficient native experience whom I could spare to send on a mission to explain and make clear to the kings the purport of the Ordinance. I shall be glad to have your leave to delay entrusting its ample powers to the kings until I receive your reply to this despatch. The expectation of the stipends would influence the way in which the kings administer the Ordinance and render them more sensible to any observations on the subject which the Governor might feel at any time called upon to make to them.

Two modes of determining the relative amounts of the stipends present themselves. The one is to make the stipends proportionate to the distance from the seat of Government; that is, inversely to the influence that can be exercised by the Government over the territories of the several kings.

The other mode is to proportion the stipends to the importance of the kings and of the services which they are able to render to the Government. There are, however, objections to both modes. The first mode is open to the objection that some of the kings resident near the seat of Government exercise influence over the more distant kings, which is admitted by those kings themselves, and it would not do to pay the inferior king more than his superior. The second mode is objectionable by reason of the jealousies that would be occasioned among the kings, extent of territory and number of subjects being by no means always commensurate with the value of the king's services.

I therefore incline to think that the better course is to begin by giving all the kings the same stipend, fixing it at a minimum of £40 per annum, but this should not be considered a permanent arrangement as it will be liable to be modified by increasing the amounts to deserving recipients or by adding to their number.

I submit for your approval the kings of Apollonia, Denkera, Tchuffel Denkera, Western Wassaw, Eastern Wassaw, Ahanta, Chama, Elmina, Assin, Cape Coast, Anamaboe, Gomoah, Winnebah, Mankessim, Agoonah, Adjumaco, Ekoomfie, Western Akim, Eastern Akim, Aquapim, Accra James Town, Accra Ussher Town, Christiansborg, Eastern Croboe, Western Croboe, Addah, Ahwoonah, as those to whom the stipend should first be granted. The state of the revenue would seem to justify the expenditure.   [C.O.96/125]

321 LEES TO HICKS-BEACH NO. 231.
ACCRA, 18 NOVEMBER, 1878.

Sir,

I have the honour to acknowledge the receipt of your despatch Gold Coast No. 138 of the 30th September, and with reference to the last paragraph[1] to say that, bearing in mind the opposition made to the poll tax which was imposed some years ago, and to the fact that the collection of any direct taxation would be most difficult without the concurrence and co-operation of the kings and chiefs, I have though it desirable to postpone recommending such a measure until you have decided whether or not the kings and chiefs should receive the stipends as recommended in my despatch, Gold Coast No. 230 of 18 November 1878.   [C.O.96/125]

322 HICKS-BEACH TO LEES
31 JANUARY, 1879.

. . . With regard to the proposed acquisition of the Afflahow coast, I should wish, before coming to a decision on the subject, to receive from you a more definite opinion as to the precise amount of territory which it will be necessary to take in order to secure the object aimed at. . . .

You will, of course, bear in mind that Her Majesty's Government are averse to any unnecessary extension of territory, and the responsibilities which it implies, on the West Coast of Africa; and that unless some spot can be found, the possession of which would enable the Gold Coast Government effectually to check the importation of contraband goods, the only result will be that the traders will again remove their factories beyond British jurisdiction, and the same process would have to be repeated indefinitely.

I observe that Captain Hay is of opinion that the occupation of the coast up to and

including Bagadah would suffice for the purpose, as this would enable the Government to prevent the passage of smuggled goods through the lagoons, which, from the sketch map enclosed in your despatch[1] apparently terminates a short distance beyond Adaffia.

You point out in your despatch that Elmina Chica and Adaffia appear to have been occupied under the Treaty of Peace with the Ahoonahs, to whom, however, these places did not belong, and you suggest that the kings and chiefs of Agbosomeh, who are the rightful owners, should receive some satisfaction and be induced to acquiesce formally in our occupation.

I do not gather from your despatch that the Agbosomehs have as yet made any complaint or protest on the subject, and I should be glad to know in what way you would propose to open communications with them. It appears to me to be undesirable without good reason to raise a question of difficulty and importance, and to make it known that we had occupied and collected duties at those places by virtue of a treaty which did not give us the right to do so. It would seem better, in the absence of any complaint from the Agbosomehs, to treat the annexation of Elmina Chica and Adaffia as an accomplished fact which the Government is under no necessity to explain or justify. . . .   [C.O.96/125]

323 HICKS-BEACH TO LEES
13 MARCH, 1879.

Sir,

I have the honour to acknowledge the receipt of your despatch No. 6 of 12th January, forwarding a Petition from the king and chiefs of Agbosomeh, in which they complain of the annexation of their territory, and desire that the detachments of Houssas now stationed there may be withdrawn.

It appears from the enclosures to your despatch that a somewhat similar representation was made to Sir Sanford Freeling

---

[1] Inviting him to consider 'the question how far it may be possible to impose any direct taxation upon the native inhabitants of the Colony and the best means of doing so'. Hicks-Beach had raised this earlier in his despatch No. 4 of 8 February, 1878.

[1] No. 252 of 18 December, 1878.

in April 1877, and that you afterwards, at a personal interview with the representatives of the Agbosomehs, arranged the matter apparently to their satisfaction. You ought to have informed me of these proceedings in your despatch No. 252 of 18th December last, as my reply (No. 212 of 31st January) was founded upon the assumption that no protest against the occupation of the sea-board of their territory had ever been made by the Agbosome people.

I have now to instruct you to inform the king and chiefs that I have received and considered their petition: but that the British Government, having deemed it necessary for the peace and welfare of the Gold Coast Colony, to incorporate in the Protectorate the portion of the sea-board over which they claim authority, it is not possible now to relinquish or withdraw from it. You will add that Her Majesty's Government nevertheless desire to remain on friendly terms with the Agbosome chiefs and to secure their co-operation in the maintenance of peace and order and the prevention of smuggling; and that with this view the Government of the Gold Coast will pay to the principal chiefs an annual stipend, the receipt of which will, however, be conditional upon their good behaviour.

I think it desirable to leave it to your local knowledge and experience to decide as to which of the chiefs should have stipends assigned to them, and the amount which should be given in each case. You will, of course, report to me the arrangements which you may make.

The petitioners should be further informed that Her Majesty's Government regret to hear complaints of the misconduct of the Houssa police, and have already issued instructions to the Colonial Government which, they hope, will prevent any repetition.

I shall hope to receive from you an early report as to the proposed extension of jurisdiction beyond Adaffia, in reply to my despatch . . . of 31st January last.

I have etc.   [C.O.96/126]

324 HICKS-BEACH TO LEES
23 APRIL, 1879.

Sir,

With reference to Sir S. Freeling's despatch No. 143 of 19th May, 1877, on the subject of the encouragement of schemes for gold exploration in the Gold Coast Colony, I have the honour to transmit to you a copy of a letter from Lieutenant Colonel Wray asking for countenance and recognition for the African Gold Coast Company, who are now engaged in working mines at Tarqua in the neighbourhood of Axim. I also enclose a copy of the reply which by my direction was returned to Colonel Wray, and of a further letter which he has addressed to this Department.

I have to request that you will give your attentive consideration to this question, and report to me whether, in your opinion, the countenance and reasonable assistance of the Colonial Government may properly be extended to the operations of the Company.

I am disposed to think that circumstances have somewhat altered since Sir S. Freeling's report was written, and the fact that the African Gold Coast Company appear to have obtained a regular and bona fide concession for working the mines, from the native chiefs, would seem to have removed one of the principal difficulties which, in his opinion, were likely to hinder the successful prosecution of gold-seeking enterprises.

If on political grounds there is no objection to be taken to the operations of the Company, their action in introducing capital and machinery, and to a certain extent opening up the country, must, I think, be beneficial to the commercial and social interests of the Colony.

I have etc.   [African (232)]

325 HICKS-BEACH TO LEES
25 APRIL, 1879.

Sir,

I have to acknowledge the receipt of your Despatch No. 32 of the 25th of February, reporting that the king of Ashanti had been interfering in the affairs of Adansi, and that you had sent Captain Hay on a mission to Adansi in consequence.

You likewise enclose a copy of a letter which you had addressed to the king of Ashanti, in which you protest against the acts of his servants in Adansi, contrary to the Treaty of Fommanah, and call upon him at once to fulfil his treaty obligations by withdrawing his messengers and discontinuing to interfere in the internal affairs of Adansi.

You add, in the letter to the king, that Captain Hay, should he find Ashantees remaining in Adansi against the wish of the king, is to request them to return to their country.

I trust that if any such request is made, it may be peaceably complied with, and that the king himself will recognize the propriety of observing the Treaty of Fommanah entered into by his predecessor with Sir Garnet Wolseley.

But the action which you took upon this occasion was of a character which might possibly have placed the local Government, and ultimately the Imperial Government, in some embarrassment, should the Ashantis decline to comply with the demands made upon them. In dealing with savages, the refusal of a demand can seldom be left unnoticed; and demands should not therefore be made unless there is a settled purpose beforehand to enforce them, directly or indirectly, in the event of their being refused.

Adansi is not within the Protectorate, and the question of requiring the observance of the 3rd article of the Treaty of Fommanah is one of external policy, on which the Government of the Gold Coast should refrain, unless in case of urgent necessity, from definite action, until Her Majesty's Government had decided whether the action proposed was proper and opportune, having regard to the general interests of the Empire. I have to request that in future you will bear this caution in mind; and that you will take no further steps in

the matter now under consideration, without the previous sanction of Her Majesty's Government.

I have etc.

[C.3064, A & P (1881) lxv]

326 H. T. Ussher to Sir M. Hicks-Beach

ACCRA, 18 JULY, 1879.

Sir,

Referring to Sir S. Freeling's despatch, Gold Coast No. 143 of the 29th May, 1877 . . . on the subject of the concessions of land made by native chiefs to the African Gold Coast Company, and to an opinion of the Acting Chief Justice, in which he agrees with those views . . . I am constrained humbly to differ from them, at all events as to their practical bearing on the case now before me. . . .[1]

It is, as the Acting Chief Justice states, undoubtedly difficult to realise the extent and value of these concessions, but that argument must be held to apply with equal force to the Company, who may fail to make their speculations remunerative, and who have commenced operations by disbursing heavy sums on the mere chance of success. And although King Ango[2] and his chiefs are stated to have been unable to comprehend the possible benefits hereafter to accrue to them from the 3% royalty, the fact of that consideration having been extended to them still remains and, if the mines prosper, the solid results will tend to induce their successors to keep to the bargain.

The difficulties that may hereafter arise in this matter can scarcely at this time, and in the present transition state of native law and customs, be correctly anticipated, and I think that they should be taken and dealt with in a proper spirit of justice, in the law-courts, as from time to time they may arise. If companies commencing undertakings of a beneficial character to this Settlement are

[1] The application of the African Gold Coast Company for the countenance and reasonable assistance of Government in their activities.

[2] Ango of Apinto was an important sub-chief of Wasaw-Fiasi.

to be hampered at the outset by these and similar considerations, it will prove an effectual obstacle to future enterprise. A certain risk must necessarily be incurred in so good a cause by both parties to the agreement — the companies and the native authorities, who are by no means so foolish as might be supposed, and whom I hold to be capable, as a rule, of looking after their own interests. It might *prima facie* be conceded that the kings and chiefs making these concessions knew what they were about; and so, in an equal degree, must I consider the Company to have known these possible difficulties beforehand.

After a review of all the circumstances, I am of opinion that it would be injudicious to raise any questions in advance, unless in a case clearly shown, of real injustice or oppression. The raising of such points would possibly involve the Government in disagreeable complications, and perhaps necessitate lengthy and costly enquiries and missions, and even troublesome legislation at an inconvenient time. It would simply amount to inviting complaints from one side or the other, whereas as far as I can learn just now, none exist. Doubtless these and many other important matters concerning native law and custom will come eventually before the courts of justice and will have to be dealt with by the Government: but to raise them at present, by interfering unsolicited between either party in this case, would be more likely to create difficulties and raise a feeling of general discontent than to effect any permanent good.

As far as concerns Colonel Wray's request for special countenance and recognition to be accorded by Her Majesty's Government to the African Gold Coast Company . . . I see no reason for treating this differently to any other commercial undertaking. Such an enterprise should undoubtedly enjoy the full amount of protection and encouragement which would be afforded to any other legitimate attempt to develop the resources of the Settlement, but no more; for any exceptional favour in the

way of the remission or refund of duties, for instance, would surely open the door to requests which might be of an embarrassing nature and prove inconvenient precedents.

It must, however, be borne in mind, that in the interests of the public peace, in the event of a large influx of people consequent upon the well-established success of the mines, it may be necessary to take additional measures for the due preservation of life and property, and that it may hereafter be advisable to establish at the principal mining centres a District Commissioner, with a competent police force, to keep order and suppress lawlessness. . . .

[C.O.96/126]

327 USSHER TO HICKS-BEACH

24 JULY, 1879.

[The Ashantis had withdrawn from Adansi before his arrival on the coast.]

. . . The attitude of Gaman and possibly of Shawi[1] towards Ashanti is threatening; and there is no doubt in my mind that Ashanti unaided would be eventually crushed in a contest with these states. Hostilities of a desultory nature are, I am given to understand, still in progress. But beyond maintaining friendly relations with Gaman and Shawi, for the purpose of keeping open the roads to the interior in the north west, I see no reason for intervention of any kind. The friendship of Gaman is of high importance to this Colony, and will probably eventually exercise a great and beneficial influence upon our trade.

I found that in the early part of this year, three hundred rifles had been permitted to pass up to Ashanti through Cape Coast. They were at first detained, but subsequently permitted to be sent on. In a similar manner, the Ashantis have been permitted, it would appear, to purchase powder and lead.

There can be no reasonable doubt that the king of Ashanti is and has been for some time collecting a body of Houssas, whom, with Prince Ansah's assistance, he is

[1] Sefwi.

endeavouring to drill. But I believe that that monarch's object, both in purchasing the rifles and munitions of war, and in intriguing with Adansi, was simply to strengthen himself against Gaman, and that he is fully aware of his complete powerlessness against the British Government, and would far rather be upon friendly terms with it, trusting possibly to our mediation in the case of his being worsted by his native foes.

At the same time, the integrity and independence of Adansi must be supported by all the means in our power of a pacific nature. If once any important ally of the Ashantis be, by intrigues, threats or promises, induced to return to its old allegiance, a danger will exist of others following suit, and Ashanti might after a lapse of years again find itself in a position to attempt to reassert its supremacy and reoccupy its old obstructive and menacing attitude towards the Protectorate.

I therefore am disposed respectfully to suggest that this Government should for the present remain passive, and not attempt any interference, but at the same time endeavour to observe a friendly neutrality to all those tribes; and I do not see, now that Ashanti has ceased to trouble Adansi, any necessity for a suspension of the freedom of importation of the ordinary arms and munitions supplied to the natives. And while on this subject, I may point out that the matter lies absolutely in our own hands, the old road to the coast to Krinjabo and Assinee, by which Ashanti once received large quantities of warlike stores, being blocked by unfriendly tribes. . . .

[C.O.96/126]

328 USSHER TO HICKS-BEACH
ACCRA, 21 JANUARY, 1880.

[Advises against any attempt to levy direct taxes.] . . .

It must moreoever be remembered that when Governor Hill imposed the Poll Tax, there was practically no other taxation worth considering, and the total revenue of

O

the Settlement rarely exceeded £5,000 or £6,000 per annum. . . . At present the natives complain of the, to them, heavy import duty on their favourite articles, rum, guns, and tobacco. The duty on spirits in 1856 was two pence per gallon: in 1880 it is two shillings and sixpence. . . . [Now] the Colony has a surplus of nearly £60,000, and I doubt whether the proceeds of a Poll Tax would, with the only mode of collection now possible, be worth the risk and trouble of attempting it under present conditions. . . . I do not think *a fortiori* that I need inquire into the feasibility of applying the far more complicated system of direct taxation in the Senegal, disclosed by the papers . . . in your despatch.[1]

With regard to the stipends of the chiefs, you only consider them as part of a scheme of direct taxation, and therefore . . . I would recommend its abandonment for the present. . . . But the question of the Native Jurisdiction Ordinance opens up a prospect of great difficulty, at least under our present system of government.

When slavery was abolished on the Gold Coast, and abolished, in my opinion, after too rapid and peremptory a fashion,[2] it was, I presume, thought necessary to give in some measure to the native chiefs, a substitute for the powers that, by the Ordinance abolishing slavery, they were summarily deprived of. Another object was doubtless to encourage them to educate themselves by degrees and relieve the courts of the coast of a considerable pressure of work, while raising the status of the chiefs and natives themselves. The scheme is feasible and can be carried out, but not in the manner intended, nor with the means at my disposal.

This scheme properly carried out, direct taxation can hereafter be attempted and probably with success. Under the present conditions of Government, both are out of the question; and you will find that each Governor has shrunk, as I do, from

[1] Hicks-Beach to Ussher, No. 354, 6 September, 1879.
[2] Cf. the Colonial Office minute by Hemming (6 February, 1875) that it had been 'somewhat precipitate' (C.O.96/115).

attempting to set in motion the Native Jurisdiction Ordinance. . . . Practically, the interior kings and chiefs have made little or no progress towards civilization. Their courts are as venal, their decisions as unjust, and they themselves as superstitious and ignorant as they were twenty, or for that matter, one hundred years ago. Each king or chief has generally some hanger-on, in the shape of an educated native, who writes letters and transacts what business he may have with the white man. This person, the only link binding him to the coast, is generally a fugitive from the Settlement who has received a scanty education at one of the missionary schools. His mind is on the same level with that of the king or chief, and he is probably more dishonest than the uneducated native, on account of his contact with the rogues of the coast. He deceives his master habitually, and of course falls in with all the native evil customs, bringing in addition a stock of cunning and fraud which his slight knowledge of figures and writing enables him to utilize.

Simple as is the wording of the Ordinance, to understand it would be utterly beyond the power of the native chief, if left to interpret it either by the aid of a hasty visit from the Commissioner from the coast, or at the doubtful hands of the person of the type above described. There are certain technicalities in it; more than that, certain principles underlying it, which would have to be carefully explained to the king or chief, and his practice of them would have to be subjected to careful supervision: but that would not now be possible. He should be required to exercise his jurisdiction under the constant or frequent care and direction of competent officers, and such officers must be appointed.

This . . . brings me to the suggestions which I have the honour to submit to you for the better government of the Gold Coast Settlement in its interior districts. . . .

While taxes, or rather import duties, heavy in comparison with those formerly levied on the Gold Coast, have been imposed, realising a reasonable and, for present purposes, ample revenue; and while the sufferance of powers only is left to native chiefs in the interior, it cannot fail to be remarked that next to nothing has been done to ensure to the poor and helpless inhabitants of that interior, the comparatively just and upright rule and the efficient protection of the law, which is accorded to the natives of the coast. . . . Our educational vote for the year 1880, including a sum of £300, granted in aid of missionary schools, amounts to but £991; our estimated revenue being £82,345, which is likely to be exceeded. The entire remainder of our expenditure, with the exception of a few occasional small payments in the shape of casual missions, and a vote of £800 for 'Aborigines' — the latter being mainly used as contingent expenses, presents to native chiefs &c. — is devoted to the benefit of a narrow strip of coast line.

Nothing is done for the interior worthy of the name. The chiefs are expected to keep up certain roads in their districts, which they rarely do, in consideration of a remuneration, in a few instances, of ten shillings per mile — a sum totally inadequate for the requirements of the roads in question; and if they neglect to do it, they are liable to be fined. But they complain, not without reason, that in taking away their slaves, their power to carry out the orders of the Government in this and other respects is practically removed; and doubtless it is hard to combat this theory, however well it may be known that for their own purposes they evade and break the law against slavery. A sum of £300 is voted for the Aburi and Prahsue roads, and occasionally, within a mile or two of the coast, other roads are cleared from time to time at a trifling expense: but with these few exceptions, the whole of the Gold Coast expenditure is devoted to the coast establishments and staff. . . .

The only road to improvement is to bring the European into immediate contact with the natives of the interior. A certain number of District Commissioners should be appointed, whose sole charge it should be, in conjunction with the native chiefs, to rule certain districts, hereafter to be formed, in nearly the same manner as they now, under the Government, rule the coast stations.

These Commissioners should be charged to sit periodically with the native kings and chiefs of their district in their due turn, explaining to them the working of the Native Jurisdiction Ordinance; seeing that justice is administered as far as may be without corruption; that the court fees and fines are duly collected and properly . . . accounted for; to be devoted to their separate districts, and, in fact, supervising, in a general way, the affairs of the provinces to which they may be appointed; remedying immediately abuses, complaints, and injustice, and reporting periodically to Headquarters.

Such officers would enable the well-disposed chiefs to become efficient rulers, and they would effectually check, and, if need be, cause to be removed, the unjust and law-breaking class of whom we have now too many. These officers, being also constantly on or about the frontier, would prove a valuable check to disputes with neighbouring tribes, and would protect the frontier line and symbolize British power as effectually within the interior limits of the Protectorate as on the coast.

They would greatly lessen the work of the coast Courts, and they would relieve the native of the interior from the obligation he is now under, either to travel many miles to obtain justice, or to do without it. In nine cases out of ten, the inhabitant of the remoter provinces prefers to suffer injustice at the hands of his chief, rather than undertake so doubtful and lengthy a journey; and the greater part of those aborigines are probably ignorant that justice can be obtained easily and inexpensively. I can get, as a rule, no complaints from Akim and other places, on the part of the subjects of those native chiefs of whom I complain. These matters only come to me at second and third hand, and for one complaint brought to me, dozens are never heard of.

The credulity, simplicity and ignorance of the interior native are incredible; and the clumsy devices by which he is ruthlessly plundered, too often by native officials of the lowest class and most contemptible acquirements, would excite laughter, did they not produce a feeling of depression and disappointment. . . .

When the authority of the proposed District Commissioner shall have been established, it will be time to carry out an improved scheme of native jurisdiction and direct taxation, the proceeds of which, together with the fines and fees of court, will cover all expenditure including reasonable stipends to the chiefs. . . .

[C.O.96/130]

329 USSHER TO HICKS-BEACH
ACCRA, 10 MAY, 1880.

. . . The reports of ill-treatment of the natives by the white and coloured traders, on and about the Volta, have now been confirmed by facts. A warrant was issued for the apprehension of an European clerk in the employ of Messrs F. & A. Swanzy, for brutally flogging an African at Amedica, and thereby endangering his life. . . . Mr. Turnbull, the senior agent of the firm, who came to see me on the subject, . . . pleaded that this was the universal custom, and that the king, Sackitey,[1] was powerless. This is true, for Sackitey has, on more than one occasion, begged for help against these turbulent characters. Mr. Turnbull also stated that it was a common practice to flog women for bringing impure oil, and to ill-treat them in other ways. . . .

I trust that on receiving this information, you will no longer hesitate to authorize me permanently to establish a District Commissioner and customs staff along the River Volta and its adjacent districts. The fact is that what I have repeatedly told you has come to pass. Possibly and probably the immediate reason is the annexation of Afflowhoo and Agbosome; viz. that the River Volta is developing large trading

[1] Konor of Manya Krobo, 1867–92.

proportions, and, as a natural consequence, a number of lawless and greedy traders are accumulating there and taking matters into their own hands. In answer to the accusations of cruel and arbitrary conduct towards the natives, they ask, 'Who are we to go to? The native chiefs have not the power, if they have even the will, to decide our cases, and we must take the law into our own hands. Send us a European magistrate, and it will cease.' This is the language of both Europeans and Africans.

Unless a competent District Commissioner be immediately appointed, I cannot well be answerable for the maintenance of order in the district to which I refer. I believe one native chief, indignant at his treatment, said, 'If the Government will not interfere, I must right myself', and, it is reported, has marched 200 men to attack a factory where one of his retainers was ill-treated.

I have said nothing, moreover, of the necessity for checking, in some measure, the steady and continuous persistence of slavery in most of its forms, which is encouraged by the freedom of trade with Salagha — in itself a most desirable thing, but, like many other good things here, bringing with it concomitant evils. . . .

In order to prove the . . . sympathy with which slavery is still regarded, I may mention that King Amoacoo Attah of Eastern Akim was deliberately acquitted, a few days since, by an educated jury, and in the face, to use the Queen's Advocate's own expression, of "uncontradicted and clear evidence", of two important charges of slavery and breach of the Slavery Abolition Ordinance. Had I relied on these cases alone, he would have escaped. . . .

[C.O.96/131]

330 H. T. USSHER TO THE EARL OF KIMBERLEY

ABURI HOUSE, 25 SEPTEMBER, 1880.

. . . Tarquah in the west, Mansue in the centre and Volta in the east, will serve as starting-points for an essay of the Native Jurisdiction Ordinance. In the case of the Volta division, the only one comparatively in a state of completion and about to be worked, your Lordship will perceive, from my despatch Gold Coast No. 236 of the 11th instant, and enclosing a proclamation on the subject, that the Civil Commissioner, whose headquarters will be at Odumasi in Eastern Krobo, will from time to time visit sundry other districts, or rather countries, at convenient periods. He will hold a court of appeal (and, if necessary, of first instance) wherever he goes, thus enabling native suitors to appeal at once on the spot, without proceeding to Accra — a troublesome proceeding for them. He will also be enabled, by selection of fitting chiefs, to make the first essay of introducing the Native Jurisdiction Ordinance, and of reporting thereon after a time.

From what I see up here and in Aquapim, the measure of introducing Europeans into the interior is looked upon with favour by the people. To the traders, it is, of course, distasteful, as many convenient little practices will have to be discarded; and lynch law, which doubtless exists, especially in and around Kpong, a receptacle for all the rascals in the eastern division, will be checked. The Civil Commissioner will also guard the revenue along the Volta frontier, and I expect will prove of great service in this respect.

As far as Tarquah is concerned, I am credibly informed that an accumulation of bad characters, escaped felons, and others of the Settlement, is already to be found there; and that a population of some seven or eight thousand people are at the mining centre. Here again, I believe, some of the employees and owners in the mines are very much averse from the appointment of a Commissioner; but I need not descant upon its utility, not to say necessity. The Civil Commissioner at Tarquah can keep an eye upon the two Wassaws, and the Axim and Apollonia districts; and he should have power, if need be, to supervise the proceedings of the District Commissioners of Axim and Dixcove.

With respect to the third Commissioner, whom I propose your Lordship should appoint for central Fanti, that officer's special seat of jurisdiction should be the countries lying along and near the main artery of the Prahsue road, the way to the Ashanti frontier, or rather that of Adansi. While, in a similar manner to his colleagues of Tarquah and the Volta, he shall exercise certain judicious powers, having a fixed place for headquarters, the Commissioner could watch the proceedings of Ashanti along the frontier; superintend the erection of the block-houses, suggested to be placed along that road; and see that the road itself is kept free and open.

All these officers should, of course, periodically, or as occasion may require, report to the Governor on the general state of affairs in and about their districts, and keep him well informed. Authentic intelligence is difficult to obtain from native sources. . . .

While I am on the subject of Commissioners, I must point out to your Lordship that the growing importance of the settlement at Addah will soon demand the rule, in that district, of a competent European, and I may say the same of Axim. . . .

[C.O.96/132]

331 KIMBERLEY TO USSHER

19 NOVEMBER, 1880.

Sir,

I have received your further despatch No. 243 of the 25th September, in reference to the appointment of Civil Commissioners in certain interior districts of the Gold Coast Protectorate.

Although I fully recognize the importance of the appointment of Civil Commissioners at such places as Tarquah and the Volta, I entertain doubts as to the expediency of creating such an office for the interior Fantee District. . . .

The appointment of a Commissioner in this district must, as it appears to me, involve a considerable amount of that interference with the authority of the native chiefs, which I have explained to you in my despatch[1] to be contrary to the policy which Her Majesty's Government are anxious to see carried out in the Protectorate; namely, that the local administration should, as far as practicable, be left in the hands of the native chiefs, and their authority supported within reasonable limits. If the Protectorate were to be divided into separate districts, each under the control of a European Commissioner, not only would the direct responsibility of the Government be largely increased, but progressive augmentation of expenditure would be certain to follow, both of which results would, in my opinion, be very undesirable.

Unless, therefore, you are able to show some further reason for the appointment of the Commissioner on the Prahsue road, I am not prepared to approve of the proposal.

I have etc.

[C.O.96/135]

[1] No. 68 of the 16 July, 1880.

24 Troubles in Ashanti, 1881–1883

THE policy of non-intervention in Ashanti, resumed after Wolseley's march to Kumasi, survived the defeat of Juabin in 1874 (314), and Ashanti interference in Adansi in 1879 (327). Even a threatened invasion of the Protectorate itself in 1881 brought no change (332). The military measures then adopted by the Earl of Kimberley hardly went beyond those recommended by Cardwell in 1864 (333); and although he was prepared to approve periodic missions to Kumasi, he was anxious to avoid even the appearance of encouraging Ashanti's neighbours and enemies (334). When Captain Lonsdale was sent up twice in 1882 to Kumasi, the second time to investigate a boundary dispute between Ashanti and Gyaman, Kimberley disapproved of any British officer arbitrating in such a question (335), and refused to consider the possibility of appointing residents in Ashanti and beyond.

The Earl of Derby reiterated this refusal in the following year (336), but he could not continue to ignore events across the Pra. In the course of 1883, Ashanti affairs became increasingly confused. Partly because he was judged too subservient to the British, one Asantehene (Mensa Bonsu) was deposed in February 1883. The divisions in the kingdom were bad for trade, and for that reason, a mission of observation was sent up (338) to report on the situation (339). As a result, the British Government brought itself to agree to assist with the enstoolment of a new Asantehene: but with many reservations aimed at evading any new responsibilities for the future (340). Then the one candidate who commanded wide-spread support died, and the confusion in Ashanti was worse than ever. But by that time, the British authorities had more pressing problems to face elsewhere.

332 W. B. GRIFFITH[1] TO THE EARL OF KIMBERLEY

CAPE COAST, 24 JANUARY, 1881.

. . . It is with the deepest regret I have to state to your Lordship my belief that the Ashantis intend to force another war upon the Gold Coast Colony, and that they may commence hostilities at any moment. On 18th January, an Ashanti prince, who had escaped from Coomassie, entreated British protection; next day, a messenger from the king of Ashanti, bearing his gold axe, and accompanied by ambassadors, one being Saibie Enquie who signed the treaty of peace with Sir Garnet Wolseley at Fommannah, requested an audience, when they demanded that the refugee should be given up to them. I declined, whereupon Enquie, supported by others, stated that if I did not surrender the man, the king of Ashanti

[1] On Griffith see p. 427 and n.

would attack Assin. I called Enquie's attention to the Treaty, Articles 1 and 3, and warned him that the consequences of breaking them would be very serious. The messenger and suite then left, but subsequently I instructed them to remain at Cape Coast until today, considering it best to put my reply to the king's demand in writing.

The refusal of a demand from Ashanti accompanied by the gold axe, means war on the part of the Ashantis; that they will cut their way to the accomplishment of their purpose. The gold axe was sent down in 1863 and 1873 and war followed. All chiefs, public officers and respectable merchants, warn me to prepare for war with the Ashantis, and that it is imminent. I am very loath to believe it, but nevertheless am taking every available measure and precaution in my power for the protection of the Colony. I shall carefully avoid provoking hostilities, and shall act strictly on the defensive. . . .

[C.3064, A & P (1881) lxv]

333 THE EARL OF KIMBERLEY TO SIR S. ROWE [1]

DOWNING STREET, 15 FEBRUARY, 1881.

Sir,

I have the honour to acknowledge the receipt of Lieutenant-Governor Griffith's Despatch of the 24th January, confirming his telegram of the same date, furnishing the evidence upon which his apprehension of an outbreak of war with Ashanti was founded, and reporting the steps which he had taken in consequence.

I have to express my approval of the energetic measures adopted by Mr. Griffith to meet the emergency which had arisen.

He was undoubtedly right in refusing to comply with the demand of the king of Ashanti for the surrender of the Gaman Prince Owoosoo, and the Assin trader Amangkrah, and I approve of the letter which he addressed to the king in reply to his message.

Mr. Griffith will, however, have learnt from my telegram of the 7th instant, that I am of opinion that it might be judicious to remove Owoosoo from the Gold Coast. If you find that this has not been done, you will, of course, be guided by the state of affairs on your arrival in determining whether it is expedient to remove him.

You will use every endeavour to induce the native tribes within the Protectorate to combine for their own defence, and in organising their forces you will have the assistance of the officers who have been placed at your disposal for special service.

The Houssa Constabulary, from its peculiar constitution and mobility, will afford a valuable means of establishing a nucleus round which the native levies may rally.

But in any measure which may be taken,

[1] Sir Samuel Rowe (1835–88); served in the army and colonial medical service; served in the Ashanti war of 1874; Governor of Gambia (1876), Sierra Leone (1877) and Gold Coast (1881–4).

you should bear in mind that it is of the utmost importance that the safety of the forts and coast towns should not be imperilled, and no operations should therefore be contemplated which, in the event of failure, would leave those positions unprotected.

In the event of an invasion of the Protectorate by the Ashantis, you will place the whole of the forces of the Colony, native levies as well as Houssas, under the Officer commanding Her Majesty's troops, whose duty it will be to decide, in consultation with you, what operations it may be necessary to undertake. I may observe, however, that Her Majesty's Government are of opinion that the duty of defence must in the first instance devolve upon the native levies, with such assistance in the way of arms and munitions of war, and the counsel and direction of white officers as the Colonial Government are able to afford, and with the support of the Houssa Constabulary and possibly some small contingent of West India troops, if, in the opinion of the Officer commanding they can be employed without in any way compromising the security of the forts on the coast.

This is in accordance with the principles laid down by Lord Cardwell in his despatch of 23rd June, 1864, to which I have to refer you for your guidance.

The Secretary of State for War has, as you are aware, arranged to send direct from Barbados to the Gold Coast, about 500 officers and men of the 2nd West India Regiment, to reinforce the troops already there. Colonel Justice will accompany them from Barbados, and on arrival will assume the military command. I have no doubt that he will cordially co-operate with you in any action which may be required for the defence of the Colony, and you will be careful to consult fully and freely with him on all occasions.

Should it be determined that he should take the field for active operations with Her Majesty's troops, you will, of course, render him every assistance in your power, and place at his disposal, so far as may be consistent with the essential requirements of your Government, all the resources of the Colony.

But Her Majesty's Government earnestly hope that the necessity for hostile operations may after all not arise, and that you may be able, by timely communications with the king of Ashanti, to prevail upon him to observe the engagements of the Treaty of Fommanah, and to refrain from making war upon the British settlements or the protected tribes.

In the event of your efforts in this direction proving successful, and a war being averted, Her Majesty's Government are of opinion that it will be desirable to endeavour to make arrangements for periodical meetings, once perhaps in every year, between the king of Ashanti and the Governor of the Gold Coast, or his representative, at some convenient place, so that there may be an opportunity for free and friendly discussion of any points which either party may desire to bring forward.

It is possible that these meetings might with advantage take place at Coomassie itself, and that it might be well to send an annual or biennial mission to that city, in charge of some officer of high rank attached to the Gold Coast Government.

I shall be glad to receive an expression of your opinion on this point after you have had time fully to consider it.

I am etc.   [C.3064]

334 KIMBERLEY TO ROWE
15 MARCH, 1882.

Sir, I have the honour to acknowledge the receipt of your despatches . . . reporting the efforts which you have made to encourage communication and open up trade with the tribes in the interior beyond the Gold Coast Protectorate.

I approve of your endeavours in this direction, which I trust will be productive of good results.

There is, however, obviously a danger that these proceedings should give rise to the belief that the Gold Coast Government

is seeking the alliance of the tribes bordering on Ashanti, with a view to future operations against that kingdom, and that the result might be to encourage those tribes in hostile design against their neighbours, and at the same time to awaken alarm and suspicion in Ashanti itself.

I perceive from . . . your despatch of the 18th January, that you are conscious of this, and I have observed with satisfaction, the pains which you took to impress upon the representatives of the tribes westward of Ashanti, that Her Majesty's Government have no intention of attacking the Ashantis, and that the differences which recently existed have been amicably settled.[1]

I am confident that you will continue to exercise the same discretion in your dealings with these tribes.

I have etc.
[C.3386, A & P (1882) xlvi]

335 KIMBERLEY TO ROWE
12 DECEMBER, 1882.
Sir,

I have received Captain Moloney's despatch of the 12th September, enclosing a report by Captain Lonsdale[2] of his recent mission to Ashanti and Gaman. . . .

Captain Lonsdale's suggestions as to the employment of Consuls or Residents in Ashanti and other interior countries, could not, in my opinion, be adopted with advantage. Such appointments, besides the expense which would be incurred in maintaining the necessary establishments, would involve grave responsibilities, in the event, which in such barbarous countries cannot be considered improbable, of these officers suffering any outrage or indignity at the hands of the native chiefs.

I gather from Captain Lonsdale's report, that he has to a certain extent committed

---

[1] In June 1881.

[2] Captain Rupert LaTrobe Lonsdale; served in the Gaika and Zulu wars; sent on mission to Kumasi and Salaga, October 1881–February 1882 to open trade routes; mission to Kumasi and Gyaman, April–August 1882 (Report in C.3687) to investigate boundary dispute; went on third mission to Kumasi in 1887.

the Government of the Gold Coast to an undertaking to settle the disputes between Ashanti and Gaman. Such an undertaking appears to me to be open to very serious objection, and if you have reason to believe that Ashanti and Gaman regard what Captain Lonsdale said as constituting a distinct engagement on the part of the Colonial Government, and are expecting its fulfilment, I should wish you to consider whether they should not be informed that even if you should send up an officer to act as arbitrator and arrange the disputes between them on this occasion, it must be clearly understood that the Government will not be bound to enforce the observance of the agreement, or to assist either party in the event of the other violating its conditions. . . .

[C.3687, A & P (1883) xlviii]

336 THE EARL OF DERBY TO SIR S. ROWE
30 JANUARY, 1883.

Sir,

I have received Lieutenant-Governor Griffith's despatch of the 22nd ultimo and its enclosures on the subject of the state of trade between the countries in the interior and the coast.

As regards the suggestion offered by certain merchants of Cape Coast, that a British Resident should be appointed at Coomassie, I am of opinion that there are strong reasons of policy and prudence against any such appointment, and the proposition is one which Her Majesty's Government cannot entertain.

I have etc.

[C.4052, A & P (1884) lvi]

337 ROWE TO DERBY
CHRISTIANSBORG CASTLE, 14 FEBRUARY, 1883.

. . . Mr Bowden[1] stated to me that he was authorised to see me as the representative of the whole of the companies engaged in mining enterprise at Tarquah. . . .

[1] Manager of the Tarkwa and Abosso Gold Mining Company.

The point which he appeared most wishful to impress on my mind was the necessity of the construction of a road from Axim to Tarquah. He stated that the managers of the companies had found by experience that it was impossible to obtain satisfactory results from their mines without the use of much heavier machinery than they have hitherto been able to carry up to them.

He stated that there is no doubt that the gold ore at the mines is rich enough to yield a handsome return if it be properly worked. At the present cost of working, the yield of 5 dwts in America gives a better return than 15 dwts would give at Tarquah. The heaviest weight of the machinery at present working at Tarquah is 3 cwt. But he wishes to introduce stamps of double this weight.

He states that he calculates the distance of Tarquah from Axim direct is about 31 British statute miles. This is according to the calculations of Commander Cameron and of Mr Barham who was sent to Tarquah to survey the country with the view to ascertain the possibility of the construction of a line of railway from the coast to the mines. That although a part of this journey can be completed by river, reducing the land journey to one and a half days . . . from Tomento to Tarquah, he . . . is of opinion that the uncertainties of the Ancobra bar, the inconveniences attending the transport of machinery from Axim overland to the Ancobra, its embarkation from the mouth of the river, and its debarkation from the river at Tomento or Bonsah, make it practically undesirable to use the river as a means of transport; and that so soon as a good road is constructed, the river will not be used as a highway for the transport of any stores or persons to places so far from the river bank. . . .

I told Mr Bowden in reply that Her Majesty's Government in England are anxious to do everything in their power to develop legitimate industry in any part of the coast; that they will be exceedingly pleased to see the gold mines yielding good returns on the capital invested: but I added that I did not think, considering the present demands on the revenue of the Colony, that it would be thought fitting at present to alienate so large a sum[1] from the general revenue . . . for the construction of this road; still I would very carefully consider the question. . . .

[C.4477, A & P (1884–5) lv]

338 SIR S. ROWE TO CAPTAIN KNAPP BARROW[2]   CHRISTIANSBORG CASTLE, 31 MARCH, 1883.

. . . In consequence of the disturbed and depressed state of the trade of the western district of the Colony (especially with regard to that of the town of Cape Coast Castle), which is said to result from the complication at present existing in the affairs of the kingdom of Ashanti, consequent on the determination of certain tribes, formerly feudatories of that kingdom, to no longer submit to the authority of the king, I have decided upon sending an officer to visit the king of Ashanti, to ascertain for me the true state of affairs in his kingdom. . . . Relying . . . on your past experience in the conduct of interior missions, I select you for this duty. . . .

Should you succeed in seeing the king, . . . you will be careful . . . not to say anything that may lead the king or his people to suppose that, on coming at his request, to hear from him what are, in his opinion, the causes of the differences which at present exist between him and his people, you are prepared in any way to attempt to enforce any compliance with his wishes.

I strongly impress on you that it is necessary that you should exercise, during the whole of your journey on this mission, the utmost care and circumspection, so as to ensure that you do not say anything or do anything, which could, by any possibility, be made to appear or give cause to anyone to suppose, either that Her

[1] The estimated cost was £17,500.
[2] Joined the Gold Coast Artillery 1862; served in the war of 1863–4 and at Ikorodu (1865); Governor's A.D.C., 1879; Assistant Colonial Secretary, 1882; Colonial Secretary, 1884–7.

Majesty's Government desires to interfere in the internal affairs of the Ashanti kingdom, or that they will take any action in the reported quarrel between the king and his subjects.

I desire again to impress upon you, that your visit is one made solely with the view to gather information, which you will submit for my consideration. . . .[1]

[C.3687]

339 CAPTAIN KNAPP BARROW: REPORT ON HIS MISSION TO ASHANTI

5 JULY, 1883.

. . . Before leaving [Fomena] . . . I had an interview with King Inkansah, and drew his attention, and also that of his chiefs who were present, to the disturbed state of their neighbouring country, Ashantee; and impressed upon them how needful it was for all of them to abstain from any conduct which might in any way compromise the present position of affairs, and I implored them to open their roads in the interests of trade and civilisation.

It was reported to me that some Adansis had plundered traders on the open roads, and that there was a dread on the part of some people to travel the Adansi paths. The king and chiefs denied any knowledge of this state of things, and since then I have been confirmed in the opinion formed at the moment, that these robberies which produced stoppages of the roads, were the acts of 'young men', possessing a little education, absentees from the towns on the coast-line, who had settled themselves in the villages round about, levying blackmail ('settling palavers' as it is called locally) upon the more inoffensive and innocent dwellers in the villages, by representing themselves as armed with some kind of authority from our Government, which these simple and unsuspecting villagers believed, and thereupon admitted them to their private meetings, placed implicit confidence in all that they told them, supplying

[1] The instructions were approved by Derby, 25 March, 1883. *Ibid.*

them with food and money in return, and paying the greatest respect to their evil and corrupt counsels. Thus these villagers were often led astray and often into rebellion and hostility with their lawful or properly constituted kings and chiefs. A discharged Fantee policeman, who when serving may have happened to have gone to these people on duty, is the instrument usually selected by these scholars to accompany them to the scene of their depredations, chosen because he will be recognised by the native people there as one who was in the Government service, and so by them is therefore presumably thought to be so still; hence the credence bestowed on the fabrications of the 'scholar'. In the Ashanti country, as I afterwards heard, there are many of this sect of people scattered over its provincial towns and villages, doing a vast lot of harm to the extension of trade: but in the present state of the Ashantee country . . . it would be difficult to deal with them, the obstacle being the absence of supreme ruling authority in the country. . . . [The Adansi chiefs were urged to take action against these elements.]

[At Amoafu, he learned that] King Mensah of Ashantee, upon receiving news of the death of the old king of Bequoi, in the form in which such events are communicated in the Ashantee country, sent a discourteous reply by the messengers who had borne him the news, which was most hurtful to the feelings of the Bequoi people, and to the deceased king's relatives, including Osai Yaow, the nephew, the present king: but I did not discover that this was the reason for the revolt of Bequoi against the Coomassie ruler, but apprehend, from all that I was enabled to gather together, that this revolt of Bequoi was the result of a determination on the part of the king of Bequoi to throw off an allegiance to a yoke under which his country had never prospered, in favour of an adoption of the more civilized and just laws of the constitution which he had heard the people enjoyed who lived on the other side of the Prah under British rule. His observation, repeated a

dozen times at least, was, 'I and my people, we all wish to be under the British Government.'

The chiefs of Dadiassie (Kokofu province) and of Daniassie[1] (under Coomassie town) both made the same remark, viz., that they wished 'to come under the British Government.' . . . Amuafa, chief of Dadiassie, explained that the rule of Ashantee was so cruel and severe that he could serve under it no longer; and upon no account would he ever serve under any king in alliance with the Ashantee monarch, either now or hereafter. He informed me that his immediate king, Osai Yaow, king of Kokofu, was in the habit from time to time, of disclosing to King Mensah of Ashantee, the names of the people in Kokofu province who had made money ('riches'); that then King Mensah would devise some pretext to find fault with them as a justification, from his point of view, for the imposition of a fine upon them, and that when the fine thus inflicted was paid, Mensah returned one half thereof to Osai Yaow, retaining the other half himself. . . .

The chief of Dadiassie, quoting his own words, as rendered to me by the interpreter, said impressively, 'I am tired of being plundered and pillaged,' and added, 'I ask for that intercession from the British Government which will be a "back stay" against such tyranny.' And he proceeded to say that unless he was freed from such oppression, he would run away with all his people to the coast, where he would settle and live.

I told him that there were two sides to every question, and that I should endeavour to ascertain what the king (Mensah) said. Meanwhile, I observed, 'You are making matters worse than they need be by closing your roads against all trade with the coast, which does harm to yourself, to the people who are under you, and I hear that you are preparing to attack

[1] Dadiasi lies four miles east and Denyiasi a mile west of Bekwai (with which Amoafu is now contiguous — they were a mile apart in 1874).

Osai Yaow, your king, by force of arms, which means bloodshed, and can never make you a king. Refrain from all these bad ways, leave your king alone unless he attacks you, open your roads, and encourage trade with the coast towns. . . .' Subsequently I discovered he had opened his roads as [he] promised. . . .

The chief of Daniassie, Awoosoo . . . said that he was one of the principal chiefs under King Mensah, but that ever since the accession to the 'Stool' of that monarch, he had been the victim of never-ceasing fines, which had reduced him to abject poverty. . . . Under no pretence whatsoever would he ever serve the Ashantee king again, or any king of Coomassie, and added that unless he was released from such cruel tyranny he would move down to the coast with all his people. . . . I reminded him that I had merely come to his country to gain information . . . as to the disturbed state of Ashantee, and that as I had written down what he had related to me, the best thing probably for him to do, under the circumstances, was to remain perfectly quiet until he knew more. . . .

On arriving at the village of Agemmam, [I] found Osai Yaow, the king of Kokofu, and the queen (his wife) awaiting my arrival. . . . He is an old man, and impresses one as possessing superior abilities to most native chiefs. . . . Of course he was anxious to hear what I was going to Coomassie for. At once I gave him an outline [of the reasons] for my being sent, but made him clearly to understand that he was not to imagine that the British Government was interfering in the affairs of Ashantee, or that it contemplated doing so. . . . The king then said that the country was in a bad state, and he hoped your Excellency would put some king on the 'Stool' of Ashantee in order that all the subordinate kings and chiefs might live at peace with the king of their country and with one another, and that order and stability may be restored, by those in rebellion being induced to come back again under their former allegiance. . . . He tried very hard to induce me to send messengers to his chief Amuafo, requesting him to return to his allegiance to him, but I declined. . . .

All the towns and villages throughout our route from Esang Quantah to Karsi[1] included, had revolted against the king (Mensah), but in each one . . . we were received with the most kind and welcome attention. . . . At the same time, the whole of the distance from the Prah to this evinced a total absence of traders and of persons passing up and down the road, owing to the fear felt by the people of leaving their dwellings and their families during the present disorganised and unsettled state of affairs in the Ashantee country. . . .

[He reached Kumasi on the 26th April.] The whole town was en fete in demonstration of the joy they felt at some one having been sent to them in their trouble. King Mensah was absent in retirement at his village called Abodie. I learnt privately that the elders and chiefs had decided not to send for Mensah. . . . Each day that I was in Coomassie, an interview took place between the chiefs or one of them and myself. . . . It would be wearying to detail the conversations which were thus held, but a summary of them established the fact that King Mensah was deposed and left Coomassie on the 8th of March; consequently, up to the date of my arrival in the town . . . he had been away forty days, an unprecedentedly long period for the 'Stool' to remain unoccupied, the average time, I was told, being about ten days. The elders and chiefs accounted for the wretchedly unclean sanitary condition of the town and for its streets being overgrown with grass, to the circumstance of there being no kingly authority in the country. It would appear that, in the absence of a king, there is no power vested in anybody to attend to these necessary measures for promoting the health and comfort of the people. . . .

[1] Esiankwanta, seven miles south of Bekwai; Kasi, two miles south of Kumasi.

It was an object with me . . . to endeavour to obtain interviews with as many kings and chiefs from the provinces and outlying towns and villages as was possible, if for no other reason than that of ascertaining the political relations to each other of the tribes forming the Ashantee kingdom. Towards this end I despatched messengers to Mampong, Insutah, Argoonah,[1] and other towns. . . . The general purport of the replies was that the kings would like to see me, but in the present unsettled state of their country, they could not leave their homes to join me in Coomassie or to meet me on the way down, and they wished me to go and see them instead. This I could not do, owing to the long time I had been out, and the bad state of the roads beyond and outside Coomassie. The king of Inquanta[2] . . . sent messengers [to say] 'that he could not go to Coomassie; that he will never do so; that he was the first to revolt, and that he wished to be under the rule of the British Government.'

The present position of the Ashantee country may be described as one replete with embarrassment and anxiety. A civil war has been averted by the happy circumstance of the mission from Accra arriving in Ashantee just in time to induce the elders and chiefs of Coomassie to desist from their . . . intention of putting the young Quacoe Duah on the 'Stool' of their country. This act would have enflamed the adherents and supporters of the ex-king Koffie Kalkali to hostile measures for his removal. The fire once kindled would soon have spread.

It is known that there are three candidates for the 'Stool' . . . Mensah has no supporters, is not likely to receive any, and may be said to entertain no hope of re-election. He is in bondage as a sort of state prisoner . . . in the village of Abodie. . . . He complains of being kept without

food, and he asked me to take him down to the coast. . . . It would be an act of charity if Her Majesty's Government could receive him, some provision being made for his maintenance.

The supporters of ex-king Koffee Kalkalli are uncertain in name and in numbers, and are likewise very wavering and fickle. He has, however, fewer now than he ever had. . . . When I left Coomassie, he was supported . . . by the provinces of Coranza, Mampong, Nsuta, Kokofu, and many smaller bodies such as Argoonah and Inquanta: . . . but they have all, according to the latest advices . . . seceeded from him, and he is now . . . a suppliant to your Excellency to support him in his candidature. The Argoonahs are reported to be his only supporters now. . . .

Quacoe Duah is supported by all the elders and chiefs in Coomassie. His candidature has never been canvassed outside Coomassie, but from all that I could learn on the road . . . there is no reason to suppose that there would be any opposition to his election . . . except perhaps the instances of Bequoi, Danyassi, Dadiassie and now Inquanta, but these . . . could be satisfactorily disposed of in 'Durbar' at Prahsue. . . .

The general feeling of the people being opposed to heavy fining, human sacrifice and panyarring . . . they are anxious for the abolition of these customs. They are favourably disposed to general trading, increasing their agricultural callings, and to the undisturbed trading facilities with the coast, and unquestionably seek such a better form of government as will yield them what they want. They court and solicit your Excellency's intercessions towards these ends. . . . They say they cannot do it themselves, and that nothing but the British Government can. . . . All urged me to beg your Excellency to come to their assistance, to put their country straight for them, so that they may all be 'of one mind' as in the time of Governor Maclean whom they still revere and call to this day 'Obrodie Badaie' which means, 'The time

---

[1] Mampong, Nsuta and Agona, north-east of Kumasi, were three of the principal divisions of Ashanti.

[2] Manso-Nkwanta, a principal sub-division under Kumasi, 30 miles south-west of that city.

of the white man when everybody slept sound.'

[C.4052, pp. 32–59]

340 DERBY TO ROWE

31 OCTOBER, 1883.

[Acknowledges receipt of Barrow's report.] . . .

I gather from the various despatches and reports which I have received that there is no prospect of any settled peace in Ashanti until a king has been chosen who is accepted, if not unanimously, by at all events the greater part of the nation. It appears from your despatch of 7th September, that Coffee Kalkalli has been completely defeated and captured by the party of Quacoe Duah, and that a messenger had come down from the latter and the chiefs of Coomassie, to request you to send someone to help them 'to place Quacoe Duah on the Stool and to arrange for the proper management of the affairs of Coomassie.'

It is, of course, not desirable that any premature action should be taken, but at the same time, the re-establishment and maintenance of peace is of such vast importance to the trade and revenue of the Gold Coast Colony, that no opportunity of furthering the attainment of that end should be lost.

I think, therefore, that if you are able to satisfy yourself that Quacoe Duah is likely to establish himself firmly in power, and to be acknowledged by the bulk of the Ashanti tribes as King, you would do well to take measures for at once attaching him to the British Government, by making him suitable presents, and further express your willingness to meet him with the representatives of the nation at Prahsue (or such other place as you may consider convenient and suitable) and there proceed to ratify his election and instal him on the throne.

If such a meeting should take place, it would be desirable that it should be held with as much formality and dignity as possible. All the neighbouring kings and chiefs should be invited to be present at it, or to send representatives, and you should endeavour to arrange terms of peace and amity between them, embodying the whole in a treaty which they would sign in your presence, and you would ratify and confirm by your signature.

Of course, it would have to be clearly understood by the contracting parties, that the Governor, as representing Her Majesty, by signing the treaty undertook no responsibility towards any of them, but was acting only as a witness to the fact that they, in his presence, had made certain engagements with each other. . . .[1]   [C.4052]

[1] The Governor did not act on these instructions and Kwaku Dua was finally enstooled without his assistance on 27 April, 1884. Unfortunately he died of small-pox on 10 June.

25 The German irruption and the separation from Lagos 1883–1886

FOR some time the conviction had been growing in the Colonial Office, as they watched the energetic advance of the French into West Africa, that serious attempts would have to be made to reach an understanding with that country, 'for drawing a line of demarcation between the portions of the African coast over which respectively' the two Powers 'should be at liberty to acquire and exercise political influence'. It was coupled with a realisation that, 'as in the case of the Sibylline books, the longer we delay coming to a settlement, the higher will be the price we shall have to pay'.[1]

By 1883, too, British merchants, who had been among the foremost opponents of the attempt to reach a similar understanding in 1876 (315), were demanding action by the Government to prevent further annexations by foreign powers, of the coast between Lagos and the Gold Coast (341). As, in the same breath, they went on to deprecate the union of Lagos and the Gold Coast, the force of this recommendation was rather lost. The British Government did, however, open negotiations with the French, imposing a standstill on further annexations until these conversations should have issued in some definite result (347). Neither they, nor the merchants, nor indeed anyone else, were prepared for the sudden appearance of Dr. Nachtigal off the beach of Togoland, and his proclamation of a German Protectorate over that country in July 1884 (344).

This particular intervention may well have been inspired by the actions of the Gold Coast Government itself, which, ever since 1878, had been extending its frontiers in the direction of Togo (322–3), in order to prevent losses of revenue through smuggling. In 1884, Governor Young had already initiated negotiations (342), and his agent had even secured a provisional agreement (345) with the chiefs concerned, when the Germans stepped in. In spite of its annoyance at the manner of the German intervention, the Colonial Office did not think Togo worth a quarrel (346), especially when it secured its far more important Nigerian objectives at the Berlin West African Conference in December (348).

But an inevitable consequence was the separation of the two portions of the now bisected Colony (349). This was effected with the issue of new Letters Patent in January 1886 (350). In spite of the busy schemes of 1883–4 for partitioning the African coast, the Government remained as opposed as ever to pleas (351) for intervention in Ashanti (352). And although they were now aware of the need for forestalling the Germans (353) in key areas like the Volta (354a), they were not prepared to do so on *any* terms (354b).

[1] Minute by Hemming, 28 December, 1882. C.O.147/52.

341 MEMORIAL OF MERCHANTS IN THE CITY OF LONDON ENGAGED AND INTERESTED IN THE TRADE WITH THE GOLD COAST AND LAGOS   LONDON, 7 DECEMBER, 1883. Respectfully showeth,

That the following questions in connection with the Colony of the Gold Coast particularly call for the attention of Her Majesty's Government, and that were the views expressed in this Memorial carried out, the interests of trade and civilization would be promoted and the welfare of the community advanced.

1. That whereas in consequence of the

disturbed state of Ashantee and the neighbouring countries, the trade of the Gold Coast has lately been seriously affected, and whereas numbers of chiefs and their followers, only desirous of being left at liberty to live in peace and security, have petitioned his Excellency Sir Samuel Rowe, to come under British protection, the time has arrived when the question should be reconsidered of establishing a Resident at Coomassie, who would watch over and further British interests, and advise the king of Ashantee in matters connected with the internal government of his country.

2. That it is desirable Her Majesty's Government adopt measures to prevent the further annexation of any of the countries between the Gold Coast possessions and Lagos by any other European Power.[1]

3. That the Lagos Colony having since 1874 been placed under the Government of the Gold Coast, has produced serious inconveniences and has created in the minds of the merchants an earnest desire that the administration of the two colonies should again be separate and distinct.

4. That in each British possession on the West Coast of Africa there should be a separate and distinct Legislative Council, on which the commercial interests should be adequately represented by non-official members.

5. That the condition of the finances of the Colony calls for inquiry. The revenue now collected is fully treble what it was in 1872 and previous years, but nothing more is done for the benefit of the community and for the interest of trade. The enormous expenditure is mainly due to the large staff of officials necessitated by the system of short service. If their term of residence on the coast were for a longer period, the result would be considerable saving in expenditure and greater efficiency in the administration of the Colony.

6. That, as regards the Gold Coast proper, it is desirable the *ad valorem* duty

[1] In April 1883 the French had re-established themselves at Porto Novo and proclaimed a protectorate over Kotonu.

on manufactures &c, revived at the time of the Ashantee war and then increased to four per cent as a war tax, be repealed, and they be admitted free as formerly.

7. That there is urgent necessity for an inquiry into the condition and constitution of the Houssa force. With their want of discipline and character for plunder and insubordination, they are positively an element of danger and disturbance to the Colony.

8. That it is desirable that more attention be paid to the sanitary condition of the principal towns, and that much ought to be done to improve the condition of their streets and the approaches to them.

9. That the Gold Coast, being entirely without beasts of burden, or means of water intercommunication, there can be no real or important development of its resources or trade without the formation of railways.

That therefore it is desirable Her Majesty's Government give their support to the construction of a railway between Assin, Denkera and Cape Coast Castle, as recommended by the deputation of merchants and others that waited on Sir Samuel Rowe on the 2nd March last, respecting which, papers are already in the hands of your Lordship.

10. That with a view to furthering the development of the gold-mines in Wassaw district, the project for the construction of a railway between Axim and Tarquah is also deserving of the consideration of Her Majesty's Government.

11. That whereas immense risks are run to life and property by the present lax system of storing gunpowder, Her Majesty's Government should adopt the suggestion to erect a Government magazine, made by the merchants of Cape Coast, in a petition presented to Sir Samuel Rowe in June last, and that in addition to Cape Coast Castle, Government magazines be also erected at Axim and Accra.

12. That whereas at the present time great inconvenience is caused to merchants and others by the same persons being con-

tinually called to serve on juries, inquiry be made as to the way the lists are arranged. The existing Ordinance on the subject appears to be totally disregarded.

And your memorialists will ever pray.

Alex. Miller Brothers & Co., Fred. J. Crocker, Edmd. G. Gunnell, Wm. Cleaver, A. Hutton, Walter Griffiths, Chas. Sevin, F. Swanzy, C. Lintott, W. H. Selby, Alfd. Lintott, G. H. T. Lyall, Francis W. Macan, Banner Bros.

[C.4052. Rowe's reply to these and allied representations is in C.4477, No. 51, Rowe to Colonial Office, 10 August, 1884]

342 W. A. G. YOUNG[1] TO THE EARL OF DERBY   ACCRA, 30 JUNE, 1884.
. . . I find that the Customs Revenue from Quittah has been steadily declining for the three previous quarters and there can, I think, be but little doubt that the cause is the smuggling carried on from Beh Beach. In a recent report, Mr. Firminger[2] says that 'the trade of Beh Beach and Bageidah is daily increasing, and although the consumption of tobacco and gunpowder in my district must be very considerable, yet but little of the former, and not a keg of the latter has been sold here for the last four months, and the Customs Revenue of Quittah for May has fallen to £112. 19. 1d.'

I have already addressed your Lordship in my despatch No. 255 of the 29th April 1884, upon the expediency of acquiring territorial rights over Beh Beach, and I am anxiously awaiting your Lordship's reply. . . . Mr. Firminger is sanguine that for a stipend of about two hundred and fifty pounds per annum we can obtain this concession from the chiefs. . . .

[C.O.96/158]

343 YOUNG TO DERBY
                ACCRA, 8 JULY, 1884.
. . . I have the honour to forward herewith the copy of a report dated the 3rd July

[1] Government Secretary of British Guiana prior to his appointment as Governor of the Gold Coast.
[2] R. E. Firminger; assistant-inspector Gold Coast Constabulary, 1880; District Commissioner at Axim, 1880–1 and Keta, 1882.

1884, from Mr Inspector Firminger, detailing the result of his interviews with the chief people of BEH and with King Mensah of PORTO SEGURO, and communicating the promise which they have made concerning the cession of their territory to Great Britain.

Late yesterday evening I received a further report from Mr Firminger, dated 5th July 1884, 9-30 pm., in which he states that King Lawson of LITTLE POPO had been taken prisoner by the Commander of the German Man-of-War 'Moewe'; and that he had received information that the German officers of the 'Moewe' had landed at BAGEIDAH and BEH, and had endeavoured by threat and persuasion to force the people to sign a Treaty ceding the seaboard to the German Government, but without success.

As I consider that such a cession of territory would, if brought about, not only greatly complicate our political relations on this coast, but would be disastrous to British prestige on this coast, I propose despatching Captain Barrow, the Colonial Secretary, at the earliest moment possible, to proceed to the locality, and in conjunction with Mr Firminger, to complete the work which Mr Firminger commenced last month, and conclude provisional treaties with the BEH and BAGEIDAH people for the cession to Great Britain of their seaboard, and two miles inland from the shore. . . .

Unfortunately there is no Man-of-War at Accra at present, and some delay must inevitably occur in waiting for the Mail Steamer. This is annoying, as I fear that the people of BEH may at any moment be overcome by the persuasion or coercion of the Germans. . . .   [C.O.96/159]

344 YOUNG TO DERBY
                ACCRA, 9 JULY, 1884.
My Lord,

Referring to my despatch of yesterday's date . . . I have the honour to forward herewith a further letter, dated 6th July, 1884, which I have this morning received from Mr Inspector Firminger, enclosing a letter addressed to him by Dr Nachtigal, informing him that, duly authorized by his Government, he had concluded with the king of TOGO and his chiefs, a Treaty of Protection, which places the whole country of King Mlapa of TOGO (with BEH Beach or LOME, BAGEIDAH &c) under the protectorate of His Majesty the Emperor of Germany.

This action on Dr Nachtigal's part, cannot, I assume, be ratified at home. As a matter of international courtesy and good faith, it must, I apprehend, be repudiated by his Government. The very arguments he is reported to have used with the BEH and BAGEIDAH people . . . would prove that he was aware of the negotiations carried on by a representative of this Government, and consequently that he deliberately, as he represents on behalf of his Government, obtained a treaty from those people by inducing them to commit a gross breach of faith against the Government of a friendly Power. . . . The tenor of the communications made to the Foreign Office, forwarded to me in your Lordship's despatches No. 585 of the 25th April, 1884, and No. 613 of the 19th May, 1884, would lead to the inference that in this arbitrary annexation of territory, Dr Nachtigal could scarcely be acting upon other than his own responsibility. The least he could have done, in common courtesy, when he became aware of how the matter stood, was to have communicated with me before he concluded a treaty, or hoisted and saluted the German flag.

I notice that Dr Nachtigal proposes to address me at the earliest opportunity. I shall, of course, not attempt to enter into any controversy with him. I enclose herewith the copy of a letter which I propose to send to him by the first opportunity, in reply to his letter to the District Commissioner.

In that letter, your Lordship will observe, I take the grounds that the treaty which Dr. Nachtigal has concluded cannot affect BEH Beach or BAGEIDAH, inasmuch as that territory had already been virtually ceded to Great Britain; and the hoisting of the German flag I acknowledge as a Consular act; and I assure Dr Nachtigal of my readiness to acknowledge him in his Consular capacity. Mr Firminger does not mention in his official letters that he had actually reduced the terms of his Agreement with the chiefs to writing, and had obtained their signatures. But I learn this morning, from an unofficial letter which Mr Firminger addressed to Captain Barrow, that he actually did so, although he regarded it at the time merely as an aide-memoire. The document, however, if so desired, can no doubt be made of value. It certainly is substantial evidence of prior action. . . .

[C.O.96/159]

345 PROVISIONAL AGREEMENT WITH TOGO CHIEFS   23 JUNE, 1884.

Provisional Agreement between Reginald Edward Firminger, First Class Inspector of the Gold Coast Constabulary, Justice of the Peace and District Commissioner of Quittah, representative of Her Britannic Majesty's Government on the one part, and ABDODGA TABEH ALAHGRO, ASHIGBENO GAHJOKOR, and TSATSHA, Fetish chiefs and priests of Togo on the other part.

We the afore-mentioned chiefs and priests agree to cede to Her Britannic Majesty's Government, the seaboard of our country of Beh, extending from the frontier of Porto Seguro on the east to the British flagstaff on the west, under the following conditions viz:—

If at the expiration of one month from this date we are unable to induce, by fair and just means, the merchants and traders at Beh Beach or Lomeh and Bagaidah to leave our country.

[Witnesses' signs and signatures.] . . . Porto Seguro, 23 June, 1884.

[Confidential Print,[1] African (West) No. 411, West African Treaties, London, 1892, p. 331]

----
[1] Cited below as C.P.: P.R.O. series C.O.806.

346(a) MINUTE BY J. ANDERSON[1]
COLONIAL OFFICE, 4 AUGUST, 1884.

. . . As to the annexation of Beh Beach, the subsequent telegram of 10th July relieves us of the necessity of discussing it. We objected to the Portuguese levying toll on the interior trade through the Congo, but I suppose we have a divine right to levy toll on all trade with those parts of the interior which are reached through the Gold Coast or the neighbouring seaboard. The Germans naturally fail to see that we have any right to levy toll and obstruct trade with places which we do not either protect or govern, and if the French or Portuguese were in our position I have no doubt we should not much object to the annexation of Beh Beach. Before we annex more territory, and obstruct or kill trade with customs duties, we ought to do something more for the trade we already tax so heavily, by opening up roads and improving the landing places. It is difficult to say what service we at present render even the inhabitants of the protectorates in return for the taxes we levy. . . .

[C.O.96/158]

(b) MINUTE BY E. FAIRFIELD
COLONIAL OFFICE, 19 AUGUST, 1884.

This is rather a worse case than the Angra Pequena one, and we would have a right to remonstrate very strongly, but I think it would not, on the whole, be a bad thing to leave the Germans wedged in between us and the French, and that Beh is not worth a long quarrel, but should be used as an argument to prove how strangely and wantonly the Germans are trying to aggravate us.

It is plain that the Beh trade is in German hands, and that the German traders have brought about this annexation in order to protect themselves against our high tariff. Our tariff is at the bottom of all our

---

[1] John Anderson (later Sir); entered the Colonial Office, 1879; Secretary to the Colonial Conferences of 1897 and 1905; Permanent Under-Secretary, 1911–16.

troubles. We should point out, in the first instance, that we had a prior arrangement with the Beh people, and at the same time complain of the language alleged to have been used by Dr Nachtigal, and the treatment of our protegee King Lawson, who, if not a British subject, is a grandson of one of our oldest and most respected officials on the coast.   [C.O.96/158]

347 COLONIAL OFFICE TO FOREIGN OFFICE
12 SEPTEMBER, 1884.

Sir,

With reference to the letter from this Department of the 30th June, I am directed by the Earl of Derby to transmit to you, to be laid before Earl Granville, copies of despatches from the Governor of the Gold Coast, respecting the action of Dr Nachtigal at Beh Beach.

This territory, as was stated in the letter from this Department already referred to, lies just outside the limits of the Gold Coast Protectorate. For some time past goods have been extensively passed direct into the Gold Coast Protectorate from Beh Beach without paying duty, to the great detriment of the Colonial Revenues, and, with a view to put an end to this state of things, Governor Young in his despatch of the 29th of April, already communicated to you, proposed to negotiate for the annexation of the sea-board to the Gold Coast Colony. In view of the negotiations at present pending with the French Government, as to the territories lying between the Gold Coast proper and Lagos, Lord Derby was unwilling to sanction anything which might disturb the *status quo*, which it has been agreed between the French and English Governments to respect while the negotiations are proceeding; and he therefore in his Despatch of the 11th of July, declined to authorise Mr Young to take the steps which he had proposed. It appears, however, that Mr Young, without waiting for a reply to his Despatch of the 29th of April, had instructed Mr Firminger, District Commissioner of Quittah, which borders on the

Beh territory, to proceed to that place and endeavour to make an arrangement with the chiefs for the cession of their seaboard. In accordance with his instructions, Mr Firminger proceeded to Porto Seguro and concluded a provisional arrangement with the chiefs to the effect that if within one month from the date of his visit, the 23rd July, they had not by fair means induced the Beh traders to remove from Beh, they would cede their seaboard to the English Government.

The mere fact that, in view of the negotiation with France, Lord Derby had refrained from authorizing Governor Young from taking action at present, would not of itself prevent his Lordship from ratifying the action which he has actually taken, in the absence of orders, were it not for the following considerations.

In the first place, there is some doubt as to whether Dr Nachtigal's proceedings amount to the establishment of a territorial and political protectorate or merely a personal protectorate, within certain limits, of threatened German interests; and, in the next place, the terms of the agreement made by Mr Firminger are not such as would have been suggested by Her Majesty's Government, and are such as can scarcely now be approved in the absence of further explanations. The agreement with the Beh natives was not one for the cession out and out of their territory to Her Majesty, but one for its cession in the event of the natives failing, within one month, to induce the merchants and traders at Beh Beach or Lomeh and Bageidah, to quit the country. No mention was made of compensation, nor was the time allowed apparently sufficient to admit of the merchants getting rid of their stocks, or even transferring them to some other seat of commerce, and Mr Firminger seems to have considered that the requirement as to the means being fair and just was sufficiently met by what, according to him, was a notice to quit by the 6th of July, under the threat that otherwise the roads would be closed.

According to a telegram from Berlin in the 'Times' of the 21st ultimo, the natives went further, threatening to 'destroy the factory of the Hamburg firm Walber and Brohm, unless the owners departed within a week,' and Dr Nachtigal, in his letter of the 9th of July to Governor Young, speaks of himself as having acted in the interests of life and property. Even allowing for exaggeration in the German description of the attitude adopted by the natives, the agreement made by Mr Firminger is not one which, in the absence of further explanations, Lord Derby thinks could be ratified, in view of the principles which should guide the action of Her Majesty's Government towards the subjects of a friendly power, nor does he see that under the circumstances, any valid objection be taken to the action of Dr Nachtigal in safeguarding the lives, stores and stocks of his fellow countrymen.

He would suggest that inquiries should be made in the first instance, as to the character of the protectorate established by Germany. It will be perceived that passions have been aroused on each side, and that the store of an English firm, Messrs Swanzy, has been attacked by an excited mob of pro-German negroes. If the protectorate is merely over Germans and German interests, it will be for Her Majesty's Government to punish and prevent such outrages at Beh and Bageidah by the usual means: but if the German protectorate is territorial and political, that Government will no doubt take measures to provide its representatives on the spot with the means of repressing disorder and with instructions to use those means impartially.

It will be observed that it is also believed that the German traders have given reprehensible counsel to the smugglers who are their customers, namely to go into the British Protectorate in large parties and armed, and to fight the English police if they interfered with them, and that in anticipation or conformity with this advice a band of 200 of these marauders have murdered an English policeman and cut off his hands and otherwise mutilated the body. The attention of the German Government should, in Lord Derby's opinion, be at once drawn to these allegations, as it will no doubt be anxious to inquire into them, and, if they prove well-founded, relieve Her Majesty's Government of the duty primarily devolving on it, in the absence of a German Protectorate, of avenging in the amplest manner, the murder and mutilation of one of the Queen's servants.

In conclusion, I am to draw attention to the statement in Mr Firminger's general report, dated the 1st August, that the German flag had been hoisted at a point overlapping the eastern limit of the English protectorate. The settlement of this particular point does not seem urgent and may await the solution of the other questions raised by the action of Dr Nachtigal. Lord Derby has no doubt that the German Government intends to respect the limits of the existing English protectorate, and will direct its flag to be hauled down at any point where its hoisting may be inconsistent with previously acquired rights.

I am etc.

R. H. Meade.[1]

[C.P. African 283, p. 136]

348 THE EARL OF DERBY TO W. A. G. YOUNG   26 DECEMBER, 1884.

Most confidential. . . .

The course of proceedings in Berlin[2] has been very favourable, on the whole, to British interests on the West Coast and in the Bights, and Her Majesty's Government are well satisfied with the result. If Germany has gained something, Great Britain has gained much more, and Her Majesty's Government have no disposition to dispute the German acquisitions, or criticise further the mode in which they were obtained. It

is of no use, for instance, to discuss whether a particular king who signed a treaty with the Germans has any objective existence, or whether another has a respectable following.[1] In the interests of British traders, putting aside the question of international policy, it is best to treat the Germans in the most friendly way possible, and to drop all further controversy. I am happy to believe that, now that the first alarm is over, the most intelligent English traders have made up their minds that they have nothing to fear from German rule, and that they only desire to see it become more and more of a reality.

These confidential instructions are not to be taken as implying that you are, in cases which may *hereafter* arise between your Government and the German representatives, to abate the assertion of British rights, or observe any different attitude from what your own experience and judgement would dictate to you, were you serving in any other part of the world, and were the question to arise with the representatives of any other power than Germany. . . .

[African 283]

349 COL. F. A. STANLEY[2] TO W. B. GRIFFITH   14 OCTOBER, 1885.

Sir,

As you are no doubt aware, the question of the separation of Lagos from the Gold Coast, and its erection into an independent Government, has for some time past been under the consideration of Her Majesty's Government.

Experience also has gone far to show that owing to the nature of the climate, to the difficulties of communication, and to the

---

[1] Sir Robert Henry Meade (1835–99); entered Foreign Office, 1859; private secretary to Earl Granville in the Colonial Office, 1868; Assistant Under-Secretary for Colonies, 1871; delegate to the Berlin Conference, 1884; Permanent Under-Secretary, 1892–6.

[2] i.e. at the West African Conference.

[1] Young (to Derby, 6 November, 1884) had asserted that there was no such person as King M'lappa, with whom Nachtigal concluded his treaty, and that King Garsoo of Bageidah, another of the alleged signatories, had been dead for some years.

[2] Sir Frederick Arthur Stanley (later 16th Earl of Derby) (1841–1908); served in the army, 1858–65; Conservative M.P., 1865–86; Secretary for War, 1878–80; Secretary for the Colonies, 1885–6; Governor General of Canada, 1888; succeeded his brother as Earl of Derby, 1893.

many important matters requiring his constant presence and attention at Accra, it is
not easy for a Governor of the united
colonies to give to the affairs of Lagos that
personal supervision which is necessary and
desirable.

In these circumstances, Her Majesty's
Government have decided to recommend to
the Queen that the Charter constituting the
Gold Coast Colony should be amended,
and that Letters Patent should be issued,
providing for the administration of the
Gold Coast and Lagos as separate Colonies,
each with its own executive and legislature.

Her Majesty has been graciously pleased
to approve of this recommendation and the
necessary instruments to give effect to it
will accordingly be prepared and passed.

In view of this decision, it becomes necessary now to consider the best means of
providing for the administration of the two
colonies, and the establishments which will
be required for the purpose.

I have given this matter my best attention, and in the result, I entertain considerable doubt whether it will be possible, looking to the nature of the climate and the
requirements of the leave system, to effect
much reduction in the present staff of the
Gold Coast, without imparing its efficiency
and hindering the conduct of public business.

On the other hand, the establishment of
Lagos must, of course, be considerably
increased.

Her Majesty has been pleased to approve
of your appointment as Governor of the
Gold Coast, at the present rate of salary
and allowances. . . . The Gold Coast will
retain its present Colonial Secretary, but I
am of opinion that in the altered circumstances, three instead of four assistant
colonial secretaries should be sufficient.
. . . The arrangement recently made at the
Gold Coast for the division of the offices of
Treasurer and Collector of Customs, will
not be disturbed. . . . I think that, at all
events for the present, it will be unnecessary
to incur the expense of separate establishments for the audit of the accounts of the

two colonies. I therefore propose that
there shall be only one audit office for the
Gold Coast and Lagos. . . . I am of
opinion that the Gold Coast should retain
its present Surveyor-General and Assistant
Surveyor, but some reduction may be made
in the number of foremen of works by transferring one or more of them to Lagos. . . .
The Chief Justice and one Puisne Judge
will, I think, suffice for the requirements of
the Gold Coast, and the other Puisne Judge
will become judge at Lagos. . . . It will be
desirable that the Supreme Court of the
Gold Coast should be made an appeal court
for Lagos. . . .

It is somewhat difficult to decide what
arrangements should be made with regard
to . . . [the constabulary] and I shall
refrain from coming to any decision until
I am in possession of your views on the
matter. As at present advised, I am disposed to think it will be best, if possible, to
maintain the force as one regiment, the
officers and men of which will serve either
at the Gold Coast or Lagos as may be
required. . . .   [C.O.96/165]

350 LETTERS PATENT

13 JANUARY, 1886.

Letters Patent passed under the Great Seal
of the United Kingdom, constituting the
office of Governor and Commander-in-
Chief of the Gold Coast Colony, and providing for the Government thereof.

Victoria, by the grace of God, of the
United Kingdom of Great Britain and
Ireland, Queen, Defender of the Faith,
Empress of India: to all whom these
presents shall come, greeting.

Whereas our Gold Coast Colony, as now
constituted, comprises our Settlements on
the Gold Coast and at Lagos, lying between
the fifth degree of west longitude and the
fifth degree of east longitude: And whereas
by letters patent, under the Great Seal of
our United Kingdom of Great Britain and
Ireland, bearing date of Westminster, the
twenty-second day of January, 1883, we
did constitute the office of Governor and

Commander-in-Chief of our Gold Coast Colony, and did provide for the Government of our said Colony: and whereas we are minded to separate the Government of our Settlement at Lagos from the Government of our Settlements on the Gold Coast, and to make further provision for the Government of our said Settlements on the Gold Coast:

Now know ye that we do, by these presents, revoke and determine our said letters patent of the twenty-second day of January 1883, but without prejudice to anything lawfully done thereunto: and further know ye that we do, by these presents, order and declare that our Gold Coast Colony shall henceforth consist of our Settlements on the Gold Coast, as hereinafter described, and that there shall be a Governor and Commander-in-Chief in and over our Gold Coast Colony, and that appointments to the said office shall be made by commission under our sign manual and signet.

2. Our Gold Coast Colony (hereinafter called the Colony) shall, until we shall otherwise provide, comprise all places, settlements, and territories belonging to us on the Gold Coast in Western Africa between the fifth degree of west longitude and the second degree of east longitude.

3. We do hereby authorize, empower, and command our said Governor and Commander-in-Chief (hereinafter called the Governor) to do and execute all things that belong to his said office, according to the tenor of these our letters patent, and of such commission as may be issued to him under our sign manual and signet, and according to such instructions as may, from time to time, be given to him under our sign manual and signet, or by our Order in our Privy Council, or by us through one of our principal Secretaries of State, and to such laws as are now, or shall hereafter be, in force in the Colony.

4. And we do by these our letters patent declare our will and pleasure as follows:—

5. Every person appointed to fill the office of Governor shall, with all due solemnity, before entering on any of the duties of his office, cause the commission appointing him to be Governor to be read and published at the seat of Government on the Gold Coast, in the presence of the Chief Justice, or of some other judge of the Supreme Court, and of such members of the Executive Council of the Colony as can conveniently attend, which being done, he shall then and there take before them the oath of allegiance in the form provided by an Act passed in the Session holden in the thirty-first and thirty-second year of our reign, intituled, 'An Act to amend the Law relating to promissory Oaths'; and likewise the usual oath for the due execution of the office of the Governor, and for the due and impartial administration of justice, which oaths the said Chief Justice or judge, or, if they be unavoidably absent, the senior member of the Executive Council then present, is hereby required to administer.

6. The Governor shall keep and use the public seal of the Colony, for sealing all things whatsoever that shall pass the said seal: and until we shall otherwise direct, the public seal hitherto used for our Gold Coast Colony aforesaid shall be used as the public seal of the Colony.

7. There shall be an Executive Council for the Colony, and the said Council shall consist of such persons as we shall direct by Instructions under our sign manual and signet, and all such persons shall hold their places in the said Council during our pleasure.

8. There shall be a Legislative Council in the Colony, and the said Council shall consist of the Governor and such persons, not being less than three at any time, as we shall direct by any Instructions under our sign manual and signet, and all such persons shall hold their places in the Council during our pleasure.

9. In pursuance of the powers vested in us by an Act of the Imperial Parliament, passed in the sixth year of our reign[1] . . . we do hereby commission the persons who shall from time to time compose the said Legislative Council, and we do hereby

[1] See document 139.

delegate to them full power and authority, subject always to any conditions, provisoes, and limitations, prescribed by any Instructions under our sign manual and signet, to establish such Ordinances, not being repugnant to the Law of England, and to constitute such Courts and Officers, and to make such provisions and regulations for the proceedings in such Courts, and for the administration of justice, as may be necessary for the peace, order and good government of the Colony.

The Governor shall have a negative voice in the making and passing all such Ordinances.

10. We do hereby reserve to ourselves, our heirs and successors, full power and authority and our and their undoubted right to disallow any such Ordinances, and to signify such disallowance through one of our principal Secretaries of State. Every such disallowance shall take effect from the time when the same shall be promulgated by the Governor in the Colony.

We do also reserve to ourselves, our heirs and successors, our and their undoubted right, with the advice of our or their Privy Council, from time to time to make all such laws or Ordinances as may appear to us or them necessary for the peace, order and good government of the Colony.

11. In the making of any Ordinances the Governor and the said Legislative Council shall conform to and observe all rules, regulations, and directions in that behalf contained in any Instructions under our sign manual and signet.

12. The Governor, in our name and on our behalf, may make and execute, under the public seal, grants and dispositions of any lands within the Colony which may be lawfully granted or disposed of by us: Provided that every such grant or disposition be made in conformity either with some law in force in the Colony, or with some Instructions addressed to the Governor under our sign manual and signet, or through one of our principal Secretaries of State, or with some regulation in force in the Colony.

13. The Governor may constitute and appoint all such Judges, Commissioners, Justices of the Peace, and other necessary officers and ministers, as may be lawfully constituted or appointed by us, all of whom, unless otherwise provided by law, shall hold their officers during our pleasure.

14. [Suspension of officers.]

15. [Grant of pardons. Remission of fines . . .] provided always that the Governor shall in no case, except where the offence has been of a political nature unaccompanied by any other grave crime, make it a condition of any pardon or remission of sentence that the offender shall be banished or shall absent himself or be removed from the Colony.

16. [Succession to the Government. Lieutenant-Governor; Administrator; Senior Civil Member of the Executive Council.] . . .

17. [Powers and authorities of Administrator to include] . . . such of the powers hereby vested in the Governor, except the powers of suspension and pardon, as the Governor shall think fit to assign to him or them. . . .

18. [Officers and others to obey the Governor.]

19. In the construction of these our letters patent, the term 'the Governor' unless inconsistent with the context, shall include every person for the time being administering the Government of the Colony.

20. And we do hereby reserve to ourselves, our heirs and successors, full power and authority from time to time to revoke, alter, or amend these our letters patent as to us or them shall seem fit.

21. [Proclamation of letters patent.]

22. In witness whereof we have caused these our letters patent to be made patent. Witness ourself at Westminster, the thirteenth day of January in the forty-ninth year of our reign.

By warrant under the Queen's sign manual.

Muir Mackenzie.

[Ordinances of the Gold Coast, 1903, vol. 2, p. 1327]

351 RESOLUTION OF THE LONDON CHAMBER OF COMMERCE   22 APRIL, 1886.

That in view of the serious consequences to the trade of Cape Coast Castle and other places on the Gold Coast, resulting from the unsettled state of Ashanti, and the petty wars so frequently waged between one and another of the inland tribes, this Committee is of opinion that more constant communication should be maintained with the interior, and that the influence of the Colonial Government should be more effectually exercised in the settlement of native disputes, and the preservation of peace, with a view more particularly to preventing any hindrance to the free intercourse of the interior tribes with the coast. With these objects in view, the Committee considers that a competent Commissioner should be appointed, either to reside at Coomassie, or to make frequent visits to that place, as well as other important centres in the interior.

[C.4906, A & P (1886) xlvii]

352 COLONIAL OFFICE TO THE LONDON CHAMBER OF COMMERCE   28 MAY, 1886.

. . . The Governor of the Gold Coast has not lost sight of the desirability of taking such steps as may be possible to remove the hindrances to trade which now exist, and with this view, he has sent an officer (Inspector Firminger) up to the frontier with a proposal to mediate between the Adansis and the Becquais, who are at war. . . .

It appears that he was unsuccessful in his efforts to induce the contending tribes to make peace, and had been compelled to return to Prahsue. . . .

In these circumstances, Lord Granville does not see that any further action can at present properly be taken, as, of course, active measures for coercing either of the hostile tribes (who are beyond British jurisdiction) to make peace, are out of the question. . . .

With regard to the appointment of a Resident at Coomassie, Lord Granville agrees with the Committee that more constant communication with the interior is desirable, but he remains of the opinion, expressed by the Earl of Derby in 1883, that there are strong reasons of policy and prudence against such an appointment, and that the proposition is one that Her Majesty's Government could not entertain.

Lord Granville thinks that it will be preferable to send as frequently as circumstances permit, an officer on a special visit, and his Lordship proposes to ask the Governor whether he is of opinion that it would be desirable to appoint an officer whose special duty it should be to pay such visits to the various tribes bordering on the Gold Coast Protectorate in order to promote and maintain friendly relations with them, and keep the roads open and free for traders. . . .   [C.4906]

353 MINUTE BY THE EARL OF KIMBERLEY   20 JUNE, 1886.

It is safe to assume that the German Govt. will annex anything which is not claimed by some other Power on the ground of prior annexation.

Therefore we should make up our minds promptly as to any territory we really want, and take it at once, or, if for any reason it is not thought desirable to extend our territory, then we should acquiesce cheerfully in the German acquisition. Otherwise we merely invite snubbing. . . .

[C.O.96/176]

354 MINUTES ON THE PROPOSED TREATY WITH AKWAMU[1]   SEPTEMBER, 1886.

(a) A. W. L. H[emming] 14 September, [1886].

The Germans have occupied Beh beach and are, as we know, pushing their Protectorate into the interior, with, it has been said, the object of reaching the Volta and setting up their authority on the left bank of that river.

[1] The Akwamus had asked to be taken into the protectorate and signed a treaty with the Gold Coast Government (printed in Sarbah, *Fanti National Constitution*, p. 157) on 27 July, 1886.

This they could do only by acquiring the Aquamoo territory, and we may be sure that if we refuse to take it under our protection we shall shortly find it in the hands of Germany. The presence of the Germans on the Volta would be extremely inconvenient, and injurious to our trade and revenue, and would probably lead to many complications. . . . [The land between Akwamu and Anlo must also be secured.]

It seems clear . . . that Aquamoo — and also Crepee — have been held to be included in the territories handed over by Denmark in 1850, and by approving the present treaty we shall be only confirming and strengthening the title we already possess.

(b) R. W. W. H[erbert][1]

It is of real importance that we should hold sufficient control over both banks of the Volta to protect the trade of the Gold Coast Colony from interference by Germany or any other foreign Power, and from this point of view there is much to be said in favour of 'protecting' the Aquamoo people and territory.

But this treaty does much more; it purports to cede Aquamoo to Her Majesty 'so that the same shall become and form part and portion of the Gold Coast Colony'. This would compel us to govern the whole territory as British soil — slaves would be free throughout it, and much larger responsibilities than those of a mere 'protectorate' would be incurred.

I think the treaty in its present form cannot be sanctioned for the above reason, and if it is not ratified, I should be inclined to assent to nothing more than a renewal of the treaty with the Aquamoos of 1874; . . . undertaking on our part friendship and good advice rather than 'protection' and on the part of the Aquamoos, the freedom of navigation and promise to make no treaty with a foreign power except with H.M's consent.[1]   [C.O.96/176]

---

[1] Sir Robert George Wyndham Herbert (1831–1905); Colonial Secretary of Queensland, 1858; Assistant Under-Secretary for the Colonies, 1870; Permanent Under-Secretary, 1871–92.

[1] The treaty was accordingly replaced by a declaration of 9 May, 1887 (also printed by Sarbah, op. cit., p. 159).

1887–1918

THE AGE OF EXPANSION

BOOK VIII

THE FIRST PHASE OF THE 'SCRAMBLE' 1887–1894

26   The Gold Coast Administration under fire
1887–1889

THE later eighties on the Gold Coast, the central period of Sir William Brandford Griffith's long service as Lieutenant-Governor and Governor,[1] have very much the appearance of an interlude.   There is a lull in the diplomatic activity, started by the French and German advances of 1883–4, and to be resumed even more feverishly in the nineties.[2]   The emphasis now is on internal developments.   The brief agitation in Accra at the end of 1886 (355) and the more significant movement for municipal government in Cape Coast (357) which was sympathetically (358) if inadequately (359) received by the British Government, link the protagonists of the Fanti federation with the later opponents of the Land Bills.

But economic rather than political matters weigh most.   A set-back in trade after 1885[3] revived earlier demands for road (357) and rail (341) development by the Government (356): this especially on the part of the European commercial interests, whose growing demands on Government are a salient feature of the new imperialism.   The decline in trade also attracted attention in Downing Street, if only because it meant a loss of revenue, which, coinciding with an expanding programme of public works, meant a series of budget deficits.[4]   The Secretary of State re-opened the case for direct taxation through the native authorities, but, like his predecessors, Griffith would not look at any form of direct tax, whether on land, huts, heads or income, and urged instead that *ad valorem* duties should be re-introduced and increased.[5]   Ultimately, after a visit to England in 1889, he convinced the Secretary of State of the wisdom of this policy, and the new duties were introduced at the beginning of the following year (363); thereby setting the fiscal pattern for some years to come.

The Governor also encouraged the educated African to interest himself in the economic progress of his country.   One result was the 1889 Report on Economic Agriculture (361).   Griffith did not agree with all the findings of this Report (362), which perhaps did less than justice to the considerable development which had taken place during his tenure of office.[6]   Inevitably, as he himself realised, the more that was done, the more were new needs created.   This had, in fact, been his great argument for seeking a permanent increase in the revenue.

But the most important achievement of the eighties is noticed only, as it were, in a footnote (362a).

---

[1] Griffith first took office as Lieutenant-Governor on 1 December, 1880, became Governor in January 1886, and held the post until April 1895.

[2] An Anglo-German Agreement (No. 359) 'neutralized' much of the basin of the middle Volta.

[3] Cf. Appendix D.

[4] The average annual deficit between 1881 and 1888 was £3,374.

[5] See the confidential despatches, Griffith to Knutsford, of 24 November, 1888 and 15 June, 1889 (C.O.806/318, C.P. African (West) 379).

[6] Particularly notable was the formation of new departments in this period: Sanitary (1888), Roads (1890), Education (1890), Telegraph (1891), Prisons (1891).

355 W. B. Griffith to E. Stanhope[1]
Accra, 28 January, 1887.

Sir,

I have the honour to acknowledge the receipt on the 15th instant of your telegram of 14th of January, informing me that a telegram had been sent to Her Majesty the Queen on the 9th of January, under the names of the king, chiefs and people of Accra, complaining of my conduct; and instructing me to inform them that if they wished to make representations, they must do so in the usual manner, through me; and directing me to report to you fully by post, the situation of affairs at Accra, and the grievances alleged. . . .

I have the honour to report for your information that there is nothing unusual in the situation of affairs at Accra at present, nor has there been since September last. About the middle of that month there was some irritation and excitement consequent on the imprudent action of the District Commissioner[2] and of circumstances connected with it, but the measures which I took to maintain order quickly allayed these feelings.

With regard to the alleged grievances you direct me to report upon, I regret that I am unable to give you any positive information, as they have not been represented to me by the parties who sent the telegram. Indirectly, however, I have heard that efforts are being made under the auspices of a Mr Brew,[3] the editor of a newspaper called the 'Western Echo', and Mr Edmund Bannerman,[4] a solicitor of Accra, aided by a few traders here, to raise funds to send a deputation to England, to represent the grievances of the people and the changes they desire to see accomplished.

With this ostensible object, I learn that they have sent to all of the kings and principal chiefs in the Colony and Protectorate, to subscribe money to pay the expenses of the proposed deputation, and I have been informed that they have studied the weaknesses and pecularities of the various parties addressed, in order to gain their support, or, more correctly speaking, to obtain their subscriptions.

In this way they have sent messages to some kings that they propose to get them reinstated in their former rights; that they will endeavour to get the British Government to pay them for the slaves who were emancipated; to permit the renewal of domestic slavery, and to allow them to purchase and sell slaves. To the Awoonahs they have promised, in addition, the disbanding of the Houssa force; to the coast towns they have held out the hope of getting the duty on spirits reduced, and to the Accras, that people from the rivers shall not have their baggage searched. . . .

The kings of Christiansborg and Akropong both counsel that if there is any cause for complaint, it should be brought to the notice of the Governor before taking the matter to England. In a letter from the District Commissioner of Quittah . . . it will be observed that a part of the inducement held out to the Awoonahs for their subscriptions, is the disbandment of the Constabulary, and that the emissaries of the Accras had placed the names of certain chiefs of Quittah to a document in spite of the protests of their messengers. . . .

[C.O.96/179]

[1] Edward Stanhope (1840–93), Secretary of State, 3 August, 1886, to 14 January, 1887.

[2] Some high-handed action by the police, and an insult to King Tackie in the D.C.'s court, produced some excitement and stone-throwing. Young Mr Hutton Mills lost his post in the Queen's Advocate's Office for shouting imprudent slogans.

[3] See No. 394 n. The Western Echo appeared between September 1885 and December 1887.

[4] Edmund Bannerman (1832–1903); son of James Bannerman; D.C. at Keta, 1858, and at Winnebah, 1860; lawyer and journalist.

356 The Manchester Chamber of Commerce to the Colonial Office
8 February, 1887.

Sir,

On the occasion of the Deputation of this Chamber to the Colonial Office on the 19th ultimo, circumstances prevented the full development of the representations which the Board desires to make, relative to West African Colonial affairs. I am therefore now desired by the President to

draw your attention to the present condition of trade with the Gold Coast, complaining of the apathy and inactivity of the
Government of the possession.

In January, a memorial was received
from Cape Coast which, this Chamber was
informed, was unanimously signed by every
merchant of position trading in that
Colony. The purport of these communications is that the Government of the Gold
Coast is responsible for the decline in the
trade, in consequence of no serious steps
having been taken to maintain proper
authority, both within and on our borders,
and to keep a clear highway for the trade
into the interior; and further that, owing
to the continued depredations of the tribes
on the frontier of the Gold Coast territory,
it is feared that British influence is declining, and that trade is passing to the territories of other countries.

With respect to the information submitted to the Chamber, that proper authority is not maintained within our borders,
it is asserted that the Adansi tribe — who
were driven by the Bequahs out of Ashanti
and have taken refuge on British territory
— have been attacking and robbing the
native traders on their way down from the
interior to the coast; and that although
complaints have been addressed to the
Government, no adequate measures had
been taken to suppress such outrages.

In further support of the complaints of
the merchants that the interior trade paths
outside our borders have been stopped, a
copy of a memorial addressed by them to
the Governor of the Gold Coast has been
received by the Chamber. It relates to
their trade with Gaman and other interior
tribes, which had been stopped by the
Saifwhies, through whose country, lying
between our western border and the adjoining French Settlement of Assinie and
Grand Bassam, the Gamans and other
traders from the interior have been in the
habit of passing, in order to reach the
British Settlements on the coast.

The Chamber of Commerce is informed
that Her Majesty's Government has already received a copy of the memorial
referred to, and that their attention is being
given to these representations: but I
would respectfully remark that when Her
Majesty's Government assumed the responsibility of destroying the power of the
kingdom of Ashantie in 1874, thereby
rendering independent the various tribes
composing that kingdom, they have never
since recognized or acted under the duty
which devolved upon them, of taking
adequate steps to maintain that free and
peaceful trade which formerly passed
through these tribes to the British Settlements on the coast; and yet frequent
appeals have been made by the chiefs of
these people to the Government to 'put
their country in order'.

The attention of the African Committee
of this Chamber has been called to the
despatches in the Blue Book of September
1886, from which it appears that there has
been great apathy on the part of the
Government of the Gold Coast. That
territory is about three hundred miles in
length, and because the trade of one part of
the territory, producing palm oils and
kernels, had increased in 1884, and because
the increased imports of spirits, tobacco,
&c had brought in £19,000 more customs
duties, the Governor, from a letter addressed to the Earl of Derby on the 9th
June, 1885, seemed to think that 'the
general prosperity of the Colony does not
appear to have been affected by the decline
of the trade of Cape Coast.'

The Governor of the Gold Coast cannot
be ignorant of the fact that the principal
trade of the Cape Coast district is the import of cotton goods and other British
manufactures. The so-called prosperity of
the Colony can only relate to an increase
in the revenue through imports of foreign
spirits, tobacco, arms and ammunition, on
which a heavy duty is levied, but of which
the imports neither contribute to the
advancement and prosperity of the Colony,
nor to the development of British commerce.

I am desired respectfully to remind the
Colonial Office, that although formerly

there was a steady increase in the annual exports of British cotton goods to the Gold Coast, and to the other British settlements on the west coast of Africa, there has, during the last two years, been a considerable decrease. Twenty years back, the exports there of British cottons amounted to £300,000 per annum; ten years back they had risen to £550,000; and in 1884 to £591,000: in 1885 they declined to £388,000 and in 1886 to £318,000 — the falling off in quantity also approaching that in value.

I would also remark that in 1885 the total import trade of the Gold Coast amounted to £466,000, upon which customs duties of £114,000 were levied, and of this a sum of about £60,000 was paid in maintaining an unnecessary and expensive staff of officials, while scarcely anything was done for the development of trade or for the good of the people who were thus heavily taxed.

Ten years back, the imports amounted to £446,000, and a customs revenue of £51,000 then sufficed to pay for the administration of the country, which was quite as efficient and was less grievous to the people than the present system of administering the government.

This Chamber cannot but feel that considerable apathy has been shown by the Gold Coast Government in regard to the commercial interests of that Colony. The Blue Book shows that with a very large staff of officials, the Government of that Colony allowed eight months to elapse before replying to a letter of the Secretary of State of July 1885, asking for information as to the condition of Ashantee, and on the future policy of the Government with respect to that country. This letter was only acknowledged and answered on the 1st of April, 1886, and no opinion was even then given as to future policy. . . .

The merchants trust that Her Majesty's Government will accept the responsibility of assisting them in the development of their trade; and that they will recognise that there is a duty owing to them, and also to those natives who come from the interior

behind the British territories, and who thereby promote the extension of commerce with our possessions, and contribute materially to the revenue.

Whenever these native tribes on our borders seek our sympathy and advice, and whenever they are desirous of being brought under our influence, it will conduce to the maintenance of peace and to the development of British commerce, if their prayers that their country 'be put in order' be no longer disregarded by Her Majesty's Government.

In such case they will not be driven to seek aid from other powers in obtaining the fulfilment of their desires, nor will they incur the risk of sacrificing the independence of their country to the advantage of others and to the exclusion of British interests.

I have etc.

J. Fox Turner, Secretary.

[C.5357, A & P (1888) lxxv]

357 PETITION OF THE CAPE COAST CHIEFS
CAPE COAST, 18 MAY, 1887.

. . . The internal state of the town in almost every respect has not been that which it should have been under proper management. Owing to the chiefs having lost their control over the people which they possessed in past times, the companies have very frequently been on the verge of coming into collision with one another and, had not the educated community stepped in between them, there can be no doubt that all the efforts of the District Commissioners here would have proved unavailing, and that blood would have been shed. In proof of this assertion, we would respectfully refer your Excellency to the communication which Mr Commissioner Forbes addressed to Governor Griffith on the occasion of the disturbance which took place here during his term of office. Even the other day, on the occasion of the last fracas between some of the companies here, the educated classes strove in like manner to prevent bloodshed, and they met with success in their efforts. . . .

Further, the sanitary reforms, such as they are, at present being carried out, are not so carried out as to meet local requirements. Here again we have reason to believe that the services of the educated community would be of material assistance to the Government and the carrying out of the necessary measures; and with a proper scheme, supported by your Excellency, we have no doubt much more could be achieved in that direction than has hitherto been done.

We are aware that the Government is making some attempt in that way, but the poor state of the roads and the streets of the town, together with the inefficient lighting up of it at night, has called our attention, and we have endeavoured to ascertain how best the same may be improved without entailing on the Government duties which it is apparently unable to perform, and which, in other countries, fall to be discharged by local municipal institutions.

Again, matters for litigation crop up between natives, which the British courts are unable to determine on. If they do so, they do so in a manner which causes a vast amount of dissatisfaction, and thus breeds much of the ill-will which is frequently exhibited in various ways. Such matters are more easily disposed of and determined by native tribunals.

In consequence of the foregoing, we deemed it advisable to convene meetings of the seven companies in the town here, to see how best we could remedy things as they stood. The result of these meetings have been that the seven companies have elected seven chiefs, each company having now a chief as its representative, who will be responsible for the due observance of law and order by his company. Following this, the seven companies proceeded to elect one chief as the head-chief, known as Master of Arms from time immemorial. The seven companies then proceeded to elect from among the educated classes, seven gentlemen as councillors, who will represent the town and be responsible for

P

the due preservation of order, under a system similar to that which obtains in municipalities, taking as their guide the Municipal Ordinance of 1858. . . .

As your Excellency will perceive . . . it was even then deemed fitting that we should have municipal institutions among us. In taking the step, therefore, which we have done, we have but been reverting in a measure to the old order of things, and we feel the weight of the obligations which we have thus voluntarily incurred. But we are buoyed up with the hope that your Excellency will accord us every support in our humble effort to train up our people in the art of self-government, since that is professed to be the primary object which tbe British Government has in view.

We can assure your Excellency, that in thus acting, we have as our sole object the amelioration of our race and country, and that our loyalty to the Government is as firm as ever.

[Signed by 5 chiefs of Cape Coast: Kofi × Sackey, Kofi × Yammi, Cudjoe × Essell, J. S. Watts, and R. Dawson.

7 chiefs of companies: Quow X Arkoon, Quamin × Awordue, W. B. Acquay, Cudjoe × Korsah, J. B. Hagan, J. P. Brown, Jos. N. Daniel, H. Brew, Master at Arms.

7 representatives of companies: F. C. Grant, J. Sarbah, J. W. Sey, A. Q. Yarquah, W. E. Pietersen, James Sago, T. F. Jones.

Other signatories include: Brew of Dunquah, J. E. Ellis, J. W. D. Johnson, W. E. Johnson, C. F. Turkson, J. E. Biney, J. Emml. Hayford, S. R. Hansen, T. Anan, T. Laing, Francis Williams.]

[C.O.96/182]

358 SIR H. T. HOLLAND[1] TO COL. F. B. P. WHITE 5 SEPTEMBER, 1887.

Sir,

I have the honour to acknowledge the receipt of your despatch No. 246 of the

[1] Sir Henry Thurston Holland (later 1st Viscount Knutsford) (1825–1914); Legal adviser to the Colonial Office, 1867; Assistant Under-Secretary, 1870–4; Conservative M.P., 1874–88; Secretary of State for the Colonies, 1887–92.

5th of July last, transmitting a petition from various chiefs and other inhabitants of Cape Coast, requesting authority for the formation of a local municipal board for the administration of the affairs of that town.

The formation of a board of chiefs and councillors by an unauthorised election was, as you properly pointed out, not warranted by law, as the Ordinance of 1858 on the subject of Municipalities has never been brought into force. Your action in dealing with this matter has accordingly my approval and I am glad to note that it evoked expressions of loyalty and intelligent obedience from the chiefs and people whom you addressed.

It is, however, pleasing to Her Majesty's Government to find the leading inhabitants of Cape Coast Castle taking such an energetic interest in the affairs of that important town. So far as concerns what may be called municipal affairs, their complaints and their criticisms appear to be moderate and reasonable, and such as will doubtless already have received attention at your hands.

It must, however, be obvious, that it is not possible for the Colonial Government properly to attend to all the minor details of local administration in so large a Colony as the Gold Coast, and the Public Works Department in particular, is naturally quite unable to carry out promptly all the numerous small sanitary and other works which are urgently required. It has therefore always been the policy of my predecessors to encourage the formation of municipalities in the larger towns of the Colony, and the attention of various Governors has been drawn to the subject at different times. It has sometimes been feared that there would be a want of sufficient interest in such institutions, which are, of course, somewhat alien to the habits of the people. But the recent occurences at Cape Coast lead Her Majesty's Government to hope that this will not be found to be the case, and to think the present a favourable opportunity for the creation of a local municipal board in that town.

Such an institution could, I need hardly say, greatly relieve the present strain on the various departments of the Colonial Government, by undertaking the supervision of all local sanitary matters, and it might at the same time be of great educational value in accustoming the inhabitants to take part in public administration.

A Municipal Body would doubtless need some careful advice and guidance at first, and it is possible that its action may not always be in accordance with the opinion of persons of greater administrative experience. The condition of the town may, for some time, not be much better under an elected board than under a District Commissioner, but the people will have the remedy in their own hands, and I do not doubt that their representatives will soon endeavour to make such arrangements as will satisfy their constituents. It is to be hoped that the new Board will secure the cordial co-operation of all the inhabitants of the town, whether of European or of African race, and that such persons as have gained any commercial and official experience will assist the new body by participating in its deliberations.

It will, I presume, be necessary that an ordinance should be passed to regulate the formation of municipalities, but upon this point I request that you will at once consult your legal advisers, and that you will cause the necessary steps to be taken with the least possible delay.

I think it will be necessary for the Board to be under the presidency of the District Commissioner, and for it to consist partly of elected members. It will probably be found convenient to cause the election to take place by tribes or companies as is contemplated by section 9 of the Ordinance of 1858, and as seems to have been the case in the informal elections lately held. It will be for consideration whether the Governor should have power to nominate a small proportion of the Board, in order that Europeans and others not voting in the tribes or companies may be properly represented.

It should be made clear that the Board will have authority over nothing but local affairs relating to sanitation, water supply, cleaning and lighting the streets, and the supervision of the markets and similar purposes, but that it will have no civil or criminal jurisdiction, nor any control over the Courts or the police.

The Board should have power to levy a local rate or hut tax, and you should consider whether there are no minor sources of local revenue, such as fees, licenses, or market dues, collected within the town, which could properly be transferred to it. Provision should be made for proper accounts being kept by the Board's officers and regularly submitted to the Local Auditor for audit, and for the accounts and the Local Auditor's report upon them to be published. . . .

A draft should be submitted to me before the bill is introduced into the Legislative Council. . . .   [C.O.96/182]

359 Joint Recommendations of the British and German Commissioners, with regard to the future limits of British and German Protectorates and spheres of influence in the territories lying in the interior of the Gold Coast Colony and the German Togo Protectorate   September 1887.

1. That the boundary line laid down in the Agreement signed by the German and British Commissioners on the 14th July, 1886, should be continued in such a manner as to include within the German Protectorate the territories of Towe, Kowe and Agotime, and to leave within the British Protectorate the countries of Aquamoo and Creppe (or Peki). The exact definition of this boundary to be hereafter determined, if necessary, by a joint commission on the spot.

2. That between the northern limit of the territory of Creppe and the mouth of the River Daka, the river Volta shall form the line of demarcation between the spheres of influence of the two countries, Great Britain undertaking not to acquire any protectorates to the east of that river, and Germany entering into a similar agreement with regard to the territories to the west.

3. That a conventional line be drawn on the latitude of the mouth of the River Daka, and that the two Governments shall mutually agree to regard the territories lying to the north of this line, within the limits marked on the accompanying map,[1] as neutral ground, and to abstain from seeking to acquire within them protectorates or exclusive influence.

4. If the second of these recommendations is adopted, the Commissioners are of opinion that an agreement might properly be concluded that, in the event of Germany extending her protectorate up to the River Volta, within the limits mentioned, the Imperial Government will engage not to levy duties upon goods in transit, nor to place any other impediment in the way of trade between the British Protectorate and the interior; the British Government undertaking on their part, *in the event of the extension of the German Protectorate above-mentioned*, not to levy transit duties within their Protectorate east of the River Volta upon goods passing from the German Protectorate into other districts east of the Volta, not being British, or from the same into the German Protectorate.[2]

[Hertslet, Map of Africa by Treaty, vol. 3, p. 890]

360 Legislative Council Debate Christiansborg Castle, 5 April, 1889.

Present:

His Excellency the Governor, Sir W. Brandford Griffith, K.C.M.G.

His Honour the Chief Justice, J. T. Hutchinson, Esquire.

[1] The northern limit of the 'neutral Zone' was fixed at 10 degrees north, and its eastern and western limits at c. 0 degrees 33′ east and 1. 27′ degrees west longitude (Greenwich).
[2] It was approved by the British Government on 12 March and by the German Government on 14 March, 1888.

The Honourable the Colonial Secretary, F. M. Hodgson, Esquire.

The Honourable the Queen's Advocate, Gerald H. Cowie, Esquire (acting).

The Honourable the Treasurer, Charles Pike Esquire, C.M.G.

The Honourable John Sarbah, Esquire, Unofficial Member.

Absent:

The Honourable the Officer Commanding the Troops of the Gold Coast, Major Bingham.

The Honourable C. W. Burnett, Esquire, Unofficial Member. . . .

The Governor read two despatches from the Secretary of State for the Colonies, No. 227 of 5th September, 1887, and No. 175 of 25th May, 1888, upon the subject of the Municipalities Bill. His Excellency stated that the Bill was the outcome of certain representations which had been made to Colonel White when administering the Government in the year 1887, by certain of the inhabitants of Cape Coast; that Colonel White had communicated with Her Majesty's Government on the subject and had received instructions to cause a draft Bill, based upon specified lines, to be prepared and submitted to the Secretary of State for His Lordship's approval before enactment; that the draft Bill in question had been so prepared, and after amendment in accordance with the views of Her Majesty's Government, was introduced and read a first time in Council on the 10th July, 1888. Since then the Governor added that he had had copies printed and circulated among the principal people at Cape Coast and that he had also had the opportunity of consulting with Mr F. C. Grant on the 17th January, as representing the views of the community at Cape Coast with regard to it; and that Mr Grant had expressed his approval of all its provisions with the exception of those relating to the rating of the town for revenue, which he thought should, in the first instance, be provided by a subvention from the General Revenue.

The Chief Justice moved the 2nd reading of the Bill.

Seconded by the Treasurer and agreed to.

The Bill was read a second time.

The Chief Justice moved that the Council do now go into Committee on the Bill.

Seconded by the Treasurer and agreed to.

Clauses 1 to 4 passed the Committee.

At Clause 5, Mr Sarbah stated that he wished to record his objections to the principle of Municipal Assessment; that the Bill was not what was required at the present time; that municipalities would be better able to administer the existing expenditure from General Revenue at the different towns than the Government; and that by this course the people might be better educated to govern themselves. He added that he strongly objected to direct taxation in a Colony which was in a sound financial position and had incurred no debt as yet, but that he would formally record his objections by moving an amendment at a later stage.

Clauses 5 to 46 passed. . . .[1]

[Leg. Co. Debates]

361 REPORT ON ECONOMIC AGRICULTURE ON THE GOLD COAST. . . .   1889.

[The principal export was palm oil, the trade in which was harmed by the adulteration resorted to by Gold Coast producers.] . . .

To show the effects of the adulteration, nothing more is necessary than to compare the position of Lagos oil (which is the purest known) with that of Gold Coast oil, on the European market. When Lagos oil sells for £22. 10s. per ton, Accra oil (which includes Addah and Quittah sorts) fetches £19. 10s., and Saltpond (including Winnebah, Appam and Chama sorts), £18 only, or 20 per cent less than Lagos sorts. . . .

The average export of oil from the Gold Coast, taking the exports from 1882 to

---

[1] The Bill received its third reading on 9 April, Mr. Sarbah handing in a statement of his views for transmission to the Secretary of State. For the later history of this measure see No. 464 below.

1888 as a basis, is 3,276,000 gallons, which, allowing two gallons per tree, would be the product of 1,638,000 trees, probably not more than one half of the trees actually existing in the Colony. Allowing one fourth of this deficiency (a large estimate) for home consumption, we have nearly one and a quarter millions of gallons of the value of £51,700, as lost to the Colony every year. A large quantity of the oil in the nuts subjected to manufacture, is wasted, owing to the defective methods employed, but a still larger quantity there is no attempt to use, it being allowed to fall from the trees and rot on the ground.

It is impossible to pass from this subject without referring to the fluctuations in the price of palm-oil which have occurred during the past few years (the effect of which is seen in the diminution of the exports during 1886–7, while the price was steadily falling, and in the increase in 1888, owing to a recovery of the market), and considering the prospect, in view of the competition of tallow, petroleum and other oils, and the increased production which would be caused by the adoption of improved methods of cultivation, manufacture and transport, there can be no hesitation in saying that, given a cheap method of transport, palm oil can be profitably produced on the Gold Coast, even though prices should fall considerably below their present level. It is the difficulty of transport that keeps the price on the Gold Coast at such a height as renders the present state of the markets in Europe unprofitable to the exporter, although the grower can produce it at a cost which would enable him to sell it with profit at 3d to 4d per gallon. Allowing 300 gallons to the ton, the cost to the exporter would be £3. 15s. to £5 per ton, which, after paying for the caskage, shipping &c, and allowing £1 per ton for transport from the plantation to the beach, would enable him to place it on the European market at £13 a ton. In view of the increasing use of other fats, displacing palm oil in many directions, the inhabitants of the Colony

have to face the probability of the price of palm oil touching £15 to £14 per ton, and have the right to call upon their Government to perform its obvious duty by putting the roads in such a condition as to enable them to transport their produce at a reasonable cost, and to prevent their staple product being driven from the market, to the ruin of their trade. . . .

After the manufacture of the oil, the nuts are still valuable as they contain the well known palm kernels. For every ton of palm oil, there should be 2½ tons of clean palm kernels, and yet we find that the exports of this article are much below those of the oil. . . . The direct loss to the Colony is enormous, and arises from the same causes as diminish the export of oil. Machines have been invented, by Gunnell and others, for the purpose of rapidly breaking the nuts, but they can never come into general use until it is possible to move large weights in carts along roads adapted for the purpose, as will be evident when it is considered that under present conditions, four men are required to carry on their heads sufficient nut (two cwts) to produce 56 lbs of kernels, the value of which varies from 1s 9d to 2s 3d. Owing to this cause, £100,000 worth of this one article are annually wasted. . . .

The cocoanut is largely grown, every town and village along the coast having its grove of palms at the edge of the beach . . . but very little commercial use is made of the fruit, the exports of copra reaching barely £1,000 per annum. . . . It is astonishing that no effort to utilise this source of wealth has ever been made by the laying out of plantations and the establishment of a trade in the produce of the trees. . . . The coast of Guinea is as well adapted for the production of this valuable palm as [either the East or West Indies] . . . and it depends upon the inhabitants of the Colony whether they will gather the wealth that is within their reach from this source. . . . The capital required is small, and the labour of cultivating the trees and collecting the nuts need not interfere with the cultivation of . . . foodcrops. . . . No fear need be felt of over-stocking the market, as the civilized world of the temperate zone can absorb all the oil and fibre the tropics are likely to send, for generations to come. . . .

Although the youngest of our industries, the manufacture of india-rubber is now second only in importance to that of palm oil. Attention was first drawn to this valuable product by Mr Alfred Moloney . . . when administering the Government of the Gold Coast in 1882, by letters to the local press. The first practical experiments were made by Mr F. C. Grant of Cape Coast, whose example was quickly followed by others, and, the undertaking proving remunerative, the collection of rubber began in every part of the Colony, and the quantity now produced annually ranges from £30,000 to £40,000 in value, although in the meantime the price has fallen considerably. . . . The preparation is slovenly, and a wet process is usually allowed, resulting in an inferior, wet, and ill-smelling article. . . . The wet process causes the product to lose greatly in weight in the process of manufacture in Europe, which tends, of course, to lower the value still further. . . . The German traders obtain a higher price for the rubber shipped by them, by cutting it into small pieces, pressing between grooved steel rollers, to express the non-coagulated juice, washing it to get rid of foreign matters, again passing it through the rollers, and finally drying it. The process is long and tedious, but raises the value of the product by fifty per cent. All this trouble would be avoided by proper treatment of the milk in the first instance. . . . It is to be feared that the present methods of collecting the milk is by cutting the vines instead of tapping them, and that this will lead to an early exhaustion of the supply. Already the collectors have been compelled to move to a considerable distance from the sea and the ports, the forests near the coast being exhausted. If it is impossible to regulate the mode of collection (as in Assam),

steps should be taken to keep up the supply by planting. . . .

The forests of the country form an untouched mine of wealth which only requires the introduction of a cheap method of transport to be developed. A large export trade might be carried on after all local wants are supplied, and yet the Colony is at present actually importing timber from the United States for building purposes. . . .

Coffee has long been grown in the Aquapim district under the auspices of the Basel Mission, who introduced the seed from the West Indies in 1843. The early plantations were destroyed by the Ashantees in 1869, but were (at least in part) re-established, and nothing but perseverance and capital are required to develop this culture. . . .

Cocoa . . . is another product worthy of every attention. Attempts on a small scale have been made to introduce it into the country, but no information is obtainable as to the results. The culture is cheap, and the preparation simple, so that it should receive the attention of small cultivators.

Although the Gold Coast Colony is adapted for the raising of almost any tropical growth, it exports hardly any agricultural produce save palm oil and kernels. . . . The question naturally arises why, with a fertile soil, an enormous extent of forest, and an agricultural population, is there not a large trade in timber and other products of the country? It is too often taken for granted that the fault lies with the natives of the Colony; that they are too lazy to work. This has a specious air of truth. The native of the Gold Coast is indolent because he has few wants, and these being easily gratified, he has small inducement to continuous labour: but . . . the rapid development of the trade in india-rubber is a proof that the natives of the Gold Coast are capable of taking advantage of their opportunities when they are made aware of them . . . if they see promise of adequate return. . . .

The principal reason for the neglect of native products is the difficulty of transporting cumbersome goods, which arises from the want of roads as, too often, the vendor, having collected his produce and brought it to market, finds the value is swallowed up by the cost of transport. . . . All the produce that is exported is brought down on the heads of men and women, and in every case, the cost of transport at least doubles the cost. This gives his opportunity to the middleman who steps in and makes his profit out of producer and exporter, and injures the trade of the country by adulteration.

The first step towards developing the resources of the country must be the establishment of good roads between the producing districts and the ports of shipment. . . . The direction which these roads should take is pointed out by the present trade routes. There are eight principal lines of trade, having their outlets at Dixcove, Chama, Elmina, Cape Coast, Salt Pond, Winnebah, Akusi and Quittah. . . .

Improved means of communication will lead to a great and immediate increase in the exports of palm-oil and kernels, but the country's prosperity will always be subject to violent shocks while it rests on a single product. Efforts should be made, therefore, to render it independent of the state of any single market, by broadening the basis of trade by the introduction of foreign products and the exploitation of native growths. . . . No better means can be used than the establishment of experimental gardens under trained botanists . . . [which also] should be utilised as training stations for young natives, to teach them civilised methods of cultivation, to enable them either to cultivate the soil for themselves, or to take charge of plantations established by others. This is the more important in view of the unsuitability of the climate for the prolonged residence of the natives of northern climates. While 'petite culture' will no doubt be largely followed by natives, large plantations must for many years be dependent on European

capital, but no European will think of starting a plantation unless he is able to find someone to take charge of it when he is obliged to leave the Colony for his health's sake. No greater boon could be bestowed on the country than such an opening for the employment of its youth, who now flood the clerical market. . . . All our towns are filled with young men seeking in vain a livelihood in clerical offices, while vast fields of labour are left untouched. . . .

[C.5897, A & P (1890) xlviii]

362 GRIFFITH TO KNUTSFORD
10 NOVEMBER, 1890.

. . . The Report refers to the loss sustained by the fruit of the oil palms 'being allowed to fall from the trees and rot on the ground, because, owing to the want of cheaper transport than that afforded by the native carriers, it will not pay to bring it to the towns on the coast,' and it is urged that the Government should put the roads in such a condition as to enable the people to transport their produce at a reasonable rate. [But roads alone will be very little use because draught animals will not live on the Gold Coast.] . . .

The Government has not been unmindful of the responsibility which devolves upon it to keep the principal trade roads open, and to improve the communication between the important towns inland and those on the seaboard, and towards this end an inspector of interior trade roads has been specially appointed. . . . The Colony is only in the sixteenth year of its existence, and doubly and trebly more has been done in the last five years to advance its substantial interests than was attempted in the previous eleven years. . . . Roads for carriage traffic will be all very well in their way, when it is shown beyond doubt that such traffic can be steadily maintained, but it appears to me that the real improved communication which is required between the seaboard and the interior is that to be afforded by the introduction of railways. . . . The introduction of light railways between Accra and Krobo, Anamabu with Saltpond towards Akim Swaydru and Insuaim, and Cape Coast and Elmina to the countries behind them . . . will do more towards the rapid opening and development of the interior, and place it far more promptly in touch with the commercial seaboard than the slower and uncertain process of carriage transport by cattle. . . .

[The Aburi[1] station was designed to provide the sort of agricultural training mentioned in the Report.] . . . The Curator has succeded fairly well with the cocoa seeds I supplied to him, and more will be furnished as soon as I can procure them from Fernando Po. 1,900 seeds were sent from Trinidad, but the voyage appears to have been too long for them, as they were dead before arrival. It may interest your Lordship to be informed that the king of Western Akim has requested me to allow him to purchase 100 cocoa plants from Aburi, and to inform him as to the mode of culture. . . . [They had also experimented with Liberian and Akwapim coffee, Egyptian cotton, and coconuts.]

The rubber industry referred to in the Agricultural Report has recently developed amazingly. . . . It appears that the first attempt to export rubber from the Gold Coast was made in 1880. The following figures supply the quantities and values shipped in the undermentioned ten years:—

1880	1,200 lbs [Valued at] £	43
1881	555 ,,	31
1882	70 ,,	1
1883	57,913 ,,	2,372
1884	223,843 ,,	13,620
1885	548,474 ,,	26,175
1886	1,549,121 ,,	69,911
1887	1,306,252 ,,	62,430
1888	878,387 ,,	38,048
1889	1,241,628 ,,	55,198

. . . . .

The Report alludes to 'the present method of collecting the milk' from the rubber vine and tree by cutting either

[1] Opened the previous year.

down instead of resorting to the tapping process. This was brought to my notice about two years ago, and I at once took steps to communicate [with] . . . the kings and chiefs whose countries were the principal rubber producers, and to point out to them the folly of the action of the rubber gatherers. In several instances the native authorities exerted themselves to put a stop to the partial destruction of the rubber trees and vines, but they reported to me that, looking to the vast area over which rubber was grown, it would be simply impossible to prevent the cutting of the trees and vines altogether. . . . There are two circumstances from which comfort may be derived in this matter; first that the rubber family plants are virtually inexhaustible, and second, that if a tree or vine is cut down, the part remaining in the ground sends up new shoots which grow rapidly and in due time are again operated on. . . .

As to the resources of the people having been diminished by a long period of depression which has checked their spirit of enterprise so that it requires nursing, I would call attention to the . . . figures indicating the imports and exports of the colony . . . from 1875 to 1889 . . . showing the total average annual trade of the Colony as £804,772, which might be considerably increased if the average native was less indolent and apathetic. . . .

With regard to the reporter's idea that pecuniary aid should be afforded by the Government to private undertakings of an agricultural or other character, I am decidedly in conflict with him. The Government could not afford such aid without steady supervision, and it could not undertake the responsibility and anxiety which obviously would be the result of any such commitments as I have referred to. . . . In a country where for thousands of years the people have been accustomed to look up to their own kings and chiefs for direction and action, exercising no volition of their own, it is not singular that . . . their descendants should be so disposed to look to the Government to do . . . more than the Government should commit itself to. If the Executive were to undertake all that the people would desire it should, one of the almost certain consequences would be, not only to prevent the people from exercising self-reliance, but it would make them more helpless and dependent. Gradually, as education, civilization, and agricultural and commercial enterprise expand, the people will no doubt strike out paths of action for themselves, instead of leaning with so much expectation, as they do at present, upon the Government. . . .

[C.6270, A & P (1890-1) lv]

362a CURATOR OF GOVERNMENT GARDENS TO GOVERNOR [Enclosed in **362**]

ABURI, 22 AUGUST, 1890.

. . . I went to Mampong . . . and saw the cocoa plantation belonging to a man called 'Tetti Quashi'.[1] He has about 300 trees, ranging from two to four years old. They look extremely healthy, and many of the larger trees have as many as fifty large, healthy pods on each; some of the two-year-old trees have a few pods on, and the three-year-old trees were bearing well. From the results of this plantation, it is proved beyond a doubt that cocoa will grow well here. These trees had received very little attention and cultivation; the land had not been properly cleaned, and the bananas were growing up and spoiling the shape of the trees, besides taking the substance from the soil. The rank grass and bush were about three feet thick over the whole plantation, still the trees looked healthy. . . . [C.6270.]

363 A NOTE ON FINANCE.

The revenue of the colony is almost entirely derived from a specific duty of 1s a gallon (old wine) on wines and malt

liquors and 2s 6d a gallon (old wine) spirits, and from a 10 per cent ad valorem duty which has been imposed upon the principal imports since the 1st January 1890. There are also specific duties on tobacco, cigars, gunpowder, cartridges, lead, percussion caps and guns; stamp duties; and a tax upon the sale of liquors.

Until the 1st January 1888, there was an ad valorem duty of 4 per cent upon all imports with but few exceptions other than wine, malt liquors, spirits, tobacco, gunpowder and guns, upon which specific duties were levied: but Ordinance No. 2 of 1877, imposing these duties, was repealed by Ordinance No. 5 of 1887, the chief feature of which was the abolition of the ad valorem duty of 4 per cent, and an increase in the specific duties on wine, malt liquors, tobacco and cigars. The revenue at once fell from £122,350. 10s. 6d. in 1887 to £97,806. 19s. 5d. in 1888, and although in 1889 it rose to £111,386. 6s 7d., . . . it became patent that the fiscal change was unlikely to provide sufficient revenue to admit of works for the development of the Colony being undertaken, and that it was on that account not a success. Hence the reversion to, and an increase of, the previous ad valorem duty, from 1st January 1890.

In that part of the Protectorate which lies to the eastward of the River Volta, the duties upon spirits, tobacco, gunpowder, and guns, were, from the 1st May, 1890, considerably reduced, and at the same time all merchandize which was elsewhere subject to the ad valorem duty of 10 per cent was then entirely exempted from duty. It was found that trade was being attracted to the neighbouring Colony of Togoland in consequence of the comparatively low import duties levied in that Colony, and the reduction of the duties eastward of the Volta was therefore a measure of self-defence. It has answered all expectations, the trade at the ports of Ada and Kwitta, and more especially the latter, having increased enormously since the step was taken. . . .

[1] Tete Kwashi (c. 1842-92); brought his cocoa pods from Fernando Po where he worked from 1870-6.

The items of revenue for each year [1889–92] can . . . be shown as follows:

ITEMS OF REVENUE	1889 £	1890 £	1891 £	1892 £
Specific Duties. . . .	95,371	110,619	135,550	133,448
Ad Valorem Duties	—	22,728	32,445	28,322
Liquor Licenses	4,000	3,905	5,185	5,597
Stamps. . . .	2,769	5,564	6,410	6,686
Other items.	9,247	13,630	8,430	9,019

It does not appear that the imposition of a 10 per cent ad valorem duty has in any way hampered the trade of the Colony in goods subject to that tax. The tax is a very proper tax, because it reaches every person in the Colony in a manner which is not felt. . . . There is no other way by which the native can so easily be reached. Direct taxation is impossible excepting in the towns. There such taxation lies ready for municipal purposes when the time arrives for the formation of municipalities.

The population of the Colony being 1,473,882 and the Revenue from taxes in 1892 being £178,978. 12s. 1d. . . . it follows that the taxation amounts to 2s. 5d. per head. It is clear, therefore, that the natives of the Gold Coast have, in comparison with the population of other countries all over the world, a very light burden of taxation, and are wholly without any just grounds for complaint in that respect. In Sierra Leone and Lagos the taxation per head is very much higher, in the former nine times, and in the latter seven times as high. . . .

[Report on the Blue Book for 1892.[1]]

[1] This extract from the Blue Book has been used rather than the longer statements on which it is based, in Griffith's despatches to Knutsford of 24 November, 1888, and 15 June, 1889. It must not be inferred, from the heading of this chapter, that criticism of Griffith's adminstration necessarily declined after 1890. On the contrary, the re-imposition of the specific duties produced a monster protest petition in 1892, with over 500 signatures. See C.7225, A & P (1893–4) lx, 651.

27   The Partition of Krepi and Gyaman, 1889–1891

AFTER the demarcation of the coast-line with the Germans and French in 1884, the partition of the coastlands fell to be considered. With the French, at first, there were no difficulties, and an agreement of 1889 fixed the western frontier of the Colony as far as Nugua (364). In the east, however, the conflicting aims of the British and Germans centred on the question of the precise extent of the 'kingdom' of Krepi or Peki (365), with which Britain had long-standing relations. The compromise agreement reached in 1890 (366), if slightly more favourable to the Colony than at one time seemed likely (367), was very unpalatable to the eastern chiefs (368).

In the case of Gyaman, which the British were anxious to hold as a cover to the Ashanti hinterland (370), their position was weakened by the fact that, while their relations with Gyaman went back earlier than those of the French, the latter were the first to conclude a definitive treaty with that country (369). Again a compromise partition was agreed in principle (371): but it was only implemented, after further differences (382), in 1893 (385).

Griffith's appointment as Governor coincided with a renewed outbreak of hostilities in Ashanti, which resulted in the Adansis, 'a troublesome and useless set of filibusters', being driven across the Pra into the Protectorate, whence they continued to molest Ashanti traders. Then in April 1888 a new Asantehene was at last enstooled. Kwaku Dua III, better known as Ajiman Prempeh, after having to fight and expel the Kokofus in order to establish himself, set on foot something of an Ashanti revival. This does not seem to have pleased Governor Griffith. In 1891 he sent a mission to Kumasi (372), to warn Prempeh not to attack Attabubu, which was rather hurriedly taken under British protection, and invited him to accept a British Protectorate over Ashanti (373).

The invitation was neither accepted by Prempeh nor approved by the British Government (375).

364 ARRANGEMENT CONCERNING THE DELIMITATION OF THE ENGLISH AND FRENCH POSSESSIONS ON THE WEST COAST OF AFRICA

SIGNED AT PARIS, 10 AUGUST, 1889.

The undersigned, selected by the Government of Her Majesty the Queen of Great Britain and Ireland and by the Government of the French Republic, for the purpose of preparing a general understanding with a view to settle all the questions at issue between England and France with regard to their respective possessions on the West Coast of Africa have agreed on the following provisions.

[Articles 1 and 2 relate to Senegambia and the northern boundary of Sierra Leone.] . . .

Article III, Sec. 1. On the Gold Coast, the English frontier shall start from the sea coast at Newtown at 1,000 metres to the west of the house occupied in 1884 by the English Commissioners. It shall thence go straight to the Tendo lagoon. The line shall then follow the left bank of that lagoon and of that of Ahy and the left bank of the River Tanoe or Tendo, as far as Nougoua.

The French Government shall undertake to allow England full liberty of political action to the east of the frontier line, particularly as regards the kingdom of the

Ashantees: and the English Government shall undertake to allow France full liberty of political action to the west of the frontier line.

The French frontier shall, in like manner, start from the seashore at Newtown at a distance of 1,000 metres to the west of the house occupied in 1884 by the English Commissioners. After having reached in a straight line the Tendo lagoon, it shall follow the right bank of that lagoon and that of Ahy, as well as that of the River Tanoe or Tendo, and terminate at Nougoua, the point at which the two lines of frontier shall unite.

Sec. 2. In the event of the Gold Coast Government thinking proper to establish a Custom House at the mouth of the River Tendo, the French Government will not object to the English authorities requiring from French boats, certificates of destination for goods going up the Tendo, in which certificates it shall be specified that the duties payable on goods imported into the French Colony have been paid in full.

The navigation on the Tendo and Ahy lagoons and on the River Tendo shall be free and open to the boats and inhabitants of the two Protectorates.

In the event of the French authorities thinking proper to establish a Custom House for the purpose of keeping a similar supervision over the English boats coming from the direction of Apollonia, as that exercised over French boats at the mouth of the Tendo, the English Government will raise no objection.

Sec. 3. The acceptance of the English Government of the above-mentioned lines of frontier remains subject to the adoption by the French Government of a Customs tariff to be established at Assinee, in which the duties upon spirituous liquors shall not be less than 40 fr. the hectolitre for alcohols and trade liquors of less strength than 25 degrees; than 60 fr. the hectolitre for alcohols of 25 to 49 degrees; and 100 fr. the hectolitre for alcohols of 50 degrees and over.

Duties upon tobacco in leaf and manufactured shall not be less than 80 centimes the kilogram.

Cotton goods shall be liable to a duty of 15 per cent *ad valorem*. . . . [Article IV deals with the Slave Coast between Porto Novo and Lagos.] . . .

Article V. The two Governments reserve to themselves the right of nominating Special Commissioners of Delimitation to trace upon the spot, wherever they may consider it necessary, the line of demarcation between the English and French Possessions, in conformity with the general provisions which are set forth above.

In witness whereof the undersigned Delegates have drawn up and signed the present Agreement, subject to the approval of their respective Governments.

Done at Paris in duplicate, the 10th day of August, 1889.

> Edwin H. Egerton.
> Augustus W. L. Hemming.
> A. Nisard.
> Jean Bayol.

Annex . . . Sec. 1. As far as regards the frontier line between the sea and Tendo lagoon, the expression 'straight' shall be taken to mean straight towards the true north.

The 'map showing the towns and villages visited by the Assinee Boundary Commissioners in December 1883 and January 1884', has served for the description of their part of the frontier as far as Nougoua.

[Hertslet, *op. cit.*, ii, 730]

365 MEMORANDUM BY A. W. L. HEMMING, ON KREPI

COLONIAL OFFICE, 11 DECEMBER, 1889.

The history of this matter is briefly as follows:—

In 1884 an officer was sent down by the Gold Coast Government to negotiate with the chiefs of Beh Beach, a district lying to the east of the Colony, for the cession of their territory, with a view to the suppression of the smuggling trade which was being carried on there to the detriment of the Colonial Revenue. The German traders, who were the principal smugglers, hearing of the negotiations, and being alarmed at the prospect of losing their gains, sent word to Dr Nachtigal, who happened to be on board a German man-of-war in the neighbourhood. He landed near Beh Beach, and getting hold of some of the chiefs, forced them to sign a treaty of cession to Germany, and hoisted the German flag.

Although there was clear evidence that the treaty was not signed by the chiefs who really had authority in the country, and in spite of the unfriendly nature of the act of thus taking possession of a country for which negotiations had actually been opened by a British officer, Her Majesty's Government at the time, anxious to show that this country had no jealousy of the desire of Germany to establish colonies, did not dispute the German occupation. Difficulties, however, soon occurred, owing to the German Protectorate being used as the basis for smuggling operations, of which it had always been a hot-bed, as Herr Richter recently stated in the Reichstag. In 1886, it became necessary to fix the boundary on the coast between British and German territory, in order that the Gold Coast police, in pursuing smugglers, might not infringe the border, and this was accordingly done.

Shortly after, the Germans began to push into the interior, and seized Agotime, which was a part of Crepee hitherto always regarded as being under British protection. Again, Her Majesty's Government, not wishing to be accused of checking German Colonial enterprise, acquiesced in the occupation of this territory.

As, however, the Germans continued to advance, the anxiety of the Colonial Government was aroused, and, fearing further encroachments on British territory, Her Majesty's Government informed Prince Bismarck, through Sir E. Malet, on 17th December, 1886, that 'the territories of Aquamoo and Crepee were among those which formerly recognised the authority of

the Danish Crown, that they were therefore included in the purchase of the rights and possessions of Denmark by Great Britain in 1850, and have ever since been under British Protectorate.'

No communication was received from the German Government until 23rd April, 1887, when, without referring to the above-mentioned note, they asked for some further information as to the British claims, and suggested a definition of the respective spheres of influence of the two countries.

The necessary information was furnished, and further correspondence ensued, which resulted in its being decided that Dr Krauel and Mr Scott should discuss the matter with a view to arriving at a settlement, and . . . the negotiations resulted in joint recommendations being agreed to by the British and German Commissioners.[1] . . .

The recommendations were accepted by the two Governments in February and March 1888, but the conclusion of a formal arrangement was deferred until Her Majesty's Government could decide upon a proposal which had been put forward by the German Commissioner that the whole of the territory east of the Volta, should be ceded to Germany. In November 1888 the German Government was informed that this proposal could not be acceded to.

Her Majesty's Government considered that the Agreement of December 1887 had definitely settled the questions at issue, and they would have been prepared to proceed to a delimitation of the frontier in accordance with it. But the German Government, apparently on the strength of information with respect to the position of the native tribes which was furnished to them by some of their authorities on the Coast, have put an interpretation on the agreement so wholly at variance with the understanding of Her Majesty's Government, and so contrary to the well known and long recognized facts, that in the present position of affairs it is impossible for a Boundary Commission to be appointed with any chance of success.

[1] No. 359 above.

The points in dispute between Her Majesty's Government and the German Government are practically two, viz.:

1. Whether Crepee (or Peki), mentioned in the agreement of 1887, means the whole of the territory known as Crepee, which formed part of the Danish possessions in 1850, or only the small district of Peki.

2. Whether the two districts known as Panto and Inkonia, in the northern part of Crepee, are integral portions of that kingdom, and of the British Protectorate.

With regard to (1), the German contention is that the Commissioners in 1887 had no intention to recognise the kingdom of Crepee as within the sphere of British influence in the whole extent which it attained under the Danish dominion, and that the word 'Peki' was added in the agreement to show that only that territory was assigned to the British sphere of influence, and in Count Hatfeldt's note of 9th August, and the map which accompanies it, they propose to reduce the area of the British Protectorate to the most insignificant proportions.

The answer of Her Majesty's Government is, that they purchased the whole of the Crepee territory from Denmark in 1850; that by the Convention of 17th August, 1850, the King of Denmark ceded all his Possessions, property and territorial rights whatever to Her Majesty; that their claims have from the first been founded on that Convention; that this is shown by the whole of the correspondence which led up to the meeting of the Commissioners in 1887; that the King of Peki has always been recognised as the paramount chief over the whole of Crepee; and that the word 'Peki' was only introduced into the agreement because it was understood by the British Commissioner that the Germans designated Crepee by that name, using the title of the paramount king or chief to designate the whole.

(2) The Germans contend that Panto and Inkonia do not form part of Crepee, but are independent territories. They have furnished no evidence of this beyond certain assertions of Herr von Puttkamer and Captain von Francois.

Her Majesty's Government, on the other hand, have produced reports of Captain Lonsdale, written in 1882, when there was no question of any other Power seeking to establish itself in these territories, which show that Panto certainly was then under the supreme authority of the king of Peki, and that the king and chiefs also signed a declaration of allegiance to Her Majesty before Captain Lonsdale; also a treaty of 1886, and a declaration of fealty to Her Majesty, signed by a number of the kings and chiefs of Crepee on the 15th June, 1887, six months before the agreement made at Berlin. The king of Peki signed as 'Head Chief of Crepee' and among the other signatories were the king and chiefs of Panto and the king of Inkonia. By this act these kings and chiefs distinctly acknowledged the paramountcy of the king of Peki.

But even supposing that the king of Peki is not the suzerain of these kings and chiefs, the rights of the British Crown rest upon their direct declarations of allegiance to Her Majesty, as made in the case of the king and chiefs of Panto in 1882, and again in 1887, and in the case of Inkonia in 1887.

The German Government desire that the Boundary Commission should be directed to investigate the question of the inclusion of Panto and Inkonia in the British Protectorate, but Her Majesty's Government hold that there is no room for inquiry as the Commissioners cannot be allowed to go behind the formal documents above mentioned, executed before the date of the agreement of 1887, and therefore constituting such prior claims as, Dr Krauel told Mr Scott, his Government desired scrupulously to respect. . . .

The importance of Panto and Inkonia to the Gold Coast Colony is very great. The former is a converging point for the trade routes from the interior, and the possession of these places would enable the Germans to divert to Lome a very large portion of the trade which now passes through British territory to the sea coast.

The German Government have recently suggested that the question of the northern boundary might stand over, and that the Commission should proceed to delimit the frontier to the east of Crepee. But, as has been shown in the letter from the Colonial Office of 29th ultimo . . . the divergence of the views of the two Governments is as great on the east as on the north, and the Boundary Commission, if it were to meet under present circumstances, would be stopped by this divergence at the very outset of their work.

Her Majesty's Government have already made very considerable concessions to Germany by surrendering their undoubted claim to Agotime, as a part of the territory acquired from Denmark in 1850, and by consenting to allow the extension of the German Protectorate up to the River Volta, between the north of Crepee and the River Daka, and they cannot, without giving up territory which has been in the uncontested possession of Her Majesty for nearly 40 years, and thereby seriously affecting the interests of the old-established British Colony on the Gold Coast, accept the proposals for the limitation of the British Protectorate which have been advanced by Count Hatzfeldt's note of 9th August.

[C.P., African (West) No. 384]

366 AGREEMENT BETWEEN THE BRITISH AND GERMAN GOVERNMENTS, RESPECTING AFRICA AND HELIGOLAND

BERLIN, 1ST JULY, 1890.

[Art. I relates to East Africa; Art. II to Witu; Art. III to German South West Africa.] . . .

Article IV. In West Africa —

1. The boundary between the German Protectorate of Togo and the British Gold Coast Colony, commences on the coast at the marks set up after the negotiations between the Commissioners of the two countries of the 14th and 18th of July, 1886; and proceeds direct northwards to the 6. 10′ parallel of north latitude; thence it runs along that parallel westward till it reaches the left bank of the River Aka; ascends the mid-channel of that river to the 6. 20′ parallel of north latitude; runs along that parallel westwards to the right bank of the River Dchawe or Shavoe; follows that bank of the river till it reaches the parallel corresponding with the point of confluence of the River Deine with the Volta; it runs along that parallel westward till it reaches the Volta; from that point it ascends the left bank of the Volta till it arrives at the neutral zone established by the Agreement of 1888, which commences at the confluence of the River Dakka with the Volta.

Each Power engages to withdraw immediately after the conclusion of this Agreement all its officials and employees from territory which is assigned to the other Power by the above delimitation. . . . [Section 2 concerns the Rio del Rey; Article V, the Benue; VI to X are general, and XI relates to Zanzibar and Mafia.]

[Hertslet, op. cit., iii, 903]

367 KNUTSFORD TO GRIFFITH

DOWNING STREET, 18 JULY, 1890.

. . . The line which has been agreed upon as the boundary between the Gold Coast Colony and the German Protectorate of Togo, is almost identical with that which was proposed by the German Ambassador in his note of the 9th of August, but you will see that it is slightly more favourable to the Colony. I regret that it was impracticable to have the places mentioned in your telegram of the 24th of June[1] included within the limits of British jurisdiction. You will, however, have learnt from my telegrams of the 18th and 27th of June, that it was considered necessary to accept the German proposals in this matter, as part of a general scheme for the settlement of the many territorial questions in dispute between the two Governments. . . .

[African (West) No. 384, p. 74]

[1] Waya, Adaklu, Ho and Tavieve.

368 GRIFFITH TO KNUTSFORD

Confidential.

CHRISTIANSBORG CASTLE, 12 SEPTEMBER, 1890.

. . . Chief Odonkor[1] seemed very much distressed at the information conveyed to him. He said the transfer of certain portions of Krepi, inclusive of Panto [Kpandu], to Germany, would cause the strongest possible feelings of irritation and annoyance amongst the people who would have to pass to a foreign Power, and he thought it would lead to bloodshed, when they would be murdered, as the Germans had rifles and the natives only trade guns.

He stated that many of the districts to be transferred were the most valuable portions of Krepi, because there were mines there in which gold was to be found, and a greater part of the rubber obtained in Krepi was grown in the districts of Adaglu, Ho, Tavieve, Madzi, and other places that were to be transferred. He said that the English, in taking this step, had acted towards them as if they were slaves, like one slave master transferring his slaves to another slave master, and he asked, 'What has come over the English that they give up everything to the Germans? Why', he said, 'it looks as if the English were afraid of the Germans in giving them everything.' . . . He said the Germans . . . were brutal and cruel in their treatment of the natives . . . that the natives would not submit to them at first, but would retaliate, and then the Germans would bring an army and kill them all.

He added that Akuse and Kwitta would lose much of their trade in consequence, especially if the Germans built a railway from Beh Beach to Panto, which it was said they intended to do. . . . He said if Panto could have been retained, they would not mind so much, for that was the key to the whole position, but now the Germans had got that, they would secure the

Salagha trade, and they had only to make the communications easy to Bagida, to reduce the markets of Akuse, Krepi, and Kwitta to nothing, because, he said the Germans would probably take steps to prevent any traders in their new territory from going to Kwitta.

I told him that . . . even supposing that policy were undertaken and allowed, nevertheless it appeared to me it would be impossible to guard the long stretch of country from Panto to Bagida so closely that if the natives wanted to take their produce into British territory the Germans would be able to prevent them; that I should make good roads close up to the frontier line . . . and that if Her Majesty's Government were pleased to accept the Protectorate of Atabubu which had been offered,[1] I should then make good roads from Atabubu to Abetifi in Kwahu, and thence by way of Begoro and Kebi, to meet the new road in Western Akim, to which I should add another road shortening the distance to Accra, and by that means, I thought it was not impossible that a portion of the Salagha and Kintampo trade would be diverted to the Gold Coast.

I advised him, at all events, not to be downcast nor to lose heart. . . . He said he would do his best to carry out my wishes, but that the English Government had acted very cruelly towards them, and that he must say again, he could not but think that they had exceeded their right in transferring Krepis to another Power without consulting them at all in the matter, and that this would be the prominent feeling in the Krepi country, and would tend to create a strong feeling of irritation at the manner in which they had been treated by the Government. . . .

[African (West) No. 384, p. 106]

[1] Early in 1890. Cf. Hodgson to Knutsford, 14 January, 1890 (C.O.96/208), G .E. Ferguson was sent up to conclude a treaty, signed at Atatubu on 25 November, 1890.

[1] Chief of Kpong.

369 THE MARQUIS OF SALISBURY[1] TO LORD LYTTON[2]

FOREIGN OFFICE, 21 MARCH, 1891.

. . . It cannot be denied that, whereas the 3rd Article of the Convention of August 10, 1889 provided that the frontier in the rear of the Gold Coast should be fixed in the interior in accordance with the various treaties which had been respectively concluded by the two Governments with the natives, France possesses a concluded treaty with Gaman antecedent to the treaty concluded on behalf of this country. At the same time, it may fairly be contended that the king of Gaman, having engaged in a signed paper to accept the British flag, was incapacitated from negotiating with the representatives of another Power, and that a treaty signed by him under such circumstances is invalid.

Her Majesty's Government cannot but think that the French Government, if they had been aware of the facts, would not have authorised M. Treich la Plène to open negotiations with a chief who had already placed himself under the British flag. It may reasonably be urged that a treaty concluded under these conditions is invalid, and that the conclusion of the subsequent British treaty must be taken in connection with the previous acceptance of the flag, being, in fact, part of a continuous transaction.

Taking this view, I concur with Lord Knutsford in the opinion that the neutralisation of a portion of Gaman would not be a satisfactory solution. If Her Majesty's Government are to give way as to Bondoukou, the territory to the east of the line of demarcation should be included in the British sphere. Neutralization would be no protection. The predominating influence at Bondoukou would, if the

[1] Robert Arthur Talbot Gascoyne Cecil (3rd Marquis of Salisbury) (1830–1903): M.P., 1853–68; Foreign Secretary, 1878–80, 1885–6, 1887–92, 1895–1900; Prime Minister, 1885, 1886–92, 1895–1902.
[2] Edward Robert Bulwer Lytton (1st Earl Lytton) (1831–91); poet and diplomat; Viceroy of India, 1876–80; British ambassador at Paris, 1887–91.

counter-influence of the British authorities were excluded from the other side of the frontier, carry all before it in the so-called neutral territory, in spite of protests, which would be our only weapon. . . .

[C.P., African (West) No. 389, p. 96]

370 E. H. EGERTON[1] TO LORD LYTTON

PARIS, 23 MARCH, 1891.

. . . The practical object respecting Gaman is to stop further advance of the French eastwards behind Ashantee and our Gold Coast Colony, whilst retaining the trade of that district and the interior. After consideration it seemed to me better to neutralise (as in the case of the not far distant Salaga) the portion which we wished to withdraw from the French, than to claim it for the British Protectorate. Neutralization would be equally efficacious as stopping the French advance, less likely to cause friction, and entailing to the Gold Coast Colony less expenses and responsibility. The trading facilities being fully secured, not only by the roads to the coast being thus free from the exclusive French influence, but the town of Bondoukou being also open and free to trade, the Gold Coast will thus have full commercial communication through it with Kong and the interior. In accordance with instructions, however, I will now claim for the British Protectorate what it was proposed to neutralise. . . .   [*Ibid.*, p. 98]

371 FOREIGN OFFICE TO COLONIAL OFFICE

21 APRIL, 1891.

. . . Although it was, in Lord Salisbury's opinion, desirable to advocate in the negotiations, as strongly as possible, the claims of this country over Gaman, his Lordship is not surprised that the attempt to enforce them has failed. The position of Her Majesty's Government was materially weakened by the fact that Her Majesty's

[1] (Sir) Edwin Henry Egerton (1841–1916); Secretary at the Paris Embassy 1885–92.

Commissioners of 1889, while accepting the principle of delimitation according to concluded treaties, laid down in Article III of the Agreement of August of that year, did not make any reserve as to the position of Great Britain in Gaman, which rested on the initial agreement of Corporal Van Dyke, as opposed to the subsequent treaty concluded by Captain Binger.

That the Agreement was considered by the Governor of the Gold Coast only as a step towards a treaty is proved by the instructions given by his Excellency in 1888 to Mr Lethbridge,[1] which clearly show that he did not then consider that the king of Gaman had concluded a treaty nor had accepted British protection. In [these] . . . instructions, Mr Lethbridge was directed to enter into a provisional treaty, and . . . was told to base his action on the contingency of the willingness of the chiefs to accept Her Majesty's protection. On the other hand, it cannot be denied that M. Treich la Plène did conclude a treaty.

It is not easy under these circumstances to answer satisfactorily a contention on the part of France, that when Mr Lethbridge arrived with the object of negotiating a treaty, he found a French treaty already concluded, and that the British Commissioners of 1889, who were aware of all the facts, would have made a special reservation when accepting the principle of concluded treaties, if they had intended to dispute the validity of the French treaty, and to set up against it the initial Van Dyke arrangement.

Lord Salisbury is therefore disposed to agree that, in view of the above consideration, the line sketched out by Captain Binger . . . might be accepted as the basis of a frontier, if better terms cannot be obtained, provided that the territory to the east of it is absolutely secured to Great Britain.

His Lordship entirely agrees with Lord

[1] H. Bridgman Lethbridge; served in the army, 1877–84; assistant-inspector, Gold Coast Constabulary, 1886; on special mission to Akim, 1887, and Gyaman, 1888.

Knutsford that Kwobyn must be placed within the British sphere. His Lordship also concurs in the view that France cannot reasonably claim compensation for the proposed Gaman arrangement [on the frontiers of Sierra Leone.] . . .

[African West No. 389, p. 102]

372 SIR W. B. GRIFFITH TO LORD KNUTSFORD

CHRISTIANSBORG CASTLE, ACCRA, 19 MAY, 1891.

. . . It appeared to me to be matter for serious consideration whether the time had not arrived to pursue a firm, decided and strong policy on the part of the Government with regard to [Ashanti] . . . for the following reasons. . . .

For some time past, since the present king was elected, this Colony has often been put to great and costly inconvenience in dealing with refugees from, and preventing raids on Ashanti, by those who have fled from it for safety to the Protectorate, and in sending missions of inquiry for the benefit of the authorities in Kumasi: but it is clearly not in the interests of this Colony that [this] procedure . . . should be continued indefinitely.

So far as I can judge from the information in my possession, the indications are that Ashanti as a whole, besides being gradually broken up, is steadily retrograding, both in its entirety as it now remains, and in the portions which have separated themselves from the nominal government at Kumasi, which is powerless to check the downward tendency mentioned, and has latterly been weakened by coolness between Kumasi and Bekwai, and by a disposition on the part of Yow Sapon of Juabin, to desert his allegiance if he can obtain admission into the Protectorate, whilst Bekwai, almost the only province of Ashanti which has steadily supported the young King Kwaku Duah at Kumasi, would gladly see the British flag planted throughout Ashanti. At present Adansi, owing to the absence of population, is rapidly resuming its forest character. . . . Kokofu and Dadiassi are quite neglected, cultivation has diminished, trade has fallen away, the roads to Gaman and Bontokoo are virtually closed, and Ashanti as a whole appears to be gradually falling into decay. . . .

I considered that if Ashanti was taken under British protection, it was, in the circumstances of the case, naturally to be expected that a great and beneficial change would very probably be the result. The fact of itself would gradually dispose those who have deserted their particular localities to return and re-inhabit them. Some twelve to fifteen thousand Adansis would again be spread over their country. About twenty thousand Kokofus and Dadiassies would seek their former homes. . . .[1]

I formed the opinion that . . . the best policy for this Government to pursue, would be to propose to the Ashantis, through the authorities at Kumasi, to place their country under British protection; to take action in the matter while it was still possible to do this before the rainy season started in the interior; and, in the event of the Ashantis agreeing to the proposal, to leave it open to Her Majesty's Government to ratify or disapprove of the . . . treaty. [The Executive Council concurred in these views, and Mr Hull left Accra on his mission on 12 March.] . . .

Your Lordship will observe that the position of affairs was such as to demand, as I considered, immediate action on my part, and I therefore assumed the responsibility of communicating with the king, without first submitting the course I have taken, for your Lordship's instructions thereon. . . .

[C.7917, A & P (1896) lviii]

373 TERMS OFFERED TO ASHANTI   1891.

Article 1

The King of   for himself, and his lawful successors, together with the kings,

[1] The Kokofus and Dadiassies took refuge in the Protectorate in 1888.

chiefs and principal men of that country, whose names are hereinafter signed and seals affixed, for and on behalf of themselves and their successors and the people of   , hereby place their country and themselves under the protection of Great Britain, declaring that they have not entered into any treaty with any other Foreign Power.

Article 2

[Acceptance by Great Britain.] . . .

Article 3

It is hereby agreed that the King [&c] of   , will not enter into any war or commit any act of aggression on any of the chiefs bordering on their country, by which the trade of the country shall be interrupted, or the safety and property of the subjects of Her Majesty the Queen of England . . . shall be lost, compromised or endangered, and that the said King . . . hereby undertakes to refer to the Governor of the Gold Coast Colony, acting on behalf of Her Majesty, for friendly arbitration, any trade or other disputes or misunderstandings in which they may become involved before actually entering upon hostilities, in order to avoid the same.

Article 4

Should any differences or disputes accidentally arise between the King . . . and any of his kings, chiefs and principal headmen, it shall be referred to the Governor or to the nearest British authority of the Gold Coast Colony for the time being, whose decision shall be final and binding upon all parties concerned.

Article 5

British subjects shall have free access to all parts of   and shall have the right to build houses and possess property according to the laws in force in the Gold Coast Colony; and they shall have full liberty to carry on such trade or manufacture as may be approved by the Governor of the Gold Coast Colony, or by any officer appointed for the purpose by Her

Majesty's Government. Any difference or dispute which may arise between the aforesaid British subjects and the King [&c] . . . shall be referred to the officer mentioned in Article IV, whose decision shall be binding and final. And it is hereby agreed that the King [&c] will not extend the rights hereby guaranteed to British subjects to any other persons without the knowledge and consent of such officer as aforesaid.

Article 6

In consideration of the protection guaranteed on the part of Great Britain to the King [&c] of   , they hereby bind themselves, their heirs and successors, to keep their main roads in good order, that they will encourage trade and give facilities to traders; and will not cede their territory to, or accept a protectorate from, or enter into any agreement, arrangements, or treaty with any other foreign power, except through and with the consent of Her Majesty, the Queen Empress.

Article 7

The Government of Her Majesty the Queen Empress will not prevent the King of   or his kings, chiefs, and principal headmen from levying customary revenue appertaining to them according to the laws and customs of their country nor in the administration thereof; and Her Majesty's Government will respect the habits and customs of the country so far as they do not militate against the dictates of humanity, but will not permit human sacrifices.

Article 8

It shall be competent for Her Majesty the Queen-Empress to appoint a Commissioner to reside in   , who shall assist the King by his advice, with a view to composing differences and securing the just administration of the law and the maintenance of order in the country; to directing the proper clearance of the roads; to promote the trading interests of the country; and to act in accordance with instructions which may be issued to him from time to time by the Governor of the Gold Coast. Her Majesty may further direct that   may be visited by a Travelling Commissioner of the Gold Coast Colony, when it shall seem fit to the Governor of the said Colony to despatch such an officer to that country for the purposes hereinbefore mentioned.

Article 9

This treaty shall come into force from the date hereof, but power is expressly reserved to Her Majesty the Queen-Empress to refuse to approve and ratify the same within one year from the date hereof. . . .   [C.7917, p. 52]

374 AGREEMENT BETWEEN GREAT BRITAIN AND FRANCE FOR THE DEMARCATION OF SPHERES OF INFLUENCE IN AFRICA (MIDDLE AND UPPER NIGER DISTRICTS AND GOLD COAST)

SIGNED AT PARIS, 26 JUNE, 1891.

The undersigned Plenipotentiaries charged in execution of the Declaration exchanged at London on the 5th August, 1890 between Her Britannic Majesty's Government and the Government of the French Republic to proceed to the laying down a line to delimit the respective spheres of interest of the two countries in the districts south and west of the Middle and Upper Niger, have agreed as follows:—

[Provisions for the definition of the eastern frontier of Sierra Leone.] . . . The Technical Commissioners who are nominated by the two Governments in accordance with Article III of the Agreement of the 10th August 1889, shall be instructed to trace the frontier in accordance with the following indications taken from M. Binger's map:—

The line would follow the frontier of Nougoua on the Tanoe, between Sanwi and Broussa, Indenie and Sahue, leaving Broussa, Aowin and Sahue to England; the frontier would then intersect the road from Annibilekrou to Cape Coast Castle, midway between Debison and Antieben-dekrou, and follow the direct road from Annibilekrou to Bondoukou, by Bodomfil and Dadiasi, at a distance of 10 kilometres to the eastward. It would then pass Bonko, so as to strike the Volta at the spot where that river is intersected by the road from Bandagadi to Kirkindi, and would follow that river as far as the 9th degree of north latitude.

[Signed] Edwin Henry Egerton
    Joseph Archer Crowe[1]
    Gabriel Hanotaux[2]
    Jacques Haussman.

[Hertslet, Map of Africa, vol. 2, p. 743]

375 COLONIAL OFFICE TO SIR W. G. GRIFFITH   3 SEPTEMBER, 1891.

Sir,

I am directed by Lord Knutsford to acquaint you that he had had under his consideration your Despatches . . . in which you report the circumstances under which you had sent Mr H. M. Hull to Ashanti, to propose to the King the conclusion of a treaty placing his country

[1] Sir Joseph Archer Crowe (1825–96); journalist and art historian; British commercial attaché in Paris, 1882–96.
[2] Albert August Gabrielle Hanotaux (1853–1944); Secretary in the French Ministry of Foreign Affairs, 1879; Minister for Foreign Affairs, 1894–5 and 1895–8.

under the protection of Great Britain, and the refusal of the King to accept the proposal and sign the treaty.

Lord Knutsford desires me to state, that whilst he is fully aware that you were actuated in the course you adopted by a sincere desire for the welfare and advantage of the Gold Coast Colony, and although he appreciates the force of many of the reasons which you have assigned for it, he regrets that he is unable to approve of the action which you took in the matter.

Looking to what has passed with respect to Ashanti, his Lordship cannot consider that you were justified in proposing to the King of Ashanti, without previous authority, a treaty which, if it had been accepted, Her Majesty's Government could hardly have declined to approve.

I am to point out that there does not appear to have been any special urgency in the matter, and that in a question of such importance, you should have telegraphed for permission to proceed, if you considered that too much delay would have been caused by correspondence.

I am to add that Lord Knutsford will be glad to receive from you an expression of your views as to the policy which should be adopted in future towards Ashanti.

I am etc.

R. H. Meade.

[C.7917, p. 74]

28 The Ferguson Missions, 1892-1894

THE growing anxiety of British merchants about French[1] and German plans in West Africa (376), carried to the pitch of demanding that all the land up to the Niger should be secured to the Gold Coast Colony (377), led Governor Griffith in 1892 to despatch an African agent, G. E. Ferguson, to the Ashanti hinterland, with instructions to conclude commercial treaties with the more important tribes outside the Neutral Zone (378). The Home Government was still, at this stage, more interested in a link-up with the Niger Company's territories, through Borgu (379).

Ferguson was successful in his negotiations, but his treaties were primarily commercial agreements (381), and their political value was further impaired by the very doubtful status and inter-relationships of the interior tribes (383). In 1894, he was therefore sent on a further mission to supplement the work of the first (387), and ultimately got as far as Wagadugu and Chakosi (390). Britain's hold on the Brong tribes (386) and the regions beyond, however, was necessarily tenuous as long as she had no agreement with Germany or France, and as long as the Home Government declined to sanction the use of force (388) to back up their attempts to persuade Ashanti into accepting a British Protectorate.

[1] In particular the travels of Captain Binger, who in 1888-9 visited Wagadugu, Mamprusi, Dagomba, Salaga and Kintampo, on his way from Bamako to the sea; and of Captain Monteil, who, in 1891, also visited Wagadugu, where he was (erroneously) believed to have secured a protectorate treaty, before striking east to Say and Bornu.

376 DEPUTATION ON THE BOUNDARIES OF THE WEST AFRICAN COLONIES

COLONIAL OFFICE, FEBRUARY, 1892.

. . . Your Memorialists respectfully reiterate their opinion that steps should immediately be taken to protect the interests of British Commerce in the countries adjacent to Sierra Leone which are still free from foreign European control, and, they may add, in other countries adjacent to the British possessions on the West Coast of Africa, where efforts are being made by rivals to close long-established avenues of trade with the interior, as your Memorialists believe that unless freedom of trade with the interior is secured, either by treaty, or by the establishment of British spheres of influence, the colonies of the coast must ultimately become valueless for commerce. . . .

Mr. Swanzy: . . .

Other speakers have referred, more especially the President of the Liverpool Chamber, to the comparative importance of the trade of the West of Africa with that of the East,[1] and I do claim that, as he said, the general question of spheres of influence should have your Lordship's attention. He and other speakers have referred to the activity of the French and Germans in the districts on the West Coast. . . . As representing the Gold Coast and the interests there at stake, I may mention that Captain Binger penetrated to the back of the Gold Coast, and if, as I understand, the French Under-Secretary of State is prepared to support the treaties made by that gentleman with some sort of force or moral support, we shall have something of this sort at the back of the Gold Coast.

As regards Grand Bassam and Assinee, we are very largely interested in those

[1] Commercially, West Africa was, of course, far more important than East: but between 1885 and 1900 British Governments tended to favour territorial expansion in East even at the price of concessions in West Africa.

places, and your Lordship is probably aware that there are large merchants trading from Bristol also interested in that line of coast, and I would mention that even in these French possessions themselves, we hold the large majority of the trade. And bearing upon that point I may mention that we are threatened at the present time by something like a Chartered Company. I believe there is a party in the French Ministry that are in favour of the establishment of chartered companies, and if that is the case, our interests in these French places, and the interests of other British merchants, will be affected. Again, if the French are allowed to penetrate to the back of the Gold Coast, the fact of a chartered company carrying on trade in places adjacent will affect the Gold Coast itself.

Again, I would point out to your Lordship, that on the east of the Gold Coast we have the Germans penetrating into the interior. We felt rather sore in connection with that Anglo-German agreement, that the Germans were allowed to get a footing much further down the Volta than we thought they should be allowed to get. They have penetrated as far as Salaga. I do not know to what extent they have secured the trade of those districts, or the kindly feeling of the chiefs, but anyway, as representing those districts, I would impress upon your Lordship the necessity of keeping open the communication with the interior and of protecting our Hinterland in every possible way. It may not affect the immediate present, but as trade increases, and as we get better communication, possibly by railway, with the interior, it is of primary importance that this Hinterland should be secured. . . . Not only is the Gold Coast increasing in prosperity, but the people are becoming more civilized, and I think it would be a very serious matter indeed if this growing trade, and the success of this promising colony, should be affected by a little laxity on the part of Her Majesty's Government. Previous speakers have referred to

the laxity of previous Governments on this point. I think merchants have been in a great measure to blame for their laxity. The point is this; we have not sufficiently appreciated, in years gone by, the effect of other nations coming; we did not consider, I suppose, the prospect of other nations coming and interfering alongside of us. . . .

Lord Knutsford: . . . I come to the . . . question . . . of enlarging the British sphere of influence behind the Gold Coast Colony in the direction of the Niger. As to that, by the agreement of 1889 and a further agreement of the 20th June last, the whole of the territory behind the Gold Coast Colony, as far as the 9th parallel of latitude, has been secured to the British sphere of influence, and the French are excluded from it. One gentleman mentioned Salaga, and I may say that by the agreement of 1887 with Germany, Salaga and a considerable extent of country round it, has been neutralised, and therefore remains free and open to British trade. The Niger Company have also by treaty secured their influence over all that large portion of country, Gurma and Borgu. That region is therefore secure from French or German influence. . . . Certainly, the endeavour of Her Majesty's Government has been to make the best of the state of things as we found them, and to prevent, by the treaty of 1889, any advance of foreign influence. . . .

[C.P. African (West) No. 421]

377 RESOLUTION OF THE WEST AFRICAN SECTION OF THE LONDON CHAMBER OF COMMERCE

BOTOLPH HOUSE, EASTCHEAP, LONDON, 8 MARCH, 1892.

Resolved. . .

That the necessity be strongly urged upon Her Majesty's Government of securing to the Gold Coast Colony, without delay, the territory as far as back as the Niger, which is the natural boundary to the north of the ninth parallel of north latitude, as a British sphere of influence, treaties for that territory not having been made by any other power, and that the said territory should be protected from behind from the encroachments of Foreign Governments. That to this end, the Gold Coast Government be telegraphed to equip and despatch Government Officers to make treaties with the native tribes between the said parallel of north latitude and the meridian of longitude of the coast limits of the Colony.

That it be recommended to Her Majesty's Government that British interests generally should be secured in the territories of West Africa where British trade predominates, and which are unappropriated by any European Power, by arranging that such territories shall become British spheres of influence.

That in any other territories, arrangements should, if possible, be made, that no differential duties prejudicial to British trade, shall exist or be imposed in the future, the claim to such privilege being based on the fact that Great Britain opened up the West African territories to commerce, by exploration and by the abolition of the slave trade. . . .

      [C.P. African (West) No. 448, p. 3]

378 SIR W. B. GRIFFITH TO G. E. FERGUSON[1]

ACCRA, 25 APRIL, 1892.

Secret.

Sir,

It has been decided that steps should be taken to secure British influence over the territory in the rear of the Gold Coast Colony beyond the 9th parallel of latitude, where such territory is not clearly proved to have been already placed under the protection of a foreign Power. I have selected you for the purpose indicated, and I now instruct you to proceed as promptly

[1] George Ekem Ferguson (1864–97); clerk in Government service; later took up surveying; on special mission to Krobo and Akwamu (1886), Kwahu and Atabubu (1890); on Anglo-German Boundary Commission, 1891.

as you possibly can, to execute the mission entrusted to you.

You will endeavour to make treaties with the native authorities of the following countries, viz.:—

> Dagomba,
> Gonja,
> Gourounsi, and
> Mossi.

I append a copy of a treaty such as it is desirable you should obtain and have formally executed. You will observe that it does not imply the protection of the countries referred to, as that would be simply impossible, looking to their distance from the Gold Coast, but that it is a treaty of friendship and freedom of trade, with a binding engagement by the native chiefs that they will not make any treaty with, or accept the protection of any other Power, without the consent of Her Majesty's Government.

You are well aware of the fact that Great Britain cannot, under treaty arrangements, exercise any exclusive right over territory situated within the Neutral Zone of the agreement made at Berlin in 1888. It will be for you, therefore, to consider as to the best course for you to take in proceeding to the countries indicated. . . . You will, of course, understand that you must not make treaties with native chiefs whose territories lie entirely within the Neutral Zone. But you would not be debarred from making treaties with chiefs having territory lying partially within it, as you would be free to negotiate with them respecting those portions of their territories situated outside of it. Any such treaty must then contain a clause stipulating that territory within the zone is not affected by it. . . .

After the conversations we have held upon the subject matter of this communication, it appears to me unnecessary to do more than again impress upon you . . . the absolute necessity of your proceeding to the localities where your operations are to be carried out, with the utmost promptitude, as the matter is of much urgency, and should be carried out at once. . . .

[African (West) No. 448, p. 13]

379 THE MARQUIS OF SALISBURY TO E. C. H. PHIPPS[1]   FOREIGN OFFICE, 6 JULY, 1892.

. . . Her Majesty's Government have given their most careful consideration to the report . . . of the first meeting of the Anglo-French Niger and Lake Chad Commission.

It is stated in that report that the French Commissioners said that the line they proposed for the delimitation of the French and British spheres of influence to the west of the Middle Niger, would start from Say, passing the north-west limit of the so-termed Neutral Anglo-German zone, about the tenth parallel of latitude, crossing the ninth parallel where it is intersected by the Black Volta, and terminating at Bondoukou.

I enclose for the information and guidance of Mr Phipps, copies of a letter from the Colonial Office, and of a memorandum by the Intelligence Department, which show that it is considered in both quarters that the proposal forms a basis for negotiation. In this view I concur.

We could not agree to a line drawn direct from Say to Bondoukou deviating only so as to leave the Neutral Zone . . . intact; but we should be prepared, in view of Captain Monteil's reported action,[2] to leave Mossi to the French side. The Commissioners may discuss the question of an alternative boundary on the basis of the line suggested in the letter from the Colonial Office,[3] with some modification in order to prevent the division of the territory of Gourma, which must remain on the English side.

The alternative line, starting 20 miles

[1] Edmund Constantine Henry Phipps (later Sir) (1840–1911); entered Diplomatic service, 1858; First Secretary (1890); Minister Plenipotentiary at Paris (1893); British delegate on West African Boundary Commission (1893).
[2] See note p. 452.
[3] Printed in African (West) No. 418, p. 137.

due west of Say, would run northward, keeping always at a distance of 20 miles from the Niger, till it reaches the 14th degree of north latitude, and would follow that line of latitude westwards as far as the meridian 0 of Greenwich, would run along that meridian to about 10. 30′ north latitude, and thence bend due west to about 1. 30′ west longitude, thence continue in a south-westerly direction till at the ninth parallel of latitude, it would reach the frontier of June 26th, 1891. . . .

Too much stress should not be laid upon an attempt to limit the French sphere of influence to the eighth parallel of latitude behind Dahomey or Porto Novo, although the Commissioners should be careful that it is clearly secured that the French Government abandon any claim whatever to the hinterland of Dahomey. . . .

It is possible that the natural frontier behind Dahomey, indicated by Monsieur Hanotaux, a little above the eighth parallel, may actually exist, and in that case it could be accepted: but as its existence is problematical . . . it would be essential to stipulate that in case of Perthe's map being in error, the geographical parallel on which it places the range will form the frontier unless a natural frontier in its immediate vicinity should be discovered on survey and accepted by both Powers.

Having seen Sir George Goldie, you are acquainted with his views, which are that the proposed delimitation would be acceptable to the Niger Company, provided that there is no doubt as to the retention in the British sphere of the hinterland of Dahomey and the French possessions.

[C.P. African (West) No. 435, p. 2]

380 FERGUSON TO GRIFFITH
CHRISTIANSBORG, 19 NOVEMBER, 1892.

Secret.

[Announces the signature of treaties with Bole, Daboya, Dagomba and Bimbla.] . . .
According to Binger's map of 1890, the

French influence is limited more or less to the River Akba or Como. The countries of Mosi, Gurunsi, Gonja, Dagomba, Lobi &c are not, so far as I could ascertain, under any territories to the west of the Como river as his map suggests.

Lobi on the east of this river is an independent state trading with Bona at the Jilasu market. It is reported very rich in alluvial deposits of gold. The people are inhospitable but possess great predilections for trade.

Bona, an Ashanti country, is an important centre at which the caravan routes from Bontuku and Kong meet and go from there to Wa and Yariba.[1]

Wa is a very large Dagari town with a Mussulman population. Routes from Bole, Bona, Lokosu, Daboya converge here. Wa, though a state in the Dagari (Gurunsi) country, suzerainty has been claimed over it by Gonja since Gardiari attacked it and Bole went to its protection.

The portion of Gurunsi country between the 11th and 12th parallels of latitude is occupied by Gardiari, a slave hunter who is much dreaded by neighbouring tribes. He is at present settled at Sati and holds a large market at Yariba, at which guns, gunpowder, kola nuts and horses are exchanged for, principally, slaves and a little ivory and gold; while a large quantity of shirting from Salaga and Bontuku also finds its way there among his Mussulman adherents. Gardiari himself is dead, though the camp is known by his name. He has been succeeded by his two sons, Isaka and Barbutu, who, from all accounts, are desirous of direct trade with us ('the white man who conquered Ashanti').

Yariba and Walembele, both feudatories to Daboya, were represented in the treaty with Daboya.

Dagomba has an organised despotic monarchical government, the king residing at Yendi. . . . Mamprusi, a Gurunsi tribe, and Chakosi, a colony of Sefui people, together with Pampamba, are feudatories

[1] Mod. Yagaba.

to Dagomba. Sansane Mango and Pampamba have often tried to assert their independence of Dagomba, and it is only recently that the king of Yendi returned from punishing the latter country.

Salaga is the great market for kola nuts and coast goods. Three fourths of the European goods I found there to be of British manufacture. Nearly all of the brass and copper rods imported into the Gold Coast find their way to Mosi and neighbourhood. I understand that the king of Mosi considers it undesirable to have a market near his capital, as he is desirous to monopolise the Salaga trade by sending as heretofore his four or five great caravans every year, and selling the goods he receives to neighbouring tribes. Mosi, Dagomba and Gruma speak dialects of the same language.

As regards the boundary suggested with France in the hinterland of the Gold Coast . . . the treaties attached secure to us the trade of the countries exterior to the Neutral Zone. By adopting the lines proposed, we will lose the centres of trade in our rear and the rich auriferous deposits which appear to extend from Wassaw, through Gaman, to Lobi. In my opinion, the River Akba or Como presents the most natural boundary, looking to the trade which we have hitherto enjoyed with Mosi and other caravans at the Salaga and Bontuku markets; to the fact that the people themselves are strongly opposed to a division or disunion of their dominions; and to the fact also that the French influence is limited more or less . . . to River Como. France has not enjoyed trade with Mosi owing to the political state of the region, occupied by Gardiari, sometimes known as Zambrama. On the other hand, the former visits of 'the white man who conquered Ashanti' to Bontuku, Kintampo, Salaga and Yendi, I ascertained, produced a feeling of confidence in the interior, and invited more trade from Mosi and Niger territories to the Gold Coast, an oath to trade being sworn eventually between Salaga and Mosi.

[African (West) No. 448, p. 35]

381 TREATY WITH DABOYA

8 JULY, 1892.

. . . .

Article 1

The king of the country of Daboya, otherwise called Wasape, for himself and his lawful successors, together with the chiefs and principal men of the country, for and on behalf of themselves and their successors, and the people of Daboya, otherwise called Wasape, hereby declare that they have not entered into any treaty with any other foreign power with regard to that portion of their country which is not included in the section of territory belonging to them and known by the British and German Governments as the Neutral Zone, which last-mentioned territory is not included in this treaty.

Article 2

There shall be friendship and freedom of trade between the king, princes, chiefs, and principal headmen and people of Daboya, otherwise called Wasape, and the subjects of Her most Gracious Majesty the Queen Empress, and it is hereby understood and agreed between the contracting parties to this treaty that British subjects shall have free access to all parts of the country of Daboya, otherwise called Wasape, exterior to what is now known as the Neutral Zone and is not included in this treaty, and shall also have the right to build houses and possess property according to the laws of the country of Daboya, otherwise known as Wasape, and they shall have full liberty to carry on trade or manufacture, and should any difference or dispute arise with regard to any trading transactions or other matters between the subjects of Her Majesty residing or carrying on business in that portion of the Daboya country included in this treaty and the people of that country, the same shall be decided by the proper local authorities according to the customs and laws existing in that country. The king, princes, chiefs and principal headmen of Daboya, also declare and engage that they will not extend the rights hereby guaranteed to British subjects, to any other persons without first communicating to the Governor of the Gold Coast Colony their intention to grant such rights to persons other than British subjects who may apply to them to be admitted to the same privileges as British subjects in that part of the country exterior to what is now known as the 'Neutral Zone', and is not included in this treaty.

Article 3

The king, chiefs, princes, and principal headmen of the country of Daboya, otherwise called Wasape, in consideration of their friendly connection with Great Britain and the Gold Coast Colony, by virtue of this treaty, hereby promise to have their principal trade roads in those portions of their country lying exterior to what is now known as the 'Neutral Zone' and is not included in this treaty, kept in order for the advantage of traders passing through, and to the general advantage of the people of the country; that they will encourage trade; and they likewise hereby undertake and bind themselves not to cede their territory to, nor accept a protectorate from, or enter into any agreement, arrangement, or treaty with any other foreign power, with regard to that portion of their country lying exterior to what is now known as the 'Neutral Zone' except through and with the consent of the Government of Her Majesty the Queen Empress.

Article 4

This treaty shall come into force the date hereof, but power is hereby expressly reserved to Her Majesty the Queen Empress to refuse to approve and ratify the same within 18 months from the date hereof. . . .

Done at Daboya, in the country of Gonja . . . this 8th day of July in the year one thousand eight hundred and ninety-two. . . .

[African (West) No. 448]

382 COLONIAL OFFICE TO FOREIGN OFFICE
15 DECEMBER, 1892.

Sir,

With reference to previous correspondence respecting the delimitation of the Anglo-French Boundary to the west of the Gold Coast Colony, I am directed by the Marquess of Ripon[1] to transmit to you, to be laid before the Earl of Rosebury,[2] a copy of a despatch from the Governor of the Gold Coast, forwarding the report of Captain Lang, R.E., the British Boundary Commissioner.

As Lord Rosebery is already aware, the proceedings of the Joint Commission were abruptly terminated before the work of delimitation was completed, and Captain Lang states very fully and clearly the circumstances under which Captain Binger broke off communications with him. There is therefore no joint report of the Commissioners, and Her Majesty's Government can only consider the questions at issue by the light of the information furnished by Captain Lang.

It appears that with regard to the frontier up to Nougoua, no dispute has arisen. It is at and from that point that the difficulty begins. . . . By an oversight, no provision was made in either [the 1889 or 1891] Agreement as to the actual possession of Nougoua itself, and it was on this point accordingly that the first difference between the Commissioners arose. . . .

The evidence taken by the late Lieutenant Pullen in 1883–4 and by Captain Lang entirely agree as to Nougoua having always been subject to and having formed a part of the kingdom of Apollonia, and if this can be considered as proved, there can be no doubt that it ought to be assigned to Great Britain. . . . Lord Ripon is not disposed to think that the actual possession

of Nougoua itself is of very great importance, but it is stated to govern the control of the territory lying within the loop of the Tanoe River between Nougoua and Alacuabo . . . and it would be impossible to surrender this to France, as it would form a wedge between the British territories of Brissam and Apollonia, and . . . would cut off Brissam and Aowin from communication with the coast.

Lord Ripon is therefore of opinion that upon these grounds, Her Majesty's Government should claim that Nougoua must remain within the British sphere. . . . If, however, it should prove impossible to retain Nougoua, Lord Ripon would be prepared to concede that the line should be drawn from a point west of Ferraferraco Hill in a north-westerly direction to the west of Acouacrou.

It is no doubt a weighty argument against this last proposal that it would inconveniently divide the territories of the chiefs of Nougoua, but this would seem to be of less consequence inasmuch as, owing to the incorrect geographical information upon which the Agreement of 26th June 1891 was drawn up, this sort of arbitrary partition of Native States must go on all along the boundary line as there laid down. At the same time, Lord Ripon feels the grave objections which must always exist to such partition of native states, and is of opinion that every effort should be made to avoid them.

The next, and perhaps most important point at issue, is the question of the boundaries of Brissam and Aowin, both of which, under the Agreement, belong to the British sphere.

It appears from . . . Captain Lang's report of 12th July, that all the existing maps are wrong in representing Aowin as being another name for Brissam, the former being really the name of a large kingdom embracing at the present time, Brissam, Indenie, Dadiassa and Assikasso. It is true that on Captain Binger's map, by which the negotiators of the Agreement of June 1891 were guided, Aowin and Brissam

---

[1] George Frederick Samuel Robinson (1st Marquis of Ripon) (1827–1909); Liberal statesman; Governor-General of India, 1880–4; Secretary of State for the Colonies, 1892–5.

[2] Archibald Philip Primrose (5th Earl of Rosebery) (1847–1929); Foreign Secretary, January–June 1886, and 1892–4; Prime Minister, 1894–5.

(Broussa) are put down as distinct, while the former is given as only a small territory.

Lord Ripon regrets that he cannot but entertain the idea that Captain Binger, knowing that Aowin was British, designedly minimised its extent upon his map, as it is difficult to believe that, having travelled all through the country, he was ignorant of the fact that Indenie and Assikasso, which he marks as large and apparently independent districts, were in reality dependencies of the king of Aowin, and integral parts of his kingdom. But however this may have been, it is certain that the British Commissioners in 1891 were misled by the map into agreeing to the assignment of Indenie and Assikasso to France, which of course they would never have done had they been aware that they belonged to the kingdom of Aowin, with which Great Britain had long-standing treaties.

The error of the Agreement is undoubtedly unfortunate, but it is now impossible for Her Majesty's Government to go behind it, or to press any claims to Indenie or Assikasso. But Lord Ripon considers that under the circumstances, Captain Lang . . . was perfectly right and justified in desiring that the question should be reserved for the decision of the two Governments. . . .

With regard to Gaman, I am to call Lord Rosebery's attention to paragraphs 66 and 67 of Captain Lang's report, which show the gravity of the situation which is likely to be created if it is attempted to define the boundary in accordance with the Agreement of 1891. . . . Lord Ripon, however, fears that it is hardly open to Her Majesty's Government to demand a rectification of the Agreement of 1891, on the ground that M. La Plène was misled by his interpreters into the belief that the king and chiefs of Gaman understood the nature of the treaty they were signing, whereas they now unanimously assert that they only intended to give a permission to trade, and had no idea of placing their country under French protection.

The foregoing remarks are based upon the view that the French Government will insist upon a literal fulfilment of the terms of the Agreement of 26th June 1891, but the difficulties and complications which are likely to arise from the adoption of such a course are so great that Lord Ripon has carefully considered whether it might not be possible to propose some other arrangement in the form of a compromise, which might prove acceptable to both parties.

A division of territories acknowledging as their head the same king or chiefs, such as it now appears the boundary fixed by the Agreement of 1891 would affect, not only in the case of Gaman but also in that of Aowin, cannot fail . . . to prove unsatisfactory, and must in the future produce serious trouble and inconvenience. It would therefore seem much better for each Power to take the whole of a state rather than partition it between the two.

With this view, Lord Ripon would suggest . . . that it should be proposed to the French Government that they should take the whole of Aowin, as it is shown by the evidence taken by Captain Lang now to exist, whilst Great Britain should retain all Gaman. In this event, any difficulty as to the disposal of Nougoua would be got rid of, as it would naturally fall to France, which would obtain the natural boundary of the Tanue River up to the frontier of Sefwhi.

If the French Government should altogether decline to entertain such a proposal, Lord Ripon would be willing to consent to an alternative offer being made to them, that they would give up the whole of Aowin and obtain in exchange the entire country of Gaman. . . . But this latter arrangement should not be so satisfactory, for the following reasons.

If Great Britain possessed Aowin, and France Gaman, the free communication of the latter with the coast at Assinee would be to a certain extent interrupted, but if the position were changed, we should have free access to Gaman, as the roads through Sefwhi and Ashanti would be in our hands.

The French also would not lose their communication with the interior, as they would keep the Comoe River (or the right bank of it) and the country to the west, and, in accordance with Great Britain's general policy of allowing full freedom of trade, no hindrance would be placed in the way of their traders passing freely through Gaman. . . .[1]

[African (West) No. 435, p. 55]

383 OBSERVATIONS BY THE DIRECTOR OF MILITARY INTELLIGENCE ON MR. FERGUSON'S REPORT

QUEEN ANNE'S GATE, 28 FEBRUARY, 1893.

. . . By comparing Mr Ferguson's map with his itinerary, it will be seen that, with the exception of Bole, the headquarters of all the chiefs with whom he made treaties, lie within the Neutral Zone.

The political value of these treaties as regards territory without the Neutral Zone, depends entirely upon the extent of the territory immediately under the sway of the treaty chiefs and upon the political relations existing between those chiefs and the neighbouring tribes. On this point, Mr Ferguson is not very explicit, and the evidence he does adduce in support of his views is not very convincing. While it may be accepted that Mr Ferguson's treaties render it impossible for the French to establish their influence in any part of the Neutral Zone, it is not so clear that they establish British influence without that Zone to the extent claimed by Mr Ferguson.

The following points appear to require further consideration:

Bona is described as an Ashanti country, but it is not stated whether it is feudatory to Ashanti; as it is separated from Ashanti by Gaman, the probability is that it is not so. As Bona is an important trade centre, it seems very desirable that steps should be taken to prevent the French establishing their influence there.

[1] Ripon's proposal was not proceeded with, as the Foreign Office (to C.O. 6 February, 1893) saw no prospect of the French agreeing to it.

Wa is described as under the protection of Bole, to which state it annually pays tribute; this protection is, however, of recent date, and our influence over Wa would be more satisfactorily established if we had a separate treaty with it. Wa is an important place to us for two reasons:

(a) Its geographical position immediately west of the north-western corner of the Neutral Zone. The occupation of Wa by the French would effectually cut off our connection between the Gold Coast and the Niger Company's territories.

(b) Wa is an important trading centre and junction of roads leading from Bole, Bona, Lokosu and Daboya. Its commercial importance is manifest.

Lobi is an independent state, and there is no evidence that a treaty has been concluded with it. For political and commercial reasons a treaty is desirable.

Walembele was represented in our treaty with Daboya, as a feudatory of that state, but in . . . his report, Mr Ferguson includes it among the 'little states more or less independent' which comprise the Gurunshi state.

As in the case of Wa, the control of Walembele is particularly important to us as it is situated immediately to the north of the north-west corner of the Neutral Zone. If any uncertainty, therefore, exists as to its political relations with Daboya, a separate treaty should be concluded with it.

Yariba. The remarks on Walembele apply almost equally well to this tribe also.

Mamprusi, Chakosi and *Pampamba* are stated to be tributary to Dagomba, but as they do not appear to have been represented in our treaty with that State, definite evidence that they are so is all the more necessary, as they complete the connection between the Neutral Zone and the Niger Company's territories. . . .

[African (West) No. 448, p. 82]

384 RIPON TO GRIFFITH
DOWNING STREET, 10 MARCH, 1893.

Secret.

. . . I am disposed to think that it would be desirable, if possible, to send Mr Ferguson again to the interior to complete his work by getting treaties with Bona, Wa, Lobi, and, if necessary, Walembele and Yariba.

It would be much to be regretted if, after the trouble and expense which has been incurred, it should ultimately be found that the object of securing the Hinterland of the Colony against the encroachments of foreign powers had not been fully attained. . . .

[African (West) No. 448, p. 83]

385 AGREEMENT BETWEEN GREAT BRITAIN AND FRANCE FIXING THE BOUNDARY BETWEEN THE BRITISH AND FRENCH POSSESSIONS ON THE GOLD COAST
SIGNED AT PARIS, 12 JULY, 1893.

The Special Commissioners nominated by the Governments of Great Britain and France, in accordance with Article 5 of the Agreement of the 10th August 1889, having failed to trace a line of demarcation between the territories of the two Powers on the Gold Coast in conformity with the general provisions . . . of the said Agreement, and . . . of the Agreement of the 26th June 1891, the undersigned Plenipotentiaries, charged in execution of the declarations exchanged at London on the 5th August 1890, between Her Britannic Majesty's Government and the Government of the French Republic, to proceed to delimit the respective spheres of influence of the two countries in the districts south and west of the Middle and Upper Niger, have agreed to fix on the following conditions the line of demarcation between the French and British Possessions on the Gold Coast:—

1. The British frontier . . .[1] runs along the left bank of the Tanoe or Tendo river as far as the village of Nougoua, which, being on its right bank, Great Britain consents to recognise as belonging to France. . . .

3. Thence the British frontier continues to follow the left bank of the Tanoe or Tendo river for a distance of five English miles above the present residence of the chief in the village of Nougoua. At the five-mile point it crosses the river and becomes the common frontier indicated below. . . .

4. The common frontier then leaves the River Tanoe and strikes northwards to the centre of Ferra-Ferrako Hill. Thence passing two miles to eastward of the villages of Assikasso, Sankaina, Asambosua, and Akuakru, it runs 2 miles to the eastward of the road leading from Suakru to the Boi river, reaching that river two miles to the south-eastward of Bamianko, which village belongs to France. Thence it follows the thalweg[1] of the Boi river and the line traced by Captain Binger (as marked on the annexed map), leaving Edubi, with territory extending 1 mile to the north of it, to France, until it reaches a point 16,000 metres due east of Yau. Thence it coincides with the line traced by Captain Binger (as marked on the annexed map) to a point 1,000 metres to the south of Aburaferassi, which village belongs to France. Thence it runs 10 kilom. to the eastward of the direct road from Annibilekrou to Bondoukou, by Bodomfil and Dadiassi, passes midway between Buko and Adjamarh, runs 10 kilom. to the eastward of the road to Bondoukou via Sorobango, Tambi, Takhari, and Bandagadi to Kirhindi. Thence it follows the thalweg of the Volta to its intersection by the 9th degree of north latitude. . . .

Signed. E. C. H. Phipps
J. A. Crowe
Gabriel Hanotaux
J. Haussman.

[African (West) No. 435, p. 88]

[1] As in Article III, Sec. 1 of No. 364 above.

[1] Or valley line: the line joining the lowest points along a river course.

386 MEMORANDUM ON THE BRONG TRIBES,
BY G. E. FERGUSON

24 NOVEMBER, 1893.

. . . Nkoranza, Atabubu, Gwan Basa,
Yeji, Prang and Abeasi comprise the Brong
tribes. They speak a dialect of their own,
which is slightly different from Ashanti
proper. They are in league together for
offence and defence against a common foe.
That league is founded on the greatest
oath. They may be described as lying to
the north and east of Ashanti, and occupying the country bounded on the south by
the Sene River, on the north by a large
tributary of the Volta, which, taking its
rise from the Gaman country, curves
northward to join the 'Daboya-Kraki-Ada'
Volta. Kraki is on the eastern or left
bank of the Volta. Banda lies between
Gaman and Nkoranza. The king of
Nkoranza possesses the territory to the
west and north-west of Atabubu, while
Mampon and Nsuta are situated to the
south-west of Atabubu. . . .

Nkoranza and Ashanti proper were
formerly separate kingdoms. They were
brought together by an alliance formed
between Opok Wari, the king of Ashanti,
and Bafu Pim, king of Nkoranza, when the
Ashantis asked the Nkoranzas to assist
them in a war against a king of Takiman,
called Ameo. From an ally, the Nkoranza
kingdom developed into an Ashanti
province. All the countries referred to in
the preceding paragraph were formerly
under the sway of the king of Ashanti.
His conquests extended as far as the
Gonja and Dagomba territories, and from
all these countries also he received yearly
tributes. Salaga was the only market then,
and from there tolls were collected for him.
. . . But the Fetish Dente of Kraki was
already recognised, and appeal was made
to it from Ashanti and surrounding
countries in matters relating to fetish and
religion . . . but there was no trade done
in Kraki.

Like most other savage tribes, Ashanti
did not keep a standing army, but for the
maintenance of authority, one country was
deputed to punish another, and about the
middle of the present century an expedition
commanded by Dewia, the king of Atabubu, was conducted against Kojo Gyeyini,
the Fetish Priest of Kraki, to subjugate the
Krakis who had revolted. Kojo Gyeyini,
the father of the present priest, was taken
prisoner and slain by the king of Atabubu.
Between all these several tribes there are
also accounts of great and bloody wars,
and shortly before the Kumasi war of
1873–4 one of these ensued between Gaman
and Banda, in which . . . the inhabitants
of the latter country were driven from their
ancient habitat to take refuge in the
Nkoranza territory. The Bandas then
formed an alliance with the Kumasis. . . .

When . . . the British forces entered
Kumasi in 1874 . . . the bonds which
united the various countries to Ashanti
were loosened. Atabubu with the other
members of the Brong tribes, except
Nkoranza, threw off their allegiance to the
king of Kumasi, and formed a confederation with the priest of the Fetish Dente of
Kraki at the head. The Gonjas killed all
the Ashantis in their territories, and
Dagomba made captives of those in that
territory. . . . Nkoranza, though one of
the Brong tribes, remained under an indifferent sort of subjugation to Ashanti.
In fact it preferred to be independent, and
it is stated that Atafa, the king of Nkoranza,
never, after the Kumasi war, set foot in
Kumasi, though messages were exchanged
between the monarchs of the two countries.
Markets were established, one at Kun-
tampo by Atafa, and another at Atabubu
by Jan Kwaku the king of Attabubu, from
which the kings derived a handsome
revenue.

After the Kumasi war, the fetish priest
of Kraki and the confederate kings sent
tusks of ivory to the Governor of Accra.
The native expression of this act is 'Mako-
tao aban mu', meaning, 'I have deposited
in the fort', a token of acknowledgement
of fealty to the conqueror. In fact the
argument used by the natives runs thus:
'The Ashanti monarch was formerly our

master. The English fought with him and entered his capital. Ashanti with all that pertains to it became the trophies and captives of the conqueror. We can assert our independence of Ashanti, but will only serve the English who delivered us from the tyrannical rule of a blood thirsty African monarch.' Such is the prestige which was gained by the Ashanti war of 1873–4. . . . [C. 7917, A & P (1896) lviii]

387 F. M. HODGSON[1] TO G. E. FERGUSON
                    9 JANUARY, 1894.

. . . As soon as you have completed what I may call the political work with which I entrusted you in connection with the despatch of an expeditionary force into Attabubu; that is to say, the making of treaties of friendship and freedom of trade with the kings and chiefs of the Brong tribes, as regards the country or countries on the right bank of the Volta, and outside the neutral zone, and with the king of Nkoranza, or have brought them to a point where they can conveniently be taken up by another officer, I desire you to proceed to *Bona* for the purpose of concluding a treaty with the king and chiefs of that country. You will move thence to *Lobi* and *Wa* and make treaties with the kings and chiefs of those places.

You should then proceed to make treaties with tribes to the northward of the neutral zone. The explanatory statements which you have made as regards the relations of Walembele and Yariba towards the king of Daboya, with whom a treaty has already been concluded, are regarded as satisfactory, and it is not now considered necessary that separate treaties should be made with the kings and chiefs of those countries, but this is not so in the case of Mamprusi, and a separate treaty should, if possible, be made with the king and chiefs of that country.

[1] Frederick Mitchell Hodgson (later Sir); entered the Colonial Service, 1869; Colonial Secretary of the Gold Coast, 1888; Governor, 1898–1900; later Governor of Barbados (1900–4) and British Guiana (1904–11).

Q

From Mamprusi, or if you think it best, from Wa or Lobi, leaving Mamprusi to be dealt with on your return journey, I desire you to make your way, if you can possibly do so, to Wagadugu, in order to get a treaty signed with the king and chiefs of Mossi, having treaties signed also, if possible, by the kings and chiefs of tribes not clearly and without doubt feudatory to it, between that country and Mamprusi.

It is not, I may state, considered to have been clearly shown that the countries of Chakosi and Pampamba are dependent upon Dagomba, but as neither of these countries is specifically mentioned in the telegraphic instructions from the Secretary of State, and as they appear to lie to the north-east of the neutral zone, I feel myself precluded from definitely authorizing you to make treaties with the kings and chiefs of those countries. At the same time, I may be wrong as regards the geographical position of Chakosi, and it may be within your knowledge that a portion of the country lies due north of the eastern limit of the zone. In that case you might conclude a treaty with the king and chiefs. I think there can be no doubt, however, as regards Pampamba.

In connection with the new treaties which you are now commissioned to make, it will be necessary for you to satisfy yourself in each case beforehand, that the king and chiefs of the country have not entered into an agreement or treaty with any other foreign Power. If they have done so, you must not take any action. . . .
                    [African (West) No. 448, p. 116]

388 THE MARQUIS OF RIPON TO F. M.
HODGSON   30 JANUARY, 1894.
Sir,

I have had under my consideration your despatches . . . furnishing information with respect to the relations of the Colonial Government with Ashanti, and the condition of affairs in the interior, and urging that the time has arrived when action should be taken with a view of bringing Ashanti under a British Protectorate.

In reply I have to acquaint you that Her Majesty's Government, while fully appreciating the ability and judgement which you have displayed, and the clearness with which you have placed your views before them, are not inclined to adopt the policy which you advocate, which they consider would greatly increase the responsibilities of the Gold Coast Government.

Moreover Her Majesty's Government could not sanction the adoption of any course which might involve the employment of British troops, and as, in your despatch of 18th November, you stated that 'such a contingency has to be provided for', and that you are 'not prepared to advocate the despatch of a further ultimatum to Kumasi unless it is', they find it impossible to authorise you to send such an ultimatum, or to entertain the question of assuming a Protectorate over Ashanti by force.

At the same time, they are fully alive to the risk which, under present conditions, constantly exists, of Attabubu and other territories which are under the protection of Her Majesty, being invaded by the Ashantis, and they are therefore anxious to ascertain whether some *via media* cannot be found whereby the object of controlling the power of Ashanti may be attained without the use of force.

I have therefore to request you to consider and report to me, whether, in your opinion, it would be possible to get the king of Kumasi and the principal chiefs to accept stipends, which might be fixed at a liberal rate, on condition that they should consent to receive a British Agent at Kumasi, and should agree to refrain from making war upon or disturbing any of the tribes, beyond a certain frontier which should be laid down by the Governor of the Gold Coast, and which should exclude from Ashanti the Nkoranzas, Bekwais, and other tribes who have asked for British protection.

In case of any dispute between the king of Kumasi and any of these outside tribes, the matter should be referred to the agent, who should enquire into it and give his decision, and if he found that the Ashantis were in the right, the question should be referred to the Governor of the Gold Coast, who would require the offending tribe to make such reparation as he might deem expedient.

The Agent would, of course, have a strong guard of Houssas, under one or more white officers, for his own protection, but it would be clearly understood that he must interfere as little as possible with the domestic affairs and policy of the country, but would confine himself to the duties . . . of inquiring into disputes between the Ashantis and tribes beyond the border, of preventing the outbreak of war and disturbances, and of using his influence and authority to promote the development and security of trade.

I have to request you to communicate your views on these proposals, if possible by telegraph, and, pending a decision, I have to authorise you to exercise your discretion as to keeping the expeditionary force in Attabubu, or withdrawing it. In the event of its withdrawal, you should send a messenger to the king of Kumasi, saying that this step has been taken on the faith of his assurance that he has no intention of invading any portion of the British Protectorate; he must, however, understand that the question . . . of what action should be taken in the future has been referred to the Queen, and that her decision will, to a great extent, depend upon the king's conduct, as he cannot be allowed to continue with impunity to make war upon and destroy his neighbours, and that if he desires in any way to avoid Her Majesty's serious displeasure, he must remain quiet and desist from further warlike operations.

[C.7917, p. 147].

[These terms were sent to Kumasi (23 February, 1894). C.4917, p. 167].

389 FERGUSON TO GRIFFITH

GAMBAGA, MAMPRUSI, 7 JUNE, 1894.

Sir,

. . . I have the honour to report . . . that treaties have been concluded by me:—

(a) With Bona, at Bona on the 12th April, 1894. The Lobis exist in family communities; they have no king. As a tribe they are under the influence of Bona, and thus Lobi, to say the least, becomes our sphere of interest by treaty with Bona.

(b) With Dagarti, at Wa on 4th May 1894.

(c) With Mamprusi, at Gambaga, on 28th May 1894.

No explorer nor an agent of a foreign power had succeeded in reaching Bona before my arrival there on the 30th March 1894, though attempts have been made by the French from Bontuku and Kong. However, on the 17th April, that is, five days after the treaty with Bona had been made and the British flag delivered to the king and people, a certain Monsieur Moskovitz arrived at Bona from Bontuku. . . . He represented that he was *not* a political agent; that he was . . . interested in . . . certain geographical matters; that he had ascended the Komoe River . . . to decide whether the river Ise or Komoe is the main feeder of the Grand Bassam lagoon. . . . I left Bona on the 21st April. The political horizon was clear, the king and chiefs acknowledged the responsibility they incurred by the treaty with England, and I received their assurance that they are true friends to the English Queen.

As no traveller or political agent had ever visited Wa and Dagarti, the treaty was concluded by me, and [the] British flag hoisted there.

As regards Mamprusi, no political results were connected with Monsieur Binger's visit to Walewale. Von Francois reached this place, Gambaga. He tried to come to some arrangement with the king, but the king refused to see him. He attempted to persuade the Alimani of Gambaga to accept a German flag, but he was unsuccessful. The king and chiefs declared and gave me every assurance that they made no arrangement with him, and accordingly I executed treaty with Mamprusi. Von Francois also attempted to push his way to Wagadugu, but he was compelled to turn back from Zurma owing to the hostile attitude of the barbarous tribes between Mamprusi and Mossi.

At present all the direct routes to Wagadugu are closed by a belt of hostile barbarous tribes, Talensi, Kusasi, Bus-sanga;[1] the last account we heard being that a caravan consisting of about 1,000 traders with Magudu Osuman at its head, came to grief when proceeding to Beri on the way to Wagadugu. Just now, Mossi traders steal their way to Wagadugu via Kupela, with a great deal of risk.

Immediately after despatching this letter, I leave for Mossi. Its importance tempts me to risk the Kupela road. It is the caravan-producing country of our hinter-land, which ought not to be conceded to any foreign power. But not wishing to carry all my eggs in one basket, I enclose herewith the duplicates of the treaties made with Bona, Wa and Gambaga. . . .

[C.P. African (West) No. 479, p. 2]

390 FERGUSON TO GRIFFITH

YENDI, DAGOMBA, 18 AUGUST, 1894.

Secret.

. . . I have the honour to report that I arrived at this place yesterday . . . having treated successfully with the authorities of Mossi on the 2nd July, and with Chakosi on the 8th of August. I beg to submit the duplicates of the treaties made with those countries. The English flag was also handed to the treaty kings.

I ascertained that previous to my arrival at Wagadugu, three visits had been made by different explorers to Wagadugu, but that their visits were unattended with political results. As regards Chakosi, I

---

[1] Bussansi.

was the first to penetrate into that region of our Hinterland. . . .

In connection with the subject of the *condition of the people of* the Hinterland, there are three principal factors, viz. (1) countries with organized government, (2) barbarous tribes; and (3) a Neutral Zone agreed to between England and Germany. . . .

Under the first division . . . come Mossi, Mamprusi, Gruma, Borgu, Chakosi, Dagomba, Bona, Wa (Dagarti), Gonja, Bimbla, Banda and Nkoranza. They possess a government of some sort, however imperfect the system may be. In Mossi and Dagomba, the Government is more despotic, and the subjects of the former have almost a superstitious reverence for the person of the king. The king of Yendi exercises a deal of influence over Bimbla. In all the countries mentioned, there are frequent civil wars between rival claimants for regal ascendancy, such as the one which has destroyed the market of Salaga lately. In many cases, however, they are willing to submit their feuds to arbitration. The trading community is composed chiefly of persons professing the Mahommedan creed. They all demand European commodities and comforts, but the numerous princes who seize goods from traders are a pest to the community and put restrictions on trade. With the exception of Nkoranza and Banda, the more northern communities raid their weak neighbours for cattle and slaves. Caravans are furnished by Mossi, Gruma, and Hausa; the transport is conducted by means of slaves, horses, donkeys and oxen, and their commodities are exchanged mostly for kola nuts, which they take to their countries. Salt, brass and copper rods, guns, gunpowder, and cotton goods &c which they also purchase, are often bartered to the barbarians on the way. . . .

The second division . . . comprises those portions of Pampamba, Kusasi, Busansi and Grunshi which have not been assimilated with Dagomba, Chakosi, Mamprusi, Mossi and Daboya. They live mostly in family communities, and resist intercourse, even among their own selves, with showers of arrows. These people, together with Lobi, Dafina, Nieniege and Kaprisi,[1] move about in perfect nudity, their lips, noses, and ears are pierced, into which straws and beads are inserted as ornaments. Some of them, principally those through which caravans fight their way, live in village communities with a strong man (who has arrogated to himself the position of a chief) as the head of the community. He demands transit dues and makes various extortions which are often the cause of the fight. As a tribe or district, none of them is capable of negotiating with a European power and can only be civilised by force of arms. Their country is rich. Gardiari has a camp at Sati, for slave-raiding in Gurunshi, but their more powerful neighbours do not consider it to their interest to enter into war with them for the purpose of either punishing them for these extortions or of making the trade roads safe.

The third factor is . . . the Neutral Zone. It is composed for the most part of Gonja and Dagomba countries, and is one in which England and Germany refrain from exercising exclusive influence. Most of the people affected by this arrangement do not know of its existence. Considering the political condition of the people, the arrangement is unfavourable to the civilization of our Hinterland. . . .

In the present condition of our Hinterland, I consider the political procedure of Germany more formidable than French, and any concessions to the former should be well considered. The strip of country which is owned by Dagomba and Bimbla between the eastern boundary of the Neutral Zone and the Oti River, is one of great strategic importance. If we concede it to Germany, after the trouble and expense incurred in concluding treaties with Dagomba and Bimbla[2] in 1892, the

---

[1] Probably all Bobo groups located west of the Upper (Black) Volta in Ferguson's 'Gurunsi'.

[2] Bimbilla, capital of the Nanumba.

treaty made with Chakosi this year will be of little or no value at all; we will be cut off from direct communication with our Niger territories, and Germany will command the principal caravan route from the Hausa countries to Salaga and the neutral zone. Moreover, to make friends with native kings respecting their territory (a portion only in the present instance) and then give it over to another Power, produces not only distrust for English promises and assurances, but contempt towards us, and with it our prestige, which, as I have pointed out, exists in the Hinterland, will be compromised — a compromise which is ominously suggested in your Excellency's letter of 31st May.[1] In the event of such a compromise, Germany will virtually have the Daka for its boundary, and will be in a position to influence the king of a large territory, Dagomba. . . .

With regard to the French on the West, their object, I believe, is to get a way from Kong and Bontuku, through Bona and Walewale, to Wagadugu and the Niger. If they succeed, the trade to our Colony from the north and east will be interrupted and diverted into French channels. However, by the priority of the treaties which have been concluded with Bona, Dagarti and Mamprusi, as well as Mossi, and the cordial relations which have subsisted between me and the contracting parties, the Hinterland has, I hope, been saved from such a plight. . . .

For trade and economic purposes, the Colony may be divided into three provinces — eastern, central and western — with markets situated in the Hinterland at Salaga, Kintampaw and Bontuku respectively. The present overland route to Salaga passes through German territory. Access to Kintampaw is not always insured, and is rendered precarious by the political condition of Ashanti, with its oft-recurring intestinal feuds. The market at Bontuku and the facilities offered by the road passing through that town to Bona,

[1] Reporting proposals for a partition of the Neutral Zone.

are both in danger of falling into French hands, owing to previous concessions. Kintampaw and Salaga are both now composed mostly of ruins, and the large nomadic population which settled in those markets are also dispersed in all regions. It is represented on the one hand that French intrigues are responsible for the market of Kintampaw being destroyed, while, owing to the observance of neutrality on the other, we were prevented from stopping the fight which has laid Salaga in ruins, when our forces were at Atabubu, and we had the opportunity of doing so.

The above facts show that our interior is wanting in commercial stability, but the causes of that instability suggest the remedy: to interfere with barbarous practices and native customs which put restrictions on the interior trade; to render the roads safe for caravans and traders; to put a stop to the [de] predations of the Dagombas in the Neutral Zone; to civilize the barbarous tribes . . . [to occupy Ashanti; and to confine the French and Germans west of the Comoe and east of the Oti respectively].

[African (West) No. 479, pp. 21–6]

391 MEMORANDUM OF CONVERSATION WITH DR. KAYSER ON FRENCH SCHEMES IN THE HINTERLAND OF DAHOMEY, AND ANGLO-GERMAN RELATIONS IN AFRICA

BERLIN, 30 AUGUST, 1894.

Dr Kayser took an opportunity at my last interview with him to refer to the general relations of England and Germany in Africa.

After repeating his favourite axiom, that there are but three Powers in Africa — England, France and Germany — two of which must inevitably combine against the third, he said it was for Her Majesty's Government to decide whether Germany goes with or against them.

In reply to my remark that I had not observed, during the last six months, much inclination on the part of the German colonial authorities to make things easy for

British interests in Central Africa,[1] Dr Kayser replied that he had every wish to work with us, and, as an illustration of his good will, he warned me that he foresaw difficulties which would shortly arise in the Dahomey Hinterland.

The French are already pushing on northwards, and unless the spheres of interest of the three Powers were quickly delimitated in those regions, Borgu, which lies north of Dahomey, would be lost to England.

'If only Her Majesty's Government would consent to cede to us the coast line up to the mouth of the Volta, Germany would agree to anything England wished with regard to the Neutral Zone and Tchancholand.'

I replied that this proposal had been made more than once, and that I had no

[1] i.e. over the Anglo-Congolese agreement of April 1894.

reason whatever for believing that Her Majesty's Government had any intention of reconsidering their refusal to entertain this proposal. I believed their decision on this point to be absolute.

Dr Kayser replied, 'Well then, I suppose matters must be left to take their course, but rest assured that the French have their eyes on Borgu.'

I concluded from the drift of Dr Kayser's observations, that unless Germany can obtain the left bank of the Volta mouth, she will do nothing towards checking an advance of the French through Borgu in the direction of Say. . . .

Martin Gosselin[1]

[African (West) No. 479, p. 4]

[1] Martin Le Marchant Hadsley Gosselin (later Sir) (1847–1905); entered the Diplomatic service, 1868; Secretary of the Brussels Conference on the Slave Trade, 1890; Secretary to the embassy at Berlin (1893–6) and Paris (1896–8); Assistant Under-Secretary for Foreign Affairs (1898–1902).

BOOK IX

THE WINNING OF THE NORTH, 1895–1902

29 The first Land Bill and the occupation of Kumasi, 1895–1896

EVER since the first influx of mining prospectors in the late seventies had given rise to the first concessions, the Government, in England and on the Gold Coast, had been exercised by the twin problems of how to secure adequate titles for industrial undertakings while guarding against the reckless alienation of tribal lands and the wanton dissipation of the forests and their natural products (318). In the nineties, official opinion favoured vesting all 'waste' lands in the Crown, and a Bill to achieve that object was introduced in the Legislative Council in 1894.

It at once provoked violent protests from the Africans (394). These protests were indeed discounted by the new Governor, W. E. Maxwell, who succeeded Griffith in 1895, but he himself objected to the Bill on technical grounds (395), and secured leave to withdraw it. In 1897, to anticipate, he tried again (407) with a second Bill which was vigorously opposed in the Legislative Council (418). The Gold Coast Aborigines' Rights Protection Society was formed to fight this measure, and, in 1898, prevailed upon Mr. Chamberlain to withdraw it. The Gold Coast Government thereafter contented itself with a Concessions Ordinance (426), which established a not very satisfactory machinery for scrutinising concessions (444) and said nothing about the ultimate ownership of land. The Aborigines' Rights Society basked in the afterglow of this two-edged triumph for the next twenty-five years.

By 1894, even the Liberals thought a Protectorate over Ashanti was desirable (388) but they hesitated to take steps to secure one. Griffith's final arguments for intervention (392) would have been more applicable to the situation five or six years earlier. It was not really the situation inside Ashanti, or any deeds or misdeeds of Prempeh, whom the Colonial Office now affected to recognise only as King of Kumasi (393), that dictated the final intervention; and the Ashanti embassy in Britain in 1895 was therefore worse than futile (400). It was, as Governor Maxwell pointed out (396), the advance of the French and Germans on either side of Ashanti, that induced the British Government to present an ultimatum to Prempeh (398), even at the risk of appearing unjust to him. The ultimatum was backed by a determination to use force (400), to depose Prempeh (399), even to seize the Golden Stool (402), if any of these appeared necessary for the firm establishment of British control.

Kumasi was occupied in January 1896. There was no resistance, even when the Governor, who had chosen to superintend the operation himself, decided also to remove Prempeh to the coast. The Ashanti, it seems, were not so much overawed by the considerable military retinue that accompanied the Governor, as completely taken unawares by this deposition. In turn, the several Ashanti states concluded Protectorate treaties with the British Government (404).

From the international point of view, it was not a moment too soon. The French had already shown what they thought of Ferguson's treaties, and had their own political missions at work to the immediate north of Ashanti (397). The Germans also were reaching out towards the Niger, and failure to reach an agreement with them, in November 1895 (401), clearly presaged a new struggle for vantage points in the Neutral Zone and beyond. The final 'Scramble' was on.

392 MEMORANDUM ON RELATIONS WITH KUMASI [BY SIR W. B. GRIFFITH]

ACCRA, 25 OCTOBER, 1894.

[Reviews events since 1881.] . . .

In September 1893, information was received by the Government that the Ashantis intended to attack Attabubu, as it was alleged that it had given assistance to Nkoranza. Attabubu was under British protection, but it was stated that the Ashantis thought we should take no steps to hinder their design, as we did nothing when they drove the Adansis out of Adansi.[1]

Prompt steps were taken to send a force of about 350 Housa to protect Attabubu from the Ashantis. This had the desired effect, and the Ashantis repudiated having entertained any designs against Attabubu.

At present, it appears that there is a general feeling in Government, native and commercial circles, that Ashanti might be taken without a blow. The question for consideration and decision is, what policy should the Gold Coast Government adopt in the circumstances described?

It would appear to be neither humane nor politic to continue the policy of non-intervention. It has had a fair trial and has not succeeded, and further non-intervention will mean constant interference with the trade of the Gold Coast, frequent costly missions to Ashanti, a never-ending state of disorder in that country, one district flying at another's throat, or Kumassi and other districts warring against a recalcitrant state. Bloodshed and disorder has been our experience of non-intervention. A further result . . . will be loss of influence which might be exercised for good.

It is needless to consider rebuilding Ashanti so as to make it independent and self-reliant. That would require a military organisation, which would be used against us and our protected states. Indeed, we cannot suffer Ashanti to remain independent of us, as it commands our trade routes; and our previous relations with it

[1] In 1886. The war with Nkoranza took place in 1892–3.

entitle us to take this position, while we cannot with safety to the peace of the Protectorate permit Ashanti to continue to occupy the position of a country in a state, more or less, of antagonism to the interests of this Colony, whilst its barbarous and cruel customs are a disgrace to, and an outrage upon humanity; and all parties in the Colony are unanimous in the opinion that we must not aid Ashanti to attain to any part of its old position of dominance.

I am convinced that by far the best solution would be to include the several tribes forming the Ashanti combination, in the protected territories, and this could be accomplished practically by annexing its several sections in detail, or by at once asserting our power over the whole country. And it seems to me that the last will be the most sagacious and least troublesome course to take. . . .

After the treaty of Fomana, by which Ashanti lost the Adansis, the Kwahus threw off the yoke of Kumasi, and subsequently came under British protection. The Juabins followed suit, but, becoming involved in war with Kumasi, and being defeated, the greater part of them came into the protected territories. Then the Kokofus and Dadiassies, being also defeated by the Kumasis and Bekwais, came into the protected territories, but before these occurrences, Gaman also had thrown off its allegiance to Kumasi. Quite lately, Nkoranza strove in vain to make itself independent. From our experience of Ashanti, we know that as soon as any chief thinks himself able to do so, he forthwith sets himself up as independent, and thereupon Ashanti ranges itself into two camps, one in favour of such chief, and the other for the authority of Kumasi.

Their union in arms was the only bond which formerly held together the various Ashanti tribes. As long as they had a common enemy, viz. the Fantis, or the Denkeras, or one or other of the tribes now under British protection, they were able to keep together. But now things are changed. All their former foes are under British protection. The bond which formerly bound them together no longer exists, and it is contrary to experience to expect them to hold together. It must be remembered that they have no special language, or dress, or habits, or religion; they are practically the same . . . as the Accras, Fantis, Denkerahs, Assins, and other tribes in the protected territories, except that the Accras speak a language of their own. . . .

In these circumstances, I am of opinion that it will be false policy to continue to treat Ashanti as a compact state. We should recognise the fact that it is only composed of a bundle of states, kept together by no common interest, but which, by their internal wars and intrigues, menace the interests and security of the trade of the protected territories. I would therefore submit for consideration the adoption of either of two lines of action with regard to Ashanti; first, the policy of accepting any advances from any of these tribes, and if they ask to be taken under our protection, I consider it would then be our duty to extend it to them; and, as to the second line of action, where no such offers were made, then we should exercise our power, and compel obedience to it, by bringing recalcitrant tribes under our supreme control. . . . I am most strongly of opinion that the wisest, safest, and most prudent and inexpensive course of action, will be to pursue a resolute policy, and if the sections of Ashanti which are still independent of the Gold Coast decline to accept its rule, they should be compelled to do so.

[C.O.96/248. C.7917, pp. 224–7]

393 THE MARQUIS OF RIPON TO W. E. MAXWELL[1] LONDON, 15 MARCH, 1895.

. . . As you are about to assume the administration of the Government of the

Gold Coast Colony, I desire to put you in possession of the conclusions at which Her Majesty's Government have arrived with respect to the relations between the Colonial Government and the King of Kumasi.

As you are aware from the papers which have been furnished you, those relations have for a long time been very unsatisfactory, and have recently assumed a threatening aspect.

In February 1894, Mr Hodgson, then Acting-Governor, sent, under instructions from Her Majesty's Government, a message to the king, inviting him to accept a British agent to discharge certain duties at Kumasi, and to observe certain conditions which it was considered necessary to lay down for the preservation of peace, and for promoting the development and security of trade.

To this message no reply has been returned, but the king sent down to the coast certain messengers, whom he styled ambassadors, with instructions to proceed to England to see Her Majesty the Queen.

The Governor was thereupon directed to inform the messengers that if they came to England, they would not be received, and a mission was sent to Kumasi to tell the king that the Queen would only communicate with him through the Governor of the Gold Coast Colony, who is Her representative, to whom therefore, he should at once reply to the message sent to him, and that in no case would Her Majesty receive a mission from a ruler who is accused, on apparently good grounds, of allowing human sacrifices.

The mission was treated with marked discourtesy by the King, whose final answer was that his messengers at Cape Coast Castle were in possession of his reply to Mr Hodgson's letter of 23rd February 1894, which would be delivered to the Queen of England, in England.

Under these circumstances, Sir W. Brandford Griffith submitted in his telegram of 12th ultimo, his views of what

[1] William Edward Maxwell (later Sir) (1846–97); served in the Malay States, 1865–94; Governor of the Gold Coast, 1895–7.

should be done, and strongly recommended that an expedition should at once be sent against Kumasi, to enforce the conditions laid down by Her Majesty's Government.

The policy advocated by Sir B. Griffith has received the serious and careful consideration of Her Majesty's Government, but, for various reasons, and particularly in view of the very limited time available for active operations before the commencement of the rainy season, they have felt themselves unable to authorise any action which might involve the immediate despatch of an expedition, and a telegram to this effect was accordingly sent to Sir B. Griffith on the 1st instant.

They, however, fully recognize that matters cannot be indefinitely left in their present unsatisfactory position, and they entertain the conviction that your long experience in dealing with natives elsewhere will enable you to bring a fresh and practised eye to bear upon the whole subject, and to furnish them with a valuable and trustworthy opinion as to the course of action which it will be most desirable to adopt.

I have therefore to instruct you, on your arrival at the Gold Coast, to make a careful examination of the questions pending with the King of Kumasi, and of the policy which it would be best to pursue in regard to them, and to report fully on the subject.

As it would now be impossible for any military expedition to be undertaken for some months, ample time is afforded for a careful and judicious consideration of the various questions which are involved.

Her Majesty's Government would desire to avoid the necessity of warlike operations if possible, and you should therefore direct your first attention to the possibility of bringing about a peaceful settlement.

If, however, after due consideration, you should be of opinion that there is no chance of accomplishing this desirable object, Her Majesty's Government consider that, before taking hostile action, it would be right to make a further communication to the King, setting out their causes of complaint against him, and his breaches of the Treaty of Fommanah of 1874, in not paying the indemnity stipulated for, and in continuing to allow and encourage the practice of human sacrifices, calling upon him to fulfil his obligations, and demanding an immediate and explicit reply, to be delivered within a fixed time of reasonable duration, addressed to you as Governor.

If the reply should be unsatisfactory, or not be sent within the time allotted, it will then become necessary to send a military expedition to enforce compliance with the demands made. You should, therefore, in your report, go fully into the questions of the strength and cost of such an expedition. Its strength should be amply sufficient to ensure success, as any check or failure would be very injurious, and much more costly in the end. The expense of the expedition would have to be borne entirely from colonial funds, and you will, of course, bear this in mind in framing your arrangements.

You are aware that although Prempeh styles himself 'King of Ashanti' he does not legally hold that position, as, by the custom of the country, he cannot occupy the 'Golden Stool' of Ashanti unless placed there by the king of Kokofu and the king of Mampon, both of whom are, at the present time, refugees within the British Protectorate. Prempeh is therefore, only King of Kumasi, and Her Majesty's Government do not recognise him as possessing any other title. . . .

I need scarcely, perhaps, impress upon you, that no ultimatum must be sent without direct authority from the Secretary of State, and that no steps must be taken towards the preparation of an expedition without his knowledge and approval. . . .

[C.O.96/255, C.7918, A & P (1896) lviii]

394 J. H. BREW[1] TO THE MARQUIS OF RIPON   LONDON, 22 MARCH, 1895.

My Lord,

It is incumbent on me, owing to information received from the Gold Coast . . . to address you on a question of vast importance, which has been raised by the contemplated passing of an Ordinance regarding what is termed in it the 'Waste lands, forest lands, and minerals' of the territory.

It is historically true to say that the Gold Coast Protectorate stands on a footing different from that of any dependency of the British Crown. Its position is unique. It has not been acquired either by conquest, cession, or treaty; and although the British Government have exercised certain powers and jurisdictions, it possesses no inherent legal right to deprive us of our lands, as is contemplated in the proposed Bill, whatever it may have done in countries such as South Africa, Tasmania, New Zealand, East Africa, and elsewhere.

It is not shewn that the natives desire legislation on the lines of the proposed Ordinance to protect them from the grantees or lessees to whom they have granted or leased land. It is not proved that they are incapable of ascertaining what rents should be paid to them for their lands, nor can it be said that undue advantage has been taken of them, such as has occurred in other dependencies of the Crown, to which the Government itself has been more or less a party. What then, with all due deference, have we done that this attempt should be made to deprive us of our lands? . . .

The people of the Gold Coast are the original owners of the land, and were not settled thereon by the British Government. Governor Griffith, it is said, remarked to a deputation which waited upon him in

[1] James Hutton Brew (1844–1915); 'Prince Brew of Dunkwa'; solicitor; assistant-secretary of the Fanti Federation; Editor of the *Western Echo*; went to England in 1889 and remained there until his death. (Cf. Sampson, Magnus, *Gold Coast Men of Affairs*.)

reference to this Ordinance that 'in 1874 . . . the whole of the lands of the Gold Coast Colony became the property of the Government by right of conquest.' One can hardly believe that Sir Brandford Griffith can have made such observation in earnest, for its absurdity is too apparent. Up to now, not an inch of our land is owned by the British Government . . . although it does own some land by purchase. The jurisdiction, rights, and powers hitherto exercised by the Government over and in the Gold Coast Protectorate have been 'by usage, sufferance, or usurpation,' not by cession, treaty, or by conquest. . . . This is a fact which is recognised in the correspondence which passed between the Colonial Office here and the Government of the Gold Coast at the time of the creation of the Colony and the abolition of slavery; the only instrument upon which the Government can base any show of right so to act, being the Bond of 1844 . . . which was not executed by all the kings and chiefs of the Protectorate.

It may be here mentioned that the country fully recognises the benefits of British administration, and the relief given in 1873–4. But whilst thus appreciating the good offices and general administration of the British Government, it is not prepared to assent without a murmur, as is testified by the movements now going on at home against the proposed 'Crown Lands Ordinance', to the strange assumption of rights now put forward for the first time by the Local Legislature. . . .

[C.P. African (West) No. 513]

395 MAXWELL TO RIPON

ACCRA, 9 MAY, 1895.

. . . The African view of the position is, apparently, that within the Protectorate, the Colonial Government may collect a revenue on imports (paid in the first instance by merchants upon the coast, and therefore not understood by the African consumer to really fall upon him), provide the necessary machinery of administration, make roads and maintain order. But anything like direct taxation is resented, and sovereign rights are claimed over land, the rights of Her Majesty being denied in respect of any land not purchased from a king, chief, community or individual.

Now this is a situation which can hardly be accepted. It is not tolerable that the protected African chief and tribe should receive everything and yield nothing. The very theory of a protectorate seems to imply something in the nature of sovereign rights in the protecting power. As soon as protectorates were established in the Malay peninsula, the native rulers were taught that the advice of the protecting authority must in future be obtained before any act of sovereignty could be performed by them. From the first, no grant or concession, made by a native ruler, after the date of the establishment of a protectorate, was recognised unless it was counter-signed by the chief British resident authority. This, I humbly conceive, is what should have been done here as soon as concessions in the Axim district commenced (in 1890) to cause embarrassment. It would not have been difficult, I think, to declare, without any immediate recourse to legislation, that no grant by an African 'king' or chief, would be recognized unless it should bear the necessary evidence of having been approved by the Governor of the Colony, as the representative of the Protecting Power.

It can hardly be conceded that notwithstanding the sacrifices made by the British Government in freeing the Protectorate from the Ashanti invasion in 1873–4, claims to full sovereign rights over the forests, waste lands and minerals, on the part of these petty chiefs, are to be recognised. . . .

It appears to me that British interests, and the interests of the Gold Coast Colony, demand that the relative position of the Colonial Government and the native population, in respect of real property, should be clearly laid down by law, and I entertain no doubt whatever, that it is

right and politic to restrict the power assumed by certain native 'kings' and chiefs to deal with waste lands, forests and minerals. In the absence of definite orders and laws upon the subject, supposed rights have in some districts been acquired from native 'kings' by speculators; in others, the development of tracts known to contain metalliferous deposits, has been retarded by the cupidity of the local native authority; while the Colonial Government is in the ridiculous position of being unable to erect a building, or lay out a road, on waste land, without having to go through a tedious legal process, concluding usually with payment to some individual or community, whom the prospect of gain has prompted to lay claim to the land. If it were decided, at some future time, to import Chinese or Indian coolies, for public works or as settlers (a scheme which has its advocates),[1] I should, under the present condition of things, be unable to allot them land for building and cultivation without applying to some native authority for permission!

Again, the title to property is most unsafe. 'Native Law', to which such frequent allusion is made in Sir Joseph Hutchinson's Bill,[2] apparently favours joint ownership by numerous members of a family, their interest being proportionate to the degrees of consanguinity. The purchase, therefore, by a European merchant, of a house and land, in this Colony, is not unlikely to be followed by litigation, in which members of the vendor's family, of varying degrees of remoteness, will seek to establish a claim to a share in the property, or its equivalent in money. . . .

It may be admitted at once, that the difficulty of dealing with this subject has been enhanced by delay, and by the quasi-recognition, on the part of the Colonial

---

[1] Chinese immigration had been recommended as early as 1879. Cf. Ussher to Hicks-Beach (No. 294 of 27 November, 1879).

[2] Sir Joseph Turner Hutchinson (1850–1924); Queen's Advocate, Gold Coast, 1888; Chief Justice, 1889–94; Chief Justice, Windward Isles (1895), Cyprus (1898) and Ceylon (1906–11).

Government, of grants and concessions. . . . It is by no means too late to take action, and I am of opinion that something in the nature of Sir Joseph Hutchinson's Bill is much required.

There are details, however, in this measure, which are open to objection from the administrative point of view. . . . Nothing but a complete survey of the Colony would make it possible to say what land is beneficially occupied at the present time. . . . Here, any expenditure on survey, except in the towns, would be thrown away. There is no land revenue to be collected, and the cultivation practised by the African negro is of the very rudest. The system is that which is known in India as 'shifting cultivation,' and is practised there by the most backward tribes. . . . Under the proposed Bill, any attempt by Government to take possession of a piece of waste land just outside Accra as Crown land . . . might be defeated on the production of witnesses to swear that they took a crop of yams or cassava off it within the last 30 years. There can be little doubt that the witnesses would always be forthcoming.

Again, I take exception to the recognition in the Bill, of something quite unknown in the shape of 'Native Law'. If, as no doubt is the case, there are certain useful and beneficial native customs which ought to be preserved, let us ascertain what they are, and enact them as part of the measure. But I should be sorry to imperil the working of any system by making it liable to be modified at any time by any proposition or doctrine accepted by a judge as 'Native Law.'

With your Lordship's permission, I will defer, for some time longer, acting upon the permission given to my predecessor, to pass the Crown Lands Bill. . . . I may possibly ask your Lordship's permission ultimately to withdraw this Bill and substitute another for it. . . .

In the meantime, the answer to those who hold the opinions advanced by Mr Brew . . . is, I submit, that no interference of any kind is contemplated with the free use of land by Africans, for all the purposes for which they used it before the establishment of the Protectorate. They will be deprived of nothing which is the result of industry, but the right of the paramount authority to deal with natural products, and with land which has not been turned to account, will be declared and asserted. Sir Joseph Hutchinson . . . says, 'the right — if it exists — of making grants to strangers, particularly to Europeans, of waste lands and of minerals and of concessions of forest land, will be taken away. The practice of making such grants and concessions is quite modern, and is probably illegal according to Native Law and Custom.' Native chiefs are entitled to the protection which they receive only so long as they accept and act upon the advice of the controlling power. The chief who asserts an authority inconsistent with his duty towards the Protectorate, will be liable to forfeit his position. A declaration of this kind by your Lordship would greatly strengthen my hands in dealing finally with this troublesome question. . . .   [C.O.96/257.]

396 MAXWELL TO RIPON
CHRISTIANSBORG CASTLE, 13 JUNE, 1895.

. . . The difficulty of getting information about anything that goes on in Ashanti is extreme. As your Lordship is aware, this Government has no qualified agents in the interior. Our stations are almost all small coast ports, and with the exception of two native District Commissioners (one at Tarkwa and the other at Akuse) we have no representatives in the interior at all. Again, the European public servants here are, with two or three exceptions, wholly ignorant of the native languages, and are not, therefore, in confidential communication with the natives of any class. Not only, therefore, is little intelligence received, but it is not easy to judge of the value of the statements which may be made.

The examination which I have made of

the questions pending with the king of Kumasi, suggests certain reflections which I will lay briefly before your Lordship. It is necessary for the peace and welfare of this Colony, which has constantly been disturbed by the occurrence of petty warfare beyond our borders, begun or fomented by Kumasi, that the neighbouring tribes should be allowed to live unmolested. It is desirable in the interests of humanity, that the horrible practice of sacrificing human victims should be stamped out wherever our power can reach, as without this, the work of Great Britain in suppressing the slave trade, is incomplete. And, finally, at a period when the French are advancing inland on both sides of us, it is not, I submit, to be tolerated, that the opening up of the interior of this part of Africa to British commerce, should be prevented by the pretensions of a petty despotism, from which no decent government is to be expected, on whose protestations no reliance can be placed, and whose history is a chronicle of deceit, cruelty, and breach of treaty engagements. Further, it is not possible, without preparing for ourselves grave trouble in future, to recede from the position already taken up, or to allow matters to remain as they are. As it is, the return of the Hausa force from Attabubu last year has been misunderstood, and those in power at Kumasi affect to believe that this column was withdrawn without striking a blow in Ashanti because it was recognised that the power of the king of Kumasi is too formidable.

The refusal of the king of Kumasi to give a direct answer to our demands of February 1894, makes it difficult to say what part of those demands may be acceptable and what unacceptable. Native opinion here seems to be that, while there is comparatively little objection to the establishment of a British resident at Kumasi, universal fear is entertained that the establishment of British protection will result in the manumission of slaves. This I believe to be the main difficulty. Of course, the spokesmen of the deputation sent by the king of Kumasi to England are astute enough to keep in the background a motive, the avowal of which would horrify public opinion in England. They merely claim independence in general terms. . . .

I find it difficult to submit for your Lordship's approval a sketch of the policy which I should propose to pursue, pending the return of the deputation from England. From your Lordship's despatch of the 14th May, 1895, I have learned that the messengers have been refused an interview with your Lordship, and have been referred to me. They will, I assume, before returning to Africa, visit Paris and Berlin, and it may be expected that they will endeavour there to ascertain whether they can obtain the protection of either France or Germany, retaining full liberty to do as they have been accustomed to do in all matters relating to slaves. In Paris, they will no doubt be informed that the French Government recognise Ashanti as being exclusively within our influence, while in Berlin, they will learn, if they do not know it already, that the German sphere of influence lies exclusively to the eastward of the Neutral Zone.

Returning, as they must, disappointed with the failure of their mission, they will, I trust, eventually address themselves to me, with no unreasonable expectations, and it will be my very earnest desire to bring about a peaceful settlement of all matters at issue. As they are not under instructions from the king of Kumasi to present themselves here, it may be that they will return to Ashanti before seeking to open negotiations with me. However this may be, my present intention is, subject to your Lordship's approval, to tell them, if I have the opportunity, that in my opinion, the proper place for the discussion of the future of Ashanti is Kumasi itself, and that I shall be willing to go there to treat with the King in person, on being invited by him to do so. I should, of course, take a sufficient guard of Hausa Constabulary and a few civil officials selected for their experience of native affairs. The recent experience of Lagos shows the good results which may be accomplished by an expedition headed by the Governor himself.

The subjects for negotiation are:—

Acceptance by Kumasi and by all Ashanti tribes of British protection and flag to such extent as your Lordship may direct.

Free trade between Ashanti and the coast and vice versa.

Free passage through Ashanti for goods from the interior on their way to the coast.

Protection for missionaries.

Abolition of human sacrifices.

Appointment of a British Resident with an adequate guard.

Guarantee by Kumasi to abstain from warfare with neighbouring tribes, not to close trade roads, and to refer all disputes to the Governor.

Payment by Colonial Government of stipends to certain persons, should these be acceptable.

As to these, I believe that I am fully in possession of the views of Her Majesty's Government. There remains the claim of the British Government to the balance of the 50,000 oz. of gold remaining unpaid under the Treaty of Fommanah. Probably this claim can remain in abeyance, if a peaceful settlement can be arranged as regards the other subjects.

The return of the messengers from Europe cannot, I suppose, be very long delayed. In any case, I feel that, while their mission continues, no fresh representations at Kumasi, unaccompanied by a display of force, can be of the slightest use. If, after their return, the king of Kumasi fails, within a reasonable time, to give a satisfactory answer to our letter of February 1894, or if negotiations, whether carried on at Kumasi or at Accra, prove, in spite of all my efforts, that a peaceful settlement is impossible, the time will have come for the despatch of an ultimatum to king Prempeh, in accordance with your Lordship's instructions. . . . The period within which compliance with the request

of Her Majesty's Government is demanded should terminate not later than the 31st October, so as to allow the whole of the intervening dry season for military operations, if necessary. . . . [It is impossible to say whether the Ashantis will resist or not.]   [C.O.96/258. C.7918]

397 LES MISSIONS DU HAUT-DAHOMEY
'FIGARO', 12 AOUT, 1895.

[Two missions had been sent to link up Dahomey with the French Sudan and with the Ivory Coast. The first, under Decoeur and Ballot, reached the Niger between Say and Boussa.] . . .

La second des missions fut celle des lieutenants Baud et Vermeersch, qui, au lieu de rentrer en Europe, reçurent l'ordre de rejoindre la colonne Monteil à Kong. Le but de cette nouvelle expédition était de limiter au plus près l'hinterland des colonies anglaise et allemande dans les parties insuffisamment circonscrites par Decoeur. Il s'agissait, en un mot, de resserrer les mailles du filet.

En conséquence, les traités furent multipliés, surtout dans le Mampoursi, region où les Anglais avaient expédié un nègre nommé Fergusson, avec prescription de devancer les officiers français.

Ce nègre avait une manière toute spéciale de conclure les pactes d'alliance. Il déposait le long de son itinéraire et chez les chefs qui le recevaient, des papiers au sujet desquels il ne fournissait aucune explication. C'étaient, en réalité, des conventions amicales et commerciales rédigées en langue anglaise! Bonne précaution prise contre la curiosité ou l'indiscrétion des destinaires.

Ceux-ci acceptaient le pli entre un ballot de cotonnades de Manchester, et un paquet de couteaux de Sheffield, et le conservaient, croyant qu'il s'agissait d'un certificat de bonne hospitalité.

Fergusson avait pris soin de représenter par des croix de diverses tailles, les signatures des chefs auxquels il remettait ses petits papiers. Or, les intéressés saient tous écrire en arabe, à plus forte raison tracer leur nom. Jugez de leur stupéfaction quand le lieutenant Baud leur donna connaissance des poulets qu'ils détenaient.

À côté des croix, le diplomate de couleur avait ajouté des cachets de cire de grosseur proportionnée a l'importance du personage supposé signataire. Pour le roi, l'empreinte était produite avec le pommeau d'une canne ou d'un parapluie strié; pour les marabouts et les simples princes, on s'était contenté d'appuyer le pouce mouillé sur les cachets.

Inutile de dire que le mission des lieutenants Baud et Vermeersch s'empressa de conclure des traités en bonne et due forme, revêtus d'authentiques signatures, qui remplacèrent les prospectus de Fergusson.

Ces documents sont actuellement entre les mains de M. le ministre des colonies, qui, nous aimons à le croire, n'aura pas de peine a en établir la valeur vis-à-vis des chancelleries étrangères.

Actuellement, le but poursuivi par la France depuis la chute de Behanzin est atteint. Les colonies de la côte d'Or et du Togoland sont cravatées d'un chemin de ronde qui nous appartient, et ce résultat est d'autant plus méritoire qu'il a été obtenu sans effusion de sang, sauf l'échauffourée du moyen Niger, et sans perte d'aucun soldat français.

> Guy Tomel.
> [African (West) No. 496, p. 19]

398 J. CHAMBERLAIN[1] to W. E. MAXWELL
             6 SEPTEMBER, 1895.

Telegraphic.

. . . Her Majesty's Government have had under their careful consideration your Despatch of 13th June, and in accordance with their decision, I have to instruct you to send a message to the King of Kumasi to the following effect:—

[1] Joseph Chamberlain (1836–1914); Municipal reformer and Lord Mayor of Birmingham; President of the Board of Trade, 1880–5; led the Liberal-Unionist opposition to Home Rule for Ireland; Secretary of State for the Colonies, 1895–1903.

Her Majesty's Government are satisfied from the evidence submitted to them that the King has violated the Treaty of Fommanah by the encouragement and practice of human sacrifices, by placing hindrances in the way of trade and by not carrying out the guarantee contained in article VII with regard to the maintenance of the road from Kumasi to the Prah River. He has also made attacks upon tribes with whom the British Government are in friendly relations, and who have sought the protection of the Queen.

By his conduct and the state of warfare and unrest in which it has involved the country, the development of trade and free communication between the colony and the interior has been checked and interfered with.

Her Majesty's Government regard this condition of things as intolerable and they cannot allow it to continue.

They must therefore require the King to carry out his treaty engagements and to refrain from making attacks upon his neighbours, and, in order to effectually secure these objects, it is necessary that he should consent to a British Resident being established at Kumasi, who will exercise control over him in these respects, but will not otherwise interfere with the administration or institutions of the country.

You may also remind the king that the indemnity of 50,000 ounces of gold which was stipulated for in the Treaty of Fommanah has not yet been paid. . . .

> [C.O.96/258.   C.7918]

399 COLONIAL OFFICE TO WAR OFFICE
             9 NOVEMBER, 1895.

. . . In reply to your question as to the exact objects to be attained by the [proposed Ashanti] expedition, I am to observe that, if the king had accepted the terms offered to him in the ultimatum, Her Majesty's Government would have been satisfied with the establishment of a Resident at Kumasi, leaving the government of the country in the hands of the present King. But as it has become necessary to take the extreme step of sending up an armed force to compel compliance with the reasonable demands of Her Majesty's Government, it will in all probability be no longer possible or desirable to allow the King, Prempeh, to retain the position which he now occupies. The Governor will, however, be called upon to submit his proposals as to the future administration of the country. In the meantime it will be necessary that Kumasi should be occupied, and a detachment of the Houssa Constabulary will be left there at the termination of the operation. . . . It is not anticipated that it will be necessary to detain any of Her Majesty's Regular Troops at Kumasi. . . .

[C.O.96/262]

400 CHAMBERLAIN TO MAXWELL
22 NOVEMBER, 1895.

Confidential.

Sir,

I communicated to you by telegram on the 21st instant the substance of a correspondence between this Department and Mr Thomas Sutherst with respect to the Ashanti Messengers now in England, and their desire to make submission on behalf of the King of Kumasi, his chiefs and people, to the terms of the ultimatum of 23rd September.

I now transmit for your information and guidance, copies of the correspondence, from which you will learn exactly what has passed.

You will observe from these letters that I feel no confidence in the ability or bona fides of these messengers, and that I have only accepted their assurances for what they may be worth, and that I have distinctly informed them that the King's submission must be made to you, and that it is by and with you only that a treaty embodying the terms of Her Majesty's Government can be negotiated.

I have from the first refused to recognise the so-called Ambassadors. It now appears that none of them, with the exception of John Ansah, produce any credentials at all, and the chiefs who do not speak English appear to regard the Ansahs only as their interpreters. But in spite of all this uncertainty as to their position, I could not, when so many valuable lives are at stake, stand upon formalities and refuse to listen to their intermediary or to examine into the reality of the submission which they offered on behalf of their King.

The result is not conclusive, and you will see that I have clearly stated that the expedition will proceed; that, under any circumstances, such a force as may be considered desirable and sufficient, will go to Kumasi; and that the King will be required to pay the costs which have been or may be incurred in connection with the expedition.

The composition of the force will be discussed by you in consultation with Sir F. Scott, who has been instructed to report the result for the approval of the Secretary of State for War. In view of the uncertainty as to whether the King will adopt the promises of submission made in his name, the escort should under any circumstances be amply strong enough to defend itself against attack.

As there is no likelihood of the King in any event coming to the Prah to meet you, I do not desire that you should yourself proceed to Kumasi to negotiate with him. This duty may be entrusted to the Commander of the expedition, but you should detach some capable officer of the public service to assist him in the preparation of the necessary agreement or treaty. At the same time, if you should be of opinion that it would be better for you to go there yourself, you are at liberty to do so, informing me by telegram.

In drawing up a treaty, the terms of the letter of February 23rd, 1894, and of the ultimatum of the 23rd of September last, will of course be adhered to, except that the subsidies mentioned in the draft prepared by Mr Hodgson should not now be offered. The clearest language should be used, so that there may be no doubt or mistake hereafter as to the precise nature of the engagements entered into by the King.

It will be necessary to include a provision with regard to the payment by the King of the expenses of the expedition, an estimate of which I shall send to you as soon as possible. If it appears to you that the finances of Ashanti make it impossible to pay the whole amount, you may arrange to compound the claim for a sum proportioned to the resources of the King.

You will also consider whether it will be desirable that the sum in question should be paid at once, or be divided into fixed instalments, to be paid at intervals, the period of which should, of course, be definitely fixed.

In consideration of the payment of the cost of the expedition, Her Majesty's Government will not insist upon the discharge of the debt of 50,000 ounces of gold stipulated for in the Treaty of Fomanah. . . .

Her Majesty's Government will be glad, as you will fully realise, if the King's submission should render all fighting unnecessary, but it is absolutely essential to secure such a complete and efficient British control at Kumasi, as will prevent a recurrence of the difficulties and disturbances which have caused so much trouble in recent years; will put a stop to the practice of human sacrifices, and other atrocities; will ensure freedom of trade and communication throughout the country; will afford an opportunity for the introduction of civilizing influences, and the improvement of the people and their institutions; and will relieve the Gold Coast Government from the anxiety and useless expenditure which the state of unrest in Ashanti, and the intrigues and hostile proceedings of the king, have so frequently forced upon the Colony.

If the necessary arrangements for these objects cannot be obtained by the peaceable submission of the King, recourse must be had to force, and the future conditions of the Kingdom of Kumasi will then be dictated by Her Majesty's Government.

[C.O.96/262]

401 MEMORANDUM OF THE NEGOTIATIONS OF NOVEMBER 1895, IN REGARD TO AN ARRANGEMENT RESPECTING THE 'HINTERLAND' OF THE BRITISH AND GERMAN POSSESSIONS ON THE GULF OF GUINEA.

Count Hatzfeldt[1] and Sir Percy Anderson[2] met on the 15th November.

Count Hatzfeldt produced the map, published in Germany, illustrating Dr Gruner's expeditions.[3] He said that Germany claimed the whole territory marked in red on the map. It comprised the region to the north-west of Togoland, including parts of the Neutral Zone; Gambaga and Karga[4] to the north of the zone; the eastern portion of Mossi; the whole of Gurma, the frontier of which was carried to Gomba on the Niger; Gandu to the east of the Niger; the right bank of the Benue; Ilorin and part of Nupe on the right bank of the Niger. . . . Count Hatzfeldt stated that the cession of the territory belonging to the Gold Coast Colony on the left bank of the Volta, though not marked as a German claim on Dr Gruner's map, would be included in the German demand. . . .

The next meeting took place on the 18th November, when Sir Percy Anderson told Count Hatzfeldt that Lord Salisbury confirmed the view, which he had expressed at the previous meeting, that German claims to the east of the Niger, and those to the west based on Dr Gruner's treaty with Gandu, could not be discussed. . . . Sir

[1] Count Paul von Hatzfeldt-Wildenburg (1831-1901); German ambassador in London, 1885-1901.

[2] Sir Henry Percy Anderson (1831-96); entered the Foreign Office, 1852; Assistant Under-Secretary for Foreign Affairs, 1894.

[3] Gruner left Misahoe in November 1894, and visited and made treaties at Yendi, Sansanne-Mango, Matschakuale and Gando, returning in April 1895.

[4] Karaga was in fact within the Neutral Zone.

Percy Anderson gave his Excellency, confidentially, the following Memorandum recording the suggestions which he had made:—

'1. Germany undertakes not to interfere with the exercise of British influence on the west of the Niger, to the east of a line commencing with the frontier between Dahomey and Lagos, which was drawn from the sea to the 9th parallel by the Anglo-French Agreement of the 10th August 1889, and following from the 9th parallel the meridian adopted in the above-named arrangement to the parallel of Gomba. From that point, the line of demarcation shall follow the last named parallel to the right bank of the Niger at Gomba, where it shall terminate. The line shall, if necessary, be deflected so as to leave the territory of Nikki within the British sphere.

2. Great Britain undertakes not to interfere with the exercise of German influence on the west of the Niger to the north of Gomba, nor in the territory between the line defined in the preceding paragraph and that defined in the following paragraph.

3. Great Britain undertakes not to interfere with the exercise of German influence to the east, and Germany undertakes not to interfere with British influence to the west, of a line which, commencing with the boundary between the Gold Coast Colony and Togoland, defined in article IV of the Agreement of the 1st July 1890, shall proceed northward, following approximately the 0° meridian to the 10th parallel, but deflected so as to leave Yendi to Germany and Salaga to Great Britain.

From the above parallel it shall follow the 0° meridian to the parallel of Say, where it shall terminate.

This Agreement terminates the arrangement made in 1888 constituting a Neutral Zone.

4. The preceding paragraphs refer only to territories west of the Niger.

5. Germany recognises the exercise of British influence over the territories to the east of the Niger, bounded on the east by the Anglo-German boundary between the Rio del Rey and Lake Chad, and on the west by the Niger from the parallel of Say to the mouth of the river.

6. The two Powers agree that in the territories affected by this Agreement over which they may exercise influence, there shall be no differential treatment in matters of trade of their respective subjects.'

The next meeting was on the 23rd November.

Count Hatzfeldt said that he had received a telegraphic reply from Berlin which confirmed his view that the Volta stipulation was a *sine qua non*. . . .

At a further meeting on the 26th, Sir Percy Anderson said that he was instructed that the proposal for the cession of the Volta could not be accepted. He said that an arrangement had been offered as regards the interior, in which the two Powers were free to advance or retire, of a character which was as liberal as it could be made, and which seemed to give both countries room to move independently; but that Lord Salisbury could not entertain a suggestion for handing over a territory which had been for nearly 50 years a dependency of the Crown, which measured nearly 2,000 square miles, contained 600,000 inhabitants, registered in its ports a third of the tonnage of the Colony, and contributed on important articles of import, half the total revenue.

Count Hatzfeldt replied that this was the only point under discussion to which any value was attached. Pointing to the Say–Gomba line on the map, he observed, 'Do you think if we had it we could ever hold it?' If the Volta was refused there was an end of negotiations. . . . He went on to observe that it was unfortunate that an arrangement had not been made, as now Germany must go to France, and Great Britain might find some points not settled to her satisfaction. . . .

[African (West) No. 496, pp. 103–6]

402 CHAMBERLAIN TO MAXWELL
                    12 DECEMBER, 1895.

Confidential.

Sir,

I desire to submit for your consideration certain suggestions which have been made to me as to action which it might be advisable to take in the event of hostilities with the Ashantis actually taking place; in which case, as stated in paragraph 15 of my confidential despatch of 22nd ultimo, 'the future conditions of the Kingdom of Kumasi would be dictated by Her Majesty's Government.' You will understand that I do not press them upon you, but leave it to your judgement to adopt or not as you think best.

1. That it would be desirable to instruct Sir F. Scott to seize and bring away the Golden Stool of Ashanti, as the possession of this Stool will strengthen the Government in the eyes of the natives, and render easier the task of controlling the tribes.

2. That Yao Sapon, King of Juabin, should be bribed to remain neutral by the promise of the return to him of the Royal Stool of the Juabin tribe which is held by the Gold Coast Government.

3. That Ya Kia, the Queen Mother, who is a noted intriguer and a power in Ashanti, should be brought down to the coast.

4. That Atcheriboanda, who is likely to be pliable in the hands of a strong Resident, should be made King of Kumasi, on condition that he discloses and gives up the buried treasure of King Kofi Kalkalli, of which he is believed to hold the secret.

                    I have etc.
                    [C.P. (African West 500)]

403 COLONIAL OFFICE TO FOREIGN OFFICE
                    20 JANUARY, 1896.

Sir,

I am directed by Mr Secretary Chamberlain to state that he has had under his consideration your letter of 21st ultimo, submitting certain unofficial suggestions made by Dr Kayser, in conversation with Mr Gosselin, for an arrangement in the 'Hinterland' of the Gold Coast Colony and Togoland, of which the principal points were that the free navigation of the Volta should be secured to Germany, and that there should be such a partition of the Neutral Zone as would place Salaga as well as Yendi within the German sphere.

I am to request you to inform the Marquis of Salisbury, that Mr Chamberlain would strongly object to any arrangement which would give Salaga to Germany, and he would in fact deprecate any alteration of the Agreement of 1887–8 by which the Neutral Zone was established.

The object of that arrangement was to secure that the Gold Coast should not lose the trade of Salaga and the neighbourhood, and that neither Power should be enabled to close that important centre against the other. Great Britain does not desire to acquire any exclusive influence or trade privileges in any part of the zone, and there appears to be no reason, except with the object of shutting out British trade, why Germany should seek to do so.

As regards the free navigation of the Volta, Mr Chamberlain cannot but fear that its concession would be injurious to the interests of the Gold Coast Colony, but at the same time he feels that it would hardly be consistent with the general policy of this country to refuse it altogether, and he would therefore be prepared, in case a satisfactory arrangement was arrived at, to undertake that, whenever the river (the navigation of which above Pong is at present impeded by rapids) is opened up, free transit should be allowed to German vessels, on such conditions and under such restrictions as have been imposed in similar circumstances elsewhere.

But in the event of this important concession being granted, it would be necessary that the German Government should be willing to give fair and reasonable compensation in some other direction.

Referring to this last suggestion, I am to observe that Mr Chamberlain has been struck by the almost entirely one-sided nature of the proposals which have been put forward in connection with these negotiations.

Her Majesty's Government have been asked to make most important and valuable concessions, to abrogate an agreement with which they are well satisfied, and to which the German Government readily consented in 1888, and to give Germany free rights of navigation over a river, the full possession of which was guaranteed to Great Britain by the Agreement of 1890, both banks being ours, under that Agreement, from the Neutral Zone to the sea.

On the other hand, the German Government has offered absolutely nothing at all, beyond perhaps, the withdrawal of certain unsubstantial and inadmissable claims based upon alleged treaties made by Dr Gruner in territories with which Her Majesty's Government already had long-standing and undeniable treaties.

Unless the German Government are prepared to accept the principle laid down by Prince Bismarck, of 'Do ut des', Mr Chamberlain thinks that it would be better for this country to adhere absolutely to the status quo.

> I have etc.
> R. H. Meade.
> [African (West) No. 507, p. 3]

404 Treaty . . . with Nsuta

30 January, 1896.

Treaty of Friendship and Protection made at Kumasi this thirtieth day of January, one thousand eight hundred and ninety-six, between Her Most Gracious Majesty Victoria, Queen of Great Britain and Ireland, Empress of India, &c, Her Heirs and Successors, by Her subject, His Excellency William Edward Maxwell, Companion of the Most distinguished Order of Saint Michael and St George, Governor and Commander-in-Chief of the Gold Coast Colony, on the one part, and the King, Chiefs, and Principal Headmen of the country of Insuta on the other part.

Whereas Edu Egay, King of the country of Insuta, and the Chiefs and Principal Headmen of that country, for and on behalf of themselves, their heirs, successors, and people, have presented to the Governor of the Gold Coast Colony a request that their country should be placed under the protection of Great Britain, and have agreed to enter into a Treaty with Her Majesty the Queen of Great Britain and Ireland, Empress of India &c &c, Her heirs and successors on the other part, do hereby enter into this Treaty containing the following articles.

Article 1

The King of the country of Insuta, for himself and his lawful successors, together with the Chiefs and Principal men of the country of Insuta, whose names are hereinafter signed and seals affixed, for and on behalf of themselves and their successors and people of Insuta, hereby place themselves under the protection of Great Britain, declaring that they have not entered into any treaty with any other foreign Power.

Article 2

Her Majesty's subject, the Governor of the Gold Coast Colony, for and on behalf of Her Majesty the Queen of Great Britain and Ireland . . . Her heirs and successors, hereby takes the country of Insuta under the protection of Great Britain.

Article 3

It is hereby agreed that the King, Chiefs and Principal Men, together with the other people of Insuta, will not enter into any war or commit any act of aggression on any of the Chiefs bordering on their country, by which the trade of the country shall be interrupted, or the safety and property of the subjects of Her Majesty the Queen of England and Empress of India shall be lost, compromised or endangered, and that the said King, Chiefs, and Principal Men of Insuta hereby undertake to refer to the Governor of the Gold

Coast Colony, acting on behalf of Her Majesty, for friendly arbitration, any trade or other quarrels in which they may become involved before actually entering upon hostilities.

Article 4

Should any difference or dispute accidently arise between the King of Insuta and any of his Chiefs and Principal Headmen, or between any of the Chiefs and Principal Headmen, it shall be referred to the Governor of the Gold Coast Colony, or to the nearest British authority for the time being, whose decision shall be final and binding upon all parties concerned.

Article 5

British subjects shall have free access to all parts of Insuta, and shall have the right to build houses and possess property according to the law in force in the Gold Coast Colony; and they shall have full liberty to carry on such trade or manufacture as may be approved by any officer appointed for the purpose by Her Majesty's Government, and should any difference arise between the aforesaid British subjects and the King, Chiefs or Principal Headmen of the country of Insuta, as to the duties or customs to be paid to the said King, Chiefs or Principal Headmen of the towns in that country by such British subjects, or as to any other matter, that the dispute shall be referred to the officer mentioned in Article 4, whose decision in the matter shall be binding and final, and that the King, Chiefs, and Principal Headmen of Insuta will not extend the rights hereby guaranteed to British subjects to any other persons without the knowledge and consent of such officer.

Article 6

In consideration of the protection guaranteed on the part of Great Britain to the King, Chiefs and Principal Headmen and the people of Insuta, they hereby bind themselves, their heirs and successors, to keep their main roads in good order; that they will encourage trade, and give facilities to traders; and will not cede their territories to, or accept a protectorate from, or enter into any agreement, arrangement, or treaty with any other foreign Power, except through and with the consent of the Government of Her Majesty the Queen Empress.

Article 7

The Government of Her Majesty the Queen Empress will not prevent the King of Insuta, or his Chiefs and Principal Headmen, and their lawful successors, from levying customary dues appertaining to them according to the laws and customs of their country, nor in the administration thereof; and Her Majesty's Government will respect the habits and customs of the country, but will not permit human sacrifice; and slave dealing, when brought to the notice of the Government, will be punished according to the laws of the Gold Coast Colony.

Article 8

This Treaty shall come into force from the date hereof, but power is expressly reserved to Her Majesty the Queen Empress, to refuse to approve and ratify the same within one year from the date hereof. In witness whereof the parties to this Treaty have hereunto set their hands and affixed their respective seals.

Done in triplicate at Kumasi, in the country of Ashanti, this thirtieth day of January of the year one thousand eight hundred and ninety-six, in the fifty-ninth year of the reign of Her Majesty the Queen Empress. . . .

[C.P. African (West) No. 1010.]

30   The Race for the North, 1896–1899

WHEN, in January 1896, negotiations with France were resumed, for a settlement of West African boundaries, Chamberlain at the Colonial Office (406) was noticeably stiffer in his terms than Salisbury (405).   He was not prepared to cede France access to the lower Niger, or a protectorate over Mossi; and as a settlement without one or the other of these concessions was evidently improbable (408), it was necessary to make sure of Britain's claims on the spot (410).   The Germans were already in possession of Sansanne-Mango (409), and the first critical position was therefore Gambaga (411), which Captain Stewart managed to occupy in December 1896 (412).   The status of Wagadugu was still held to be in doubt (413), in spite of a flying visit by a French force, but Stewart, on his way thither, fell in with a French column at Tengrugu, and there concluded what proved to be a decisive local agreement with the French commander (414).

Effective occupation on the spot was now what counted, and, while Salisbury remonstrated with the French about their cavalier attitude to British treaty rights in the hinterland (419), Chamberlain was preparing, in the West African Frontier Force, an instrument for taking counter-measures within the French sphere of interests (417).   He hoped in this way to improve his bargaining position in respect of Mossi and sundry Nigerian questions at issue.   But, besides the French, there were the Germans to be reckoned with.   Their conduct in Dagomba, made necessary counter-measures within the Neutral Zone (416), and these detracted from the forces available for action elsewhere.   On the west, the officer sent to occupy Bona and Wa, found himself, for a time, a prisoner of Samory's war bands.

Samory, nearing the end of his ten-year struggle against the French, was an awkward problem for the incipient British administration of the Northern Territories (421).   In so far as he was anti-French, Chamberlain was even prepared to make overtures to him (417): but while there was every reason for avoiding a conflict with him, if possible, protection against the raids of his war bands was the chief inducement to the other tribes of the north to sign treaties with the British authorities (420).   Eventually Samory drew away to the south-west, where he was finally rounded up by the French on the borders of Liberia.   The permanent result of his sojourn in Bontuku in 1897 was the loss to the Gold Coast of some of the hinterland Chamberlain had hoped to secure in the direction of the Comoe river.

From the summer of 1898 the tension began to relax.   In June, the British and French at last reached a compromise agreement (423).   The German problem was less serious, if only because they were not present in such force as to make a conflict likely; while with them there was no point at issue comparable in importance to the lower Niger question, which had brought Britain and France so nearly to blows.   The bargaining, though protracted, was over small details, and the final agreement of 1899 (425), scarcely differed in any essential from the offer made by Britain two years before.[1]

---

[1] Cf. Salisbury to Gough, 9 December, 1897, in African (West) No. 538, p. 332.   The Germans made a final but unofficial bid to secure a footing on the navigable Volta by offering to accept the Oti as the frontier north of 9 N, which would have avoided partitioning Dagomba; cf. African (West) No. 651, pp. 53–4 and map.

405 THE MARQUIS OF SALISBURY TO THE MARQUIS OF DUFFERIN[1]

7 FEBRUARY, 1896.

My Lord,

As your Excellency is aware, the agreement signed in London on the 15th ultimo by M. Courcel and myself[2] which chiefly concerned the affairs of Siam, contained an article in the following terms:—

'The two Governments agree to name Commissioners delegated by each of them, who shall be charged to fix, by mutual agreement, after examination of the titles produced on either side, the most equitable delimitation between the British and French Possessions in the regions situated to the west of the Lower Niger.'

I informed your Excellency on the 31st ultimo that Sir Augustus Hemming, Governor of British Guiana, would be associated with Mr H. Howard as British Commissioner, and received on the 3rd instant your Excellency's Despatch stating that the French Government had named MM. Larrouy and Roume as their Commissioners, and that there was no reason why they should not meet the British Commissioners in Paris during the present week.

The negotiations are . . . to be considered, as regards the Niger, as a resumption of those which took place between Mr Phipps and M. Hanotaux in 1894, the bases of which were sent home in Mr Phipps's Despatch No. 266, Africa of the 9th October of that year. . . .

As regards the hinterland of the Gold Coast north of the 9th parallel, Mr Phipps reported in October 1894 that M. Hanotaux had informed him in a private conversation, that he would agree to a line drawn due westward from the north-west corner of the neutral zone, and ending at the 3rd meridian. If by this the 3rd

meridian west of Greenwich was meant, such an arrangement would bring the western boundary nearly up to the river Komoe, and the Commissioners might, in the first place, suggest that river as the limit in that direction. But in the probable event of its not being accepted, and of their being also unable to obtain the line of the 3rd meridian as far north as the 11th parallel, they are authorised to accept a line, commencing at the present limit, or parallel 9, and extending direct to the north as far as the 11th parallel. From this point the line should be carried eastwards so as to include in the British sphere the territory of Mamprusi and Gambaga, or, failing this, in a direct line along the 11th parallel till it reaches the eastern boundary of the neutral zone, and should thence be continued due south till it touches the northeast corner of the same zone at the 10th parallel. It will be seen that any of these proposals entail a sacrifice by Great Britain of large territories with which Her Majesty's Government have treaties, including in any case the valuable district of Mossi, and possibly that of Lobi, a tributary of Bona. . . .

[C.P. African (West) No. 506, p. 30]

406 COLONIAL OFFICE TO FOREIGN OFFICE

13 JULY, 1896.

Sir,

I am directed by Mr Secretary Chamberlain to inform you that he has read the reports of the British Representatives on the Niger Commission, which were enclosed in your letters of the 30th of May and previous dates, and that he desires to offer, for the consideration of the Marquess of Salisbury, the following remarks and suggestions with reference to the territories to the west of the Niger, in which the Colonies of the Gold Coast and Lagos are more particularly interested.

The proposal of the French Commissioners that the boundary behind Lagos should start from the eastern frontier of Dahomey at its intersection with the 8th

---

[1] Frederick Temple Hamilton-Temple Blackwood (1st Marquis of Dufferin and Ava) (1826–1902); diplomat and writer; Governor-General of Canada, 1872–8; ambassador at St. Petersburg (1879) and Constantinople (1881); Governor-General of India, 1884–8; Ambassador at Paris, December 1891–October 1896.

[2] Cf. Hertslet, Map of Africa, vol. 2, p. 765.

degree of north latitude and follow that parallel eastward to the Niger, is, of course, wholly unacceptable, as Lord Salisbury has stated in his Despatch of the 12th of May; and Mr Chamberlain agrees with the British Commissioners in considering that, even with the modification suggested by the French Commissioners at the meeting of the 22nd of May, this proposal cannot fairly be taken as a basis for discussion.

With regard to the boundary behind the Gold Coast, I am to state that, in Mr Chamberlain's opinion, it is of great importance that Mossi and Gurunsi, as well as Bona and Lobi, should, if possible, be secured to Great Britain. [The proposals] in Lord Salisbury's despatch of the 7th of February last . . . would entail the sacrifice of Bona, Lobi, Mossi, and a portion of the Gurunsi country; and since it was decided to give these instructions to the British Commissioners, Sir W. Maxwell has pointed out that, as many of the Hausas who compose the Gold Coast Constabulary are recruited from Mossi and Gurunsi, the moral effect on the force would be grave, if those districts were handed over to France, and it is also necessary, in order to secure the full advantage which should be derived from the heavy expenditure recently incurred on the Ashanti expedition, that the French should not be able to divert the trade of Mossi and the neighbouring countries to their own possessions, as they are doing in the case of the countries behind Sierra Leone.

For these reasons, Mr Chamberlain is anxious that no effort should be spared to strengthen our position to the north of Ashanti and the Gold Coast. It seems not improbable that the French Government will endeavour to repudiate Mr Ferguson's treaties, on the ground that he is a native of West Africa; and a further complication is introduced by the presence of Samory with whom the French are doing their best to make peace. Samory is stated in the French newspapers to be stipulating for a

retention of territory, and the situation would become very difficult if he were allowed to occupy Bona and other places in the vicinity.

I am therefore to suggest, for Lord Salisbury's consideration, that a white officer should be sent, without loss of time, to Wagadugu, accompanied by some of the natives who went there with Mr Ferguson, or (if possible) by Mr Ferguson himself, to get the King of Mossi to confirm Mr Ferguson's treaty and accept another British flag, and that detachments of the Gold Coast Constabulary should be sent to occupy Bona and visit Wa and other neighbouring places with which we have treaties. The French Government would have no ground for objecting to our taking this action, as it has been established that Bona is north of the 9th parallel, and that they have no treaties either with Bona or with Wagadugu.

I am etc.

John Bramston.[1]

[African (West) 506, p. 134]

407 House of Commons Debate

28 July, 1896.

Mr. D. F. Goddard[2] (Ipswich): I beg to ask the Secretary of State for the Colonies whether he is aware that in a recent speech at Liverpool, Sir William Maxwell, K.C.M.G., Governor of the Gold Coast, stated that it would be proposed to make it impossible for the native chiefs to make any concession of land without the concurrence of the Governor; whether the native chiefs will be consulted before such a proposal becomes law; and whether the Colonial Office has sanctioned this policy?

The Secretary of State for the Colonies (Mr J. Chamberlain, Birmingham, W.): Yes Sir: I have sanctioned this policy, and there are good reasons for it. ('Hear,

---

[1] Assistant Under-Secretary of State for the Colonies, 1876–97.
[2] Daniel Ford Goddard (later Sir) (1850–1922); Liberal M.P. for Ipswich, 1895–1918.

hear!') The land laws and land customs of West Africa are different from the law of land tenure in England, while the concessions are framed in the language of English conveyancing, and purport to convey the fee simple, or to grant a lease with the conditions which are incident to such transactions here, but are probably unintelligible to the native signing the instruments. It is uncertain how far native chiefs possess the right of making alienations of this character for their own benefit, and in some instances, concessions have been brought to the local Government for approval which have proved to be signed by men who had no title in the land. In the interests of all the native tribes and chiefs, as well as of British investors, it is essential that the local Government should be able to see that such transactions are made in good faith and on reasonable terms, and that the conditions are thoroughly understood by the natives. ('Hear, hear!')

[Hansard, 4/43/819]

408 MEMORANDUM
BRITISH EMBASSY, PARIS, 5 AUGUST, 1896.
Confidential.

With reference to the Franco-British frontier in the immediate vicinity of the Niger, I fear that there is but little chance of any proposal being made by M. Hanotaux on the subject of the same which will not include a demand on the part of France for access to the navigable portion of the river below the rapids. For Her Majesty's Government ever to make such a concession would, I am convinced, be disastrous; for the French, once on the lower navigable Niger, would be the source of immense and never-ending trouble.

As to the hinterland of the Gold Coast Colony, the French, I believe, will never *willingly* consent to Mossi remaining British. They have always considered Mossi as properly belonging to their sphere of influence, and — probably owing to a false report that a treaty had been concluded with that country by Colonel Monteil — it was proposed to be given to France during the Anglo-French negotiations of 1892 and 1894. Rightly or wrongly, the French will always contend that Mossi should be theirs, and I feel sure that unless it is given to France, no general agreement such as was contemplated being effected by the present Niger Commission, or even a separate one dealing only with the Hinterland of the Gold Coast Colony, will ever be arrived at. It is for Her Majesty's Government to decide whether they will cede Mossi, so as to arrive at the above-mentioned general or separate agreements, should such a cession make either of the latter possible, or whether, Mossi having become too valuable in their estimation to be abandoned, they prefer to retain it at all costs.

Whatever their decision may be, and whatever proposal M. Hanotaux may make hereafter, I am distinctly in favour of all territories which Her Majesty's Government really intend to retain, and to which they have indubitable rights, being occupied, or at all events, revisited, at the earliest possible date, provided that the missions sent to the territories in question be accompanied by a force sufficiently strong to prevent any possibility of a repulse or failure. I believe that the undoubted success of the recent French missions in the bend of the Niger, was principally due to the great daring of their leaders and the great force that the latter had at their disposal. A repulse or a failure, in Mossi especially, would . . . be certainly held to justify the assertions of the French Commissioners that Mr Ferguson's success was owing to his colour. . . .

Henry Howard.[1]

[African (West) No. 506, p. 176]

[1] Henry Howard (later Sir) (1848–1921); entered the Diplomatic Service, 1865; envoy extra-ordinary and Minister-Plenipotentiary at Paris, 1896.

409 MEMORANDUM BY WILLIAM EVERETT[1]
LONDON, 7 SEPTEMBER, 1896.

Sansanné Mangu[2] is the capital of Chakosi, and, being situated north of 10 north latitude, is without the Hinterland of Togo as defined by Dr Kayser. . . . Chakosi is situated on the caravan route from the Haussa states to Salaga and the Neutral Zone. The object of the Germans is, therefore, very probably, to tap this trade. At the same time, it should be borne in mind that Sansanné Mangu is also a station on the road to the Niger via Pama and Kankantjari. . . . Its occupation may therefore be also the initial step of the policy of the German Colonial Party . . . [for] the extension of the Togo Hinterland northward to the Niger. . . .

[The possibility of a diversion of trade is not serious, as Britain commands the supply of kola nut, and the overland trade is likely to die out when the Niger Company starts direct shipments to Boussa.] The expansion of German Togoland northward to the Niger does not concern us, provided it is not extended beyond the right bank of that river.

Although by the instructions given to Her Majesty's Commissioners for the delimitation of the British and French spheres of influence in the neighbourhood of the Niger, Great Britain would appear to have no further interest in Sansanné Mangu, it was also laid down in those instructions that the territory of Gambaga should, if possible, be included in the British sphere. Now the country of . . . Mamprusi, of which Gambaga appears to be the capital, lies immediately to the westward of Chakosi, and since Germany asserts that she has a treaty with Gambaga, it seems not improbable, that in course of time we may hear of the occupation of this place also, together with Karga, a district immediately to the south, and the greater

portion of which lies to the north of the Neutral Zone. It is, I think, most important to guard against this step. It may fairly be assumed that in any future negotiations with Germany which may include a further delimitation of frontiers in these regions, an equitable partition of the Neutral Zone will be a matter for consideration, and it is evident that the position of the point where this dividing line, starting in the south from the junction of the Volta and Daka rivers, is to emerge from the Zone on its northern frontier, will be appreciably influenced by the amount of territory to the north of the Zone which is found to be in possession of the Contracting Parties at the time. If then, at the time, Germany is occupying territory to the north of the Zone from Sansanné Mangu as far west as Gambaga and Karga, this occupation, together with her treaties with the King of Yendi, i.e. Dagomba, the first of which is dated in 1888, will constitute pretensions to a claim for the Volta as a continuation of the frontier northward from its junction with the Daka. . . .

[The German claim to Sansanné Mangu rested on their treaty with its Yendi overlord.] The principle that a treaty with the ruling power covers its dependencies, has been steadily adhered to by Her Majesty's Commissioners, during the recent negotiations at Paris. Only by asserting this principle could the claims of the Niger Company be possibly upheld, and this same argument has still more recently been made use of in addressing a remonstrance to Germany respecting her treaty with Sugu. On this occasion, Her Majesty's Government pointed out that, according to Kiepert's map, Sugu was included within the limits of Borgu, and that, therefore, under the Niger Company's treaty with that country, we had a prior claim.

It becomes, therefore, I think, a question for consideration, whether it would be advisable to address a remonstrance, or even an inquiry, to Germany respecting the occupation of Chakosi, especially as it

---

[1] Director of Military Intelligence, War Office.
[2] A German force under Lt. von Carnap had established a post at Sansanné Mangu in the spring of 1896. This was announced in the Kolonialblatt of 15 August.

is exceedingly improbable that any representation we might be able to make would induce her to withdraw from that territory. At the same time, for the reasons given above, it is of great importance that we should take measures to protect ourselves from any encroachment on territory lying to the westward of Chakosi, and I am therefore strongly of opinion that our best reply to the occupation of Sansanné Mangu is the occupation by ourselves of Gambaga, at an early date. By this step, not only should we acquire all the territory lying immediately to the north of the Neutral Zone that is necessary to the development of the Gold Coast Hinterland, but our position, both as regards any future negotiations with Germany respecting those regions and our present negotiations with France, would be greatly strengthened. . . .

[African (West) No. 507, p. 89]

410 CHAMBERLAIN TO MAXWELL

3 OCTOBER, 1896.

Confidential.

Sir,

I have the honour to inform you that Her Majesty's Government have decided that a European officer of the Gold Coast Government should be sent without loss of time to Wagadugu, accompanied by some of the natives who went there with Mr Ferguson, or perhaps by Mr Ferguson himself, to get the King of Mossi to confirm Mr Ferguson's treaty and accept another British flag, and that detachments of the Gold Coast Constabulary should be sent to occupy Bona and visit Wa and other neighbouring places with which we have treaties. It has been established, as you are aware, that Bona is north of the 9th parallel, and that France has no treaties either with Bona or with Mossi.

Her Majesty's Government have also decided that it is desirable that Gambaga should be occupied by the Gold Coast Government.

I have to instruct you, therefore, if, on your arrival, you are still of opinion that this can be done by means of a peaceful mission, to take the necessary steps to carry out these decisions with as little delay as possible. The cost will be defrayed from Gold Coast funds.

I am etc.

[African (West) No. 506, p. 193]

411 INSTRUCTIONS TO CAPTAIN D. STEWART[1]

. . . I am directed by the Governor to inform you that the following telegram has been despatched today to Prahsu with instructions that it shall be sent on to you by special runner:—

'To be kept secret.

'Information received of the occupation of Mossi by the French. You will proceed Gambaga at once with one company of Haussas, one European officer, and Dr Coker. You must occupy that place. British flag to be hoisted. You should take 100 rounds of ammunition per man, also one Maxim with ammunition, and sufficient sum of money pay Haussas and carriers for three months. . . . No time should be lost in starting for Gambaga by quickest route, passing through Daboya, Yariba and Walewale. All these places under treaty — salute the flag. Avoid collision with French or Germans. You are aware that Sansanné Mangu already in occupation of German Commissioner. Hope you will accomplish occupation of Gambaga without opposition, and await further instructions there; but if you find that French or Germans have arrived, you had better withdraw to Walewale, or elsewhere, and apply for instructions. . . .'

[African (West) No. 506, p. 270]

---

[1] Captain Donald Stewart (later Sir); entered the army, 1879, and served in Afghanistan, the Transvaal and the Sudan; Political Officer with the Ashanti expedition, 1896; Resident of Kumasi, 1896–1904; later served in East Africa.

412 CAPTAIN D. STEWART TO F. M. HODGSON

GAMBAGA, 29 DECEMBER, 1896.

Sir,

I have the honour to report for the information of his Excellency the Governor, that I arrived at Gambaga on the 24th December and saluted the British flag which was flying, I having sent on two Haussas overnight to hoist it at day-break. . . .

The 28th December was the day appointed for me to see the king, but being ill myself, I sent Captain Hawtrey and Dr Coker, with presents from the Government. The king, who lives in the village of Nalierigu, about 1¼ hour's march from Gambaga, was delighted to see them, and said he was under the English and only under them. A British flag was given him and raised in his presence, the escort saluting the flag on its being raised, the king saying that was the flag he served under.

I am placing a picket of Hausas at Morozagu on the Gambaga-Sansanné-Mangu road, to prevent further encroachments by the Germans on Mamprusi country, they having already got a picket at Yensomboru, which village belongs to Mamprusi; also another at Zendsah on the Gambaga–Yendi road, to prevent further encroachment from that side. We were only just in time in reaching Gambaga, as evidently Dr Gruner intended to occupy this place in a few days, from all the information we can get. . . .

The news from the Moshi country, which I believe to be fairly correct, having heard it from several sources, is as follows:—

One French expedition, consisting of two white officers and 400 soldiers, arrived at Wagadugu three months ago and said they wanted the king of Moshi, as he had been making human sacrifices (which is true). The king, on hearing he was wanted on this charge, ran away to a village called Numgani. The French followed, and he then ran to Kunda, where he now is. The

French burnt the king's palace, but did no harm to the people or the remainder of the town. They stayed 30 days and retired to Marne, from there to Yariga, about seven days from Wagadugu, where they are at present.

Yariga is not in Moshi country, and no troops or even a representative of the French was left in the country. While the French were at Wagadugu, they had a flag flying. Though they have since withdrawn from Moshi country, I have decided to wait here for further instructions re my going to Wagadugu. As far as the Moshi people are concerned, they will be delighted to see us there. I shall be glad if full instructions can be sent, especially with regard to treaties. I think all these countries could be got to sign the same treaty as the Ashantis, if his Excellency would authorise my making the treaties with them.

The Grunshi country has no treaties with us, I believe, and should be visited, I think, as soon as an officer can be sent. I shall go as far as Tengrugu, the capital of the Busiansi country, and try and make a treaty of friendship and commerce with them. These people are under Mamprusi and will round off the north-east corner of the Mamprusi boundary. . . .

[C.P. African (West) No. 529, p. 45]

413 HODGSON TO STEWART

10 FEBRUARY, 1897.

. . . You ask for fresh instructions regarding Wagadugu, in view of the fact that the French have been there and have had their flag flying, though they have since withdrawn from the Mossi country. You, no doubt, received, shortly after the date of your report under acknowledgement, my letter of the 5th December, in which I said that 'If they (the French) are not in occupation of Wagadugu, you may proceed there at once, leaving such men as you can spare at Gambaga, and enter into a treaty of protection with the king and chiefs, confirmatory of Mr Ferguson's treaty of

1894 which is still in force. Your treaty will be one of protection, whereas his was for friendship and commerce.' Supplementary instructions were sent to you on the 24th December in the Governor's semi-official letter of that date. In that letter, the following passage occurs: 'In that case (i.e. that there is no French post at Wagadugu) you can of course go on to Wagadugu and, if the chiefs and people are friendly and renew the treaty which they entered into with Ferguson, establish a British post there.' . . .

The occupation of Mossi, which you have been directed to carry out, is founded upon our treaty rights of 1894. These have not been in any way disturbed or prejudiced because a French expedition has, improperly, as it must be contended, made its way to Wagadugu. If the French had remained in possession of Wagadugu, it would have been undesirable that you should have come into contact with them, but as they have retired to Yariga, there is no reason why Wagadugu should not be occupied and our claim asserted to the protectorate of the whole of the Mossi country. If this has not yet been done, no further time should be lost. . . .

You have stated in your semi-official letter to the Governor, of December 29th, that you do not know what our policy in the Hinterland is. I am to explain, therefore, briefly, that the object of the Governor is to secure for the trade of the Gold Coast as much as possible of the Hinterland, and that the territory claimed as belonging to the British sphere of influence includes Mossi up to Jilgodi,[1] and all the territory between that country and Ashanti. The boundary on the west may be taken to be the Komoe and Lokhosi rivers, slightly west of longitude 3 W., and the boundary on the east, the neutral zone up to the 10th parallel of north latitude. North of the 10th parallel no indication can at present be given of what may eventually be claimed towards the eastward, but the opening of a route to the Niger through

[1] c. 14° N.

Gurma, to which you refer . . . is not at present within your instructions.

The peace of the Gold Coast Hinterland is at present disturbed by the slave raids of Samory's Sofas,[1] who have occupied Bona, behaving there with great cruelty, and who are believed to have designs upon Lobi. It will be necessary, before long, to take decisive action to put down raids of this kind, and the Governor is in communication with the Secretary of State on the subject. . . . You should, as far as possible, encourage and assist the protected [tribes] of the Hinterland, to resist the attacks of the Sofas, and you should report what, if any, aggression on the part of the latter is expected. It will, perhaps, be necessary to establish a post at Daboya in order to maintain communication both with Gambaga and Wa. As to this you should report. It must be remembered, however, that the Gold Coast Constabulary is below its strength, and that the Kumasi garrison demands at all times a strong detachment. The Governor is, therefore, very anxious to learn from you what are the chances of recruiting in the north, and whether the Gonja, Dagomba, Gurunsi and Mossi tribes can furnish men who, if drilled and armed and led by British officers, would act on the defensive against the Sofas.

I have etc.

[African (West) No. 529, p. 67]

414 Colonial Office to Foreign Office
6 April, 1897.

Sir,

I am directed by Mr Secretary Chamberlain, to transmit to you, to be laid before the Marquess of Salisbury, with reference to the letter from this Department of the 22nd of March, the accompanying copy of a further telegram from the Governor of the Gold Coast, in which it is stated that Lieutenant Voulet with a French force, met Captain Stewart at Tengrugu, on the 6th of February.

[1] i.e. war bands.

It will be seen that M. Voulet notified to Captain Stewart that Mossi and Gurunsi had been occupied by the French, and claimed Tengrugu as being a part of Mossi; that he protested against any British occupation of Dagomba (Yendi), Gambaga, Buale, or Bona; and that he laid claim to Sansanne-Mango, Gurma, and Wa; but that, at Captain Stewart's suggestion, it was agreed that both parties should withdraw from Tengrugu, and refer the question to their respective Governments, and that M. Voulet accordingly returned to Wagadugu, while Captain Stewart went back to Gambaga.

Mr Chamberlain proposes, with Lord Salisbury's concurrence, to approve of Captain Stewart's action in making this arrangement, but he trusts that Lord Salisbury will intimate to the French Government that it has been made simply in order to avoid any risk of collision between the British and French forces, and that it does not imply any doubt as to the validity of the British claim to Mossi, and that his Lordship will press for the evacuation of Mossi as soon as instructions to that effect can reach the French officer in command there.

With regard to the other places mentioned by Lieut. Voulet, I am to observe that the French have either no treaties at all with them, or treaties of later date than those concluded by Mr Ferguson, and that it seems to Mr Chamberlain to be desirable to remind the French Government, without delay, that Her Majesty's Government claim these places and that they do not admit the claims put forward by M. Voulet.

I am &c

Selborne.

[African (West) No. 529, p. 95]

415 COLONIAL OFFICE TO FOREIGN OFFICE
27 APRIL, 1897.

Sir,

I am directed by Mr Secretary Chamberlain to transmit to you, to be laid before

R

the Marquess of Salisbury . . . the accompanying copy of a telegram from the Governor of the Gold Coast, reporting that a treaty was concluded by Mr Henderson with the new King of Bona, and the British flag hoisted in Dokita, on the 16th of March, and that he had great hopes of being able to occupy Bona shortly.

Lord Salisbury will recollect that among the telegrams of which copies were enclosed in the letter from this department of the 12th instant, was one stating that the main body of the Sofas had left Bona.

I am to suggest, for Lord Salisbury's consideration, that as soon as Bona has been occupied, it would be desirable to notify to the French Government, that Bona, Wa, and Gambaga, have been taken under British protection and occupied by the forces of the Gold Coast Government; that Mossi (including Tengrugu) is claimed under the treaty of the 2nd of July 1894, and that the Gurunsi country is also claimed as belonging naturally to the British sphere of interest.

It appears to Mr Chamberlain to be imperative that something should be done, without delay, to induce the French Government to put a stop to the proceedings of French officers in Mossi and other territories whose inhabitants have grounds for looking to Her Majesty's Government for protection. . . .

[African (West) No. 529, p. 118]

416 COLONIAL OFFICE TO FOREIGN OFFICE
13 MAY, 1897.

. . . It appears to Mr Chamberlain, that if Germany is to be prevented from reaping the advantage of the unscrupulous proceedings of German officers, Her Majesty's Government must, without delay, denounce the Agreement of 1887, and authorize the Governor of the Gold Coast to occupy Yendi and other places in the Neutral Zone. So far as this Department is concerned, the only question is whether the Gold Coast Government is in a position to occupy these places before the Togoland

Government can do so, and, on learning that Lord Salisbury sees no objection to the denunciation of the Agreement, Mr Chamberlain will consult Sir W. Maxwell, as to the possibility of effecting the occupation. The latest reports with regard to Mr Henderson are of a reassuring character,[1] and there is some ground for hoping that it will not be necessary to employ the whole of the available forces in repelling the attacks of the Sofas.

[African (West) No. 529, p. 179]

417 CHAMBERLAIN TO MAXWELL

4 JUNE, 1897.

Confidential.

Sir,

You are aware that the French have recently occupied not only Mossi but also Boussa and other places with which treaties had previously been concluded by agents of the Gold Coast Government and the Royal Niger Company, binding the kings and chiefs not to accept the protection of, or to make any treaty with another Power without the consent of Her Majesty's Government.

When the terms of these treaties were settled, it was considered that they would be sufficient to bar the conclusion of subsequent treaties by agents of a foreign Government; but although the French Government have not expressly repudiated this view, they have not as yet made any reply to the remonstrances which have been addressed to them by Her Majesty's Government, with reference to the occupation of Mossi and Boussa, and in the French newspapers it is openly stated that no treaty with native authorities will be respected unless it has been followed up by effective occupation.

[1] Lieutenant Henderson (R.N.) was sent in November 1896 to occupy Bona, Bole and Wa, where his force was attacked by Samory's *Sofas*. Henderson decided to visit Samory in his camp, and was there detained, though well treated, until his release on 4 May. His force in the meantime retired from Bona, was attacked by the Sofas, and Ferguson killed.

It has been a source of weakness to Her Majesty's Government in all the negotiations which have taken place with regard to West Africa, that the French have usually been in occupation of the principal places in dispute, and it was therefore decided, when the negotiations in Paris last year were suspended, that British officers should be despatched by the Gold Coast Government, to occupy Gambaga, Wa, Bona, and, if possible, Wagadugu. Captain Stewart succeeded in occupying Gambaga, but the French had seized Wagadugu before he could get there, and Mr Henderson has been prevented by the Sofas from remaining in occupation of Wa and Bona.

The situation is, therefore, a difficult one, as we have to deal with the Sofas as well as the French, and it has been made still more complicated by the action of the Germans, who are intriguing against us in the Neutral Zone, and supplying the Sofas with arms and ammunition.

I have learnt with much satisfaction from your telegram of the 31st of May, that Mr Henderson has been released, and is now on his way to the coast with a letter from Samory. It appears to Her Majesty's Government that, while the tribes with which we have made treaties of friendship or protection must be protected against Sofa raids, it would not be advisable to commence military operations against Samory without the strongest cause, and without a very clear perception of the results to which they might lead. An expedition against him would be a very serious undertaking, and it is to be feared that the French would derive more advantage than we should from the sacrifices which such an expedition would entail upon us. You have suggested that the French Government might be invited to join with us in breaking Samory's power, and I am awaiting the remarks which, as stated in your telegram of the 23rd of May, you are sending to me by post, with regard to making representations to them on the subject. I think, however, that joint action would be attended with great difficulties, and, in particular, that it would tie our hands in asserting our claims to Mossi and other countries which the French are endeavouring to secure for themselves. It would certainly lessen our prestige with the natives and our own subjects, who would suppose we were unable, without assistance, to assert our authority. If, therefore, it should ever unfortunately become necessary for us to break the power of Samory, I am of opinion that we shall have to carry out this operation with our own resources. But upon this point I will not express a final opinion until I am in possession of your views.

If, however, as I hope, a satisfactory arrangement can be made with Samory, the most urgent question for you to consider will be the arrangements to be made in view of the recent aggressions of the French and Germans. As regards the latter, I shall address you in a separate despatch, but in respect of the former, I am disposed to think that you should, if your forces are sufficient, immediately occupy all the important places in the Gold Coast hinterland, which can be claimed as properly belonging to Great Britain, and which are not already in the occupation of the French.

It remains to consider what measures can be taken to procure the evacuation of those places which have been occupied by them in violation of the rights which we have acquired by treaties. They have no doubt been encouraged in their action by the belief, based on their experience of the facility with which we have yielded to their demands and abandoned our rights on other similar occasions, that we were not in earnest in urging our claims, and that we should not be willing to incur any expense to make them good by effective occupation; and the best evidence of our determination to adopt a different course, in the present instance, will be the presence of a force superior to theirs. . . .

It is possible that on finding themselves confronted by a superior force, and being made aware that we are determined and prepared to substantiate our claims, the French might withdraw from places which we claim under treaties with native authorities . . . but in case they do not do so, I wish you to consider whether there are any places which it would be practicable for us to seize and hold as a material guarantee for dealing with the French seizures of Mossi and Boussa, when negotiations are resumed with the French Government.

You will, of course, understand that French rights in any place like Bontuku, which has formed the subject of an agreement between the two countries, must be scrupulously respected, but to the north of the 9th parallel, there is nothing to prevent our seizing any place outside the Anglo-German Neutral Zone, which would answer our purpose, with the exception of such places as are included in the agreement which Captain Stewart made with Lieutenant Voulet at Tenkrugu. . . . It is open to you, without offering any explanations, to occupy any places north of the 9th parallel, to the west as well as to the east of the Komoe River, or in the Gurunsi country, or (if you should be strong enough to do so) in Gurma. The chief point to consider is whether the importance of the places to the French is such that they would be induced by our occupying them to relinquish their hold on those which we claim.

You will also, of course, understand that you are not to take the offensive against French troops. The discretionary permission accorded to you in this despatch, to advance to and occupy places claimed by the French as theirs, does not apply to any town or village garrisoned by French regular troops, or in which a French officer is stationed.

To carry out this policy it will be necessary that a strong force should be raised, and I hope that it may be possible to get recruits through the Royal Niger Company, in addition to those whom you may be able to obtain on the spot. The chief difficulty will, I am afraid, be to get the men. I am prepared to apply to the War Office for more officers, as soon as I learn from you that they are required. The question of expense must not be allowed to stand in the way of dealing effectively with the present emergency. It is proposed that the force, although raised in the first instance by the Gold Coast Government, should eventually be employed in occupying the territories claimed as British, not only behind the Gold Coast, but on the Niger, and in that case, Lagos and the Niger Coast Protectorate, and the Royal Niger Company would be called upon to contribute towards the cost of what would be, in effect, a small West African army.

[African (West) No. 529, p. 238]

418 LEGISLATIVE COUNCIL DEBATE
ACCRA, 29 JUNE, 1897.

Mr Bannerman.[1] . . . The Chiefs have a right, an immemorial right, to their lands, and are perfectly justified in giving away their lands to any person they wish. . . . These grants which have been made by native kings and chiefs have always been recognised by the Supreme Court of the Gold Coast Colony. . . . The present Bill really aims at taking away the right which has always been observed as belonging to the native chiefs . . . and though it is the intention . . . of your Excellency and the Legislative Council, to protect, in a certain measure, the lands of the people of the Gold Coast Colony, yet I say, according to native ideas, the taking away, in such a manner, of their lands, will be a violation on the part of the Government of the trust reposed in it by the people. . . . It is stated in your Excellency's message of the 10th March, that the Bill which was introduced in 1894 has been the subject of criticism, and, under the direction of the Secretary of State, has been abandoned. . . . We cannot say that this Ordinance of 1894 is not the same, in form, as the

[1] C. J. Bannerman. He speaks here as counsel for the chiefs.

present Bill. I say this is another way of getting into the room through the window if the doors are closed.

The Governor: . . .

It is alleged that the Bill encroaches upon the rights of chiefs and people, and that it takes away their lands. What it does is this: it distinguishes between public rights and private rights. It recognises the fact that the stool lands of a tribe are really public lands which ought to be administered for the benefit of the people, and it gives, in respect of those lands, concurrent rights to the Governor with the native headmen. I have stated what the powers of the chiefs are, and in all that concerns the dealings of a chief with his own people, in accordance with native custom, this Bill does not interfere with them. The Bill continues to the Chief, power to authorize the occupation by a native of public land, as the site of a habitation, or for permanent agricultural or industrial or trading purposes, or for shifting cultivation. In that respect, therefore, the existing rights of the chief are not prejudiced. For shifting cultivation, which is the primitive kind of cultivation practiced in this Colony, a chief may, in future, as heretofore, allot any portion of the common land of the tribe to any individual or group of his people. In that respect, therefore, his rights are not touched.

When, however, it comes to his dealing with foreigners, and to the making of concessions, then, I admit, this Bill does curtail, not the real rights of the chief, but the rights which he has usurped. Accordingly, it is laid down, in section 10 of the Bill, that in future 'it shall be unlawful for any native chief or other native authority to create by any instrument in writing, or by any other method, any private right in public land, without the previous consent thereto in writing by the Governor.' This is the chief respect in which a right claimed by a native chief, or a power at present exercised by him, is curtailed.

Now let us consider what I have called 'inferior rights'.

In future, as in the past, any native with the customary right to do so, may take up what land he requires for 'shifting cultivation' . . . [&c]: but it is laid down that a man does not, simply by resorting to a piece of land for 'shifting cultivation', acquire any title in that piece of land, or any interest therein beyond the ownership of the crops which he plants. It would be monstrous if it were laid down by law, that because a man plants a crop of yams or cassava on a piece of public land and then abandons it, he may, nevertheless, at any time, return and lay claim to it, and may stand by, in the 'dog in the manger' attitude, and say that nobody is henceforward to take any crop off it, because he once did so. . . . In Section 18, it is laid down that land which has been taken up for residence or for cultivation, or for industrial purposes, and is then abandoned for three consecutive years, ceases to belong to the person who occupied it, and becomes again public land. . . . The Bill says 'three years': Mr Sarbah says 'ten years', and if three years seems to be a short term, I take it that the Council will consider the advisability of modifying that section in this respect. . . .

The learned Counsel who has addressed the Council today has commented upon Section 20, where it is laid down that 'the transfer of a settler's right by a native to any person other than a native, shall be subject to the approval of the Governor, or the person to whom he may . . . delegate his power of approval.' This provision is for the protection of the natives themselves. I want to give to the natives of this country the right of proprietorship, which, in many cases, especially as regards people who have had, or whose forefathers have had, the status of slaves, they have not got. I should like to see every man with a proprietary tenure and in a position where he will be safe from any oppression on the part of any native authority: but, on the other hand, I do not think that he ought to be in a position to part with his right of occupancy to a foreigner. Let him part

with it to a native by all means, but not to a foreigner, without the permission of the Government. We must not do anything which would lead to collusion between natives with customary rights and foreigners without any. Otherwise, land might be temporarily taken up by natives simply in order to have something to sell to a white man. . . .

The learned counsel have used the word 'immemorial' a great many times: but have they really studied the history of their country? . . . [Reindorf's History] leaves upon the mind the impression of a number of tribes, more or less migratory, which have really only settled down in a quiet way and have abandoned war and tumult under the influence of European Governments. . . .

I claim that the right of the Paramount Power established here is to exercise any and every right which may be exercised by any chief. I claim as the Governor of this Colony, and as the representative of Her Majesty, to have in this Colony, any and every power which may be lawfully exercised by native custom by any chief; and, further, I consider that there is an obligation upon this Government . . . to see that native chiefs do not abuse their position, and exceed their powers, by encroaching upon the rights of those for whom they are really trustees, and by dealing illegally and improvidently with stool lands, which are, in other words, the public lands of the tribe.

If chiefs find themselves inconvenienced because they are no longer allowed to do what they have been doing, and to continue to create, irregularly, all kinds of vague claims, all over the country — claims which will cause infinite trouble and expense before they can be examined — they have only themselves to blame. They have been led away by offers which may have seemed to them at the time to be tempting . . . and they have committed acts which are really illegal. If objection is taken to the position which I claim on behalf of the Government, that the Governor has, as the representative of Her Majesty, a concurrent right with any chief to create rights in public lands (to be evidenced in future by Land Certificates), that objection is one which I cannot entertain. I believe the principle to be thoroughly sound, and I am sure that the Legislative Council will do wisely in accepting it. . . .

[Gold Coast Government Gazette, 13 August, 1897]

419 THE MARQUIS OF SALISBURY TO SIR E. MONSON[1]

FOREIGN OFFICE, 4 SEPTEMBER, 1897.

. . . What are the facts? In Bona, in Dagarti and Daboya, in Mamprusi and Mossi, in Gurma and in Borgu or Boussa, British agents concluded treaties . . . of unquestionable prior date to any obtained on behalf of France, giving to Great Britain certain rights over these territories, and binding the chiefs with whom they were contracted, to abstain from making treaties with other foreign Powers, without her consent. These treaties were communicated to the French Government. They have not been renounced by Great Britain, and she retains the right to enforce their observance.

The Agreement signed by Baron de Courcel and myself on the 15th January 1896, contained an Article in the following terms:—

'The two Governments agree to name Commissioners delegated by each of them, who shall be charged to fix by mutual agreement, after examination of the titles produced on either side, the most equitable delimitation between the British and French possessions in the region situated to the west of the lower Niger.'

The Commissioners met in February of the same year, and proceeded to discuss in great detail the titles produced on either side. The discussions continued till the month of May, when the French Com-

missioners put forward a proposal that a line starting from the eastern frontier of Dahomey at its intersection with the 8th degree of north latitude, should follow that parallel eastward to the Niger, and thence ascend that river to Say, the right bank falling to France and the left to Great Britain.

As I stated in my despatch to the Marquess of Dufferin, No. 139 Africa of the 12th May 1896, this line would have deprived Great Britain of the whole of her sphere of influence to the west of the Niger north of the 9th parallel. It substituted absolute surrender by one party, in place of an amicable arrangement between the two Powers. It could not be discussed by Commissioners, and could only be treated direct between the two Governments. These views were communicated to the French Government, and at the meeting of the 23rd May, the French Commissioners made [a] further proposal [which] . . . differed only in degree from that of the 8th May. The British Commissioners were unable to accept it, and the meeting adjourned in order that the French Commissioners might receive fresh instructions. The Commission has not since reassembled, although Her Majesty's Government have more than once expressed their readiness to renew the meetings.

The French Government have, however, sent expeditions into the very territories covered by the British treaties, and their officers, arrogating to themselves the right to settle these disputed points in their own favour, have forced or persuaded the chiefs into denials and repudiations, have concluded other treaties with them, and have been supported by their Government in attempting to establish French supremacy. France now claims as hers by occupation nearly all the territories under discussion. . . .

The Government of the Republic cannot however, fail to realize the lengths to which the theory of occupation against prior treaty rights, now advanced on their behalf, may lead in Africa. At the Conference of

[1] Sir Edward Monson (1834–1909); entered the Diplomatic Service, 1856; British Ambassador in Paris, 1896–1904.

Berlin, Her Majesty's Ambassador proposed that the principle of effective occupation, established for the coast-line of Africa, should be extended to the interior of Africa: but Baron de Courcel, on behalf of the French Government, resisted the proposal, and it fell to the ground.

The system of spheres of influence has since been applied with success. It is evident that, in the present state of communications with the interior of Africa, effective occupation is extremely difficult to maintain, and that there must be many districts adjacent to European posts which are by no means effectively occupied. It is unnecessary to point out the state of political chaos which must ensue, if every European Power considers itself at liberty to plant military or civil posts within such districts, in entire disregard of the rights of neighbouring Powers; but that result will inevitably follow in disputed territories, if the theory of effective occupation is pushed to extremes.

Her Majesty's Government have already, though with great reluctance, found themselves compelled, in consequence of the adoption of this theory by France, to push forward in the rear of the Gold Coast, and to occupy certain posts in order to save the Colony from the consequences of the French advance. The protests with which their actions have been met by the French Government appear to show that the latter only apply the theory of occupation to the French advance, and that, while British treaties are held to be invalid against subsequent French occupation, French treaties of whatever date are to debar Great Britain from any forward movement.

In the opinion of Her Majesty's Government, the intentions of the Powers assembled at the Conference of Berlin and Brussels, and their efforts for the welfare of the African races, can only be fulfilled if the Powers territorially interested in that continent agree to work in separate spheres for the common end, arranging those spheres by mutual concession. A contrary policy, involving as it must, rival

military expeditions, can only ruin commerce and create confusion and distrust among the natives; whilst, however anxious the Governments may be to localise the complications which must ensue, they may find it impossible to avoid their reacting on the higher interests of European policy.

[C.P. African (West) No. 538, p. 17]

420 MAXWELL TO CHAMBERLAIN
BONTUKU CAMP, 13 OCTOBER, 1897.

Confidential.

. . . It is perfectly clear that any peaceful understanding between the British Government and Samory would be intensely distasteful to the Gamans, and there can be little doubt that this feeling would be universal among the tribes of the Hinterland. . . . Samory is now feared as much as, or more, than any king of Ashanti ever was, and the tribes in the Hinterland will give their adherence and allegiance to the Power which saves them from him. If the idea should become general that we are the friends of Samory, while the French are ready to attack and punish him, the result is likely to be unfavourable to our prestige and influence.

Her Majesty's Government have laid down that the tribes with which we have made treaties of friendship or protection must be protected against Sofa raids, and I am only waiting for the . . . reply of Samory to my demand for the evacuation of Bona, before moving to the vicinity of that town, the force now concentrated at Bontuku. Should the reply of Samory be unsatisfactory or evasive (which is not improbable), I shall not refuse to allow the Gamans to raise an armed native contingent, to accompany the Colonial force; though I shall not, of course, demand native levies in French territory. If, on the other hand, Samory withdraws his troops from Bona, in accordance with my demand, and undertakes to respect our frontier, it will be possible to give the tribes with which we have treaties, all the protection to which they are entitled, without actual hostilities with the Sofas.

[African (West) No. 538, p. 355]

421 CHAMBERLAIN TO MAXWELL
15 OCTOBER, 1897.

Confidential.

Sir,

I have the honour to inform you, with reference to my telegram of the 24th of September, that it has been decided that the title of the appointment which Major H. P. Northcott has been selected to fill, should be that of 'Commissioner and Commandant in the Northern Territories of the Gold Coast,' and I have to request that you will appoint him formally to that office, in the usual manner. He will have the rank of Lieut.-colonel while holding the appointment.

As Her Majesty's Government have agreed to resume negotiations with the French Government, you should not attempt to occupy any places except those which are in the Hinterland of British possessions and are claimed as British under treaties prior in date to any French treaties; but in other respects, the instructions contained in my confidential despatch of the 4th of June remain in force.

You should therefore inform Major Northcott that he may occupy any places in Mossi or Gurunsi, or elsewhere, which are in the direct 'Hinterland' of the Gold Coast, which we claim under treaties, and which are not occupied by the French when he reaches them. He must be positively instructed, on no account and under no circumstances, to initiate a conflict with the French. I do not think it possible that the French will attack him or any detachment of British troops, but if they should unfortunately take the aggressive, he will, of course, defend himself, and act afterwards as circumstances may dictate; *but the French must clearly be the aggressors*, and he will take care immediately to report all the circumstances, with the greatest fulness, in order that representations may at once be made to the French Government.

The people of Mossi have suffered much at the hands of the French, and the King has sought the protection of the British forces. I approve of a proposal which Major Northcott has made, that he should endeavour to get the King to accompany him and use his influence in solving the question of transport and native supply, as well as that of a remount establishment. The people of Mossi would also be invaluable in collecting information as to the whereabouts of the French, and would be of some use as auxiliaries to the expedition.

If he meets with French officers, and they complain of his having advanced into Mossi, or any of the territories which he has been authorized to occupy, he should reply that he is where he is under instructions from Her Majesty's Government, and in virtue of treaties with the native authorities, and that their complaints should be made through the French Government to Her Majesty's Government in England, but that he will report their complaints to the Governor of the Gold Coast, for the information of Her Majesty's Government.

He should bear in mind the necessity of keeping on good terms with all chiefs, including (if possible) Samory. With reference to Samory, he should receive instructions on the lines laid down in my despatch of the 4th of June, subject to any modifications which your communications with that chief may render necessary. He should also be given, if possible, precise instructions as to the boundary east of which Samory's followers are to be treated as enemies. . . .

[African (West) No. 538, p. 130]

422 TREATY WITH NADAWLE
11 JANUARY, 1898.

. . . .

Article 1

The King, Chiefs and Principal Headmen of Nadawle, having declared that they have not made any treaty with any other Power, do hereby voluntarily place their country under the protection of Great Britain.

Article 2

Her Majesty's subject, Lieutenant-Colonel Northcott, for and on behalf of Her Most Gracious Majesty Victoria, Queen of Great Britain and Ireland, Empress of India, &c, &c, hereby takes the country of Nadawle under the protection of Great Britain.

Article 3

In consideration of the protection guaranteed by Great Britain, the King, Chiefs, and Principal Headmen of Nadawle undertake to keep their main roads in good order, to encourage trade, and to give facilities to traders being British subjects; and not to cede their territory to, or enter into any agreement, arrangement, or treaty with any foreign Power, except through and with the consent of the Government of Her Majesty the Queen Empress.

Article 4

The King, Chiefs and Principal Headmen of Nadawle agree to refer any dispute that may arise between themselves and any chief bordering on their country, or amongst themselves, to such officer as the Commissioner and Commandant, Northern Territories, Gold Coast, shall, from time to time appoint, and to accept his decision as final and binding.

Article 5

[As in Article VIII of No. 404 above.] . . .
[African (West) No. 1010.]

423 CONVENTION BETWEEN THE UNITED KINGDOM AND FRANCE FOR THE DELIMITATION OF THEIR RESPECTIVE POSSESSIONS TO THE WEST OF THE NIGER, AND OF THEIR RESPECTIVE POSSESSIONS AND SPHERES OF INFLUENCE TO THE EAST OF THAT RIVER
SIGNED AT PARIS, 14 JUNE, 1898. . . .

Article I. The frontier separating the British colony of the Gold Coast from the French colonies of the Ivory Coast and Sudan, shall start from the northern terminal point of the frontier laid down in the Anglo-French Agreement of the 12th July 1893, viz., the intersection of the Black Volta with the 9th degree of north latitude, and shall follow the thalweg of this river northward up to its intersection with the 11th degree of north latitude. From this point it shall follow this parallel of latitude as far as the river shown on Map No. 1 annexed to the present Protocol, as passing immediately to the east of the villages of Zwaga (Souaga) and Zebilla (Sebilla), and it shall then follow the thalweg of the western branch of this river, up stream to its intersection with the parallel of latitude passing through the village of Sapeliga. From this point, the frontier shall follow the northern limits of the lands belonging to Sapeliga, as far as the river Nuhau (Nouhau), and shall then follow the thalweg of this river, up or down stream, as the case may be, to a point situated 2 miles (3,219 metres) eastward of the road which leads from Gambaga to Tenkrugu (Tingourkou), via Bawku (Baukou). Thence it shall rejoin by a straight line the 11th degree of north latitude, at the intersection of this parallel with the road which is shown on Map No. 1 as leading from Sansanne-Mango to Pama via Jabigu (Djabiga). . . .

Article IX. Within the limits defined on Map No. 2 which is annexed to the present Protocol, British subjects and British protected persons, and French citizens and French protected persons, as far as regards their persons and goods, and the merchandize, the produce or the manufacture of Great Britain and France, their respective colonies, possessions and protectorates, shall enjoy, for thirty years from the date of the exchange of the ratifications of the Convention . . . the same treatment in all matters of river navigation, of commerce, and of tariff and fiscal treatment and taxes of all kinds.

Subject to this condition, each of the two Contracting Powers shall be free to fix, in its own territory, and as may appear to it most convenient, the tariff and fiscal treatment and taxes of all kinds.

In case neither of the two Contracting Powers shall have notified, twelve months before the expiration of the above-mentioned term of thirty years, its intention to put an end to the effects of the present Article, it shall remain in force until the expiration of one year from the day on which either of the Contracting Powers shall have denounced it. . . .

(Signed) Martin Gosselin
William Everett
Rene Lecomte
G. Binger.
[C.9334, A & P (1899) cix]

424 COLONIAL OFFICE TO FOREIGN OFFICE
2 NOVEMBER, 1899.

Secret.

. . . With regard to the Neutral Zone and the territories to the north of the Zone, I am to state that Mr Chamberlain agrees to the proposal that the Daka river should be the boundary, from its confluence with the Volta to the point of its intersection with the 9th parallel of latitude; and I am to submit that, as in the case of the Volta, the boundary should be drawn along the left bank of the Daka.

It is proposed by the German Government, that, from the 9th parallel, the boundary should be continued in a straight line to the north, but Mr Chamberlain is unable to agree to this proposal, as such a line would pass through Mamprusi . . . and would give a portion of the territory of Mamprusi to Germany. Mr Chamberlain would propose that the boundary should follow the eastern arm of the Daka up to its source, and that it should then be drawn in the direction of Morozugu; or, if the German Government would prefer it, he would be willing to agree the boundary should be drawn in the direction of

Morozugu[1] from the 9th parallel, and he understands that the German Government would be prepared to agree to such a modification of their proposal. In either case, it should be stipulated that, although the general direction of the boundary would be straight from one or other of the points mentioned to Morozugu, which should in any case be British, it should be delimited on the ground so as to follow, as far as possible, natural physical features, or well-known tracks, until it reaches the southern limit of Mamprusi and Chakosi (of which country Sansanne Mango is the chief town), and that it should then be drawn so as to leave the whole of Mamprusi to Great Britain and the whole of Chakosi to Germany, in accordance with the provisional arrangement recently made by the representatives of the two countries on the spot.

It will be seen that the boundary proposed, whether it is drawn as suggested by the German Government, or as suggested in this letter, will divide the Dagomba country into two parts, of which the western portion would be British, while the eastern one (including the chief town, Yendi) would be German. As the German Government use the expression 'territory of Yendi', it is, in Mr Chamberlain's opinion, of great importance that there should be no misunderstanding on this point. Lord Salisbury will recollect that the arrangement of 1887–8 under which the Neutral Zone was established, gave rise to a dispute between the British and German Governments as to the meaning of the expression 'the countries of Aquamoo and Creppe (or Pekki),' which was only settled by Her Majesty's Government consenting

[1] The identity and location of Morozugu was uncertain at this time. It had been indicated as an important position by Ferguson, who however did not visit it. When the frontier came to be delimited in 1903, Morozugu (or Mossiegu) was discovered to be a settlement of 60 huts, rather less than half-way along the track from Gambaga to Sansanne-Mango, and of no economic or strategic value. The attempt to maintain its connection with British territory to the west, by a strip of land 17 kilometres long and 2 wide, was thereupon abandoned.

to relinquish a much larger extent of country than they had contemplated when the arrangement was agreed to, and I am therefore to express Mr Chamberlain's hope that the vague and incorrect term 'territory of Yendi' will not be used in the arrangement now about to be made. . . .

[C.P. African (West) No. 631, p. 31]

425 Convention between Great Britain and Germany for the settlement of the Samoan and other questions Signed at London, 14 November, 1899.

· · · · ·

Article 5

In the neutral zone, the frontier between the German and English territories shall be formed by the River Daka as far as the point of its intersection with the 9th degree of north latitude; thence the frontier shall continue to the north, leaving Morozugu to Great Britain and shall be fixed on the spot by a Mixed Commission of the two Powers, in such a manner that Gambaga and all the territories of Mamprusi shall fall to Great Britain, and that Yendi and all the territories of Chakosi shall fall to Germany.

Article 6

Germany is prepared to take into consideration, as much and as far as possible, the wishes which the Government of Great Britain may express with regard to the development of the reciprocal Tariffs in the territories of Togo and of the Gold Coast. . . .

[African (West) No. 631, p. 34]

426 J. Chamberlain to Sir F. M. Hodgson   22 December, 1899.

Sir,

When you were last in this country, advantage was taken of your presence to discuss with you the subject of the legislation required for regulating concessions of rights relating to land by natives of the Gold Coast.

I have now the honour to transmit to you the draft of an Ordinance which is the outcome of these discussions.

As the basis of this draft is materially different from that of the Lands Bill which was under consideration during the administration of Sir William Maxwell, I do not think it necessary to refer to that Bill, beyond observing that, in considering this question, I have had regard to the representations made by the Deputation which came to this country in 1898. While I consider it absolutely necessary for the Colonial Government to supervise grants of land, so as to protect all parties against fraud or misrepresentation, to secure to them the rights given or reserved, to guard against results prejudicial to the public interests, and to obtain for the Government a reasonable income from profitable operations; at the same time I do not wish to make any 'fundamental alteration in the rights of the natives', such as was apprehended by the Deputation. The draft accordingly does not purport to confer on any Government authority the right of claiming or making grants of any land whatsoever, which is owned by natives of the Gold Coast, and the idea of vesting any unoccupied land in the Governor, as public land, has been abandoned. The native owner is left free, as now, to make his own bargain, if he wishes to sell to a European; and the benefit of his bargain is not interfered with, but, on the contrary, more effectually secured to him, by the conditions which the Bill imposes on the grantee. I should be glad if you would take an opportunity of explaining this character of the Bill.

The draft provides for the establishment of a Concessions Court in the Colony, to which every concession granted by a native will have to be notified, together with particulars of the concession and the documents on which the claimant relies in support of his claim. The Court will have power to certify the concession to be valid or invalid, except that any concession dated before the 10th of October 1895, duly registered and undisputed, would be certified as of course to be valid, if the Court be satisfied that the rights granted under such concession have been in fact exercised, and that the natives resident in the locality have known of, and acquiesced in, the exercise of such rights.

The Ordinance provides that the term of a concession is not to exceed 99 years, nor that of a prospecting licence, three years.

The Ordinance restricts the area of single concessions to 5 square miles, in the case of mining rights, and 20 square miles in the case of rights to take timber, or rubber, or other products of the soil. No one person or corporation is to be allowed to hold, at one time, concessions the aggregate area of which exceeds 20 square miles, in the case of mining rights, or 40 square miles in the case of rights relating to timber, rubber, or other products of the soil. The provisions of this and the preceding paragraphs, do not, however, apply to any concession dated before the 10th of October 1895.

The Ordinance provides for the levying of a tax of 5 per cent on all profits made by the holder of a concession from the date on which the Ordinance comes into force. Prospecting licences are to be subject to a stamp duty of £1 per square mile. . . . [He discusses certain criticisms made by various commercial bodies in England to the draft.]   [C.O.96/346]

31 The Ashanti Rising and the Orders in Council, 1900–1901

WITH international complications out of the way, it was time to consider the future administration of Ashanti and the north (428). Inevitably, this involved steps for raising a revenue to defray the cost of government, and Sir Frederick Hodgson was authorised to announce the Government's proposals, early in 1900 (427). His visit to Kumasi in March was the signal for an armed rising by several of the Ashanti tribes. A message which was bound to be unpalatable to the Ashantis was not improved by the Governor's presentation of it, or by his ill-conceived attempt to seize the Golden Stool (430). While this touched off the rising (429), what the insurgents really wanted was the restoration of Ashanti independence (431). Fundamentally, the revolt was against any form of British rule (434), and would have taken place more logically in 1896 when that rule was first imposed. This was the theme developed by Chamberlain in the House of Commons, when he defended his Ashanti policy and even the Governor's indiscretions, which had to some extent been condoned in anticipation by his own despatches (433).

Once the protracted resistance of the insurgents had been broken (432) it was, therefore, the Government's aim, while eschewing vindictive retaliatory measures (435), to put its position as Paramount Power beyond all doubt. This was the object of the Orders in Council, which annexed to the British dominions Ashanti (436) and the former Protected Territories on the Gold Coast (438), and empowered the Governor of the Gold Coast to administer and legislate for the Northern Territories Protectorate (437).

427 CHAMBERLAIN TO HODGSON

19 FEBRUARY, 1900.

Confidential.

Sir,

I have the honour to acknowledge the receipt of Mr Low's[1] Confidential despatch of the 6th of January 1899 and of your Confidential despatch of the 12th of September, relating to the question of raising a revenue from the people of Ashanti.

Captain Stewart proposes, in his letter of the 28th of November 1898, that a revenue of £12,500 a year should be raised by means of a direct tax, which would amount to about 4/- a head of the male population, and that it should be collected

[1] W. Low, Colonial Secretary, Gold Coast, 3 August, 1898–20 November, 1901.

by the kings and chiefs of the various Ashanti tribes, on the understanding that they are to receive 10% of the collections. He proposes that it should not be called a tax or tribute, but interest on the debt incurred for the war of 1874 and the expedition of 1896, and he states that the Ashantis will understand this as a perfectly just and legitimate debt.

I observe that you concur in these proposals, and that you also agree with Captain Stewart in thinking that the collection of this revenue is not likely to cause any serious trouble.

In these circumstances, I approve of these proposals and of your visiting Coomassie in accordance with your suggestion, as soon as you can conveniently do so, and explaining to the kings and chiefs what is required, leaving the actual work of collection to be commenced when Captain Stewart returns from leave of absence.

I have etc.   [C.O.96/343]

428 CHAMBERLAIN TO HODGSON
19 FEBRUARY, 1900.

Confidential.

. . . The questions which have now to be determined are what form of administration should be established in Ashanti and the Northern Territories; whether they should be treated in the same way or differently, and how Quahoo (and ? Sefwi and Attabubu) should be treated. With regard to the 'Protected Territories', that is to say, the territories south of Ashanti, I am inclined to think that, although the existing system is not altogether satisfactory, no change is required, as provision has already been made for the exercise of Her Majesty's jurisdiction in them, and they do not appear to have yet reached the stage at which they could properly be annexed to the Colony.

With regard to Ashanti, I have had the advantage of considering the views expressed both by you and by Sir William Maxwell. I understand that you recommend that the position of Ashanti should be assimilated to that of the Protected Territories to the south of it, and in particular, that you see no objection to requiring the people of Ashanti to bring their cases to the Courts of the Colony. Sir William Maxwell, however, pointed out, in his despatch of the 28th of January 1896, that the unrestrained exercise of the jurisdiction of the Supreme Court has its inconveniences, and that it was undesirable that the local chiefs and their people should be placed at the mercy of the traders from the coast towns who, in case of trade disputes, would threaten to have them brought down to the coast by a summons from the Supreme Court. He expressed the opinion that, for some time to come, the Resident could be trusted to administer justice on ordinary principles of equity and common sense, and

proposed that, for the present, the jurisdiction of the Supreme Court should be limited or taken away altogether in all places north of the Prah. It might, he observed, be enacted that actions should be brought and prosecutions instituted, in matters arising in those places, only with the leave of the Governor first obtained.

I have come to the conclusion that it would not be advisable to extend to Ashanti the system in force in the Protected Territories, but that it would be preferable that the Resident should be entrusted with judicial as well as executive functions, and that the Governor of the Gold Coast should have power to legislate by proclamation for Ashanti. I should, however, be prepared to approve of its being provided that certain cases or classes of cases might, with the concurrence of the Governor, be referred by the Resident to the Supreme Court of the Colony for trial. It will certainly be necessary that the provisions of the Concessions Ordinance should be applied to Ashanti, and for the purposes of this Ordinance, the judges of the Supreme Court, who constitute the Concessions Court, must have jurisdiction there.

I propose, therefore, that an Order in Council, similar to the Northern Nigeria Order in Council, 1899, (a copy of which is enclosed) should be passed to provide for the exercise of Her Majesty's jurisdiction in Ashanti, but the Order, in place of providing for the appointment of a High Commissioner, as in Northern Nigeria, will provide that all Her Majesty's powers in Ashanti shall be exercised by the Governor of the Gold Coast; and the first duty of the Governor, after the passing of the Order, will be to issue a legislative proclamation, providing for the administration of justice, and defining the powers of native authorities and British officers. I enclose, for your assistance in drafting such a proclamation, copies of the Gambia and Sierra Leone Protectorate Ordinances: but you will, of course, understand that these laws are only sent to you in order to indicate, in a general way, what subjects you should deal with in the Ashanti Protectorate Proclamation.

I have to request that, unless you desire first to consult me further on any points, you will have the draft of an Ashanti Protectorate Proclamation prepared and submitted to me, and that you will also furnish me with a description of the boundaries of the Ashanti Protectorate, for insertion in the Order in Council. You should also consider and report to me, your opinion upon the question whether Quahoo, Attabubu, Sefwi, and any other territories adjacent to Ashanti, should be included in the new Protectorate of Ashanti, or in the old Gold Coast Protectorate.

With regard to the Northern Territories, I have decided not to proceed with the scheme for appointing an administrator, but that they should be constituted merely as a division or province, like Ashanti, of the Gold Coast Protectorate under a Commissioner or Resident. I am disposed to think, subject to any observations which you may have to make upon the subject, that it would not be practicable for the Resident of Ashanti to take charge also of the Northern Territories, and that it is therefore necessary to form these territories into a separate division. It appears to me also, that, in some respects, the form of administration should be different. The administration of the Northern Territories should, for the present, be conducted upon the lines sketched out by Colonel North-cott, in his despatch of the 31st of July 1898. I agree with him in the opinion that, in the present condition of the country, the application of a rigid and minute system of administration would be impolitic, even if it were practicable. The agency of the native chiefs should be employed to a greater extent than in the districts nearer the coast, and their power should, during good behaviour, be uniformly supported, except in respect of intertribal relations, and offences of a capital nature, which should be reserved for decision by a British officer.

Speaking broadly, the functions of the Resident or Commissioner in the Northern Territories, will for some time to come be largely of a semi-military character, while the Resident in Ashanti will be occupied with questions connected with the development of the gold-mining industry. I think, however, that their legal powers should be similar, and the Order in Council which will be required to provide for the exercise of jurisdiction in the Northern Territories, should be in the same terms as the Ashanti Order: but the Protectorate Proclamations in the two divisions must be different, and I should be glad to receive a draft, or at least an outline of the Proclamation which you would propose to enact in the Northern Territories. . . .   [C.O.96/349]

429 TELEGRAM RECEIVED FROM GOVERNOR OF GOLD COAST. . . .   7 APRIL, 1900.

Telegram begins:—

Arrived Kumasi 26 March. All native chiefs were present. *Held meeting of native chiefs 28 March when I explained arrangements approved in your Confidential despatch of 19 February and pointed out the Queen is paramount power and they must not look out for return of Prempeh. Presents were distributed to native chiefs.* On 31st March from information received, sent detachment under Inspectors Armitage Legget make an attempt to obtain Golden Stool. Quest failed. In the meantime Kumassis *discontented at proposed annual payment &* having obtained knowledge of quest, organised opposition. It was too late recall detachment cancel instructions, and letter of advice sent to Armitage failed to reach. Regret to report occurrence of collision of forces. One Constabulary killed, one missing, two dangerously wounded, nineteen slightly wounded including Armitage and Legget. . . .

At present native chiefs express loyalty to British Government and decline to join Kumassis. Have ordered Commissioner and Commandant Northern Territories send 1 Company for purpose of increase of garrison here and have ordered 1 Company from Accra. Hope to effect peaceful settlement and obtain all ringleaders. Active operations not necessary for the present. *In any case could not be carried out till after rainy season ended September.* Will stay here pending settlement which doing all in power to arrive at. Hopeful of satisfactory result. Will report result by telegraph. Telegraph interrupted between here and Accra. Hodgson.

Telegram ends.

[C.O.96/359.]

[Passages in italics omitted from Press release]

430 HODGSON TO CHAMBERLAIN

KUMASSI, 7 APRIL, 1900.

Confidential.

[After describing his arrival at Kumasi on the 26th March:] . . .

The kings and chiefs had been summoned to meet me at 4 p.m. on Wednesday [28 March]. I transmit a copy of the shorthand writer's notes of my remarks to them. In addition to making an announcement to them as regards the payment of interest upon the sum due to the British Government under the Treaty of Fomena and the expenses incurred in connection with the expedition of 1895-6, I had decided — as I was well aware that the Kumassis, and their immediate adherents, the Ejisus and Ofinsus, were nursing the idea that Prempeh would sooner or later be restored to rule over them, while others thought the return of Atcheri-boanda was only a question of time — to tell them definitely and decisively that they were not to expect either one or the other, and that the Queen is now the paramount power in Ashanti. Although I felt sure that this announcement would not be a palatable one to many, it appeared to me to be necessary to make it, having regard to the large number of Gold Mining Concessions which are being obtained and also worked in Ashanti, and so that there might be no misapprehension in the minds of the kings and chiefs, as to the position which the Government holds towards them.

I referred also to the Golden Stool which I now feel certain exists, and which is in the custody of the Kumassis. It is, I consider, much to be regretted that when the troops occupied Kumassi in force, the Kumassis were not made to produce the stool. It forms a rallying point for malcontents against the Government, and I am certain that until the Government possesses this symbol of power, which is regarded by all Ashantis with the utmost veneration, it will not be wholly secure against intrigues and trouble. It is the possession of the Stool which enables the Kumassis to maintain a spirit of defiance, which is only kept in subjection by the presence of an armed force and the armament of the fort.

There is no doubt whatever, and now that I have seen matters for myself and come into immediate contact with the kings and chiefs I can speak with knowledge, that the force now garrisoning Kumassi is wholly insufficient, and dangerously so. It consists of a company and a half of Houssas, nominally 225 Privates, but the Companies are not at their full strength, and some of the men are on detachment duty in Attabubu and British Gaman. The result is that not more than 130 Privates are actually available for garrison work. The fort must always be manned, and, this being so, there is no available force of sufficient over-awing strength to send through the country, if a demonstration in force at any place should be required. In fact, the Ashantis are not over-awed, as they ought to be and must be. . . .

I was informed on the 4th instant, by the king of Mampon, that the notification as to the payment of interest was most distasteful, and had been received with intense dissatisfaction. It appears that after the Public Meeting on the 28th instant, he and the kings of Juabin, Kumawu and others suggested a meeting among themselves to discuss the situation, but the Kumassis declined to attend, and stated that as they now knew that Prempeh would not be restored to them, they were not going to discuss the question of payment, but would at once arm themselves and set themselves in opposition to the British Government. They were, I have since discovered, joined by the Ejisus and Ofinsus, and had also persuaded the Kokofus to act with them, by promising King Asibi, who it appears is the nearest blood relative to Prempeh, that he should be placed on the Golden Stool.

I come now to the occurrences which gave rise to a collision between a detachment of Hausas on the one hand, and the Kumassis, Ejisus and Ofinsus on the other, in the bush villages of Atchima, with the serious and very regrettable result reported in my telegram. In December last, an Ashanti lad came down to Accra to report to the Government that he had been sent by his father, Kwasi Ta, one of the guardians of the Golden Stool, to reveal the Stool to the Government, and to give it up with such treasure as is buried with it, if the Government would ensure the lives of the guardians and reward them handsomely. He said that they had been guarding the Stool in the bush for four years and were tired of the work. Upon consideration, I determined to make an effort to get the Stool, and sent my private secretary, Captain Armitage, by a circuitous route, to the spot. He failed. . . .

I brought the lad with me to Kumassi disguised as a Hausa. It appeared to me desirable, if the Acting Resident were of the same opinion, that the Atchima villages of Bali and Nkwanta should be visited from Kumassi in force, in order to let the people there see that the Government had its eye upon them, and would not tolerate their becoming a menace to the peace of Ashanti by arming themselves and collecting munitions of war in large quantities. I thought that it might be possible, if the village were visited, to give the lad another chance of revealing the hiding place of the Golden Stool. . . . [The expedition miscarried and came into collision with the Kumassis and Ejisus who had meantime assembled at Atchiassi near Nkwanta.]

What should be done, of course, is to send a punitive force against the Kumassis and their allies, surround them in their bush villages, break up their strength, and read a lesson to the Ashanti tribes generally. It is very bitter to me to be unable to adopt this course on account of the weakness of the garrison here. . . . I have had no alternative but to fall back on diplomacy and use the kings of Mampon, Juabin, and Kumawu, as well as the king of Aguna, who has joined them, to bring the matter to an end. . . . The king of Mampon . . . asked me to annul the announcement as regards the annual payments to be made by them, and then stated that he and the other kings were prepared to assist the Government against the Kumassis. I informed them, in reply, that I would take care that the representation they had made with respect to the annual payments should be brought to your notice, and at the same time, their loyalty to the Queen, and that I should not order the collection of the interest until after I had received your further instructions. . . .

The kings say that the Kumassis and their allies will, under their orders, disperse, but I consider it very doubtful if the chiefs will come in. They must come sooner or later, voluntarily or compulsorily. I am rather hoping that they may not come in voluntarily, as the Government can then, when it has a sufficiently strong force at hand, have an excellent reason for dealing with the Kumassis once and for all, and reading them a lesson. This is essential in the interests of Ashanti generally. . . .

The discontent of the Kumassis and of their adherents, the Ejisus and Ofinsus, is not a sudden creation. It has, I find, existed from the first, and has only been kept in check by the fort and garrison, and by their firm belief in the return of Prempeh at no distant date. I am strengthened in my view by remarks made to me by Captain Davidson-Houston[1] who tells me that rumours of threatened risings were heard of in April 1896, when Captain

[1] Acting Resident of Ashanti.

Larymore C.M.G. reported that the Achimas were disaffected; that again in June–July 1897 similar reports were bruited; that in December 1898 the kings of Bekwai and Mampong informed Captain Stewart that the Kumassis talked of taking up arms against us, and, further, that in November last (1899) the rumours seemed so authentic that he called all the Kumassi and Achima chiefs to Kumassi and made them all swear oaths of loyalty to the British Government through the Native Committee. This latter affair was not, I regret, reported to me. . . .

[Cd. 501, A & P (1901) xlviii]

431 HODGSON TO CHAMBERLAIN
THE FORT, KUMASI, 16 APRIL, 1900.
Confidential.

. . . On the 14th April, the kings of Mampon, Juabin and Kumawu asked specially to be allowed to go to Dentasu, a place just outside Kumassi and where, from time immemorial, meetings have been held, to hear what the rebel chiefs had to say — the latter having asked them to come. I consented. On Sunday evening, the 15th instant, they reported that they had just returned from a meeting at which most of the rebel chiefs were present. The king of Mampon, acting as spokesman, said that the rebel chiefs and their people were divided into two parties. One, headed by Osei Kanyassi,[1] was desirous of laying down their arms and returning to their allegiance, if they could be pardoned. The other and larger party had determined to fight, unless the Governor complied with the following conditions which they had been requested to state:—

1. Prempeh to be given back, and to regulate and collect any annual payment to be made.
2. Permission to buy and sell slaves as in the old time.
3. To be free from demands for carriers.

[1] i.e. chief of Kanyase (Ahafo). Probably Osei Kojo Krum.

4. To be freed from the obligation of building houses and supplying thatch.
5. All huxters and strangers to be sent away.

I told the king of Mampon that I was surprised that he had dared to bring such a message to the Governor. . . . I said to the three kings, that if any of the rebel chiefs wanted to come in, they would have to treat with me and agree to terms which I would name. That as regards the terms proposed, they were, on the face of them, absurd. Prempeh, I had stated at the meeting held on the 28th March, would never come back to rule over Ashanti, and that statement was a correct one and would not be changed. That as regards the buying and selling of slaves, black men might regard themselves as no better than cattle, to be bought and sold as opportunity offered or as circumstances dictated, but that the white man did not and would not so regard them. They had been told, when Kumassi was occupied in January 1896, that slavery had ceased, and that announcement would never be cancelled or altered. They would not be freed from the obligation of supplying carriers or finding labour and material for house-building, but that in the matter of carriers, I had found, since I had been in Kumassi, that there was some hardship caused, and that I intended to find a remedy. That as regards huxters and strangers, Ashanti was a portion of the British Empire, in which all persons are free to live and trade where they please, and that no exception would be made in the case of Kumassi. . . .

It is, I think, clear, from the terms sent to me by the Kumassis, that the rebellion had been brewing for some time, and I think this is made clear from the letter addressed by the king of Juabin to the Acting Resident on the 27th March.[1] I

[1] The operative sentence in this message runs: 'I learned clearly from the Kumassi people, that they would not accede to what the Governor is coming to relate them. But if he persists to force them about them, they will . . . fight his Excellency.'

regret to say that I hear that the Nkoranzas have joined the rebels, as well as the Tekimans and Bechem Ahafus. . . . The Kokofu tribe seems to be divided in its allegiance. The young King Asibi leans towards the rebels, the more so now that he was compelled by his principal chiefs to abandon the offer made to him by the Kumassis, that he should be placed on the Gold Stool. They have secretly decided to depose him when the troubles here are over, and I think he has heard this. . . .

The force here upon the arrival of all the troops ordered up will be as follows:—

Governor at Kumassi (including Haussas brought up by the Governor)	150
Detachment under Captain Middlemist	100
Detachment from Lagos under Captain Aplin	200
Detachment from Jebba	150
Detachment from Northern Territories.	300
	900

. . . . [C.O.96/359]

432 CAPTAIN DONALD STEWART TO MAJOR M. NATHAN[1]

KUMASSI, 14 JANUARY, 1901.

Sir,

I have the honour to forward for the information of his Excellency a short report on the state of affairs in Ashanti, up to the present date. On my arrival in Kumassi towards the end of September, I found military operations still going on. They were absolutely necessary, as the enemy, though driven away from round Kumassi, still had large numbers of men in the field.

After the fight at Abuasu[2] on the main road to Berekum, which ended with the complete defeat of the enemy, I consulted

[1] Matthew Nathan (later Lieutenant-Colonel Sir) (1862–1939); entered the army, 1880; Acting-Governor of Sierra Leone, 1899; Governor of the Gold Coast (1900–3), Hong Kong (1903–7), Natal (1907–9) and Queensland (1920–26).
[2] 30 September, 1900; the last serious action of the war.

with Colonel Willcocks[1] as to sending out messengers to the rebel chiefs, and endeavouring to get them to accept the terms offered to them by Her Majesty's Government. For this purpose I chose Chief Osei Kenjassi, an influential Kumassi chief, who was a prisoner in the stockade, as the bearer. This man took my message and a letter explaining the terms to the rebel chiefs, but he was unable to persuade them to come in and surrender. I fancy their principal objection was that nearly all of them had been mixed up in different murders of prisoners, and were afraid of the consequences. The message, however, did its good work, as the young men, who were fighting under the chiefs' orders, were informed that they would be safe as far as their lives were concerned, for fighting against the British Government.

As this news got spread about, so the chiefs' armed forces dwindled away, the young men deserting and returning to their villages at every opportunity, until the ringleaders could not muster 50 armed men between them. News was then brought to me that they were seeking assistance from the French, and that they proposed retiring into the Kingabo district. If this move had been carried out they would always have been a thorn in our side; so I held a meeting of all the loyal kings and chiefs I could collect, and explained to them the serious state of affairs, calling on them to give me every assistance in the capture of the rebel leaders. Orders were issued, and four or five large armed parties proceeded to the district where the rebels were hiding, namely in the dense forest of Ahafo. The whole country was cleverly surrounded, all roads guarded, Sefwhis, Wams, Berekums, and Ahafos warned to watch their roads, in case they tried to break out towards the French boundary. The cordon was daily drawn closer and closer, until the chiefs were located by hunters, and then arrested

[1] James Willcocks (later General Sir) (1857–1926); 1899 Colonel-commandant West African Frontier Force; led the force which relieved Kumasi in July 1900.

by the different parties sent out. Very few chiefs got away, and these I hope to arrest shortly. The work was excellently carried out, and all the principal leaders are now prisoners in Kumassi prison. . . .

There are many kings' Stools vacant, that I propose to elect a candidate for. After having gone into their respective claims, their names and claims for the vacancies will be sent to his Excellency . . . for final approval. The Stools vacant are . . . Adansi (rebel leader), . . . Kokofu (rebel leader) . . . Insuta (dead) . . . Borumfa Ahafu, Bechim (rebel leader) . . . Inquanta (rebel leader), Abodom (rebel leader) . . . Egisu (rebel leader) . . . Offinsu (rebel leader) . . . Wenchi (rebel leader) . . . the six sections into which Kumassi is divided. . . . Besides these, there are the sub-chiefs of all the rebel tribes. . . .

The Golden Stool . . . and its sub-stools is looked upon as the great fetish of Ashanti, and I don't believe that any Ashanti king, chief, or man, even if they knew where it was put, would ever give the Government the slightest help to seize it. Even our most loyal chiefs and kings dislike immensely any allusion to the Stool . . . at the same time denying all knowledge of its whereabouts. . . .

Everywhere things are quiet, and the whole country settling down. The rebels will be disarmed gradually as we find them, and I have given orders that no arms are to be carried in the rebel districts for the future. As soon as the new kings and chiefs have been elected, and the people know exactly whose orders they have to obey, Ashanti will resume its ordinary status. . . .

C.O.96/377. Cd. 938, A & P (1902) lxvi]

433 HOUSE OF COMMONS, COMMITTEE OF SUPPLY   18 MARCH, 1901.
[There was some criticism of the handling of Ashanti affairs, and Mr Buxton,[1] the

[1] Sydney Charles Buxton (later Earl Buxton) (1853–1934); grandson of Sir Thomas Fowell Buxton; Liberal M.P. for the Poplar Division of Tower Hamlets, 1886–1914; Under-Secretary for the Colonies, 1892–5; Governor General of South Africa, 1914–20.

Member for Poplar, had argued that with a little tact and less readiness to interfere with Ashanti customs, the rising of 1900 might have been averted.]
Mr. Chamberlain: . . .

What is the theory of the Hon. Member for Poplar? It is that all these colonies were enjoying a sort of Elysian happiness; that these natives . . . were engaged in peaceful innocent pursuits; that the colonies were progressing gradually towards a higher civilization, and that if they had only been left alone, no evil consequences could have resulted. And then upon this picture a baneful shadow is cast — the shadow of the Colonial Secretary. Everything is changed. War takes the place of peace and harmony, and that Ashanti who was no doubt ploughing his furrows and living under his own vine and fig tree, is suddenly interfered with, his Golden Stool taken from him, and all sorts of outrages are perpetrated on him in his domestic and political life, and his constitutional customs are interfered with. . . .

What are the real facts? . . . The facts are these. Africa, as far as we were concerned with it, was, some ten or twenty years ago, a mere question of outposts. We and other European nations had stations on the coast, and the great interior was left to itself. . . . But about that time began what has been called the Scramble for Africa, and that scramble was going on during the period when the Hon. Member for Poplar was Under Secretary for the Colonies. What action did the Colonial Office take in these circumstances? Their action was characterised by 'tact', 'discretion', 'patience', and 'non-interference': in other words, they did nothing. In the most critical stage of our history as an empire in Africa, the Colonial Office was silent and inept, and the result was that our colonies in West Africa and elsewhere were being surrounded and their value destroyed by the advance of other nations. . . . The danger was serious, that in a very short time we should find all our colonies on this coast enclosed and depreciated, just as our colony of Gambia had been many years ago.

Well, when we came into office, we found every important and critical question left unsettled. Of course there was no war in times like that. When the policy is one of avoiding war at all costs, it is easy enough to keep the peace — for a time: but meanwhile you are losing your position. Our position was in danger, and we had to take serious steps. I am not going into details of our relations with foreign countries, but we had to raise a considerable force, the West African Frontier Force. At that time we had no force whatever worth the name that could protect our rights and position in West Africa, while foreign countries had large forces at their disposal. We had to create a force; and let me say I rejoice that Hon. Members opposite agree with me in praise of that force and of the way in which it has been conducted by Sir James Willcocks, who was senior officer under General Lugard....

We had at the same time to negotiate with Germany and France. We have made arrangements which have not excited much public attention, but as to which I will only say that I think they were fair arrangements, in which we gained all, or nearly all, that we hoped to gain, and perhaps as much as we could expect to gain in peaceful and friendly negotiation with other Powers. We have secured, therefore, vast hinterlands for these colonies which otherwise would have been shut in, and which have now become spheres of influence or British protectorates. And we have no longer, I am happy to say, an international question. . . .

But the moment we had defined boundaries, internationally agreed upon, we entered upon a new series of obligations and responsibilities. For my part, I am perfectly ready to agree with anyone who would say that it would have been better for other countries as well as for us, if this scramble for Africa had been still further postponed. But it was not we who began the scramble, and we could not fail to take

our part in protecting our interests. But from the moment that this new condition of things was established, we had to deal with protectorates and spheres of influence for which, hitherto, we had no responsibility.

The Hon. Member for Poplar complained of the present colonial policy because, forsooth, he said that we were interfering with the customs of the natives. What are the customs . . . with which we are interfering? Human sacrifice is one, fetishism of all kinds is another, and slavery is another. . . . We have declared in all these places that the legal status of slavery shall be abolished. . . . The consequences are war. It is not a question of tact, discretion, or patience. When you say to these savage tribes, who for centuries have exercised these rights of slave-raiding, who regard labour as something discreditable, and to whom it is necessary they should have slaves in order to preserve their personal dignity: 'From this day, when the British flag and the British protectorate come, there is an absolute prohibition of slave-raiding,' then you have to fight for your principles. . . . It is on that account that we find ourselves in frequent contest with some of these native populations.

That is the general statement. Now apply it to this case of Ashanti. . . . They are a brave and gallant native race. They have been the predominant race in that part of Africa: but what is the result of being the predominant race? They themselves would do no work whatever. They insisted upon having slaves and were constantly attacking the tribes in their neighbourhood. There was no peace or security for life or property within reach of them, and trade was impossible throughout the territory. They maintained themselves by a tyranny which was natural to them as a great African tribe, but which we could not tolerate from the moment we had any responsibility. . . . The Hon. Member speaks of these savage tribes as though he were speaking of a modern

European Power. He talks of the Ashantis fighting for their 'constitutional rights'. The Ashantis, if they understood what constitutional rights meant, would explain that their constitutional rights were to exercise absolute power and authority over all neighbouring tribes, to make slaves of them, to procure from them all the labour they required; and, if they did not get it, and tribute also, whenever they desired it, to torture them, sacrifice them to their fetish, and generally treat them with the utmost barbarity. Seeing the condition of civilization in which they were, we may make allowances for the Ashantis, that they know no better: but it is absurd to treat these tribes as if they were members of a civilized community; and nothing of the kind was attempted.

The Hon. Member has spoken of the Ashantis as having been British subjects for twenty-five years: but in this he is absolutely and entirely mistaken. We never claimed any authority over them until recently. That we claimed their territory as within our sphere of influence, excluding the influence of other European Powers, is true: but we claimed nothing in the nature of sovereignty over them. They were an independent power, under treaty with us, made after the original expedition (of 1874) to which the Hon. Member has gone back, and under which they were to pay us a certain indemnity. They have never paid that indemnity.

In the time of Sir William Maxwell, the question of that indemnity came up. . . . That is really ancient history. It is now five years ago that Sir William Maxwell went up to Coomassie. He was not opposed on the route, and a great palaver of chiefs was called. He explained his demands, and those demands were refused. . . . Sir William . . . removed Prempeh to the coast, as the king who had refused his terms. The expedition accordingly was so far successful that it was concluded without a single drop of blood having been shed. And when you come to ask, what is the cause of the subsequent disturbance,

I have no hesitation in saying that it was the bloodlessness of the previous expedition. The people of Ashanti, in common with every savage tribe, hold it to be a point of honour to fight for their chief, and to fight for their cause. They are ready to accept defeat, but they are not ready to accept the consequences of defeat without actual conflict. If you want to get at the bottom of the recent disturbance, you will find it in the fact that these people were called upon to suffer the consequences of defeat without having been defeated. The result was they nourished the intention of rising on the first opportunity, and anybody who reads the Blue-book will see that preparations were being made, and it was quite certain that sooner or later the Ashanti warriors would desire to try conclusions with the British, before they finally submitted. . . .

[On receipt of the message about the Golden Stool] Sir Frederick Hodgson decided to go up to Coomassie. He went up with a small force, not a provocative force, and called a meeting of the chiefs, to whom he desired to explain the intentions of the Government. Let me first deal with the incident of the Golden Stool. That really is of collateral and not of very great importance. Sir Frederick Hodgson did not ask my permission to go for the Golden Stool, but, speaking now, after the event, I entirely approve of his attempt to secure it. . . . It is not loot in the sense the Hon. Member supposes. It has no great pecuniary value. If we got it, we should not have melted it down for bullion. But in the opinion of the tribe, and according to the custom of the tribe, the possession of the Stool gives supremacy. And if, therefore, we could secure this Stool, we should be doing more for the peace of Ashanti than, probably, by any armed expedition. Therefore it was of the greatest importance to get hold of this symbol of sovereignty, if we could possibly do it. . . . No Governor would be justified in neglecting the information which was sent to him that he could have this emblem if he sent for it. Sir Frederick Hodgson did send for it, but the expedition failed because, as we understand, the chiefs themselves became afraid and refused to deliver up the Stool. . . . To say that the Governor was wrong in seeking for it is altogether a mistake, considering the extreme importance which a symbol of this kind has among a savage population.

The second complaint . . . is that Sir Frederick Hodgson asked for interest for the expenses of the wars of 1873 and 1896 and the present expedition. . . . [He] did nothing of the kind. . . . When we undertake responsibility for these protectorates, when we have to prevent slave raiding, to interfere with native customs, we must establish a police force and get some kind of income from the people. The chiefs before us got a tribute. Our tribute is, at all events, regularly paid, it is not exorbitant, and is not capable of being made an engine of extortion by the chiefs. . . . We decided to ask for £12,500 a year as a direct tax of about 4 shillings per head on the male population, to be collected by the kings and chiefs of the various tribes, on the understanding that they were to receive 10 per cent for the collection. That is a condition to which I attach the greatest importance. We do not want to destroy the authority of the native chiefs, but to regulate it. We are not making these vast territories parts of our colonies, but protectorates over which our control is more or less indirect. We desire to govern through the chiefs, to regulate their action, but not to interfere with their dignity and position. . . .

Sir Frederick Hodgson . . . suggested that it should not be called a tax or a tribute, but interest on the debt incurred in the wars of 1873 and 1896, which, he said, the Ashantis would understand as perfectly just. . . . We had to collect revenue . . . for the . . . government of the protectorate, and the question was by what name it should be called — a direct tax, or tribute, or interest. We took local opinion, and that local opinion was to the effect that under the latter name it would be more acceptable to the Ashantis. I dare say the Ashantis, like most other people, objected to any tribute or tax: but was that the real cause of the outbreak? Certainly not. In the statements some of them made to our agents on the Gold Coast, they put, as the first reason for their objection to British rule, our interference with slavery. . . .

It is not to be supposed that native wars such as this in which we have been engaged are the peculiar result of the presence in office of the Colonial Secretary. . . . There have been, I think, five native wars in countries which are under the Foreign Office. Surely . . . there must be some general influence at work. It is not due to the peculiar iniquity of the Colonial Secretary. What the general influence is, I have endeavoured to represent to the Committee. It is that this Government has decided, from the first, to deal with a strong hand with those questions which the party opposite allowed to drift. We have settled those questions of boundaries and spheres of influence in West Africa satisfactorily and peacefully, so far as European Powers are concerned. That was a gigantic work. But from the moment we undertook responsibilities for those spheres of influence, it became necessary, unless we were to take the advice of Hon. Members opposite, not to interfere in native customs, that we should be prepared for the attacks of native tribes whose customs we had interfered with. For one man . . . that is killed in a war of this kind, hundreds of men will, in future generations, have life, and peace, and security for their possessions.

The great continent of Africa possesses every advantage for the races native to it. Why have the native inhabitants not multiplied? Why are they still so largely out of proportion to the gigantic extent of the continent? It is because for centuries, possibly for thousands of years, there have been going on these internecine contests between different tribes, attended by terrible loss of life. First one tribe assumes superiority; then another, equally arbitrary, cruel and tyrannical, obtains the primary position. That state of things has been put a stop to. The moment we came into our sphere of influence or protectorate, we made it our business to establish, once and for all, that great *Pax Britannica* which we established in India, where similar conditions existed before our rule was firmly established. We have had to go through trials and difficulties and bloodshed before that rule was established: but once it was established, there was ample compensation for all we suffered, and ample compensation to the natives who will benefit by our more generous and more just rule.

It has been said that the colony is a burden to the United Kingdom; that this vote of £400,000 which the war has cost must be borne by the Imperial Exchequer. I have not the slightest doubt that the whole of it will be repaid. It is, properly speaking, a loan, though, in accordance with precedent, it is put down as a grant-in-aid. . . . We have not only secured the boundaries, but we have undertaken development of the territories within those boundaries. Within five years we have added 446 miles of railway to the West Coast of Africa. Within the same period, the exports of British produce — produce of British origin, not of foreign manufactured goods passing through Great Britain — have increased from a little over £2,000,000 a year to over £3,000,000. That is to say, we have increased the exports of this country to the colony by 50 per cent. That is not a bad record. It is one of which I am not at all ashamed.

[Hansard, 4/91/349 ff.]

434 NATHAM TO CHAMBERLAIN
KUMASI, 19 MARCH, 1901.

. . . I should say that the real origin of the rising is a profound dislike on the part of the chiefs and leading people of Ashanti to British rule. This dislike is not unnatural. We take away from them all they care about, and given them in place, conditions of life which have no attractions to them. We have deprived them of the power of making war on each other and on neighbouring tribes, of the power of keeping their people in order by barbarous punishments, and of the power of recruiting their labour with slaves. We try to give them protection from external aggression, peace within their own boundaries, law enforced by our own civilized methods, and opportunities of making wealth by labour. The Ashanti was perfectly able to protect himself from the aggression of the surrounding tribes, before we came to his country, having, for 200 years, prosecuted a series of successful wars against his neighbours, all the facts of which are well known to him. Peace within the country has no attractions to a man whose title to respect and whose recognised source of power and wealth are in feats of war. Humane punishments for offences and particularly for offences against the power and dignity of big men, are to his mind ridiculous, as well as unsatisfying to the pleasure he derives from seeing blood flow. Personal labour of any kind is beneath the dignity of the Ashanti, and a wage which has to be slowly accumulated before it reaches such a sum as he could obtain from a day's loot in an enemy's town, is no compensation for labour.

I fear that the only things which European ilisationciv has brought him which he really appreciates are spirits and powder. The chiefs like, no doubt, velvets and silks, but the use of them is confined by native custom to a comparatively few leading people. The toga which forms the sole dress of the bulk is rightly regarded by the ordinary Ashanti as superior when made of native cloth to when it is made of Manchester cotton. Native custom as a rule restrains them from building any but the simple huts in which their race have always lived. It is true they like jewellery, but of this the big men have plenty made by native workmanship from their accumulated hoards of gold.

A complicated system of administration, hallowed by antiquity and historic precedents, which our ignorance and policy have alike tended to break down, and a deep-rooted superstition which we are unable to understand and from which our presence in the country has detached a portion of the people, further help to make our rule distasteful to the Ashanti.

I may, incidentally, summarize his character by saying that he is cruel, unmerciful to his enemies, disloyal to his friends, deceitful, suspicious and intemperate. On the other hand, he is brave, dignified, respectful, commercially honest, clever, and obedient to the laws and order he receives from an authority he recognizes.

The tribes that originally joined in the rising were the Kumassis, Offinsus, Atchimas, and Ejisus. A small proportion of the Kokofus were disloyal under considerable pressure from the Kumassis. Later on, the Adansis joined, and the rising spread to the Ahafus, Wankis, Bechims and Inkwantas. The people of Mampon, Juabin, Insuta and Aguna, whose kings were detained within the fort, did not join in the rising. Bompata on the east, Kumawu and Attabubu on the north-east, and British Gaman on the north-west, remained loyal. N'koranza wavered, but ultimately declined to throw in its lot with the Ashantis.

The principal instigators of the rising appear to have been the members of the Native Committee,[1] Opoku Mensah, Kwami Elfilfa, and Kwoku Nenchie, of whom the first named is dead. The military organisation was mainly in the hands of Kofi Kofia, a chief of no great importance except by reason of his military capacity. Ya Asantiwah, the queen-mother of Ejisu, is said to have been made leader of the insurrection. . . .

[C.O.96/378. Cd. 938, p. 12]

[1] Set up by Governor Maxwell in 1896 to help the Resident administer Kumasi. Kwaku Nantwi was a Kumasi linguist and Kwame Afirifa chief of Atwima.

435 NATHAN TO CHAMBERLAIN
KUMASI, 20 MARCH, 1901.
Sir,

I have had under consideration the question of the advisability of making changes in the ownership of land in Ashanti, as a result of the rising of last year. Two ways of making such changes have been suggested: first, the taking by the Crown of lands of the tribes that rose against British rule; and, secondly, the transfer to loyal tribes of lands of disloyal tribes.

In your instructions to Captain Donald Stewart, you stated that lands belonging to rebel tribes might be confiscated to the Crown unless such a course was clearly repugnant to native custom or tribal practice, and you directed the Resident to submit recommendations on the matter. I have discussed it fully with him, and we are of opinion that the confiscation proposed would not be desirable. The profits derived from the lease to European mining communities of stool lands will, in the future, be an important and legitimate source of revenue to the native chiefs. For the present we are not in a position to dispense, over any considerable part of Ashanti, with the assistance of these chiefs, in its administration. It is therefore our interest to support their position. At the same time, it has been necessary to take from them some of their sources of wealth and therefore of power. They can no longer increase their riches by raiding their neighbours for slaves and loot, and even in their courts of justice they cannot get the large fees and fines they formerly obtained. By putting them in a position to get considerable rents for their lands, we compensate them, to some extent, for depriving them of less legitimate sources of revenue. It must also be borne in mind that we have secured to the Government, by the provisions of the Concessions Ordinance, a good revenue from the mines, apart from any rents of lands, should the mines eventually prove a financial success.

Leaving to the chiefs their lands and the

rents they will derive from them, will give them a special interest in keeping their countries quiet, and will be a guarantee for their good conduct. It will also assist the mining companies; for if the lands were taken over by the Government, the chiefs would not help these companies in getting labour, and would put every obstruction in the way of their carrying out their work.

Another reason against the confiscation of the lands of the rebel tribes, and preventing these lands being a source of revenue to them, is the fact that we are now, with your approval, imposing a direct tax on the tribes. The Ashantis are neither agricultural nor industrial; and though I believe them to have a considerable amount of accumulated wealth, I also think it would be unfair to make them contribute directly to our revenue and, at the same time, cut off an important source from that of the native chiefs.

Yet another, though a less important, reason against the confiscation of the lands of the rebel tribes is that, in the absence of any reliable survey, and with the incomplete information we have as to present ownership, it would be difficult to define and demarcate them. We should be further involved in the land palavers which are now a constant source of dispute between the native tribes, and which we are, in present circumstances, often able to settle as a disinterested arbiter. All we should gain would be the rent from concessionaires. We already take from the Ashantis any lands required for Government purposes, without any question on their part.

With regard to the second part of the question, viz.:— the transfer to loyal tribes of lands of disloyal tribes . . . you will see that Captain Stewart is strongly opposed to allowing the claims of the king of Denkera to land on the north and east of the Offin River, claims based on an ownership lost in war 70 to 80 years ago, which had not been put forward until the king of Denkerah, living on the coast, thought the lands could be made a source of profit by leasing them to concessionaires eager to buy and not unduly particular as to title. The loyal king of Bekwai feels equally strongly with the Adansis against the Denkeras being allowed to come to the north or east of the Offin. The king of Denkera has a large tract of country both in the rear of Cape Coast and in Upper Denkera, between the Offin and the Ancobra. This country is very badly looked after, roads and towns being reported to be in a disgraceful state, whilst the king lives intemperately at Cape Coast. I do not propose that the claims of the Denkeras to lands north and east of the Offin should be recognised. . . .

[A] correspondent states that what the natives consider direct confiscation of the northern portions of Denkera will 'produce another uprising among the Denkeras.' I trust that the course which it is proposed to pursue will not produce that result, though if the Denkeras are given support against the Government by Europeans and natives at Cape Coast, it is quite possible that trouble may arise. I do not believe that these people desire to embarrass the Government in its attempts at a lasting solution of the many difficult problems that are produced by the conflicting claims of native chiefs, but undoubtedly the readiness with which concessions are purchased at Cape Coast, and the efforts made to back their validity when there are conflicting claims to the ownership of the lands they represent, must occasionally put the concessionaires in the position of giving support to a policy different from that which the Government is pursuing. . . . It is the earnest desire of this Government to give all assistance and facilities to the mining companies, to which we look for the future development of the country. If the companies will recognise this and refrain directly or indirectly from any interference with the policy of the Government, I do not anticipate any trouble arising.

Reverting to the question of the transfer

of lands from disloyal to loyal tribes, I decided to give to the king of Bekwai the villages of Chinabusu and Odumasi. These villages were asked for by him as part of his reward. They adjoin his territory, and the Bekwais have some claim to them. I announced at a public palaver on the 14th, that the villages were taken from Adansi as part of the punishment of that people for their disloyal and treacherous conduct. The king of Bekwai had also asked for the Kokofu villages of Duasi and Ankankasi, but I decided, on the Resident's advice . . . that this transfer was not desirable. The only other change I am making in territorial jurisdiction[1] is to place Agogo, formerly under a disloyal chief of Kumasi, under the loyal chief of Bompata. The Resident ascertained for me that the change would be acceptable to the Agogo people. . . .

Cognate to the question of future ownership of land in Ashanti is that of the proposed future boundary of the country. . . . No advantage would be gained by including Kwahu and Sefwi in Ashanti for administrative purposes. They would be under different systems of jurisdiction which would create inconvenience. The arrangement would be likely to be misunderstood by the chiefs and people in Kwahu and Sefwi, who consider that they have been freed for ever from their connection with Ashanti. . . .

British Gaman, Wam and Ahafu should certainly be under the same jurisdiction and administration as Ashanti. They are peopled by Ashantis having intimate relations with the chiefs in and near Kumasi, and have no natural connection with the Sefwis from whom they are separated by a thick belt of forest only inhabited by a few hunters.

On the other hand, Upper Denkera,

[1] Nathan's restraint was not copied by his successors. Cf. Tordoff, W., *The Exile and Repatriation of Nana Prempeh I* in Trans. Hist. Soc. of Ghana (1960), iv, part 2, p. 44. A number of Kumasi divisions (Ahafo, Bompata, Dengiase, Mansu-Nkwanta and Obogo) became Bekwai dependencies.

lying on the right bank of the Offin, which is populated by Denkeras, and to which the Ashantis have no claim, should be included in the Colony (probably as part of the Sefwi district). . . .   [Cd. 938, p. 21]

436 ASHANTI ORDER IN COUNCIL
26 SEPTEMBER, 1901.

Ashanti. Order of His Majesty the King in Council. At the Court of Saint James's, the 26th day of September, 1901.

Present: The King's most Excellent
Majesty.
Lord George Hamilton.
Mr Chamberlain.
Mr. St. John Brodrick.
Sir Charles Scott.

Whereas the territories in West Africa situate within the limits of this Order, heretofore known as Ashanti, have been conquered by His Majesty's forces, and it has seemed expedient to His Majesty that the said territories should be annexed to and should henceforth form part of His Majesty's dominions, and that provision should be made for the peace, order, and good government of the said territories in manner hereinafter provided:

Now, therefore, His Majesty, by virtue and in exercise of the powers in His Majesty vested, is pleased, by and with the advice of His Privy Council, to order, and it is hereby ordered, as follows:—

1. This Order may be cited as the Ashanti Order in Council, 1901.

2. Until further provision be made in respect thereof, the limits of this Order are the territories which are bounded as follows — on the south by the Colony of the Gold Coast; on the west by the line of the frontier between the British and French possessions from a point on the frontier 1,000 metres to the south of Aburuferasi to the point where the frontier cuts the eighth parallel of north latitude; on the north by the eighth parallel of north latitude; and on the east by the line of the frontier between the British and German

possessions from the point where that frontier cuts the eighth parallel of north latitude to a point on the left bank of the Volta due west of the village of Krobo.

3. In this Order, unless the subject or context otherwise requires —

'His Majesty' includes His Majesty's heirs and successors.

'Secretary of State' means one of His Majesty's Principal Secretaries of State.

'Treaty' includes any existing or future Treaty, Convention, Agreement, or Arrangement, made by or on behalf of Her late Majesty Queen Victoria or His Majesty with any civilized power or with any native tribe, people, chief, or king, and any Regulations appended to any such Treaty, Convention, Agreement, or Arrangement.

'Gazette' means the Gold Coast Government Gazette.

'Governor' includes the Officer for the time being administering the Government of the Gold Coast Colony.

4. From and after the coming into operation of this Order, the aforesaid territories shall be annexed to and form part of His Majesty's dominions and shall be known as Ashanti.

5. The Governor of the Gold Coast Colony may, on His Majesty's behalf, exercise all powers and jurisdiction of His Majesty within Ashanti, and to that end may take or cause to be taken all such measures, and may do or cause to be done all such matters and things therein as are lawful, and as in the interest of His Majesty's service he may think expedient, subject to such instructions as he may from time to time receive from His Majesty or through a Secretary of State.

6. Subject to the approval of a Secretary of State, the Governor may appoint a Chief Commissioner and so many fit persons as, in the interest of His Majesty's service, he may think necessary to be Commissioners, Judges, Magistrates, or other Officers, and may define from time to time the districts within which such Officers shall respectively discharge their functions.

Every such Officer may exercise such powers and authorities as the Governor may, with the like approval, assign to him, subject nevertheless to such directions and instructions as the Governor may from time to time think fit to give him. The appointment of such Officers shall not abridge, alter, or affect the right of the Governor to execute and discharge all the powers and authorities hereby conferred upon him.

The Governor may, subject to confirmation by a Secretary of State, remove any officer so appointed.

7. In the exercise of the powers and authorities hereby conferred upon him, the Governor may, amongst other things, from time to time by Ordinance provide for the administration of justice, the raising of revenue, and generally for the peace, order and good government of Ashanti, and of all persons therein, including the prohibition and punishment of acts tending to disturb the public peace.

The Governor, in issuing such Ordinances, shall respect any native laws by which the civil relations of any native chiefs, tribes, populations under His Majesty's protection are now regulated, except so far as the same may be incompatible with the due exercise of His Majesty's power and jurisdiction, or clearly injurious to the welfare of the said natives.

8. Every Ordinance of the Governor shall be published in the Gazette, and shall, unless otherwise provided, thereupon come into operation and thereafter shall, until disallowed by His Majesty or repealed or modified by any subsequent Ordinance, have effect as if contained in this Order, and the Governor shall take such measures as he thinks proper for giving due publicity thereto within Ashanti.

9. His Majesty may disallow any such Ordinance wholly or in part, and may signify such disallowance by Order in Council or through a Secretary of State, and upon such disallowance being notified in the Gazette, the provisions so disallowed shall, from and after a date to be

mentioned in such notification, cease to have effect, but without prejudice to anything theretofore lawfully done thereunder. Due notification shall be publicly made by the Governor within Ashanti of the disallowance of any such Ordinance.

10. The Governor shall use the Public Seal of the Gold Coast Colony for sealing all things whatsoever relating to Ashanti that are required to be under the Public Seal.

11. The Governor may, upon sufficient cause to him appearing, suspend from the exercise of his office any person holding or exercising any office within Ashanti, whether appointed by the Governor, or under and by virtue of any Commission or Warrant granted or which may be granted, by His Majesty, in His Majesty's name, or under His Majesty's authority, which suspension shall continue and have effect only until His Majesty's pleasure therein shall be signified to the Governor by a Secretary of State. The Governor in proceeding to any such suspension, shall observe the directions in that behalf given to him by any instructions from His Majesty or signified through a Secretary of State.

12. The Governor, or, in the absence of the Governor from Ashanti, the Chief Commissioner, may, as he shall see occasion, when any crime has been committed within Ashanti, or for which the offender may be tried therein, grant a pardon, in His Majesty's name, to any accomplice, not being the actual perpetrator of such crime, who shall give such information and evidence as shall lead to the apprehension and conviction of the principal offender; and further, may grant to any offender convicted of any crime in any court, or before any Judge, Justice, Magistrate, or other Officer within Ashanti, a pardon, either free or subject to lawful conditions, or any respite of the execution of the sentence of any such offender, for such period as the Governor, or in the absence of the Governor from Ashanti, to the Chief Commissioner, may seem fit, and

may remit any fines, penalties, or forfeitures, which may become due and payable.

13. This Order shall be published in the Gazette, and shall thereupon come into operation, and the Governor shall give directions for the publication of this Order at such places, and in such manner, and for such time or times, as he thinks proper for giving due publicity thereto within Ashanti.

14. His Majesty may from time to time revoke, alter, add to, or amend this Order.

And the Right Honourable Joseph Chamberlain, one of His Majesty's Principal Secretaries of State, is to give the necessary directions herein accordingly.

A. W. Fitzroy.

[Gold Coast Government Gazette, 1 January, 1902]

437 NORTHERN TERRITORIES ORDER IN COUNCIL   26 SEPTEMBER, 1901.
Northern Territories. Order of His Majesty the King in Council. At the Court of Saint James's, the 26th day of September, 1901.

· · · ·

Whereas by the Foreign Jurisdiction Act, 1890, passed in the reign of Her late Majesty Queen Victoria, it was amongst other things enacted that it should be lawful for Her Majesty to hold, exercise, and enjoy, any jurisdiction which Her Majesty then had and might at any time thereafter have within a foreign country, in the same and as ample a manner as if Her Majesty had acquired that jurisdiction by the cession or conquest of territory:

And whereas the territories of West Africa, situate within the limits of this Order, as hereinafter described, are under the protection of His Majesty the King:

And whereas by treaty, grant, usage, sufferance, and other lawful means, His Majesty has power and jurisdiction in the said territories:

And whereas it is necessary to provide for the peace, order and good government of the territories aforesaid:

Now, therefore, His Majesty, by virtue and in exercise of the powers by the Foreign Jurisdiction Act, 1890, or otherwise in His Majesty vested, is pleased, by and with the advice of His Privy Council, to order, and it is hereby ordered, as follows:

1. This Order may be cited as the Northern Territories Order in Council, 1901.

2. Until further provision be made in respect thereof, the limits of this Order are the territories which are bounded on the south by the eighth parallel of north latitude; on the west and north by the line of the frontier between the British and French possessions; and on the east by the line of the frontier between the British and German Possessions.

The territories so bounded shall be known as the Northern Territories of the Gold Coast, and are hereinafter referred to as the Northern Territories.

3. [As in No. 436.]

4.–13. [As in sections 5–14 of No. 436 above, reading 'Northern Territories' for 'Ashanti'.]   [*Ibid.*]

438 GOLD COAST ORDER IN COUNCIL
                   26 SEPTEMBER, 1901.

Order in Council defining boundaries of the Gold Coast Colony and annexing all Territories within such Boundaries hitherto unannexed. . . . Saint James's, 26 September, 1901.

[Recites Letters Patent of 13 January, 1886.] . . .

And whereas it is expedient that the boundaries of the Gold Coast Colony should be further defined and that all such portions of the territories on the West Coast of Africa within the limits hereinafter defined which have not already been included within His Majesty's dominions, should be annexed to, and should henceforth form part of, the said Gold Coast Colony:—

Now, therefore, His Majesty is pleased, by and with the advice of His Privy

Council, to order, and it is hereby ordered, as follows:—

1. This Order may be cited as 'The Gold Coast Order in Council, 1901.'

2. The limits of this Order shall be the territories on the West Coast of Africa which are bounded as follows, namely:
On the south by the Atlantic Ocean; on the west by the line of the frontier between the British and French possessions from the sea to a point on the frontier 1,000 metres to the south of Aburuferasi; on the north by a line drawn from the last mentioned point through the point where the road from Wam to Patubuso crosses the Tano River, to the right bank of the River Ofin, then along this bank to the confluence of the Ofin with the River Prah, then along the left bank of the Prah to the point where the road from Obo to Bompata crosses the river, then due north until it meets the parallel of latitude which passes through Agogo, then straight to the point where the road from Abetifi to Attabubu crosses the River Sumi near Sumisu, then straight to the village of Achrinang, and then straight to a point on the left bank of the Volta due west of the village of Krobo; and on the east by the line of the frontier between the British and German possessions southwards to the Atlantic Ocean.

3. All such parts of the territories within the limits aforesaid as have not heretofore been included in His Majesty's dominions shall be, and the same are hereby annexed to His Majesty's dominions, and the whole of the said territories are declared to be part and parcel of His Majesty's Gold Coast Colony in like manner, and to all intents and purposes as if all such territories had formed part of the said Colony at the date of the said Letters Patent of 13th January, 1886.

4. It shall be competent for the Governor of the Gold Coast Colony, by and with the advice and consent of the Legislative Council of the said Colony, to make laws for the peace, order and good government of the said territories.

5. As and from the date of the coming

into operation of this Order, all laws and Ordinances which shall at such date be in force in the territories heretofore known as the Gold Coast Colony, shall take effect within the limits of this Order, and shall remain in force therein until the same shall have been altered or repealed by the Governor of the Gold Coast Colony, by and with the advice and consent of the Legislative Council, or by His Majesty.

6. This Order shall come into operation on a day to be fixed by the Governor of the Gold Coast Colony by a Proclamation published in the Gold Coast Government Gazette.[1]

And the Right Honourable Joseph Chamberlain, one of His Majesty's Principal Secretaries of State, is to give the necessary directions herein accordingly.

A. W. Fitzroy.

[Ordinances of the Gold Coast, 1903, ii, p. 1347]

[1] The Order came into operation on 1 January, 1902.

BOOK X

EXPANSION IN PEACE AND WAR, 1902–1918

32 Economic Expansion, 1902–1913

THE definitive occupation of Ashanti in 1901 opened the way for a decade of commercial progress. The railway, pushed on for strategic as well as economic reasons, reached Kumasi in 1903 (440). The gold prospecting of the nineties now showed the first considerable returns (439), and, by 1906, gold was by far the most important export of the country. The recovery of the trade in rubber — the characteristic export of the nineties (441) — was more than matched by the growth of cocoa shipments (443).

Behind the comforting export statistics lay problems of labour supply and transport (443), and, in the case of the rubber and timber trade, more serious questions of how best to prevent the country's resources being recklessly squandered. Problems of this order spilled over into politics, particularly where the ownership or control of land were involved. Attempts to make a start with forest conservation by ordinance were made after an exhaustive enquiry in 1912 (444), but foundered in the face of local opposition. The Land Bill agitation had set the pattern for an undeviating and unreasoning opposition to any Government measures connected with land. Opposition to the Palm Oil Bill of 1913 — an attempt to introduce large scale capital enterprise into the declining Palm Oil industry was perhaps better founded. At all events, it was an issue on which European and African unofficials in the Legislative Council could unite (445).

At the end of a decade of peaceful development the Gold Coast was prosperous as never before. 1912 was a record year for gold production, but, even so, the exports of cocoa, of which the Gold Coast was now the premier world producer, were more valuable. With substantial revenue surpluses behind him, the Governor, in 1913, could look forward to a great expansion of the Colony's transport system (446).

439 EXTRACT FROM THE ANNUAL REPORT FOR THE GOLD COAST FOR 1902

. . . The fall in the export trade of the Colony, which had been continuous since the year 1899, was arrested. This was due partly to the gold mining, which had in previous years taken labour from other industries, beginning to be itself productive, partly to the rapid growth of the cocoa industry, and partly to the year having been a very good one for palm oil and palm kernels. The export, however, of timber and rubber further declined. . . .

Since its discovery by Europeans in the fifteenth century, the Gold Coast has continuously exported gold to Europe. The available records, prior to 1850, of this exportation, are intermittent and meagre, and from that year till 1880, there are wide gaps in them, the values of exportations during the period fluctuating between £24,000 and £175,000. These figures refer, however, only to British Settlements, and it should be borne in mind that up to the year 1872 shipments of gold must also have been made from the . . . Dutch Settlements on the Gold Coast, and that there is evidence of a large quantity of gold dust having been exported from Ashanti to Yendi and Kong, and, via Timbuctoo, to the countries on the Mediterranean seaboard. The industry was practically in the hands of the natives, and it was not till 1874 (with the exception of old Portuguese and Dutch enterprises, traces of which still exist, and which it is said ended in the annihilation of the whites by the natives) that the first European Company was formed for gold mining in West Africa. It apparently did little beyond exploration, but the foundation of a second Company in 1879 resulted in some mining operations in the Tarkwa region, and the records of 1880 to the present time, which are continuous, cover the period in which the exportation of gold dust, the product of native mining, was replaced by that of gold bars, the result of European operations.

The export of gold increased from a value of £33,865. 12s. 9d. in 1880 to one of £89,981. 4s. 2d. in 1885. From that year to 1897 it fluctuated between values of about £77,000 and £103,000, the lowest return being that of 1894, the highest that of 1889. The year 1901 witnessed a remarkable . . . 'boom' in the West African mining market. The Colony was overrun by prospectors, and during the year no less than 2,825 concessions were taken up and filed in the Colony. Many of these were, however, abandoned on the collapse of the 'boom' towards the end of that year. . . .

The whole export of 1902 was due to the Ashanti Goldfields Corporation and to its offshoot the Ashanti Sansu Mine, with the exception of a shipment of £2,000 in value, made in the last month of the year, which was the first of the 'Bibiani Goldfields', a Company working in Sefwhi, and except £35. 11s. 3d. worth of gold dust received in trade with natives. . . .

Gold is generally diffused throughout the Colony, Ashanti, and a small part of the Northern Territories, and appears in Quartz formation and alluvial deposits, and in the Wassaw District there is a conglomerate, or 'banket' formation. The rivers of the Colony are said to be rich in alluvial deposits.

From reports at present available, the only mining being carried on in the Sefwhi District are those of the Bibiani Goldfields. Actual mining operations are being conducted on [11] . . . out of 71 mining properties in the Wassaw District and eight properties are being prospected. In the Dixcove District there are 21 mining properties, in none of which actual mining operations are proceeding. In the Axim District there are 14 properties, on two of which prospectors are working. The Goldfields of Eastern Akim are engaged in transporting machinery to five properties in Eastern Akim, and general prospecting is being carried on in connection with them and with the properties of one or two other Companies. . . .

[The reports] of the Ashanti Goldfields Corporation and the Ashanti Sansu Mine recorded active mining operations; the former with 65 stamps having crushed 16,348 tons of ore, yielding $16,407\frac{7}{10}$ oz. of gold; the latter with 20 stamps, 8,223 tons yielding $9,948\frac{3}{4}$ oz. of gold. Pending the completion of the Tarkwa–Kumasi extension of the Government Railway, other mining Companies in Ashanti have confined themselves to development work. . . .

[Cd. 1768. 2, A & P (1904) lvii]

440 EXTRACT FROM THE GOLD COAST ANNUAL REPORT FOR 1903

. . . Construction of the Government Railway was commenced at Sekondi in August, 1898, the first rail being laid in December of that year. During 1900 and the early part of 1901, construction was interrupted by the Ashanti disturbances which practically put a stop to the importation of labour. Thus it was not until May, 1901, that the first section, Sekondi–Tarkwa (40 miles) was completed. From that time, however, better progress has been made, and the Tarkwa–Obuassi section was finished in December, 1902, Kumasi, the present terminus, being reached in October, 1903. . . . The Sekondi–Obuassi section, 124 miles, was taken over by Government from the Construction Department in July 1903; the Obuassi–Kumasi section is to be taken over on the 1st of April, 1904. . . .

The amount expended on construction up to the 31st of December, 1903, was £1,796,203 1s. 8d., or approximately £10,700 a mile, which included the cost of permanent bridges, offices, quarters for staff, hospital, rolling stock, and landing jetties at Sekondi.

Funds were raised for construction mainly by the issue of Inscribed Stock, partly by advances made by the Crown Agents for the Colonies against scrip of an unissued Gold Coast loan, and partly by advances made by the Colony. . . . It is not yet possible to give exact figures of the total cost of construction, but it may be put down approximately at £1,820,000. The length of the line Sekondi–Kumasi is 168 miles, the gauge 3 feet 6 inches, the permanent way laid with 50 lb. steel rails on steel trough sleepers. The heaviest type of locomotive used, including tender, weighs 60·5 tons. The steepest grade is over the Adjah Bippo rise between the 45 and 49 mile, where it is 1 in 46 on both sides. The total number of changes of grade, below 1 in 100 is 400. The total number of curves is 690; and there are 157 with a radius of 5 chains. . . . The most noticeable fact in connection with the goods traffic is that 98 per cent. is in the up direction. Efforts are being made to develop the downward traffic by carrying export produce, such as rubber and cocoa, at low rates. . . .

[Cd. 2238. 3, A & P (1905) li]

A number of papers on early railway projects have been collected and printed in African (West) No. 451, C.O.806/362.

441 [STATE OF TRADE IN 1904. GOVERNOR'S STATEMENT TO LEG. COUNCIL, 16 OCTOBER, 1905.] . . .

The total trade of the Colony in the past year amounted to £3,341,883, as against £3,063,486 in 1903; the imports being valued at £2,001,857 and the exports at £1,340,026. Imports . . . show a decrease of £80,687 as compared with the previous year, while exports show an increase of £359,084. . . . The total trade figures for the year 1894 amounted to £1,663,173, so that the volume of trade has since that date rather more than doubled. . . .

Referring to imports . . . the principal decreases occur in Machinery £82,748; Provisions £62,874; Building Materials, £18,027; and Rum, £11,752. The first three items are clearly due to the completion of the Government Railway, and of the milling machinery on several of the principal mines in 1903; and partly to the fact that some of the mines have found it necessary to close down. . . .

The principal increases in the Imports are Gin [£14,442] . . . Cotton Goods, £35,715; Wearing Apparel, £10,025; Perfumery, £4,724; Specie, £22,844. It is, I think, obvious that the increase in the first four items tends to show that the natives are prosperous and have more money to spend on clothing, spirits, and a luxury like perfume.

With reference to Exports, the principal items of increase are those of Rubber, £164,144; Cocoa £113,775; and Gold, £90,817. It is satisfactory to find that Rubber has now resumed the first place in the list of articles of Export from which it fell in 1900 in consequence of the Ashanti disturbances. The success of the Cocoa trade is a matter on which the native farmers of the Eastern Province of the Colony are to be congratulated; the value of the exports of this article was more than doubled in 1904 when 11,451,458 lbs. were shipped, as compared with 5,104,761 lbs. in 1903. In connection with this industry, however, I must impress on both the growers and purchasers of this product, the necessity of shipping, as far as possible, Cocoa of the best quality that can be grown here, and not mixed consignments containing a large proportion of immature, unclean, or improperly prepared beans. I am informed that there is no reason whatever why Gold Coast Cocoa should not realize a price fully equal to that grown at St. Thome, of 52/- a cwt, instead of 30/- to 46/- as at present. It would be a matter for regret if, in the early days of what promises to become a great and profitable industry, Cocoa from this Colony were to be classified as a second or third rate article on the London and European markets. The Chambers of Commerce have approached the Government with a view to the introduction of legislation on the subject on the lines of the Ordinance to provide for the Prevention of the Adulteration of Palm Kernels of 1898; but I trust that such a measure will not be necessary. The remedy appears to lie chiefly with the Merchants themselves, as it is evident that the native producer would not go to the trouble and expense of bringing low-grade cocoa to the markets for sale if there were no demand for it.

The value of the Gold exported, which amounted to £345,608 shows an increase of £90,817 which though not so large as was anticipated early in the year, is an indication that steady progress is being made. . . .

Eighteen properties are now producing gold as against five in 1903 and thirteen in 1904. The value of the gold won during the first six months of the present year is £300,617, which compares very favourably with the total amount, £345,608, exported in 1904. . . .

It cannot fail to be a source of gratification to all who are interested in the progress and development of the Gold Coast to find that the marked improvement which has taken place in the general health of the Colony and Protectorate in recent years has been well maintained; this is especially noticeable in the case of Europeans. Both the death and invaliding rates amongst the Government Officials show, I regret to observe, a slight increase as compared with the year 1903. On the other hand the percentage of deaths amongst the employees of the Mercantile Firms has decreased from 35·82 to 9·83 per 1,000 for the same period. The death rate amongst the employees of the Mining Companies in 1904 was 10·63 as against 19·17 in 1903 and the invaliding rate 79·37 as against 88·20. . . .   [Leg. Co. Debates]

442 MINUTES OF A MEETING OF THE LEGISLATIVE COUNCIL HELD AT GOVERNMENT HOUSE, ON MONDAY THE 2ND DAY OF SEPTEMBER, 1907 AT 10 A.M.

Present:

His Excellency the Governor,
Sir John P. Rodger, K.C.M.G.[1]

His Honour the Chief Justice (Sir William Brandford Griffith, Kt.)
The Honourable the Colonial Secretary (Major Herbert Bryan, C.M.G.)
The Honourable the Attorney-General (A. Willoughby Osborne, C.M.G.)
The Honourable the Treasurer (C. Riby Williams, Esquire, C.M.G.)
The Honourable J. M. Sarbah[2] (Unofficial Member)
The Honourable Giles Hunt[3] (Unofficial Member)
The Honourable J. P. Brown[4] (Unofficial Member)
The Honourable W. H. Grey[5] (Unofficial Member). . . .

. . . The Attorney General moves the second reading of a Bill intituled 'An Ordinance to make better provision for the exercise of powers and jurisdiction by Native Authorities,' with regard to which a Memorial has been presented by Mr. Brown; and states that he proposes, as briefly as possible, to refer to the difficulties in connexion with the question of Native

[1] Sir John Pickersgill Rodger (1851–1910); served in the Malay States, 1888–1903; Governor of the Gold Coast, 1903–10.
[2] John Mensah Sarbah (1864–1910); son of John Sarbah of Cape Coast, merchant and M.L.C.; educated in England; first Gold Coast barrister; founder-member of the Gold Coast Aborigines' Rights Protection Society, 1897; M.L.C., 1900–10; author of *Fanti Customary Laws* (1897) and *Fanti National Constitution* (1906); educationist and co-founder of Mfantsipim School, 1904.
[3] An English barrister practising in Cape Coast, M.L.C., 1903–13.
[4] Joseph Peter Brown (1843–1932); born at Dixcove; served in Ashanti War of 1873; agent of F & A Swanzy; co-founder of G.C.A.R.P.S., and member of delegation to the Colonial Office, 1898; M.L.C., 1904–8.
[5] Chief Agent for Swanzy & Miller Bros., M.L.C., 1906–18.

Jurisdiction, and to the circumstances under which the Bill has been introduced.

As Honourable Members are aware, Native Tribunals have existed from ancient days; their efficacy, however, had decreased as the power of the British Government has increased. As to their inherent jurisdiction, the Commission appointed in 1894 to enquire into the question of Native Jurisdiction generally, and to report on the constitution and Jurisdiction of Native Tribunals reported that, under the native law, there were no cases, civil or criminal, beyond the jurisdiction of a native Head Chief's Court, but the idea in the native mind that all cases of killing must be tried in the English Courts was general; and the dread of doing anything to incur the displeasure of the Government induced most Chiefs to refer criminal cases of a serious nature to the English Courts for trial. They also reported, incidentally, that a Chief had jurisdiction over strangers temporarily residing in his territory.

At the time that report was made, only a small part of the territory which is now the Gold Coast Colony was the Colony proper — the rest was a Protectorate. Before then a series of inroads had been made into the inherent rights of the Native Tribunals. He refers to an Ordinance which was passed in 1878 and was subsequently repealed, its principal features being re-enacted in the Native Jurisdiction Ordinance No. 5 of 1883, now in force, under the provisions of which it is competent for the Governor in Council to place any Head Chief's division; and states that certain portions of the Protected Territory prior to 1902 were from time to time placed under this Ordinance. He refers also to the Native Prisons Ordinance,[1] which practically took away from the Native Tribunals their effective power of punishment by imprisonment; and states that under this Ordinance only licensed native prisons are allowed, and that no punishment by imprisonment for more than a period of one month in a

[1] No. 23 of 1888.

native prison can be inflicted on pain of a penalty of £100. Moreover, there was the strong possibility of an action for heavy damages in the Supreme Court against the Chief concerned, in the event of a breach of this provision.

On the first January, 1902, an important constitutional change was effected by the Gold Coast Order in Council passed by His Majesty in Privy Council in September, 1901, which, after defining the limits of the Colony as practically including all land south of the territory of Ashanti, goes on to annex to the British Dominions all such parts of the territory south of Ashanti as have not heretofore been included in His Majesty's Dominions, and to declare them to be part and parcel of His Majesty's Gold Coast Colony, as if they had formed part of the said Colony at the date of the Letters Patent of the 13th January, 1886.

The effect of that Order in Council was that Natives who were originally protected aliens became British subjects. Many legal questions were raised by this Order in Council, on the question of Native Tribunals generally, as, for instance, the effect it had on the criminal and civil jurisdiction of tribunals not under the Native Jurisdiction Ordinance, which exercised their inherent jurisdiction; and also upon the Courts which were placed under the Native Jurisdiction Ordinance before and after the 1st January, 1902. There were many legal difficulties and it was inevitable that some of them should come before the Court for decision.

He refers to the case of Gambra v. Num, in which Mr Justice Pennington decided that the effect of the Imperial Order in Council, combined with sections 12 and 13 of the Criminal Code, was to remove from Native Tribunals not under the Native Jurisdiction Ordinance, all criminal jurisdiction whatsoever.

With regard to the civil jurisdiction of Courts not under the Native Jurisdiction Ordinance, he states that the question was raised in the case of Bainyi v. Dantsi and Bainyi v. Appiah, in which the presiding

Judge, Mr Justice Morgan, stated a case to the Full Court who were asked to express an opinion as to whether the Native Kings and Chiefs could exercise in their jurisdiction the powers and functions vested in them by native law and custom, subject to the limitations imposed by the Native Prisons Ordinance. The Full Court, composed of four Judges, was equally divided on the question — two of the Judges deciding in the affirmative and the other two in the negative. There was at that time no casting vote, and consequently there is no express decision of the Full Court on the subject. He thinks, however, that if the question were ever to go before the Privy Council, it might possibly be held that although in the protected territory the Crown has power to set up British Courts, co-existent with the ordinary Courts of the country, in the British Dominions the Crown is in strict law the only fount of justice, and every Court of law must derive its authority from the Sovereign, or else cease to be a court of justice, and to become a mere voluntary tribunal of arbitration to which natives may continue to resort as a result of long tradition, but which has no legal power to compel appearance before it, or to enforce its awards. . . .

He has said enough to show that the position of Native Tribunals not under the Native Jurisdiction Ordinance is one of great doubt and difficulty. The conditions of the tribunals under that Ordinance are also very unsatisfactory.

It has been urged that the present system under which every application for an appeal must go before the Secretary for Native Affairs, thus involving a waste of time in correspondence, is cumbersome, and that greater facilities are wanted. There is no doubt that the natives are not familiar with the procedure which certainly acts in some cases as a deterrent to appeal against wrong decisions.

No action has ever been taken to regulate the fees charged by native courts, which are sometimes in excess of all reason.

Further, there is no recording of judgements in the native courts, with the result that when the judgement of a native court is brought up for review in the Supreme Court, there is nothing to show what that judgement really was. Another great drawback is that the chiefs have no means, under the Native Jurisdiction Ordinance 1883, of enforcing their judgements, and certain chiefs have applied to the Government to be given the same power as the Supreme Court has to enforce their judgements, e.g. by the sale of land.

One of the Unofficial Honourable Members, whose position as a Barrister of long standing and a native of the Colony, entitles him to be heard with great respect on all questions of native jurisdiction, has suggested that the solution of these difficulties is to be found in repealing the Native Jurisdiction Ordinance 1883, and enacting a new Ordinance, applying to the whole Colony, comprehensive, explicit, and complete in itself, which should define the powers and jurisdiction possessed by Native Chiefs, should regulate the exercise thereof, and the Court fees and fines for breaches of oath, and should, by facilitating appeals from inferior courts to that of an Omanhene, and thence to a Divisional Court, establish a perfect system of connection between the lowest and highest tribunals in the Colony.

To that suggestion, the Bill before the Council is, in some sense, an answer. . . . He is aware that there are many details of a very controversial and contentious nature in the Bill, but it is going to be referred to a special Committee of the Council, composed of the Chief Justice, the Colonial Secretary, the Attorney-General, the Secretary for Native Affairs . . . and three Unofficial Members — two of whom are natives — who will be given full power to amend the Bill as they may consider necessary. As Honourable Members are aware, the sole aim of the Government in introducing the measure, is to establish on a sound basis, an efficient system of co-operation by Native Chiefs in the impartial administration of justice, but at the same time it is desired, as far as consistent with the public welfare, to preserve native law and procedure. . . .

[Leg. Co. Debates]

The Special Committee failed to agree and the Bill was abandoned.

443 STATE OF TRADE IN 1906
SIR JOHN ROGER: STATEMENT IN LEGISLATIVE COUNCIL, 30 SEPTEMBER, 1907.

. . . The revenue for the year 1906 amounted to £683,101, as compared with £586,221 in 1905; while the expenditure only amounted to £628,906, as compared with £616,118. . . .

The following returns show the comparative value of trade during the last two years:—

	IMPORTS	EXPORTS.
1905	£1,486,068	£1,646,145
1906	2,058,939	1,996,412

The principal increases in imports from the United Kingdom were those of coal (£20,445), Cotton Goods (£7,153), and Machinery (£103,036); while the principal increases in Exports were those of Cocoa (£149,460), Gold (£225,442), Palm Oil (£36,649), and Rubber (£10,730). No change was made in the Customs Tariff, and the total receipts from Import Duties in 1906 amounted to £386,344. . . .

The following statement shows the quantity and value of gold exported during the last two years:—

	OZ.	£
1905	158,736	596,583
1906	217,288	822,025.

The supply of native labour is now fairly plentiful and the Secretary for Mines reports very favourably on the first batch of mining labourers from the Northern Territories, which ought to form a valuable recruiting ground.

The construction of a branch railway from Tarkwa to Prestea will afford transport facilities for an important mining district, and the reductions in the cost of

coal and in railway freight have improved the financial position of all mines served by the Sekondi–Kumasi Railway. Two of the principal mining companies have declared dividends at the rate of 10% each. . . .

[In Agriculture] the principal feature of the year was the rapid development of cocoa plantations, which now extend from the western side of the Aburi hills, through Akim and Kwahu, until they reach and even cross the borders of Ashanti. The export returns for the last two years were as follows:—

	lb.	£
1905	11,407,608	186,809
1906	20,104,504	336,269

Five motor lorries are now employed in bringing cocoa from Dodowa (26 miles) and Ayimensa (18 miles) to Accra, and this number will shortly be increased; while machinery for drying the beans is being erected both at Accra and Dodowa. . . .

I regret that it has not yet been found possible to obtain the services of a qualified Forest Officer, as a Forestry Department is greatly required in this Colony. When travelling in the Western Province, I was impressed by the large increase in the export of mahogany, and by the fact that the timber was frequently immature. I was also informed . . . that rubber was being collected without any regard to the manner in which the trees were tapped, with the result that many of them were already either dead or dying. Unfortunately, many native chiefs appear to sell or lease, both to Europeans and natives, rights to fell timber and collect rubber on 'Stool' lands, which they hold as tribal trustees, without imposing any conditions as to the manner in which such rights may be exercised. To prevent the continuance of this reckless improvidence, which threatens to destroy all accessible mahogany and native rubber trees within the next few years, a Bill, amending the Concessions Ordinance, has been introduced to regulate the felling of timber and collecting of uncultivated rubber on land granted under concession. . . .

[Leg. Co. Debates, 1907]

444 REPORT ON THE LEGISLATION GOVERNING THE ALIENATION OF NATIVE LANDS IN THE GOLD COAST COLONY AND ASHANTI . . . BY H. CONWAY BELFIELD, C.M.G.[1]

. . . A review of the period embracing the last twenty years, during which the value of land in the Central and Western Provinces of the Colony for commercial purposes has been proved by the operations of European capitalists, discloses the existence of some diversity of opinion with respect to its ownership. An effort was made in 1897 to establish the right of the Crown to all land in the Colony which was not at that time beneficially occupied, but for reasons to which it is unnecessary to refer here, that contention was eventually abandoned. . . .

Prior to the advent of European enterprise in the inland districts . . . the land was of little or no value in the estimation of the people of the country. It is true that the occupation of land was a necessity to them . . . but the area available was so largely in excess of their requirements that there seems to have been no necessity for apportioning the land amongst the various tribes. Gradually, however, as the disposition of the people became less nomadic, and as they settled down to the occupation of different districts, it became an understood thing that the chiefs and members of the tribe had acquired a right of possession in the land which they had for generations been occupying.

The next step no doubt was that the people should look to the chiefs and elders chosen by themselves to administer the land on their behalf, for the purpose of ensuring that each family should obtain what was necessary for its own use and sustenance, whereupon the chiefs, having allotted such areas as were sufficient to meet the requirements of all divisions of the people, held the remainder in reserve against the further needs of the future, setting aside portions of it for religious purposes, and generally controlling it in the capacity of trustees for the tribe. It was doubtless in some such manner that what is known as 'stool land' came into existence.

Notwithstanding the communal principles on which the native system of land tenure was based, and the unquestionable right of every member of the tribe to participate in the use of the land and in the profits accruing from it, the result of the administration of the reserve land by the chiefs and headmen has been that they have by degrees arrogated to themselves the profits arising from such administration, until, at the present time, the mass of the people derives from it no advantage other than the privilege of cultivating allotted portions, and any revenue which is obtained from it is absorbed by their superiors.

The fact that in early times the whole of the land in the country was gradually appropriated by, and divided among, the various tribes, constitutes the foundation of their claim that every acre of land is the property of some tribe, family, or individual. Certainly boundaries were ignored in the past as being of no importance, and there is a general inability to describe them definitely even at the present day, but the people unquestionably know the approximate limits of their respective territories, so far as topographical features can settle them; the rectitude of their claim has been admitted by all who have studied the subject during the last ten or twelve years, and I can find no reason for disputing it. It must, therefore, in my opinion, be taken to be established that all land belongs to the people which has not been acquired by other parties by specific process, such as cession, purchase, exchange, or inheritance; consequently such general appropriation by the Crown

---

[1] Henry Conway Belfield (later Sir) (1855–1923); served in the Malay States, 1888–1911; Governor of the East African Protectorate, 1912–18.

as was contemplated by the Land Bill of 1897 is, in my view, out of the question. . . .

When the resources of the country began to attract the attention of European miners and capitalists, and the chiefs were approached with requests that they would alienate land for industrial purposes, in respect of which substantial sums would be paid, they were quick to recognise the advantage which would accrue to themselves from the exercise of their right of the disposition of the Stool land. Their sense of obligation to the tribe in respect of their trusteeship was frequently obscured by their greed for money, and some cases have certainly occurred where the proceeds of concessions granted have been misappropriated to their own personal use. Such fraudulent action has, however, been invariably resented by the tribe, and has resulted in the removal of the offender from the Stool.

As a general rule, therefore, and particularly in later years, the chiefs who have granted concessions have been careful to effect the distribution of the proceeds in a manner conformable to the rules of the tribe, but the fact nevertheless remains that in consequence of their own ignorance, and the reluctance of the tribe to press their elders unduly, concessions have been granted upon terms which are unfavourable to the people.

This is particularly noticeable when inquiry is made concerning the areas granted. The chiefs and their advisers have no idea, even at the present time, what extent of country is contained in a given number of square miles. They always imagine that what they are granting is a mere fraction of the area which they actually dispose of. . . . The inability of the mass of the people to share either directly or indirectly in the revenue accruing from concessions, is an objectionable feature of the present system, and an improvement would be effected if part of the money were set aside to be expended on works for the public benefit of the community. . . .

On no account must the fact be lost sight of that the land is the property of the people; that a concession is a contract between the land-owners and the applicant, to which the Government is no party; that intervention must therefore be limited to supervision and guidance only, to the end that improvident alienation may be prevented and only such terms sanctioned as will ensure adequate protection of the rights and requirements of present and future generations. . . .

The extent of land which has been alienated to Europeans in the Colony up to the present time bears no more than a very fractional proportion to the area which remains. . . . I believe it will be found that misconception with regard to the area alienated has arisen in the minds of people in England through inability to distinguish between those lands the disposition of which has been finally completed by the issue of certificates of validity and those which are locally referred to as being 'under notice'. . . . In the vast majority of [the latter] no further action is contemplated, and they continue to congest the Court records only because no efficient machinery has been provided for their removal. . . .

I understand that suggestion has been made to the effect that the process of acquisition of land by Europeans is unduly contracting the area which should be retained by the natives, and that such contraction may result in partially depriving them of their legitimate and principal means of subsistence. Also that the contention that they may suffer such deprivation is based on the assumption that the population is increasing.

To deal with the latter point first, I have obtained no information which I can accept as reliable evidence that such increase is taking place. . . . It is possible that some increase may be taking place in the more flourishing agricultural districts of the Eastern Province, but I consider that no ground exists for the belief that there is a general advance in the numbers of the community throughout the Colony as a whole. . . .

I have no hesitation in expressing the opinion that the extent of the forest and bush lands now available for exploitation by the native farmers is far in excess of anything which they can possibly make use of for very many years to come. Unless indeed the population doubles or trebles itself and the permanent cultivation of large areas is substituted for the present practice of scratching minute lots, I see no prospect that the land in beneficial occupation by natives will ever be more than an unimportant part of the whole area available.

Moreover, it must not be assumed that the disposal of lands for mining concessions has deprived the people of the use of them. It is incumbent on the Judges of the Supreme Court to satisfy themselves that continued use of the surface for cultivation, hunting, and other purposes is assured to the native population, and it appears to be the fact that, in some cases, such as that of the Prestea concession, the advantage offered by the proximity of a market for their produce has caused the people to come in and cultivate the ground within the limits of the conceded area in far greater numbers than ever occupied it before the industry of the white man created a centre of attraction. . . .

It is a matter of complaint that the people of the country do not seek employment in the mines to the extent that the companies would like, and that the labour force is for the most part composed of foreigners brought in from other parts of the continent. A large number are nevertheless attracted from the villages in the Central and Western Provinces by the high rate of wages. . . .

The necessity of formulating some scheme whereby the disposition of land by native owners should be regulated and controlled, was made apparent in the course of the discussion which followed the introduction of the Land Bill of 1897, but it is not clear why the unusual course was taken of placing the jurisdiction in matters of land administration in the hands of the Judicial rather than those of the Executive Authority; that being a course which . . . has not been adopted or found necessary in any other Colony or Dependency of the Empire. . . .

I believe . . . that defects do exist in the Ordinance which seriously detract from its efficiency. . . . Those whose opinions on the subject are of the more value are unanimous in adverse criticism of the prevailing system, the only noteworthy exceptions being the Attorney-General . . . and the chiefs and educated Africans of the Central Province, who openly express their distrust of any action taken by Government in relation to land. . . .

The outline of the present system is that the Court inquires into and approves concessions conveying the right to work minerals, and to collect natural forest produce — that the Governor approves agricultural concessions exceeding one square mile in area, but is not directed to make any inquiry into the terms and conditions agreed upon; and that concessions for agricultural purposes not exceeding one square mile in area are subject to no inquiry and require no approval by anybody. . . .

I believe that the work can be performed more effectively, more expeditiously, and more economically, if entrusted to executive officers, and I recommend that a system of land administration by the executive be substituted for that which at present prevails. . . .

The Forest Ordinance.

The movement which was commenced in 1911, in opposition to the introduction of the Forest Ordinance, had its origin in the Central Province, and it was only at Cape Coast Castle that objections to the measure were urged upon my attention. Elsewhere the subject was not propounded to me as a matter of importance, and I have no reason to presume that a desire for its withdrawal is general throughout the Colony. This view is to some extent supported by the fact that the Unofficial Members of the Legislative Council, representing interests in other parts of the country, saw no reason for witholding their assent to the introduction of the measure. Moreover, in no instance did any of those in Cape Coast Castle who opposed the Bill, suggest that the views they expressed were commonly held throughout the Gold Coast. They appeared to consider it sufficient that they themselves object to its adoption.

Cape Coast Castle is the headquarters of the Gold Coast Aborigines' Protection Society, which came into existence in the year 1898 after the successful opposition offered in London to the Land Bill of 1897. It appears that the chiefs, being possibly elated by the result of their intervention in that instance, expressed a desire for the formation of a body which should watch their interests and ensure united action in the event of any policy being proposed in the future to which they might see fit to object. The Society is composed of the Chiefs of the Central Province, in association with a number of educated native traders and lawyers resident in Cape Coast.

It is generally believed by those who have not closely examined its constitution, that the educated members in Cape Coast really dictate the policy of the Society, and that the chiefs have little or no voice therein, and are admitted to the privilege of membership principally for the purpose of providing it with funds. I found this to be by no means the case. At least three or four of the chiefs readily speak, read and write English. Almost all of them take in the 'Government Gazette' and follow the actions of Government with accuracy and intelligence. There is no doubt that the inception of the Society was due to the expressed wish of the chiefs themselves, and that they take as active a part in its proceedings as any of the educated members.

It exists for the avowed purpose of opposing and blocking any action by the Government or by any persons, which may, in the opinion of the members, be subversive of their interests, or likely to be prejudicial to their native customs or their canons of land tenure. Funds are subscribed by the chiefs only, no payment being made by the Cape Coast members, but such of them as are lawyers, give their services without fee, receiving only their actual travelling expenses. . . .

The objection offered to the Ordinance by the chiefs and other members of the Society was similar in every instance. Specific objection to any particular section or word was not, as a rule, taken, but strong opposition was offered to the assumption by Government, of power to take over any portion of their tribal lands, even though with the declared intention of administering it for the benefit and profit of the community. It was urged . . . that the Ordinance is, in effect, an endeavour to attain the same object as that attempted by the Land Bill of 1897. . . . They point out that, if it becomes law, the Government may assume possession on the plea of establishing a system of conservancy, and then put it to other uses, even alienating it to third parties for commercial purposes, and thus arrogating to itself the rights and privileges of ownership which are vested only in the tribe. No one of all the persons who gave evidence before me, could be induced to show the smallest interest in the preservation of forests, or to admit, when the system was explained to him, that the country would be any better for its introduction. . . . The answer invariably made, was to the effect that if Government wants the forests preserved, it should give them the necessary instruction and leave them to do it for themselves. . . .

The suggestion made by the chiefs that the forests should be left in their own hands, and that Government intervention should be confined to teaching them how to manage them, is not a practical proposal worth serious consideration. There is no real desire on the part of the people to conserve the forest land — they are naturally careless and wasteful in their methods of dealing with it. . . . Even, therefore, if it were possible to organise a system of instruction which would instil into the chiefs a knowledge of the elements of forestry, nothing short of the strictest supervision and direction, amounting in practice to compulsion, would suffice to ensure the effective application of that knowledge by the present generation. . . .

I look upon the opposition offered by the chiefs as devoid of any substantial foundation, other than the apprehension that Government may be intending to vest interests in reserved areas in third parties. I think that the knowledge that such power has not been taken, would go far to modify that opposition, and I advise that the Ordinance be passed and put into force after it has been amended in the manner which I have indicated.[1]

[Cd. 6278 of 1912, pp. 7–13, 15–16, 23, 37–8, 41, A & P (1912–13) lix]

445 THE PALM OIL BILL 1913.

[a] Debate on the Second Reading. Leg. Council, 28 January 1913.

The Colonial Secretary[2] states:—

After an interval of nearly six months, the Palm Oil Ordinance comes up for second reading. In the interim, the Bill has been subjected to a good deal of criticism by question and answer across the floor of the House of Commons, and in the Press. As one of the results of these criticisms, the Government will move several important amendments at the

---

[1] . . . 'The Bill . . . should be so altered that its scope may be limited to the selection, demarcation, constitution, and maintenance of reserves, and no terms should be incorporated which, by expression or implication, will confer upon Government the power of dealing with reserved areas in a manner not essential to the formation of an effective system of conservancy.' . . . Para. 156, *ibid.*

[2] Major Sir J. H. Bryan, Colonial Secretary, 1904–14.

Committee stage. . . . It is proposed to omit all reference to railways . . . and the power to grant exclusive rights in railways. . . .

I venture to think that if the amendments which I have indicated should be made in Committee, cause for much hostile criticism will be removed. Briefly, the Bill is framed with a view to revive an old established Gold Coast industry by encouraging capitalists to erect modern machinery for the expression of oil from the pericarp of palm fruits. It is hoped that by the establishment of such machinery, perennial markets within palm-bearing areas will be afforded to natives who will not have to travel so far afield as at present to sell this form of produce. The Bill does not restrict or interfere in any way with existing native rights with respect to local products; the cultivators of the soil will remain free to sell when and where they like; no interest, right, or property in land or the products of the soil is taken; not an acre of land can change hands under the Bill. Native farmers will be under no compulsion to sell palm fruits to the owners of the mills. If the mills are in a convenient position, and adequate prices are offered, one may reasonably suppose that natives will sell their produce to the capitalists; but if they should elect not to do so, or to revert to the former primitive methods, there will be nothing to prevent them. Experience shows that the native farmers of the Gold Coast are sufficiently alive to their commercial interests to take their produce to the most accessible market at which they can obtain fair prices, and it will be for the owners of the projected mills to secure the goodwill and custom of the natives by treating them fairly and even liberally.

If the installation of modern machinery and labour-saving appliances should prove successful in reviving and developing the palm fruit industry, the project should have the effect of releasing, for productive purposes, a considerable proportion of the labour now employed in expressing the oil by hand and in conveying it to distant markets.

I beg to move that the Bill be now read a second time.

Mr Grey moves that the Bill be not read a second time at this sitting of the Council and states:— . . . As no copies of the Government proposed amendments have been supplied to Unofficial Members, it is impossible for me to form an opinion upon them, and so far as the Unofficial Members are concerned, the Bill I am now objecting to appears to allow the Government to grant monopoly of areas of approximately 300 square miles, including the sole right of constructing and working railways within the area. I suppose the whole palm-oil tree area in the Colony is between 3,000 and 4,000 square miles . . . so I think ten concessions of monopoly areas would comprise the whole of the palm-tree area of the Colony.

I think the Hon. Giles Hunt could give your Excellency some idea as to how easy it will be to render ineffective the clause prescribing the area grantable under this Ordinance. A similar clause was inserted in the Concessions Ordinance under which no mining company could hold more than 20 square miles. Nevertheless, in *Gazette* No. 94, published recently, you will see that one concern under various names, has passed through the Concessions Court no less than 27 concessions, equal over 130 square miles, although the law allows the holding of only 4 concessions or a total of 20 square miles.

The Bill states that only one concession shall be allowed, but it will be very easy, however, for powerful companies like Messrs Levers, or Messrs Brunner-Mond & Company to take up, under various names, the whole of the palm tree area of the Colony, and the Government will be unable to enforce the clause limiting the number of concessions, as it has undoubtedly been unable to enforce a similar clause in the Concessions Ordinance.

The Colonial Secretary also states that the Bill is intended to encourage and revive an old Gold Coast industry. I do not think the Palm Oil Industry requires reviving. It is at present in a fairly flourishing condition, notwithstanding the labour and transport difficulties resulting from the competition for labour with the cocoa industry and mines. There is undoubtedly room for increased exports, but I do not think a monopoly is necessary in order to encourage any industry in this Colony. I think a monopoly will have exactly the reverse effect.

The sole reason why machinery has hitherto not been used in the palm oil industry is that no satisfactory machinery has existed, and experiments on a large scale have only taken place during the past two years. There is at present one experimental plant in use by Messrs Levers at Adjuah, and I have it on authority that the machinery is not satisfactory and that Messrs Levers propose to adopt a new method altogether. Moreover, the exports from Adjuah during the last 18 months indicate that the experiment is not successful. . . . Another Company, Messrs Apol Limited, controlled by Brunner-Mond & Company, has made arrangements for erecting machinery near Dixcove; this machinery is also of an experimental nature. It is, however, considered to be of a more advanced type than Levers', and similar machines have proved fairly successful in the German Cameroons. A machinery at Lome . . . of the same type as Messrs Levers has not proved successful. I can speak with authority regarding this machinery as my Company is financially interested in it. In Lome, the German Government have not considered it necessary to grant a monopoly, neither have they been asked for one, and as soon as it is proved that oil-extracting machinery is commercially successful, several companies will put up machinery for dealing with palm fruit without asking for the grant of a monopoly. . . .

So far as native rights are concerned, we are told that the Bill does not affect them.

This, however, is not the opinion of Unofficial Members. . . . You propose to grant a monopoly of 300 square miles over native lands. That means that native farmers who could afford to do so will be prohibited by the Concessionaire to treat their crops by means of machinery. If the Government were to grant a concession in the Krobo district, for example, that single concession will embrace all the palm-bearing lands of the district, and the consequence will be that Chief Mate Kole, who can afford to do so, will not be allowed to use machinery himself, but will have to continue primitive methods of extracting oil from the pericarp by hand labour. This is a serious point. It is bad enough to eliminate competition by granting exclusive rights to a concessionaire as against other European companies, but it is worse still to stop the native owner of palm trees from employing machinery for treating his products. . . .

The effect of the Bill will be that the concession holder will be able to go to the native farmer and say, this is my price for your produce, and if you do not sell it to me, no one else near your land will be allowed to purchase it from you. The concession holder will naturally offer the lowest price possible, as he will have no competitors. Is it right that in this Twentieth Century you should say to the native farmers, you will only allow them to treat their products in the same way as their forefathers, and that if machinery is discovered which will allow of large profits being made out of the products of their land, you will not allow them to use it? . . .

I am opposing the Bill because I want it to be withdrawn, not amended. The Bill gives the company holding the monopoly practically the sole trading rights over the area conceded, because anybody possessing the transport will also posses the trade. . . . By giving a company power over transport you are placing every inhabitant of the area under the control of the Company. . . .

The reason this Bill has been placed before the Council is said to be to encourage Companies to come into the Colony to take up concessions and erect machinery for the extraction of palm oil. No reason however is given why companies already in the Colony have not been asked to put up machinery for the oil extraction. A new company has practically been told, 'Go in, we will give you concessions and all possible facilities.' I do not know what Messrs Levers have done for this Colony that they should be given a monopoly, or why they have the ear of the Secretary of State. In Parliament it has been suggested that these concessions on the Gold Coast and Sierra Leone are to be given in return for bribes Messrs Levers have contributed to the cause of the Liberals. . . .

The motion is put and carried, Messrs Grey, Hutton-Mills and Mate Kole voting in the minority. . . .

[b] Proceedings in . . . Legislative Council, 4 July, 1913.

Mr Hutton-Mills[1] moves that Mr E. J. P. Brown, Barrister at-law, be permitted to address the Council, as Counsel on behalf of the Aborigines' Rights Protection Society, with regard to the Palm Oil Bill, and, on the suggestion of the Governor, proceeds to give some information as to how the Bill is considered to affect the Society's interests. The Aborigines' Rights Protection Society, he states, was formed in the year 1897, when the attempt was made by Government to pass the Lands Bill, and that it was due to the opposition instituted by that Society on behalf of the Colony generally, and in particular the Amanhin, Ahinfu and the Manchemei of the three provinces, that the Bill in question was withdrawn.

The Society has a constitution of its own. One of its primary objects is to assist the Government as much as possible in carrying out administrative measures, and since the year 1897 it has been the

[1] Thomas Hutton-Mills (1865–1931); born at Accra; lawyer; member of Legislative Council 1898–1904 and 1909–14.

mouthpiece and organ of the people. As the petition just presented demonstrates, the Society is interested on behalf of the Amanhin, Ahinfu, Manchemei and the people of the Colony; and he asks the privilege of being heard by Counsel, which was accorded it when the Lands Bill of 1897 and the Forest Bill were before the Legislative Council, be extended to it on the present occasion. . . .

Mr Brown: . . .

This Bill is without a preamble. It is respectfully submitted, Sir, that it is becoming a practice to pass measures in skeleton with reservation of enormous powers in the Governor to make rules, amendments and alterations. Sometimes these amendments go beyond the scope of the measure, and clothe it with a new scope and purview which varies with the original objects and the reason for its promulgation. . . . A measure such as this, which proposes to affect private rights, should not be elastic and ambiguous, since it would be inimical to the interests of owners of oil-palm lands to restrict their rights of user indefinitely without setting forth clearly the scope of the measure, in a preamble, so as to govern and restrict its provisions accordingly. . . .

The tenure of land in this country is allodial; that is to say, the people do not hold their lands of any superior person, whether such land-owners be individuals, families, or tribes. The chiefs designated as Tribal Authorities in the Bill, do not own the lands of this country. It sometimes happens that some chiefs own no lands . . . and such being the case, their powers are not based on territorial rights but upon the consent and wish of the people, for administrative purposes. In other words, the sovereignty of this country is in the people. . . .

The term tribal authority would appear to be loosely used in connection with the Bill, without regard to the fact that the tenure of land . . . is allodial. . . . It would be . . . unjust if the Government are

going to assume that the consent of tribal authorities is essential to the grant of the contemplated exclusive rights without the consent of the landowners. Of late, native kings and chiefs have been erroneously assumed to be trustees of all the lands in this country. They are not trustees, but joint owners with their families, and cannot deal with the lands without first obtaining the consent of the other joint-owners. . . .

The interposition of an Executive Officer between the licensee and the so-called Tribal Authority, instead of the licensee going direct to the land owner, gives the petitioners just cause to apprehend a serious invasion of the use of, and the free enjoyment of proprietary rights in land, which, in practical politics, amounts to an extinguishment of such rights. There should be nothing to prevent the licensee from acquiring a concession of oil-palm lands as an agricultural concession in the ordinary way; that is, by going direct to the landowner and subsequently to the Concessions Court, so that the restriction can be made to apply only to the area acquired. On the other hand, if the parties in whose interest this Bill is being promulgated, desire to protect their machinery, they should apply for a patent under the Patent Ordinance of this Colony.

To make the measure affect the lands of other people unconnected with the transaction, would appear to be neither legal nor equitable. Not legal, because the Government are granting to outsiders, rights which do not exist in themselves, nor in the so-called Tribal Authorities, who are not owners of the proposed area. It is inequitable, because the owners are not parties to the transaction, and receive no compensation for the 21 years, the life of the grant, and the renewal for a further term of 21 years, during which the licence is to operate. . . .

It is . . . reasonably to be apprehended that the proposed measure will ultimately kill native enterprise in the oil-palm industry, in the same way as the introduction of European gold mining, with the

...uent promulgation of the Gold ...ng Ordinance, is gradually killing the native gold mining industry. Today there is scarcity of gold dust, and goldsmiths work jewellery with gold coins (sovereigns) instead of gold dust as before. ...

The proposed measure raises the same point which had been threshed out in connection with the Crown Lands Bill 1893, Lands Bill 1897, and recently the Forest Bill, which is under consideration — namely, the dealing with our lands and our rights thereover as if we hold them of the British Crown. The frequent recurrence of this point, raised by such measures, naturally perturbs the people, and entails great expense in sending Deputations to England to interview His Majesty's Secretary of State for the Colonies. ... It would be a breach of faith with the people of this country, on the part of the Government, in face of the several treaty obligations with, and assurances to the people to leave intact their immemorial rights in their land, to restrict in any way the free enjoyment of their proprietary rights in, and user of, land. ...

On the question being put that the Bill be read a third time, the Council divided as follows:—

Noes	Ayes
Mr Howie	The Principal Medical
Mr Hutton Mills	Officer
	The Treasurer
	The Attorney-General
	The Acting Colonial
	Secretary.

The motion is carried and the Bill is read a third time and passed as Ordinance No. 10 of 1913.

[c] Statement by Sir Hugh Clifford.[1] Legislative Council, 3 October, 1913.

[1] Sir Hugh Charles Clifford (1866–1941); served in Malay States, 1883–99 and 1901–3; Governor of N. Borneo and Labuan, 1899–1901; in West Indies, 1903–6; Colonial Secretary of Ceylon, 1907–12; Governor of the Gold Coast (1912–19), Nigeria (1919–25), Ceylon (1925–7); Governor of Straits Settlements and High Commissioner to the Malay States, 1927–9.

... The object of this Ordinance is to encourage capitalists to invest money in machinery for the more scientific expression of oil from the pericarp of the palm fruit, by securing to them, for a period of years, the sole right to erect and work such plant, within an area of ten miles from a given centre. For this purpose the Ordinance empowers the Governor, in certain circumstances, to issue a licence to an approved applicant. ...

As originally drafted, the Ordinance was open to the objection that it empowered the Governor to grant these licences on his own responsibility, and without reference to the inhabitants of the localities concerned. This defect was pointed out in this Council by several Unofficial Members, and was felt by me and by my advisers, to be a serious flaw in the Ordinance as originally drawn. Full consideration was given to the matter, and finally an amendment was introduced by Government, and adopted by a majority of this Council, limiting the power of the Governor to grant a licence conferring this exclusive right, to localities where the proposed issue of a licence had received the consent of the Tribal Authorities, or a majority of them, and after these Authorities had satisfied the Governor that the owners of palm-bearing land in the vicinity, or a majority of them, had approved. ...

[Leg. Co. Debates, 1913]

446 STATE OF TRADE IN 1912
SPEECH OF SIR HUGH CLIFFORD IN LEGISLATIVE COUNCIL, 3 OCTOBER, 1913.

... The revenue for the year 1912 amounted to £1,230,850. ... Some peculiar circumstances have combined to reduce unduly the revenue of the current year, but ... I am of opinion that the estimated revenue for 1914 can safely be placed at £1,387,200. ... To this total it is anticipated that Customs Receipts will contribute £825,000 and the Railways £396,000, leaving £166,200 only to be drawn from all other sources of revenue.

. . . In a country such as this, the Government Railway must be regarded, not only as a public convenience and a means of transport, but also as a direct engine for taxation. . . . Any comparison between the interest which the revenue of the Railway is able to pay, as a return upon the capital expenditure, and a similar figure for railways in lands where extensive systems of direct taxation are in vogue, must at once be regarded as fallacious.

The expenditure for which Honourable Members were invited to provide in the estimates for the current year amounted to £1,263,250. The revised estimate of the sums which will actually be disbursed up to December 31st next, now places the probable expenditure of the year at £1,225,800. . . .

At the end of 1912, the net excess of Assets over Liabilities amounted to £939,568, and by the end of the current year it is anticipated that this sum will have been increased to approximately £1,005,000. . . . The accumulation of the[se] large balances . . . cannot but be viewed with mixed feelings. Rightly understood, their existence is mainly to be attributed to the inability of the Government to expend upon much-needed public works, and upon other services of general utility, the funds which this Council has from time to time placed at its disposal. . . . . I am of opinion that, in the present stage of the Colony's development, every available shilling of the public revenue should be invested in works which are needed to accelerate that development, and to consolidate the prosperity of the people. Until the resources of the Colony have been opened up far more effectually than is today the case, it will be impossible to regard steadily growing accumulations of unexpended money with anything resembling complacency. . . .

The trade of this Colony has never before attained to such proportions as those which exist today. . . . The progress of recent years has not only been steady but rapid:—

	IMPORTS	EXPORTS[1]
1910	£2,618,982	£2,613,919
1911	2,762,946	3,471,258
1912	3,140,786	4,004,294

From this it will be seen that the total trade of the Colony for 1912 was £7,145,080, as against £5,232,901 in 1910 — an increase of £1,912,179, or over 36½% in two years.

The exports of cocoa in 1912 amounted to 86,568,481 lbs., valued at £1,613,468 in 1911. It is anticipated that the exports of cocoa during the current year will show a very considerable increase. . . . Today . . . this Colony occupies the position of the premier cocoa-producing country of the world. . . .

During 1912 the shipments of palm kernels amounted to 14,628 tons valued at £202,365, an increase of 10% in quantity and of 17% in value compared with the exports in 1911. It is believed that this increase will be maintained during the current year, and the great interest which various large firms of soap-boilers are manifesting in this product will, it is hoped, lead to a considerable expansion of the industry in the immediate future.

The shipments of rubber in 1912 amounted to 1,990,699 lbs, valued at £168,729, a decrease of 25% in quantity and 23% in value as compared with 1911. These are the lowest figures shown during the last nine years, except in 1908 when they were about the same level. This decrease, it is suggested, is due to the low prices ruling in the European markets, the practical extinction of the market for the lowest grades of native rubber, and the diversion of local labour to more profitable occupations. Some of the new rubber plantations in the Western province have now begun to make shipments. The high cost of wages which rules in this Colony, as compared with the pay earned by labourers in the principal rubber-producing

[1] These figures differ from those of the Colonial Office List quoted in Appendix E, which are inclusive. The figures quoted here would appear to exclude specie and re-exports.

countries of the East, combined with the difficulties and expense of transport, must inevitably place rubber-growers in this Colony at a serious disadvantage at a time when competition, based on cheapness of production, is annually becoming more and more acute.

The quantity of kola nuts shipped in 1912 amounted to 7,133,165 lbs., valued at £135,231, which is an increase of 23% in quantity and 44% in value over the previous year, and is the largest quantity ever exported during any one year. This does not take into account exports of this commodity across the inland frontiers of the Colony of which no exact record can be maintained.

The exports of timber during 1912 also constituted a record for the Colony. They amounted to 23,573,651 square feet, valued at £228,745, an increase of 69% in quantity and of 65% in value as compared with the figures for 1911. There is every prospect of this record being surpassed during the current year. The bulk of the mahogany exported is absorbed by the American market.

The gold exported from the Colony and Ashanti during 1912 amounted to 377,659 oz., valued at £1,439,267, as against 280,060 oz. valued at £1,057,692 in 1911. . . . It is hoped that this, the largest export of gold on record for this Colony, will be materially exceeded during the current year, the value of the gold exported from the 1st January to the 30th of June last having amounted to £840,099. . . .

The economical development of the Northern Territories . . . must necessarily be a slow and protracted process. So far as is at present known, the resources of the Protectorate are purely agricultural; and the possibility of an export trade in agricultural produce hangs mainly on the two questions of population and transport. The population, as shown by the census of 1911, is not large, having regard to the area it inhabits; and transport to the Northern Territories is peculiarly difficult and expensive. The Protectorate, more-

over, is not known to possess any natural advantages of soil or climate which render it more suitable for agricultural enterprise than are the numerous rich and comparatively-speaking accessible areas in the Colony and Ashanti which still await development. In these circumstances, therefore, there is little prospect of an export trade in agricultural produce assuming any notable proportions until such time as transport facilities — and in this Colony, I am persuaded, efficient transport facilities mean the construction, not of roads, but of railways — can be provided. In this matter, however, the Northern Territories must be content to await its turn. At the present time . . . many of the richest and most developed districts of the Colony and of Ashanti are still without any efficient means of transporting their produce to the coast; and it is not until these districts have been opened up by railway extensions that the provision of similar facilities for the Northern Territories can be regarded as a question of practical politics. . . . The Government of the Colony must be content for years — it may be for decades — to recognise the Northern Territories as a direct and unremunerative source of expenditure. In 1912, for example, the revenue of the Protectorate amounted to £2,994 and the expenditure to £78,894. However, the work which is being carried on so ably by Captain Armitage, Major Irvine, and their colleagues in the Northern Territories, is not, I consider, to be judged by the kind of test which a balance-sheet supplies. A population of over 360,000 people has been rescued from the tyranny of slave-raiders, from the horrors of frequent inter-tribal conflicts, and from the miseries and privations which these things were wont to bring in their train. The very meaning of peace and security has only during the past few years dawned upon the understandings of the majority of these people; and already the native population is showing its appreciation of the changed conditions and of its new found liberty. The people come and go freely without fear of molestation. The chiefs are learning to realise their powers and responsibilities, and are ranging themselves on the side of law and order. Serious crime is decreasing and that at a time when our administrative officers are annually getting into closer and closer touch with the natives, and crime is, therefore, more easily detected and less easy to conceal.

I feel sure that Honourable Members will agree with me that a rich and prosperous Colony, such as ours, may well congratulate itself upon having a share in the furtherance of work of this description, and need not grudge the expenditure which, for many years to come, will be required, in order to enable it to go forward without check or interruption. . . .

One of the questions which first engaged my attention after my arrival in the Colony was the problem of transport, upon which, in my opinion, the moral and intellectual progress of the native population, no less than their material and economic advancement, and the efficient administration and development of the country will be found primarily to hinge. In this connection the rival merits of roads and railways, having regard to the peculiarities of local conditions, called in the first instance, for careful study, and upon this subject I have formed some very definite opinions; . . . that wide roads of any description are only required in this country for the accomodation of motor-propelled vehicles; that they are not needed for hand-carts or for cask-rolling; that metalled roads are in this country extraordinarily expensive, and again are only needed for motors; that broad roads inflict great hardship upon the bearers of head-loads; and that the existence of a made road in a country which is possessed neither of traction animals, nor of an indigenous wheeled traffic, does not necessarily tend to the immediate solution of existing transport difficulties. Railways, on the other hand, are, viewed from this stand-point, roads ready equipped with the vehicles which on the majority of our existing roads are so few in number, and so comparatively ineffective in capacity. By means of railways, moreover, main arteries of traffic can be driven through the more populous and productive districts, which will supply efficient transport, not only to the country actually tapped, but, by curtailing the distances over which goods have been transported by primitive methods, throughout an extensive area on each side of the line, will tend to reduce the labour and cost of transport over a wide belt of country.

Early in March, therefore, I addressed the Secretary of State on this important question, and warmly advocated a vigorous policy of railway extension. The main principles which I then advocated, and which have met with a measure of general approval from the Secretary of State, may be shortly stated as follows:—

1. That the surveys for projected lines should be run with a greater regard to the centres of existing population and cultivation, than with the object of securing the most direct route between the starting point and the ultimate objective, their primary aim being rather to open up the country en route, than to afford rapid means of locomotion between any given points.

2. That the policy of running railway lines mainly in a direction at right angles to the coast, should be abandoned.

3. That in the first instance, the country to be developed should be the districts situated between the Sekondi–Kumasi and the Accra–Akwapim railways; and that the railway system should be based on the two ports of Accra and Sekondi, upon the improvement of the harbours of which places, large sums of public money have been and are being spent.

4. That the survey of one line from Komfrodua to Kumasi, via Tafo, Anyinam, the foot of the Kwahu plateau, and Bompata, should be immediately undertaken.

5. That the survey of a second line from Accra to some point yet to be determined on the Sekondi–Kumasi Railway — the effect of which will be to bring the towns of Cape Coast, Saltpond and Winnebah into closer touch with the railway system of the Colony, and at the same time to afford efficient transport facilities to the inhabitants and for the produce of the country between the Birrim River and the sea — be also undertaken.

6. That after the line which each railway will follow has been determined with more or less certainty by means of a flying survey, survey operations should be carried on simultaneously from Komfrodua, Kumasi, Accra, and the point of junction of the new line with the Sekondi–Kumasi railway respectively, and working plans prepared.

7. That in each case construction should follow hard upon the heels of survey, the completed line being handed over to the Railway Department and opened to traffic in short convenient lengths, while the work of construction still proceeds on a further section of the projected line. . . .

[Leg. Co. Debates, 1913]

33   The Gold Coast at War 1914–1918

GOVERNOR CLIFFORD'S programme was rudely interrupted by the outbreak of the World War in August 1914. But the Colony, in spite of many new handicaps, continued to advance, both politically and economically.

Military operations did not touch the Gold Coast very closely. A sharp campaign, in August 1914, brought about the surrender of the Germans in Southern Togoland (448), while in the north, a British occupation was welcomed as re-uniting the Dagomba peoples (447); but not until 1918 did the Government make tentative enquiries into the wishes of the population of Togoland, preparatory to a permanent settlement (456). Gold Coast troops after 1914 served in the Cameroons and in East Africa (454).

The economic effects of the war threatened to be more serious, since Germany had been one of the best markets for Gold Coast cocoa (448): but loss of the German market was more than made good by the enhanced value of Gold Coast products, and by the development of trade with the United States (454). Even the cessation of railway building in the Colony was effectively counterbalanced by the advent of the light motor lorry (456), which was to pave the way for the great economic expansion after the war. On the other hand, some of the measures adopted by the Entente Powers, to cripple the German economy, might well have compromised the welfare of the Gold Coast, and, on that account, were opposed by the Governor (453).

Governor Clifford was also responsible for the first notable constitutional advances (449), which, modest as they were, were almost too much for a hesitant Secretary of State (450). Not the least important feature of his proposals was the attempt to secure representation for the tribal masses as well as the educated few (452). Clifford was the first to direct attention to the problem of adapting tribal institutions to the requirements of a modern democracy. Until some solution had been found to that problem, there could, in his view, be no advance to a system of elective representation — which the literate minority were already demanding before the end of the war (457).

---

447 SIR HUGH CLIFFORD TO LEWIS HAR-COURT[1]   ACCRA, 14 SEPTEMBER, 1914.

Sir,

I have the honour to forward, herewith, a copy of a report from the Chief Commissioner of the Northern Territories, Captain C. H. Armitage, C.M.G., D.S.O., with reference to the occupation[2] of

[1] Lewis Harcourt (later 1st Viscount Harcourt) (1863–1922); son of Sir William Harcourt; Liberal M.P., 1904–16; Secretary of State for the Colonies, 1910–15.
[2] On 14 August.

Yendi by the Northern Territories Constabulary.

It will be observed with satisfaction that no opposition was offered, and that the entry of the British forces was welcomed by the native population.

Yendi is the chief town of the Dagomba portion of the Sansanne-Mangu district of Togoland; and it will be within your recollection that I arranged with the Lieutenant-Governor of Dahomey that the Dagomba portion of this district should be administered by the British during the military occupation of Togoland. This has been approved by both the British and the French Governments, and I have now, with the concurrence of the Lieutenant-Governor of Dahomey, instructed the Chief Commissioner of the Northern Territories to depute a District Commissioner of experience, to settle, in conjunction with the French Administrateur at Sansanne-Mangu, the provisional boundaries of the areas to be temporarily administered by our respective Governments. . . .

On my arrival at Accra on the 28th August, Mr Robertson[1] informed me that he had learned from the Chief Commissioner of the Northern Territories that he had concluded a treaty with the chief of Yendi. The Acting-Governor had at once telegraphed to the Chief Commissioner, saying that such action was undesirable, and I also wired to him endorsing this communication.

A copy of the treaty forms an enclosure to Captain Armitage's report, and it will be seen that this document is less in the nature of a treaty than of a petition for protection and for the unification, under British rule, of the Dagomba country, which was bisected when the Anglo-German boundary in the Northern Territories was determined. I do not think such a document can be held to be binding either upon the Chief or upon the Government of the Gold Coast; but it should, I think, be noted for future reference, that any attempt once more to divide the Dagomba country in a manner which is opposed to the ethnological distribution of the native population, will be keenly resented by the chiefs and people both in the Northern Territories and in the Sansanne-Mangu district of Togoland.

The foregoing remark applies with equal force to the feeling of the natives in the Peki and Misahoe districts, and to the Awuna population in the Keta and Lomeland districts. . . .

[Cd. 7872, A & P (1914–16) xvii]

[1] Acting-Governor, May–August 1914.

448 LEGISLATIVE COUNCIL PROCEEDINGS
26 NOVEMBER, 1914.

Present:

His Excellency the Governor, Sir Hugh Clifford, K.C.M.G.
The Honourable the Colonial Secretary, A. R. Slater, Esquire.
The Honourable the Attorney-General, W. R. Townsend, Esquire.
The Honourable the Treasurer, E. B. Reece, Esquire.
The Honourable the Principal Medical Officer, Dr. F. G. Hopkins,
The Honourable W. H. Grey ⎫
The Honourable T. Hutton-Mills ⎪
The Honourable Emmanuel Mate Kole (Konor of Eastern Krobo) ⎬ Unofficial Members.
The Honourable J. D. McKay ⎭

. . . . .

The Governor: . . .

The Gold Coast was the first of Great Britain's Colonial Possessions to take an active part in the war. The armed Forces of the Colony, acting in co-operation with those of the French Colony of Dahomey, — the whole under Lieutenant-Colonel Bryant of the Gold Coast Regiment — invaded the neighbouring German Colony of Togoland within a few days of the declaration of war, and before the end of August the enemy was compelled to surrender. Simultaneously a detachment of the Northern Territories Constabulary under Major Marlow occupied Yendi, the capital of the Dagomba country, without resistance; and another detachment of the same force penetrated unopposed to Bismarcksburg. The campaign in southern Togoland, which entailed an advance upon Atakpame, distant by rail 101 miles from Lome, the capital, was pushed forward with great vigour, and, after several sharp engagements, the enemy was forced to retire to Kamina. Here, after destroying the huge wireless installation, which had recently been completed at a cost of nearly a quarter of a million sterling, the enemy unconditionally surrendered. . . .

Everywhere in Togoland our coming has been welcomed by the native chiefs and people; and in the country now in the occupation of the Allies, provisional Governments have been established in the two spheres of administration which, for immediate purposes only and without prejudice to any settlement which may hereafter be arrived at, have been temporarily arranged between the allied Governments of Great Britain and France.

The decision of the Government thus to take an active part in the war, has locally met with universal approval; and the destruction of the great wireless installation erected by the German Government at Kamina, which was the real *raison d'être* of the expedition, was a matter of considerable service rendered to the Empire.

The cost of the invasion of Togoland is estimated to amount to between £60,000 and £65,000 sterling; and this Council, acting on behalf of the people of the Gold Coast, has recently undertaken, as our local contribution to the expenses of the Imperial Government in connection with the war, to charge the entire cost of the expedition upon the Colonial Revenue. This offer has been accepted by His Majesty's Government with warm expression of appreciation.

The Government had also despatched a fully equipped force, under the command of Lieutenant-Colonel Rose of the Gold Coast Regiment, to aid in the operations now being conducted by the Allies against the German Government in the Kameruns. . . .

The exports of cocoa from the Gold Coast . . . represented during 1913, more than 20% of the total production of the world. . . . Had circumstances remained normal, it was to be anticipated that the exports of cocoa during 1914 would have slightly exceeded the amount exported in 1913, which . . . was rather more than 50,550 tons. The cocoa market, however, has been considerably affected by the war. Not only has Germany in the past consumed some 15,000 tons annually, of the cocoa exported from the Gold Coast, which will now have to be sold elsewhere, but the value of cocoa is largely dependent upon a cheap and abundant sugar supply. It is estimated that the world's production of sugar during 1913 amounted to approximately 18½ million tons, of which 7¼ million tons, or more than 39%, was produced in Germany, Austria, Russia, France and Belgium, all countries whose agricultural activities have been seriously affected or restricted by the war. It is therefore probable . . . that a certain shortage will make itself felt, and that a portion of the present cocoa crop will have to be stored and held for a period more or less prolonged. . . . These considerations, added to the stringency everywhere prevailing in the money markets of the world, have necessarily resulted in a serious fall in the price of cocoa, and a weakening of the inducements to local farmers to pick and market their crop. . . .

[Leg. Co. Debates, 1914]

449 SIR HUGH CLIFFORD TO LEWIS HARCOURT

ACCRA, 15 APRIL, 1915.
Confidential.

Sir,

I have the honour to address you on the subject of the existing constitution of the Executive and Legislative Councils of this Colony.

The Executive and Legislative Councils are established under clauses 7 and 8 respectively, of the Letters Patent, issued by Her late Majesty, Queen Victoria, under date the 13th January 1886.[1] . . .

It is not, I think, necessary that I should discuss in detail the alterations which have been made from time to time, by successive Royal Instructions, in the constitution of the Executive and Legislative Councils: but I may here note that the most recent

[1] See No. 350 above.

alterations have been that on the retirement of Sir W. Brandford Griffith from the Chief Justiceship in 1911, the holder of that office ceased to be a Member of the Legislative Council, and that in the same year, the Principal Medical Officer was appointed an *ex officio* member of the Executive and Legislative Councils. Both these alterations were steps in the right direction, as is, I think, universally admitted.

At the present time the Executive and Legislative Councils are constituted as follows:—

EXECUTIVE COUNCIL

The Governor.   (President)
The Colonial Secretary.
The Attorney-General.
The Treasurer.
The Principal Medical Officer.

LEGISLATIVE COUNCIL

[As above] . . .
and four nominated Unofficial Members (two European and two native members).[1]

The Executive Council forms a compact and convenient body, and there is only one respect in which I consider that it requires to be strengthened. No one of its members is usually possessed of any intimate knowledge of native affairs or of first-hand experience in local provincial administration; and it has not infrequently happened that when, e.g. Mr. W. C. Robertson was Clerk of the Council, I have found it necessary to invite his opinion on occasions when I and my colleagues were considering matters connected with native affairs. It is, of course, possible for the Governor to require the attendance of any officer whose advice on any particular question may prove useful to the Executive Council in its deliberations; but though this

course is easy to adopt when Customs, Public Works, or any similar technical matters are under discussion, I do not think that this expedient works in an equally satisfactory manner when native affairs are under discussion. What is required, in my opinion, is that one member of the Council should invariably be in a position constantly to watch the action proposed to the Council from the standpoint of the native population and of the provincial administration, and to advise the Governor and the other members thereon.

To this end, therefore, I have the honour to recommend for your consideration and approval that the Secretary for Native Affairs should be appointed an *ex officio* Member of the Executive Council. At the present time the office of Secretary for Native Affairs ranks junior to that of Provincial Commissioner, though the emoluments are in each case the same. I, however, regard the post of Secretary for Native Affairs as one of very great and growing importance in this Colony, and I shall not be sorry to see this publicly attested by the holder of that office being granted the precedence and standing of a Member of the Executive Council.

The reforms which I am about to propose in the constitution of the Legislative Council are of a much more extensive character: but before I submit these recommendations to you in detail, I should like, in the first instance, very emphatically to express the opinion that it is essential, having regard to the present state of development attained by the Colony and its population,

(a) that the Government should have and should maintain an official majority, and

(b) that all Unofficial Members should, as at present, be nominated by the Governor, subject to the approval of His Majesty the King.

The first of these points is, I think, self-evident, and upon the necessity for an official majority I need not here enlarge.

[1] This had been the position since 1886. Before that, Unofficial representation in the Legislative Council was very irregular. There were never more than two unofficial members at a time, and between 1853–61, 1874–8, and 1881–5 inclusive, there would appear to have been none.

With regard to the second point, a few of the educated natives at Cape Coast have from time to time agitated for the recognition of the elective principle: but I am convinced that the vast majority of the general public of this Colony has not yet reached such a stage of intellectual development as would enable them to exercise the franchise with wisdom and discrimination and in the best interests of the community as a whole. . . . In the case of the Legislative Council, moreover, racial and tribal animosities and rivalries would not improbably be excited were any attempt made to confer the franchise upon the native population, and if its members were taught efficiently to exercise it. It would be possible to deal with this question in much greater detail and to apply to the proposal a mass of destructive criticism, but as I do not anticipate that you are likely seriously or favourably to consider the substitution of elected for nominated members in the Legislative Council of this Colony, I will not further labour the point at the present time.

If then, it be accepted, that a permanent Government or official majority should be maintained, and that all the Unofficial Members should be nominated, I need only lay before you in this despatch my views with regard to the present constitution of the Legislative Council; my reasons for thinking that reform is necessary; and my recommendations which are designed to strengthen it both on the official and unofficial side. . . .

I may say at once that I do not consider that on either its official or unofficial side it is sufficiently strong and representative.

Taking first the unofficial representation, the interests of the various communities, European and native, and of all the diverse tribes and peoples of this large Colony, are entrusted to the care of two European and two native members only.

The two European members selected for nomination are ordinarily drawn from those best fitted to speak for the mercantile and mining interests respectively. Each member so selected is wont to view all public questions from a somewhat special and exclusive standpoint. I consider that the unofficial element upon the Council would be materially strengthened if a third European member were to be appointed who should, when possible, be chosen from those Europeans who in this Colony are in a position to take a more independent view of public questions than is possible for either the merchant or for the spokesman of the mining interest. For instance, if this addition were to be made to the Council at the present time, I should recommend the District Manager of the Bank of British West Africa for appointment, and I feel certain that such a selection would prove to be very useful. Moreover, as I propose to recommend very considerable numerical additions to the native element upon the Legislative Council, I think it will be recognised that it is advisable simultaneously to strengthen the European unofficial representation thereon.

The native members of Council at the present time are Mr Hutton-Mills, the lawyer, of Accra, and Konor Mate Kole of Eastern Krobo. Both these gentlemen are natives of the Eastern Province and belong to the Adangme-speaking stock, in spite of the fact that these tribes form only a small minority of the native population of the Gold Coast. The Twi-speaking people of the Eastern Province are without an accredited representative on the Council, and the Fanti and Twi-speaking people of the Central Province, and the numerous native tribes of the Western Province are, at the present time, similarly unrepresented.

I consider that the basis of the representation of the native tribes and of the three provinces should be greatly extended, and that special representation should also be accorded to those sections of the native community who have received an European education and belong to the professional classes.

As regards the representation of the native tribes and the three provinces, I consider that the members selected for nomination should, as far as possible, be drawn from the ranks of the Paramount Chiefs, who are the natural leaders of the people, live in close communication with them, and are intimately acquainted with their needs and interests. I would only qualify this by stating my opinion that it is essential that every nominated member should have a good command of the English language; but fortunately, at the present time, there is a considerable number of literate chiefs, both in the Eastern and the Central Provinces, and the tendency throughout the Colony is markedly in the direction of the annual increase of that number.

My proposals, therefore, are as follows, as regards the representation of the native tribes in the various Provinces:—

Eastern Province:
one Paramount Chief of Adangme-speaking stock; one Paramount Chief of Twi-speaking stock.

Central Province:
one Paramount Chief of Fanti-speaking stock.

Western Province:
one nominated native member to represent this province, until such time as a suitable literate Chief is available for the purpose.

The population of the Eastern Province is divided between the Adangme-speaking and the Twi-speaking tribes. Each, in my opinion, should be represented on the Council; and as the Twi-speaking Chiefs who are also literate are at present found in greatest numbers in the Eastern Province, I consider that, in the first instance, the Twi-speaking representative should be chosen from among their number. There are a large number of Twi-speaking people in the Central Province and in parts of the Western Province, and if at any future time a Paramount Chief living in either of these Provinces was regarded as the best available representative of the Twi-speaking tribes, there would, of course, be no objection to his nomination.

The strongest element in the Central Province is the Fanti population, and I consider that a literate Fanti Chief should be chosen to represent this portion of the community.

The Western Province, which possess a very heterogeneous population, has so far produced no Paramount Chief who is at once literate and representative of the Province. At the same time, I consider that the natives of this part of the Colony should have their accredited spokesmen in the Legislative Council, and no difficulty, in my opinion, would be experienced in selecting for this post an educated native possessed of a close knowledge of the affairs of the province.

I do not mean to suggest that the Governor should be bound by any hard and fast rule confining his selection of native provincial representatives in the manner set forth above. I submit, however, that the principle of local and tribal representation should be recognised as one which it is expedient to establish, and that, provided suitable men are available, representatives of each province and of each of the principal sections of the population, should ordinarily be chosen for nomination.

As regards the representation of the native professional and educated classes, the two principal centres in which this portion of the native community resides are Accra and Cape Coast; and I propose that an educated native gentleman should be selected from the inhabitants of each of these towns to act as the spokesmen of their class in the Legislative Council.

If these proposals be approved, the Unofficial Membership of the Council would be as follows:—

Three European Members.
Two Paramount Chiefs of the Eastern Province.
One Paramount Chief of the Central Province.

One native representative of the Western Province.

One representative of the educated native community of Accra.

One representative of the educated native community of Cape Coast.

The Unofficial Members would, therefore, be nine in number.

Turning now to the consideration of the official element on the Council, it will be noted that the same weakness with regard to first-hand knowledge of native affairs and provincial administration as I have noted when writing of the present constitution of the Executive Council, is once more apparent. Moreover, it will be observed that all the official members are drawn from the Headquarters Staff, resident in Accra, at least two of whom — the Attorney-General and the Treasurer, — have not necessarily any personal knowledge of the Colony outside the immediate neighbourhood of Accra, though this remark does not chance to apply to the present holder of the last-named office. In addition to this, such important technical advisers of Government as the Comptroller of Customs and the Director of Public Works have no seat on the Council, and the Central and Western Provinces are also without their official representatives. I am very strongly of opinion that on its official side, the Legislative Council, if it is to be made a really efficient engine of Government, requires, at least as urgently as does the unofficial element, to be strengthened and to be rendered more fully representative.

In these circumstances, I have the honour to recommend that the following public officers should in future be appointed *ex officio* members of the Legislative Council:—

The Governor or Officer Administering the Government (President).

The Colonial Secretary.

The Attorney General.

The Treasurer.

The Principal Medical Officer.

The Secretary for Native Affairs.

The Commissioner of the Eastern Province.

The Commissioner of the Central Province.

The Commissioner of the Western Province.

The Comptroller of Customs.

The Director of Public Works.

If this recommendation be approved, the number of official members would be eleven.

I trust that you will be able to see your way to advise His Majesty the King to issue his Royal Instructions with a view to effect being given to the above proposals. In a Colony such as this, there is only a weak Press in existence, and where public opinion is necessarily to a great extent inarticulate, I attach very special importance to the Legislative Council being made as representative of all elements of the population and of all interests of the various communities as circumstances render possible; and I submit that this object will be attained in a satisfactory manner if the scheme which I have ventured to lay before you be approved and adopted.

I have etc.

[Gold Coast Sessional Paper 2, 1916–17]

450 A. BONAR LAW[1] TO SIR HUGH CLIFFORD

DOWNING STREET, 30 OCTOBER, 1915.

Sir,

I have the honour to acknowledge the receipt of your confidential despatch of the 15th of April last, in which you discuss the question of the constitution of the Executive and Legislative Councils of the Gold Coast. I have given prolonged and careful consideration to the important points raised, and have had the advantage of

[1] Andrew Bonar Law (1858–1923); Conservative M.P., 1900–23; Secretary of State for the Colonies, May 1915 to December 1916; Chancellor of the Exchequer, 1916–18; Prime Minister, 1922–3.

personally discussing the matter with you while on leave in England.

As regards the Executive Council, I agree that the addition of the Secretary for Native Affairs as an *ex officio* member is desirable and would be of advantage to the Council.

In the case of the Legislative Council, the changes which you propose are of a far-reaching character and have received much consideration. You propose to increase the Council from four official members (not including the Governor) and four unofficials, to ten officials and nine unofficials, the latter being selected so as to represent, to some extent, the views of the different sections of the native community, a third European member being added to the existing two. The new *ex officio* members proposed are the Secretary for Native Affairs, the Comptroller of Customs, the Director of Public Works, and the Commissioners for the Provinces.

I feel some doubt as to the advisability of making so large an increase immediately. In particular, I would suggest that the obligation to attend debates, which, in a council of the size proposed, will, of necessity, tend to be more lengthy than in the past, will be a severe tax upon the time of the official members, especially upon the three Provincial Commissioners, who will also, if they are to attend Council, be absent from their Provinces for prolonged periods, which may prove a source of difficulty.

Taking everything into consideration, and recognising that a good case is made out for an increase in the Council, I am inclined to consider that, as a first step, the membership should be raised to fourteen, excluding the Governor, by the addition of three officials and three unofficials. The three official members, in that case, would be the Secretary for Native Affairs, the Comptroller of Customs, and the Director of Public Works, all of whom may well be added to the Council.

The unofficial membership might then be increased by the addition of a third European member and two native members, to be selected from the various sections of the community mentioned by you. There would thus be four native and three European unofficial members.

If, however, on full consideration, you are of opinion that there is necessity, on political grounds, for the larger body which you recommend, I shall be prepared to accept your view.

I shall await the receipt of a reply to this despatch before taking steps to prepare amended Royal Instructions for submission to His Majesty the King.

I have etc.　　　　　　　[*Ibid.*]

451 Sir Hugh Clifford to A. Bonar Law　　　Accra, 25 November, 1915.

. . . Were the suggestion contained in your despatch to be adopted, either the natives in the Western Province would have to be left without a representative, or the same fate would befall one or other of the three great agglomerations of tribes which speak respectively the Twi, Fanti, or Adangme languages. Either of these eventualities appears to me to be highly impolitic.

The second object of the scheme submitted by me is to secure to the educated native community, adequate direct representation, independently of the rest of the native population. At the present moment these sections of the native population are represented in the Legislative Council by Mr Hutton-Mills, a barrister who resides at Accra. In many ways, however, the educated natives of Cape Coast are the most active section of their community; and if adequate direct representation is to be accorded to this portion of the population, it is essential, in my opinion, that the educated natives of Accra and Cape Coast should each be separately represented on the Council. Were one member only to be appointed to the new Council to represent the educated native population, much heartburning would be caused, either at Accra or at Cape Coast, according to which community chanced not to be selected to supply the required member; and if the latter were drawn from Cape Coast, it might happen that no educated native member would be present at some of the Council's debates. Moreover, seeing that under the new scheme increased representation is being given to the European and general native communities, the educated natives would certainly feel aggrieved if they alone were excluded from the enjoyment of increased representation. I am particularly anxious that the new Council should not be so constituted as to afford plausible grounds for discontent to any section represented upon it, and this end can best be attained by the appointment of two educated native members to represent Cape Coast and Accra respectively. . . .   [*Ibid.*]

452 SIR HUGH CLIFFORD, SPEECH IN LEGISLATIVE COUNCIL
                    25 SEPTEMBER, 1916.
. . . For the first time since the Gold Coast Colony came under British rule, an institution which may be regarded as really representative of the people has been established in our midst. . . . In the old Legislative Council, beyond the Members of my Executive Council, we had on the Council one European Unofficial Member who represented the interests of the mercantile community and another European Unofficial Member who represented the mining industry. We also had one native Unofficial Member who represented the educated classes in the Colony, and one Native Chief from the Eastern Province who represented the chiefs and people of the Colony.

Today the Council, as reconstituted, has been strengthened on the official side by the addition of the Secretary for Native Affairs, native affairs being, in my opinion, the most important matters which should engage the attention of this Council, and of the Government of the Colony; by the

addition also of the Comptroller of Customs, the Director of Public Works and the General Manager of Railways . . . and further, by the addition of the three Provincial Commissioners, each of whom is, in a sense, the impartial spokesman of the Province over the affairs of which he presides.

On the Unofficial side, a third European Member representing neither the mercantile nor the mining interest has been added; and this third Unofficial European Member has been selected in the first instance, from the Bank of British West Africa, which necessarily sees a great deal of the business conditions of the Colony as a whole. . . .

The Council has had added to it three Paramount Chiefs. . . . The Omanhene of Akim Abuakwa[1] belongs to a Twi-speaking tribe, and as such may be held to represent the Twi-speaking tribes throughout the Colony. . . . The Omanhene of Anamabu . . . will fill a similar office for the Fanti-speaking peoples, and the Fia of Awuna Ga, whose people at the time of the Togoland campaign so specially distinguished themselves . . . has been appointed to represent the Ewe-speaking people of the Colony.

The special object with which this Council has been enlarged, is to enable the Government of the Colony to obtain advice from as many varied quarters as possible. We have also added to the Council, two other Members, both of them well-known throughout the Colony . . . .[who] can speak, one [E. J. P. Brown] for the Central Province and the other [J. E. Casely Hayford] for the Western Province. . . . The selection of the Honourable Members whose names I have mentioned has been made with a single aim, namely, to obtain the best spokesmen for the various interests which they are appointed to represent, and the choice has fallen upon those who are most likely to be acceptable to the communities for whom they will speak. There has been no attempt to

[1] Nana Ofori Attah. See note on p. 607.

pack this Council with Government partisans. . . .

I would point out to you, however, that the alteration which has been made in the Legislature is not . . . one of kind but one of degree. Nobody who has studied the Colony closely, or has been associated with its Government would suggest that the time has yet come for anything in the nature of a relaxation of the central control of Government, or that the responsibility vested in the Governor and his official advisers, for the ultimate decision in any given matter, should be weakened. If you will examine the history of the Gold Coast, you will find that in the last year of the last century, the Colony's development was still in an embryonic state, and that it was only during the last fifteen years that the great prosperity and development which today mark the history of the Colony, have manifested themselves; and no thinking man can reject the opinion that, left entirely to its own devices, the Gold Coast Colony, without any control or assistance from outside, could not have attained the position which it holds today. . . .

At the present time there is no intention in any way to relax the existing system of Government control in any of its fundamental principles. His Majesty's Government holds strongly, and I personally fully share the opinion, that the present stage of peaceful development on the Gold Coast still requires the maintenance of the Crown Colony system of Government, which is of a paternal rather than of a democratic character. Such a Government cannot but be burdened by a sense of the heavy responsibilities confided to it. . . . It is therefore its constant object to ensure that no step should be taken which may prove detrimental to the interests of any section of the community. I therefore felt, during my first year of administration of this Colony, that it was extremely difficult, with the Legislative Council as then constituted, for any measure brought before it to receive that minute criticism

from all points of view that it might often demand. . . .

It struck me as a very interesting phenomenon that in the Gold Coast constitutions of a purely native growth are based on democratical, and not on autocratical or oligarchical principles, as is usually the case with the forces of government that have been evolved for themselves by other tropical races. This fact at any rate encourages us to hope that in the fullness of time, and as education spreads among the masses, it may be found possible in this Colony, to give to the people of the Gold Coast a greater measure of self-government than has been won for themselves by their fellows in other tropical countries of the Empire. But I am firmly convinced that the time for any such development has not yet come.

Anybody, however, who studies the native institutions will find that though in theory they are democratical, in practice they are often oligarchical or even autocratical; and he would be a bold historian who attempted to describe Osei Tutu Kwamin or Kofi Kari Kari as constitutional monarchs. You will also find that, up to very recent times, the rank and file of the native population in each Tribal division has exercised very little power save as an endorsing body: but it seems to me that with the great social revolution which today is in progress in the Colony, something very much in the nature of a political revolution is quietly and silently taking place among some of the tribes, and that the rank and file of the native population are beginning, to an extent not known before in their past history, to assert their political rights.

I foresee that the very partial application of the democratic principles on which the theory of local native constitutions rests, which has been accepted without demur in the past, is likely in the near future to be seriously challenged, and I foresee the probability of various Tribal divisions experiencing during the next few years considerable difficulty in adjusting the ancient machinery of Tribal government to the changed conditions with which they are now beginning to be confronted. While these inevitable adjustments and adaptations in the native political system are in progress, chiefs and people alike will stand in a greater need than ever before of the assistance and guidance of the Government. . . .

There is a great difference between a Legislative Council and a House of Parliament. . . . In a Legislative Council, no question of party government arises. There is no such thing . . . as a Government and an Opposition — instead we have to realise that we form a single corporate body, all of whose members are working equally for the attainment of a single end — the prosperity of the Gold Coast Colony — and to that end we should endeavour, according to our experience and our conscience, to place upon record the opinion which we hold as to whether any measure should or should not be passed into law, and to draw attention to the manner in which its operation will affect the various interests concerned, not in a spirit of captious criticism, but with a view to the law under discussion being framed in the manner best adapted to local needs. . . .

[Leg. Co. Debates, 1916–17, pp. 16–22]

453 SIR HUGH CLIFFORD TO W. H. LONG[1]
ACCRA, 15 AUGUST, 1917.

Confidential.

Sir, . . .

You have invited me to express my opinion with regard to the Recommendations of the Paris Conference,[2] in so far as their adoption is calculated to affect the interests of the Gold Coast and its dependencies. . . .

I submit . . . that if the larger and far more complex interests of the United Kingdom and of the self-governing Dominions demand that a protective policy should be adopted, in order to divert the Empire's supplies of raw materials to their manufacturing centres, it would appear, from the point of view of the Gold Coast, at once more logical and more appropriate that the measures designed to effect this end should be taken, and that the resulting sacrifice should be borne, exclusively by those countries which stand to benefit by the policy in question, and not by the producing Colonies whose interests are bound to be injured by its adoption.

I further venture to submit that this matter raises the whole question of Great Britain's responsibility toward the tropical populations of the Empire. Our system of Government in these Colonies is of a kind that enables us, in the last resort, to take any legislative action that may appear to us to be expedient, no matter how strong may be the local opposition thereto. Having regard to the peculiar psychology of the natives of the Tropics, experience has shown that this system of Government is the one best suited to their character, and that it is also best calculated to serve the general interest of these communities. I venture to suggest, however, that the fact that we have assumed and possess this power, makes it all the more incumbent upon us to see that any legislation which we may propose is primarily framed in the interest of the native population concerned, and that no departure from this principle should be made without the deepest consideration, and a full appreciation of its probable effects, moral even more than material. A perusal of the Memoranda furnished by the native unofficial members of Council . . . will show that the natives themselves are keenly alive to this aspect of the question.

Finally, in this connection, I venture to point out that, during the period of more than three years which have elapsed since the declaration of war, the native population of the Gold Coast and Ashanti has manifested an ardent loyalty to the Empire,

---

[1] Walter Hume Long (later 1st Viscount Long) (1854–1924); Conservative M.P., 1880–1921; Secretary of State for the Colonies, 1916–18.
[2] Of June 1916. Cf. Cd. 8271.

T

and has contributed, so far as has lain in its power, both men and money to the success of the common cause. I do not propose here to go into details on this subject, nor can I pretend, of course, to be able to prophesy how far local enthusiasm will continue to stand the strain of an indefinitely prolonged trial of faith in our ultimate ability to defeat our enemies. I may, however, mention that, for instance, this attitude of the natives has rendered it possible, since the beginning of August, 1914, continuously to denude the Colony and Ashanti of the troops which, even in time of peace, are ordinarily maintained in them; that the Colony has thus been able to despatch expeditionary forces successively to Togoland, to the Kameruns, and to East Africa; and that these forces have been kept up to more than normal strength by repeated drafts of voluntary recruits supplied by the chiefs and people of the Colony and its dependencies. I am not in the least disposed to exaggerate the material value of the assistance which has thus been afforded to the Empire by the Gold Coast and its dependencies. On the other hand, I do attach very great importance to the spirit of loyalty and devotion which, up to the present time, has thereby been manifested by the native population; for I believe that it is mainly to be traced to an appreciation by them of the fact that British rule secures to them justice and fair-play, and of the further fact that, though the Government possesses very extensive and arbitrary powers, it is scrupulous in their use, and never employs them save in the interest of the people whose affairs have been committed to its charge. I submit that it is most important that, in devising a scheme for the economic organisation of the Empire, no line of action should be adopted of a kind calculated to shake this confidence in the essential justice and disinterestedness of our rule. Immediate financial advantages, by whomsoever reaped, would, I think, be dearly purchased at such a price. . . .

[He goes on to discuss the proposals for economic measures against Germany and her allies after the conclusion of peace.] . . .

It is, of course, no part of my province to express an opinion as to whether, when peace is eventually concluded, it will be found possible and expedient thus to prolong international strife by transferring its incidence to what the Paris Conference names 'the economic plane'. From the point of view of this Colony, however, it is important, in this connection, to ascertain how far we are likely to benefit by, and to what degree it is probable that we shall suffer from the pursuance of such a line of policy. . . .

To deal first with cocoa. . . . The cocoa exports of this country rose between 1909 and 1914 from 20,213 tons in the former to 52,888 tons in the latter year. Simultaneously, the quantities shipped respectively to Great Britain, Germany and France, rose between 1909 and 1913 in the following manner:

	1909	1913
Great Britain	10,232	26,652
Germany	7,459	15,460
France	2,519	8,441

The total quantities exported from the Gold Coast during these two years amounted to 20,213 tons and to 50,554 tons. Of this, in 1909, Great Britain was taking approximately one half (50·57 per cent), Germany was taking rather more than a third (36·9 per cent) and France slightly more than one eighth (12·46 per cent). By 1913, on the other hand, Great Britain was taking 52·7 per cent, Germany 30·6 per cent, and France 16·7 per cent of the Gold Coast export of cocoa.

These figures would lead one to infer that between 1909 and 1913 Great Britain and France had both somewhat increased the percentage of our crop with which they were prepared to deal, while in the same space of time, Germany, though nearly doubling the quantity which she could annually consume, was taking a smaller percentage of the entire crop. In this connection, however, the figures which I have quoted are somewhat misleading, for though only 30·6% of the 1913 crop was exported from the Gold Coast direct to Germany, while 52·7% was imported into Great Britain, I have it on the authority of Mr J. H. Batty, the Managing Director of several of the most important mercantile firms now operating in this Colony, that in pre-war times, British manufacturers purchased less than 25% of the Gold Coast Crop. Our cocoa, as you are aware, is of a somewhat low grade, and it finds only a limited market among manufacturers of cocoa and chocolate in Great Britain and France. Large quantities of the cocoa imported into England from the Gold Coast were annually re-shipped to Holland and Germany. The importance of these outlets, from the point of view of the Gold Coast cocoa farmer, was emphasised during 1914 and 1915, when trans-shipments of cocoa to neutral ports, whence it found its way into Germany, were subject to comparatively slight restrictions. During that period, good prices ruled, and the local industry throve in spite of the war: but when, in 1916, it was decided to deprive Germany of her supplies of cocoa, Gold Coast produce became to some extent a drug on the market, in spite of the fact that a new outlet had been found for it in the markets of the United States of America.

With regard to this latter market for our cocoa, though in existing conditions it is affording us a certain limited measure of relief, it cannot be regarded as a satisfactory substitute for that of Germany. Gold Coast cocoa, in spite of its low quality, possesses, over its competitors, the advantage of being the most cheaply produced cocoa in the world. This is due to the fact that it is grown by a very large number of native peasant proprietors, who incur in its production none of the expenses incidental to the management, supervision and control of an European enterprise. The Gold Coast moreover, having regard to its tropical situation, is less remote from Europe than are many other cocoa-producing countries. On the other hand, many of the latter are situated in much closer proximity to the United States of America, and though the market furnished by the latter may prove to be an outlet of some value to this Colony, our cocoa placed upon it inevitably competes with the produce of Central America and of the West Indies, at a considerable disadvantage, not only as regards its quality, but also on account of the much longer transit by sea. . . .

Making full allowance, therefore, for the quantity which, in the future, the markets of the United States of America may be able to absorb, it must be admitted . . . that any attempt to restrict or impede the exportation of Gold Coast cocoa to Germany — either direct or via Great Britain or Holland — will result, less in injury to our present enemies, than in the acute depression of this Colony's staple industry. . . .

Turning now to the question of Palm Kernels and Palm Oil . . . of the total output of palm kernels from the Gold Coast in 1909, Great Britain took only 1,575 tons, and France only 45 tons, while 9,978 tons — representing 86% of the total quantity exported — was absorbed by Germany. During the same year Great Britain took 1,502,127 gallons of palm oil from the Gold Coast, 305,740 gallons went to France, and only 199,429 gallons, or 9·93% to Germany. By 1913, Great Britain was taking 2,601 tons of our palm kernels, France 738 tons and Germany 6,405 tons — equivalent to rather more than 65·7% of the total quantity exported. During the same year, Great Britain took 591,378 gallons of our palm oil, France 212,057 gallons, and Germany only 56,720 gallons, or only a little more than 6·59% of the whole quantity exported.

During the five years immediately preceding the outbreak of war, therefore, Germany was much the largest consumer of our palm kernels, while the quantity of palm oil which she took from us represented an insignificant fraction of our total export.

The fact that so large a percentage of our palm kernels went to Germany, must not, however, be regarded as an indication that she had, in any sense 'captured' this trade, in so far as the Gold Coast was concerned. On the contrary, the business of purchasing and exporting palm kernels and palm oil was mainly in the hands of British firms; and the latter shipped kernels to Hamburg and oil to Liverpool solely because these ports afforded respectively the best market for these two commodities. . . . It was shown by the evidence taken before [the Steel-Maitland] Committee that German manufacturers were enabled to handle palm kernels more advantageously than their British rivals, partly on account of cheaper landing-charges and transport, partly because they possessed machinery better adapted to the extraction of the oil than was ordinarily to be found in Great Britain, and partly because they had developed a satisfactory market for the palm oil cake for cattle fodder, which had no counterpart in England or Scotland. . . .

The Committee . . . recommended . . . that an export duty of £2 per ton should be imposed by the West African Colonial Governments upon palm kernels which were not exported under a guarantee that they would be crushed in Great Britain. . . . The grounds upon which I opposed the imposition of this tax in November last were that, having regard to the circumstances of the local trade in this product, the export duty could not fail to depress the prices which the merchants would offer to the native producers for their palm kernels, and that this would probably deal the *coup de grace* to an industry which has been steadily declining for several years. . . .

I may add that the produce trade, and indeed the whole commerce of the Gold Coast is largely controlled by a very strong group of firms — *viz*. Messrs F. & A. Swanzy, Messrs Millers, the African Association and the Basel Mission Factory — which adopt towards one another a reciprocal policy, and conduct their business in close combination. I think it must be obvious that the existence of such an association makes the regulation of the purchasing price to be locally offered for any commodity, a matter of comparatively small difficulty; and that in this instance, the opportunity and the temptation to drive prices down to a bedrock footing will alike present themselves. It should also be borne in mind that the native producer is not in a position to ship his kernels on his own account, and that in this matter he is utterly at the mercy of the European merchant. . . .

If it be desired, in the interests of Great Britain, to establish a kernel-crushing industry in England, on a firm basis, and if it be considered that, in order to achieve this end, it is necessary to afford the British crusher an effective measure of protection against his German competitor, I suggest that such protection should be secured to him by the imposition of import duties on the articles manufactured from palm-kernels, or by some other means, but that the native producer in the Gold Coast cannot equitably be called upon to pay, by the restriction of his market, for the establishment of an industry from which he stands to derive no benefit, direct or indirect. . . .

[As to the question] to what extent and by what means the resources of the Empire should and can be developed . . . I have one or two suggestions to make, to which I attach considerable importance. So far as a Colonial Administration is concerned, the development of the resources of the territory under its charge should not, as a rule, I consider, be attempted by it directly, nor should it seek to apply artificial stimulants to private enterprise by the granting of subsidies or the like. Experiments of this kind which have been made from time to time in the Colonial Possessions of other European nations, have not been attended by results of a kind to encourage a departure from the British policy of non-interference under which our own Crown Colonies have thriven and flourished.

The contribution to the work of development which can be made by a Colonial Government in the Tropics, should take the form . . . of the construction of railways, roads, harbour-works, the provision of such works of public utility as pipe-borne water-supplies, drainage systems, etc. . . . Some of these works, such as a railway, for instance, can usually be made to be directly remunerative. Many others, on the other hand, e.g. roads, cannot be expected to yield a direct revenue: but even these . . . will eventually produce a substantial return on the capital expended, in the shape of stimulated production . . . and the expansion of trade in imported articles. . . .

However buoyant the revenue of a Tropical Colony may be, however, it cannot hope to defray the cost of development for any very protracted period, out of its ordinary income. . . . This being so, I submit . . . that the first and most important step that should and can be taken to develop the resources of the Tropical Colonies of the Empire, is to facilitate the flotation of the loans, upon the issue of which, on reasonable terms, that development must be seen mainly to depend. . . .

In conclusion, I should like to say that, though the questions at issue have been dealt with in this despatch exclusively from the point of view of the Crown Colonies, and especially, of course, from that of the Gold Coast, I do not wish to be understood as ignoring the school of thought which holds that the Tropical Dependencies of the Empire should be required to submit to material sacrifice in the interests of the United Kingdom, in return for the protection afforded to them. I contend, however, that, as matters stand at present, the United Kingdom already obtains a very material return from her Crown Colonies. The bulk of their trade is with her; and I submit that the adoption of any policy which is calculated to depress that trade, or to retard the development of her Tropical Colonies, cannot fail in the long run, to react no less unfavourably upon the United Kingdom herself, through her commercial interests, even though the latter may stand to gain some immediate, direct advantage from the action taken.

I have etc.

[G.C. Sessional Paper 2 of 1917–18]

454 Sir Hugh Clifford, Speech in Legislative Council

25 October, 1917.

. . . Very shortly after my arrival in England in December 1916, it became evident . . . that the mobilisation of the available man-power of the Empire, on a scale hitherto without precedent, was demanded, in order that the war might be energetically prosecuted, and that, in view of this necessity, projects which would entail the employment of large labour forces would everywhere have to be postponed. . . .

Early in 1917 . . . it became evident that an attack of a wholesale and organised character was about to be delivered by the submarines of Germany against the shipping, not only of the belligerent powers, but of the whole world. This . . . made it necessary for His Majesty's Government to take immediate steps to husband available shipping resources. To this end, decisions were arrived at, determining the amount of space which could be allotted to each of the various products of the Empire. These decisions were based upon the relative importance to the United Kingdom, in existing circumstances, of the raw materials with which her Colonies have been in the habit of supplying her. . . . At the moment, the stocks of cocoa in Great Britain were large, but she stood in great need of vegetable oils, and accordingly the imports of the former had to be restricted . . . in order to enable as large a quantity of the latter as possible to be brought to the ports of the United Kingdom. In February of the current year, therefore, the cocoa shipped from this Colony to Great Britain, was limited, in the case of each individual exporter, to half the quantity which the latter had shipped from Gold Coast ports during the preceding twelve months. . . .

This action has, of course, resulted in a great depression of the local cocoa market. . . . The prices which cocoa farmers have recently been able to obtain have been so small that it is to be feared that, in many cases, they fail to repay the labour of picking and transporting the crop. . . .

When, in February last, it became evident that it would not be possible to carry out the programme of railway extension and other public works for which provision had been made in the Estimates for the current year, it was decided, by a unanimous vote of this Council, to invest £500,000 in the new War Loan. . . .

A similar sentiment was manifested when . . . the Acting Governor appealed to the chiefs and people of the Gold Coast and its Dependencies, for recruits to supply drafts for our Expeditionary Force, which left the Colony in July 1916, to take part in the campaign in East Africa. . . . Many of the chiefs and people of the Eastern and Central Provinces are to be congratulated upon the response which they made to his appeal. The chiefs and people of Ashanti also furnished a contingent; and no difficulty has been experienced in meeting all the demands for reinforcements which the War Office has so far addressed to us. Nothing in the nature of compulsory conscription was attempted or contemplated, and it must be frankly admitted that, having regard to the size of the population in the Colony and Ashanti, the number of recruits who volunteered might easily have been much larger than it actually was. On the other hand, it must be borne in mind that, since the beginning of the present century, the natives of the Gold Coast and Ashanti have experienced a social revolution of a kind that could not fail to leave its impress

upon their character and upon their outlook on life. They have learned to appreciate the peaceful conditions to which they are now habituated. . . . The majority of the native population . . . are today bound to their homes by ties and interests which are much stronger than any that existed twenty years ago. . . .

In times of peace, the population of the Northern Territories have usually furnished the bulk of the recruits to the Gold Coast Regiment, the balance being made up of immigrants from neighbouring Colonies, and in August 1914, not a single native of the Gold Coast Colony, or of Ashanti, was serving in the Regiment. Since the war began . . . the Northern Territories has continued and is still continuing to supply the majority of the recruits required.[1] . . . The military quality of the men whom the Northern Territories have produced leaves nothing to be desired. In Togoland, in the Kameruns, and in East Africa, they have greatly distinguished themselves. . . .

Judged from a purely financial standpoint, the year 1916 was easily the most prosperous that this Colony has yet experienced. . . . The revenue collected . . . was the largest ever recorded in the history of the Colony. It amounted to £1,835,989, a sum which exceeded . . . the receipts for 1915 by £379,860. . . . On the other hand, the Expenditure was reduced to £1,465,946. . . . The total revenue collected on account of Customs Duties during 1916 amounted to £1,131,426, an increase of £303,326 over the receipts on the same account during 1915, or rather more than 36%. Of this sum, £32,568 only was derived from the export duty on cocoa.[2] . . .

The total value of the trade of the Colony during 1916, including dutiable imports across the inland frontiers, amounted to £11,827,576, as against £10,461,034 in 1915. The former figure exceeds the value of the Colony's total

[1] Over 90% of all troops raised.
[2] Imposed by Ord. 19 of 1916.

trade for 1913 — which has hitherto constituted a record — by £895,375. The total value of our commercial exports amounted in 1916 to £5,576,134, a decrease of £238,676 as compared with the figure for 1915. This decrease was more than accounted for by the fact that a large quantity of the gold won during the year was still awaiting shipment on the 31st December. . . . In spite of this, the value of the year's commercial exports exceeded that for the year 1913 by more than £790,000. The value of the total commercial trade of the Colony amounted to £10,458,054. This shows an excess of £1,526,584 over the corresponding figures for 1915, which in part is no doubt to be attributed to the enhanced value of all imported goods, but which is to be ascribed in an even greater measure to an actual expansion of trade. . . .

The most notable feature of the year's trade is the great expansion of our commercial relations with the United States. Seven years ago, the value of the goods imported into the Gold Coast from America amounted to £20,141 only, whereas during the same year (1910) Germany supplied us with goods to the value of £324,670. By 1913 the value of our imports from America had risen to just over a quarter of a million sterling, while those from Germany were valued at £386,670. . . . In 1916, however, our import trade from the United States took a sudden leap forward, and the value of goods imported during that year amounted to £751,225, representing 15% of our total imports.

Simultaneously, our export trade to the United States has undergone a corresponding, though not quite equal expansion. In 1910 the value of our export to America amounted to £40,272. By 1913 it had risen to £101,055, and after declining to £93,383 in 1914, it rose to £329,466 in 1915, and in 1916, to the imposing total of £603,772, representing 12% of the total value of our exports for that year.

Our import trade from France has never been large, but during the war its value has risen from £44,299 in 1913 to £77,089 in 1916. On the other hand, the value of our exports to France has more than trebled during the same period. It stood at £455,593 in 1913, and by 1916 had risen to £1,374,815, which is equivalent to 24% of the value of our total exports. In this connection it is worth noting that the value of our exports to Germany, which reached its culminating point in 1913, never amounted to more than £899,468, which was equivalent to only 17% of the total value of our exports during that year. It is also satisfactory to note that, in spite of the vicissitudes of the war, and the great expansion of our trade with the United States and of our export trade to France, the United Kingdom during 1916 contrived to maintain its predominating position in our markets, and supplied us with 75% of our imports, and absorbed 62% of our exports. . . .

The year 1916 marked the completion of a period of a quarter of a century since cocoa first began to be regularly exported from this Colony. The present, therefore, may be regarded as an appropriate moment at which to glance at the rapid and phenomenal development of that industry, and at the effect which it has had upon the social advancement of the people.

In 1891 a consignment of locally grown cocoa, weighing 80 lbs and valued at £4 sterling, was exported from the Gold Coast. Some years earlier another small consignment had been shipped, but it had no successor until 1891. From that date onward, however, shipments of cocoa were made annually, and at the end of the first decade . . . in 1901, their volume had risen . . . to 960 tons, valued at £42,827. The completion of that first decade synchronised with the last of the many Ashanti wars, and inaugurated a reign of peace which has since suffered no local interruption. The succeeding decade, therefore, constituted a period during which the natives of the Gold Coast, secured for the first time in their history from the danger of raids or disturbances from without, had the best opportunity for advancement that had yet been afforded to them. During that decade too, railway construction was at last begun in earnest, a beginning was made of a proper road system, and the permanent cultivation of cocoa-gardens was each year undertaken on an increasingly large scale by the rural population. By 1911, therefore, we find the 960 tons of cocoa exported in 1901, swollen already to 35,261 tons, valued at £1,613,468 sterling.

During the next half decade the advance of the industry was greater and more rapid than ever before. The culminating point was reached in 1915 when 77,278 tons of cocoa, valued at £3,651,341 were shipped. For reasons already noted, the export of cocoa during 1916 fell to 72,161 tons, though the crop itself was larger than that of the preceding year. The value of the shipments during 1916, on the other hand, amounted to £3,847,720, or nearly £200,000 in excess of the corresponding figure for 1915.

Now an examination of the Customs returns for 1891 shows that the total value of the distinctively native products exported from the Gold Coast during that year, amounted to £527,000. The principal items were palm kernels and palm oil, the aggregate value of which was £282,441, rubber which was shipped to the value of £89,600, and monkey-skins, an article of commerce which has long ceased to figure in our returns, but of which in 1891 over 30,000 were exported, valued at a pound apiece. I have excluded gold and lumber from this calculation as both were mainly financed by European capital and were worked almost exclusively under European management, and we are here concerned with purely native industries. Calculated on a similar basis, the value of distinctively native exports in 1916 amounted to nearly £4,200,000, and of this only about £350,000 represents the value of native produce other than cocoa. The exports of palm kernels, for instance, had declined from

12,927 tons in 1891 to 5,857 tons in 1916; palm oil from 3,894,369 gallons in the former to 450,360 gallons in the latter year; and rubber from 2,946,913 lbs in 1891 to 2,215,973 lbs in 1916. From the last named figure, moreover, a deduction must be made on account of plantation rubber which is mostly in the hands of European companies, of about 112,000 lbs.

These figures will serve forcibly to bring home to us the extent to which the spread of cocoa cultivation has caused older native industries to decline during the last quarter of a century. . . . In spite of the falling off . . . it will be seen that the income of the natives of the Colony was approximately eight times as great in 1916 as it had been in 1891.

This increase, as I have indicated, is entirely due to the spread of cocoa cultivation: but I question whether it is at all generally appreciated how very radical a change was wrought in the social scheme of the people of the Gold Coast by the introduction and growth of this new industry. . . . Up to 1891, in fact, the trade of the Gold Coast was restricted to natural jungle produce; and though the natives had learned to work their rubber and their palm trees to satisfy a commercial demand, their agriculture was confined to the primitive stage represented by the cultivation of temporary food-patches. To them, therefore, the planting and maintenance of permanent cocoa-gardens were an entirely novel experiment, which was without parallel or counterpart in the past experience of their race, and their adoption of this unfamiliar industry entailed a great revolution in their social structure. It brought to them, among other things, an entirely new conception concerning the value of land. In the past there had been room and to spare for all, and tribal boundaries were loosely marked by natural features visible from the paths ordinarily frequented by wayfarers. Very soon, however, these rough delimitations proved to be inadequate to the changed conditions, and the result has been innumerable inter-tribal boundary disputes which have caused so much protracted and regrettable litigation. Similarly, though all land still theoretically belongs to the Stool, the vested interest of the cocoa farmers has brought into being a measure of individual property in real estate, such as was never contemplated by ancient tribal customs. The acquisition of considerable wealth by individuals who would otherwise enjoy no high status in the tribe to which they belong, is also a new feature in the social life of the native communities, and the political results which this shows signs of producing should be jealously watched by all who desire to see the tribal constitutions, which their ancestors have evolved, preserved from the disintegrating forces of too rapid innovation. . . .

Personally . . . I have a strong faith in the ability of the people of the Gold Coast to . . . prevent [these changes] from destroying the social fabric which their forbears have bequeathed to them. . . .

They should realise, however, that while the labour of a people is the original source of their wealth, the quality and the energy of that labour in the end mainly determine the amount of their wealth and the permanence of their prosperity. Fixed cultivation is . . . a new departure in the history of the people of the Gold Coast, and though cocoa growing is one of the least laborious of its forms, it calls for attention of a much closer and more exacting description than is demanded by the planting of temporary food-patches. The decline of other native industries which has kept pace with the rise of cocoa growing shows that the latter is specially attractive because it entails less physical toil: but this is mainly the case because only the barest minimum of cultivation is spared to his garden by the average farmer. A habit of patient and regular industry, such as permanent cultivation requires, can only be a gradual growth among a people whose past history has made in them no preparation for the changed agricultural conditions which pre-

vail today. If the prosperity which they have recently enjoyed is to be permanent, however, this habit must be developed, for should they fail to rise to the occasion before it is too late, it is to be feared that the cocoa industry will decay almost as rapidly as it has arisen. . . .

[Leg. Co. Debates, 1917–18]

455 SIR HUGH CLIFFORD TO W. H. LONG
ACCRA, 29 APRIL, 1918.

. . . It should be borne in mind that ever since British authority was established in the western portion of Togoland in August 1914, by the provisional agreement entered into by M. Noufflard, the Lieutenant-Governor of Dahomey, and myself, and subsequently approved by our respective Governments, the natives of our sphere of occupation have consistently had it impressed upon them that no annexation of territory has taken place, and that the destiny of their country will not be finally determined until the conclusion of hostilities. This being so, the people in the British sphere of occupation have always had before their eyes the *possibility* of His Majesty's Government eventually restoring Togoland to Germany; and the chiefs on our side of the border, who have sought territorial re-union with portions of their divisions from which the decisions of the Anglo-German Boundary Commission of the 14th and 28th July, 1886, caused them to be severed, have been throughout informed that such matters cannot be considered or decided until the war has been fought to a finish.

In these circumstances, it will be realised that the people of Togoland, who have now been invited to express their personal wishes on the subject of the future administration of their country, are inevitably placed in a position of some embarrassment. They realise their own impotence, and they realise too, that a desire to maintain the *status quo* will be, in the eyes of their former German masters, a dire offence. . . . When these facts are taken into consideration, the frankness with which they have expressed their opinions, and the practical unanimity of their decision, tend to demonstrate the genuine character of their feelings in this matter. . . . In spite of the appreciation of their own impotence, which is shown in the . . . statements made by the chiefs on behalf of and in the presence of their assembled people, very little hesitation is evinced . . . in expressing a strong aversion from German methods, and an equally strong preference for British rule.

The former sentiment is not the result of prejudice, but of experience; and the grounds upon which it is based are clearly and forcibly set forth in statements which come from all parts of the occupied territory visited by Mr Furley.[1]

The grievances of the bulk of the population are:

1. The imposition of a head tax of 6 marks per adult male *per annum*.
2. Forced labour, and the restrictions which were thereby placed upon the ability of the people to earn their livelihood, and which caused their young men to emigrate to the Gold Coast in quest of money and freedom.
3. Expropriation of land.
4. The constant use of the whip.
5. The meting out of punishments without investigation.
6. The ignorance in which the people were kept of the criminal code under which they were liable to floggings, imprisonment, &c.

To these grievances must be added the system designed to make trade as far as possible a European monopoly, and the impossibility of securing justice for a native *vis à vis* a white man, both of which are special complaints of the educated classes among the natives of Togoland. . . .

The natives of Togoland are no less explicit in the explanations they give to

[1] J. T. Furley (1878–1956), G.C. Civil Service 1902, Provincial Commissioner 1911, Secretary for Native Affairs 1917–23.

account for their preference for British rule. . . . Most of these reasons are based upon practical considerations, but a strong sentimental feeling is also manifested. In this connection I should remind you that when the Ashantis launched their great attack upon the coast country in 1873, their invading armies advanced in the form of an immense crescent, the western horn of which penetrated to Elmina . . . and the eastern extremity to the Peki country beyond the Volta River. A large portion of what is today western Togoland was at that time part of the Peki division, whose Paramount Chief, Kojo Dey, is frequently referred to in the[se] statements. . . . The Ashantis advanced as far as Ho, which they sacked and burned; but the British expeditionary force under Sir Garnett . . . Wolseley, delivered the natives, who had made a gallant stand, from further danger. This fact is remembered with gratitude and appreciation, as is shown by the frequent mention of their deliverance which occur in the statements. . . .

It is also borne in mind by the people throughout this part of Togoland that friendly relations had been entered into with the British Government long before the arrival of any Germans on the scene. As Professor Ramsey Muir has said: 'The German colonial empire was the result of force and design, not of gradual evolution. . . . It fell almost wholly within regions where, until its acquisition, Germany had been practically without any material interests.' (The Expansion of Europe . . . London, 1917, pages 140 and 149.) This was the case in Togoland, which today includes within its boundaries large areas whose people had voluntarily placed themselves under British rule, and who protested vehemently against their transfer by Great Britain to Germany. Strong representations upon their behalf were made at the time by the Government of the Gold Coast, but the then Prime Minister had publicly declared that if Germany wished to acquire colonies 'her co-operation in the work of civilization would be welcomed.' The Colonial Government was accordingly instructed to make things as easy for the German empire-builders as possible, and to refuse to entertain the protests of the natives who raised strenuous objections to the friendly international agreement of which they were at that time the victims. . . .

With reference to the frequent allegation made by the natives of Togoland that under the German system of administration the exactions of the Government left them little time for their own work, I was able to report to your predecessor, in my Despatch of 5th September, 1916, that it was estimated then, after barely two years of British occupation, that there was already 33 per cent more land under cultivation by the natives in the British sphere than there had been at any time under German rule. It was also noticeable that whereas the natives formerly cultivated land at as great a distance as possible from Europeans, they are now tilling land in close proximity to the railway and high-roads, thus saving much labour formerly wasted in head-carriage of their produce. This is due to the fact that they no longer fear molestation by white officials. . . .

[Cd. 9210, A & P (1918) vi]

456 Sir Hugh Clifford, Speech in Legislative Council

28 October, 1918.

. . . At the beginning of 1913 . . . the solution of the transport problem appeared to me to lie almost exclusively in the construction of main railway lines, from which, at a later period, a network of light rail or tram lines might be made to radiate into the more remote cocoa districts. Later in that year, however, the enterprise of the firms at that time locally controlled by Mr, now Major-General Grey, C.B., C.M.G., had brought about the introduction into the Colony of light Ford motor-lorries, which have since wrought what amounts to a veritable revolution in the transport

problems of the Gold Coast. It is not too much to say, moreover, that their advent, and the banishment of heavy motor-propelled vehicles from our roads, have saved the situation for us during these years of war, which have witnessed the cessation of further railway construction, and have seen our annual exports of cocoa increase from 50,553 to 90,964 tons. Save in some special instances, the tram or light railway, as a feeder of a main railway system, may be regarded as a project of the past, so far as this Colony is concerned. Roads in the Gold Coast have suddenly acquired a new and unprecedented value, since they can be used by vehicles which are far more efficient, and not much more destructive, than the bullock-cart of the East or the mule-waggon of the West Indies, and which are not affected by *tse-tse* fly or by trypanosomae.

The condition to which those of our roads were reduced, over which, in 1913, the heavy unwieldy motor-lorries then in use, were accustomed to ply in any number, demonstrated the sheer impossibility of maintaining, at any save a prohibitive cost, even a partial equilibrium between the devastation wrought by these vehicles and the pathetic efforts of the Public Works Department to repair the damage done by them. The appalling condition of the road-surfaces, moreover, so shortened the lives of the motor-lorries which floundered over them, that it was seriously debated whether motor-transport was not, on this account, a too expensive substitute for head carriage. The introduction of the light Ford *chassis*, however, has completely revolutionised the position. The standardisation of their parts and the simplicity of their construction render it easy and cheap to maintain these vehicles in a good state of repair. The comparatively slight wear and tear which they inflict upon our roads, make the task of upkeeping the latter, one which can be performed at once efficiently and at a reasonable cost. Most important of all, perhaps, it has been found that these light cars can run with safety over tracks which the local tribal communities are capable of constructing for themselves, with very little extraneous aid or supervision from the Government. This has led, during the last five years, both in the Colony and in Ashanti, to what I can only describe as an extraordinary development of our rural road-system throughout the cocoa districts. . . . Accordingly, though the war has prevented my railway scheme from maturing during the period of my administration, the transport difficulties which today exist in the Gold Coast and Ashanti are infinitely less serious than they were six years ago. . . .

[Leg. Co. Debates, 1918–19, p. 86]

457 Legislative Council Debate

Victoriaborg, Accra, 2 November, 1918.

Mr Casely Hayford:[1] . . .

Your Excellency will allow me to mention that . . . at the time you assumed the reins of Government, the state of public feeling was one of great discontent and tension due to the fact that various Bills had been promulgated which were exercising the public mind to a great extent. The interest that Your Excellency and Lady Clifford show in the affairs of this Colony and in the welfare of the people, has since served to expel all doubt and all fears. . . . This administration . . . marks a distinct landmark in the annals of the Gold Coast Colony. One great step that has been taken by this administration had been the enlargement of the present Legislative Council . . . and this is due to Your Excellency, to whom the Colony is grateful. . . .

I am in great hope that though we have achieved so much, we shall not stand there

[1] Joseph Ephraim Casely Hayford (1865–1930); born at Cape Coast; barrister and journalist; Unofficial Member Legislative Council, 1916–26; Municipal Member of Legislative Council for Sekondi, 1927–30; author of *Gold Coast Native Institutions, Ethiopia Unbound, The Truth about the West African Land Question* (cf. Sampson, *op. cit.*).

but go still further . . . until we have a full representative Assembly, representative of all interests and all claims. Sir, with the coming of peace there will be as certain as possible, what has been termed an 'economic war', and in that economic war we may be quite certain that this country will play a very great part, by reason of the rich resources at our disposal. That being so, we must take cognizance and notice of any suggestions that may serve the purpose in view, *viz.*, the free co-operation of the people of this country in the further development of its resources. For this reason, I am so glad that the views of the Empire Resources Development Committee, which seem to militate against the free development of any Colony or Dependency, have not received the encouragement or sanction of His Majesty's Government. I believe, Sir, that both now and hereafter, the principle that the resources of a country are to be developed by the state for the state, and not by the native for the native, must not stand. . . .

Mr E. J. P. Brown: . . .

I now come to the important question of elective representation to which reference has been made by the Honourable Mr Casely Hayford. The feeling in the country is, Sir, that an Unofficial Member is a Government nominee, and that however honest and well-directed his intentions may be, he is not looked upon as the people's representative, because they do not elect him to the Council. Naturally enough, they have little or no confidence in his representation. Many reasons have been given against elective representation, and one I have heard is, 'the country is not united; it is divided into many factions, and feuds, quarrels and disputes among them are so rife, that the idea of giving them the right to elect their own men to the Council is not feasible.' I think, Sir, that that view may now be dispensed with, for though some grounds exist for some of these reasons, unfriendly chiefs, tribesmen and factions have always met on common ground and taken united action in safeguarding their immemorial rights and customs. I think, Sir, that the people should not be pre-judged without a fair trial. . . . I feel sure, Sir, that if the present number of aboriginal unofficial members is allowed to be selected and returned to the Council by the people, it will be one step forward in representative government.

Since the establishment of the Town Councils in the Colony, no appreciable effort has been made by the Government to give the people a fair chance of training themselves for municipal government. Our Town Councils are evidently Government-controlled institutions. The Official and Unofficial Members are in equal number, the President being always an Official with a casting vote. . . . But I am not sure that an injustice is not sometimes done by European Official Members who, as 'birds of passage' cannot be expected to know the right opinion of the people, the exact local conditions and the true state of affairs as the Unofficial Members who should have a more effective voice in the management and control of their own municipal affairs. . . . Political liberty is denied our people, and if their persistent agitation for its grant has hitherto availed nothing, surely the spontaneous practical loyalty displayed by them in this War should appeal to the Government to reconsider its inflexible decisions refusing them the franchise. . . .

Sir Hugh Clifford: . . .

I fully agree that in the fullness of time it is probable that every part of the British Empire will be as completely self-governing as are the Dominions today, but that can only come about as the culmination of a slow and gradual development, which in turn must keep pace with the educational, social, and political advancement, not only of a small and specialised section of the community, but of the bulk of the native population. I say emphatically that, in my opinion, the progress and development achieved by the great masses of the population in the Gold Coast, are not yet sufficient to render it possible for them safely or wisely to govern the affairs of the Colony.

Honourable Members will recall that when I came here six years ago, the Legislative Council was a body which enjoyed scant repute in this Colony, which carried on its deliberations in a more or less hole and corner fashion, exciting very little public interest and inviting no criticisms of the action of the Government. . . . In those days, I am given to understand, the only effective means which Unofficial Members possessed of making their presence felt upon the Council was to make what General Grey used to describe as a 'row'. Well, as the Honourable and Gallant Member told us just now, the legislative machinery of the Gold Coast has advanced a long way since those days, and I say without hesitation, that this Council, as it is constituted now, is an infinitely more representative institution than was any legislative body that preceded it. . . .

Having regard to the complete absence of all interest which is manifested in selections of Unofficial Members to the Municipal Councils — the total number of votes recorded on any occasion can usually, so far as my experience goes, be counted on the fingers of one or at most of two hands — I do not consider that the bulk of even the urban population is, or for a long time to come will be, educated to the pitch of taking an intelligent interest in such a thing as an election. So few people could do so at the present time, that the grant of the franchise would quite certainly result in Members of this Council being elected by a small and specialised class, whose ideas had been borrowed from the political atmosphere of Europe, without regard to local conditions in the Gold Coast, and the members so elected would possess no possible claim to speak for the bulk of the population, who would not, as a matter of fact, have had any hand in their election. They would only be the nominees of a class instead of the nominees of the Governor, and as such, they would be bound exclusively to advocate the interests of that particular class. I consider that the people must be educated to take a keener interest in municipal elections and must learn to make a real use of them, before the much more important task of selecting Members of this Council can wisely or safely be entrusted to them.

There is another point. I have heard and read a good deal of rather loose talk on the subject of representative government in the Gold Coast, but I have never seen any attempt made to formulate any scheme which would be applicable to local conditions. I should very much like to see such a scheme put forward if only as a basis of discussion. It would afford me even greater pleasure to criticise it. There are, in the Gold Coast, certain special circumstances which render the adoption of any such scheme a matter of peculiar difficulty. The Gold Coast . . . is not a single entity, but is instead a mosaic composed of a number of mutually independent, and often mutually antagonistic, Native States, who derive such cohesion as they possess from their common loyalty and allegiance to His Majesty the King. If each of these little States were to send a member to the Council, the latter would be a body almost as numerous as the House of Commons. If several States were to be grouped together for the purpose of electing a member of the group, how could this grouping be effected, having regard to the rivalries and animosities which so often divide one State from another? For even in the minor affairs of these communities, sections of one and the same tribe have often shown, of late, a very uncompromising spirit.

For these and other reasons, I feel that the political development of the Colony is such that if you were to attempt, at the present time, to give the right of election to the native population, that right would be exercised only by the classes who have obtained an European education, and who have, with it, imbibed ideas of government which are peculiar to Europe, but which, at the present stage, make no appeal whatsoever to the man in the cocoa-garden or the man in the palm-grove, whose interests, under such a system, would not secure the same attention as is accorded to them today. . . .

[Leg. Co. Debates, 1918–19]

1919–1957

THE AGE OF FULFILMENT

BOOK XI

GUGGISBERG 1919–1927

34 Post-war projects 1919–1923

THE years immediately after the war saw much planning and speculation about the future of the Gold Coast. The new Governor, Sir F. Gordon Guggisberg, saw in the improvement of transport — harbour, railways and roads, in that order — the key to all other development (458). As the focus of, and indispensable threshold to the new transport system, he planned to construct a deep-water harbour, a site for which was eventually selected, not without some murmuring, at Takoradi (460). Although not opened for traffic until after he had left the country, Takoradi is the fitting memorial of Guggisberg in the economic field.

Economic progress to him was the necessary prerequisite of educational and political progress. At the end of the war, the local 'intelligentsia' tended to reverse the priorities. Casely Hayford founded his West African National Congress (in spite of its name a predominantly Gold Coast affair) to demand a substantial measure of elective representation in the Legislative Council (461), real municipal self government in the chief towns, and a West African university. There was little likelihood of Lord Milner at the Colonial Office entertaining such proposals (462), and Guggisberg himself had cause to be critical of the policy of the Congress (463). While material grievances were not wanting, as in the Palm Kernels Ordinance of 1919[1] and others were threatened by the extravagances of the unofficial Empire Resources Development Committee, which did not fail to attract attention on the coast (457), the main inspiration of the Congress, as its name implies, was the post-war ferment in India. Like Clifford, Guggisberg found such claims quite inappropriate to the state of society as it then existed in the Gold Coast. Nevertheless he encouraged the African members of the Legislative Council to study the country's needs in education and local government. An excerpt from the report of the Educationists Committee of 1920, even if it had less influence on actual policy than its successor, provides a convenient summary of the past educational history of the Colony (459). The report of the Town Councils Committee of 1922 was characteristic of local political thinking in its combination of a desire for municipal self government with a reluctance to pay for it (464); an attitude which was to postpone any real achievement in that field for another twenty years.

[1] Cf. Casely Hayford's protest on 'the grave constitutional principle involved by the . . . Secretary of State for the Colonies directing the passing of this Bill into law notwithstanding the unanimous vote of the Unofficial Members of Council against it' and Clifford's protest (no. 453 above) — Legislative Council Debates, 20 October, 1919.

458 THE TEN YEAR DEVELOPMENT PROGRAMME

LEGISLATIVE COUNCIL, 17 NOVEMBER, 1919.

. . . *Governor* [Brigadier-General F. G. Guggisberg, C.M.B., D.S.O.[1]] . . .

[1] Brigadier-General Frederick Gordon Guggisberg (later Sir) (1869–1930); Born in Toronto; entered the army 1889; engaged in survey work in the Gold Coast (1902–8); Surveyor-General of Nigeria 1910–14; served in France 1914–18; Governor of the Gold Coast 1919–27; Governor of British Guiana 1928–30.

A great revival in trade this year . . . has resulted in our accumulated balance at the end of this year being estimated at over 1¼ millions. Much as I dislike the principle of accumulating balances to this extent, I consider that the country is to be heartily congratulated for many reasons on having such a good start for the year 1920. . . . (i) In this balance we have a safeguard against a slump in cocoa. In this country we have nearly all our eggs in one basket. . . . We have many products, both actual and potential, but insufficiently developed. . . . Our balance will help us through this time of preparation. (ii) We want this balance as a 'capital' on which to start our great and extensive scheme for the provision of those things which are directly essential to the progress of our people; our system of colleges, technical schools, secondary education, water-supplies, electric lighting, drainage, re-layout of congested areas.

Now both the original cost and future maintenance of these systems is going to be very great. They are, with few exceptions, non-productive as regards revenue. And it is out of revenue that they must be paid for. How are we going to produce this revenue? The answer is:— (a) By increasing our trade. (b) by lessening the cost of production of our exports. (c) by lessening the price of imports.

The solution of these three problems lies, as far as we are concerned, in the word TRANSPORTATION.[1] Shipping certainly enters largely into the first and third, but this is a matter which *for the moment* is out of our control. We cannot, however, solve any of the three problems without a deepsea harbour, and a great extension of our railways and roads.

The harbour will earn a direct revenue of no inconsiderable value. Its indirect value will be enormous in saving time, labour, freights, and cost of shipping and landing; *without it we shall never appreciably increase our trade.*

The extension of our railways will cheapen transportation and will open up country rich in produce but at present too distant to permit of paying trade. The principle of low charges for long distance

[1] Capitals and italics in the Guggisberg extracts as in the original.

freights will be adopted, but even with this concession the railway will *and must*, be the chief revenue earning department of the country. *Without extension of our railway system we cannot appreciably increase our trade.*

Finally come the roads. From every point of view except one, roads are the most difficult item of transportation where weather conditions render upkeep ruinously expensive. But the one point above referred to outweighs all others — they must be kept up to feed the railways.

Of the three items of transportation, we can build our roads out of revenue. But the cost of the harbour and railway extension will be too expensive to meet out of revenue unless we spread their construction over at least 20 years — 20 precious years during which trade will be retarded — years moreover, during which all the revenue would have to be devoted to engineering construction instead of to our water-supplies and education. It is therefore essential that we should have at the earliest possible date, a good loan for the rapid construction of our harbour and railways. Negotiations for this loan are under the consideration of the Secretary of State. . . .

The programme of work for 1920 is based on a *10 year programme for development of the country*. The programme, divided into 10 main headings is as [shown on page 577].

. . . The survey party to select the site for the harbour and to prepare plans and estimates embarks this month. It will make first investigations at Seccondee; but these are by no means limited to that place. I have simply chosen Seccondee as being the most likely, owing to the lie of the land and the nature of the bottom. No construction will be begun until we are as satisfied as is humanly possible, that the site chosen is the most suitable on the coast line. Already there are cries from Accra and Cape Coast; I expect other towns to join in the chorus, each demanding the deep-sea harbour. . . . Honourable

Unofficial Members of this Council naturally will look at the question with an open mind. . . .

The staff for the completion of the Tafo–Coomassie Railway is now being engaged. The re-alignment of the worst parts of the Seccondee–Coomassie line, is already being carried out. . . . The location and building of new lines will depend to a certain extent on the site of our future harbour. . . . The general lay-out of our whole system of transportation is to be the subject of enquiry and report by a special transportation committee. This Committee will include those Europeans and Natives, officials and un-officials, whose knowledge of requirements will be of most value. . . .

Next to harbour works, there is in this country no more difficult engineering question than the selection of the right source for water-supply. A special staff of experts is being formed in the Public Works Department for the necessary investigations. . . .

In drawing up a programme for the construction of public buildings, we are faced by an extraordinary difficulty. We know what buildings we want but we are unable to estimate their exact final cost. The reason for this is the present cost of materials and of sea-transport [see Table].

With regard to the buildings themselves, they include such items as Native Hospitals, Secondary and Technical Schools, Prisons, Police Barracks, Courts of Justice, Town Halls, Post Offices, Market Places, Quarters for the official staffs, and Technical buildings such as workshops, Custom houses, etc. For example, in Accra we badly require many buildings of which the most important are a new Supreme Court, a new Town Hall, a new Prison, more schools. . . . We also require a Native Hospital. This we have placed at the top of the list as it is the most urgent human

Expenditure based on a loan of £4,000,000

Item No	Construction	Anticipated total expenditure £	From loan funds first four years £	From revenue first four years £	Req. expenditure for second 6 yrs. (Approx) £
I	Harbour	2,000,000	1,000,000		1,000,000
II	Railways	14,581,000	3,000,000		11,581,000
III	Roads	1,000,000		500,000	500,000
IV	Water Supply	1,790,000		200,000	1,590,000
V	Drainage	1,350,000		200,000	1,150,000
VI	Hydro-electric Works	2,000,000		170,000	1,830,000
VII	Public Buildings	1,100,000		1,000,000	100,000
VIII	Town Improvements	500,000		250,000	250,000
IX	Telegraphs & Telephones	90,000		80,000	10,000
X	Maps, Political & Industrial	200,000		100,000	100,000
		24,611,000	4,000,000	2,500,000	18,111,000
			6,500,000		
	Grand Total	24,611,000			24,611,000

requirement in the country. . . . Next, we have placed the schools . . . next the prison. . . . Neither the Supreme Court nor the Town Hall can be begun this coming year. . . .

I would draw your attention [to] . . . *the increase in European officials*, and especially in the technical departments. From every point of view — continuity of service, cost of passages, and progress, — I should like to see 50 per cent. of the present European staff in technical departments replaced by natives. Speaking perfectly frankly, that is, at the present time, quite impossible. We have not got the qualified men . . . so for the moment we must have a very large proportion of Europeans. That is essential. If you want the work done which is necessary for progress you must have the men. Our policy is to employ every qualified native that we can and to assist the (at present) inadequate technical schools by training them within the departments. As soon as they become sufficiently qualified, and show that they are capable of bearing responsibility, they will replace certain classes of Europeans. I regard this policy as essential to progress. . . .

[Leg. Co. Debates, 1919–20, pp. 5–13]

459 REPORT OF THE EDUCATIONISTS' COMMITTEE APPOINTED BY HIS EXCELLENCY THE GOVERNOR ON 5 MARCH, 1920, TO ADVISE THE GOVERNMENT ON EDUCATIONAL MATTERS. . . .

It has generally been considered that the pioneers in educational work in this Colony were missionaries sent out under the Society for the Propagation of the Gospel at the request of the 'Royal African Company' stationed at Cape Coast. The first missionary under that society who proceeded to this country was the Rev. Thomas Thompson, who arrived in 1751, just 50 years after the Society had been founded. He remained in the country for five years, but was then obliged to leave on account of ill-health. Three of his native pupils were afterwards sent to England to study, and though two of them died there, one returned and established a school at Cape Coast[1] which was afterwards carried on by his successors. This school was eventually taken over by the Government and today it is one of the largest schools in the Colony.

The Basel missionary Society founded in the year 1815 began work in this country twelve years later, and one of their first missionaries was employed in a school started by the Government. Every year saw the extension of the educational work of this Society, and in the year 1881 there were nearly fifty Basel Mission Schools throughout the Colony. During the first 60 years of its establishment in this country nearly 100 of the European missionaries died.

In 1834 the Wesleyan Mission started educational work in the Gold Coast and before the passing of the first Education Ordinance in 1882 it had over 80 schools in the country. During the first eight years of the establishment of this Mission, it sustained the loss of 14 missionaries.

The Bremen Missionary Society began work . . . in 1847 and in the year 1881 had established four schools in the Colony.

The Roman Catholic Mission did not start educational work in this country until May 1881. . . . This mission made its first settlement at Elmina. . . .

The cost of maintaining the Government Schools in 1880 was between £800 and £900. The grants paid by Government to the various Missions for their educational work were £150 to the Basel Mission, £200 to the Wesleyan Mission, and £75 to the Bremen mission. The Roman Catholic Mission first applied for aid in 1883.

The majority of the Basel and Wesleyan Mission schools were scattered over the interior, the Wesleyan schools being chiefly in the Central Province while those of the Basel Mission were entirely

[1] Philip Quaque (1741–1816). Cf. F. L. Bartels, *Philip Quaque*, in Transactions of Gold Coast and Togoland Society, i, 153–77.

confined to the Eastern Province. The Bremen Mission established schools on the eastern side of the Colony, bordering on Togoland.

Most of the teaching in these schools was in the vernacular, and very little proficiency had so far been obtained by the children in English. The systems of management of the Mission schools differed very widely, and it was chiefly on this account that the Government drew up the first Education Ordinance under which rules were afterwards formulated. . . .

In May 1882 the first Ordinance for the promotion and assistance of Education was passed in Council. It may be briefly summarised as making provision for the following:—

(1) The appointment of a General Board of Education consisting of the Governor as President, the Members of the Legislative Council, and not more than four other members nominated by the Governor.

(2) The formation of Local Boards . . . to report to the General Board on the advisability or not of establishing new Government schools;

to ascertain that the conditions on which the grants-in-aid were to be allowed were fulfilled. . . ;

to grant certificates to teachers.

(3) The appointment of an Inspector of Schools

[And provisions for syllabus and religious instruction]

Later in 1882 an Amending Ordinance was passed repealing the provision as to the issue of certificates by Local Boards and enacting that the Governor alone should have power to grant certificates. . . .

In his report for the year 1886, the Inspector of Schools (the Rev. M. Sunter) gave forcible expression to his dissatisfaction with the existing state of educational matters in the Colony, the blame for which he ascribed principally to the difficulty of working the 1882 Ordinance satisfactorily. 'I cannot,' he wrote, 'too strongly express my regret that no proper Ordinance has yet been passed; after the lapse of nearly four years an unworkable and ridiculously complicated Ordinance remains a dead letter. . . . Till an Ordinance of a workable kind is passed no school can qualify, in the proper sense, for a grant. . . . Under it (i.e. the 1882 Ordinance) the machinery was never completed, so far as even Government was concerned for . . . a secretary was appointed without salary . . . the General Board was . . . never completely filled in as to members . . . the Local Boards never took tangible form. . . .'

In 1887 during the Administration of Sir William Brandford Griffith, a new Education Ordinance . . . was passed. . . . In 1890 . . . the report of the Inspector showed that progress in Education had been made, as regards both the proficiency of the children and the number in attendance at the various Government and Assisted Schools. The number of children on the roll and the average attendance . . . for that year were as follows:—

	No. on Roll	Avge. Attendance.
Government Schools	884	665
Wesleyan Mission Schools	1,807	1,157
Basel Mission Schools	1,777	1,335
Bremen Mission Schools	85	78
Roman Catholic Mission Schools	471	365
Hausa Military	52	44
	5,076 (of whom 1,037 were girls)	3,641 (of whom 712 were girls)

These figures are in respect only of Government and Assisted schools; there were in addition a large number of Mission schools not in receipt of Government aid and definite particulars relating to them are unobtainable. . . .

Early in 1902 more definite and detailed Rules were drawn up and approved by the Board of Education. These rules, with schedules of work attached thereto, were based on the code in force in England some years previously and very little attempt appears to have been made to adapt the courses of instruction to local conditions. The schedules of work tended to encourage memory work. Grants were paid 'on results.' Thus a grant of 2/- per head was awarded for each 'pass' in Arithmetic, Reading and Writing; while grants varying from 6d to 2/- per head *on the average attendance* were awarded in each of the other subjects (except Industrial Training) on the result of a few minutes' questioning by the Inspector at the annual examination. One result of this system was to encourage Managers to overload the time-table in the hope of obtaining a small amount of grant for each subject. In the 1902 Rules, an attempt was made to encourage Industrial Training by the offer of grants varying from 1/- to 10/- per head on the average attendance. School gardens (or plantations as they were then described) were started, but except at a few schools, the *training* was non-existent. . . . At this time two weeks' notice of a visit by the Director of Education for the purpose of holding the annual examination had to be given, and in that time many hours' strenuous work was performed to put the plantations 'in order'. . . .

The Education Rules of 1902, defective as they were, considerably improved education and are worthy of note as making provision for the first time for the award of grants to Training Institutions for Teachers (the only Training Institutions at that time being those of the Basel Mission at Abetifi and Akropong).

In July 1902 two Mohammedan schools were subsidized by the Government . . . at Ekrofu and Kroboase, and an additional one at Ekotsie in the following year, all these schools being situated in the Fanti district. Very great difficulty was experienced in conducting these schools. The priests were very suspicious and afraid of the effects of allowing instruction to be given in the schools by teachers who were not of their own faith, there being no Mohammedan teachers in the Colony qualified to give instruction in English. In the following year only one of these schools remained, and though one was reopened later, the last of them was eventually closed in 1907.

Education had hitherto been almost entirely primary in character. There were no secondary schools under the Board and apart from the two Seminaries of the Basel Mission . . . there were only four schools in the Colony which claimed to give an education other than elementary. These were the Accra Grammar School, the Cape Coast Graded School, the Wesleyan Collegiate School, Cape Coast, and a school opened in the same town by the Fanti Public Schools Company. There were no Europeans on the staff of any of these schools except for short periods in the Wesleyan Collegiate School, and they could hardly be regarded as secondary in more than name. . . .

In 1909 the Accra Government Training College for Teachers was opened . . . which received students from any Mission school as well as from Government schools. The original staff consisted of one European and one West Indian . . . in 1912 the staff was increased to five Europeans in addition to the West Indian Teacher and a native teacher. Students entering the College are required to give a bond for £30 with two sureties to complete the course of instruction and to teach in a Government or Assisted School for a period of five years. The College accomodates about 80 students. It was the first and still is the only Government Training College for teachers established in West Africa.

In the same year the Accra Government Technical School was opened. This school was the first of its kind established in the Gold Coast, although the Basel Mission Workshops at Christiansborg had given a somewhat similar training for many years previously. . . . In 1909 the Mfantsipim School, a Non-Assisted Secondary School at Cape Coast formed by the union of the

Wesleyan Collegiate School and the Fanti Public School was reorganized on Secondary lines under a European graduate. . . . In 1910 the S.P.G. Grammar School was started under a European headmaster. The number on the roll of the two schools at that time was about 150. . . .

In June 1916 the German Missionaries belonging to the Bremen Mission were deported and all the schools of that Mission came directly under the control of the Education Department.

In December 1917 and January 1918 all Missionaries belonging to the Basel Mission were deported. The schools and Teachers' Training Institution at Akropong were taken over temporarily by Government. . . .

This outline history of Education in the Gold Coast would not be complete without reference to the hundreds of non-assisted schools dotted over the country. Usually the number of pupils on the roll is between 10 and 25, though there are some much larger schools which are non-assisted because of the difficulty of getting certificated teachers to bring them up to the efficiency required by the Education Rules. As official returns of these schools are not compulsory, detailed statistics are not available, but it is estimated that above one-fourth of the children attending school in this country are in non-assisted schools. Usually these schools are conducted by catechists or evangelists who have also religious work to perform. Needless to say, these teachers are generally untrained (and their methods far from ideal) but the pioneer work they are doing is most valuable. . . .

[Gold Coast, S.P.4 of 1919–20]

460 REPORT BY MESSRS. STEWART AND MACDONNEL . . . EMBODYING RECOMMENDATIONS FOR THE CONSTRUCTION OF A DEEP SEA HARBOUR AND RAILWAY TERMINUS AT TAKORADI

24 SEPTEMBER, 1920.

. . . We understand it is the intention of the Government — in which we fully concur — that the projected deep-water harbour is to be the central terminal base of the Colony's railway system, and that it is in contemplation to take up the development of the latter concurrently with the construction of the former. If this be the case, it would appear advisable to us to concentrate expenditure on the development of the deep-water harbour and its tributary railways, rather than to distribute the resources of the Colony in any attempt to improve the existing facilities of a number of the smaller surf-boat and lighterage ports.

The existing coastal settlements, viz., Axim, Dixcove, Ajua, Sekondi, Elmina, Cape Coast, Anomabo, Salt Pond, Appam, Winneba, Accra, and Addah on the Volta, owe their existence primarily not so much to the ability of their immediate neighbourhood to originate exports and business generally, as to their selection in the Middle Ages as convenient points at which to establish offensive and defensive posts by the various adventurers from different European countries, which though nominally at peace in European waters, were constantly at war on the West African Coast when competing in the slave trade and barter for gold with the natives.

There is a comparatively unproductive coastal zone of several miles in depth which produces little for export. Each of the above-named coastal settlements, however, acts as a point of export for the hinterland to the north of it, since the present high cost of inland transportation, combined with inadequate facilities, renders it at present more expedient for merchants to use the nearest point at which a surf-boat service, however risky, is available, than to forward goods to be shipped from the existing lighterage ports of Sekondi and Accra, except from the hinterland immediately tributary to these two points, or tapped by the existing railways leading to them.

We are of opinion that harbour works of even a very minor character, to improve the existing conditions at any of the surf-boat and lighterage ports of the Colony . . . would be of a very expensive nature, and that the advantages to be gained would be of relatively little value, as the situation should alter entirely when the deep-water harbour and radiating railway system come into operation, especially if a belt line is built parallel to, and at some distance back from the coast, connecting with the lines running north from Sekondi and Accra. Such a line should carry all the export freight originating between it and the sea, either to the deep-water harbour in the neighbourhood of Sekondi or to the lighterage port of Accra. The amount of cargo to be exported or imported at the intermediate points would then be reduced to that required to meet purely local requirements.

The dominant factors which would govern the diversion of the exports or imports from the intermediate surf-boats and lighterage points to the deep-water harbour, in which ships could lie alongside wharves and work cargoes are as follows:—

(a) The cost of rail transport as compared with motor transport; — existing rates average (about) in the proportion of 1 to 10.

(b) The elimination of risk of loss or damage to merchandise. . . .

(c) The reduction of ocean freight charges, which should correspond to the reduction of demurrage costs incurred by the frequent delay in obtaining surf-boats or lighters to work cargo, and the slow rate at which cargo can be worked when surf-boats or lighters are available (viz. 300 tons per ship per day). . . .

On the understanding that the deep-water harbour is to be the terminal base of the railway system, it clearly should be located as centrally as possible on the seaboard of the Colony. On the other hand, owing to the physical difficulties to be overcome, the selection of the most suitable harbour site must be the governing factor.

Salt Pond is geographically the most central point of the coastline, but from that place eastward to the boundary of the Colony (with the exception of the Volta mouth . . .) and westward to the entry of the Prah River into Shama bay, the coast is unsuitable. The shore is practically one continuous sandy beach, shoaling very gradually from deep water. The natural and shallow indentations such as are found at Elmina and Appam are small . . . and no deviation corresponding . . . is found in the five fathom contour, which . . . does not appear to be anywhere less than 1,200 feet from low-water mark in the area under discussion. . . .

From east of the mouth of the Prah River to Cape Three Points, the general trend of the coast is from N.E. by E. to S.W. by W. There are several localities such as Akwida, Ajua, etc, to the eastward of Cape Three Points, which afford considerable shelter from the prevalent swell, but the two pronounced recessions . . . forming Takoradi and Sekondi Bays provide more natural protection than is to be found at any other points on this section of coast.

Other features in favour of the Takoradi–Sekondi area are:—

(a) It is closer to the centre of the Colony's coast line than the other points referred to above.

(b) The existing facilities, such as the lighterage harbour, railway facilities, roads, water supply, electric current and light . . . at Sekondi would materially aid in the construction of a harbour in this vicinity. . . . [After survey of the area, they preferred Takoradi to Sekondi.]

We felt that a site selected a few years ago as capable of being developed to meet such probable requirements of the Colony as could then be foreseen, might prove today inadequate to meet the extraordinary increase which has taken place during the last five years in the agricultural and mineral export business of the Colony. . . .

At Sekondi, as there is no natural protection [like the Takoradi reef] we consider that it would be necessary . . . , to construct a breakwater of a heavier and more expensive type than we propose for Takoradi. . . .

A ship would approach the entrance to the proposed harbour at Takoradi head on to the sea, with ample room to leeward . . . whilst at Sekondi a ship making the entrance would have the swell nearly abeam, with restricted sea room to leeward of the harbour. . . .

The Takoradi site is the more favourable for the extension of the breakwater and construction of additional piers . . . and at the same time would provide ample room for corresponding developments on shore. . . . Similar and equal facilities are not found at Sekondi, either on land or sea. . . .

[The] protected and sheltered sea area would . . . be enclosed by two converging breakwater arms; the main arm running along the south side and also curving round to form the east side; and the secondary or leeward arm running east by south from the shore in a straight line, and, together with the harbour entrance, forming the north side. . . .

The location of the main arm of the breakwater is designed to obtain the maximum advantage offered by the natural reef. Only about a quarter of its length is located in deep water; and practically all of this . . . is . . . at an oblique angle to the direction of the heavy and prevailing waves, and covered to windward by the outer end of the reef. . . .

[Enclosure in G.C.S.P. 8 of 1920–1.]

461 PETITION OF THE NATIONAL CONGRESS OF BRITISH WEST AFRICA
19 OCTOBER, 1920.

To his most Gracious Majesty George the Fifth, King of Great Britain and Ireland, and the Dominions Beyond the Seas in council.

The Humble Petition of the National Congress of British West Africa by its delegates now in London,
Sheweth:

That your Petitioners are the accredited representatives of the National Congress of British West Africa, which was brought into being after the first Conference of Africans of British West Africa,[1] for the purpose of continuing and perpetuating the work of the Conference.

That your Petitioners would respectfully seize the opportunity of expressing their loyalty, devotion, and attachment to Your Majesty's person and throne and would further beg to refer to the sentiment of the Conference in one of its Resolutions, to the effect 'That this Conference desires to place on record the attachment of the peoples of British West Africa to the British Empire, and their unfeigned loyalty and devotion to the throne and person of His Majesty the King-Emperor, and direct that copies of these Resolutions be forwarded in due course to His Majesty's Principal Secretary of State for the Colonies and to each of the Governors of the several Dependencies.' Further it may be noted that the policy of the Congress is 'to preserve strictly and inviolate the connection of the British West African Dependencies with the British Empire and to maintain unreservedly all and every right of free citizenship of the Empire and the fundamental principle that taxation goes with effective representation.' . . .

That your Petitioners desire to bring to the notice of Your Majesty, that the administrations of the several British West African Dependencies are composed of Executive and Legislative Councils. The Members of the Executive Councils are all Government officials who also, together with Members nominated by the Governors, compose the Legislative Councils. As such the nominated members do not really represent the people, and they are not directly in touch with them. . . .

That apart from the fact that the National Congress of British West Africa

[1] Held at the Accra Native Club from 15 to 23 March, 1919. There were 42 Gold Coast Delegates, 6 Nigerian, 3 Sierra Leonean and 1 (?) Gambian.

represents substantially the intelligentsia and the advanced thought of British West Africa, and that the principles it stands for are some of those fundamental ones that have always actuated communities that have arrived at the stage of national consciousness, it also represents the bulk of the inhabitants of the various indigenous communities and with them claims, as sons of the soil, the inherent right to make representations [as] to existing disabilities, and to submit recommendations for the necessary reforms.

That your Petitioners would respectfully beg leave to point out that in asking for the franchise, the people of British West Africa are not seeking to copy a foreign institution. On the contrary, it is important to notice that the principle of electing representatives to local councils and bodies is inherent in all the [political] systems of British West Africa, which are essentially democratic in nature, as may be gathered from standard works on the subject.

That, further, according to the African system, no Headman, Chief, or Paramount Ruler has an inherent right to exercise Jurisdiction unless he is duly elected by the people to represent them, and that the appointment to political offices also entirely depends upon the election and the will of the people.

That such being the British West African system of representation, the arrangement by which the Governor of a Crown Colony nominates whom he thinks proper to represent the people, cannot but strike them as a great anomaly and does constitute a grievance and a disability which they now respectfully pray may be remedied. . . .

That in order that Your Majesty may appreciate how detrimentally the present system of appointment to the Legislative Councils by Government nomination works, attention is respectfully drawn to the passage of the Palm Kernels Ordinance against the will of the people. . . .

That your Petitioners, therefore, humbly pray your Majesty to grant an amendment of the existing letters patent for the several British West African Dependencies whereby the present system of Government may be altered so as to provide for the reconstruction of the several Legislative Councils by giving the people the right of electing one-half of the Members thereof, and by the constitution of Houses of Assembly which shall be composed of the Members of the Legislative Council besides six other financial representatives elected by the people, who shall have the power of imposing all taxes and of discussing freely and without reserve the items on the annual estimates of revenue and expenditure prepared by the Governors in the Executive Council and approving of them. . . .

That your Petitioners would respectfully submit that the time has come for the establishment of Municipal Corporations in all the principal towns of British West Africa with full power of local self-government, and that the people may have the power of electing four-fifths of the Members thereof and the remaining one-fifth nominated by the Government, such elected and nominated members having the power of electing the Mayor of the Corporation, who, however, must be an elected member.

That your Petitioners desire the establishment of a British West African University, and are prepared to promote the necessary funds for its establishment, supported by Government subsidies.

That in the opinion of your Petitioners the time has arrived for the introduction of Emigration Laws so as to keep out 'undesirables', and the opinion of Your Majesty's Government is invited as to whether Syrians are not 'undesirables'. . . .

That your Petitioners view with marked disfavour the scheme of the Empire Resources Development Committee, and regret that British publicists should be found capable of advocating a policy which, if adopted, would bring Imperial Britain on a par with pre-war German attitude with regard to African Proprietary rights.   In this connection, it is submitted that the principle of Trusteeship may easily be made to operate detrimentally to African proprietary rights, and that the people are well able to control their own lands and to watch and protect their proprietary interests. . . .

That Your Majesty's Petitioners view with grave alarm the right assumed by the European Powers of exchanging or partitioning African countries between them without regard to the wishes of the people, and beg leave respectfully to request that the partitioning of Togoland between the English and the French be reconsidered. . . .

Signed for and on behalf of the National Congress of British West Africa.

T. Hutton-Mills . . . Barrister-at-Law, . . . President . . .

Casely Hayford, M.B.E., M.L.C., Barrister-at-Law, Vice President . . . and Gold Coast Delegate.

Edward Francis Small, Gambia Delegate.

Henry Maurice Jones, Merchant, Gambia Delegate.

Fred. W. Dove . . . Merchant, Sierra Leone Delegate.

H. C. Bankole-Bright, Physician and Surgeon . . . Editor 'Aurora', Secretary London Committee, Delegate Sierra Leone.

H. Van Hien, Merchant . . . Treasurer . . . Gold Coast Delegate.

J. Egerton-Shyngle . . . Barrister-at-Law . . . Nigeria Delegate.

Chief Oluwa, of Lagos . . . Nigeria Delegate. . . .

[G.C., S.P. 7 of 1919–20, pp. 21–26]

462 COLONIAL OFFICE TO H. C. BANKOLE-BRIGHT 26 JANUARY, 1921.

Sir,

I am directed by Viscount Milner to acknowledge the receipt of your letter dated the 30th of October last, in which was enclosed a petition signed by yourself and eight other persons on behalf of 'The National Congress of British West Africa.'

Lord Milner has laid the petition before the King and has received His Majesty's commands to reply to it.

His Lordship has received from the Governors of Nigeria[1] and the Gold Coast information which shows that 'The National Congress of British West Africa' is in no way representative of the native communities on whose behalf it purports to speak, that its pretensions in this respect are expressly repudiated by the most authoritative exponents of native public opinion (including practically all the Chiefs in the Gold Coast), and that the scheme put forward by the Congress would in their opinion be inimical to the best interests of the community. Lord Milner has no reason to suppose that any different opinion is held in Sierra Leone or the Gambia.

The Secretary of State has, however, carefully considered the petition, and as a result His Lordship had advised the King that the time has not yet come for the introduction in any of the West African Colonies and Protectorates of the principles of election to the Legislative Councils and of unofficial majorities on those Councils. Nor does he consider that the legal changes suggested in the petition would improve the administration of justice and be in the interest of the great bulk of the native populations. He has accordingly been unable to advise His Majesty to grant the prayers of the petitioners on these points.

Of the other matters referred to in the petition, some relate to all the British West African Colonies and Protectorates, some to only one or two, while their relative merit varies greatly. With regard to these matters, the Secretary of State will consult the Governors of the several Colonies concerned and request them to report in due course what action, if any, is in their opinion possible and desirable.

I am to take this opportunity to acknowledge the receipt of the letter of the 11th instant signed by you and by Mr. Hayford,

[1] Sir Hugh Clifford.

and in reply to state that Lord Milner does not consider that any useful purpose would be served by his granting an interview to the Delegates now in London with the object of discussing with them the salient points in the petition.

I am etc.

H. J. Read.　　[*Ibid.*, p. 61]

463 GOVERNOR'S SPEECH IN LEGISLATIVE COUNCIL　　27 APRIL, 1921.

. . . No one denies the right of the educated natives to take a part in Government; the more educated natives we have in Government the better. No one, moreover, denies the fact that every African in the Gold Coast belongs, or should belong, to one of the Stools. However, though they may have full claims to belong to the Stools, the fact remains that in this country there are such things as Chiefs, elected by the people, and it is not in my opinion a fair thing for the people of the Stools to be approached by a political party on any big public question in any other way than through the Chief and his Councillors.

Any attempt to get at the people behind the backs of the Chiefs and their Councillors will be bound in this country to create unrest and enormous opposition from those who support the maintenance of national institutions. . . .

Now I wish to speak plainly to Honourable Members. The attitude adopted by the journals and newspapers of this Colony is very much to be deprecated. It has come on gradually since the formation of the National Congress, and the bitterness of these journals has increased rapidly since the Honourable Nana Ofori Atta perfectly justifiably denied the claim of the Congress to represent the chiefs of West Africa. The inference is perfectly clear; that these journals are acting on behalf of the Congress, that they are publishing the propaganda of the Congress. That is the inference; if that is so, the National Congress of British West Africa is com-

mitting a deadly sin against the Gold Coast. They are at the present moment . . . widening day by day and month by month, the gap between the black man and the white man; they are increasing and creating this racial feeling. It is getting worse and worse. Ask any intelligent man today what he considers to be the attitude of the black man towards the white man compared with what it was six months ago. It is greatly to be hoped that this attitude on the part of the journals and newspapers in this country will be abandoned. Because, believe me, no success will be obtained except by bitter fighting . . . and much damage, moral and material, to the various peoples of this country, unless the black man and the white are going to co-operate together for the good of the country. There is no white man who has thought seriously of this question, who has ever denied to the black the prospect of taking over Government at some time or other in the history of their country. There is no white man who has thought out this question who is not willing to give greatly increasing powers to the black man. If the Congress is going to continue to widen this gap between the races, it is going to do irreparable damage. It is going to prolong the time before the black man of this country gets a real voice in the Government; far longer than it would be if there was good co-operation. . . .

[G.C., S.P. 10 of 1920–21, pp. 16–17]

464 REPORT BY THE TOWN COUNCILS COMMITTEE ON THE CONSTITUTION AND WORKING OF . . . TOWN COUNCILS IN THE COLONY. . . .　　ACCRA, 26 MAY, 1922.

[Opens with a review of the abortive experiments in 1858 and 1887.] . . .

The present ordinance [No. 17 of 1894] was drafted and passed through the Legislative Council by Mr — afterwards Sir Alexander — Ashmore, who was then Colonial Secretary. . . . Mr Ashmore had apparently taken as his model the Municipal Ordinance of Ceylon, as then in force.

The principal feature of the Ordinance was that the Government should have upon each Town Council so constituted a permanent official majority, while the Chairman also would always be a Government official

There was great dissatisfaction with and opposition to the Bill, and protests were received from the Manchemei and people of Accra . . . and a deputation was appointed to wait upon the Governor and to protest against the Ordinance being put into force. . . . [And its application was postponed.]

It is interesting to note the grounds of objection of the unofficial population, both European and African, to the new law, which were . . .

(1) That it imposed a direct house tax, which was hateful in itself.

(2) That such taxation was not necessary, having regard to the fact the Gold Coast was at that time in possession of an annual surplus, and had been able to lend funds to . . . Sierra Leone.

(3) That the projected Town Council was a sham in that the District Commissioner or some other official nominated by the Governor, was to be ex-officio President and Treasurer; that half of the Council was to be composed of members nominated by the Governor, who were to hold their seats during his pleasure; and that the . . . elected members would be in a permanent minority, owing to the possession by the official President of a casting vote.

(4) That the Government officers who would thus command a majority of votes on the Council were not householders, and would therefore be levying a house rate which they themselves would not be called upon to pay.

(5) That the community as a whole was not sufficiently advanced in enlightenment and civilisation to . . . appreciate the advantages of municipal institutions. . . .

Mr Joseph Chamberlain . . . on the 23rd December [1895] . . . issued a circular Despatch on the subject of Municipal Government in the Crown Colonies. In this despatch he stated . . . That the system of charging the community at large with the cost of a local scheme, does not conduce to economy or prudence in the administration of that scheme, or the fostering of a due sense of responsibility on the part of those who administer the affairs of a locality that is allowed to draw upon the whole community for contributions to local undertakings. . . . That he was anxious to encourage and develop the Municipal spirit in all the larger towns of the Crown Colonies, but that he held it to be of the first importance that such a spirit should aim from the first at being self-supporting.

This was a high ideal to work up to, and we venture to think that . . . Mr. Chamberlain was better acquainted with the constitution and conditions of life in England than with those on the West Coast of Africa, and did not realise that any attempt to draw a parallel between them could not but give fallacious results. . . .

The Ordinance was first put into operation in May 1898, when the towns of Accra and Christiansborg were brought within its provisions. There was considerable opposition, principally on the ground of the House Rate, but the educated natives paid the rates due from the Manchemei, and very shortly thereafter all outward opposition to the establishment of the Council broke down; but it cannot be denied that bringing this law into force provoked intense resentment. However, the smouldering discontent which it left behind appears to have almost disappeared, judging from the unanimous desire from both African and European for the reorganisation of Municipal Government.

The provisions of the Ordinance were extended to Seccondee in 1904 and to Cape Coast in 1906, but not without opposition from the Chiefs and inhabitants of these towns. . . .

In our opinion there is no doubt whatever that a mistake was made in drafting the present constitution by the introduction of an official majority with power to impose rates. . . . Town Councils were born in an atmosphere of ill-will and sullen resentment, which resulted, for a considerable period, in a lack of interest in their proceedings and work, whilst the aspect of their work with which the African came into most direct contact, viz., the raising of revenue by house and land taxes, aroused his active hostility. We feel that had the Councils commenced their career either with an African majority, or, as was probably necessary at the time, an official majority but no direct taxation, they would probably have been a success from the outset.

Despite these very serious handicaps, however, the Councils have certainly done good work, and the superiority of the three towns which possess Councils over those which do not, particularly in regard to sanitation, is very marked. This has been gradually borne in upon the inhabitants so that there is now general agreement as to the utility of Town Councils and a strong desire for their reorganisation and the extension of their powers. . . . If the people are placed in control of spending their own money, we confidently anticipate that development of interest in the Councils and their work, and of a civic sense amongst the population, will be rapid. . . .

The oldest Town Council in the Colony (Accra) has only existed for 24 years and the other two . . . for 18 and 16 years respectively. We should therefore be blind to the teachings of history if we proposed to engraft on to a community with such small experience of English municipal institutions and with the manifest educational drawbacks [that] exist on the Gold Coast today, the British system of Local Government in its entirety. . . . In Accra (the seat of Government) the last census showed that 75 per cent. of the population is illiterate, and of the remaining 25 per cent. it can be safely said that only a very small minority have any knowledge or experience of municipal institutions.

The grant of full democratic institutions to a community before the general body of the people is fit and ready to exercise its powers and duties is a very dangerous proceeding. It frequently results in the concentration of power in the hands of a few persons who have neither the training nor traditions behind them which would enable them to administer the Government as trustees of the people and not for their own ends; while the people themselves are divorced from the guidance of their natural rulers.

Conditions today, however, differ in one very important respect from those obtaining . . . in 1894. The boom in the Colony's trade and the spread of education are beginning to have much the same effects as the industrial revolution . . . produced in England. The population is commencing to migrate. The young men are no longer content to remain in the country villages and are flocking to the large towns to take up work as clerks, mechanics, shop assistants, etc. They are seizing the opportunities of intercourse and mutual education which concentration in large communities in touch with the outside world affords them. The influx into the towns is not composed solely of natives of the rural districts of the Gold Coast, but comprises many immigrants from other West African Colonies . . . and they also are demanding a share in the government of their adopted country.

The young African is asserting in no uncertain manner his claim to independence of thought and action. This tendency will probably increase, and as time goes on, the inhabitant of the towns will inevitably demand a political system which will afford him scope for the exercise of his newly found liberties. This, we consider, he will find in a wide and generous measure of local self-government. . . . Our task therefore has been to devise a scheme which will give that fuller responsibility without which further progress is impossible, and at the same time provide that experience, advice and guidance which it is admitted are essential and can only be provided by Government. . . .

In order, therefore, to give to the African citizen real responsibility for the management of his own affairs, we recommend that the franchise be extended to all ratepayers, male and female, of the age of 21 years, possessed of, or occupying land or buildings of the annual value of not less than £5, and that the majority of the Council be elected by the ratepayers, either as one body for the whole town, or by wards, as local circumstances dictate. . . .

To provide Government experience, it is proposed that members be appointed by the Governor, up to one-third of the total of elected members. Further, to ensure the representation of the European mercantile community, the Chambers of Commerce, where such exist, should appoint a number not exceeding one-sixth of the elected members. . . .

We are . . . of opinion that the time has arrived when the Governor's power of appointing an ex-officio President and Treasurer should be abolished and that the title of President should be changed to Mayor. We recommend that the Mayor should be elected by the Council from amongst the unofficial members . . . and the office of Treasurer should be a paid appointment in future. [Several witnesses, however, took exception to this proposal.] . . .

There is no doubt that if Municipal Councils are to be a success in the future, and are to carry out the duties imposed upon them, that the maximum rate, viz.: five per cent. on the annual value, permitted to be levied under the 1894 Ordinance, will require to be increased. This rate at present is ridiculously small, and certainly does not pay for the many services rendered to the inhabitants of a Town by its Town Council. . . . [They proposed to empower the Council to levy a graduated rate.]

At the same time, however, we consider it inopportune that the first few years of municipal administration should witness a heavy increase in the rates imposed upon the population of the towns. We therefore suggest that the Government should continue the present grants-in-aid to the Municipal Councils for a few years after the proposed Ordinance comes into force. At the end of a fixed term of years, the grants-in-aid should be annually reduced as circumstances permit. Even when they are abolished as regular annual payments, they may be required from time to time to meet special purposes. . . .

We are of opinion that the work of the reorganised councils will be closely watched by the people of the more important towns, and if successful in one town, then application will no doubt be made for the provisions to be extended to other towns. [One witness] . . . suggested that the Ordinance should be applied to the towns of Accra, Cape Coast, Seccondee, Koforidua, Winnebah and Axim, but after giving this question very careful consideration, we have come to the unanimous conclusion that the bill . . . should be applied in the first instance to Accra only. . . .

If our proposals are looked upon in the light of an experiment in the practical political education of the African we think that will be the correct angle from which they should be judged. A great mass of theory of English political and municipal institutions has been absorbed by the educated African in recent years, but he has not been in a position to gain much practical experience of their working. The time has now arrived when he must 'try out' his theories in practice, and apply them to the benefit of his own people. In our opinion it would be as fatal to deny all rights of local self-government because the people are not yet fitted for complete autonomy, as it would be to grant that, in one act, before [the] general populace is ready for it. . . .

As new people and nations have come within the orbit of the Empire, they have come under the influence of its political institutions and as they have fitted themselves for these institutions, so have their privileges been extended to them. The process to be sure, must be gradual, but at the same time it must be steady and continuous, and it must incorporate the best features of the indigenous institutions of the nations concerned. These principles have guided us in the preparation of our report. If, as the result, one step in the march of civilization in Africa is recorded, our purpose will have been achieved. . . .

> [Signed] John Maxwell (Chairman)
> Casely Hayford.
> T. Hutton-Mills.
> E. J. P. Brown.
> J. Glover Addo.

[G.C., S.P. 17 of 1922–3, pp. 23–4, 36–7, 39, 68]

465 THE BRITISH MANDATE FOR TOGOLAND
[20 JULY, 1922]

The Council of the League of Nations:

Whereas by Article 119 of the Treaty of Peace with Germany signed at Versailles on June 28th, 1919, Germany renounced in favour of the Principal Allied and Associated Powers all her rights over her overseas possessions, including therein Togoland: and

Whereas the Principal Allied and Associated Powers agreed that the Governments of France and Great Britain should make a joint recommendation to the League of Nations as to the future of the said territory; and

Whereas the Governments of France and Great Britain have made a joint recommendation to the Council of the League of Nations that a mandate to administer, in accordance with Article 22 of the Covenant

of the League of Nations, that part of Togoland lying to the west of the line agreed upon in the Declaration of July 10th, 1919, referred to in Article 1, should be conferred upon His Britannic Majesty, and

Whereas His Britannic Majesty has agreed to accept the mandate in respect of the said territory, and has undertaken to exercise it on behalf of the League of Nations in accordance with the following provisions;

Confirming the said mandate, defines its terms as follows:

Article 1.

The territory for which a mandate is conferred upon His Britannic Majesty comprises that part of Togoland which lies to the west of the line laid down in the Declaration signed on July 10th, 1919, of which a copy is annexed hereto.

This line may, however, be slightly modified by mutual agreement between His Britannic Majesty's Government and the Government of the French Republic, where an examination of the localities shows that it is undesirable, either in the interests of the inhabitants or by reason of any inaccuracies in the map Sprigade 1 : 200,000, annexed to the Declaration, to adhere strictly to the line laid down therein. . . . [Provides for delimitation.]

Article 2.

The Mandatory shall be responsible for the peace, order and good government of the territory, and for the promotion to the utmost of the material and moral well-being and the social progress of its inhabitants.

Article 3.

The Mandatory shall not establish in the territory any military or naval bases, nor erect any fortification, nor organise any native military force except for local police purposes and for the defence of the territory.

Article 4.

The Mandatory:

(1) Shall provide for the eventual emancipation of all slaves, and for as speedy an elimination of domestic and other slavery as social conditions will allow;

(2) Shall suppress all forms of slave trade;

(3) Shall prohibit all forms of forced or compulsory labour, except for essential public works and services, and then only in return for adequate remuneration;

(4) Shall protect the natives from abuse and measures of fraud and force by the careful supervision of labour contracts and the recruiting of labour;

(5) Shall exercise a strict control over the traffic in arms and ammunition and the sale of spirituous liquors.

Article 5.

In the framing of laws relating to the holding or transfer of land, the Mandatory shall take into consideration native laws and customs, and shall respect the rights and safeguard the interests of the native population.

No native land may be transferred, except between natives, without the previous consent of the public authorities, and no real rights over native land in favour of non-natives may be created except with the same consent. The Mandatory shall promulgate strict regulations against usury.

Article 6.

The mandatory shall secure to all nationals of States Members of the League of Nations the same rights as are enjoyed in the territory by his own nationals in respect of entry into and residence in the territory, the protection afforded to their person and property and acquisition of property, movable and immovable, and the exercise of their profession or trade, subject only to the requirements of public

U

order, and on condition of compliance with the local law.

Further, the Mandatory shall ensure to all nationals of States Members of the League of Nations, on the same footing as to his own nationals, freedom of transit and navigation, and complete economic, commercial and industrial equality, except that the Mandatory shall be free to organise essential public works and services on such terms and conditions as he thinks just.

Concessions for the development of the natural resources of the territory shall be granted by the Mandatory without distinction on grounds of nationality between the nationals of all States Members of the League of Nations, but on such conditions as will maintain intact the authority of the local Government.

Concessions having the character of a general monopoly shall not be granted. This provision does not affect the right of the Mandatory to create monopolies of a purely fiscal nature in the interests of the territory under mandate and in order to provide the territory with fiscal resources which seem best suited to the local requirements; or, in certain cases, to carry out the development of natural resources either directly by the State or by a controlled agency, provided that there will result therefrom no monopoly of the natural resources for the benefit of the Mandatory or his nationals, directly or indirectly, nor any preferential advantage which shall be inconsistent with the economic, commercial and industrial equality hereinbefore guaranteed.

The rights conferred by this article extend equally to companies and associations organised in accordance with the law of any of the Members of the League of Nations, subject only to the requirements of public order, and on condition of compliance with the local law.

Article 7.

The Mandatory shall ensure in the territory complete freedom of conscience and the free exercise of all forms of worship which are consonant with public order and morality; missionaries who are nationals of States Members of the League of Nations shall be free to enter the territory and to travel and reside therein, to acquire and possess property, to erect religious buildings and to open schools throughout the territory; it being understood, however, that the Mandatory shall have the right to exercise such control as may be necessary for the maintenance of public order and good government, and to take all measures required for such control.

Article 8.

The Mandatory shall apply to the territory any general international conventions applicable to his contiguous territory.

Article 9.

The Mandatory shall have full powers of administration and legislation in the area subject to the mandate. This area shall be administered in accordance with the laws of the Mandatory as an integral part of his territory and subject to the above provisions.

The Mandatory shall therefore be at liberty to apply his laws to the territory subject to the mandate with such modifications as may be required by local conditions, and to constitute the territory into a customs, fiscal or administrative union or federation with the adjacent territories under his sovereignty or control, provided always that the measures adopted to that end do not infringe the provisions of this mandate.

Article 10.

The Mandatory shall make to the Council of the League of Nations an annual report to the satisfaction of the Council, containing full information concerning the measures taken to apply the provisions of this mandate.

Article 11.

The consent of the Council of the League of Nations is required for any modification of the terms of this mandate.

Article 12.

The Mandatory agrees that if any dispute whatever should arise between the Mandatory and another Member of the League of Nations relating to the interpretation or the application of the provisions of the mandate, such dispute, if it cannot be settled by negotiation, shall be submitted to the Permanent Court of International Justice provided for by Article 14 of the Covenant of the League of Nations.

The present instrument shall be deposited in original in the archives of the League of Nations. Certified copies shall be forwarded by the Secretary-General of the League of Nations to all Members of the League.

Done at London, the twentieth day of July, one thousand nine hundred and twenty-two.

For the Secretary-General, League of Nations,

Rappard.

Director of the Mandates Section.

[Cmd. 1794. British Mandates for the Cameroons, Togoland and East Africa, pp. 10–13]

466 Togoland under British Mandate, Order in Council 1923.

At the Court at Buckingham Palace, the 11th day of October, 1923. . . .

3. (1) Togoland under British Mandate shall be divided into two sections; to be named the Northern Section and the Southern Section respectively.

(2) The boundary line between the two sections shall be the following.* . . .

(3) The following divisions are in the Northern Section: Tapa, Apai, and Delo Lolo (Ntsibu); and the following divisions are in the Southern Section: Bowiri, Wora Wora, and Guamen.

[* Details in Laws of the Gold Coast, 1936, iv., 99. The order was amended by the Togoland under British Mandate Order in Council, 1934, *loc. cit.* p. 102, to bring it into line with the Gold Coast Colony, Ashanti and Northern Territories Orders in Council of that year.]

4. Subject to the provisions of the mandate, the Northern Section shall be administered as if it formed part of the Protectorate; and, subject as aforesaid . . . the Southern Section shall be administered as if it formed part of the Colony, and, until the Government shall by Proclamation issued with His Majesty's approval, signified through a Secretary of State, otherwise ordain, as if it formed part of the Eastern Province thereof.

5. So far as the same may be applicable, the law for the time being in force in the Protectorate shall, as from the date of the commencement of this Order, apply to and be the law in force in the Northern Section, but it shall be lawful for the Governor from time to time, by Ordinance to modify or amend any provision contained in such law in its application to the said Northern Section or to exclude any such provision from application thereto and the Governor shall have full power by Ordinance to make all such provision as may from time to time be necessary for the administration of justice, the raising of revenue, and generally for the peace, order and good government of the said Northern Section: Provided always that, should any such law so applied as aforesaid be repugnant to any provision of the mandate, such law or Ordinance shall to the extent of such repugnancy, but not otherwise, be and remain absolutely void and inoperative.

6. [Repeats for Southern Section, reading 'Colony' for 'Protectorate'.]

7. The Supreme Court of the Gold Coast shall have and exercise throughout the Northern Section the like jurisdiction as it has and exercises in the Protectorate and as if the said Northern Section formed part of the Protectorate; and shall have and exercise throughout the Southern Section the like jurisdiction as it has and exercises in the Colony, and, subject to the terms of any Proclamation issued under Article 4 of this Order, as if the said Southern Section formed part of the Eastern Province of the Colony. . . .

35 The Guggisberg Achievement 1923–1926

THE early nineteen-twenties saw a tremendous expansion of the Gold Coast economy, and by 1924, sufficient progress had been made with the Ten Year Development Plan (467) for the Governor to turn to what he always regarded as the most important aspect of his policy — education, and particularly higher education, where his name will always be associated with the founding of Achimota. Here, and in his pronouncements on the Africanisation of the civil service, he could command the general and almost unqualified approval of African as well as European.

The constitutional problem was more difficult. In 1924, by way of preliminary, a Municipal Corporations Bill was introduced, which, it was hoped, would give a real measure of self government to the principal towns, and serve as a basis for their elective representation in a reformed Legislative Council. Success here proved more elusive than the Governor expected. His chief concern was with the problem indicated by his predecessor; how to devise a basis for elective representation of the tribal masses. In the new constitution which Guggisberg introduced in 1926, the central feature was the election, by newly constituted provincial councils, themselves drawn from the traditional authorities of the country, of six head chiefs, who would speak for the rural population, as the three municipal members would speak for the towns and the intelligentsia (468).

467 GOVERNOR'S ADDRESS TO LEGISLA-TIVE COUNCIL   6 MARCH, 1924.

. . . Since Council last met, a memorable and successful year has passed by. In the first place, with the exception of the fallacious results of the great boom year,[1] we have made the biggest revenue in the records of the country, exceeding by nearly half a million the amount originally estimated.

Secondly, we exported more cocoa in 1923 than in any previous year, namely 197,000 tons — exceeding 1922 by more than 40,000 tons, and the great boom year itself by 20,000 tons.

Thirdly, we have dealt with the greatest tonnage of trade in the history of the country, namely 637,000 tons — exceeding the record of 1922 by over 100,000 tons.

Fourthly, an event that will, I believe, give great satisfaction to the African Unofficial Members — Government has formulated definite proposals for the appli-

[1] 1920.

cation of the principles of elective representation and the increase of African representatives on this Council.

Fifthly, we have opened, what is by common consent judged to be the finest hospital in the whole continent of Africa,[1] and thereby taken the first practical step towards the wide extension of medical science and sanitation throughout the country.

Sixthly, we have opened an additional pipe-borne water supply at Winnebah, which is proving a boon and a blessing to the inhabitants of that prosperous town, who in the past have suffered much from the lack of pure, wholesome drinking water.

Seventhly, before the end of this session of the Council, I hope to turn on the Electric Lighting for the town of Accra. This public utility is long overdue. . . .

And finally, before this month is at an end, we shall have laid the foundation stone for what I believe is destined to be

[1] Korle Bu Hospital, Accra.

the greatest institution for the higher education of the native races of Africa.

Education, as I never lose an opportunity of reminding Members, education of the right sort — education of the mind as well as of the hand and brain — is the keystone of the edifice forming Government's main policy. . . . Definite progress . . . has been made, but at the usual cost. Honourable Members will remember that last year I warned them that every year they must be prepared to vote an increase of ten to fifteen thousand pounds for education. This year I am asking them for close on £120,000 for the Education Department alone, exclusive of any new buildings. Last year it was £106,000. This time next year it will be £140,000. . . .

I lay stress on this fact, thus early in my message, because the necessity for providing the funds for our steady expansion of education should be in the minds of Honourable Members during the discussion of the whole of the budget, and especially those estimates connected with harbours, railways and roads, with cocoa sanitation, agricultural experiments, and forest reserves. For it is on two chief things that the educational progress of this country depends — the cheapening of transportation, and the development and the protection of our agriculture. . . .

Twelve months ago, considerable doubt existed regarding our trade prospects for the year through which we have just passed. . . . Actually, our revenue, which is an index of the volume of trade, has exceeded the estimate by about £487,000 and our sea-borne trade showed an increase of nearly £2,000,000 on the previous year. . . . The total tonnage of our maritime imports and exports in 1923 reached 637,540 tons and was the highest on record . . . as the following table will show:—

	IMPORTS	EXPORTS	TOTAL.
1913	224,000 tons	181,000 tons	405,000 tons
1914	263,000 ,,	167,000 ,,	430,000 ,,
1915	182,000 ,,	154,000 ,,	336,000 ,,
1916	196,000 ,,	170,000 ,,	366,000 ,,
1917	116,000 ,,	203,000 ,,	319,000 ,,
1918	79,000 ,,	149,000 ,,	228,000 ,,

	IMPORTS	EXPORTS	TOTAL.
1919	133,000 tons	260,000 tons	393,000 tons
1920	223,000 ,,	237,000 ,,	460,000 ,,
1921	178,000 ,,	200,000 ,,	378,000 ,,
1922	185,000 ,,	358,000 ,,	543,000 ,,
1923	248,635 ,,	388,775 ,,	637,540 ,,

As usual, cocoa was responsible, both directly and indirectly, for the increase in trade. Over 194,000 tons left our ports, which with some 3,500 tons exported overland, makes a total of between 197,000 and 198,000 tons for the year. . . . When it is remembered that during the greater part of the year, the market price was lower than it was before the war, the increase of 38,000 tons recorded in 1923 must be regarded as an amazing achievement, and the present seems a fitting opportunity to review the wonderful growth in our exports of cocoa since 1905. These have been, in round numbers:—

1905	7,000 tons	[£	187,000]
1906	8,000 ,,	[£	336,000]
1907	10,000 ,,	[£	515,000]
1908	13,000 ,,	[£	541,000]
1909	21,000 ,,	[£	755,000]
1910	22,000 ,,	[£	866,000]
1911	41,000 ,,	[£ 1,613,000]	
1912	39,000 ,,	[£ 1,641,000]	
1913	52,000 ,,	[£ 2,489,000]	
1914	53,000 ,,	[£ 2,194,000]	
1915	78,000 ,,	[£ 3,651,000]	
1916	73,000 ,,	[£ 3,848,000]	
1917	92,000 ,,	[£ 3,147,000]	
1918	67,000 ,,	[£ 1,797,000]	
1919	176,000 ,,	[£ 8,278,000]	
1920	125,000 ,,	[£10,056,000]	
1921	133,000 ,,	[£ 4,764,000]	
1922	159,000 ,,	[£ 5,841,000]	
1923	197,000 ,,	[£ 6,567,000]	

Altogether, our exports for 1923 amounted to 388,000 tons valued at £8,328,000, an increase over 1922, in spite of the lower price of cocoa, of £832,000.

The most striking increase was in manganese, 136,000 tons being shipped as compared with 61,000 in the previous year. Next year we anticipate a still further increase, as our railway is at present dealing with over 18,000 tons a month, and we have been requested to increase this to 20,000 tons. When it is considered that the manganese trade is labouring under the most adverse conditions of shipment . . . it will be seen that the future of this great industry when Takoradi is opened is most promising.

It is gratifying to note that our exports of palm oil increased by 148,000 gallons and palm kernels by 728 tons. . . . It is still more gratifying, in view of the serious shortage of raw cotton in the United Kingdom, that our modest export of cotton lint increased from 6,000 lbs in 1922 to 37,000 lbs in 1923. . . .

On the other hand there were decreases in two of our main exports. In view of the necessity of preserving our forests, I cannot regard the first of these with any regret, namely, the decrease of one million cubic feet in our shipment of mahogany. The other decrease, however, causes me great concern, as it consists of 13,165 ounces of gold. . . . The decrease in the export of gold is practically entirely due to the difficulty of obtaining labour for the intensely unpopular underground work. It is a peculiar fact that the Ashanti Gold-fields Corporation does not seem to have the same difficulties as the companies in the Tarquah district, but I think that the Chamber of Mines will be the first to recognise that Government has spared no effort short of compulsory enlistment to assist them in recruiting on a voluntary basis in the Northern Territories. . . .

As in the case of the Injurious Pests Ordinance . . . no conflicting opinion exists among either Europeans or Africans in this country on the necessity for preserving sufficient forests to safeguard the whole source of our trade and wealth. It is, as with the Pests Ordinance, the remedy and the method of applying it, on which past Governments and the people have not seen eye to eye. Fully recognising the people's apprehensions, and also the responsibility I was personally incurring by deferring the definite action urged on me by my expert advisers, I deliberately adopted the method

of trusting the chiefs and people, four years ago. As I stated in enunciating our forest policy, I still repose my trust in them; but as the time for inaction has passed, I have laid down the period during which I consider that my confidence should be justified. It now depends entirely on the chiefs and their people as to whether a Forestry Ordinance shall be or shall not be passed during 1926 or 1927. . . .

With regard to railways . . . the number of miles opened for traffic in 1923 was 394, as compared with 269 miles in 1921. The opening of the Tafo–Coomassie line early in the year resulted in a heavy increase of cocoa exports, while the completion of the Seccondee–Dunkwa deviations has resulted in traffic being dealt with at such a rate that the port of Seccondee became at intervals hopelessly congested. . . . In December no less than eleven trains of cocoa vans were lying idle, owing to the inability of the merchants and shipping agencies to deal with them successfully. . . . The Accra railway during the past year has consistently dealt with more cocoa than can be handled at the port. In December last, 19,214 tons were railed to Accra and during that period, 11,165 tons were actually shipped. . . .

By the end of this month, the total number of miles of road constructed and repaired by the Public Works Department is 1,212, an increase of 103 in the year, while the length of the pioneer roads constructed by chiefs and Political Officers, on a number of which motor traffic is subject to interruptions during the rains, amounts to something over 2,600 miles. The total of our motor and motorable roads is, therefore, about 3,800 miles, which means that 2,600 miles of road have been constructed in the last five or six years. . . .

The great progress made in the 'Ten Year Development Programme' of harbours, railways and roads, the public spirit of the chiefs and people, and the willing manner in which the already over-burdened Political Officers have added to their work in helping the hardworking engineers of the Public Works Department, have almost brought in sight the moment at which we may consider our cocoa trade safe against competition. Takoradi and the Central Province Railway should both be opened in the last half of 1926, and in view of the road extensions that will have been completed by that time, I believe that we shall then have consolidated our position against all attacks. . . .

I now arrive at the subject to which my remarks on finance, trade, agriculture and transport have merely been leading — Education. In view of my frequent utterances on the importance of this subject, there should be little doubt in the minds of Honourable Members as to education and the progress of the people being Government's chief policy. . . .

Here I would like to point out to those who are clamouring for us to do more than we are doing, that any delay that has occurred is not on account of financial stringency; we have the necessary funds at our disposal, and in that respect the people of this country are at an advantage as compared with those elsewhere. The stumbling-block to greater progress in education is the lack of sufficient African teachers with the necessary educational attainments and qualities of character that are necessary for the efficient training of both the youth and the young manhood of this country. . . .

It is not fair to make too sweeping a denunciation of our present system of education, for it has undoubtedly done a certain amount of good, but I am certain that, if continued, it will lead to disaster in the not distant future. Putting the case briefly, we are at present turning out annually some 4,000 to 5,000 boys who are only fitted to be clerks and, what is worse, the majority of whom could not, from their education, be anything but inferior clerks. We are flooding the market with semi-educated youths for whom, owing to their disdain of manual labour, there is annually less employment. . . . Failing employment in an office, and strongly imbued with an unhealthy dislike to manual labour, they fall a natural victim to discontent and consequently to unhappiness. We are, in fact, repeating here the history of educated India, which has long suffered from the adoption, years ago, of an incomplete European system. . . .

The worst feature . . . of the situation today is that we have no system of training African leaders in thought and industry. Lack of the qualities of leadership, which in all cases involves the bearing of responsibility and in many also the power of command, is a pronounced defect among the races of the West Coast of Africa. Those citizens of the Gold Coast who have developed the qualities I have mentioned, have done so by their own individual efforts, and in spite of our system of education; and the majority of them only after residence in Europe. . . . We are annually turning out a mass of semi-educated youths and have made no provision for the training of leaders. This is a most serious state of affairs, for without the willing and efficient co-operation of African leaders, we shall not be able to fulfil the sacred trust imposed on us — 'the well-being and development of peoples not yet able to stand by themselves.' . . .

The solution undoubtedly lies in the institution of secondary schools. Convinced as I am, however, that secondary schools are necessary, I am equally confident that to start them at the present moment would do more harm than good. In the first place, we have not got enough Africans, sufficiently highly educated, to staff efficiently the primary schools alone. Secondly, if these secondary schools are to produce leaders, they must be residential schools where character-training takes the first place in the curriculum; and here there is at present a total deficiency of Africans qualified to undertake the work. . . .

There are others who hold that the solution of the educational problem of the Gold Coast lies in the formation of a university. My remarks on secondary schools apply here with even greater force. Like secondary schools, the university must come in due course, but the time is not yet ripe for it. Even if we combined with other West African Colonies, I believe that we should not find enough sufficiently educated students to fill it at this particular period. . . .

Accepting the fact that we must eventually provide both secondary schools and a university . . . our chief task today lies in increasing the efficiency of education in our primary schools, sufficiently to ensure a flow of suitably educated scholars to the higher institutions of tomorrow. It is obvious, therefore, that the first step to be taken is to raise the educational standard of African teachers for the primary schools. . . .

What is really required is an institution at which our future teachers can obtain a higher education before actually learning how to teach. . . . It is highly important . . . that we should, as soon as possible, provide some facilities for higher education locally, so as to obviate the necessity for Africans proceeding to England . . . for wherever one turns, one is faced by the necessity to fill appointments, hitherto occupied by Europeans, with Africans possessing a better education than it is at present possible for them to obtain. . . .

Writing some years ago on Egyptian education, Lord Cromer makes some remarks on the subject of secondary education that may well serve as a solemn warning to us. He points out that the intellectual phase through which India is now (1907) passing, stands before the world as a warning that it is unwise to create too wide a gap between the state of education of the higher and lower classes in an oriental country governed under the inspiration of a western democracy. He points out that higher education cannot and ought not to be checked or discouraged, and that the policy advocated by Macaulay is the only policy worthy of a civilised nation. If, however, it is to be carried out without danger to the state, the ignorance of the masses should be tempered with the intellectual advance of those who are destined to be their leaders. . . .

Lord Cromer points out that 'it is neither wise nor just, that the people should be left intellectually defenceless in the presence of the hare-brained and empirical projects which the political charlatan, himself but half-educated, will not fail to pour into their credulous ears. In this early part of the twentieth century there is no possible general remedy against the demagogue except that which consists in educating those who are his natural prey to such an extent that they may at all events have some chance of discerning the imposture which but too often lurks beneath his perfervid eloquence and political quackery.'

Lord Cromer's words apply with great aptness to this country. In spite of the existence of one or two educational institutions of a secondary nature, the intellectual gap between the African who has completed his education at an English university and the semi-educated African of our primary schools, is dangerously wide. No one is more ready than I am to sympathise with the legitimate aspirations of the African for advancement and for a greater share in the government of his country, but if we are to help him to do this, if we are to protect the masses from the hasty and ill-conceived schemes of possible local demagogues, we must hasten, as rapidly as our means will allow, to fill up the gap between the two classes.

Our first step in filling this gap will be taken this year in the building of Achimota College. This will be an institution at which the African youth will receive, first and foremost, character-training of such a nature as will fit him to be a good citizen; and secondly the higher education necessary to enable him to become a leader in thought, in the professions, or in industry, among his fellow-countrymen. . . .

Achimota, as I see it, will be more of the nature of a university college than of a secondary school. It has been suggested that this is putting the cart in front of the horse, that we should have our secondary schools first and our university college afterwards. Theoretically the suggestion contains some truth, but in view of the chief factor in the educational situation at the moment, the entire absence of suitable African teachers for secondary schools, the arrangement may be regarded as a practical and satisfactory compromise, pending the introduction of an extended secondary school system of education. It is therefore obvious that one of the first tasks of Achimota will be to give general education and technical training to the teachers on whom we must rely for staffing our secondary schools and for improving our primary schools sufficiently to render the former a success.

Achimota College is the stepping stone towards the university which it is the ardent desire of the Africans to have, and which it is the undoubted duty of the Government to take a share in giving as soon as . . . the time is ripe. Further, there is no reason whatever why Achimota should not itself expand into a university when it has done enough to enable sufficient secondary schools to be started. . . . In planning the administration I have, therefore, thought it advisable to consider the prospect of the College eventually becoming a University. Such a reservation as to its future does not affect the organisation and administration of the intervening period; but, in view of the great cost of providing the highly qualified staff required by a university, it is more than likely that when the time comes, the people of the Gold Coast will not be the only ones who will welcome the idea of a university in West Africa.

If Achimota does become a university, it should be endowed and managed by a Board independent of Government. For this reason I feel that it would be inadvisable to place it under the control of the local Education Department. From the very beginning, Achimota will be entirely independent, and will be organised in such a manner that it can, when the time comes, be transferred to the control of whatever board or authority that by then may be considered the most suitable to take charge of the university into which it will blossom.

For the present, therefore, I propose that the College should form a separate and special department of Government. Its finances will be dealt with by the Treasury and audited in the usual manner, but its internal economy and administration will be in the hands of a carefully selected headmaster, who will be directly responsible to the Governor. . . . I hope that Honourable Members will assist in laying the foundation-stone of this important building before the end of this month. It is difficult, however, to see how construction can be completed before December 1925 . . . .

The Educationists' Committee of 1920 recommended the formation of a Training College for Women teachers to provide the staff for our Girls' Schools, and to replace the men at present in charge of infant classes. In forming the 1922 Committee I drew their attention especially to this recommendation, and asked them to consider the question of co-education generally, and especially the provision at Achimota of a block of buildings in which women students could live under the care of their mistress and take part in the general classes of the College. . . .

It appears that the Committee are not wholly opposed to the introduction of co-education, provided that it begins in the primary schools. . . . They express the hope that if this is done gradually, the time will come when Achimota can open its doors to girls. . . . So great is the importance of educating the women of the Gold Coast [that] I cannot but feel that we should take the slight risk that will be run by combining the education of the sexes at Achimota. In view, however, of the consensus of native and European opinion against it, I do not feel justified in adopting this course at the moment, but I hope that public opinion will become more enlightened in the course of the next few years . . . for there can be no real civilisation if the women of the race are left uneducated. . . .

Honourable Members during the present session will have the important and exacting task of examining and passing the new Municipal Corporations Bill, which will be put into effect at Accra during the coming year. The proposed legislation will, as Honourable Members know, practically confer municipal self-government on the citizens of Accra. I regard this as the biggest step in political advancement ever taken by the inhabitants of this country. . . . We intend to apply the Ordinance to Accra, to begin with, for neither the Town Councils of Seccondee or Cape Coast consider that the time is ripe for [it] to be applied to them. In this I believe their decision to be wise. . . .

During the past year, I and my advisers have been giving the most careful consideration to the subject of the representation of Africans and the non-official members of the European community on this Council. I have been greatly assisted by members of the Aborigines' Rights Protection Society, and the Political Officers have conducted careful enquiries in their respective administrative areas. . . . I have never been against the principle of elective representation. My chief anxiety has been to give it wider application than has hitherto been adopted in other West African countries. The most careful enquiries were therefore necessary in order to evolve a practical working scheme that would apply not only to the educated communities of the seaport towns, but also to the native stools and the non-official European Communities. I am not at liberty to divulge at present the recommendations which I have made to the Secretary of State, nor can I hope that they will satisfy everyone, but I believe that they form a solid stepping-stone on the path of political advancement. . . .

[G.C., S.P. 3 of 1924–5, pp. 28–130]

468 SPEECH OF SIR GORDON F. G. GUGGISBERG IN LEGISLATIVE COUNCIL. . . .

22 FEBRUARY, 1926.

. . . [a] Government's General Policy. . . .

If the peoples of the Gold Coast are ever to 'stand by themselves', it must be by the gradual development of their own institutions and customs to meet the demands of more modern and advanced civilisation. That is the experience of every country, as history shows, and I do not see why or how the Gold Coast can be the solitary exception. Now in the south, the inhabitants of the coastal belt have been for several centuries in contact with the civilisation and customs of European peoples, and the advent of education and European trade has long imposed a severe strain on their original institutions and customs. This strain is most acute in the larger southern towns, but the gradual extension northwards of education, trade, and mining operations has been, and is still exercising a disintegrating influence on the institutions and customs of the interior. So much so is this the case, that there is a danger that what are called Western civilisation and Western customs will swamp the natural institutions and customs of this country. That, Honourable Members, is a very grave peril, which, if not averted, will result in the serious deterioration of the national characteristics of the African race and this . . . would be entirely inimical to progress.

Government by itself cannot avert this peril; that is the task of the inhabitants of this country. In order to preserve their nationality, their racial characteristics, their institutions and customs, and yet at the same time to retain their position as a free people in the world, it is essential that the African should absorb only what is best in Western Civilisation — what is best calculated to enable his country to cope with the Western methods of life which are slowly penetrating to all parts of the land. . . .

[b] Government's policy in regard to the employment of Africans.

Government's policy is to employ Africans who are suitably qualified by education and training in any appointment in any branch of the Government Service. Two reservations only are made — the Political Service is not open to Africans as they have opportunities of serving their country in the Oman Councils of the Stools to which they belong; while the Secretary of State does not at present contemplate the appointment of African judges. . . .

Government's policy of employing Africans in its service is necessary for two reasons. Firstly, it is dictated by the spirit of justice, for it is only fair-play to give those inhabitants of the country who are properly qualified for the work, an opportunity of entering, and eventually advancing to the highest appointments in the Government Service. Secondly, the policy is dictated by hard fact, namely, the necessity of reducing expenditure on the present costly system of staffing the Senior Service by Europeans. . . . Government is . . . faced with an automatic increase in expenditure of £267,000 in connection with its staff only, by 1935–36. . . . If the establishment which is necessary for efficient administration in every direction is to be maintained, some form of economy is essential. The most effective, is to fill vacancies in European appointments, with Africans, and to create posts for Africans instead of Europeans when an increase in staff is necessary. . . . From all causes, it may be taken that there will be a total average reduction of expenditure of approximately £500 per annum for every African employed instead of a European. . . .

Honourable Members will find attached to the printed copy of my address a progressive programme of African appointments in the Government Service, covering the next twenty years. Two points should be noted about this programme.

(i) The programme does not contain *all* the appointments in the Government Service, but merely those in which it is considered that definite progress can be made in the next twenty years in employing Africans;

(ii) The number of appointments shown are those which should be filled by Europeans and Africans respectively, but if qualified Africans are available earlier, they should be employed before the date given. . . .

Summarised, the table provides for the following appointments:—

Number of appointments provided in		Europeans	Africans.
Estimates	1925–6	481	28
Proposed appointments by	1926–7	496	31
Proposed appointments by	1930–1	467	76
Proposed appointments by	1935–6	396	148
Proposed appointments by	1945–6	319	229

. . . In concluding my remarks on this subject, I will deal briefly with three objections which have from time to time been advanced against the general policy of employing Africans instead of Europeans.

The first objection is that there will be a general loss of efficiency. I do not believe that this loss should be appreciable in the case of a well-organised Department which arranges for good supervision. Even if there is a slight loss to begin with, I see no reason why full efficiency should not be restored in due course.

The second objection is that there will be a serious loss of efficiency when Africans occupy Staff Appointments. I do not see that this objection can be justified. A Staff Appointment is given by selection and not by seniority, and so long as this system of promotion continues, Government is bound to select the best qualified man — whether he be an African or a European — for promotion to a Staff post.

The third objection is that racial feeling will be created if and when the senior African in any Department is passed over for promotion to a Staff Appointment. This will inevitably be a political cry in the distant future, but it will only need serious consideration if the passing over is an unjust act. Neither an African nor a European will have any claim to promotion to a Staff Appointment on account of his colour, but because he is the best man for the appointment. The African cannot expect to be specially favoured because he is an African, nor do I believe that his solid thinking countrymen in twenty years' time would support him if he did. . . .

[c] The New Legislative Council. . . .

The new constitution of the Legislative Council of the Gold Coast Colony is inseparably bound up with two other steps which have been taken simultaneously for the progress of the Africans in Native Administration and in Municipal Government respectively. Any criticism of the new constitution must therefore take [these] into consideration. . . .

The new Council will consist of the Governor as President, and fifteen Official and fourteen Unofficial Members, as against the present eleven and nine respectively. The former consist of the five senior members of the Executive Council, namely,

The Colonial Secretary.
The Attorney-General,
The Treasurer,
The Director of Medical and Sanitary Services,
The Secretary for Native Affairs,

and the following ten officials:—

The Comptroller of Customs,
The Director of Public Works,
The General Manager of Railways,
The Commissioners of the Eastern,
    Central and Western Provinces,
The Surveyor-General,
The Director of Education,
Two nominated Official Members.

With regard to the above, the only important changes lie in the four last-named members. The Surveyor-General becomes a member as arrangements are being made to include the office of Com-

missioner of Lands in this appointment, on account of the increasing importance of land questions in the Colony. The Director of Education naturally becomes a member owing to the paramount importance of education to the progress of the African peoples, while the two nominated Official Members give the Governor an opportunity of appointing any two officials whose sympathy with, and knowledge of, native questions and institutions, make their advice particularly valuable to Government.

It is in the new appointments of Unofficial members of the Council, however, that the most appreciable change in the constitution of that Chamber has been introduced. These members consist of:—

Six African Provincial Members,
Three African Municipal Members,
Five European Unofficial Members.

With regard to the six African Provincial Members, these will all be Head Chiefs. They will be elected in the following manner. In each province of the Colony, a council called 'The Provincial Council of Head Chiefs' will be formed. These Councils will meet at some central place in their respective provinces to elect their members. In the event of their failure to do so, the Governor has power to nominate a Head Chief as a Provincial Member. The population of the Eastern Province is three times, and that of the Central Province twice, the population of the Western Province. The Provincial Council of the Eastern Province will therefore elect three Head Chiefs, that of the Central Province two, and that of the Western Province one. In the Eastern Province, the Provincial Council will be divided into three sections according to the vernacular, namely those representing the Ga-Adangme, the Ewe, and the Akan languages respectively. No such division of the Provincial Councils of the Central and Western Provinces is necessary.

In electing the Head Chiefs, each member of a Provincial Council will have one vote for every ten thousand inhabitants or part thereof in his division or stool. No Head Chief will be eligible for election unless he is able to read and speak the English language sufficiently well to take an active and intelligent part in the proceedings of the Legislative Council. . . .

Although in the first place the Provincial Councils have been formed to elect Head Chiefs to the Legislative Council, it is intended to develop them still further by encouraging each Provincial Council to meet and confer on the general welfare of the divisions comprising each province. It is hoped in this way to provide the chiefs with an opportunity to unite in defence of native rule and institutions against the disintegrating effects of modern civilisation, while at the same time giving them an opportunity of conferring on the problems which the advent of modern civilisation must inevitably introduce into any country. . . .

It will be seen that the introduction of Provincial Councils is a most important innovation, and is likely to lead to the betterment and strengthening of the rule of the Chiefs and their Councils, without in any way interfering with native institutions. When the new constitution was first discussed, it was suggested that the people of each division should themselves elect a member to the Legislative Council, but as these people practically elect — by recognised native custom — their own Head Chiefs, and are as yet not sufficiently advanced to make a satisfactory use of the system of election by ballot, it was considered advisable, for the present at any rate, to let the Head Chiefs, sitting in Provincial Councils and themselves elected by the people, elect their own representatives to the Legislative Council.

It is contended in some quarters that the new constitution violates and is likely to weaken native institutions. . . . It is said — and this is an old contention, familiar to all of us — that by native custom no Chief is allowed to speak in public except through his Linguist, and in

the vernacular of his Stool. . . . The native custom of a Chief speaking in public through his linguist and in the vernacular is . . . very necessary to the efficiency of his rule over his particular people. It will, no doubt, be observed in the Provincial Councils, but to apply it to such a gathering as the Legislative Council would effectually prevent a chief becoming a member of this assembly. And who have more right to represent the people in this Council than their own properly elected Chiefs? Indeed, the non-observance of this native custom in the Legislative Council in the past, is a sufficient proof that the Oman Councils of the country wisely recognise the desirability of their local tribal constitutions possessing the elasticity necessary to enable them to adapt themselves to the changes which time and progress must inevitably bring.

It has been further stated that the formation of these Provincial Councils of Head Chiefs generally weaken native institutions. It is difficult to see on what grounds such a vague statement can be based. . . . The general functions of the Provincial Councils must inevitably tend to unity among the Head Chiefs. This unity is essential to the defence of native institutions. . . . To take one instance only, the sovereignty of a Head Chief — such as an Omanhene — over the Chiefs of his division, is clearly recognised in the native constitution. As Honourable Members are aware, many of these chiefs have broken away in the past, and are attempting to break away today, from such control of their Head Chiefs as has been recognised from time immemorial. Each secession violates the native constitution, and moreover tends to further weakening of various native institutions. If the process continues indefinitely, it will inevitably lead to the complete loss of power by the Chiefs, and to the substitution of direct for indirect rule, a change that would be entirely contrary to Government's policy. In their respective Provincial Councils, the Amanhin and other Head Chiefs of the country will, I hope, be able to advise on such measures as will lead to the entire stoppage of such secession, and will moreover be able to advise the Government on any claim that is made by a Chief that he is not subordinate in his own jurisdiction to any other Chief.

I will now turn to the next important innovation, namely, the appointment of three African Municipal Members. The new constitution permits of the election of an African member for each of the towns of Accra, Cape Coast and Sekondi. In these towns the populations have advanced sufficiently in modern civilisation to justify the adoption of the system of election by ballot. . . .

This introduction of the elective system of representation is, however, by no means the most important feature of this section of the new constitution. It is true that, for the first time, power is given to the people to elect educated Africans to represent them in the Legislative Council, but this power is only granted to those towns which show themselves capable of municipal self-government. . . .

Although [a new Municipal Corporations] Ordinance was passed in 1924, careful examination into the many objections raised, chiefly by the illiterate sections of the community, has prevented its being applied as yet to any one town. These difficulties are now well on the way to being solved satisfactorily, and it is intended during 1926 to make a start by applying the ordinance to Accra, which town will in due course be followed by Cape Coast and Sekondi. As the ordinance is applied to each town, that town will then become eligible to elect its own member to the Legislative Council. . . .

The new constitution is a carefully planned attempt by the Gold Coast Government to give the African a stepping-stone towards the assumption of greater responsibility than he has borne in the past. It is true that the official majority on the Council has been retained, but the time is not yet ripe for any change in that respect. It is not expected that the new constitution will be received with satisfaction in all quarters, for the minds of some Africans are still set on the early grant of self-government. Their consolation and their encouragement should be that they have made a definite step forward, a step that has been earned by the progress made since 1916. It is probable that the next step will be the extension of the franchise now given, either by adding to the number of towns, or by increasing the number of municipal members. It is on the work done by the Chiefs in their Provincial Councils, and by the Municipal Councillors in their towns, that future changes will depend. . . .

[Leg. Co. Debates, 1926-7, pp. 10, 17-19, 21, 25-36.]

The 1926 constitution is printed in M. Wight, *The Gold Coast Legislative Council*, London, 1947, pp. 208-38

36   Views and Reviews 1926–1928

WITH the publication of the 1926 constitution, Guggisberg's administration had passed its zenith. For a time the promise of constitutional advance had won over the leaders of the politically minded 'intelligentsia', but the form taken by that advance, and the greater weight given to the rural representation did not meet with their approval (469a). The Municipal Corporations Ordinance also aroused more and more criticism and Guggisberg, confessing to his 'only real disappoint-ment' as Governor, withdrew it and amended the 1926 Constitution accordingly (471).

On the other hand, the new constitution won him the staunch support of Nana Ofori Atta, Omanhene of Akim Abuakwa, the largest state in the Colony, and himself a far bigger man than any of his rivals among the 'intelligentsia' (469b). Like Guggisberg, this chief saw the need for revitalising native institutions if they were to meet the demands likely to be made of them in the years ahead; and in 1927 he was allowed to introduce a new Native Jurisdiction Ordinance worked out by the chiefs themselves (472). To Ofori Atta, this was something like a last chance for the chiefs to put their house in order. The new measure did not make good the past failures of Government to grapple with this problem, without meriting all the abuse poured on it by the self-appointed spokesman for African tradition in the coast towns.

The most important document on Gold Coast affairs in these years was, however, the report by the Under-Secretary of State for the Colonies (the Hon. W. G. Ormsby-Gore) on his visit to West Africa in 1926 (470). This covers all aspects of government activity, and is typical of the more scientific approach then being made to questions of tribal custom and institutions and those of health and housing: but the great emphasis is still on problems of production (now, especially, the need for more scientific methods) and, as in the extracts here, on problems of trans-portation.

469 PROCEEDINGS IN LEGISLATIVE COUNCIL
18 MARCH, 1926.

. . . .

a. *Mr. Casely Hayford.* . . .

There was very great enthusiasm when a year or two ago Your Excellency was in a position to announce that as far as the Gold Coast was concerned we were also going to enjoy the benefits of elective representation. But I regret to say that the enthusiasm . . . has turned to a kind of despair, and the great anticipation that was then entertained has now pro-voked a certain amount of unrest. It is my duty . . . to bring to the notice of

Government the cause of the present situation. . . .

In 1920 there was considerable agitation in British West Africa as regards the actual extension of the franchise. That was the time the Congress met and sub-mitted representations. To put the matter shortly, about that time Nigeria received a new constitution, which was followed by one to Sierra Leone. . . . To compare the scheme put into operation in these two places, in Lagos alone there are three educated members appointed to represent the population of Lagos, which I believe is not larger than the population of Accra. . . . Then also in Sierra Leone we know

605

they have three Urban Members for the town of Freetown. It seems to me that . . . in the Gold Coast . . . [where] we have got to deal with Accra, Cape Coast, Sikondi, Winneba, Appam, Saltpond, Elmina, Dixcove, Keta and other places . . . the Southern portion of this Colony is very meagrely represented in this measure, and we humbly suggest that in this case, this matter may receive further attention on the part of Government.

My second point is that this measure is conditional. In other words, there is no certainty that the three Municipal Members will be returned to the Council by election. . . . We shall be *in statu quo* until and unless Accra, Cape Coast and Sekondi have adopted the Municipal Corporations Ordinance. Therefore . . . it seems to me that although we have been given Elective Representation, it is more like our getting the shadow rather than the substance. . . .

Then again . . . this measure has a kind of damper upon educational progress. . . . It strikes me that in the period of our educational progress, it would have been an encouragement to the literate class to feel that they would be adequately and unconditionally represented in the Legislative Council. . . . [We] who have worked hard on this Council for the past ten years . . . had hoped that the result of our work would be such as to encourage Government to extend the Franchise to more educated Africans to be able to serve their country. This is not the case under the present measure. . . .

Again, this measure makes unwholesome differentiation between Municipal and Provincial Members. . . . In my humble opinion, the representation of the people of this country should be one and the same — there should be no attempt to divide the people, as it were, into sections, because from the practice of our own constitution — from our own usages . . . — we are one people. The division . . . between educated and uneducated is a false one, because if education is good for the country we must not *at any time* seek to divide the educated from the uneducated. We go together. . . .

I may say that the Chiefs of this country are not of a hereditary caste. . . . Until the day the people put you on the stool, you are an ordinary commoner. Therefore, Sir, it is to my mind somewhat unfortunate that we institute, as it were, by this measure, a hereditary house composed of Amanhene by themselves, and to elect members to this Council from among themselves. Because when once we do that, we establish a hereditary caste, and since there is no such caste, we think it unworkable. . . .

Another point I should like Your Excellency to note, is that this measure restricts the people's power of choice. The choice of men elected to the Legislative Council should be the choice of the people and not the choice of the Amanhene. According to this measure, not only do the Amanhene exercise the right of choice, but they also have to choose from among themselves. . . . I am submitting that [it] should be left to the people to select any eligible person, whether he be an Omanhene or a commoner, and they should not be restricted to the circle of Amanhene. . . . If this restriction is imposed, it will lead to a good deal of discontent; we want harmony between the Amanhene and the people, and I say, Sir, as a responsible man, that if the people's right of choice is restricted to the Amanhene, it would create confusion worse confounded, and it would bring trouble.

Then again . . . the powers of the Governor under this scheme are repugnant to the principle of elective representation because . . . there is to be a list of Amanhene, and whoever is an Omanhene has got to be so declared by Government. Where the very electors are men who cannot exercise their functions except under the sanction of Government . . . who stand to be deposed or suspended by Government, they are not free electors. . . .

b. *Nana Ofori Atta:*[1]

We have been told . . . that Provincial Councils, if brought into existence, will be a breach of native constitution. I am asking those people who are opposed to the scheme not to be biased or prejudiced because the proposal has not been the product of their political sagacity. . . . There is nothing to fear as to the Provincial Council breaking the constitution, or the institutions and customary laws of this Country. On the contrary, it will tend to the solidarity of the Native Administration. . . . The Provincial Council will work steadily towards the uplift of the Native Administration and render the institutions capable of not only resisting but of defeating its enemies from within and without. That is the object of the Provincial Council in its administrative aspect. . . .

We are told that the fact that Paramount Chiefs are going to meet without the Aman is a breach of native custom. . . . That the Paramount Chief, being merely a figurehead, is not the proper person to voice the wishes of his people. . . . What does Mr Casely [Hayford] say of the Paramount Chief? I am now quoting from his book:—

'At the head of the Native State stands 'prominently the *Ohin* (King) who is the 'Chief Magistrate and Chief Military 'Leader of the State. He is first in the 'Councils of the country, and the first 'Executive Officer. His influence is only 'measured by the strength of his character. 'He it is who represents the State in all its 'dealings with the outside world; and, so 'long as he keeps within constitutional 'bounds, he is supreme in his own 'State.' . . .

Why then suggest now that an Omanhene cannot constitutionally represent his

[1] Nana Ofori Atta (later Sir); Omanhene of Akim Abuakwa (1881–1943); enstooled 1912; nominated unofficial member of Legislative Council 1916–27; provincial member Akan section of Eastern Province 1928–43; unofficial member of Executive Council 1942; knighted 1928.

state in its dealings with other States or with the Government? If he is the first Executive Officer, if he is supreme in his own state, why suggest now that it will be a breach of custom when an Omanhene with the knowledge of his Oman meets his fellow Amanhene or Government as a representative of his State? It is an invention. . . . I am appealing to my brother rulers not to be duped by those who have their own axe to grind, and who will continue to live comfortably well if your Stool falls into an ignominious position. I know . . . that the same old game is on; the usual tactics. The Chiefs are being told: 'If you follow Ofori Atta you will surely find yourself under him; the Government would make him paramount over you all.' It is wicked to say these things. . . .

But let me make it also clear that within the State the State Council is the governing body over which the Paramount Chief presides; the Paramount Chief and the Council working together. . . . The Council is open to any other African, not necessarily a stool holder, be he educated or uneducated, and if you get the will to help your country, and your Stool considers you fit, the appropriate place for the educated African is to seek a seat at the Council of his Oman. . . . I am suggesting that it is only by striving to become a member of the Oman Council . . . that the educated African can do much to help his people and his country. . . .

Anyone perusing the new Constitution must be struck with one fact, that is, the new Constitution recognises to the full extent the basic principles of the Constitution of this country. That . . . is a matter of much gratification. . . . We are satisfied, Sir, that the preservation of the principles of our Native Administration are so essential to the true progress of the Gold Coast that we are anxious that they should be preserved not only today but in its advancing stages. That is so well expressed in the new Constitution that we are deeply grateful for it. . . .

The question as to whether or no it is unconstitutional for a Paramount Chief to hold a seat on the Legislative Council is so very important that I should like to deal with that first. It seems to me most extraordinary for a suggestion of this kind to come from those who profess to be progressive. . . . In other words, the intelligentsia want the chiefs to remain unprogressive. . . . [The objection is refuted by Sarbah and Casely Hayford's own writings] Mr Casely Hayford says all measures affecting the people must be passed *with the consent and direct co-operation of the Chiefs themselves.* [His] book was published in 1903 while the cry for elective representation had been on 10 years already. . . . What should be borne in mind is that the object of these books was to educate the Government in the matter of the proper administration of the country . . . and surely Mr. Sarbah and Mr. Casely Hayford knew at the time that if the Chiefs came on the Legislative Council as advocated by them, they would not speak through linguists. Why all this talk now?

I come now to the question of the Provincial Council constituted as [an] electoral body. If every State in the country was to send its representative to the Legislative Council then it would be reasonable to expect the Oman Council meeting at a place 'where the King-Paramount would sit in solemn conclave with his vassals and finally dispose of the matter.' But in this case, where several States are to send one representative . . . to represent a particular tribe, how can that be done? There can be no other way than the way laid down by the Order in Council. . . .

The second objection is [to] the preponderance of Chiefs over the intelligentsia. . . . We have got to remember that the Intelligentsia have some few years ago set up a claim [quoting the Petition of the National Congress] . . . that they are the proper persons to represent the people of this country. That claim without a shadow of doubt knocks the chiefs out of the show altogether. The Chiefs are not wanted. That is a claim which must not be allowed to stand, because the educated community are members of Stools and belong to the different Stools in the country. . . . Some years ago when this question came up, it was pointed out that the claim was wrong . . . but . . . has that claim been renounced by the Intelligentsia who put it up, so that confidence could be restored in them? Nothing of the sort has been done. It is this claim that is at the root of the objection to the new Constitution in so far as the Chief's side is concerned. So I maintain that the new Constitution as it is now granted should not be disturbed in any way, at any rate for the present. . . . Until the intelligentsia prove, not only by word of mouth but by deed and action, that they do not consider the Native Administration to be a humbug, until they satisfy us that they are in true sympathy with the needs and wants and aspirations of the masses of the people, until we are satisfied that they do inspire confidence . . . the question of delegating powers to them must be a matter of remote contingency.

Now whatever inconvenience my brother Native Rulers may be put to, I am submitting to them respectfully that they have got to realise . . . that the easy-going days are gone, and they must be prepared to march with the times. . . . There was a time when an illiterate chief thought it was no good to send his heir to school. That has very nearly brought us to the verge of ruination and complete national disaster. The effect was discovered just in time, and the need for sending heirs to schools to be given as much education as possible is much more emphasised. So I am inviting critics of the Constitution not to think of it [in terms of] today, and say that the Paramount Chiefs are not sufficiently highly educated today, so every chance of their advancement must be blocked. . . . If the Gold Coast [is to] remain under the present system of monarchical democracy and not come under republican democracy, then I should submit that the principle of the new Constitution is a perfect one. It gives the people of this country a chance to develop through their own system of rule. That is the excellent part of the whole constitution, and as our system of rule has been tested and found to be the best suitable to the people of this country, we should aim at all times at its preservation. [Leg. Co. Debates, 1926–7, pp. 316, 318–24, and 345–6, 350–1, 354–9]

470 REPORT BY THE HON. W. G. A. ORMSBY-GORE[1] (PARLIAMENTARY UNDER-SECRETARY OF STATE FOR THE COLONIES) ON HIS VISIT TO WEST AFRICA DURING THE YEAR 1926. . . .

[a. The scientific approach.

The many differences among West African peoples require scientific study.] . . . If we are to succeed in our duties towards these peoples as rulers or as missionaries, or as instruments for their advance or civilisation, we must study them objectively, and base our policy on real understanding acquired not only from personal contact, but from scientific study of their mental language and traditions. Native methods of agriculture, native arts and crafts, should be examined scientifically before any attempt is made to supersede what we find existing.

Herein lies the importance of anthropological work, an importance which it is difficult to over-estimate. The wider the knowledge of the elements of anthropology amongst the administrative staff, the better. . . .

At the same time, this study of the indigenous population should not lead us to adopt any unduly conservative attitude. . . . We cannot impede the spread of civilisation — indeed, we should fail in our duty if we allowed the vast economic

[1] William George Ormsby-Gore (later 4th Baron Harlech); born 1885; Conservative M.P. 1910–38; Under-Secretary of State for the Colonies 1922–24 and 1924–29; Secretary of State for the Colonies 29 May, 1936–16 May, 1938.

potentialities of one of the richest continents of the world to lie fallow. In short, our methods should be evolutionary rather than revolutionary.

The idea that the African, if left to himself — a thing impossible in modern international conditions — will by himself evolve into the 'gentle savage' of Rousseau's imagination, is an assumption untenable in the light of history. The condition of Nigeria a generation ago has only to be considered. Benin was running with the blood of human sacrifice, and the Northern Emirates were the scene of wars, slave-raiding and slave-trade on a scale and of a character which the world rightly held to be intolerable.

Those people who, though they have never been in Africa, are apt to talk about oppression should be the first to realise that if it had not been for our rule, these intolerable conditions would still remain. . . . No one could maintain that, in the event of the removal of European guidance and control, there would not be a return to the old conditions, and no serious student of Africa can view with equanimity such a possibility. . . .

[b. Transport Policy.]

The Gold Coast . . . possesses no natural harbour, and as yet no harbour at which ocean-going vessels can be berthed alongside a wharf. All traffic on the Gold Coast has to be conveyed to and from ships lying in open roadsteads, and all the shore work at Accra and the smaller ports, is done in native surf-boats under the most difficult and dangerous conditions. At Sekondi there is a small breakwater, and the use of tugs and lighters has been possible. The marvel is that . . . the Gold Coast has been able to develop in the manner that it has with such primitive and inadequate facilities. I wish to record my opinion that, however costly the construction of the new harbour at Takoradi may prove to be, the policy of its construction is sound. My only regret is that it was not possible to commence it sooner. I should further add that I am convinced that Takoradi is the one and only place on the Gold Coast where a modern harbour with adequate facilities could have been constructed. . . .

The development of the railway systems of British West Africa is still in its infancy. . . . The Gold Coast, with approximately the same area as England and Wales and a population of about two and a half million, has 495 miles of railway. . . . The Gold Coast system does not go further north than Kumasi . . . consequently two-thirds of the country is beyond the reach of this form of transport. . . .

Railways by themselves can only open up a very limited area of the country. Feeder roads to the railway system are quite as important as railways themselves, and the programme of road development should go hand in hand with any programme of railway development and should be considered in relation to it. With the possible exception of the Gold Coast, the development of the road systems of British West Africa lags behind requirements. The mileage of roads possible for motors . . . in January, 1925, in Nigeria was only 2,596. In the Gold Coast the total mileage of roads in 1925 was 4,734, as against 1,300 miles in 1919. That is to say that in the six years since the war, 3,434 miles of roads possible for motor traffic have been constructed in the Gold Coast. This is a very remarkable achievement, and the increasing trade and revenue of the Gold Coast is largely attributable to this fact.

In British West Africa the distinction between a road which can be used by motors and one which cannot, is vital. . . . It must be remembered that, except in parts of Northern Nigeria and in the Northern Territories of the Gold Coast, animal transport is non-existent on account of the tsetse fly. Even in the areas where animal transport is possible, the cost per ton mile of such transport is very little cheaper, if cheaper at all, than mechanical transport, and as an offset to any lower cost per ton mile must be set, first the greater rapidity of mechanical transport, and secondly, the necessity of mechanical transport for the conveyance of such heavy and bulky produce as cotton bales. . . .

In West Africa the most notable development of motor transport is found in the Gold Coast. In March, 1926, there were no less than 2,401 motor lorries in use in the Gold Coast. In giving this figure I should like to emphasise the lamentable fact that of this total only 139 were of British make, while 1,541 were American. . . .

The construction of motorable roads in British West Africa presents many difficulties. Throughout a large part of the area, the annual rain-fall is high and everywhere it is of a torrential character. Rivers and streams rise and fall with great rapidity, and consequently the main item of cost in road construction is the cost of bridging. Bridge building is the bottleneck of all road development, but over and above [this] . . . is the problem of road surface in African conditions. The cost of maintenance varies greatly according to the amount of traffic and the rainfall. . . .

Throughout the greater part of British West Africa, laterite is generally used as a road-building material. It makes an adequate surface in the dry season when most of the transportation takes place, but is liable to rapid deterioration during the rains. Real metal for road construction and road surfacing is scarce and expensive. . . . All these circumstances have made it necessary for the West African Governments to limit the maximum axle load of mechanical vehicles, and to limit the speed of such vehicles, for it is the speed even more than the weight of motor lorries which damages the roads. . . . In the Gold Coast Colony . . . the cost of maintaining those laterite roads where the traffic is heaviest during the cocoa season has driven the Government to partial metalling. The method adopted and so far found very successful is locally known as 'Tarmet.'

Apart altogether from the supreme

importance of roads as the first essential in developing modern and more economical means of transport, the civilising influence of the road is a paramount consideration. . . . The road more than anything else tends to break down the narrowness and the circumscribed life of the African native. . . .

I should perhaps add one word as to the general policy of alignment of railways and roads in any comprehensive scheme for the opening up of an undeveloped continent, which . . . have not always been observed. Railways should run, as far as possible, straight inland from the selected ports. Main roads should run at right angles to them so that they do not tap the same country. . . .

While these should be the governing principles, they must be subject to the common modification that disconnected and isolated sections of railway or road are not economical and the various systems must be connected up. . . . Colonial railways cannot afford the isolation of their rolling stock or separate construction and repair shops, unless distance demand it. . . .

The railways in Africa almost without exception are state owned. . . . Where a country is undergoing rapid development both politically and in trade, the direction of railway policy is necessarily intermingled with the general needs and responsibilities of the Government. . . . In the distant future, it may become possible to lease the railways to private enterprise, as in India. But at the present stage I do not consider that this is practicable.

In regard to the question of railway rates, I think that the general principle should be laid down that while a Railway Department should not be regarded as revenue earning, it should not on the other hand be subsidised from general revenue. The rates should be fixed so that all expenses are covered . . . as nearly as possible. . . . I am convinced that in the special circumstances obtaining in Tropical Africa today, particularly in connection

with the labour problem, construction by Government is to be preferred to construction by outside contractors. Personal knowledge of the African climate and African labour is essential. . . .

The experience of both Nigeria and the Gold Coast tends to show that it does not pay to build an inferior railway in the first instance to be 'improved' later as traffic develops. The high cost of making the deviations on the Sekondi–Kumasi line, and the grave limitations imposed on the more economic working of the whole Nigeria system by the character of the Baro–Kano section . . . are only too apparent today. This is not so much a question of the weight of rail, but a question of curves and grades. All new branch lines should be built to conform to the standard curves and grades of the system. . . . Modern railway science has taught us the immense economy of the big locomotive and the heavy train. The difficulty in reducing rates on the British West African railways is due in no small part to the limitation of the size and consequently of haulage capacity of the locomotive that can be used over a great part of their systems. This limitation . . . is the result of initial weaknesses of construction in the matter of curves, grades, and bridges. Experience shows that the enormous cost of regrading and re-building bridges is out of all proportion to the saving on the original construction. The building, therefore, of cheap pioneer railways has proved a penny wise and pound foolish policy in West Africa. . . .

The tonnage and value of sea-borne trade handled at Gold Coast ports has been expanding very rapidly, as may be seen from the following table:—

YEAR	TOTAL TONNAGE.	VALUE IN £
1921	378,000	12,419,000
1922	542,807	13,311,000
1923	637,540	15,306,000
1924	785,653	15,961,000
1925	920,000	17,788,000

The main increase in the tonnage of sea-borne trade in the Gold Coast has been due to the rapid increase in the output of manganese ore from 7,195 tons in 1921 to 340,000 tons in 1925.

Of the total tonnage handled in 1925, no less than 559,058 tons passed through the port of Sekondi. . . . From the point of view of value — but not tonnage — the trade of Accra is still approximately equal to that of Sekondi. It is apparent that quite apart from the question of Takoradi, the main development of the future will be at the western rather than at the eastern port, because of the development of the mining industries, the opening of the Central Province railway . . . and the extension of the cocoa output of Ashanti and the Western Province, as against the probable decline of tonnage of cocoa produced in the Eastern Province. . . .

It is no part of my duty to re-open the various controversies that have ranged round the construction of a harbour at Takoradi. . . . The decision to construct this harbour was taken by the late Lord Milner. . . . The bottle-neck, all along, has been the quarry, both as regards the quantity and size of the granite required. . . . The contract date for the final completion of the harbour is 31st December, 1928. . . . The two breakwaters when completed will enclose an area of 200 acres available for anchorage. The deep-water berths . . . will be located along the inner side of the lee breakwater, and provide berths for two large general cargo steamers and one berth for manganese ore export, affording a depth alongside of from 25 to 32 feet at low water. . . . The total cost of Takoradi harbour and port works is estimated at between £3,000,000 and £3,250,000. . . .

In 1924, investigation was directed by the Government into the possibility of branch lines in the Western Province of the Colony. Detailed economic and traffic surveys . . . established that the population and prospects of the country west of the line between Sekondi and Kumasi were far too scanty (short of any further outstanding mineral discovery) to warrant the construction of a railway. . . .

The Northern Territories Railway is the chief problem before the Gold Coast Railway Department. The distance in a direct line from Takoradi . . . to the northern frontier is roughly 440 miles. At present the railway only goes as far north as Kumasi, 168 miles by rail from the coast. . . . The whole of the Northern Territories with an estimated population of half a million is quite outside its reach. The density of this population, very sparse in the neighbourhood of the Ashanti boundary, increases as the northern frontier is approached, while immediately to the north of British territory lies the most densely populated part of the whole of French West Africa, with an average density of 9·3 per square kilometre. The total population of French West Africa is a little over twelve millions, with an average density of 2·6 persons per square kilometre. This Haute Volta area is not at present served by any of the French railway systems.

The Northern Territories of the Gold Coast approximate, in climate and conditions, to much of Northern Nigeria, and may be suitable for the cultivation of ground-nuts and American cotton. The bulk of the area is free of tsetse fly, and cattle are fairly numerous. The meat supply of the Gold Coast Colony is obtained from the Northern Territories and French territory beyond them. The present wastage of cattle driven down on the hoof is at least 50 per cent.

Consequently the Gold Coast cannot be said to have been fully developed until the railway to the Northern Territories has been constructed. That it is the duty of Government to construct such a railway as soon as the financial situation permits, is, I think, clear. It would increase the variety as well as the total of the economic products of the country, would improve and cheapen the supply of locally-grown food, especially meat, and would increase the supply and mobility of labour.

All authorities are agreed that if and when the railway is constructed, it would be of no real value unless it was carried right through to Navoro,[1] the principal trade centre in the extreme north. Alternative routes are now being surveyed. . . . In any case I do not think construction should be commenced before 1929, when Takoradi is complete and open. Only then can the financial position of the Colony be fully appreciated, and the practicability of raising another large loan . . . be decided. . . .

Manganese ore and wood (firewood and timber props) for the gold mines constitute over 50 per cent. of the total tonnage hauled by the railway. Unfortunately these are all 'short hauls.' . . . The approximate average rate charged by the railway on both categories of goods is 2d. a ton mile. Coal is carried to the mines at an even lower rate, viz., 1·4d. per ton mile. At the present scale of rates the railway is just paying. . . . It would appear that unless there is an increase in the tonnage carried over the longer hauls, and unless the railway system expands so as to secure more economical working, there is no possibility of further reductions in railway rates.

Cocoa, and cocoa alone, at present enables the railway to pay its way, and the rate on this commodity varies from 9d. down to 5d. per ton mile. In the neighbourhood of Accra, fierce competition obtains between the railway and motor transport for the carriage of cocoa and of the more expensive articles of import. Any further attempt of the railway to meet this competition by special local reduction of rates would, to my mind, be undesirable. If motor transport in this particular area can beat the rail — let it. . . .

I have already alluded to the special Tarmet roads of the Gold Coast, and the strain put upon the roads by the rapid expansion of motor transport. Undoubtedly the wear and tear to the roads, especially in the height of the cocoa season,

[1] Navrongo.

is very great, and . . . there has been a tendency to overload and over-drive all forms of motor transport. . . . Further, there has been a good deal of cut-throat competition between the lorry owners during the last two years, and rates have been cut so low that in many cases no allowance has been made for depreciation. . . . While fully recognising the great part played by motor transport in the recent development of the Gold Coast, one cannot help feeling that the business has yet to be brought on to a sound commercial basis. . . .

[c. Agriculture.]

The wealth of British West Africa lies primarily in its agricultural and forest products. The Gold Coast contains important assets in the way of manganese, gold, diamonds, and bauxite. . . . But valuable as these minerals are, the economic progress of the Colonies depends on the development of their vast agricultural and sylvicultural resources.

The foundation of sound agricultural policy must necessarily begin with the production of the food of the people. . . . The development of economic crops at the expense of production of food for local consumption is most undesirable. . . . There can be no doubt that in the cocoa-producing areas of the Gold Coast and in the Coast towns, the supply of locally grown foodstuffs is frequently inadequate and consequently expensive. The result of such a state of affairs is two-fold. In the first place, an appreciable number of the people are receiving an inadequate diet, and secondly the cost of living, and therefore the rate of wages, and the costs of production, are automatically raised. . . .

The capacity of labour . . . is bound up with the question of food. There are few parts of the world where the study of dietetics is more important than in Africa. It affects not only the question of the efficiency of labour, but also public health, and particularly infant mortality. I think there can be no doubt that the progress of many native races is bound up with the improvement of their present food supplies and diet.

Owing to the prevalence of tsetse fly there are vast areas where the only local meat supply is wild game, and, partly as a result of this fact, there are many areas, such as . . . the Colony of the Gold Coast, where game is to all intents and purposes extinct already. In many parts . . . the production of cereals presents great difficulties, and in these areas the main food of the population consists of root crops such as yams and cassava, with a high content of starch, but deficient in other essentials. For continuous work such foods are an inadequate substitute for cereals. . . .

Particularly in the Gold Coast towns, the marketing of such food supplies as do exist, is most unsatisfactory, and the unreasonably large divergence in the price obtained by the producer and the price charged to the consumer is even more marked than it is in Great Britain. . . . The distribution side . . . of the problem requires immediate attention. I found that the same size of yam as was fetching 2s. 6d. in Accra was fetching 6d. in the southern parts of British Togoland. . . . One of the chief reasons why the wages of unskilled labour are anything from two to three times as much in the Gold Coast as they are in Nigeria is due to this question of the cost of food. . . .

The Gold Coast Colony and Ashanti are at the present time entirely dominated by cocoa. The Gold Coast . . . is producing very nearly half the world's total supply. . . . I heard the opinion frequently expressed that cocoa production in the Gold Coast is now reaching, if it has not actually reached, its possible maximum. The area of suitable land with the requisite rainfall and necessary forest protection has nearly all been brought under cocoa. Certain new areas, however, still remain to be developed in the Western Provinces of the Colony and in Western Ashanti, but in both these the population is sparse. In the Eastern Province, where the industry has been long established, there are signs of a falling off in the production per acre, due in part to a development of disease among the older trees. How far this is due to senility and how far to exhaustion of the soil is not yet clearly established.

Little or nothing has been done in the way of manuring, and it may well be that the native farmers will have to adopt more scientific methods if they are to maintain their past yields. Hitherto the cocoa farmers of the Gold Coast have been singularly fortunate in happening upon a crop which seems to have been ideally suited to the local conditions, and also remarkably free from insect pests and fungi. They have been able to produce a high-priced crop, with comparatively little effort, requiring no very great skill. In these circumstances it is perhaps natural that the maintenance or development of any alternative crops is no easy matter. . . .

Formerly the oil palm industry in the Gold Coast was considerable. The exports . . . some forty years ago were worth about £1,000,000, but they are now only about one-tenth that sum. . . . The decline . . . is entirely due to the success of cocoa, in which the labour is less arduous and the returns greater. . . .

The forests of the Gold Coast are a rich asset to the country. Apart from their value both for the export trade and for internal use, the security of the cocoa crops depends on adequate forest protection. The establishment of a Forestry Department . . . [dates] only from 1908. A Forestry Ordinance submitted to the Legislative Council in 1910, met with such opposition that it was withdrawn and another less satisfactory Ordinance substituted which, however, though passed, was never brought into effect. In 1919 the . . . Department was reorganised. . . .

Before the war, its policy had been largely directed towards the productive side of forestry. It, however, became apparent that deforestation was becoming a serious problem, due not only to the spread of cultivation, but also to the steady advance of the savannah area of the coastal belt. There has, however, been great difficulty in persuading chiefs to set aside reserves. It is almost impossible to persuade the native that it is essential for the future of the crops and water supply of his country that certain forest areas should be maintained. . . .

In 1923 a campaign for the establishment of adequate forestry reserves for protective purposes was launched. In that year there were two reserves covering 111 square miles, and there are now twelve reserves occupying approximately 450 square miles, though this represents less than half the total required. . . . Full warning has been given to all concerned that if reserves are not voluntarily set aside, new legislation would have to be undertaken. In the Governor's speeches on the Estimates in 1924, 1925 and 1926 this warning was clearly repeated. I think the time has now come when legislation can no longer be safely postponed, and I strongly recommend that it should be put in hand forthwith. . . .

[d. Land legislation.]

I am convinced that any radical alteration in the general policy of the Government in regard to the land is neither practicable nor desirable, but . . . I do not wish to be understood to mean that the present situation is satisfactory. At present litigation about land is a curse to the country. . . . Boundary disputes have become increasingly frequent, and the result is that many of the stools have been seriously impoverished, while some have been reduced to a condition of bankruptcy. The subjects of the stools are submitted to heavy levies to pay lawyers' fees, and this is one of the chief causes of discontent among the poorer peasantry. . . .

The introduction of the concepts of English law, frequently at variance with native custom, is producing a modification if not an elimination of transactions under native custom. The first cause of this is economic, namely, the introduction of permanent crops on agricultural land, and the growth of land values in urban areas. The second cause is the direct and indirect influence of members of the legal profession trained in the English law of real property. . . .

There is no legislation applying the statute of limitations, which is an important feature of the law of real property in England, to suits respecting land in the Gold Coast, with the result that there is no finality to any decision given in the courts. . . .

I am fully satisfied that the time has come for definite action by the Gold Coast Government in these matters. There is ample evidence in existence regarding the lines upon which legislation could be based, and in my opinion there is no necessity to wait for any further commissions or enquiries. . . .

Leases of land can be obtained for the furtherance of non-native enterprise in the Gold Coast under a Concession Ordinance. . . . At present valid concessions cover 677 square miles in respect of timber and rubber, 151 square miles in respect of agricultural and surface rights, and 193 square miles in respect of oil-palms. Of these three categories, 603, 118, and 143 square miles are today being effectively worked. The number of valid mining concessions is 346 of which 267 are today effectively worked.

Apart from these, there is a concession in Ashanti . . . for a lease for 99 years of an area of between 6,000 and 7,000 acres near Akrokerri . . . for the purpose of growing cocoa on plantation lines. This is the only cocoa plantation in Ashanti under European management. . . . A large cocoa plantation being developed by Messrs. Levers on similar lines is situated in the Eastern Province of the Colony near Bosuso. . . .

[Cmd. 2744 (1926), pp. 13, 25–8, 31–4, 48–55, 77–9, 82–3, 140, 145–7, 149, 152–3]

471 Speech of Governor Sir F. G. Guggisberg in Legislative Council

3 March, 1927.

. . . The Order of the King in Council, providing for the constitution of this Council, in section 20 makes provision for the towns of Accra, Cape Coast and Sekondi each to be represented by one Municipal member. If the Municipal Corporation Ordinance has been applied to any of these three towns, provision is made for the election of the representative; otherwise the representative is to be nominated by the Governor. I have, in fairness to the people of the three towns concerned, recommended to the Secretary of State the removal of the restriction above mentioned. My recommendation has been accepted and the Order-in-Council is in course of being amended. The three towns will therefore in due course be able to elect one representative each to this Council. I am prepared to give the necessary authority for the elections to proceed when the necessary arrangements have been made, and when the necessary vacancies among the Municipal Members now on the Council have been created by either the expiration of their terms of service or by their resignation.

The reason for this early change in the Constitution should be clearly understood by this Council. As Honourable Members are aware, I have never made any secret of the great value which I attach to Municipal self-government by Africans. It is the field of training in the responsibilities of wider Government; it is the acid test of fitness of the citizens of our urban areas to take a greater share in the government of the country. I use the word 'acid' advisedly, after the experience of the past few years, for municipal government in this country requires far greater resolution than it does in the more advanced countries of the world.

The recent history of municipal government should be well known to Honourable Members. When legislation was being drawn up, and when the Municipal Cor-

porations Bill was passed in this Chamber, it received the whole-hearted support of the African Members who represented Accra, Cape Coast and Sekondi. When it was known that it was to be applied to Accra, it aroused such a local storm of protest as to necessitate Government enquiring into the objections. These, as a rule, were trivial and were easily disposed of. The enquiry revealed the fact, as Sir James Crawford Maxwell[1] pointed out in this Council, that the African Members who supported the Municipal Corporations Ordinance appeared to have spoken for themselves and not for the townspeople that they represented.

Early in 1925 I held a conference which was attended in force by the representatives of this town, Cape Coast and Sekondi. The result of this conference clearly showed that Africans, however much they have desired to have a majority on the Municipal Councils, as provided for in the Bill, were not yet ripe for such a change. Since the passing of the 1924 Ordinance, the gradually growing opposition of the less advanced native communities in Accra showed that great strength of will, and the sacrifice of much private time, would be required of the future Municipal Councillors in carrying out what would be a very important duty, namely, the raising of the rates.

The general result of the opposition led to such delays that, when finally the new Order-in-Council was received, it early became apparent that the rights of electoral representation to this Council would have to be long postponed. After several conversations with African citizens, I conferred on the subject with my advisers, and finally, when in England in the summer of 1926, I recommended the alteration referred to above.

This failure to make municipal self-government a stepping-stone, as far as the seaport towns are concerned, to elective representation on this Council, has been the only real disappointment which I have

[1] Colonial Secretary of the Gold Coast 1922-7.

had as your Governor. . . . Anyway, seeing that the citizens of our sea ports think as they do, it would not be right at the present moment to force the responsibility of local municipal self-government on them. . . . Municipal self-government must come, and that it will come soon is my hope. In the meantime, certain amendments will be introduced into the present Town Councils Ordinance, and Government with its official majority on the Town Councils, will have to take the responsibility of raising the rates at an early date.

In concluding my remarks on this subject, I should like to allude briefly to the idea which seems to prevail, that the populations of Accra, Cape Coast, and Sekondi are large enough to justify more than a total of three members being elected for these towns. Their combined population does not exceed 75,000 souls, whereas the population of the Colony was 1,171,913 at the last census, 1921. There therefore does not appear to be any present justification for increasing the numbers, but I have no doubt that, in due course, the number of Municipal Members will be increased, when self-governing municipalities come into existence and show, by their work, that the 'commoners' of the country are capable of taking higher responsibility. . . .

The success of the Provincial Councils has, if possible, exceeded my anticipations. It has given me the keenest personal satisfaction, for I have never concealed my conviction that it is on the native institutions of this country, with the exception of the necessity of giving certain populous municipalities a voice — that the gradual development of the Constitution must be founded. It was at the preservation of native institutions that I aimed when devising what is the outstanding feature of the new constitution — the Provincial Councils. These Provincial Councils are really the breakwater defending our native constitutions, institutions and customs against the disintegrating waves of western civilisation. They are the chief means by which the nationality of the Africans of the Gold Coast will be built up out of the many scattered tribes; for it must be remembered that although each Council functions for its own Province, yet arrangements have been made by which these Councils can meet and discuss common questions, as has already been done in the case of the Native Jurisdiction Bill. . . .

No nation of the world, however much it may have retained its nationality, has ever succeeded in preserving intact its own particular institutions and customs throughout the ages. . . . So long as the changes are gradual and come from within, national character cannot be injured, and it is precisely here that I attach such paramount importance to the Provincial Councils — they are the machinery for such gradual evolution of native institutions as the people may find necessary to enable their country to retain its place in an ever-advancing world. . . . The new constitution, whatever may be its defects . . . is far more solidly based on the institutions which the people of this country have found best suited to them, and far more likely to develop into something bigger and wider, than any mushroom constitution based on the ballot-box and the eloquence of politicians over whom the people have no control except at election time. . . .

[Leg. Co. Debates 1927, separately printed under title: *The Gold Coast. A Review of the events of 1920–26 and the prospects of 1927–8.* Accra 1927]

472 SPEECH OF NANA OFORI ATTA ON THE NATIVE JURISDICTION BILL

19 APRIL, 1927.[1]

Your Excellency, I have the honour to move that an Ordinance to define and regulate the exercise of certain powers and jurisdictions by Native Authorities and to

[1] The first time an Unofficial Member introduced a Bill into the Legislative Council. Cf. Wight, *op. cit.*, p. 138.

assign certain functions to the Provincial Councils . . . be read a second time. . . .

What happened in this Council Chamber in November, 1922, is fresh in the minds of all. The Paramount Chiefs saw fit, on that occasion, to oppose the measure [introduced by Government] . . . not because they did not want a new Native Jurisdiction Bill, but they felt the country had long passed the stage at which that measure sought to put it. They also felt that the measure did not support the authority of the Chiefs and of the Oman in a way we had a right to expect. Your Excellency sympathised with the objections brought forward and had the measure withdrawn. . . .

The Government, after their experience of the 1922 measure, felt disinclined to introduce . . . another bill to remedy the defects generally felt under the present Ordinance. . . . In February, 1925, Your Excellency thought fit to make the position quite clear, and you laid down one stipulation: that is, the Government would only move when the Paramount Chiefs and their State Councils moved first in the matter of a new Native Jurisdiction Ordinance. . . . Well, the Paramount Chiefs on the Council in 1922 felt they were under an obligation to the Government and to the people in this regard. Having taken active part in opposing the Government measure and destroying it, they naturally felt it was up to them to do something to replace it. . . . So, a question having been put, during the said session, and an answer given whereby the Government expressed its willingness to permit the introduction of a Bill by an Unofficial Member, when the terms of the Bill had been considered and approved by Government, we set to work very earnestly. The Paramount Chiefs on the Council had several conversations, and in that way were very ably assisted by our friend the Honourable E. J. P. Brown. . . . Certain proposals were made and certain principles were then decided upon. Other Paramount Chiefs throughout the country were informed and their views were in-

vited. Following that . . . a conference was held at Nsawam . . . from the 2nd to the 15th May (1925), and the ideas and principles upon which a Bill could be prepared were discussed and laid down. These proposals were communicated to all the Paramount Chiefs and other bodies in September. . . . I may say in passing, that the conference held at Nsawam met in certain quarters with the foulest criticism. The scolders — I should not call them critics — condemned the Chiefs who met there, in the most uncompromising language, because it was alleged that the act of the Paramount Chiefs in meeting at Nsawam to confer on a matter of such importance, was unconstitutional. . . . Well, of course, I should only say here, that all that was a terminological absurdity. Those Chiefs who met at Nsawam returned to their homes without the aid of the police and without the aid of any other authority, which meant that the States concerned approved of their actions in this direction. . . . Much more time than was anticipated . . . had to elapse before another meeting was held, because we thought that ample opportunity should be given to every Paramount Chief to consult his State Council, in order to discuss the whole matter thoroughly and and then come to definite conclusions. . . .

The next meeting . . . was, as far as the Eastern Province was concerned, held at Nsawam in May 1926. On this occasion the Paramount Chiefs attended the inauguration ceremony of the Provincial Council, and were accompanied by a good many of their respective important Chiefs, who took part in the discussions and expressed their views. After that, Sir, one of the Paramount Chiefs was charged with the consolidation of the views that had been expressed. The draft of this was not ready until July. The Paramount Chiefs of the Eastern Province met at Bososo in the early part of July, 1926, for the consideration of the draft Bill and the same was approved by them. The draft Bill was sent at once to the Provincial Council,

Central Province, and copies were also sent to all the Paramount Chiefs of the Western Province. . . . After that . . . the Government asked the Provincial Council of the Eastern and Central Province to appoint some of their number to meet the Committee which has been appointed by Government to go into the matter. This was done and several meetings were held with the result that this Bill now before Council is one which has been agreed to. . . .

For the past two years, Sir, the proposals and principles upon which this bill is now based have been within the knowledge of all the Chiefs and people of this country. Well, some of them may have ignored the proposals; if that is so, it is their own fault and they have themselves to blame. As far as I know, I can tell you Sir, it is only in one or two instances that I have been asked to refer the matter to the Aborigines' Society. Certainly there was one from Sekondi and I think one from the Central Province. All the other Paramount Chiefs warmly acclaimed the measure. . . .

I will now proceed to deal with the Bill. Looking to the Objects and Reasons we find a statement therein of the principles to which the Bill seeks to give effect, namely:—

'1 The recognition of the customary rights and powers of the State or Oman Councils in the management of affairs connected with Stools.

2 The Government as Central Authority to have the final decision in regard to all political differences and disputes affecting Stools within the legitimate purview of recognised native institutions and customary law.

3 The regulation and placing on a sound basis of the powers and jurisdictions of the Tribunals, in their order of precedence and within their territorial limits, with necessary powers for enforcing their judgements and verdicts.

4 The facilitation of the means for preventing and checking abuses in the Tribunals, by Government, through its Commissioners.

5 The utilisation of the Provincial Councils, recognised by the Gold Coast Colony (Legislative Council) Order in Council 1925, for administrative and judicial purposes, the decisions of such Councils being subject, categorically, to the Executive Government and to the Judiciary.

6 To provide means for codifying the Native Customary Laws. . . .'

I have . . . come across certain things which are said to be objections to the Bill by . . . some people. The first allegation is, our Bill 'takes away the traditional safeguards of the people against the development of our national system of democratic monarchical rule into a system of autocratic rule.' That is a very serious allegation to make. . . . I challenge anyone to point out any single thing in this Bill which makes the Paramount Chiefs autocrats. . . . If that man will probe into the Bill a little deeper . . . he will find that the Bill is a State Councils' Bill and not a Chiefs' Bill. The whole power is left in the hands of the State Council, that is, the people, and rightly so. . . .

Secondly, it is alleged that the Bill 'confers upon our Paramount Chiefs rights which never belonged or could belong to them under the constitution of our native states.' This is very funny, and I say it must come from a man who is absolutely ignorant of our constitution. . . . The party may have been looking at the Ordinance of 1883 and the 1910 Ordinance, and seeing that this Bill goes further than those Ordinances, he jumps to the conclusion that the Paramount Chiefs are creating for themselves powers they never had. . . . If he only knew that in ancient times the Paramount Chiefs and State Councils had even the right and power of 'life and death', he would not have made these suggestions. Here we come before a Government which is noted for its sense of justice and fairplay. I do not think the British Government would tolerate any class of people exercising any sort of oppression over any class of people within the jurisdiction of His Majesty. . . .

The third allegation is [that] our Bill reduces the position of the Sub-Chiefs or Chiefs or Head-Chief from the position of equals of the Paramount Chiefs in matters affecting the regions over which their respective Stools are supreme. . . . [There is no such equality.] In every state you have one who is the Paramount Chief or Head of the State; he is the first servant of the State and then we have under him Chiefs and Sub-Chiefs and other people holding other offices according to our customary laws. That is our constitution.

Fourthly, it is alleged that the Bill 'confers on Political Officers, rights which could not have been intended by the late Queen Victoria that they should enjoy or exercise.' I have endeavoured to explain this morning that the Chiefs like to be guided in their administration of justice, as far as possible, by the advice of Government's representatives. We have . . . deliberately made provisions which enable a District Commissioner to enquire into any act of a Tribunal if a complaint is brought to his notice that some injustice has been done by that particular Tribunal. We think we are right in doing this, and have done it in the interests of the people. We have done that after experience, and I say to the man who is responsible for this allegation that an ounce of experience is worth a ton of theory. . . .

It is now my duty to deal with one point which has come up since this Bill came before the Council — the proposed amendment to the definition of 'Native.'[1] I must say at once, Sir, that the definition we have in the Bill is one which is acceptable to the Chiefs and people of this country. We cannot for any reason exempt Africans who come from any part of Africa — black as we are — coming into this country to take residence here, mingling themselves freely with the people, according to the customary law, from being dealt with as though they were non-natives, to enable them to go and tell the Chiefs, after all 'you have no jurisdiction over us' . . . I would never bother about people living the life of a non-native, well apart from the confines of the native customary laws; they will never come under the native tribunals. . . . I am submitting very seriously that we should not entertain any amendment to this definition, otherwise you will have to tell these people they cannot buy lands, they cannot marry our women in the way most of them do. . . .

[Leg. Co. Debates, 1927–8, pp. 460–3, 482–7. For a criticism of the Ordinance cf. Lord Hailey, *Native Administration in the British African Territories*, London, H.M.S.O., 1951, iii, 203.]

[1] 'A person of African descent, ordinarily residing within the Gold Coast Colony, Ashanti, the Northern Territories of the Gold Coast, or the British sphere of Togoland, and includes mulattoes; but it does not include persons ordinarily passing as Europeans.'

BOOK XII

MARKING TIME 1928–1939

37   Hard Times 1928–1934

BY the late twenties some of the old certainties wore a queer look, particularly as regards railway construction.   Guggisberg's Central Province Railway never paid its way (473), and work on the Northern Territories railway, recommended so warmly by Ormsby-Gore, in 1930 was put aside indefinitely (474).   Later that year the world slump halved the price of cocoa and with the old prosperity went much of the harmony between Government and Governed that marked the Guggisberg era (475).   When in 1931 Governor Slater tried to introduce income tax, rather than cut too drastically the votes for social services (477a), Africans in the Legislative Council were opposed to a man (477b), and their dissatisfaction was as nothing to that demonstrated outside (478).

Like his predecessor, Sir Shenton Thomas had to contend with difficult economic conditions, and in such circumstances his hope of more harmonious relations in the Legislative Council was over-optimistic (479).   He was chiefly instrumental in bringing about the restoration of the Ashanti Confederacy, although this was not finally effected until after he had left the Colony (480).

473 SPEECH OF GOVERNOR SIR R. SLATER [1]
IN LEGISLATIVE COUNCIL
26 SEPTEMBER, 1929

. . . The question of Railway Rates in this Colony has always been a subject of considerable controversy.   The question was last raised in 1925 when Sir Gordon Guggisberg considered whether railway rates should not be generally reduced.   But at that time there seemed to be a certain amount of doubt as to whether cheap motor transport had come to stay, and Sir Gordon considered it desirable to make no move in the matter until Takoradi had been opened.

Last year, as you are aware, the rates on the Central Province Railway were drastically reduced, as it had already been found, even before the opening of Takoradi, that cheap motor transport had undoubtedly come to stay, and the Central Province Railway was making no headway at all in securing the traffic in that district.   Notwithstanding the reduction of rates that

was then made, the Central Province Railway has still failed to attract traffic in that district. . . . Consequently, at the beginning of this year, I asked the General Manager of Railways to review the whole position and to make recommendations.

The General Manager of Railways in his reply pointed out that there were two ways of dealing with the question; either to enforce purely competitive rates between particular points or tackle the question on a bolder front and make a general reduction of railway rates.   The General Manager of Railways had no hesitation in recommending the bolder line.   With the concurrence of the Executive Council, I put the whole question in detail before the Secretary of State and recommended the bolder policy.   By the mail received the day before yesterday, I received the Secretary of State's despatch approving my recommendation. . . .

[The proposed rates] will mean that on commodities such as clothing, hardware, silk goods etc., which I imagine form a very large part of the trade of the country, the rates from Sekondi to Kumasi will be roughly halved. . . . [There will be] a substantial reduction in the railway rates

[1] Sir Alexander Ransford Slater (1874–1940); Colonial Service in Ceylon, 1899–1914; Colonial Secretary of the Gold Coast, 1914–22; Governor of Sierra Leone, 1922–7; Governor of the Gold Coast, 1927–32; Governor of Jamaica, 1932–4.

X

on spirits [which] will bring the traffic in those commodities within the profitable reach of the railways. . . . I have more than once announced, in this Council, that I was reluctant to reduce the railway rates on spirits, because I was reluctant to do anything that would make spirits cheaper. The argument that high railway rates mean high priced spirits was perfectly sound theoretically, but in practice the high rates had just the opposite effect as they drove the traffic into the hands of the lorry owners who could carry the stuff for very low rates. . . .

It may also be argued that Government in making these drastic cuts in railway rates is aiming an unfair blow at motor transport in this Colony. I do not think that that argument can be fairly urged against us. . . . In proof of our favourable attitude towards motor transport, I should like to remind the Council that we are providing, at no little expense, fresh outlets for motor transport in the roads we are building in the Western Province, in the Northern Territories, and between the Northern Territories and the Colony. Take, for example, the big trunk road we are building from Insu to Enchi, at great expense. . . . Moreover, Government is contemplating extending the Dunkwa–Wioso road to the more distant parts of the Western Province. We are also improving or are about to improve the trunk road from Tamale to Navrongo. We also intend to build a new road from Bamboi Ferry to Wenchi, so as to avoid the long detour via Kintampo. We also intend to improve the road on the east side of the Northern Territories between Kete Krachi and Kpandu. . . .

Another aspect of the new rates is that they will enable Government definitely to abandon the policy known as the 'road gap' policy. As long as the railway has high rates on spirits and other commodities, it is necessary to give it artificial protection against the competition which naturally springs up; that is why there exist certain places where there is a gap between two means of communication,

because if those gaps were linked up and closed, the railway would lose more and more traffic to the roads. Now that railway rates are about to be reduced, with the effect, we hope, that the railway will regain some of its legitimate traffic, it will no longer be necessary to regard every road proposal to the same degree as we have done in the past, from the angle of 'railway v. road.'

I must, however, make it quite clear that the abandonment of the road gap policy does not mean that Government will forthwith proceed to tarmet the road from Accra to Kumasi, as some of our friends — especially those in the Kumasi Chamber of Commerce — appear to think we ought to do. I do not regard it as reasonable that Government should be expected to make the Accra–Kumasi road, which runs parallel with the railway, a road for heavy goods traffic, though I hope that, as funds permit, it will be possible to improve the road for passenger traffic. With the reduction of railway rates between Accra and Kumasi, I consider that all legitimate demands for cheap transport have been ment. . . .

[Leg. Co. debates, 1929–30, pp. 308–12]

474 Speech of Sir R. Slater in Legislative Council 17 February, 1930

. . . The Northern Territories Railway.

I have seen no reason to change the opinion recorded in my last Address that the construction of a railway to the Northern Territories would not be a paying project in the near future. I summed up this proposition as follows in a despatch which I addressed to the Secretary of State in June, 1929:—

'Railway construction in the Gold Coast has hitherto been carried out in comparatively short sections, e.g.:—

Sekondi–Tarkwa	39 miles	(1898–1901)
Tarkwa–Obuasi	85 ,,	(1901–1902)
Obuasi–Kumasi	64 ,,	(1903–1904)
Accra–Akwapim	65 ,,	(1909–1917)
Tafo–Kumasi	125 ,,	(1920–1923)
Central Province Railway	99 ,,	(1922–1927)

and the maximum capital cost incurred on any one of these sections was £2,141,896. All these railways serve thickly populated areas and a thriving cacao industry. The projected Northern Territories Railway — of unprecedented length, viz.: 350 miles — is estimated to cost 50 per cent. more than the most expensive of any previous railway built in the Gold Coast, would pass through country where the population is only about one-third as dense as in the Colony and round Kumasi, would serve an area where cacao can never be grown, and where there are as yet no certain prospects of alternative traffic other than such as is likely to be adequately provided for by motor transport.' I added:— 'I wish to make it clear that the proposed postponement of a Northern Territories Railway as a project of the near future will by no means mean a postponement of the development of the Protectorate. The extent to which the Northern Territories is served by excellent motor roads cannot be realised by anyone who has not travelled round the Protectorate. There are now 2,124 miles of such roads, and it is safe to say that no town or village of any importance is without good motor communication. Moreover, there are three trunk roads running due north and south, viz.:

(1) Navrongo–Tamale–Kumasi.
(2) Lawra – Wa – Bole – Kintampo – Kumasi.
(3) Djereponi–Yendi–Kete Krachi.

My policy is to develop these roads as follows:—

(1) To make the Navrongo–Tamale road an all-weather road by replacing the "drifts" at Nasia, Pwalagu, etc. by bridges or ferries.
(2) To extend the Lawra–Bole–Bamboi road direct to Wenchi.
(3) To extend the Yendi–Krachi road to link up with the old German road from Kpandu to Wurupon. . . .
To make all these three main arteries of traffic capable of carrying lorries at all times

of the year, and at the same time to improve the cattle routes (a work which is in hand), will involve expenditure amounting to only a fraction of the cost of a railway.'

Lord Passfield expressed his agreement with the view 'that circumstances at present do not justify the construction of such a railway, which must accordingly be postponed and need no longer be regarded as a project to be taken up in the near future.'

Subsequently, the Chairman of the United Africa Company wrote both to the Colonial Office and to me urging the construction of the railway, basing his arguments on the potentialities of the shea nut and groundnut industries.

The chances of rapid development of an export industry in shea-kernels or shea-fat seem to me to be slight. It is true that the total annual weight of kernels produced in the Northern Territories has been estimated at 150,000 tons and that of this total it is estimated that 50,000 could be collected by the existing population of women. But both the population and the shea trees are scattered widely over an area of 29,000 square miles (say 300 by 100) so that the problem of centralisation, even with good results and a railway, would be extremely difficult and . . . probably very expensive. Moreover, the yield per acre, as determined by the Agricultural Department (under conditions better than the average), is about 45 lbs of kernels, compared with an average yield of 800 lbs per acre of groundnuts. . .

As regards groundnuts . . . I am aware of the successful groundnut industry which followed the extension of the Nigerian railway to Kano, and I agree that there is a possibility of similar success being achieved here. A railway to the northern Territories, however, could not depend for its revenue on the success of one low-priced product, and I remain of the opinion that it would be imprudent for Government to assume, at this juncture, heavy additional debt charges (amounting to over £200,000 per annum) for a project of which so many of the factors are uncertain. . . .

[Leg. Co. Debates, 1930–1, pp. 138–40]

475 SPEECH OF GOVERNOR SIR R. SLATER IN LEGISLATIVE COUNCIL
4 DECEMBER, 1930.

. . . A grave situation has arisen in the local cacao industry. The prices for Gold Coast cacao (f.o.b. Accra), quoted in the London and New York cocoa exchanges, have declined steadily from a mean of £67 to £68 a ton in 1927 to £26 and even less today: the prices offered to the farmer have necessarily also declined to an equally disconcerting extent. So largely is the prosperity of the Gold Coast dependent on the prosperity of the cacao farmer, that the result of this decline has been to cause great depression in all branches of trade, and all classes of the community have suffered and are suffering severely. . . .

Although it is common knowledge that the prices of other tropical products, e.g. rubber, sugar, palm oil and kernels, have also experienced an equal or even greater decline, the cacao farmers are evidently of the opinion that they are being exploited by the buying interests, and they have formed themselves into a Federation, the members of which have resolved not to sell their cacao for less than 25s. a load, or rather more than double the average price now being offered by the buyers. As a result, business has been almost at a standstill for the past six weeks — weeks which are ordinarily among the busiest in the season. Notwithstanding the hold-up, the market price has fallen.

Government's attitude towards this movement may be summed up as follows:—

1 We regard the formation of the Federation as a perfectly legitimate move on the part of the farmer. Provided that it is honestly and wisely guided . . . such a combination of farmers should be able to do a great deal to place the cacao industry of the Gold Coast and Ashanti on a sound footing.

2 In the controversy as to what is, and what is not, a fair price for the cacao farmer to receive for his cacao at this time, Government can take no part. . . . One thing is certain: Government cannot fix prices and compel buyers to pay those prices. . . . However Government may deplore the present low prices, it is not practical politics to attempt to improve them by legislative or executive orders. To you, Honourable Members, this is a platitude, but it may not be so to some of the farmers, and I appeal to you to remember your responsibilities and use your influence in explaining to them the true position.

3 But while Government maintains . . . a strict neutrality in the trade dispute between the sellers and buyers of cacao, it has kept, and will continue to keep in close touch with both parties in an endeavour to promote as full as possible a measure of understanding of the contending points of view. The Colonial Secretary is ready to preside, if so requested by both parties, at a meeting between representatives of the Chamber of Commerce and the Federation. . . .

4 Government is not limiting itself to this watching function; it has a constructive policy for helping the cacao industry. . . . Briefly our policy is:—

(a) To participate in a publicity scheme for stimulating the consumption of cacao in the United Kingdom.

(b) To eliminate as many as possible of the wasteful expenses that now deprive the farmer of no inconsiderable part of his legitimate profit: to effect this by assisting the farmers to form co-operative societies for marketing their cacao.

(c) To enhance the reputation of Gold Coast cacao, and so to enable it to compete more successfully in the world's markets, by a scheme of inspection and certification. . . .

One feature of the situation has caused me . . . grave concern. . . . It is reported, so commonly that I can hardly question the substantial correctness of the reports, that individuals who, for various reasons, have sold or tried to sell their cacao, even though they cannot get the price laid down by the Federation for its members, have been haled before the Native Tribunals and have been fined, or otherwise punished by those tribunals. Now I wish to state clearly that for a Chief or State Council to proclaim that people who sell their cacao below a certain price, or people who buy certain imported goods, will be liable to be punished by a tribunal purporting to exercise jurisdiction under the Native Administration Ordinance, is an interference with legitimate trade which no Government in a British Colony can tolerate. . . .

If . . . this interference with the liberty of the subject continues, Government will feel obliged, and will not hesitate to use its supreme authority and legislate so as to make it a punishable offence for any chief, whether by way of claim to make an order under the Native Administration Ordinance or in fulfillment of a Stool-oath, or on any other ground whatsoever, to prohibit any person from buying or selling any articles from or to any other person on any terms upon which the parties agree. . . .

From the day that I took over the administration of this Colony, I have given my whole-hearted support, often in the face of much opposition and criticism, to my predecessor's native policy, as enshrined in the Native Administration Ordinance. That measure was admittedly not perfect in all its details, and both its authors and Government have found it necessary to amend it in various respects, and doubtless further amendments will be necessary. But in its basic principles, I, for one, still firmly believe, and I am anxious that the State Councils of the Gold Coast shall not, through an illegitimate exercise of the power which the Ordinance confers on them, constitute a case for any substantial restriction of those powers.

[Leg. Co. Debates, 1930–1, 11, 380–4]

476 Speech of Nana Ofori Atta in Legislative Council
23 February, 1931.

. . . At the end of the last Estimates Session, the Governor appealed to the Chiefs of this country to co-operate with Government; and in your address this time we have the same appeal. In his last speech, the late Governor called his Government a 'Government of co-operation,' and what he said was 'I make one claim, and that is, the Government of 1919–27 has been a Government of co-operation, as far as any Government can justifiably be of that nature.' . . .

A Governor who, on the last day of his term of office, was able to declare to this Council that his Government was a Government of co-operation, and that statement was not challenged, must be a Governor who will be remembered as long as memory lasts. Can the present Administration be called a Government of co-operation? I deeply regret, Sir, to have to make these remarks. Sometimes one feels one ought to be blunt. I am not here to say things and go and talk differently to the people. Whatever views I express are with a genuine desire to bring forward matters which I hope Government will consider. . . .

We have on three successive occasions brought to the notice of Government their lack of co-operation with the Unofficial Members. We had occasion to complain at the time we were called upon to make some big payments to the Commonwealth Trust and the Basel Mission Factory. On that occasion a very large sum was to be paid, yet nothing was said in the Governor's Address to the members previous to this, and it was just when the whole thing had been completed, that we were invited here and asked to vote the money. Another occasion was the reduction in the initial rates of the salaries of the African subordinates. There again we felt that we were not taken into confidence of the Government. On this present occasion, we have had cause to complain about

Government not consulting us in matters incidental to the Loan Bill.

I am submitting, seriously, Sir, that if you will take the Unofficial Members into confidence of Government, you will not in any way be embarrassed. On the contrary, you will see that they will give you all due assistance. To have to give our formal consent to matters which involve a very great consideration, is unfair; we are not given sufficient opportunity to consider these matters. I can assure your Excellency, we will not prove ourselves a stumbling block to the progress of the people of this country. If the Government will try to consult us in any matter, you will see that we shall endeavour to offer useful suggestions. . . .

[Leg. Co. Debates, 1931–2, pp. 241–2]

477[a.] SPEECH OF SIR R. SLATER
24 SEPTEMBER, 1931.

[Reviews the financial position and proposed economies (summarised below).]

. . . Even when all the proposed retrenchments have been carried into effect, and even if the increase in import duties and certain licence fees produces the estimated additional revenue, there will still remain an adverse balance of some £400,000. . . .

As it is impossible to rely on an improvement in trade conditions to provide a solution of the Colony's financial difficulties, it will be necessary to take steps to bridge the gap between revenue and expenditure with a structure which will probably be built, in part of further economies, and in part of new forms of taxation. There are some who will say that economy is the only material which should be used in the construction of the bridge, but those who so argue have possibly not considered carefully the nature of the commitments from which Government would have to withdraw, at least partially, in order to give effect to such a policy. . . .

To take education first. . . . The situation with regard to expenditure on education allows of two alternatives only. One

is further to reduce the grants-in-aid, a course which will most certainly result in the closing of the majority of the Mission schools, which even with the grant assessed on the present scale are kept open only with the greatest difficulty, owing to the serious declension in the financial assistance received from other sources. The other alternative is to devise means whereby the general revenue may be maintained at a figure which will permit of the continuance of the payment of grants at the present scale.

The extent to which the educational system in the Gold Coast has been developed during the past few years, either by Government or by Missionary Societies with the aid of Government, can best be gauged by comparing the grants-in-aid paid in Nigeria — with a population six times as large as that of the Colony — with those paid in the Colony. The figures given in the current estimates are £82,500 and £96,600 respectively. . . . In addition there is the endowment of Achimota College, which represents a charge on our revenue of £68,000 per annum. . . .

To judge from the remarks of the African Members of this Council at the last Estimates Meeting, the introduction of economies which would have the effect of restricting the existing educational facilities — which even now are considered by many to be inadequate — and thus of reducing the general standard of education, would meet with the condemnation of the mass of the people of this country. If, therefore, it is their desire that a system which was built up during years of prosperity should be fully maintained, they must be prepared to assist in providing the funds to meet the expenditure involved. The maintenance of the system will assuredly demand from them individually a larger contribution than they have been accustomed to make in the past. . . .

As in the case of education, so in the case of roads, we may profitably draw a comparison between the Gold Coast and Nigeria. . . . The central Government of

Nigeria spends £170,000 only on the maintenance of roads [compared with the current Gold Coast estimate of £174,905]. It must not be concluded from this statement that there are fewer roads in Nigeria, or that they are generally speaking inferior to those in the Gold Coast. Such is not the case . . . but . . . in that country all the roads other than those between Lagos and Port Harcourt and between Lagos and Ibadan are maintained by the native administration. . . .

Those who have studied the situation will agree that the future of the cacao industry largely depends on cheap transport, as, with the price of cacao at the present figure, the cost of head loading for any except the shortest distances would exceed the profit which the producer obtains. . . . Therefore no further economies can be expected, in respect of road maintenance, without endangering the one industry from which the greater part of the Colony's revenue is derived, directly or indirectly. . . .

At the last Estimates Meeting, the African Members of this Council criticised Government for reducing expenditure on the Medical and Sanitary Services during the current financial year, even after it had been explained that the Gold Coast continues to spend considerably more per head of population (e.g. 3s. 2d. as compared with 6¾d. in Nigeria) on Medical services and public health than any other African Colony. . . . It is clear from the attitude of African Members that those whom they represent are averse to any further decrease of the vote for Medical and Health Services. . . .

To recapitulate: of a total estimated revenue of £2,300,000, the votes for education, medical facilities and roads . . . absorb no less than £845,118 which is made up as follows:—

Education   £275,661
Medical facilities   364,819
Roads   204,638
[plus £174,905 for supervision]

Thus more than 33⅓ per cent. of the estimated revenue for the current year (the actual revenue will almost certainly be much less) is devoted to three services which it will not be possible to maintain on even the present reduced scale unless new courses of revenue are tapped.

Probably some will say that the deficit should be made good by increasing indirect taxation through the import duties which, it may be remarked, produced no less than 77 per cent. of the Colony's revenue in 1930–31.

But this method of balancing revenue and expenditure cannot continue to be employed indefinitely. Sooner or later the point must be reached — in the opinion of some it has been reached already, when an increase in import duties will not only hamper trade, and prevent, or in any event delay, its return to normal conditions, but will actually result in a fall of revenue. . . . Is it a wise or economically sound policy to allow the revenue of the Colony to be harnessed for all time to one product, the price of which fluctuates from year to year, and is outside our control? . . . The necessity for direct taxation has been recognised by every Government in British and foreign tropical Africa, with the one exception of the Gold Coast, and the time has come, in my considered judgement, when the Gold Coast Government also must, in the interests of the people themselves, fall into line with the other administrations. . . .

In deference to the wishes of the Africans . . . Government introduced legislation in 1929 and 1930 to restrict the sale and increase the cost of all spirits, and in the case of gin, gradually to decrease imports until in ten years' time they will cease altogether. As a result . . . the revenue derived from the imports of potable spirits decreased from £1,456,161 in 1928 to £625,939 in 1930, a loss of £830,222. A portion of this loss at least must be made good from other sources of taxation. . . . I confidently hope . . . that those who advocated the change in liquor policy . . . will, therefore, appreciate the necessity for the introduction of direct taxation in the form of an income tax, and will lend it their support. . . .

Income tax, far from being contrary to the principles of progressive states[1] is the concomitant . . . of progress. . . . Government fully understands and appreciates the objection which the people have to a poll-tax, and a hut-tax, and I assure the African Members that Government has no intention of introducing either of these forms of tax. The Bill which Government contemplate . . . provides for the imposition of a tax of 6d. in the pound on all income of or over £40 per annum. . . .

I will end this part of my message with a quotation from the 'Dual Mandate', which, as you know, was written by Lord Lugard, shortly after his retirement from the Governorship of Nigeria. He says: 'There is no civilised State in the world where direct taxation has not been found to be a necessity, and African communities which aspire to be regarded as civilised, must bear the common burden of civilisation.' I doubt whether in any part of tropical Africa are the benefits of civilisation available in as great a degree as in the Gold Coast, or whether in any part have the people displayed so great a desire to make use of them as have the people of the Gold Coast. In the days of trade prosperity it was possible to provide those benefits without calling upon the individual to contribute directly towards their cost. But conditions have changed; the individual must now learn to realise his duty to those who will come after him, and by making a small sacrifice, to ensure that the benefits which he now enjoys will be available for them. . . .

Let me now sum up my review of the financial position:—

(1) The revenue of the Gold Coast which reached high water mark in 1927–28 at £4,121,523, had sunk by 1930–31 to £2,572,976, and the revised estimate for the current year is only just over £2,000,000.

[1] An African Member in February had described income tax as 'humiliating' and 'against the principles of progressive states.'

(2) In consequence of this rapid and complete reversal of the Colony's wonted financial prosperity, our surplus assets will, unless special steps are taken, have wholly disappeared by the end of the current financial year. On the other hand, our Reserve Fund, which at present amounts to some £1,300,000, remains intact.

(3) The estimated Recurrent Expenditure was reduced from £2,977,250 in 1930–31 to £2,733,433 in the current year's budget, i.e. by £243,807. As a result of the efforts made by Heads of Departments and the Economy Committee, further reductions have been ordered which when wholly effective will aggregate some £270,000. Against this there will be a set-off of about £15,000 on account of additional pensions and gratuities, but altogether it may be said that during the last nine months, reductions in current expenditure have been ordered to the extent of approximately £500,000.

(4) Having regard to the probability that the Colonial Treasury will again have to carry in 1932–33 a Railway deficit which may extend to over £100,000, it is clear that the prospective gap between revenue and expenditure in 1932–33 is still so large that the deficiency cannot prudently be met entirely from the Reserve Fund.

(5) Consequently some additional taxation is inevitable and the proposals of Government involve the imposition of additional taxation to the extent of some £240,000. In the execution of this decision, Government has taken the utmost pains so as to adjust the new taxation that its incidence on the poorer classes should be almost negligible.

(6) The savings effected by retrenchment (£500,000) are more than double the additional taxation (£240,000). In other words, recourse has not been had to new revenue measures until every avenue of economy had been closely explored.

(7) If the world depression continues, it will inevitably be necessary, not only to make a third retrenchment in personnel — a retrenchment which will have to embrace

all Departments without exception — but also to have further recourse to inroads on the emoluments of the public service. A substantial, but not necessarily large, improvement in cacao prices, would probably obviate these unpleasant contingencies. . . .

[Leg. Co. Debates, 1931–2, pp. 276–82]

[b.] SPEECH OF DR. NANKA BRUCE
24 SEPTEMBER, 1931.

. . . The people have developed that sort of irritated militant spirit which is quite foreign to them and quite unknown to myself. I do not blame them, Sir. These people have no knowledge of the laws of supply and demand. They do not know why the price of cacao has gone down; they have no knowledge of the so-called 'gold-standard', and I myself know nothing about it and cannot explain it to them. They cannot fathom the reason why things are so bad with them. The only way in which they can give vent to their feelings is to say that Government is against them; that the merchants and the Pool are up to a work of mischief, and they must find a way out; and the only way is certainly to find a man who is prepared to fight Government. So I put it to you very clearly, Your Excellency, that the spirit in which the people to-day are existing is not a very healthy one in which to go and propose to them new taxation. . . .

It is really sad and distressing to find the Colony in such a position with its finances, but I must confess, as one who has taken keen interest in the affairs . . . of this country, that I am not at all surprised. To my mind, Government has been gallivanting with the finances of this country. In and out of season, we have been preaching retrenchment. Long years before Your Excellency came here, we saw that the development of the Colony was proceeding at such a rate that there was difficulty ahead . . . and we preached that in vain, [for] of course, with Colonial Governments everything is nothing so long as it is not Government's proposition. . . . I take it that

Government had sufficient warning in 1928 to put its house in order.

And what was the position when I came out? I met Government building palatial bungalows at the rate of £130,000 a year, bringing out officials in large numbers, notwithstanding the protests of Unofficial Members and public opinion published in the press, as if nothing had happened; so I say with all earnestness, that the people of this country are not to blame . . . for what has happened, and they are not likely to sympathise with the steps that are being taken by Government to remedy the situation. . . .

Retrenchment has not gone as far as we should like. . . . Your Excellency maintains that the present salaries of officials should be left intact. I submit, Sir, that that is a very difficult position to take. . . . Officials have to concede something, and it will just meet the point if you will just put a small 'axe' into the amount of emoluments stated in this paper. Just 10 per cent. will satisfy everybody, and I think we shall balance our budget without giving anybody trouble at all. [What little remains to be found] . . . can be found very easily by resorting to the Reserve Fund. This Reserve Fund, as the Honourable the Provincial Member for the Central Province has pointed out, was expressly created for this emergency . . . and now that the crisis has come, I am asking Your Excellency to fall upon this fund for balancing our budget, instead of resorting to fresh taxation. . . .

We are willing to pay taxes, but we have not got the money. Our people contribute most liberally to the taxes of this country. . . . Your Excellency will appreciate that when you compare this country with Nigeria, when you consider the size of Nigeria and the revenue of the two Colonies. Here our revenue rose to nearly four million and a half. In Nigeria, with a population of nearly 20 million people, the revenue rose as high as five million pounds. It shows how easily we contribute to the revenue of this Colony [when we have money]. . . . But we have not got it . . .

and with the family system strained as it is we Africans have to undertake the burden of looking after other members of the family, even including their wives and children, who are in want, and that is the reason why the people of this country have not clamoured for any Poor Law and Insurance laws, notwithstanding, as I said, the liberal way in which they put taxes into Government's chest.

I know a good deal of expenditure has gone in good education, in Achimota, good hospitals and roads. But I believe, Sir, that if that matter is pushed too far forward and the people asked to choose between all these things and Income Tax . . . they would say that they would do without them. . . . Our people are averse to direct taxation, no matter in what particular form — Poll Tax or Income Tax. We know nothing about Income Tax. There is a history about Poll Tax in this country, and we know something about that. . . .

I say, Sir, that if direct taxation was a remedy for all financial ills, England would not be in a position such as she is today. . . . . What Government has failed to see is, there is a point beyond which Government expenditure cannot go, and that is the point we have now reached, and it behoves our Government to retreat carefully. . . .

With regard to the views of Lord Lugard . . . I would say this: that if I met the Noble Lord and put the corollary of equal representation with direct taxation, he would only say: 'You are a denationalised African. You have no business in this country.' We must not take the views of the Noble Lord, no matter how experienced he may be. There is no need in this country to have direct taxation. In every country where direct taxation is imposed there must be equal representation. I will only put this proposition: Is Government prepared to give to this country full representation, and is Government prepared to give the control of our finances to the people of this country? If not, it is better that we remain where we are and

try to balance our budget in some other way.

[Leg. Co. Debates, 1931–2, pp. 380–5]

478 GOVERNOR SIR R. SLATER'S SPEECH TO LEGISLATIVE COUNCIL   1 MARCH, 1932.

. . . The Question of Direct Taxation.

Hitherto, with rare (but I am happy to say, gradually more frequent) exceptions, the Chiefs and people have looked to Government to bear the financial burden of practically all local improvements (except roads). . . . In the changed financial conditions that now obtain, the Central Government cannot possibly continue this policy, and local development must either practically cease, or be financed from local funds. The Chiefs and people have, to their great credit, rapidly learned to appreciate this fact, as is proved by a recent resolution passed by the Provincial Council of the Eastern Province, which was later endorsed by the Joint Conference of Provincial Councils. The Councils ask 'That Government should introduce measures enabling the States to assume properly and adequately the requisite responsibilities' so that 'the duties and responsibilities of Government towards such states may be lightened.' . . . It is my intention to invite the Provincial Councils to appoint representatives, to discuss with the Secretary for Native Affairs and other Government officers, the principles of a Native Administration Revenue Bill, which is the principal measure required for the establishment of local government in the various states. . . .

The most important condition for the proper development of native administrations is the delegation to the Native Authorities of financial responsibility, which can only be fully exercised if the duty of raising revenue locally, as well as of disbursing it, is entrusted to them. I wish particularly to emphasize the words 'raising revenue' as there are some who apparently hold the view that the Native Administrations should be financed by grants from general revenue. Such a method of providing funds for local government, apart from the fact that it would provide no relief to the Central Government, is to be condemned, because it does not impose on the Native Authorities a responsibility which they must learn to bear if any real progress in self-administration is to be made. . . .

I come now to the publication of the Income Tax Bill last September. . . . To my regret, and to the regret of all persons who are jealous of the reputation of the Gold Coast peoples, the Bill evoked in certain quarters outside this council, instead of dispassionate study, sheer invective and abuse. . . . The critics intemperately asserted, ignoring published facts, that the need for further revenue was either nonexistent, or could be met by a levy on official emoluments, and other measures of further retrenchment. These appeals to prejudice had the not unnatural result that the uninstructed classes in Sekondi, Cape Coast and elsewhere, were inflamed, and committed acts of violence which served merely to besmirch the good name of the Gold Coast. I am glad to say that the people of Accra dissociated themselves from this policy of unruly demonstrations, and the majority of their leaders consistently advocated constitutional methods of protest. . . .

Income Tax in the Gold Coast was never intended to be, and those who consider the difficulties of its assessment and collection will realise that it could not be, a complete scheme in itself. It can never be more than supplementary to a Native Administration Revenue Ordinance. . . . The principal object of direct taxation is to provide funds for the development of Native Administrations, and, subject to any recommendations which the representatives of the Provincial Councils may make . . . I propose that . . . all persons who are subject to the Native Administration Ordinance shall pay their direct tax to the Native Authorities. . . . It would be manifestly unjust to exempt Europeans and other non-natives from a form of taxation to which natives are subjected, and I therefore see no reason

whatever to withdraw the Income Tax Bill unconditionally. The Income Tax Ordinance will be applied to the Europeans and non-natives, wherever they may be, and it will also apply to natives resident within the boundaries of towns already possessing a form of local government. . . . No one will be called upon to pay both income tax and a tax under the proposed Native Administration Revenue Ordinance. But the Income Tax Ordinance being . . . supplementary to the Native Administration Revenue Ordinance, I have decided to postpone its introduction until the latter measure is ready so that the whole scheme may come into operation at the same time. . . .

Cacao.

The maritime exports of cacao in 1931 amounted to 237,534 tons, valued at £5,379,454, as compared with 186,772 tons valued at £6,865,374 for the year 1930. The quantity is the highest ever exported, but the increase was entirely due to the 'hold-up' which lasted from the end of October, 1930, to the beginning of January, 1931. . . . Unfortunately, the record export in quantity coincided with the lowest average f.o.b. value ever recorded in this colony. In 1931 the f.o.b. value per ton was £23. In 1918 the similar value was £27, which until last year was the lowest annual f.o.b. value recorded. Although the quantity exported in 1931 was 50,762 tons higher, the value of the year's exports was £1,485,920 less than in 1930, and it is this basic fact which makes the revenue prospects for 1932–33 so unpromising in so far as they depend on Customs import duties. . . .

The exports (including exports overland) of cacao for the last ten years have been as follows, together with their values. . . .

	TONS	VALUE (F.O.B.) £
1922	159,000	5,841,000
1923	198,000	6,567,000
1924	223,000	7,250,000
1925	218,000	8,222,000
1926	231,000	9,181,000

| TONS | VALUE (F.O.B.) |
| | £ |

1927	210,000	11,728,000
1928	225,000	11,230,000
1929	238,000	9,704,000
1930	191,000	6,970,000
1931	244,000	5,493,000

In spite . . . of our record export in 1931, it is difficult to resist the conclusion that the peak year of cacao exports from the Gold Coast has been passed. . . . Nevertheless . . . in 1929 a survey of Western Ashanti alone showed that 130,000 acres (30,000 tons) had not yet come into bearing. It is clear that under the stimulus of high prices, exports might increase to figures considerably greater than our present 210,000 to 220,000 tons. . . .

The maritime exports of cacao for the years 1931 and 1930 were distributed as follows:—

	1931 tons	1930 tons
Holland	61,828	39,753
United Kingdom	56,065	42,486
United States	55,469	37,129
Germany	50,812	56,285

Particulars are given hereunder of the ports of shipment of Gold Coast cacao in 1931 and 1930.

	1931 tons	1930 tons
Accra	112,772	80,251
Takoradi	74,997	67,132
Winneba	27,089	18,132
Saltpond	12,523	12,558
Cape Coast	9,381	6,272
Ada	772	1,240

Northern Territories Protectorate. . . .

This part of the Gold Coast has for some thirty years been administered almost entirely on the principle of Direct Rule. That form of administration has not been unsuccessful in so far as it has secured tranquility, but it has no future: tranquility is not development, and sooner or later there must needs come restlessness, with the spread of civilisation, unless the Chiefs are educated to take some real share in the government of their tribal areas.

During the past two years, the Administrative Officers in the Northern Territories have devoted considerable time and patience to inquiries into the constitution of the three states, namely Gonja (Gbanya), Dagomba (Dagbon) and Mamprussi, which comprise the greater part of the Protectorate. At fully representative conferences, which were held, in the case of the Dagomba state at Yendi, and of the Gonja state at Yapei, the constitutions of those states were recorded, and their relations *inter se* defined. I have, on the advice of the Chief Commissioner, enacted a Native Authority and a Native Tribunal Ordinance, the first of which places on the Native Authorities certain executive duties and responsibilities, while the latter confers on them the right of jurisdiction over natives in certain cases. . . .

In November last I enacted the Northern Territories Land and Native Rights Ordinance to replace Cap. 11 of the Protectorate. . . . The objects remain the same: namely (a) to preclude the natives from the temptation to dispose of their lands outright, without regard for the requirements of their descendants, and for totally inadequate payments; (b) to ensure that such profits as are derived from the land arc used for the benefit of the community as a whole and not of any particular section or individual member of it; and (c) to minimise the possibility of ruinous litigation. It cannot be gainsaid that, had a similar Ordinance been applied to the Gold Coast Colony some forty or fifty years ago, certain of the States would now be in a far more prosperous and happier condition than they are today. . . .

Under the Ordinance, the Governor becomes the representative of, and trustee for, the people, and, as such, it will be his duty to see that the land is developed to the best advantage. The Crown acquires no title to the lands: they remain the property of the people, but are placed, for their protection and proper development, under the control of the Governor, in so far as applications by non-natives for concessions and plots of land are concerned. . . .

[Leg. Co. Debates, 1932–3, pp. 20–4, 28–30, 72–6]

479 Speech of Governor, Sir Shenton Thomas[1] in Legislative Council
22 March, 1933.

. . . In this, my first Address to you, it is perhaps appropriate that I should say a few words about the Legislative Council itself. . . . You will remember that the Ordinances passed in this Council commence with an enacting clause reading 'Be it enacted by the Governor with the advice and consent of the Legislative Council.' The point that I wish to make is that a Legislative Council does not, as is sometimes supposed, consist of a Government and an Opposition, but is one body of persons authorised to do such things as are necessary for the good government of the Colony. The unofficial members of this Council, therefore, share the responsibility for the administration of the Colony, in accordance with the authority vested in them by His Majesty. They are entitled — and indeed are expected — to offer criticism and advice and to oppose any measure with which they do not agree; but I deprecate any suggestion that they should regard themselves as a sort of official Opposition. It shall be my aim, by taking all its members into my confidence, and asking for theirs in return, to promote unity in this Council, so that we may all work together for the common good.

It may be said that the majority of the members of this Council are officials and that therefore criticism on the part of unofficial members is unavailing. I reply that, so far as my memory serves me, I can recall no occasion since 1921, when I first came to West Africa, where the Governor of a West African Colony has refused to listen to the unanimous advice of the unofficial members. I quote here from a speech by Sir Hugh Clifford in the Legislative Council of Nigeria, in 1924: 'In the event — the very unlikely event — of my

[1] Sir Thomas Shenton Whitelegge Thomas; born, 1879; Colonial Service in East Africa, 1909–18; and Nigeria, 1923–7; Colonial Secretary of the Gold Coast, 1927; Governor of Nyasaland, 1929; Governor of the Gold Coast, 1932–4; subsequently Governor of the Straits Settlements.

Government majority on this Council finding itself opposed by a solid wall of opposition from the unofficial members, I think I can undertake to say that, as soon as the vote has been registered, no action will be taken on the matter until further consideration has been given to it, or reference had to the Secretary of State for the Colonies.' I desire also to say that, in the ordinary course of events, reasonable latitude will be allowed in the matter of the vote to official members, when, in my judgement, the interests of the public service do not forbid the expression of a diversity of views among its officers. I should like the Legislative Council to regard itself, not as a machine assembled for the automatic registration of [measures decided by] me and my Executive Council, but as a body of persons called together freely and frankly to debate the *pros* and *cons* of any measure that may be brought before it, in the best interests of the Gold Coast. So used, a Legislative Council can be the means of promoting trust and confidence between all sections of the community to the enhancement of the prosperity of the country and its better government. . . .

Native Administration.

By the Native Administration Ordinance of 1927, the Government divested itself, to all intents and purposes, of the authority to supervise the working of the State Councils and the native tribunals. The experience of the past five years has shown that this abrogation was premature. A few of the tribunals have worked well . . . but it would be idle to deny that, in parts of the country, there is much dissatisfaction at the manner in which the Ordinance has been enforced. . . . It is not the duty of Government to bolster up corrupt and inefficient tribunals and to put money into the pockets of the members. . . . It will be necessary, therefore, for me to take power to exercise proper supervision over the working of the tribunals and the expenditure of stool revenue. . . .

There can be no doubt whatever that in

tropical Africa the most effective channel of communication between the Government and the people is through the Native Authorities, and nothing that I have said must be construed to mean that I wish to weaken the Native Authorities. On the contrary, I desire to strengthen them. By the provisions of the Ordinance, the Government agreed to stand aloof, leaving the Chiefs and their State Councils with their own responsibilites. We have now seen that in many cases the action taken was too abrupt, and in future I intend to stand by their side, helping and advising them in the way of good government, so that eventually they may be better able to stand by themselves. . . .

I may add that, to be of any value, a Native Authority must be a real authority in the minds of the people affected, which they are willing to obey. Educational facilities in this country are increasing, and it is not to be expected that a people thus becoming enlightened will continue faithful to a Native Administration which is reactionary and repressive in its tendencies. . . .
[Leg. Co. Debates, 1933, i., pp. 3-4, 16-17]

480 SIR SHENTON THOMAS TO SIR PHILIP CUNLIFFE-LISTER[1]

ACCRA, 1 MARCH, 1934.

. . . The restoration of the [Ashanti] confederacy has . . . always appeared to me to be inevitable after the release of Prempeh I from his exile [in] the Seychelles. In the eyes of the Government he returned as a private citizen, and it was not until two years later[2] that he was given even the subsidiary office of Kumasihene, but in the eyes of the Ashanti, it was their Asantehene who had come back to them; the Golden Stool had once more an occupant and the

---

[1] Sir Philip Cunliffe-Lister (later 1st Earl Swinton); born, 1884; Conservative M.P., 1918-35; President of the Board of Trade, 1922-3, 1924-9, 1931; Secretary of State for the Colonies, 1931-5; Secretary of State for Air, 1935-8; Resident Cabinet Minister in West Africa, 1942-4.
[2] 1926.

people had once more their supreme spiritual head. I have often wondered, therefore, whether to the Ashanti the return of Prempeh had greater significance than would the restoration of the confederacy with official recognition of the Asantehene, and when in Kumasi recently I asked the Kumasihene. He told me that, although the decision to allow Prempeh I to return was of course 'a great thing', yet it still left Ashanti incomplete, and that therefore the present proposal is the greater. . . . Without an Asantehene there can be no confederacy. . . .

The question is not, therefore, merely one of according official recognition to an office which the Ashanti in spite of all past vicissitudes have never ceased to recognise: it is rather one of restoring nationhood to a people and of making Ashanti once more complete. I offer the following reasons why this should be done.

First, the great mass of the people earnestly desire it, and it is a principle of modern Colonial policy that people should be governed so far as is possible in accordance with their wishes. . . . It is remarkable that the opponents of the scheme should be so few. After all these years of independence it might have been supposed that many of the chiefs would have been swayed by motives of self-interest, but it is not so. Their allegiance to the Golden Stool is as strong as ever. I have taken the utmost care to ensure that no pressure of any sort, no advice as to the nature of their reply, has been placed upon or given to those who have been asked to record their decision, and I am quite sure that the replies convey the genuine desire of the signatories. . . .

Secondly, by their behaviour during the last 30 years, the Ashanti have earned the right to be given what they want. They are a thoroughly loyal, law-abiding, and progressive people. The relations between them and the Government are, and have been for years, excellent. In the Great War they gave two aeroplanes to the Imperial Government and made other substantial contributions. During the past few years they have, by reason of their distance from the sea, suffered more severely by the fall in cocoa prices than their neighbours in the Colony; yet they have been steady and sensible. In the attempted hold-up of cocoa three years ago, they took no part, and no doubt they profited accordingly. There need be no fear that they will use the restoration to cause embarrassment to the Government: on the contrary, I am sure that it will intensify their loyalty.

Thirdly, the restoration will render administrative progress more easy. With an Ashantehene, it will be possible to discuss Ashanti affairs as a whole, and there will be a common meeting-ground in the Confederacy Council in which these matters can be ventilated. I submit that an Administration which refuses without good cause to give official recognition to the essential elements in the faith of a people must necessarily be defective.

On the administrative side, it is proposed . . . that the Asantehene shall be assisted by a Confederacy Council of the Amanhene of all the constituent divisions together with a chief of each of the seven Kumasi clans. In the first instance, therefore, the members of this Council will be 15 in number plus seven from Kumasi . . . ; if at some later date the remaining Brong divisions of Wam-Pamu, Techiman, Nkoranza, Atebubu, Jaman, Abease and Berekum . . . apply to join and are admitted, the Council will be 29 in number. To us, such a body might seem unwieldy but to the Ashanti this would not be so. . . . The Kumasi-hene himself, with whom I discussed the matter recently, is very strongly in favour of a Council as proposed in the Memorandum.

There may be some who will say that the Brong divisions were not an integral part of the old confederacy and that therefore they should not be admitted to the Council of Ashanti. Rattray . . . says that 'the Brongs, on conquest, became vassals of the confederacy,' and they were called upon in time of war. There is reason also to believe that they, with the Ashanti, are of the same stock. If, therefore, they or any of them now desire a closer association with the Ashanti, and the Ashanti agree, I know of no reason why the wishes of the two parties should not be met. The political amalgamation of the Ashanti and the Brong will make for a stronger State, and will make administration easier.

It may also be suggested that the Kumasi clan chiefs should not be members of the Confederacy Council. . . . As the Kumasi-hene was also the Asantehene under the old regime, it is clear that the chiefs of the Kumasi clans, apart from the power derived from their purely territorial position, must have risen greatly in influence and prestige, from the fact that their own chief was also King of Ashanti. Today they still retain much authority, and some of them at least control a much greater population than do some of the Amanhene of the other divisions. . . . In the old Ashanti Confederacy the principal Kumasi chiefs were the Adamfo, that is 'friends at Court,' of the territorial Amanhene . . . who could not approach the Asantehene except through their respective Adamfo. . . . For a quarter of a century prior to the return of Prempeh I and his subsequent restoration to the Golden Stool, these important chiefs were members of the Council of Chiefs which Sir Francis Fuller inaugurated in 1905 to assist him in administering Kumasi affairs. . . . In Ashanti these clan chiefs have always been regarded both by the administration and in the eyes of the people, as being in status only a point below the independent Amanhene, and as holding a position of much greater dignity than do the ordinary chiefs of the second class. . . .

For this cause alone it is natural, therefore, that the Kumasihene should press for their inclusion in the Confederacy Council; but there is also the obvious argument that, sitting as he will as President in his capacity of Asantehene, he should have some one other than himself to express the views of the Kumasi division. It is important that his impartiality should not be called in question.

The inclusion of the Kumasi clan chiefs will therefore strengthen the hands of the Asantehene. I put it to the Kumasihene that the other chiefs might demur on the ground that Kumasi would thus be too fully represented on the Council, but he did not agree. His point was that, in dealing, as Kumasihene, with the affairs of the Kumasi division, he would have his own divisional council; but that, in the Confederacy Council, he would be dealing with the affairs of Ashanti as a whole, and that decisions would be taken in the light of the general opinion, expressed by the various Amanhene, whose places in the confederacy are perfectly well known and understood. It would not be possible, he said, for the views of the Kumasi clan chiefs to over-ride the opinion of the Amanhene.

[Papers relating to the Restoration of the Ashanti Confederacy, Accra, 1935. The restoration of the Confederacy was announced at a Durbar in Kumasi on 31 January, 1935.]

481 THE GOLD COAST ORDINANCES ORDER IN COUNCIL   1934.

At the Court at Buckingham Palace, the 9th day of November, 1934. . . .

[Recites Gold Coast Colony (Legislative Council) Order in Council of 8th April, 1925, the Ashanti Order in Council, 1934 and the Northern Territories Order in Council, 1934.] . . .

And whereas it is expedient to provide for the enactment of laws for the peace, order and good government of the Gold Coast and Ashanti as though they were a single territory, and for the enactment of laws for the peace, order, and good government of the Gold Coast Colony, Ashanti, and the Northern Territories of the Gold Coast as though they were a single territory:

Now therefore, His Majesty, by virtue and in exercise of all powers enabling Him in that behalf, is pleased, by and with the advice of His Privy Council, to order, and it is hereby ordered as follows: . . .

[Title and definition of terms.]

3. It shall be lawful for the Governor, with the advice and consent of the Council, from time to time by Ordinance to provide for the peace, order and good government of the Colony and Ashanti, and of all persons therein, provided as follows:

(a) That such Ordinance shall be subject to the advice and consent of the Council only so far as the provisions thereof relate to the Colony, and such Ordinance shall be expressed to be enacted by the Governor of the Gold Coast, with the advice and consent of the Council, so far as the provisions thereof relate to the Colony, and the provisions of the Gold Coast Colony (Legislative Council) Order in Council, 1925, or any Order in Council adding to, amending, or substituted for the same, relating to the making and establishment of Ordinances by the Governor of the Gold Coast with respect to the Colony, shall apply to such Ordinance.

(b) That subject to the foregoing proviso, the provisions of the Ashanti Order in Council, 1934, relating to the making and establishing of Ordinances by the Governor of the Gold Coast with respect to Ashanti, shall apply to all Ordinances made under the authority of this Article in all respects as if they were made under the authority of the said Ashanti Order in Council, 1934.

4. It shall be lawful for the Governor, with the advice and consent of the Council, from time to time by Ordinance to provide for the peace, order, and good government of the Gold Coast, and of all persons therein, provided as follows:—

(a) That such Ordinance shall be subject to the advice and consent of the Council only so far as the provisions thereof relate to the Colony, and such Ordinances shall be expressed to be enacted by the Governor of the Gold Coast with the advice and consent of the Council, so far as the provisions thereof relate to the Colony, and the provisions of the Gold Coast Colony (Legislative Council) Order in Council, 1925, or any Orders in Council adding to, amending, or substituted for the same, relating to the making and establishing of Ordinances by the Governor of the Gold Coast with respect to the Colony, and shall apply to such Ordinances;

(b) That subject to the foregoing proviso, the provisions of the Ashanti Order in Council, 1934, relating to the making and establishing of Ordinances by the Governor of the Gold Coast with respect to Ashanti, and the provisions of the Northern Territories Order in Council, 1934, relating to the making and establishing of Ordinances by the Governor of the Gold Coast with respect to the Northern Territories, shall apply to all Ordinances made under the authority of this Article in all respects as if they were made under the authority of the said Orders in Council respectively.

5. Nothing in this Order contained shall be construed to diminish or affect the powers of making Ordinances conferred upon the Governor with the advice and consent of the Council, with respect to the Colony, and upon the Governor with respect to Ashanti or with respect to the Northern Territories or with respect to Togoland under British Mandate, or to confer upon the Council the power of making any Ordinance affecting Ashanti or the Northern Territories or Togoland under British Mandate, save as provided in the two immediately preceding Articles, or upon the Governor, without the advice and consent of the Council, of making any Ordinance affecting the Colony. . . .

[Laws of the Gold Coast, 1936]

38 Hard Feelings, 1934–1939

IN the financial conditions of 1934, it seemed not unreasonable that the water supply of Accra should cease to be a charge on the general revenue: but the Waterworks Bill of that year, coupled with a Sedition Bill, touched off a fresh explosion of Gold Coast opinion. Chiefs and 'intelligentsia' united in opposition to these measures, and Ofori Atta accompanied a delegation to London to demand their removal and a greater share for Africans in the government of the Gold Coast (482). The 1934 programme combined what Casely Hayford had asked for in 1920, with the rural majority in the Legislative Council which Ofori Atta had defended ever since 1926. It was a sign of the times that they also sought to bring in some consideration of Ashanti grievances, and to secure some remedy for the depressed state of the cocoa trade. They were listened to by the Secretary of State, but that was the extent of their success (482c). The Aborigines' Society, not to be outdone, also submitted a petition which did not get so far (483). It was their swan-song, and fully in character, with its long historical digressions and its over rigid definition of somewhat amorphous native constitutional 'law'.

A trade revival, largely based on mineral development, made Sir Arnold Hodson's succession easier (484), and by 1936 chiefs and intelligentsia were once more divided over the old question of Native Policy (485). But there was still general dissatisfaction at the rate at which the civil service was being Africanised, where progress fell short of Guggisberg's schedule (486). And in a country where cocoa was so overwhelmingly important, there could be no real recovery as long as the cocoa trade was in difficulty. At the end of 1937 a buying agreement between the big European firms provoked a counter hold-up of supplies by the producers. Sir Arnold Hodson handled this crisis with conspicuous impartiality, but the report of the subsequent Commission foreshadowed the end of the time when Government could dissociate itself from problems of marketing (487).

482 PETITION OF THE DELEGATION FROM THE GOLD COAST AND ASHANTI 1934.

[A] *To the King's Most Excellent Majesty in Council.*

The Humble Petition of

The Honourable Nana Sir Ofori Atta, Knight Commander of the Most Excellent Order of the British Empire, Omanhene of Akim Abuakwa, Member of the Legislative Council of the Gold Coast; the *Honourable Frederick Victor Nanka Bruce*, M.B. Ch.B. (Edin.), Member of the said Legislative Council; the *Honourable Kobina Aaku Korsah*, M.A., B.C.L., LLB., Member of the said Legislative Council, Barrister-at-Law; *Akilagpa Sawyerr*, B.A., Barrister at Law; *Joseph Boakye Danquah*, Ph.D., LLB., Barrister-at-Law; *James Mercer*, Licensed Surveyor and Auctioneer; *Edward Ochir Asafu-Adjaye*, B.A., LLB., Barrister-at-Law and *Isaac Kwadjo Agyeman*, Esquire; for and on behalf of the Paramount Chiefs, Chiefs and People of the Gold Coast Colony and Ashanti, whose duly accredited delegates and representatives they are *sheweth* as follows:—

1. YOUR Petitioners respectfully take this opportunity of expressing their unwavering loyalty and attachment and the unwavering loyalty and attachment of the populations represented by them to Your Majesty's Person and Throne.

2. BY a Mandate signed by Paramount Chiefs and Chiefs, whose names are set out in the First Schedule hereto, represent-

ing the Paramount Chiefs, Chiefs and people of the Gold Coast Colony and Ashanti, your Petitioners were appointed and constituted a Delegation to England on their behalf to present a Memorial to the King's most Excellent Majesty in Council through the Right Honourable the Secretary of State for the Colonies PRAYING that his Majesty may be pleased —

(1) To disallow the Criminal Code (Amendment) Ordinance, 1934 and the Waterworks Ordinance, 1934, both of which were recently passed by the Legislative Council of the said Gold Coast Colony, and

(2) to grant certain reforms in the constitution and in the administration of the said Gold Coast Colony,

and further to interview on their behalf the said Right Honourable the Secretary of State for the Colonies for the purpose of laying before him the grievances of their people.

3. YOUR Petitioners desire to state shortly in the body of their Petition the nature of the relief which they seek from Your Majesty in Council, leaving the several subject matters to be developed in detail in Schedules appended hereto.

4. African sentiment has been deeply stirred by the Ordinances spoken of in the Mandate. The people, and above all the women, have treasured the promise made to them 20 years ago, in circumstances of special solemnity, by the Governor, when water was first laid on, that the public fountains would be free to all, and a threatened breach of such a promise, touching them so nearly, will cut at the root of confidence, above all at a time of narrowing means when every extra charge hits the poor hard. It is a part of our Mandate to give voice to their protest where we trust it will be heard.

We humbly submit that a promise from the Governor should remain, as it has always been thought to be, beyond the possibility of question; if it is not, the people may fear anything.

5. THE sedition clauses in the Criminal Code (Amendment) Ordinance deeply offend the sense of the people.

In the first place, the people claim to be loyal and trustworthy, and they point to their absolutely clean record, in proof of this. To their minds, the clauses cast a slur upon their good name, and are felt as an insult; what have they done to deserve to have this scourge held over them? In the second place, the clauses are the cause of uneasiness and fears; any man may find himself called upon to stand his trial for some seditious writing with which he has no sympathy. Governors and officials come and go and know little of the people, and the people have no certain knowledge how these things may at any time be used.

6. THE passing of these Ordinances and a number of other matters in which the African population is greatly interested, have brought to a head the feeling that has been growing in the minds of the leaders of the people, that the time has now fully come when the African people should be given a greater share in the internal legislation and administration of the Colony, and that until this happens, African sentiment does not and will not carry its due weight in the Colony.

7. THE existing Constitution was admittedly planned 'to give the African a stepping stone towards the assumption of a greater responsibility.' (Sir Gordon Guggisberg when Governor, in 1925.) In the meantime, the African people have become more fit to take a leading part in the internal government of their country, whereas the European trading community has become less adapted to take a useful part therein. Where formerly there were independent traders with some personal interest and permanence in their relations with the country, there are now largely servants of great companies, working at a salary and at the expense of their companies.

8. THE African population has nine representatives among the 14 unofficial members of the Legislative Council, and the European community has five; the official members number 15, and the total mem-

bership numbers 29. In fact, however, the five European unofficial members do not represent any independent opinion or feeling upon any matter affecting the African community, and they have neither the African sentiment nor the local experience to enable them to investigate and pass an independent vote upon such matters. In the result, they do not attempt to do so, but generally follow the lead of the official members, so that their presence on the Council is of little value to the African community. On the contrary, owing to their presence, a strong unofficial minority appears always to approve of official measures.

Your Petitioners and those whom they represent, humbly submit that the African representatives on the Legislative Council should be increased to one-half of the whole number.

9. THE African population has at present no representation whatever on the Executive Council, which controls the administration of the Colony and which initiates legislation in the Colony; thus they practically have no control over the expenditure of public money, no initiative in reform, and no voice when legislative proposals are first taking shape.

YOUR Petitioners humbly submit that they should have a part in all these matters. It is important that African feeling should be represented at the earliest moment in the initiation of legislation, particularly fiscal legislation, and that African sentiment should not be disturbed by such proceedings as the erection of new residences for officials, for which they see no necessity, at a time of diminishing trade and revenues, and increasing poverty. It is hoped, further, that the representations of the African population on the Executive Council would add driving force to studies and investigations having the object of instituting reforms and relieving distress.

10. TO your Petitioners and the population represented by them, the European officials who control the Government of the Colony are only short-term visitors to Africa, whose honesty and goodwill they do not question, but whose interests are not their interests, but in conflict to some degree with theirs, and who cannot see with their eyes.

This consideration adds force to the desire of Your Petitioners for an effective part on the government, and for this reason it would give satisfaction to the Colony if (pending wider constitutional reforms) they could be assured that no measure of a fiscal nature which was opposed by not less than two-thirds of the African members of the Legislative Council, would receive the assent of the Governor until the opposing members had had an opportunity (if they desired it) of presenting a Memorial of their views to Your Majesty's Right Honourable Secretary of State for the Colonies, and of having their views placed before him.

11. THERE are other matters of administration in which the native inhabitants are interested and which Your Petitioners humbly pray should form the subject of inquiry with a view to modifications and improvements. These matters include the very important question of the employment of Africans in the Civil Service and the terms and conditions of such employment and of their superannuation or pension allowances; public health, and particularly sanitation, medical services, dispensaries and hospitals; education, both elementary and secondary, and grants in aid thereof; the administration of forests and the application of the Forestry Ordinance; agriculture, trade and industry and improvements therein.

Your Petitioners would be anxious to render their utmost assistance in connection with any such inquiry. The application of the Forestry Ordinance, in particular, has caused a great deal of difficulty and led to great differences of view-point between the African Chiefs and the official members of the Legislature.

12. A Memorandum on 'Cocoa and other Industries,' a Memorandum on 'Trade and Industry', and a Memorandum on 'Education', which have been prepared

by members of the Delegation, are submitted herewith in order to shew the views of African leaders upon these topics.

13. IT is recognised that, in the main, these matters require to be dealt with in the Colony; but in relation to Cocoa, it is felt that the Home Government can render important service by pressing on a Conference of the world's producers, with a view to concerted action. Some measure of general control appears to be necessary for restoring reasonable prosperity to the industry, and in the meantime it is submitted that steps should be taken to organise the industry in West Africa. Co-operative marketing in some form appears to promise the best results, but it is necessary in the interests of the farmers, who are largely without capital, and living from day to day, that some part of the value of their produce should come to them at an early stage after the crop is ready, either through the instrumentality of Agricultural Banks, or in some other way. The farmers as a class cannot, without financial assistance, afford to hold back their crops and wait for the first return from them until a reasonable price is offered, particularly at a time when a small excess of supply over demand, either in West Africa or other producing districts, may result in their being left at the end with their crops unsold and unsaleable. Thus, in present conditions, pressure to sell seriously depresses prices all round. Some appropriate organisation with a financial backing might distribute fairly among the farmers the burden of any unsold crop surpluses, and secure to them some immediate return and an ultimate better price for the marketed proportion.

It is strongly urged that the West African farmer should be represented at any general conference by one or more of their number.

14. THOSE of the Delegation who represent the Ashanti territory have proposed a Memorandum which is set out in Schedule V. . . .

15. THE Africans whom they represent are seriously concerned with the land question of Kumasi, the Ashanti capital town. The land within a mile radius of the centre has been for a long time treated as Government property. It is felt, however, as a grievance, that ground rents should within that area be raised to the point of making it difficult or impossible for native residents to retain their houses in competition with wealthier aliens.

It is felt as a greater grievance that the action of the Town authorities of Kumasi in extending (as they have done) the limits of Municipal Government outside the mile radius, should result not only in the imposition of rates for municipal revenue outside that area (which is only a fair return of Municipal Services) but should also result in the imposition of ground rents upon the landowner for Government purposes, amounting to a practical confiscation of their titles.

The land outside the mile radius never was and is not now Government property and its treatment as Government property threatens the whole security of tenure of land in Ashanti.

YOUR PETITIONERS HUMBLY PRAY that Your Majesty in Council will take account of this Petition and grant such relief in relation thereto as may seem expedient. AND Your Petitioners as in duty bound will ever pray &c.

[B Extract from Schedule IV. . . .]

It is humbly submitted that the . . . defects in the 1925 Constitution would be remedied by the introduction of amendments to the following effect, namely:—

(1) The composition of the Legislative Council to be changed so as to consist henceforward of the following members in addition to the Governor as President, viz.,

15 official members as heretofore
15 unofficial members made up as follows:—

12 Provincial Members, namely six for the Eastern Province, four for

the Central Province, and two for the Western Province.

Three Municipal Members as heretofore, namely one each for the towns of Accra, Cape Coast and Sekondi.

The six members of the Eastern Province to be elected by the whole Provincial Council and not by sections as heretofore.

(2) The Provincial Councils to be empowered to elect as Provincial Members of the Legislative Council any persons who are certified as able to read and speak the English language sufficiently well to enable them to take an active and intelligent part in the proceedings of the Council, irrespective of whether or not such persons are Chiefs.

(3) The Governor to have a vote in the Legislative Council upon questions of imperial concern only, and to have no vote upon questions of domestic concern to the Colony.

(4) In case of the votes cast for and against any Ordinance before the Legislative Council being equal, such Ordinance to be deemed not to have been passed unless and until it shall have been sanctioned by the Secretary of State for the Colonies.

(5) Any 10 unofficial members to be empowered to veto a financial measure before the Legislative Council, subject to review by the Secretary of State for the Colonies.

(6) The composition of the Executive Council to be altered by the addition of two unofficial members, such unofficial members to be selected by the unofficial members of the Legislative Council or a majority of them from amongst such unofficial members. . . .

(10) It is the duty of each Paramount Chief in his own State or 'Stool' to maintain the dignity of his position, to carry out all necessary operations relating to public health and sanitation, to maintain public buildings and works, to assist poor and aged subjects, and gener-

ally to conduct the administration of the native affairs of the Stool. For these purposes, it is essential that the Chief should possess an assured revenue of substantial amount. In fact, however, the only revenue available to each Chief consists of such small and intermittent sums as he may derive from rent of alienated land and from fines imposed by him as President of a Legal Tribunal or a State Council. This revenue is wholly insufficient and expensive to collect, involving frequent expensive litigation.

(11) In the foregoing circumstances, it is humbly submitted that arrangements should be made whereby each Chief may receive a regular grant from the central revenues of the Colony, sufficient to enable him to carry out the duties of his office.

(12) The question of financing the 'Stools' has long been a burning question in the Colony, and it is felt that its settlement is a matter of primary importance which, it is humbly submitted, might well be the subject of special inquiry at the instance of the Secretary of State. . . .

[C] Sir Philip Cunliffe-Lister's reply:
[1. On the Waterworks Question.]

There are really two questions here. The first is a broad question of equity and justice; the second, the interpretation of a statement made by Sir Hugh Clifford. Let me deal first with the question of justice and equity. On that I do not think there can be two opinions. To say that people who benefit by an exclusive service for a particular area should have the whole of the cost of that service carried by the general community of tax payers is one which, in equity, it would be impossible to support. . . . The principle which has always operated and has never been challenged (i.e. in England) is that where a special benefit is created, it is the primary duty of the people for whom that benefit is created to pay for the benefit. . . .

But now it is said that there is something in the statement made by Sir Hugh Clifford, which precludes the Government from taking what is the plain and just course towards the whole of the inhabitants. . . . In this matter, it is very relevant to consider the action of Sir Hugh Clifford at the time when this pledge, so called, this statement, was fresh in everyone's mind, including his own. . . . It is perfectly plain, from the recorded documents, that not only Sir Hugh Clifford, but the Committee (set up to draft a Water Works Ordinance), took the view that what this declaration meant was, that a general water rate was not only permissible, but was indeed necessary, but that special steps ought to be taken to exempt the poorest people from having a particular levy of this kind made upon them. . . . I am bound to say that, reviewing this entirely independently, I come to exactly the same conclusion that Lord Passfield came to, and there is nothing in this statement of the Governor to prevent the ordinary and just course from being followed, at such time as the Governor on the spot thinks is the fair and right time for it to be enforced. . . .

[2. On constitutional proposals.]

Let me say at once that I could not contemplate an alteration in the Constitutional system under which the Governor had not the power to pass whatever legislation he thought was right in the public interest. That being so, I do not think that it is a matter of great importance how many people sit on a Council. What you really want to be sure of, in a Council of that kind, is that you have competent people who can express the different points of view which it is desirable should be expressed, and I do not really think that, as long as your system ensures that the best people for that purpose are there, the actual numbers are of any great importance. . . .

Now as regards the Provincial Councils, I will consider the suggestion which is made to combine the sections of the Council of the Eastern province. I should like to consider that further. I should also like to consider further, and in due course an answer will be returned through the Governor, the question of electing persons other than Chiefs. At first blush, I feel this about it. Great care was taken in the building up of the Provincial Councils and in securing, through the Provincial Councils, the representation on the Legislative Council. The Chiefs sit in the Provincial Councils because they have the confidence of the people and they are really the representatives of their people. Now it seems to me that you are proud and rightly proud of that system. You have built up your own institutions in this system of indirect rule, basing them on past tradition. I would suggest this to you. Be careful you do not undermine that. . . . Suppose you elect somebody who is not a Chief to go and sit on the Legislative Council, may it not be that that would rather undermine the power of the Chief and his authority? You want to consider that point. I have an open mind about this, but I should like to be sure that it had been considered very carefully from that point of view. . . .

Now as regards the financing of the Stools. The measure of administrative authority in any area must depend on proved capacity, and Government cannot abandon or abrogate its position as a Trustee; but I am bound to say, and here I am voicing what has been the experience everywhere throughout the great Colonial Empire, that the local Native Administration should, in so far as it requires finance, be financed through its own local taxation. That has been the regular practice. It is certainly not financially possible today; I doubt whether it is economically desirable or administratively desirable, even if it were possible, that Stool Treasuries should exist on grants-in-aid coming from the central revenue; but I should consider favourably proposals for the raising of local revenue, consistently, of course, with efficient financial administration. As each State increased its revenue it would then take a greater share in providing local services for the benefit of the people. . . .

[Sessional Paper No. 11 of 1934]

483 GOLD COAST ABORIGINES' RIGHTS PROTECTION SOCIETY PETITION
NOVEMBER 1934.

To His Most Gracious Majesty, the King of Great Britain and Ireland, and the Dominions beyond the Seas in Council,

The Humble Petition of the Gold Coast Aborigines' Rights Protection Society by its duly authorised Delegates now in England Sheweth:—

That the Petitioners . . . are the duly constituted and sole authorised representatives of the Kings, Rulers and Chiefs of the Gold Coast, being such Kings, Rulers and Chiefs according to the recognized native laws, customs and usages of the Gold Coast in West Africa, and being the lineal and/or lawful successors in office as such to their respective peoples and tribes, elected and succeeding according to the immemorial traditions and customs of such peoples and tribes, such laws and customs being unbroken subsisting and intact to the present time, except in so far as these may have been, as Your Petitioners humbly submit, wrongly and mistakenly, and to the great sorrow and grief of your Petitioners, disturbed or lessened by the acts of Your Majesty's Government on the Gold Coast. . . .

[From 1898 to 1932, successive Governors had given] recognition and acceptance of the status of Your Majesty's Petitioning Society as truly representative of the natural Chiefs and Rulers . . . of the whole of the . . . Gold Coast. . . . Non-recognition by the Government took, however, a definite shape in the early part of the year 1932 [when it was] . . . averred that the policy of the Government, since the inception of the Native Administration Ordinance (which came into force in 1927), and of the Provincial Council System, had been consistently to communicate with the people of the country, upon matters affect-

ing their welfare, through the medium of the Provincial Councils. . . . And finally, on the 21st of March, 1932, Your Petitioning Society was informed by the Commissioner of the Central Province . . . that 'Government does not recognise your Society as the medium of communication between Government and the Chiefs and people.' . . .

Your Petitioners beg humbly to point out to Your Majesty in Council, that neither in the Native Administration Ordinance, 1927, nor in any of its amending Ordinances, is there any provision prescribing such functions for the Provincial Councils, nor enabling them to exercise them. . . . Your Petitioners cannot but observe that the 'policy' of the local Government . . . is illustrative of that tendency to autocracy and high-handedness latterly exhibited on the part of the Government, which profoundly disturbs their happiness under, and content with, the Administration, and tends to alarm the people as to the future. . . . Instead of being educated and trained to govern themselves, they are being governed without any adequate joinder of themselves in the government of themselves. It is a melancholy and depressing reflection for them to perceive that their prospects of self-government . . . seem to be in inverse ratio to their progress under tutelage in European civilisation.[1] . . .

The main objection made by Your Petitioners in 1926 to the provisions of the Order in Council of 1925, were that it was conceived in a most illiberal spirit. That it conferred but a restricted measure of electoral representation of the people; that it struck a deadly blow at the federal union of the Native States,[2] and at the indepen-

[1] I have omitted a very long historical account of the retrogression from the 'enlightened and liberal views' of the Select Committee of 1865, in which great prominence is given to the events of 1874 and 1901.

[2] The Petition puts some stress on Sir Hugh Clifford's description of the Gold Coast (*Enc. Britt.* 12th ed.) as 'an agglomeration of small, self-contained and mutually independent Native States, each of which is under the immediate management of its own tribal organisation.'

dence of the Chiefs; that it violated the Customary Law in its most vital particulars; that it tended to divide the Head Chiefs from the Sub-Chiefs, Linguists, Councillors, and the general mass of the people, promoting friction between the Head Chiefs on the one hand and their Sub-Chiefs on the other; and that, if unamended, it would result in the disintegration of the Native States. . . . [It was contrary to native custom for Chiefs to sit on the Legislative Council or speak apart from their Linguists and Elders.] To establish, therefore, a Council, in which the Head Chiefs of the various divisions are to meet to perform so solemn a public act as the election of a member to represent their people on the Legislative Council, without the Sub-Chiefs . . . and their Elders and Councillors, is so revolutionary a proposal, that the people would only submit to it through fear of the strong arm of the Government, and that if persisted in, it would shake to their very foundations the Constitution of our Native States. . . .

The next step in the direction of disintegration of the Stool system . . . was the introduction of the Native Administration Ordinance, 1927. . . . This Ordinance was the subject of strong protests, at the time, by Your Petitioning Society, which were embodied in a Petition against the Bill lodged with the Secretary of State on the 29th September, 1926. . . . The Bill was passed through a Legislative Council which had overwhelming power by reason of the weight of its Official Membership thereon to pass anything.

The creation of a different and higher status for the Paramount Chief . . . was new and entirely unknown to . . . native law and custom, . . . and is mischievous in its tendency, and subversive. The exercise, and attempted exercise of these new powers by self-seeking and ambitious Chiefs . . . has led to oppression and infinite trouble, and to much litigation between a Paramount Chief in the Eastern Province and some of the Divisional Chiefs of the State in which he is for the time being

Paramount Chief,[1] and to acts of aggression and oppression on his part, which afterwards formed part of the subject matter of an arbitration inquiry held by Mr. Justice Hall . . . resulting in a very serious and damaging Report or Finding against the said Paramount Chief. . . .

[The Petition goes on to complain of the Waterworks Ordinance, the Criminal Code Amendment Ordinance, and the Labour Ordinance.]

Your Petitioners therefore humbly pray as follows:

(1) That Your Majesty may through Your Majesty's Principal Secretary of State for the Colonies, graciously be pleased to direct Your Officers administering the Government of the Gold Coast, to resume the practice inaugurated in 1898 and continued up to 1926 . . . of treating Your Petitioning Society as the acknowledged medium of communication between the Government of the Colony of the Gold Coast and the Natural Rulers and Chiefs who are constituent members of Your Petitioning Society, in all matters affecting the welfare, interests and concerns of such Natural Rulers and Chiefs, and of the indigenous people of the Gold Coast.

(2) That Your Majesty may be graciously pleased to direct full, independent and impartial inquiry, or inquiries, at which Your Petitioning Society may be represented, into the following matters:—

(a) The nature of the true relations between the British Crown [&c and the Gold Coast] from the year 1821.

(b) As to the validity and true intention and effect of the Imperial Orders in Council of the 26th September, 1901 and the 2nd October, 1906. . . .

(c) As to the desirability or otherwise of the revocation or amendment of the Gold Coast (Legislative Council) Order in Council of . . . 1925 . . . in the matter of the representation of Africans on the Legislative Council of the Colony,

[1] Akim Abuakwa.

and the proportion thereof to the Official and European representation, and as to the justice and expediency of granting representation of the indigenous population on Your Majesty's Executive Council of the Colony by members of the indigenous population. . . .

(d) Into . . . the Native Administration Ordinance, 1927. . . .

(e) Into the instances of discrimination or victimisation of Paramount Chiefs. . .

(f) Generally into the administration of the country, with especial reference to the system of decentralisation now proceeding, resulting in whole districts being ruled by junior and inexperienced officials, with no real opportunities of getting redress from the Central Government, and

(g) To inquire into other matters and disabilities affecting the indigenous population, such as the Education Ordinance. . . .

(3) That Your Majesty may be graciously pleased to direct the repeal of the Criminal Code Amendment Ordinance, in so far as it deals with 'sedition' and the repeal of the Waterworks Ordinance, or its amendment so as to relieve the poorer classes from the burden of paying water rates. . . . [Gold Coast Aboriginies' Rights Protection Society Petition, 1934, pp. 1, 5–7, 21–2, 27, 30, 37–8.]
There are 77 pages in the original. The deputation was not received at the Colonial Office.

484 ADDRESS OF GOVERNOR, SIR ARNOLD HODSON,[1] TO THE LEGISLATIVE COUNCIL
20 FEBRUARY, 1936.

. . . The country's commerce showed a very welcome revival [in 1935]. The value of the sea-borne trade in 1935, at 16¾

[1] Sir Arnold Hodson (1881–1944); served in the Transvaal, 1902–4; Bechuanaland, 1904–12, and Somaliland, 1912–14; consul in Abyssinia, 1914–26; Governor of Falkland Isles (1926–30), Sierra Leone (1930–4) and the Gold Coast, 1934–41.

million pounds, was 36 per cent. in excess of that of 1934. In tonnage, the corresponding increase was 20 per cent. Both tonnage and value were the highest achieved since 1930. Our imports increased rather more than did our exports, but we nevertheless preserved a healthy favourable trade balance of two million pounds. . . . Our exports reached the value of just over 9¼ million pounds, for nearly 5¼ million of which cocoa was responsible. Increases were shown in respect of gold, cocoa, manganese, timber, kola nuts, and in the products of the palm and lime tree. Timber exports, mainly mahogany, were the largest since 1929; and the palm kernel figures were nearly double those of last year. The export of gold bullion, valued at nearly 2¾ million pounds, was more than 20,000 fine ounces in excess of the previous year's exports. It is now approaching this country's record figure of 416,000 fine ounces, which was set up in the year 1915. The relative values of our main domestic exports were, cocoa, as usual first, accounting for 55 per cent. of the total, gold 30 per cent., manganese 7 per cent., diamonds 6 per cent., and timber 1 per cent. . . . The production of cocoa for the crop year ending in September last was an outstanding record for the Gold Coast. The total crop has been estimated at 276,000 tons. . . .

Taking the mining industry as a whole . . . statistics for 1935 are well in advance of those for any previous year. During the year, the total production of gold amounted to 358,835 fine ounces, valued at £1,524,180 (at par), as compared with 326,040 fine ounces and £1,385,026 respectively, during 1934. . . . At the end of the year, there were 7 producing, 15 developing, and 29 prospecting mines in operation. . . . Gold mining companies employed, on all operations, a daily average of 718 Europeans and 26,814 Africans throughout the year, as compared with 456 and 18,419 respectively in 1934. The total amount of diamonds exported during 1935 was 1,349,847 carats, valued at £546,094.

These figures compare with 2,391,609 carats and £756,816 respectively [in 1934]. . . . The decrease can be attributed entirely to the price factor, and to an abnormally large shipment by one of the bigger companies during the first half of 1934, when higher prices were ruling. There are five diamond-producing companies in operation, and they employ a daily average of 59 Europeans and 4,300 Africans throughout the year; an increase of six Europeans and 76 Africans over 1934. The total quantity of manganese ore exported amounted to 398,718 dry tons, valued at £612,170, as compared with 339,385 tons and £480,880 respectively in 1934. . . . There was, as in previous years, only one mine producing manganese ore, that at Nsuta, the property of the African Manganese Company, which employed a daily average of 33 Europeans and 1,312 Africans, as compared with 22 and 921 respectively in 1934. . . . There were employed on all mining and prospecting operations a daily average of 810 Europeans and 32,506 Africans; an increase of nearly 40 per cent. on the figures for 1934. The yearly expansion of mining activities is shown by the following comparative statistics:

YEAR	AVGE. NO. PER DAY EUROPEANS	AFRICANS.
1931	237	11,889
1932	244	11,940
1933	323	14,939
1934	532	23,642
1935	810	32,506

When the Estimates for the current year were passed in Council last March, a small surplus of £994 was expected. The revised estimates of revenue and expenditure show that the year will end with a surplus of £365,290. . . . In addition . . . the Railway accounts are expected to show a surplus of £81,256, instead of a deficit of £10,969. . . . But it must not be overlooked that there will still be at 31st March, 1936, an undischarged liability of £352,476, in respect of suspended contributions to the Railway Renewals Fund. We have been warned that very heavy expenditure on renewal of rolling stock, machinery and

track, during the period 1936–45, amounting to over £850,000 will be necessary. . . .

The current year's revenue estimate was on a conservative basis. We could not possibly foresee such a remarkable trade revival. The results of the year, however, give us more confidence for 1936–37, and consequently next year's revenue is estimated in a much more optimistic frame of mind. . . . We have been able to provide for much needed medical and other services, while development works, particularly railway, roads and other public works, show increases of over £350,000, without taking into consideration a sum of £75,000 for aerodromes, and £46,280 contribution to the Sinking Fund. . . . Briefly, revenue is expected to yield £2,985,753, and expenditure is estimated at £2,975,280. . . . The Railway estimates show an expected surplus of £92,805, and those in connection with Takoradi harbour also exhibit a small surplus. . . . This is the first time the Harbour estimates have ever shown a balance on the right side. . . .

[Leg. Co. Debates, 1936, i., pp. 5, 7, 18–19, 21–3]

485 DEBATE ON THE NATIVE JURISDICTION AMENDMENT ORDINANCE

25 FEBRUARY, 1936.

[A] *Mr. Kojo Thompson:*[1] . . .

With regard to clause 18, sub-section 2 (s), which reads, 'The imposition of levies or tribute by a Paramount Chief with the concurrence of the State Council, the fixing of the amount to be raised by means of such levies or tribute, and the methods of the collection of such levies or tribute,': I am asking, Sir, that the whole of this section be deleted. . . . When there is going to be imposition of taxes, then there must be representation. The subjects of the Chiefs who are going to be taxed, I say, Sir, are not represented on this Council; they have no knowledge of this bill, and the principle of it is against native custom. We all

[1] Lawyer and Municipal Member of Legislative Council for Accra, 1936–44.

know, Sir, that at the present moment the people of this country are sufficiently taxed, and this is borne out by the fact that only recently when the introduction of the water-rate bill was brought into this Council, a delegation was sent to England, because the inhabitants of the Gold Coast were not in a position, financially, to pay further taxation. . . .

Nobody knows where this is going to end; but I warn the Government, that if any attempt [is made to raise levies] the people will come in conflict with the chiefs; there will be trouble in the whole country. . . . We know, Sir, at the present moment it is stated that this levy is optional. . . . What guarantee have we that it will ever remain optional? Apart from this, the people who are going to be taxed are not represented; but assuming that the Provincial Members represent the people, since this proposal is in their interest, is it likely that they will object to it? Surely not. Nor can it be said that they are here representing their subjects so far as this particular question of levy is concerned. . . .

[B] *Nana Sir Ofori Atta.* . . .

If I listen to these barristers, I often wonder what they really think of the Chiefs. One day they would say to the Chiefs 'you are our Almighty God,' and the next day, the Chiefs would not be worthy of the respect due to a scavenger. I say that some sort of consideration is due to the Paramount Chiefs in the Gold Coast. No Paramount Chief dares, Sir, impose a levy on his own authority, or impose a levy because he wants money. I simply cannot contemplate that. I remember, Sir, that a few years ago, when the Native Administration Revenue question came under consideration, we had the same agitation, before the people knew what was going on, with the result that some of the Stools today . . . have fallen absolutely into ruin, and it pleases some of the members of the educated community to see that the Chiefs are ruined. . . .

I say, Sir, that a Chief or Paramount Chief and his State Council, when they so decide, should be able to impose [a] levy without having to face the ordeal of law court proceedings. . . Speaking as the Omanhene of Akim Abuakwa, I say that we are not very much interested in the matter of general levy. But we say that the Chiefs and State Councils should have some sort of means, if they so wish, to establish Stool Treasuries. . . .

[C] *Nene Nuer Ologu V.*[1] . . .

In 1934 when the Sedition Bill came up . . . a Committee of Twelve was formed in Accra, and we, the Chiefs, were approached to aid them to send a deputation to England. . . . We did not disappoint them. We helped even with money collected from our States. Now, if there appears to be a question of raising funds from our own people for the benefit of the State and for the benefit of the people, he stands here and says this question will cause commotion over the whole of the Gold Coast. The Chiefs are at a loss to understand this. When they are in difficulties they know that we are fathers, but once they are free, they become like children quite independent. Now, if my memory would serve me well, during the Sedition Bill, the Municipal Member for Accra was one of the Committee of Twelve, and he took part in any meeting we convened. And if he took part in these meetings of the Sedition Bill at the time when he knew that the Chiefs represented the people, why today should he say that this levy will cause commotion? . . .

The Municipal Member should not forget that before any of the Chiefs could come here and say anything about their States, it is usual that every State must be consulted by the Head of that State, and we are not here only to say what will suit us, but what will suit our States. Now, could the Municipal Member believe that presently I am representing about six states? If I were to ask him to tell me the views of the

[1] Konor of Yilo Krobo; member of Legislative Council, 1934.

Manya Krobo State on the question of this levy, or the views of the Ada State . . . or the views of the Shai State, or . . . of the Osudoku State on this levy question, he would simply say, 'I do not know what you have decided on this matter': and why should he come and say that this matter will cause commotion all over the country. The Municipal Member has no authority to come and say this at all. . . .

[Leg. Co. Debates, 1936, i., pp. 77–8, 81–2, 88]

486 SPEECH OF MR. A. KORSAH[1] IN LEGISLATIVE COUNCIL 23 MARCH, 1937.

. . . On the question of the employment of Africans in the Government Service, I wish to place on record that we have rather a serious and legitimate complaint, but I must first of all say that it would be foolish for any African to expect that Government would employ every educated member of the community. . . . What we do say is that Government has failed to maintain that progressive programme of African appointments which was approved of by the Secretary of State in the year 1926, and of which His Excellency Sir Gordon Guggisberg spoke to the members of this Council. . . .

According to this programme, the year 1935–6 ought to see 148 Africans holding what we . . . call European appointments. Instead of that number, we have 28 appointments. . . . Well, this is getting rather serious, because we do know that over 1,000 Africans have got to their maximum in the second division. Some of them have been in their maximum for over 10 years. They have qualified for promotion. They have been told that there is nothing against them, but your brother in the first division is not dead or has not retired, and until somebody goes away you have got to remain on the other side. . . .

[1] Kobina Arku Korsah (later Sir); born, 1894; lawyer; member of West African Congress, and Aborigines' Society; member of Legislative Council for Cape Coast, 1928–40; member of Executive Council, 1942.

I . . . believe that the real cause of this delay is the fact that the Service is divided into two main classes — one is the Senior Service, known as 'European appointments,' and the other, the Junior Service, known as 'African appointments.' Every African is bound to join the Junior Service and not the senior, and if you are lucky you may get promotion to the senior. Now what I . . . wish to suggest . . . is that Your Excellency may be pleased to recommend to the Secretary of State, that the time has arrived for that distinction in the Gold Coast Service, based on race or colour, should be abolished, and that the Service be divided into two main branches — the senior and the junior. When an African is qualified to enter into the Senior Service, he should sit . . . the same examination, and pass the same test as a European. . . . I ask that equal opportunities may be given to Africans as well as Europeans in the Service. . . .

[Leg. Co. Debates, 1937, i, pp. 96–8]

487 REPORT OF THE COMMISSION ON THE MARKETING OF WEST AFRICAN COCOA 1938.

. . . Early in November 1937, as a result of Buying Agreements entered into in respect of Gold Coast and Nigerian Cocoa by all but one of the important European firms trading in the two dependencies, a general hold-up of cocoa, accompanied by a boycott of certain European goods, was started by Gold Coast and Ashanti farmers. The hold-up and boycott were so effective as to bring both the export and the internal trade in the Gold Coast practically to a standstill; only small quantities of cocoa were marketed, and imported merchandise accumulated unsold in the firms' stores and in the Customs sheds. In spite of efforts made by Government to effect a compromise, neither the farmers nor the firms appeared to be prepared to withdraw from the position which they had taken up. No serious agitation against the Agreement occurred among producers in Nigeria and the Nigerian crop was marketed as usual; but in the Gold Coast the deadlock continued into the spring of 1938. At the instance of the Governors of the Gold Coast and Nigeria, therefore, your predecessor[1] decided to appoint a Commission to inquire into the situation and at the same time to examine the whole question of the marketing of West African cocoa. . . .

[World consumption of Cocoa]

By far the largest single market for cocoa is in the United States of America. This market has increased in relative importance over the [last 11 years] . . . and took nearly 45 per cent. of total supplies of 1936–37 as compared with 38 per cent. in 1926–7. The United Kingdom has shown a considerable proportional increase as a consumer since the last industrial slump, and Canadian consumption is increasing rapidly: but in the important Continental markets there has recently been a tendency for consumption to fall either absolutely or relatively.

It is clear . . . that the prosperity of the cocoa industry is closely linked with the trend of consumption in the United States, which in turn depends very largely on general business conditions. The business setback which occurred in the United States at the beginning of 1937 had a serious effect on cocoa prices through a slump in demands from manufacturers. . . .

Prices

Two main types of cocoa are recognized on world markets; cocoa known commercially as 'fine', which . . . is the type produced in Ecuador, Venezuela, Trinidad, Ceylon, and the Netherlands East Indies; and that known as 'ordinary' or 'bulk,' which is made up of the coarser 'Forastero' varieties and is the type produced in West Africa, Brazil and San Domingo. . . .

[Returns of] . . . the annual average

[1] Rt. Hon. W. G. A. Ormsby-Gore. The report is addressed to the Rt. Hon. Malcolm MacDonald.

price of Accra cocoa between 1921 and 1931 on the old basis of 'Fair fermented, f.o.b.' . . . [show] that until the great depression, prices were never lower than 30s per cwt. and actually rose as high as 64s per cwt. in 1927. The fall of price which began soon thereafter continued with minor interruptions until December 1933. [The revision of the Basis of Accra quotations to 'Good Fermented, c.i.f. London', in 1931 disguises a further real fall in price of roughly four shillings per cwt.] The improvement up to the end of the 1935–6 season was very gradual but sound. . . . The rapid rise in the first four months of the 1936–7 crop year was however . . . unhealthy. . . . The period was one of booms in all commodity markets . . . and an excessively speculative view of the cocoa market was encouraged by the forecast of a small crop in the Gold Coast. . . . Later forecasts of a heavy, rather than a short crop in the Gold Coast, combined with the general business setback . . . led to a sharp fall in price after January 1937; by the end of June the whole of the earlier advance had been lost. . . .

Organisation of cocoa trade . . .

Thirteen European firms shipped, in 1936–7, approximately 98 per cent. of the cocoa exported. All of these firms, with the exception of the English and Scottish Joint Co-operative Wholesale Society, Limited, whose exports were slightly under 4 per cent. of the total exports, entered into the Buying Agreement. By far the most important shipper is the United Africa Company, Limited, a private Company formed in 1929 by an amalgamation of the Niger Company, the African and Eastern Trading Corporation and a number of other smaller firms, and controlled as to 80 per cent. of its share capital by Messrs. Lever Brothers Limited and Unilever Limited and as to the remainder by the African and Eastern Trading Corporation.

The firms exporting cocoa may be classified into three groups; (i) merchant firms with a business in imported merchandise; (ii) merchant firms with no import business at all; and (iii) manufacturing firms which themselves consume the bulk of the cocoa which they buy on the coast, and do not engage in the merchandise trade. The 13 large European organisations fall into either group (i) or group (iii). In the former group fall, in order of the importance of the cocoa business, the United Africa Company, Limited (which also has by far the most important merchandise business); Messrs. G. B. Ollivant, Limited; the Compagnie Française de l'Afrique Occidentale; the Union Trading Company; Messrs. John Holt and Company (Liverpool) Limited; Messrs. Busi and Stephenson, Limited; the Swiss African Trading Company; the Société Commerciale de L'Ouest Africain; Paterson Zochonis and Company, Limited; and Messrs. W. Bartholomew and Company Limited. In 1936–7 these merchant firms together exported nearly 76 per cent of the total Gold Coast crop.

The manufacturing consumers established in the Gold Coast are Messrs Cadbury Brothers, Limited (who buy in association with Messrs J. S. Fry and Sons, Limited); Messrs J. Lyons and Company, Limited; and the English and Scottish Joint Co-operative Wholesale Society Limited. These manufacturers together exported nearly 22 per cent. of the 1936–7 crop. . . .

Conditions of Production

A survey made in Ashanti some years ago by the Department of Agriculture on farms of 1,250 farmers, showed the average area per farmer to be 2½ acres. The size of farms varied from a fraction of an acre to 27 acres, and 60 per cent. were under one acre. For the cocoa districts as a whole, the number of farms is estimated . . . at 300,000, and the acreage under cocoa at somewhere between 1,250,000 and 1,500,000 acres. With production at the 1936–7 level of about 300,000 tons, the average output per farm would work out at one ton. . . .

'In a typical cocoa village with a popula- 'tion of 1,181 in the Western Akim district 'of the Central Province, 201 families, living 'in 153 separate compounds, produced and 'sold 5,451 loads of 60 lb. each in the crop 'year 1934–5. The number of farmers was '174 males and 180 females, giving a pro- 'duction per head of 924 lb. of cocoa, 'worth, at the then average season price of '7s. 7d. per load, about £5. 16s. . . .'

The original conception of the Gold Coast farmer . . . is of a peasant cultivator who, with his own labour and the help of his family, grows his food and tends an acre or two of cocoa trees. This picture is no longer true of more than a minority of farms, and these of the smallest size. The employment of labour has become a regular feature of cocoa growing, even where the owner resides on his farm. Multiple and absentee ownership has also developed, involving the complete use of hired labour. In actual fact very many so-called farmers neither grow nor market their cocoa.

There is little indigenous labour available for hire in the cocoa districts; and although there are now fairly large settlements of outside labourers in the districts of heavy cocoa production, farmers are dependent mainly on migrant labour which comes in from the Northern Territories, where money crops are inadequate, or from neighbouring French colonies, where money is a necessity to meet direct taxation. There is normally a great annual ebb and flow of such labourers, who tramp down to the cocoa districts from the north for the cocoa season and return by lorry to their homes and families in the food-planting season.

Only the initial labour of clearing the bush and starting a new farm is paid on a piece-work basis. Once a cocoa farm is in bearing, it receives little or no attention during a large part of the year and to that extent the hired labourers responsible for it seem to carry out the somewhat vague duties of retainers and custodians rather than those of employees who are expected to give their whole energies to manual work. Wages for cultivation vary considerably and are usually less in Ashanti than in the Colony. Rates of £6 to £12 together with food and shelter, or a maintenance allowance in lieu, were mentioned to us, but it appears that wages are sometimes based on the price realised for cocoa and may even be paid in cocoa.

Multiple and absentee ownership is now common. The native small capitalist becomes possessed, either directly by purchase of land . . . or indirectly through the widespread custom of pledging farms for monetary loans, of numerous farms, often widely scattered. . . . Absentee proprietors may employ a head labourer and assistants under their own periodic or occasional supervision; more commonly they adopt some system of share-cropping. A usual arrangement is that a relative occupies the farm as tenant or bailiff, hires the necessary labourers, and returns to the owner one-third of the crop or its proceeds. The system known as 'Abusa', by which one-third goes to the landowner, one-third to the farmer, and one-third to the labourers, is apparently traditional, and tribal lands are often farmed on this basis without previous purchase beyond various dues to the Chief. . . .

There is as yet little evidence regarding the maintenance of yield and the duration of the farms. Beyond the periodic cutting of the undergrowth necessary for access, and apart from the collection of the crop, the trees are left to nature. The measures which are standard on a well-conducted plantation — draining, pruning, manuring, and pest control — are unknown. . . .

An industry in the condition just described would seem to be ripe, in fact considerably over-ripe, for agricultural education. . . . We found none. . . . One serious difficulty is obvious. So many farms are left more or less completely in charge of migrant labourers, and so many are in the hands of receivers whose only interest is to gather the crops, that there is nobody, in a large number of cases, permanent enough to receive education or to apply it. . . .

The Agreement and Hold-Up.

It is natural, in view of the many trade understandings which existed on the Gold Coast before the War, that cocoa should have been included within their scope. We have had described to us a cocoa agreement entered into in 1903 by the leading exporters in the Gold Coast, which had certain similarities, including the division of purchases, to the Buying Agreements with which we are concerned. Although the 1903 Agreement was apparently limited to one year, subsequent agreements were made in 1904, 1905 and again for a period of five years in 1906. . . . From 1910 there followed a period of cocoa buying and selling agreements (i.e. agreements including provision for the pooling of sales as well as purchases) which lasted until 1917. After the War, probably owing to the efforts at amalgamation between the two largest concerns, agreements were less common, but a cocoa Agreement of the earlier type was in force between 1925 and 1927; and a cocoa buying and selling Agreement operated during the first three years of the United Africa Company's existence.

We have been told that Gold Coast producers resorted to a hold-up of supplies on several occasions before the war, and we have taken evidence on the attempted hold-up and boycott which occurred in 1930–1. The latter was organised at the start of the 1930–1 crop season, when low prices had succeeded a period of high prices as in 1936–7, by a 'Gold Coast and Ashanti Federation'; but it was not fully effective, especially in Ashanti, and collapsed early in 1931. The Federation was dissolved shortly thereafter. . . .

The cardinal principles of the Buying Agreements [of 1937] were: (i) the division of the total purchases of cocoa by all members and the allocation to each of an agreed proportion, based on past performance; and (ii) the payment . . . of a uniform 'limit' price by all members, based on the world price ruling from time to time, less an agreed amount to cover costs of collecting, handling and shipping cocoa from the Coast to world markets, and a reasonable profit to the firms. . . . In practice . . . the Agreements removed the incentive of competition between the member firms. It is, however, the contention of the parties to them, that the producer was assured the highest possible price for his cocoa by the methods of price-fixing adopted. . . .

We wish to record here . . . the view, that so far as the Gold Coast was concerned, the signatory firms committed an error of judgement in attempting to introduce the Agreement in such haste, particularly in view of the fall in the price of cocoa which had taken place since the end of the previous main buying season. . . .

The great majority of the firms' witnesses expressed the view that the hold-up was not a spontaneous movement of the farmers. They attributed it on the one hand to the activities of the Chiefs, backed or led by influential brokers and 'agitators' and by a hostile Press campaign, and on the other to the Gold Coast Government's failure to perform its duties of giving the people a lead and of suppressing lawlessness. . . . The coincidence of a falling price for cocoa with the introduction of the Agreement was considered by the firms' witnesses to have been a powerful weapon in the hands of the leaders of the hold-up and indeed to have provided the only motive for the farmers' opposition. 'The price and not the Pool was behind all the trouble.' . . . . The firms' witnesses, in alleging that the Chiefs engineered the hold-up suggested that they had two important motives. One was that 'the majority of Chiefs are directly interested in the cocoa trade, many are themselves actual middlemen, many indulge in large-scale loans on the farmers' crops, and conversely, others are heavily in middlemen's debt. Very largely then, their interests are identical with those of the middlemen — i.e. to force up the price of cocoa.' The fall in the price of cocoa which preceded the 1937–8 season threatened considerable losses, the argument runs, to those middlemen who had made

Y

advance purchases of cocoa from farmers on the basis of the previous season's high prices; the Chiefs, therefore, declared the hold-up in the expectation that the price would be forced up thereby.

A second motive suggested by the firms was that the Chiefs seized this opportunity of making a display of their strength in order to dissuade Government from embarking on certain reforms in the political system which are known to be under consideration. One important firm's witness said: 'Although outwardly the present crisis appears to be a commercial dispute, my personal view is that the root cause of all recent trouble is the reinforcing of the power of the Chiefs under the Native Administration Ordinance.' The absence of a comparable movement in Nigeria was attributed, in part at least, to the different political status of the native rulers in that dependency. . . .

The whole problem of the marketing of West Africa cocoa is dominated by the fact that the bulk of the crop has to be bought within a period of approximately three months. About 22 per cent of the Gold Coast crop is bought by consumers . . . the remainder being taken over by merchants. One of the Agreement firms has expressed the view that 'the outstanding service which the merchants have rendered to the producers and the trade as a whole . . . has been their shouldering the risk of spreading over twelve months, to meet consumers' requirements, a crop the marketing of which is compressed into five months.' . . . It was, however, admitted that on occasion the carrying of stocks might prove a profitable policy.

We accept the contention that it would be to the detriment of producers if the whole weight of the crop were forced on to the world markets as soon as it passed into the hands of merchants. We have, in fact, no doubt that the policy of merchants in carrying stocks of unsold cocoa has at certain times been of great value, as they claim, to the industry as a whole. . . .

We are convinced on general grounds,

and our opinion is supported by the weight of evidence, that the Buying Agreements did not confer upon members any power as individual firms to exert an influence over world prices which they had not previously possessed. . . .

Conditions of marketing before the Buying Agreements.

We reached conclusions regarding conditions of cocoa marketing on the West Coast which may be summarised as follows:—

(1) That the trade has not in general been remunerative to the buying firms in recent years;

(2) that this was largely due to intense competition between the firms on the Coast which led

to their offering prices frequently out of parity with current world prices;

to various forms of increases of the remuneration paid to middlemen;

to an increase in the advances made to middlemen and the extension of the period for which they were allowed to remain outstanding (especially in the Gold Coast); and

to the free and even unscrupulous interpretation, largely tolerated by the firms, of certain conventions under which middlemen were entitled to declare purchases whenever a price change was made;

(3) that as a result of these circumstances, the cost of buying cocoa on the Coast and of shipping it to world markets, frequently, and even usually, exceeded the price that would be realised on an immediate sale, so that a conservative marketing policy became impossible; and

(4) that a number of practices and conditions existing in the trade must

be regarded as undesirable, notably:

the sale of badly prepared cocoa by producers, especially in Nigeria;

the fact that producers are not generally paid at different rates for cocoa of different qualities;

the purchase of cocoa in advance of the season by African money lenders and middlemen at fixed prices, allowing a large margin of profit;

the pledging of farms as security and of crops as interest for loans;

the use of false weights and measures by African Buyers;

the issue of large advances to middlemen with cash advanced by the firms, in the form of over-declarations on a rise; and similar speculation by sub-buyers with the advances passed on to them;

the use of expedients such as a temporary and artificial lowering of prices by the firms in order to induce declarations of middlemen's purchases before a genuine rise occurred;

the conditions of strain created for firms' agents and middlemen caused by the rivalry for tonnage, the fear of defaults on advances, and generally the intense competition; and

the danger that the remaining small firms might be unable to stand the pace set by competition and be forced to leave a still larger share of the trade in the hands of two or three firms.

Recommendations. . . .

In all the circumstances, it is our opinion that the Agreements should be finally withdrawn. . . .

It would be preferable, other things being

equal, that a plan of re-organisation should be built and operated on an entirely voluntary basis; but we feel that in the circumstances this is impracticable. We therefore recommend instead, the adoption of the expedient which in recent years has been increasingly used in the United Kingdom, in the Dominions and in foreign countries, namely, the association of the whole body of producers of a commodity within a statutory marketing scheme. . . . The 300,000 cocoa farmers of the Gold Coast certainly stand in no less need of organisation. . . . The hold-up has proved the existence of remarkable capacities among the mass of farmers for joint action, and among their leaders for organisation. . . .

Democratic methods of organisation and procedure . . . would certainly be inappropriate in the Gold Coast, where the ballot-box is not a commonplace of public life; and we do not envisage that either the question of initiating a scheme or matters involved in its operation should be put to the general vote of producers. We have nevertheless recognised that public support is necessary in recommending that African leaders be invited to assist in the drafting of a scheme, and in . . . providing for African representation in central and local bodies. . . . It is evident that the collaboration of the chiefs must be secured. . . .

We attach great importance to our recommendation that Africans should be employed wherever possible. . . . It is even more important in the interests of the farmers, however, that efficiency should be maintained. In making appointments the requirements of business should not be outweighed by racial interests and sympathies, and when suitable African candidates did not present themselves, Europeans should be appointed.

[Cmd. 5845, pp. 1, 7–10, 17–22, 49–51, 65–6, 129–30, 135, 147–8, 151, 158, 162, 165–6. Para. 515 outlines the sort of scheme proposed]

BOOK XIII

THE ADVANCE TO INDEPENDENCE, 1940–1957

39　The Second World War, 1939–1945

THE first World War had seen the first important constitutional advances on the Gold Coast; it had ended with the National Congress demanding fully representative government.   The second World War inevitably was a time of even more searching proposals; and while the future of the country was the theme of several discussion groups and Youth Conferences, official policy was also undergoing notable changes.

Considerations of Welfare were assuming increasing importance; and hard upon the Inquiry into Cocoa marketing, from which stemmed the later Cocoa Marketing Board, came inquiries into the conditions under which industrial labour was recruited and employed.   The Orde Browne Report (488) was the fountain head of a rapidly growing corpus of social and industrial legislation.

In 1941 it was still possible for a Governor to contemplate the then existing Gold Coast Constitution with something more than complacency (489): but from the time of the introduction of unofficials into the Executive Council by Sir Alan Burns (490), expectation of far reaching constitutional changes quickened. As always, the question of direct taxation — finally carried by Sir Alan in 1943 (491), was linked, in the minds of the Gold Coast intelligentsia, with representative government, and they were further stimulated by discussion of the freedoms then being announced to the world in the Atlantic Charter (492).   Although the Governor was at pains to make clear that he could give no pledge, Income Tax was accepted by the African Members of the Legislative Council in the belief that it in fact presaged a substantial measure of elective representative government (494).

Towards the end of 1944, after measures had been passed for the reform of native administration (495) and municipal self-government, the Governor was able to announce the main features of the proposed new constitution.   For the first time, Ashanti was to be included with the Colony in the Legislative Council, which was to have a majority of elected unofficial members (496).   It was a logical corollary of these political proposals that a Committee of Educationists appointed by the Imperial Government recommended the establishment in the Gold Coast of a University College (497).

---

488 LABOUR CONDITIONS IN WEST AFRICA
REPORT BY MAJOR G. ST. J. ORDE BROWNE,[1]
O.B.E.

. . . Originally mainly agricultural, the mineral resources of the country have proved increasingly valuable during recent years.   By far the most important crop is cocoa, which in 1926 was estimated to have produced over eleven million pounds for the agricultural community.   The value of the crop fluctuated violently, falling in

[1] Labour Adviser to the Colonial Office since 1938.

1933 to approximately two and three-quarter million pounds; the figure continues to be erratic. . . .

The opening up of the various mines has thus introduced a valuable alternative to agriculture; payment to Government by the mines for royalties and services amounted in the year 1938–39 to £779,309, salaries to Europeans £671,868, and wages to Africans £1,180,940. . . .

There is accordingly a satisfactor balance between peasant-farming and wage-earning; the mine employees are almost

661

all land-holders in their own homes and alternate between the two forms of occupation. There is also a small proportion of the labour working under the peculiar system known as 'tributing.' . . .

Food

The greater part of the Gold Coast affords a considerable variety of foodstuffs and actual hunger must be comparatively rare. . . . The diet is varied but distinctly lacking in animal protein, the latter being supplied by fish and the occasional consumption of domestic animals. Generally, therefore, the Gold Coast native may be regarded as fairly well nourished for life in his own village, but insufficiently so for hard work such as mining. No rationing exists among the mines, the employees buying their own food, with the implication that the best use is not always made of the money expended. This system is well established and it would be difficult to change over to the ration system, desirable though this might be. . . .

As in other parts of West Africa, the situation might be materially improved by greater exploitation of the available fish supply. At present this trade is in the hands of fishermen and petty traders working on a very small scale. Organisation, possibly on co-operative lines, should do much to improve the product and increase the range of supply. . . .

Housing

Housing on the mines has greatly improved during recent years, and the most recent accomodation may be considered quite satisfactory. . . . There is, however, an evil legacy from the past in the shape of old villages which came into existence many years ago, often under the auspices of companies now defunct. Where these villages are on land under the control of the mine management, the problem is . . . comparatively simple. . . . Far greater difficulties exist in the case of the 'mushroom village' which usually

springs up in the neighbourhood of labour lines, but outside the mining area. . . . A community soon springs up, the composition of which varies from comparatively respectable petty traders, down to gamblers, prostitutes, drug-sellers and criminals. Houses are naturally badly built and maintained, no regular lay-out is followed and sanitary arrangements are non-existent. The whole community is a parasitic one of evil influence, while the material conditions constitute a sort of rural slum. . . .

In all the principal towns there is, of course, the inevitable legacy from a heedless past; in the older towns, substantial buildings frequently present a serious obstacle to any clearance scheme. Overcrowding exists in varying degrees and proper supervision is difficult; rents are usually unduly high. In Kumasi considerable progress has been made with a rebuilding scheme. . . . In Accra the progress of slum clearance and rebuilding was greatly accelerated by the earthquake in 1939, which destroyed or rendered unsafe a large part of the town. . . .

Migrant Labour

Labour for the various employment centres is largely migrant, the bulk of it coming from the Northern Territories, Nigeria, or the French colonies. The reasons governing this movement are the general shortage of money and the seasonal scarcity of food in the north. Fairly definite labour routes seem to be followed, though the detailed information necessary to determine their exact course has yet to be collected. . . . Kumasi forms an important centre through which the principal routes run. Since there is no recruiting and no contract, the men have to make their own way and pay their own expenses on the journey; no medical inspection is carried out and no facilities for repatriation exist. The travellers support themselves on the journey by providing themselves with a little food with which to start out, and by carrying fowls and other local products to trade on the road: beyond this they have to depend upon casual employment and the conspicuous hospitality of the country people. A journey of four or five hundred miles in such conditions is naturally a severe ordeal and a large proportion, therefore, arrive at their destination, worn out and emaciated. . . .

The hardships entailed present a difficult problem; some appreciable help can be given, however, by the establishment of rest-camps. . . . Nine camps of varying types are already in existence, and nine more . . . are approved for the year 1940–41. . . . The accomodation should be provided free, first-aid remedies should be available, and dressers should be maintained at the more important camps. Consideration should also be given to the supply of the ordinary native food at cheap rates, with arrangements for a free issue in the case of destitutes. All such arrangements will require both money and organisation. The revenue drawn from the mines by Government should admit of the former, and the recently created Labour Department should provide for the latter.

. . . The recruitment of labour is at present carried out in a haphazard manner by messengers working without official authorisation. This naturally leads to many irregularities, both labourers and employers being unscrupulously deceived and cheated; there have also been instances of exploitation of the capitation fee by a recruiter, who has arranged for the labourers to leave work as soon as he has received payment. If organised recruiting proves to be really required, it certainly needs regulation. . . . Generally the rules might be modelled on those in force in Tanganyika Territory. . . . The introduction of such methods would be a novelty in West Africa, but it would constitute a great advance upon the existing situation, where the travelling labourer suffers great hardships, possibly even dying of starvation by the roadside, while constantly running risk of being deceived and exploited by unscrupulous touts. . . .

Conditions in the Mines . . .

Dealing first with gold, this industry may be divided into (a) producing companies, numbering some 15, thirteen of which are producing from lode mines and two from alluvial operations; (b) properties in course of development, at present seven in all; (c) alluvial mines, of which there are four, two of these being engaged in dredging operations; and (d) prospecting companies, of which there are eighteen for lodes and three for alluvial. Of the foregoing enterprises, several are different forms of activity on the part of the same company. The circumstances of these properties vary considerably; some of the earlier ones have passed through various vicissitudes, including bankrupt and derelict periods. Others have only recently been developed and have, therefore, no inheritance of old-established villages, etc. to embarrass the lay-out of their properties. Their financial situation again differs widely; certain mines are of proved value with a considerable life before them; others have a more precarious existence, depending largely upon the maintenance of the present high price of gold and the satisfactory demonstration of a considerable body of paying ground. While, therefore, certain companies are quite in a position to provide ample accomodation and amenities for their work-people, others can hardly be expected to attain the same standard on account of their limited resources and the unknown life expectancy of the mine.

The producing mines have as a whole made considerable strides during the last few years. . . . In the cases of some of the newer properties, certain difficulties arise owing to the fact that the exact distribution of the metal is not yet sufficiently established to admit of decision as to the sites for labour lines. . . .

Working conditions on the mines are as a whole satisfactory; numerous shafts of several hundreds of feet exist and the underground workings are extensive. . . .

Lighting and ventilation are carefully considered, sanitation receives proper attention, and first-aid stations are maintained at the principal stations. Wages were as a whole adequate, although they varied considerably. In the majority of cases they were from 50 to 100 per cent. above the total cost of living for the locality. Skilled labourers are able to earn good wages and in many instances prove to have been in the same employment for a considerable number of years. . . .

Developing mines are in a somewhat different position . . . since they are mostly still experimental in their arrangements. . . . The alluvial type of mining is apt to be unsatisfactory, regarded from the point of view of labour conditions. Considerable doubt usually exists as to the whereabouts and value of the deposits, and work in any particular spot may continue for a few weeks or many months. Expenditure on accomodation, sanitation, etc., is, therefore, usually grudged and the labour is to be found housed in makeshift huts; these may be admissible when new, but with continued occupation they rapidly become most objectionable. . . .

The Gold Coast ranks as one of the largest producers of diamonds in the world, the value being nearly £600,000 annually. The nature of the work is agreeable, operations all being conducted within a few feet of the surface without the use of shafts; at the same time it is somewhat arduous, consisting of the continuous digging out of the diamondiferous earth. I visited the principal mine and found conditions there distinctly good. . . . The sole point on which improvement seemed desirable was the food supply. . . . The normal diet cannot be considered adequate for a man employed in hard work. Rations are not supplied and would almost certainly prove unpopular. . . .

The Gold Coast produces large quantities of manganese ore, the value being £681,188 for 1938–39, as compared with £1,166,175 for the previous year. Only one company is operating. . . . A feature

of the mine is the division of the labour into Company's employees, working chiefly in connection with the machinery, and the contractors' employees, engaged in the simple manual work of lifting the overburden; of these the latter form about one-third of the total number employed. Their position has in the past been unsatisfactory since the Company did not recognise their claims under the voluntary workmen's compensation scheme. . . . Under the terms of the Workmen's Compensation Bill now before Council the ultimate responsibility will be placed upon the Company. . . .

Trade Unionism

Trade unionism is still in its infancy in the Gold Coast. An Ordinance to regularise its position is now before Council and has every prospect of becoming law at an early date; this provides protection against torts and legalises peaceful picketing.

Certain embryo trade unions already exist in the shape of the Ashanti Motor Transport Union, the Gold Coast Railway African Workers' Union, and the African Civil Servants' Association; other small groups are still in process of formation. . . . An interesting alternative to these modern methods of organisation exists in the shape of informal groups of workers under tribal leaders; the unsophisticated tribesman finds great difficulty in expressing himself through an alien leader, so a headman from his own people makes an acceptable mouthpiece. . . . This system . . . is of course inapplicable to the detribalised worker from the south of the country. . . .

Labour Legislation

. . . in the Gold Coast may be regarded as satisfactory and up to date when certain measures now under consideration have become law. . . . The main body of legislation dealing with labour consists of the Master and Servant Ordinance (Cap.

70 of the Laws), as amended by Ordinance No. 19 of 1940. . . .

[Cmd. 6277, pp. 87–93, 96–9, 101–3]

489 GOVERNOR SIR ARNOLD HODSON'S SPEECH IN LEGISLATIVE COUNCIL
27 FEBRUARY, 1941.

. . . Certain Colonies have stated that it is their policy, in the course of time, to give *all* European posts to Africans. This is not my policy, and I am quite convinced that it is not the wish of the Africans themselves. After all, Africans are very fair . . . and I feel certain they realize the immense debt of gratitude they owe to Europeans for the work they have done, and are doing, in the Gold Coast, and they also realize that without the Imperial Government, they would not be able to retain the independence of the Gold Coast against foreign Powers who covet its riches. . . . Again I feel sure you will agree with me that the Service is infinitely stronger with Europeans serving in it, than without them. . . . My view is the same as that expressed by the Honourable and Municipal Member for Cape Coast [G. E. Moore], namely, that Europeans and Africans should hold the senior posts on a fifty-fifty basis. This has always been my policy. . . . It will have to come gradually and by degrees, and no good can come by trying to force the pace. . . .

Another delicate point I should like to touch on, is how this country should be governed in the future. It is a fashion, I am sorry to say, in certain quarters, to criticize the present form of Government, but I maintain . . . that ninety-nine per cent of the inhabitants of the Gold Coast are perfectly satisfied with the Government in its present form. The views of the one per cent who want a change are being continually aired in the Press and elsewhere, whereas the ninety-nine per cent. contented people do not air their views. The result is that people in England who read our newspapers are apt to get a wrong impression. . . .

Let us examine, for a moment, our present Legislative Council. It is true we have an official majority, but that, in my opinion, is absolute necessary in a country like the Gold Coast which does not consist of one people but several distinct races, speaking different languages, and with their own customs. It is a mistake . . . when certain people state that the unofficial members have absolutely no authority and are like sheep in a pen. Nothing can be farther from the truth. The unofficial members have a very real authority and their wishes are in most cases carried out. . . . Any member of the community can always air his views through one of the unofficial members, so that Government is well informed of public opinion. I should not have the slightest objection to increasing the unofficial members of the Legislative Council, but it appears to me quite unnecessary for the reasons I have given above, and the larger the assembly the longer it takes to transact business.

The Opposition in the Mother of all Parliaments in London is infinitely worse off than the unofficial members out here. Their views are not treated with the sympathy that your views are, and their speeches . . . have no effect on the passing of a Bill. One thing I must make quite clear is that I do not look upon the unofficial members here as the Opposition, but rather as part and parcel of the Government. . . .

Time and tide stand for no man, and I am aware that in years to come our constitution is bound to change. People never know when they are well off. You may then have election campaigns and party factions, and politicians seeking election for their own advancement, and not really for the good of their country. When that time comes, look back on the present, and, I feel certain, you will say in your heart that the change has not been for the best, and you will pine for the peace and security of our present form of Government. . . .

[Leg. Co. Debates, 1941, i, pp. 116–17]

490 GOVERNOR SIR ALAN BURNS,[1] SPEECH
IN LEGISLATIVE COUNCIL
29 SEPTEMBER, 1942.

. . . There is an announcement I have to
make to you. As you are aware, the
Royal Instructions regulating the constitution of the Executive Council provide
that the Council should consist of certain
official members and such other persons as
may from time to time be appointed by
His Majesty's Instructions or appointed
by the Governor in pursuance of instructions received from the Secretary of State
for the Colonies. The Executive Council
at the present time consists of certain
official members who are my special advisers on all matters of administration.

The Secretary of State for the Colonies
has now approved my recommendation
that the Executive Council should be
strengthened by the addition of two unofficial members. The unofficial members
who will serve on the Executive Council
will do so in their personal capacity and
not as representing any race or any
interest, but will be gentlemen in whose
character and ability I can have confidence
and on whom I can rely as my personal
advisers. I have received instructions
from His Majesty the King, through the
Secretary of State for the Colonies, to
appoint the following gentlemen to be
members of the Executive Council, for a
term of three years: the Honourable Nana
Sir Ofori Atta, K.B.E., and Mr. K. A.
Korsah, O.B.E. . . .

This is not a budget session of Council,
and I do not want to weary you with a long
address, but there is one other matter which
I feel I should refer to today, the first
opportunity I have had to speak to the
Legislative Council since my arrival in the
Colony. As a newcomer to this country
I have been struck . . . by the large
number of interminable stool disputes

[1] Sir Alan Cuthbert Burns; born, 1887; served
in West Indies, 1905–12 and 1924–8; in Nigeria,
1912–24 and 1928–34; Governor of British
Honduras, 1934–40; Governor of the Gold
Coast, 1941–7; U.K. representative on the
Trusteeship Council, 1947–56.

which disturb the peaceful life of the community. From inquiries I have made I
learn that within the last ten years no less
than 22 Paramount Chiefs have been destooled, in addition to 22 others who have
abdicated in that period — in most cases to
forestall de-stoolment; that seven stools of
Paramount Chiefs are now vacant, and
that in many States no Paramount Chief
has succeeded in maintaining his place
on the stool for more than a very short
time. In the case of subordinate chiefs, I
understand that the position is as bad or
worse, and since my arrival in the Colony,
rioting has occurred in small villages in
stool disputes. Now I want to make it
quite clear that such disorders will not be
permitted and will be put down with a
strong hand. It is intolerable that the
peaceful life of the community should be
disturbed by irresponsible minorities or
by a few irreconcilables who will agree to
no reasonable solution of any problem,
however trifling. . . .

[Leg. Co. Debates, 1942, ii, pp. 2–4]

491 SPEECH OF GOVERNOR, SIR ALAN
BURNS, IN LEGISLATIVE COUNCIL
23 FEBRUARY, 1943.

. . . I have now been able to visit all of
the Districts throughout the Colony,
Ashanti, the Northern Territories and
Togoland. . . . My brief visits have . . .
enabled me to form an impression of the
country as a whole and to realise more
clearly some of the more pressing problems.

I am convinced that there is an urgent
need for the development of our educational and medical services, and of social
services generally.

I am fortunately in possession of a
valuable report made by the Education
Committee appointed by my predecessor, a
report with which I am in general agreement. Steps have already been taken to
implement many of the suggestions contained in the report, and although progress
must inevitably be delayed by war conditions, I am determined to push on as

fast as possible with the educational development which I consider so essential.

I am equally concerned with the inadequacy of hospital accommodation and health measures in the Gold Coast. . . . I am making certain recommendations to the Secretary of State on medical and health matters, which I consider absolutely essential, and I trust that funds will be forthcoming to implement these recommendations.

I am also recommending to the Secretary of State that a temporary Water Supply Department should be set up to press on with the provision of water supplies in the Northern Territories, on the Accra plains, and in other parts of the country. This is an urgent matter which even the war should not be allowed to hold up.

I am also considering a scheme for rehousing. . . .

I am considering what steps can be taken to improve, after the war, the economic condition of the Gold Coast, and I am in correspondence with the Secretary of State for the Colonies on this subject. Apart from major questions which need examination, it appears to me that there are numerous small industries which could be developed to the benefit of this country.

In the Estimates for the coming financial year of 1943–44, we have budgeted for a revenue of £3,707,710 and an expenditure of £4,042,126, a deficit of £334,416. This deficit is caused partly by the reduction in the amount of export duty on gold, which is inevitable in view of the closing down of some of the gold mines, and by increased expenditure which is unavoidable, owing to rising costs, if we are to continue the policy of maintaining our social services, as far as possible at pre-war level. It would be a tragedy indeed if we had to reduce the standard of these services. I shall not be satisfied until that standard has been considerably improved.

But we must face the fact that we are budgeting for a deficit, and although our existing reserves permit us to do so for a time, this cannot continue indefinitely. The only possible alternative to the cutting down of expenditure, which can only be effected by an undesirable reduction in public services, is additional revenue from taxation.

It has been decided that income-tax must be imposed in the Gold Coast, and a bill for this purpose will be introduced into Legislative Council at its next session. As you are aware, the people of Great Britain are paying to-day an income-tax of no less than 10s. in the pound, and no large units of the British Empire, except the Gold Coast and Sierra Leone, are free from this form of taxation. It has been paid for some years in Nigeria and in the Gambia, and it has now been decided that the Gold Coast and Sierra Leone must follow suit. . . .

I do not suppose that income-tax will be popular in the Gold Coast; it is unpopular everywhere. But it is one of the inevitable results of civilisation, which demands that the richer people should pay more towards the cost of Government than their poorer brethren. . . .

The rates proposed for income tax in the Gold Coast are, moreover, extremely moderate. . . . In the first place there is a personal deduction of £150 which everyone gets the benefit of; then there is an extra deduction for a married man of £200; a deduction of £25 in respect of each of the first three children below a certain age; and a deduction in respect of any insurance premiums that are paid. . . . The rates of tax will, of course, be higher on the higher incomes. Thus on the first £200 of chargeable income the rate of tax is . . . only 3d. in the pound. On the next £200, it is 6d in the pound. On the next £200 it is 9d. in the pound. On the next £200, it is 1s. in the pound. On the next £400 it is 2s. in the pound. On the next £800 it is 3s. in the pound, and so on. . . . So much for the individual. But there is a very important matter that I have left to the last. At the present time, none of the companies operating in this country pays any income-tax at all to the Gold Coast Treasury in respect of its profits (except for the tax of 5 per cent. imposed under the Concessions Ordinance on the profits of mining companies who are holders of concessions). All the tax most of the companies pay goes to the Imperial Treasury, although the profit is made in respect of their business in the Gold Coast. Under the proposed new law, all such companies, mining companies or trading companies, or any other kind of company, will pay income-tax to the Gold Coast Government of 5s. in every pound of its profits. This involves a loss to the Imperial Treasury of an equivalent amount, but it is a loss which the British Government willingly accepts. And the loss of the British Government in this case will be the gain of the Gold Coast, which will obtain from this source additional revenue with which to carry out those improvements on which I am so anxious to make a start. . . .[1]

[Leg. Co. Debates, 1943, i, pp. 5–8]

492 Speech of Mr. G. E. Moore[2] in Legislative Council

3 March, 1943.

. . . Your Excellency, at a meeting of this Council last year, Your Excellency spoke strongly about stool disputes and destoolments of Chiefs. These are still going on, and will continue to go on because we have not applied the remedy to the cause. I some time ago in this Council placed the cause of these stool disputes at the door of the Political Officers. I have not changed my mind. If the Political Officers will cease to interfere in the election or destoolment of chiefs, which is after all the internal affair of the State Councils, and quite within their competence, we will hear very little of these disputes. . . . I beg

to refer in this instance to the case of Winneba, where, I am told, there is now a complete deadlock. I am of opinion that in that matter, the Governor was wrongly advised to interfere at the time he did, when he referred the case to the Provincial Council. . . . What I would respectfully but strongly emphasize is that Government should in every case respect the unanimous or majority decision of the State Council. . . . From time immemorial, in all our States, matters affecting our rulers or otherwise have been and are decided by the unanimous or majority vote, and Government will be well advised to govern accordingly by this rule which is practised in all democratic and civilised states.

There is a widespread demand for a better constitution for this country, a constitution that would give the natives of this country an effective voice in the administration of their country. Last year Your Excellency went a step forward by your recommendation which resulted in the appointment of two Africans to the Executive Council . . . but there is still the need and room for more . . . improvements. In short, we want a constitution liberally conceived, a constitution by which Africans in the Executive Council would be the representatives of the people. . . .

Whilst on this it may not be out of place to state that rumour is current that Africans or member countries of the Empire outside Europe and the Dominions have no share in the good things provided for in the Atlantic Charter. In this connection I beg to refer to a column in the *Church Times* . . . under date December 4 1942 and headed JUSTICE FOR THE AFRICAN:— . . . 'Mr. Churchill, in a statement quoted in full appears to have limited the scope of the Charter to "nations of Europe now under the Nazi yoke"; whereas President Roosevelt has affirmed that it "applies not only to the parts of the world that border the Atlantic, but to the whole world." The American committee feels that Mr.

---

[1] The Income Tax Ordinance received its third reading on 20 August, 1943.
[2] Municipal Member of Legislative Council for Cape Coast, 1941.

Churchill's view of the matter is not representative of the British people in general. . . . If the "aggrandisement, territorial or other", of the United Nations, and "territorial changes that do not accord with the freely expressed wishes of the people concerned" are wrong in Europe, they are equally wrong in Africa. If it is "the right of all peoples to choose the form of government under which they live," it is a right which the Africans share, and the trustee Powers are bound to do everything possible both to fit them to exercise it and to give them the opportunity of doing so. . . .' I am sure, Sir, that you will agree with me that it will be a great relief to us if Government would make a statement as to where we stand regarding the Atlantic Charter.

A wave of relief ran through our hearts when, on Tuesday the 23rd February, 1943, Your Excellency made the announcement . . . that the Native Administration Ordinance had become unsuited to the needs of the country, and that a draft Native Authority Ordinance, which it is proposed will replace [it] . . . is under consideration. The Native Administration Ordinance was, from the time of its promulgation in 1927, found by the reflective among us to be unsuitable and almost the whole country rose against it. With the exception of the present session, there has not been a meeting or session of the Council at which amendments . . . have not been made and passed. . . .

Whilst on the question of the need for a better constitution for the country, you will agree with me that it is equally important and necessary that the Town Councils Ordinance which has outlived its day, should be replaced with a better Ordinance which will give the ratepayers who contribute the funds of the Councils, control over their own affairs. I dwelt fully upon . . . this very important question . . . at the last Estimates Session of this Council. . . . Instead of Government giving a sympathetic attention to this, the only reply was the scathing speech of the

Honourable Attorney-General [in which he described] . . . Cape Coast as 'the focus of non-co-operation in the Gold Coast.' . . .

I say, Sir, that Cape Coast is not the focus of non-co-operation in the Gold Coast. Cape Coast, the state that first came into contact with British influence, diplomacy and civilization, and played not a little part in the introduction of these into the other states of this country, is conscious of her responsibilities. Cape Coast has a sacred trust, a responsibility to see that the rights of the people of this country are conceded to them and are protected from foreign interference and encroachment. Cape Coast knows that the lowest and humblest subject of the King has rights and Cape Coast expects, and considers it her duty to see that the rights of the inhabitants of this country are respected by all. . . .

Nevertheless, it is the belief of the people of Cape Coast that their desire for a more suitable municipal constitution . . . is under consideration . . . and that belief is further strengthened by Your Excellency's gracious act in offering to provide for the inhabitants of Kumasi a new Municipal Constitution, which as seen in the draft, is second to none in West Africa, and far in advance of what is in force in the Gold Coast proper, with its decades of municipal experience in advance of Ashanti. . . .
[Leg. Co. Debates, 1943, i, pp. 135–8, 152–3][1]

493 SPEECH OF NANA SIR OFORI ATTA IN LEGISLATIVE COUNCIL 4 MARCH, 1943.

. . . One of the great aims of the Native Administration Ordinance was to check the numerous attempts on the part of sub-chiefs to break away from their superior or Paramount Chiefs. That was becoming too frequent, and it constituted a very great problem, a very real danger. . . .

[1] Accra Town Council Ordinance (No. 26 of 1943) reformed that municipality with an elected majority, and the Cape Coast Town Council Ordinance (No. 18 of 1944) did the same for that town. Cf. Wight, op. cit., 51–2.

There is nothing more ruinous to a state. . . . If the Native Administration Ordinance has succeeded in checking these evils, which would have hastened the collapse of Native Administration, I think it can be said that it has served a good purpose. . . . So if anybody is annoyed with us, it is only because we have attempted by the Native Administration Ordinance to secure the solidarity of the States.

Can it properly be said that it is the Native Administration Ordinance which has caused trouble — Stool disputes — in the Ga State as well as in the other Adangme States? I entirely disagree. We have in this Council a member representing the Ga–Adangme States. We have also in the Provincial Council representatives of the Ga and Adangme States, and I can tell you that there has not been a single occasion when the Ga–Adangme Member has complained in this Council that the Native Administration Ordinance is responsible for trouble in any of the said states. A few months ago the matter of an alleged deposition of a Manche of one Adangme State was enquired into by the Provincial Council. After exhaustive inquiry we found that the custom of deposition did not exist in this particular state, and yet by misconstruing the provisions of the Native Administration Ordinance they had applied and forced upon themselves this custom, which I say did not exist in that State, and we had to tell them so. . . .

The Honourable the Municipal Member for Cape Coast . . . started by saying that Your Excellency was wrong in referring the Winneba Stool dispute to the Provincial Council. . . . I should ask those people, the so-called guardians of native customs, if they are sincere, to agree with me that whenever it was thought possible and necessary that in the interest of the country there should be a development of native constitution or custom, we should not falter about it. But to say that the old and ancient customs which had been found to be incompatible with the present state of affairs should remain without any change could only mean one thing. All that such people would want to do then is to render us impotent, and to make it impossible for us to march with the times, so that they can override us and put us under their feet. I submit, Sir, that the Provincial Council system is a development of native constitution . . . and it has come to stay. . . .

What is the position of the State Council before whom the accused Paramount Chief is to appear to take his trial? The members are the very people who have framed charges against him. . . . The poor Paramount Chief . . . goes before his accusers who are backed by the Asafo. . . . If the Honourable Member wants us all to enjoy the benefits of the administration of justice, then he must agree that no one should be a judge of his own case. Should a Chief be denied justice just because he is a Chief? And even then, Sir, in our native institutions, it is not a wholly mischievous thing for a matter in which a Chief is involved to be referred to an impartial body — a body which has no knowledge of the proceedings in the first instance. I invite the Honourable Member to examine the procedure with regard to the deposition of a Divisional Chief. The charges are framed and served by his elders, but they do not try him. He is rather to appear before the State Council composed of his Paramount Chief and the other Divisional Chiefs of the State . . . and there will be an impartial decision. And if it is admitted, Sir, that the Provincial Council is a development of our native institutions, as I have just said, then I think it must also be admitted that it is the only body — an impartial body — which is competent to hear a case against a Paramount Chief at the instance of the State Council. I am therefore submitting, Sir, that it was right for Your Excellency to have referred the Winneba dispute to the Provincial Council. . . . If the State Council of Winneba knew they had a good case against the Paramount Chief, what was their fear for having to appear before the Provincial Council? The mere fact that they refused to go made it plain that they could not support the case which they thought they had. They had not complied with custom in their act. It would be a very bad thing for a chief to be treated unjustly, simply because a body like a State Council, meeting, apparently under the influence of some ill-disposed person or persons — so desired it. . . . I submit, Sir, that if Your Excellency had not acted in the Winneba affair as you have done, you would have capitulated to mob violence — mob rule. . . .

It has been said that the Native Administration Ordinance is responsible for the increase in de-stoolments of Chiefs. In the Honourable the Secretary for Native Affairs' reply yesterday, he told us that the number of de-stoolments from 1928 to date is, I think, 42 in the case of Paramount Chiefs. We have on record a statement by the Acting Secretary for Native Affairs in March, 1924 to the effect that from the 1st January, 1910 to the 24th March, 1924 . . . the number of destoolments was 94. . . . Has not the Native Administration Ordinance rather something to its credit? I also suggest, Sir, that too much has been said about the nature of these stool disputes. . . . I am certain that if the clique I have been told about cease to be active and the insidious propaganda against the Chiefs ceased, there will be peace.

I should like to assure Your Excellency that the Provincial Councils have an open mind altogether on the matter of replacing the Native Administration Ordinance either by a Courts Ordinance or by a Native Authority Ordinance. . . . Provided there is nothing which is in direct conflict with some of the fundamental principles of the native constitution, we will co-operate with Your Excellency in bringing up any measure which in the judgement of the Government will help to smoothen the administration of this country. . . .

[Leg. Co. Debates, 1943, i, pp. 171–6]

494 DEBATE IN LEGISLATIVE COUNCIL ON THE 2ND READING OF THE INCOME TAX BILL 18 AUGUST, 1943.

Nana Tsibu Darku IX:[1] . . .

In view of the universal demand in the country for the immediate alteration of the present constitution, and in view of the proposals of the Joint Provincial Council of Chiefs, will Your Excellency give us the lead in the matter as to what is the attitude of Government in the matter of the demand for changes in the constitution. Whether the final decision is to rest with the Secretary of State or not, there can be no doubt that the views of the Government in this, as in other matters, will weigh considerably with the Colonial Office, and an assurance by Your Excellency on the subject will afford great relief to the whole country, and in particular to the African Unofficial Members of this Council.

Governor:

I can give this assurance to the Honourable Member, that the representations of the Joint Provincial Council of Chiefs were transmitted promptly to the Secretary of State, and I have myself communicated to the Secretary of State my views on the Constitution of the Colony. It is, however, clearly impossible for me to tell the Council what I have said in a confidential document. . . . I am quite certain that, as the Secretary of State will be here next month, he will not come to any decision on the matter until he has seen the place for himself. I am afraid I cannot give any assurance on the lines requested, but I can assure you that constitutional questions have been and are receiving attention, and I would invite Honourable Members' attention to the fact that two days ago I assented to a bill which is now an Ordinance, creating a Town Council for Kumasi. You all know the terms of that bill. This morning we have passed a bill which I shall shortly assent to, creating a Town Council

[1] Omanhene of Asin Atandasu, and Provincial Member for the Central Province in Legislative Council since 1932.

of Accra, and it is no secret that proposals are now being considered for creating Town Councils in other towns.

Both these bills . . . provide for a very marked advance in municipal government. I can say nothing more than that, but I will remind Honourable Members that these bills have been brought forward by Government not in response to any explicit demand by the people concerned, but spontaneously by the Government during the last few months. They are not in fulfilment of any bargain and are not connected in any way with income tax or with any other kind of tax. . . .

[An amendment to postpone the reading of the bill until after the visit of the Secretary of State was defeated without a division.]

Nana Tsibu Darku IX. . . .

In the opinion of my Council the following points stood out clearly for discussion:

(a) Is the bill before this House necessary in view of our social and economic position?

(b) Is it equitable for the rich classes of the community to contribute now to the social and economic development of the country?

(c) Whether it is right for the mining and commercial companies to pay any portion of their profits to the coffers of this Colony?

(d) Is it not a fact that the country as a whole and the Press, our local 'Fourth Estate' in particular had advocated and championed the cause of this measure? [All answered in the affirmative. . . .]

(e) Administrative duties of the States. [A plea for subsidies for Native Administrations.]

(f) Representation on this Council. . . .

We want a more effective representation on this Council to control the distribution of the increased revenue, that is, we must have an effective guarantee that the revenue will not be spent on things we do not approve of. It is true that Your Excellency has given us an idea of what the increased revenue is required for, but this is not enough. 'No taxation without representation.' Income tax is different from an indirect tax. There is a large section of the people who are still unaware they are paying any taxes at all. An Income Tax is an admission that the citizens are responsible factors in the government of the land, and if this is so then we deserve to have a more effective representation. African members of this Council have not used their position in the Council merely for the sake of opposing. They have, if tributes paid to them from time to time are to be taken into account, shown their ability to co-operate in the higher councils of Government.

With the assurance which Your Excellency gave us this morning, we trust your recommendation would receive the favourable consideration of His Majesty's Government and that at no distant date this country would hear from Z.O.Y. that glad tidings of His Gracious Majesty's Assent to a new Constitution based on [an] unofficial majority, for the Gold Coast. . . .

Mr. Blay [Municipal Member for Sekondi]:[1]

Your Excellency, I think . . . I must follow my Honourable Friend the Provincial Member for the Western Province,[2] and say at once that I came to Accra with a mandate to oppose in the most strenuous manner the passing of this bill. I came armed with a resolution to that effect. . . . But this morning when Your Excellency . . . gave us that promise, or shall I rather call it an inkling of what was in Government's mind, I have on my own responsibility . . . modified my attitude, and that is the sole reason why I do not support the amendment that this bill be postponed. Having modified my attitude

[1] Member of Legislative Council, 1940–4.
[2] Nana Blay VI, Omanhene of Eastern Nzima, who with R. S. Blay abstained from voting.

to that extent, Your Excellency, I submit that if the demands of the people as regards constitutional reforms are not granted, it would be a breach of faith, and it would put some of us in a very awkward position with our constituencies. . . . We have seen in that sessional paper that was read to us yesterday, that certain schemes are afoot, but what guarantees have we that when, perhaps, Your Excellency has left this country . . . these schemes will be carried out. We have had many abortive schemes in this country, and we put it down to the system of government prevailing here. . . . There is no continuity of policy in this country. Under our present system of Government the bill will be passed anyway, even if all the Unofficial Members of the Council oppose it. But when it is passed, we hope that by the time it is being operated properly and revenue is coming in, the Government of this country will be so constituted as to give the people of this country a more effective representation in this Council.

Governor:

I hope the Honourable Member does not assume that I have given any pledge with regard to a change in the Constitution. . . .

Mr. Blay:

Your Excellency, I am not saying that you have given a pledge, but . . . having regard to Your Excellency's reference to the constitution that has been given to Kumasi and Accra, I think one can safely read between the lines, and I have thought it proper not to carry out my mandate. . . .
[*Ibid.* Two members opposed the 2nd reading and two did not vote.]

495 THE NATIVE COURTS (COLONY) ORDINANCE, 1944   No. 22 OF 1944.

An ordinance to make better provision for the administration of justice in Native Courts.

This ordinance may be cited as the Native Courts (Colony) Ordinance 1944; and it shall apply to the Colony but shall not apply to the Southern Section of Togoland under British Mandate. . . .

3. The Governor in Council may by order provide for the constitution of Native Courts which shall exercise jurisdiction in accordance with this ordinance within such area as may be defined in the order and may by the same or a subsequent order authorise a Native Court to sit as a Native Appeal Court. . . .

4.–9. Personnel of Native Courts. . . .

10.[–12]. Persons subject to the jurisdiction of Native Courts. . . .

13. (1). Every Native Court shall have full jurisdiction and power to the extent set forth in the order of the Governor in Council establishing it and, subject to the provisions of this ordinance, in all civil and criminal causes in which the parties are persons subject to the jurisdiction of Native Courts.

(2) . . . there shall be four grades of Native Courts. . . .

14. (1) All land causes shall be tried and determined by a Native Court having jurisdiction over the area in which the land which is the subject matter of the dispute is situated.

(2) All criminal causes shall be tried and determined by a Native Court having jurisdiction over the area in which the offence is committed.

(3) All civil causes other than land causes shall be tried and determined by a Native Court having jurisdiction over the area in which the defendant was at the time the cause of action arose.

15. Subject to the provisions of this Ordinance a Native Court shall administer

(a) the native customary law prevailing within the jurisdiction of the Native Court so far as it is not repugnant to natural justice, equity and good conscience nor incompatible either directly or by necessary implication to any ordinance for the time being in force:

Provided that in regard to criminal offences by virtue of Native customary law the Native Court shall take cognisance only of those offences set out in the first column of the First Schedule to this Ordinance and no Native Court shall impose in respect of such offences penalties heavier than such Court is, according to its grade, authorised to impose by virtue of the relevant provisions of the First Schedule;

(b) the provisions of any law binding between parties subject to the jurisdiction of Native Courts . . . [unless they agree to be regulated according to English law]

(c) the provisions of any Ordinances which such Native Court is by or under such Ordinances authorised to administer;

(d) the provisions of any Ordinance which a Native Court may be authorised to enforce. . . .

(e) the provisions of any orders or rules in force by virtue of the Native Authority (Colony) Ordinance, 1944.

16. Governor in Council may empower Native Courts to administer provisions of any ordinance. . . .

17. Pending causes and matters.

18. [–21] Officers of Native Courts. . . .

22. [–27] Proceedings in Native Courts. . . .

28. [–42] Ancillary Powers of Native Courts. . . .

43. Indemnity of members and officers of the Native Council. . . .

44. No fees or fines in excess of those authorised to be exacted. . . .

45. Corruption illegal and punishable. . . .

46. [–53] Appeals. . . .

54. [–58] Transfers. . . .

59. [–66] Control of Native Courts. . . .

67. [–71] Miscellaneous. . . .

496 SIR ALAN BURNS, SPEECH IN LEGISLATIVE COUNCIL   4 OCTOBER, 1944.

. . . I am authorised by the Secretary of State to inform you that he has given careful consideration to the amended requests put forward by the delegates representing the Colony and Ashanti at the recent conference at Government House, on the subject of the proposed changes in the Constitution.

The Secretary of State is prepared to agree in principle to seven out of the nine requests made, that is to say, he will agree:—

1. That representatives of Ashanti, elected by the Ashanti Confederacy Council, and a Municipal Member for Kumasi, elected by ballot, should be included in the Legislative Council.

2. That the Provincial Members for the Colony should be elected by the Joint Provincial Council, and that the Municipal Members for Accra, Cape Coast and Sekondi–Takoradi should be elected by ballot.

3. That the Legislative Council should consist of:—

   i. The Governor, as President;

   ii. Six Official Members, namely the Colonial Secretary; three Chief Commissioners; the Attorney-General; and the Financial Secretary;

   iii. Nine Provincial Members for the Colony; of whom five should be drawn from the Eastern Province and four from the Western Province.

   iv. Four Members for Ashanti;

   v. Five Municipal Members, namely two for Accra, and one each for Cape Coast, Sekondi–Takoradi, and Kumasi;

   vi. Six Nominated Members to be appointed by the Governor.

4. That the President of the Council and the Extraordinary Members should not be entitled to vote.

5. That the Governor should have

'reserve powers' which would permit him to over-ride a decision of the Legislative Council in the interests of public order, public faith or good government (which expressions, without prejudice to their generality, include the responsibility of the Gold Coast as a component part of the British Empire, and all matters pertaining to the appointment, salary, and other conditions of service of public officers); any such action by the Governor would be subject to revocation by the Secretary of State, except in the case of a bill which would be subject to disallowance by His Majesty.

6. That the post of Secretary for Native Affairs should be abolished and that there should be appointed a Chief Commissioner for the Colony with headquarters at Cape Coast;

7. That the present Central Province should be divided between the Eastern and Western Provinces, leaving only two Provinces instead of three in the Colony.

The Secretary of State feels unable to fetter in any way the discretion of the Governor to choose his unofficial advisers and therefore regrets that he cannot agree to the request that at least two members of the Executive Council should be appointed from among the elected members of the Legislative Council. While, however, he is unable to agree to this as a matter of right, the Secretary of State is willing to approve of my recommendation that a second elected member of the Legislative Council should in fact be appointed to the Executive Council when the new Constitution comes into being.

The Secretary of State further regrets that he is unable to agree to the request that there should be a Standing Committee of the Legislative Council for periodical consultation and discussion of measures of policy, as such a Committee would tend to ursurp the function of the Joint Provincial Council and the Ashanti Confederacy Council, as well as those of the Executive Council and the Finance Committee of the Legislative Council.

The Secretary of State will advise His Majesty to grant a revised Constitution to the Gold Coast on the lines indicated in this statement and the necessary instruments will be prepared as soon as possible.

[Leg. Co. Debates, 1944, ii, pp. 85–6]

497 REPORT ON HIGHER EDUCATION IN WEST AFRICA   JUNE, 1945.

. . . .

47. We recommend that there should now be set up a university college in Nigeria, and a university college in the Gold Coast, and that certain re-organisations and new developments of higher education should be carried through in Sierra Leone, in close connection with Fourah Bay College. The university college in Nigeria should include faculties of arts and science and the professional schools of medicine, agriculture, forestry and animal health, as well as a teacher training course. The university college in the Gold Coast should include faculties of arts and science, and an institute of education, which would provide for research in education and for teacher training courses. The university college in Sierra Leone should include courses in arts and science up to the intermediate level and a teacher training course. With this, we hope, would be associated an arts degree course intended mainly for theological students, financed by the Church Missionary Society who are the present authorities of the college. . . .

48. . . . We review the main points which have weighed with us in coming to this conclusion, namely, that advance in each major colony is necessary, as against the argument that effort should be concentrated wholly on the creation of a single central institution.

49. In the first place we must have regard to the great populations in question, and the diversity and isolation from each other of the territories. British West Africa with 27 million people comprises

nearly half the population of the colonial empire. It does not form a 'region' such as the West Indies with three million inhabitants, though these admittedly differ widely in language and race. The British West African colonies are themselves an empire. . . .

51. For advances in general education, and in particular the general education of the majority of those who are to lead in the improvement of the educational system which is so urgently required, work proceeding up to the degree levels in their own country, evoking the interest from both students and community which such work inspires, and attracting and retaining the staff who can maintain the inspiration, seems to us altogether to outweigh the advantages which would be gained by concentration. The general need of these populations cannot be met wholly by one centre of higher education even for a short time.

52. For certain professional, research, and technical schools the balance of arguments is, for the present, in favour of concentration.

53. There are also questions of general policy which cannot be ignored. We do not have before us a blank sheet. The two colleges of Achimota and Yaba were each planned and launched with the intention, publicly proclaimed in each case by the Governor at the time, that they would proceed towards university levels. . . .

54. Fourah Bay, Yaba and Achimota colleges are regarded by African opinion as symbols of future progress. Any steps taken to halt development for a generation or more, would rouse the deepest feelings, and evoke grave misgivings as to good faith, in any territory concerned. These factors, though imponderable, have to be taken seriously into account. African support, African enthusiasm, is an indispensable need if higher education in Africa is to surmount the difficulties which inevitably lie before it. It is a universal experience that local patriotism is one of the strongest factors in evoking such support. . . .

55. There is, however, the important point, on which we have had many discussions, that of 'regionalism' or 'How best can a West African outlook, such as we all desire, be achieved, which will take into account the common factors and common problems of the whole "region" of British West Africa?' The belief that educational progress in one territory was being held back to promote the success of a regional plan, might well prejudice the chance of whole-hearted support for any particular project of centralised education or research. Only if each community believes that as and when it shows itself capable of further progress, such progress will be permitted and indeed fostered, will it be possible to obtain cordial agreement upon the numerous institutions, such as the Medical School, the Education Institute, or the various researches which for reasons of staff and finance, it will be necessary, for some time, to limit in each case to a single colony.

56. The financial arrangements by which one colony would help to build up a complete university in another colony, which would eventually pass from a general West African institution into a university for that colony alone, would be complex in the extreme, and the minds of those responsible for education in the other colonies would inevitably keep looking forward to the time when they could end their contribution to the central institution, and begin to build up one of their own. A fruitful source of disagreement rather than of unity, would thus be ready to hand.

57. The lesser difficulties might be got over; but the main arguments remain. The influence of a university college outside its walls is strong, but in the nature of things it cannot reach for hundreds or for thousands of miles. . . . Institutions reaching towards university level have come into existence in each of the three colonies, not in pursuance of any abstract plan, but arising out of the facts of the case. To discourage two of the existing organisations, and, at a later date, to encourage

them again, is a proposal which might well defeat the purposes which it is designed to achieve. . . .

58. Two questions must be answered. First, are there sufficient West African students of the required quality to make a vigorous development feasible now or in the near future? Second, is it possible to find the staffs, buildings, and finance which will be required? We believe the answer to each of these questions is 'Yes.' . . .

60. . . . In fact it may well be that the secondary schools will be turning out a body of young men and women capable of taking advantage of university training in West Africa, and eager to do so, before some of the proposed institutions, even at the most rapid pace of development, are ready to receive them. . . .

68. Finance. — We consider that the expenditure involved in our proposals should be financed from the revenue of the West African Governments and from the Colonial Development and Welfare Fund. The extension of facilities for higher education is an essential part of the plans for the development of British West Africa. This is recognised both by the West African Governments and by the Secretary of State for the Colonies. It is appropriate therefore that at first the greater share of this expenditure should be out of the grant of £120,000,000 which has recently been voted by Parliament under the Colonial Development and Welfare Act. In making our proposals we have borne in mind that there are many other urgent claims on the Colonial Development and Welfare Fund from West Africa and elsewhere, that this sum is designed to serve the whole Colonial Empire. It should however be remembered that the 27 million inhabitants of West Africa comprise nearly half of that Empire.

69. The West African Governments should in our opinion, bear part of the cost of these proposals from the start; their share should increase steadily until they ultimately bear the whole burden on their own shoulders. . . .

90. It is our opinion that the Gold Coast at the present moment affords the best opportunities for the development of higher work in arts and education. Not only have arts courses been satisfactorily developed at Achimota up to the Intermediate level, but we believe that the constructive and co-operative attitude there towards social problems which has been due in no small measure to the Gold Coast Government's strong support for the development of this college, provides the favourable basis for the further development of humane studies. (It is largely owing to this spirit, which is particularly evident in the whole field of education in the Gold Coast, that we later recommend the establishment there of an institute of education to serve the whole of West Africa.) . . .

In making our recommendations for the development of university education in British West Africa we are fully conscious of the ambitious nature of the programme we have set out. We are aware that what we have proposed may to some appear incompatible with the somewhat slender foundation of primary and secondary education upon which it is necessary to build. We are, however, firmly convinced that no considerable advance in the social, economic and political development of the four dependencies is possible without the setting up of the institutions of higher learning we have proposed. A major advance in the general educational level is a pre-requisite to advances in all other directions, and little progress is possible in the lower ranges of education without a simultaneous and rapid development in these at the top. . . .

Walter E. Elliot (Chairman), J. R. Dickinson, J. F. Duff, B. Mouat Jones, K. A. Korsah, I. O. Ransome Kuti, Eveline C. Martin, E. H. Taylor Cummings, A. E. Trueman.

[a. Extract from the Minority Report.]

Our colleagues . . . propose the establishment of three separate university colleges of varying degrees of comprehensiveness.

Our proposals are on the contrary founded on the belief that the development of higher education will be best promoted by the formation of a comprehensive unitary University College for the whole of British West Africa together with a Territorial College in each of the three larger dependencies. We [hold] . . . the view that the proposal of our colleagues to create three university colleges will defer for a considerable time the provision of the type of university education which we would wish to see established as soon as possible. In our opinion, their proposals do not pay sufficient attention to the question of the number of students likely to be available, nor to the difficulty of making the necessary provision of staff, equipment and finance; they involve a diffusion of effort and resources when all the circumstances suggest to us the urgent need of concentration, if realisation is not to be indefinitely postponed; they make what we regard as a provision for quantity when we would prefer one of higher quality, more soundly based. Lastly, we believe that there is danger that such proposals will lead to a wrong emphasis in educational development which may prove detrimental to the social and economic needs of the territories. . . .

The present conditions both of secondary education and of life in West Africa . . . mean that pupils leave the schools with a general education which is far too limited for them to begin true university study. . . . This state of affairs is inevitable and it will persist until the secondary schools are able to undertake sixth form teaching as it is understood in Great Britain. . . . The present deficiencies of schooling must therefore be met by the colleges to which the students proceed on completion of the school certificate, and two years are devoted to the intermediate course which in Great Britain occupies one year. . . .

If a university is to come into being within any reasonable period of time, it is not the extent of the area to be served nor indeed the size of its population which must be considered. It is the capacity of the area to supply an adequate flow of students able to pursue successfully degree courses within the period normally allotted to these courses in universities in Great Britain. . . . [One estimate at Achimota put the annual intake of those fitted for degree work at 60 from the start.]

In our view, the urgent needs and desires of West Africa can be met only by the creation of . . . a new West African Institution, serving all the dependencies. A West African University College of this type, provided with all the material facilities necessary for a full range of studies from the start and concerned only with students of proven capacity, would succeed in attracting staff of the university experience and quality to be desired. These three factors — adequate material facilities, capable students and a staff of quality — which are all within the range of achievement in the next few years, would provide great impetus to its development both in teaching and research. . . .

We also recommend that the Gold Coast, Nigeria and Sierra Leone . . . should each possess what we shall describe as a Territorial College. . . . Each Territorial College would provide courses up to the intermediate level for potential entrants to the West African University College, for those who wished to prepare for more advanced technical and other vocational training, or to fit themselves to hold posts of greater responsibility than would otherwise be open to them. Each would become a vigorous centre for training teachers for secondary and primary schools and social welfare workers. Each would act as the centre from which extra-mural activities and extension work in the broadest sense would be conducted. In a word, each Territorial College would make itself the growing point of education in its colony. . . .

Any university education can only succeed in its educational purpose if it is comprehensive in scope. . . . Our visit to West Africa left us deeply impressed with the intense need for the development of studies in arts and sciences to the same level *side by side*. While we recognise the same desirability of providing in West Africa degree facilities in arts and science as soon as possible, we would nevertheless regard some delay in their provision as preferable to their divorce from one another.

Such developments at Achimota and Ibadan as are suggested by the majority might lead eventually to a federal type of university organisation. . . . Little if any support can be found for the federal conception among university opinion in Great Britain. In our view, it would be unfortunate if the experiences of Great Britain in this matter were repeated in West Africa. . . .

We consider that the majority proposal that degree facilities in arts and sciences should be duplicated at Achimota and Ibadan will greatly hinder the development of research activities in both these and allied fields of study. . . .

In our view, the establishment of three college centres of restricted scope, struggling at this stage to develop to university status, and providing in each colony, at an unjustifiably high public cost, courses for small numbers of students, is not the wisest use which can be made of the money available for education in general, nor is it in the best interests of the social progress of the West African peoples. . . .

H. J. Channon, Geoffrey Evans, Julian S. Huxley, A. Creech Jones, Margaret Read.   [Cmd. 6655 of June 1945]

40   From Burns to Coussey, 1946–1950

THE new constitutional proposals were implemented in the summer of 1946. Sir Alan Burns, who stayed in the Gold Coast long enough to preside at the inauguration of a constitution with the making of which he had had so much to do, rightly stressed its 'advanced' character (498). It went well beyond what the Gold Coast leaders had demanded — much less expected, ten years before. But within two years it was to be described as 'outmoded at birth'. The following year Dr. Danquah founded his United Gold Coast Convention (U.G.C.C.) to agitate for full self-government, and at the end of 1947 the post war *malaise* culminated in rioting in Accra and other towns and a clash between police and ex-servicemen at the approaches to Christiansborg Castle. A Commission of Inquiry was appointed to investigate these matters, and its report was almost more startling than the events it described. It recommended a measure of responsible government, i.e. a substantial share in the executive administration for the African, and it disregarded, almost completely, the chiefs and traditional institutions, as having no part to play in a self-governing Gold Coast (499).

Views so much at variance with those of Clifford, Guggisberg and Burns were not allowed to pass unchallenged by the British Government (500) or even on the coast, but they so far prevailed that an all-African committee under the chairmanship of Mr. Justice (later Sir Henley) Coussey, was appointed, which was to make recommendations for a new constitution. Regional jealousies began to appear, now that the time for crucial decision was at hand (501): but the Coussey Committee was unanimous in its main recommendations for a mainly African executive, to be responsible to a legislature elected by universal suffrage, through a process of indirect election (503). With some reservations, particularly on the responsibility of the executive council (505), the British Government accepted the proposals and a new constitution based on them was drawn up, to come into force in 1951. These proposals in turn were accepted by a majority of the Legislative Council as a reasonable instalment of responsible government (506).

Extremist criticisms were not lacking even in the Council, while outside, first of all in the towns, but increasingly over the country as a whole, Gold Coast opinion was being revolutionised by a new leader and a new party. The underlying philosophy of Kwame Nkrumah and his Convention People's Party (C.P.P.) was vaguely 'socialist' where earlier movements had been conventionally 'liberal': but where these had demanded more adequate representation for the 'intelligentsia', the C.P.P. demanded a root and branch destruction of 'imperialism' and set to work to indoctrinate and organise a mass following in the country as a whole. It was the first truly popular political movement in the Gold Coast. Condemning the 'half-baked' proposals of the Coussey Committee, in January 1950 it launched a campaign of 'Positive Action' (502) to achieve its goal of 'Self Government Now' (or, occasionally, 'Dominion Status Now'). The immediate result was more disorder (507) leading to the arrest and imprisonment of the C.P.P. leaders.

498 ADDRESS OF THE GOVERNOR (SIR A. C. M. BURNS) TO LEGISLATIVE COUNCIL 23 JULY, 1946.

. . . [This] is the first time in the Gold Coast, and indeed, in tropical Africa, that a Legislative Council has included a majority of elected members. It is also a historical event of some significance, inasmuch as for the first time, representatives of the Colony and of Ashanti sit together in Council, while the presence of the Chief Commissioner of the Northern Territories foreshadows future unofficial representation of these territories.

This is a very considerable political advance, and it affords an opportunity for the Gold Coast people to prove to the world that they have deserved the confidence placed in them, and are fitted to make still further steps forward on the road of democracy.

They have now the chance to prove that they are fitted for responsibility, and it is the need for a proper sense of responsibility that I wish to emphasise. . . . Power can be used in an irresponsible way . . . for the benefit of a few, for personal advertisement, for the satisfaction of private or national prejudices, and with little regard for the welfare of the majority. . . . It is not the person who talks most who does the most useful work. . . . But power used with a sense of responsibility for the welfare of the people as a whole, and with due regard to the future, evokes a feeling of respect and confidence. It is important that this Legislative Council should do all that it can to win that respect and confidence, not only from the people in this country, but from those in other lands who are watching us, for — make no mistake about it — we are being watched. And our fitness for further political advance will be judged to a great extent by the use to which you put the powers that have now been given you.

I hope there will be no misunderstanding as to the origin of this Constitution. It is not a constitution that I have invented, or that has been imposed upon us by anyone in England. It is a constitution granted to the Gold Coast Colony and Ashanti by His Majesty the King at the request of the people of the Gold Coast made through their representatives.

You will recollect that when Colonel Oliver Stanley, at that time Secretary of State for the Colonies, visited the Gold Coast in September, 1943, a Memorial was presented to him on behalf of the Colony and Ashanti, praying for certain changes in the Constitution. He was unable to agree to all the changes proposed, but I was authorised at a later date to discuss the matter further with those who had put forward the original Memorial.

I therefore invited representatives of the Joint Provincial Council and the Municipal Members of the Legislative Council, as representing the Colony, and representatives of the Ashanti Confederacy Council, to meet me in Accra, and, at meetings held in my office in July and August, 1944, the matter was very fully discussed. I was able finally to recommend to the Secretary of State for the Colonies, agreed proposals for a new Constitution, which, in its essentials, is the Constitution we have now received. It is not therefore MY Constitution, but I am glad to think of it as OUR Constitution, which we have worked out together and agreed upon. . . .

One of the proposals of your representatives with which I could not agree was that the Constitution should provide that two of the elected members of the Legislative Council should be nominated to the Governor's Executive Council. While I could not agree to this as a right, I have no personal objection, without committing my successors in office in any way, to selecting as members of my Executive Council, two of the elected members . . . and I gave such an assurance to your representatives. . . . I have gone beyond the assurance I gave by the appointment of three instead of two elected members.[1]

. . . It is perhaps desirable that I

[1] C. W. Tachie-Menson (Municipal Member for Sekondi); Dr. I. B. Asafu-Adjaye (2nd Ashanti M.L.C.); Nana Tsibu Darku (Prov. Member for Western Province).

should speak to you about the reserve powers of the Governor. . . . In this connection I would remind you that the Secretary of State acts, as regards the Colonies, on behalf of His Majesty's Government in the United Kingdom, which is itself responsible to the British Parliament, and this Parliament is the body responsible, in the last resort, for all the Colonies which have not yet attained the status of full self-government. . . . I should be happy indeed if I never have to call up my reserves, and I can give you now a promise that these reserve powers will not be lightly used. . . . Where we cannot agree I shall always be willing to give you full credit for holding an honest opinion in the matter. I hope that there will be reciprocity in this matter and that in return you will credit me with an honest conviction. If I use my reserve powers, it will only be because I feel that I cannot conscientiously do otherwise if I am to carry out my duties as Governor, as I have sworn to carry them out without fear or favour. . . .

I hope there will be no thought among unofficial members of your becoming a permanent Parliamentary opposition. That is not your function. There is no more certain way of making the Constitution a failure than by taking up an attitude of uncompromising opposition to all Government measures. It is easy for you, with your overwhelming majority, to defeat every proposal put forward by the Government, but such an attitude, which would drive the Governor to use his reserve powers, would most certainly kill any chance of a successful working of the Constitution, and equally surely kill any hope of further political advance. . . .

[Leg. Co. Debates, 1946, ii, pp. 5–9]

499 REPORT OF THE COMMISSION OF ENQUIRY INTO DISTURBANCES IN THE GOLD COAST   1948.

. . . In the main, the underlying causes may be divided into three broad cate-gories: political, economic and social. There is often no clear dividing line between them and they are frequently interrelated. . . . The remedy for the distrust and suspicion with which the African views the European, and which is to-day poisoning life in the Gold Coast, demands an attack on all three causes. None of them may be said to take precedence. . . . These may be summarised as follows:—

A. Political.

(1) The large number of African soldiers returning from service with the Forces, where they had lived under different and better conditions, made for a general communicable state of unrest. Such Africans by reason of their contacts with other peoples, including Europeans, had developed a political and national consciousness. The fact that they were disappointed with conditions on their return, either from specious promises made before demobilisation or a general expectancy of a golden age for heroes, made them the natural focal point for any general movement against authority.

(2) A feeling of political frustration among the educated Africans who saw no prospect of ever experiencing political power under existing conditions and who regarded the 1946 Constitution as mere window-dressing designed to cover, but not to advance their natural aspirations.

(3) A failure of the Government to realise that, with the spread of liberal ideas, increasing literacy and a closer contact with political developments in other parts of the world, the star of rule through the Chiefs was on the wane. The achievement of self-government in India, Burma and Ceylon had not passed unnoticed on the Gold Coast.

(4) A universal feeling that Africanisation was merely a promise and not a driving force in Government policy, coupled with the suspicion that education had been slowed up, and directed

in such a way as to impede Africanisation.

(5) A general suspicion of Government measures and intentions re-inforced by a hostile press and heightened by the general failure of the Administration in the field of Public Relations.

(6) Increasing resentment at the growing concentration of certain trades in the hands of foreigners, particularly at the increase in the number of Syrian merchants.

B. Economic.

(1) The announcement of the Government that it would remain neutral in the dispute which had arisen between the traders and the people of the Gold Coast over high prices of imported goods and which led to the organised boycott of January–February, 1948.

(2) The continuance of war-time control of imports, and the shortage and high prices of consumer goods which were widely attributed to the machinations of European importers.

(3) The alleged unfair allocation and distribution of goods in short supply, by the importing firms.

(4) The Government's acceptance of the scientists' finding that the only cure for Swollen Shoot disease of cocoa was to cut out diseased trees, and their adoption of that policy, combined with allegations of improper methods of carrying it out.

(5) The degree of control in the Cocoa Marketing Board, which limited the powers of the farmers' representatives to control the vast reserves which are accumulating under the Board's policy.

(6) The feeling that the Government had not formulated any plans for the future of industry and agriculture, and that, indeed, it was lukewarm about any development apart from production for export.

C. Social.

(1) The alleged slow development of educational facilities in spite of a growing demand, and the almost complete failure to provide any technical or vocational training.

(2) The shortage of housing, particularly in the towns, and the low standards of houses for Africans as compared with those provided for Europeans.

(3) The fear of wholesale alienation of tribal lands leaving a landless peasantry.

(4) Inadequacy of the legal powers of Government necessary to deal with speeches designed to arouse disorder and violence. . . .

In putting forward many of our proposals, particularly those dealing with political reform, we are conscious of certain risks brought to our notice by Africans as well as Europeans.

It would be idle to ignore the existence of bribery and corruption in many walks of life in the Gold Coast, admitted to us by every responsible African to whom we addressed the question. That it may spread as further responsibility devolves upon the African is a possibility which cannot be denied. No nation can rise to greatness upon any such foundations. It is a challenge, therefore, to the Gold Coast Africans to set their house in order and a challenge which we believe will be taken up under the weight of responsibility. In any event, in our view its existence cannot be accepted as a barrier on the road to self-government.

Again, in discussion with many Africans, we found a marked disinclination to face realities. A tendency existed to take refuge in ill-founded optimism that things would come right in the end, or that someone would find the answers. This was exemplified in their attitude towards Swollen Shoot, a belief that Government funds were inexhaustible, and a blithe disregard of the complexities of modern economic organisation and the like. The hard truth that every penny of Government expenditure comes out of the tax-payer's pocket, has nowhere penetrated public understanding.

Save among the older population, there is an unconfessed desire for Europeanisation, at least in many aspects. We say, unconfessed, because, while undoubtedly growing, it is not yet strong enough openly to cast off the shackles of tribalism. But the hands of the clock cannot be put back. The movement is gathering momentum, even if cloaked at times by anti-racial expressions. We doubt if it is sufficiently realised what problems these changes entail. Native authority in its widest sense is diminishing. The old religions are being undermined by modern conceptions. Earlier disciplines are weakening. Others must be devised to take their place. . . .

So far as the economic life of the country is concerned, we were struck by the high costs of production ruling in the Gold Coast. Many of the commodities, both industrial and agricultural, the export of which it is hoped to develop in the future, would be too costly to compete in world markets. It is essential, therefore, if the commercial aspirations of the people are to be realised, that productivity be increased. . . . Upon such increase depends the means to pay for all social services and for the creation of a higher standard of life. . . .

We are satisfied that in the conditions existing today in the Gold Coast, a substantial measure of constitutional reform is necessary to meet the legitimate aspirations of the indigenous population. The fact that . . . the Colony, Ashanti and the Northern Territories present, in some aspects, different problems, by reason of the varying stages of cultural, political and economic development at which each has arrived, does not in our view provide a valid excuse for delay. . . .

In so far as our proposals are acceptable, we recommend them as the basis of constitutional reform for a probationary period of ten years. At the end of that period the whole matter should be re-viewed in the light of the experience gained. We do not believe that an atmosphere of stability would be created by any shorter period of trial.

The new Constitution, ushered in with such promise in 1946, was no doubt well intentioned. Its weakness, in our view, lay in its conception. It was obviously conceived in the light of pre-war conditions. . . . In [the post-war] background, the 1946 Constitution was outmoded at birth. . . .

The concession of an African elected majority in the Legislature, in the absence of any real political power, provided no outlet for a people eagerly emerging into political consciousness. On the other hand, it provided an effective stimulant for intelligent discontent. The real and effective political government remained in the hands of the Executive Council. Composed of ex officio and nominated members, it was the instrument of power. The Legislature was largely a Chamber of Debate.

The 1946 Constitution did nothing to decentralise the machinery of government. Government continued to concern itself with the details of pre-eminently local affairs. The District Commissioner still controlled matters of local concern. Africans, thus, even at lower levels, were still deprived of the school of political experience to be found in local management.

Only in Native Administration, residing largely in a hierarchy of vested interests, jealously guarded by Chiefs and Elders, was the African provided with an approach to political expression. Even where an enlightened Native Administration admitted some fresh entrants into the fold of the State Council, it was conceded as a great privilege and not conferred as an elementary right.

We have no doubt that this policy of rule through the Chiefs possessed many advantages. But . . . great questioning has everywhere arisen, particularly among the classes with little or no say in affairs. . . . We have found an intense suspicion that the Chiefs are being used by the Government as an instrument for the delay if not the suppression of the political aspirations of the people. The fact that destooling — once the absolute privilege of a dissatisfied people . . . has been made the subject of a well-defined code, under the supervision of Government, is itself the object of grave suspicion. The view is advanced that so long as the Chief accepts and supports the Government policy he will receive Government support, however much he has become the object of dislike to his people. That there is no evidence to support this view, is beside the point. . . . Nothing impressed us so much as the volume of evidence we received, not alone from the more forward sections of the community, of the intense objection to Chiefs being elected to and sitting in the Legislative Council. We were constantly reminded that the place of the Chief was among his people. Apart from this, we found great difficulty in getting any universal agreement on the precise place to be occupied by the Chief in any new political system. . . .

While for ourselves we are unable to envisage the growth of commercialisation in the Gold Coast, with the retention of native institutions, save in a form which is a pale historical reflection of the past, we do not think we are called upon to make any immediate recommendation for the solution of a matter upon which Africans themselves are not in agreement. Our sole concern is to see that in any new constitutional development there is such modification as will prevent existing institutions standing in the way of general political aspirations. . . .

The moral justification for Britain remaining in the Gold Coast lies in this: out of a population of approximately four and a half million Africans . . . barely ten per cent. is literate. We have no reason to suppose that power in the hands of a small literate minority would not tend to exploit the illiterate majority in accordance with the universal pattern of what has happened elsewhere in the past throughout the world. His Majesty's Government therefore, has a moral duty to remain until

(a) the literate population has by experience reached a stage when selfish exploitation is no longer the dominant motive of political power, or

(b) the bulk of the population has advanced to such a stage of literacy and political experience as will enable it to protect itself from gross exploitation;

(c) some corresponding degree of cultural, political and economic achievement has been attained by all three areas, now part of the Gold Coast.

Pending the happening of these events, two matters in our view call for immediate attention:

(i) The Constitution and Government of the country must be so reshaped as to give every African of ability, an opportunity to help to govern the country, so as not only to gain political experience, but also to experience political power. We are firmly of opinion that anything less than this will only stimulate national unrest. Government through advisory committees, as a measure of reform, in our view would be quite unacceptable.

(ii) A forward policy of Africanisation must take place in the public services, so that in all appointments or promotions, having laid down the standards of qualifications, the first question to be asked is 'Is there an African capable of filling the appointment?' . . .

[Their constitutional recommendations include:

Local authorities in which provision is made for an elected element; regional councils for the Colony, Ashanti and the Northern Territories, with executive powers for, e.g. Health, Education, Housing, local communications and social services;

members to be elected by the local and town councils; an extension of town councils.

A House of Assembly of 45 elected ($\frac{1}{3}$ from each region) members and 5 nominated, as well as *ex officio* members, chosen for four years (unless dissolved earlier on advice of the Board of Ministers). A Board of nine ministers, 5 being African members of the Assembly and four *ex officio*; nominated by the Governor and approved by resolution of assembly; African ministers removable on a $\frac{3}{4}$ vote of censure.]

[Colonial No. 231, pp. 7–9, 24–6]

500 STATEMENT BY HIS MAJESTY'S GOVERNMENT ON THE REPORT OF THE COMMISSION OF ENQUIRY INTO DISTURBANCES IN THE GOLD COAST   1948

. . . It is an axiom of British Colonial policy that progress, whether political, social or economic, and whether in local affairs or at the centre of government, can be soundly achieved only on two conditions: first that it rests on the foundations of tradition and social usage which already exist, and second that changes and developments carry with them the substantial acceptance of the people. . . . A European system cannot be imposed arbitrarily on an African society; readiness to give must be matched by willingness to receive.

If some of the Commission's recommendations appear to involve radical changes of system, it is not to be implied that they have not themselves recognised the inevitability of advance by stages. Nevertheless the manner of presentation of some of their proposals may lead to misunderstanding, in that it may appear that they advocate plans which conflict with the conditions of progress laid down above. The Commission's proposals for land reform, for example, and their suggestions for fiscal arrangements as between regional and local authorities, take rather less than adequate account of the obstacles of present opinion and usage.

Again, their comments on Chiefs do substantially less than justice to the strength of the tradition and custom which a large part of the country still regards as essential to an ordered society.

A further comment on the manner of presentation of the Report is that from the extent and range of its recommendations, it may be inferred that the Gold Coast Government have, in their past actions and present plans, shown tardiness in meeting popular demand for progress. The Commission were naturally met by repeated representations from the more advanced sections of the community which is eager to accelerate the pace of political development, and have properly recorded and given weight to these representations. His Majesty's Government think it necessary . . . to emphasize that in many cases, the recommendations are in line with the course of policy which the Gold Coast administration is already pursuing. . . . The proposals to which His Majesty's Government are now announcing their willingness to agree, are not the fruits of an outbreak of disorder, but a further advance which had to a large extent already been envisaged. . . .

His Majesty's Government . . . cannot accept the criticisms of the 1946 constitution. . . . This constitution was framed in consultation with the representatives of the people of the Gold Coast; it was accepted with enthusiasm by the press and public . . . and it has been in force for two years only. His Majesty's Government have received no demands from the Gold Coast, during this period, for further constitutional reform. The Gold Coast was the first territory in West Africa to be granted an unofficial majority on its Legislative Council; this was a notable . . . and a necessary step forward. . . .

Since 1942, Africans have taken part in the formation of policy through their membership of the Executive Council. Under the existing constitution, the unofficial majority on the Legislative Council has been in a position to exercise an important influence over policy, and in the particular sphere of finance the Standing Finance Committee of the Council has shown itself willing and able to undertake effective control. The type of constitution which combines an unofficial majority on the Legislative Council with an official executive government is an essential stage in the political evolution of Colonial Territories. The very fact that it makes the business of government dependent on agreement between the executive and the legislature, is in itself an advantage; and though the system may not be perfect, it has worked well in other parts of the British Commonwealth. . . .

His Majesty's Government . . . feel it necessary to state that, while they attach the greatest importance to modernising the Native Authorities and making them fully representative of the people, they regard the Chiefs as having an essential part to play. In general, the Chiefs in the Gold Coast are the traditional leaders of the people. Their functions in regard to local administration are based upon popular support; and the transfer or delegation of any of their functions would require popular sanction, since the position of the Chiefs affects the whole system of relationships on which community life is traditionally based. Increasing numbers of Chiefs recognise the need for modernising their institutions and in this every encouragement is given to them by the Gold Coast Government and their administrative officers. Although much remains to be done, very considerable progress has already been made. . . .

In the view of His Majesty's Government and of the Gold Coast Government, the Commission's proposals must first be considered by representatives of the public in the Gold Coast itself, and for this purpose it is suggested that, subject to the agreement of the Legislative Council, a fully representative committee should be set up locally as soon as possible to examine the proposals in paragraph 122 of the Report and to consider the extent to

Z

which they can be accepted and the manner in which they should be implemented. It would be wrong for His Majesty's Government to form any final conclusions until the views of this committee are known, but if the proposals are acceptable to local opinion . . . His Majesty's Government for their part would regard them as broadly acceptable, and would be prepared to arrange for their early implementation. . . .

His Majesty's Government agree . . . that the African members of the Executive Council should be nominated by the Governor, but . . . suggest that no formal arrangements should be laid down in the first instance for the approval of appointments by the Legislative Council or for the resignation of African members, but that it should be accepted that the Governor would consult with the unofficial members of the Legislative Council before appointing African members and equally that an African member who lost the confidence of the Legislative Council should resign. . . .

His Majesty's Government suggest that, during the formative period of the building up of the new system, it would be preferable to retain the formal arrangement in the Constitution under which [the Executive Council] is advisory to the Governor. At the same time, the Executive Council would be the body where all major questions of policy would be discussed and as such the foundation from which a cabinet system would ultimately be developed. . . .

The Commission recommend that their proposals should be adopted for a period of ten years. . . . While appreciating the intention of this recommendation, His Majesty's Government feel that it is not possible to lay down in advance the pace of political development. While, therefore, they would hope that the new arrangements to be worked out by the local committee would stand for a sufficient period to give political stability to the Gold Coast, they would not wish to lay down precisely, the period within which further political advance would not be open to consideration. . . .

[Colonial No. 232]

501 LEGISLATIVE COUNCIL DEBATE
8 SEPTEMBER, 1948.

[After Nana Sir Tsibu Darku IX had welcomed the appointment of a constitutional committee. . . .]

Mr. Asafu-Adjaye:

Your Excellency, I desire to associate myself with the views expressed by the Honourable Member in regard to the setting up of a representative committee to examine the proposals for constitutional reform. But I wish to stress that in the setting up of this representative committee, regard should be had to equality of representation of the three territorial units in this country, namely, the Colony, Ashanti and the Northern Territories, and that there should be no preponderance of representation of any one territorial unit. I feel, Sir, that such a step will ensure mutual trust and confidence and dispel any dark clouds in the minds of persons in the various territories. . . .

[Other Ashanti Members spoke in the same sense.]

[Leg. Co. Debates, 1948, iii, 37–40]

502 KWAME NKRUMAH: 'WHAT I MEAN BY POSITIVE ACTION'

Party Members, Friends and Supporters,

In our present vigorous struggle for Self-Government, nothing strikes so much terror into the hearts of the imperialists and their agents than the term Positive Action. This is especially so because of their fear of the masses responding to the call to apply this final form of resistance in case the British Government failed to grant us our freedom consequent on the publication of the Coussey Committee Report.

The term Positive Action has been erroneously and maliciously publicised no doubt by the imperialists, their concealed agent-provocateurs and stooges. These political renegades, enemies of the Convention People's Party and for that matter of Ghana's freedom, have diabolically publicised that the C.P.P.'s programme of action means riot, looting and disturbances, in a word violence. . . . This is the way our struggle is being misrepresented to the outside world; but the truth shall ultimately prevail.

It is a comforting fact to observe that we have cleared the major obstacle to the realisation of our national goal in that ideologically the people of this country and their Chiefs have accepted the idea of Self-Government even now. . . . What is left now is chiefly a question of strategy and the intensity and earnestness of our demand. The British Government and the people of Britain, with the exception of die-hard imperialists, acknowledge the legitimacy of our demand for Self-government. However, it is and must be by our own exertion and pressure that the British Government can [alone be made to] relinquish its authority and hand over the control of affairs, that is, the Government, to the people of this country and their Chiefs. . . .

From our knowledge of colonial liberation movements, Freedom or Self-Government has never been handed over to any colonial country on a silver platter. The United States, India, Burma, Ceylon and other erstwhile Colonial territories have had to wage a bitter and vigorous struggle to attain their freedom. Hence the decision by the Convention People's Party to adopt a programme of non-violent Positive Action to attain Self-Government for the people of this country and their Chiefs.

We have talked too much and pined too long over our disabilities — political, social and economic; and it is now time that we embarked on constitutional positive steps to achieve positive results. We must remember that because of the educational backwardness of the Colonial countries, the majority of the people of this country cannot read. There is only one thing they can understand and that is Action.

By Positive Action we mean the adoption of all legitimate and constitutional means by which we can cripple the forces of imperialism in this country. The weapons of Positive Action are:

1 Legitimate political action.
2 Newspapers and educational campaigns, and
3 as a last resort, the constitutional application of strikes, boycotts, and non-co-operation based on the principle of absolute non-violence. . . .

Mr. C. V. H. Rao in his book entitled *Civil Disobedience Movement in India* has this to say:

'Constitutional agitation without effective action behind it of organised national determination to win freedom is generally lost on a country like Britain, which can appreciate only force or its moral equivalent. . . . An important contributory factor to the satisfactory settlement of a disputed issue, is the extent and the nature of the moral force and public sympathy generated by the righteousness of the cause for which suffering is undergone and the extent of the moral reaction it has produced on the party against which it is directed.'

The passive sympathy of the masses must be converted into active participation in the struggle for freedom: there must also be created a widespread political consciousness and a sense of national self-respect. These can only be achieved when the mass of the people understand the issue. These are not the days when people follow leaders blindly. . . .

Positive Action has already begun by our political education, by our newspapers, agitation and platform speeches and also by the establishment of the Ghana Schools and Colleges as well as the fearless and legitimate activities of the C.P.P.

But as regards the final stage of Positive Action, namely, National Non-violent Sit-down-at-home Strikes, Boycotts and Non-co-operation, we shall not call them into play until all the avenues of our political endeavours of attaining Self-government have been closed. Accordingly we shall first carefully study the Report of the Coussey Committee. If we find it favourable, we shall accept it and sing alleluya. But if we find it otherwise, we shall first put forward our own suggestions and proposals and upon refusal to comply with them we shall invoke Positive Action straight away. . . .

What we all want is Self-government so that we can govern ourselves in our own country. We have the natural, legitimate and unalienable right to decide for ourselves the sort of government we want and we cannot be forced against our will into accepting anything that will be detrimental to the true interests of the people of this country and their Chiefs. . . .

Therefore, whilst we are anxiously awaiting the Report . . . I implore you all in the name of the Party to be calm but resolute. Let us advance fearlessly and courageously armed with the Party's programme of Positive Action based on the principle of absolute non-violence.

Long live the Convention People's Party

Long Live the forward march of the people of this country.

Long live the new Ghana that is to be.
[Ghana Pamphlets No. 1. C.P.P., Accra]

503 REPORT . . . BY THE COMMITTEE ON CONSTITUTIONAL REFORM 1949.

. . . Contrary to the view expressed in the Watson Report, we believe that there is still a place for the Chief in a new constitutional set-up. . . . The whole institution of chieftaincy is so closely bound up with the life of our communities that its disappearance would spell disaster. . . . Criticisms there have been, but none coming from responsible people . . . is directed towards the complete effacement of chiefs. We cannot, therefore, accept the status which the Watson Report would assign to them. . . .

Our second set of recommendations concern Regional Administrations of which we recommend the establishment of four. . . . There are certain definite historical associations, particularly in the case of Ashanti and the Northern Territories, which it would be unwise to ignore. There is also the value of decentralisation, without which the administrative machinery of government at the centre would tend to be overburdened with routine matters. . . . Our recommendations are therefore designed to harmonise with historical realities and to provide machinery for rapid decisions by officials and councillors in close touch with the problems which they are called upon to solve. . . .

On the subject of the Legislature, our most radical recommendation is the principle of the collective responsibility of the Executive to the Legislature. As a result of earnest deliberations, we would emphasize that any proposal whereby the Executive would be responsible to the Governor is considered to be unacceptable. We put forward the principle of collective responsibility to the Legislature as being the only satisfactory method of ensuring, in the future, that executive action shall be more responsive to considered public opinion and to informed criticism in the Legislature. . . .

There is a popular cry throughout the country for universal adult suffrage. Our recommendation is for universal adult suffrage but by indirect election. . . . We feel that we can rely on the general good sense of the large majority of our people, who are by no means lacking in political understanding. Nevertheless, we have weighed the risks involved most carefully and by recommending election in two stages, except in the cases of the existing municipalities of Accra, Cape Coast, Sekondi–Takoradi and Kumasi, we have provided a means for the exercise of responsible judgement in two stages, in the election of members to the Assembly. This process of election should minimise the dangers inherent in the wide and rapid extension of the franchise before the development of that full political sense which is the true bulwark against the charlatan and the demagogue.

The proposal in the Watson Report for equal representation of the regions gave rise to much discussion. It was rejected by a majority on the ground that it would impair the unitary character of the structure of the proposed constitution and would delay the attainment of genuine manhood. Moreover, such a form of representation seems unnecessary in the light of our recommendations for Regional Administrations.

As a compromise, however, between the idea of equal representation of the three main regions on the one hand, and a more democratic representation based solely on the distribution of population on the other, we have made the recommendation [that the House of Assembly shall consist of not more than 78 members: 29 from the Colony, 19 from Ashanti, 19 from the Northern Territories, 8 from . . . Transvolta–Southern Togoland, and not more than 3 *ex-officio* members].[1] . . . It should be added, however, that the Ashanti members who have signed this report rejected this compromise, and were in favour of parity of representation between the three main regions.

Turning to the question of the structure of the Legislature, the arguments for and against a bicameral system are summarised in paragraph 353 below. The majority in favour of such a system was so narrow . . . that we feel obliged to make recommendations for the establishment of either a one chamber Legislature or a Legislature of two chambers. . . .

[In Local Government. . . .]

236. There should be established three classes of Local Authorities. . . . Class 'A' Authorities will comprise 'District Councils' and Municipal Councils; Class 'B' Authorities will include 'Urban Area' and 'Rural Area' Councils; and Class 'C' Authorities will be 'Village Area' Councils. . . .

---

[1] Inserting paragraph 373 of the Report.

248. . . . The members of the local authority who are popularly elected should be in a majority. The aim should be to have up to two-thirds of the members composed of those popularly elected and those elected from subordinate councils. . . .

252. The franchise should be given to adults who have been in residence in the locality for six months, have registered as voters, and have paid their local tax. . . .

353. After long and anxious deliberation, the Committee, by a majority of 20 votes to 19, has voted in favour of a bicameral Legislature.

(i) Some of the reasons in support were:—

(a) A second Chamber would serve as a check on hasty legislation and would enable emotional issues to be considered in a calmer atmosphere.

(b) It would enable paramount chiefs and other persons of eminence who would not be disposed to stand for ordinary election, to make a valuable contribution to the government of the country in a place befitting their rank, dignity and position.

(c) It would ensure permanence in, and respect for, the traditions of the country, by establishing a House of Elders.

(d) It would provide for equal representation of the Regions, and would permit the representation of interests which would otherwise have no voice in the Legislature.

(e) It would maintain the sovereign authority of the various states.

(ii) The arguments against the proposal stressed:

(a) the probability of friction between paramount chiefs and people if the former were confined to a Second Chamber;

(b) the added expenditure in set-ting up an additional Council for Chiefs and Elder Statesmen, involving as it would, the journey to and stay at Accra of a greater number of Chiefs, with their attendants, for long Sessions;

(c) the consequent stagnation in the immediate affairs of more states than under a unicameral system which would be affected by the absence of their Chiefs;

(d) the effect on the number and quality of members available for a first chamber, a point which may be particularly applicable to the Northern Territories;

(e) that the interaction of thought between elected members and Elders in a unicameral Chamber would not only be beneficial but would be in consonance with the accepted traditions of the country;

(f) that once a Second Chamber is established it would be extremely difficult to disestablish it, should it later be found unnecessary. The status of the chiefs might be destroyed in the process. . . .

[Or, in a unicameral system, they provide:]

397. One-third of the seats or as near as may be arithmetically possible shall be filled by members (who may be either chiefs or non-chiefs) to be elected in a manner to be determined by existing Territorial Councils in the case of the Northern Territories and Ashanti, and by states in the case of the Colony and the Transvolta.

[Colonial No. 248, London, 1949]

504 COMMISSION No. 5 OF 1949.

By His Excellency Sir Charles Noble Arden-Clarke,[1] Knight Commander of the Most Distinguished Order of Saint Michael

[1] Born 1898; served in Nigeria (1920–6), Bechuanaland Protectorate (1936–42); Basutoland (1942–6); Governor of Sarawak, 1946–9; Governor of the Gold Coast, 1949–57; first Governor-General of Ghana, 1957.

and Saint George, Governor and Commander-in-Chief of the Gold Coast.

C. N. Arden-Clarke, Governor

To Emmanual Charles Quist, Esquire and to all whom these presents shall come, Greeting:

Whereas it is provided by section 6 of the Gold Coast Colony and Ashanti (Legislative Council) Order in Council, 1946, that the Governor, with the approval of a Secretary of State, may by instrument under the Public Seal, appoint a person to be the President of the Legislative Council of the Gold Coast and Ashanti:

And whereas, with the approval of the Secretary of State for the Colonies, I have decided to make such an appointment as aforesaid:

Now therefore, in pursuance and by virtue of the authority committed to the Governor in that behalf by section 6 of the Gold Coast and Ashanti (Legislative Council) Order in Council, 1946, I, Sir Charles Arden-Clarke, Knight Commander of the Most Distinguished Order of Saint Michael and Saint George, Governor and Commander in Chief of the Gold Coast, do hereby appoint you, the said Emmanuel Charles Quist, subject to the provisions of the said Order in Council, to be the President of the Legislative Council of the Gold Coast Colony and Ashanti until the Council now in being is dissolved.

Given under my hand and the Public Seal of the Gold Coast, at Government House, Accra, in the Gold Coast Colony, this 10th day of October in the year of our Lord one thousand nine hundred and forty-nine and of His Majesty's Reign the Thirteenth.

By His Excellency's Command,
Robert Scott,
Colonial Secretary.

505 A. Creech Jones[1] to Sir C. Arden-Clarke   14 October, 1949.

. . . The observations which follow are

[1] Arthur Creech Jones; born, 1891; Labour M.P., 1935–50 and 1954– ; Parliamentary Under-Secretary of State for the Colonies, 1945–6; Secretary of State for the Colonies, 1946–50.

made with the sole object of helping and promoting the progress of the Gold Coast to responsible government within the British Commonwealth, which it is the policy of His Majesty's Government and the manifest desire of the people of the country to see achieved as soon as practicable. . . .

I have come to the conclusion that the most practical form of assistance which I can give at this stage will be to let you have immediately the views of His Majesty's Government on the more important recommendations of the Committee, so as to help forward the examination of the Report in the Gold Coast. . . .

Subject to the observations which I shall make later in this despatch, His Majesty's Government accept the proposals put forward in the Report as providing a workable plan within the framework of which constitutional development in the Gold Coast can now proceed. . . .

I agree generally with the Committee's broad conception of local government reform, although the individual recommendations will need detailed examination in the Gold Coast. . . . Now that it is recognised that radical changes in the system of local government are needed, I trust that the people of the Gold Coast will not let pass the opportunity to make them. . . .

I accept the arguments put forward by the majority of the Committee in favour of the retention and development of Regional Administrations . . . [which] at the present stage . . . have an indispensable part to play in the supervision and co-ordination of the new Local Authorities. If the Regional Administrations are to carry out their duties efficiently, it is necessary that they should be provided with a permanent staff adequate to deal with the volume of work which will inevitably grow. It is also necessary that the Central Government should be prepared to delegate authority to them, and I agree with the Committee that a very substantial decentralisation of functions should be effected. . . .

I am doubtful about the recommendation . . . that elections to the Regional Councils should be carried out in the same way as elections to the Central Legislature. The conduct of these central elections . . . will tax the administrative resources of the country very heavily, and, if similar elections are to be held for Regional Councils, I fear that the system may become too complicated. . . . I am inclined to the view that it would be preferable for the members of the Regional Councils to be elected from and by the Local Authorities themselves. . . .

I recognise the strength of the arguments both for and against a bi-cameral system, but I am particularly impressed by the third, fourth and fifth arguments against it which the Committee has recorded. . . . I feel, accordingly, that it would be advisable, certainly at this stage, to adopt a unicameral system.

I welcome the Committee's proposal . . . that, except in municipalities, an indirect system of election should be adopted for the Legislative Assembly; I feel sure that under present conditions this recommendation is sound. . . .

The Committee . . . has stated that any proposal whereby the Executive Council would be responsible to the Governor is considered to be unacceptable. It is evident that the Committee attaches great importance to this point, but I think there may be some possibility of misunderstanding on it. . . . The Committee . . . has quite properly at this stage, not proposed the granting of full responsibility to Ministers and rightly qualifies their responsibility in certain important respects. Under the recommendations of the majority report, the Executive Council would include *ex officio* members and the Governor would have reserve powers. . . . It follows that, so long as it is necessary for the Governor to have reserve powers, he must retain the ultimate responsibility. . . .

This does not mean that the members of the Executive Council would not be answerable and in effect responsible to the Assembly. The power to grant financial supply and to legislate would lie with the Assembly and members of the Executive Council would be required to answer in the Assembly for the departments of Government for which they were responsible. . . .

In the Committee's Report it appears to be implied that responsibility to the Governor and responsibility to the Legislature are inconsistent with each other; in fact they are not inconsistent but complementary. . . . If the matter is looked at from the practical point of view, it will be apparent that the substance of the Committee's recommendations will in fact be achieved.

It is a matter of experience, both in the Gold Coast and elsewhere that the Governor's reserve powers are in practice only used most sparingly. . . . The aim should be that . . . the business of government should be smoothly and efficiently carried on by consultation and agreement between the Governor, the Executive Council and the Legislative Assembly. . . .

I readily agree that there should be a majority of Africans drawn from the Legislative Assembly on the Executive Council. It would be the body where all major questions of policy would be discussed. . . . The Council should not simply, as at present, be summoned on the motion of the Governor himself, but also, as the Committee recommend, at the request of two-thirds of its members. . . . All questions proposed for decision in the Executive Council should be determined by the majority vote of the members present and voting, the Governor having a casting, but not an original vote. It would be necessary to give the Governor the right to act against the majority decision of the Council when the issue under discussion was one which fell within the scope of his reserve powers. It would be laid down that the Governor should only exercise this right (except in an emergency) with the prior approval of the Secretary of

State. . . . Normally the decision would be taken by a majority vote in a body in which elected members of the Assembly would be in the majority. Thus the Executive Council would be a very different body from the present Executive Council, which is purely advisory.

It is a corollary of this arrangement that the Executive Council should act collectively as a body and that an individual member of the Council should be under an obligation to carry out administratively, and support in the Legislature, the policy and decisions of the Council. . . .

I do not believe that the institution of a Leader of the House would work effectively in the absence of an established and well-tried party system, by which I mean a system where, through usage over a period of years, parties have become generally accepted as necessary and integral parts of the constitutional machinery of the country. In this sense there is not as yet a party system in the Gold Coast, and without it, while the member of the House of Assembly chosen as Leader would admittedly command the majority of votes on the occasion when he was so chosen, there would be no guarantee that he would continue to command a majority. If not, the efficiency of Government might be seriously hampered and the relations between the Executive Council and the Legislative Assembly impaired. . . . I suggest that the members of the Executive Council should elect one of their number for this purpose. . . .

Since members of the Executive Council (other than the *ex officio* members) would be appointed by resolution of the Assembly, I agree . . . that the Assembly should have power to initiate the steps necessary for the removal of such members . . . [though] this power should not be lightly exercised. . . . I must make it quite clear that I could not agree to any proposal for the removal of an *ex officio* member . . . on a prayer of the Assembly. . . .

I am aware that these proposals and observations will be the subject of detailed discussion and examination both by the Government and by the public in the Gold Coast and the results of such discussion and examination will of course be taken into account in preparing the instruments. My only reason for starting the process now, is my desire to avoid all delay in bringing the recommendations into effect.

I have &c.
A. Creech Jones.
[Colonial No. 250, London, 1949]

506 LEGISLATIVE COUNCIL DEBATE
12 DECEMBER, 1949.

Rev. C. G. Baeta. . . .

These past six weeks, as was to be expected, we have heard a lot of comment on the Coussey Report. Some people have criticised the committee severely for not doing what it never set out to do. . . . We know the terms of reference of the committee. They were quite specific and the import of them was that a plan of government should be devised which in the Gold Coast to-day should in the first place be workable, and then secondly should represent as great a constitutional advance as can be achieved. And, of course, the accent was on the 'workable'.

The men who were invited to serve on this committee were men who have actually lived and worked in this country and have made a mark in one way or another in their several callings. They were widely known in their own communities on that account, and it is on that account that their names came to the notice of Government. For the most part they were also men who had several other men working under them in the hum drum of every-day occupations. They were men who were responsible for the running of actual organisations and for seeing that these keep going. . . . I emphasize these points in their qualifications because I believe they are very relevant. There are a few things concerning the ways of men in every-day life which you can only learn by these means, that is, by successfully carrying out government in smaller ways. . . .

[Though there were differences of opinion] after applying themselves . . . to their task for over six months, this committee was able to sign a unanimous report, and the structure of government they recommend is in the first place workable and . . . it represents a sufficiently great constitutional advance today. It is not Dominion Status, but semiresponsible government, a half way house, if you choose to call it so. And the committee put down these recommendations without shame or apology, but with common sense and a sense of reality.

The Secretary of State has thought fit to impose a few restrictions in the matter of *ex-officio* members and the source of final responsibility for government. Mr. President, frankly, in my opinion, the amount of ink and fury which has been expended over these points is out of all proportion to their real significance in the issue today. I shall show in a moment what I consider to be the real point. . . . But it is certainly *not* whether we should have three *ex-officio* members or not, and whether the Executive should be responsible to the Assembly or to the Governor.

My point now is, however, that whereas nobody is saying that these are the ideal arrangements, the restrictions upon full autonomy are necessitated by the facts of the situation. They are the implications of our decision not to get the whole thing now, but to have a half-way house for the meantime, and I believe . . . that for the present time there are great advantages in a system of government whereby authority and responsibility are shared by the Gold Coast people with the British Government. For two reasons.

In one of the riders to the Coussey Report the statement is made that the Gold Coast peoples are a homogeneous people. Let us hope that that is so, although we all know that from time to time we have disturbing experiences as if

that were not so. But let us hope that in the future we shall see more and more, not in words only, but in fact, that we are a homogeneous people. It remains, however, true, that whatever our natural ties may be, in the decades immediately past, the bonds which have held us together were not the bonds of our natural kinship, but the Pax Britannica. . . . If some of us think that, without having previously arrived at a new understanding and agreement among ourselves, suddenly governmental orders or ministerial regulations begin to pour forth from Accra, in which orders and regulations the British Government had no hand, and we think that they will receive the same ready obedience as at present, we might find that this may not be the case. Certainly it will not be the case everywhere, and that will create considerable difficulty for all of us.

The way of wisdom, Mr. President, would appear therefore to lie in using this period of a plain and frankly-accepted partnership government to accustom ourselves to this new idea, to find a way of living together by ourselves, and to learn to recognise this new source of authority which we are creating. . . . It is not as if what is being proposed for us now is something unheard of anywhere, something undignified for us. I have heard that Malta had a similar constitution; for 16 years Ceylon had one like it, and stepped up from that to their present Dominion Status only last year. . . .

As far as our interests are concerned, surely our interests are adequately protected. I should be very sorry for *eight* African Ministers who were not able to take care of *three ex-officio* Ministers in a Council where they all have equal votes. And if by any devious means these three *ex-officio* members should try to pull more weight than is the true and legitimate weight of three, why, that should afford the most delightful platform that any politician can desire. . . . My own humble guess is, however, that whatever happens, our own men are going to be thankful for the help, support, advice and co-operation of these their colleagues.

My second point, Mr President, is that we are at present, whether we like it or not, unable entirely by ourselves to administer our essential services. Many people take this to be a small matter and say lightly that we should have the government, but we should employ experts and technical men from abroad to attend to our needs. We can do that, but if we did it we should be like a bandmaster who could not play any of the instruments himself, or a works manager who did not know anything of the job which he is supervising other people to do. You will agree that this is extremely anomalous and might yield some most painful and embarrassing situations. One of the wise men . . . said 'he who administers, governs.' I think there is truth in that. I am not saying that full responsible government should wait until we have implemented all the schemes laid before us by the Africanization Committee, but we must give ourselves time to do something about them first, so that we may know what to do if the bandsmen or the workmen begin to get recalcitrant. . . .

Mr. President, the moral of all this is simply that: (i) there is nothing at all to be gained by more haste than is necessary or by impatience of any kind and (ii) even as things are, we have more than plenty of hard work on our hands to do. There is a saying which is becoming current among us here to-day. People are saying, 'let us make our own mistakes, we learn only by trial and error.' But we must not make mistakes . . . just for the sake of making mistakes. A mistake is excusable only if we make it after having taken every possible precaution to do the right thing. . . . This is not a private matter, like a man sallying forth by himself on a little adventure of 'dangerous living', in which the consequences are personal to himself. This is something which affects five million people and their

descendants as yet unborn. We have no right to impose on them a life which is inferior in quality to that which they are leading now.

Mr. President . . . I support this motion. I know that there will be modifications of the Report — in fact I am going to suggest one myself — but I hope that the modifications will be as few as possible. In my humble opinion, if there is need for anything now, it is not for greater or more powers on paper; the need is to come down from the talking rostrum and to do a job of actual real spade work.

Mr. Obetsebi Lamptey:[1]

Mr. President, a motion like this tabled to convey the thanks of this House to His Majesty's Government of the United Kingdom for what is considered by some to be a bounty conferred upon this country, calls for a brief historical survey of Anglo–Gold Coast connection.

When a little over a decade after the abolition of the slave trade which devastated Africa and denuded this land of its human material to an extent from which she has not recovered and may never recover, Britain entered into a bond of friendship and protection with the people of this country; when on that fateful March 6 1844, on the sacred hills of Cape Coast Castle, our fathers recognised British power and jurisdiction on these shores, little did they realise that they were signing away not only their independence and sovereignty, but were also clapping their neck into the noose of another slavery more insidious, more far-reaching in its intensity, more devastating in its effects than the physical slavery that preceded it.

Britain's control of the political, cultural and social structure of this country, her monopoly of the economic resources of this land made possible by the Bond of

[1] Lawyer, member of the United Gold Coast Convention, one of the six deported to the Northern Territories after the 1948 riots; member of the Coussey Commission.

1844, has ruined this country and still rages unabated.

During the hundred years of Anglo–Gold Coast connection, Britain has extracted more gold from the bowels of the Gold Coast earth than is possible within bounds of imagination. . . . Apart from the gold to which it owes its name, the Gold Coast is the largest producer of cocoa, the second largest producer of diamonds and the third largest producer of manganese ore in the world. So fabulously rich is this country that it is revolting to think of the indigence and penury in which the people live; in spite of our natural wealth, there is perhaps more poverty in this country than any other part of the Globe. The bare necessities and essentials of life are denied us.

Take education for instance. We are all agreed that it is the duty and business of the State to provide means of education for the common people. . . . Yet for more than 100 years that Britain has ruled this country, not more than ten per cent of the total population of this country is educated. These are wrongs that cut to the very roots of human life. They must be righted, and they can only be righted when we have succeeded in removing the fountain from whence they flow — Imperialism.

Nor do we forget the appalling social conditions in this country. Take housing for instance. Some of the houses in this country are not fit for pigs, and those built by the Department of Social Welfare and Housing are no better. Those of us who live in the coastal towns may not have any idea of what conditions are in the far interior. Go to Bolgatanga . . . to Nangodi and the Kusasia country, where 50 years ago Ekyem Ferguson laid down his life to hoist the British flag and you will 'destroy your sight with another demagorgon', the squalor and abject poverty, the disease and dirt and want in which they live is too horrifying for words. . . . These are the evils of Imperialism. . . .

When Honourable Members come to consider what modifications are necessary to the Report, they will, I am sure, be guided by the knowledge of recent events. The events of 27th and 28th February, the days when Accra burnt, are still fresh in our memory. We remember also the background of that tragedy. We know that the foreign power out here for the purpose of government, some say for purpose of exploitation, was allowing the foreign merchants in our midst 75 per cent. profits on all textiles. . . . We know also that prices of essential commodities, said to be controlled, are controlled only to the privileged class — the pass-book holders. The poor illiterate woman, the peasant, the fisherman, the artisan and the labourer, who can ill afford to buy at the controlled price are forced to go to the black market, and there buy for 1s 6d. a lb. sugar which at the controlled price is sold at 8d. a lb. Now that we are called upon, as the ultimate statutory body to decide in the name of the people of this country I pray that we take a decision that will prevent a perpetuation of these social evils. . . .

Whilst . . . emancipation is in sight, let us not forget those noble sons of this land who built the foundations of the road along which we are marching. Let us not forget the gallant sons of this land who went abroad to fight for the emancipation of other lands and peoples, those who fought for democracy, freedom, and liberty, only to come back to be shot down like rats in their own home. Yes, let us not forget the boys whose blood stain[s] Christiansborg cross-roads; nor must we forget those still living who suffered exile and humiliation that this cause may prevail.

I expect when Honourable Members come to modify the Report, they will take a decision that will guarantee to this country the freedom which is hers for the asking, a freedom which will endure for all time. And I also hope that we will know what to do with that freedom. . . .

Dr. Danquah:[1]

Mr. President, the acceptance, subject to modifications, of the Coussey Report, by this Council, constitutes a remarkable triumph of democracy. It is living evidence . . . that the salvation of the people of this country rests with the people of this country — to a large extent. . . .

Just under two years ago when the United Gold Coast Convention under the leadership of that greatest of all our elder statesmen, Mr. George Alfred Grant, took it upon themselves to despatch a £30 worth of cablegram to the Secretary of State to point out that the 1946 Constitution had failed, and that a new constitution should be provided, and the government of this country handed over to the Chiefs and people, there were many prominent men in this country who thought that a great crime had been committed. . . . In fact, in certain quarters it was thought to be an act of disloyalty to His Majesty the King, and . . . certain members of our Gold Coast community, on hearing of the cablegram, sent frantic messages to the Secretary of State, professing their unstinted loyalty — as if to ask for a better system of government under British democracy was itself a sign of disloyalty.

Today we have met here to see the direct fruit and result of that historic cablegram. That false men told false stories to the Governor in consequence of which six honest lovers of their country were bundled away to the Northern Territories, the Siberia of the Gold Coast, is merely an episode that deserves mention in this connection but not to be dwelt on. I can assure Honourable Members that . . . I bear no ill-will to anyone. But there is one thing that was planted indelibly upon my soul — the bitterness of keeping wicked people as friends of those who govern. That, from now on, must be changed, and those who befriend those who govern must

[1] Dr. Joseph Boakye Danquah; half-brother of Nana Sir Ofori Atta and legal adviser to Akim–Abuakwa State Council; founder of the United Gold Coast Convention Party.

be made directly responsible for every single act they indulge in, not behind closed doors or in dark corners, but in the open daylight of the people's parliament — the Legislative Assembly.

But we have learnt great lessons from the events of the past two years. They have shown that where a people stand together united, or where a considerable body of opinion stands firm for the grant of democratic rights, under the fair play of the British, what is wanted is sweet reasonableness in the manner of your demand, and the British with their sense of fair play, will be bound to grant you something at least. , . . There is . . . every reason to believe that if we keep to that sweet reasonableness that has so far characterised sane leadership in the Gold Coast to-day, this country, Ghana, will be the first African country to reach what the Governor called 'full stature', full Dominion status.

But is there evidence that we really want self-government and that we need it? I am sorry to have to say Coussey's Report is not complete proof that all Gold Coast leaders are fully of one opinion that we want and need Dominion status to-day. Of a body of 39 Africans, only eight asked for . . . complete self-government within our Gold Coast limits. The rest . . . for one reason or another, asked that the Colonial status should be continued for a little while longer. I dare say those 31 members of Coussey have their reasons for doing so. . . . Perhaps they have not seen the great light that looms ahead on the horizon. Perhaps they are perturbed and dazzled by the brilliancy of that light. They cannot believe their own eyes that self-government is really coming, and they are apprehensive that it should come. I have in my heart no sympathy for such men. Our business from now on is not, however, to vilify them, but to try to convince them that although half a loaf is better than none, a whole loaf is better than half. . . .

I think His Majesty's Government . . . have approached the Report in a high courageous spirit. To think that only five years ago Col. Oliver Stanley did hesitate to grant our demand for an elected majority in the Legislative Council, together with a committee of policy, the latter of which was not, in fact, granted; to think that barely ten years ago, we in this country were spoken of as wards of the British, not yet able to stand on our own feet; to think that only the other day, that is to say, in 1948 when Sir Gerald Creasy was sworn in as Governor, he stated in this very King George V Memorial Hall that his policy was to secure the old indirect rule system — to think that all this was in the British mind until Imray[1] fired his shot and smashed British hopes for continuance of the old trusteeship and the new unequal 'partnership' policy, we cannot but be exceedingly thankful to His Majesty's Government that they have so quickly, and I should say, so sensibly, reacted to the new-born spirit for liberty which Imray's shot implanted firmly in the heart of the people. I am happy that the British have quietly agreed to grant us what the majority of our own African Committee demanded should be granted. . . . The attitude of His Majesty's Government in this matter is indeed a satisfying and appetitive prophylactic against suspicion and distrust. I do not of course, by any chance, say that the majority recommendations so accepted give me complete satisfaction. What will give me complete satisfaction is the acceptance of the rider by the eight . . . that the Executive Council should be wholly composed of elected members of the Assembly. . . .

[Leg. Co. Debates, 1949, iv, pp. 78–92]

507 SPEECH OF THE GOVERNOR (SIR C. ARDEN CLARKE) IN LEGISLATIVE COUNCIL 19 JANUARY, 1950.

. . . I have summoned this special meeting of the Legislative Council in response to a request made by the President and other Members of the Council who were in Accra on the 12th of January. The community is being threatened by a campaign of lawlessness and it has been necessary for me to declare a state of emergency. I was informed that this Council desired an opportunity of expressing its views and those of the country, on the present situation and the action taken to deal with it. That seemed to me a right and proper request and I have acceded to it. . . .

When I landed in this country a little more than five months ago, I found a state of affairs that caused me grave concern. The Coussey Committee — a Committee composed entirely of Africans drawn from all sections of the community and all parts of the Gold Coast and composed of men of widely divergent political views — was meeting to sign the report containing its recommendations on constitutional reform. The Gold Coast was obviously at a critical, hopeful, but anxious stage on its advance along the road to responsible government. But there was an atmosphere of suspicion and distrust abroad, a lack of confidence that the peace could or would be maintained. The lawless elements seemed to be in the ascendant. A party styling itself the Convention People's Party had announced that it proposed to achieve 'self-government' for the Gold Coast by what is called 'positive action', unless the Coussey Committee and His Majesty's Government granted it forthwith. As I travelled round the country meeting the Chiefs and people it was symptomatic of the disregard for law, order, and constituted authority that in certain places, where this party had a following, gangs had been organised to boo and barrack the representative of His Majesty on his first visit among them. In one case even, some Chiefs were intimidated into committing a public act of discourtesy.

At the same time I quickly found that there was a very large body of moderate

[1] The Police Officer who halted the Ex-Servicemen's march on Christiansborg Castle in 1948.

and responsible people who were utterly opposed to the methods of this party, and that the great bulk of the people of this country were decent law-abiding citizens. Though public confidence was returning, in the minds of many there still remained doubts as to the determination and capacity of Government to maintain peace and order and protect the property and lives of law-abiding citizens. The vigorous measures which had already been initiated to deal with this situation were continued and intensified. The moderate, responsible elements made their influence felt. The Convention People's Party on the other hand had announced that if the report of the Coussey Committee did not recommend its own version of self-government, 'positive action' would be introduced.

The Coussey Report and the statement of His Majesty's Government on it were published and the country took time to think. Whatever may be said about this or that detail of the plan of constitutional reform set out in these documents, there can be no doubt that it places the direct and immediate responsibility for the management of the affairs of this country on the shoulders of the people of the Gold Coast and that it does provide a very full measure of self-government. The Convention People's Party then submitted for its slogan 'Self-Government Now' the slogan 'Dominion Status Now' and again announced its intention of achieving its political aims by 'positive action.' 'Positive Action' was defined as 'national non-violent sit-down-at-home strikes, boycotts and non co-operation.' . . .

Despite . . . official warnings and despite the very clear indications given by the bulk of the Press, by many Chiefs and other responsible leaders, and by the Territorial Councils that this was contrary to the wishes of people of the country and could achieve nothing except to bring hardship and suffering upon them, 'positive action' was introduced. An attempt was made to call a nation-wide strike and organise a boycott.

In case any doubts still remain on the point, I wish here to state categorically that the Trades Union Congress had no mandate for a general strike and did not call a general strike. No trade dispute had been declared to exist between any of its constituent Trade Unions and the employers. The Trade Union Congress had been warned that in these circumstances, strikes would be illegal and these warnings were repeated to all Unions. From the start of the first strike the executive of the Trades Union Congress appears to have gone into liquidation. No reply could be obtained to any communication addressed to it, and no contact could be made with the majority of its members. From all the evidence at present available, it seems clear the strikes that have occurred have been engineered by certain members of the Convention People's Party who had gained positions of influence on the Trades Union Congress Executive Committee and on the committees of various of the Unions, and that they were brought about in pursuance of the Party's policy of 'positive action', and for no other reason whatsoever. These are well-known tactics advocated and practised by communists and others whose aim it is to seize power for themselves by creating chaos and disrupting the life of the community which they propose to dominate. . . .

At first the strike was confined to a few small sections of the workers, most of whom had been grossly misled. Heed was given to the repeated warnings of Government that the strike was illegal and it seemed that it would peter out. This was not to be. Much lip-service had been paid to the alleged non-violent sit-down-at-home nature of this political strike. These quickly proved to be mere empty phrases, devoid of sense and meaning, and this came as no surprise to any. Intimidation became rife and the situation deteriorated. . . .

I had been paying long-arranged visits to meet the Chiefs and people of various States in the eastern area of the Colony, returning each night to Accra to keep in touch with the situation. My meetings with the Chiefs and State Councils made it very clear that in the country places there was no support for, or sympathy with, the policy of 'positive action.' It was a different story in the larger towns, particularly in those places where for a time during the disturbances of 1948 the mob had been in command of the streets and there had been looting and arson. It seems that some of the most fervent supporters of 'positive action' thought that an opportunity would present itself of repeating past performance. On the . . . 11th of January . . . in the light of the information laid before me on my return [to Accra] I summoned a meeting of my Executive Council that night. With their unanimous advice I signed a Proclamation that as from midnight all the powers under Part 2 of the Emergency Powers Order in Council 1939, would be in operation throughout the Gold Coast. The Emergency Regulations were brought into force and such Orders under those Regulations as were deemed necessary were made. It was clear that the spread of intimidation, the rising tension and the deliberate challenge to all constituted authority, if not checked immediately, would inevitably lead to more violence and to bloodshed. It was necessary that Government should be armed with all powers needed to deal with the situation. I do not propose to describe the various outbreaks of hooliganism, lawlessness and violence that have taken place. The participants are being dealt with in the courts. The day before yesterday, here in Accra, two policemen were stabbed and killed while in the execution of their duty. The police were dispersing an armed mob by baton charges. These men died in defence of the right of the free citizens of this country to go peacefully about their business without fear of molestation. This is one of many examples of 'non-violent positive action' in practice.

Owing to the vigorous measures taken I am glad to be able to report that over the greater part of the country, conditions have returned practically to normal. There are still exceptions and these are being dealt with. The danger of further incidents has not yet passed. This matter is by no means yet concluded. . . .

This is a critical time for the Gold Coast. This country is being watched by the eyes of the world. The Gold Coast is about to make a great constitutional advance. The world is wondering if the plan now being considered is before its time. It is asking whether the people of the Gold Coast have the capacity and the determination to shoulder their new responsibilities and undertake their complex task of building up and carrying on a good government under a new constitution. It would indeed be a disaster to this country if the impression was given to the outside world that the exponents of 'positive action' are representative of the people of this country or that 'positive action' is an example of the methods of government that will be adopted under the new constitution. A bad start has been made. It is for every responsible organisation in this country, every responsible newspaper and every responsible person who has any love for his country, to give abundant proof not only by words but by their conduct and actions that the Gold Coast and its people are on the side of law and order and fully intend to abide there.

I have faith in the people of the Gold Coast, in their capacity to undertake their new responsibilities and in their determination to maintain peace, order and good government within their land. That faith is not fully shared by the outside world. What has happened in the last two years has shaken the faith of many. It is for you to restore it. Since the beginning of 1948 this country has been suffering from hooliganism, intimidation and threats of violence. Attempts have been made to subvert all constituted authority, to separate the people from their Chiefs, to bring the Chiefs and Chieftainship into disrepute and now to coerce Government by unlawful strikes designed to bring hardship and suffering on the people. This state of affairs must be brought to an end. Government will do all in its power to restore peace, tranquillity and confidence and maintain good relations, but it cannot succeed without the active and vigorous co-operation of the Chiefs and of the people. . . .

[Leg. Co. Debates, 1950, i, pp. 2–7]

41 The Government of the Convention People's Party, 1951-1957

IN 1951 the first elections under the new constitution were to be held. The C.P.P. decided to contest them. Its election manifesto (508), the first in Gold Coast history, was a comprehensive statement of the Party belief and programme. C.P.P. organisation and propaganda duly carried 34 of the 38 seats contested on a party basis, which was enough for them to dominate a House of 80, in the absence of other organised blocs. In view of its declared attitude to the new constitution, the C.P.P.'s triumph threatened a complete impasse. This, in the event, was avoided by the good sense of the Governor who released Nkrumah from prison, and of Nkrumah himself, who decided that his party would give the 'bogus and fraudulent' constitution a trial. In Party parlance, 'Positive Action' was replaced by 'Tactical Action'. Dr. Nkrumah as he now was, became the first Leader of Government Business in an Executive Council which, besides three *ex-officio* Ministers, included five other C.P.P. Ministers, with an Ashanti Minister of Local Government, and a Northern Territories Minister without Portfolio.

The new government, like Guggisberg's earlier, but to a far greater degree, entered on its duties in a boom period (510). The unprecedented prices commanded by cocoa in world markets meant that liberal provision could be made for development plans, particularly in communications and education, even if industrialisation could hardly have kept pace under any circumstances with the exuberant intentions of the Party programme (509). The spectacular Volta River Project was to be still largely a project in 1957.

The honeymoon period lasted into the summer of 1954. One by one the restraints imposed in the 1950 Constitution were relaxed. The Leader of Government Business became Prime Minister in 1952. Proposals moved in the Assembly the following year (511) envisaged the disappearance of the *ex-officio* ministers from the Executive Council, henceforward to be known as the Cabinet, and the direct election of all the members of a Legislative Assembly enlarged to 104 members (512). These proposals were accepted and at the first elections held under the changed system in 1954 the C.P.P. won 79 seats (41 Colony, 19 Ashanti, 11 Northern Territories, 8 Trans–Volta–Togoland).

Even in the debates of 1953 (511), regional tensions were becoming apparent, and a Northern Peoples' Party won a majority of the North's seats in the election of 1954. Late that year, touched off in the first instance by a dispute over cocoa prices, a more formidable brand of regionalism, which demanded a federal form of constitution as a check on the 'dictatorship' of coast politicians (and even talked of secession if it were refused), made its appearance in Ashanti. As the position further deteriorated in 1955 the services of a constitutional expert to advise on regional devolution, were offered to and accepted by the Gold Coast Government: but Sir Frederick Bourne's mission (513) was less fruitful than it might have been because the Ashanti leaders of the newly formed National Liberation Movement declined to meet him or discuss anything less than federal government. No one in England cared for a solution on such lines (514) but a further election was deemed necessary by the Imperial Government before the final transfer of power could be made. In 1956 the C.P.P. was only slightly less successful than in 1954, with a total of 71 seats. It carried all the Colony seats, 11 of 26 in the Northern Territories, 8 out of 13 in Trans–Volta, and even in Ashanti where it lost ground, it polled over 40% of the votes. It was a sufficient demonstration of the strength of the only national Party. In December 1956 the British House of Commons in a mood of sober congratulation voted the permissive bill conferring full self-government on the new state of Ghana (514). Finally, in February 1957, after the Secretary of State had visited West Africa and allayed the misgivings of the opposition leaders, the constitutional statute of the self-governing member of the Commonwealth was promulgated as an Order in Council (515), to come into effect on 6 March, 1957, the 113th anniversary of the Bond.

508 CONVENTION PEOPLE'S PARTY, GENERAL ELECTION MANIFESTO 1951.

Our Appeal to the People of Ghana to Vote C.P.P. Ghanaians!

1. If you believe in the justice of our cause.
2. If you believe that we too must be free to manage our own affairs in our own country as the British do in theirs.
3. If you believe that imperialism is a hindrance to our national progress.
4. If you believe that we too, given the opportunity, can achieve greatness for our country and leave noble heritage to our country.
5. If you believe that no foreigner, no matter how sincere he is, under an imperialist Colonial Government can make greater sacrifices than we can to improve her.
6. If you believe that our natural resources must no longer be exploited mainly for the benefit of Aliens, but for our benefit too.
7. Above all, if you believe that Self-Government is the only solution to the evils that plague us, and therefore must be fought for and won now, then your duty is clear — VOTE C.P.P. AT THE GENERAL ELECTIONS.

WHY THE C.P.P. IS CONTESTING THE 1951 ELECTION.

. . . We were not surprised when the nominated members of the Coussey Committee, in spite of hundreds of telegrams, memoranda and newspaper articles sent to them by the general public demanding immediate self-government, produced half-baked proposals which they considered acceptable as the basis for the improvement on of colonial rule. True to type, the nominated men turned deaf ear to the whole country's demand for S.G. NOW, and the people were justified for believing that 'Nominations by Colonial Governments in any shape or form are an abomination.' . . .

HOW DID THE COUSSEY COMMITTEE LET THE COUNTRY DOWN?

Among other objectionable proposals, the Coussey Committee recommended that Ghana should remain under colonial servitude and degredation for many more years.

1. That the British Governor should retain as much power as he had under the old Colonial system, by wielding the powers of *VETO* and *CERTIFICATION*; thus, bills passed by all the 75 representatives of the people could only have the force of law if the Governor agreed.
2. That the most important ministries of *DEFENCE, FINANCE* (the country's life blood) *EXTERNAL AFFAIRS* and *JUSTICE* should *NOT* be held by the people's representatives but by 'civil service ministers' who will be appointed by and be ultimately responsible to the Secretary of State for the Colonies in far-away London.

3. That the election of the representatives in all but the 4 municipalities of Accra, Cape Coast, Sekondi–Takoradi and Kumasi should be indirect, which process can easily lend itself to corrupt practices and abuse in a country where bribery and corruptions are rife.

The task of fighting to remove these objectionable proposals cannot be entrusted to the same men who framed them. . . .

WHAT DOES THE PARTY STAND FOR?

You know, we all know, the whole world knows that C.P.P. stands for full SELF-GOVERNMENT NOW and the end of foreign control of our affairs. . . . This is our native land, and we can no longer tolerate a foreign imperialist government; we are of age. . . .

OUR MESSAGE TO GHANA. . . .

Ghanaians, yours is the task of deciding whether you will be free NOW or subject yourselves to years of meddlesome, oppressive foreign colonial rule. . . . Once get the right men in, Victory will be ours at no distant date and NOT in 15 or 20 years as imperialists have been promising us.

THEREFORE

Vote wisely and God will save Ghana from the imperialist.
Long live the Convention People's Party.
Long live Kwame Nkrumah.
Long live the forward march of the common people of Ghana to their rightful and just inheritance.
SEEK YE FIRST THE POLITICAL KINGDOM AND ALL THINGS WILL BE ADDED INTO IT.

OUR PROGRAMME

. . . Our entry into the Assembly in full strength will open up better opportunities to struggle for immediate self-Government. Whilst that struggle is proceeding, the C.P.P. will do all in its power to better the condition of the people of this country; it must be pointed out however that the implementation of this development pro-gramme can only be possible when S.G. has been attained, and we are in full control of our own affairs.

(A) POLITICAL. . . .

The aim of the Convention People's Party is full SELF-GOVERNMENT NOW.
It will fight for and get. . . .

(1) A free and democratic National Assembly elected on the basis of Universal Adult Suffrage at 21 years;

(2) Direct elections with no property or residential qualifications for candidates seeking election;

(3) Not less than 100 Constituencies of about 50,000 people each to elect representatives to the National Assembly.

(4) A Senate for Chiefs. . . .

(B) ECONOMIC.

The Convention People's Party aims at launching a Five-year Economic Plan for both social and economic development of this country in order to afford the people an increasingly higher standard of living which has long been denied to them under the Crown Colony system of government. What follows is a brief account of what the Party intends to do when the country gets FULL Dominion Status and the Party is entrusted with the running of the government. . . .

The immediate materialisation of the Volta Hydro-Electric Scheme and the electrification of the whole country is one of the prime objectives of the Party. . . .

The immediate development of facilities for a modern communication and transport system . . . is another major objective. . . . The Railway system will be modernized (e.g. double track railway) and extended to the Northern Territories and Trans–Volta. Various branch lines and a coastal line extending from Half-Assini to Aflao will also be built. . . . Roads also will be modernised and extended. . . . Water transport . . . will be encouraged by the building of canals to join rivers. . . .

The party aims at a progressive mechanisation of agriculture. . . . It also aims at raising the standard of living among the peasants by bringing pipe-borne water, electric lights, good housing, education and other social and cultural amenities to the towns and villages. Special attention will be given to the Swollen Shoot Disease. . . . Farmers will be given control of the vast funds with the Cocoa Marketing Board to use for the benefit of the farmers primarily and the country in general. One of the important objectives . . . is to redeem for the farmers the numerous farms that have been mortgaged. . . .

The timber industry will be controlled and expanded for the benefit of the people. . . . A large programme of afforestation will be undertaken and measures will be taken to check and remedy soil erosion. . . . The fishing industry will be helped with the provision of canning factories . . . and modern facilities for catching fish and marketing same. . . .

The industrialisation of the country is one of the principal objectives of the Party, and under Dominion Status it will carry it out with all energy. Imperialism is incompatible with industrialisation of a colonial country. It is only under self-government that this country can be industrialised in the way it should. Under the industrialisation programme the Party envisages numerous manufacturing factories (e.g. canning, meat, electrical goods, building materials, machinery, cutlery, crockery, provision, hardwares and textile plants) springing up in all parts of the country. . . .

The retail trade in the country needs great improvement by the allowance of fair discount on wholesale prices, so that the Market women and the smaller African retailers can have a fair margin of profit. . . .

To control the economy of the country it is imperative that a National Bank be established. . . .

(C) SOCIAL. . . .

One of the first objectives of the Party is to create avenues of employment for all with good pay and better conditions of work. Jobs for all will be achieved [by the economic programme]. . . . An important innovation which the Party intends to introduce . . . is the system of weekly wages. . . . The Party will help promote Hire Purchase Systems. . . .

The country needs a unified system of education with free and compulsory elementary, secondary and technical education up to the age of 16 years. . . . The Party will bring the University College to a full university status at once. . . . The Party lays special importance on Adult Education and will see to it that a planned campaign to liquidate illiteracy from this country in the shortest possible time is vigorously undertaken. . . .

The scandalous insanitary conditions in towns and villages are some of the gravest indictments of the imperialist regime in this country and constitute one of the fundamental reasons for our demand for full self-government NOW. Imperialism . . . cannot help us. For one of the unwritten laws of imperialism is to keep colonial people poor in mind and body so as to exploit them the better. The aim of the Convention People's Party is to remove this stain; it intends to establish hospitals . . . clinics and sanatoriums all over the country and to inaugurate a Free Medical Service. . . . The C.P.P. intends as one of its principal aims to establish a country-wide network of pipe-borne water supply for use in homes and factories. At no very distant date it should be possible to see water on the tap in most homes in the country. . . .

Hard Work.

Self Government or Dominion Status by itself does not produce bread or kenkey; it only releases a colonial people from imperialist bondage and exploitation, and enables them to get work, decent wages and to attain a higher standard of living. . . .

Taxation.

Under the present Colonial rule, taxation has been most unpopular because people do not get returns commensurate with taxes they pay. Under self-government taxes would still be levied on all who should pay taxes, but the C.P.P. would see that taxation brings with it, social education, cultural and economic rewards for the whole community. . . .

Exploited and oppressed Ghanaians, this is your chance to save your country!

VOTE C.P.P. ! ! !

[C.P.P., Accra]

509 REPORT ON INDUSTRIALISATION AND THE GOLD COAST [W. A. LEWIS]

5 JUNE, 1953.

. . . 20. In unenlightened circles agriculture and industry are often considered as alternatives to each other. The truth is that industrialisation for a home market can make little progress unless agriculture is progressing vigorously at the same time, to provide both the market for industry, and industry's labour supply. If agriculture is stagnant, industry cannot grow.

21. In the Gold Coast there is very little sign of an increase in agricultural productivity, except in so far as the improvement in the world price of cocoa since the war is an increase in agricultural productivity. Physical production per man, outside the cocoa industry, is probably constant, and in the cocoa industry it is probably declining. According to the Government Statistician, about half the adult male population of the Gold Coast is engaged in food production (excluding cocoa, which absorbs only one-third as many). This half of the economy is almost certainly stagnant.

22. The most certain way to promote industrialisation in the Gold Coast is to lay the foundation it requires by taking vigorous measures to raise food production per person engaged in agriculture. . . . One way is to increase the yield per acre; the other way is to increase the number of acres worked per man.

23. To increase the yield per acre is usually the cheaper way. It requires that there should be research, to breed the most productive seeds and livestock, to discover the best use of fertilisers, to deter-

mine appropriate crop rotations, and so on. The Gold Coast Department of Agriculture has done some work in these spheres, and has no doubt made the best use of the scanty resources at its disposal. But, in one sense, the surest way to industrialise the Gold Coast would be to multiply by four or five the resources available to the department for fundamental research into food production. . . .

25. The number of acres that a man can work is a function of the amount of equipment he has. In the Northern Territories farmers are being taught to use the bullock and the plough, thereby multiplying by four the amount of land that a family can cultivate in one year. Elsewhere there are experiments in mechanical cultivation. Mechanisation is costly, especially as all its fuel has to be imported. But this is without doubt the line of progress. A high standard of living cannot be built upon an economy in which half the people are scratching the ground for food with a hoe. . . .

28. A country which lacks advantageous natural resources can compete effectively in foreign markets only on the basis of low labour costs. This way of earning a livelihood appeals, therefore, only to countries where the population is so large in relation to natural resources that even the least remunerative occupations must be fostered. The Gold Coast is not in this position. . . .

29. The Gold Coast is not over-populated, and wages are high . . . relatively to other under-developed countries. The industrialisation of the Gold Coast is not likely to be based upon importing light raw materials in order to export manufactures. . . .

30. . . . The industries which are most likely to succeed in the Gold Coast 88. . . [are:—]

Favourable Industries:

Oil Expressing	Bricks and Tiles
Canned fruit and	Cement
vegetables	Glass

Salt   Lime
Beer   Wood products
Industrial alcohol
Miscellaneous chemicals

Marginal Industries:

Biscuits   Knitwear
Soap   Weaving cotton
Confectionery   and rayon
Cigarettes   Jute bags
Boots and shoes   Foundry products
Hats and caps   Candles
Shirts   Paints and colours
     Travelling bags
     Rubber
     manufactures.

. . . .

94. There is no question that industrialisation is impossible in the Gold Coast without bringing in the knowledge of expatriates; the question is only on what terms they come in, and how much of their own capital they may invest. . . .

104. Assuming that foreign capital is required, the alternative to permitting foreign enterprise is that the Government should borrow abroad, presumably at a rate of interest lower than the profits that foreign entrepreneurs would want, and should either operate factories itself, or lend the money to African entrepreneurs. Most governments, however, need all the money that they can raise, whether by loan or by taxes, for the more urgent purpose of expanding the public services. This purpose is more urgent in a double sense. It is more urgent because the expansion of the public services is necessary if other economic activities are to be developed, so that a government is likely to contribute more to development if it expands the public services generally than if it uses the same money to build a factory. And it is more urgent also in the sense that no one but the government can expand the public services, whereas if the government does not build factories, others will. No government is so rich that it does not have to choose between alternative ways of

spending money. Even the Gold Coast Government, which seems rich to its citizens, is really very poor. If the Government were to set out to give the Gold Coast the educational system which it needs, this alone would swallow all the funds at its disposal, let alone if it were also to try to provide water supplies throughout the country, adequate medical services, properly surfaced roads. . . . There is no doubt in the writer's mind that the Gold Coast Government can do more for development by . . . expanding the public services . . . and on quadrupling that part of its agricultural services which relate to food production for the local market, than it can do by operating factories. If the Government were determined to exclude private foreign capital, it would be better to postpone industrialisation rather than to divert money to it from these more urgent purposes. For the present the Government should confine its ownership of factories to the inescapable minimum. . . .

109. Whatever the foreigner's faults may be, the fact remains that the Gold Coast needs him more than he needs the Gold Coast. Foreign capital does not need the Gold Coast. If all the foreign capital now in the Gold Coast were driven out, it would have little difficulty in being absorbed elsewhere. . . . There are many places within the sterling area crying out for capital. . . . The Gold Coast cannot gain by creating an atmosphere towards foreign capital which makes foreigners reluctant to invest in the Gold Coast. . . .

111. The issues which have to be decided are (i) from what industries foreign capital will be excluded altogether, (ii) whether foreign capitalists will be required to have African partners, (iii) what rules are to regulate employment, (iv) whether profits or prices are to be regulated; (v) whether capital and profits can be freely transferred, and (vi) what is to be the procedure on nationalisation. . . .

136. . . . When the Government has made its decisions on these six issues, it

should announce them and should stick to them. One of the essential pre-requisites of investment is confidence, and the pre-requisite of this is knowledge. Lack of confidence at present holds up investment in the Gold Coast. . . .

144. To train up African enterprise must naturally be one of the major objectives of economic policy. The role of the foreigner is that of tutor. . . . That is why foreign business men should not be allowed in this country unless they play their part in training Africans to do their job. . . .

150. Because business management has to be learnt so largely on the job, the Germans sent large numbers of their young people to work in England in the last quarter of the nineteenth century, in firms where they could acquire some administrative experience. Their example was followed a little later by Japan, whose young people were sent similarly to Germany and to the United States. The Gold Coast should follow suit. . . .

151. African enterprise cannot be built up simply by lending Africans money. To lend money to entrepreneurs who lack managerial capacity is merely to throw it down the drain. What potential African industrialists lack is not primarily money; it is rather technical knowledge, and experience of factory organisation. If the government lends money it should do this only as a supplement to rendering technical and managerial assistance. In fact the loan should be made only on condition that the borrower is willing to accept some measure of supervision.

152. This is where the Gold Coast Industrial Development Corporation went wrong. . . .

156. Another desirable shift of emphasis is away from lending people money to start new businesses, in industries of which they have no past experience, towards concentrating almost exclusively upon lending to businesses which are already in existence and which show good prospects. . . .

159. . . . One of the remarkable features of the Gold Coast is the relative insignificance of handicraft industries. . . . The only substantial trade appears to be wood-working.

160. One or two countries protect their handicraft industries because so many people are employed in them that widespread unemployment would follow if these industries were destroyed by the competition of factory made articles. There is no need to consider this in the Gold Coast. . . . Since labour is in short supply . . . and the standard of living low, it would be a dis-service to encourage handicraft manufactures of low productivity instead of factory industries of much higher productivity. . . .

253. Number one priority is therefore a concentrated attack on the system of growing food on the Gold Coast, so as to set in motion an ever increasing productivity. This is the way to provide the market, the capital, and the labour for industrialisation.

254. Priority number two is to improve the public services. To do this will reduce the cost of manufacturing in the Gold Coast, and will thus automatically attract new industries, without the government having to offer special favours. . . .

256. In order to carry out such a programme the government should

1. Establish an Industries Division in the Department of Commerce. . . .
2. Announce its willingness to give limited aid, by way of temporary protection or subsidy to newly established factories in the industries listed as 'favourable' or 'marginal'. . . .
3. Announce its attitude to foreign enterprise; welcoming such enterprise, especially if it enters into partnership with the Government or with African enterprise; guaranteeing free transfer of profits and dividends, and fair compensation independently

determined if nationalisation takes place; and safeguarding the employment of a proportion of Africans in senior posts. . . .

4. Arrange for suitably qualified Africans to be employed temporarily in industrial undertakings in other countries. . . .

5. Arrange a conference of persons engaged in labour management in the Gold Coast . . . with a view to initiating further research and teaching. . . .

6. Decide to accord priority to industry over domestic consumption in the extension of public services which are in short supply. . . .

7. Abolish import duties on industrial raw materials. . . .

8. Purchase land outside Kumasi and Accra for development as industrial estates. . . .

9. Promote and aid the establishment of a first class hotel in Accra. . . .

10. Set aside funds (a) for developing industrial estates . . .
(b) for lending to small African firms under strict supervision . . .
(c) for lending to or investing in large scale enterprise . . .
(d) for operating government factories, either for pioneering purposes or as public utilities. . . .

11. Increase the staff of the Industrial Development Corporation . . . and charge it with . . . the general duty of aiding African enterprise, and with the funds established under (10). . . .

[Gold Coast Government, Accra, 1953]

510 EXTRACT FROM THE ANNUAL REPORT FOR 1953.

. . . Total exports from the Gold Coast in 1953, at £89·8 million, were £3·8 million greater in value than the total for 1952; domestic exports totalled £87·8 million compared with £83·9 million in 1952, and re-exports £1·9 million compared with £2·1 million. The United Kingdom remained the chief consumer, taking 42 per cent of total exports. The proportion of the total exported to the dollar area fell slightly compared with 1952 to 28 per cent; exports to O.E.E.C. countries, at £19·3 million were slightly higher and comprised 21 per cent of the total.

With the exception of diamonds, earnings from exports of minerals, cocoa and timber were higher than in 1952. Cocoa exports increased by £3·6 million in 1953 despite a fall in the average f.o.b. price per ton from £248 to £237. The higher average value in 1952 reflected the higher level of world market prices owing to a smaller Gold Coast crop; prices for the larger 1952–53 crop were lower. Export values in the first three months of the 1953–54 crop year, October to December, 1953, have again been considerably higher than those for the opening months of the 1952–53 crop year. . . .

Central Government revenue continued to be derived primarily from customs duties and income tax. Of the total revenue derived from customs and excise in 1952–53, £9,544,719 was obtained from import duties and £16,827,164 from export duties. Of the latter figure the duty on cocoa provided £16,406,944, collected in accordance with the Cocoa Duty and Development Funds Ordinance. Under this Ordinance duty is paid at the rate of 10 per cent when the f.o.b. price does not exceed £100 per ton; when the price is between £100 and £120 a ton the duty remains constant at £10 per ton; and when the f.o.b. price is in excess of £120 a ton the duty is half the amount by which the price exceeds £100. The proceeds of the duty are divided in such a way that the first £20 per ton of export duty on a consignment is paid into general revenue, the next £15 per ton into the Special Development Fund, the next £10 into the Reserve Development Fund together with three-fifths of any excess of duty over £45 per ton. The remaining two-fifths of any excess of duty over £45 per ton accrue to general revenue. Both funds will be applied exclusively to such development projects as may be authorised by the Ordinance in the case of the Special Development Fund and by the Legislature in the case of the Reserve Development Fund.

Import duties are levied on a wide range of goods entering the country. While the rate of duty varies with the item, 20 per cent *ad valorem* is the rate most commonly levied, though in the case of luxury goods the rate may be as much as $66\frac{2}{3}$ per cent

ad valorem. Export duties are levied on timber, diamonds won by small operations, and kola nuts, in addition to cocoa. . . .

Total value of imports in 1953 amounted to £72,764,084, an increase of £6,279,416 or 9 per cent over the 1952 level of £66,484,668. The principal sources of supply for imports were the United Kingdom (57 per cent of total value), the Netherlands and Netherlands West Indies (11 per cent), Japan (5 per cent), the United States of America (5 per cent) and Western Germany (3 per cent). . . .

The following table shows the Gold Coast's principal imports:

	1952		1953	
		Value		Value
Goods	Quantity	c.i.f.	Quantity	c.i.f.
		£		£
Cotton Piece-Goods	72,961,099 sq. yd.	9,577,310	96,079,286 sq. yd.	10,966,248
Potable Spirits[1]	224,089 gall.	366,110	290,271 gall.	477,807
Ale, Beer, Stout & Porter	3,368,278 galls.	1,538,509	3,526,024 galls.	1,576,288
Flour	61,001,243 lb.	1,784,830	64,645,107 lb.	1,956,455
Sugar	32,614,128 lb.	1,082,079	47,060,832 lb.	1,286,327
Tobacco	3,868,217 lb.	1,923,208	3,738,603 lb.	1,894,051
Commercial vehicles*	2,941	2,120,828	4,498	2,894,635
Private Cars	2,022	1,123,518	2,658	1,390,106
Bicycles	42,258	450,358	43,051	465,200
Cement	173,650 tons	1,786,643	244,244 tons	2,092,995

[1] Gin, rum, brandy and whisky: excludes other potable spirits.
* Includes chassis with engines and tyres.

Exports.

The total value of exports in 1953 amounted to £89,781,640, an increase of 4 per cent over the 1952 figure of £86,000,103.

The principal markets for exports were as follows:

Cocoa. (Crops sales, 1952–53). U.S.A. 29 per cent; United Kingdom 27 per cent; Western Germany 10 per cent; the Netherlands 11 per cent; U.S.S.R. 7 per cent; others 16 per cent.

Gold: United Kingdom 100 per cent.

Diamonds: United Kingdom 100 per cent.

Manganese: U.S.A. 60 per cent; United Kingdom 25 per cent; Norway 15 per cent; the Netherlands 9 per cent; Western Germany 8 per cent; Italy 6 per cent; others 5 per cent.

Timber (Sawn, including veneers.) United Kingdom 68 per cent; U.S.A. 17 per cent; South Africa 7 per cent; others 8 per cent.

The following table shows actual figures of the Gold Coast's principal exports:

Goods	1952 Quantity	Value f.o.b. £	1953 Quantity	Value f.o.b. £
Cocoa	212,005 tons	52,533,085	236,634 tons	56,143,022
Gold	705,815 fine oz. troy.	9,255,704	730,156 fine oz. troy.	9,390,581
Diamonds	2,133,873 carats	5,399,885	2,164,262 carats	3,924,755
Manganese Ore	794,192 tons	8,332,847	745,990 tons	8,722,222
Bauxite	74,368 ,,	137,581	115,075 ,,	201,383
Timber: unmanufactured*	10,556,268 cub. ft.	4,157,402	15,088,860 cub. ft.	5,880,117

* This classification includes logs, sawn timber and veneers. . . .

Production. . . .

The revaluation of sterling in September, 1949, assisted the production of gold materially, but steadily rising costs soon more than outweighed the benefits of this higher production. This would have had a most serious effect on the operation of many of the mines had it not been for the relief granted by the decision of the International Monetary Fund to permit all sales to take place on the free market, and the further relief afforded by the passage of the new Minerals Duty Ordinance in 1952. The advantage afforded by the sale of gold on the free market has virtually disappeared, because the price of gold has been falling since 1949 until in 1953 there did not exist on the free market any premium over the official price. A number of mines have been operating much nearer the margin, and the fall in price of the free market gold to the official level in 1953 is therefore viewed with concern by Gold Coast mines. Total production for 1953 amounted to 730,963 fine ounces compared with 691,460 fine ounces in 1952. This figure is made up as follows:

Banket mines	188,838 fine ounces.
Quartz Reef Mines	511,363 ,, ,,
Dredging operations	30,762 ,, ,,

Production of diamonds in 1953 was at about the same rate as in 1952 which was a record year. . . . The proportion contributed by African producers was lower in 1953, but the output by the companies increased considerably and their output for the first ten months of the year was actually higher than the whole for 1952. The introduction, at the beginning of 1952, of the Prospecting and Digging Licences Regulations, has done something to regularise and stabilise conditions in the industry.

The Gold Coast has been since 1944 the world's largest exporter of high-grade manganese ore. . . .

The daily average labour force employed by the mining companies during the fourth quarter of 1953 were as follows:

	Europeans	Africans
Gold Mines	793	26,745
Diamond Mines	50	3,915
Manganese Mines	62	6,310
Bauxite Mines	24	392
	929	37,362

These figures do not include the labour engaged on small African workings. . . .

Cocoa. In recent years rather more than one-third of the world's supplies of cocoa have come from the Gold Coast which is the largest single producer. Within the Gold Coast cocoa is the basis of the national economy; since the second world war, exports of cocoa beans have averaged a little under 70 per cent of the total domestic exports and about 92 per cent of agricultural exports. Apart from a relatively small amount which is processed to produce cocoa butter in a local factory, all cocoa produced is exported as prepared beans. . . . The main cocoa harvest season usually begins in October and lasts for four or five months. A small mid-crop is also gathered in the second quarter of the calendar year.

During the 1951–52 and 1952–53 crop years the total local marketings of cocoa were 210,663 tons and 247,376 tons respectively. It is unlikely that the 1953–54 main crop will much exceed the estimate of 205,000 which together with the 1954 mid-crop should bring production for the crop year 1953–54 to around 210,000 tons.

Apart from the cocoa capsids *Sahlbergella singularis* and *Distantiella theobroma*, which have caused severe damage to cocoa since the early days, and various pod diseases, principally black pod which in some areas causes considerable losses, the industry enjoyed relative immunity from serious pests and diseases for many years. In 1936, however, it was found that large areas of cocoa in the Eastern Province were being killed by a disease (called 'swollen shoot' because of one of its characteristic symptoms) which later proved to be caused by a virus transmitted by insects called mealybugs. The disease spread rapidly in the Eastern Province, where production has since fallen disastrously, and numerous outbreaks have also been found in Ashanti and the Western Province. The effect of the grave and increasing damage caused by swollen shoot disease has to a large extent been masked in production statistics

by the coming into bearing of new farms particularly in Western Ashanti; the table [below] illustrates this point.

In spite of extensive research no cure for the disease is known and no immune varieties of cocoa have been found; efforts to control the disease have therefore been directed to preventing disease spread by removing all sources of infection; this entails the destruction by cutting out of all diseased cocoa trees and of other trees which carry the virus and from which it may be transmitted to cocoa. The method of work is to examine every cocoa farm tree by tree, to cut out every diseased tree, and to re-inspect the surrounds of every disease outbreak monthly in order that any further trees developing symptoms may be similarly and promptly destroyed. Farmers are paid compensation for the loss of the crop which the diseased trees would have borne before their death from the disease; substantial grants are also given to assist the replanting of cocoa to replace the trees lost. . . .

The start of large-scale control measures was delayed by war conditions, and the campaign was subsequently hampered and at times almost disrupted by staff shortage and opposition on the part of the farmers. There has, however, been an improvement since the middle of 1952. . . . In Ashanti all known outbreaks have been initially treated. During the survey of large acreages of cocoa during 1953 only very few isolated outbreaks have been found. In the Western Region a considerable amount of disease continues to be found around Wiawso. In the Trans–Volta area, apart

	1936–7		1951–52		1952–53	
	Tonnage	% of Total	Tonnage	% of Total	Tonnage	% of Total
Eastern Region	128,000	43	47,585	23	50,247	20
Remainder of Colony including Togoland	82,000	27	65,409	31	78,438	32
Ashanti	91,000	30	97,669	46	118,297	48
Total	300,000	100	210,663	100	246,982	100

from two single tree outbreaks in the Jasikan District, disease has been found only around Kpeve. In the Eastern Region early in 1951 good progress had been made in isolating the area of mass infection and devastation, but a hold-up lasting some months resulted in very rapid disease spread in the area north and west of the heavily diseased zone. . . .

Within the area of mass infection and devastation itself, some 31,500 farms aggregating 63,600 acres of cocoa, were initially treated by the end of 1950. Up to the end of December, 1953, the initial treatment involved destruction of 9,496,865 trees . . . and a further 5,436,358 trees were cut out on subsequent re-inspection. Many untreated farms had, however, already been replanted and swollen shoot had spread to the young trees.

Outside the area of mass infection . . . the campaign to locate and deal with swollen shoot disease outbreaks had by the end of 1953 covered nearly nine million acres of land on which approximately three million acres were found to be carrying cocoa. This disease has so far been found and located in about 30,400 farms, involving the destruction of 9,699,716 trees up to the end of December, 1953. . . .

[Gold Coast Annual Report, 1953]

511 LEGISLATIVE ASSEMBLY DEBATE
10 TO 15 JULY, 1953.

[a] The Prime Minister (Dr. Kwame Nkrumah): Mr. Speaker, I beg to move:

That this Assembly, in adopting the Government's White Paper on Constitutional Reform,[1] do authorise the Government to request that Her Majesty's Government, as soon as the necessary constitutional and administrative arrangements for independence are made, should introduce an Act of Independence into the United Kingdom Parliament, declaring the Gold Coast a sovereign and independent State within the Commonwealth; and further,

[1] *The Government Proposals for Constitutional Reform, Accra, 1953.*

that this Assembly do authorise the Government to ask Her Majesty's Government, without prejudice to the above request, to amend as a matter of urgency the Gold Coast (Constitution) Order in Council, 1950, in such a way as to provide inter alia that the Legislative Assembly shall be composed of members directly elected by secret ballot, and that all members of the Cabinet shall be members of the Assembly and directly responsible to it.

. . . Last year, I brought this House changes in the Constitution which were, at the time, regarded as of minor importance. I was accused, indeed, of personal ambition in seeking the title of Prime Minister. We can now, Mr. Speaker, see the results for ourselves. (Hear! hear!) Certainly nobody outside the Gold Coast has regarded my position as anything but what the name implies. The prestige of the Gold Coast overseas has, in fact, been enhanced by this change. Even the co-ordination of the functions of my own colleagues has been made more successful by the increase in status. I believe that there is more decision in our activities as a Cabinet than there was before, and that we are better equipped to get things done.

The freedom we demand is for our country as a whole — this freedom we are claiming is for our children, for the generations yet unborn, that they may see the light of day and live as men and women with the right to work out the destiny of their own country. Mr. Speaker, our demand for self-government is a just demand. It is a demand admitting of no compromise. The right of a people to govern themselves is a fundamental principle, and to compromise on this principle is to betray it. . . . If there is to be a criterion of a people's preparedness for self-government, then I say it is their readiness to assume the responsibilities of ruling themselves. (Hear! hear!) For who but a people themselves can say when they are prepared? How can others judge when that moment has arrived in the destiny of a subject people? What other gauge can there be?

Mr. Speaker, never in the history of the world has an alien ruler granted self-rule to a people on a silver platter. Therefore, Mr. Speaker, I say that a people's readiness and willingness to assume the responsibilities of self-rule is the single criterion of their preparedness to undertake these responsibilities.

I have described on a previous occasion in this House, what were the considerations which led me to agree to the participation of my party in the General Election of 1951, and hence in the Government of the Gold Coast, under the terms of the 1950 Constitution Order in Council. In making that decision, I took on the task of proving to the world that we were prepared to perform our duties with responsibility, to set in motion the many reforms which our people needed, and to work from within the Government, and within the Assembly, that is, by constitutional means, for the immediate aim of self-government. We have only been in office, Mr. Speaker, for two and a half years, and we have kept these objectives constantly before us. Let there be no doubt that we are equally determined not to rest until we have gained them. We are encouraged in our efforts by the thought that in so acting we are showing that we are able to govern ourselves and thereby we are putting an end to the myth that Africans are unable to manage their own affairs. . . . For despite the legacies of a century of colonial rule, in the short space of time since your Representative Ministers assumed the responsibilities of office, we have addressed ourselves boldly to the task of laying sound economic and social foundations on which this beloved country of ours can raise a solid democratic society. . . .

We have now come to the most important stage of our constitutional development; we can look back on the stages through which we have passed during these last few years: first, our discussions with the Secretary of State leading to the changes of last year; then the questions posed in the October statement, which were to be answered by all parties, groups and councils interested in this great issue; the consultations with the Territorial Councils, with the political parties, with the Trades Union Congress. . . . Every representation which we received . . . has received my careful consideration. . . . I had also received a special invitation to attend a meeting in Tamale with the Territorial Council, the Traditional Rulers and the Members of the Legislative Assembly. Naturally, I accepted the invitation, because it was clear that if I had not held discussions with the Northern Territories, the unity of the Gold Coast might have been endangered and our progress towards self-government might have been delayed. (Hear! hear!) We have adapted some of our proposals to meet Northern Territories wishes, and we have been able to set their minds at rest on several issues of the greatest importance to them, and to the Gold Coast as a whole. Mr. Speaker, sir, the days of forgetting about our brothers in the North, and in the Trust Territory, are over. (Hear! hear!)

Criticisms have been levelled against the Government for the secrecy with which these talks were surrounded, and I should like to tell the country why this was necessary. When we went to the talks, of course, the Government members had some idea of the way their collective view on the representations were being formulated. We carefully explained, however, that our views were not finally decided, and they would not be until we had had an opportunity for hearing any further views which these bodies might care to express. . . . But in order that our discussions could be of true value, frank and unreserved, I stated at an early stage that I should be grateful if the conversations could be regarded as strictly confidential. I am glad to place on record the value of the discussions which we held and the extent to which the undertaking which I was given was honoured. (Hear! hear!)

Mr. Speaker, knowing full well, therefore, the will of the Chiefs and people whom we represent, I am confident that with the support of this House, Her Majesty's Government will freely accede to our legitimate and righteous demand to become a self-governing unit within the Commonwealth.

I put my confidence in the willing acceptance of this demand by Her Majesty's Government, because it is consistent with the declared policy of successive United Kingdom Governments. Indeed, the final transition from the stage of responsible government as a colony to the independence of a sovereign state guiding its own destinies is the apotheosis of this same British policy in relation to its dependencies. . . .

There is no conflict that I can see between our claim and the professed policy of all parties and governments of the United Kingdom. We have here in our country a stable society. Our economy is healthy, as good as any for a country of our size. In many respects we are very much better off than many sovereign states. And our potentialities are large. Our people are fundamentally homogeneous, nor are we plagued with religious or tribal problems. And, above all, we have hardly any colour bar. . . .

I am confident, therefore, that I express the wishes and feelings of the Chiefs and people of this country in hoping that the final transfer of power to your Representative Members may be done in a spirit of amity and friendship, so that, having peacefully achieved our freedom, the people of both countries — Britain and the Gold Coast — may form a new relationship based on mutual respect, trust and friendship. Thus may the partnership implied in the Statute of Westminster be clothed in a new meaning. For freely associated communities make better friends than those associated by subjugation. We see today, Mr. Speaker,

how much easier and friendlier are the bonds between Great Britain and her former dependencies of India, Pakistan and Ceylon. . . . A free and independent Gold Coast, taking its rightful place in peace and amity by the side of the other Dominions, will provide a valid and effective sign that freedom can be achieved in a climate of goodwill and thereby accrue to the intrinsic strength of the Commonwealth. . . .

In the very early days of the Christian era, long before England had assumed any importance, long even before her people had united into a nation, our ancestors had attained a great empire, which lasted until the eleventh century, when it fell before the attacks of the Moors of the North. At its height, that empire stretched from Timbuctu to Bamako, and even as far as the Atlantic. It is said that lawyers and scholars were much respected in that empire, and that the inhabitants of Ghana wore garments of wool, cotton, silk and velvet. There was trade in copper, gold and textile fabrics, and jewels and weapons of gold and silver were carried. (Hear! hear!)

Thus may we take pride in the name of Ghana, not out of romanticism, but as an inspiration for the future. . . . What our ancestors achieved in the context of their contemporary society, gives us confidence that we can create, out of that past, a glorious future, not in terms of war and military pomp, but in terms of social progress and peace. . . .

[He reviews Gold Coast political and national movements from 1844 to 1951.] According to the motto of the valiant *Accra Evening News*, 'We prefer self government with danger' (*Some Honourable Members continuing*) 'to servitude in tranquillity.' Doubtless we shall make mistakes as have all other nations. . . . But we can try also to learn from the mistakes of others. . . . Moreover the mistakes we may make will be our own mistakes, and it will be our responsibility to set them right. As long as we are ruled by others we shall lay our mistakes at their door (Laughter) and our sense of responsibility will remain dulled.

And while yet we are making our claim for self-government, I want to emphasize, Mr. Speaker, that self-government is not an end in itself. It is a means to an end, to the building of the good life to the benefit of all, regardles of tribe, creed, colour or station in life. Our aim is to make this country a worthy place for all its citizens, a country that will be a shining light throughout the whole continent of Africa. . . . To Britain this is the supreme testing moment in her African relations. When we turn our eyes to the sorry events in South, Central and East Africa, when we hear the dismal news about Kenya and Central African Federation, we are cheered by the more cordial relationship that exists between us and Britain. We are now asking her to allow that relationship to open into golden bonds of freedom, equality and fraternity by complying without delay to our request for self-government. . . .

Minister of Communications and Works (*Mr. J. A. Braimah*): Mr. Speaker, I rise to second the motion, and I trust that, by doing so, I shall dispel for ever the false impression which has circulated in some uninformed quarters that the people of the Northern Territories do not want self-government. We desire as much as any man the right to govern ourselves and to enjoy our freedom. . . .

We in the North have reached this position of agreement and unity with the South, without outside influence, but not without many fears and forebodings. . . . Put briefly, the people of the Northern Territories desire, most fervently, political and economic equality with the South. By political equality I mean the assurance that in a truly democratic legislature . . . there shall be a fair proportional representation for the Northern Territories. By economic equality I mean that the resources of the Gold Coast, however localised in origin, should be used for the

good of the country as a whole. We desire to play our full part in the development of our country. We cannot offer the rich cocoa soils of the South but we can and do offer the willing labours of our sons and daughters as well as such wealth as exists in our soil. In return we ask that these offerings of our Northern resources should be utilised and paid for with a higher standard of living for our people and a full development programme for their towns and villages, their farms and forests. . . .

But . . . if the North stands back, whilst the South marches into full independence, what kind of equality shall we enjoy? We shall repeat the tragic divisions of India and Pakistan, of the Burmese and the Karens, or of the Arab world within itself. None of us desires such divisions and we realise that we must march forward with the South; but the South must make it possible for us to go with them by meeting us half way. . . .

The North has expressed the fear that too great haste towards independence would result in domination of the North by the South. We want time to make up some of the distance that separates us in levels of education and literacy. . . . The North is not yet ready to commit itself to full independence and the South, led by the outstanding statesmanship of the Prime Minister, Dr. Kwame Nkrumah, has set its face against prescribing a target for full independence. I must warn those who would like to insert such a date that they will be paving the gloomy path of national suicide; they will be driving a wedge between the North and the South; they will be sounding the death-knell of national unity and destroying the hard-won confidence of the North; and they will be ignoring the unhappy lessons so recently taught us by the news from Nigeria. . . . We in the North are most . . . sincerely grateful for the concession which the White Paper makes to our wishes in this regard. We share the desire of the South to go forward; but let us go forward together at a pace that we can all achieve. . . .

Another fear so often expressed by my countrymen from the North is the fear of an artificial division between Northern Togoland and the rest of the Northern Territories. This fear was expressed by the late Ya-Na of Dagomba [when he said] . . . 'If the new constitution will make it possible for that part of Dagomba State under the United Kingdom Administration to remain and become part of the free Gold Coast, then it may be possible for me and my people to give it our support. On the other hand, if the new constitution makes for the entire breaking away of that part of the Dagomba State in Togoland from the main part of the State which is in the Gold Coast, then of course it will only be natural for me and my people to resist any movement towards independence for the Gold Coast. For nobody will break down his own house to make it possible for somebody to build his.' . . . Honourable Members can imagine our pleasure when the Prime Minister assured us that he would never agree to our being divided by an international boundary. . . . [In the] White Paper . . . the full integration of Northern Togoland and the Northern Territories becomes the acknowledged goal and every loyal Northerner will vote for such a policy.

Another matter to which Northerners attach very great importance is the maintenance of the highest standards in every branch of Government. We will not contemplate any reduction in the levels of efficiency or of integrity. I believe in Africanisation and I long to see my fellow African taking over all the high offices of Government, but not before he is equipped . . . to do so. . . . We want to be able to trust the officers who are paid to serve us. . . . If this means the continued employment of expatriates, we in the North will welcome and indeed demand their continued employment, whilst doing all in our power to train our own sons and daughters to emulate their high example and so be worthy to inherit their

position in our national life. I venture to suggest to Honourable Members that it would be difficult to suggest any better compromise between the sometimes conflicting objectives of Africanisation on the one hand and the maintenance of standards on the other, than that incorporated in the proposals regarding the public service in this White Paper.

There is another very important matter of grave concern to the North. We do not live in isolation from the world. Nationhood in the modern world cannot mean insularity. We have our international responsibilities and we share the dangers of international politics. There could be no greater folly than to attempt to cut ourselves adrift amidst the treacherous tides and currents of international avarice and intrigue. Every thoughtful citizen will acknowledge the supreme wisdom of accepting Commonwealth and United Nations responsibilities. Moreover it does not require any very great intelligence to realise that, in the age of hydrogen bombs, jet fighters and atomic weapons, we cannot defend ourselves against a determined aggressor. We must certainly play our part. The people of the Northern Territories are proud of their contribution to defence in the past, and I, for one, look forward to the ever-expanding growth of that contribution. But it will never be enough by itself. It must be linked to the defence schemes of the Commonwealth and of the free nations of the world. That is why the Northern Territories expressed anxiety about the disposal of the portfolio of Defence and External Affairs. Those anxieties are fully and wisely allayed by the proposals incorporated in the White Paper and we of the North would not support any modification of those proposals.

There are some things we desire which are not mentioned in the White Paper, but proposals for incorporation in a constitutional document are not necessarily the best place to express all one's desires. The important question is, 'Will the new constitution provide machinery adequate for the expression of those desires and for their translation into active policies?' The answer to that question is surely in the following words from the White Paper itself:—

'The Government accepts the principle that the Northern Territories should be represented in the Assembly in proportion to their population, and adequately in the Cabinet, but does not consider that it would be in the true interests of the North or of the Gold Coast to make provision in the Constitution with regard to the special representation of any region in the Cabinet.'

That passage gives us assured democratic representation. If it differs slightly from what was asked for in the Northern Territories memorandum, we of the North will be the first to acknowledge that the process of give and take cannot be one-sided. In the interests of the country as a whole we gladly accept that proposal in the White Paper. The question as to what can be regarded as adequate representation in the Cabinet can best be left to the Northern Representatives in the new Assembly to decide. With them, too, will rest the future success of the projected arrangements for a special Development Organisation for the North. And with them we must leave all other matters upon which Northerners feel anxious or afraid. For that is the essence of democracy. . . .

Dr. J. B. Danquah (*First Rural, Akim Abuakwa*)

I beg to move an amendment . . . 'That this Assembly, having discussed the Government's White Paper on Constitutional Reform do authorise Government to *notify Her Majesty's Government of the United Kingdom that in pursuance of the general demand of the Chiefs and people of the Gold Coast for a sovereign independent State within the Commonwealth, a Declaration of Independence of the Gold Coast*
A A

shall be made by the Legislative Assembly on March 6th, 1954; and the Gold Coast Government is further authorised to take all necessary and practicable steps to secure recognition by the United Kingdom Government, in an Act of Parliament, of the Gold Coast as a sovereign independent State within the Commonwealth as a Dominion.' . . .

Why are not the Prime Minister and his colleagues . . . desirous of taking a decision here to liberate ourselves from imperialism instead of going all the way to London to beg for liberation? . . . I have looked quite carefully into the White Paper and what appears to have happened is that the Government seem to be under the impression that we of the Gold Coast are not yet fit for self-government; (Some Honourable Members: No!) that in fact we need a further preparation before we can take over complete control of our own country. That must be the case otherwise our Government would not have thought of a necessary transitional period for making constitutional and administrative arrangements for independence. That must be the case otherwise our Government would not consider it a matter of urgency to remove the subject of Defence and External Affairs from the direct control of the Cabinet and hand that subject over to the Governor alone. That must be the case otherwise the Government would not vest the control of the Public Service of the Gold Coast in the Governor within his own discretion. That must be the case otherwise our Government . . . would not . . . say that no request should be put forward for the removal of the Reserve Powers. . . .

It is our view, Mr. Speaker, that the proposals for interim changes in the constitution are a trick to keep us away from immediate self-government. . . .

Then we have just one other matter as regards detail upon which I would like to touch. I refer to the question of [a] Second Chamber. . . . In the memorandum in the White Paper all the principal parties who wrote asked for a Second

Chamber — except the C.P.P. — and of all the 131 groups which sent memoranda, only . . . seven, the C.P.P. and six other bodies, did not ask for a second chamber.[1] The Asanteman Council did so deliberately and in writing; the Joint Provincial Council did the same, the Trades Union Congress gave very cogent and sound constitutional reasons why there should be a Second Chamber. . . . We have not changed our views and we still stand firm by that view that this country, if it is to be saved from hasty legislation and from dictatorship, must have a Second Chamber. . . .

I find the first part of the Prime Minister's motion unacceptable, not because it does not set a target date, but because it does not ask for Dominion Status. What it asks for is a Sovereign Independent State within the Commonwealth. . . . A sovereign independent State within the Commonwealth can mean anything. . . . You may rely on it that if this House passes the first part of the Prime Minister's motion, what this country will get at the end is not Dominion Status, but a Malta Status — a sovereign Independent State with a Prime Minister who is not equal to the Prime Minister of South Africa or equal to the Prime Ministers of Ceylon or Pakistan; a sovereign independent state whose Prime Minister will attend the Prime Ministers' Conferences, but whose country will be merely a superior type of colony under the Colonial Office or the Commonwealth Office, but not free enough and superior enough to be a member of the United Nations. . . .

Nene Azzu Mate Kole: . . .

The part played by the natural rulers of the Gold Coast in central as well as local administration has always been taken cognizance of in every constitution that

[1] The six others being:—Juaben Local Council, Enyo-Na-Bremen Local Council, the Ghana Trades Union Congress, the Catholic Young Men's Society of Cape Coast, the Cape Coast Literary and Social Club, and the Prampram Youth Association.

the Gold Coast has had so far. Even our present Constitution, drafted under abnormal circumstances, has recognised the Chief's place and provided for it in some measure. Let us consider what has happened since the promulgation of the present Constitution Order in Council. We have passed the Local Government Ordinance which, with one stroke, revolutionised our local government system and in the process forcibly removed the Chief from his traditional place as the head of his people.

Under the law, the Chief is in name the President of the Local Council but in fact he is completely cut off from anything that is done in his area by a Local Council. . . . Thus, one may be permitted to ask where in the Central Government or in Local Administration is the Chief's place. . . ?

The views expressed by the overwhelming majority of groups and councils that submitted memoranda in reply to the Prime Minister's call in the Statement of 16th October, 1952, indicated that the Gold Coast is convinced that the Chiefs have a place and their place is with the Elder Statesmen in a Senate. . . . The Chiefs have stated that they would not like to be in politics and I believe that that statement is still valid, and that statement is neither synonymous with being cut off entirely from the Central Government, nor is it irreconcilable with the idea of a Senate. . . . If Government are decided that they do not want a Bicameral system of Legislature then it should be made quite clear that the Territorial Councils should be strengthened with a direct link to the highest governmental authority, namely the Cabinet, so that the voice of the highest traditional body could be heard in the Government and their influence felt in the whole administration. . . . I will leave the mechanics of detailed constitution drafting to the politicians, but I am convinced that we cannot afford to sow the seeds of internal strife now by displacing . . . the most vital institution in our country, namely, the Chiefs and the Stools. . . .

Mr. J. E. Jantuah (Rural Member, Kumasi North): . . .

By the proposals in the White Paper, Ashanti with an area of about 24,379 square miles and a population of about 823,000 . . . would get about 18 members only; whereas the Colony with a population of 2,000,000 concentrated in a smaller area of about 23,900 square miles, would get about 50 seats. It is my view, and it is one shared by the Asanteman Council, that a fairer approach would have been to give a range of say 25,000 to 45,000 within which to work these constituencies . . . [as was done in Great Britain]. The White Paper, the Asanteman Council argues, could have stipulated the number of seats to be allocated in each region at some figures like these:—

    35 for the Colony
    30 for the Northern Territories
    28 for Ashanti, and
    12 for Togoland

and leave the actual number of people per constituency to the proposed commission. In any case it must be forcibly stressed that population alone cannot be the basis for determining the size of a constituency. . . . [Legislative Assembly Debates, 10th–15th July, 1953][1]

512 SIR R. SALOWAY[2] TO OLIVER LYTTEL-TON[3]   9 APRIL, 1954.

. . . The most striking of the innovations suggested [concern] . . . the form of the central executive body which would be the principal instrument of policy. It is proposed that this body should in future be referred to as the Cabinet, and not the Executive Council, and that this change,

[1] The motion was carried without a division on 15 July.
[2] Sir Reginald Harry Saloway; born, 1905; Indian Civil Service, 1928–46; Colonial Secretary of the Gold Coast, 1950; Chief Secretary and Minister of Defence and External Affairs, 1951–4.
[3] Oliver Lyttelton (later 1st Viscount Chandos); born 1893; Conservative M.P., 1940–54; Secretary of State for the Colonies, 1951–4.

which reflects the present usage, should be included in the Constitution.

It is desired that the Cabinet should consist entirely of Ministers who are elected Members of the Legislative Assembly and who are collectively responsible to the Assembly. The Prime Minister should summon and should normally preside at meetings of the Cabinet, which would not be attended by the Governor except when the Governor exercised the right, which should be preserved in the Constitution, to summon a special meeting of the Cabinet and preside. All Cabinet papers should be sent to the Governor for his information at the same time as they are sent to Ministers. . . . In the appointment and dismissal of Ministers the Governor should act in accordance with the constitutional convention which is applicable to the exercise of this function in the United Kingdom by the Crown. The sole responsibility for the assignment of portfolios to Ministers should rest with the Prime Minister. . . .

The Governor should be responsible for consular matters, external affairs and the United Nations Organisation with special reference to Togoland under United Kingdom Trusteeship; naval, military and air forces, and defence and internal security. It was also accepted that the Governor should have a special responsibility in certain matters concerning the police. . . . There should be an Advisory Committee to assist the Governor in regard to the discharge of his responsibilities for these subjects. . . . The Prime Minister, the Minister of the Interior and one other Minister should be members of this Committee. . . .

As you are aware, a Commission of Enquiry under the Chairmanship of Mr. Justice Van Lare was appointed on the 1st August, 1953, to examine and make recommendations regarding representational and electoral reform. The recommendations of this Commission, with such variations as were approved in the Legislative Assembly, are now embodied in the

Electoral Provisions Ordinance. In brief, the Ordinance provides for seven municipal and ninety-seven rural electoral districts, each returning a single Member by direct election . . . the compilation of a common roll for Legislative Assembly and local government elections, and for election procedure generally. . . . The question whether the Legislature should be unicameral or bicameral has engaged the close attention of the Government, and the fullest consideration has been given to the representation of those groups or interests which favour the latter. The Government's conclusion is that the unicameral system should be given a more extended trial and that it would be imprudent at this stage to abandon this system.

It will be seen that there is no provision for the continued representation of special interests. . . . There exists a strong conviction that the retention of Special Members in the Legislative Assembly would be inconsistent with the degree of constitutional advance to which the Gold Coast now aspires. . . .

The Government holds the view that the determination of local constitutional matters . . . should be kept outside the realm of politics. . . . It is now suggested that there should be a Local Constitutional Commission established by statute, consisting of the Presidents of the four Territorial Councils or their representatives, a serving or retired judge, and one member to be appointed by the Governor on the advice of the Cabinet. . . .

With the disappearance of the *ex-officio* Ministers, the Governor would no longer have the means to ensure that measures which he considered necessary, were brought before the Legislative Assembly, unless provision to that end were included in the Constitution. Accordingly, and in pursuance of the intention . . . that the reserved powers should continue unimpaired, it is proposed that the Constitution Order in Council should empower the Governor to send by message to the Speaker the draft of any Bill or motion

which it appears to him should be introduced or proposed in the Legislative Assembly, and in the same or a later message to require that the Bill or motion shall be introduced or proposed not later than a date specified in such message. . . .

It is felt that with the adoption of the constitutional changes now being considered, it would be appropriate if the Governor were to consult the Prime Minister before exercising his powers in connection with appointments or promotions to posts of Permanent Secretary, or to posts in corresponding or higher grades. This would recognise the fact that the holders of such posts occupy a special position vis-à-vis Ministers and that, as in the United Kingdom, consultation with the Prime Minister is justified; this is not the case with posts at a lower level, and any downward extension of the practice would undermine the principle of the freedom of the Service from political influence. . . .

[Ultimately the Governor would transfer his responsibilities to a Public Service Commission. Compensation for loss of career would be introduced with the disappearance of the constitutional safeguards for pensionable overseas officers. A Judicial Service Commission would become responsible for judicial appointments.] . . .

Under the present constitution the Minister of Finance is a Civil Servant subject to the controls applicable to Civil Servants. It is now desired that he should be replaced by a Representative Minister. . . . The Constitution should provide that the Minister of Finance should be responsible for the preparation of the annual Budget, for its submission to the vote of the Legislative Assembly by means of an annual Appropriation Bill, and for the introduction of Supplementary Appropriation Bills as may be necessary; the Assembly having power to assent or refuse to assent to any Head of Estimate . . . but not to vote an increased amount, a reduced amount, or an alteration in its destination. . . .

In addition to the exclusion from the Appropriation Bill of the salaries of Members of the Public Service Commission . . . of Judges and of the Auditor-General, it should be laid down that the interest on the Public Debt, Sinking Fund payments, the costs, charges, and expenses incidental to the management of the Public Debt, the retiring awards properly payable to members of the Public Service, and such other expenditure as the Assembly may determine, should be a charge on the general revenues and assets of the Gold Coast, and should not be submitted to the Appropriation Vote of the Assembly. . . .

The present Government has no plans for nationalising industry beyond the extent to which public utilities are already nationalised. Nevertheless, in order to ensure that, if the nationalisation of a particular industry by a successor Government should be considered necessary, suitable means for guaranteeing the payment of fair compensation will be available, the Government trusts that appropriate provision for this purpose may be included in the Constitution. . . .

[The despatch ends with proposals for extending the representation of Gold Coast interests to countries other than the United Kingdom.]   [Colonial, No. 302]

513 REPORT OF THE CONSTITUTIONAL ADVISER (SIR F. BOURNE[1])
17 DECEMBER, 1955.

I was appointed by the Secretary of State at the request of the Gold Coast Government, acting under the authority of the Legislative Assembly, to advise the Gold Coast Government and all parties on problems connected with devolution to regions. To this end I arrived in the Gold Coast on 26th September, 1955. . . .

My proposals are intended to afford the means 'for diffusion of power from the

[1] Sir Frederick Chalmers Bourne; born, 1891; Indian Civil Service, 1920; Governor of Central Provinces and Berar, 1946–7; Governor of East Bengal, 1947–50.

centre' which is what I understand to be essentially what is asked for by parties in opposition to the government. The scheme I propose is what I myself consider to be justified by the facts of the situation.

In acquainting myself with the Gold Coast situation I sought information and advice very widely . . . and I was in no way limited at any time in any of my activities. In the event, the National Liberation Movement and its allies declared themselves unable to afford me the opportunity of consultation on the grounds that the recent State Councils (Ashanti) Amendment Bill directly attacked the heritage and culture of Ashanti and *pro tanto* stultified my mission.

The upshot, therefore, is that though I am aware of the Government's views on regional devolution and though I have had most fruitful discussion with the Standing Committees of the Northern Territories' Council, the Trans Volta/Togoland Council and the Joint Provincial Council, and with a very large number of Local Government bodies and other representative individuals and institutions and Government officials of all grades, I have not had the advantage of discussing their own Federal proposals with the N.L.M. and their allies. . . .

'Proposals for a Federal Constitution for an independent Gold Coast and Togoland' was published in an undated document about the middle of the current year. They were forwarded to the Secretary of State in August. The N.L.M. who were responsible for these proposals had the support of the Asanteman Council and among the signatories of the document was the leader of the official opposition, who is also chairman of the N.P.P. Another signatory was the President of the Aborigines' Rights Protection Society and others represented a number of Movements such as the Ghana Action Party, the Muslim Association Party, the Ghana Congress Party, the Asante Youth Association, the Anlo Youth Organisation and the Togoland Congress. The State Council of Akim

Abuakwa State . . . also sent a supporting memorandum dated 19th August, 1955. But the Joint Provincial Council, representing all the Chiefs in the two Colony Regions, after prolonged discussion, by a majority decision, rejected the Federal Proposals. It would be unfair for me to criticise these 'Proposals' in detail, as the authors have declined to discuss them.

Moreover, the 'Proposals' were in fact presented as an outline only; the details were left for discussion in a Constituent Assembly, and the financial arrangements in particular were to be worked out by a Finance Commission under that Assembly. The suggestion was that this Assembly should be composed of elected representatives and representatives of Territorial Councils and some other bodies selected at a preliminary conference of all political parties and movements called by Government. Under the existing Constitution, responsibility for the government of the country has been conferred on the Legislative Assembly and the Cabinet, under the general supervision of His Excellency the Governor, with reference, when occasion demands it, to the Secretary of State. This responsibility cannot be transferred to any other body, nor do I see what authority a Constituent Assembly appointed in the manner suggested would have had.

I would, however, suggest that experience in other countries has shown that fragmentation of existing States is, on general grounds, mistaken: on the contrary, the tendency has been towards greater consolidation. The 'Proposals' are based on a revolt against excessive centralisation: this can surely be corrected by less drastic administrative changes than those so far recommended by the N.L.M. The Gold Coast with its component parts working as a team has a great future not only as a prosperous member of the nations of the world, but as an example to numerous less developed communities in the African continent. The opportunities now available may not recur.

In the following paragraphs I offer such a

scheme of devolution as I have been able to devise on the evidence afforded me. They provide for a very substantial transfer of power from the centre to regions. Careful consideration of all the advice I have received suggests that they should meet the legitimate demands of all the political, social and economic conditions of the Gold Coast. . . .

[The Report envisages the establishment of four regions (excluding Togoland) each to have Assemblies (once district councils have been established), chosen for 3 years, to consist of sitting M.L.As for the region, elected representatives of district and municipal councils, and up to 20 per cent co-opted members. They would be consulted on all legislation affecting the regions, and should have considerable powers especially in development, agriculture, roads, water-supply, housing, education and health. They would have power to make regulations but not to levy taxes. To safeguard the chiefs, no legislation affecting them would be introduced without prior consultation with them.]

514 DEBATE ON THE GHANA INDEPENDENCE BILL

HOUSE OF COMMONS, 11 DECEMBER, 1956.

The Under-Secretary for Commonwealth Relations (Lord John Hope):[1]

I beg to move, That the Bill be now read a second time.

This is a historic day. The result of the passage of this Bill through Parliament, should it be passed, will be that we shall hail the first of the British dependent territories in tropical Africa to attain full self-government as a sovereign independent nation. . . .

The House will recall that in his statement of 11th May, my right hon. Friend undertook, on behalf of Her Majesty's Government in the United Kingdom,

[1] Lord John Adrian Hope; born, 1912; Conservative M.P., 1950; Under-Secretary for Foreign Affairs, 1954.

that if a General Election were held in the Gold Coast, Her Majesty's Government would be ready to accept a motion calling for independence within the Commonwealth, passed by a reasonable majority in a newly-elected legislature and then to declare a firm date for independence.

A General Election was held in the Gold Coast on 12th July and 17 July, 1956. It was observed by six Members of Parliament drawn from both sides of the House of Commons. As a result of the Election, Dr. Nkrumah's party, the Convention People's Party, was returned to power with only a slightly reduced majority, and it now holds 72 of the 104 seats in the Legislative Assembly, and it won 57 per cent. of the votes cast throughout the country.

The new Legislative Assembly was opened on 31st July, and on 3rd August the Government introduced their motion calling for independence within the Commonwealth. The Opposition Members had absented themselves from the debate and the motion was passed by 72 votes to none. The motion was conveyed to my right hon. Friend by the Governor in a despatch dated 23rd August. On 18th September my right hon. Friend published his reply, which informed the Governor that Her Majesty's Government in the United Kingdom would, at the first available opportunity, introduce into the United Kingdom Parliament a Bill to accord independence to the Gold Coast, and that, subject to Parliamentary approval, the Government intended that independence should come about on 6th March, 1957.

The Ghana Independence Bill is introduced to give effect to the undertaking by the Government in that despatch published on 18th September. It provides for the attainment by the Gold Coast of fully responsible status within the British Commonwealth, sometimes colloquially known as 'Statute of Westminster powers.'

I should, in particular, state that the Colonial Secretary has it in command from Her Majesty to acquaint the House that she has placed her Prerogative and

interests, so far as they are affected by the Bill, at the disposal of Parliament.

Before going any further, I should like to explain the relationship between the Bill and the constitution which the Gold Coast will inherit on the attainment of independence. The Bill does not deal with details of the constitution of the Gold Coast. Its main purpose is to confer on the new state of Ghana the basic powers necessary to give it the status of an independent country within the Commonwealth. The Bill also makes the necessary consequential amendments in the law of the United Kingdom and of Ghana.

As is usual, the constitution at present in force in the Gold Coast is contained in a series of Orders in Council. After the Royal Assent has been given to the Ghana Independence Bill, and before it comes into force, it will be necessary to issue a further Order in Council, to come into force on Independence Day, which will bring the existing constitution into conformity with the new status of Ghana. The final responsibility for the Order in Council rests with the United Kingdom Ministers, but the fullest account will, naturally, be taken of the Gold Coast Government's proposals regarding the constitution.

The House will know that the Gold Coast Government have recently held discussions about the Constitution with the Parliamentary Opposition and with the Territorial Councils, and that, following these discussions, they have prepared revised constitutional proposals, published in a White Paper, of which copies have been placed in the Library of this House.

The final proposals of the Gold Coast Government have only recently been received and are now receiving detailed study and legal scrutiny. It is, therefore, too early to say precisely what advice will be given to Her Majesty about the detailed terms of the Order in Council. In this connection my right hon. Friend the Colonial Secretary has asked me to say that he will take very careful note of any points about the Constitution which hon. Members may wish to raise in the debate.

The National Liberation Movement, the Northern People's Party, and the Asanteman Council have recently sent formal resolutions to my right hon. Friend the Colonial Secretary, asking for separate independence to be awarded to Ashanti and the Northern Territories, and for the appointment of a Partition Commission to divide up the assets and liabilities of the Gold Coast. The Bill which we are discussing today is in itself evidence of the intention of Her Majesty's Government to proceed with the grant of independence to the country as a whole. . . . It is our view that the partition of the Gold Coast would not be in the interests of the country as a whole, or indeed, of any of the component parts which, during the past half-century have grown steadily and strongly into a single nation.

Hon. Members will be aware that the different parts of the country are interdependent both politically and economically. Indeed, the North and the South are complementary to one another. To sever would be to cripple. The partition of the country at this stage in its history, moreover, would not only inhibit further progress, but would mean a serious falling back in the standards of life which the country has done so much to achieve during the past few years.

[He refers to clauses dealing with the name Ghana; Togoland; nationality questions; and the Colonial Development and Welfare Acts.] . . .

I come now to the question of Ghana becoming a member of the Commonwealth. There is, of course, a clear distinction between the grant of responsible self-government within the Commonwealth and full membership of the Commonwealth. The first is a matter for the United Kingdom and the country concerned, and for them alone, and the second is a matter for all members of the Commonwealth. We are looking forward to Ghana becoming a full member of the Common-wealth and at the request of the present Gold Coast Government we intend to approach the other members on the subject in the very near future. We have every hope that Ghana will become a full member on the same day as she becomes independent, namely 6th March.

When that day comes, yet another stage will have been achieved in the journey of this great Commonwealth of Nations towards its destiny. Meanwhile, we are confident that the leaders and people of the Gold Coast will rise to the opportunities which lie before them, in full awareness of the responsibilities which they are now to shoulder. We pledge to them our friendship and our support. We wish them well.

Mr. James Griffiths (Llanelly.)[1] . . . [First discussed the question of reassuring the Gold Coast Opposition by a declaration of fundamental rights.]

The second problem to which I want to refer concerns the discussion in the Gold Coast about regional devolution. Speaking for myself and, I believe, for all my right hon. and hon. Friends, may I say that we are in full agreement with, and give our fullest support to, the decision of the Government — which I think they have been wise to make plain today — that secession is not on the agenda. I beg all our friends in the Gold Coast to realise that if they now start partitioning their country, they will be rendering a grave disservice to their people . . . and they would carry a very grave responsibility if, by an action of this kind, they made it impossible for the Gold Coast to survive and become a viable state; and a grave disservice to the people in Africa and all over the world. I join with the Government in saying that we share their view and support their decision . . . that they do not propose to accept the proposal put forward for the partitioning of the Gold Coast and the acceptance or recognition of Ashanti or any other part of it as an independent state.

[1] Labour M.P. for Llanelly since 1936; Secretary of State for the Colonies, 1950-1.

That leaves the problem of regional devolution. As I understand, the argument has been as to what powers shall be vested in the regional authorities that are to be created. The Government have suggested that regional authorities shall have the same kind of authority as is now vested in the London County Council and other county councils in this country — in other words, that there shall be a form of local government — whereas, if I understand it aright, their Opposition were thinking of powers in terms of Northern Ireland. I have myself come to the view that the Government are right. There is, I think, the strongest possible argument for regional devolution. There is no argument for the creation of separate Parliaments within this small country. All the energies of the Government and of the Opposition should be directed to discovering ways and means by which these regional authorities can be made really effective bodies. [In particular, there was the question of local finance. The independence of the Judiciary also gave cause for concern.] . . .

I come now to clause 3. During the debate on the Address, I asked the Secretary of State whether he would consider telling the House before we had this Bill before us, what provisions the Government intended to make for the territories after independence day, [when they] would be excluded, as I understand, from the provisions of the Colonial Development and Welfare Acts, and, indeed, from the possible operations of the Colonial Development Corporation. . . . We should be making a grave mistake if we did not now begin to give serious thought to this problem. We should begin by making it clear that when Ghana becomes independent it is not our desire to wash our hands of it thereafter. We cannot; it is we who are responsible for conferring this independent status upon the Gold Coast. . . . We have a special responsibility. In the main, the economies of all these Colonies have been shaped and patterned by us. I

have no desire to raise old controversies, but I must say that they have been shaped and patterned to meet, not their needs, but our interests. . . . In the main the economies of our Colonies are based upon primary products and upon very narrow foundations. That of the Gold Coast is based particularly on cocoa and gold. In recent months, with the price of cocoa falling, we have seen the very serious consequences to the people of the Gold Coast. . . . In the political situation of the 1950s we simply cannot afford to go back to the economic catastrophes of the 1930s. . . . We cannot allow that to happen when all these dynamic political forces are at work in Africa, Asia and elsewhere. It is, therefore, of vital importance that there should be some form of association between us and all the other Commonwealth countries and the primary producers [to attempt to secure some measure of price stabilisation]. . . .

Mr. Lennox Boyd.[1] . . .

The right hon. Gentleman the Member for Llanelly . . . dwelt on the need to have . . . more stable prices for prime commodities like cocoa. . . . The right hon. Gentleman was quite right in saying that these are the things that really matter; and they matter very much indeed. Throughout this debate there has, I think, been a most refreshing realisation in all parts of the House of the real importance of economic advance if political and social progress is to have any basic reality. The United Kingdom, of course, consumes only a part of the Gold Coast production of cocoa. We cannot by ourselves, however much we may wish we could, alter the cocoa prices, and we can hardly buy above the world price. . . . There must be international control [and moves to investigate world production and markets are on foot.] . . .

[1] Alan Tindal Lennox-Boyd; born, 1904; Conservative M.P., 1931; Minister of State for Colonial Affairs, 1951–2; Minister of Transport 1952–4; Secretary of State for the Colonies, 1954–59.

So much of this debate has turned, as it was bound to do, on the unhappy differences of opinion that exist in the Gold Coast . . . but we all recognise that very genuine and vigorous efforts have been made to resolve those differences. . . .

I do not propose to talk much about the federal solution, because no hon. Member in the House has advocated it. I hope that that fact will be noted by our friends in Ghana. We are all anxious for a happy solution and a wise one and a statesman-like one, but no voice at all has been raised in this House in favour of a federal solution because we know the facts of life, the size of the country, the geography of the country, the consequent development of the transport of the country, and the difficulties of manning a series of Parliaments. Problems of that sort would make that a very poor solution. . . .

After Sir Frederick [Bourne's] visit and his report we had the Achimota Conference to discuss it. This was held in February of this year. Once more, I am sorry to say, it was boycotted [by the Opposition parties]. Minor modifications were introduced into Sir Frederick Bourne's report. Then the Gold Coast Government's proposals, which were a blend of Sir Frederick Bourne's report and of the Achimota recommendations were published in April this year. [Then came the pledge of the 11th May and the subsequent election.] . . . Then another attempt was made. The Governor saw the Northern Territories Council and asked for a list of safeguards which would help them. Then in September the National Liberation Movement representatives and the Northern People's Party and the Togoland Congress representatives came over and saw me. . . .

Then I came to this conclusion, which I am glad to know, has received the support of everybody, I think, in this House . . . that the best way really to bring the parties together, and to bring things to a head was to announce a firm date for independence, which I did on 18th Sep-

tember, and the date is 6th March next. Then Dr. Nkrumah, who had previously declined to meet the Opposition leaders together, changed that view and had talks with the Opposition and with the Territorial Councils. Then revised constitutional proposals were made, and these we are now giving the very closest examination.

I recognise, as does everybody in the House, that the Opposition leaders have their many anxieties. They have suggested, for example, a Council of State, to be formed of the Prime Minister, the Leader of the Opposition, the Attorney-General, and the heads of the four traditional Regions. The purpose of this Council of State would be to advise the Governor-General in the exercise of his prerogative powers, and on the public service and judicial appointments, and to act as a final court of appeal in local constitutional matters. The Gold Coast Government take the view — and I think there is some substance in this — that it is not very wise to make some of the Governor-General's functions exercisable on the advice of a body responsible neither to the Government nor to the National Assembly. They hold that a body containing political representatives is an unsuitable body to be an appeal court.

The Opposition has also suggested a Second Chamber. The view that the Gold Coast Government have taken has been that the function of reviewing legislation could be carried out better through their own proposals for Regional Assemblies and Regional Houses of Chiefs, which would be given the opportunity to examine legislation before it is introduced into the National Assembly. So the view has been that they reject the Second Chamber unless the majority of the Territorial Councils will say that they want it as a substitute for Regional Houses of Chiefs. I hope that discussion on this and other matters can still continue.

Another point raised by the Opposition was the question of the powers of the Regional Assemblies. . . . From the recent

White Paper of the Gold Coast Government, it looks as if their view is not quite the same as that of Sir Frederick Bourne regarding the form of regional power in the field of finance. It may well be that given goodwill on both sides, further progress in that field may be brought about.

The Opposition has also asked for regional control of the police. This is the only one of the nine constitutional safeguards desired by the Northern Territories, which the Gold Coast Government have not been willing to grant. The Opposition fears misuse of the police, and the Government argue that a unitary force is likely to be more efficient. . . .

A number of hon. Members have referred to the question whether or not the Regional Councils should be enshrined in the Order in Council, and whether they would follow the proposals of the Gold Coast Government on page 6 of their White Paper. The final conclusion as to what will be in the Order in Council must be left for Her Majesty's Government to decide, though it would be unwise, and very unfair, not to pay the highest possible regard to the views of the Gold Coast Government, so recently elected by a substantial majority. But it might be desirable to define the scope and continuance of these regional bodies a little more precisely. . . .

I was asked a number of questions about the amendment of the constitution. . . . As the House knows, there has been a change in regard to the Gold Coast Government's proposals for the amendment of the constitution. They originally suggested that constitutional changes should take place with the consent of two-thirds of the members present and voting. The new proposal is that two-thirds majority of all members is required.

I have listened with the very greatest interest to the speeches which have been made on this subject from both sides of the House. I recognise that the Opposition parties and people are not likely to regard the two-thirds majority criterion as being

of exceptional value when the Government in the Gold Coast at the moment, at the birth of the new constitution, already have a two-thirds majority of their own. I recognise the strong feelings that have been expressed that there should be some other additional safeguard. One hon. Member said that a two-thirds majority in two successive Parliaments should be required. Other hon. Members have privately suggested to me that the regional bodies ought to be brought in and should have a function in regard to revision of the constitution. . . .

I should not like the debate to end on a note of suspicion and uncertainty. I do not believe that these things are likely, that people will find that capital in the Gold Coast is in peril, or that British officers in the army or police will be confronted with a choice of loyalties. I am myself a believer in this great experiment. It is an experiment, but it will be helped if we enter into it, without shutting our eyes, but in high hopes that this great and romantic conception will justify the faith which so many people have put into bringing it about.

[Parliamentary Debates (Commons) vol. 562, cols. 229–326]

515 THE GHANA (CONSTITUTION) ORDER IN COUNCIL   1957.

At the Court of Buckingham Palace, the 22nd day of February, 1957.

Present,

The Queen's Most Excellent Majesty in Council.

Whereas by the Ghana Independence Act, 1957,[1] provision is made for and in connection with the attainment by the Gold Coast of fully responsible status within the British Commonwealth of Nations under the name of Ghana with effect from a day (hereinafter referred to as 'the appointed day') which, by virtue of section 5 of the said Act is the sixth day of March, nineteen hundred and fifty-seven, unless

[1] 5 & 6 Eliz. 2. cap. b.

before that date Her Majesty has, by Order in Council, appointed some other day to be the appointed day for the purposes of that Act:

Now, therefore, Her Majesty, by virtue and in exercise of the powers conferred upon her by the British Settlements Acts, 1887 and 1945,[1] the Foreign Jurisdiction Act, 1890,[2] the Ghana Independence Act, 1957, and of all other powers enabling Her, in that behalf, is pleased, by and with the advice of Her Privy Council to Order, and it is hereby ordered, as follows:—

Part I. Preliminary.

1. [Definition.]
2. [Citation and commencement.]
3. [Revocation and amendment.]

Part II. The Governor-General.

4. [Appointment of Governor-General.]
5. [Salaries of Governor-General &c.]

Part III. The Executive.

6. The executive power of Ghana is vested in the Queen and may be exercised by the Queen or by the Governor-General as Her representative.

7. There shall be a Cabinet of Ministers of not less than eight persons, being Members of Parliament, who shall be charged with the general direction and control of the Government of Ghana and who shall be collectively responsible to Parliament.

8. [Vacation of Office.]
9. [Official Oath.]
10. [Precedence of Ministers.]
11. [Summoning of Cabinet.]
12. [Presiding in the Cabinet.]
13. [Transaction of business in the Cabinet.]
14. [Assignment of responsibilities to Ministers.]
15. The Attorney-General shall be a person who is a public officer and he shall be vested with responsibility for the initiation, conduct and discontinuance of prosecutions

for criminal offences triable in courts constituted under the provisions of the Courts Ordinance[1] or any Act repealing and re-enacting with or without modification, or amending the provision of that Ordinance. . . .

16. [Parliamentary Secretaries.]
17. [Permanent Secretaries.]
18. [Secretary of the Cabinet.]
19. [Duties of Secretary of the Cabinet.]

Part IV. Parliament.

20. (1) There shall be a Parliament in and for Ghana which shall consist of Her Majesty the Queen and the National Assembly.

(2) The National Assembly shall consist of a Speaker and not less than one hundred and four Members to be known as Members of Parliament; but the number of Members may be increased from time to time by the creation of further electoral districts under the provisions of sections 33, 70 and 71, but in any event the total number of Members shall not exceed one hundred and thirty.

21. The Speaker shall be a person, not being either the holder of any public office, or a Minister or Parliamentary Secretary, elected by the Members of Parliament. . . .

22. [Deputy Speaker.]
23. [Voting at elections of Speaker and Deputy Speaker.]
24. Subject to the provisions of section 25 of this Order, any person who —

(a) is a citizen of Ghana; and
(b) is of the age of twenty-five years or upwards; and
(c) is able to speak and, unless incapacitated by blindness or other physical cause, to read the English language with a degree of proficiency sufficient to enable him to take an active part in the proceedings of the Assembly;

shall be qualified to be elected as a Member of Parliament, and no other person shall be qualified to be so elected or, having

---

[1] 50 & 51 Vict. cap. 54 and 9 & 10 Geo. 6. cap. 7.
[2] 53 & 54 Vict. cap. 37.

[1] Laws of the Gold Coast, 1951, cap. 4.

been so elected, shall sit or vote in the Assembly.

25. [Disqualifications for Members.]
26. [Tenure of office of Members.]
27. [Decision of questions as to membership.]
28. [Reporting and filling of vacancies.]
29. [Penalty for unqualified person sitting or voting.]
30. [Staff of the National Assembly.]

Part V.   Legislation and Procedure in the Assembly.

31. (1) Subject to the provisions of this Order, it shall be lawful for Parliament, to make laws for the peace, order and good government of Ghana.

(2) No law shall make persons of any racial community liable to disabilities to which persons of other such communities are not made liable.

(3) Subject to such restrictions as may be imposed for the purposes of preserving public order, morality or health, no law shall deprive any person of his freedom of conscience, or the right freely to profess, practise or propagate any religion.

(4) Any laws in contravention of subsection (2) or (3) of this section or section (34) of this Order shall to the extent of such contravention, but not otherwise, be void.

(5) The Supreme Court shall have original jurisdiction in all proceedings in which the validity of any law is called in question and if any such question arises in any lower court, the proceedings in that court shall be stayed and the issue transferred to the Supreme Court for decision.

32. (1) No Bill for the amendment, modification, repeal or re-enactment of the constitutional provisions of Ghana (other than a Bill to which section 33 of this Order applies) and no Bill to which paragraph (b) of subsection (2) of this section applies shall be presented for the Royal Assent unless it has endorsed on it a certificate under the hand of the Speaker that the number of votes cast in favour thereof at the third reading in the Assembly amounted to not less than two-thirds of the whole number of Members of Parliament. For the purposes of this subsection, the expression 'constitutional provisions' means this Order, the existing Orders and any Act (or instrument made under an Act) that amends, modifies, re-enacts (with or without any amendment or modification) or makes different provision in lieu of any provision of this Order, the existing Orders or any such Act (or instrument) previously made.

(2) Without prejudice to the provisions of subsection (1) of this section, no Bill for —

(a) the enactment, modification, repeal or re-enactment (with or without any amendment or modification) of any of the provisions of this Order specified in the Third Schedule to this Order; or

(b) abolishing or suspending any Regional Assembly or diminishing the functions or powers of any Regional Assembly,

shall be presented for the Royal Assent unless it has endorsed on it a certificate (in addition to the certificate required under subsection (1) of this section) under the hand of the Speaker that the Bill has been referred to all the Regional Assemblies, and, in the case of a Bill to which paragraph (a) of this section applies, to all Houses of Chiefs, in accordance with subsection (3) of this section and has been approved by not less than two-thirds of the total number of the Regional Assemblies (including, in the case of a Bill to which paragraph (b) of this subsection applies, any Regional Assembly affected by the Bill) and, if amendments have been made to the Bill by the National Assembly since it was so approved by the Regional Assemblies, that such amendments have been made and are not, in the Speaker's opinion, amendments of substance.

(3) [Details procedure for reference to Regional Assemblies.] . . .

33. (1) No Bill for effecting any alteration

in the boundaries of a Region which seeks to transfer an area or areas containing less than ten thousand registered electors, other than a Bill which creates a new Region, shall be introduced in the Assembly unless the alteration to which the Bill seeks to give effect has been approved by a majority of members present and voting at a meeting of the Regional Assembly of every Region whose boundaries will be affected.

(2) No Bill for effecting any alteration in the boundaries of a Region which seeks to transfer an area or areas containing not less than ten thousand registered electors shall be introduced in the Assembly unless the alteration to which the Bill seeks to give effect has been approved by referendum in every Region from which it is proposed to transfer any area and by a majority of members present and voting at a meeting of the Regional Assembly of any Region in which it is proposed to incorporate any part of the area transferred. . . .

[(4)–(7) give further details of procedure.]

34. [Compulsory acquisition of property.] . . .

35. When any Bill affecting the traditional functions or privileges of a Chief is introduced into the Assembly and is read a first time, the Speaker shall forthwith refer such Bill to the House of Chiefs of the Region in which the Chief exercises his functions as such and no motion shall be moved for the second reading of the Bill in the Assembly until three months after the day on which the Bill was introduced into the Assembly.

36. [Standing Orders.] . . .

37. [Presiding in the Assembly.] . . .

38. [The Assembly may transact business notwithstanding vacancies.] . . .

39. No business except that of adjournment shall be transacted in the Assembly if objection is taken by any Member present that there are less than twenty-five Members present besides the Speaker or Member presiding.

40. (1) Save as otherwise provided in this Order, all questions proposed for decision in the Assembly shall be determined by a majority of the votes of the Members present and voting; and if upon any question before the Assembly, the votes of the Members shall be equally divided the motion shall be lost.

(2) (a) The Speaker shall have neither an original nor a casting vote: and (b) any other person, including the Deputy Speaker, shall when presiding in the Assembly, have an original vote but no casting vote.

41. (1) Save as is provided in subsection (2) of this section, and subject to the provisions of this Order and of the Standing Orders of the Assembly, any Member may introduce any Bill, or propose any motion for debate in, or may present any petition to, the Assembly, and the same shall be debated and disposed of according to the Standing Orders of the Assembly.

(2) Except with the recommendation or consent of the Governor-General signified thereto, the Assembly shall not proceed upon any Bill, motion or petition which, in the opinion of the Speaker or Member presiding, would dispose of or charge the Consolidated Fund or other public funds of Ghana, or revoke or alter any disposition thereof or charge thereon, or impose, alter or repeal any rate, tax or duty.

42. (1) No Bill shall become a law until Her Majesty has given her assent thereto.

43. [Words of enactment.] . . .

44. [Oath of Allegiance.] . . .

45. [Privileges of the Assembly and Members.] . . .

46. (1) There shall be a session of the Assembly once at least in every year, so that a period of twelve months shall not intervene between the last sitting of the Assembly in one session and the first sitting thereof in the next session. . . .

47. [Prorogation and dissolution.] . . .

(3) The Governor-General shall dissolve the Assembly at the expiration of five years from the date of the first sitting of the Assembly after the last preceding general election, if it shall not have been sooner dissolved. . . .

48. There shall be a general election at such time within two months after every dissolution of the Assembly as the Governor-General shall by Proclamation published in the Gazette appoint.

Part VI.   The Public Service [49–53] . . .
Part VII.   The Judicature   [54–7] . . .
Part VIII.   Finance.   [58–62]
Part IX.   Regional Organisation, Local Government and Chiefs.

63. The whole of Ghana shall be divided into the following Regions:—

(a) The Eastern Region, which shall comprise those parts of Ghana which on the first day of January, 1957, were comprised in the Eastern and Accra Regions of the Gold Coast;

(b) the Western Region, which shall comprise that part of Ghana which on the first day of January, 1957, were comprised in the Western Region of the Gold Coast

(c) the Ashanti Region which shall comprise the whole of Ashanti;

(d) the Northern Region which shall comprise the whole of the Northern Territories and Northern Togoland;

(e) the Trans-Volta/Togoland Region which shall comprise that part of Ghana which on the first day of January, 1957 was comprised in the Trans-Volta/Togoland Region of the Gold Coast.

(2) In each Region there shall be a Head of the Region, who, except in the case of the Ashanti Region, shall be chosen by the House of Chiefs of the Region and shall hold office for such period as may be prescribed by Act of Parliament. The Asantehene shall be the Head of the Ashanti Region.

64. (1) For the purpose of fulfilling the need for a body at regional level with effective powers in specified fields, a Regional Assembly shall be established by Act of Parliament in and for each Region.

(2) A Regional Assembly shall have and exercise authority, functions and powers to such extent as may be prescribed by Act of Parliament relating to

(a) Local Government;
(b) Agriculture, Animal Health and Forestry;
(c) Education;
(d) Communications;
(e) Medical and Health services;
(f) Public Works;
(g) Town and Country Planning;
(h) Housing;
(i) Police; and
(j) such other matters as Parliament may from time to time determine. . . .

65. [Membership of local government councils.] . . .

66. The Office of Chiefs in Ghana as existing by customary law and usage, is hereby guaranteed.

67. (1) Within twelve months of the appointed day or as soon thereafter as may be practicable, a House of Chiefs shall be established by Act of Parliament in and for each Region. . . .

68. [Determination of matters of a constitutional nature involving chiefs.] . . .

Part X.   Elections and the Delimitation of Electoral Districts.

69. (1) Voting for the election of Members of Parliament shall be by secret ballot on the basis of adult suffrage.

(2) Every citizen of Ghana, without distinction of religion, race or sex, who —

(a) is not less than twenty-one years of age; and

(b) is subject to no legal incapacity as defined by Act of Parliament on the grounds of non-residence, unsoundness of mind, crime, or corrupt or illegal practices or non-payment of rates or taxes; and

(c) either owns immovable property within, or has, for a period of not less than six months out of the twelve months preceding the date of an application to be registered, resided within the electoral district in respect of which application is made,

shall be entitled to be registered as an elector for the election of Members of Parliament.

70. (1) For the purposes of the election of Members of Parliament, each Region of Ghana shall be divided into areas, which shall be known as electoral districts. The total number of electoral districts shall not be less than one hundred and four or more than one hundred and thirty. Electoral districts shall be so delimited that the number of persons resident in each such district at the time of delimitation is, as nearly as practical considerations admit, the same, but, in dividing any Region into electoral districts, regard shall be had to the physical features of the Region and its transport facilities and no electoral district shall be partly in one Region and partly in another Region. Each electoral district shall return one Member to Parliament.

(2) Until other provision is made in pursuance of section 33 or 71 of this Order, the number of electoral districts in the whole of Ghana shall be one hundred and four and the allocation of electoral districts between the various parts of Ghana shall remain as it was immediately before the appointed day.

71. (1) Within two years of the taking of each general census in Ghana, the Governor-General shall, in the manner prescribed in subsection (5) of this section, appoint a body to be known as the General Electoral Delimitation Commission . . . which shall review the delimitation of the electoral districts existing at the time of its appointment and shall submit a report to the Governor-General regarding the number of persons then residing in each electoral district together with such recommendations as the Commission deems necessary for a fresh delimitation of electoral districts in accordance with the provisions of

section 70 of this Order. . . . [The Governor-General may also appoint interim Commissions.]

If such Interim Commission is satisfied that the number of persons resident in [an] electoral district is, on the basis of the best available information, in excess of one hundred and seventy per centum of the average number of persons resident in each of all other electoral districts, the Interim Commission shall submit a report to the Governor-General together with a recommendation for the division of the said electoral district into two electoral districts. . . .

(5) Each General Commission, Area Committee or Interim Commission shall consist of three persons appointed by the Governor-General who shall select persons who he is satisfied are not actively engaged in politics. . . .

Part XI. Transitional Provisions. . . .

73. (1) The Legislative Assembly constituted under the existing Orders and in being immediately prior to the appointed day shall continue in being thereafter as the first National Assembly of Ghana within the meaning of subsection (2) of section 20 of this Order. . . .

85. (1) The Governor-General shall, within three months after the appointed day, or as soon thereafter as may be possible, appoint a Regional Constitutional Commission consisting of a Chairman who shall be the Chief Justice or a Judge nominated by him, two Commissioners representing each Region who shall be persons nominated by the Territorial Council of each Region and not more than six Commissioners appointed by the Governor-General.

(2) The Regional Constitutional Commission shall enquire into and report on the devolution to Regional Assemblies of authority, functions and powers relating to the matters specified in subsection (2) of section 64 of this Order and in particular, and without prejudice to the generality of the foregoing, shall make recommendations as to the composition of each Regional

Assembly, the executive, legislative, financial and advisory powers to be exercised by it, the funds required to meet the capital and recurrent expenditure to be incurred by it, the provision of such funds and the legislation required to give effect to its recommendations. . . .

The Third Schedule.

The following definitions in subsection (1) of section 1 :—

'Ashanti', 'the Assembly', 'the Consolidated Fund', 'judicial officer', 'the Northern Territories', 'Northern Togoland', 'public office', 'public officer', 'the public service', 'Region.'

Subsections (2), (3), (4), (5), and (6) of section 1.

Section 6
Section 20
Subsections (1), (2), (3), and (4) of section 31.
Sections 32 to 35.
Subsections (1) and (2) of section 42.
Subsection (1) of section 46.
Subsection (3) of section 47.
Sections 48 to 58.
Subsection (1) of section 61.[1]
Sections 62[2] to 64.
Sections 66 to 69.
This Schedule
  [Statutory Instruments, No. 1. of 1957[3]]

---

[1] Deals with the post of Auditor-General.
[2] Section 62 provides for an annual Audit of Accounts. The territorial definitions in the first subsection are those of 1950 and 1954.
[3] 47 pages in original.

APPENDIXES

Appendix A   Documents relating to the Company of African Merchants

1 AN ACT FOR IMPROVING THE TRADE TO AFRICA 1750.

Whereas the trade to and from Africa is very advantageous to Great Britain and necessary for the supplying the Plantations and Colonies thereunto belonging with a sufficient number of negroes at reasonable rates; and for that purpose the said trade ought to be free and open to all His Majesty's subjects. . . .

1. [Free trade to Africa . . . between Sallee . . . and the Cape of Good Hope.]

2. Be it enacted . . . That all his Majesty's subjects who shall trade to or from any of the ports or places of Africa between Cape Blanco and the Cape of Good Hope, shall forever hereafter be a Body Corporate and Politic . . . by the name of the Company of Merchants trading to Africa.

3. [The forts, settlements and factories etc of the Royal African Company vested in the new Company.] . . .

4. [Company prohibited to trade in their joint capacity.] . . .

5. [A Committee of nine to be chosen annually to manage the affairs of the Company. . . . No restraint to be laid on the trade or traders.] . . .

6. [Traders who shall pay 40s for the Freedom of the Company, to meet on 10 July and choose the first Committee who are to continue for one year.] . . .

7. [Elections to be held on 3 July yearly.] . . .

8. [Power to choose other Committeemen in the room of those who shall die &c. Ten days notice of such election to be given in the London Gazette.] . . .

9. [Provision if no election be made by the traders of one town.] . . .

10. [In equality of votes the Mayor[1] to determine.] . . .

11. [No order of the Committee to which all are not consenting to be valid unless confirmed at a subsequent meeting.] . . .

12. [Chairman to be chosen.] . . .

13. [Traders paying 40s on or before 30 June 1750 to be the first members.]

14. [Persons admitted after 30 June not to vote at an election for one year.] . . .

15. [Certificates to persons admitted.] . . .

16. [Sums received for Freedom to be paid to the order of the Committee &c.]

17. [Receivers to pay the same annually and to deliver lists of the Names.]

18. [List of the Company to be kept at the Office and to be printed annually before the Elections.] . . .

19. [None to be chosen into the Committee above three years successively . . . or to trade in partnership. . . .]

20. [Committee may vest the money in the purchase of goods to be sent to Africa for the use of the settlements, but not to carry on a trade to and from Africa.] . . .

21. [The Commissioners for Trade may remove any of the Committee-men, officers &c.] . . .

22. [Commissioners to summon and hear any Committee-man charged with misbehaviour.] . . .

23. [Committee to give the Commissioners an account yearly of their proceedings.] . . .

24. [Application of the monies received by the Committee.] . . .

25. [Committee at the expiration of a year to pay their accounts before the Cursitor Baron; and a copy thereof, and of their proceedings, before the Parliament and before a General Meeting.] . . .

[1] i.e. the Lord Mayor of London, or the Mayor of Liverpool or Bristol.

26. [Traders not to be obstructed. The buildings to be free for warehouses. . . .]

27. [and for the safety of their persons.] . . .

28. [Traders may build houses under the protection of the forts.] . . .

29. And be it further enacted . . . That no Commander or Master of any ship trading to Africa shall, by fraud, force, or violence, or by any other indirect practice whatsoever, take on board, or carry away from the coast of Africa, any negro or native of the said country, or commit or suffer to be committed any violence upon the natives to the prejudice of the said trade; and that every person so offending shall for every such offence, forfeit the sum of one hundred pounds of lawful money of Great Britain. . . .

30. [Instructions to be given to captains of Men of War to inspect the condition of the forts. Reports to be laid before Parliament.] . . .

31. [Officers of the Navy to inquire into the conditions of forts &c.] . . .

32. [Commissioners appointed to examine the claims of the creditors . . . of the Royal African Company. . . . Accounts to be laid before Parliament.] . . .

37. [Penalties, how to be recovered.] . . .

38. [Limitation of Actions.] . . .

39. [A public Act.] . . .

[23 Geo. 2. cap. 31]

[Passages enclosed [ ] are the marginal summaries of the Act.]

2 Instructions to Governor Torrane 1804.

Orders and Instructions by the [African] Committee to George Torrane Esqr. appointed by them to the Command of Cape Coast Castle, President of the Council, Treasurer, Warehousekeeper and Governor-in-Chief of the Forts and Settlements on the Gold Coast of Africa, and at Whydah. . . .

[The first 13 articles deal with keeping strict accounts.]

14th. You have herewith 50 copies of the Acts of Parliament, that none of the public servants may plead ignorance thereof. The Committee direct that one of each be delivered to every Commissioned Officer in the Service, and in future every officer sent from hence will have one delivered to him with his Commission, & that those Acts of Parliament be rigidly adhered to. On proof of any infringement whatsoever by any one of the Officers, dismission from the Service will assuredly follow.

15th. Much inconvenience appearing to have arisen from the powers of the Chief Governor and the Members of Council having been in some instances misunderstood, the Committee, for preventing such misunderstandings in future, direct that the Chief Governor shall have the power of convening the Council as often as he may judge fit and proper; that at all such meetings every Member shall have full liberty to deliberate, to debate, to advise, to vote & if needful, to enter a protest. This is all they have a right to do, the supreme power resting with the President, who, in cases of his dissenting from the Council, is to take the responsibility upon himself. Being in the chief direction, he can only be removed by order of the Committee.

16thly. No Governor, Chief or other officer is to quit his fort, nor during the War to sleep out of it, on any pretence whatever, without leave first obtained from the Chief Governor.

17thly. All subordinate appointments in the Service are to be filled up by the Chief Governor. He may, on these as on every other occasion, consult the Members if he sees fit, but such appointments rest with him, subject to the approbation of the Committee.

18thly. The Committee have heard with great concern the almost total neglect of all military dress by their Governors and other officers in the service; direct that in future every Commissioned Officer do on all public occasions appear in his Regimentals and Side Arms; the Committee have sent by the present store ship an ample supply of every article to enable their officers now in Africa to receive this most necessary regulation.

19thly. You have herewith a copy of a Proclamation issued by the late Governor Dalzel, bearing date, Cape Coast Castle, the 3rd of August, 1796, together with a counter-proclamation issued by the Dutch Government of Elmina, bearing date the 4th day of August in the same year. The Committee recommend it to you, as soon as may be after your arrival, to issue a Proclamation to the like effect, if you should have prevailed on the present Dutch Governor to do the same, and thereby prevent, as much as in you lies, the horrors of war extending to the settlements in Africa.

20thly. Should Cape Coast Castle, on your arrival off that place, be in the hands of the enemy, and that the Commander of the Naval Force accompanying you should find it imperative to retake it, you will in such case repairto such ot her fort as you may judge most prudent, and there land the supplies committed to your care, advising us by the earliest opportunity, that we may transmit you our further order and instructions.

21st. You will observe that the supplies and stores by the 'Trusty' are to be applied towards the expenses of the forts and settlements for the year 1805, and you are on no account to apply any part thereof, or of any future supplies which you may receive from the Committee, to the discharge of any debts due, or alleged to be due, to any of the servants in Africa.

22ndly. In times like the present, many circumstances may occur, many cases may happen, that the Committee have not provided for, whereon you will possibly be called upon to exercise your own judgement and discretion. From the opinion they entertain of your probity and honour, as well as of your abilities and local knowledge, they have not a doubt of your exerting yourself upon all such as well as upon every other occasion for the honour and interest of the Public. . . .

[T.70/148]

Appendix B British Governors and Administrators of the Gold Coast, 1807–1957

UNDER THE COMPANY OF MERCHANTS 1807–22

1805 February 8	George Torrane, President of Council, &c.
1807 December 4	Edward William White.
1816 April 21	Joseph Dawson.
1817 January 19	John Hope Smith.

UNDER THE GOVERNMENT OF SIERRA LEONE 1822–50

(a) UNDER THE CROWN

1822 March 27	Brigadier-General Sir Charles MacCarthy (Governor-in-Chief)[1]
	Major Chisholm, Commandant, 24 April, 1822,[2] from 26 May to 9 December, 1822; 17 May to 28 November, 1823; and from 21 January, 1824 conducted civil government.
	Lieutenant-Colonel Sutherland, Commandant, 18 May, 1824.
	Lieutenant-Colonel Grant (Lieutenant-Governor, Sierra Leone), Commandant, 17 July, 1824.[3]
1825 March 22	Major-General Charles Turner, (Governor-in-Chief).[4]
	Major Purdon, Commandant, 17 May, 1825.
1826 September 18	Major-General Sir Neil Campbell (Governor-in-Chief).[5]
	Major H. J. Ricketts, Commandant, 14 October, 1826.
1827 October 14	Lieutenant-Colonel H. Lumley (Lieutenant-Governor of Sierra Leone).[6]
	Capt. J. Hingston, Commandant, 9 January, 1828.
	Major H. J. Ricketts, Commandant, 5 June, 1828.

(b) UNDER THE COMMITTEE OF MERCHANTS 1828–44

1828 June 25	John Jackson, President of the Council of Merchants.
1830 February 19	George Maclean, President of the Council of Merchants.
	William Topp acted from 26 June, 1836, to 18 August, 1838.

(c) UNDER THE CROWN 1844–50

1844 February 13	Commander H. Worsley Hill, R.N. (Lieutenant-Governor).
	Dr. James Lilley acted from 8 March, 1845.
1846 April 15	Commander (later Sir) William Winniett (Lieutenant-Governor).

---

[1] Governor of Sierra Leone since 1812; date here is of arrival on Gold Coast.

[2] MacCarthy (to Bathurst, 24 April, 1822) arranged for the Officer i.c. Troops, Gold Coast to exercise Civil Govt. in absence of Gov. in Chief, as between dates following.

[3] Until 17 May, 1825.

[4] Gazetted 26 June, 1824; on the Gold Coast 22 March to 11 April, 1825.

[5] Gazetted, 13 May, 1826; on Gold Coast 18 September to 15 November, 1826.

[6] Lieutenant-Governor from 14 August, 1827, to 4 May, 1828; on Gold Coast 14 October, 1827, to 10 April, 1828.

J. C. Fitzpatrick acted from 31 January, 1849, to 19 February, 1850.

James Bannerman acted from 4 December, 1850.

1851 October 14   Major Stephen John Hill (Governor).

GOVERNORS OF THE GOLD COAST 1851–1866

J. C. Fitzpatrick acted from 7 June to 27 August, 1853.

Brodie Cruickshank acted from 27 August, 1853, to 16 January, 1854.

Henry Connor acted from 13 December, 1854.

1857 March 23   Sir Benjamin C. C. Pine (Governor).

Major H. Bird acted from 12 May, 1858.

1860 April 20   Edward Bullock Andrews (Governor).

W. A. Ross acted from 14 April, 1862.

1862 October 20   Richard Pine (Governor).

W. Hackett acted from 5 April to 1 July, 1864.

Major R. S. W. Jones acted from 13 April to 3 June, 1865.

Major W. E. Mockler acted from 3 June to 19 August, 1865.

Colonel E. Conran (Lieutenant-Governor) acted from 19 August, 1865.

ADMINISTRATORS OF THE GOLD COAST 1866–74

1866 April   Colonel E. Conran (Administrator)[1]

H. T. Ussher acted from 9 February, 1867.

1867 July 20   Herbert Taylor Ussher (Administrator).

W. H. Simpson acted from 8 August, 1868, to 3 November, 1869.

C. S. Salmon acted from July 1871 to 3 March, 1872, and from 18 May, 1872.

J. Pope-Hennessy (Acting Administrator in Chief) was in the Gold Coast from 2 to 20 April and from 2 May to July 1872.

1872 November 23   Colonel R. W. Harley (Administrator).

1873 October 2   Major-General Sir Garnet Wolseley (Administrator and Commander in Chief).

Lieutenant-Colonel J. Maxwell acted from 4 March, 1874.

Lieutenant-Colonel W. W. Johnson acted from 30 March, 1874.

C. C. Lees acted from 27 April, 1874.

Captain G. C. Strahan acted from 25 June, 1874.

GOVERNORS OF THE GOLD COAST AND LAGOS 1874–86

1874 July 25   Captain G. C. Strahan (Governor).

Charles Cameron Lees (Lieutenant-Governor) acted from 7 April, 1876.

[1] From 1866 to 1874 the Administrator, Gold Coast, was under the Governor-in-Chief, Sierra Leone. The holders of this office were: Major S. W. Blackall (February 1866, Lieutenant-Colonel Tonge acting for him from July to November 1867); Sir A. E. Kennedy (February 1868; J. J. Kendall acting for him from August to December 1869); J. Pope-Hennessy (Acting, February 1872); R. W. Keate (February 1873); (R. W. Harley was acting-Admin. in-chief from March, and G. Berkeley from August 1873.)

	Sanford Freeling (Lieutenant-Governor) acted from 30 November, 1876.
1877 June 5	Sanford Freeling (Governor).
	C. C. Lees (Lieutenant-Governor) acted from 13 May, 1878.
1879 June	Herbert Taylor Ussher (Governor).
	W. B. Griffith (Lieutenant-Governor) acted from 1 December, 1880.
1881 March 4	Sir Samuel Rowe (Governor).
	C. A. Moloney acted from 13 May, 1882.
	W. B. Griffith (Lieutenant-Governor) acted from 4 October to 24 December, 1882.
1884 April 29	W. A. G. Young (Governor).
	W. B. Griffith (Lieutenant-Governor) acted from 24 April, 1885.

GOVERNORS OF THE GOLD COAST 1886–1957

1886 January 14	W. Brandford Griffith (Governor).
	Colonel F. B. P. White acted from 11 April to 26 November, 1887.
	F. M. Hodgson acted from 30 June, 1889, to 18 February, 1890:
	12 June to 24 November, 1891:
	12 August, 1893, to 7 March, 1895.
1895 April 7	W. E. (later Sir William) Maxwell (Governor).
	F. M. Hodgson acted from 19 April to 23 October, 1896, and from 6 December, 1897.
1898 May 29	F. M. (later Sir Frederick) Hodgson (Governor).
	W. Low acted from 27 December, 1898, to 13 July, 1899, and from 29 August, 1900.
1900 December 17	Major M. Nathan (Governor).
	Captain L. R. S. Arthur acted from 30 July to 20 December, 1902.
	Major H. Bryan acted from 9 February, 1904.
1904 March 3	Sir John P. Rodger (Governor).
	Major H. Bryan acted from 10 May to 11 November, 1905:
	2 April to 1 September, 1906:
	9 October, 1907, to 28 March, 1908:
	30 March to 28 August, 1909, and from 1 September, 1910.
1910 November 21	James Jamieson Thorburn (Governor).
	Major H. Bryan acted from 5 February to 15 June, 1911, and from 29 June, 1912.
1912 December 26	Sir Hugh Clifford (Governor).
	W. C. F. Robertson acted from 1 May to 27 August, 1914.
	A. R. Slater acted from 5 May to 16 November, 1915:
	18 November, 1916, to 23 April, 1917, and from 1 April, 1919.
1919 October 9	Brigadier-General (later Sir) F. G. Guggisberg (Governor).
	A. R. Slater acted from 2 June to 6 October, 1920.
	R. W. H. Wilkinson acted from 11 July to 12 December, 1921.

Dr. J. C. Maxwell acted from 2 April to 17 August, 1923.

A. J. Philbrick acted from 18 August to 1 October, 1923.

Dr. J. C. Maxwell acted from 31 March to 1 September, 1924.

John Maxwell acted from 6 July to 1 September, 1925.

Sir J. C. Maxwell acted from 2 September to 10 November, 1925:

    11 April to 27 September, 1926:

    24 April to 5 June, 1927.

John Maxwell acted from 6 June, 1927.

1927 July 20   Sir A. Ransford Slater (Governor).

T. S. W. Thomas acted from 9 April to 11 November, 1928.

G. C. du Boulay acted from 18 April to 22 September, 1930.

G. A. S. Northcote acted from 23 September to 3 November, 1930:

    30 January to 20 April, 1931.

G. C. de Boulay acted from 8 to 14 December, 1931.

G. A. S. Northcote acted from 5 April, 1932.

1932 November 30   Sir T. Shenton W. Thomas (Governor).

G. A. S. Northcote acted from 13 May, 1934.

1934 November 23   Sir Arnold W. Hodson (Governor).

G. E. London acted from 17 June to 22 November, 1935:

    23 May to 18 October, 1938, and from 24 October, 1941.

1941 November 5   Sir Alan C. Burns (Governor).

G. E. London acted from 8 February to 28 June, 1942:

    11 October, 1943, to 1 February, 1944.

H. L. G. Gurney acted from 28 May to 18 October, 1945:

    15 August to 30 November, 1946.

R. Scott acted from 3 August, 1947.

1948 January 13   Sir Gerald Hallen Creasy (Governor).

R. Scott acted from 15 February to 27 March and from 11 June, 1949.

T. R. O. Mangin acted from 28 March to 10 June, 1949.

1949 August 11   Sir Charles Noble Arden-Clarke (Governor).

Sir T. R. O. Mangin acted from 3 June to 1 July 1950.

R. H. (later Sir Reginald) Salowoy acted from

    1 July to 11 August 1950

    21 May to 30 June 1951

    29 March to May 1952

    11 February to 20 April 1953

G. (later Sir Gordon) Hadow acted from

    29 April to July 1955

    8 February to April 1956 and 6 November to December 1956

Appendix C Gold Coast Government Treaties

YEAR	DATE	STATE	NATURE OF TREATY
1817	September 7	Ashanti (Bowdich Treaty)	Peace & Trade (see No. 33)
1820	March 23	Ashanti (Dupuis Treaty)	(Not ratified: see No. 43)
1823	December 20	States attached to British forts, with Abura, Aju-mako, 'Asonadjumacon', Denkyira, Eguafo, Ekum-fi, Gomoa, Mori, Nkusu-kum, Twifu, Wasaw	Alliance v. Ashanti (see No. 63)
1831	April 27	Abura, Anomabu, Asin, Cape Coast, Denkyira, Eja, Ekumfi, Nzima, Twifu and Ashanti	(See No. 98)
1844	March 6	Abura, Anomabu, Asin, Cape-Coast, Denkyira, Dominasi, 'Donadi'	Recognition of British juris-diction (The 'Bond') (see No. 145)
	March 12	'Braffo', Twifu	,,
	March 18	Ekumfi, 'Bentil'	,,
	March 27	Ajumako	,,
	April 12	'Assamoah-Adjumacon', Gomoa	,,
	April 22	Asikuma	,,
	May 8	James Town	,,
	May 29	'Odomtoo', Nsaba	,,
	July 22	Wasaw Amenfi	,,
	August 21	Dixcove	,,
	December 2	Wasaw Fiasi	,,
1847	March 8	Dahomey	Amity & Trade
1850	March 30	Danish settlements	Fealty (signed at Akropong)
1852	January 28	Aflao	Abolition of slave trade & human sacrifice
	January 29	Adafienu, Adina	
1858	June 17	Krepi	Agreement to pay Poll Tax
1864	December 13	Ekumfi	Allegiance
1867	August 28	Akwamu	Amity & Commerce
	November 14	Anlo	,,
1868	November 30	Ada & Anlo	Opening of Volta river
1869	March 3	Akwamu	Adherence to Volta treaty
1871	May 10	Accra, Ada, Anlo, Dzelu-kofe	Renewal of ,, ,,
	December 21	Akim-Kotoku	Submission of Kwabina Fuah
1872	August 21	Akwapim and Krobo	Peace settlement
1873	February 25	Wasaw Fiasi	Abolition of human sacri-fice

YEAR DATE	STATE	NATURE OF TREATY
1874 February 13	Ashanti	(Treaty of Fomena, No. 299)
March	Ahanta, Akwida, Axim, Bushua, Nzima, Sekondi, Shama, Takoradi	Declaration of obedience
June 15	Akwamu (at Odumasi)	Amity & Commerce & opening of Volta
June 22	Accra, Ada, Anlo, Dzelukofe (Tr. of Dzelukofe)	Amity & Commerce & opening of Volta
1876 March 8	Kete-Krachi	Freedom of transit
1879 September 24	Katanu	Protection
December 1	Aflao (provisional)	Cession of sea-coast
December 2	Agbosome	Cession of sea-coast & Abolition of human sacrifice
December 6	Aflao	Cession of sea-coast & Abolition of human sacrifice
1882 February 5	Nkonya	Freedom of transit
June 20	Akim, Akwapim (Tr. of Koforidua)	Settlement of New Juaben
1884 June 20	Beh & Togo (Provisional)	Cession of coast-line (No. 345)
1884 September 25	Little Popo	Protection
1885 November 12	Krikor (signed at Keta)	Cession
1886 July 27	Akwamu	Annexation (See No. 354)
August 12	Agrave	Cession of left bank of Volta
September 4	Bator, Mefe, Mlefi, Bakpa, Ahume, Tefle, 'Sopey' (Sakpe?)	,, ,, ,, ,,
October 7	Krepi (signed at Peki)	Annexation
1887 February 18	Sefwi (signed at Wiawso)	Protection
May 9	Akwamu	Affirmation of British Protection
June 15	Krepi	Affirmation of British Protection
July 30	Gyaman (provisional)	Protection
1888 May 5	Kwahu (signed at Abetifi)	Protection
June 2	Akim-Kotoku	Cession of Nsuaem ferry
July 3	Adaklu, Agotime, Avatime, Dzolo, Kpedze, Taingbe, Tavieve	Declaration of fealty to Britain and to King of Krepi
July 3	Anum, Buem	Fealty to Britain
July 3	Krepi	Freedom of transit
1889 January 24	Gyaman (signed at Bontuku)	Protection
1890 November 25	Atebubu	Protection
1892 June 1	Trugu & Bole (s. at Boniape)	Friendship & Freedom of Trade

YEAR DATE	STATE	NATURE OF TREATY
1892 June 13	Bole (signed at Bole)	Friendship & Freedom of Trade
July 8	Daboya (Wasape)	,, (No. 381)
August 12	Dagomba (signed at Yendi)	,, ,,
August 26	Bimbila	,, ,,
1893 December 21	Amantin (signed at Atebubu)	,, ,,
1894 January 25	Nkoranza	,, ,,
February 8	Abeasi	,, ,,
February 19	Wiase	,, ,,
February 20	Nkaneku (in Kumawu)	,, ,,
March 1	Basa	,, ,,
March 8	Eginowofi (Ayinwofi) s. at Atebubu	,, ,,
April 12	Bona	,, ,,
May 4	Dagarti (signed at Wa)	,, ,,
May 28	Mamprusi (signed at Gambaga)	,, ,,
July 2	Mossi (signed at Wagadugu)	,, ,,
August 8	Chakosi (signed at Sansanne-Mango)	,, ,,
August 31	Trugu (signed at Kombi)*	,, ,,
September 1	Salaga*	,, ,,
September 22	Debre*	,, ,,
September 29	Buipe*	,, ,,
October 5	Busunu*	,, ,,
October 12	Daboya*	,, ,,
December 5	Banda (signed at Lawra)	,, ,,
1895 October 18	Adansi (signed at Prasu)	Protection
1896 January 11	Bekwai (signed at Esankwanta)	,,
January 11	Abodum (signed at Esankwanta)	,,
January 18	Nkoranza	,,
January 30	Nsuta (signed at Kumasi)	,, (No. 404)
February 10	Mampong ,, ,,	,,
February 10	Agona ,, ,,	,,
February 10	Juaben ,, ,,	,,
February 10	Kumawu ,, ,,	,,
February 10	Ofinso ,, ,,	,,
February 10	Ejisu ,, ,,	,,
February 10	Kokofu ,, ,,	,,
1896 February 22	Bechim Ahafo (signed at Jemu)	,,
March 4	Borumfu	,,
April 21	Dormaa (signed at Pamu)	,,
May 2	Asunafo-Ahafo (signed at Kukuomo)	,,

* For areas inside Neutral Zone Subject to Anglo-German agreement.

YEAR	DATE	STATE	NATURE OF TREATY
1897	January 9	Dagarti (signed at Wa)	Friendship & Freedom of
	January 12	Mamprusi (signed at Nalie-rigu)	Trade (No. 404)
1897	February 2	'Lakhama' (signed at Dasima)	,, ,,
	February 4	'Gbelu' (Bellu?)	,, ,,
	February 6	'Achilon' (signed at Leo)	,, ,,
	February 8	Tumu	,, ,,
	February 10	'Kpan' (Kwapun/Kopun)	,, ,,
	March 16	Bona (signed at Dawkita)	,,
	June 5	Techiman (signed at Nkoranza)	,,
	July 24	Mamprusi (signed at Nalierigu)	,,
	August 9	Mossi (signed at Bawku)	,,
	August 25	Salaga	,,
	December 10	Dagarti (signed at Kaleo)	,,
1898	January 2	Doriman (signed at Pisa)	,,
	January 9	Issa (shorter form of Protection treaty)	
	January 10	Busie ,,	,,
	January 10	Wogu ,,	,,
	January 11	'Nadawle' ,,	,, (No. 422)
	January 27	'Pancheon' ,,	,,
	February 1	'Kawsau' (provisional) '	,,
	February 4	Trugu (signed at Chama)	,,
	February 9	'Gindi' (shorter form of Protection treaty)	
	July 18	Debre ,,	,,

Appendix D Gold Coast Trade and Revenue, 1853–1956

YEAR	IMPORTS £	EXPORTS £	REVENUE £
1853	60,000	115,000	13,249
1854	107,200	200,002	10,211
1855	149,587	140,697	9,830
1856	105,634	120,999	12,917
1857	118,270	124,394	7,408
1858	122,457	154,136	7,062
1859	114,596	118,563	8,286
1860	112,454	110,457	7,948
1861	162,970	145,819	9,335
1862	145,100	102,086	9,154
1863	76,955	53,764	8,547
1864			
1865			
1866			11,053
1867	206,920	160,291	10,839
1868	140,226	148,909	15,404
1869	213,491	281,913	24,127
1870	253,397	378,239	30,851
1871	250,672	295,207	28,609
1872	260,101	385,281	40,165
1873	225,525	330,624	65,706
1874	No trustworthy returns		74,868
1875	364,672	327,012	67,368
1876	446,672	465,268	64,788
1877	327,274	387,002	93,347
1878	394,153	393,457	105,092
1879	323,089	428,811	90,432
1880	337,248	482,058	119,500
1881	398,124	373,258	116,424
1882	392,975	340,019	104,817
1883	382,582	363,868	105,648
1884	527,339	467,228	125,956
1885	466,424	496,318	130,457
1886	376,530	406,539	122,531
1887	363,716	372,446	122,467
1888	432,122	381,619	97,807
1889	440,868	415,926	111,388
1890	562,103	601,348	156,449
1891	665,781	684,305	186,021
1892	597,095	665,064	183,075
1893	718,353	722,107	201,783

YEAR	IMPORTS	EXPORTS	REVENUE	
	£	£	£	
1894	812,830	850,344	218,261	
1895	924,419	877,304	230,076	
1896	905,135	792,111	237,460	
1897	907,670	857,793	237,857	
1898 [1]	1,095,864	1,992,998	258,822 [1]	
1899	1,314,922	1,111,738	322,796 [2]	
1900	1,283,343	885,446	333,283 [3]	
1901	1,795,187	559,733	471,193 [4]	
1902	2,120,433	774,186	491,755	
1903	2,082,544	980,942	554,553	
1904	2,001,857	1,340,026	650,393	
1905	1,486,068	1,646,145	572,462	
1906	2,058,939	1,996,412	673,102	
1907	2,366,196	2,641,674	703,718	
1908	2,029,447	2,525,171	752,142	
1909	2,394,412	2,655,573	778,552	
1910	3,439,831	2,697,706	1,006,633	
1911	3,784,260	3,792,454	1,111,632	
1912	4,023,322	4,307,802	1,230,850	
1913	4,952,494	5,427,106	1,301,566	
1914	4,456,968	4,942,656	1,331,713	
1915	4,509,538	5,943,630	1,456,130	
1916	5,999,749	5,816,528	1,835,989	
1917	3,386,480	6,364,925	1,624,124	
1918	3,257,591	4,472,925	1,298,674	
1919	7,946,981	10,814,175	2,601,360	
1920	15,152,145	12,352,207	3,721,722	
1921	7,661,324	6,942,197	3,016,520	1921–2
1922	7,919,339	8,343,635	3,357,196	1922–3
1923	8,448,862	8,959,213	3,742,834	1923–4
1924	8,315,234	9,914,937	3,971,187	1924–5
1925	9,782,619	10,890,223	4,116,442	1925–6
1926	10,285,876	12,104,800	4,365,321	1926–7
1927	13,770,542	14,350,355	5,217,638	1927–8
1928	12,200,045	13,824,875	4,703,967	1928–9
1929	10,082,381	12,677,716	3,397,324	1929–30
1930	8,953,770	11,287,388	3,499,418	1930–1
1931	4,803,874	9,300,620	2,284,299	1931–2
1932	5,605,219	8,348,879	2,670,786	1932–3
1933	5,543,354	8,048,484	2,684,925	1933–4
1934	4,848,800	8,117,456	2,778,055	1934–5
1935	7,956,780	9,971,535	3,268,378	1935–6
1936	11,656,719	12,636,899	3,774,746	1936–7
1937	19,228,363	16,218,193	3,791,673	1937–8

[1] The figures of revenue for 1898 to 1901 exclude imperial grants in aid: (1) £45,000 for the Northern Territories; (2) £100,000 for the Northern Territories; (3) £50,000 for the Northern Territories and £202,300 for the Ashanti disturbances; (4) £25,000 for the Northern Territories and £197,000 for Ashanti.

B B

YEAR	IMPORTS	EXPORTS	REVENUE	
	£	£	£	
1938	10,380,323	15,425,496	3,780,288	1938–9
1939	10,626,284	16,235,288	3,734,438	1939–40
1940	7,631,283	14,323,842	3,868,830	1940–1
1941	6,268,606	13,548,409	4,141,186	1941–2
1942	9,877,298	12,550,174	4,331,894	1942–3
1943	10,167,566	12,631,282	4,720,394	1943–4
1944	9,828,094	12,314,200	5,866,665	1944–5
1945	10,103,940	15,126,147	7,171,618	1945–6
1946	12,633,612	19,616,874	7,567,589	1946–7
1947 [1]	22,589,690	27,414,959	10,245,618	1947–8
1948	31,378,050	56,114,722	11,639,324	1948–9
1949	45,416,037	49,927,114	18,106,495	1949–50
1950	48,128,966	77,406,944	20,861,032	1950–1
1951	63,793,420	91,990,397	30,764,463	1951–2
1952	66,610,551	86,376,783	42,510,072	1952–3
1953	73,802,866	89,943,265	49,942,397	1953–4
1954	71,050,343	114,594,590	80,567,534	1954–5
1955	87,876,936	95,661,391	64,130,000	1955–6
1956	88,919,719	86,599,422	52,450,000	1956–7

[1] Trade figures from 1947 onwards are taken from the Office of the Ghana Government statistician, June 1957; otherwise figures are from the Colonial Office List.

Appendix E
Maps

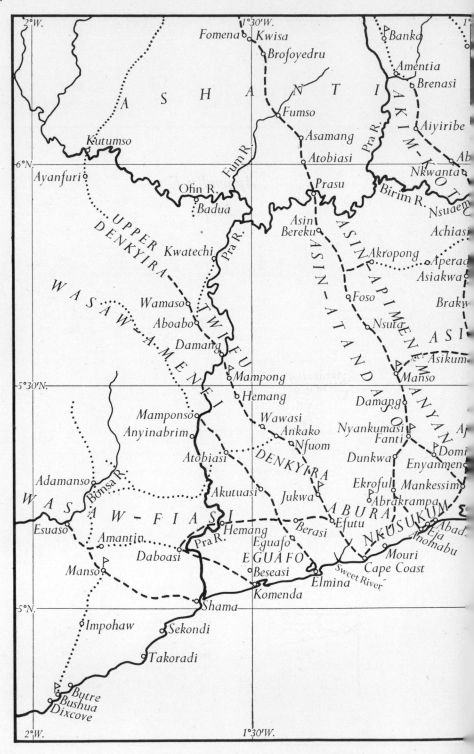

1. THE PROTEC

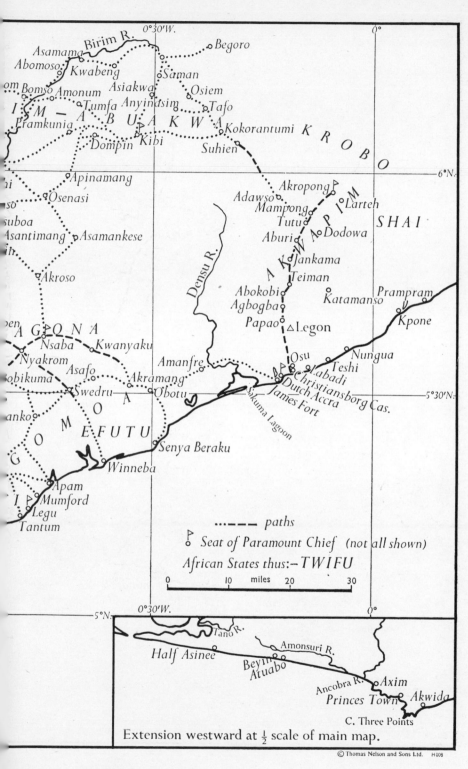

RICTS—c.1830—c.1870.

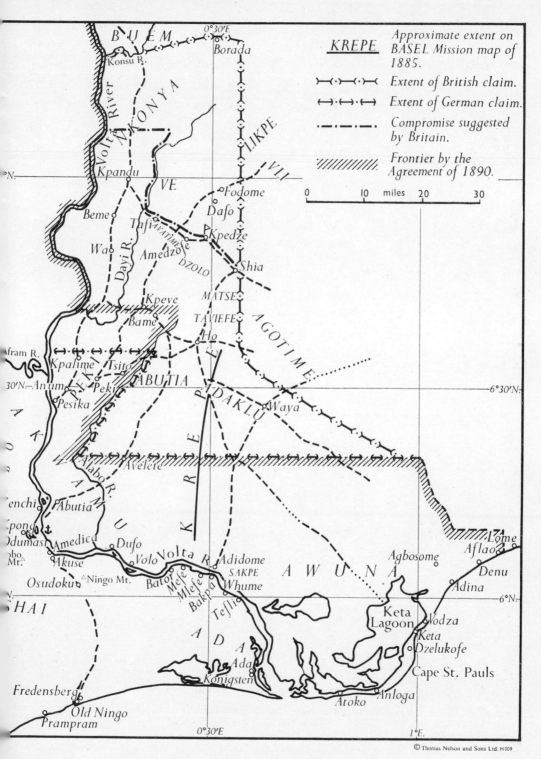

2. THE LOWER VOLTA—1890.

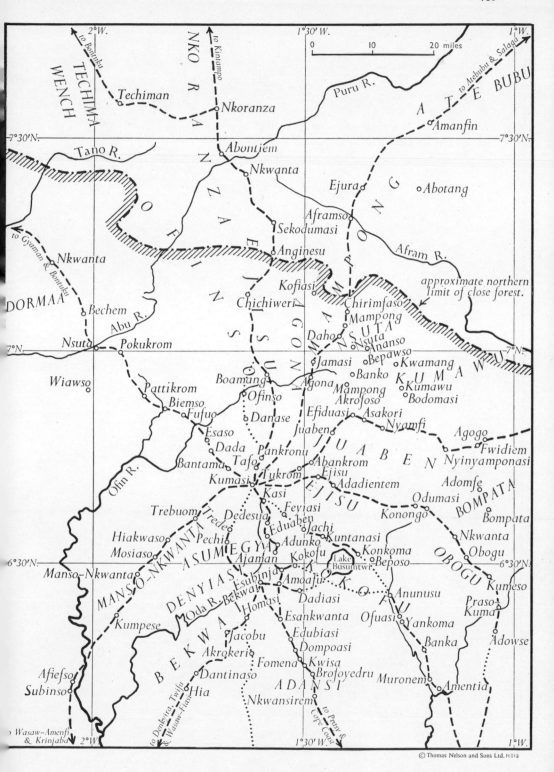

To Bontuku
2°W.
NKORANZA
to Kintampo
1°30'W.
0   10   20 miles
1°W.
to Atebubu & Salaga

TECHIMA WENCH
Techiman
Nkoranza
Puru R.
A T E B U B U
Amanfin

Tano R.
7°30'N.
Abontiem
Nkwanta
Ejura
Abotang
7°30'N.

O F I N Z A E
Aframso
Sekodumasi
Anginesu
Afram R.

to Gyaman & Bontuku
Nkwanta
Kofiasi
Chichiweri
Chirimfaso
Mampong
approximate northern limit of close forest.

DORMAA
Bechem
Abu R.
M A N S U
Daho
NSUTA
Nsuta
Ananso

7°N.
Nsuta
Pokukrom
Jamasi
Bepawso
Kwamang
7°N.

Wiawso
Pattikrom
Biemso
Boamang
Agona
Banko
K U M A W U
Mampong
Kumawu
Bodomasi
Akrofoso

Fufuo
Ofinso
Danase
Efiduasi
Asakori
Nyamfi
Agogo
Fwidiem

Esaso
Dada
Pankronu
Juaben
J U A B E N
Nyinyamponasi

Ofin R.
Bantama
Tafo
Abankrom
Adomfe
BOMPATA

Kumasi
Tukrom
Ejisu
Adadientem
Odumasi
Bompata

Kasi
EJISU
Konongo
Nkwanta

Trebuom
Tredee
Dedesua
Feviasi
Eduaben
Jachi
Kuntanasi
Konkoma
Obogu
O B O G U

Hiakwaso
Mosiaso
Pechi
Adunko
Kokofu
Beposo
Kumeso

A S U M E G Y A
Ajaman
Amoafu
Lake Busumtwi
A K O K U F U
Anunusu
Praso-Kuma

6°30'N.
Manso-Nkwanta
M A N S O - N K W A N T A
Esubinja
Bekwai
Dadiasi
Ofuasi
Yankoma
6°30'N.

Kumpese
D E N Y I A S I
Oda R.
Homasi
Esankwanta
Banka
Adowse

B E K W A I
Jacobu
Akrokeri
Edubiasi
Dompoasi

Afiefso
Subinso
Dantinaso
Hia
Fomena
Kwisa
Brojoyedru
Muronem
Amentia

A D A N S I
Nkwansirem

to Wasaw-Amenfi & Krinjaba
2°W.
to Denkera, Twifu & Wasaw-Fiasi
1°30'W.
to Praso & Cape Coast
1°W.

© Thomas Nelson and Sons Ltd. H010

3. ASHANTI.

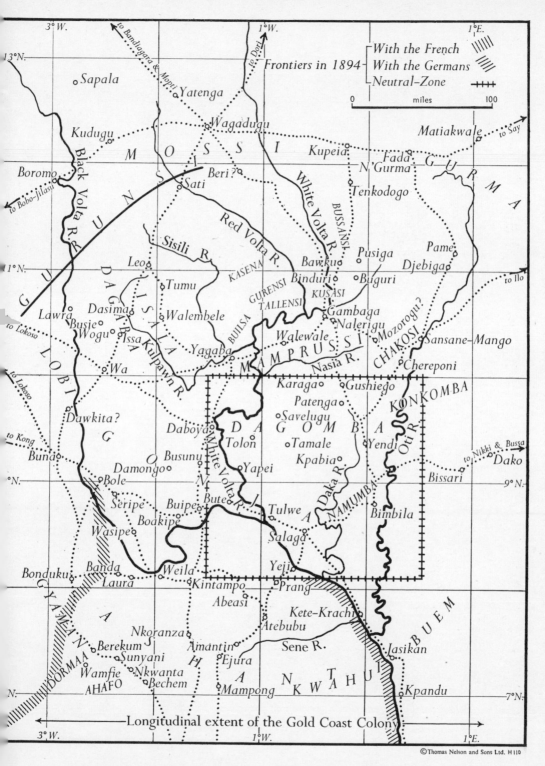

The Gold Coast Hinterland—c.1894.

Frontiers in 1894
- With the French
- With the Germans
- Neutral-Zone

0   miles   100

©Thomas Nelson and Sons Ltd. H110

4. THE GOLD COAST HINTERLAND—c.1894.

INDEX